生野 桂

This is a picture of Allen that my little brother drew. We had a big laugh about it and decided to see which of us could draw another manga artist's characters better. The last character we competed on was Goku, and I swear I won!!
— **Katsura Hoshino**

Shiga Prefecture native Katsura Hoshino's hit manga series *D.Gray-man* has been serialized in *Weekly Shonen Jump* since 2004. Katsura's debut manga, "Continue," appeared for the first time in *Weekly Shonen Jump* in 2003.

Katsura adores cats.

D.GRAY-MAN
3-in-1 Edition
Volume 4

SHONEN JUMP Manga Omnibus Edition
A compilation of the graphic novel volumes 10–12

STORY AND ART BY
KATSURA HOSHINO

English Adaptation/Lance Caselman
Translation/Toshifumi Yoshida
Touch-up Art & Lettering/Kelle Han
Design/Yukiko Whitley (Graphic Novel and 3-in-1 Editions)
Editor/Gary Leach (Graphic Novel Edition)
Editor/Nancy Thistlethwaite (3-in-1 Edition)

D.GRAY-MAN © 2004 by Katsura Hoshino. All rights reserved.
First published in Japan in 2004 by SHUEISHA Inc., Tokyo. English translation rights arranged by
SHUEISHA Inc.

The stories, characters and incidents mentioned in this publication are entirely fictional.

Printed in the U.S.A.

Published by VIZ Media, LLC
P.O. Box 77010
San Francisco, CA 94107

10 9 8 7 6 5 4 3 2 1
3-in-1 edition first printing, July 2014

www.viz.com

www.shonenjump.com

PARENTAL ADVISORY
D.GRAY-MAN is rated T+ for Older Teen and
is recommended for ages 16 and up. This
volume contains fantasy violence.
ratings.viz.com

SHONEN JUMP ADVANCED MANGA EDITION

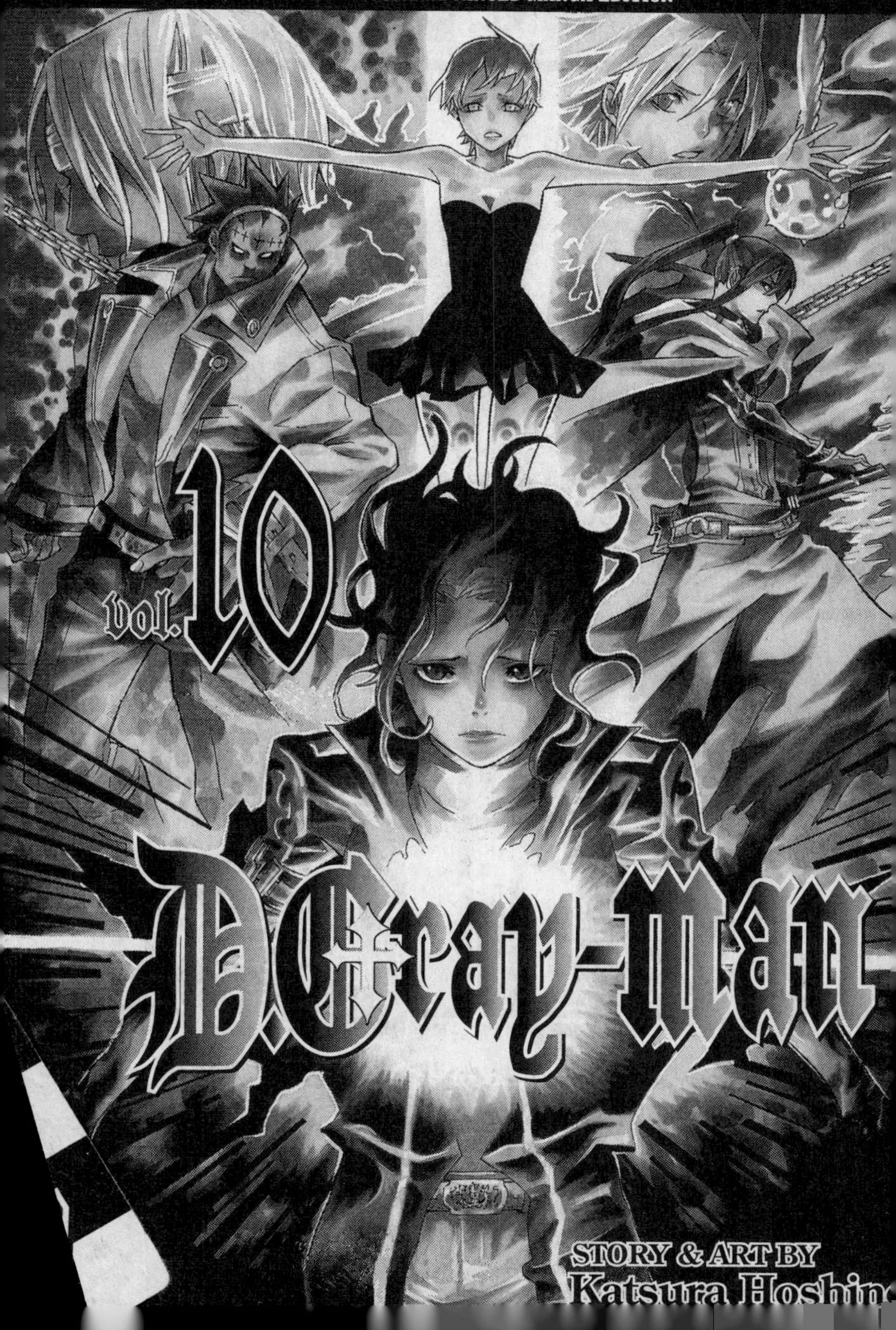
vol. 10
D.Gray-man
STORY & ART BY
Katsura Hoshin

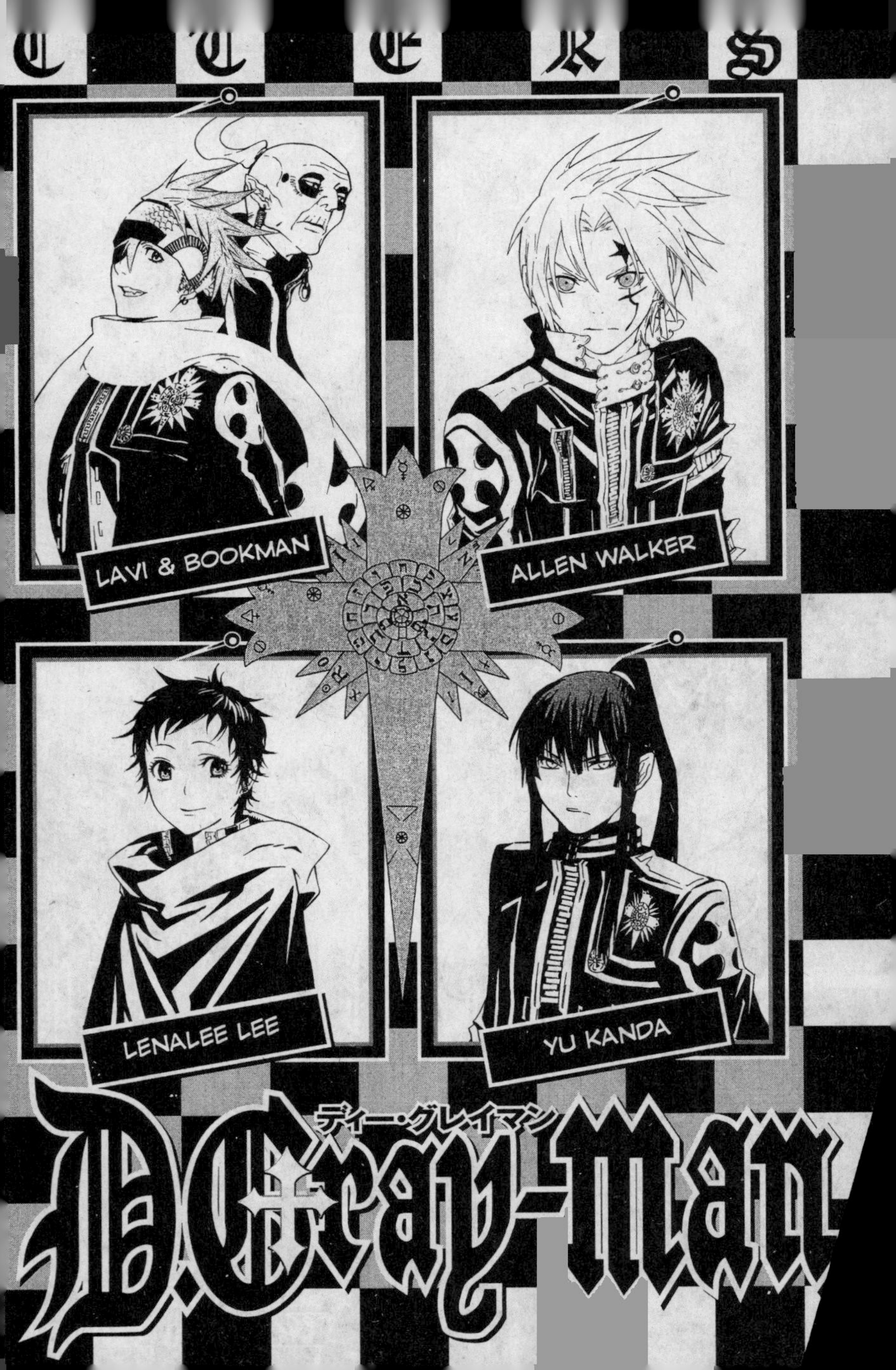
LAVI & BOOKMAN
ALLEN WALKER
LENALEE LEE
YU KANDA
ディー・グレイマン
D.Gray-man

C H A R

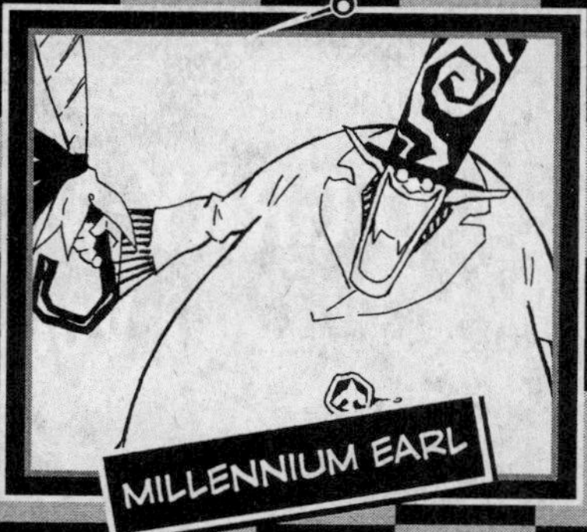

MILLENNIUM EARL

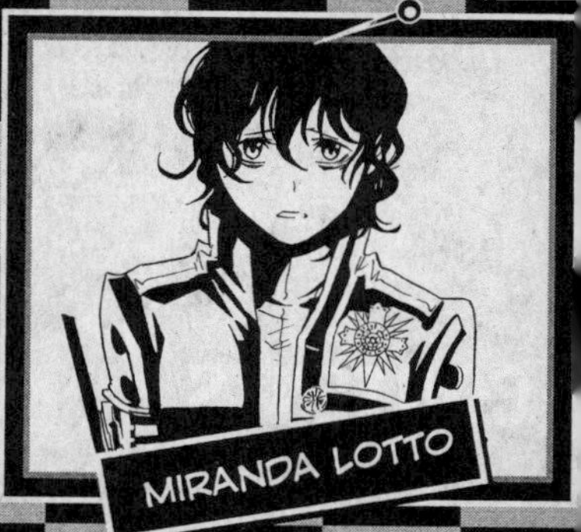

MIRANDA LOTTO

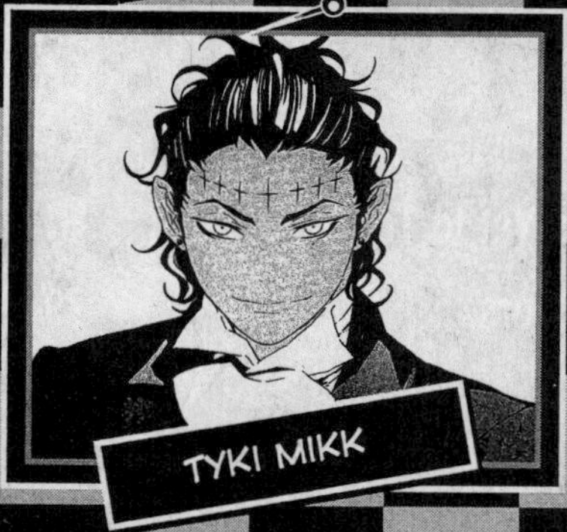

TYKI MIKK

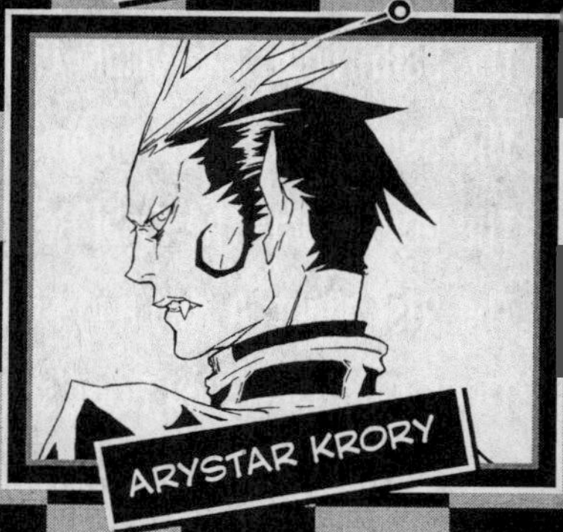

ARYSTAR KRORY

S T O R Y

IT ALL BEGAN CENTURIES AGO WITH THE DISCOVERY OF A CUBE CONTAINING AN APOCALYPTIC PROPHECY FROM AN ANCIENT CIVILIZATION AND INSTRUCTIONS IN THE USE OF INNOCENCE, A CRYSTALLINE SUBSTANCE OF WONDROUS SUPERNATURAL POWER. THE CREATORS OF THE CUBE CLAIMED TO HAVE DEFEATED AN EVIL KNOWN AS THE MILLENNIUM EARL BY USING THE INNOCENCE. NEVERTHELESS, THE WORLD WAS DESTROYED BY THE GREAT FLOOD OF THE OLD TESTAMENT. NOW, TO AVERT A SECOND END OF THE WORLD, A GROUP OF EXORCISTS WIELDING WEAPONS MADE OF INNOCENCE MUST BATTLE THE MILLENNIUM EARL AND HIS TERRIBLE MINIONS, THE AKUMA.

HAVING CROSSED THE TREACHEROUS SEAS TO JAPAN, LENALEE AND THE EXORCISTS FIND THEMSELVES UNDER ATTACK BY BOTH THE NOAH AND THE MILLENIUM EARL HIMSELF. BACK IN CHINA, ALLEN SUCCESSFULLY REACTIVATES HIS INNOCENCE AND USES THE ARK TO REJOIN HIS COMPANIONS, PUTTING HIMSELF ON A COLLISION COURSE WITH TYKI MIKK, THE NOAH WHO VERY NEARLY KILLED HIM. AND MIKK HAS HIS OWN REASONS FOR WANTING REVENGE AGAINST ALLEN...

D.GRAY-MAN
Vol. 10

CONTENTS

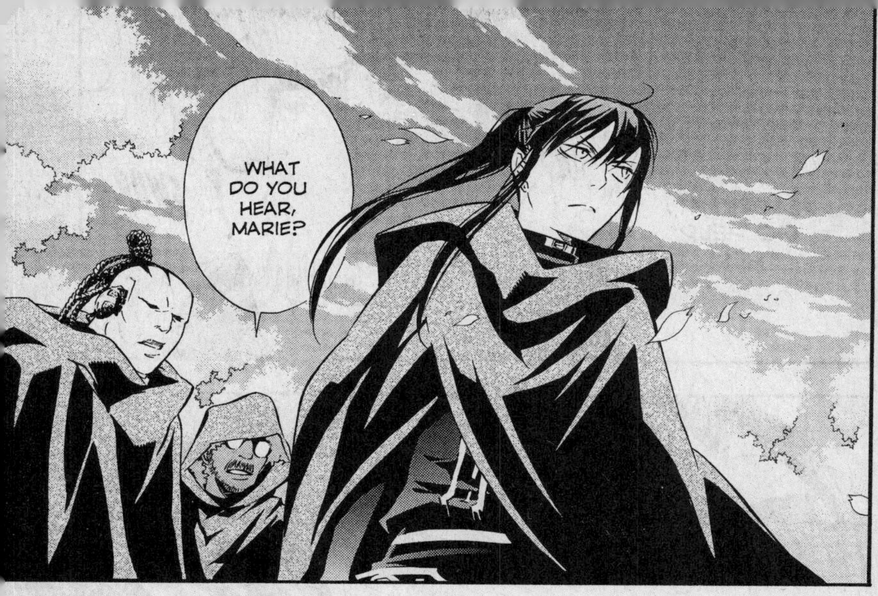
WHAT DO YOU HEAR, MARIE?

THE 87TH NIGHT: TIEDOLL'S ENTRY

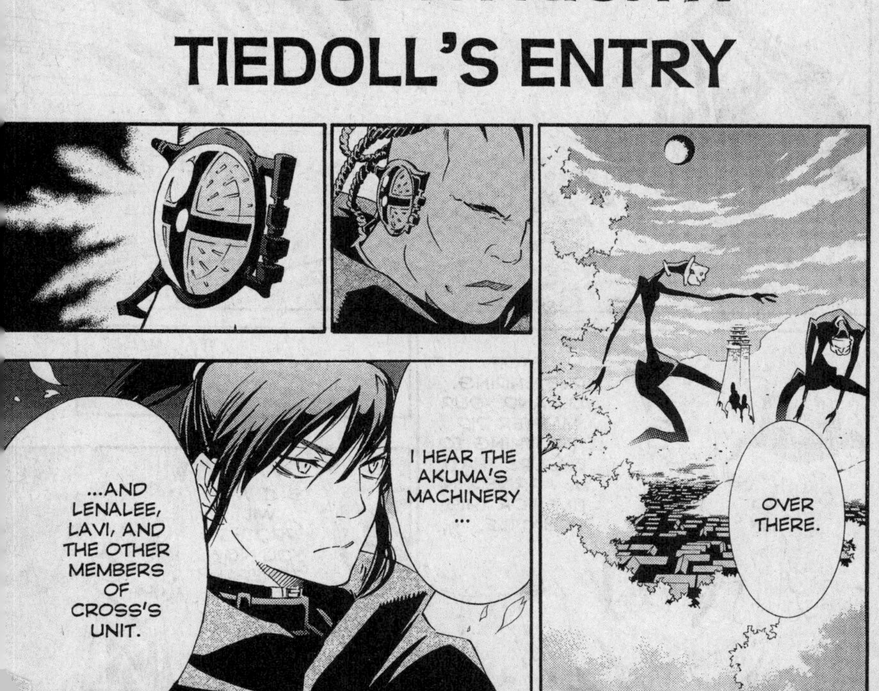
OVER THERE.
I HEAR THE AKUMA'S MACHINERY ...
...AND LENALEE, LAVI, AND THE OTHER MEMBERS OF CROSS'S UNIT.

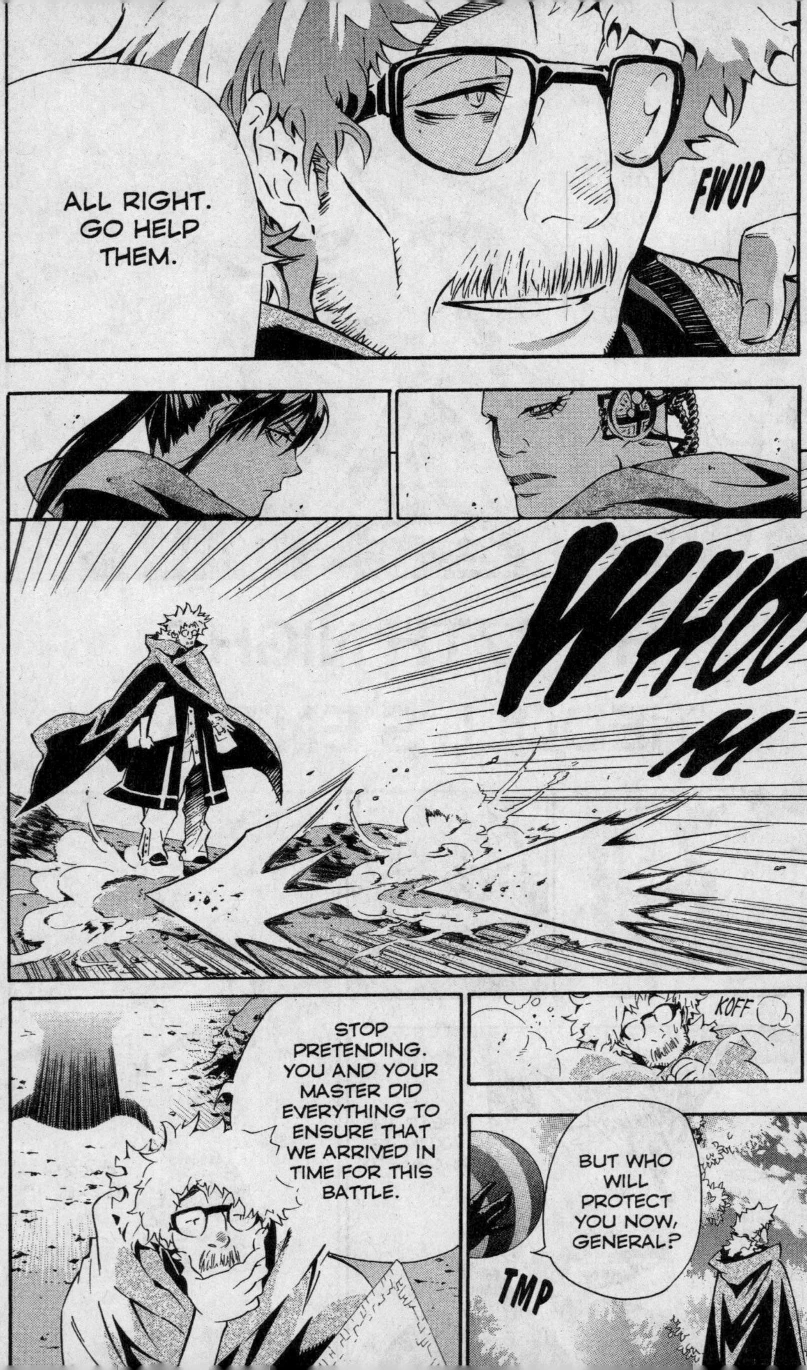
FWUP
ALL RIGHT. GO HELP THEM.
WHOOM
KOFF
BUT WHO WILL PROTECT YOU NOW, GENERAL?
TMP
STOP PRETENDING. YOU AND YOUR MASTER DID EVERYTHING TO ENSURE THAT WE ARRIVED IN TIME FOR THIS BATTLE.

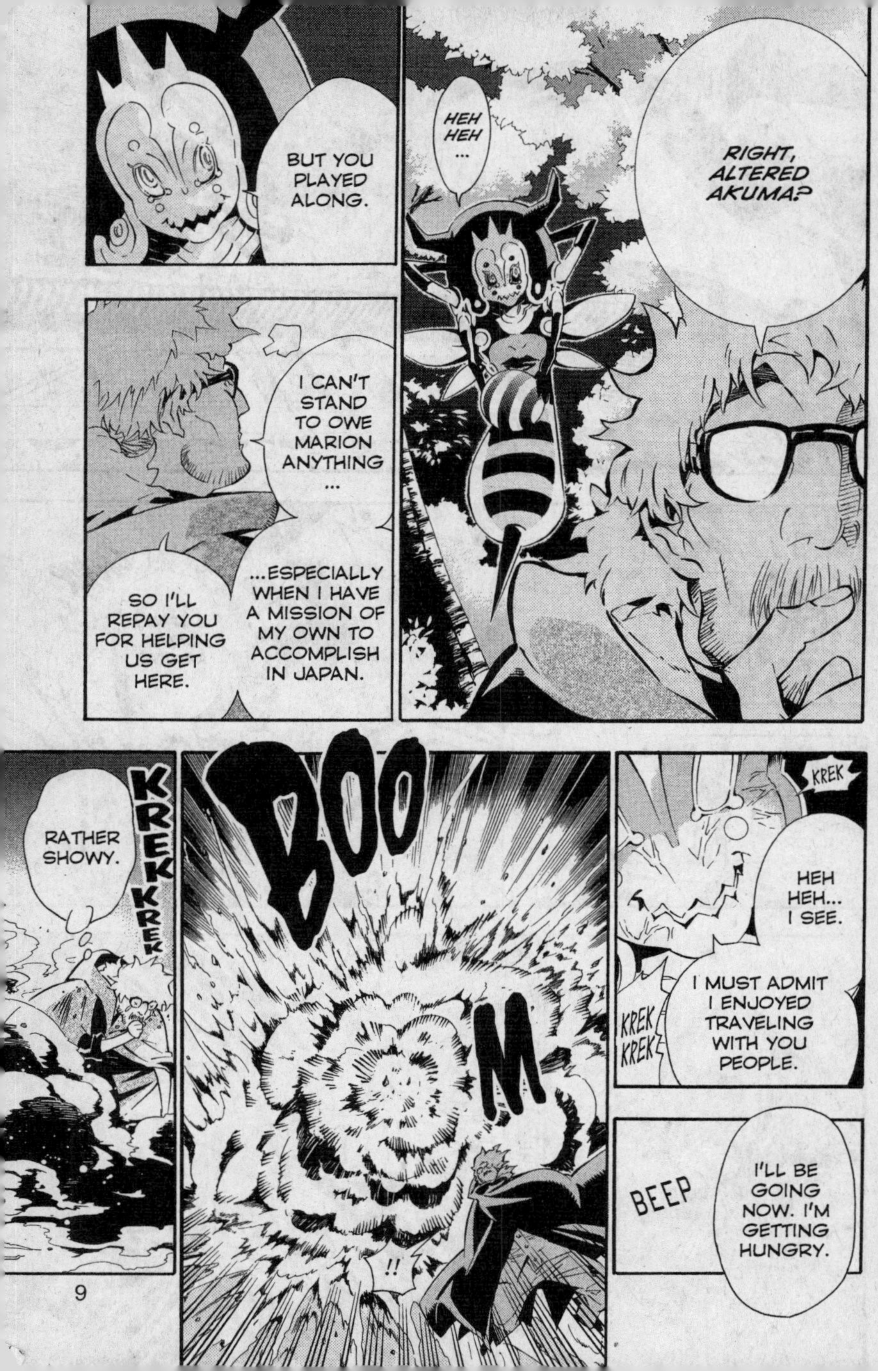
RIGHT, ALTERED AKUMA?
HEH HEH ...
BUT YOU PLAYED ALONG.
I CAN'T STAND TO OWE MARION ANYTHING ...
...ESPECIALLY WHEN I HAVE A MISSION OF MY OWN TO ACCOMPLISH IN JAPAN.
SO I'LL REPAY YOU FOR HELPING US GET HERE.
KREK
HEH HEH... I SEE.
I MUST ADMIT I ENJOYED TRAVELING WITH YOU PEOPLE.
KREK KREK
BEEP
I'LL BE GOING NOW. I'M GETTING HUNGRY.
BOOM
!!
KREK KREK KREK
RATHER SHOWY.

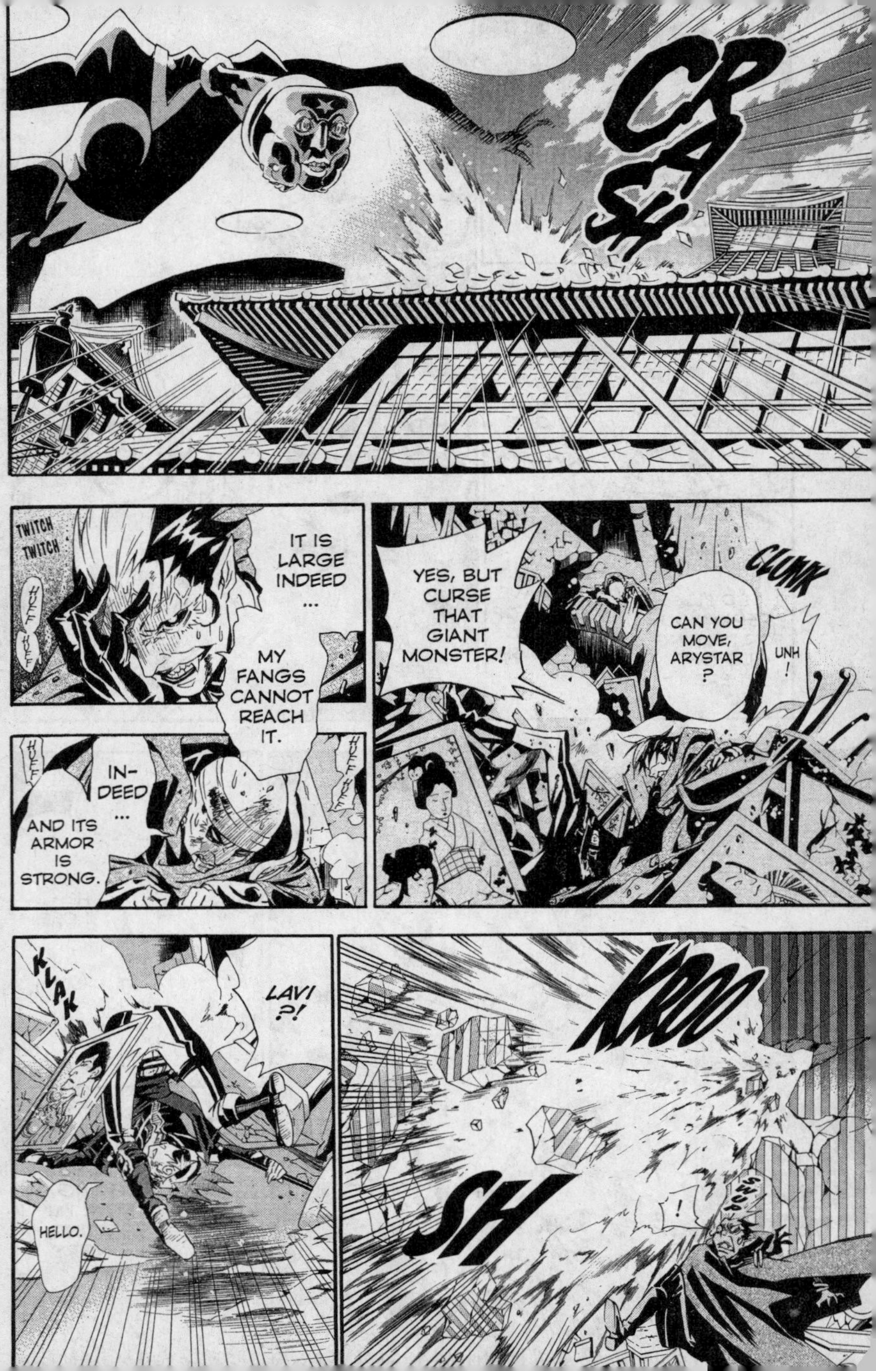
CRASH
CLUNK
UNH!
CAN YOU MOVE, ARYSTAR?
YES, BUT CURSE THAT GIANT MONSTER!
TWITCH TWITCH
HUFF HUFF
IT IS LARGE INDEED ...
MY FANGS CANNOT REACH IT.
HUFF HUFF
HUFF
INDEED ...
AND ITS ARMOR IS STRONG.
KROOSH
SWUP
!
LAV! ?!
KVAK
HELLO.

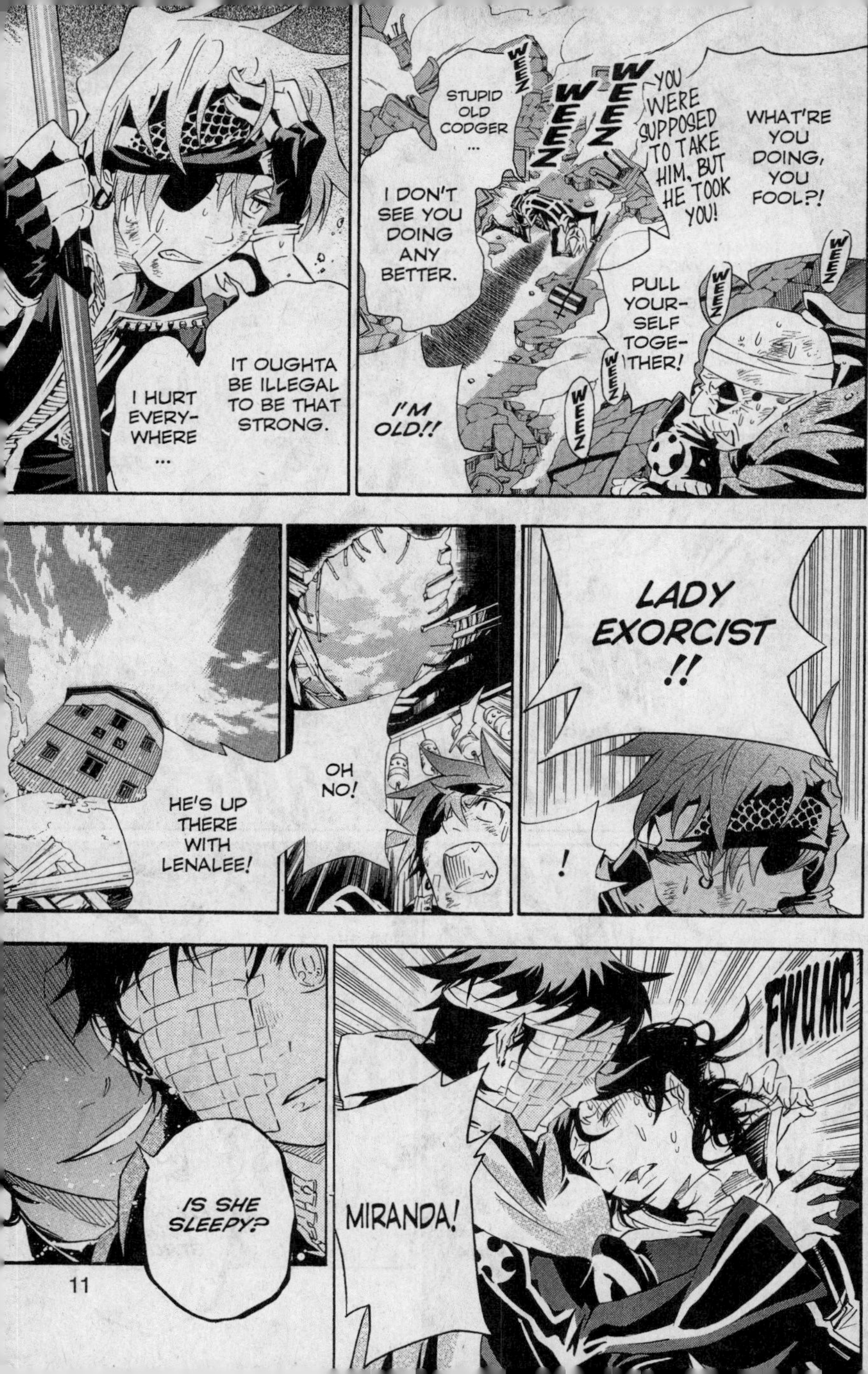
WHAT'RE YOU DOING, YOU FOOL?!
YOU WERE SUPPOSED TO TAKE HIM, BUT HE TOOK YOU!
WEEZ WEEZ WEEZ WEEZ
WEEZ WEEZ
PULL YOURSELF TOGETHER!
STUPID OLD CODGER ...
I DON'T SEE YOU DOING ANY BETTER.
WEEZ WEEZ
I'M OLD!!
IT OUGHTA BE ILLEGAL TO BE THAT STRONG.
I HURT EVERYWHERE ...
LADY EXORCIST !!
!
OH NO!
HE'S UP THERE WITH LENALEE!
FWUMP
MIRANDA!
IS SHE SLEEPY?

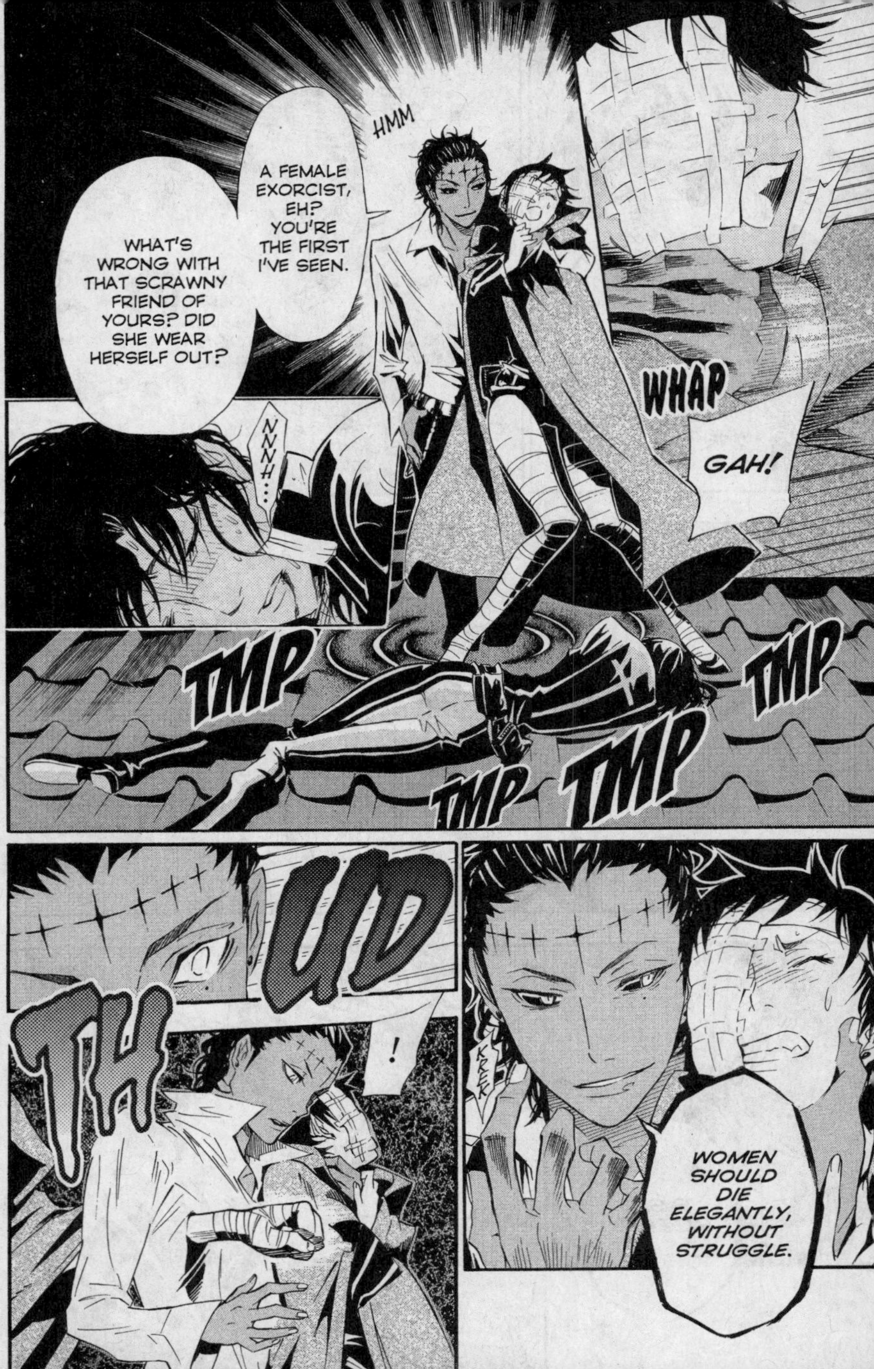
WHAP
GAH!
HMM
A FEMALE EXORCIST, EH? YOU'RE THE FIRST I'VE SEEN.
WHAT'S WRONG WITH THAT SCRAWNY FRIEND OF YOURS? DID SHE WEAR HERSELF OUT?
NNNH...
TMP
TMP
TMP
TMP
KREK
WOMEN SHOULD DIE ELEGANTLY, WITHOUT STRUGGLE.
THUD
!

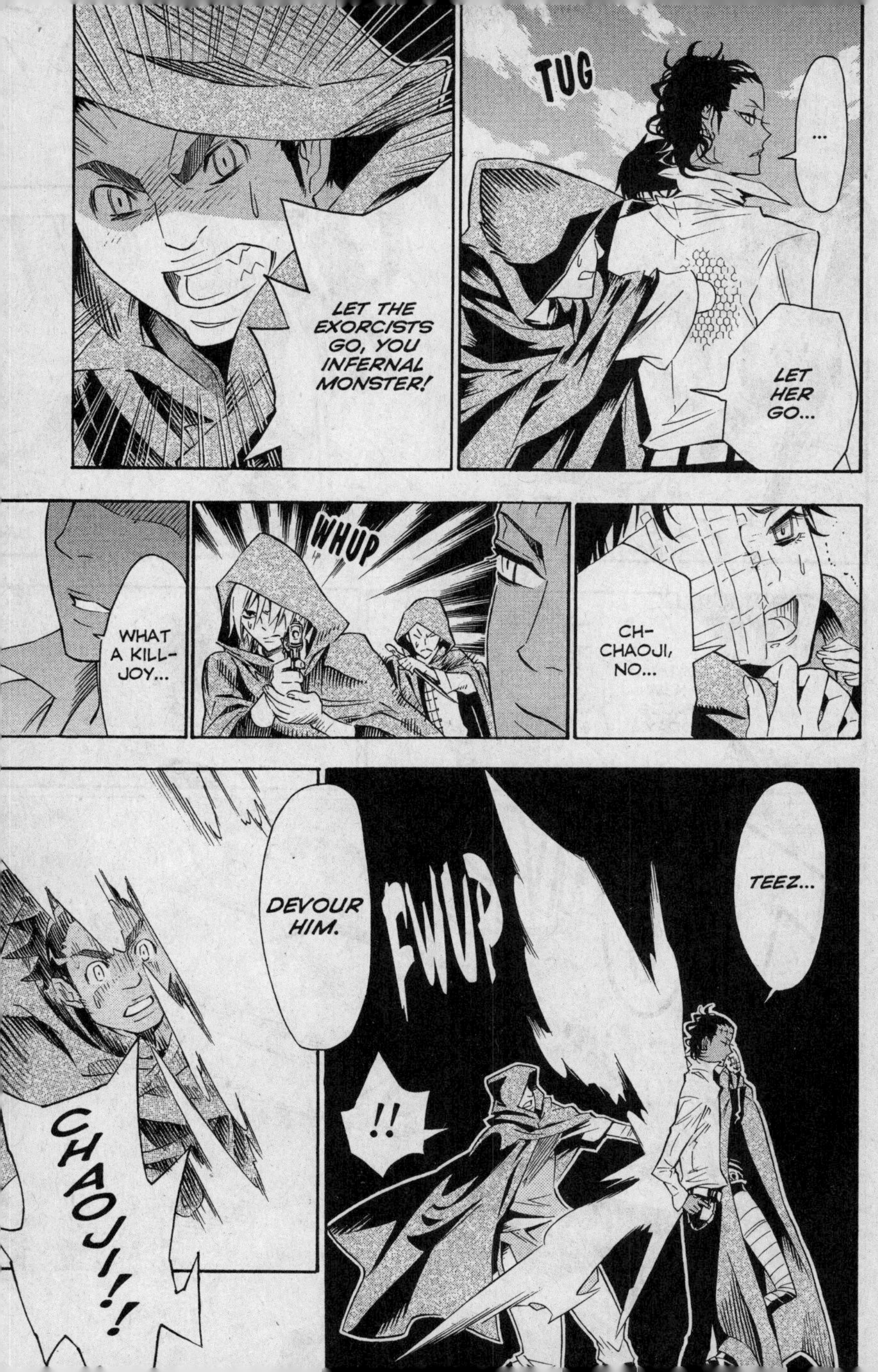
TUG
...
LET HER GO...
LET THE EXORCISTS GO, YOU INFERNAL MONSTER!
CH-CHAOJI, NO...
WHUP
WHAT A KILL-JOY...
TEEZ...
DEVOUR HIM.
FWUP
!!
CHAOJI!!!

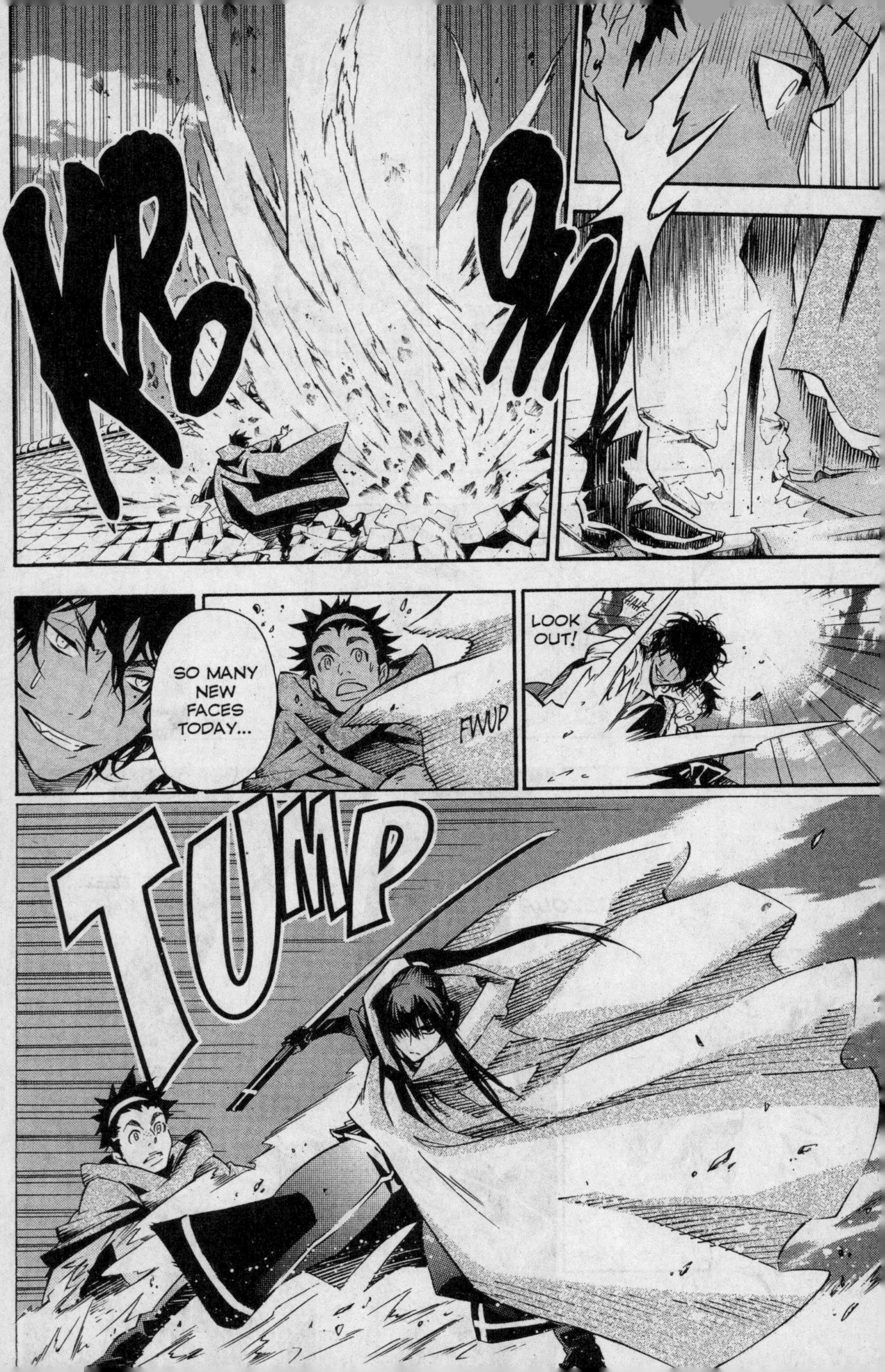
KRBOOM
LOOK OUT!
SO MANY NEW FACES TODAY...
FWUP
TUMP

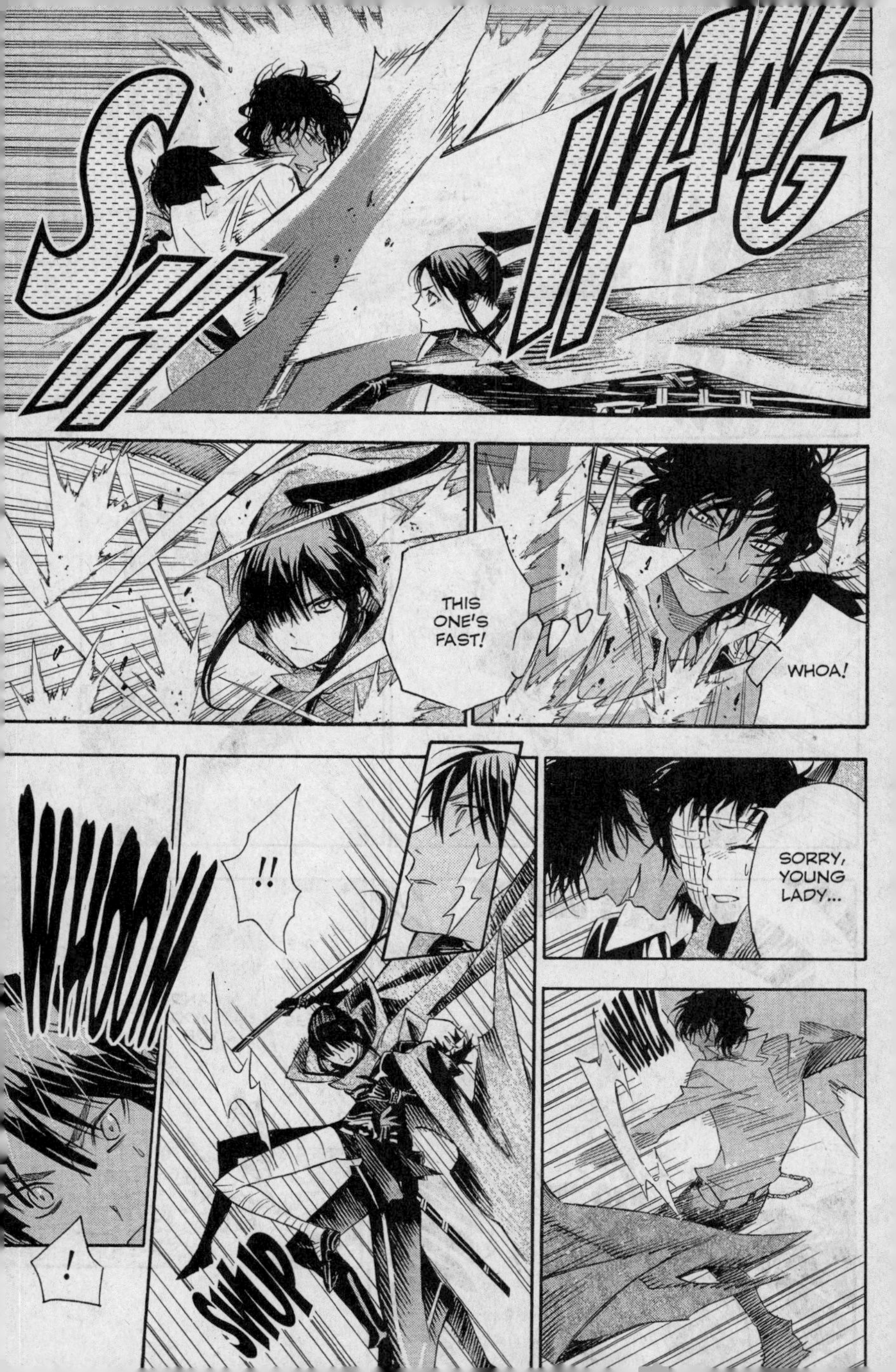
SHHANG
WHOA!
THIS ONE'S FAST!
SORRY, YOUNG LADY...
WHACK
!!
SWIP
WHOOM
!

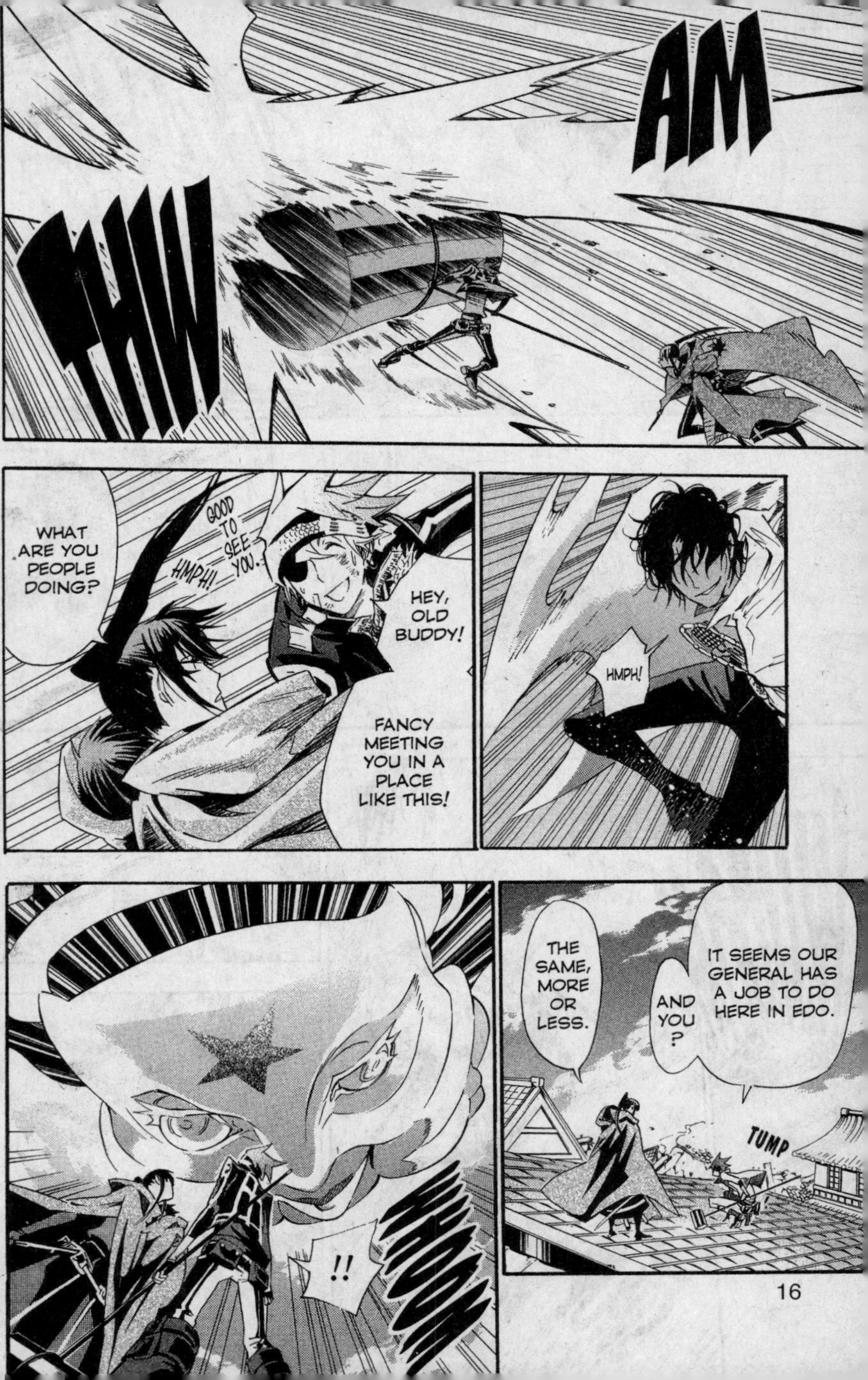
THWAM
HMPH!
GOOD TO SEE YOU.
HEY, OLD BUDDY!
HMPH!
WHAT ARE YOU PEOPLE DOING?
FANCY MEETING YOU IN A PLACE LIKE THIS!
IT SEEMS OUR GENERAL HAS A JOB TO DO HERE IN EDO.
AND YOU?
THE SAME, MORE OR LESS.
TUMP
!!

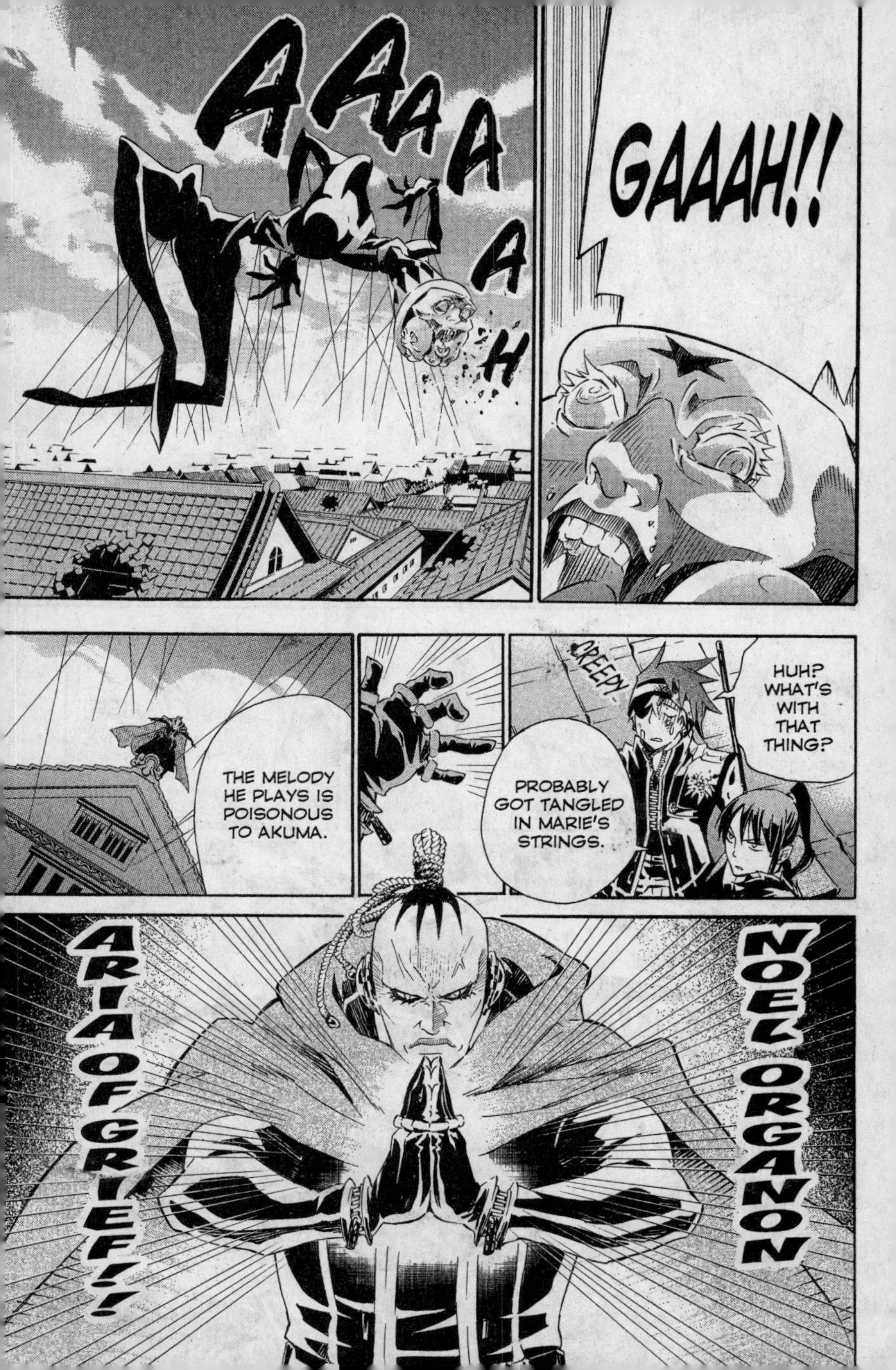

GAAAH!!
AAAAAH
HUH? WHAT'S WITH THAT THING?
CREEPY
PROBABLY GOT TANGLED IN MARIE'S STRINGS.
THE MELODY HE PLAYS IS POISONOUS TO AKUMA.
NOEL ORGANON
ARIA OF GRIEF!!

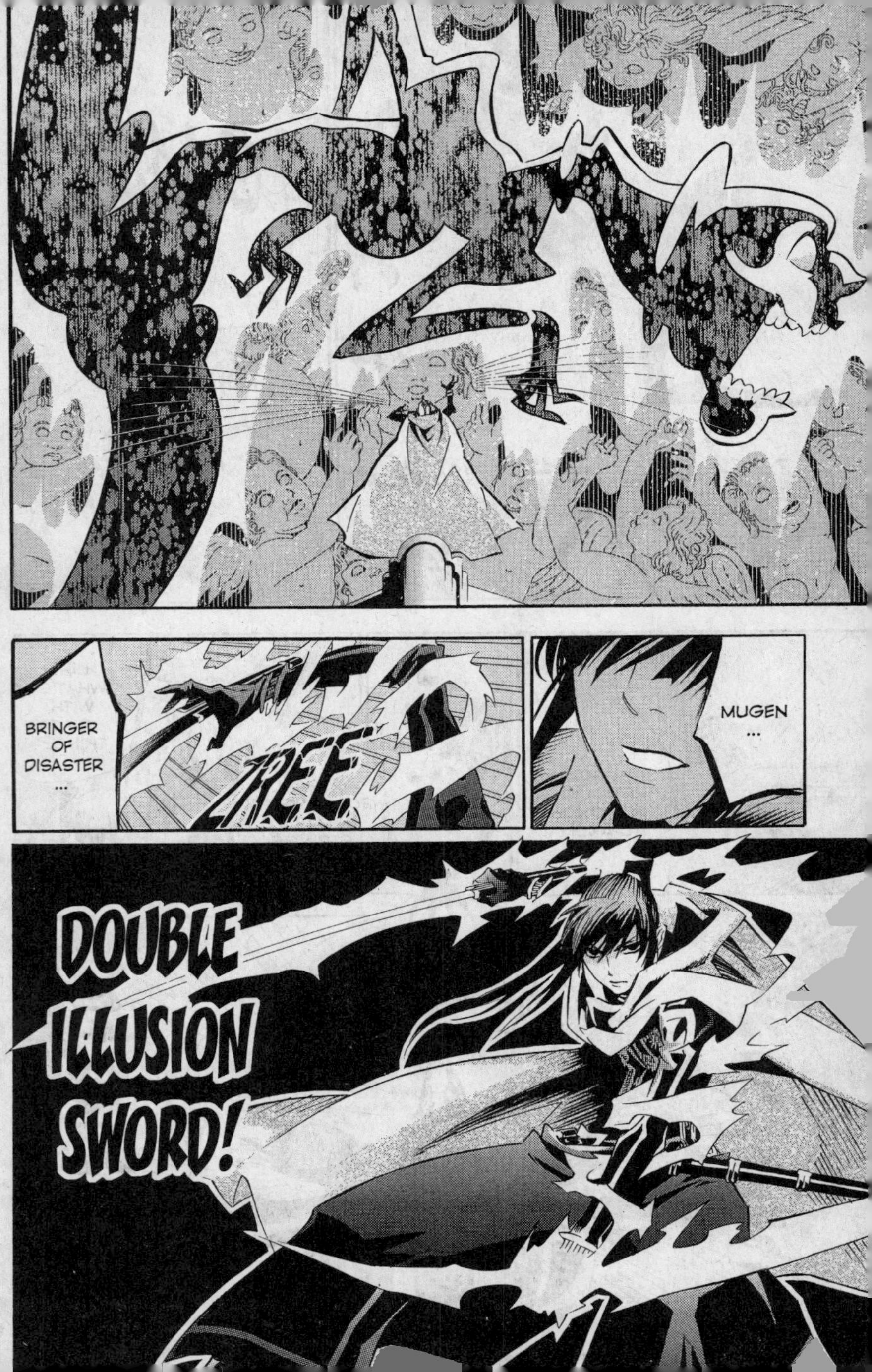
MUGEN ...
BRINGER OF DISASTER ...
DOUBLE ILLUSION SWORD!

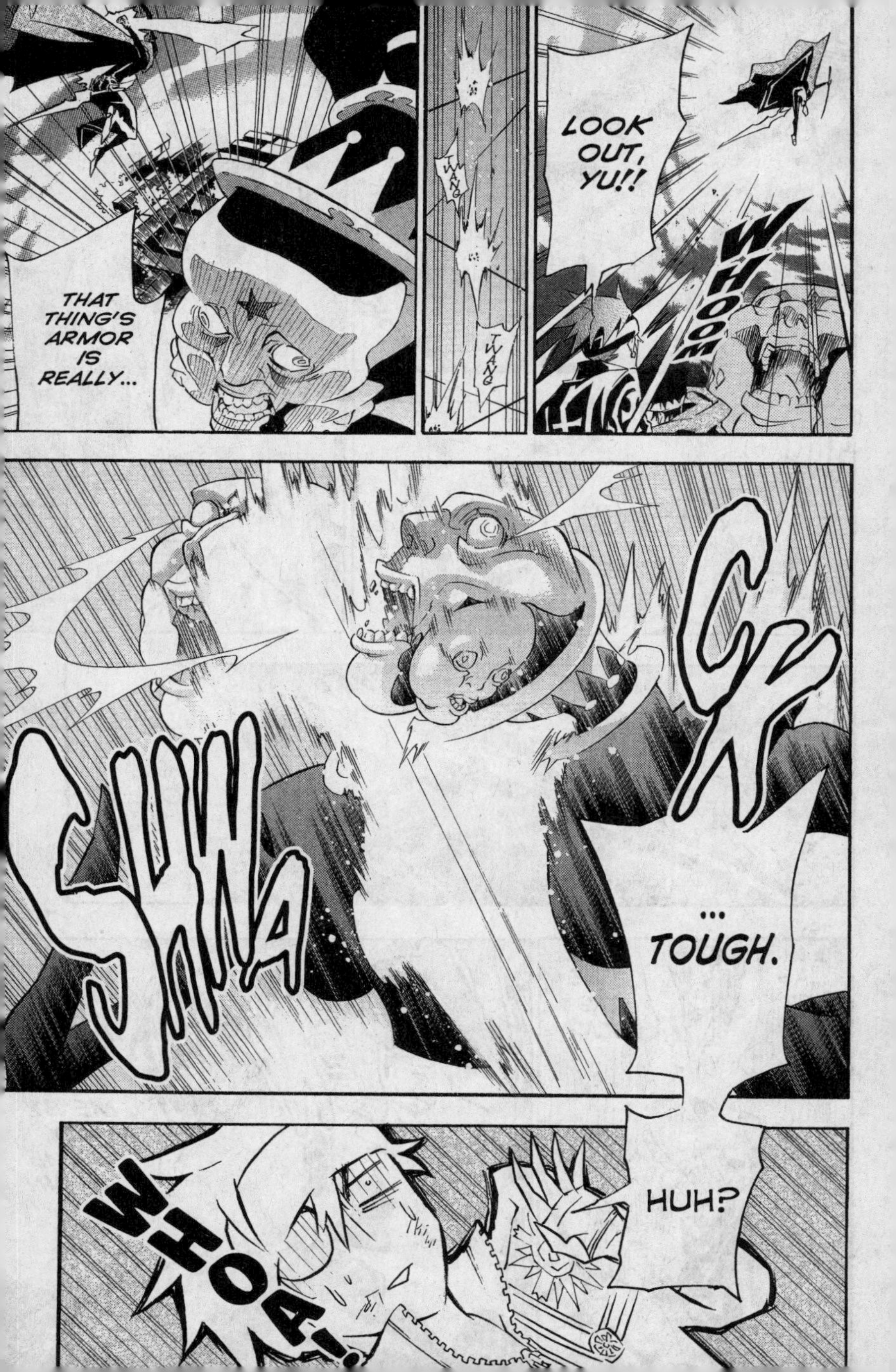
LOOK OUT, YU!!
WHOOOM
TWANG
TWANG
THAT THING'S ARMOR IS REALLY...
... TOUGH.
HUH?
WHOA!!

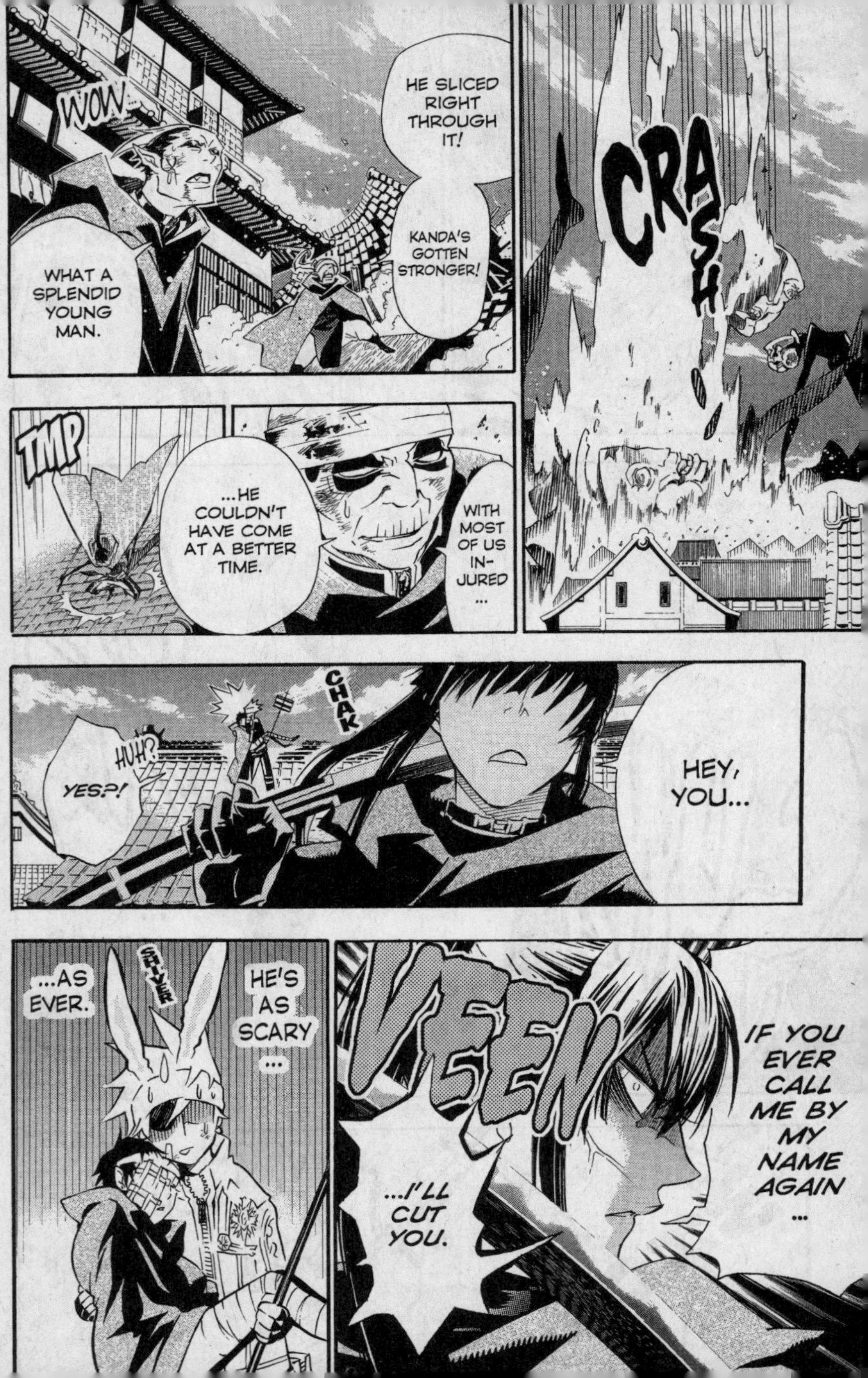
CRASH
HE SLICED RIGHT THROUGH IT!
KANDA'S GOTTEN STRONGER!
WOW...
WHAT A SPLENDID YOUNG MAN.
WITH MOST OF US IN-JURED...
...HE COULDN'T HAVE COME AT A BETTER TIME.
TMP
HEY, YOU...
CHAK
HUH?
YES?!
VEEN
IF YOU EVER CALL ME BY MY NAME AGAIN...
...I'LL CUT YOU.
SHIVER
HE'S AS SCARY...
...AS EVER.

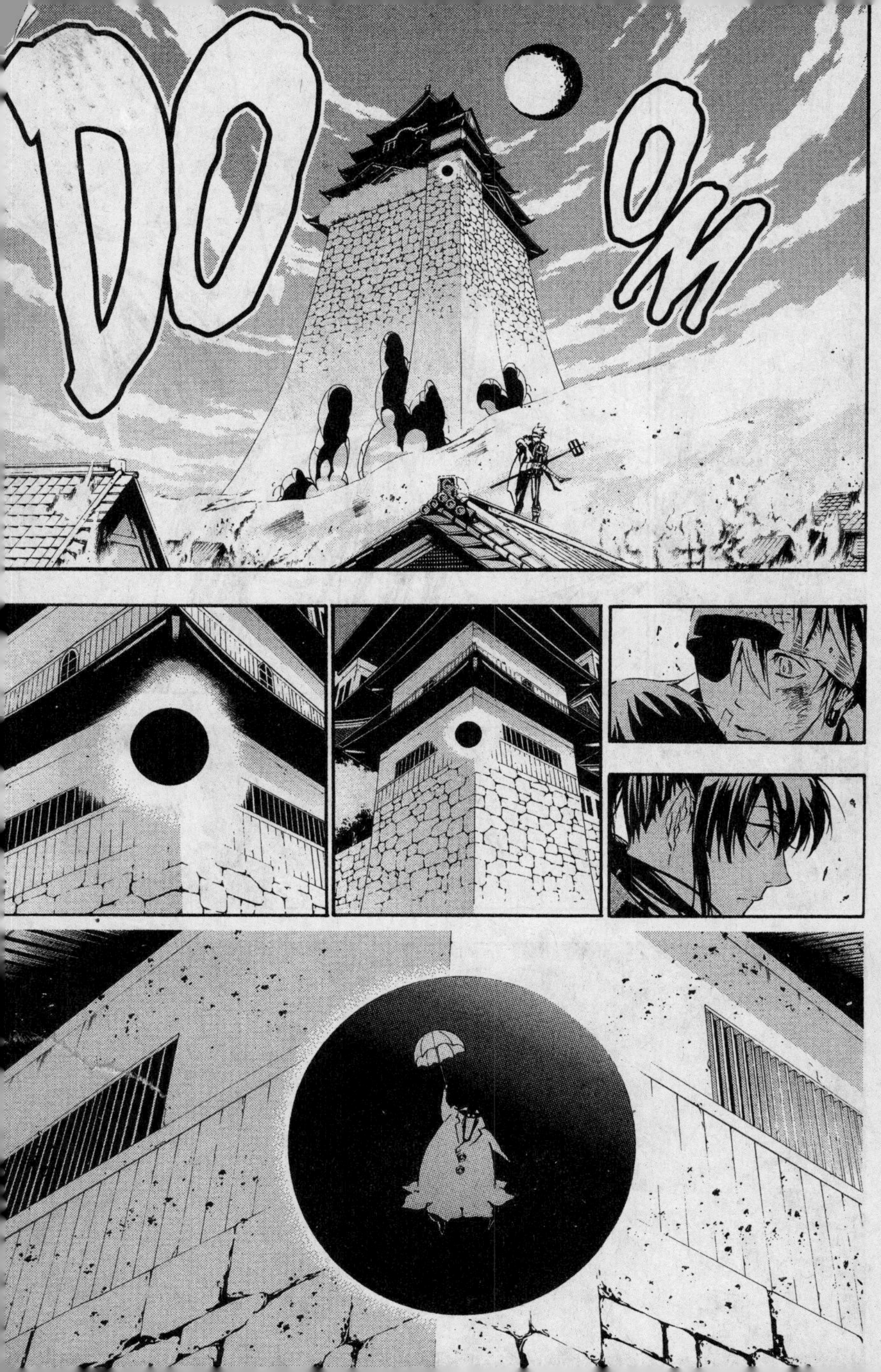
DOOM

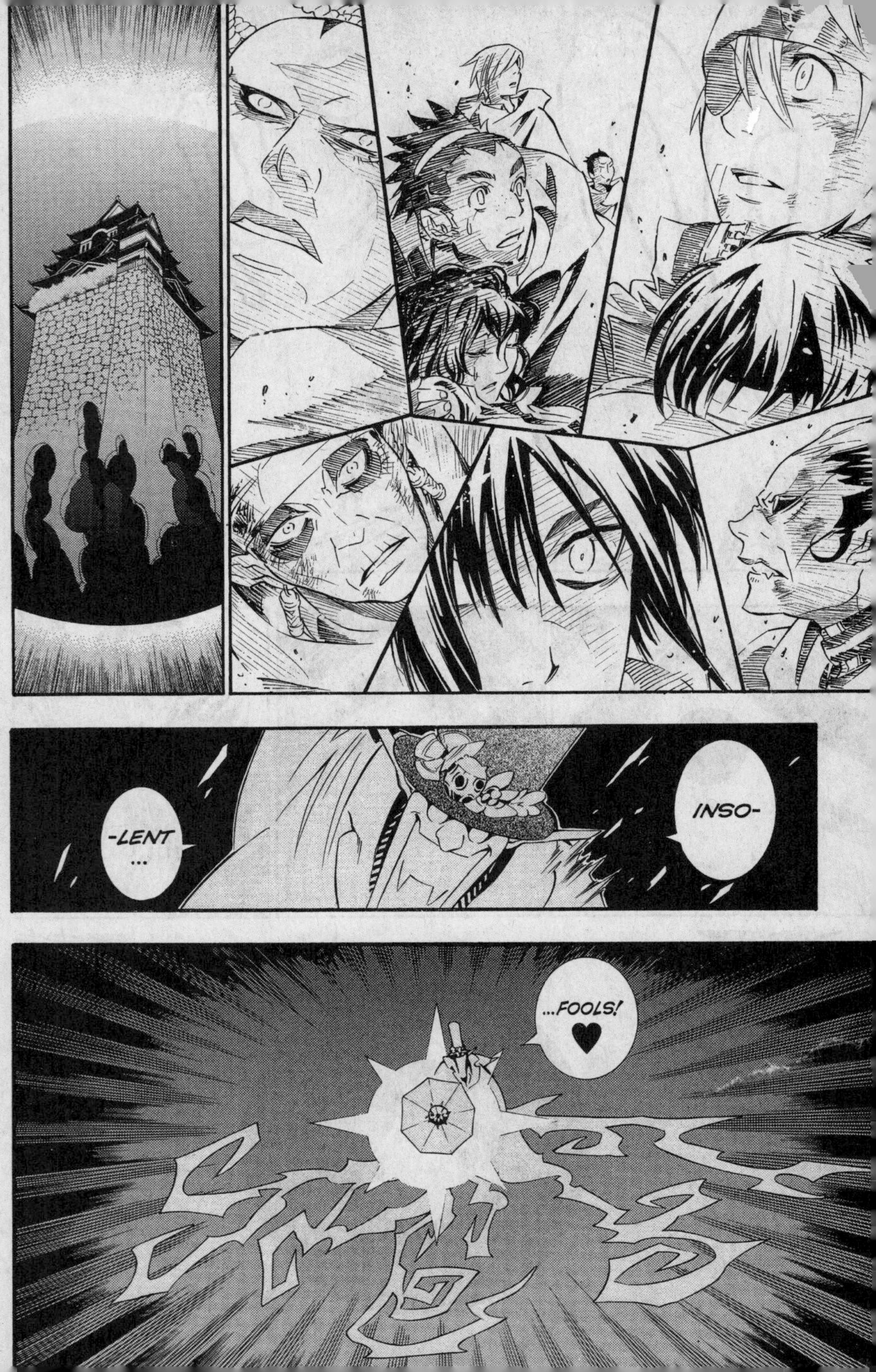
INSO-
-LENT ...
...FOOLS! ♥

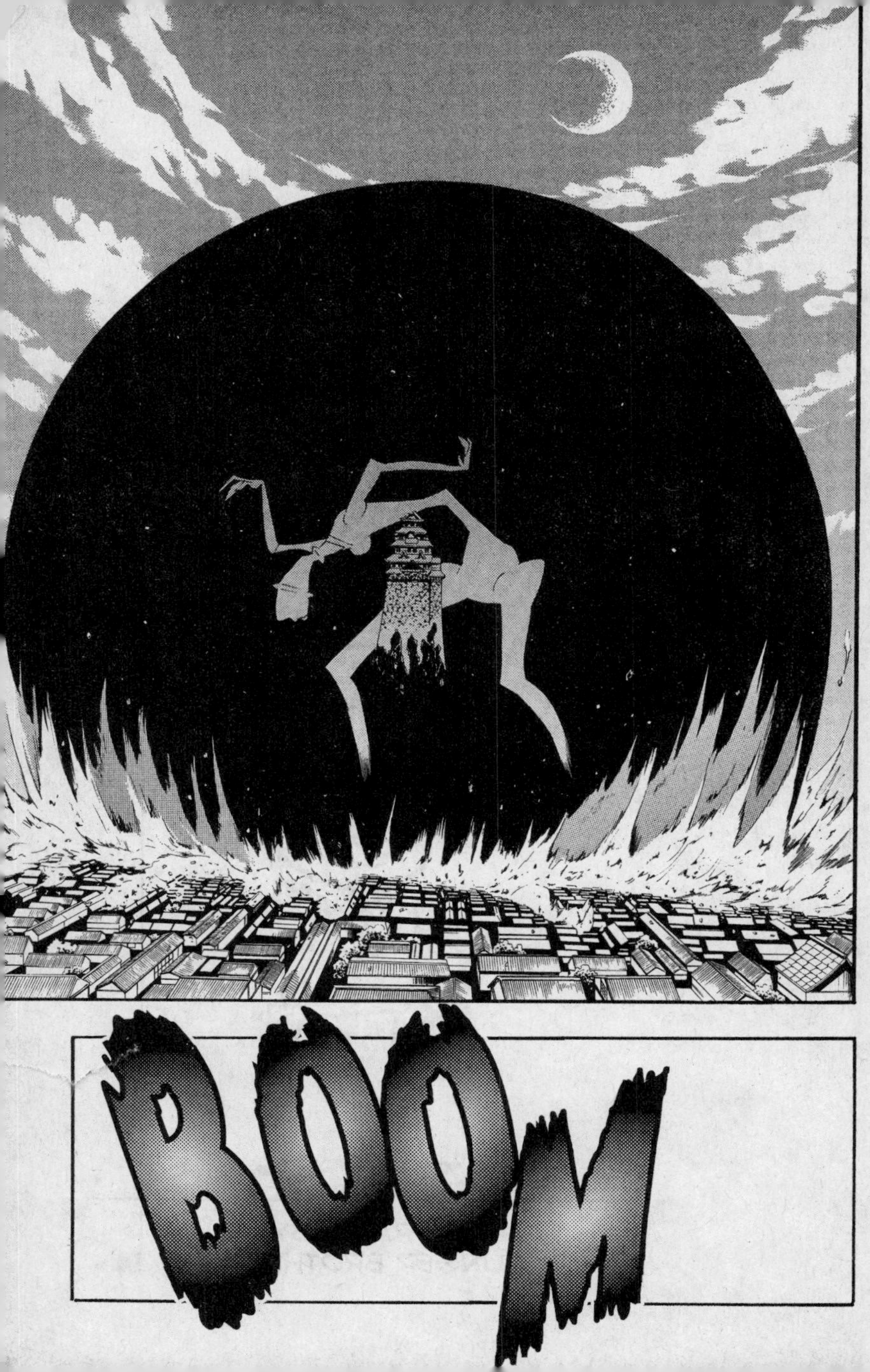
BOOM

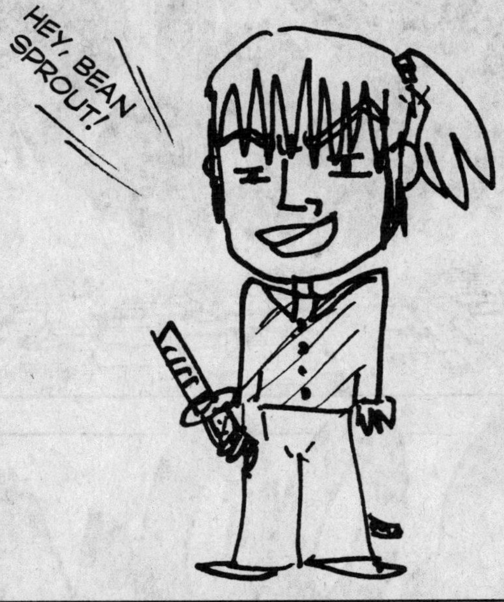
HEY, BEAN SPROUT!

KANDA (DRAWN BY MY YOUNGER BROTHER)

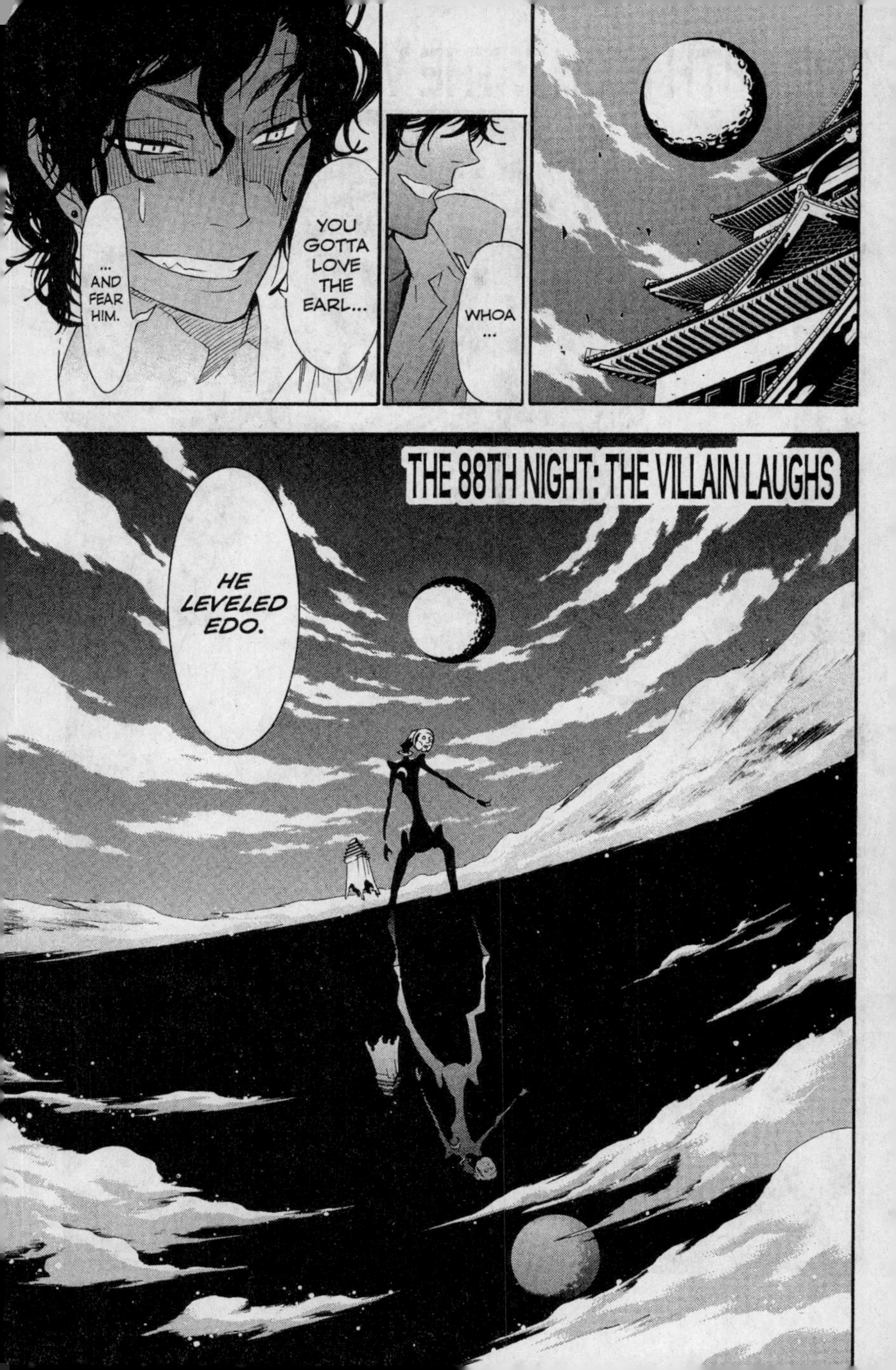
WHOA ...
YOU GOTTA LOVE THE EARL...
... AND FEAR HIM.
THE 88TH NIGHT: THE VILLAIN LAUGHS
HE LEVELED EDO.

THE 88TH NIGHT: THE VILLAIN LAUGHS

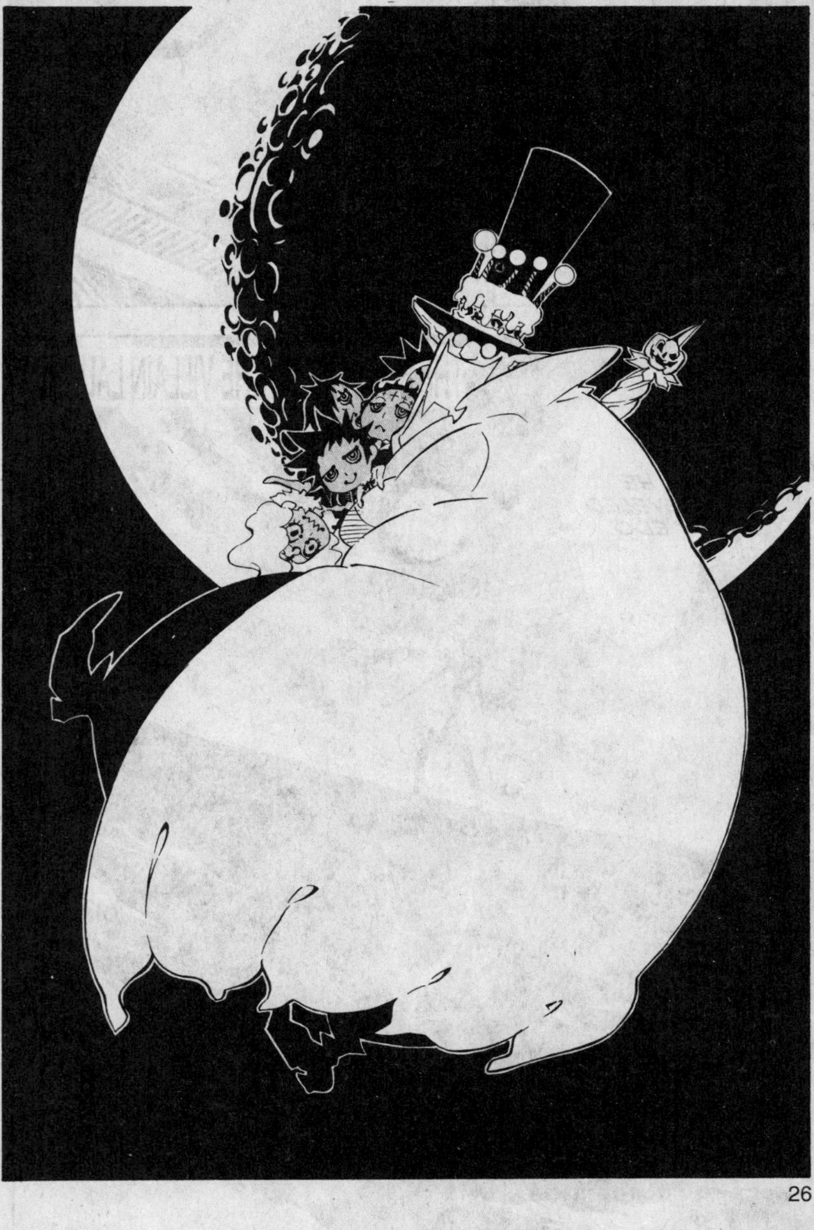

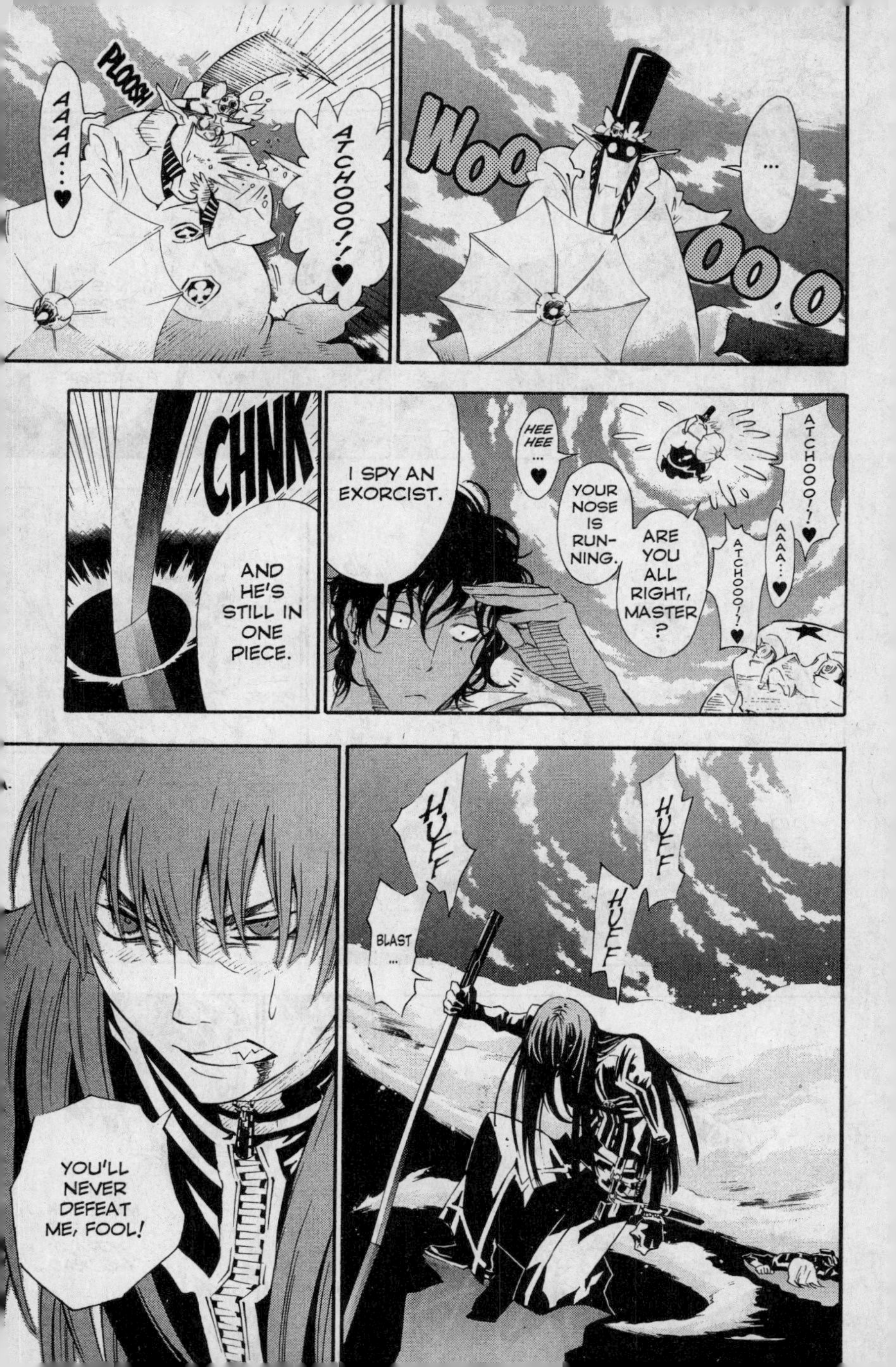
WOOOOO.O
...
PLOOSH
ATCHOOOO!!♥
AAAA...♥
ATCHOOO!!♥
AAAA...♥
ATCHOOO!!♥
ARE YOU ALL RIGHT, MASTER?
YOUR NOSE IS RUN-NING.
HEE HEE...♥
I SPY AN EXORCIST.
CHNK
AND HE'S STILL IN ONE PIECE.
HUFF
HUFF
HUFF
BLAST...
YOU'LL NEVER DEFEAT ME, FOOL!

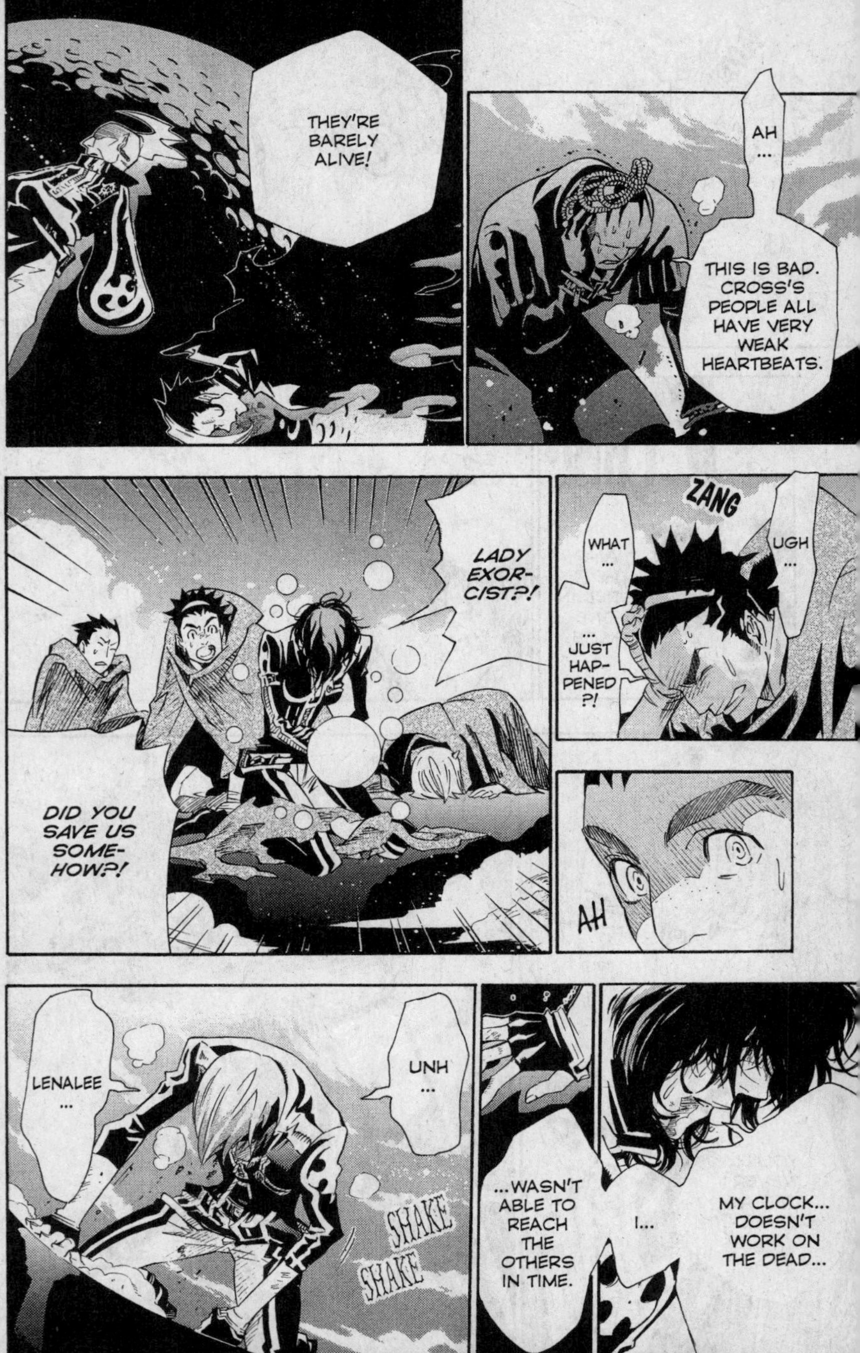
AH ...
THIS IS BAD. CROSS'S PEOPLE ALL HAVE VERY WEAK HEARTBEATS.
THEY'RE BARELY ALIVE!
ZANG
UGH ...
WHAT ...
... JUST HAPPENED ?!
AH
LADY EXORCIST?!
DID YOU SAVE US SOMEHOW?!
MY CLOCK... DOESN'T WORK ON THE DEAD...
I...
...WASN'T ABLE TO REACH THE OTHERS IN TIME.
UNH ...
LENALEE ...
SHAKE
SHAKE

LAVI...

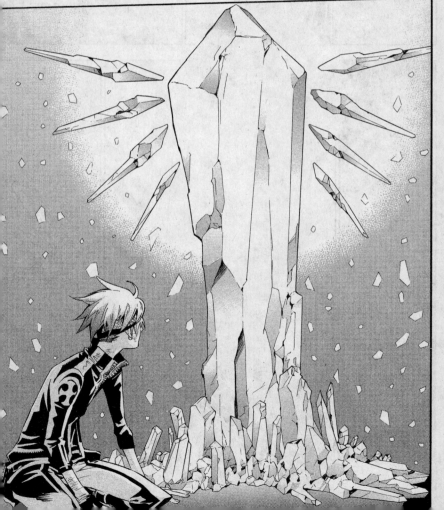

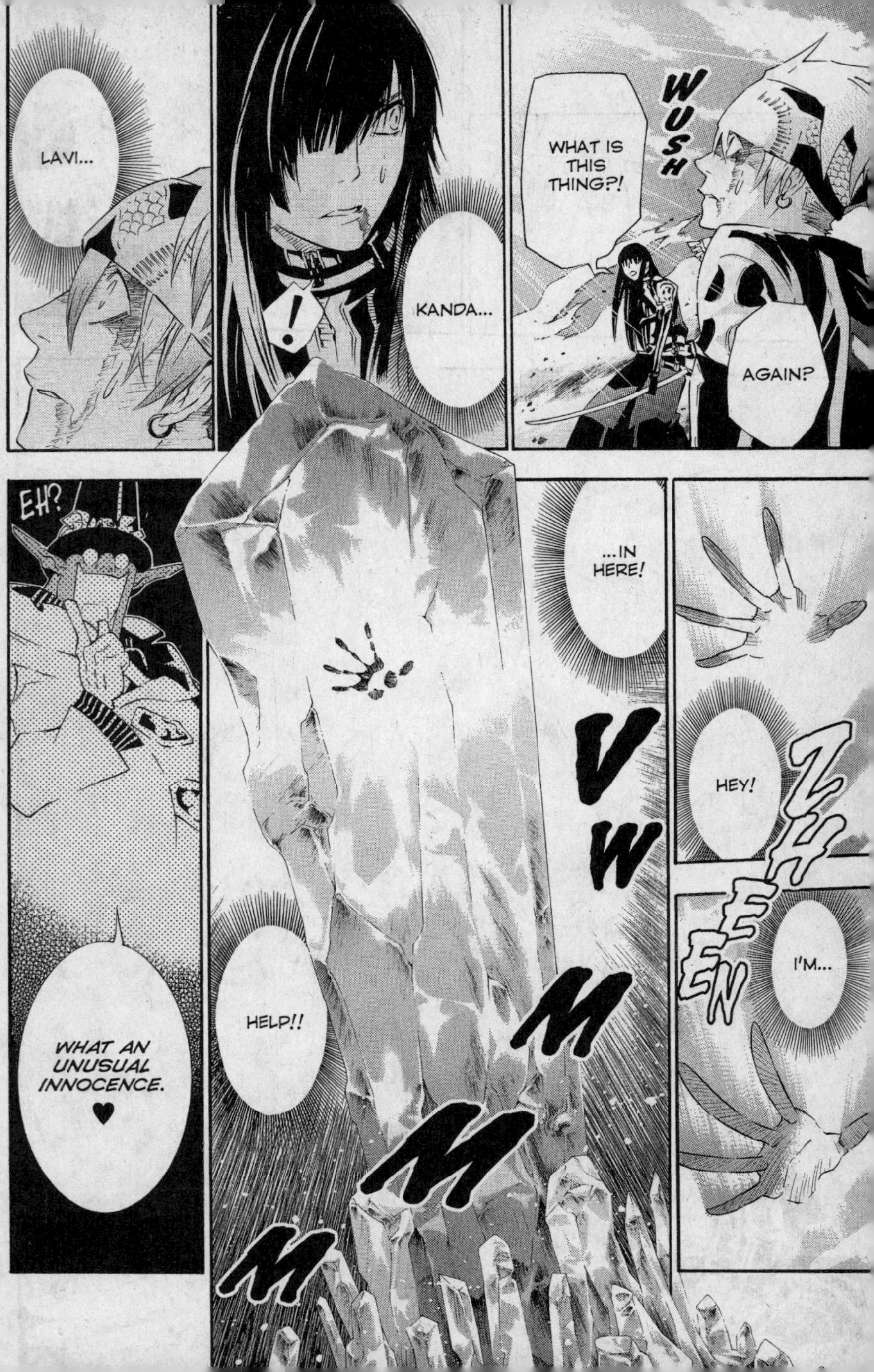
WUSH
WHAT IS THIS THING?!
AGAIN?
KANDA...
!
LAVI...
HEY!
ZHEEEN
I'M...
...IN HERE!
VWMMM
HELP!!
EH?
WHAT AN UNUSUAL INNOCENCE. ♥

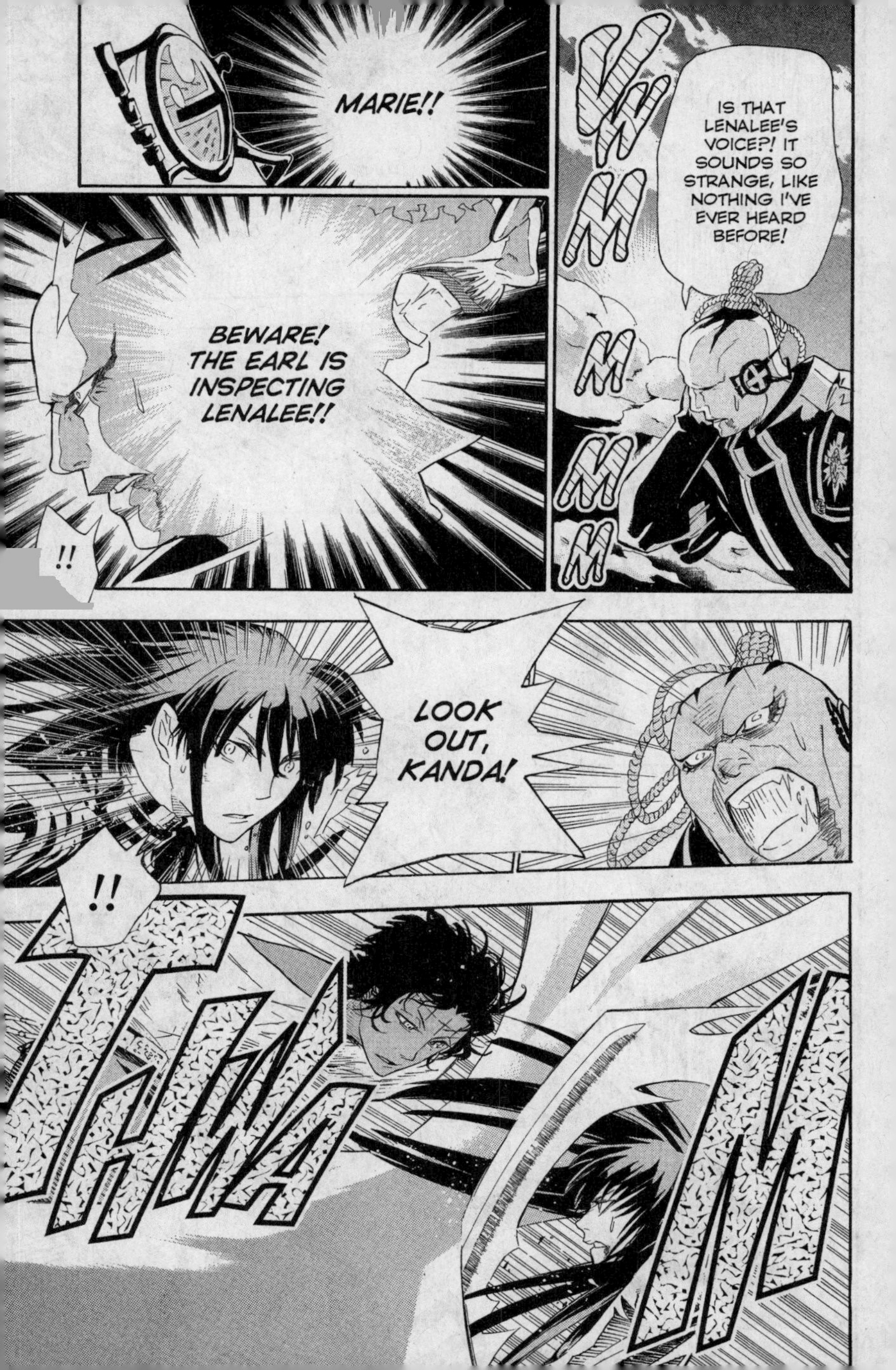
VMMMMMM
IS THAT LENALEE'S VOICE?! IT SOUNDS SO STRANGE, LIKE NOTHING I'VE EVER HEARD BEFORE!
MARIE!!
BEWARE! THE EARL IS INSPECTING LENALEE!!
!!
LOOK OUT, KANDA!
!!
THWAM

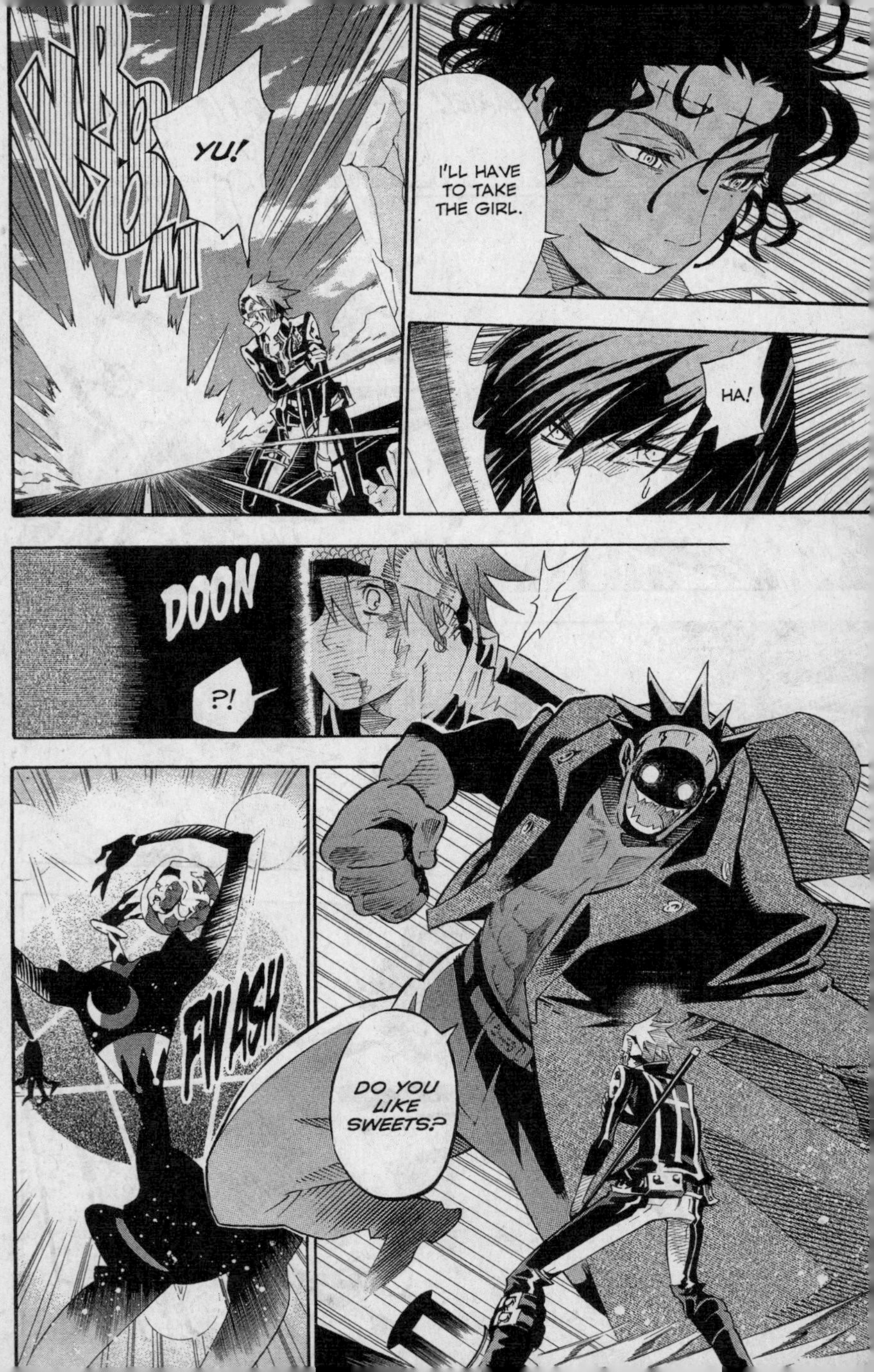

I'LL HAVE TO TAKE THE GIRL.
HA!
YU!
DOON
?!
DO YOU LIKE SWEETS?
FWASH

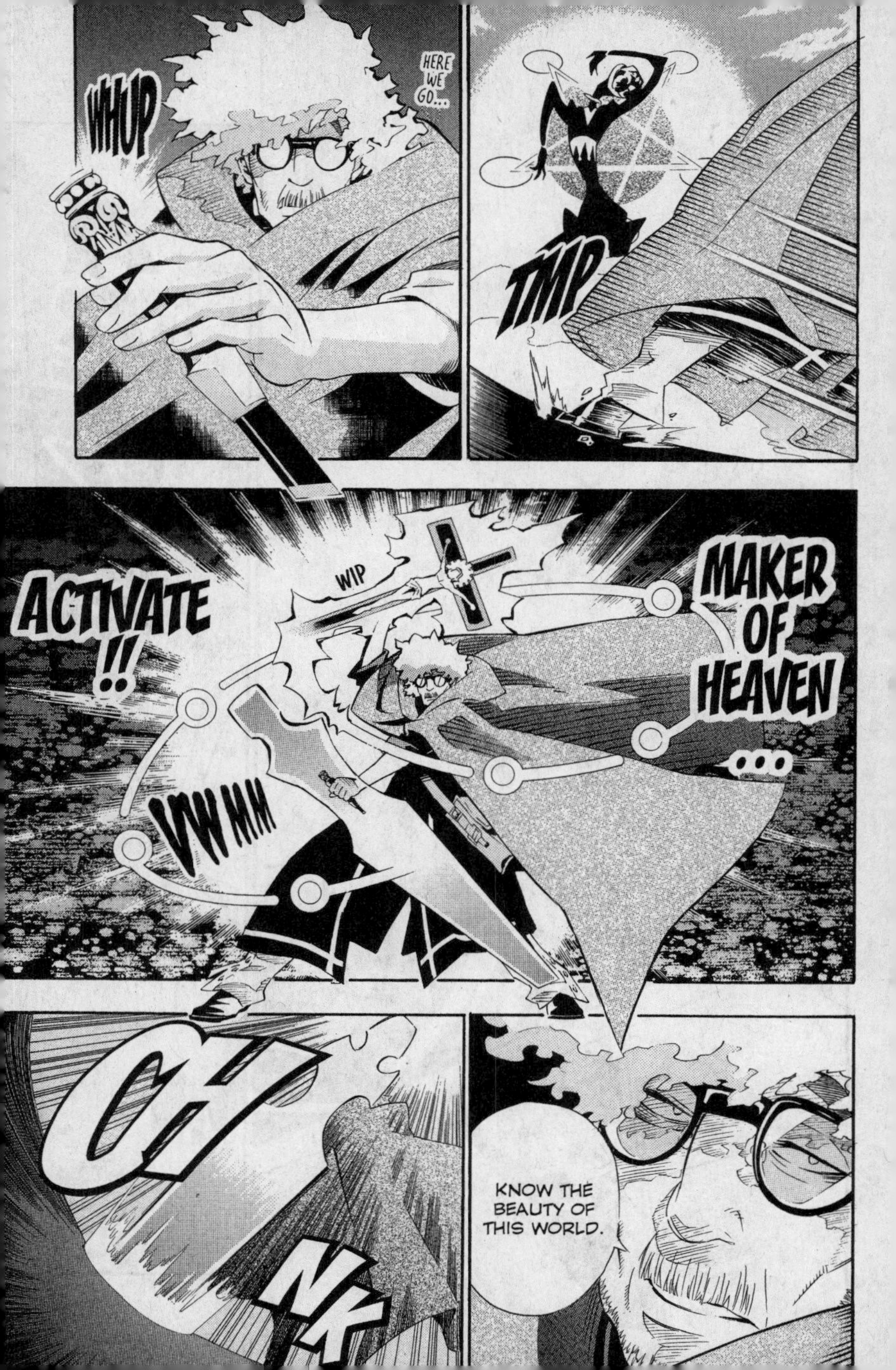
TMP
HERE WE GO...
WHUP
MAKER OF HEAVEN
...
WIP
ACTIVATE !!
VWMM
KNOW THE BEAUTY OF THIS WORLD.
CL
NK

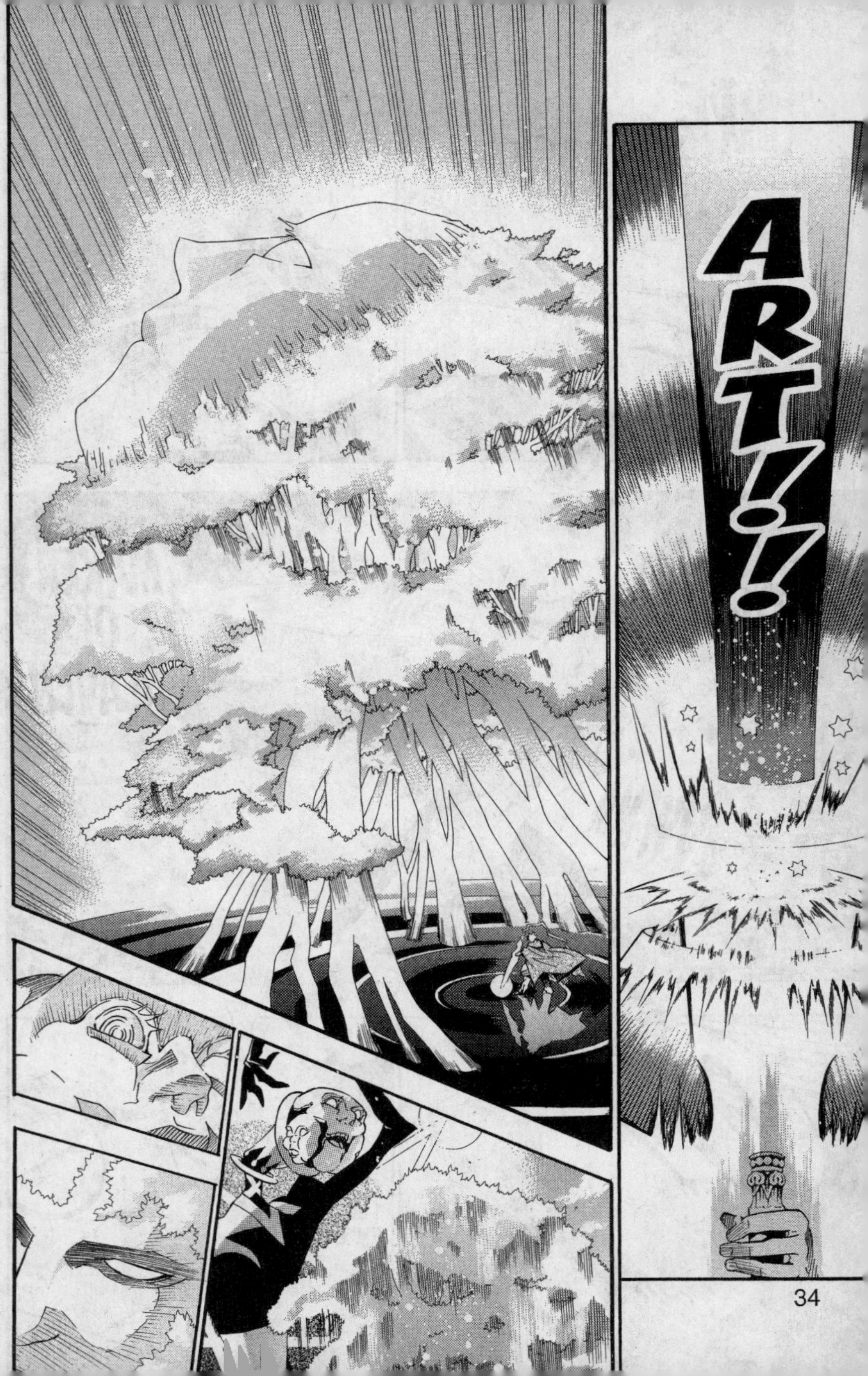

ARTIO!

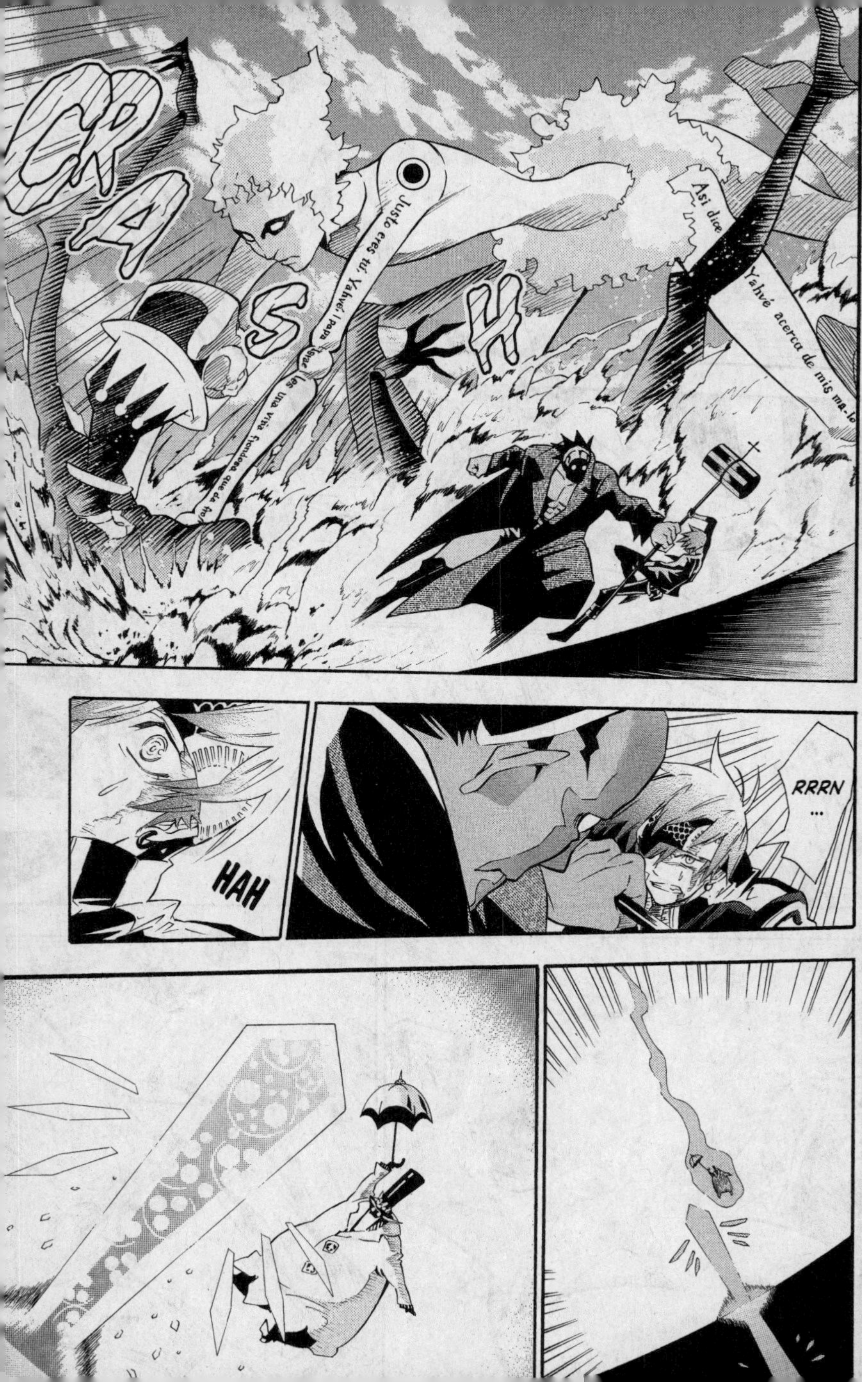

Así dice
Yahvé acerca de mis ma-lo
Justo eres tú, Yahvé! ¡Papá
les una viña frondosa que da
CRASH
RRRN ...
HAH

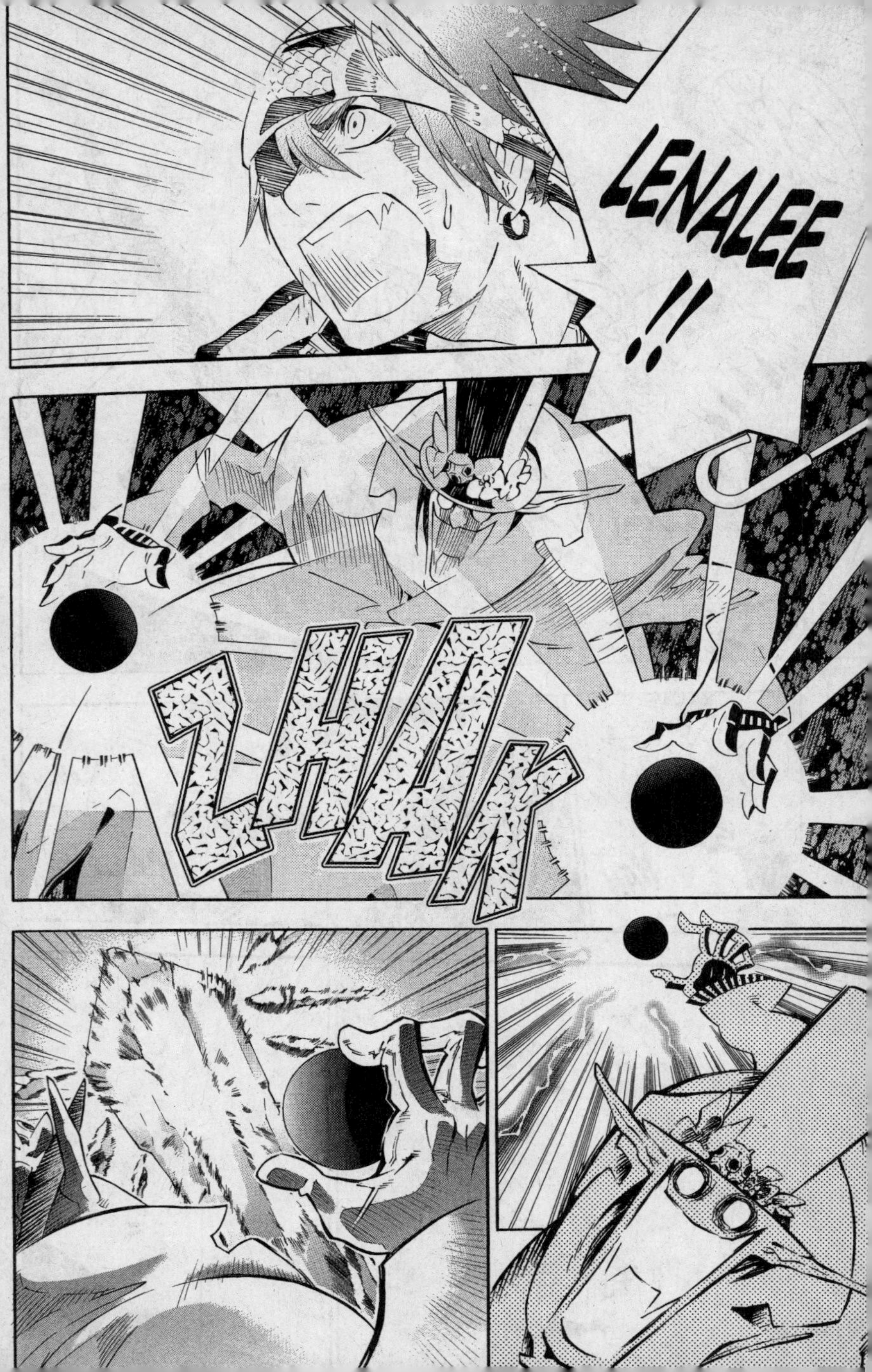
LENALEE!!
ZHAK

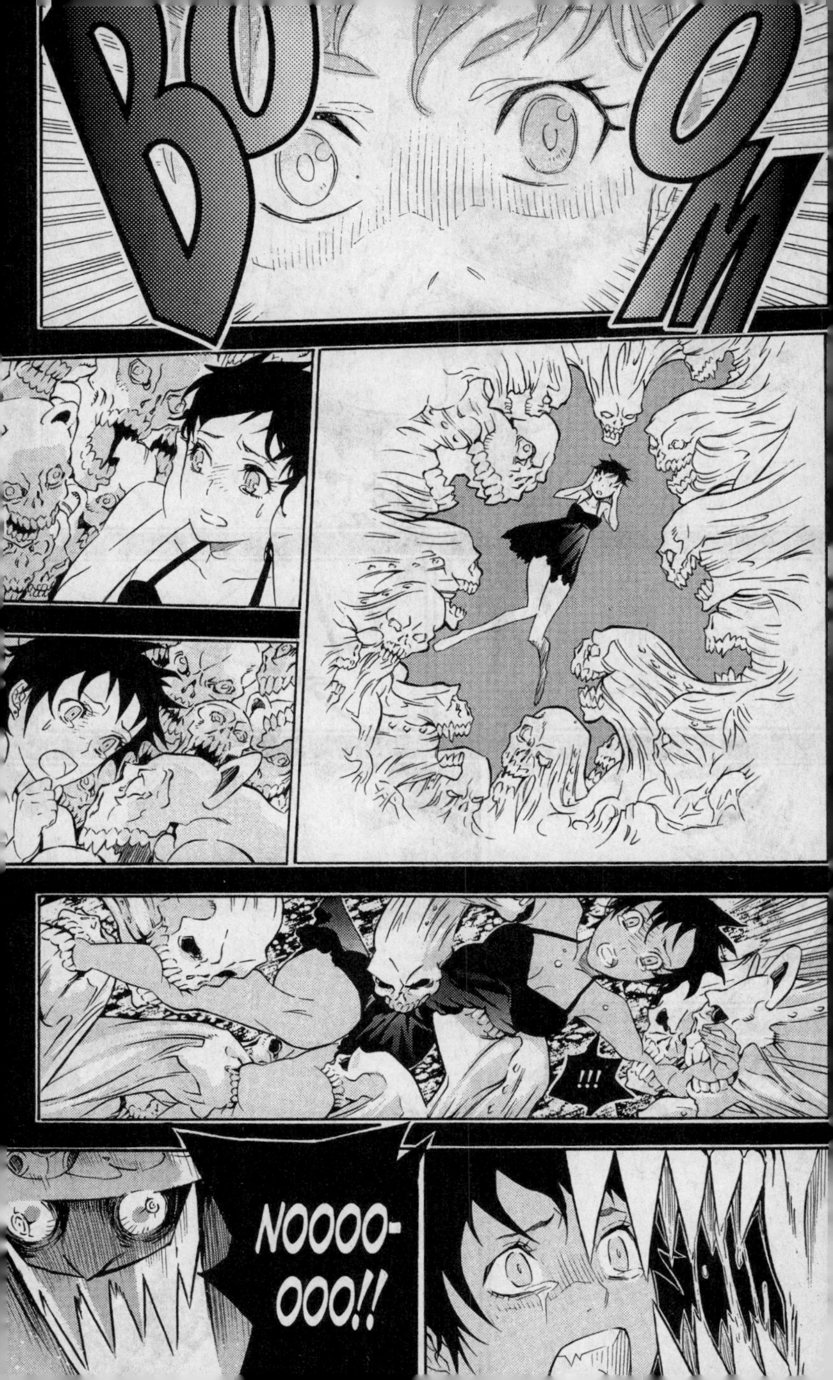
BOOM
!!!
NOOOO-OOO!!

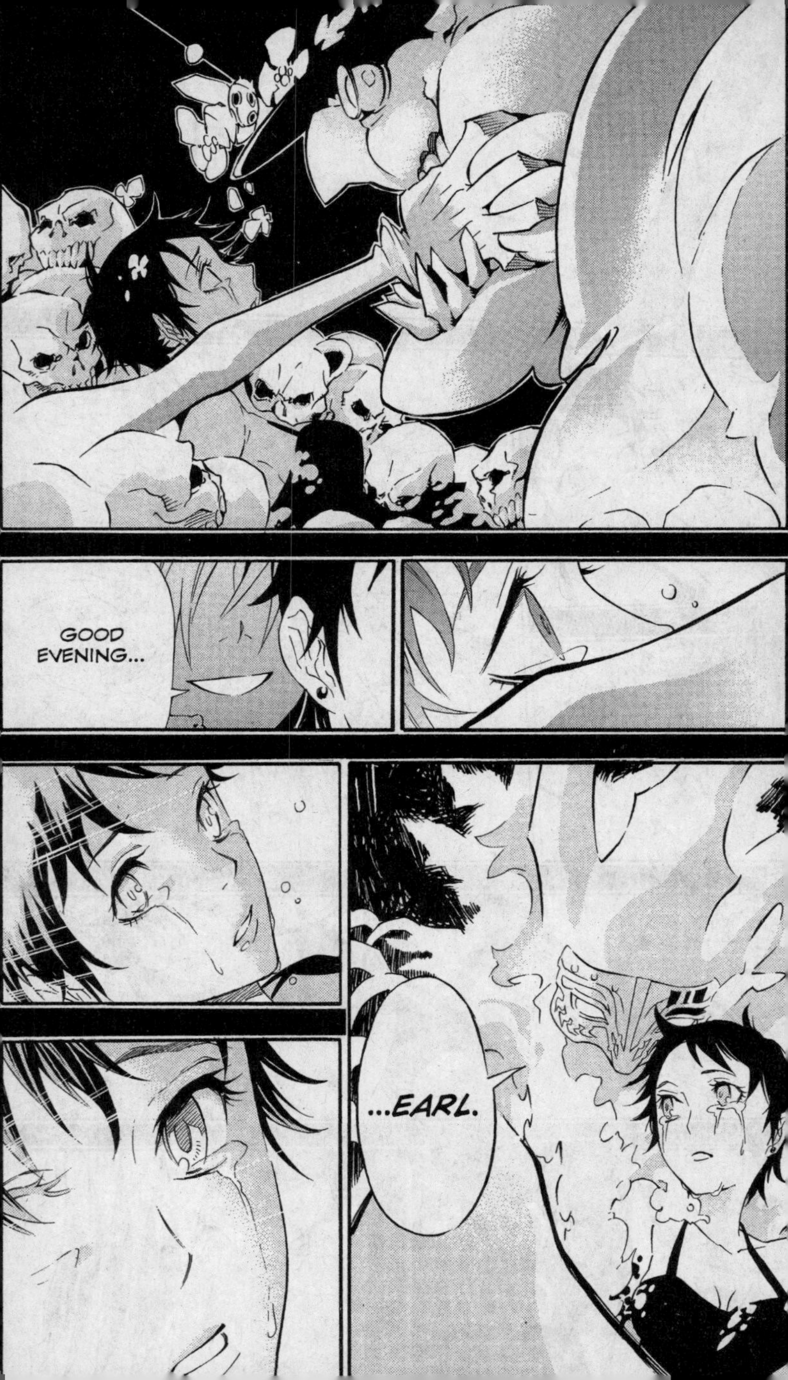
GOOD EVENING...
...EARL.

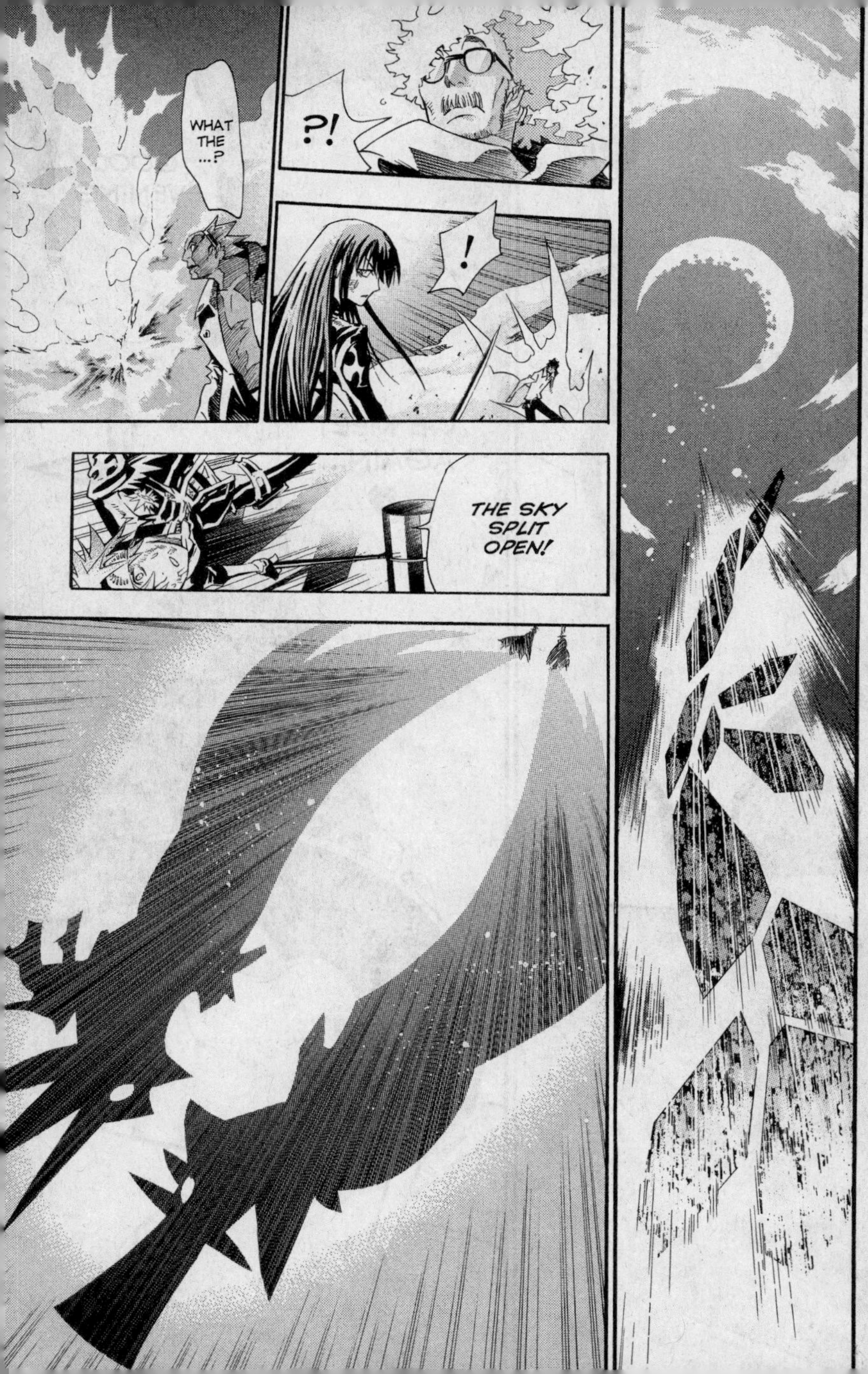
?!
!
WHAT THE ...?
THE SKY SPLIT OPEN!

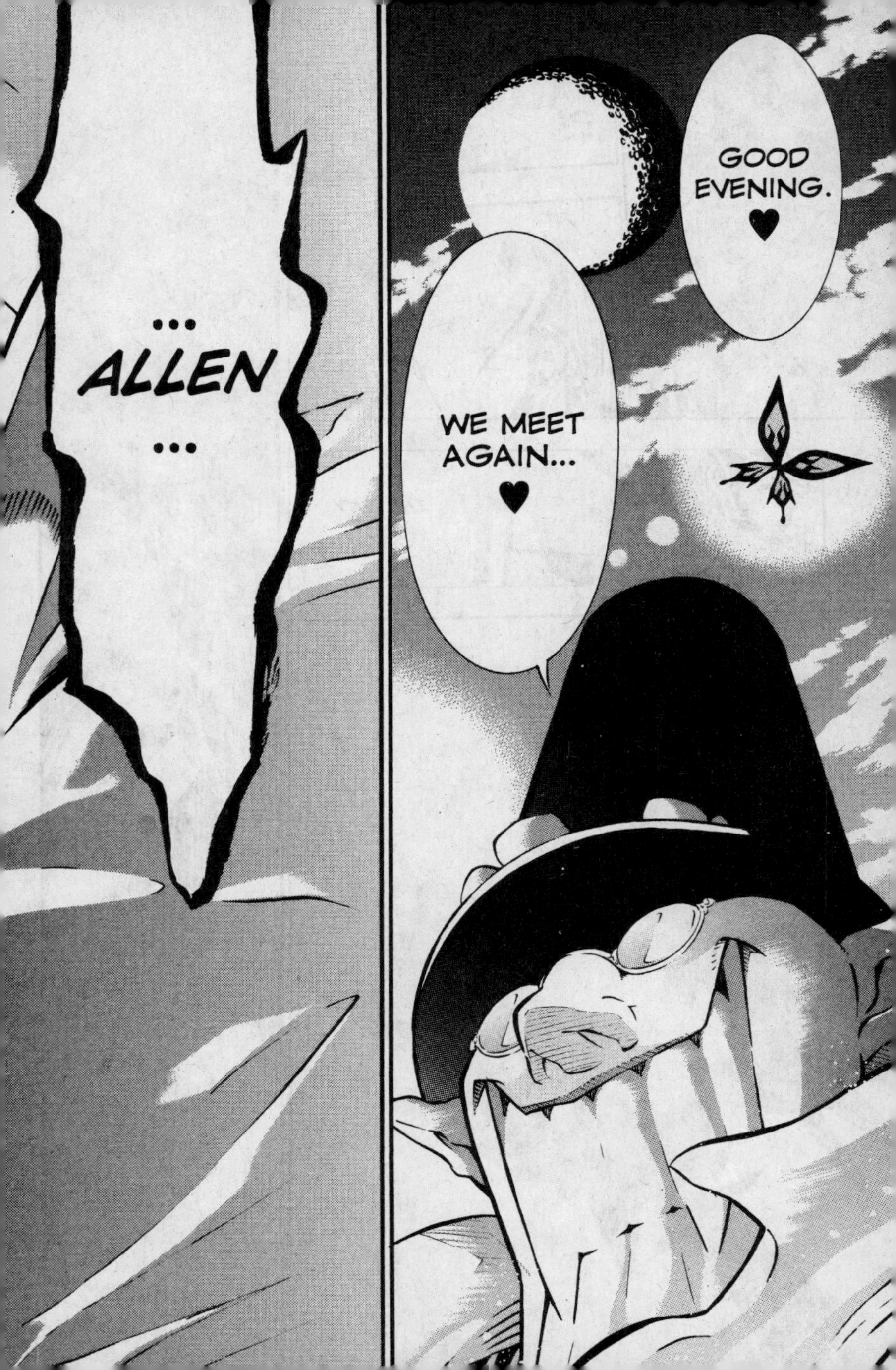
GOOD EVENING. ♥
WE MEET AGAIN... ♥
...ALLEN...

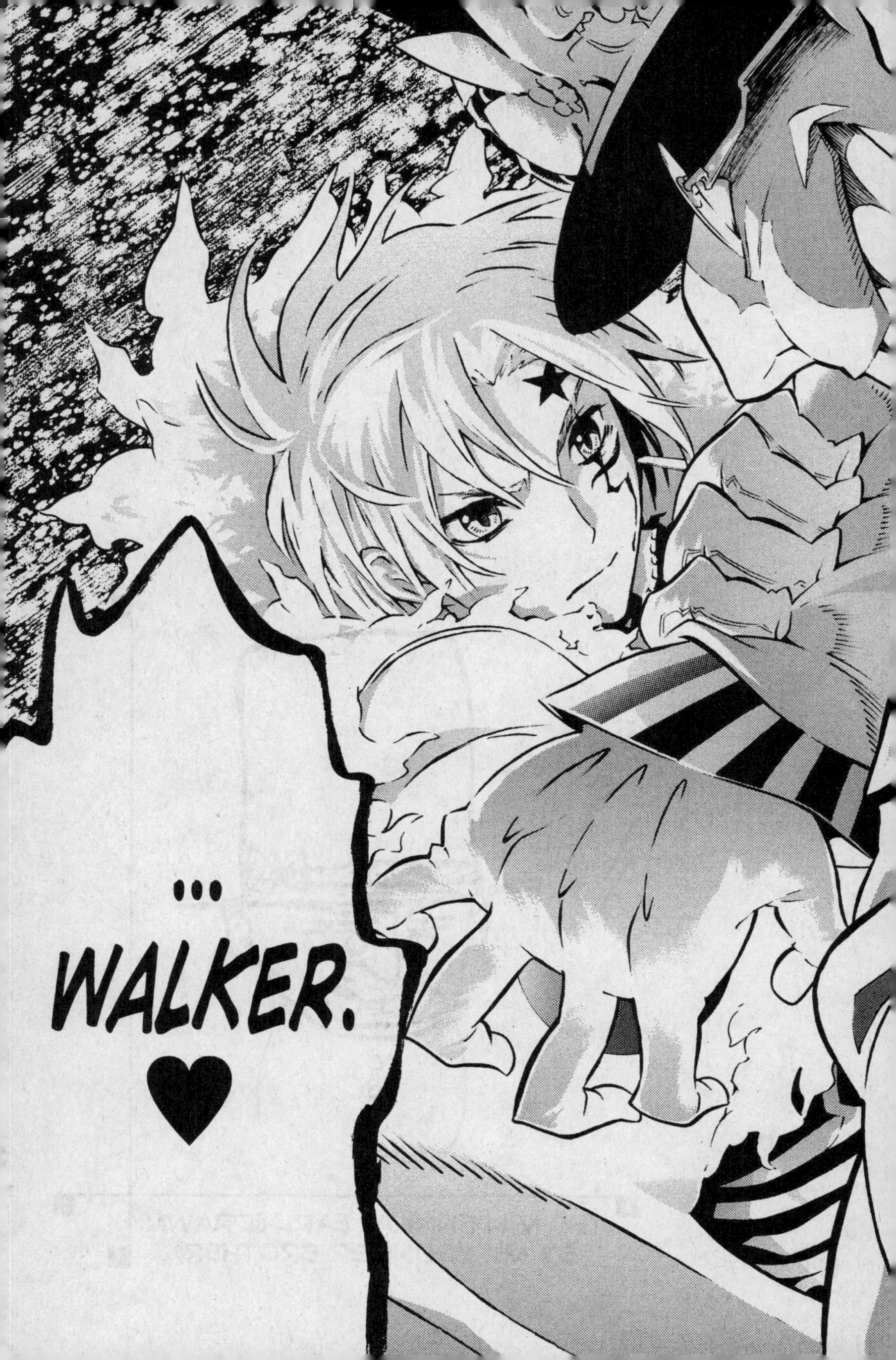
...
WALKER.
♥

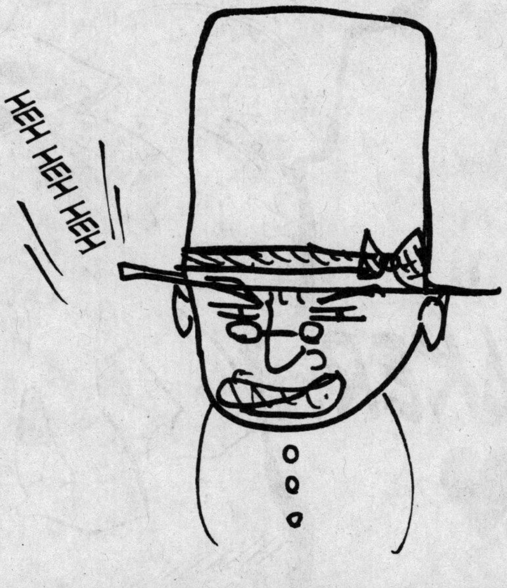
HEH HEH HEH

THE MILLENNIUM EARL (DRAWN BY MY YOUNGER BROTHER)

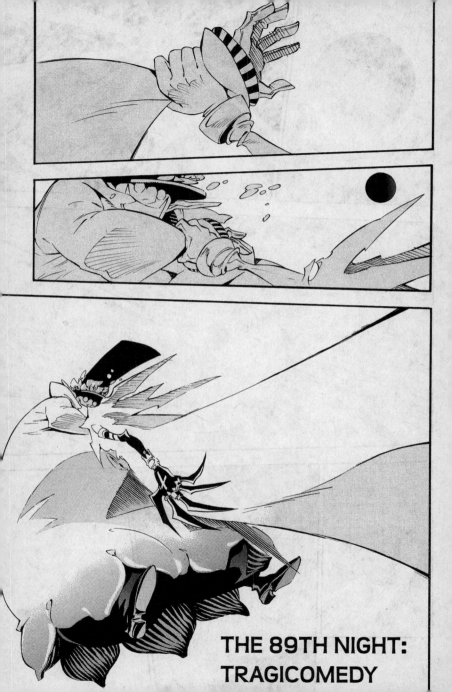

THE 89TH NIGHT:
TRAGICOMEDY

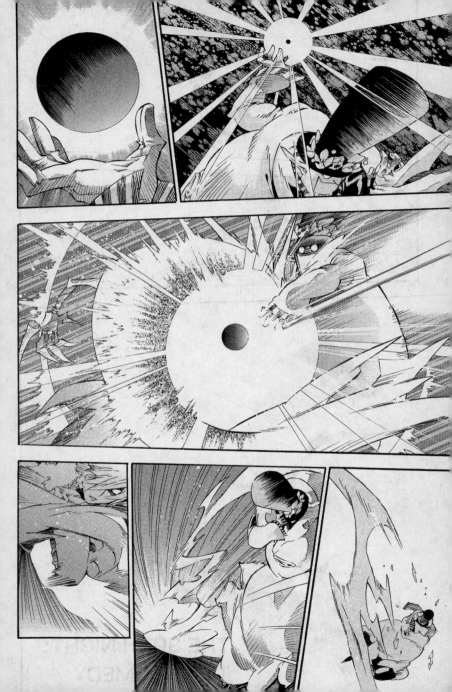

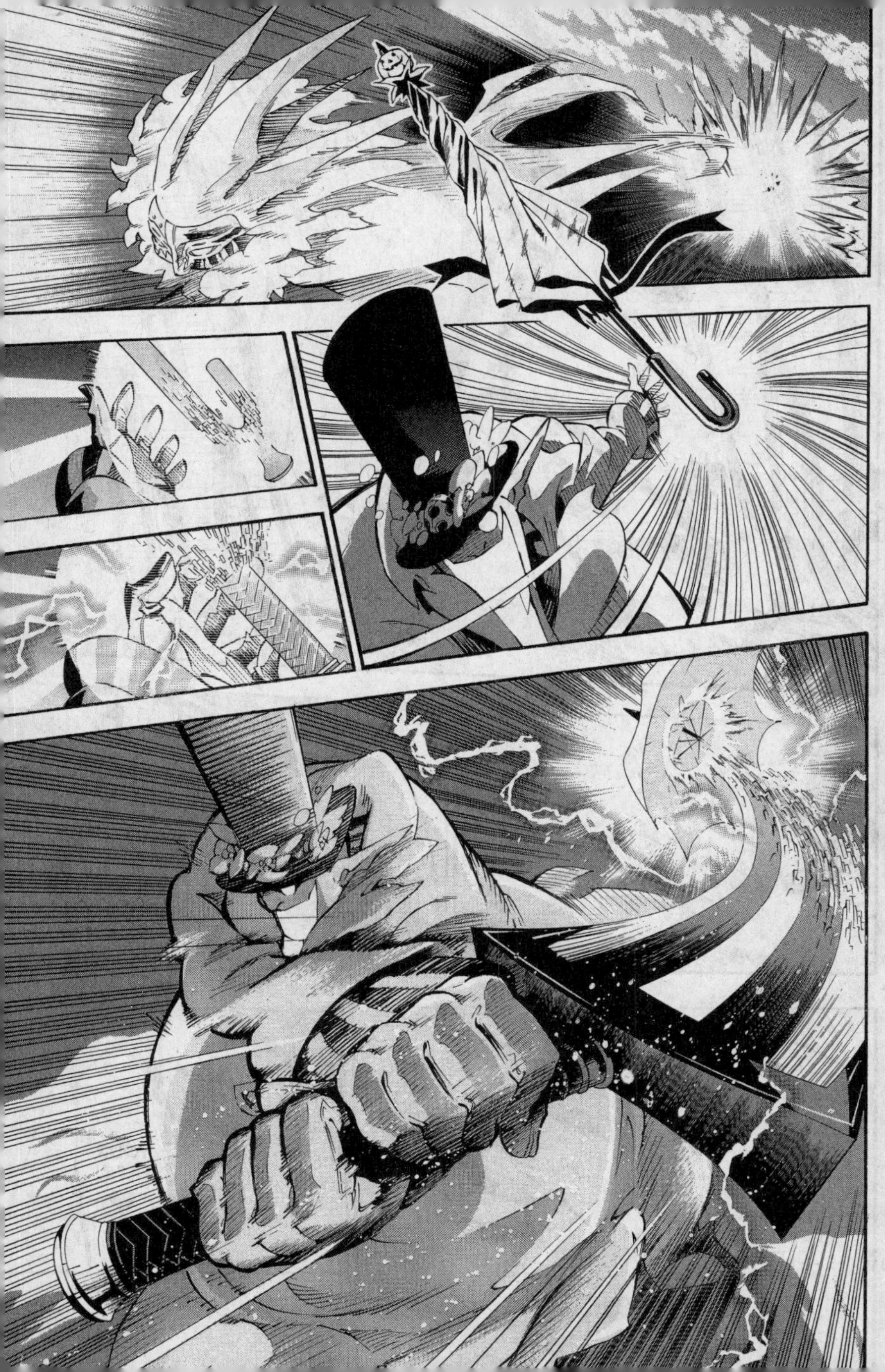

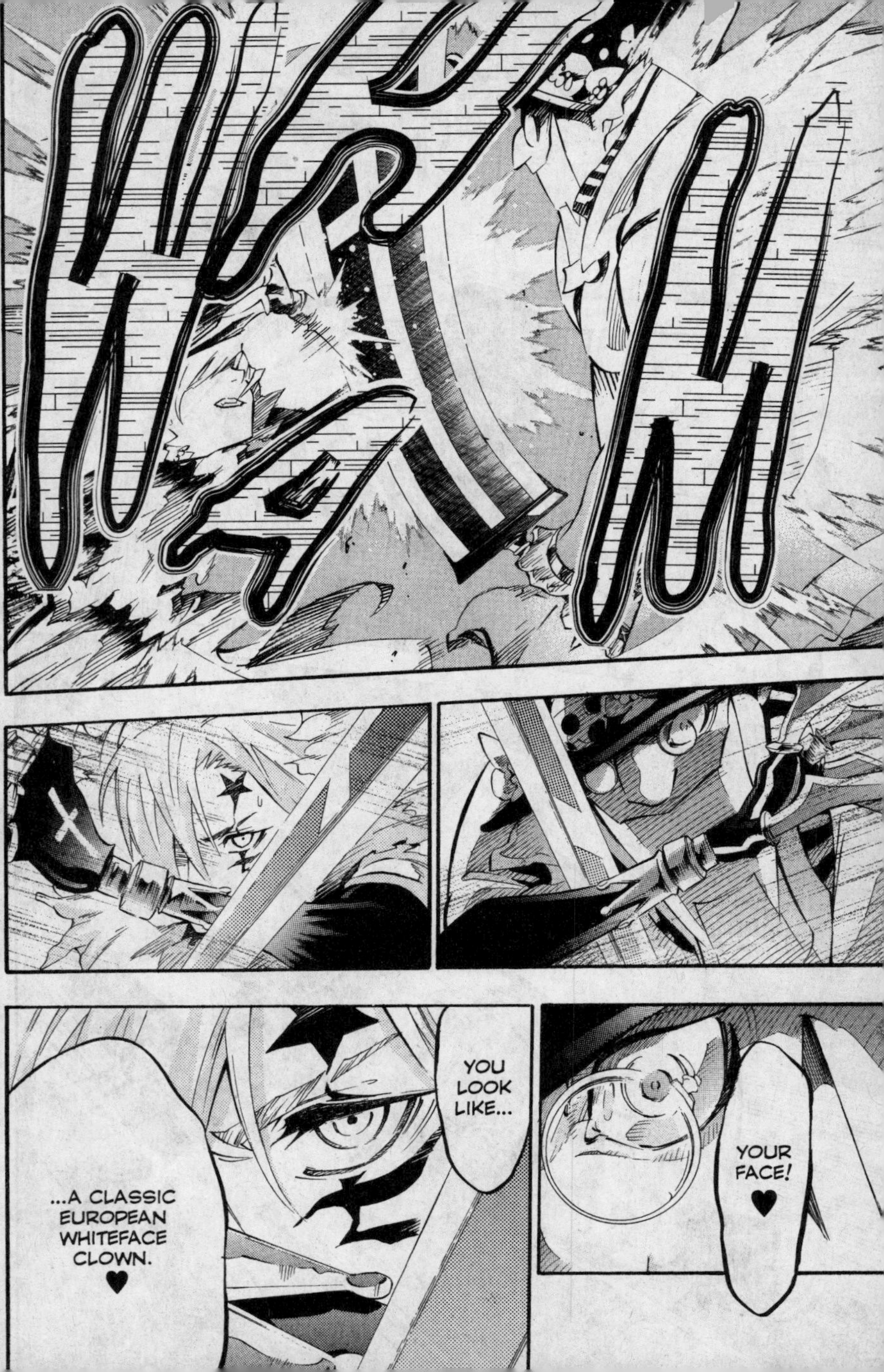
YOUR FACE! ♥
YOU LOOK LIKE...
...A CLASSIC EUROPEAN WHITEFACE CLOWN. ♥

THE 89TH NIGHT: TRAGICOMEDY

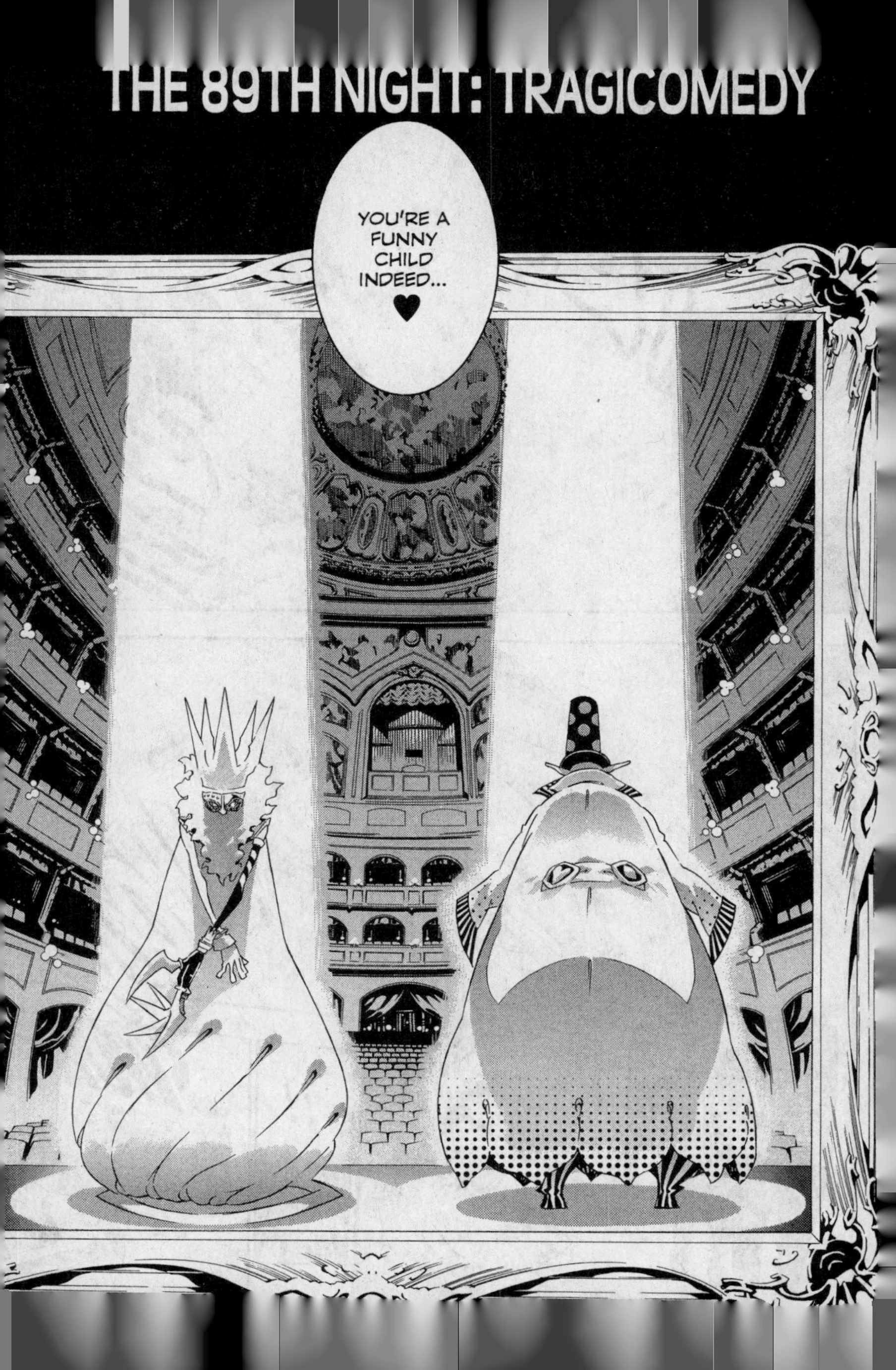
YOU'RE A FUNNY CHILD INDEED... ♥

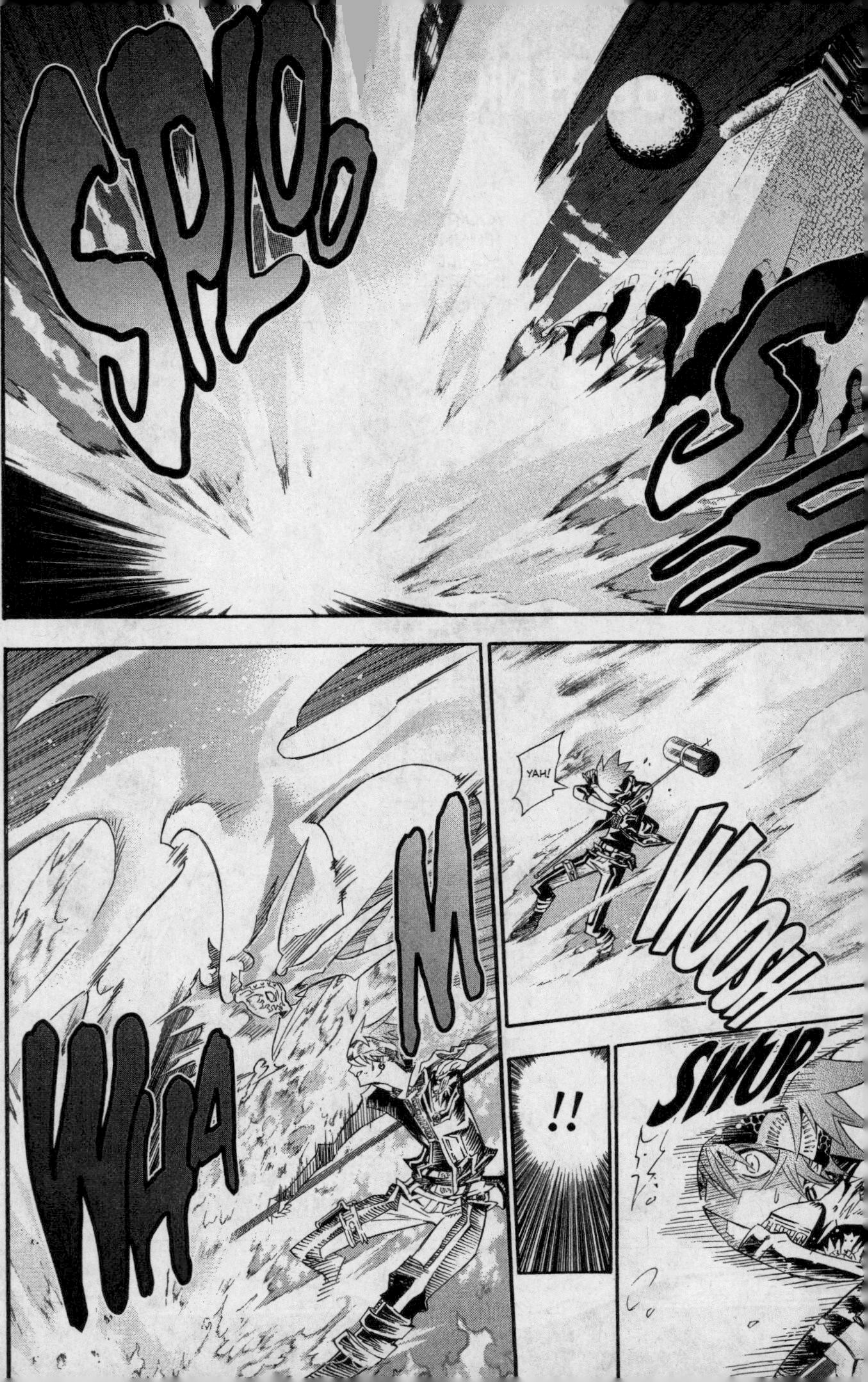
SPLOOSH
YAH!
WOOSH
SWUP
!!
WHAM

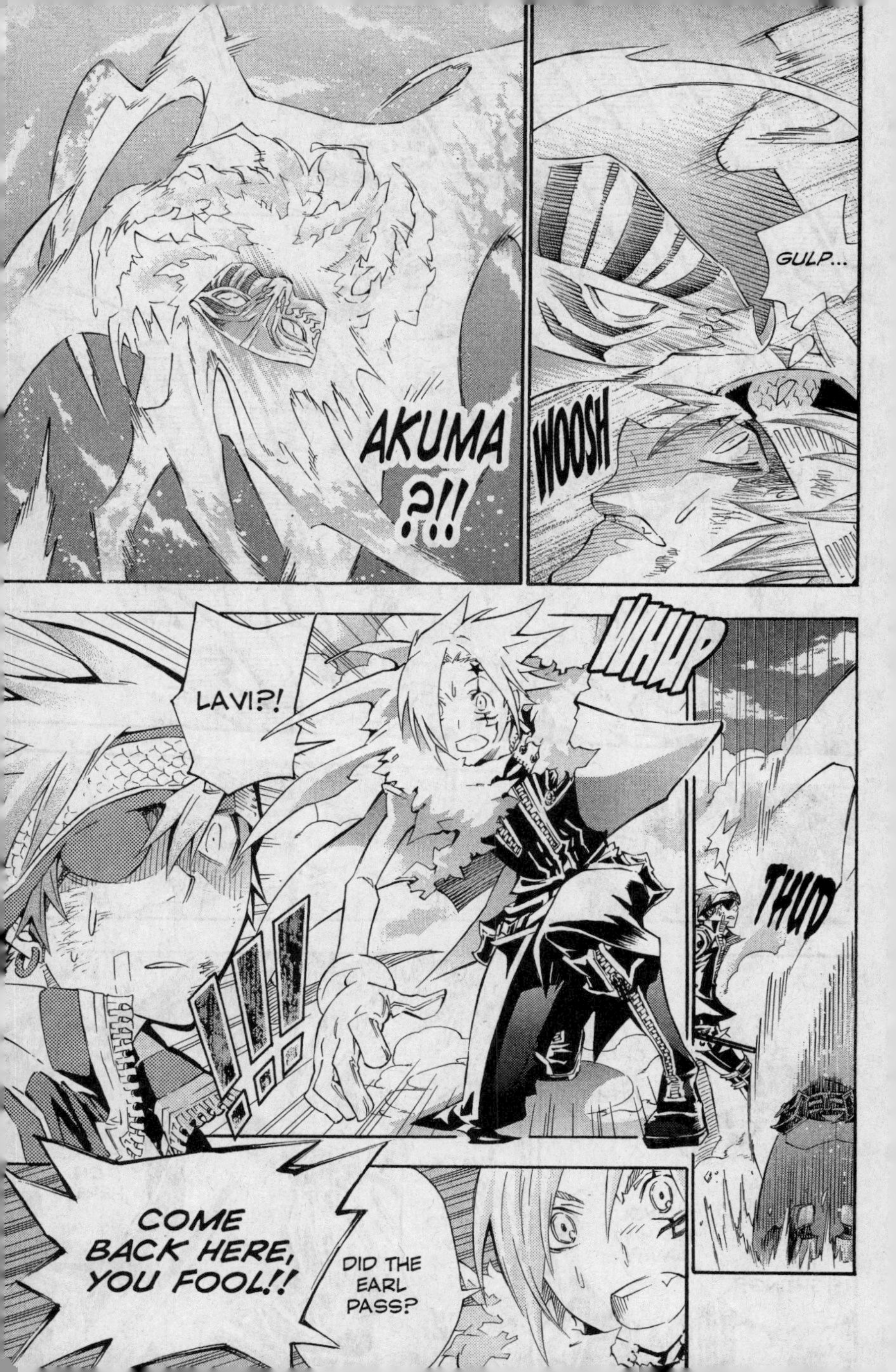
GULP...
WOOSH
AKUMA ?!!
WHUP
THUD
LAVI?!
DID THE EARL PASS?
COME BACK HERE, YOU FOOL!!

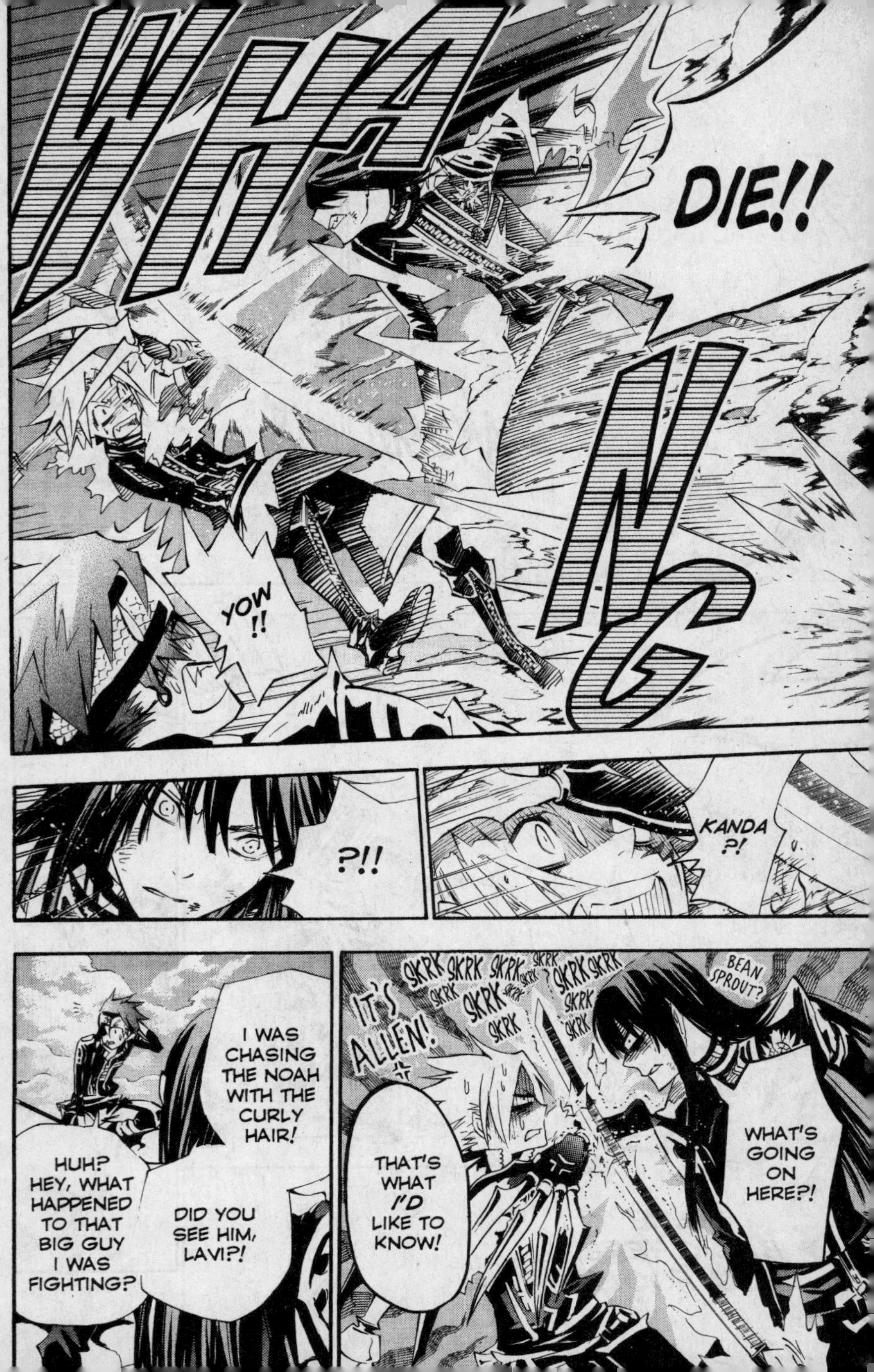
DIE!!
WHA
NG
YOW !!
KANDA ?!
?!!
BEAN SPROUT?
SKRK SKRK SKRK SKRK SKRK SKRK SKRK SKRK SKRK SKRK SKRK SKRK SKRK SKRK
IT'S ALLEN!
WHAT'S GOING ON HERE?!
THAT'S WHAT I'D LIKE TO KNOW!
I WAS CHASING THE NOAH WITH THE CURLY HAIR!
DID YOU SEE HIM, LAVI?!
HUH? HEY, WHAT HAPPENED TO THAT BIG GUY I WAS FIGHTING?

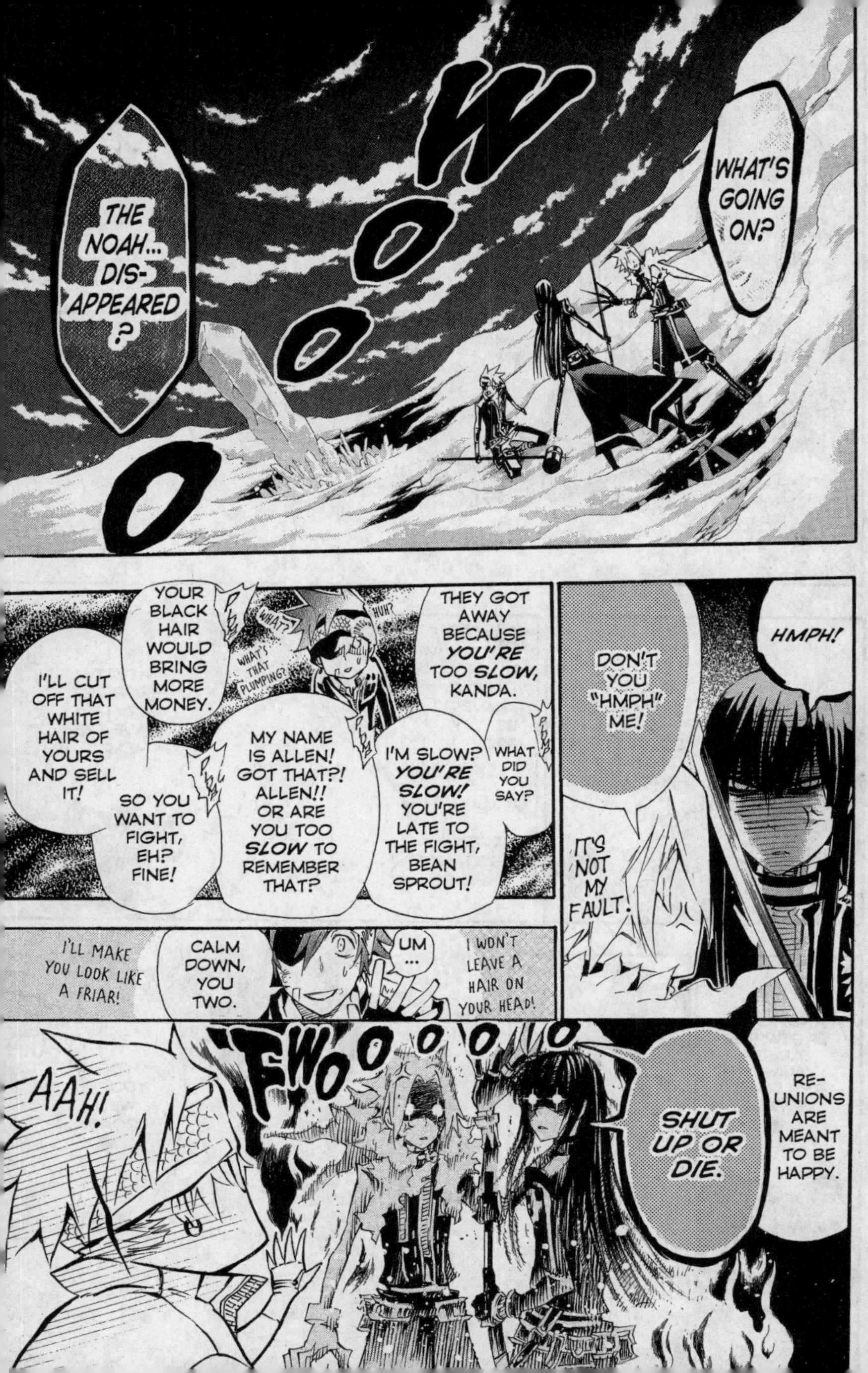
WHAT'S GOING ON?
WOOOO
THE NOAH... DIS-APPEARED?
HMPH!
DON'T YOU "HMPH" ME!
IT'S NOT MY FAULT.
THEY GOT AWAY BECAUSE YOU'RE TOO SLOW, KANDA.
HUH?
WHAT?
WHAT DID YOU SAY?
YOUR BLACK HAIR WOULD BRING MORE MONEY.
WHAT'S THAT PLUMPING?
I'M SLOW? YOU'RE SLOW! YOU'RE LATE TO THE FIGHT, BEAN SPROUT!
MY NAME IS ALLEN! GOT THAT?! ALLEN!! OR ARE YOU TOO SLOW TO REMEMBER THAT?
I'LL CUT OFF THAT WHITE HAIR OF YOURS AND SELL IT!
SO YOU WANT TO FIGHT, EH? FINE!
I WON'T LEAVE A HAIR ON YOUR HEAD!
UM ...
CALM DOWN, YOU TWO.
I'LL MAKE YOU LOOK LIKE A FRIAR!
RE-UNIONS ARE MEANT TO BE HAPPY.
SHUT UP OR DIE.
FWOOOOOO
AAH!

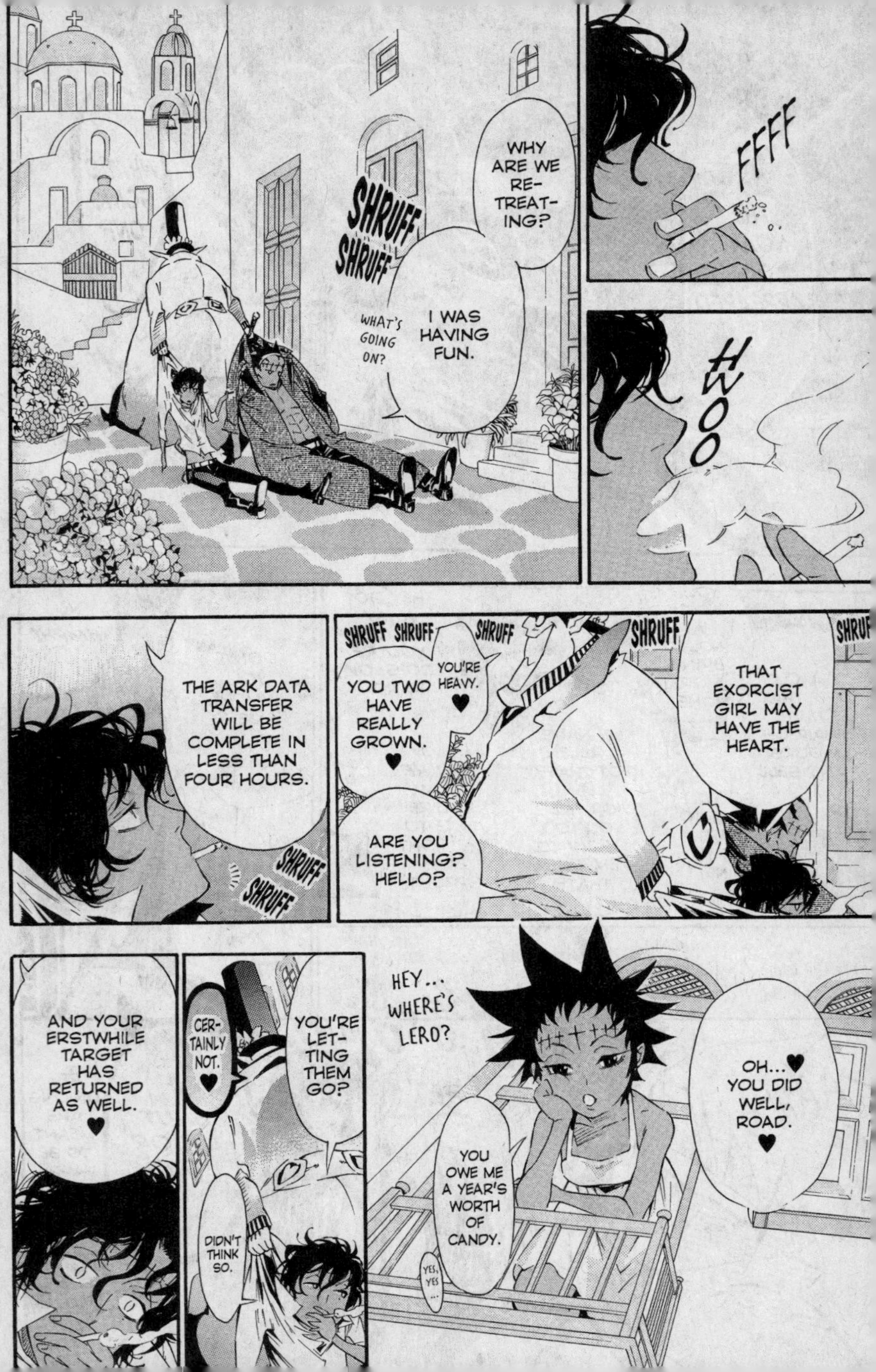
FFFF
WOO
SHRUFF SHRUFF
WHY ARE WE RE-TREAT-ING?
I WAS HAVING FUN.
WHAT'S GOING ON?
SHRUFF
THAT EXORCIST GIRL MAY HAVE THE HEART.
SHRUFF SHRUFF SHRUFF SHRUFF
YOU'RE HEAVY. ♥
YOU TWO HAVE REALLY GROWN. ♥
ARE YOU LISTENING? HELLO?
THE ARK DATA TRANSFER WILL BE COMPLETE IN LESS THAN FOUR HOURS.
SHRUFF SHRUFF
OH... ♥ YOU DID WELL, ROAD. ♥
HEY... WHERE'S LERO?
YOU OWE ME A YEAR'S WORTH OF CANDY.
YES, YES...
YOU'RE LET-TING THEM GO?
CER-TAINLY NOT. ♥
DIDN'T THINK SO.
AND YOUR ERSTWHILE TARGET HAS RETURNED AS WELL. ♥

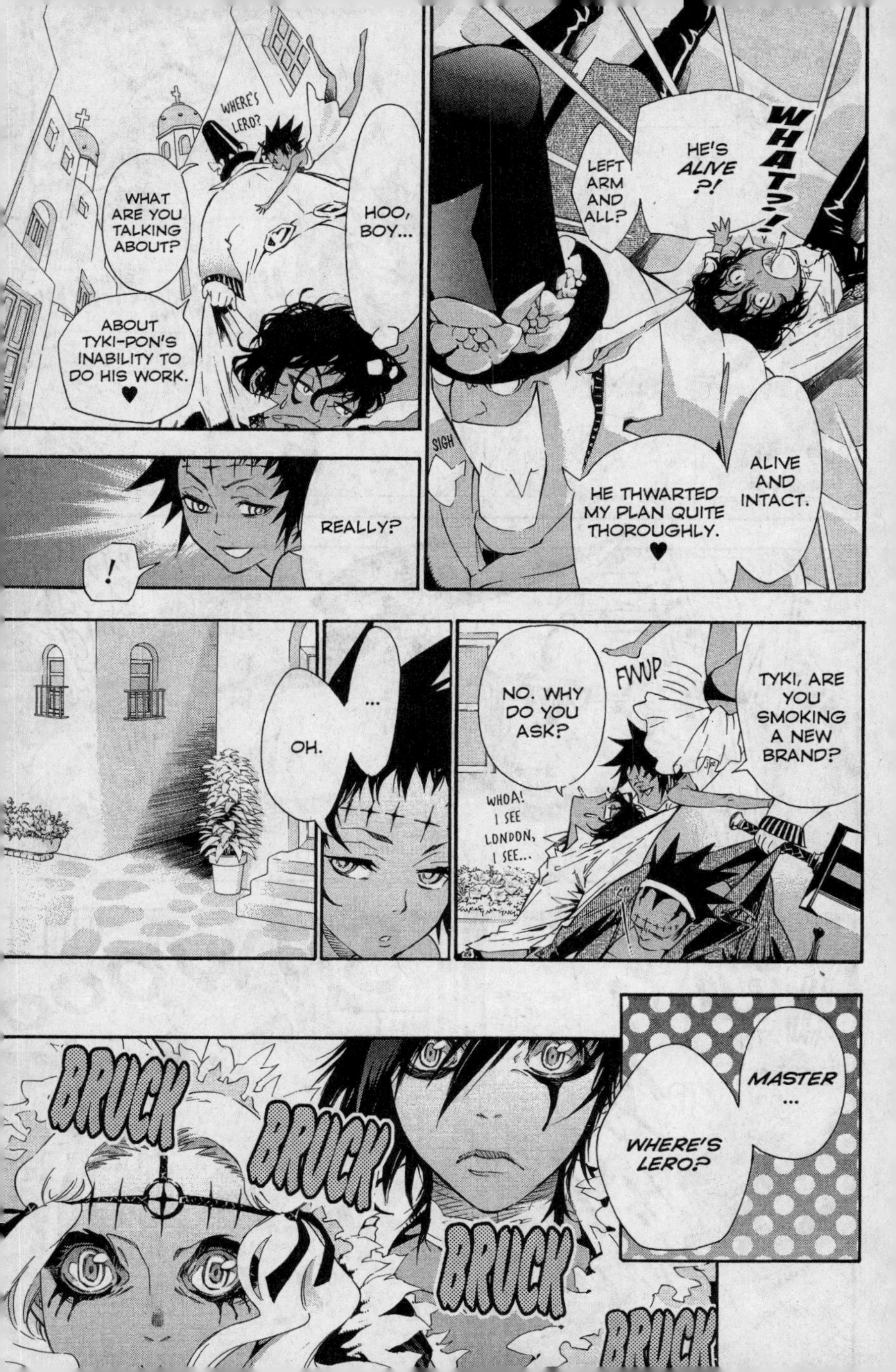

WHAT?!
HE'S ALIVE?!
LEFT ARM AND ALL?
ALIVE AND INTACT.
HE THWARTED MY PLAN QUITE THOROUGHLY. ♥
SIGH
WHERE'S LERO?
HOO, BOY...
WHAT ARE YOU TALKING ABOUT?
ABOUT TYKI-PON'S INABILITY TO DO HIS WORK. ♥
REALLY?
!
TYKI, ARE YOU SMOKING A NEW BRAND?
FWUP
NO. WHY DO YOU ASK?
WHOA! I SEE LONDON, I SEE...
...
OH.
MASTER... WHERE'S LERO?
BRUCK
BRUCK
BRUCK
BRUCK

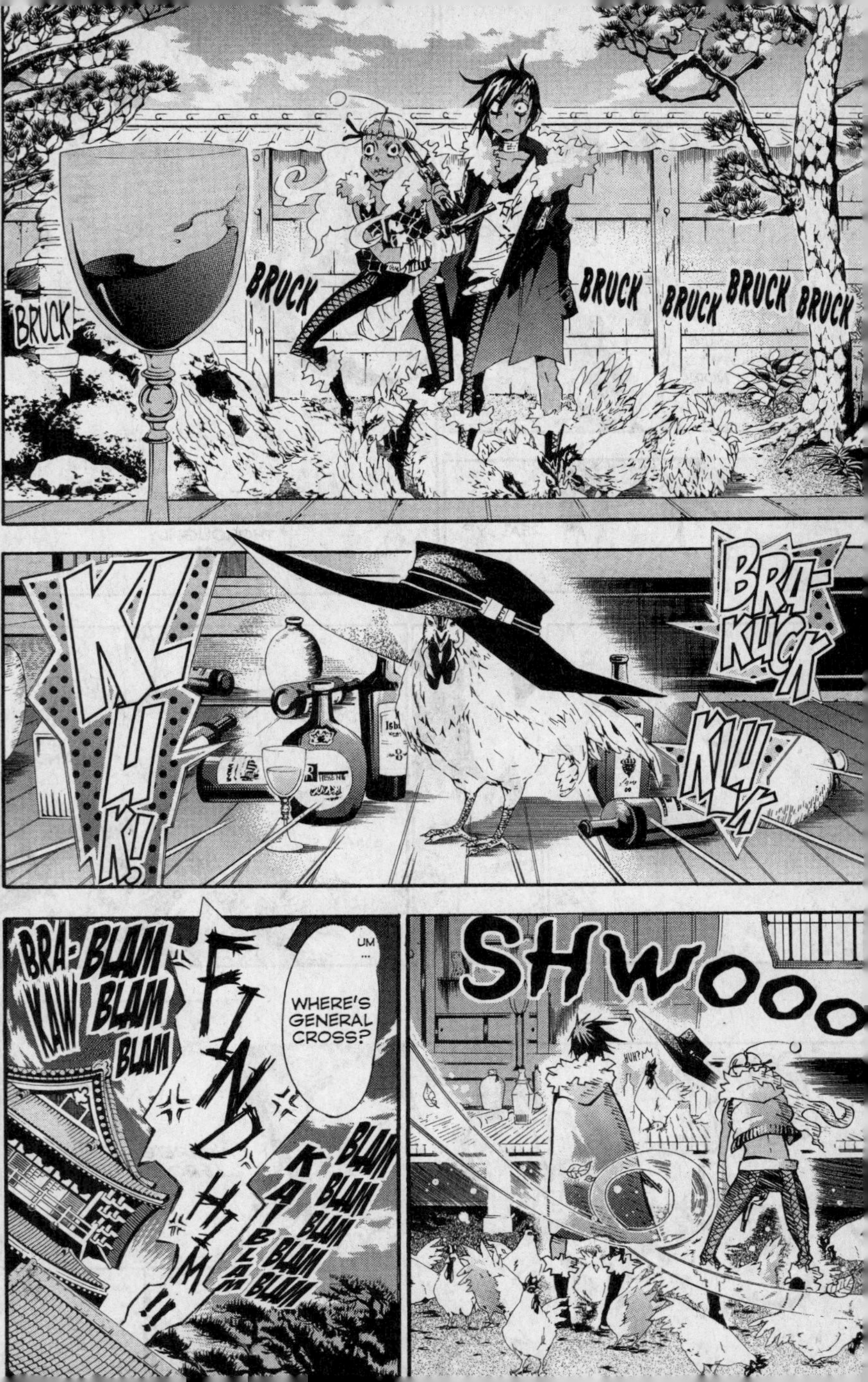
BRUCK
BRUCK
BRUCK
BRUCK
BRUCK
BRUCK
BRA-KUCK
KLUK
KLUKK!
SHWOOOO
HUH?
UM... WHERE'S GENERAL CROSS?
FIND HIM!!
BRA-KAW
BLAM BLAM BLAM
BLAM BLAM BLAM BLAM
KA BLAM BLAM BLAM

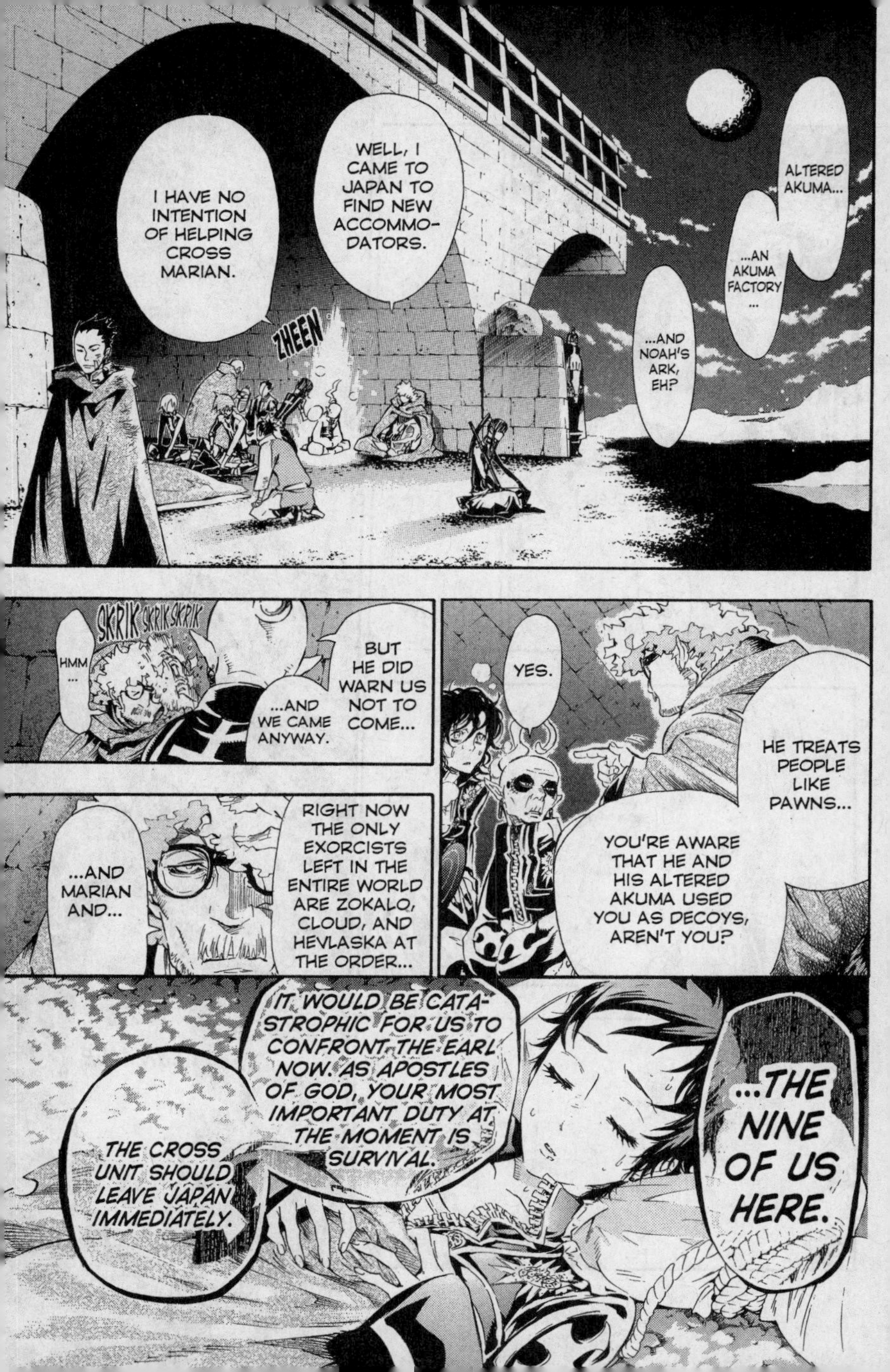
ALTERED AKUMA...
...AN AKUMA FACTORY ...
...AND NOAH'S ARK, EH?
WELL, I CAME TO JAPAN TO FIND NEW ACCOMMODATORS.
I HAVE NO INTENTION OF HELPING CROSS MARIAN.
ZHEEN
HE TREATS PEOPLE LIKE PAWNS...
YOU'RE AWARE THAT HE AND HIS ALTERED AKUMA USED YOU AS DECOYS, AREN'T YOU?
YES.
BUT HE DID WARN US NOT TO COME...
...AND WE CAME ANYWAY.
HMM ...
SKRIK SKRIK SKRIK
RIGHT NOW THE ONLY EXORCISTS LEFT IN THE ENTIRE WORLD ARE ZOKALO, CLOUD, AND HEVLASKA AT THE ORDER...
...AND MARIAN AND...
...THE NINE OF US HERE.
IT WOULD BE CATASTROPHIC FOR US TO CONFRONT THE EARL NOW. AS APOSTLES OF GOD, YOUR MOST IMPORTANT DUTY AT THE MOMENT IS SURVIVAL.
THE CROSS UNIT SHOULD LEAVE JAPAN IMMEDIATELY.

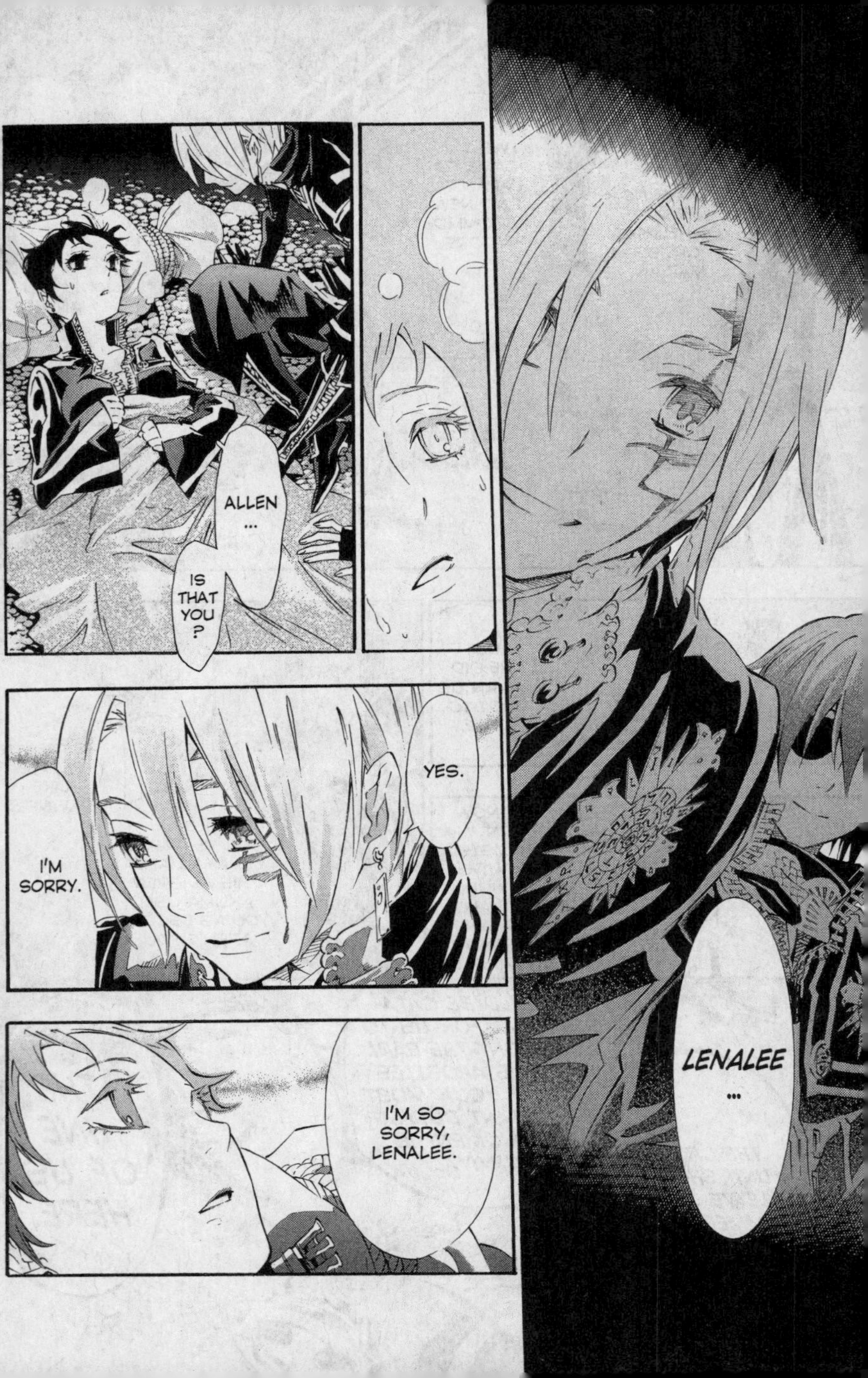
LENALEE ...
ALLEN ...
IS THAT YOU?
YES.
I'M SORRY.
I'M SO SORRY, LENALEE.

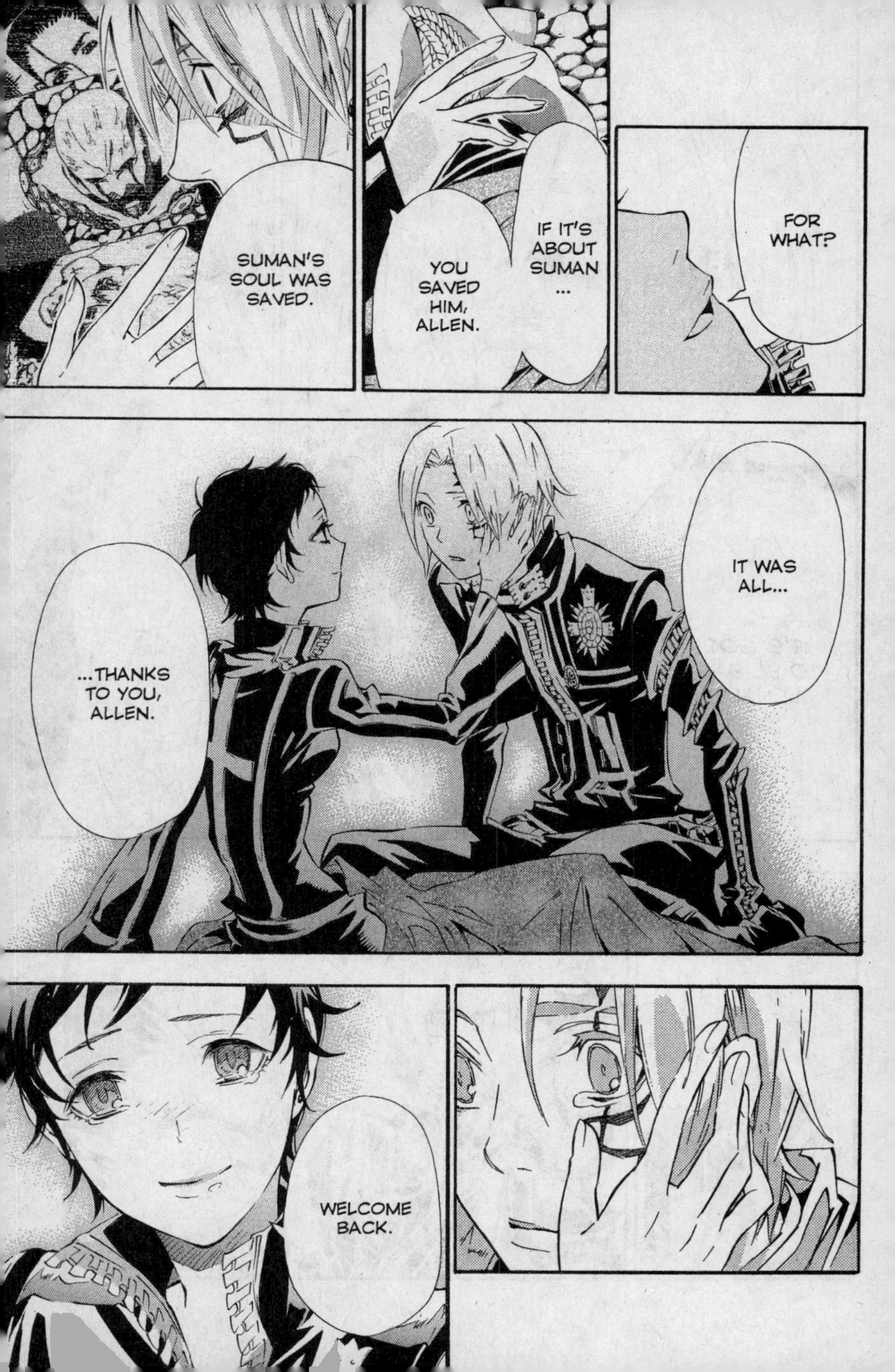
FOR WHAT?
IF IT'S ABOUT SUMAN ...
YOU SAVED HIM, ALLEN.
SUMAN'S SOUL WAS SAVED.
IT WAS ALL...
...THANKS TO YOU, ALLEN.
WELCOME BACK.

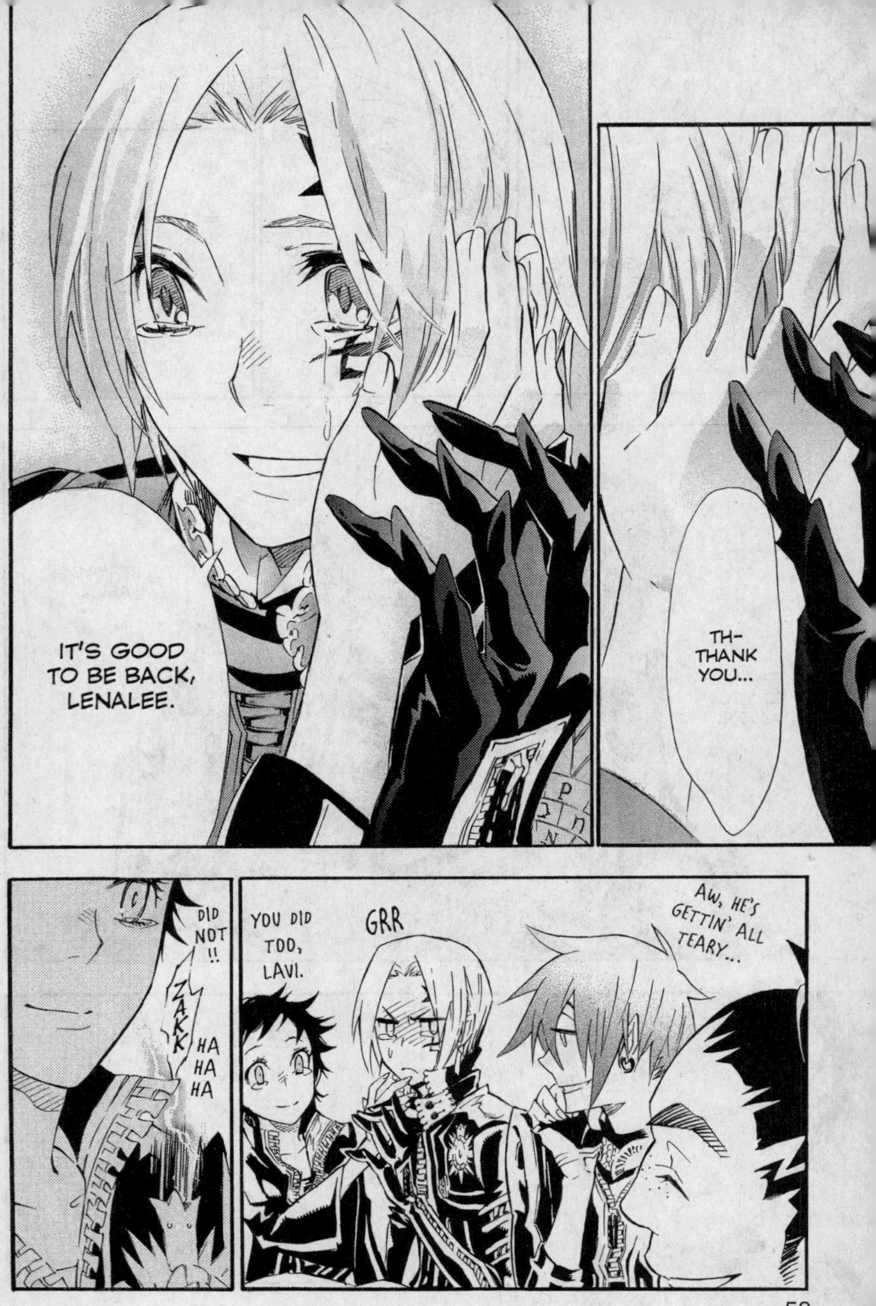
TH- THANK YOU...
IT'S GOOD TO BE BACK, LENALEE.
AW, HE'S GETTIN' ALL TEARY...
GRR
YOU DID TOO, LAVI.
DID NOT!!
ZAKK
HA HA HA

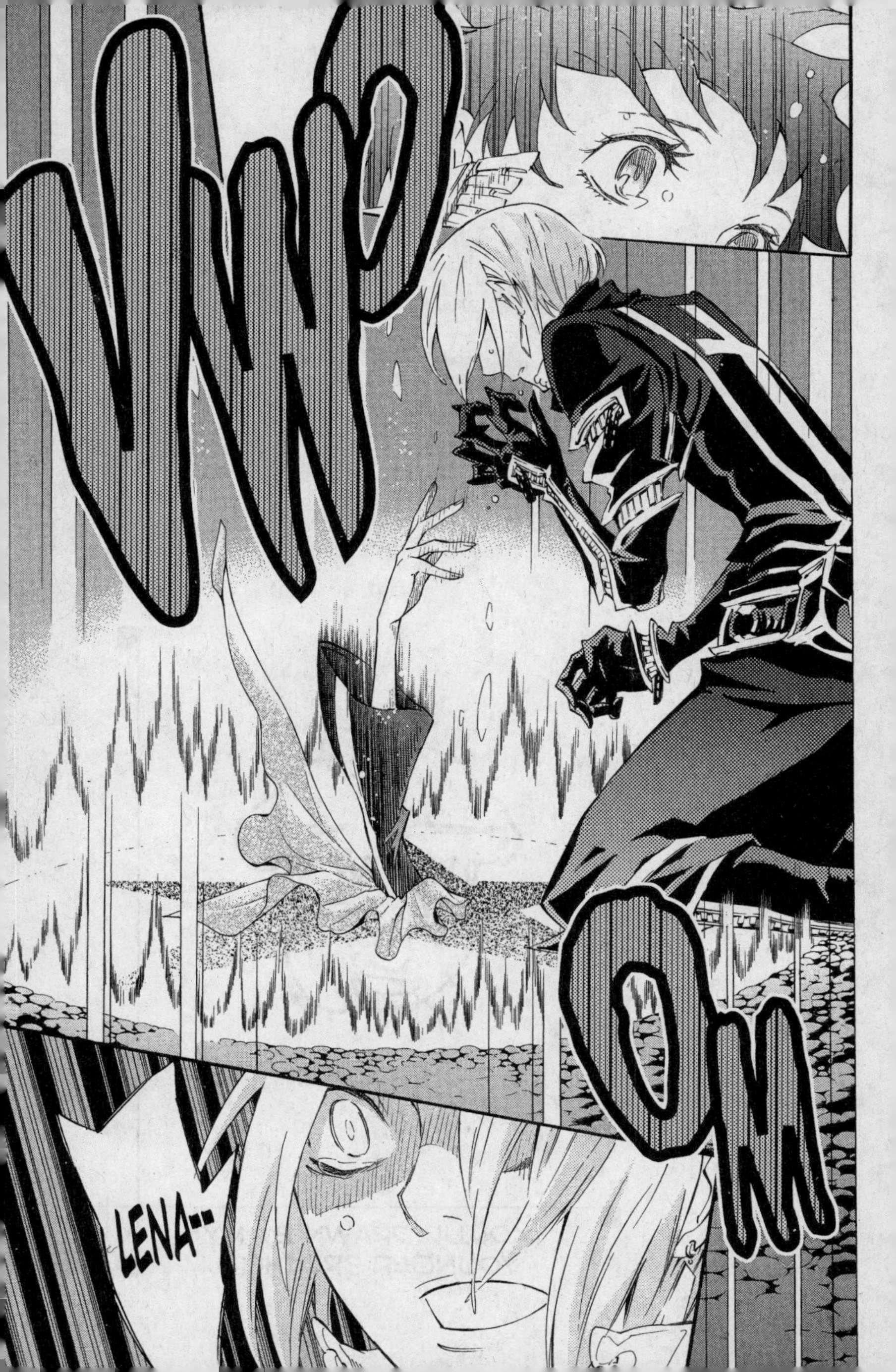
LENA..

KOMUI (DRAWN BY MY
YOUNGER BROTHER)

THE 90TH NIGHT:

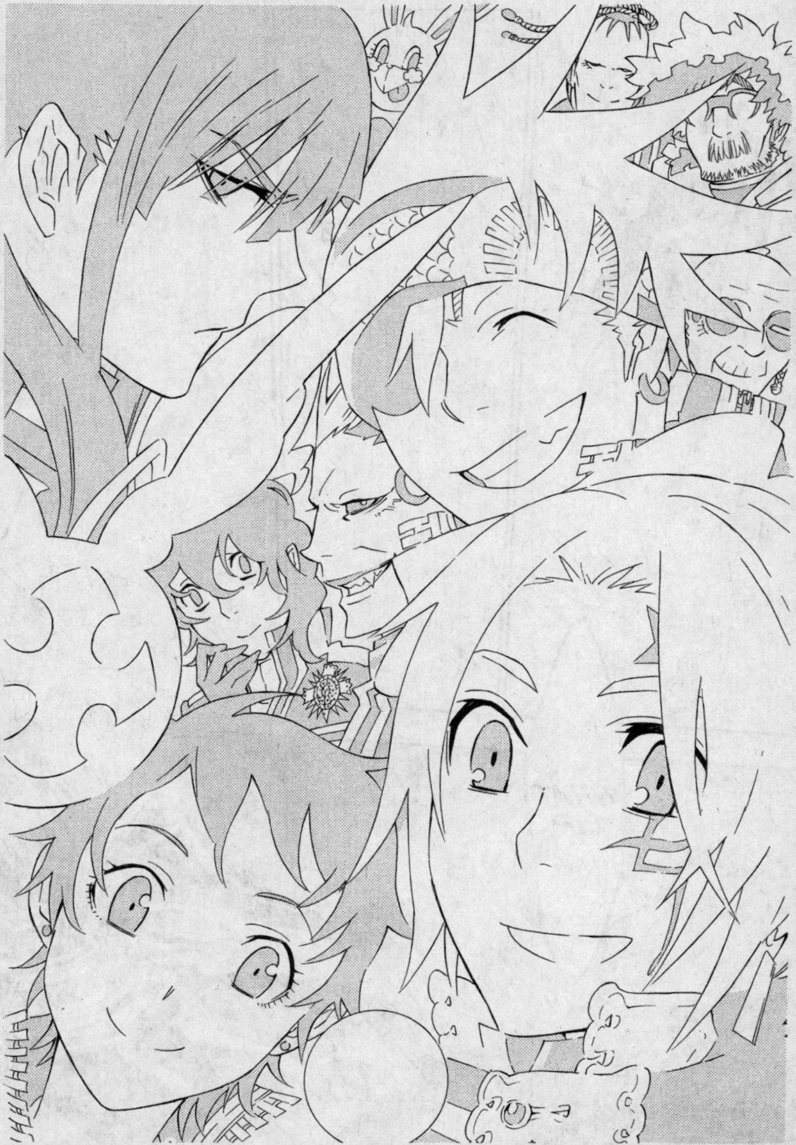

THE FINAL BELL HAS YET TO TOLL

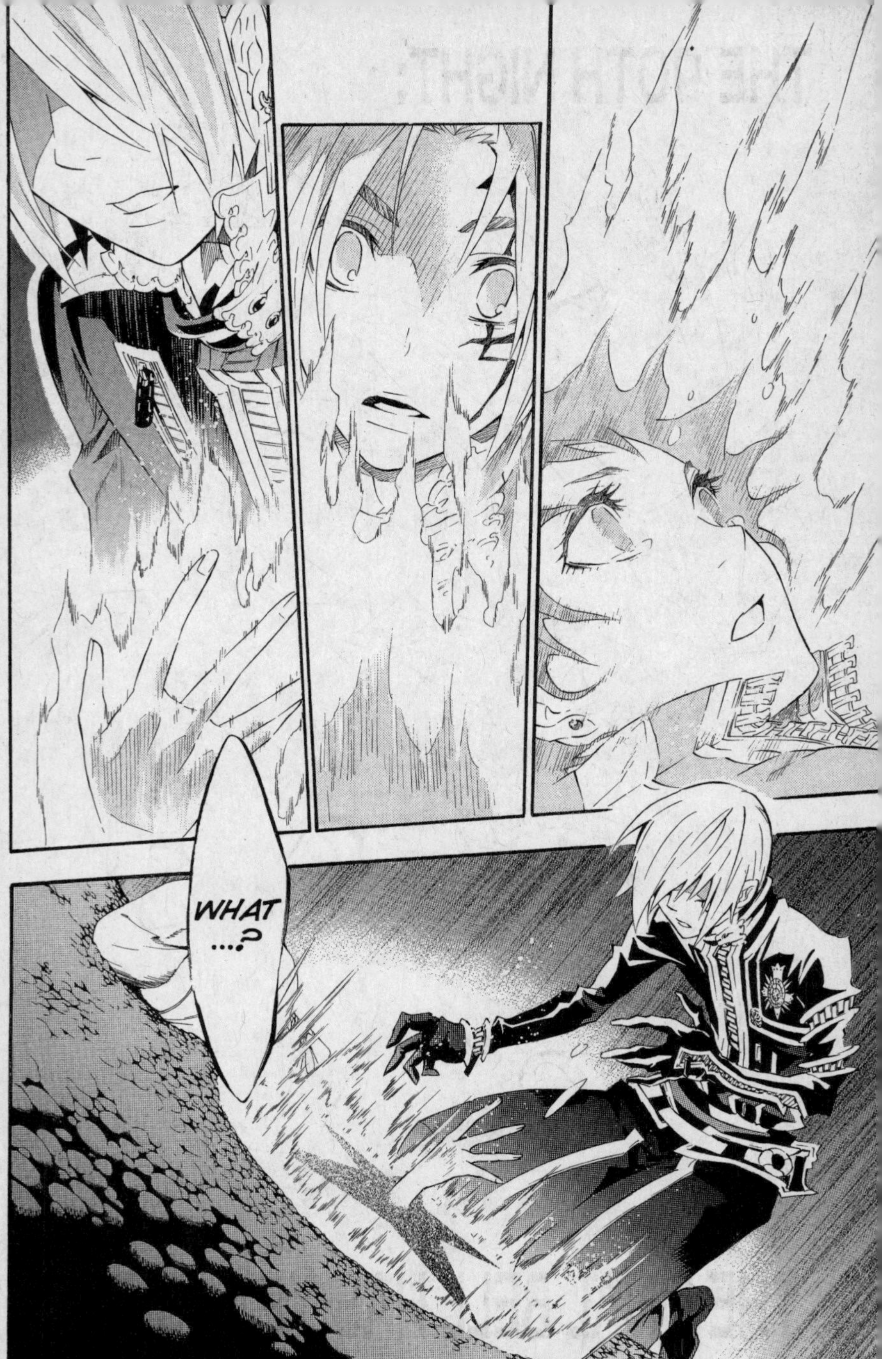
WHAT ...?

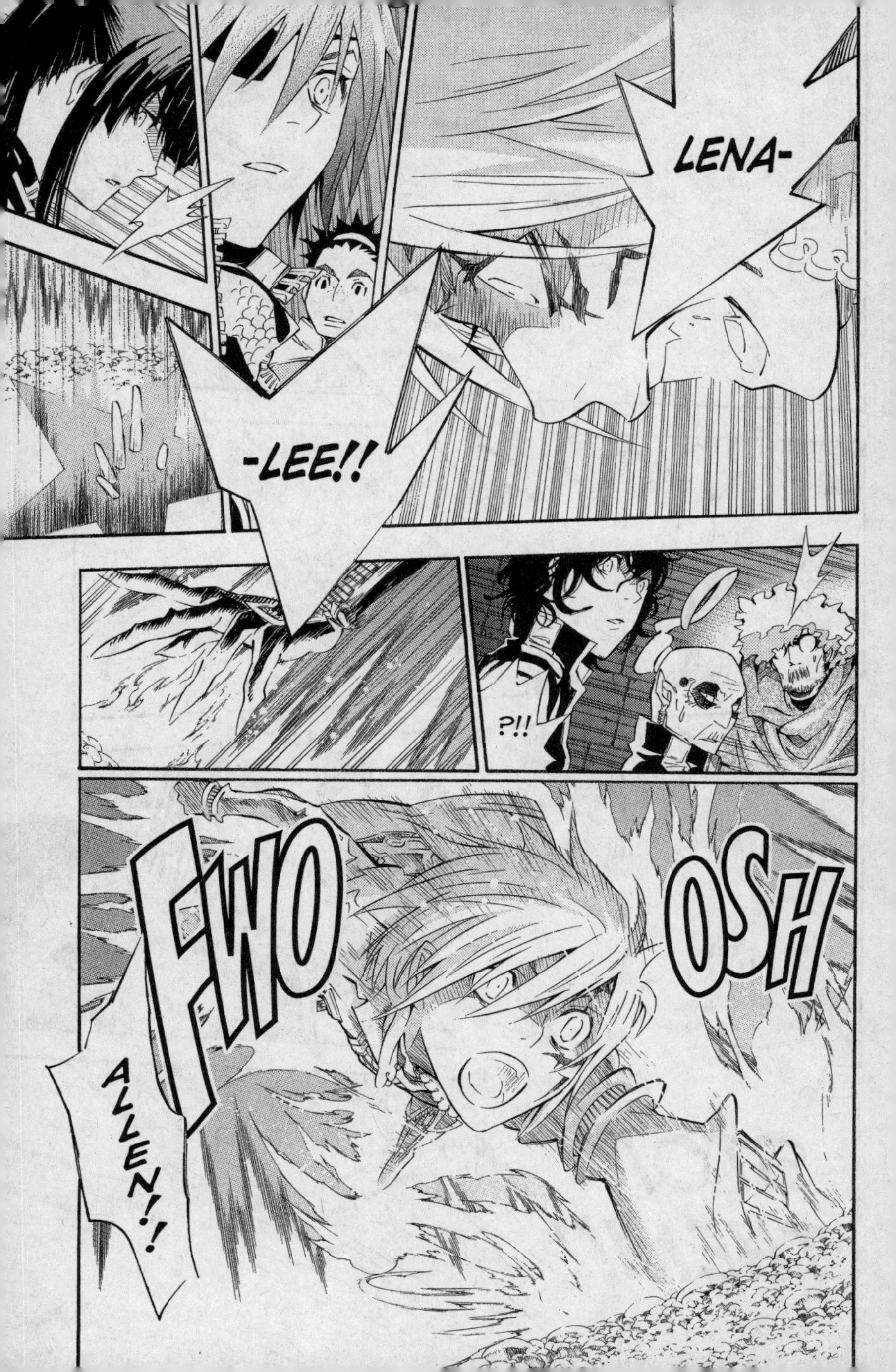
LENA-
-LEE!!
?!!
FWOOSH
ALLEN!!

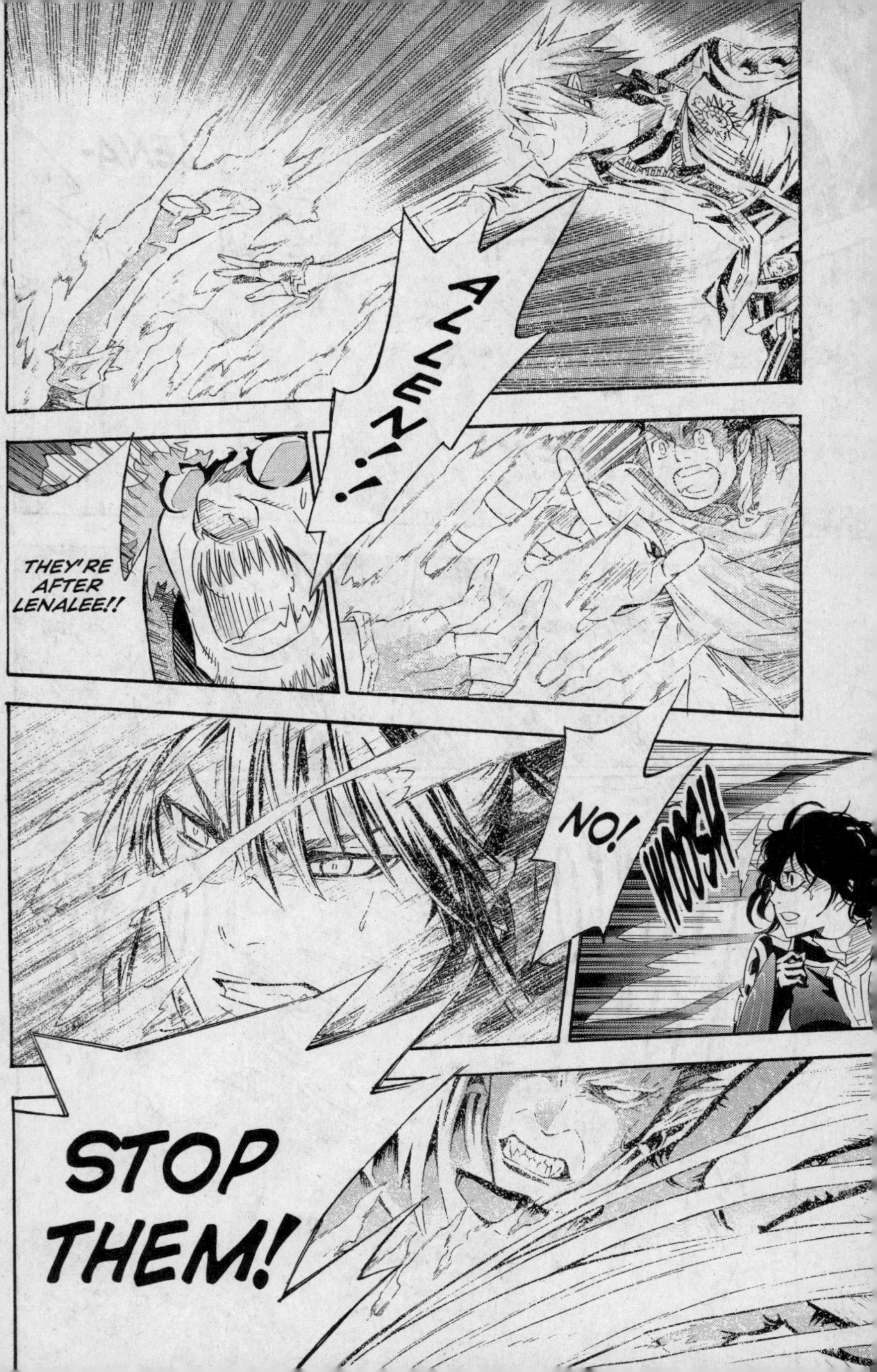
ALLEN!!
THEY'RE AFTER LENALEE!!
NO!
WHOOSH
STOP THEM!

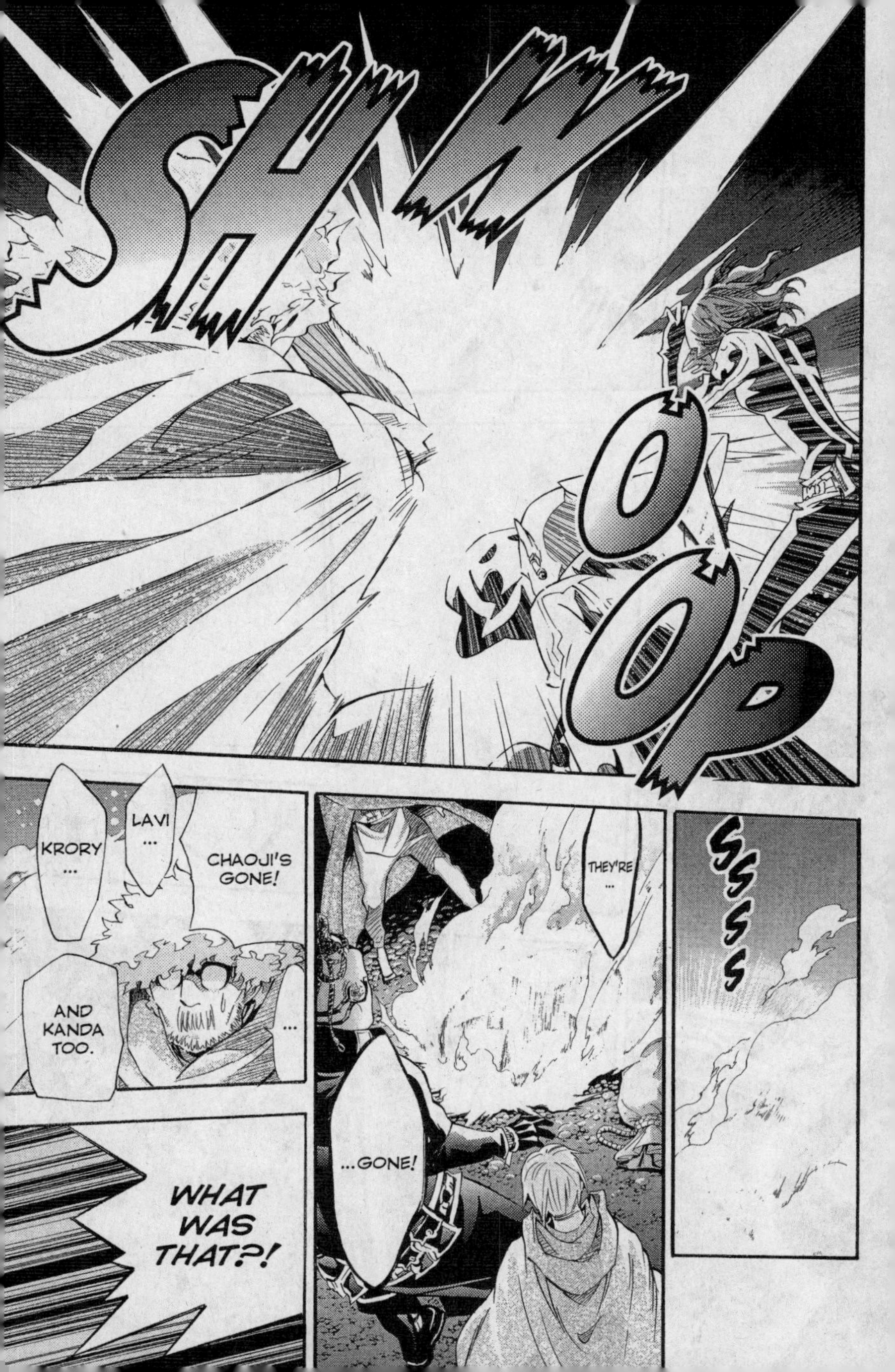
SHHOOOP
SSSS
THEY'RE ...
...GONE!
CHAOJI'S GONE!
LAVI ...
KRORY ...
...
AND KANDA TOO.
WHAT WAS THAT?!

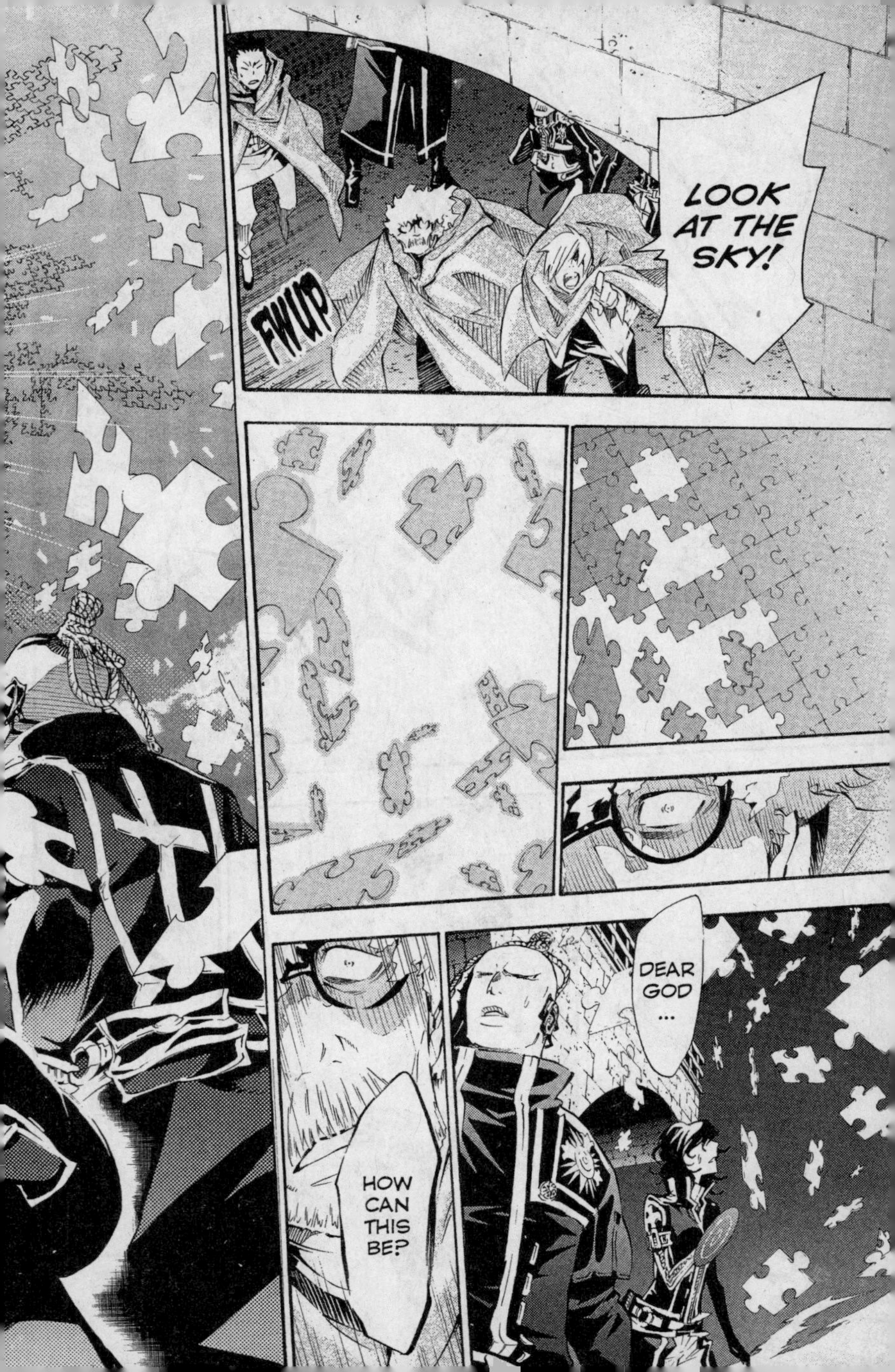
LOOK AT THE SKY!
FWUP
DEAR GOD ...
HOW CAN THIS BE?

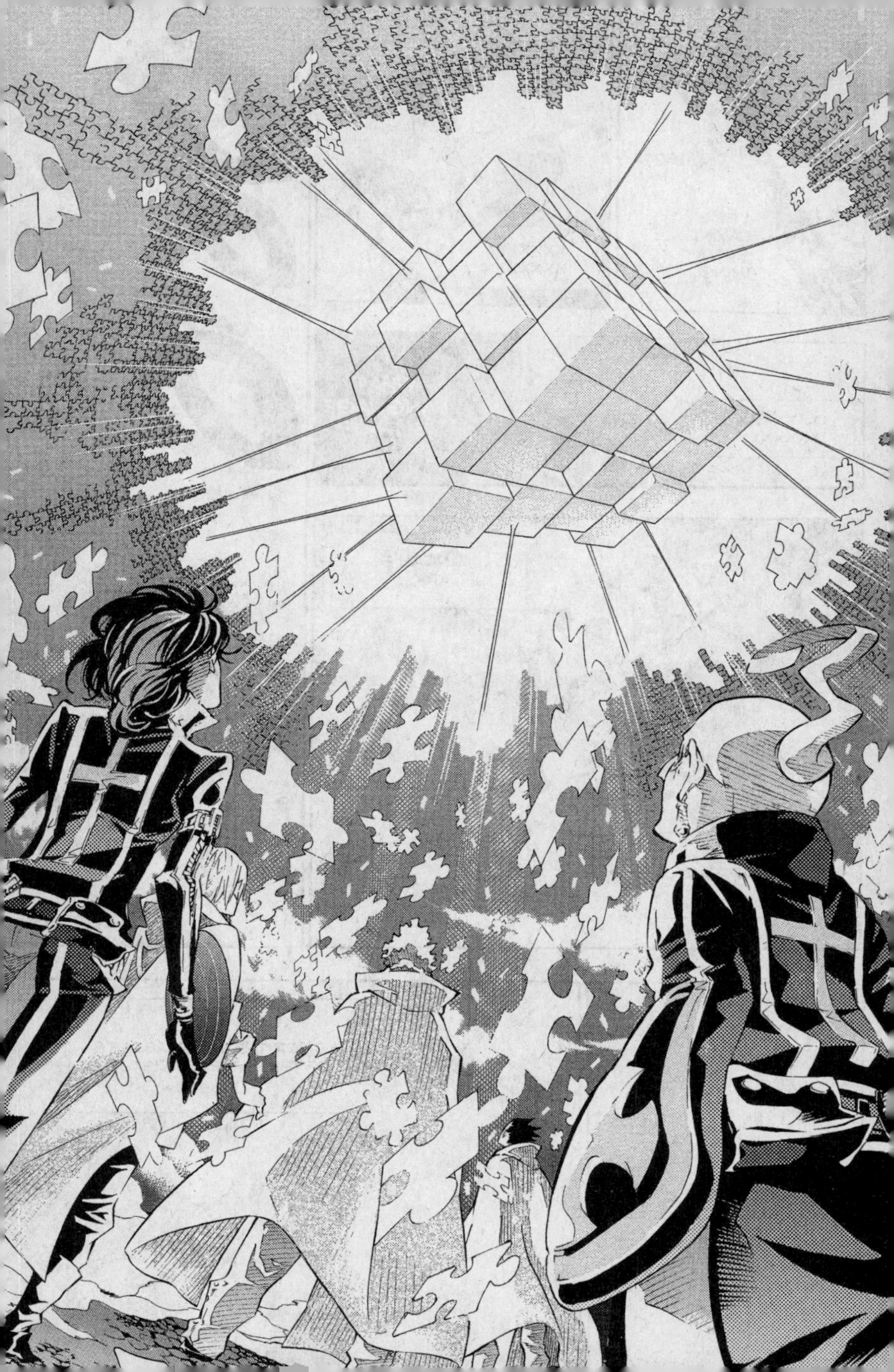

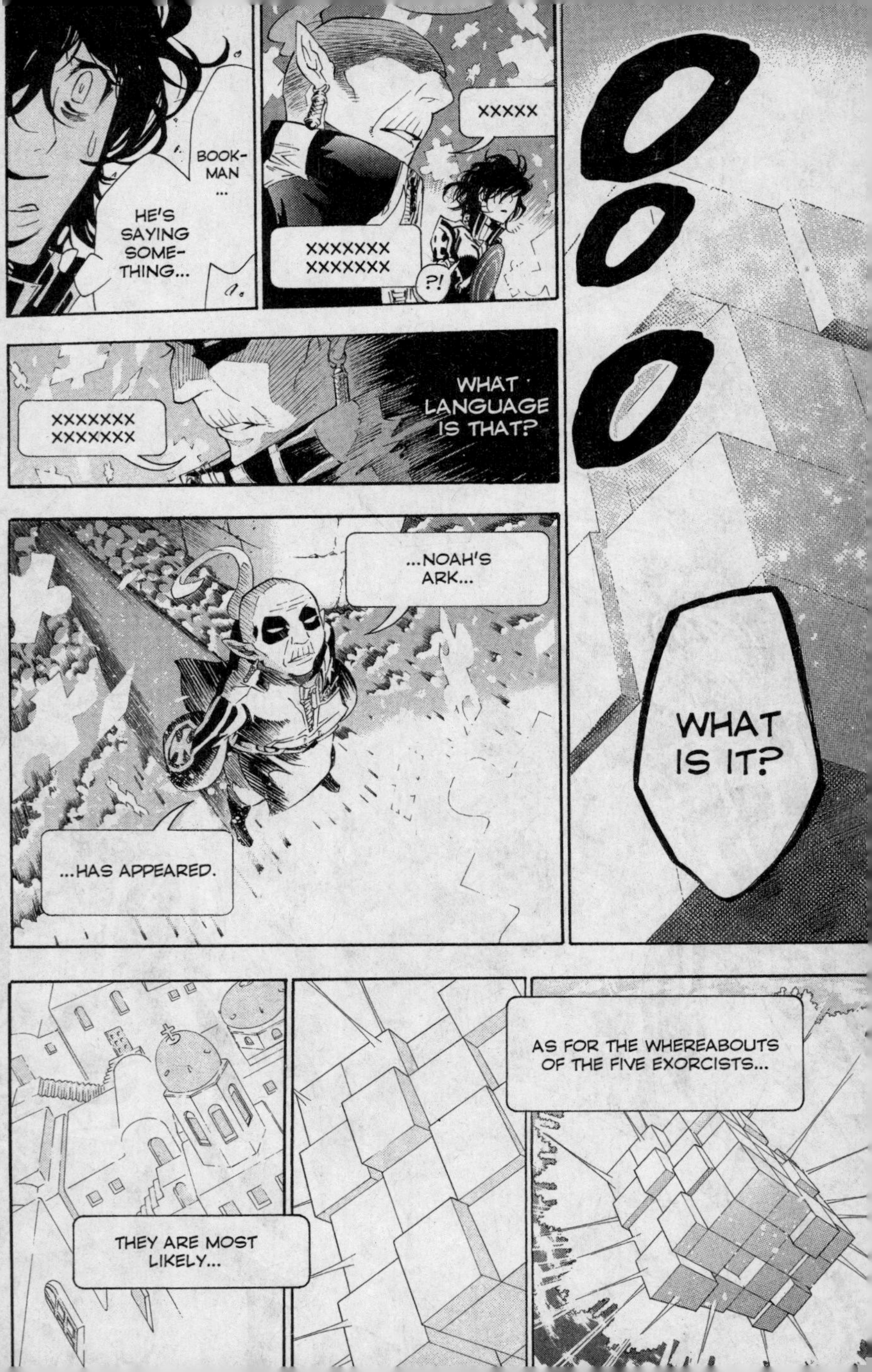

OOO
WHAT IS IT?
XXXXX
XXXXXXX XXXXXXX
?!
BOOK-MAN...
HE'S SAYING SOME-THING...
WHAT LANGUAGE IS THAT?
XXXXXXX XXXXXXX
...NOAH'S ARK...
...HAS APPEARED.
AS FOR THE WHEREABOUTS OF THE FIVE EXORCISTS...
THEY ARE MOST LIKELY...

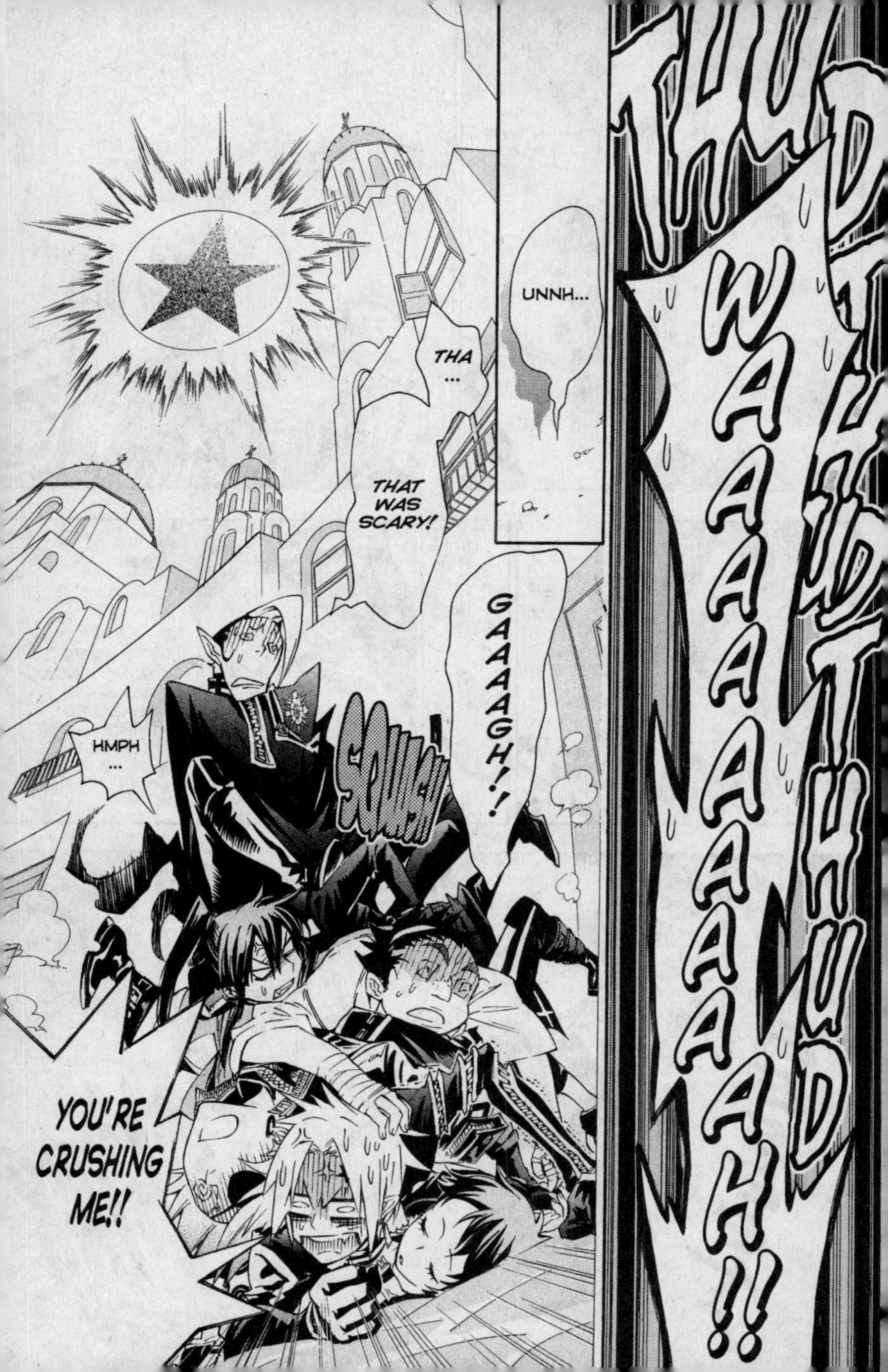
THUD
WAAAAAAAAAAAH!!
UNNH...
THA ...
THAT WAS SCARY!
GAAAAAGH!!
SQUISH
HMPH ...
YOU'RE CRUSHING ME!!

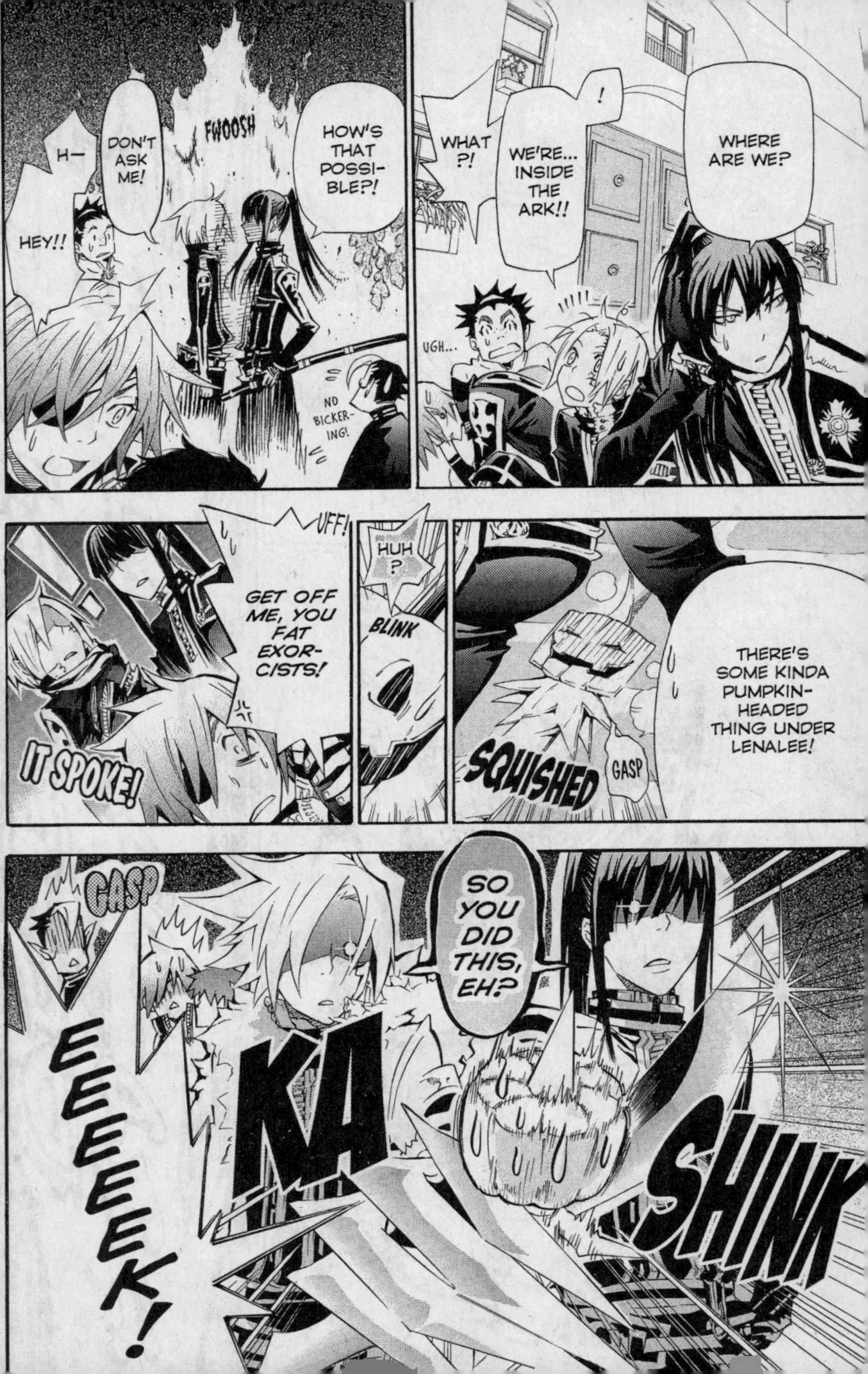
WHERE ARE WE?
!
WE'RE... INSIDE THE ARK!!
WHAT?!
UGH...
HOW'S THAT POSSIBLE?!
FWOOSH
DON'T ASK ME!
H—
HEY!!
NO BICKERING!
THERE'S SOME KINDA PUMPKIN-HEADED THING UNDER LENALEE!
SQUISHED
GASP
HUH?
BLINK
UFF!
GET OFF ME, YOU FAT EXORCISTS!
IT SPOKE!
SO YOU DID THIS, EH?
GASP
KA
SHINK
EEEEEK!

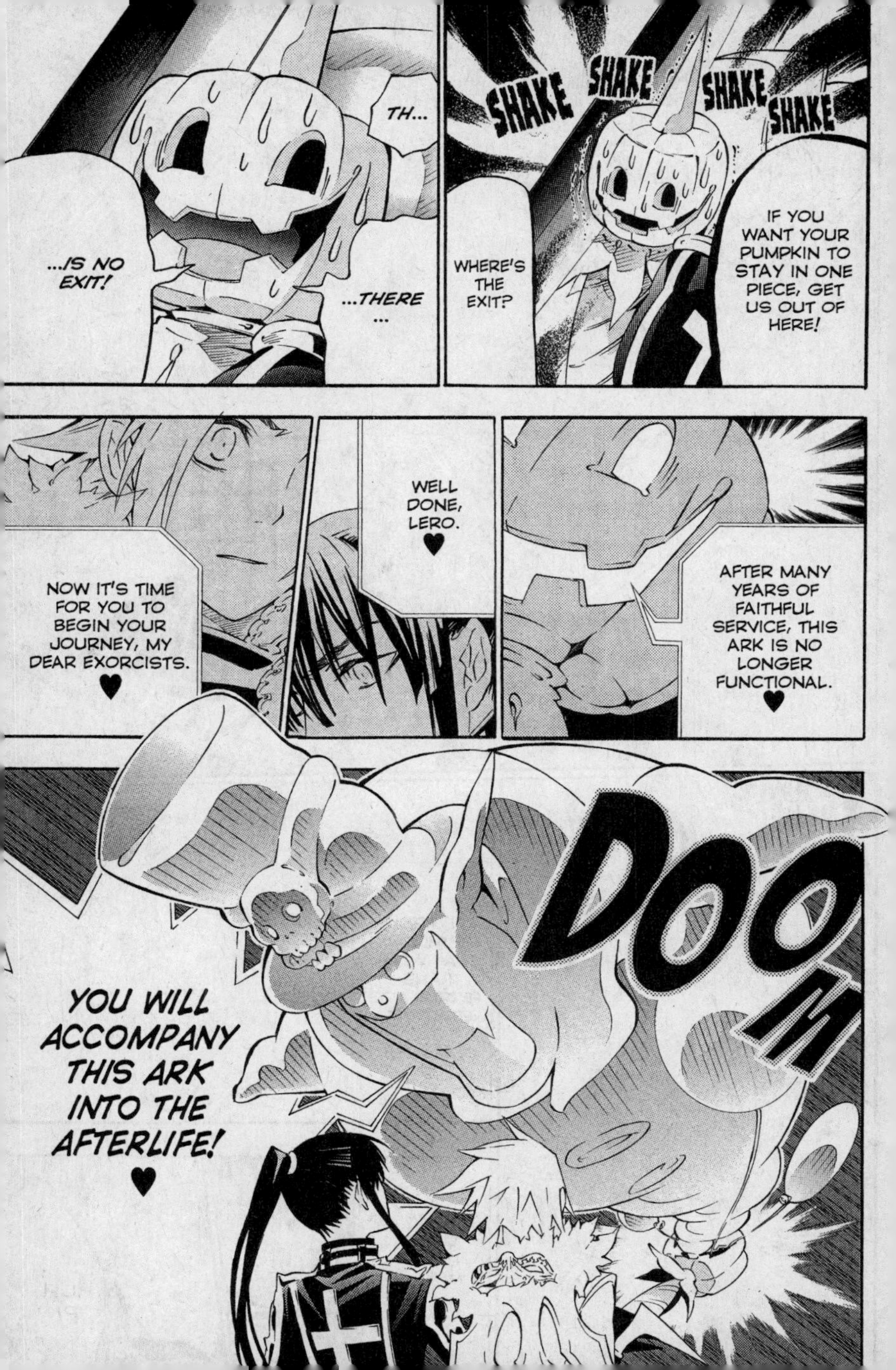
SHAKE SHAKE SHAKE SHAKE
IF YOU WANT YOUR PUMPKIN TO STAY IN ONE PIECE, GET US OUT OF HERE!
WHERE'S THE EXIT?
TH...
...THERE ...
...IS NO EXIT!
AFTER MANY YEARS OF FAITHFUL SERVICE, THIS ARK IS NO LONGER FUNCTIONAL. ♥
WELL DONE, LERO. ♥
NOW IT'S TIME FOR YOU TO BEGIN YOUR JOURNEY, MY DEAR EXORCISTS. ♥
DOOM
YOU WILL ACCOMPANY THIS ARK INTO THE AFTERLIFE! ♥

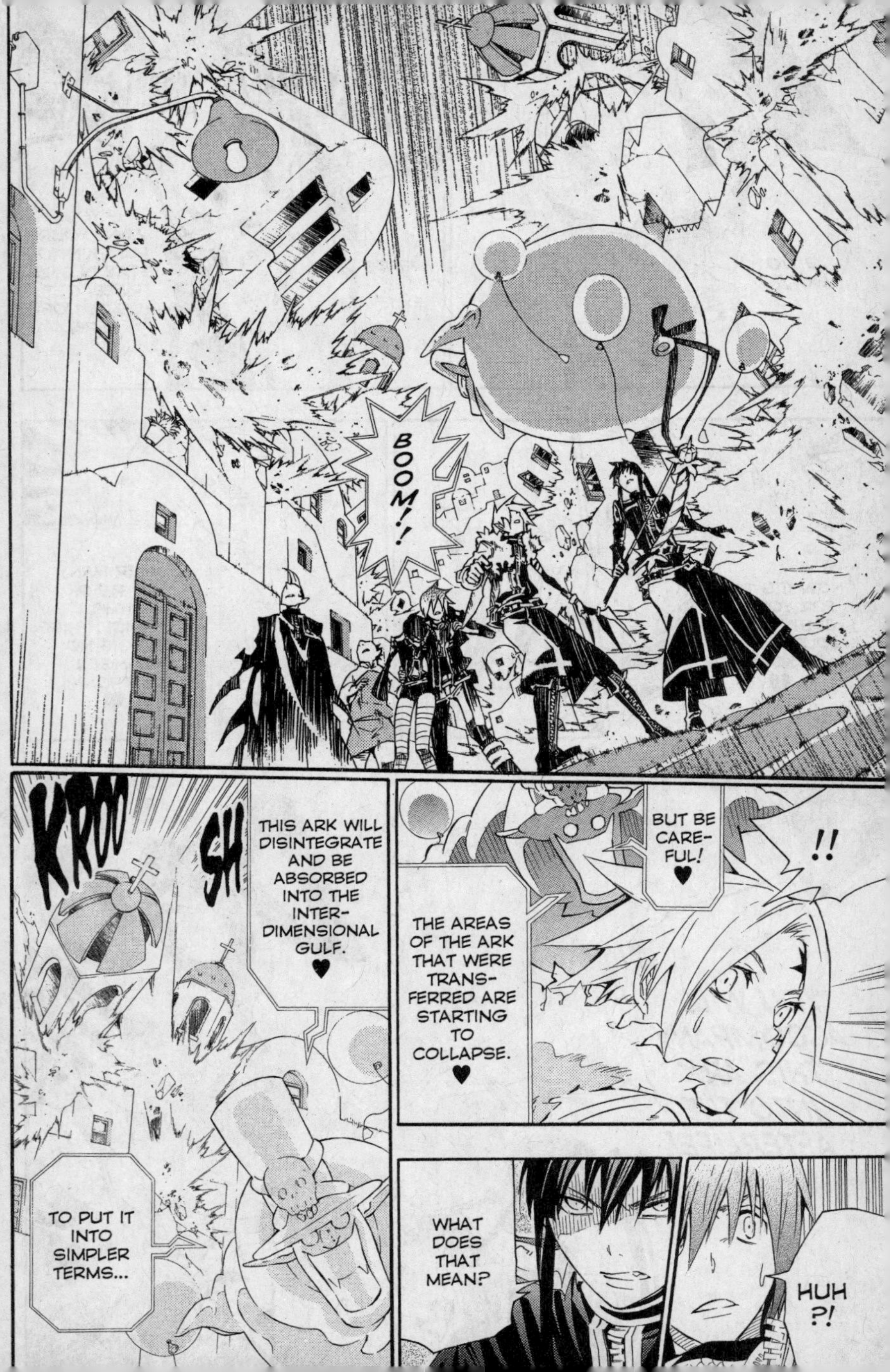
BOOM!!
BUT BE CAREFUL! ♥
THE AREAS OF THE ARK THAT WERE TRANS-FERRED ARE STARTING TO COLLAPSE. ♥
!!
HUH?!
WHAT DOES THAT MEAN?
KROOSH
THIS ARK WILL DISINTEGRATE AND BE ABSORBED INTO THE INTER-DIMENSIONAL GULF. ♥
TO PUT IT INTO SIMPLER TERMS...

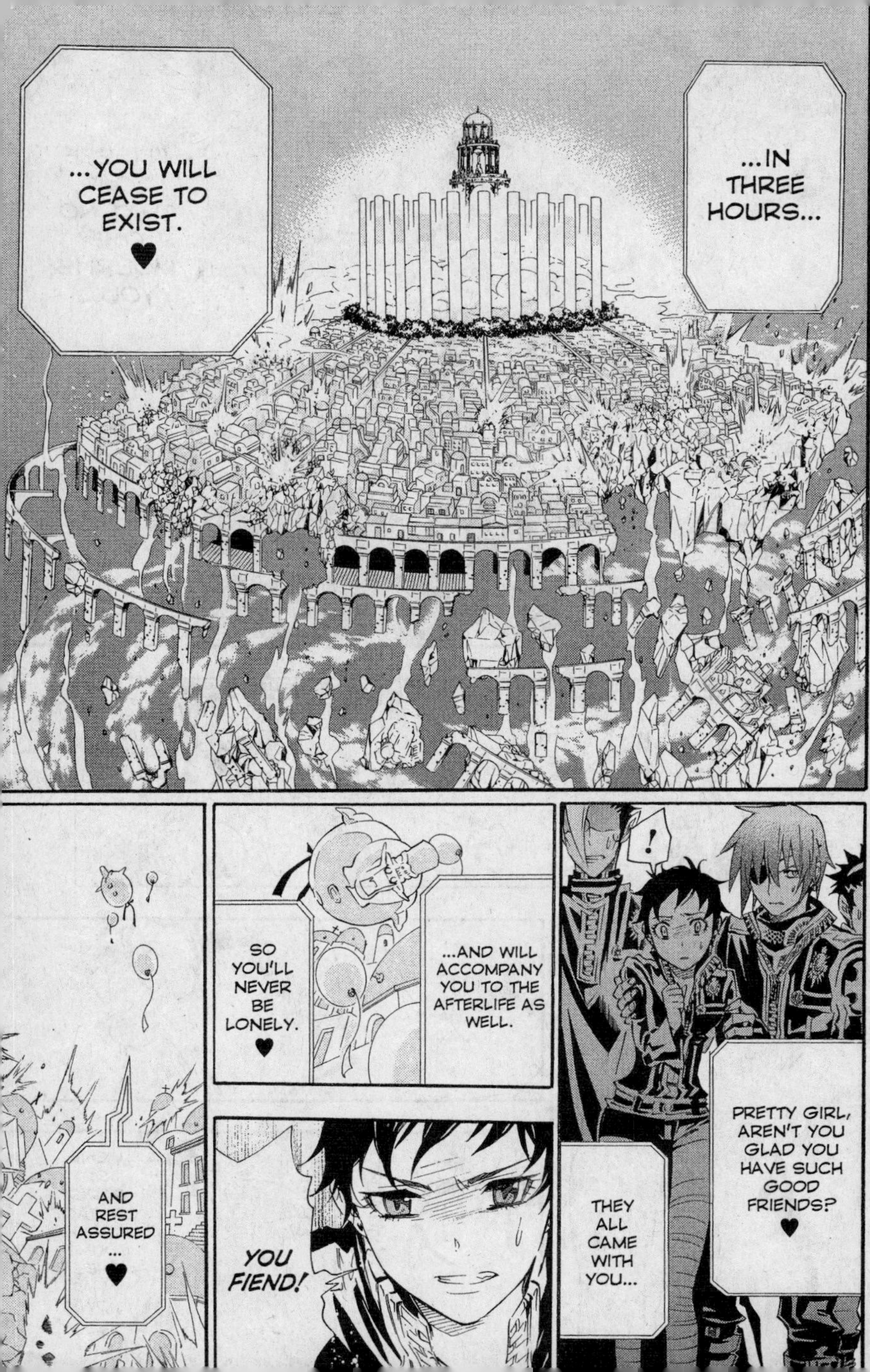
...IN THREE HOURS...
...YOU WILL CEASE TO EXIST. ♥
!
PRETTY GIRL, AREN'T YOU GLAD YOU HAVE SUCH GOOD FRIENDS? ♥
THEY ALL CAME WITH YOU...
...AND WILL ACCOMPANY YOU TO THE AFTERLIFE AS WELL.
SO YOU'LL NEVER BE LONELY. ♥
YOU FIEND!
AND REST ASSURED ... ♥

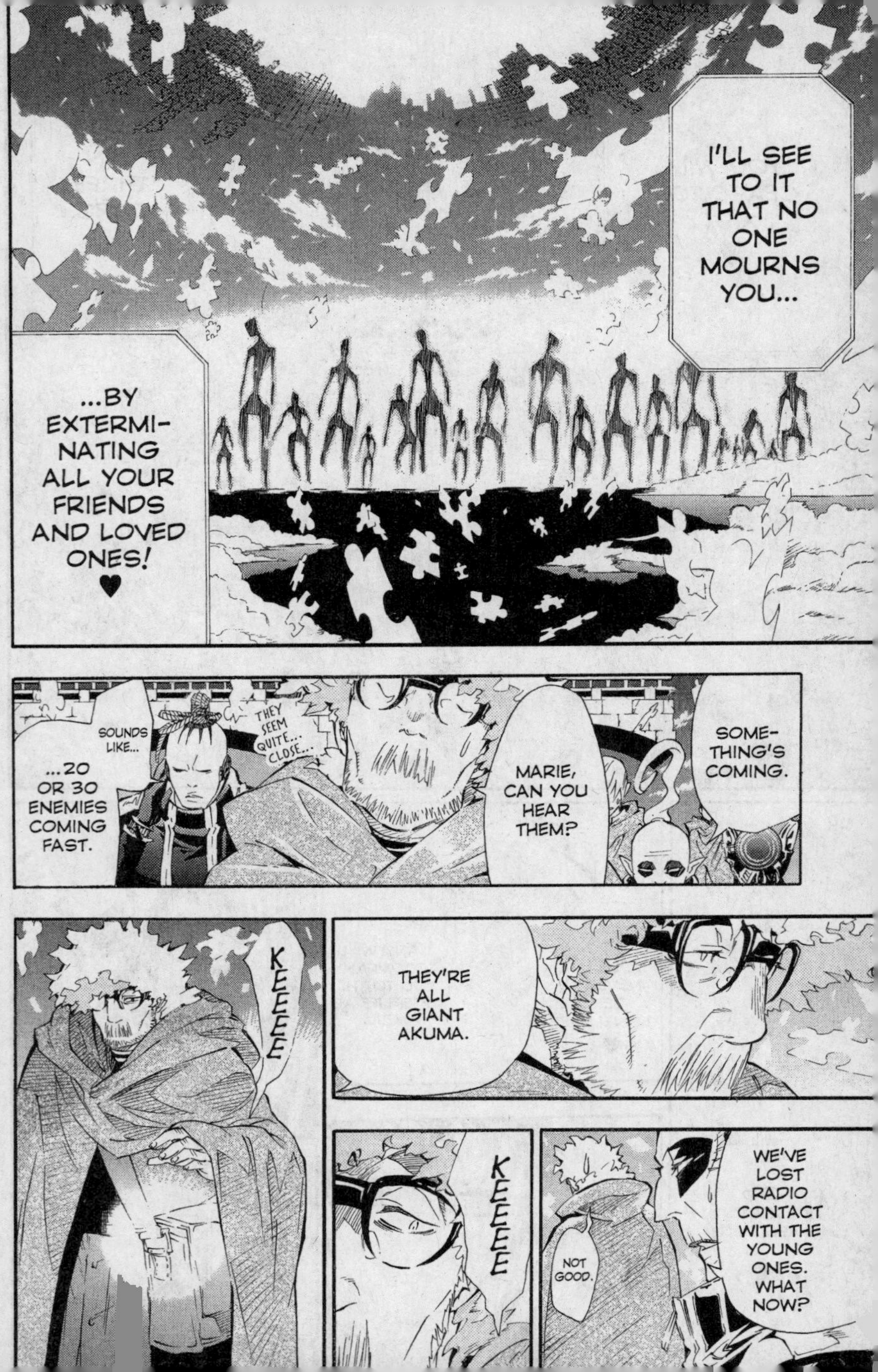
I'LL SEE TO IT THAT NO ONE MOURNS YOU...
...BY EXTERMINATING ALL YOUR FRIENDS AND LOVED ONES! ♥
SOMETHING'S COMING.
MARIE, CAN YOU HEAR THEM?
THEY SEEM QUITE... CLOSE...
SOUNDS LIKE...
...20 OR 30 ENEMIES COMING FAST.
THEY'RE ALL GIANT AKUMA.
WE'VE LOST RADIO CONTACT WITH THE YOUNG ONES. WHAT NOW?
NOT GOOD.
KEEEE
KEEEE

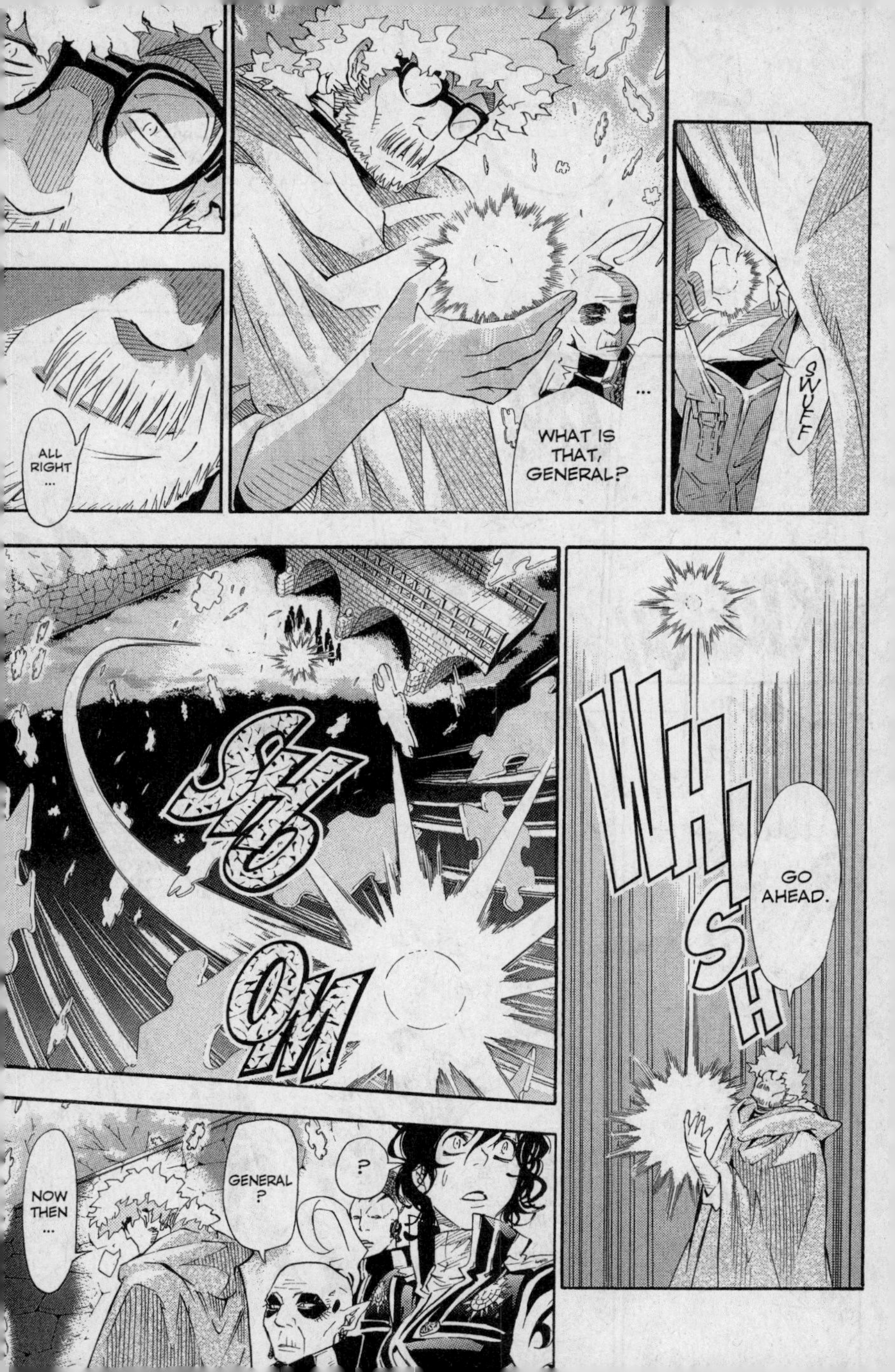

SWUFF
...
WHAT IS THAT, GENERAL?
ALL RIGHT ...
WHISH
GO AHEAD.
SHOOM
?
GENERAL?
NOW THEN ...

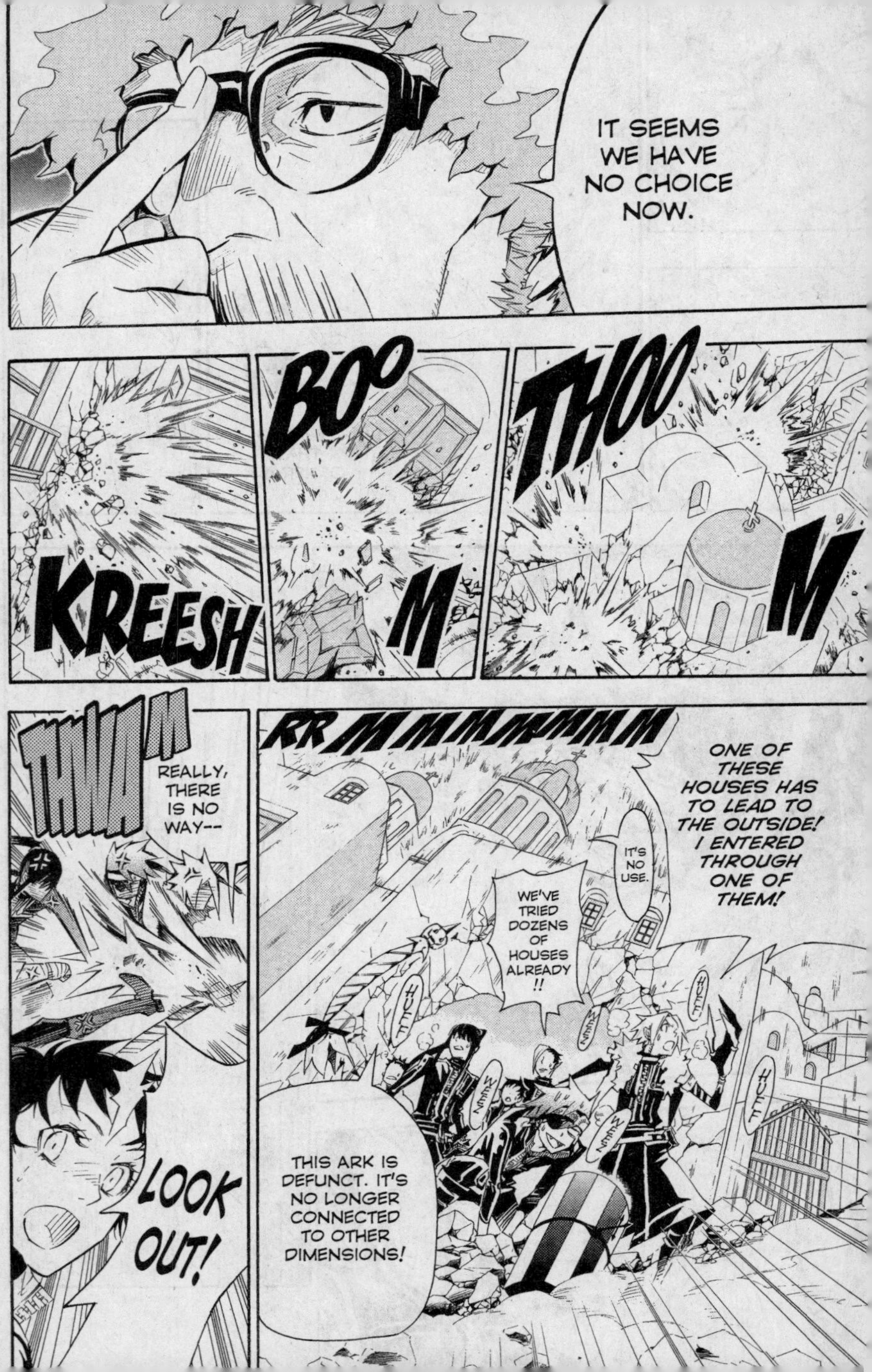
IT SEEMS WE HAVE NO CHOICE NOW.
THOOM
BOOM
KREESH
RRMMMMMMMMM
ONE OF THESE HOUSES HAS TO LEAD TO THE OUTSIDE! I ENTERED THROUGH ONE OF THEM!
IT'S NO USE.
WE'VE TRIED DOZENS OF HOUSES ALREADY!!
HUFF
HUFF
HUFF
THIS ARK IS DEFUNCT. IT'S NO LONGER CONNECTED TO OTHER DIMENSIONS!
THWAM
REALLY, THERE IS NO WAY--
LOOK OUT!

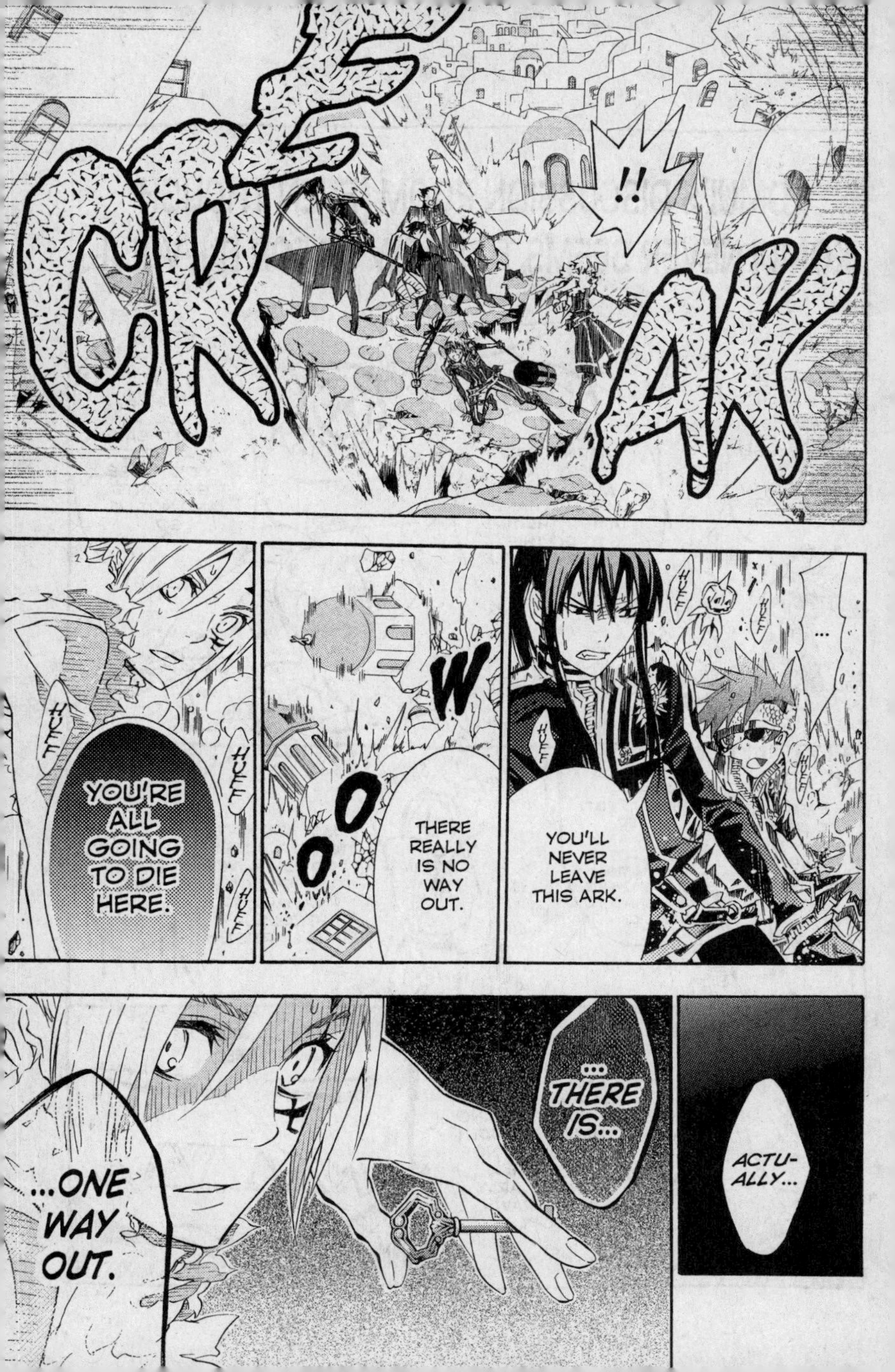
CRAAK
!!
HUFF
HUFF
...
YOU'LL NEVER LEAVE THIS ARK.
WOO
THERE REALLY IS NO WAY OUT.
HUFF
HUFF
HUFF
YOU'RE ALL GOING TO DIE HERE.
ACTU-ALLY...
...THERE IS...
...ONE WAY OUT.

KOMUI'S DISCUSSION ROOM (EVEN THOUGH KOMUI NEVER SEEMS TO SHOW UP FOR IT), VOL.1☆

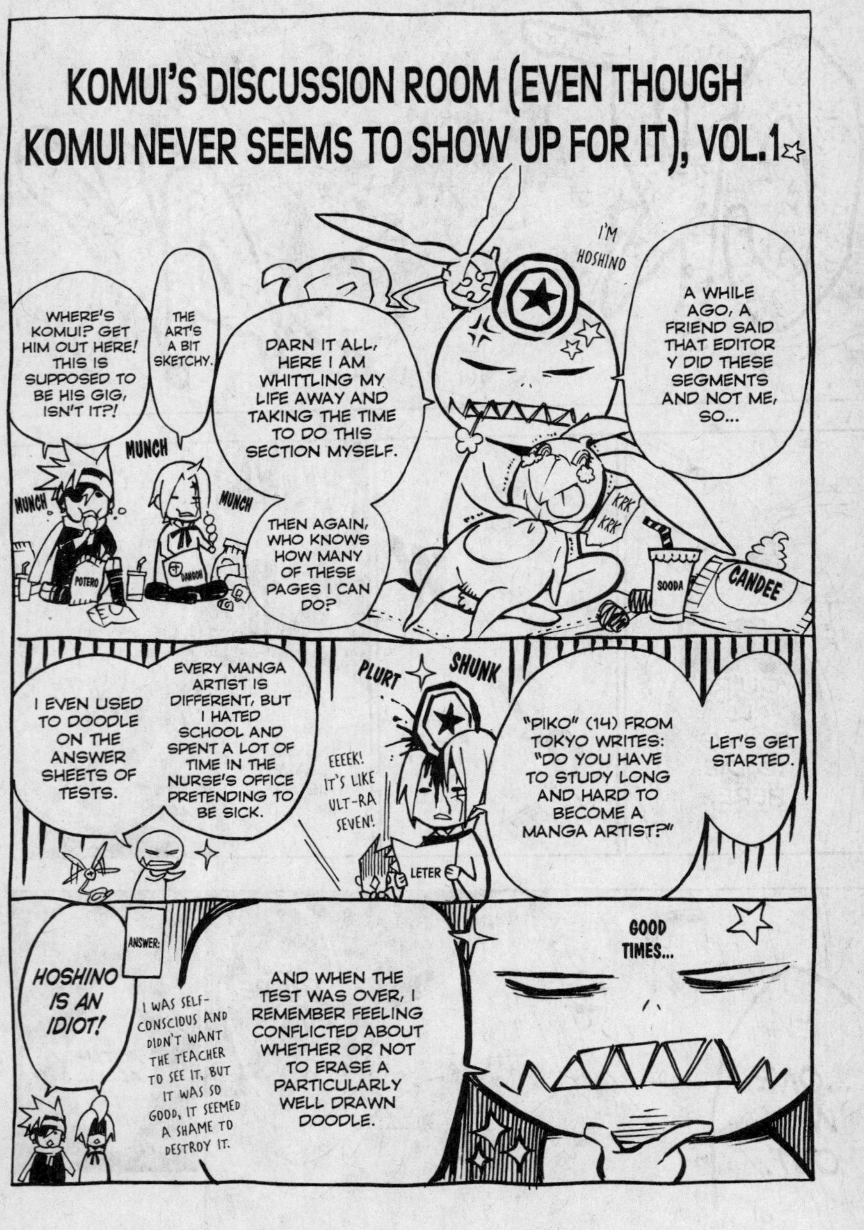

I'M HOSHINO
A WHILE AGO, A FRIEND SAID THAT EDITOR Y DID THESE SEGMENTS AND NOT ME, SO...
DARN IT ALL, HERE I AM WHITTLING MY LIFE AWAY AND TAKING THE TIME TO DO THIS SECTION MYSELF.
KRK KRK
CANDEE
SOODA
THEN AGAIN, WHO KNOWS HOW MANY OF THESE PAGES I CAN DO?
THE ART'S A BIT SKETCHY.
WHERE'S KOMUI? GET HIM OUT HERE! THIS IS SUPPOSED TO BE HIS GIG, ISN'T IT?!
MUNCH
MUNCH
MUNCH
DANGOH
POTERO
LET'S GET STARTED.
"PIKO" (14) FROM TOKYO WRITES: "DO YOU HAVE TO STUDY LONG AND HARD TO BECOME A MANGA ARTIST?"
SHUNK
PLURT
EEEEK! IT'S LIKE ULT-RA SEVEN!
LETER
EVERY MANGA ARTIST IS DIFFERENT, BUT I HATED SCHOOL AND SPENT A LOT OF TIME IN THE NURSE'S OFFICE PRETENDING TO BE SICK.
I EVEN USED TO DOODLE ON THE ANSWER SHEETS OF TESTS.
GOOD TIMES...
AND WHEN THE TEST WAS OVER, I REMEMBER FEELING CONFLICTED ABOUT WHETHER OR NOT TO ERASE A PARTICULARLY WELL DRAWN DOODLE.
I WAS SELF-CONSCIOUS AND DIDN'T WANT THE TEACHER TO SEE IT, BUT IT WAS SO GOOD, IT SEEMED A SHAME TO DESTROY IT.
ANSWER:
HOSHINO IS AN IDIOT!

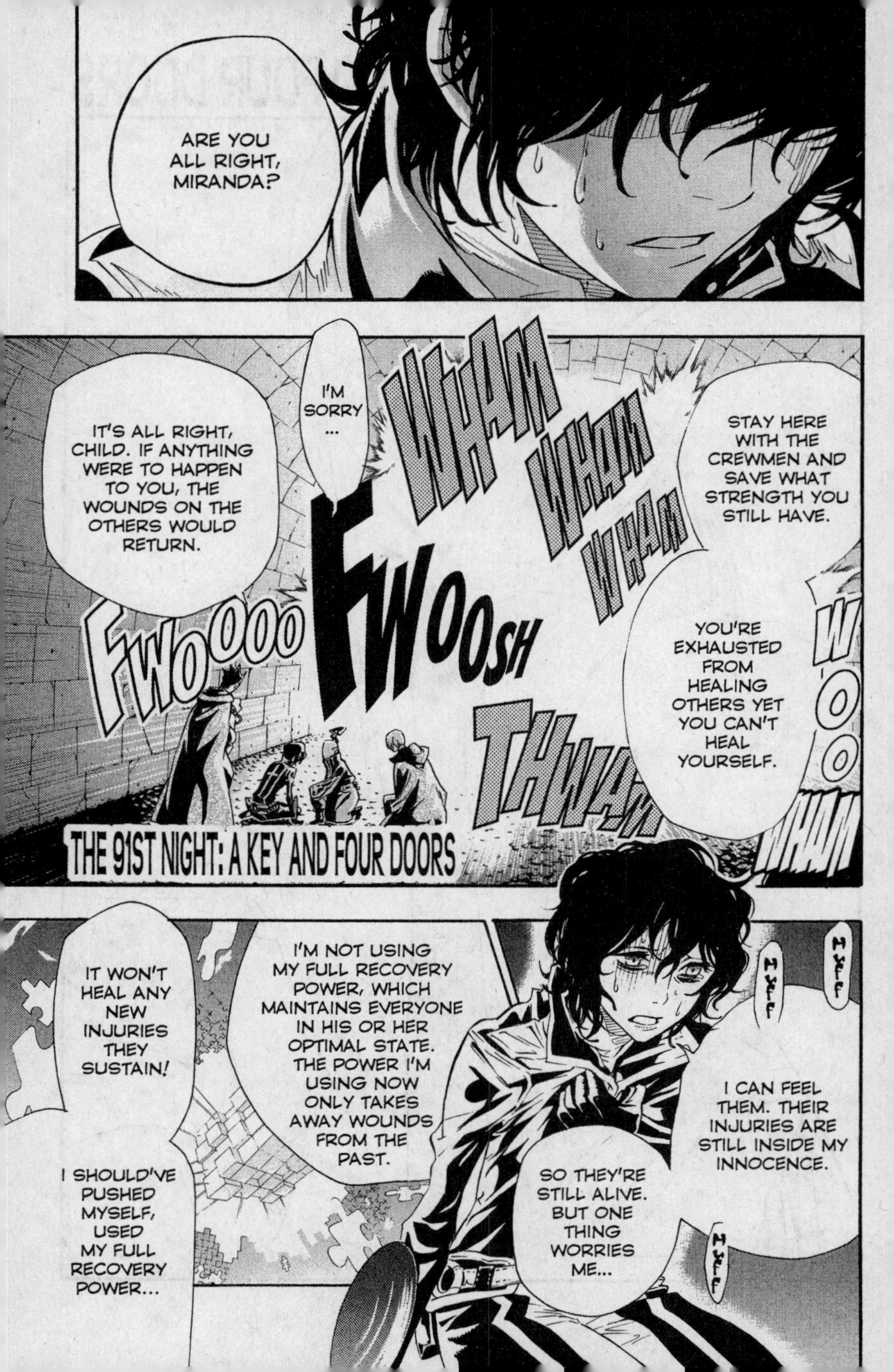
ARE YOU ALL RIGHT, MIRANDA?
STAY HERE WITH THE CREWMEN AND SAVE WHAT STRENGTH YOU STILL HAVE.
YOU'RE EXHAUSTED FROM HEALING OTHERS YET YOU CAN'T HEAL YOURSELF.
WHAM
WHAM
WHAM
THWAM
I'M SORRY ...
IT'S ALL RIGHT, CHILD. IF ANYTHING WERE TO HAPPEN TO YOU, THE WOUNDS ON THE OTHERS WOULD RETURN.
FWOOSH
FWOOOO
THE 91ST NIGHT: A KEY AND FOUR DOORS
HUFF
HUFF
I CAN FEEL THEM. THEIR INJURIES ARE STILL INSIDE MY INNOCENCE.
SO THEY'RE STILL ALIVE. BUT ONE THING WORRIES ME...
HUFF
I'M NOT USING MY FULL RECOVERY POWER, WHICH MAINTAINS EVERYONE IN HIS OR HER OPTIMAL STATE. THE POWER I'M USING NOW ONLY TAKES AWAY WOUNDS FROM THE PAST.
IT WON'T HEAL ANY NEW INJURIES THEY SUSTAIN!
I SHOULD'VE PUSHED MYSELF, USED MY FULL RECOVERY POWER...

THE 91ST NIGHT: A KEY AND FOUR DOORS

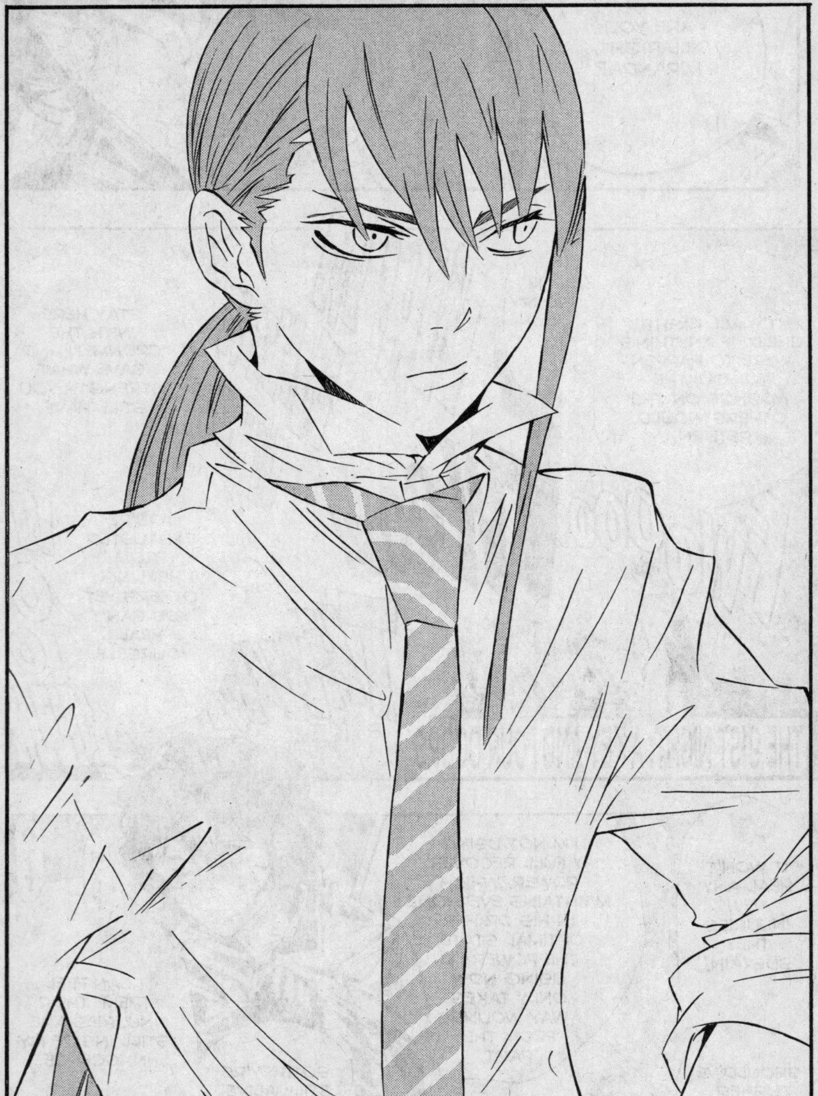

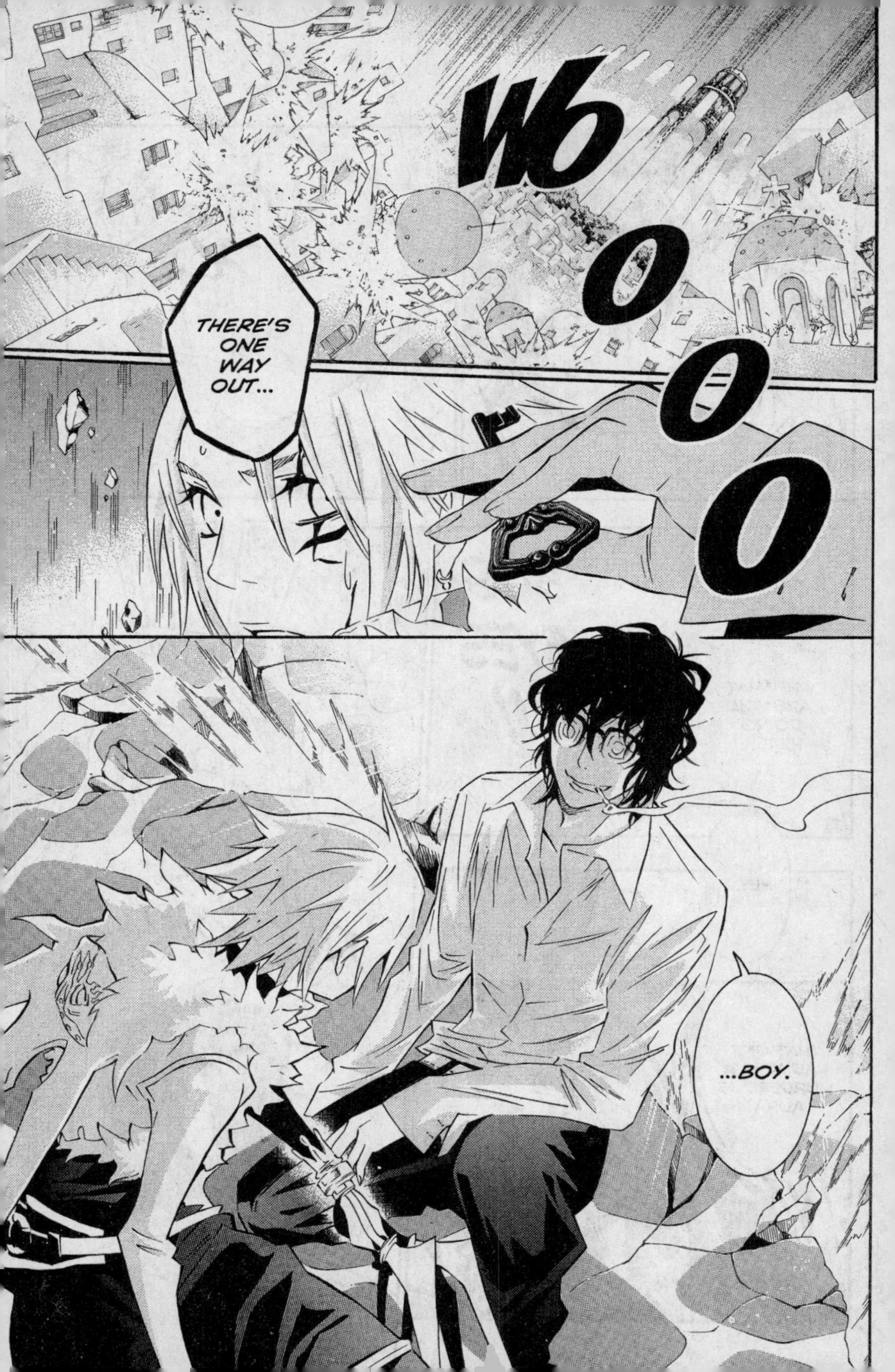
WOOOO
THERE'S ONE WAY OUT...
...BOY.

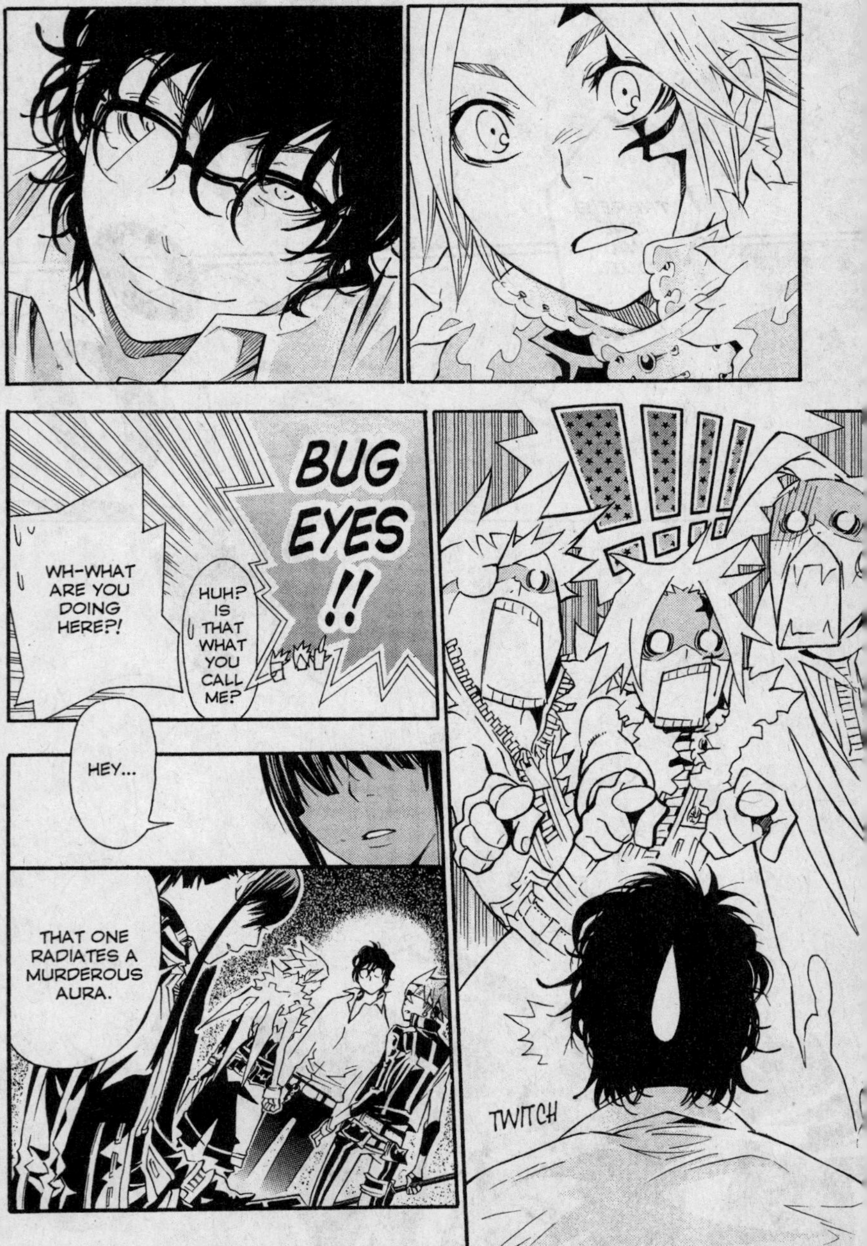
TWITCH
BUG EYES !!
HUH? IS THAT WHAT YOU CALL ME?
WH-WHAT ARE YOU DOING HERE?!
HEY...
THAT ONE RADIATES A MURDEROUS AURA.

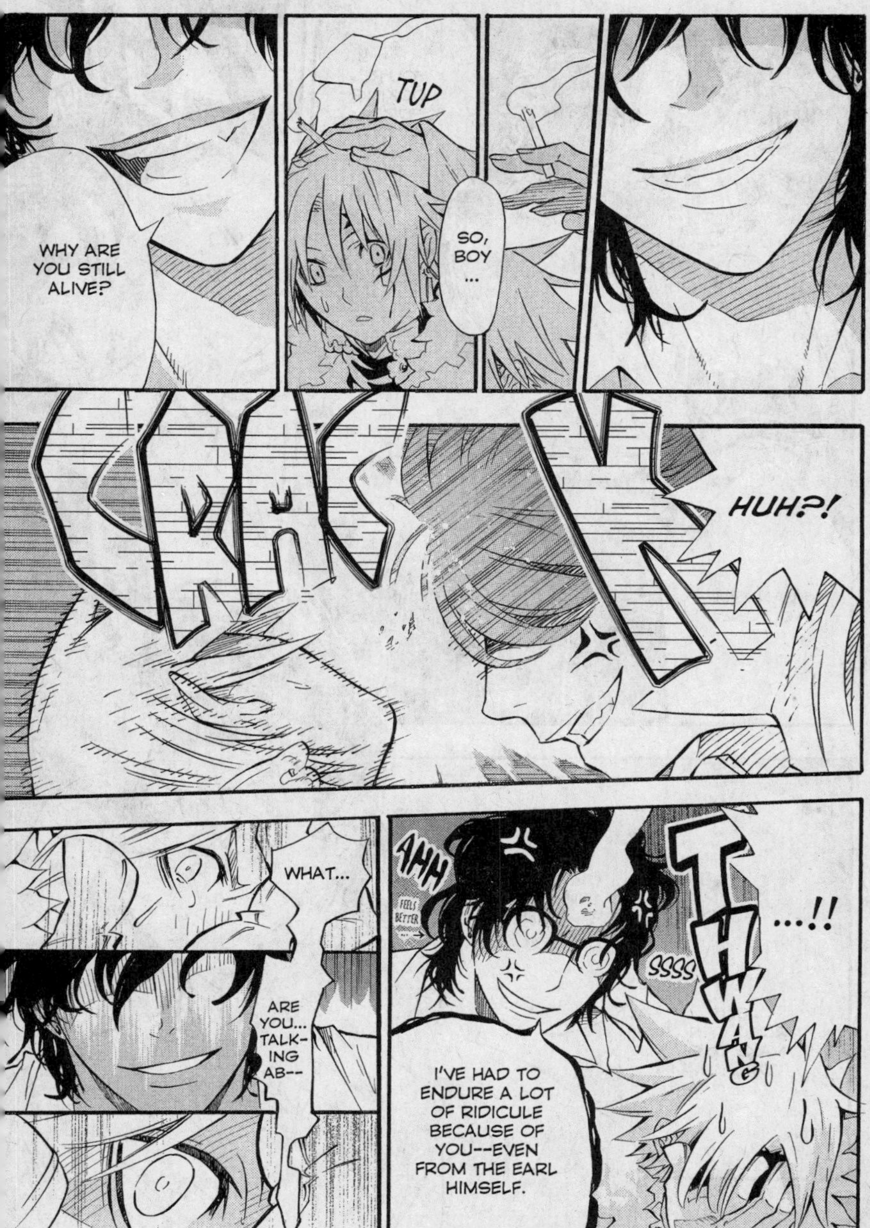
TUP
SO, BOY ...
WHY ARE YOU STILL ALIVE?
HUH?!
WHACK
THWANG
...!!
AHH
FEELS BETTER...
SSSS
I'VE HAD TO ENDURE A LOT OF RIDICULE BECAUSE OF YOU--EVEN FROM THE EARL HIMSELF.
WHAT...
ARE YOU... TALKING AB--

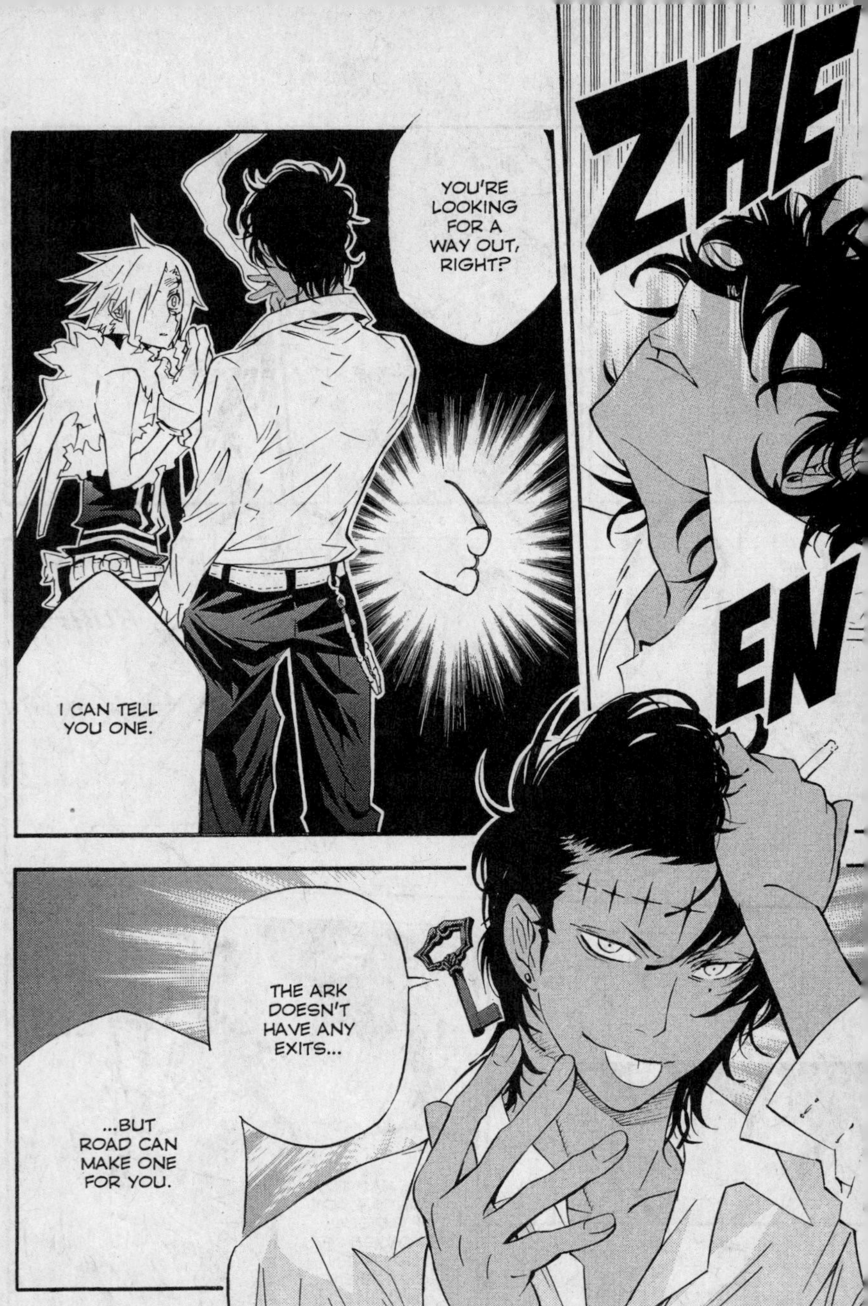
ZHE
EN
YOU'RE LOOKING FOR A WAY OUT, RIGHT?
I CAN TELL YOU ONE.
THE ARK DOESN'T HAVE ANY EXITS...
...BUT ROAD CAN MAKE ONE FOR YOU.

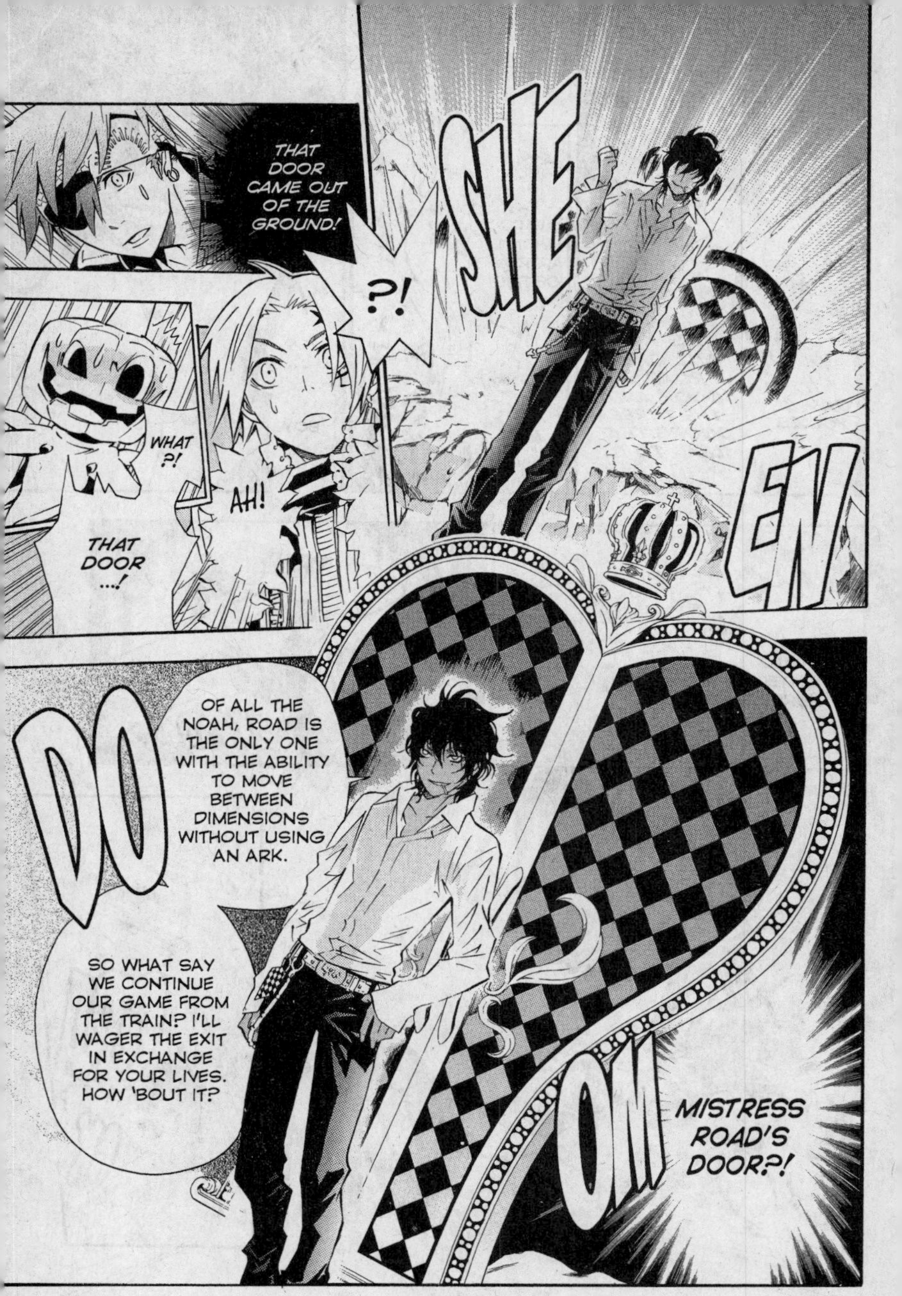
SHE
EN
THAT DOOR CAME OUT OF THE GROUND!
?!
WHAT ?!
AH!
THAT DOOR ...!
DO
OM
MISTRESS ROAD'S DOOR?!
OF ALL THE NOAH, ROAD IS THE ONLY ONE WITH THE ABILITY TO MOVE BETWEEN DIMENSIONS WITHOUT USING AN ARK.
SO WHAT SAY WE CONTINUE OUR GAME FROM THE TRAIN? I'LL WAGER THE EXIT IN EXCHANGE FOR YOUR LIVES. HOW 'BOUT IT?

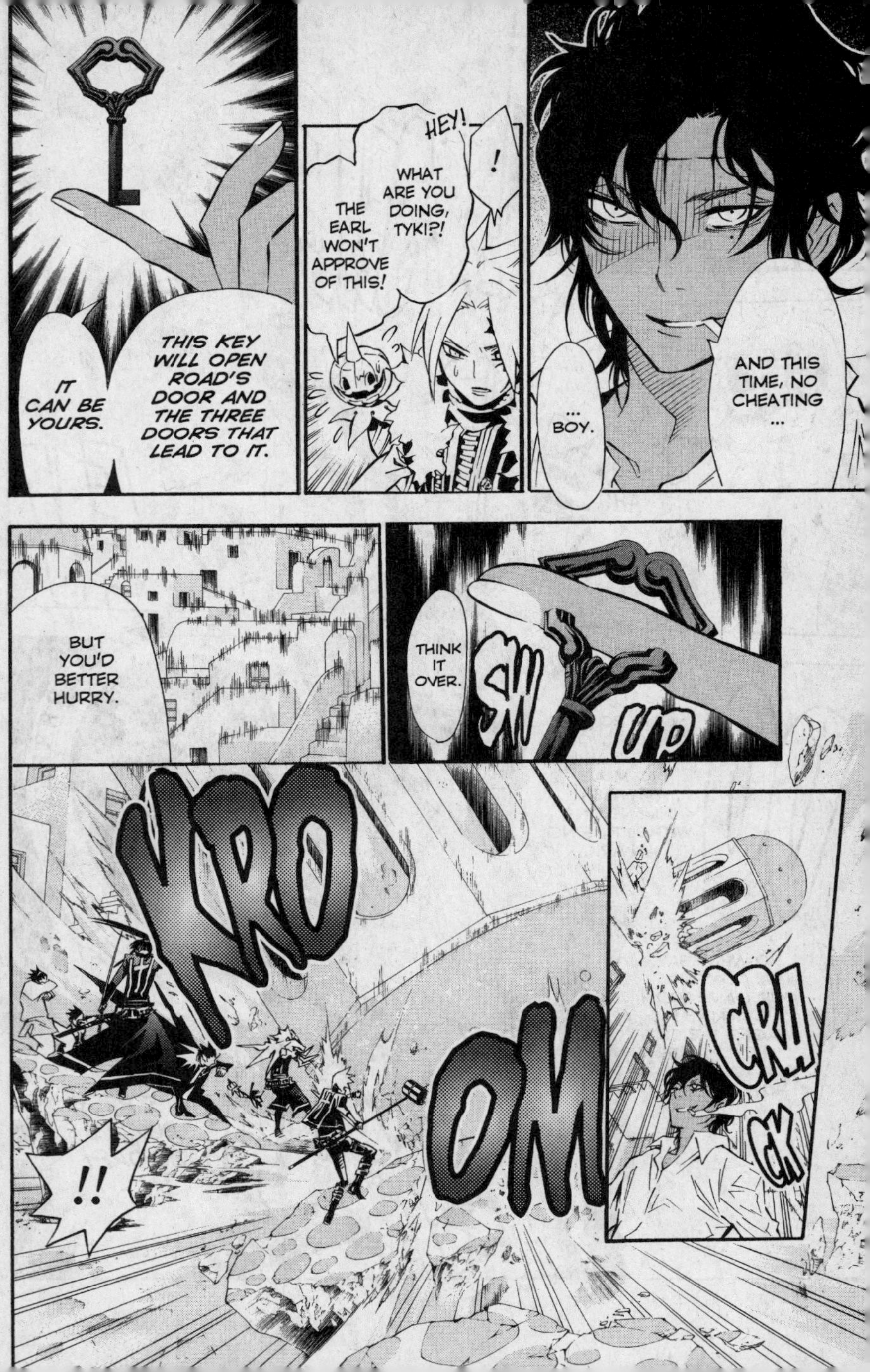
AND THIS TIME, NO CHEATING ...
... BOY.
HEY!
!
WHAT ARE YOU DOING, TYKI?!
THE EARL WON'T APPROVE OF THIS!
THIS KEY WILL OPEN ROAD'S DOOR AND THE THREE DOORS THAT LEAD TO IT.
IT CAN BE YOURS.
THINK IT OVER.
SHUP
BUT YOU'D BETTER HURRY.
CRACK
KROOM
!!

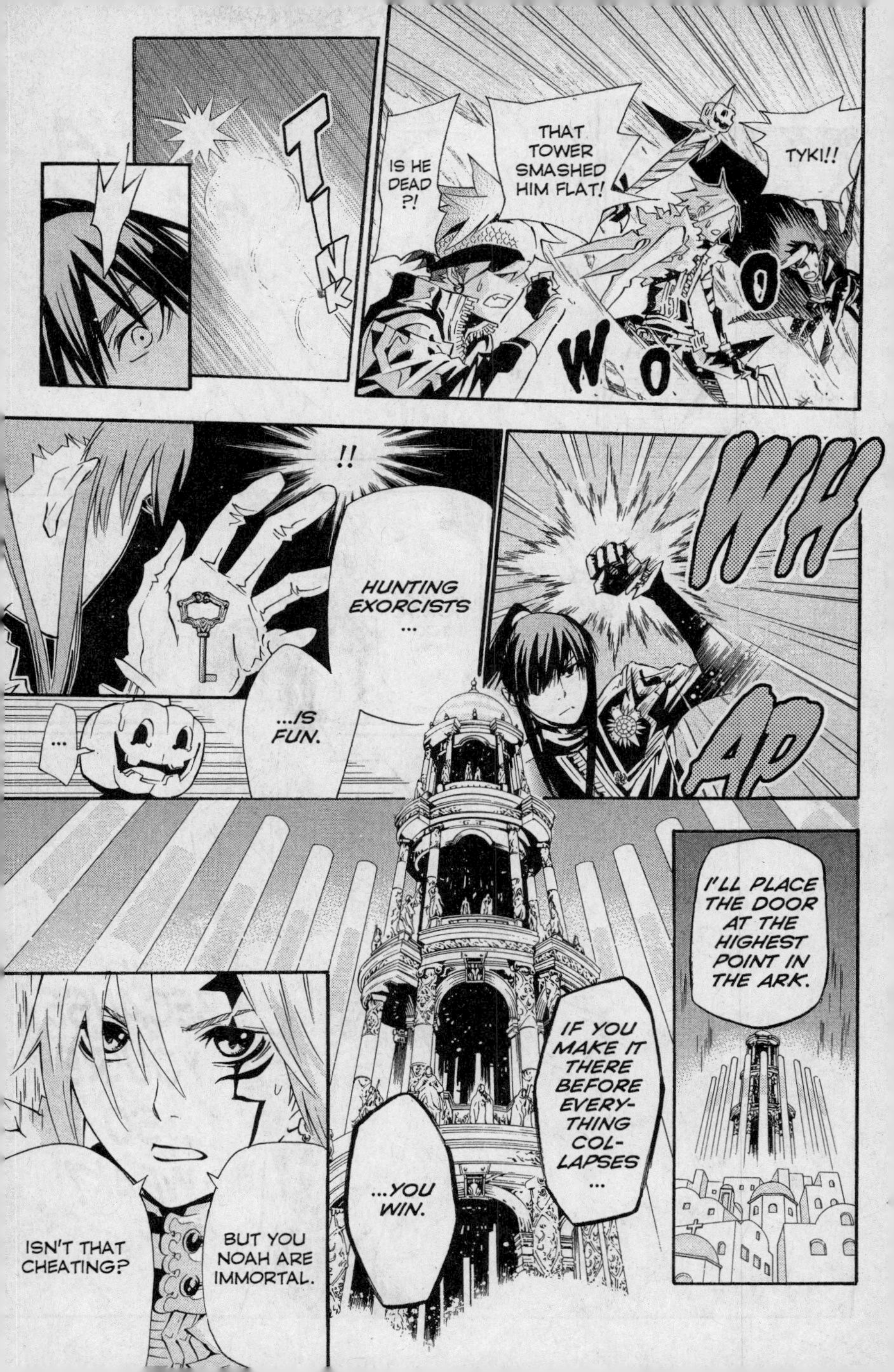

TYKI!!
THAT TOWER SMASHED HIM FLAT!
IS HE DEAD?!
WOO
TINK
WHAP
!!
HUNTING EXORCISTS ...
...IS FUN.
...
I'LL PLACE THE DOOR AT THE HIGHEST POINT IN THE ARK.
IF YOU MAKE IT THERE BEFORE EVERY-THING COL-LAPSES ...
...YOU WIN.
BUT YOU NOAH ARE IMMORTAL.
ISN'T THAT CHEATING?

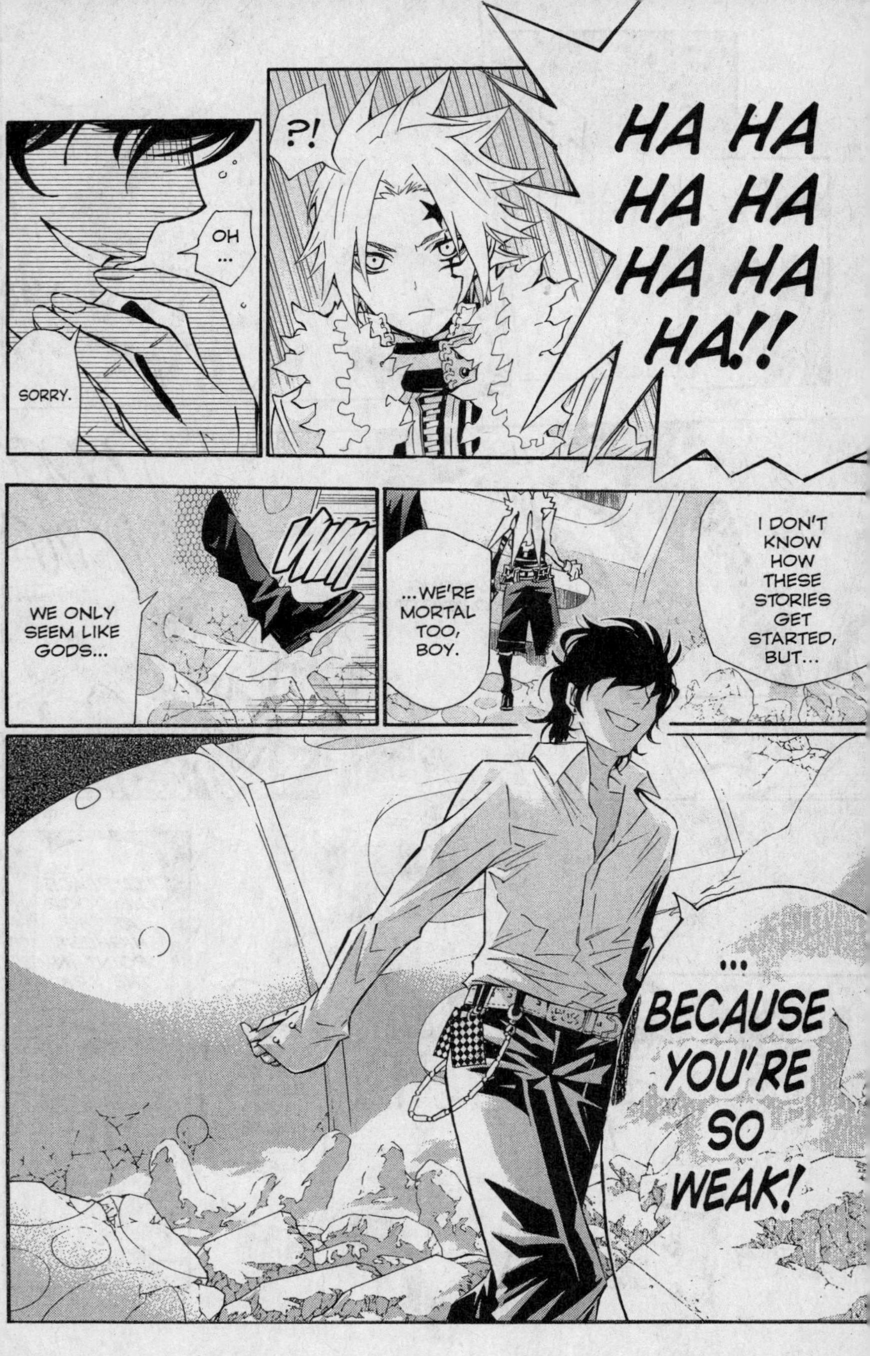
HA HA HA HA HA HA HA!!
?!
OH ...
SORRY.
I DON'T KNOW HOW THESE STORIES GET STARTED, BUT...
...WE'RE MORTAL TOO, BOY.
WE ONLY SEEM LIKE GODS...
...BECAUSE YOU'RE SO WEAK!

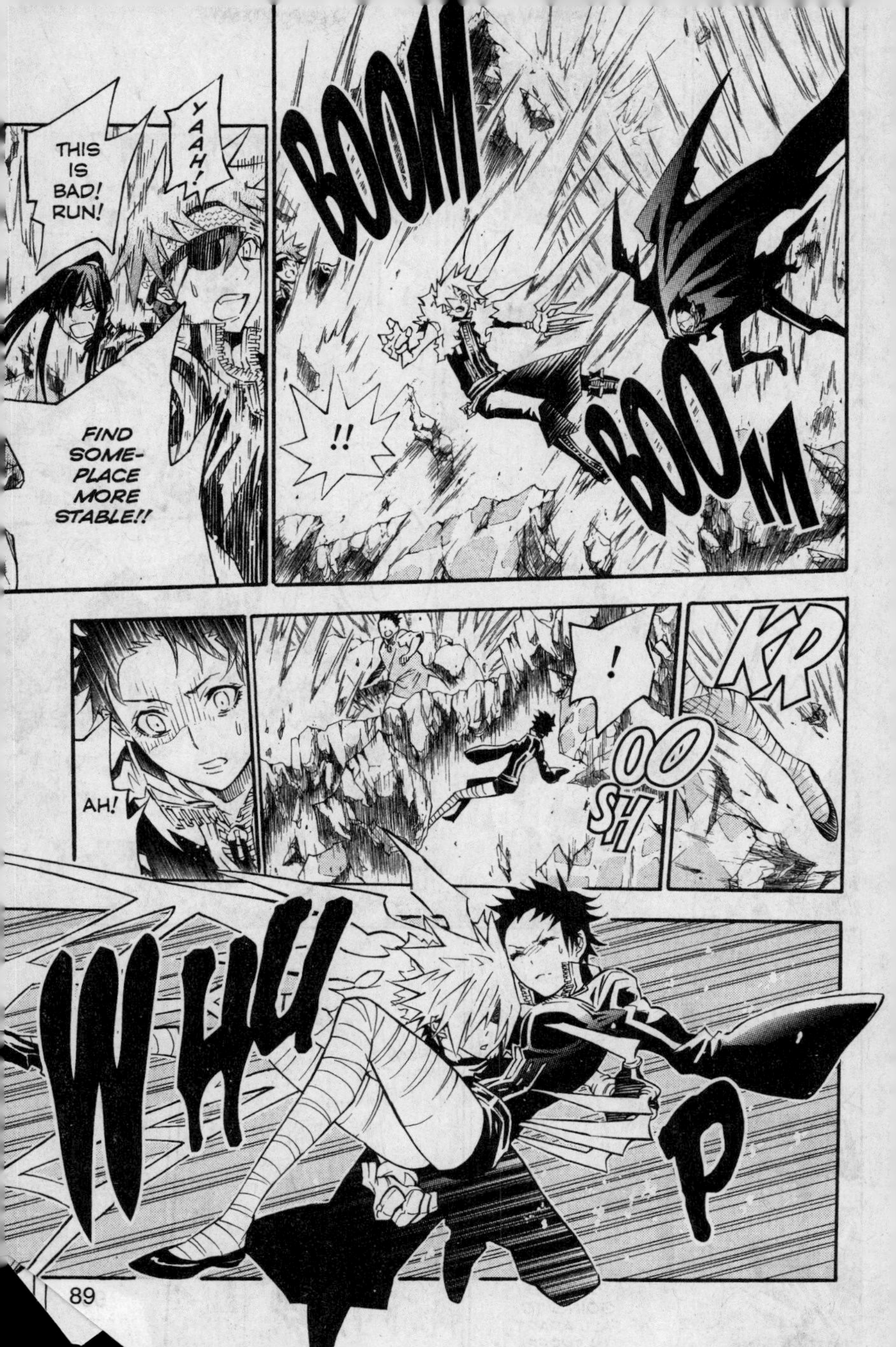
BOOM
BOOM
!!
YAAH!
THIS IS BAD! RUN!
FIND SOME-PLACE MORE STABLE!!
KR
!
OOSH
AH!
WHUP

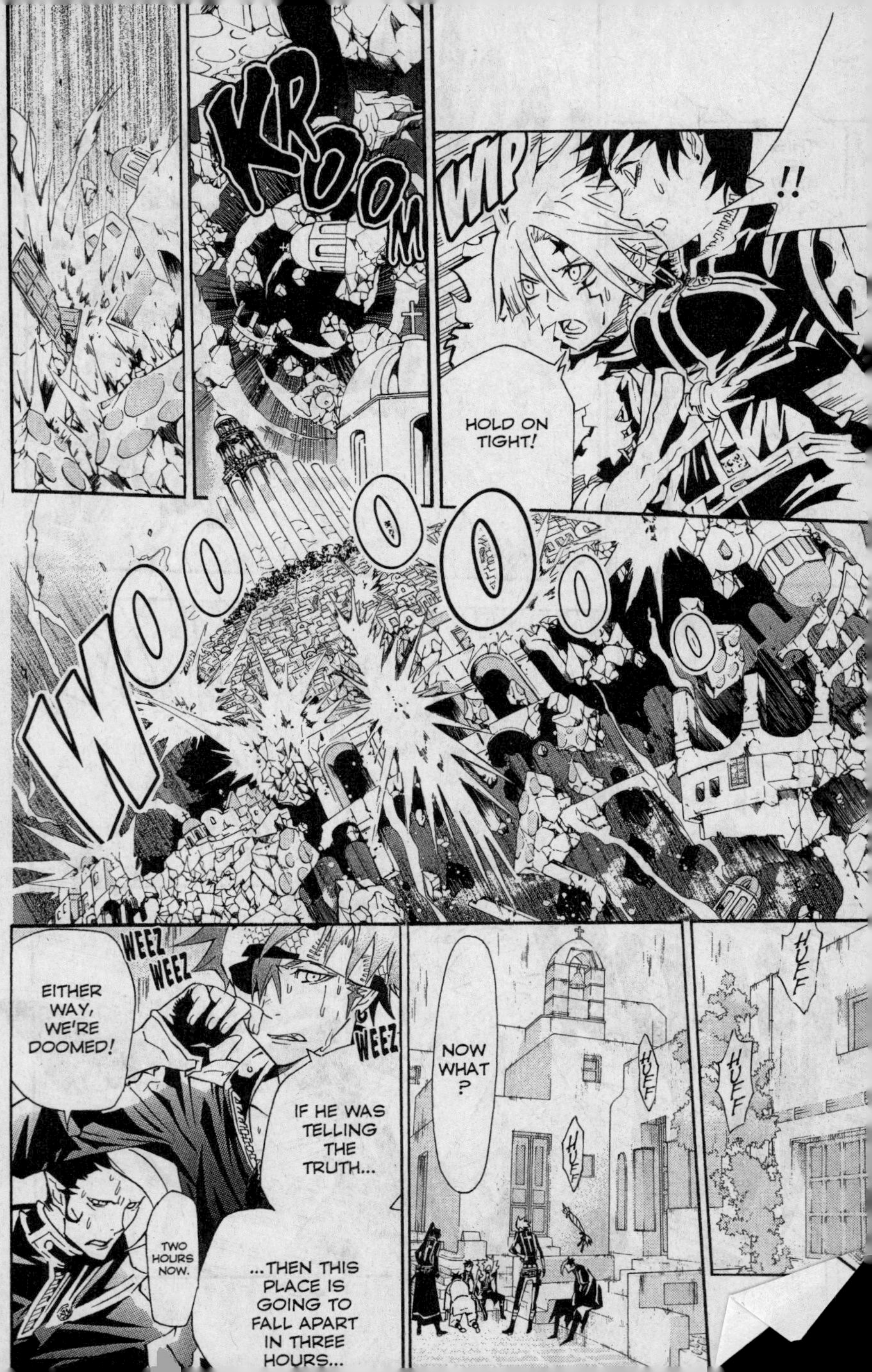

!!
WIP
HOLD ON TIGHT!
KROOOM
WOOOOOOM
HUFF
HUFF
NOW WHAT?
HUFF
HUFF
WEEZ
IF HE WAS TELLING THE TRUTH...
...THEN THIS PLACE IS GOING TO FALL APART IN THREE HOURS...
WEEZ WEEZ
EITHER WAY, WE'RE DOOMED!
TWO HOURS NOW.

READ THIS WAY

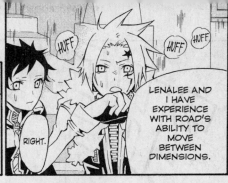

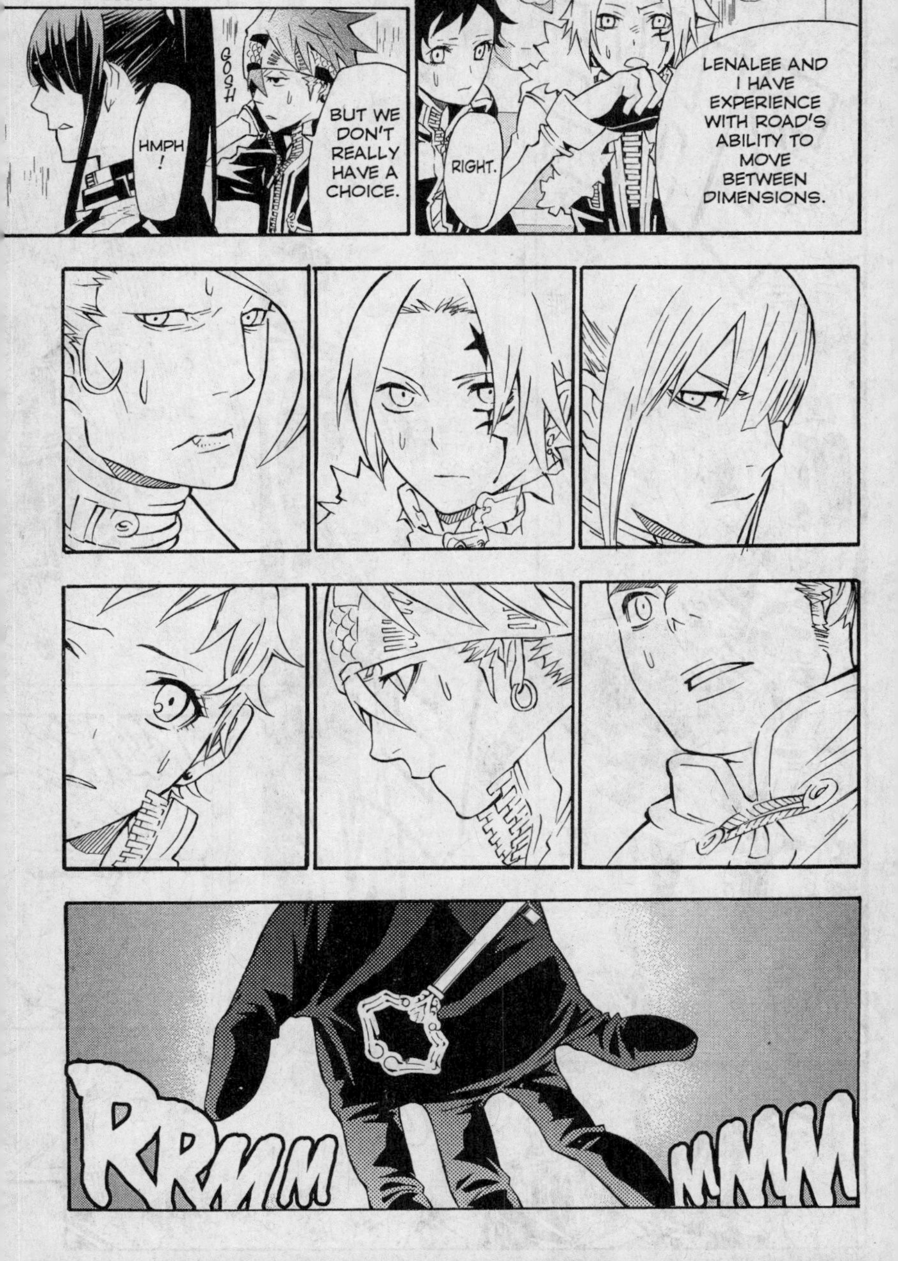
HUFF
HUFF
HUFF
LENALEE AND I HAVE EXPERIENCE WITH ROAD'S ABILITY TO MOVE BETWEEN DIMENSIONS.
RIGHT.
BUT WE DON'T REALLY HAVE A CHOICE.
GOSH
HMPH!
RRMMM
MMMM

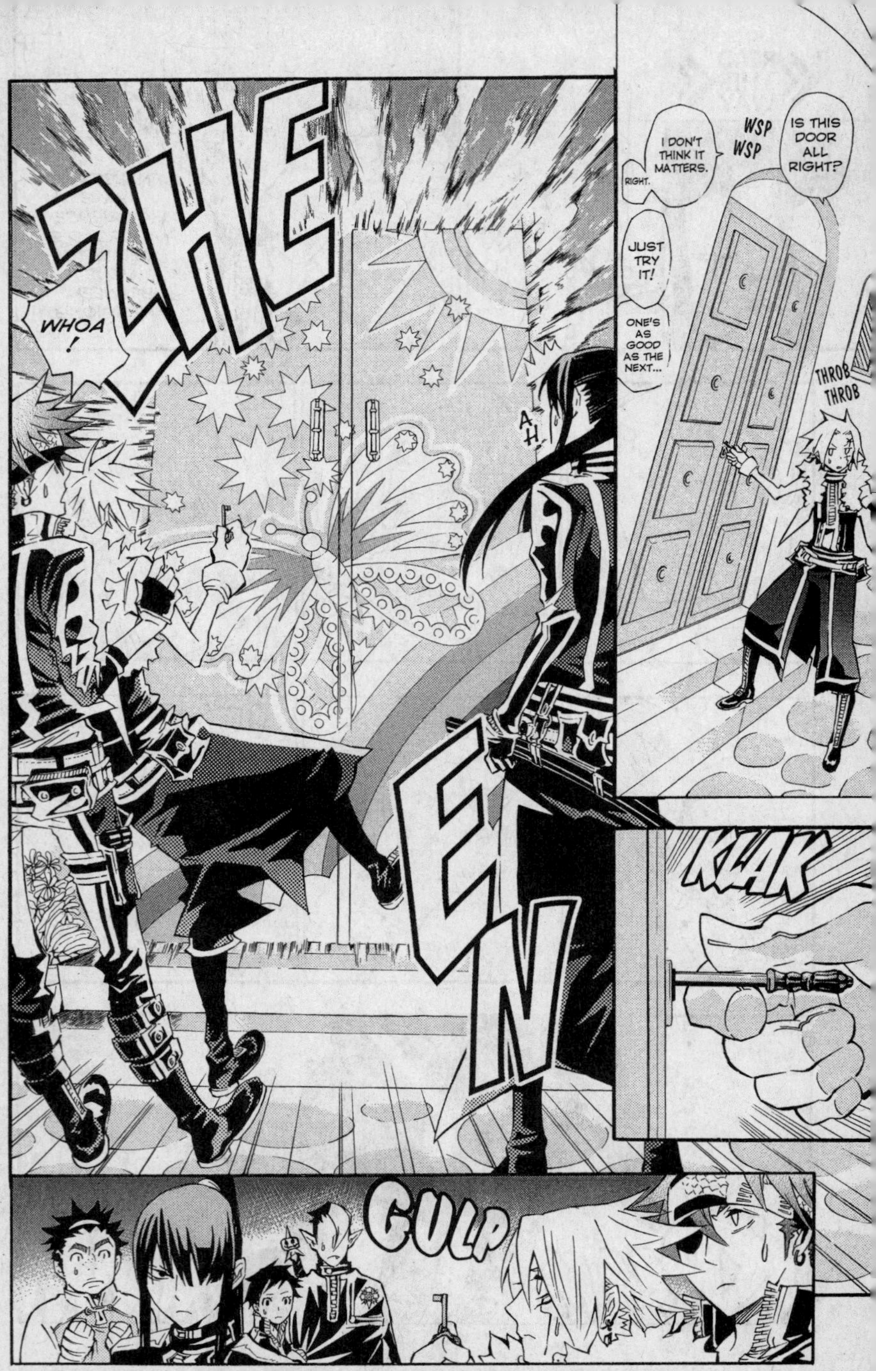
IS THIS DOOR ALL RIGHT?
WSP WSP
I DON'T THINK IT MATTERS.
RIGHT.
JUST TRY IT!
ONE'S AS GOOD AS THE NEXT...
THROB THROB
KLAK
ZHE
WHOA!
AH
EN
GULP

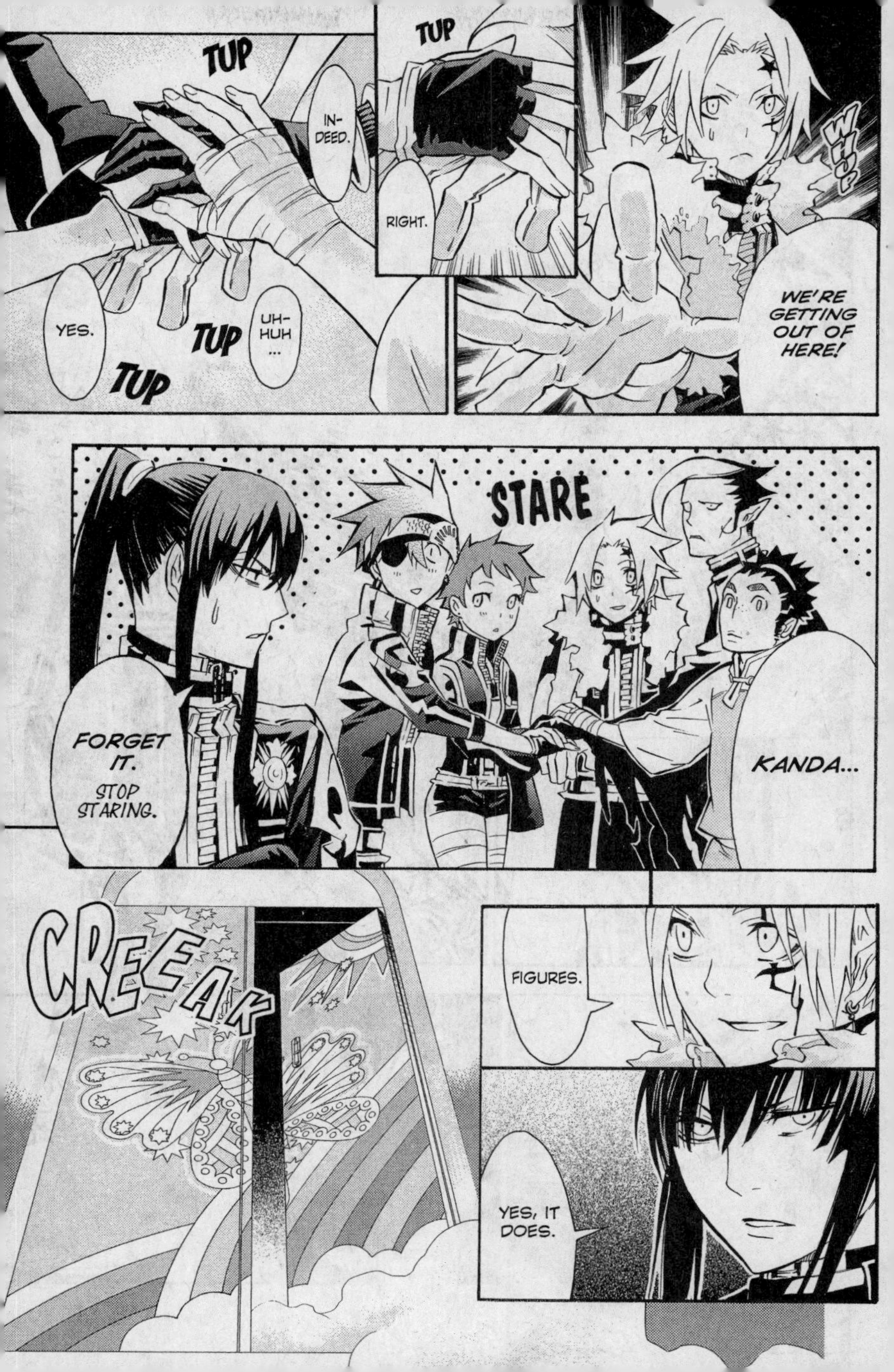
WHUP
WE'RE GETTING OUT OF HERE!
TUP
RIGHT.
TUP
IN-DEED.
UH-HUH ...
TUP
YES.
TUP
KANDA...
STARE
FORGET IT. STOP STARING.
FIGURES.
YES, IT DOES.
CREEAK

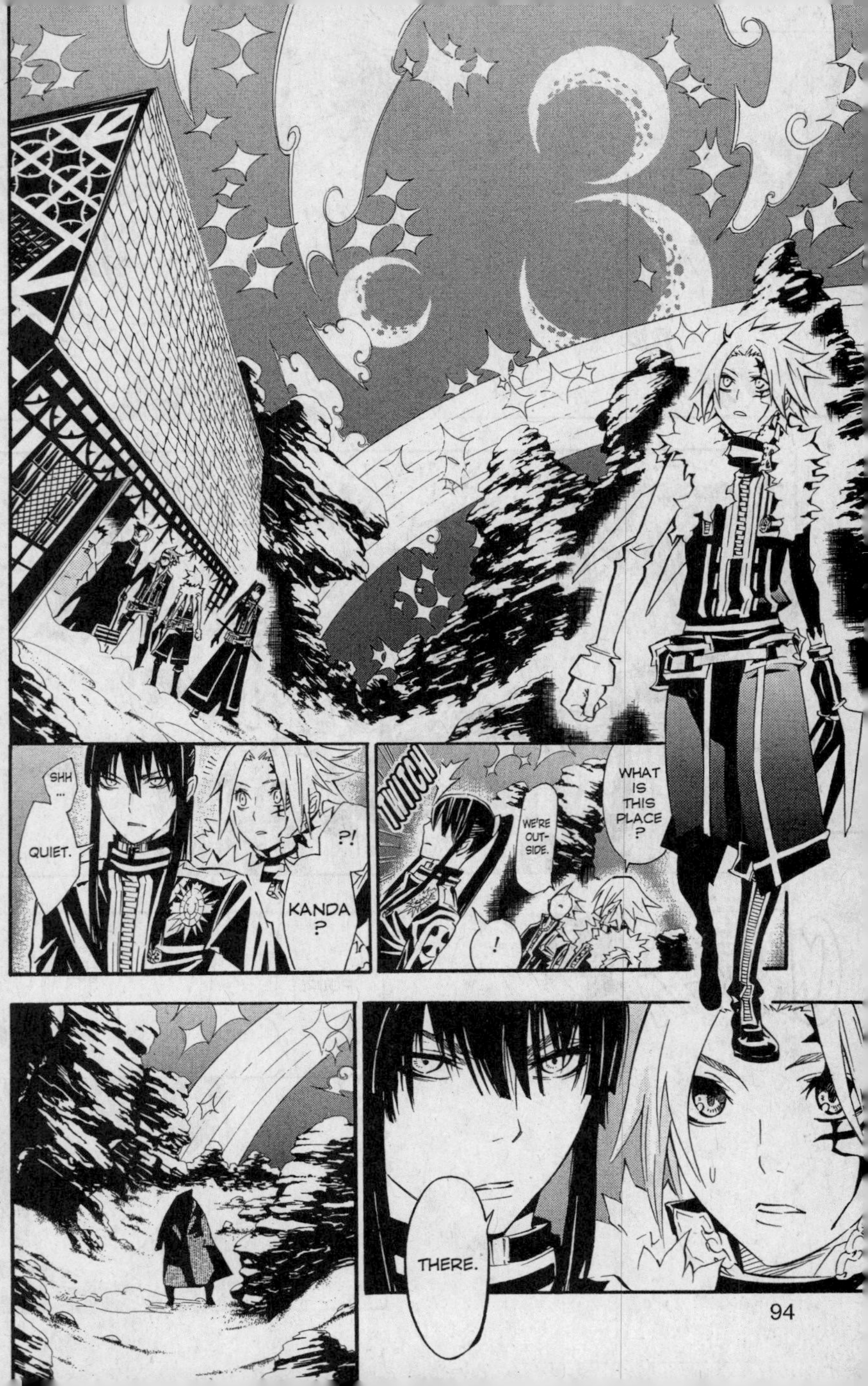
WHAT IS THIS PLACE?
WE'RE OUTSIDE.
TWITCH
!
?!
KANDA?
SHH ... QUIET.
THERE.

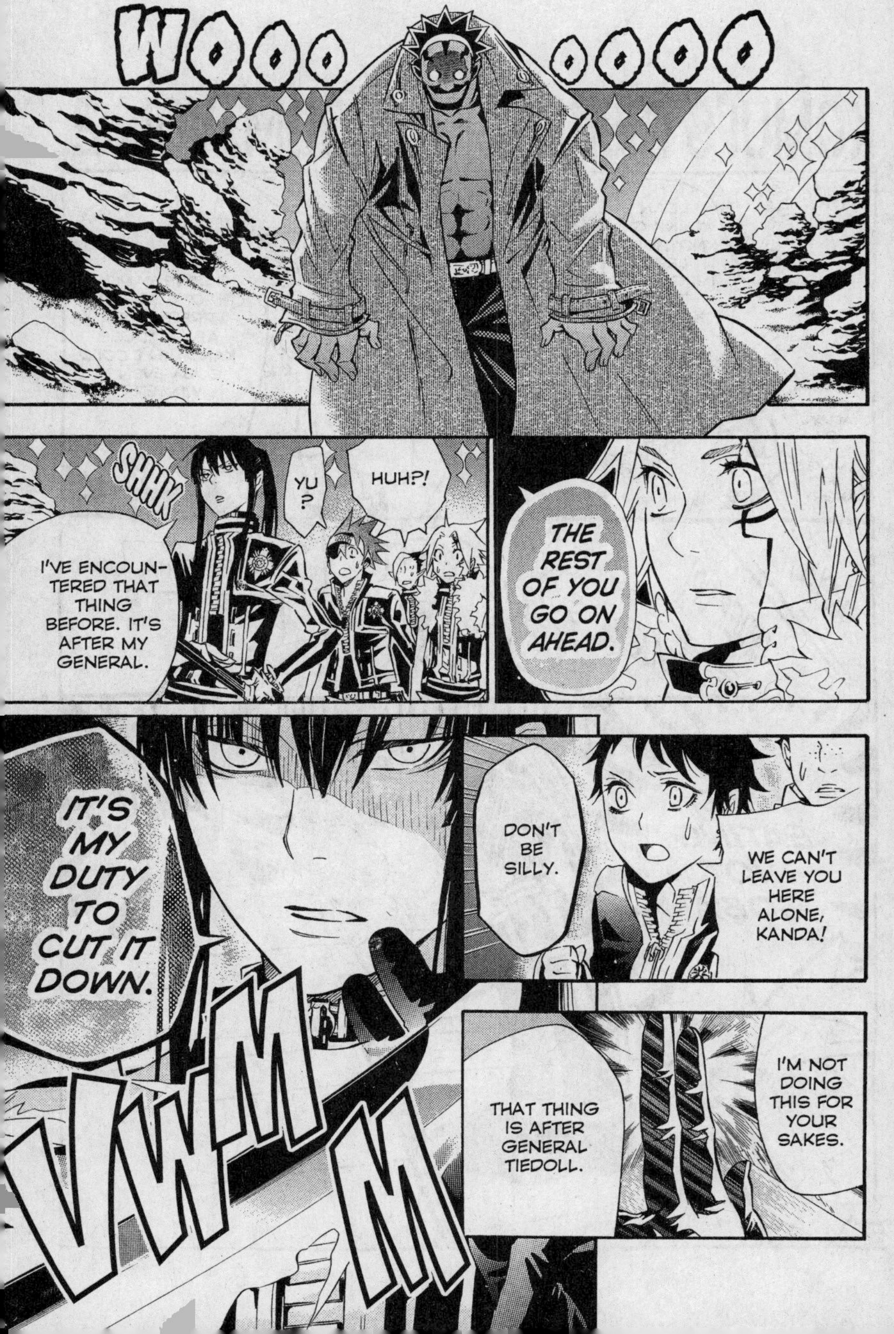
WOOOO OOOO
THE REST OF YOU GO ON AHEAD.
HUH?!
YU ?
SHHK
I'VE ENCOUNTERED THAT THING BEFORE. IT'S AFTER MY GENERAL.
WE CAN'T LEAVE YOU HERE ALONE, KANDA!
DON'T BE SILLY.
I'M NOT DOING THIS FOR YOUR SAKES.
THAT THING IS AFTER GENERAL TIEDOLL.
IT'S MY DUTY TO CUT IT DOWN.
VWMM

KOMUI'S DISCUSSION ROOM, VOL. 2

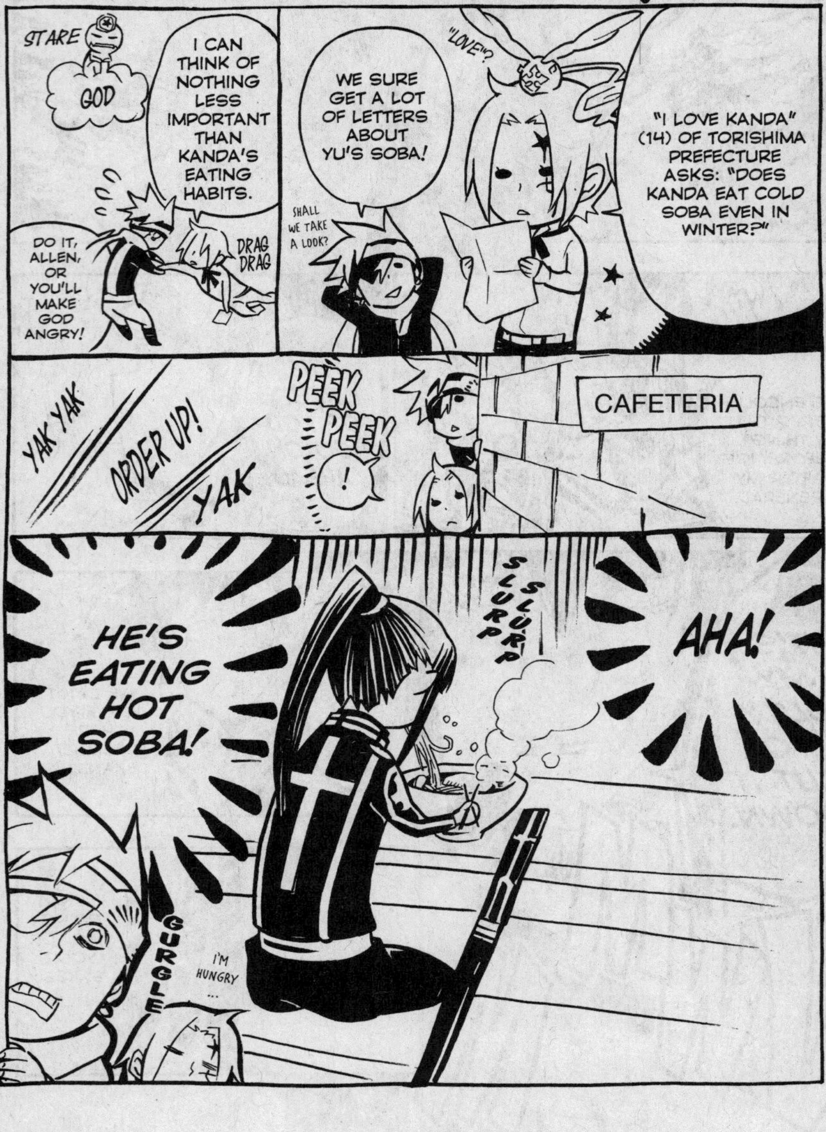
"LOVE"?
"I LOVE KANDA" (14) OF TORISHIMA PREFECTURE ASKS: "DOES KANDA EAT COLD SOBA EVEN IN WINTER?"
WE SURE GET A LOT OF LETTERS ABOUT YU'S SOBA!
SHALL WE TAKE A LOOK?
I CAN THINK OF NOTHING LESS IMPORTANT THAN KANDA'S EATING HABITS.
STARE
GOD
DO IT, ALLEN, OR YOU'LL MAKE GOD ANGRY!
DRAG DRAG
CAFETERIA
PEEK PEEK
!
YAK YAK
ORDER UP!
YAK
AHA!
SLURP SLURP
HE'S EATING HOT SOBA!
GURGLE
I'M HUNGRY ...

THE 92ND NIGHT:
SKIN BORIC'S ROOM

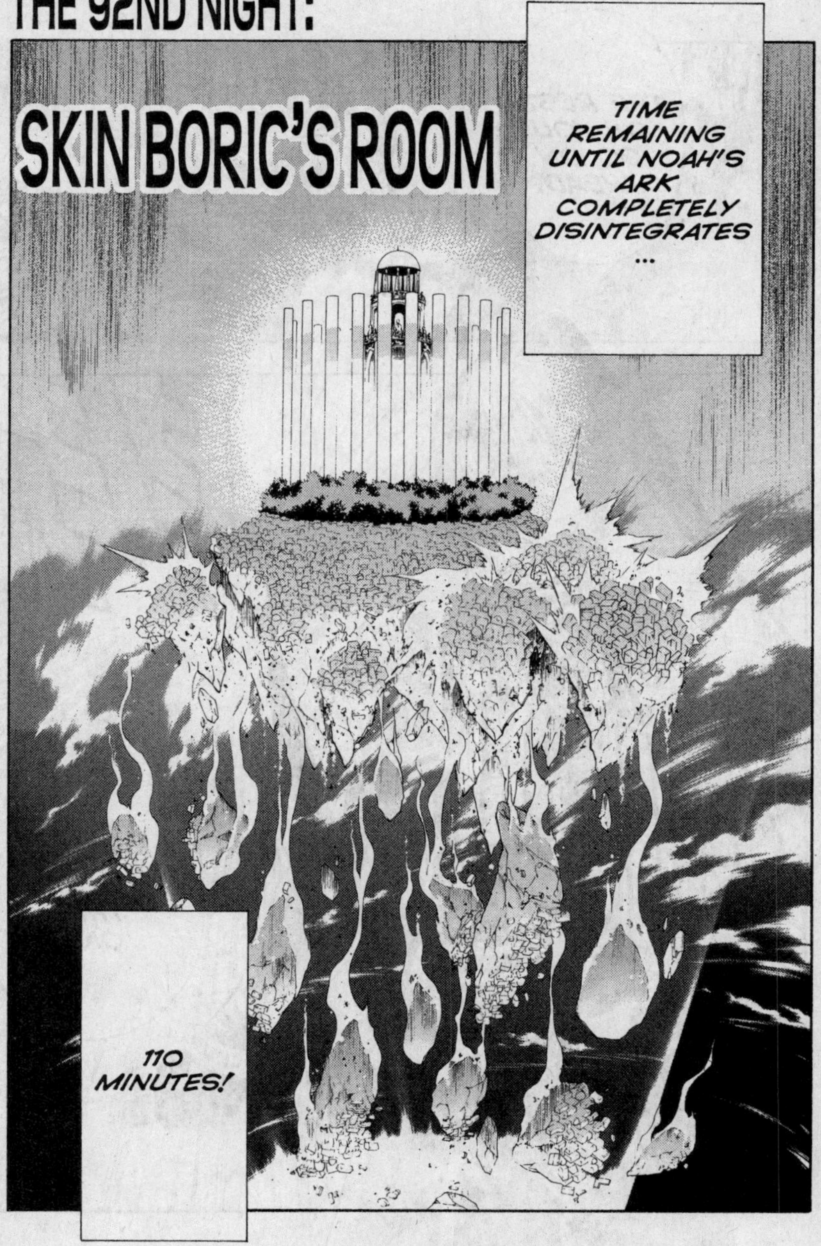
TIME REMAINING UNTIL NOAH'S ARK COMPLETELY DISINTEGRATES ...
110 MINUTES!

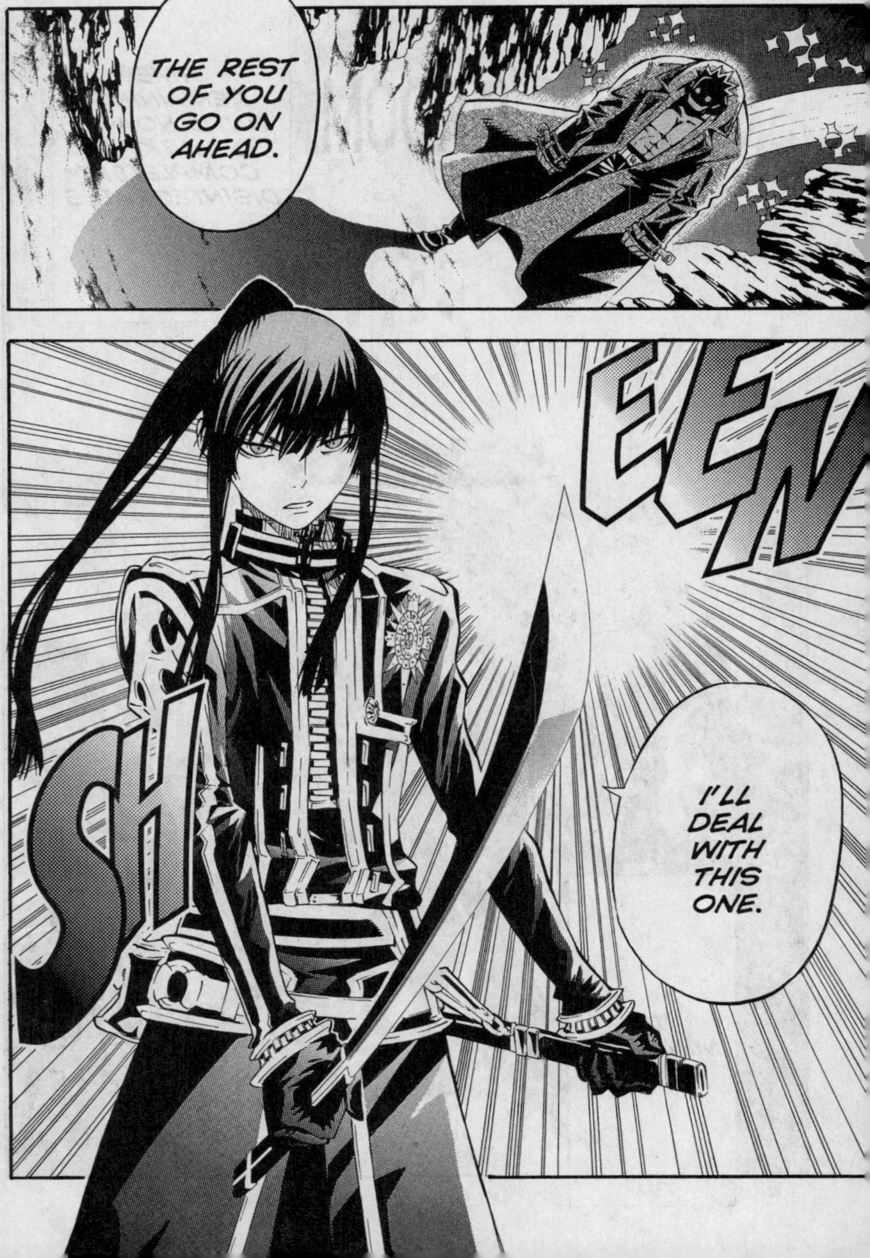
THE REST OF YOU GO ON AHEAD.
EEN
I'LL DEAL WITH THIS ONE.
SH

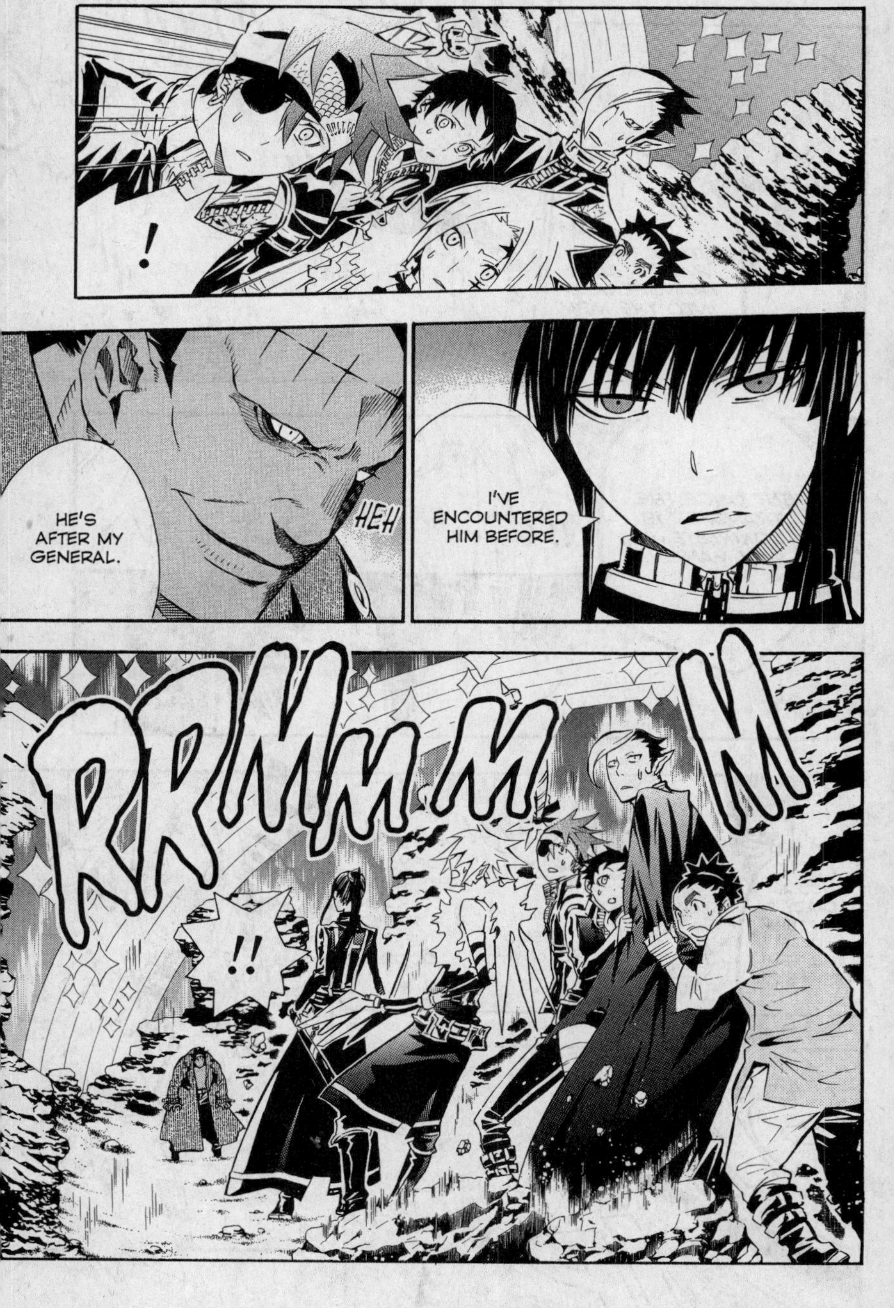
!
I'VE ENCOUNTERED HIM BEFORE.
HE'S AFTER MY GENERAL.
HEH
RRMMMMM
!!

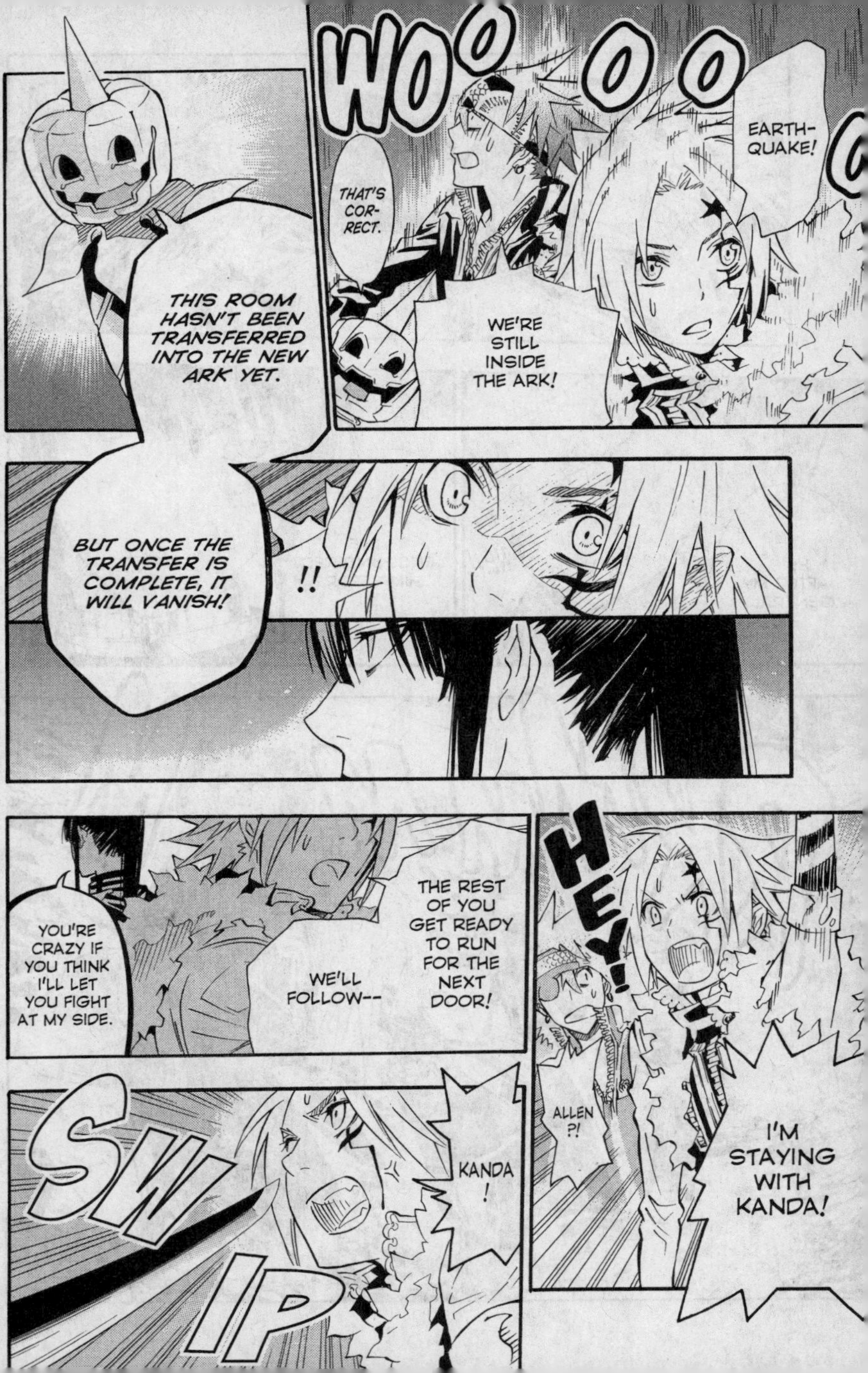
WOOOOO
EARTH-QUAKE!
WE'RE STILL INSIDE THE ARK!
THAT'S COR-RECT.
THIS ROOM HASN'T BEEN TRANSFERRED INTO THE NEW ARK YET.
BUT ONCE THE TRANSFER IS COMPLETE, IT WILL VANISH!
!!
HEY!
ALLEN ?!
I'M STAYING WITH KANDA!
THE REST OF YOU GET READY TO RUN FOR THE NEXT DOOR!
WE'LL FOLLOW--
YOU'RE CRAZY IF YOU THINK I'LL LET YOU FIGHT AT MY SIDE.
SWIP
KANDA !

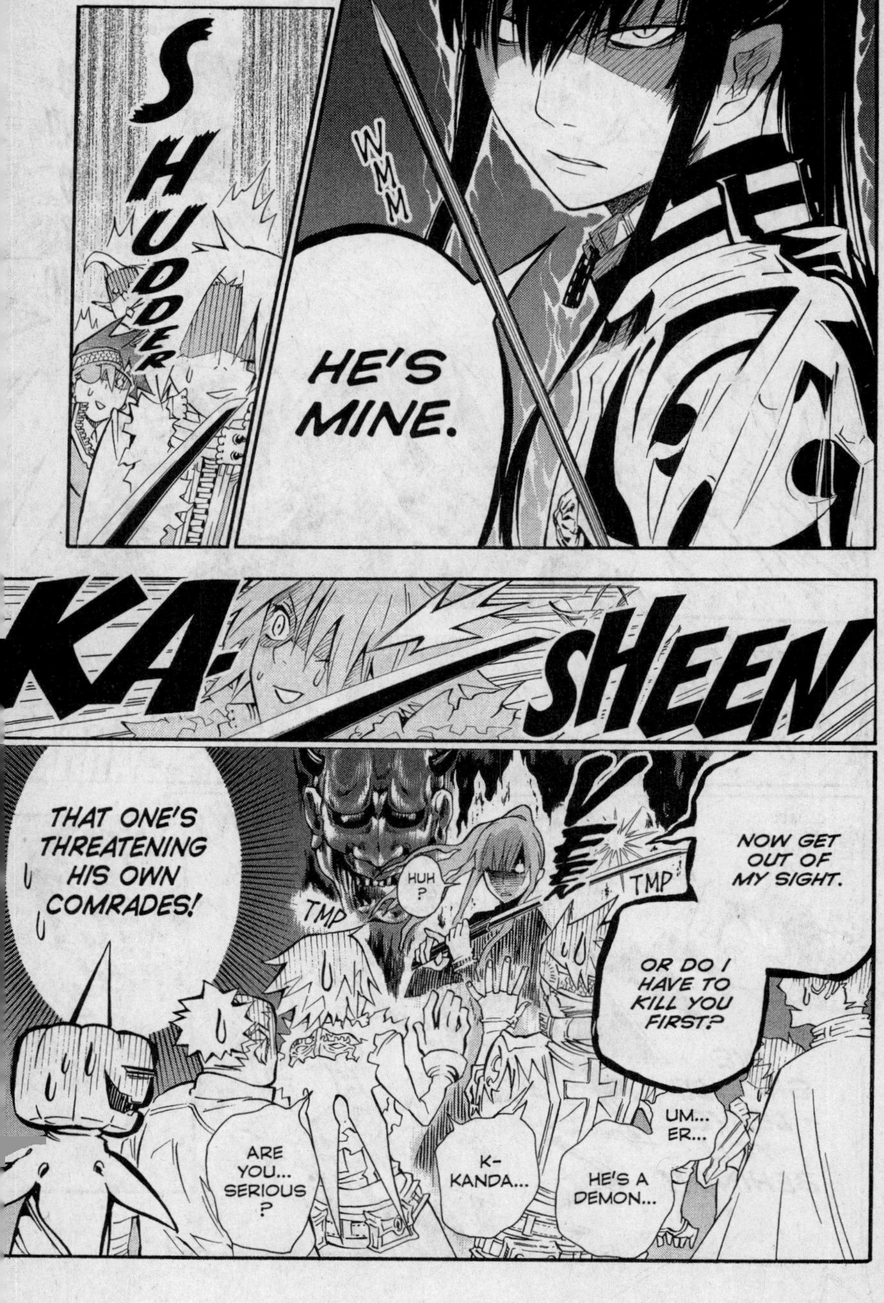
WMMM
HE'S MINE.
SHUDDER
KA-SHEEN
NOW GET OUT OF MY SIGHT.
OR DO I HAVE TO KILL YOU FIRST?
TMP
HUH?
TMP
THAT ONE'S THREATENING HIS OWN COMRADES!
UM... ER...
HE'S A DEMON...
K-KANDA...
ARE YOU... SERIOUS?

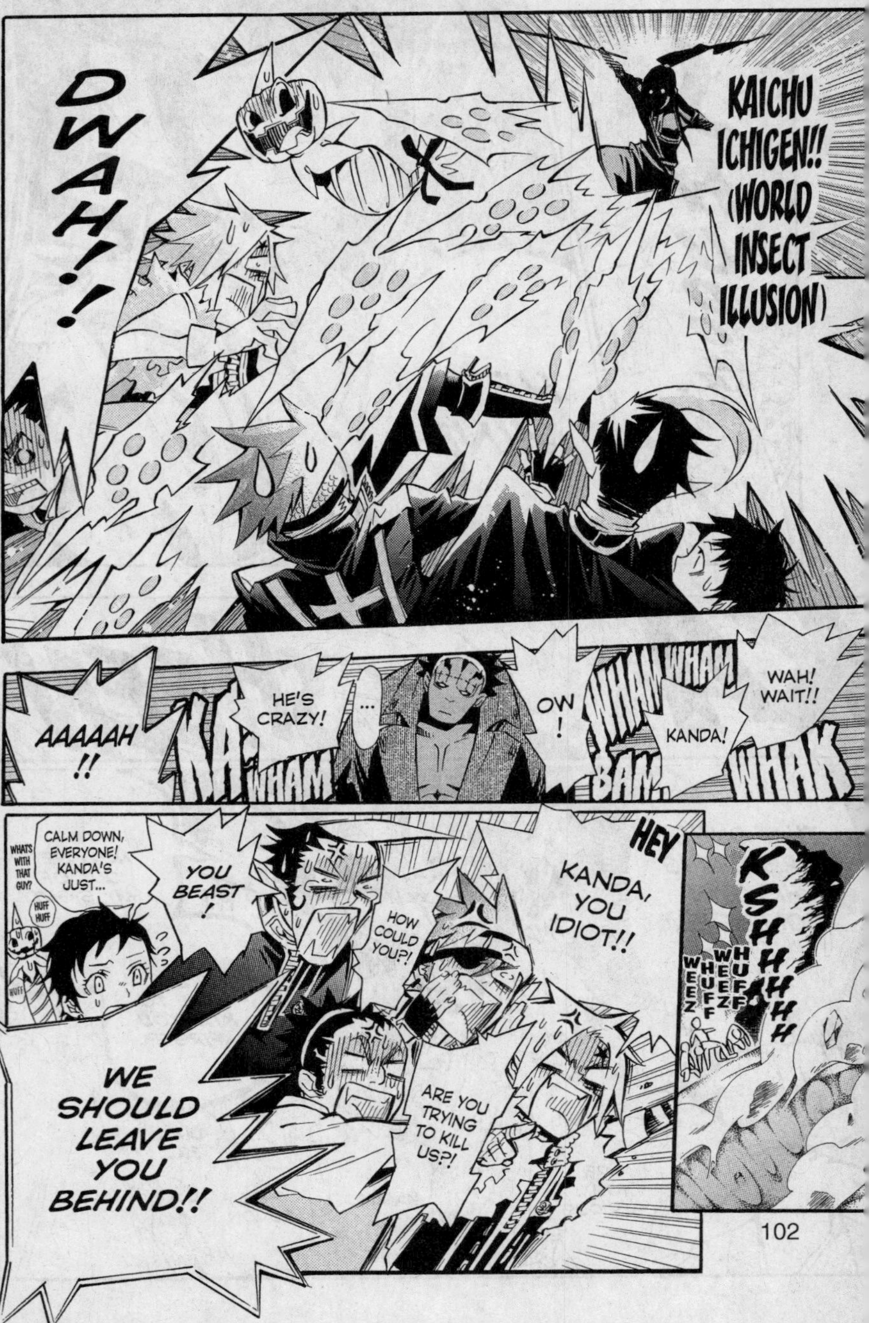
KAICHU ICHIGEN!! (WORLD INSECT ILLUSION)
DWAH!!
WAH! WAIT!!
WHAK
WHAM WHAM
KANDA!
BAM
OW!
...
HE'S CRAZY!
WHAM
AAAAAH!!
KSHHHHHHH
HUFF HUFF
WEEZ WEEZ
HEY
KANDA, YOU IDIOT!!
HOW COULD YOU?!
YOU BEAST!
CALM DOWN, EVERYONE! KANDA'S JUST...
WHAT'S WITH THAT GUY?
HUFF HUFF
HUFF
ARE YOU TRYING TO KILL US?!
WE SHOULD LEAVE YOU BEHIND!!

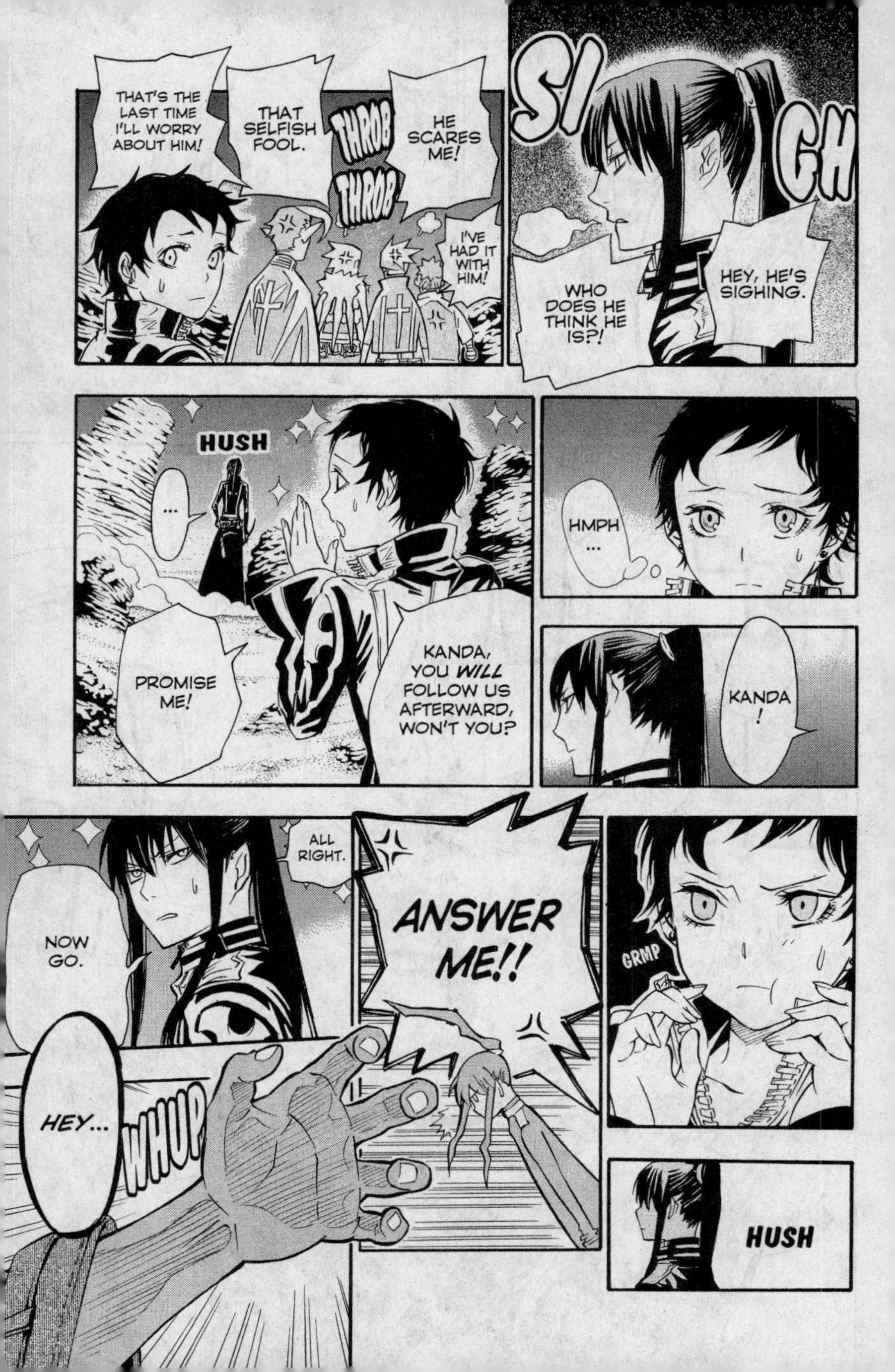
SIGH
HEY, HE'S SIGHING.
WHO DOES HE THINK HE IS?!
HE SCARES ME!
THROB
THROB
THAT SELFISH FOOL.
THAT'S THE LAST TIME I'LL WORRY ABOUT HIM!
I'VE HAD IT WITH HIM!
HMPH ...
KANDA !
KANDA, YOU *WILL* FOLLOW US AFTERWARD, WON'T YOU?
HUSH
...
PROMISE ME!
GRMP
HUSH
ANSWER ME!!
ALL RIGHT.
NOW GO.
WHUP
HEY...

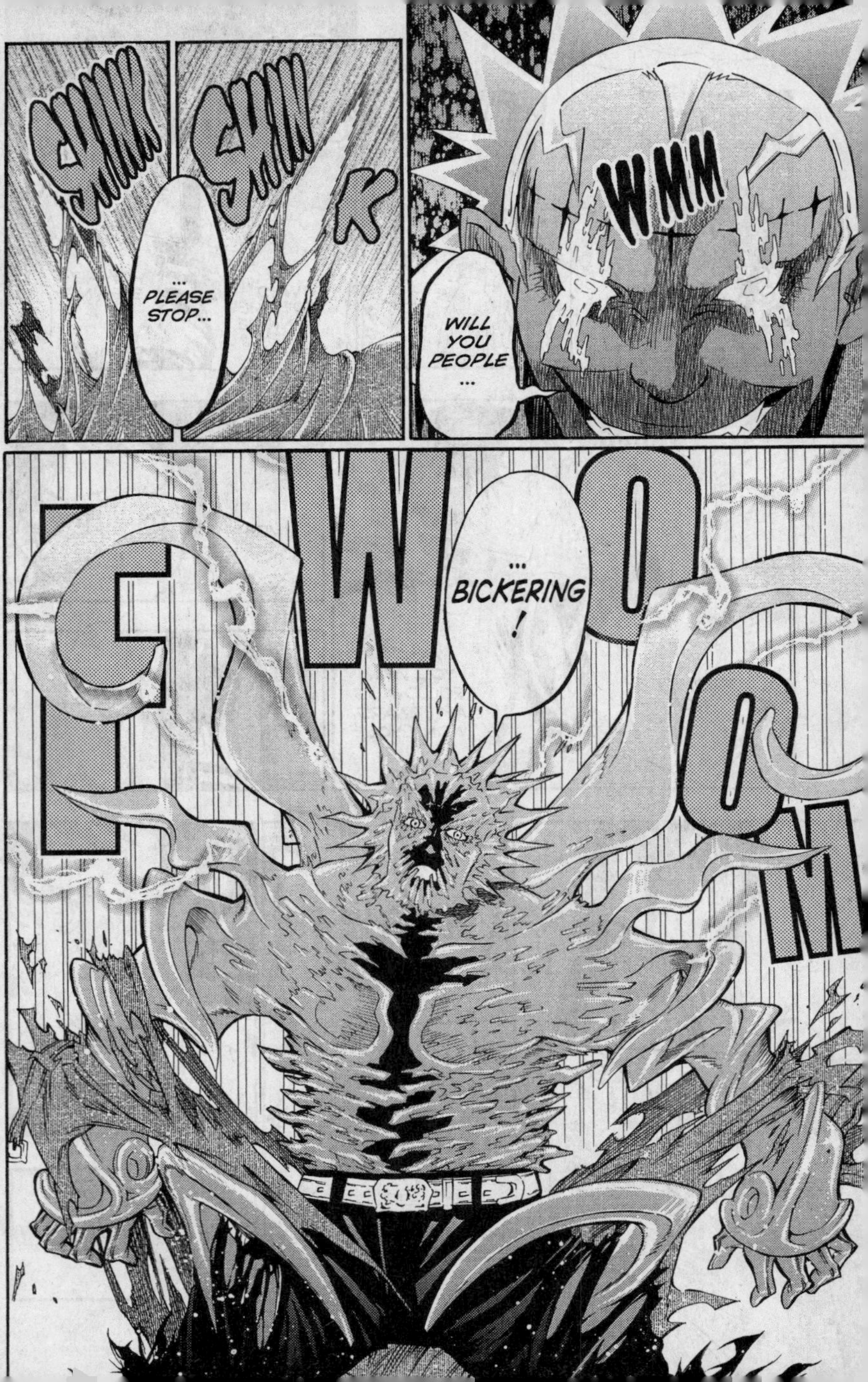
WMM
WILL YOU PEOPLE ...
SHIN K
... PLEASE STOP...
SHINK
... BICKERING !
FWOOM

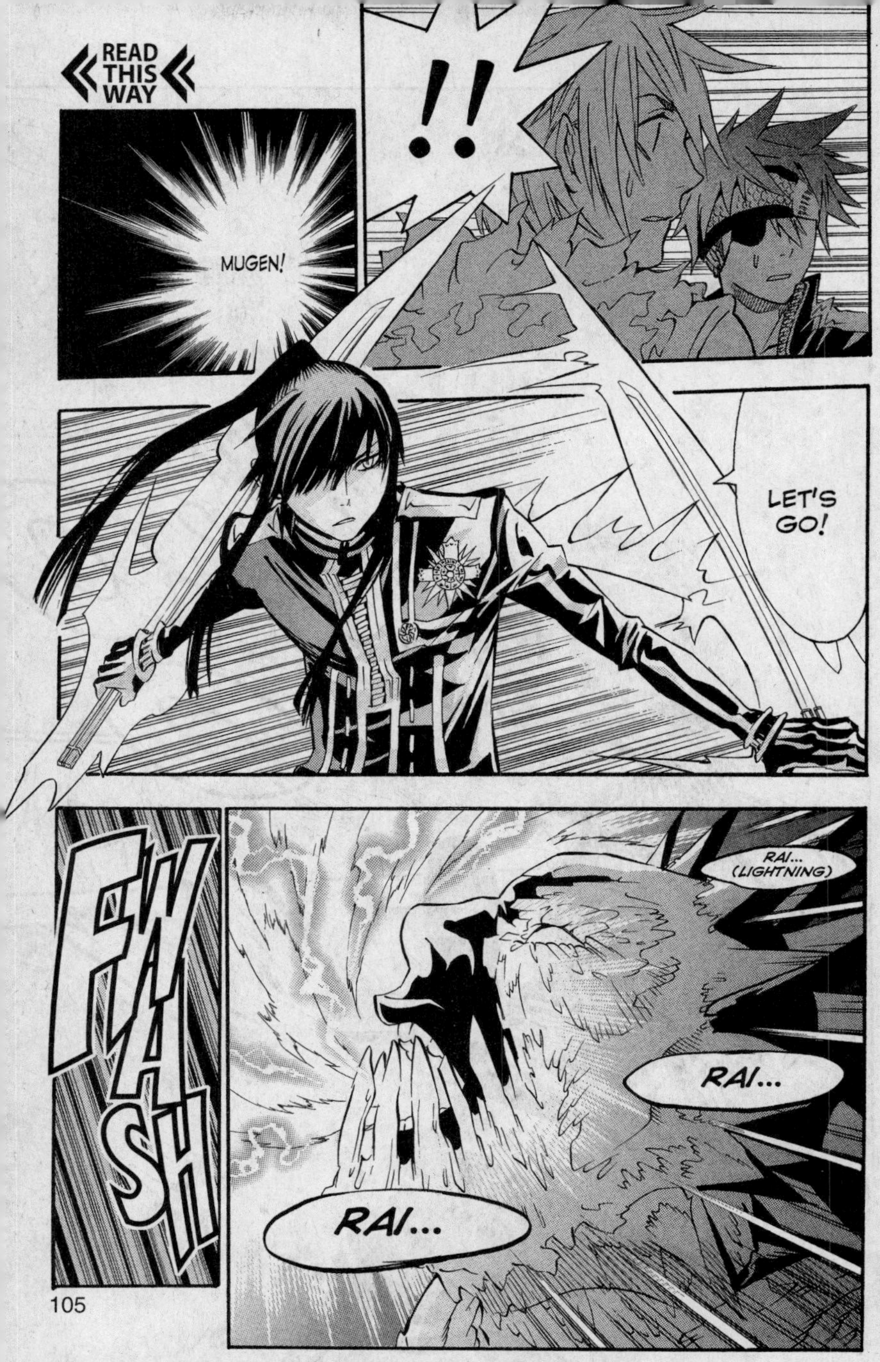
READ THIS WAY
!!
MUGEN!
LET'S GO!
RAI... (LIGHTNING)
RAI...
RAI...
FLASH

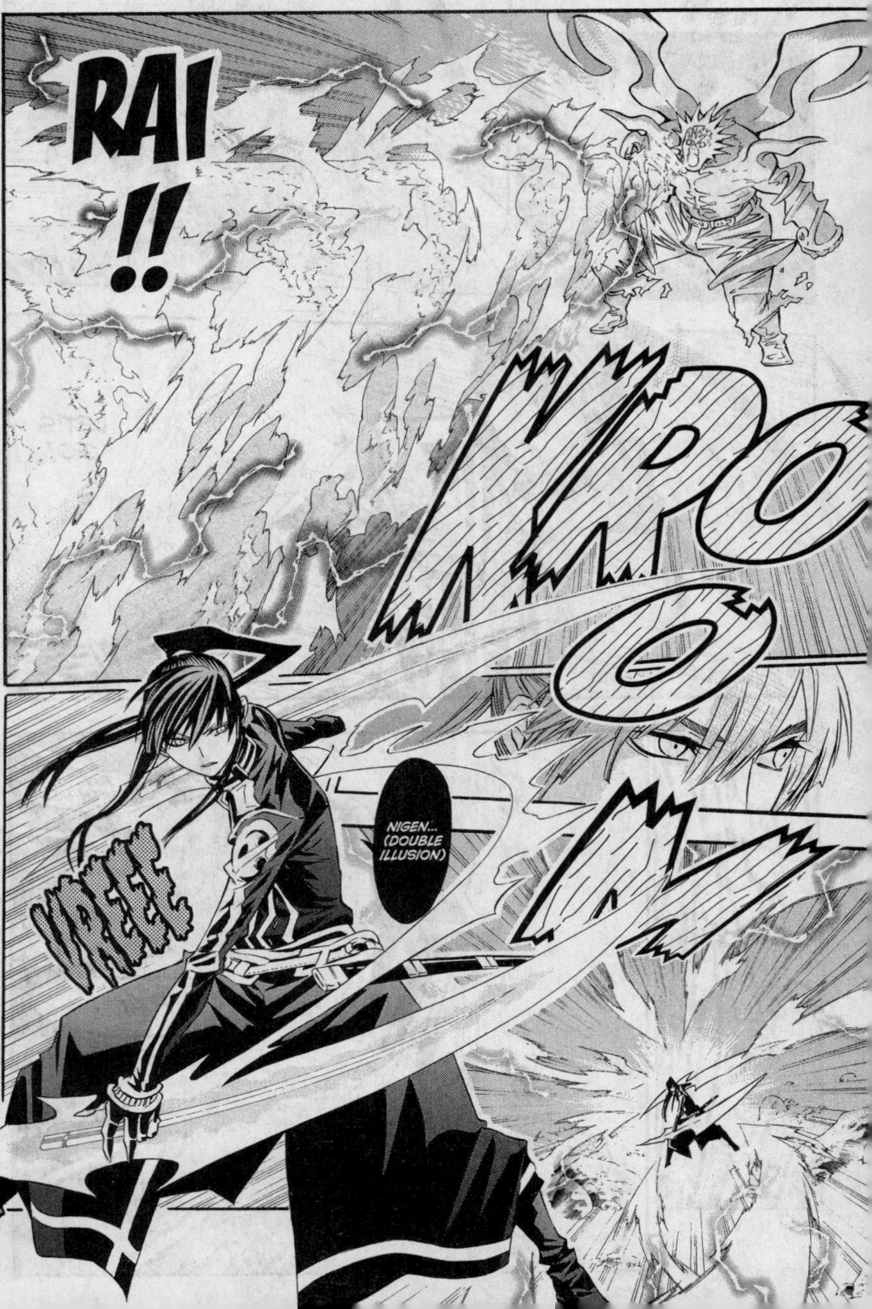
RAI!!
WROOM
NIGEN... (DOUBLE ILLUSION)
VREEE

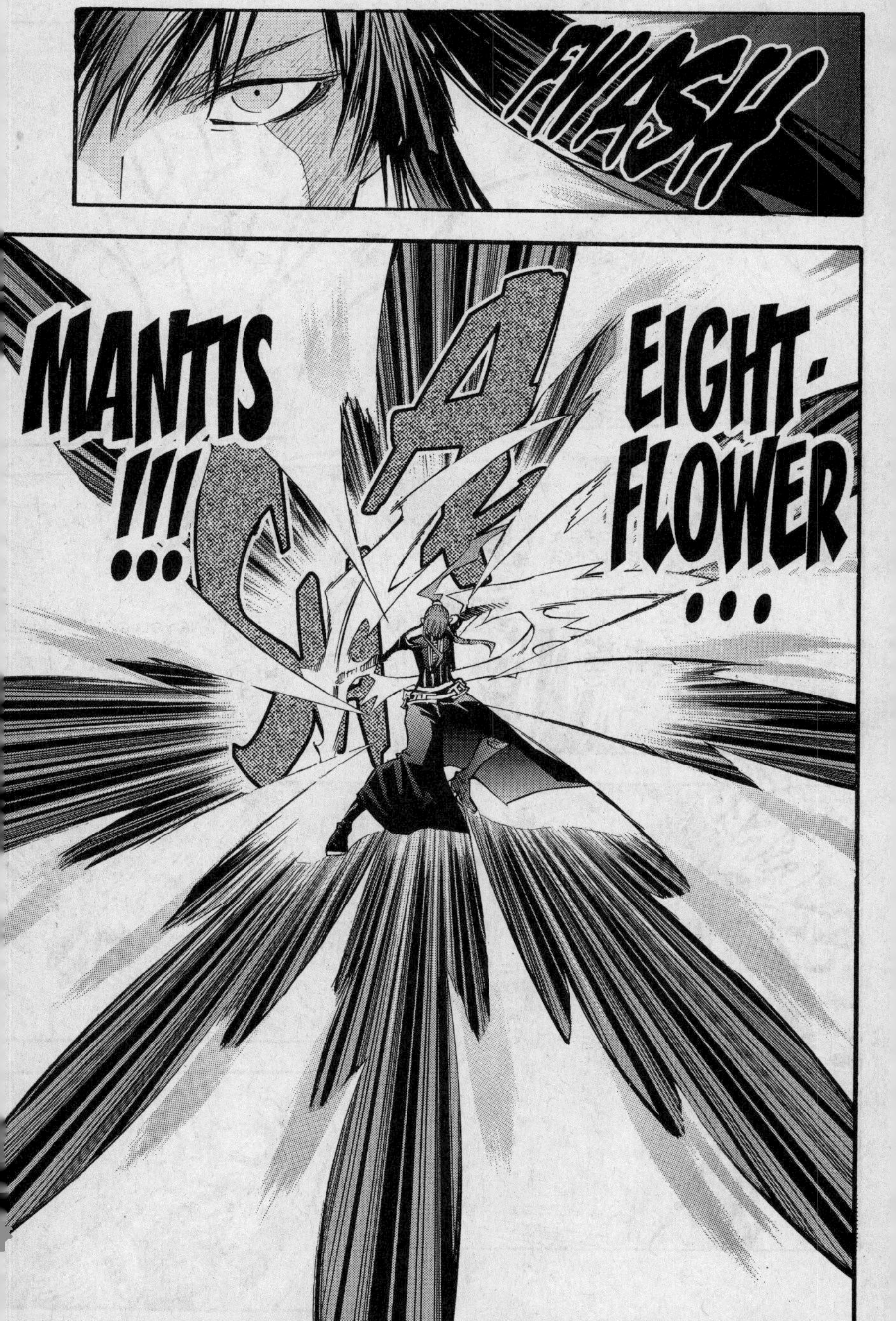
FWASH
EIGHT-FLOWER...
MANTIS!!!...

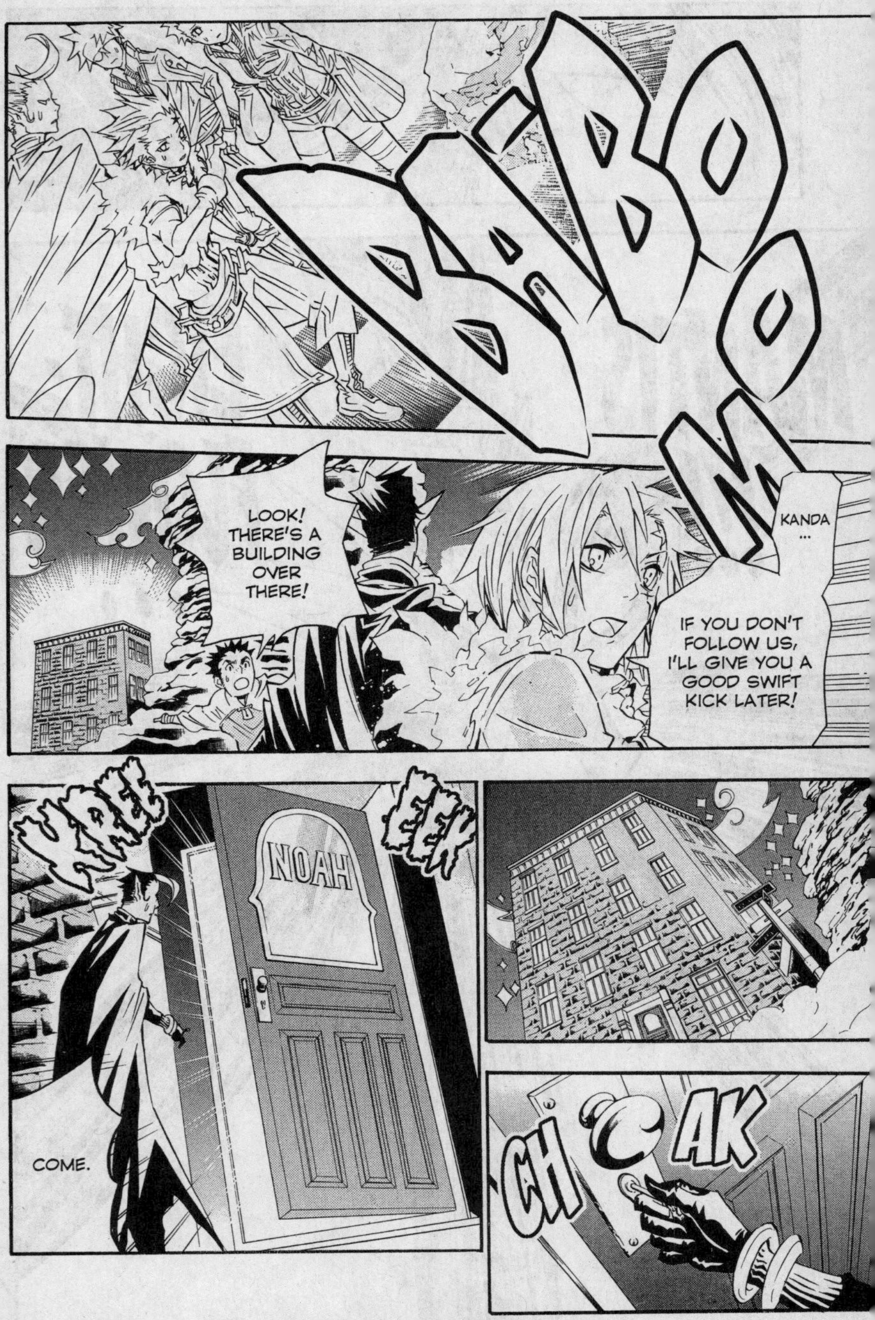
BABOOM
KANDA...
IF YOU DON'T FOLLOW US, I'LL GIVE YOU A GOOD SWIFT KICK LATER!
LOOK! THERE'S A BUILDING OVER THERE!
CH AK
EEK
NOAH
COME.

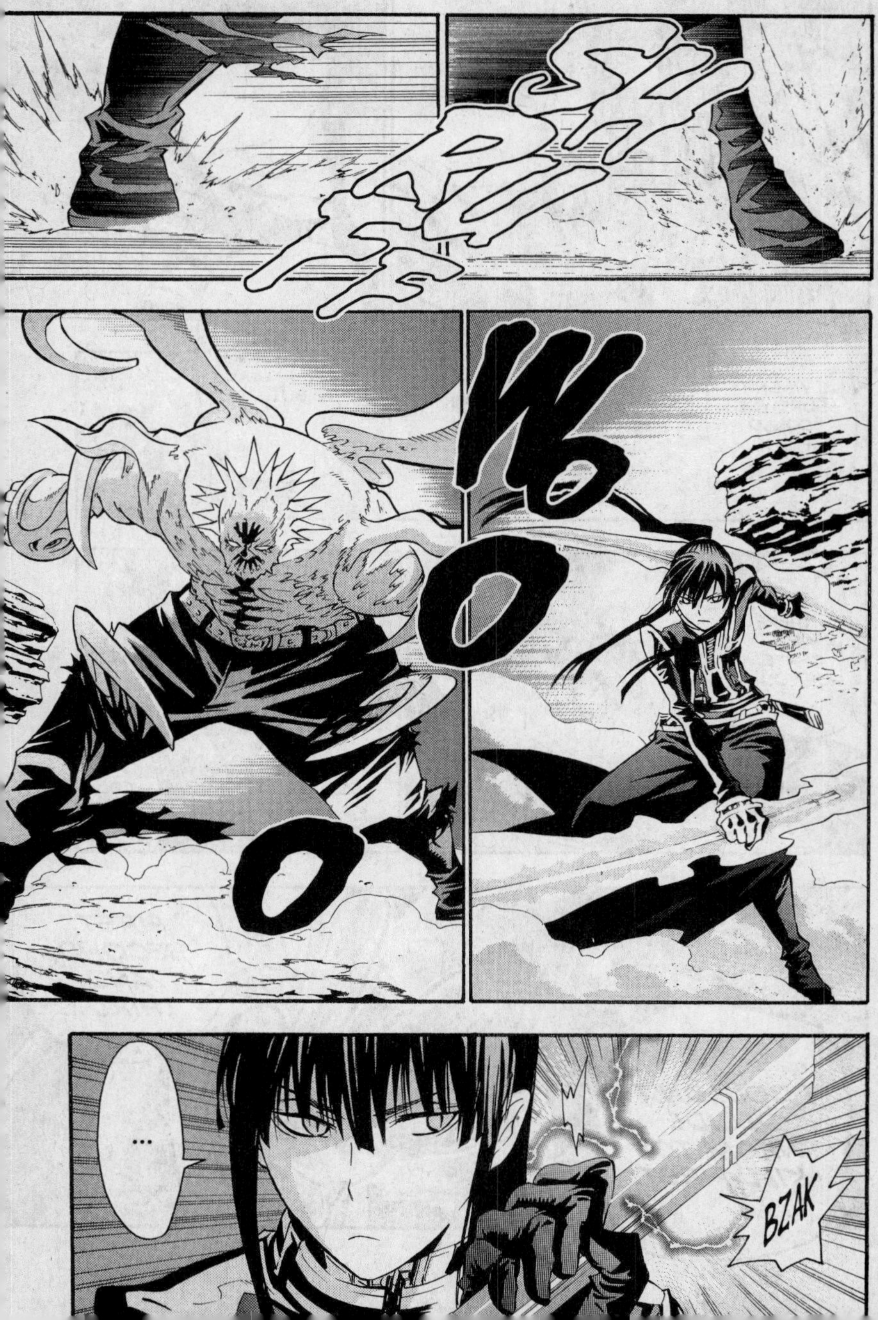
SHRUFF
WOOO
BZAK
...

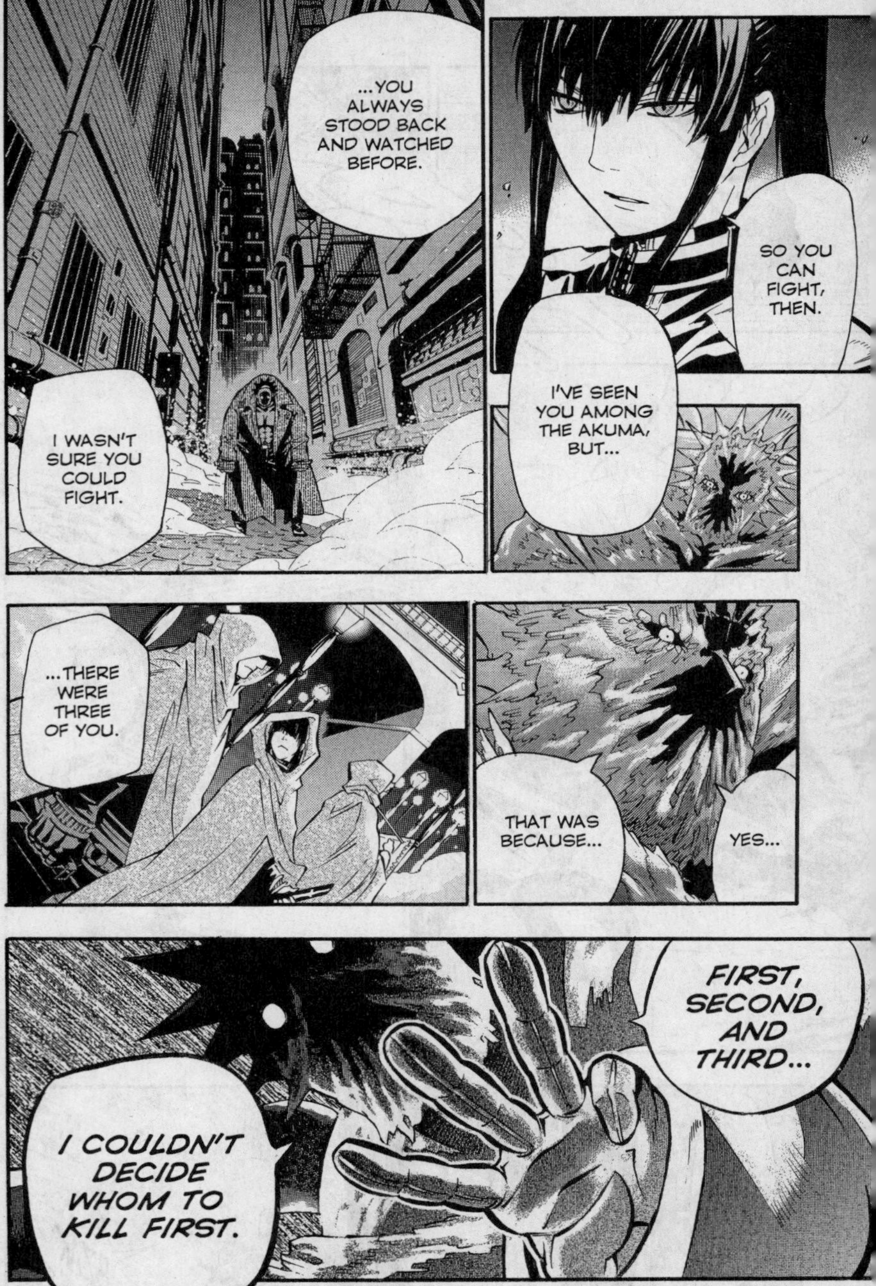
SO YOU CAN FIGHT, THEN.
I'VE SEEN YOU AMONG THE AKUMA, BUT...
...YOU ALWAYS STOOD BACK AND WATCHED BEFORE.
I WASN'T SURE YOU COULD FIGHT.
YES...
THAT WAS BECAUSE...
...THERE WERE THREE OF YOU.
FIRST, SECOND, AND THIRD...
I COULDN'T DECIDE WHOM TO KILL FIRST.

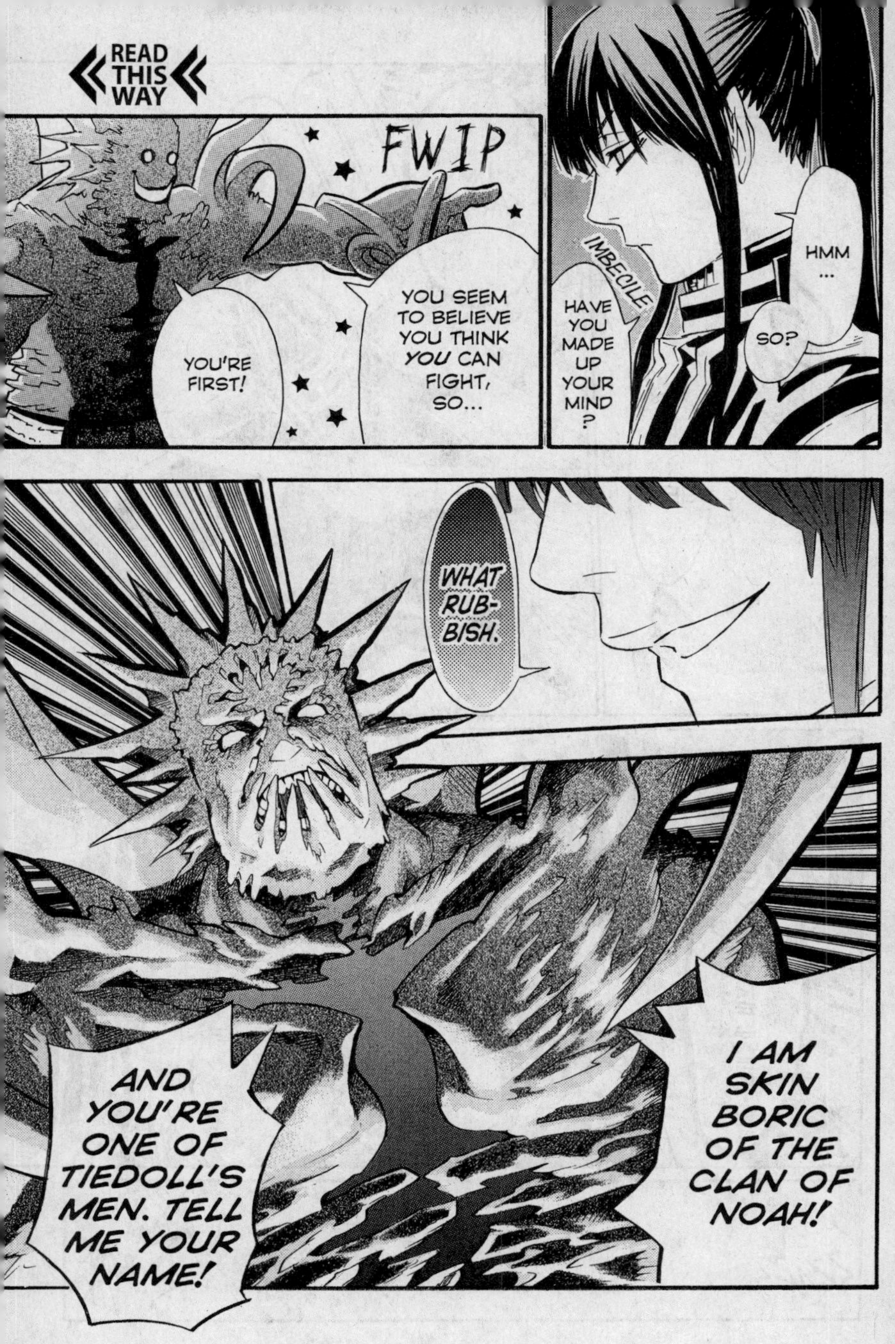
READ THIS WAY
HMM ...
SO?
HAVE YOU MADE UP YOUR MIND?
IMBECILE
FWIP
YOU SEEM TO BELIEVE YOU THINK *YOU* CAN FIGHT, SO...
YOU'RE FIRST!
WHAT RUB-BISH.
I AM SKIN BORIC OF THE CLAN OF NOAH!
AND YOU'RE ONE OF TIEDOLL'S MEN. TELL ME YOUR NAME!

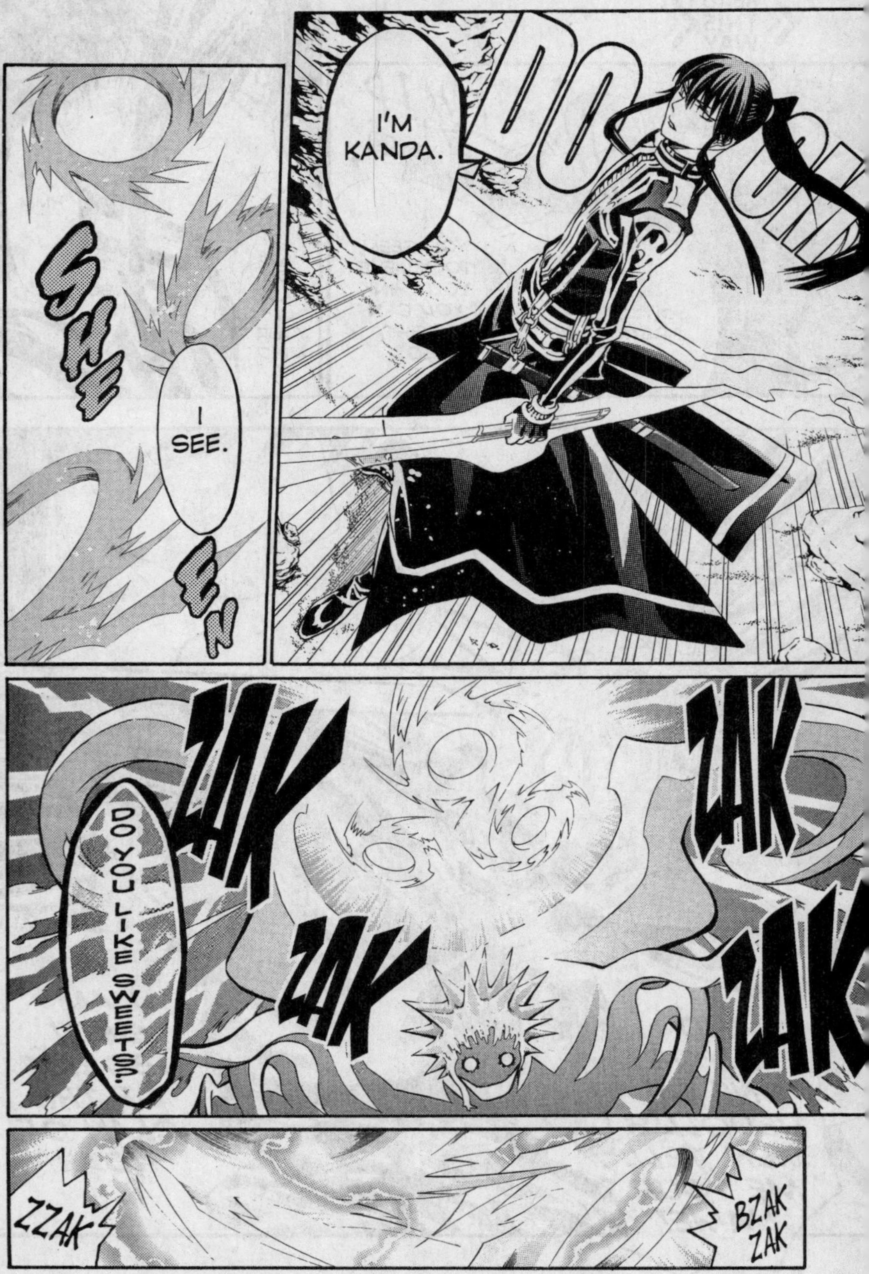
DO
I'M KANDA.
I SEE.
SHE
EN
ZAK
ZAK
DO YOU LIKE SWEETS?
ZAK
ZAK
ZAK
BZAK ZAK
ZZAK

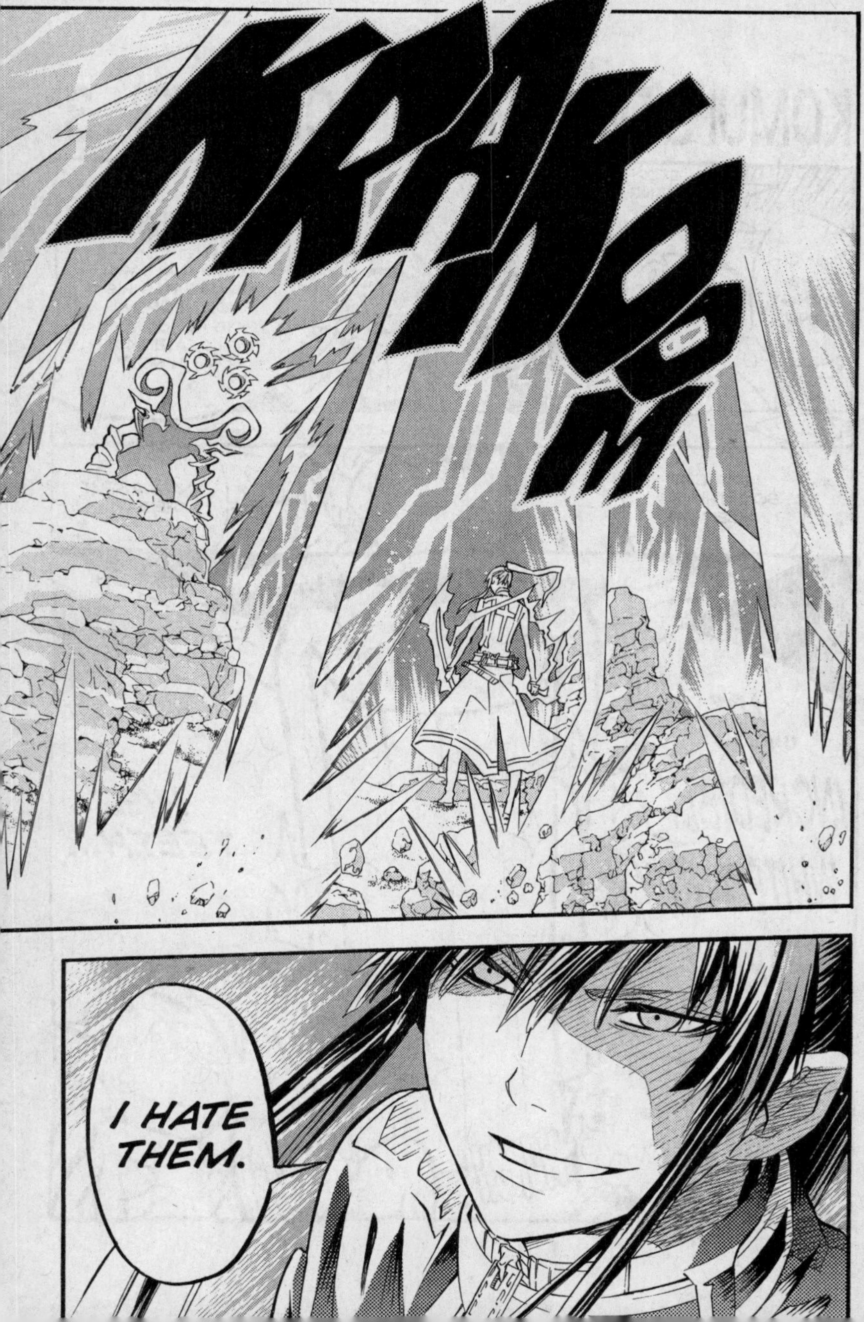
I HATE THEM.

KOMUI'S DISCUSSION ROOM, VOL. 3

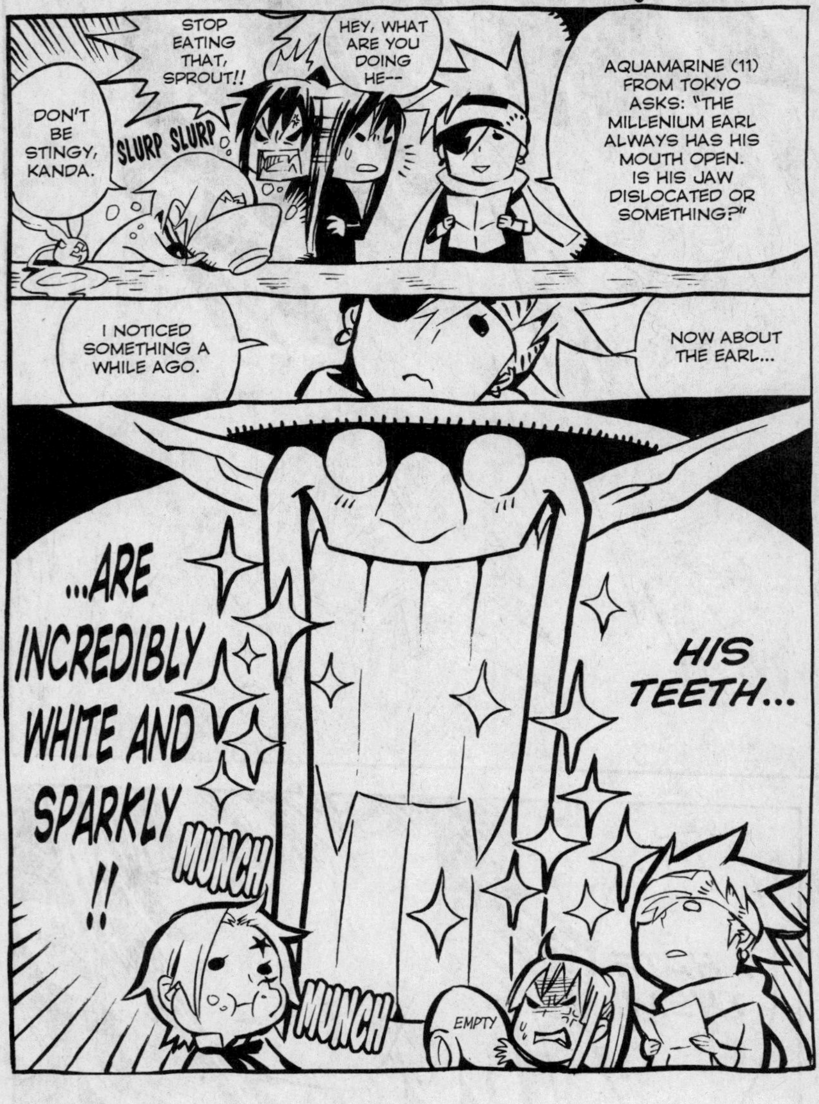
AQUAMARINE (11) FROM TOKYO ASKS: "THE MILLENIUM EARL ALWAYS HAS HIS MOUTH OPEN. IS HIS JAW DISLOCATED OR SOMETHING?"
HEY, WHAT ARE YOU DOING HE--
STOP EATING THAT, SPROUT!!
DON'T BE STINGY, KANDA.
SLURP SLURP
NOW ABOUT THE EARL...
I NOTICED SOMETHING A WHILE AGO.
HIS TEETH...
...ARE INCREDIBLY WHITE AND SPARKLY!!
MUNCH
MUNCH
EMPTY

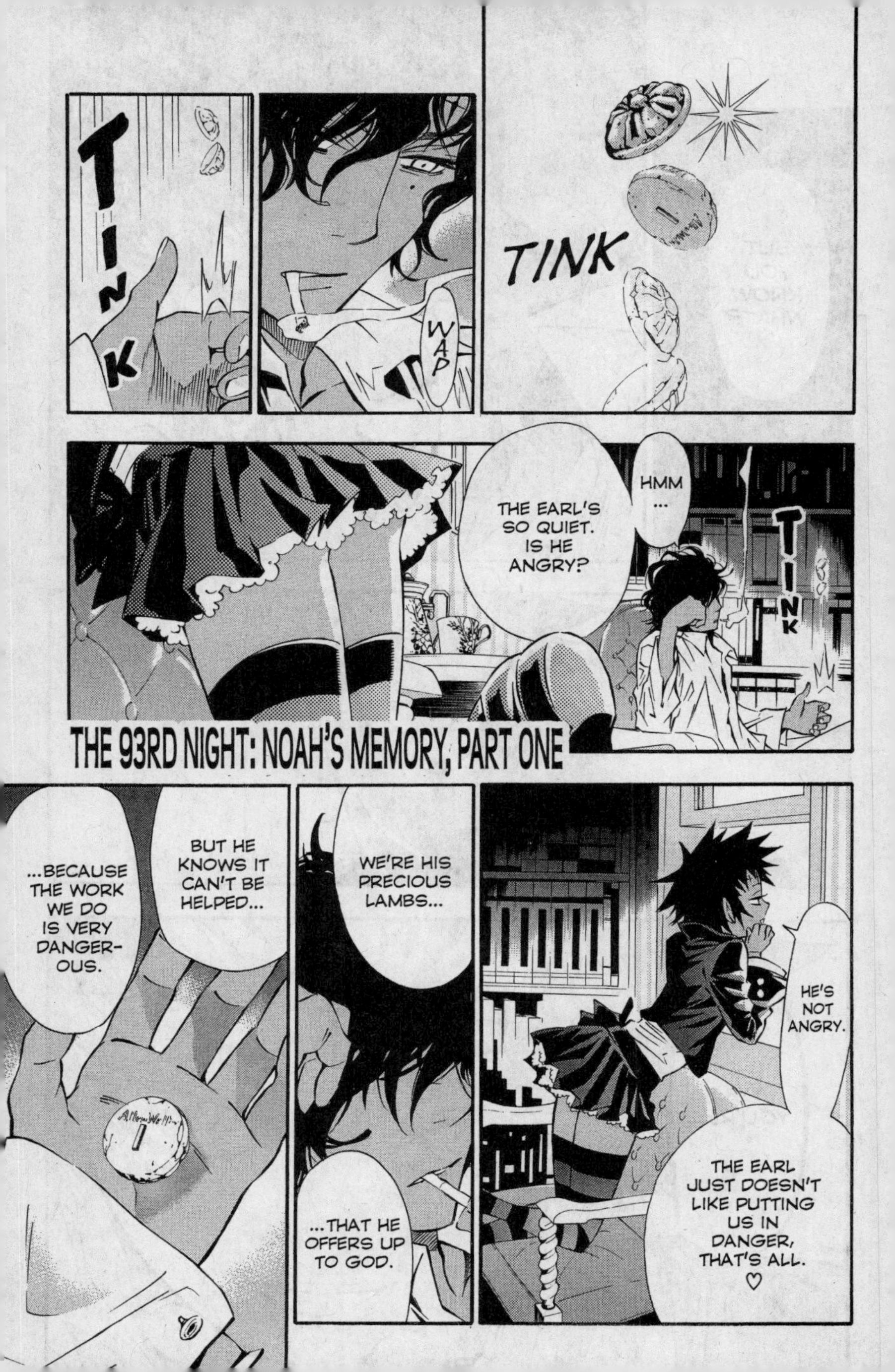
TINK
WAP
TINK
HMM...
THE EARL'S SO QUIET. IS HE ANGRY?
TINK
THE 93RD NIGHT: NOAH'S MEMORY, PART ONE
HE'S NOT ANGRY.
THE EARL JUST DOESN'T LIKE PUTTING US IN DANGER, THAT'S ALL. ♡
WE'RE HIS PRECIOUS LAMBS...
...THAT HE OFFERS UP TO GOD.
BUT HE KNOWS IT CAN'T BE HELPED...
...BECAUSE THE WORK WE DO IS VERY DANGER-OUS.

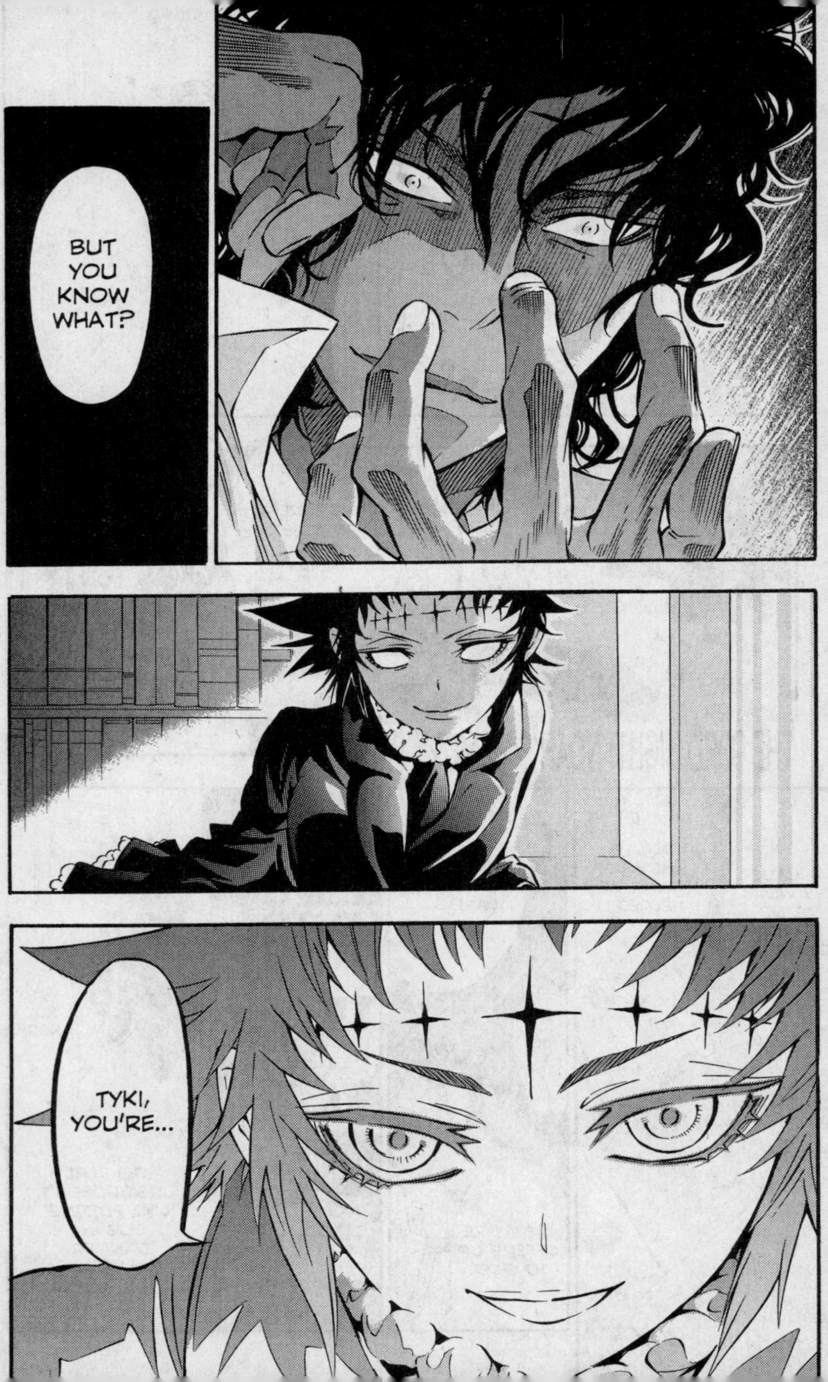
BUT YOU KNOW WHAT?
TYKI, YOU'RE...

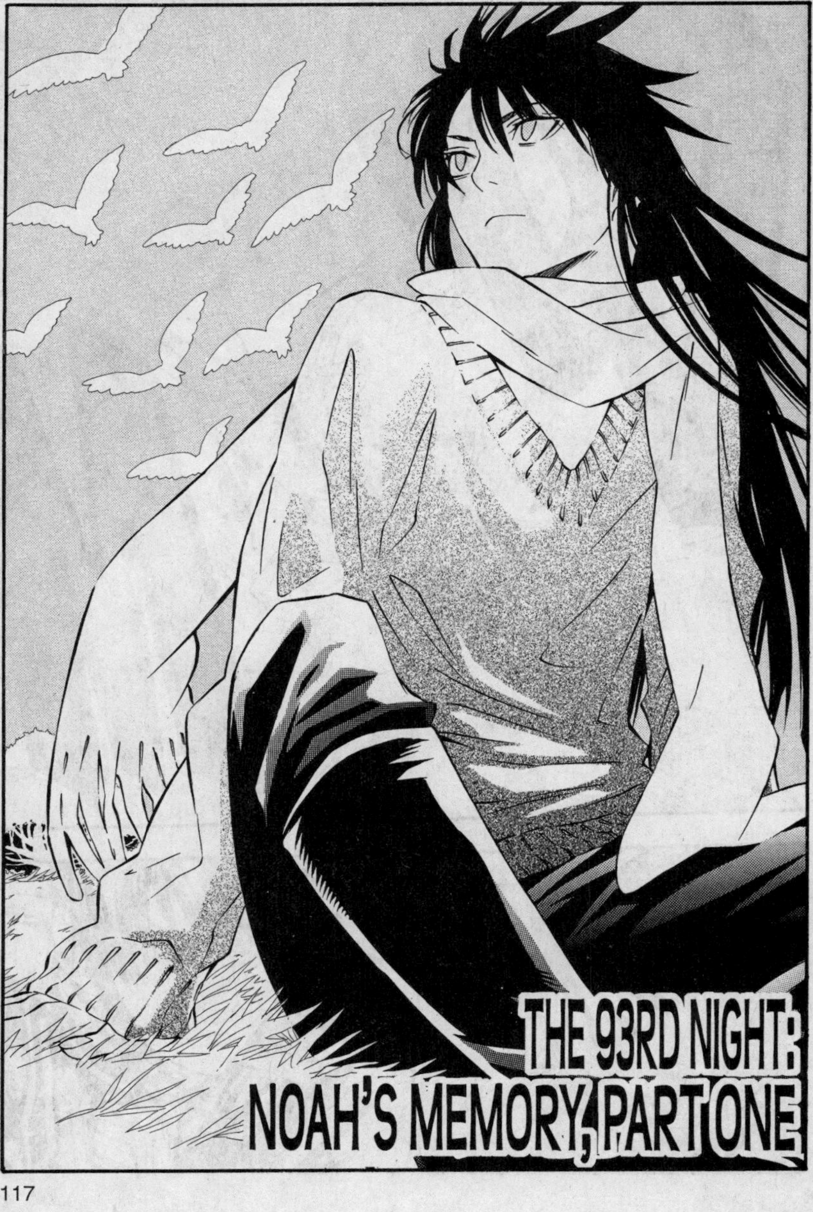
THE 93RD NIGHT:
NOAH'S MEMORY, PART ONE

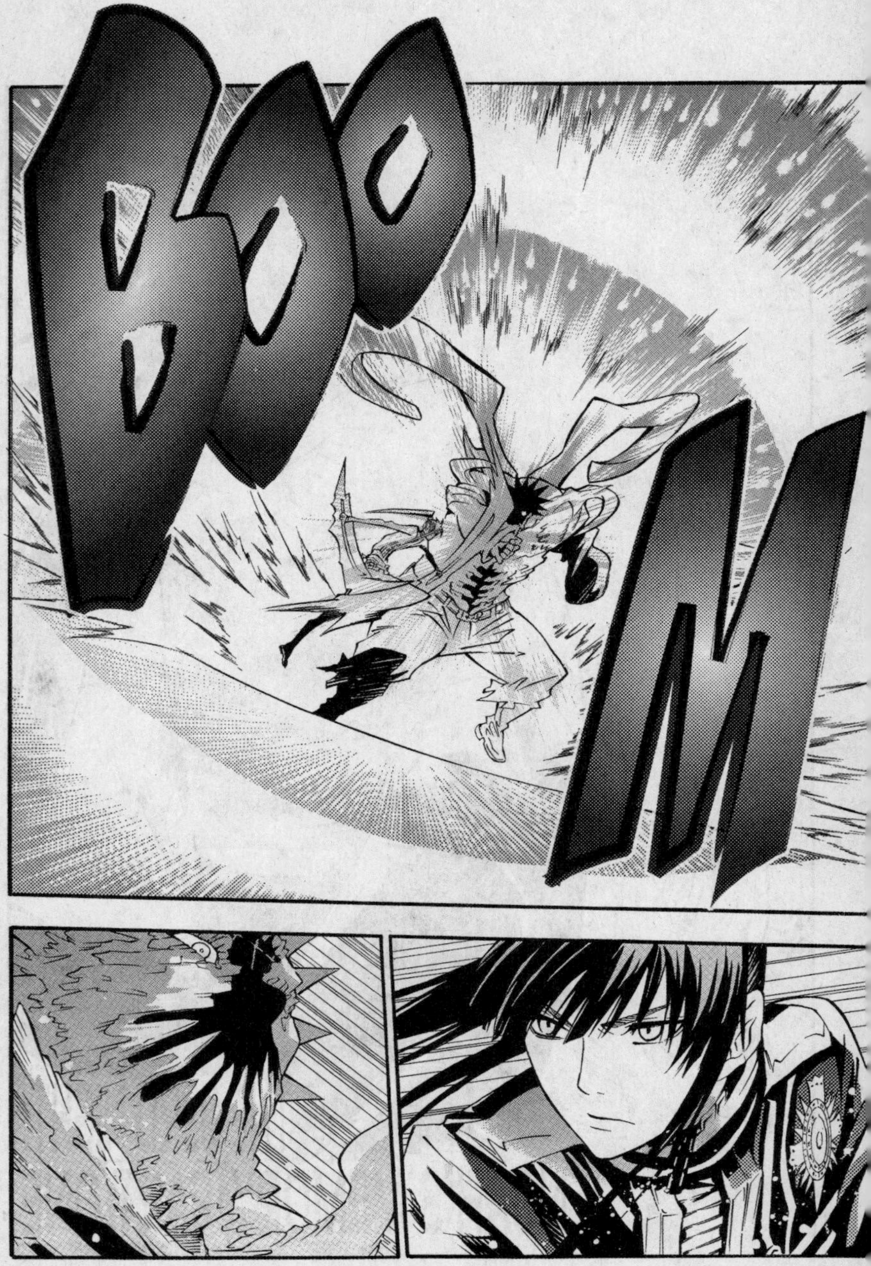
BOOM

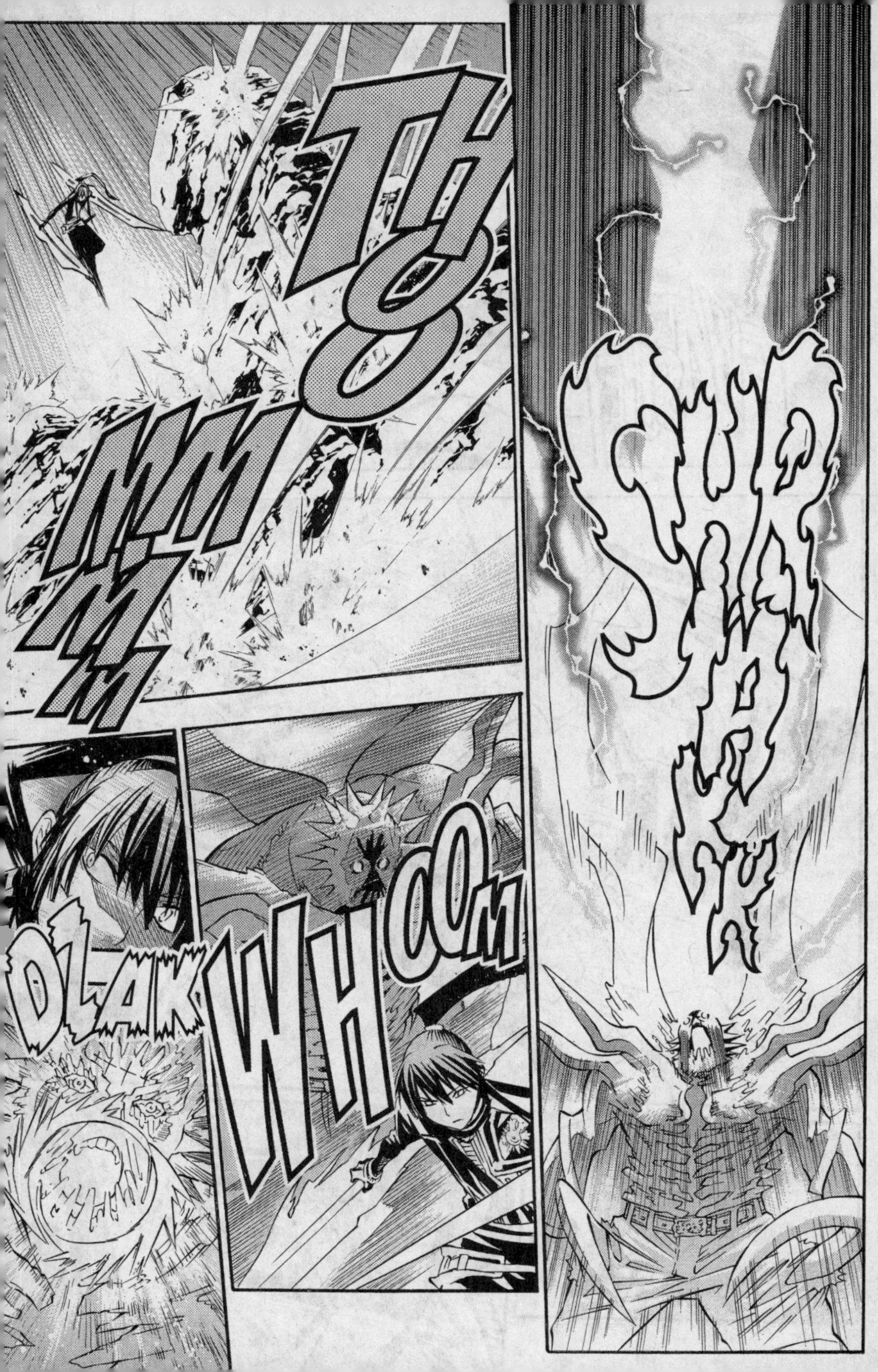
THOOMMMMMM
WHOOM
DLAK

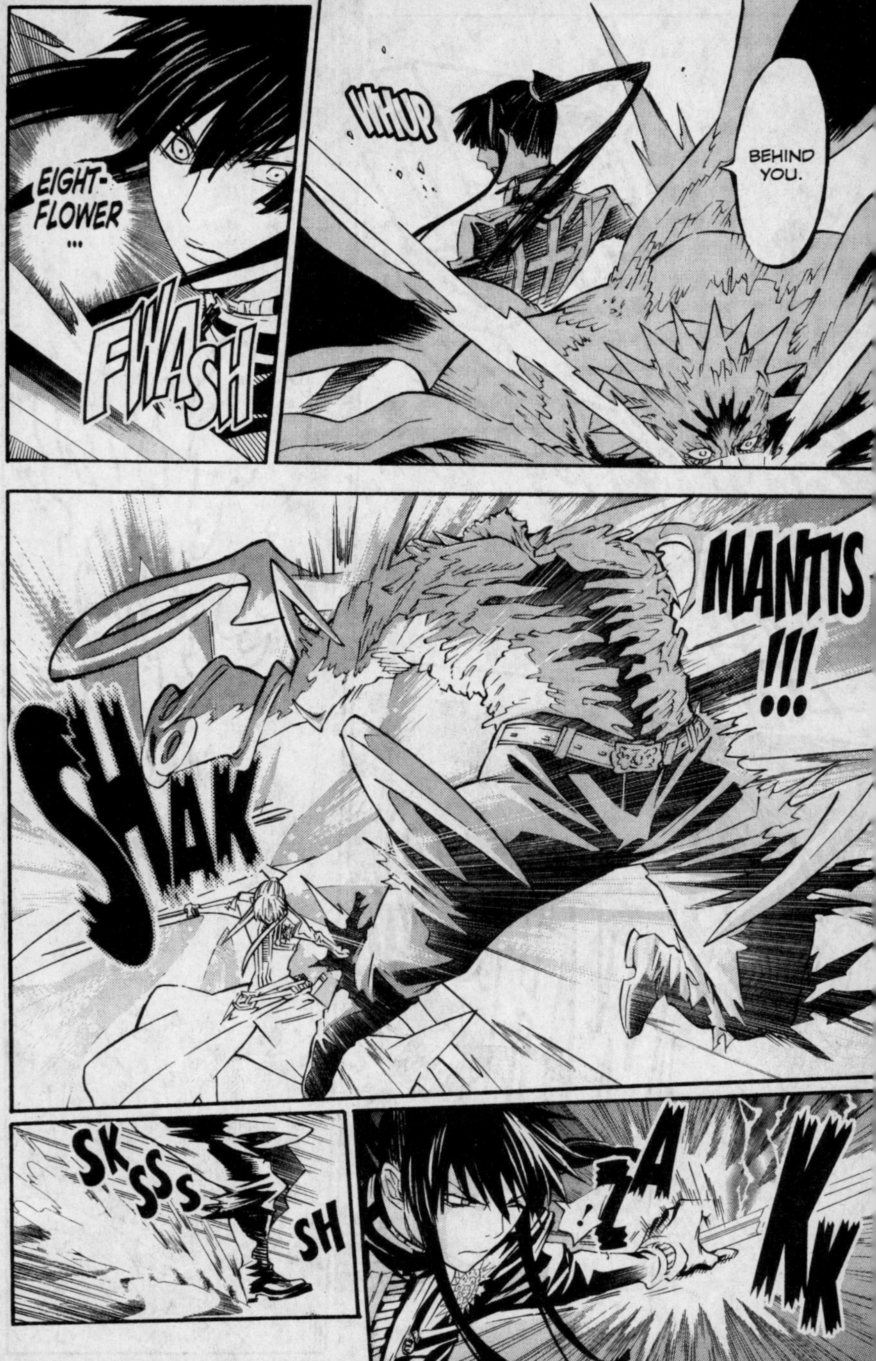
BEHIND YOU.
WHUP
EIGHT-FLOWER ...
FWASH
MANTIS !!! ...
SHAK
ZAKK
!
SKSSS
SH

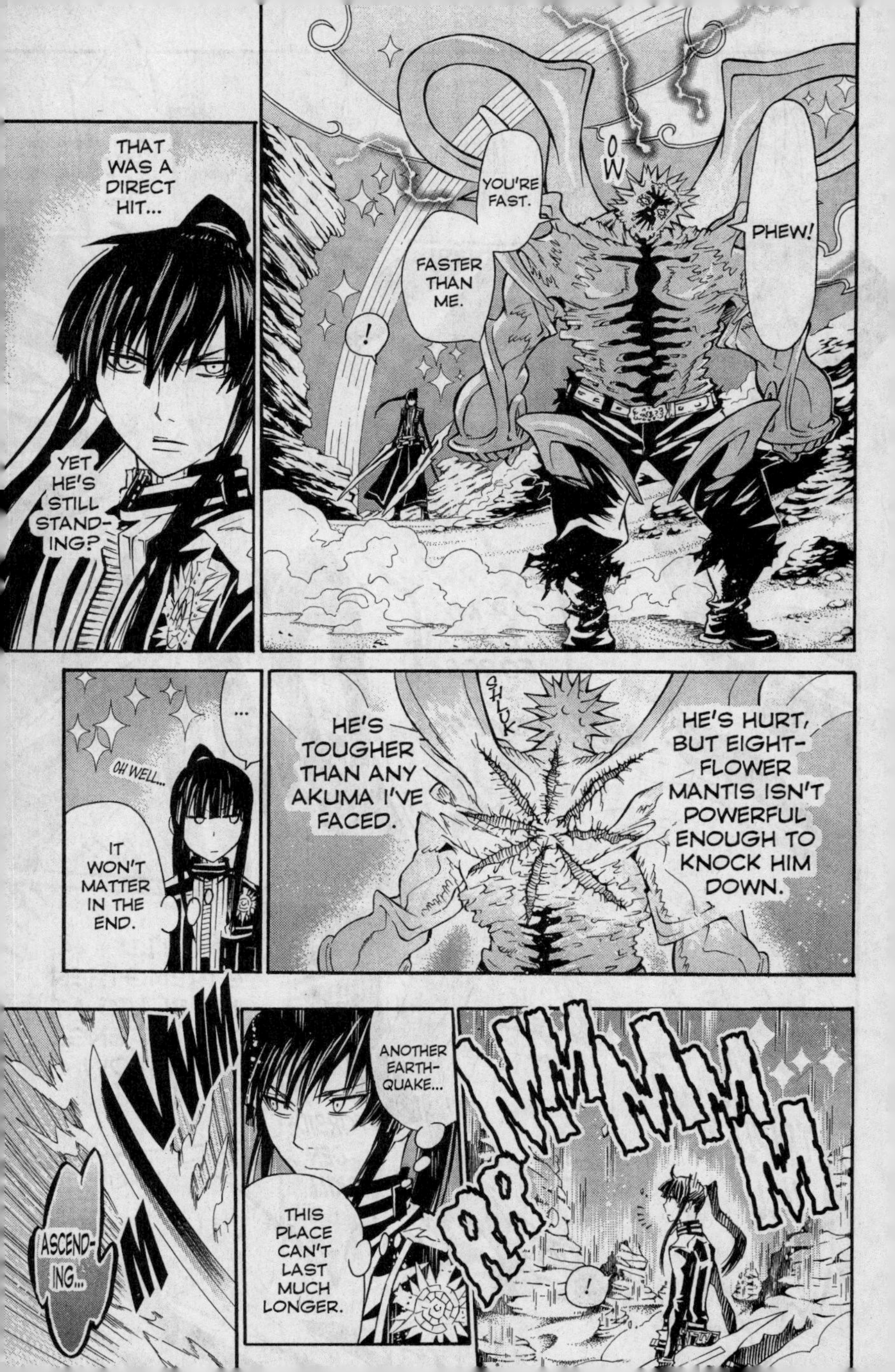

OW
PHEW!
YOU'RE FAST.
FASTER THAN ME.
!
THAT WAS A DIRECT HIT...
YET HE'S STILL STANDING?
SHLUK
HE'S HURT, BUT EIGHT-FLOWER MANTIS ISN'T POWERFUL ENOUGH TO KNOCK HIM DOWN.
HE'S TOUGHER THAN ANY AKUMA I'VE FACED.
...
OH WELL...
IT WON'T MATTER IN THE END.
!
ANOTHER EARTHQUAKE...
THIS PLACE CAN'T LAST MUCH LONGER.
ASCENDING...

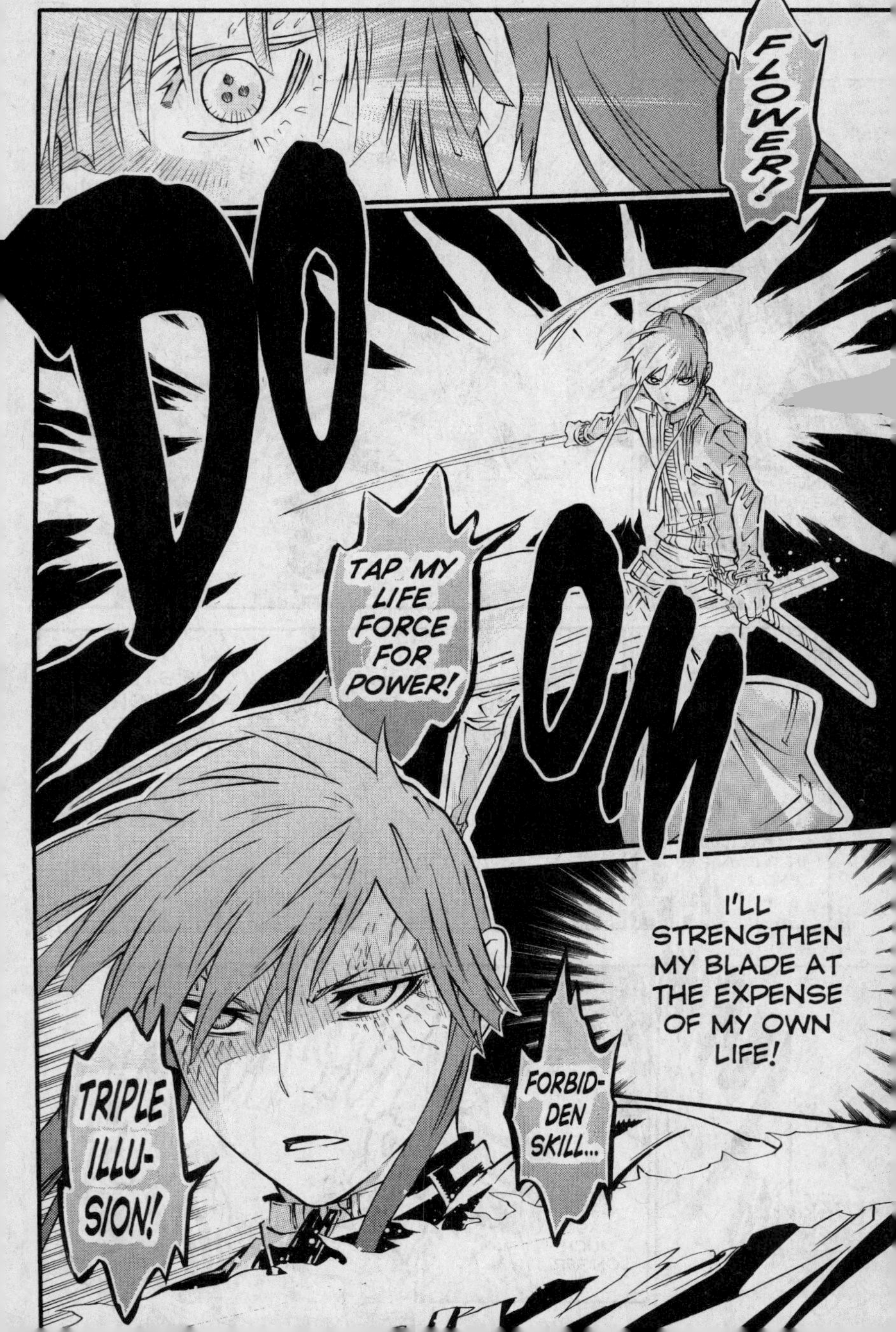
FLOWER!
DOOM
TAP MY LIFE FORCE FOR POWER!
I'LL STRENGTHEN MY BLADE AT THE EXPENSE OF MY OWN LIFE!
FORBID-DEN SKILL...
TRIPLE ILLU-SION!

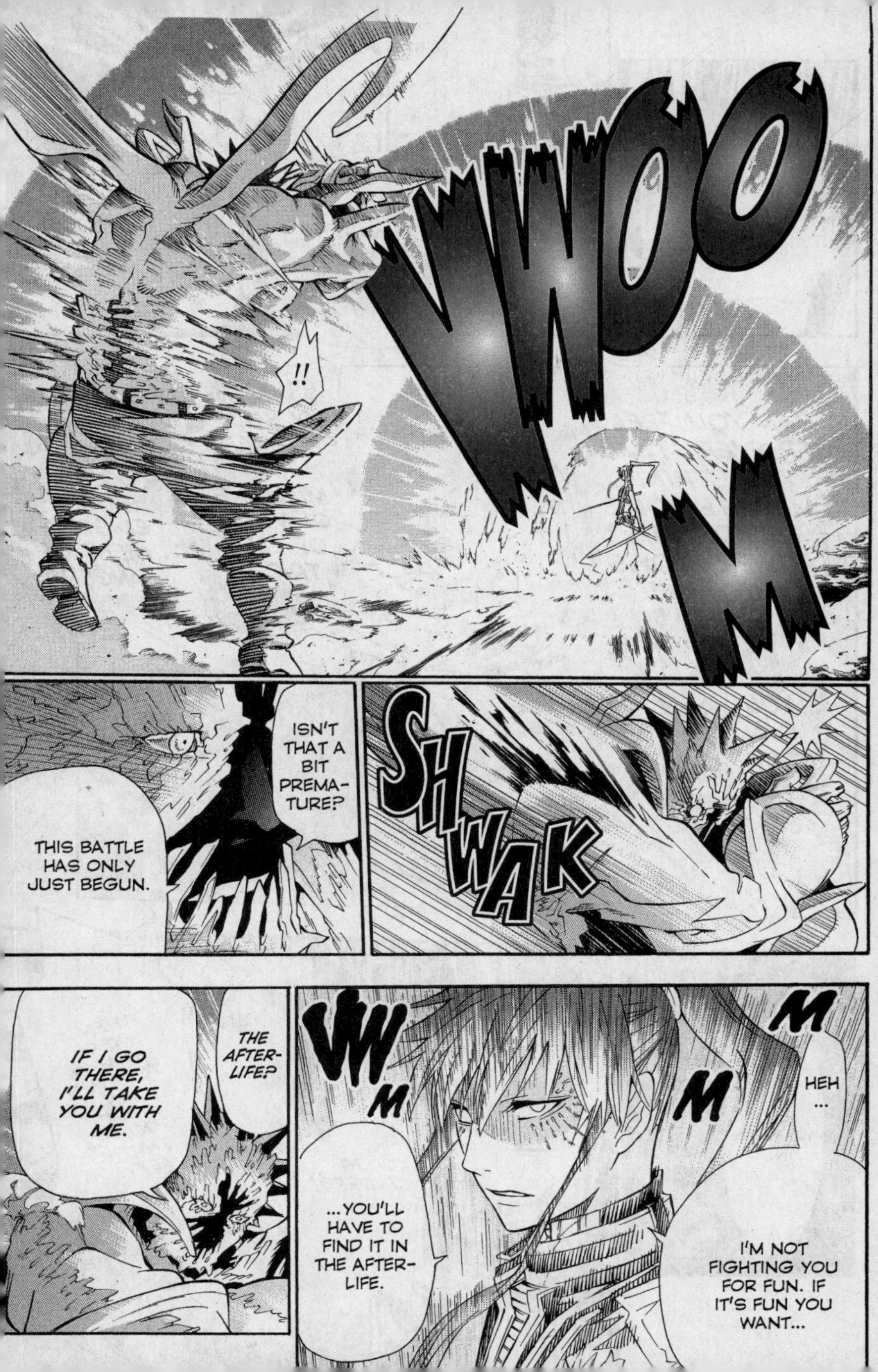

WHOOOM
!!
SHWAK
ISN'T THAT A BIT PREMATURE?
THIS BATTLE HAS ONLY JUST BEGUN.
VWMMMM
HEH ...
I'M NOT FIGHTING YOU FOR FUN. IF IT'S FUN YOU WANT...
...YOU'LL HAVE TO FIND IT IN THE AFTER-LIFE.
THE AFTER-LIFE?
IF I GO THERE, I'LL TAKE YOU WITH ME.

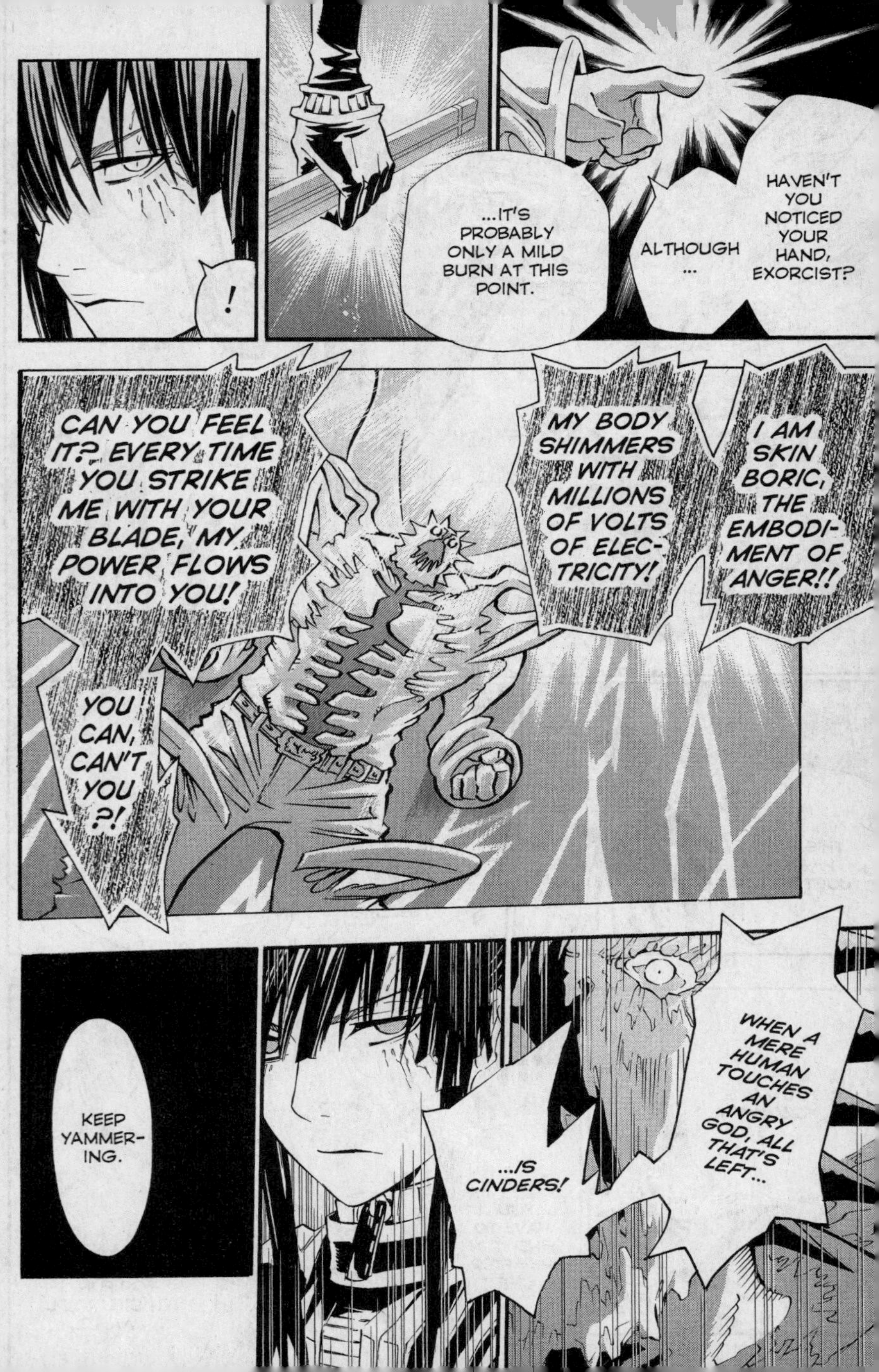
HAVEN'T YOU NOTICED YOUR HAND, EXORCIST?
ALTHOUGH ...
...IT'S PROBABLY ONLY A MILD BURN AT THIS POINT.
!
I AM SKIN BORIC, THE EMBODIMENT OF ANGER!!
MY BODY SHIMMERS WITH MILLIONS OF VOLTS OF ELECTRICITY!
CAN YOU FEEL IT?! EVERY TIME YOU STRIKE ME WITH YOUR BLADE, MY POWER FLOWS INTO YOU!
YOU CAN, CAN'T YOU?!
WHEN A MERE HUMAN TOUCHES AN ANGRY GOD, ALL THAT'S LEFT...
...IS CINDERS!
KEEP YAMMERING.

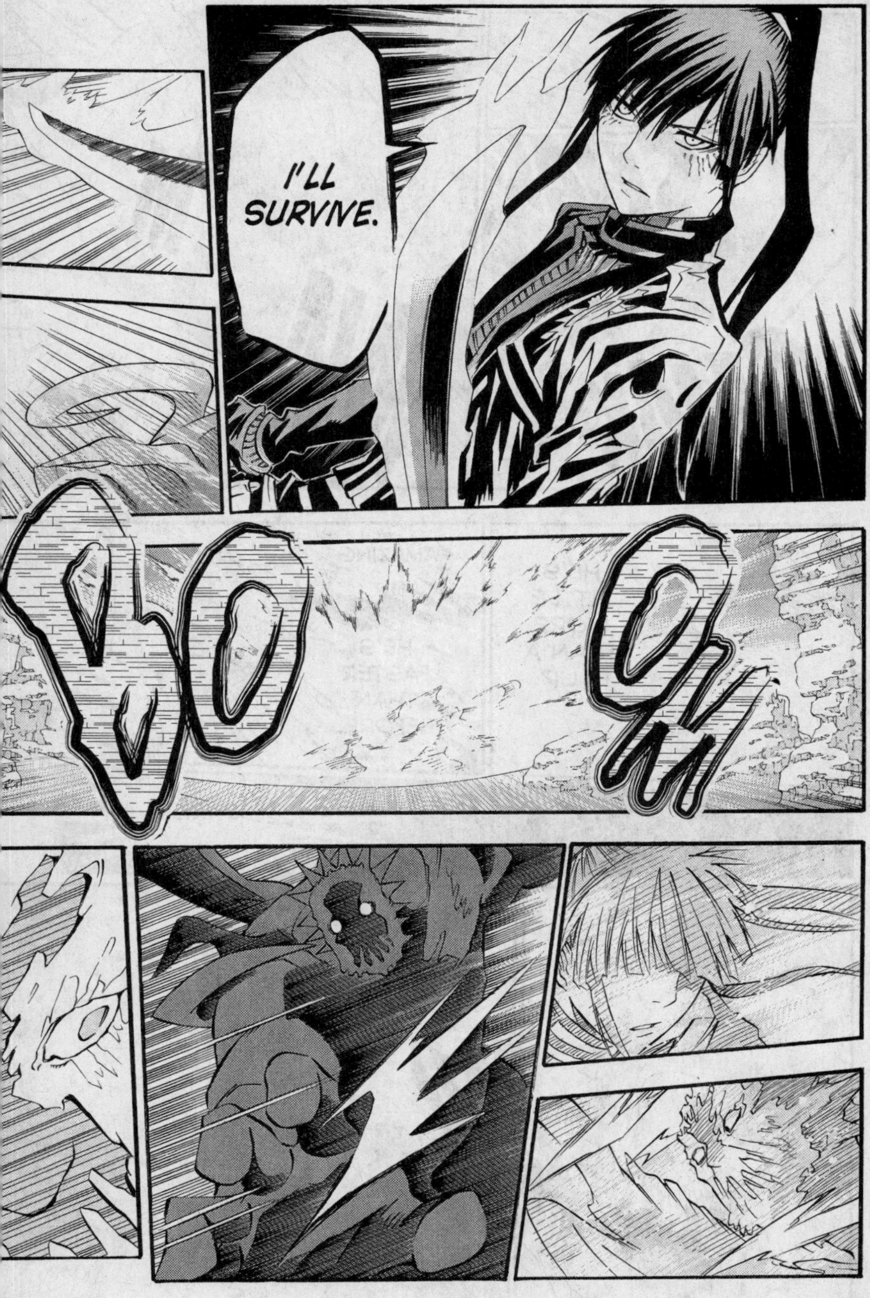
I'LL SURVIVE.
VOOM

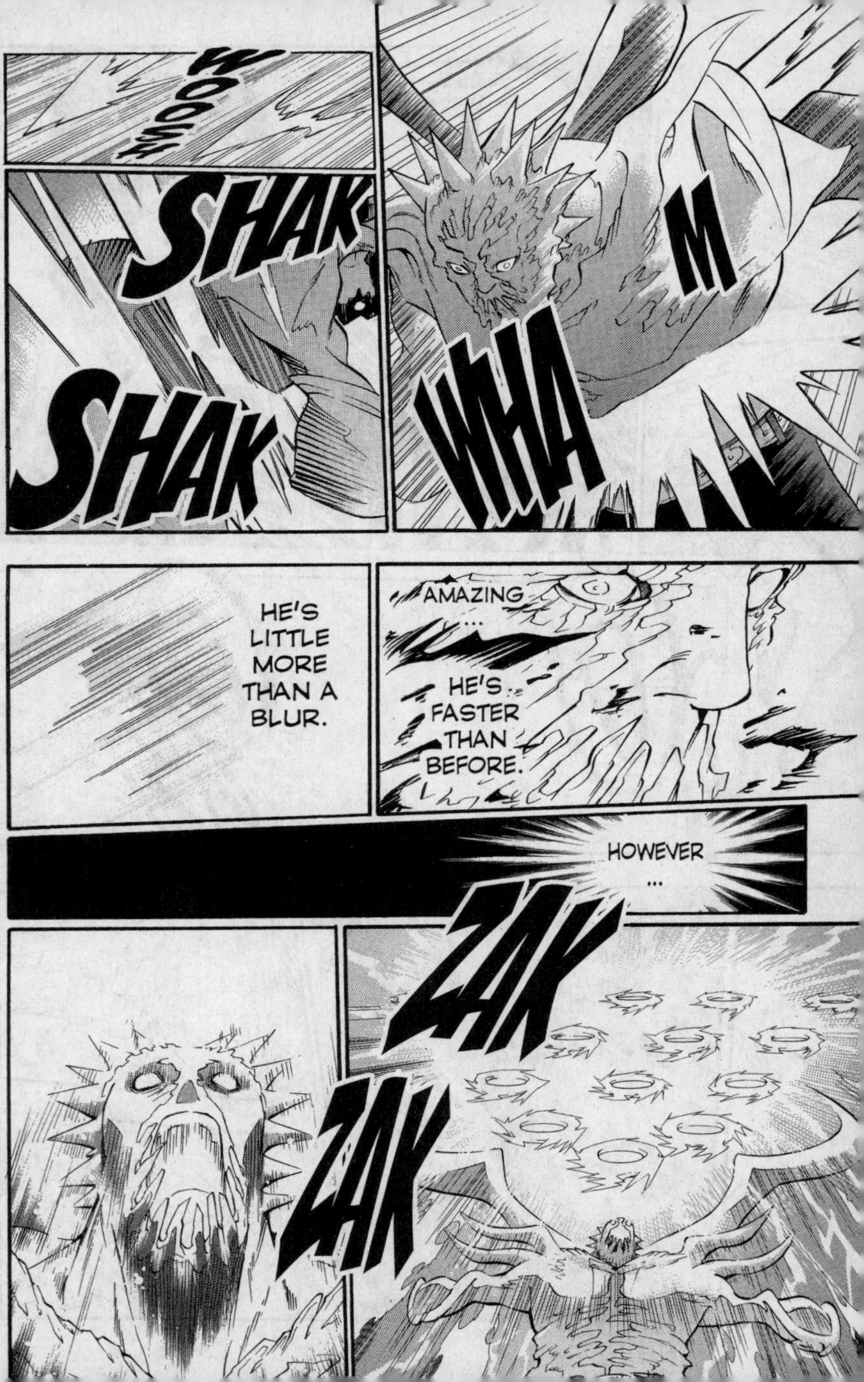
WHAM
WOOSH
SHAK
SHAK
AMAZING...
HE'S FASTER THAN BEFORE.
HE'S LITTLE MORE THAN A BLUR.
HOWEVER...
ZAK
ZAK

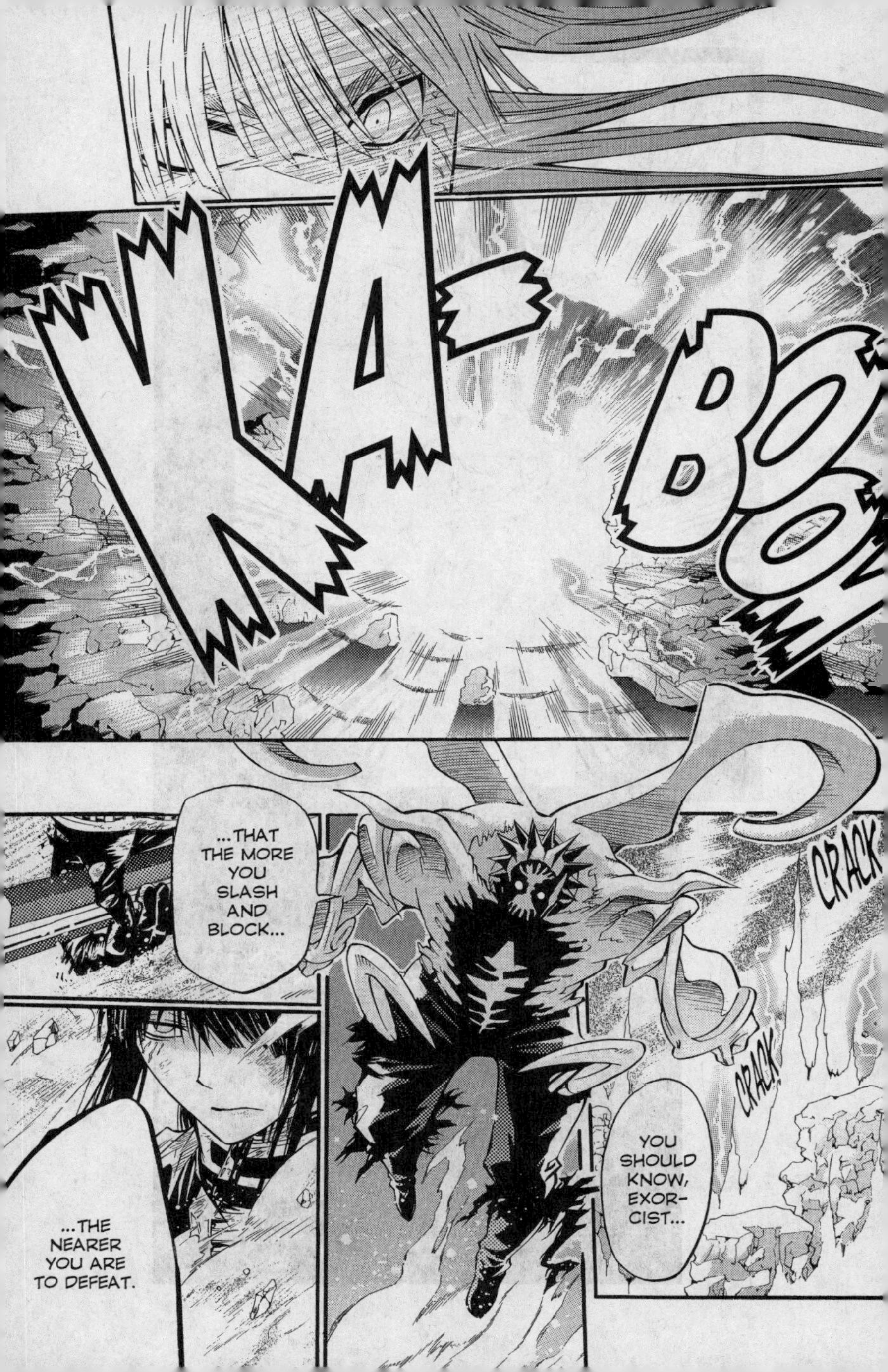
KA-BOOM
CRACK
CRACK
YOU SHOULD KNOW, EXORCIST...
...THAT THE MORE YOU SLASH AND BLOCK...
...THE NEARER YOU ARE TO DEFEAT.

UP TO NOW I'VE BEEN FEATURING
JUST ONE CHARACTER ON THE
COVER OF EACH VOLUME. BUT
DUE TO CERTAIN UNFORESEEN
EVENTS, THE COVER OF VOLUME
9 WAS DIFFERENT. SO I'M
CONSIDERING DOING THEM
LIKE THIS FROM NOW ON. ☆

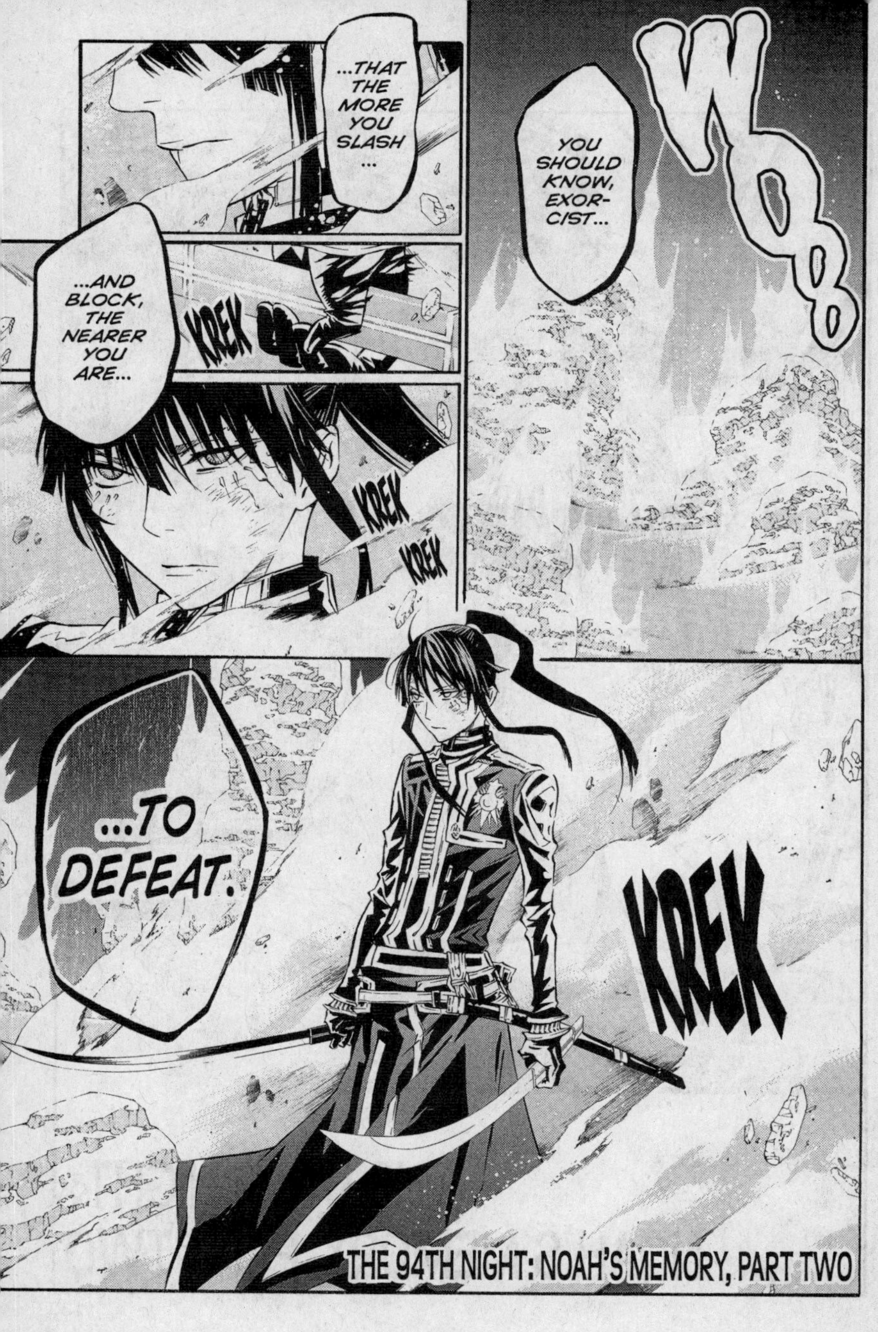
WOOO
YOU SHOULD KNOW, EXORCIST...
...THAT THE MORE YOU SLASH...
...AND BLOCK, THE NEARER YOU ARE...
KREK
KREK
KREK
...TO DEFEAT.
KREK

THE 94TH NIGHT: NOAH'S MEMORY, PART TWO

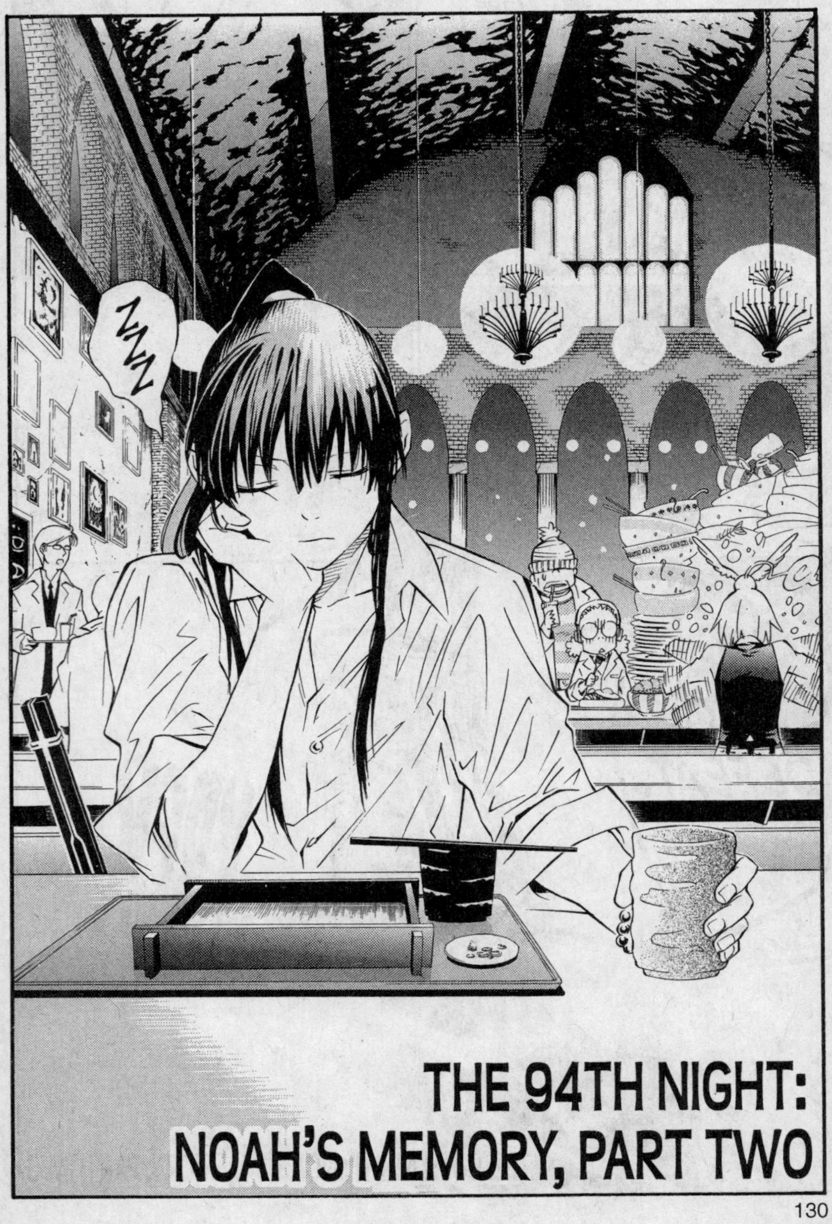
ZZZ

THE 94TH NIGHT: NOAH'S MEMORY, PART TWO

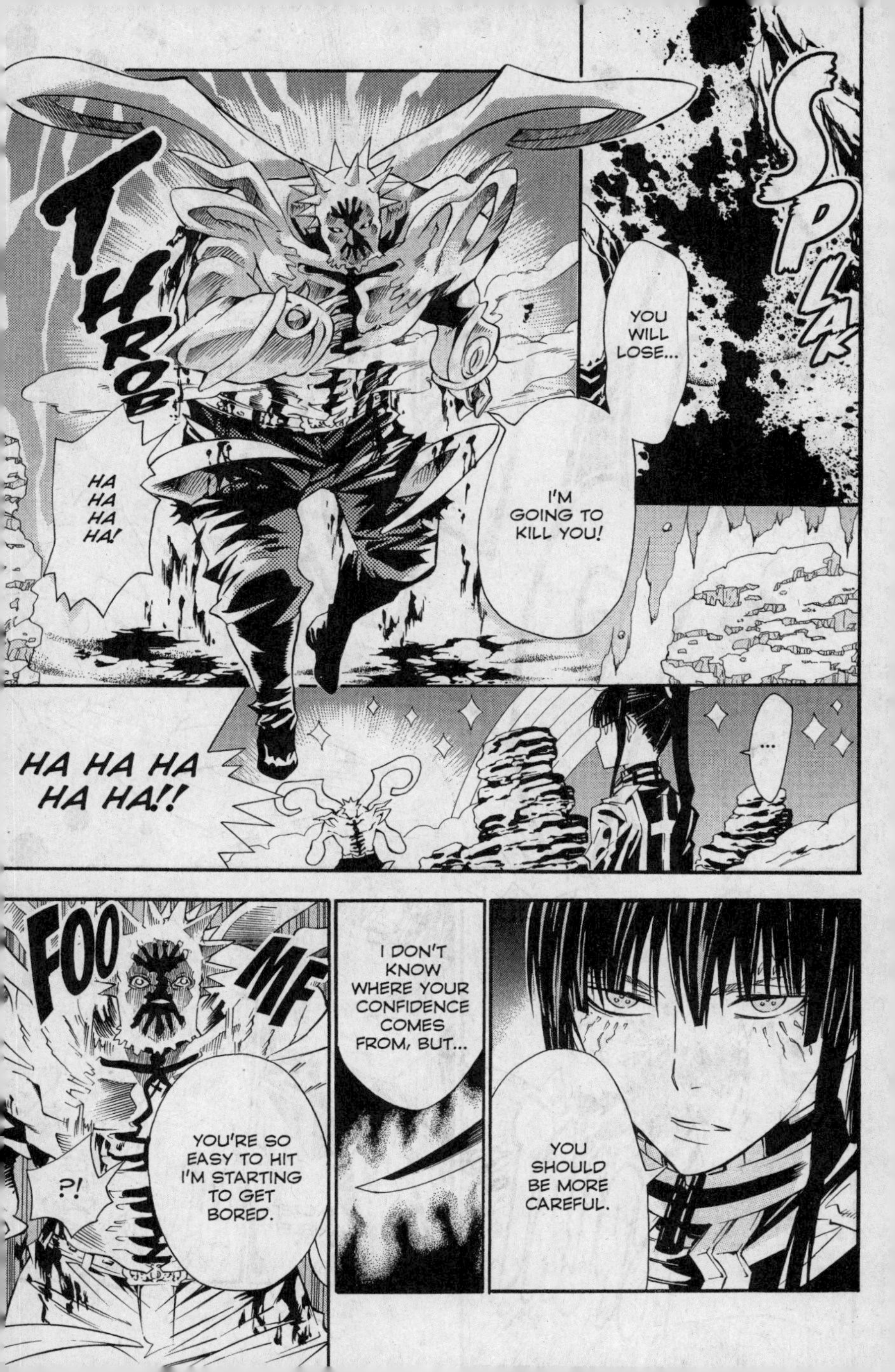
SPLAT
YOU WILL LOSE...
I'M GOING TO KILL YOU!
THROB
HA HA HA HA!
...
HA HA HA HA HA HA!!
I DON'T KNOW WHERE YOUR CONFIDENCE COMES FROM, BUT...
YOU SHOULD BE MORE CAREFUL.
FOOMF
YOU'RE SO EASY TO HIT I'M STARTING TO GET BORED.
?!

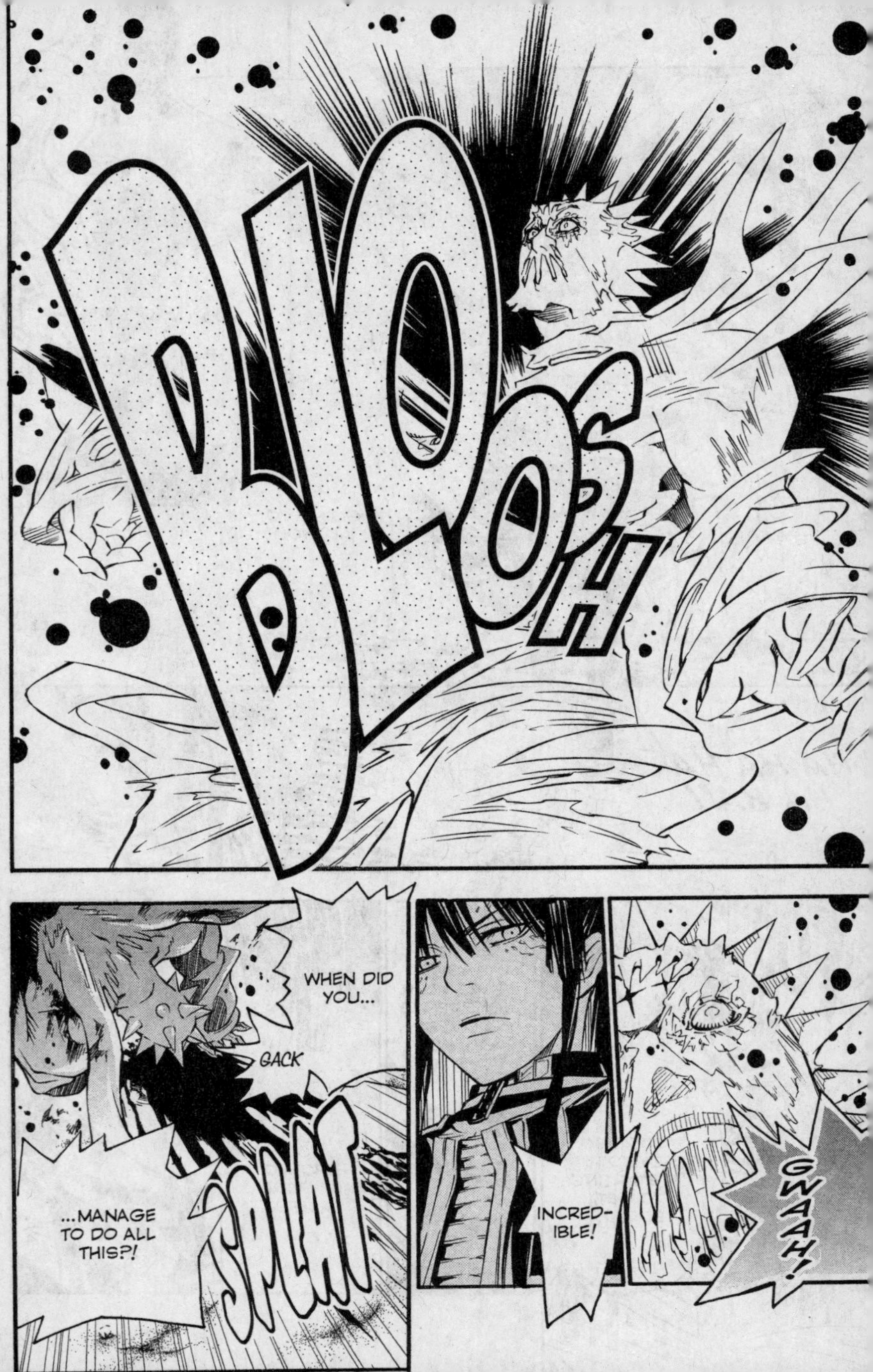
BLOOSH
GWAAH!
INCRED-IBLE!
WHEN DID YOU...
GACK
SPLAT
...MANAGE TO DO ALL THIS?!

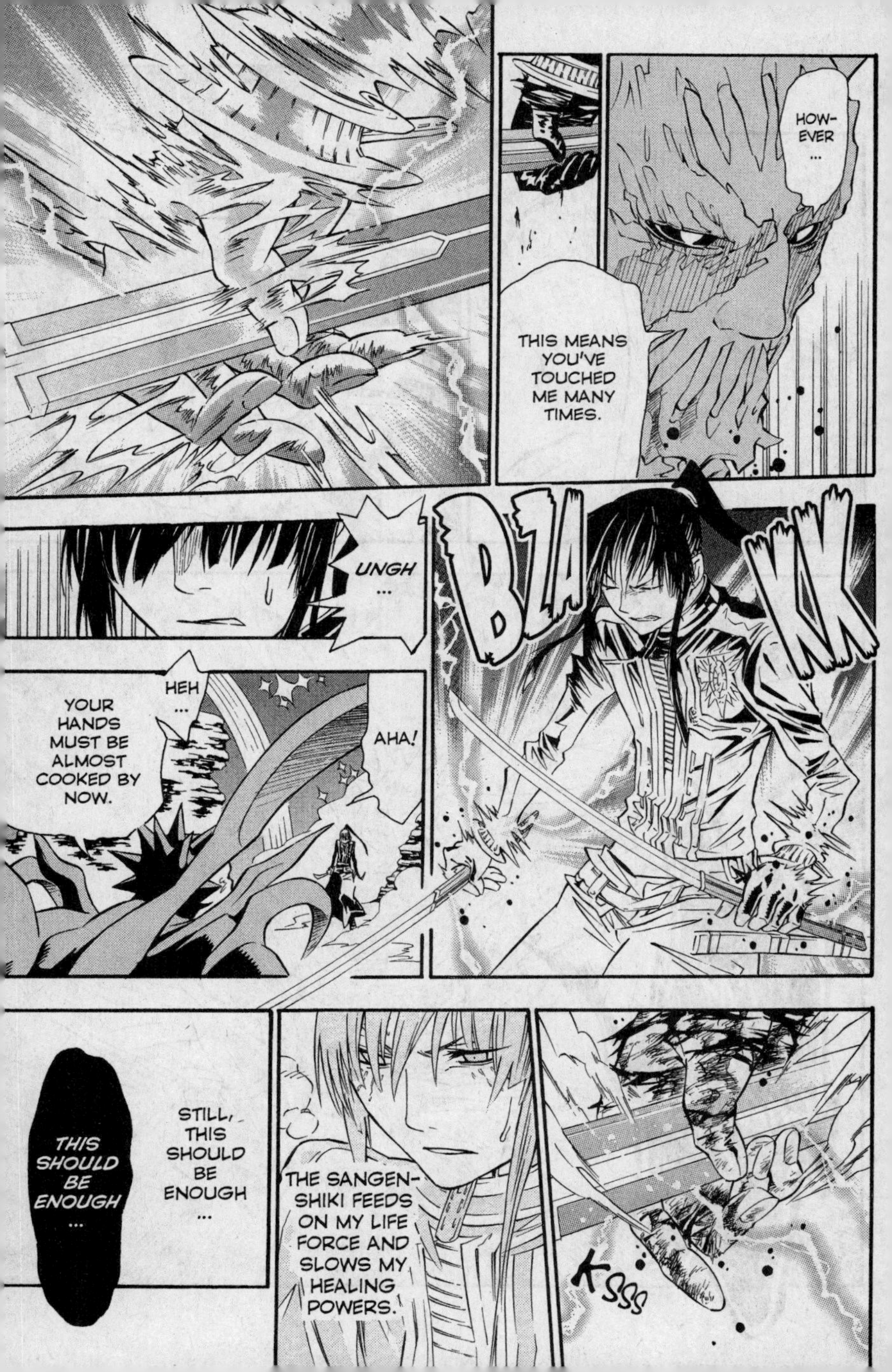
HOW-EVER ...
THIS MEANS YOU'VE TOUCHED ME MANY TIMES.
BZAKK
UNGH ...
HEH ...
AHA!
YOUR HANDS MUST BE ALMOST COOKED BY NOW.
KSSS
THE SANGEN-SHIKI FEEDS ON MY LIFE FORCE AND SLOWS MY HEALING POWERS.
STILL, THIS SHOULD BE ENOUGH ...
THIS SHOULD BE ENOUGH ...

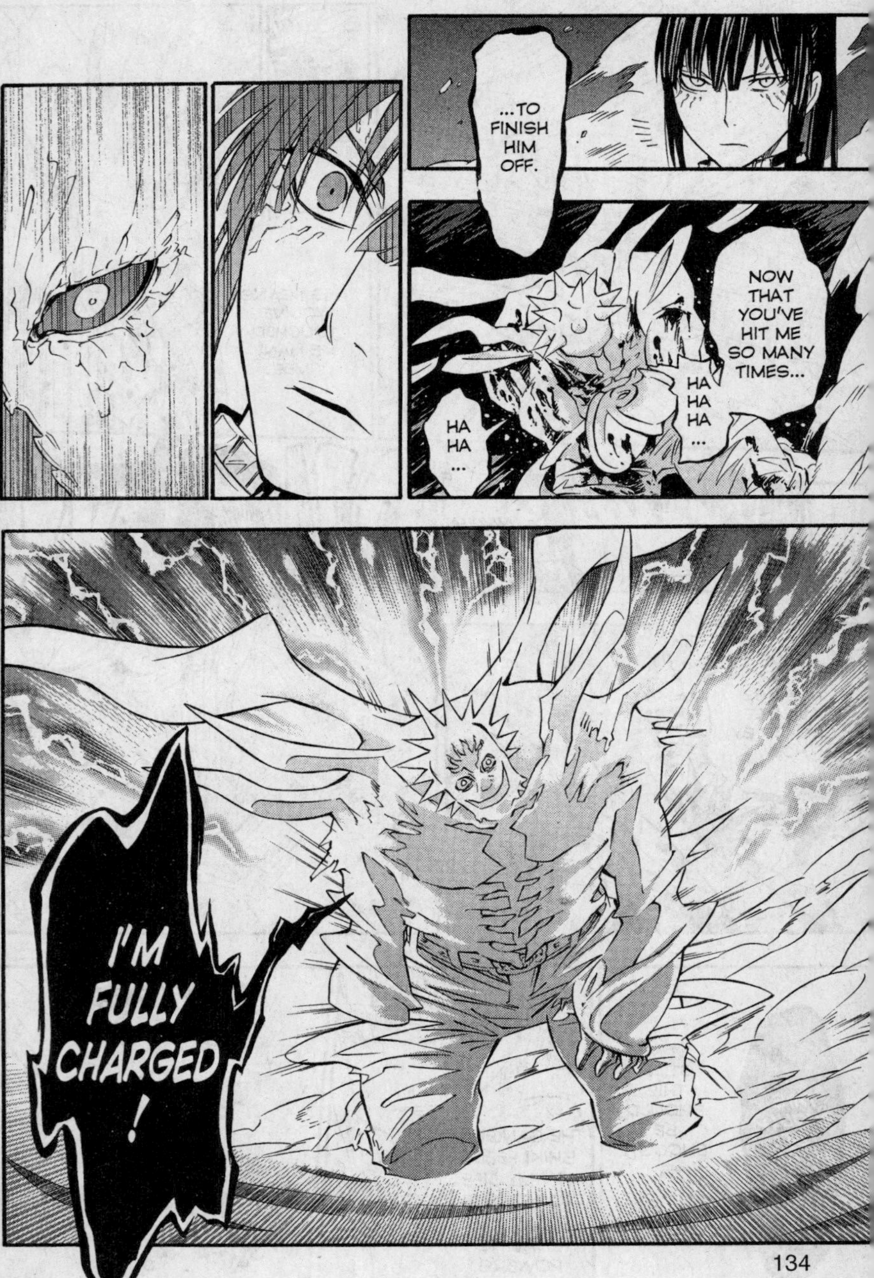
...TO FINISH HIM OFF.
NOW THAT YOU'VE HIT ME SO MANY TIMES...
HA HA HA ...
HA HA ...
I'M FULLY CHARGED!

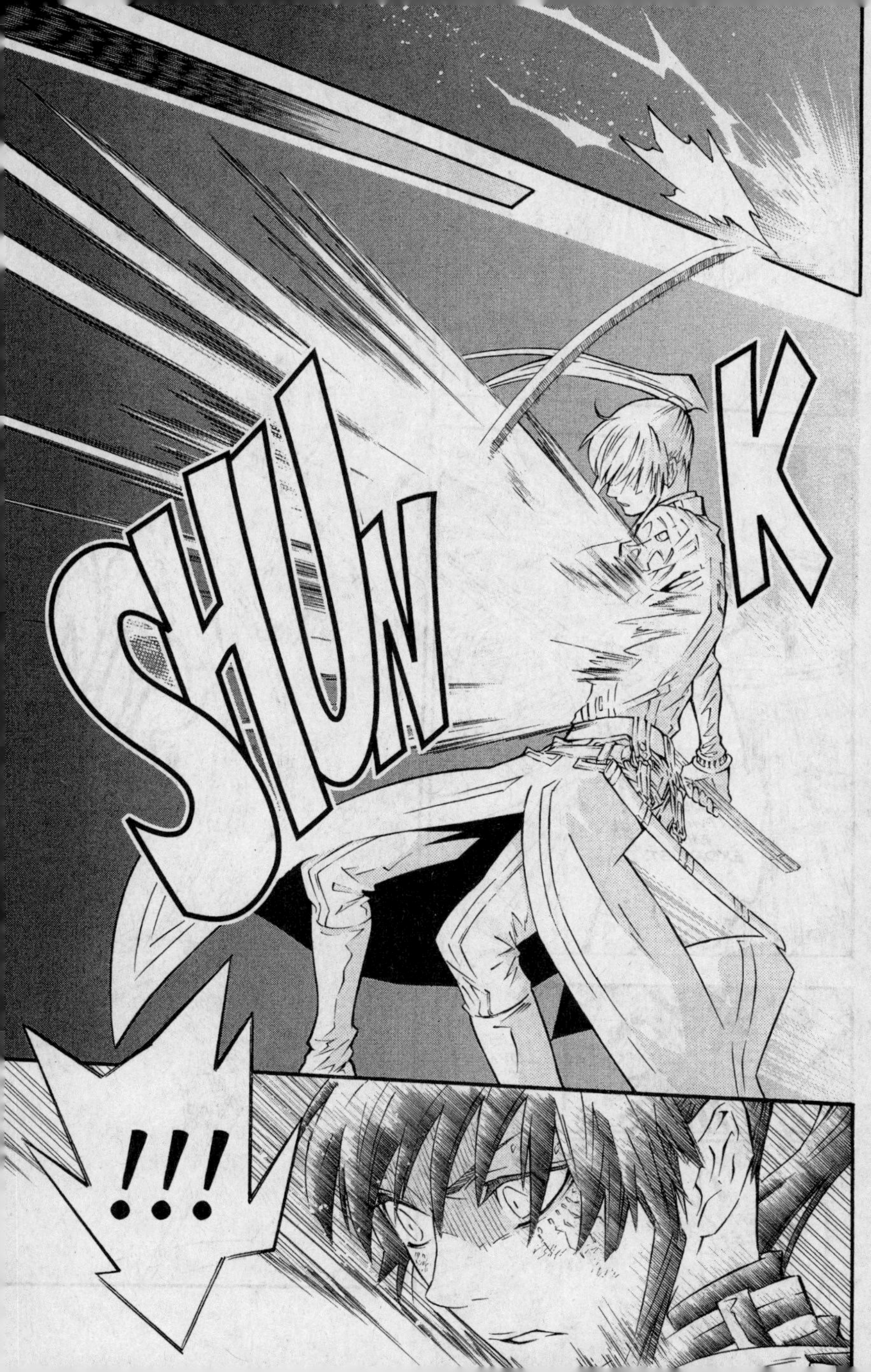
SHUNK
!!!

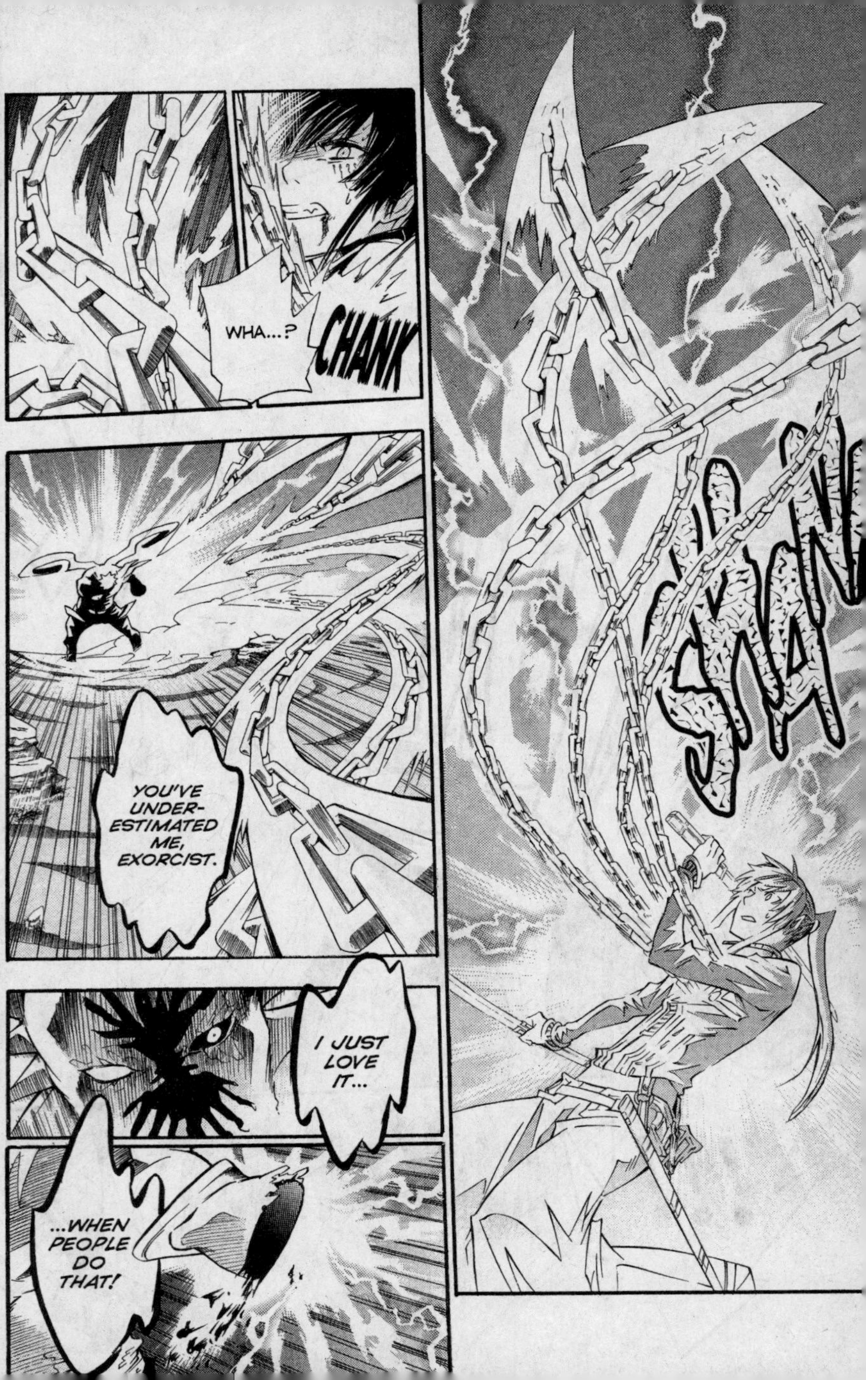
WHA...?
CHANK
YOU'VE UNDER-ESTIMATED ME, EXORCIST.
I JUST LOVE IT...
...WHEN PEOPLE DO THAT!

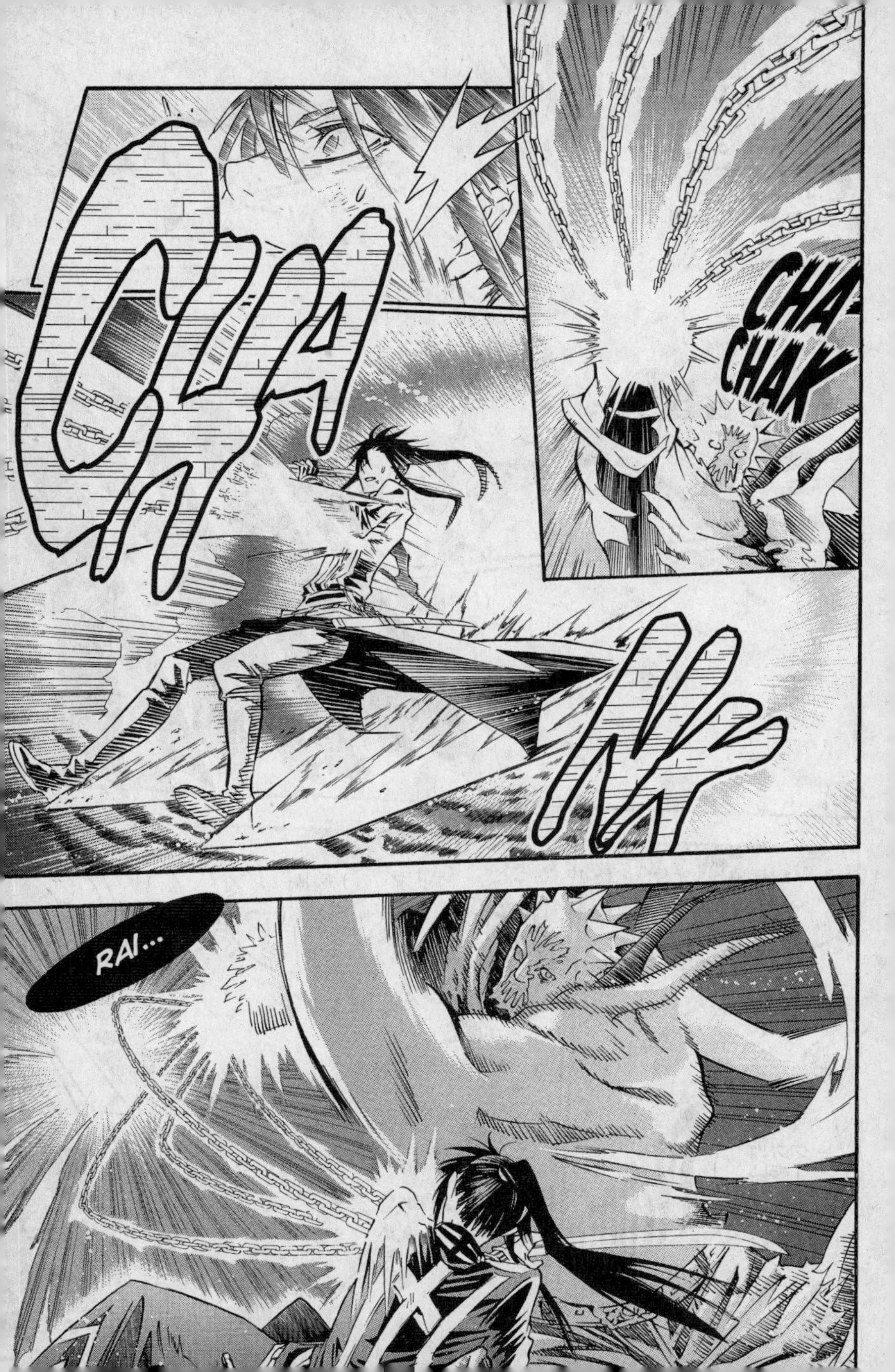
CHA-CHAK
RAI...

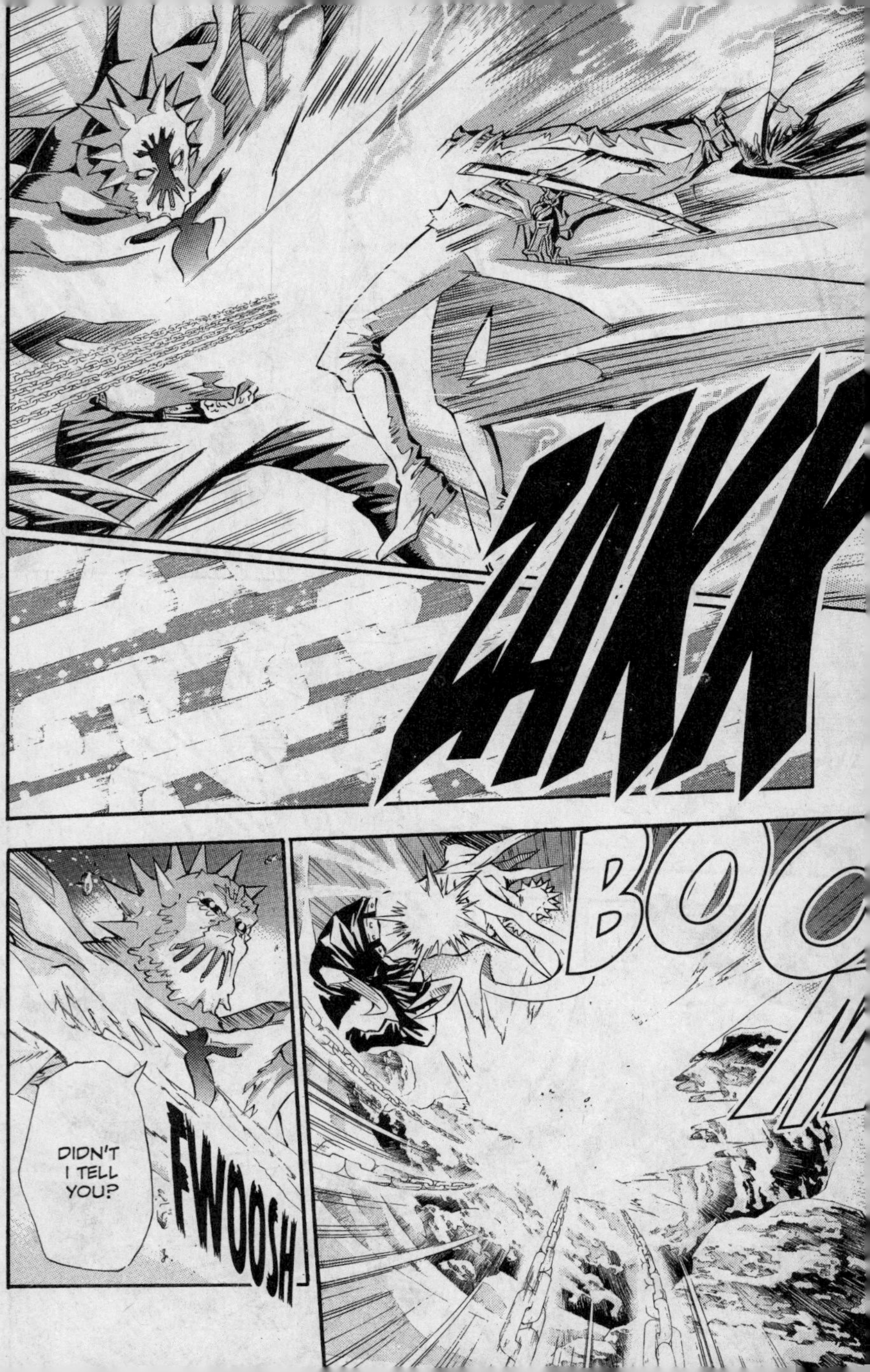
BOO
FWOOSH
DIDN'T I TELL YOU?

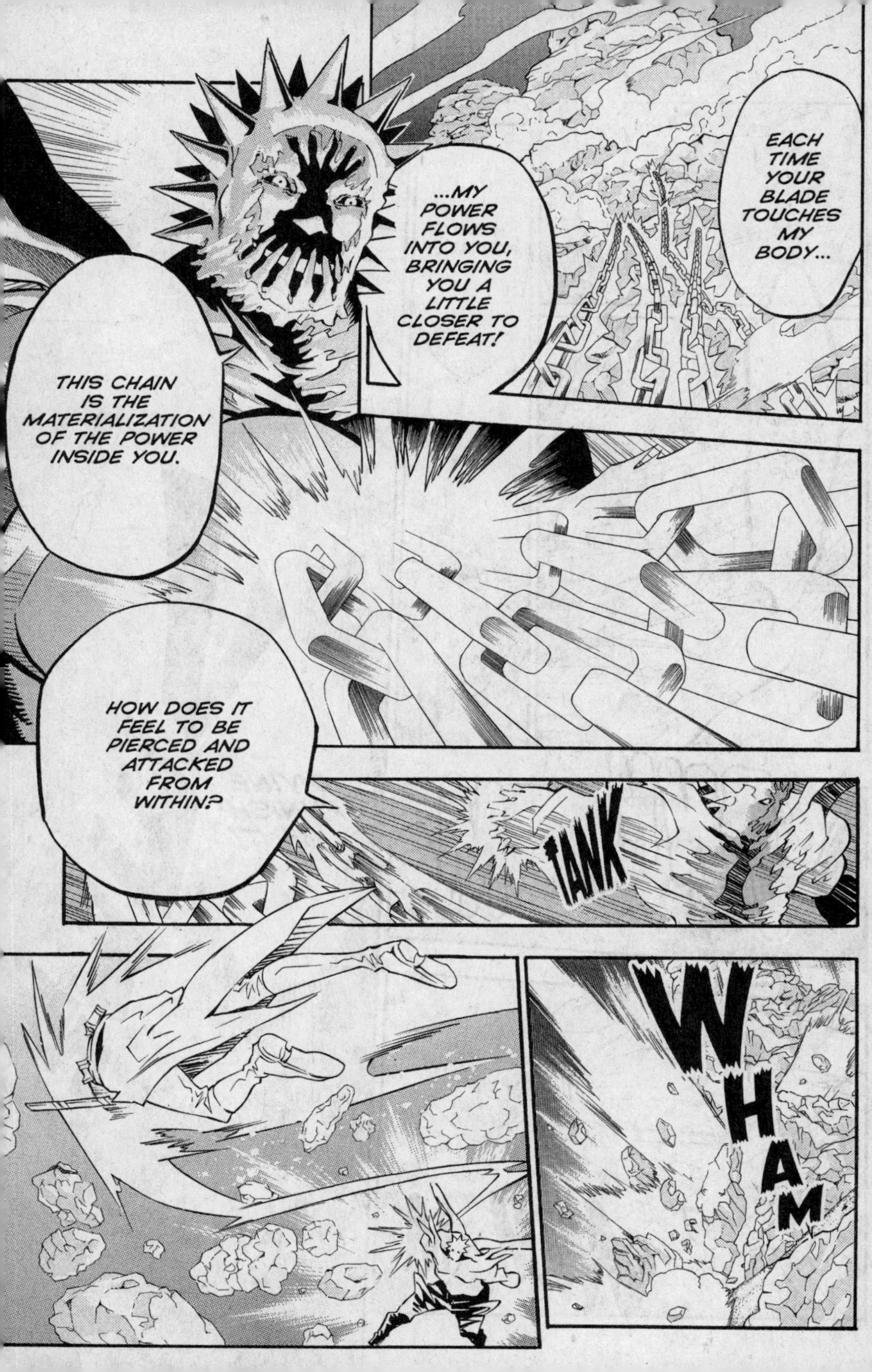
EACH TIME YOUR BLADE TOUCHES MY BODY...
...MY POWER FLOWS INTO YOU, BRINGING YOU A LITTLE CLOSER TO DEFEAT!
THIS CHAIN IS THE MATERIALIZATION OF THE POWER INSIDE YOU.
HOW DOES IT FEEL TO BE PIERCED AND ATTACKED FROM WITHIN?
TANK
WHAM

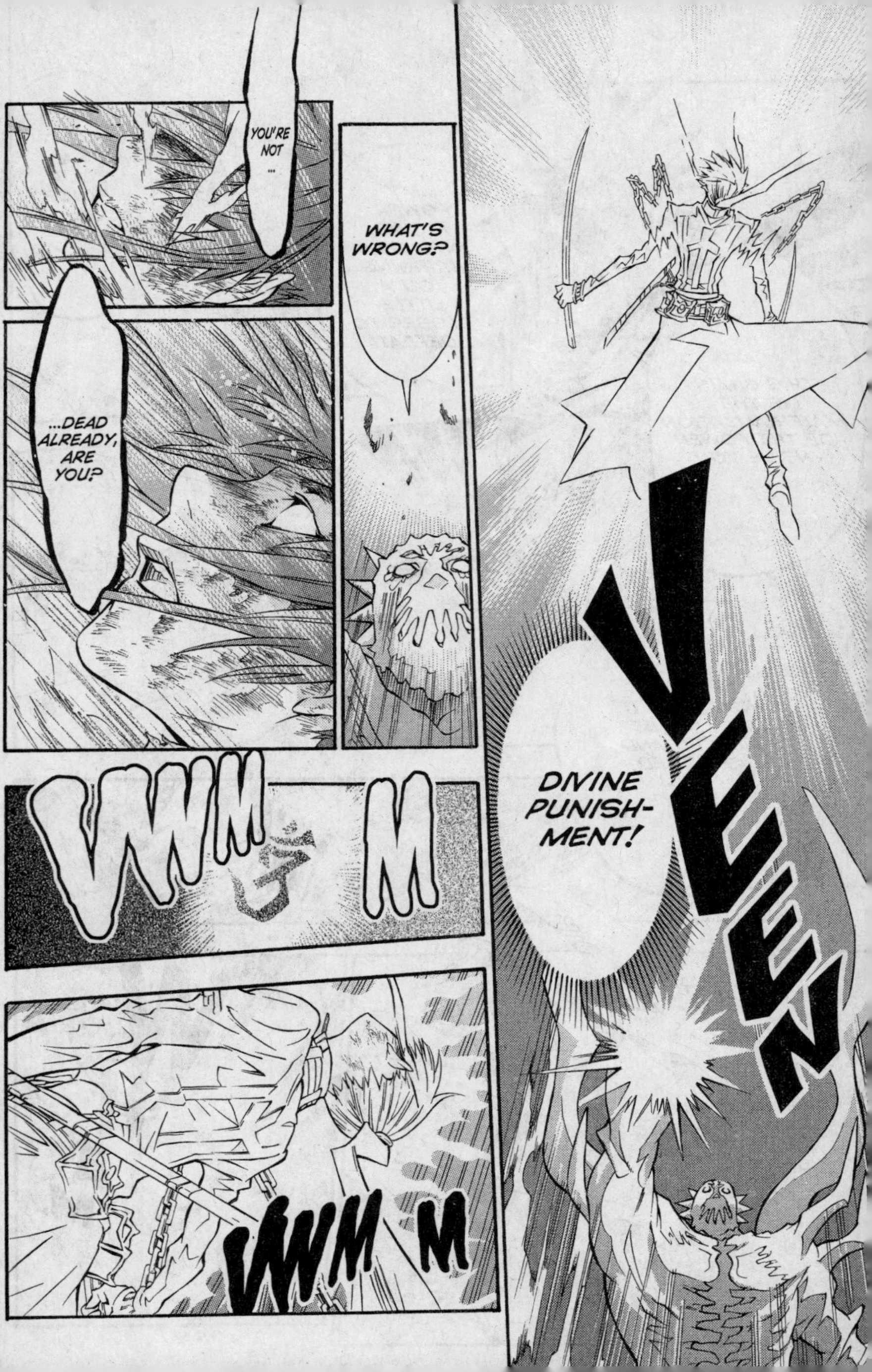
VEEEN
DIVINE PUNISH-MENT!
WHAT'S WRONG?
YOU'RE NOT ...
...DEAD ALREADY, ARE YOU?
VWM M
VWM M

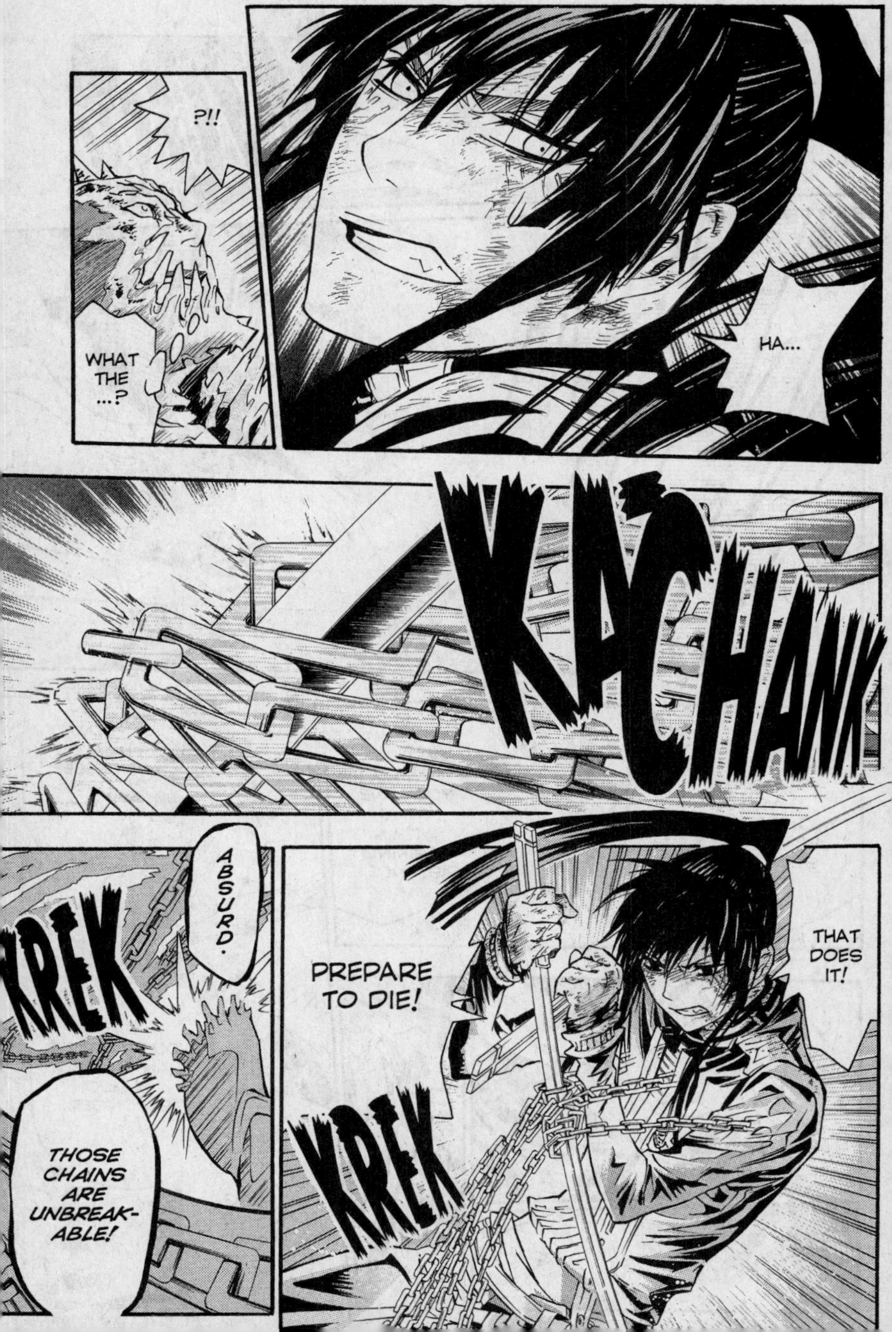
HA...
?!!
WHAT THE ...?
KACHANK
THAT DOES IT!
PREPARE TO DIE!
KREK
ABSURD.
KREK
THOSE CHAINS ARE UNBREAKABLE!

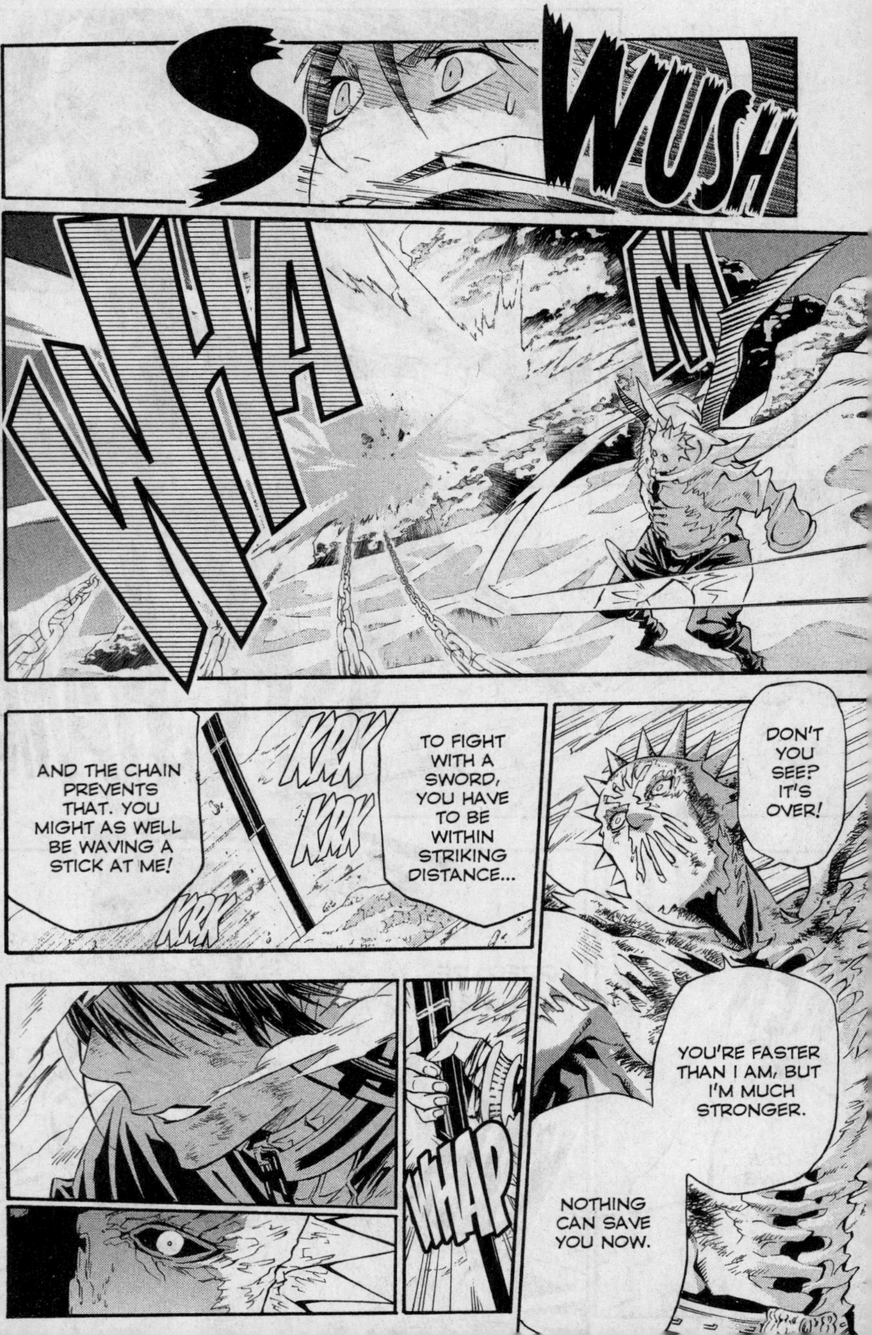
S
WUSH
WHAM
DON'T YOU SEE? IT'S OVER!
TO FIGHT WITH A SWORD, YOU HAVE TO BE WITHIN STRIKING DISTANCE...
KRK
KRK
AND THE CHAIN PREVENTS THAT. YOU MIGHT AS WELL BE WAVING A STICK AT ME!
KRK
YOU'RE FASTER THAN I AM, BUT I'M MUCH STRONGER.
NOTHING CAN SAVE YOU NOW.
WHAP

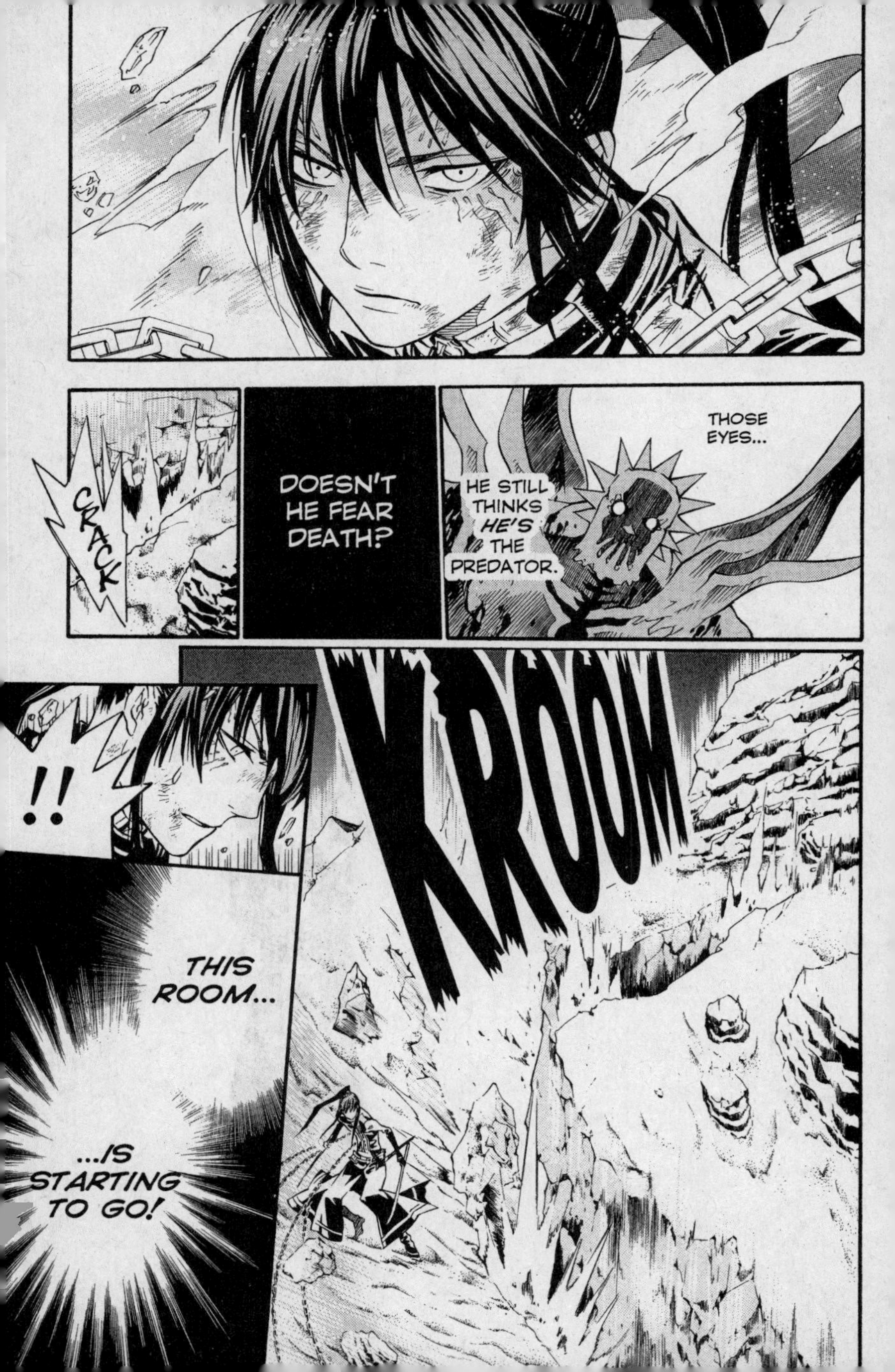
THOSE EYES...
HE STILL THINKS *HE'S* THE PREDATOR.
DOESN'T HE FEAR DEATH?
CRACK
KROOM
!!
THIS ROOM...
...IS STARTING TO GO!

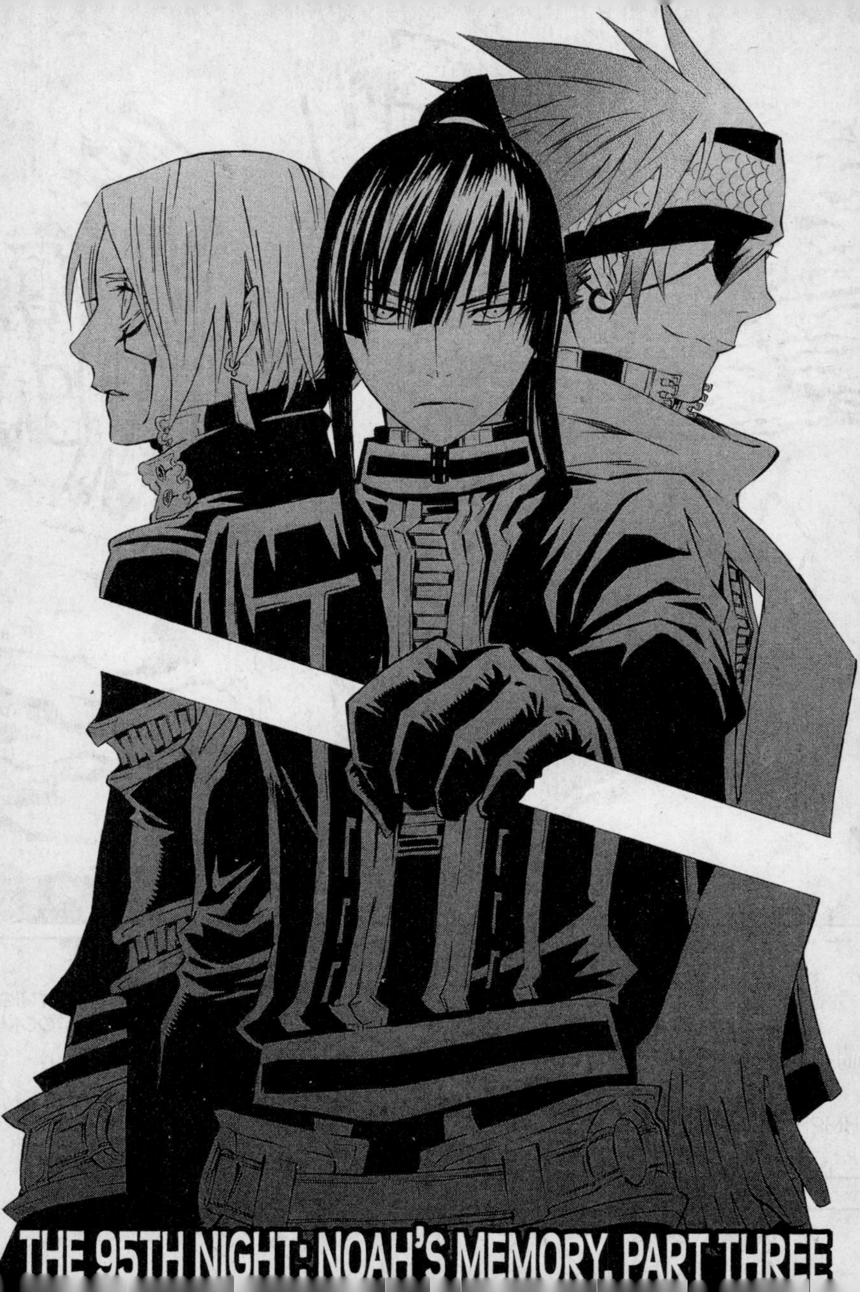

THE 95TH NIGHT: NOAH'S MEMORY, PART THREE

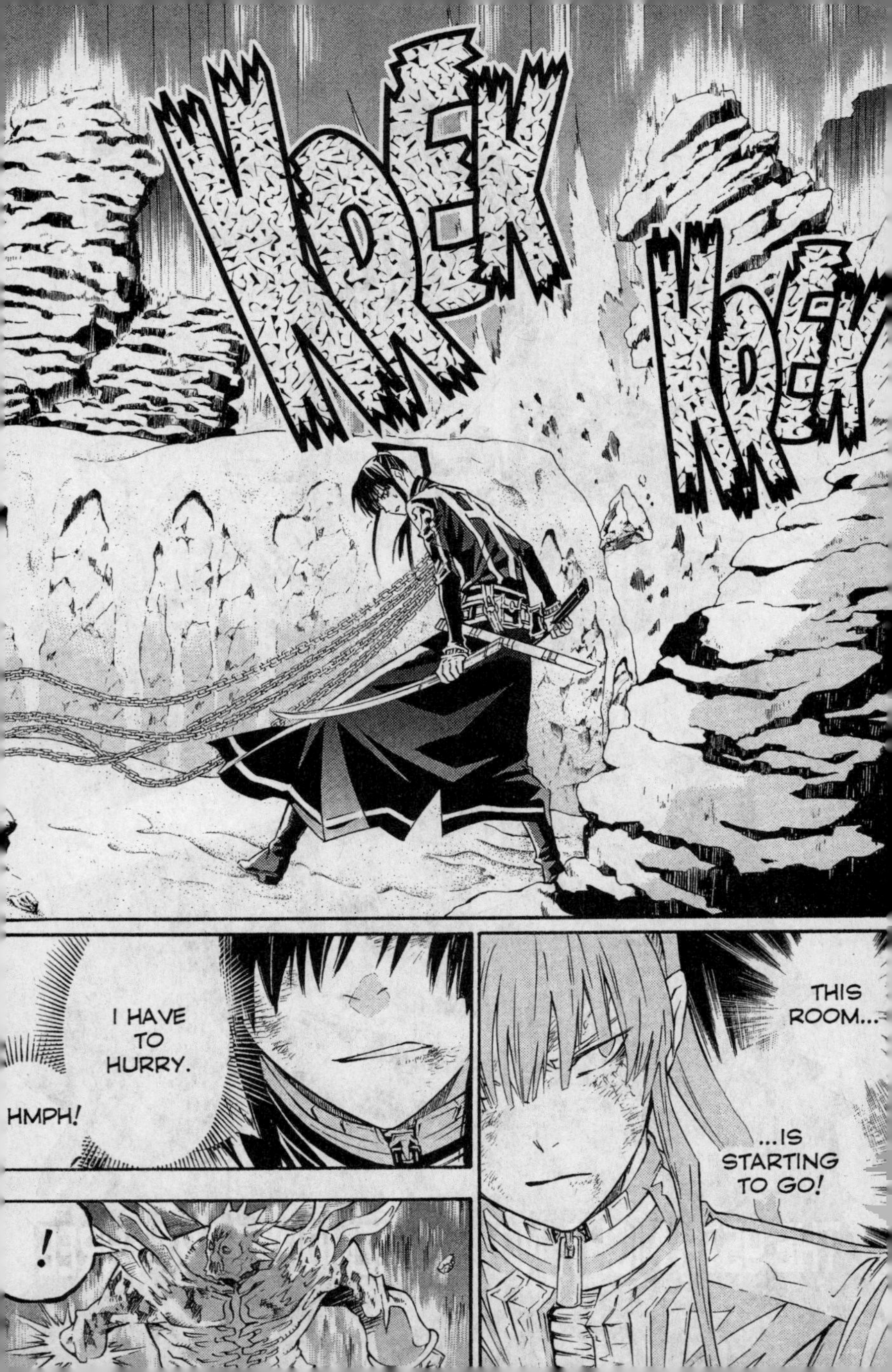
KRACK
KRACK
THIS ROOM...
...IS STARTING TO GO!
I HAVE TO HURRY.
HMPH!
!

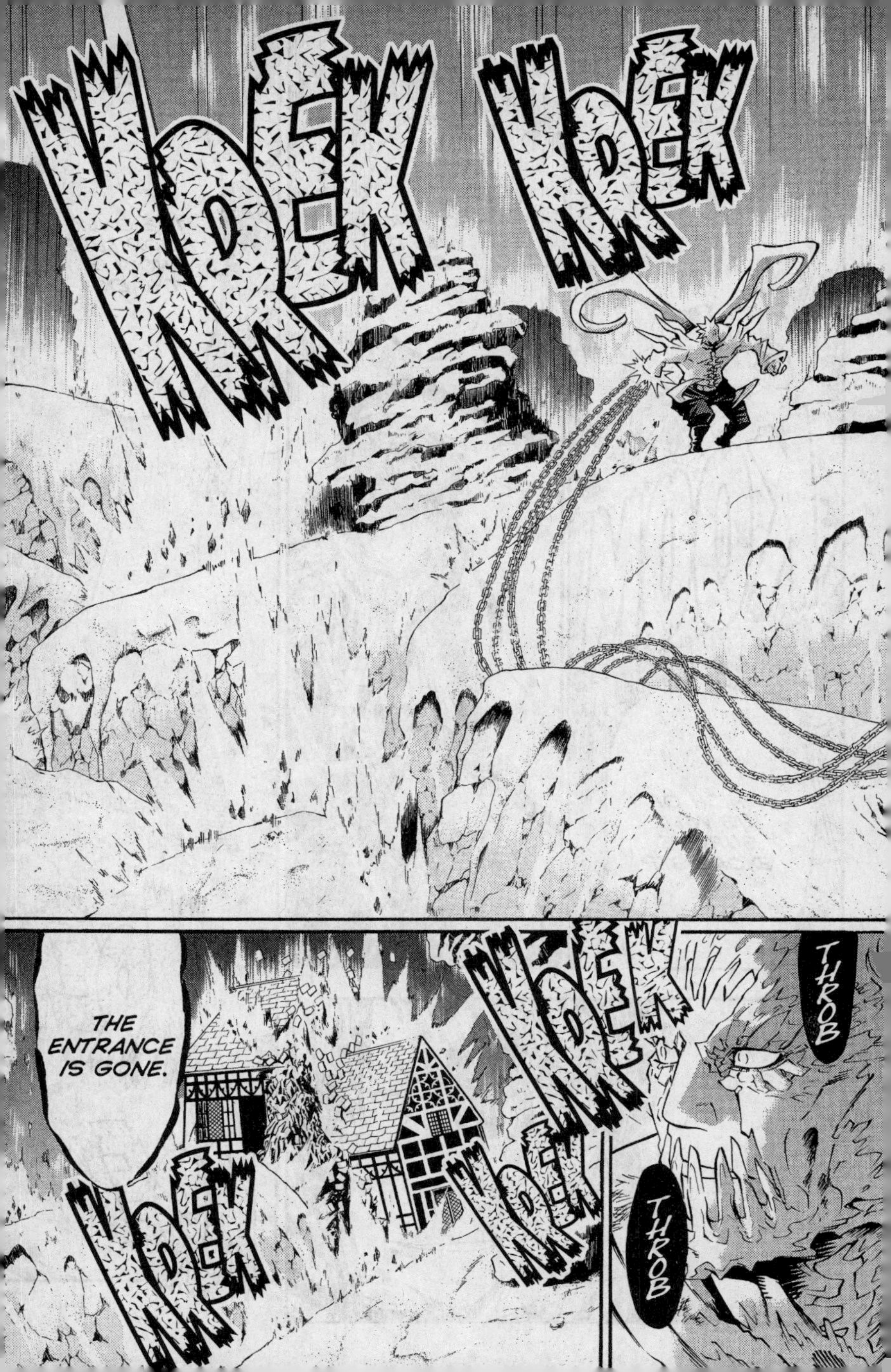
THROB
THROB
THE ENTRANCE IS GONE.

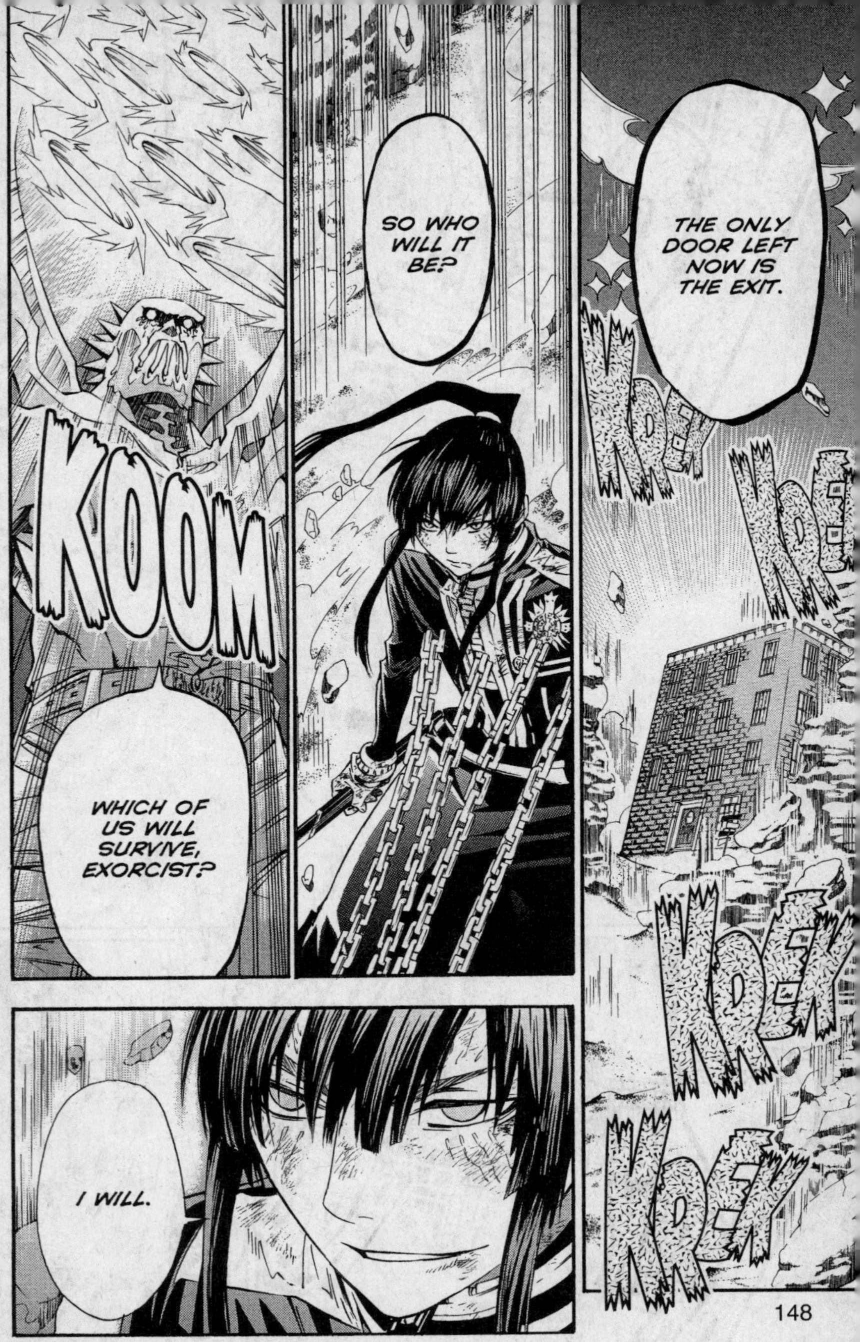
THE ONLY DOOR LEFT NOW IS THE EXIT.
KREEK
KREEK
KREEK
KREEK
SO WHO WILL IT BE?
KOOM
WHICH OF US WILL SURVIVE, EXORCIST?
I WILL.

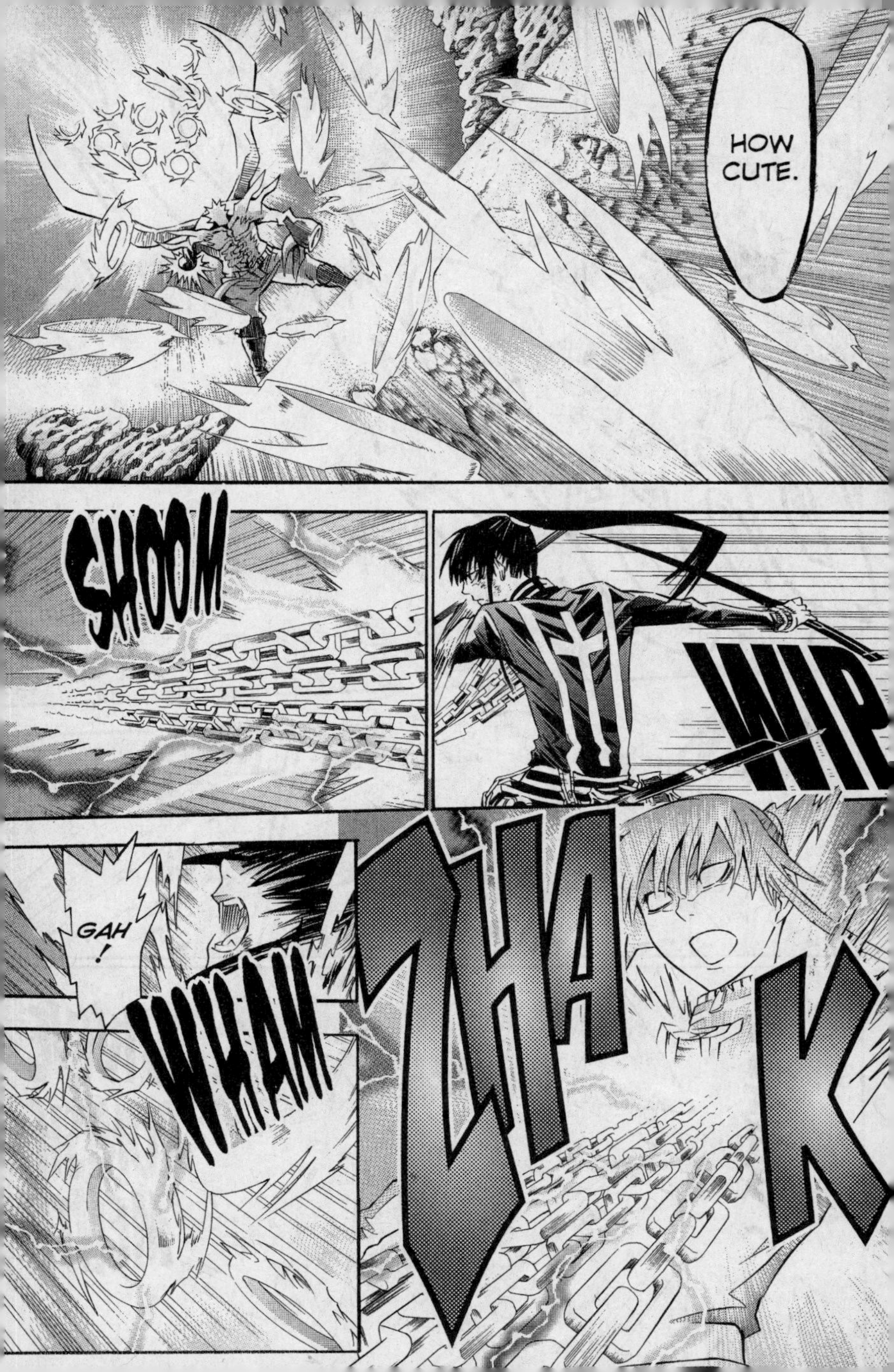
HOW CUTE.
SHOOM
GAH!
WHAM

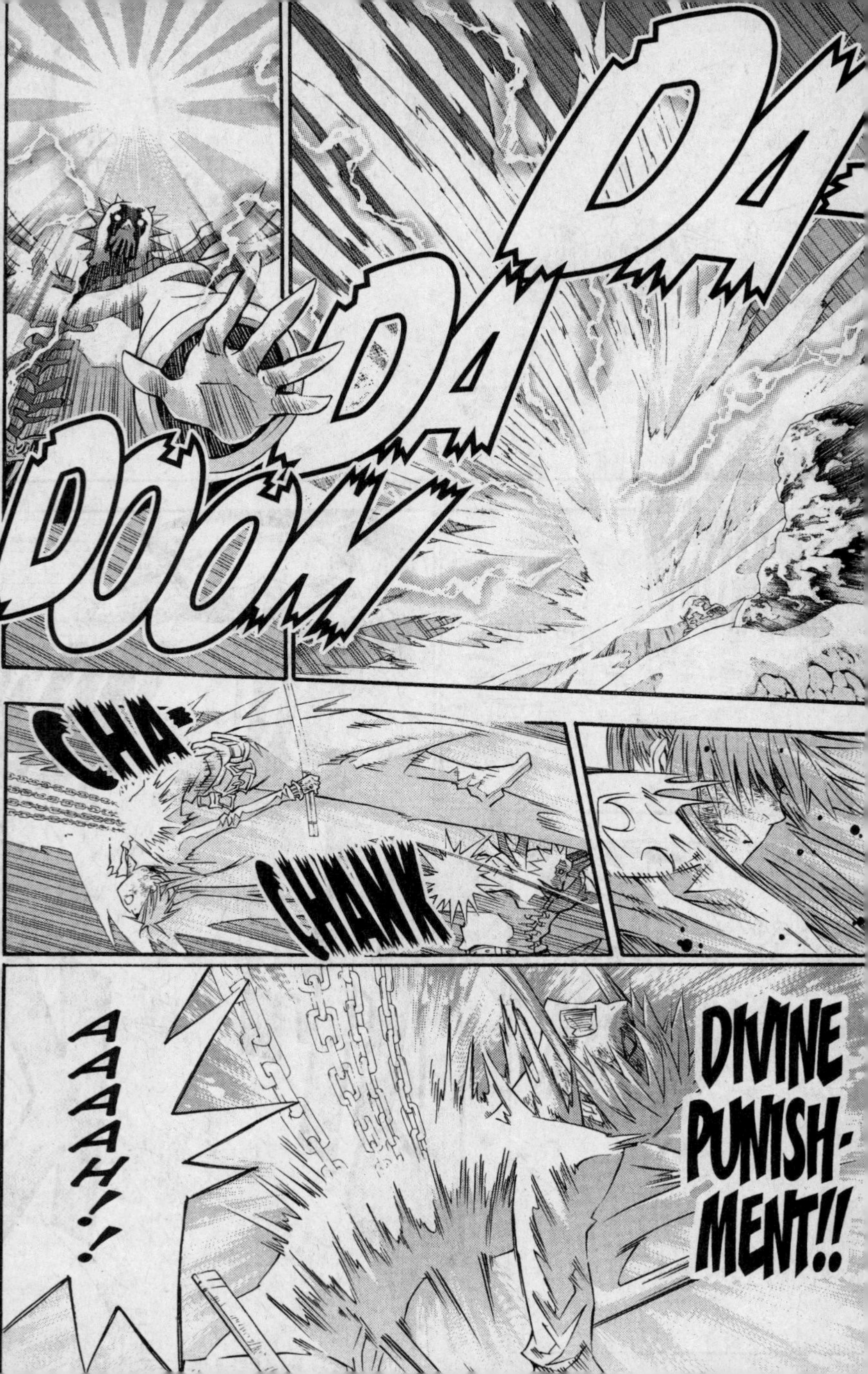
DOOOM DA DA
CHA
CHANK
DIVINE PUNISH-MENT!!
AAAAH!!

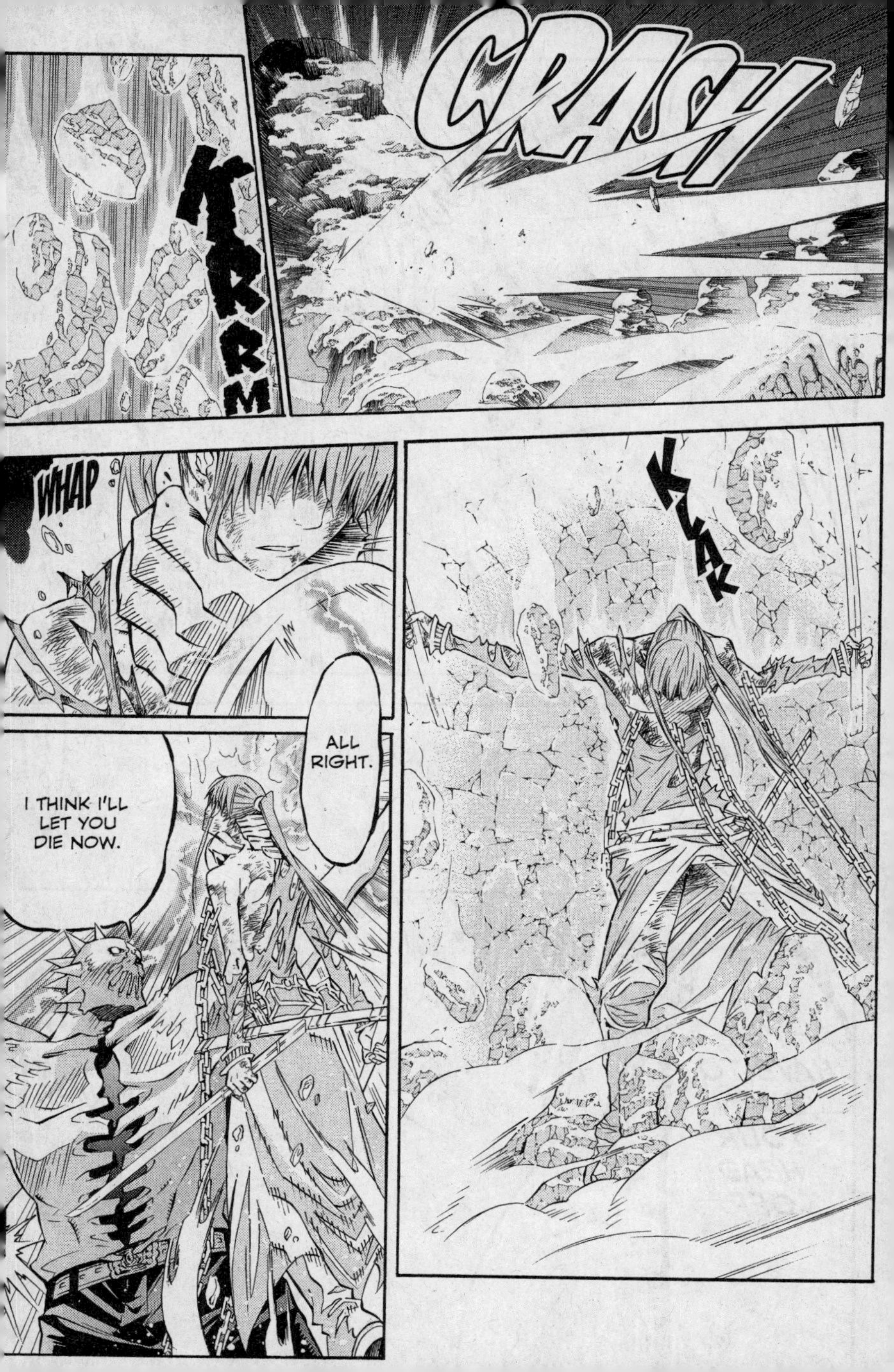
CRASH
KRRM
KWAK
WHAP
ALL RIGHT.
I THINK I'LL LET YOU DIE NOW.

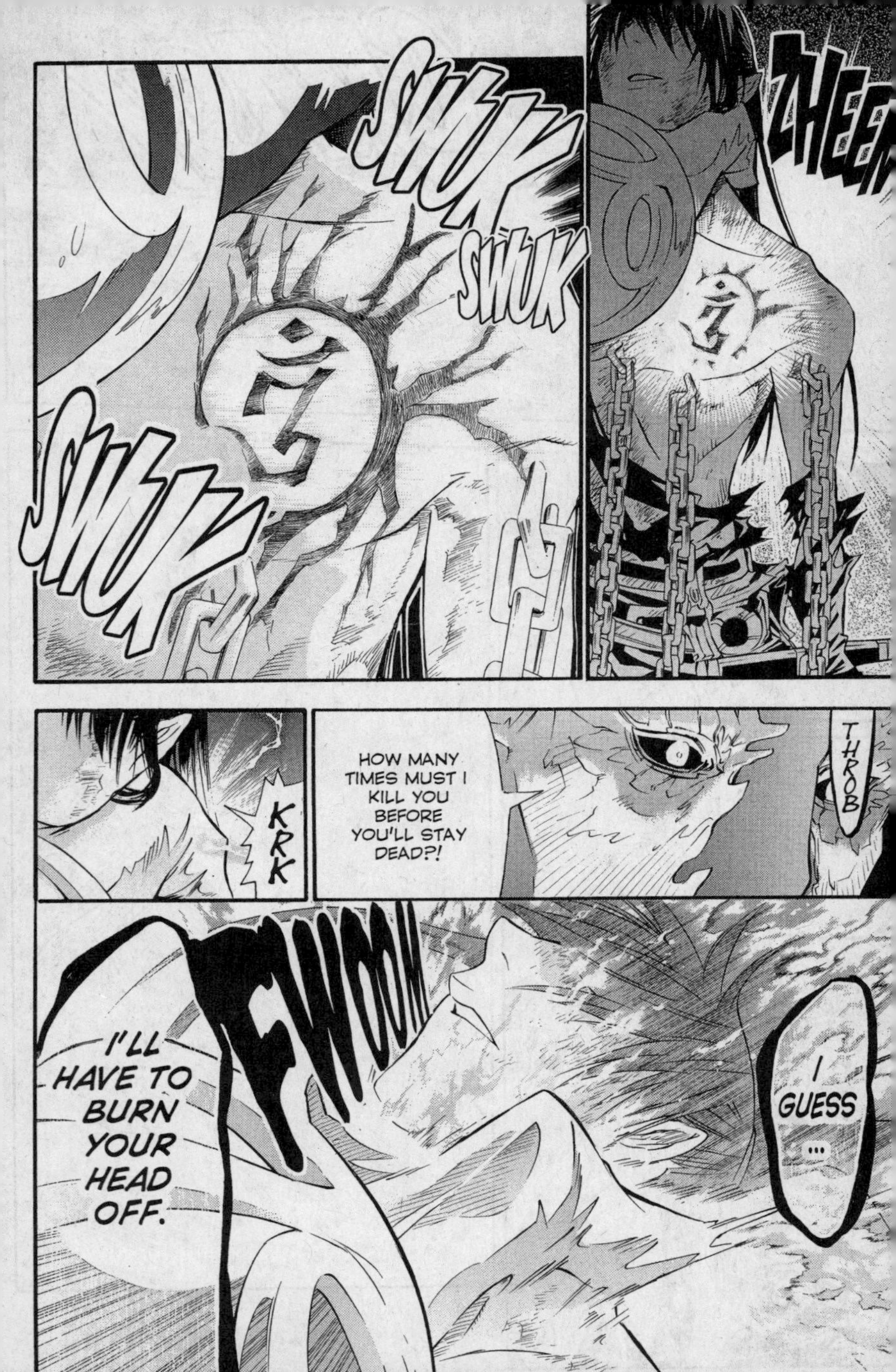
ZHEEN
SWUK
SWUK
SWUK
THROB
HOW MANY TIMES MUST I KILL YOU BEFORE YOU'LL STAY DEAD?!
KRK
I GUESS ...
FWOOM
I'LL HAVE TO BURN YOUR HEAD OFF.

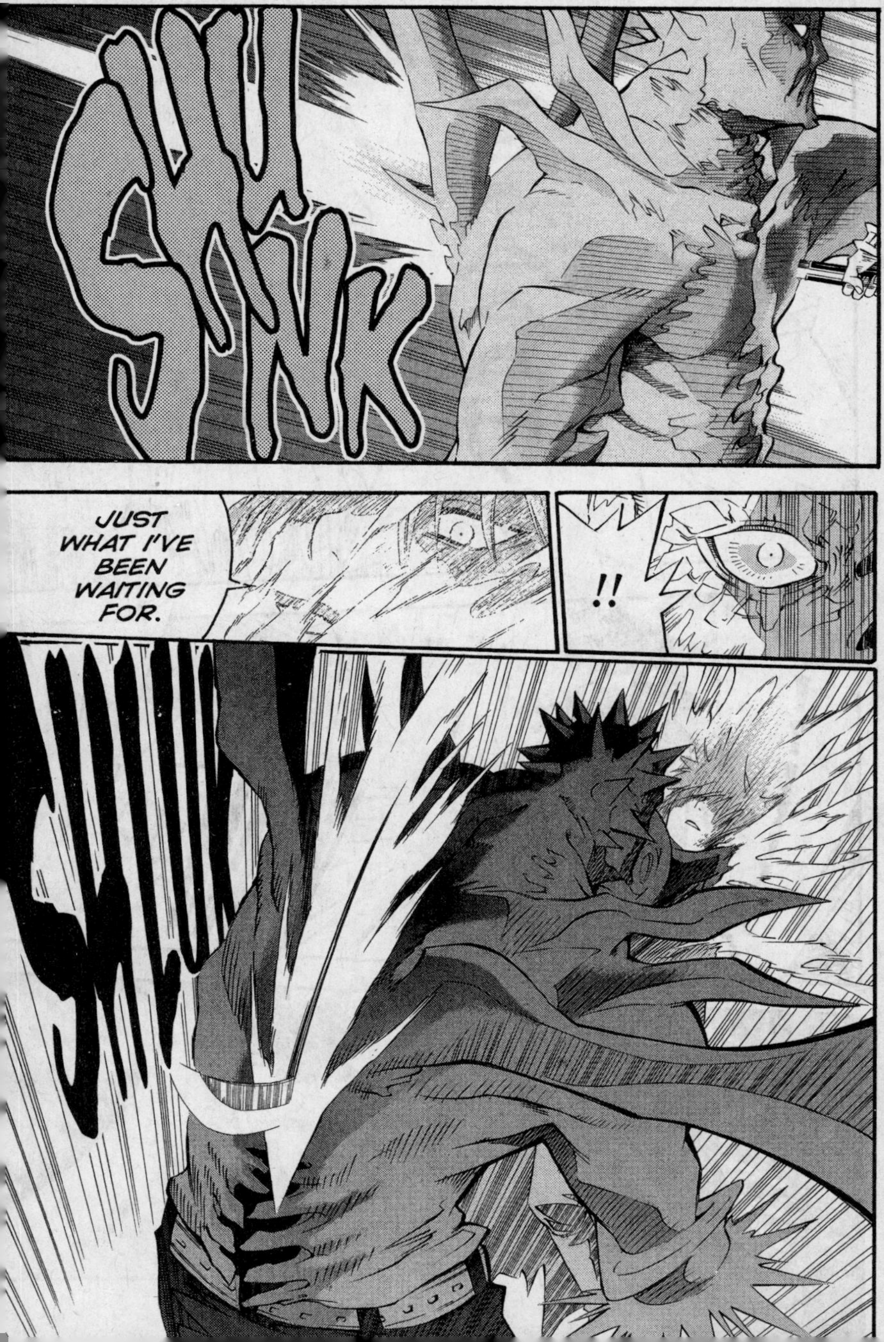
!!
JUST WHAT I'VE BEEN WAITING FOR.

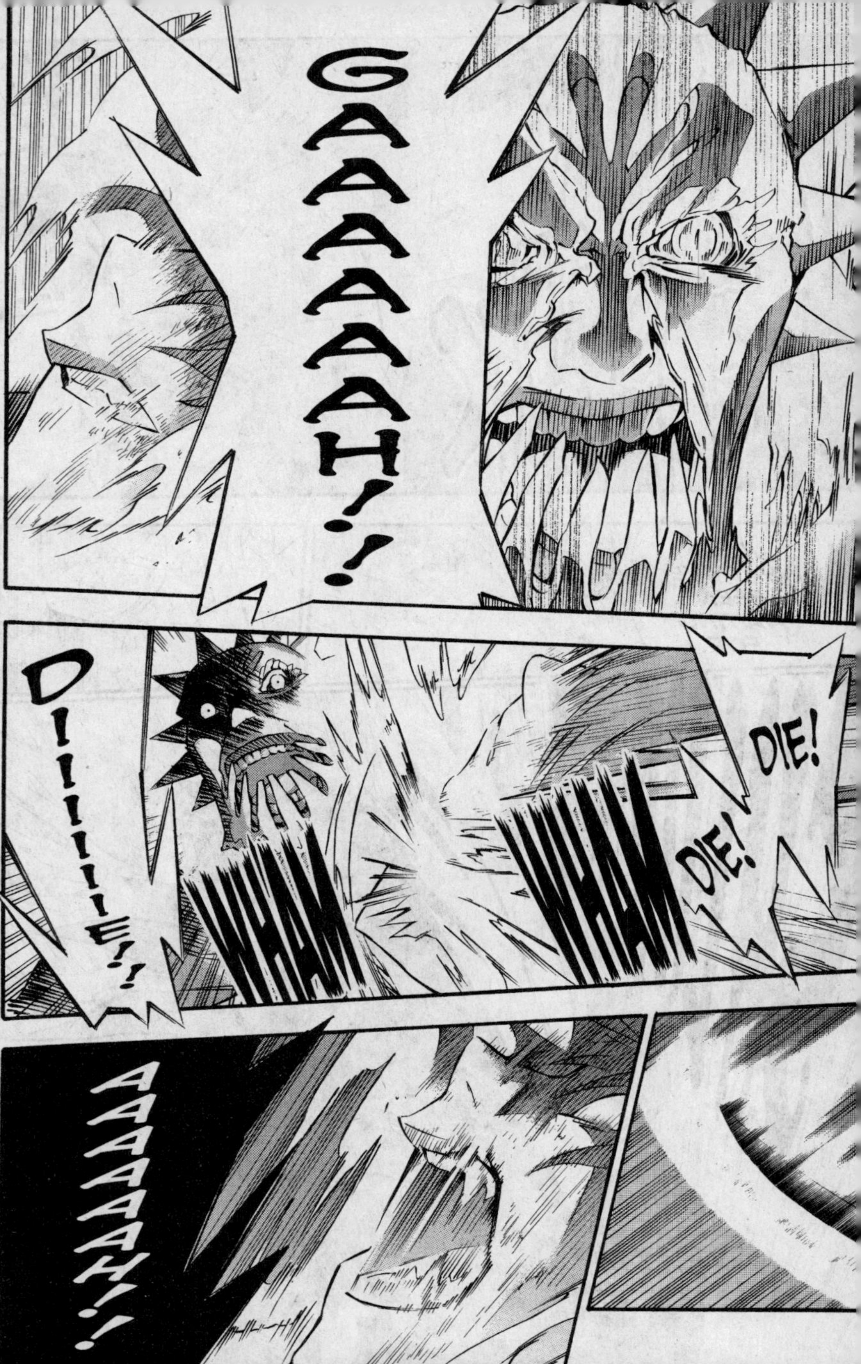
GAAAAAH!!
DIE! DIE!
WHAM
WHAM
DIIIIIIE!!
AAAAAAH!!

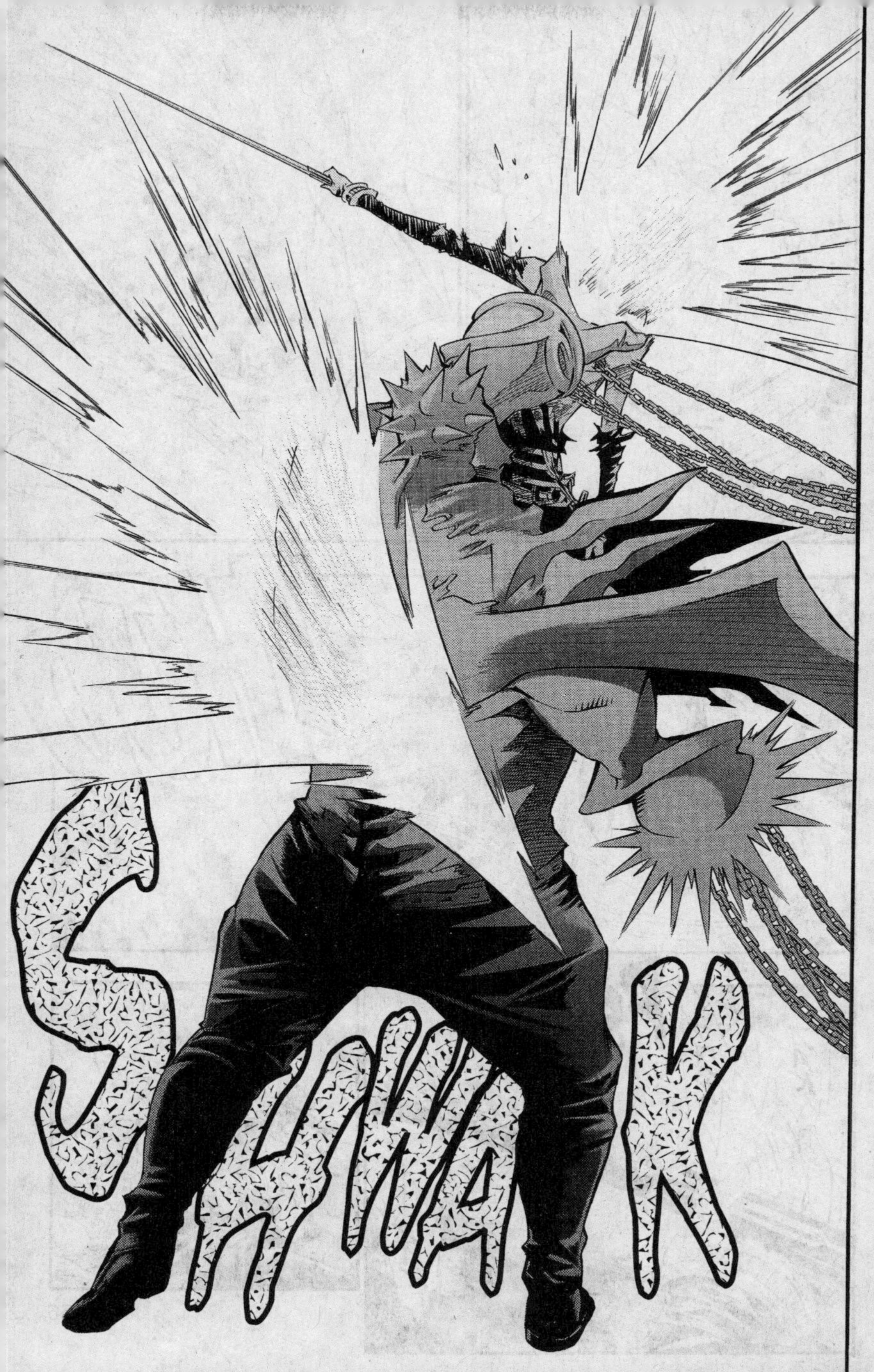
SMAK

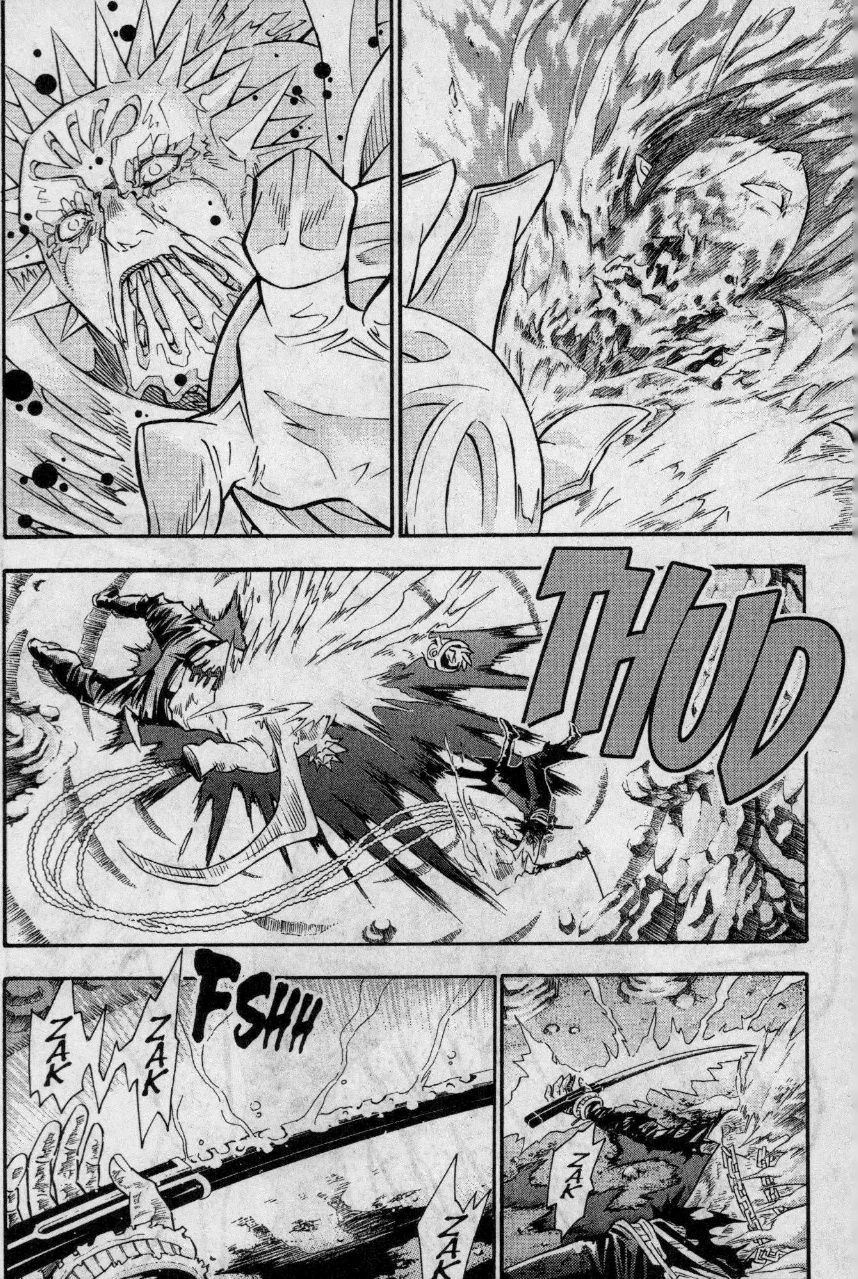
THUD
ZAK
FSHH
ZAK
ZAK
ZAK

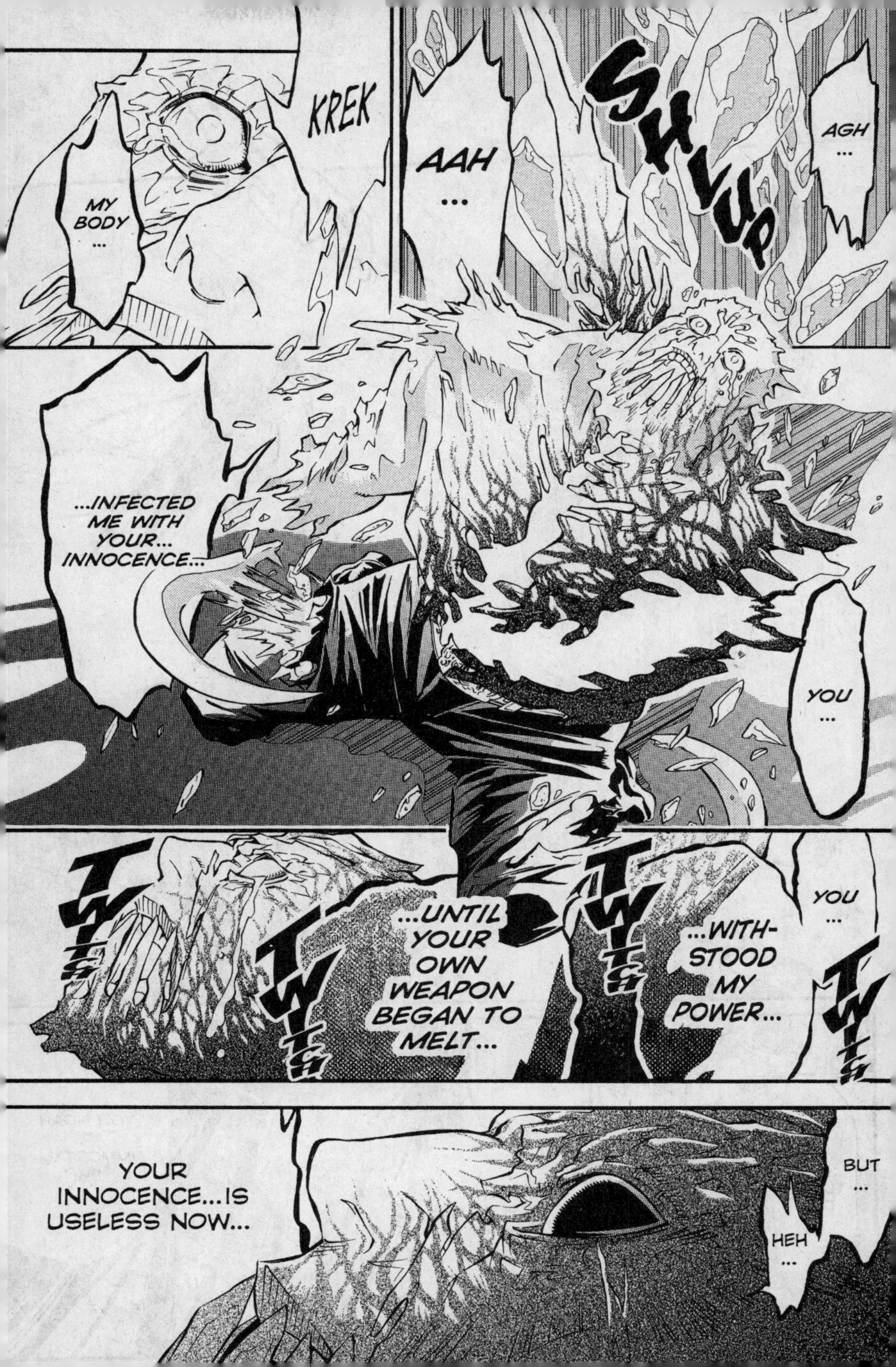
AGH ...
SHLUP
AAH ...
KREK
MY BODY ...
YOU ...
...INFECTED ME WITH YOUR... INNOCENCE...
YOU ...
TWITCH
...WITH-STOOD MY POWER...
TWITCH
...UNTIL YOUR OWN WEAPON BEGAN TO MELT...
TWITCH
TWITCH
BUT ...
HEH ...
YOUR INNOCENCE...IS USELESS NOW...

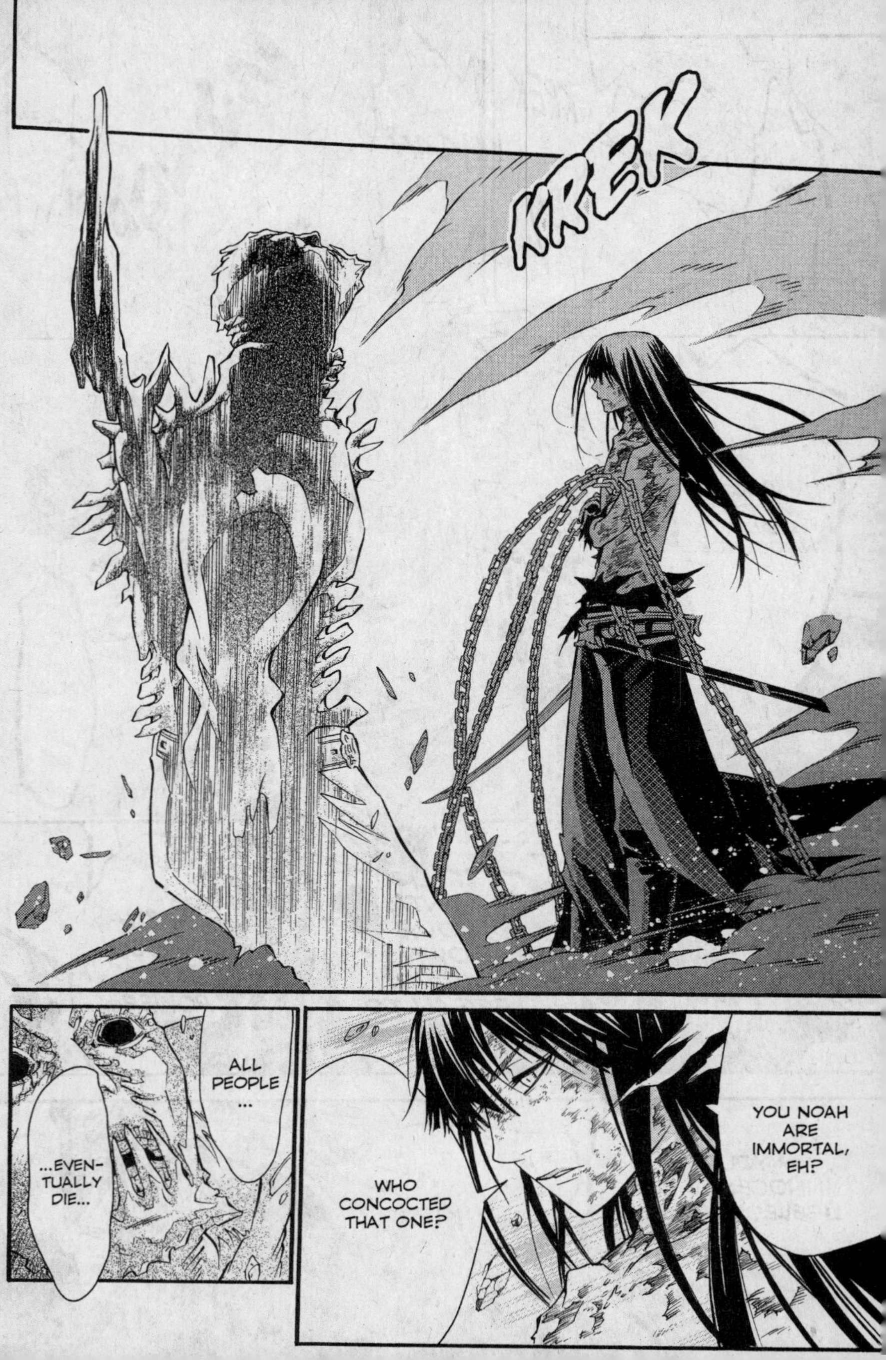
KREK
YOU NOAH ARE IMMORTAL, EH?
WHO CONCOCTED THAT ONE?
ALL PEOPLE...
...EVEN-TUALLY DIE...

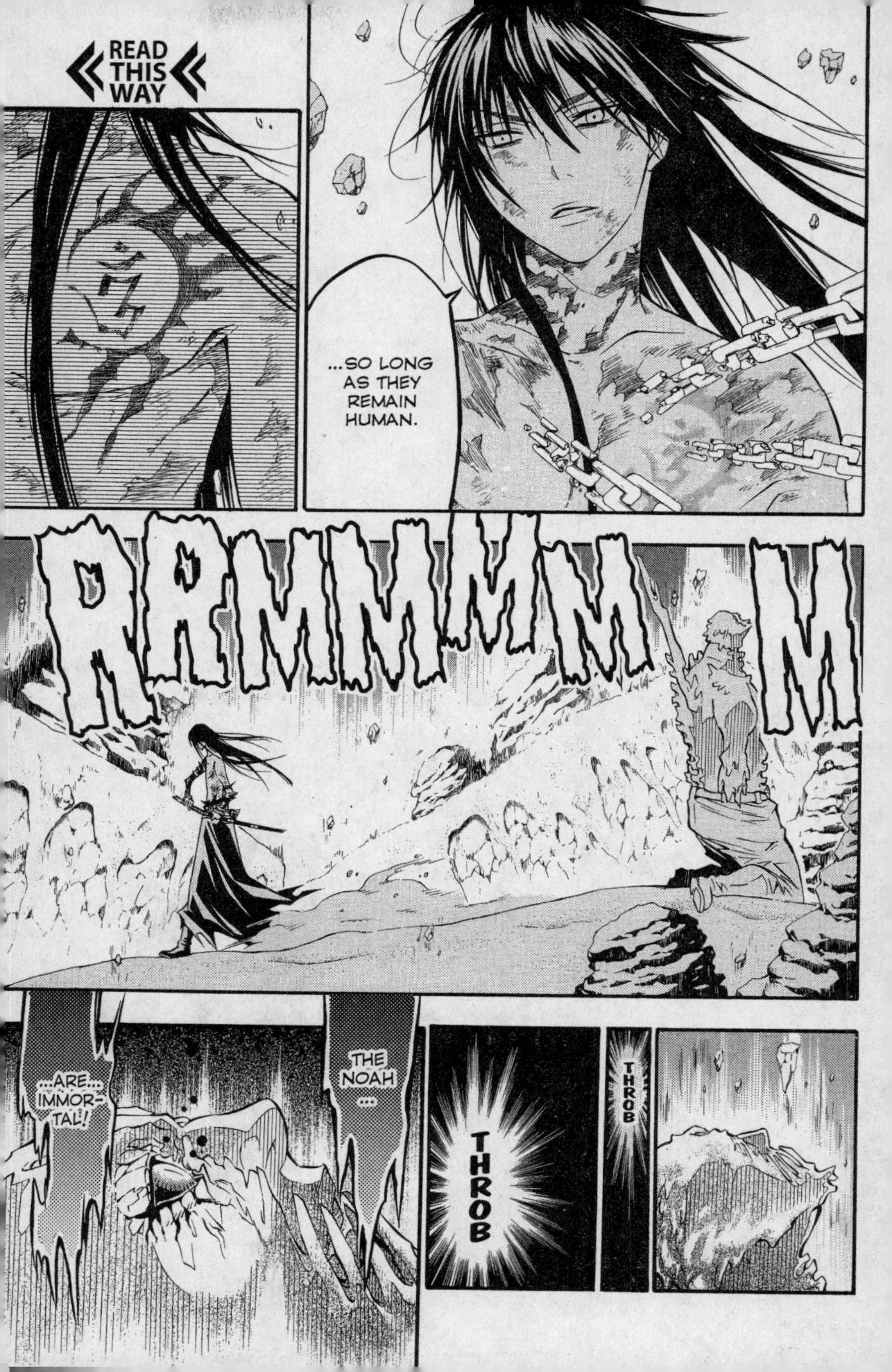
READ THIS WAY
...SO LONG AS THEY REMAIN HUMAN.
RAMMMM M
THROB
THROB
THE NOAH...
...ARE... IMMORTAL!

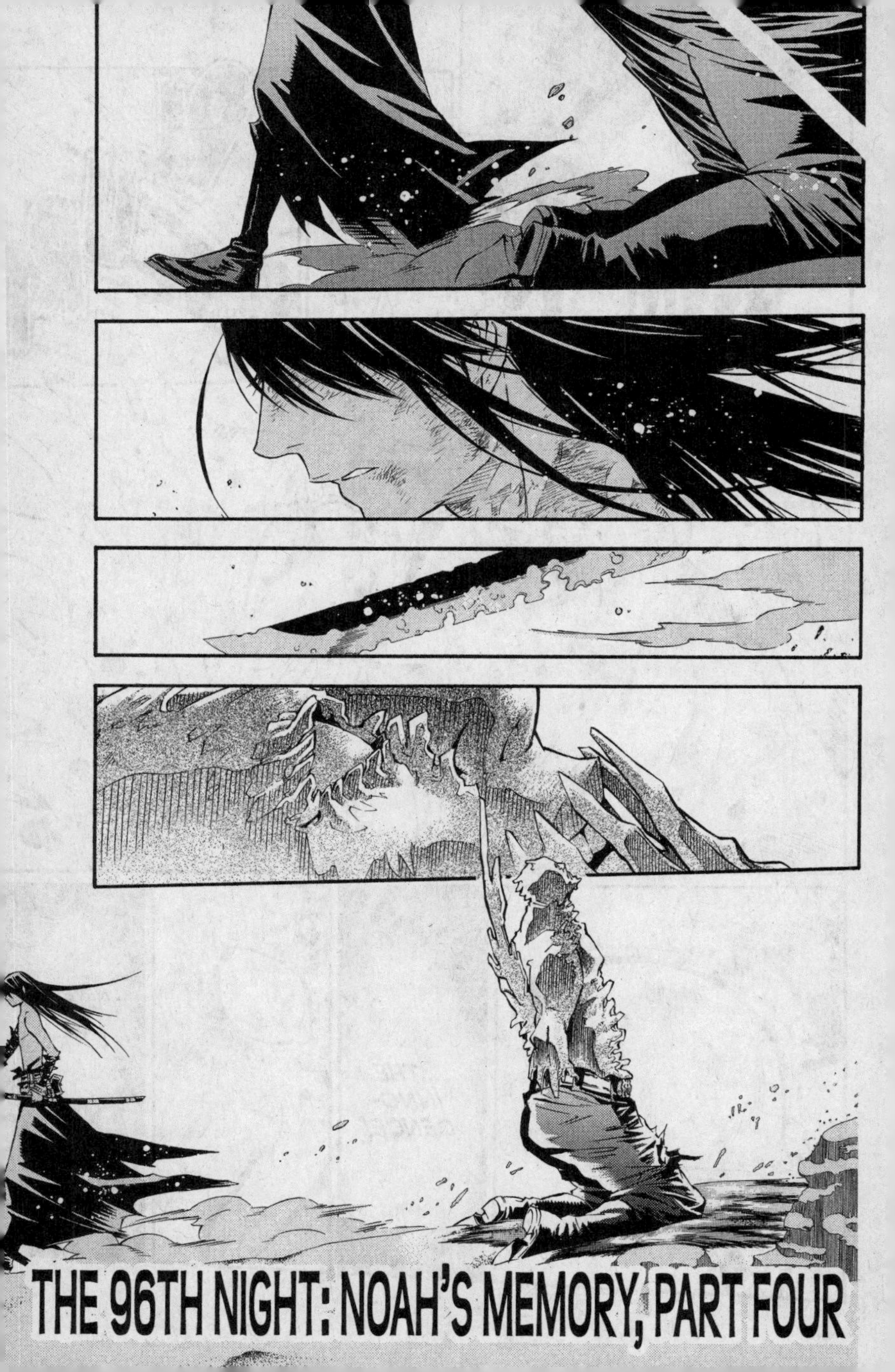
THE 96TH NIGHT: NOAH'S MEMORY, PART FOUR

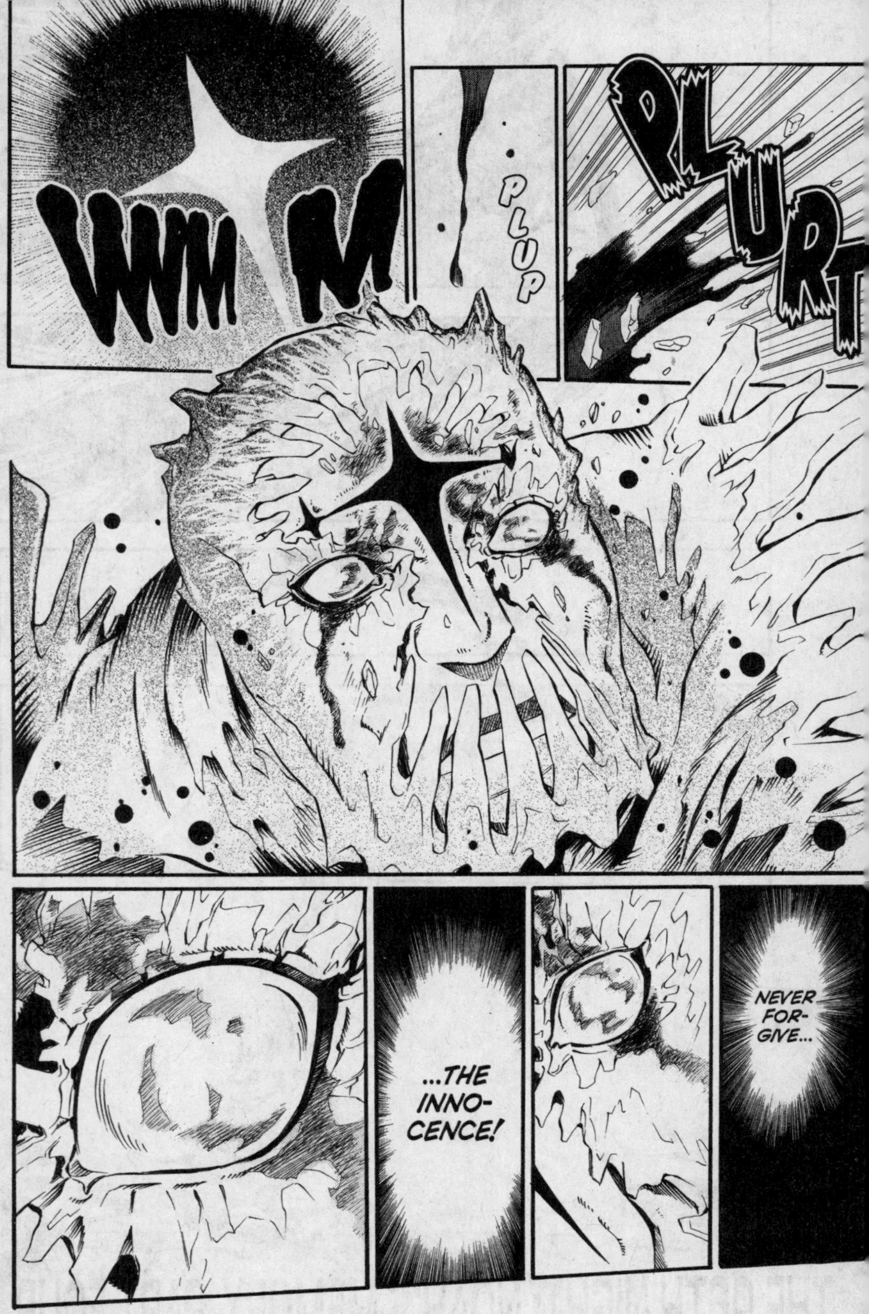
PLURT
PLUP
VWMM
NEVER FORGIVE...
...THE INNOCENCE!

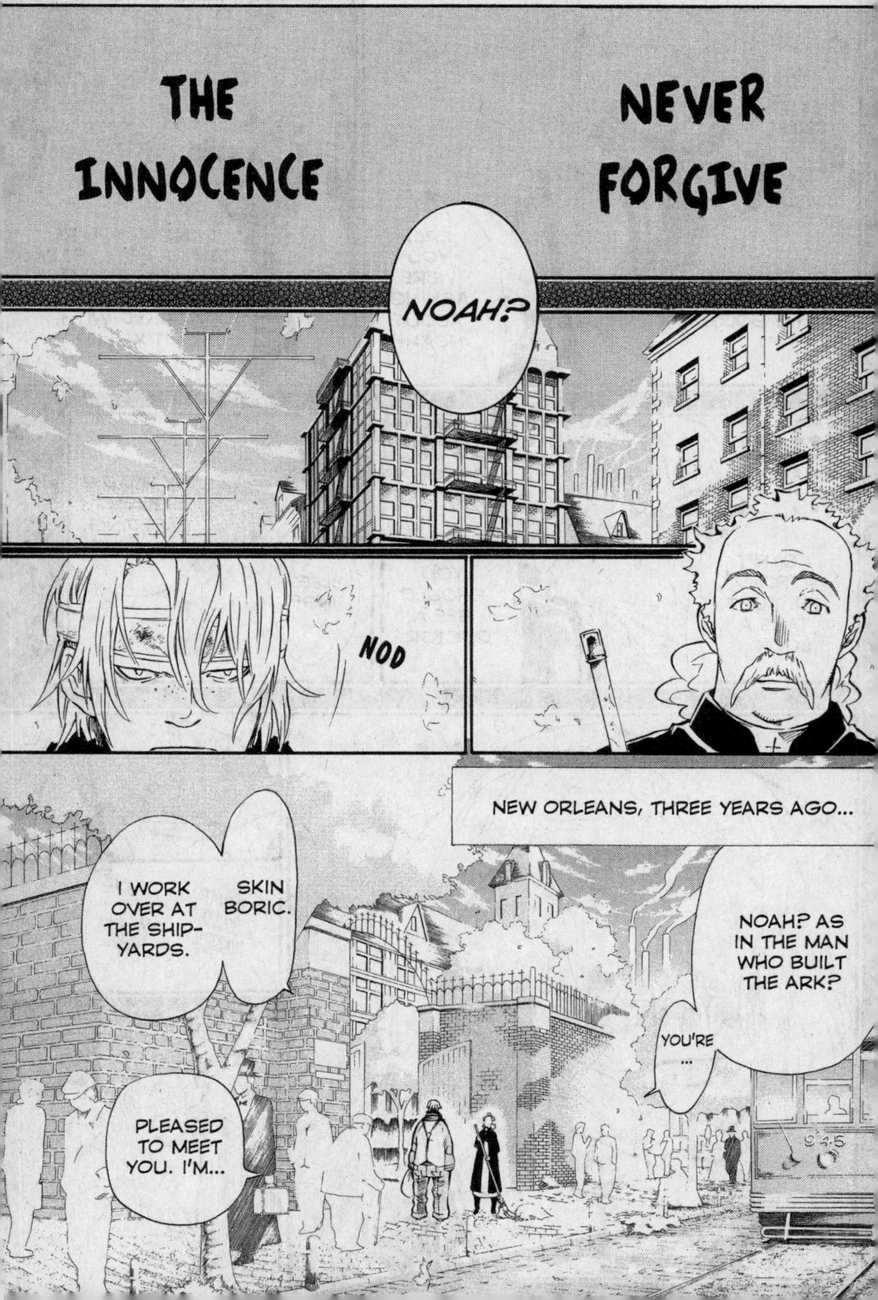
THE INNOCENCE
NEVER FORGIVE
NOAH?
NOD
NEW ORLEANS, THREE YEARS AGO...
NOAH? AS IN THE MAN WHO BUILT THE ARK?
YOU'RE ...
SKIN BORIC.
I WORK OVER AT THE SHIP-YARDS.
PLEASED TO MEET YOU. I'M...

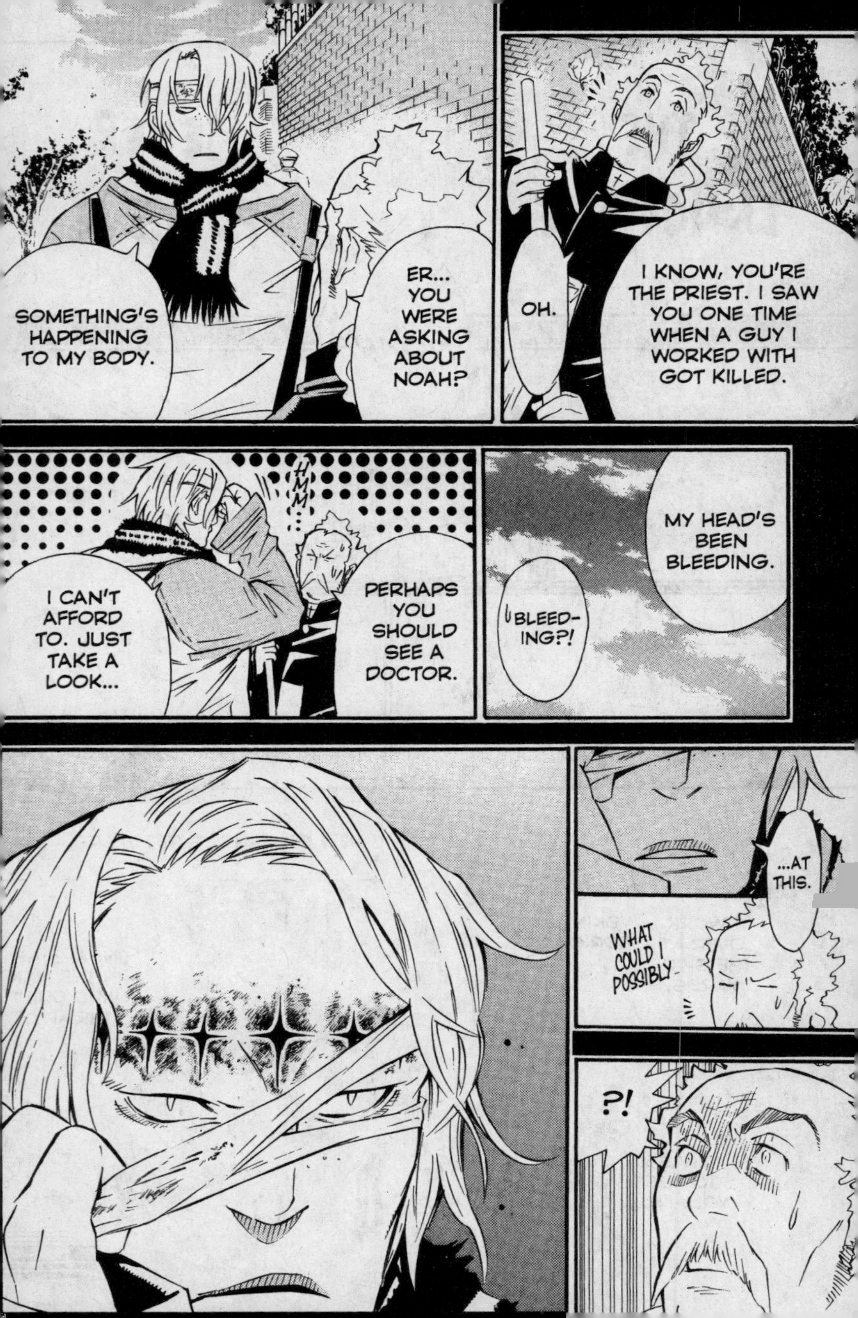
I KNOW, YOU'RE THE PRIEST. I SAW YOU ONE TIME WHEN A GUY I WORKED WITH GOT KILLED.
OH.
ER... YOU WERE ASKING ABOUT NOAH?
SOMETHING'S HAPPENING TO MY BODY.
MY HEAD'S BEEN BLEEDING.
BLEED-ING?!
HMM...
PERHAPS YOU SHOULD SEE A DOCTOR.
I CAN'T AFFORD TO. JUST TAKE A LOOK...
...AT THIS.
WHAT COULD I POSSIBLY-
?!

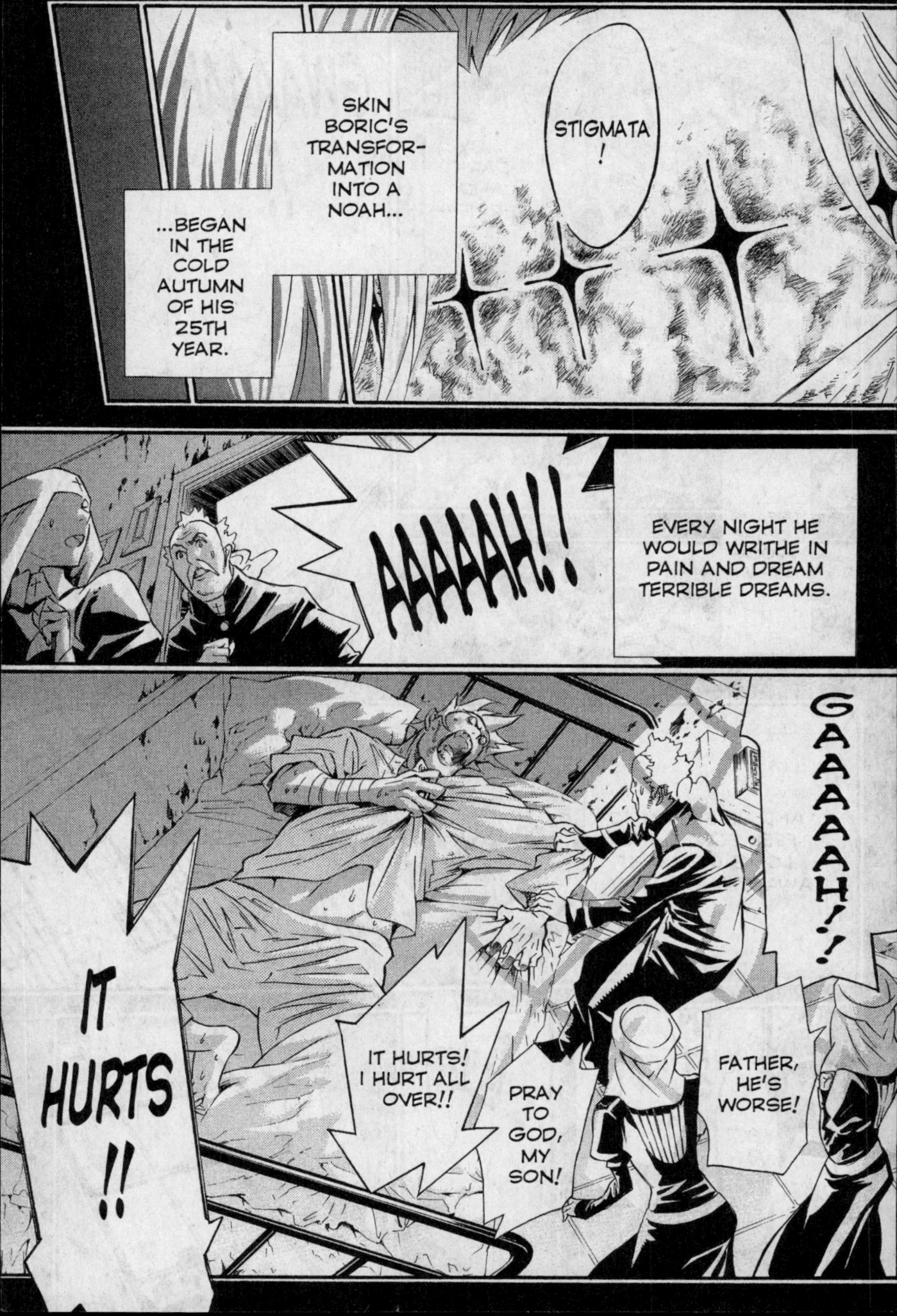
STIGMATA!
SKIN BORIC'S TRANSFORMATION INTO A NOAH...
...BEGAN IN THE COLD AUTUMN OF HIS 25TH YEAR.
EVERY NIGHT HE WOULD WRITHE IN PAIN AND DREAM TERRIBLE DREAMS.
AAAAAH!!
GAAAAAH!!
FATHER, HE'S WORSE!
PRAY TO GOD, MY SON!
IT HURTS! I HURT ALL OVER!!
IT HURTS!!

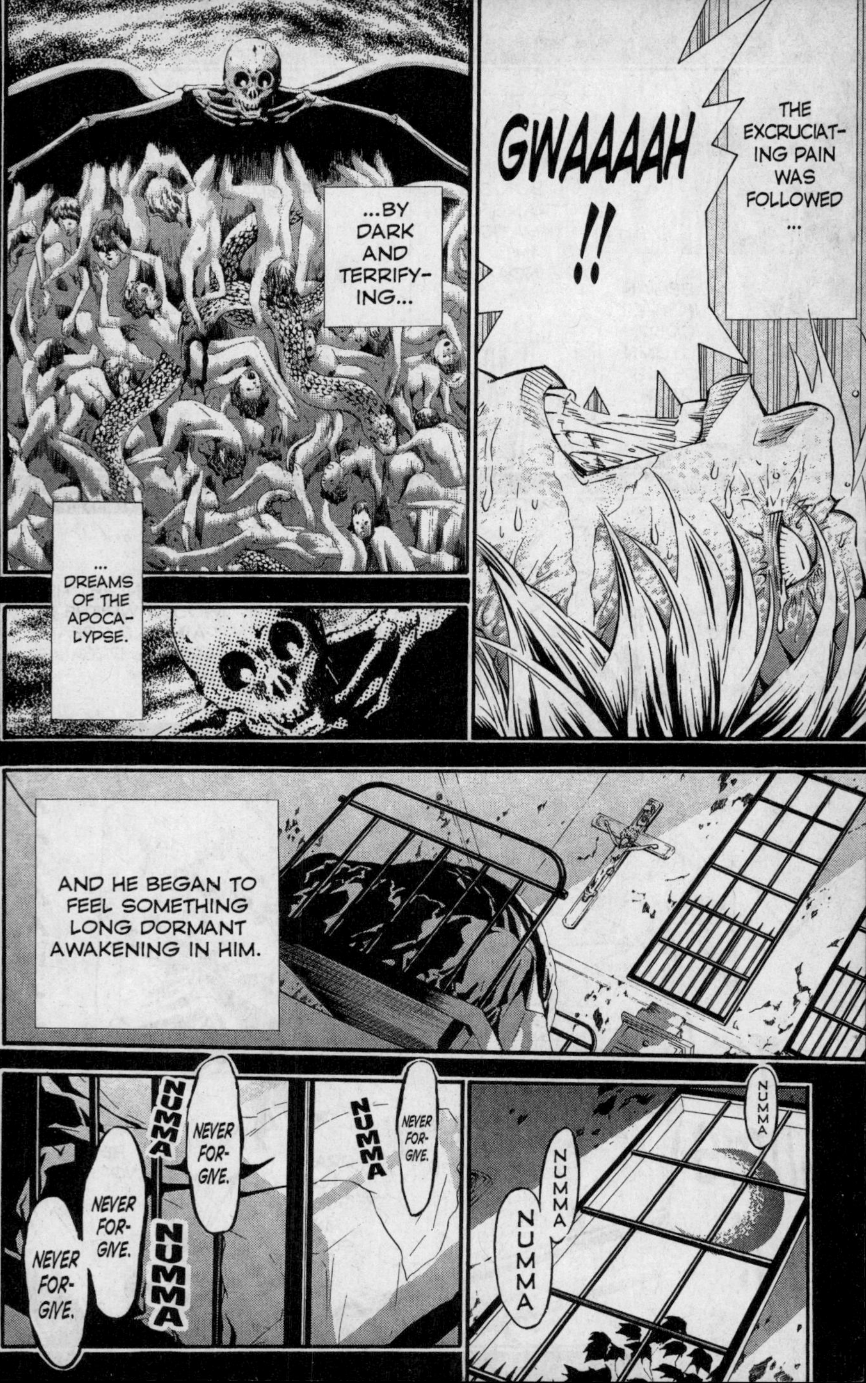
THE EXCRUCIATING PAIN WAS FOLLOWED...
GWAAAAH!!
...BY DARK AND TERRIFYING...
...DREAMS OF THE APOCALYPSE.
AND HE BEGAN TO FEEL SOMETHING LONG DORMANT AWAKENING IN HIM.
NUMMA
NUMMA
NUMMA
NEVER FORGIVE.
NUMMA
NUMMA
NEVER FORGIVE.
NEVER FORGIVE.
NEVER FORGIVE.
NUMMA

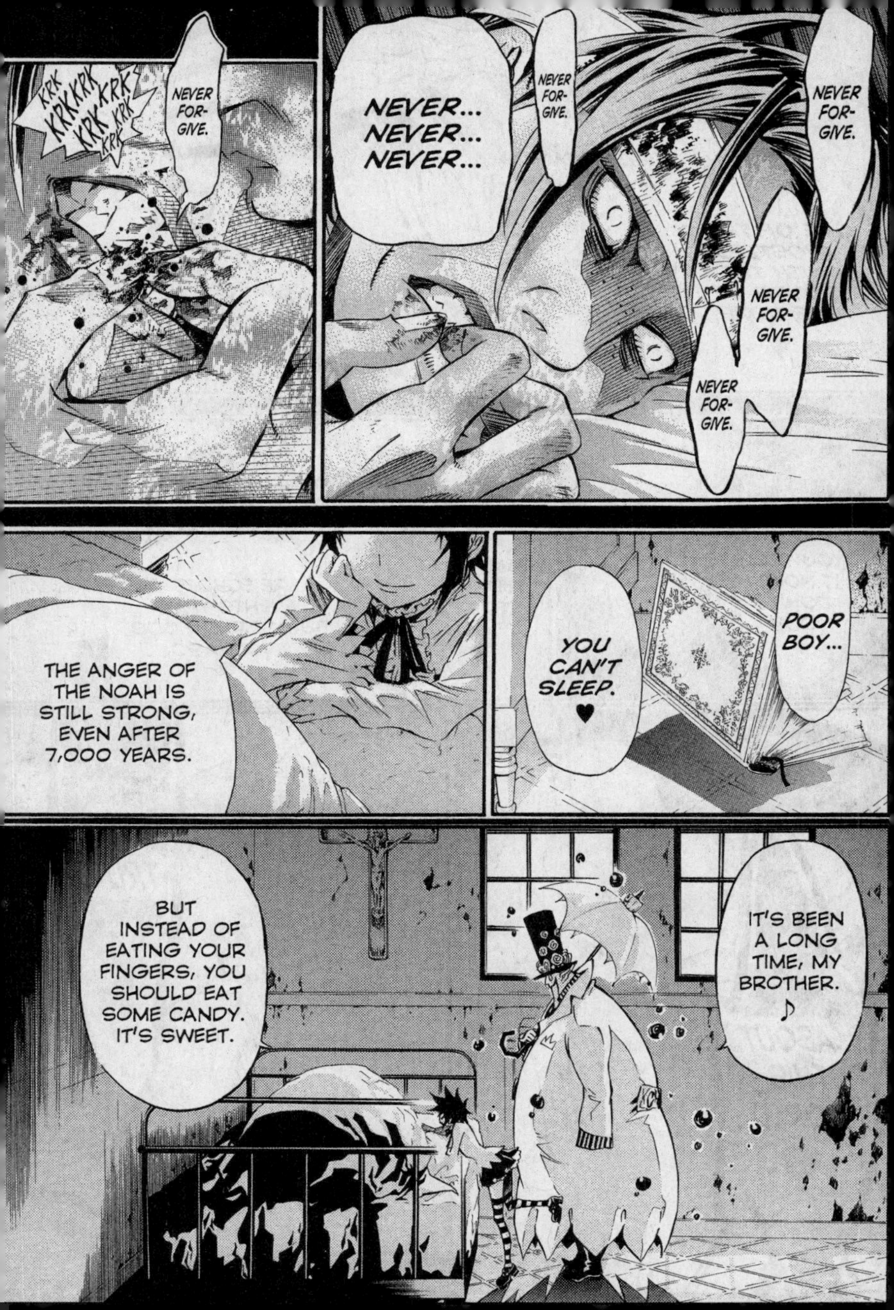
NEVER FOR-GIVE.
NEVER FOR-GIVE.
NEVER... NEVER... NEVER...
NEVER FOR-GIVE.
NEVER FOR-GIVE.
KRK KRKKRK KRK KRK KRK KRK
NEVER FOR-GIVE.
POOR BOY...
YOU CAN'T SLEEP. ♥
THE ANGER OF THE NOAH IS STILL STRONG, EVEN AFTER 7,000 YEARS.
IT'S BEEN A LONG TIME, MY BROTHER. ♪
BUT INSTEAD OF EATING YOUR FINGERS, YOU SHOULD EAT SOME CANDY. IT'S SWEET.

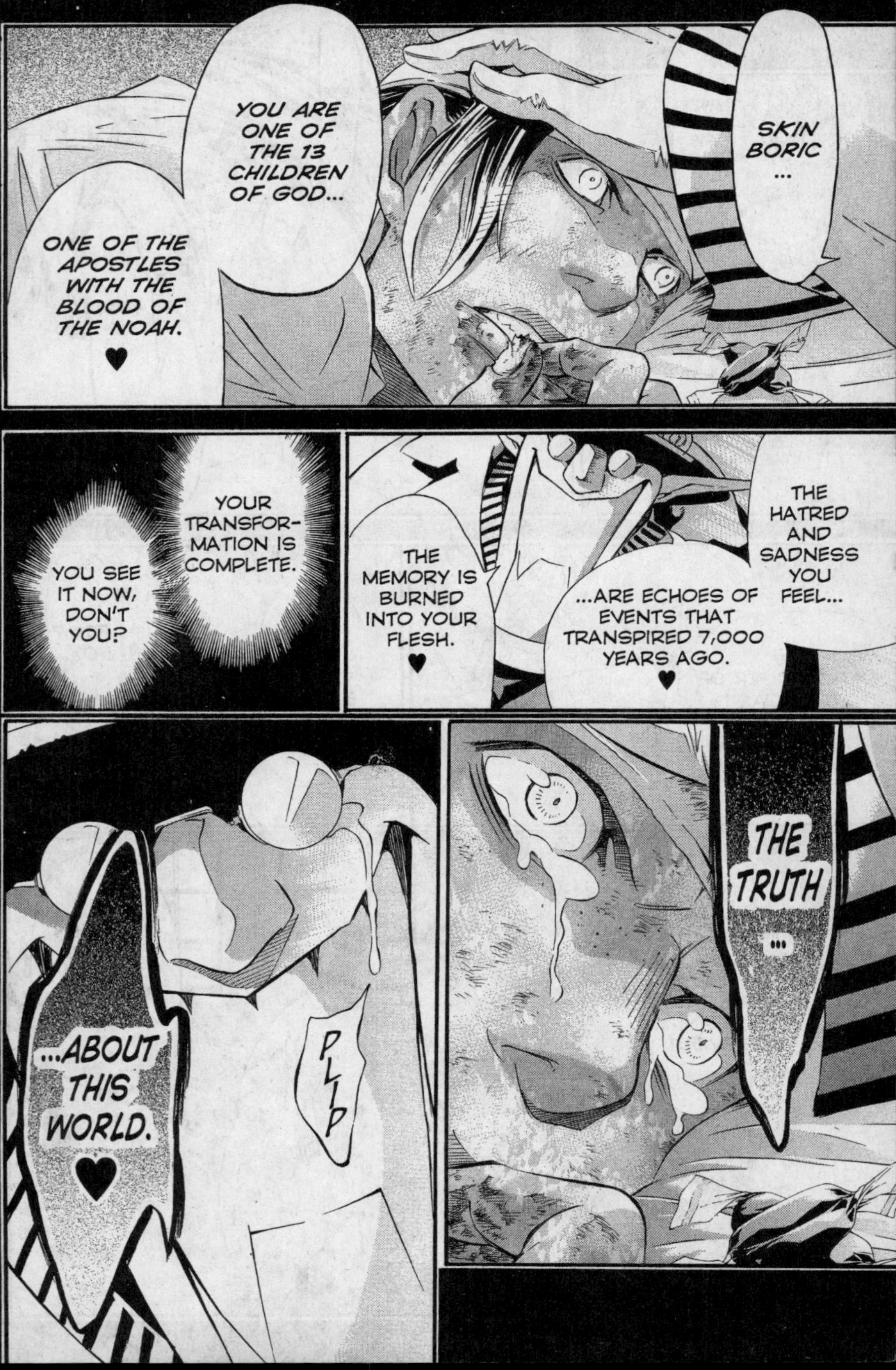
SKIN BORIC ...
YOU ARE ONE OF THE 13 CHILDREN OF GOD...
ONE OF THE APOSTLES WITH THE BLOOD OF THE NOAH. ♥
THE HATRED AND SADNESS YOU FEEL...
...ARE ECHOES OF EVENTS THAT TRANSPIRED 7,000 YEARS AGO. ♥
THE MEMORY IS BURNED INTO YOUR FLESH. ♥
YOUR TRANSFORMATION IS COMPLETE.
YOU SEE IT NOW, DON'T YOU?
THE TRUTH ...
PLIP
...ABOUT THIS WORLD. ♥

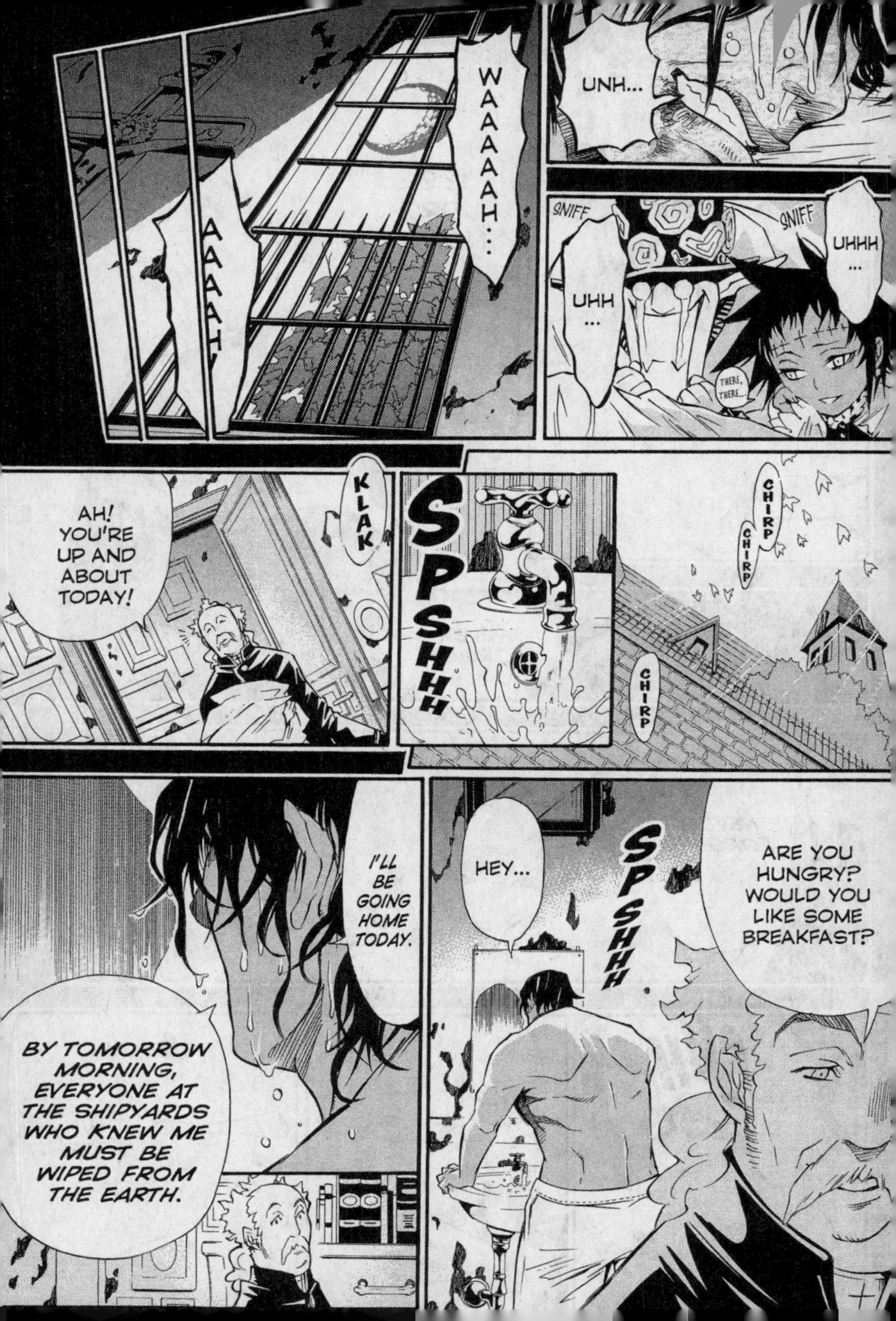

UNH...
SNIFF
SNIFF
UHHH...
UHH...
THERE, THERE...
WAAAAAAH...
AAAAAH
CHIRP
CHIRP
CHIRP
SPSHHH
KLAK
AH! YOU'RE UP AND ABOUT TODAY!
ARE YOU HUNGRY? WOULD YOU LIKE SOME BREAKFAST?
SPSHHH
HEY...
I'LL BE GOING HOME TODAY.
BY TOMORROW MORNING, EVERYONE AT THE SHIPYARDS WHO KNEW ME MUST BE WIPED FROM THE EARTH.

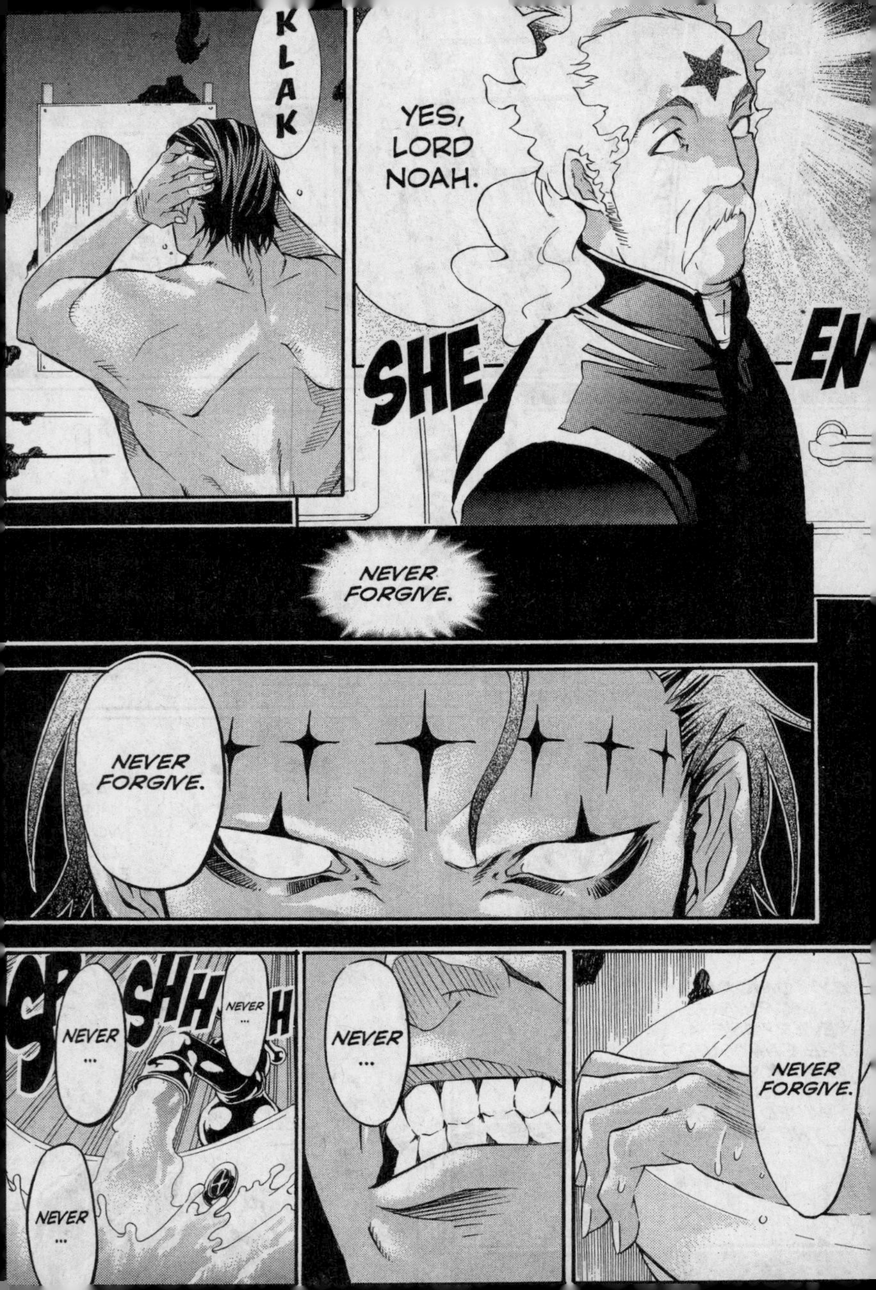
YES, LORD NOAH.
SHE
EN
KLAK
NEVER FORGIVE.
NEVER FORGIVE.
NEVER FORGIVE.
NEVER ...
NEVER ...
SHH
H
GR
NEVER ...
NEVER ...

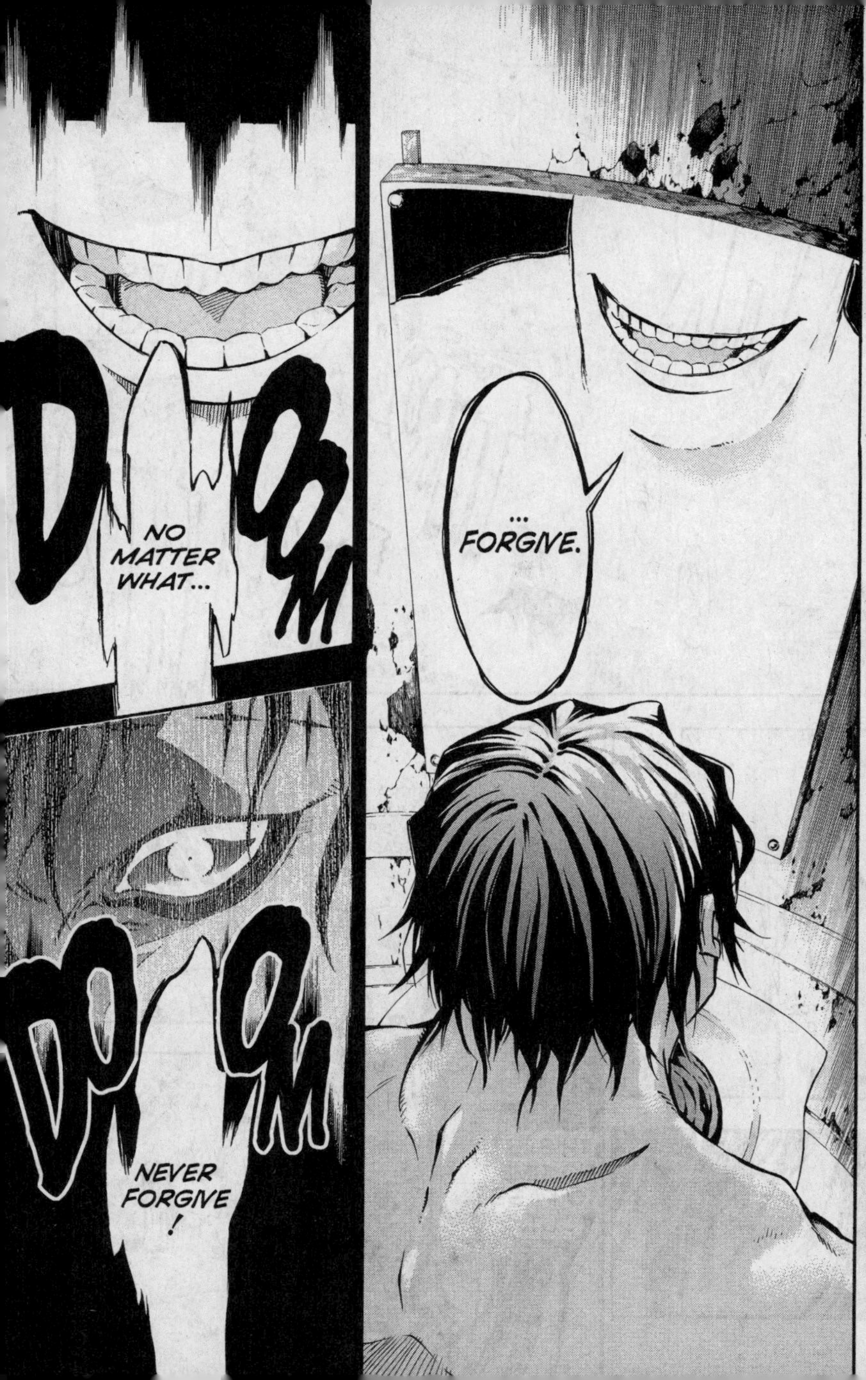
...
FORGIVE.
DOOM
NO MATTER WHAT...
DOOM
NEVER FORGIVE!

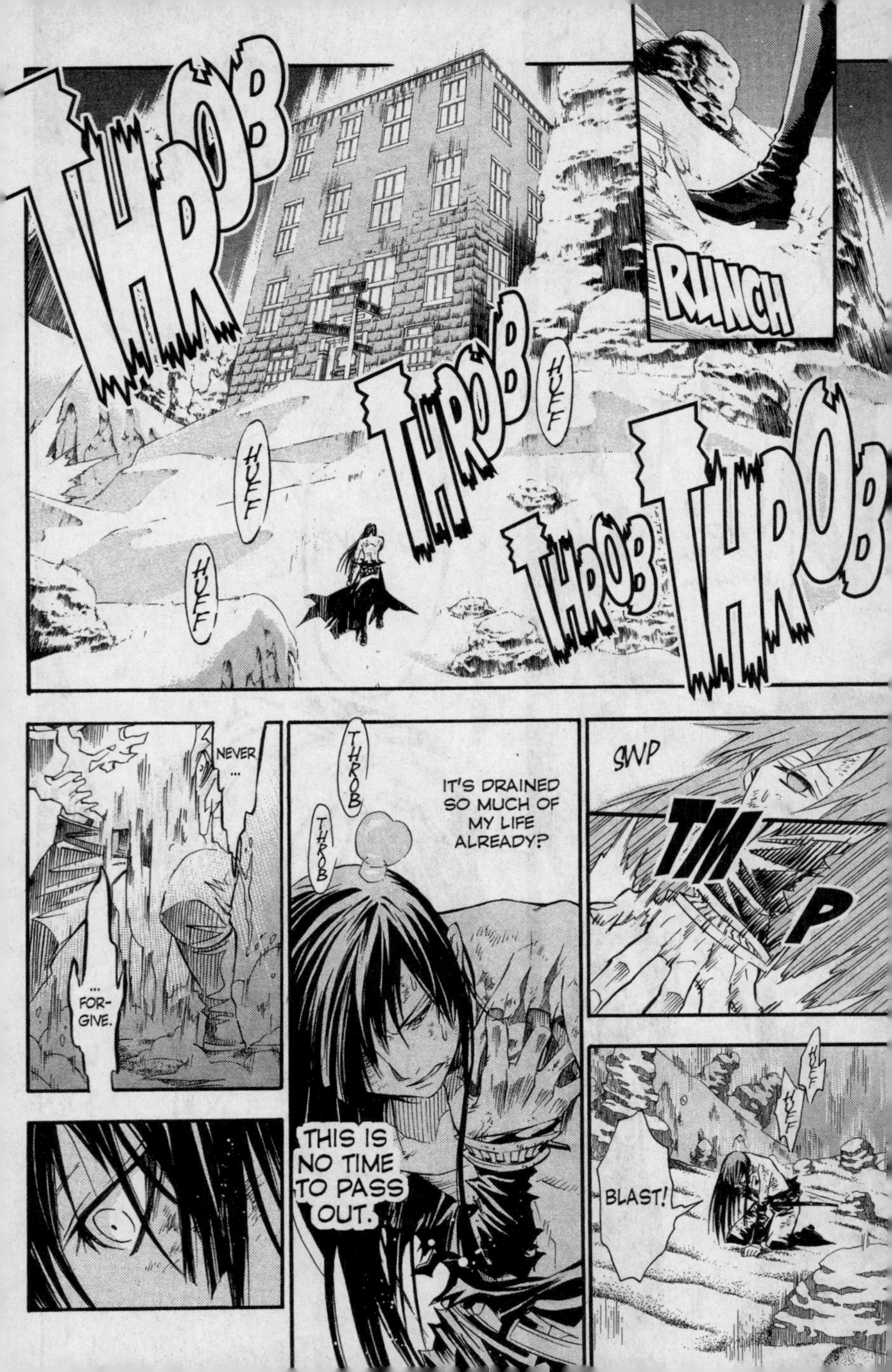
RUNCH
THROB
THROB
HUFF
THROB
THROB
HUFF
HUFF
SWP
TMP
HUFF
HUFF
BLAST!
THROB
THROB
IT'S DRAINED SO MUCH OF MY LIFE ALREADY?
THIS IS NO TIME TO PASS OUT.
NEVER...
...FOR-GIVE.

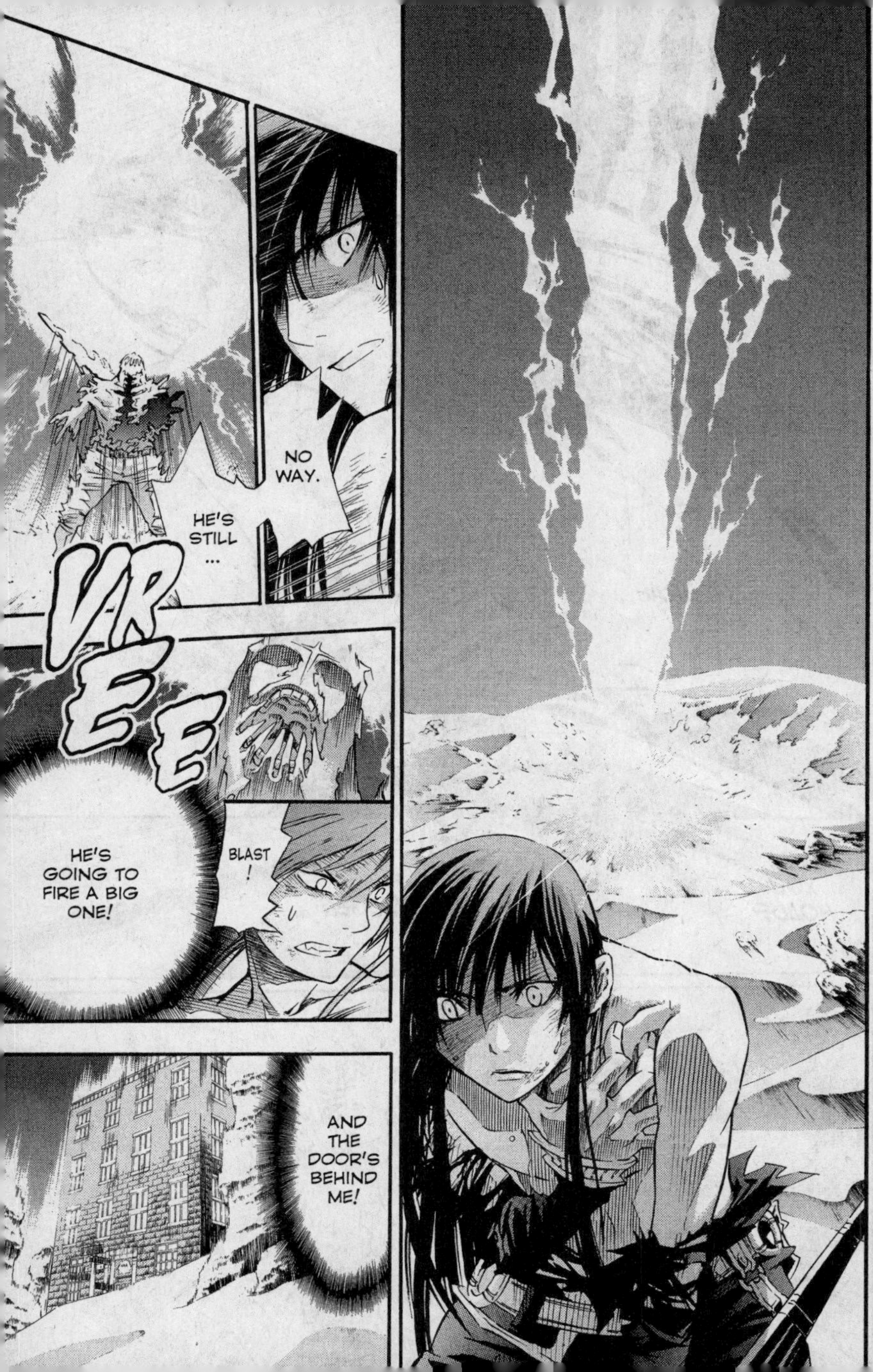
NO WAY.
HE'S STILL ...
VREEE
BLAST!
HE'S GOING TO FIRE A BIG ONE!
AND THE DOOR'S BEHIND ME!

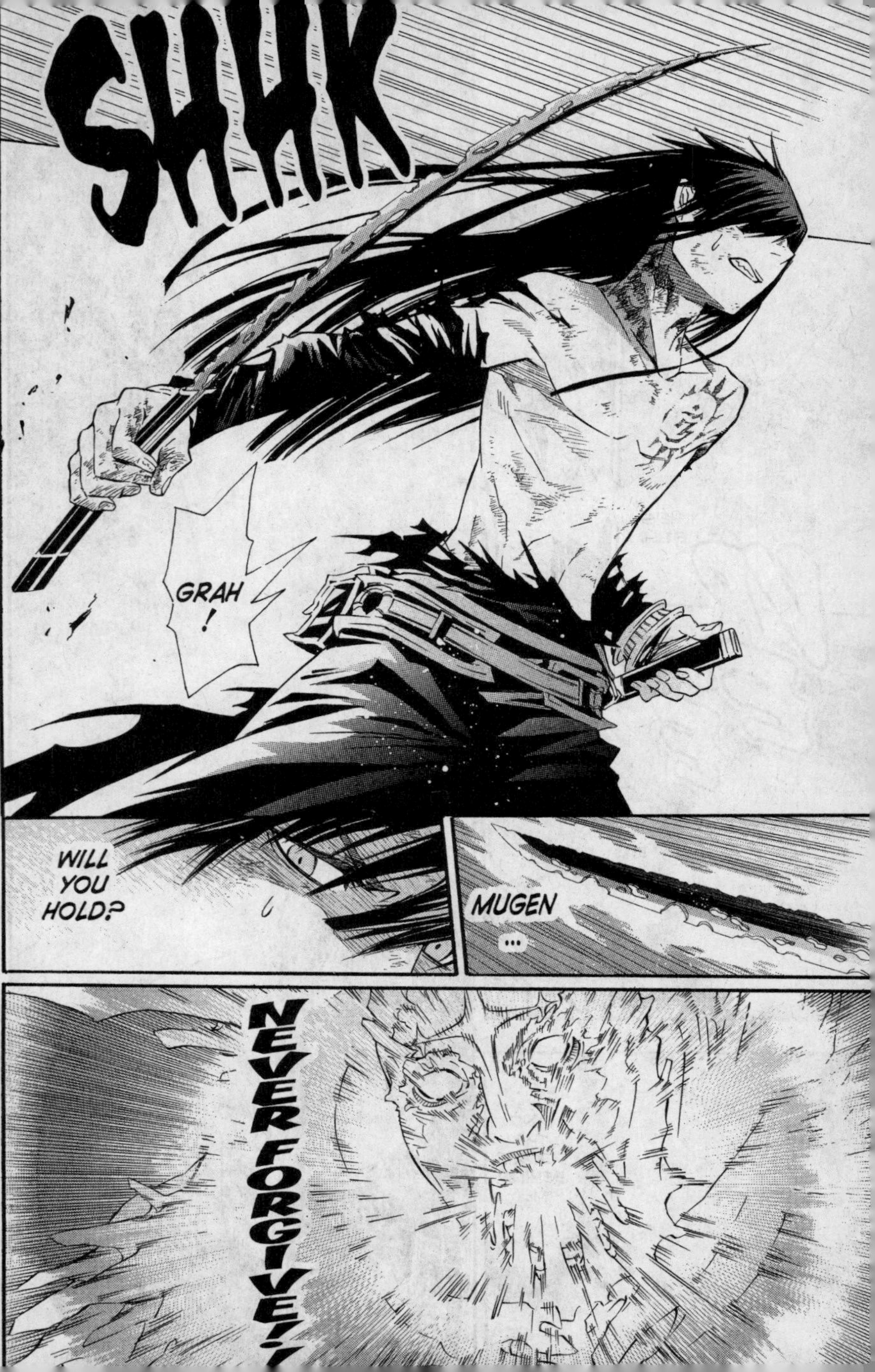
SHHK
GRAH!
MUGEN...
WILL YOU HOLD?
NEVER FORGIVE!!

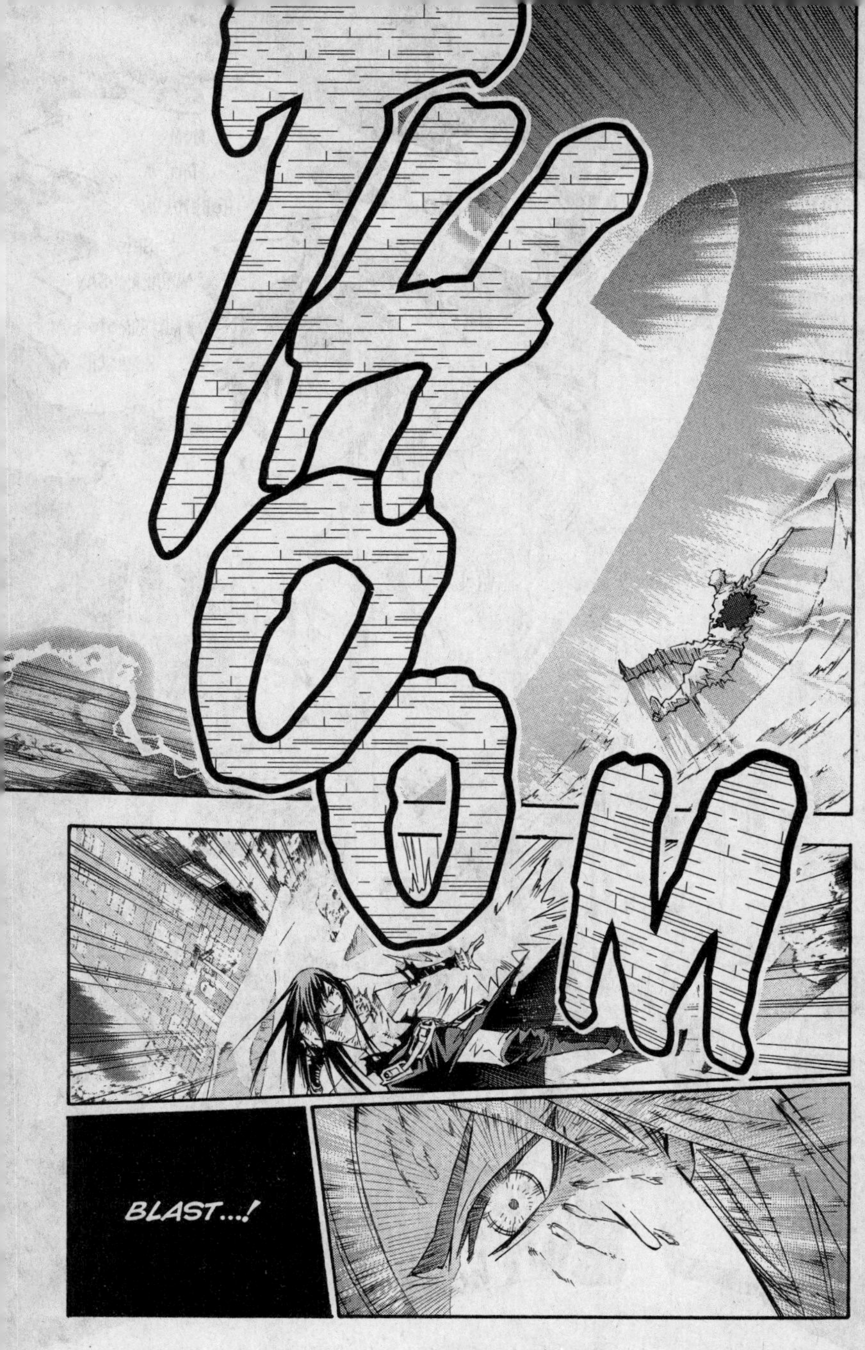
BLAST...!

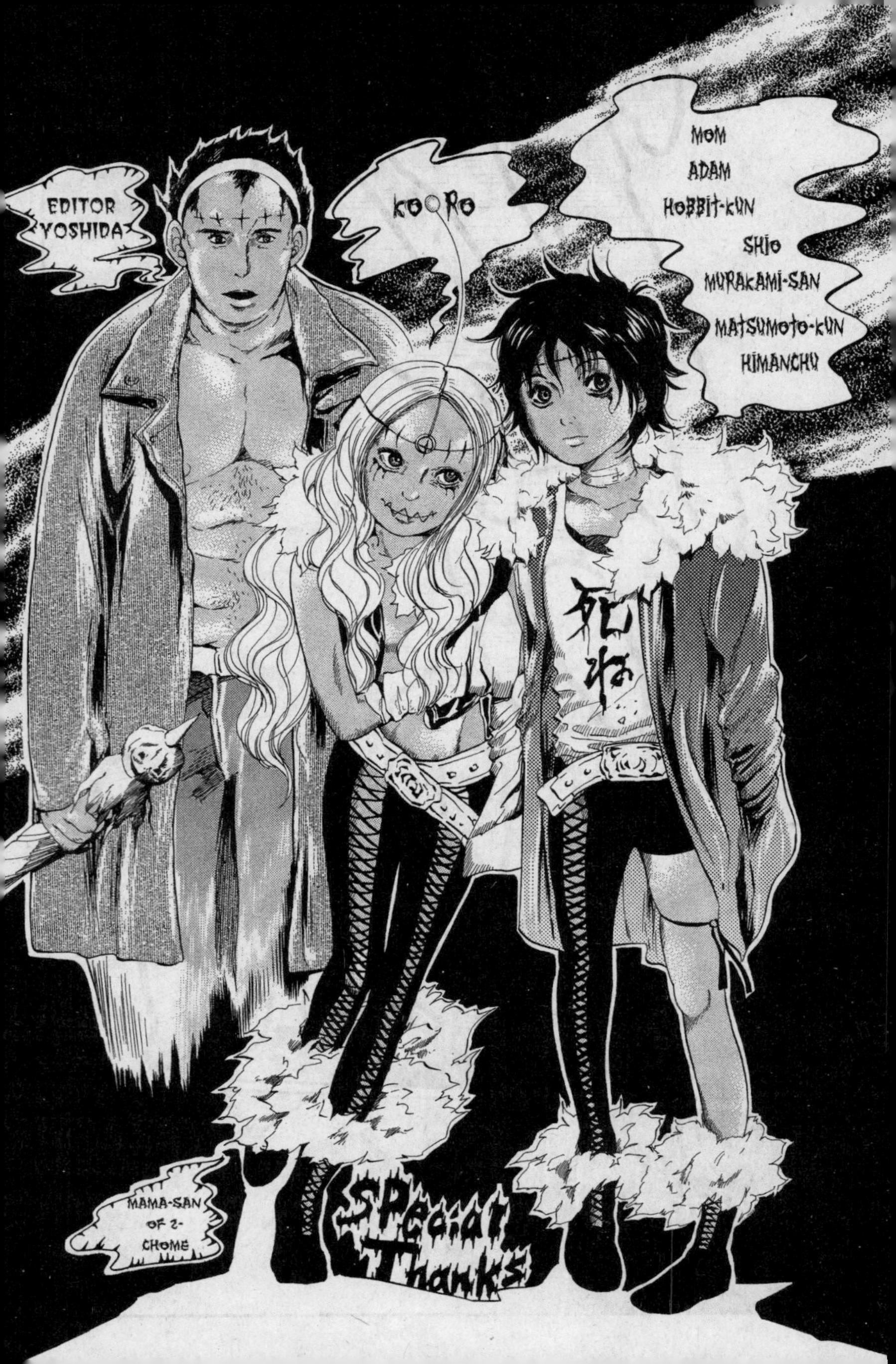
MOM
ADAM
HOBBIT-KUN
SHIO
MURAKAMI-SAN
MATSUMOTO-KUN
HIMANCHU
KO○RO
EDITOR YOSHIDA
死ね
SPecial Thanks
MAMA-SAN OF 2-CHOME

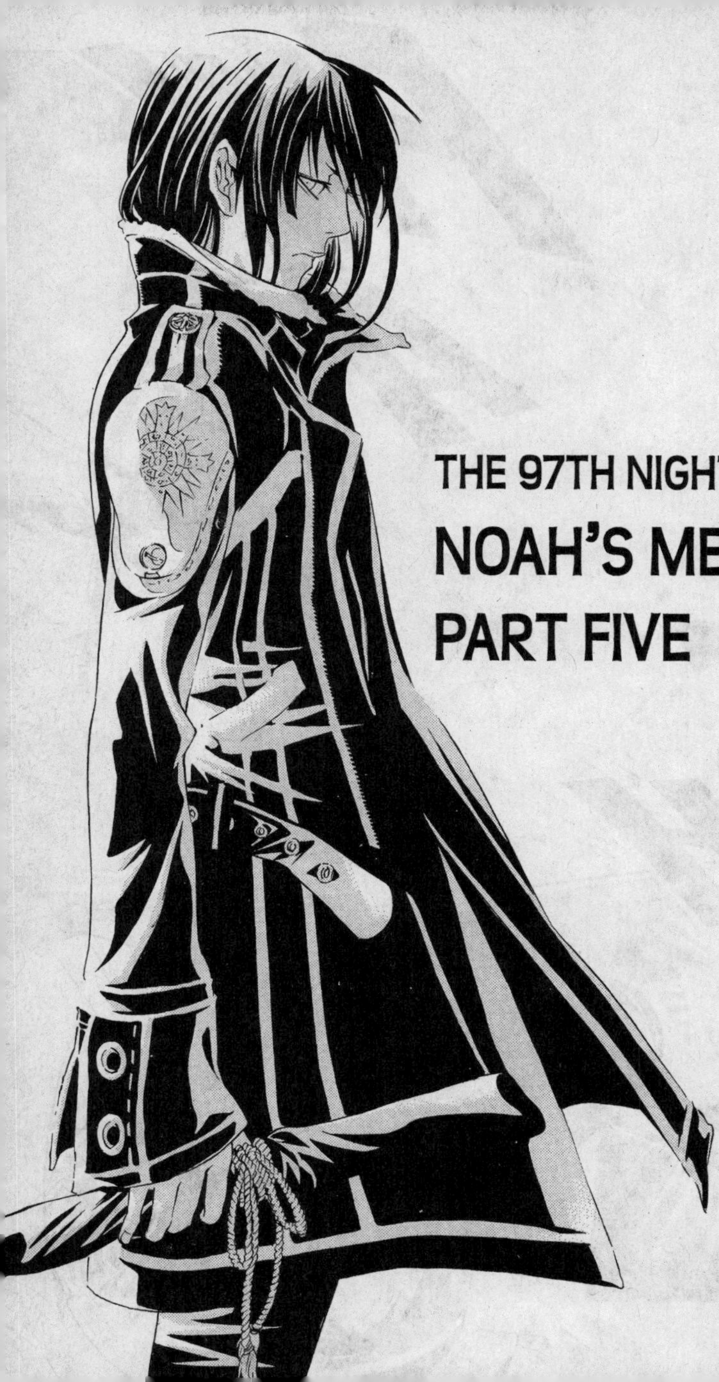

THE 97TH NIGHT: NOAH'S MEMORY, PART FIVE

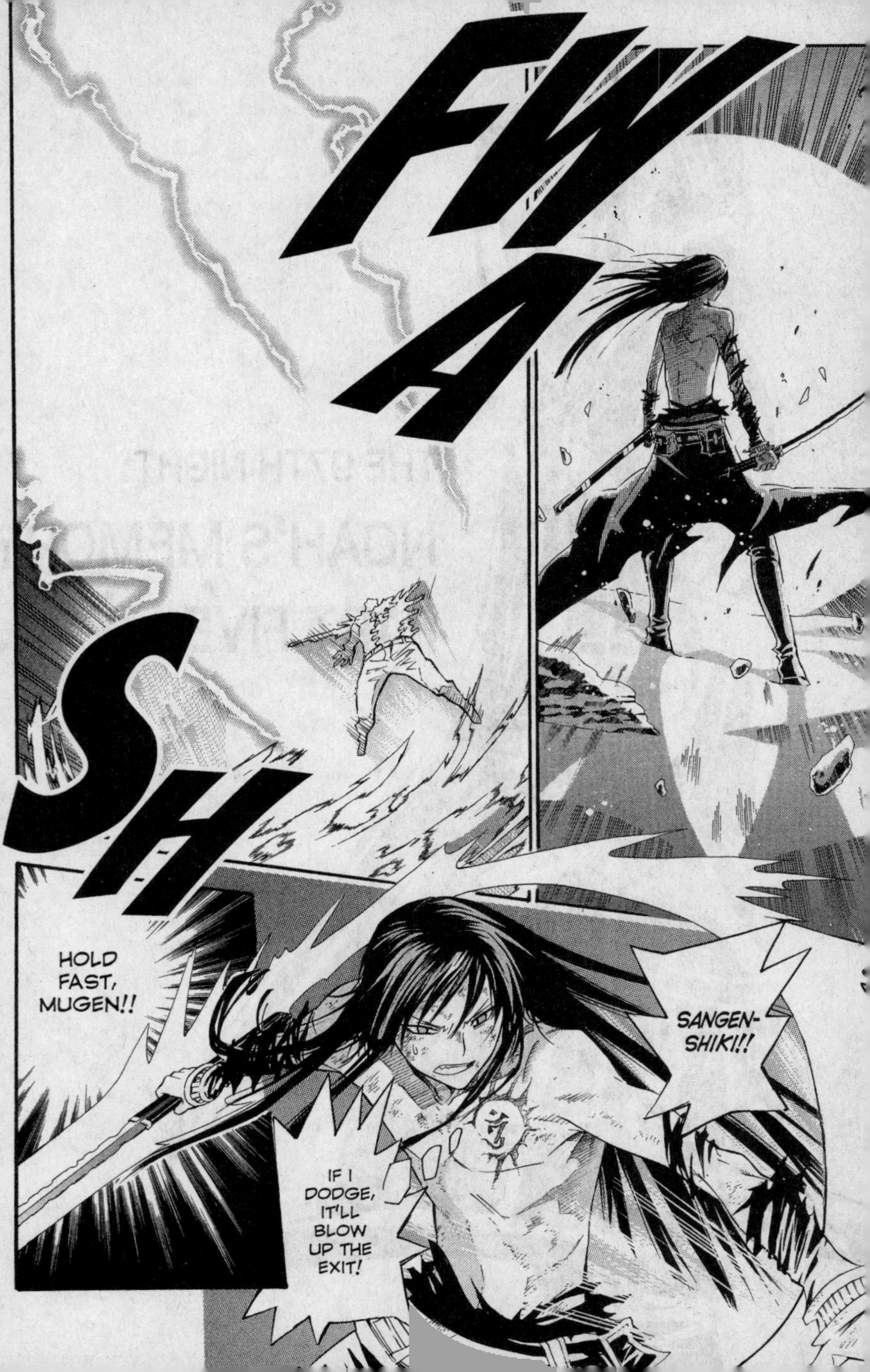
FWA
SH
SANGEN-SHIKI!!
HOLD FAST, MUGEN!!
IF I DODGE, IT'LL BLOW UP THE EXIT!

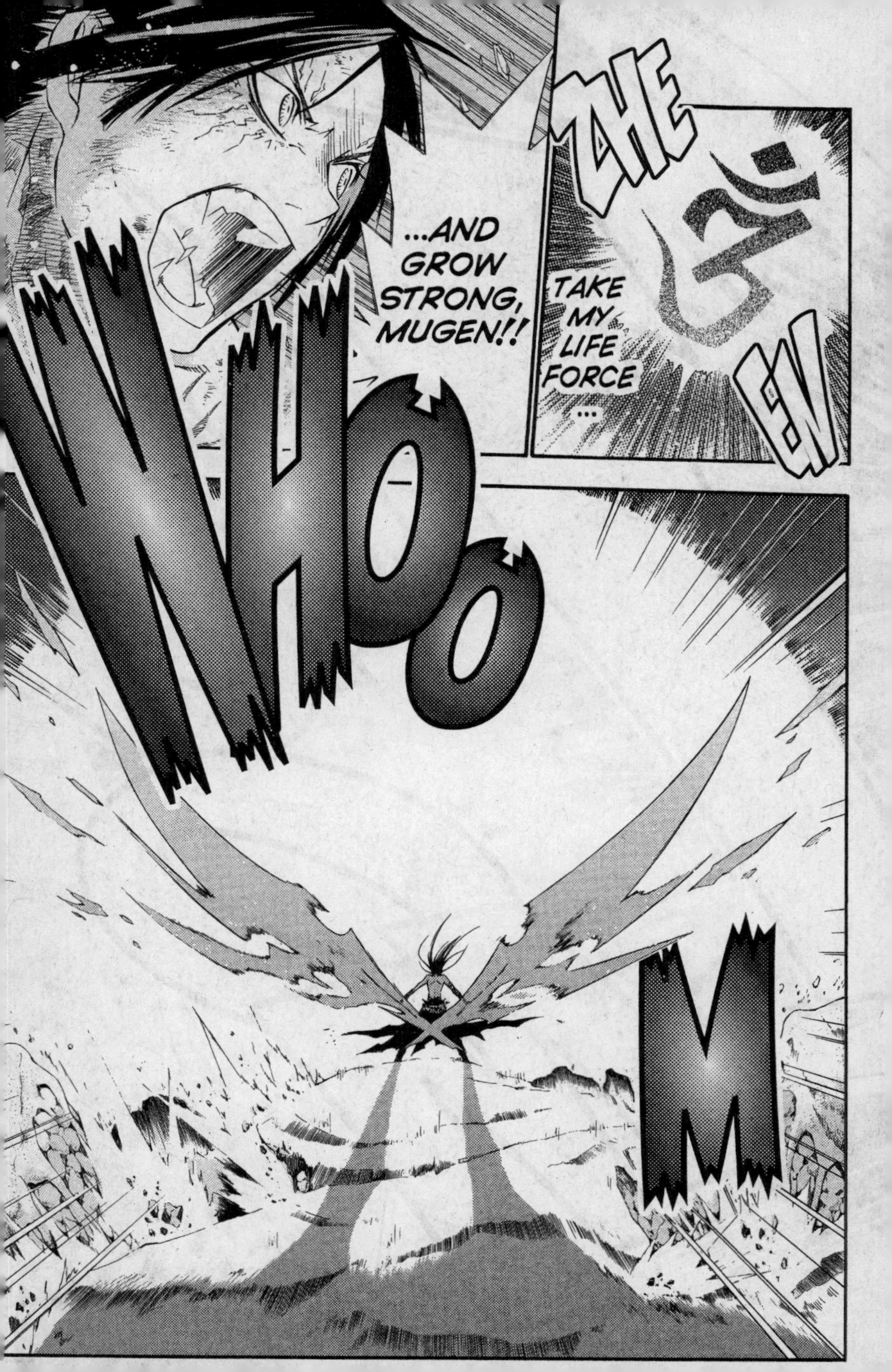
ZHE
EN
TAKE MY LIFE FORCE...
...AND GROW STRONG, MUGEN!!
WHOOM

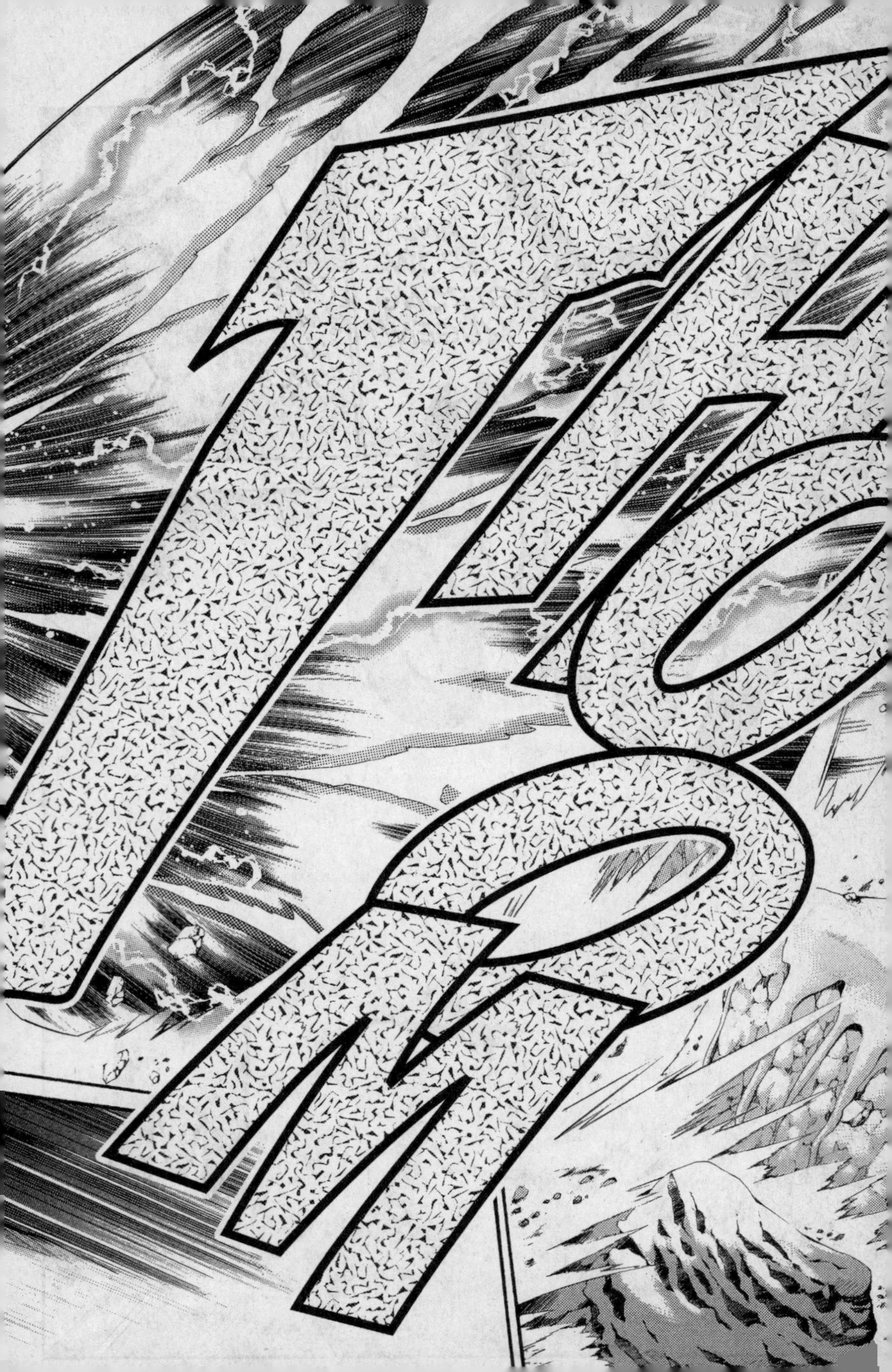

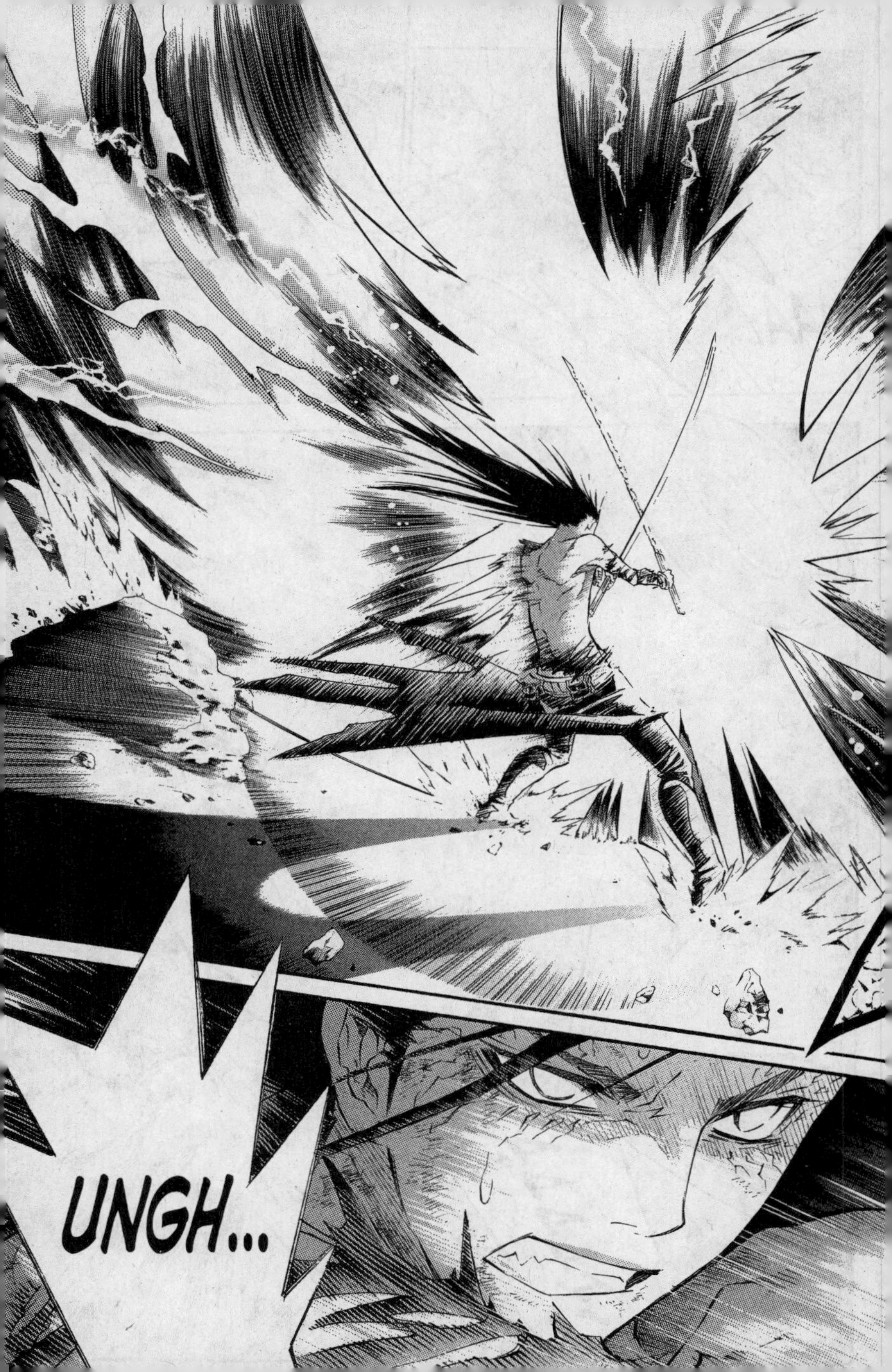
UNGH...

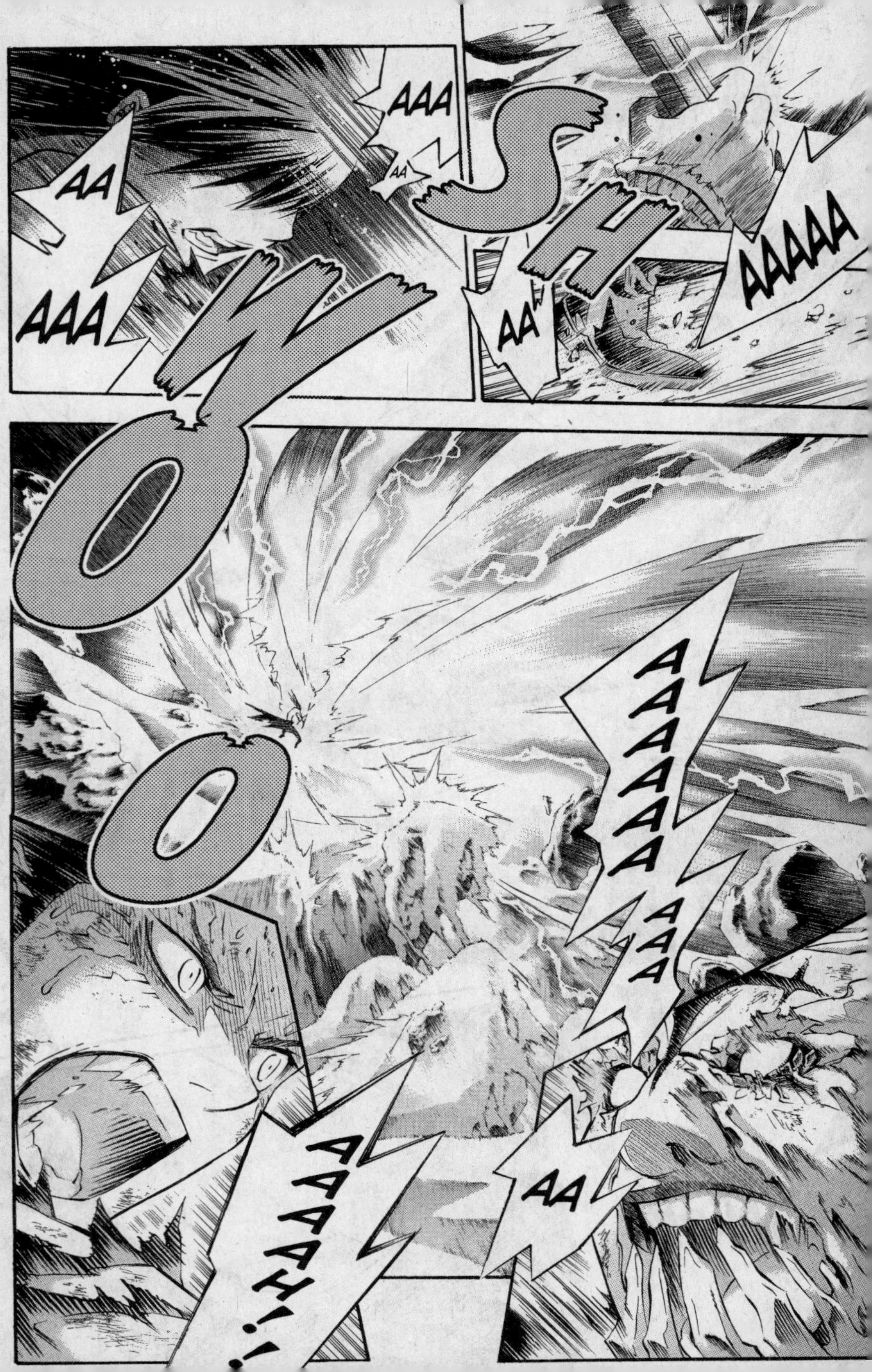
AAAAA
AA
AAA
AA
AA
AAA
SHWOO
AAAAAAAAAA
AA
AAAAH!!

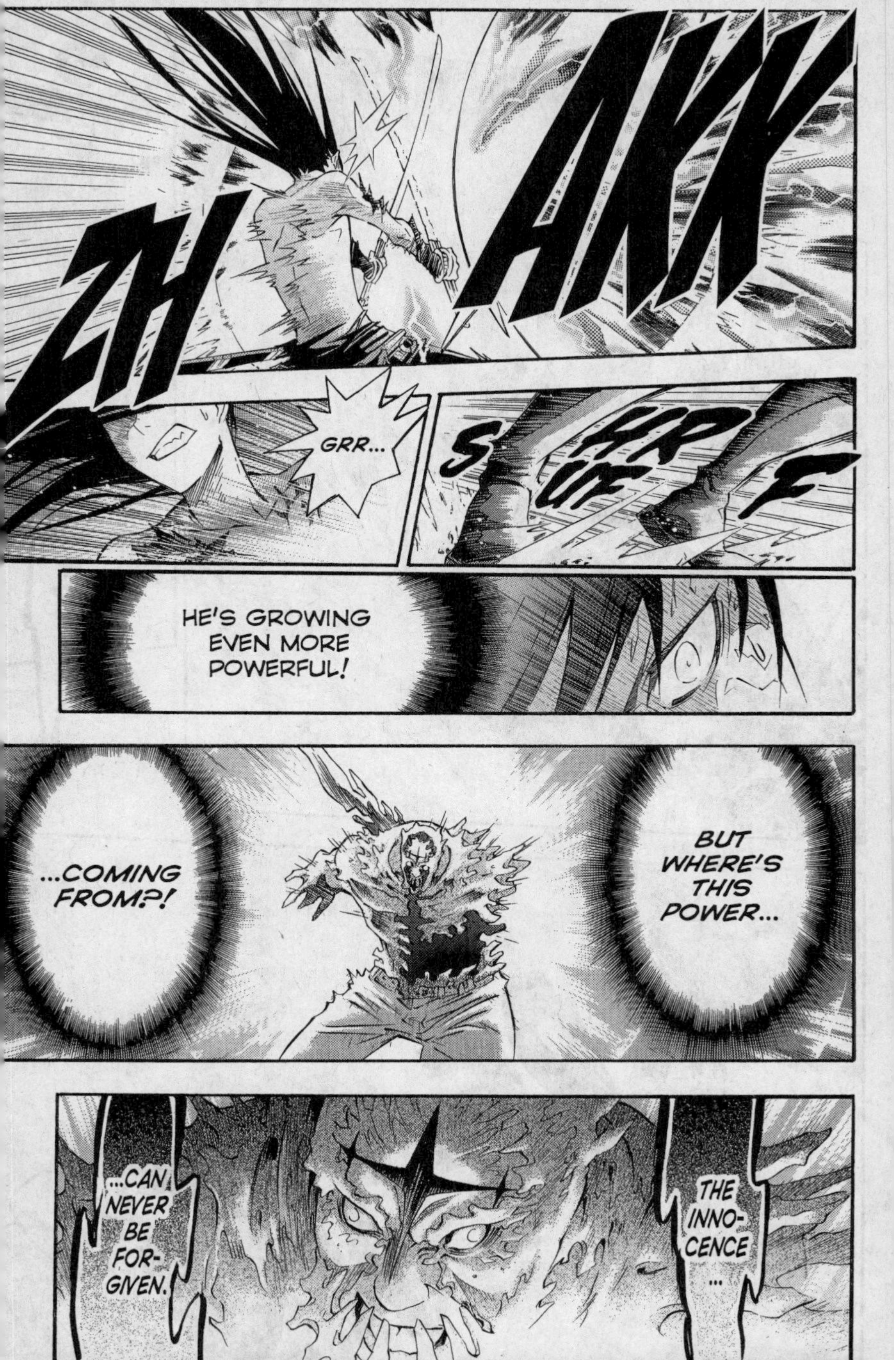
ZHANK
GRR...
HE'S GROWING EVEN MORE POWERFUL!
BUT WHERE'S THIS POWER...
...COMING FROM?!
THE INNO-CENCE...
...CAN NEVER BE FOR-GIVEN.

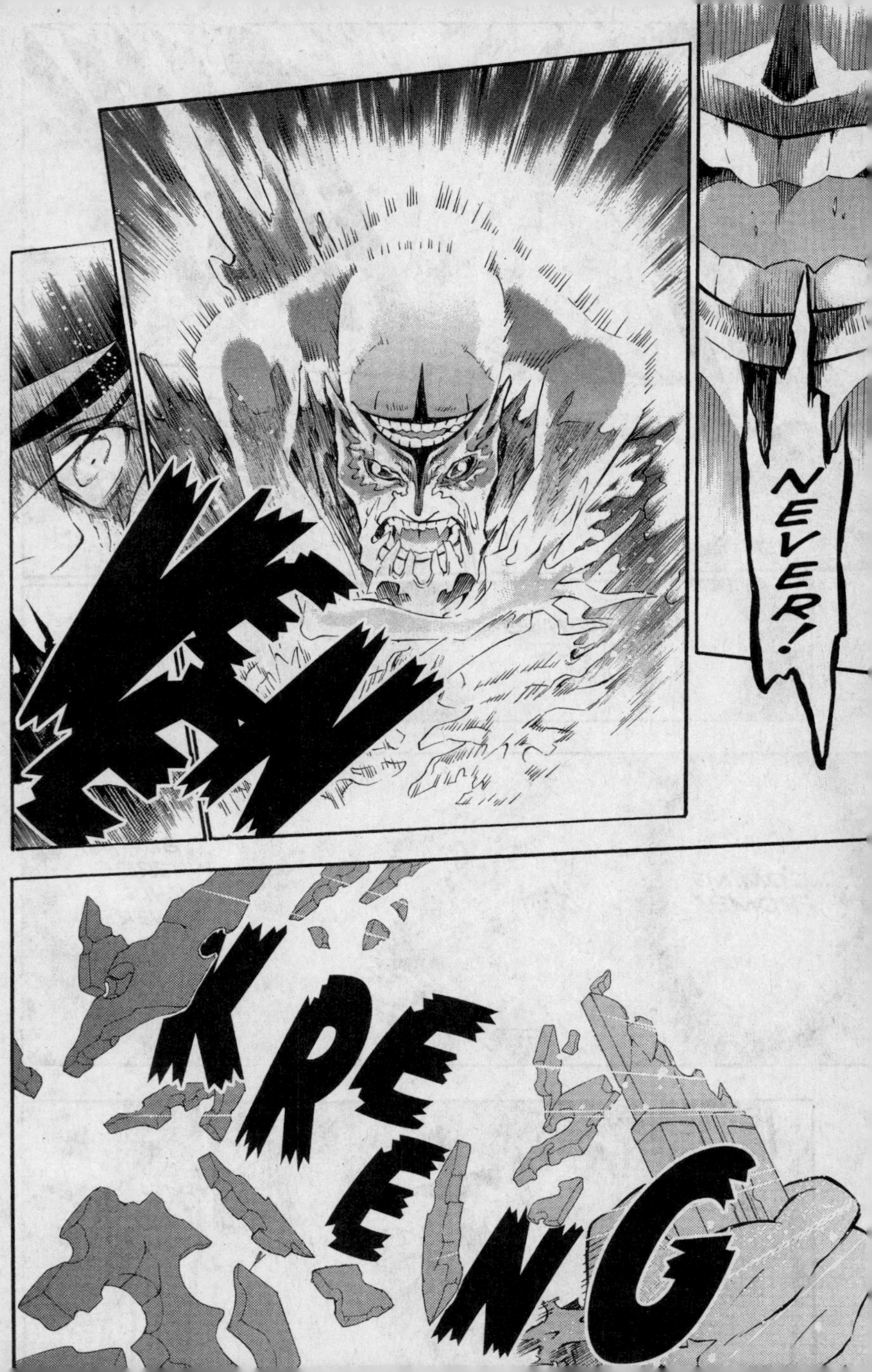
NEVER!
KREENG

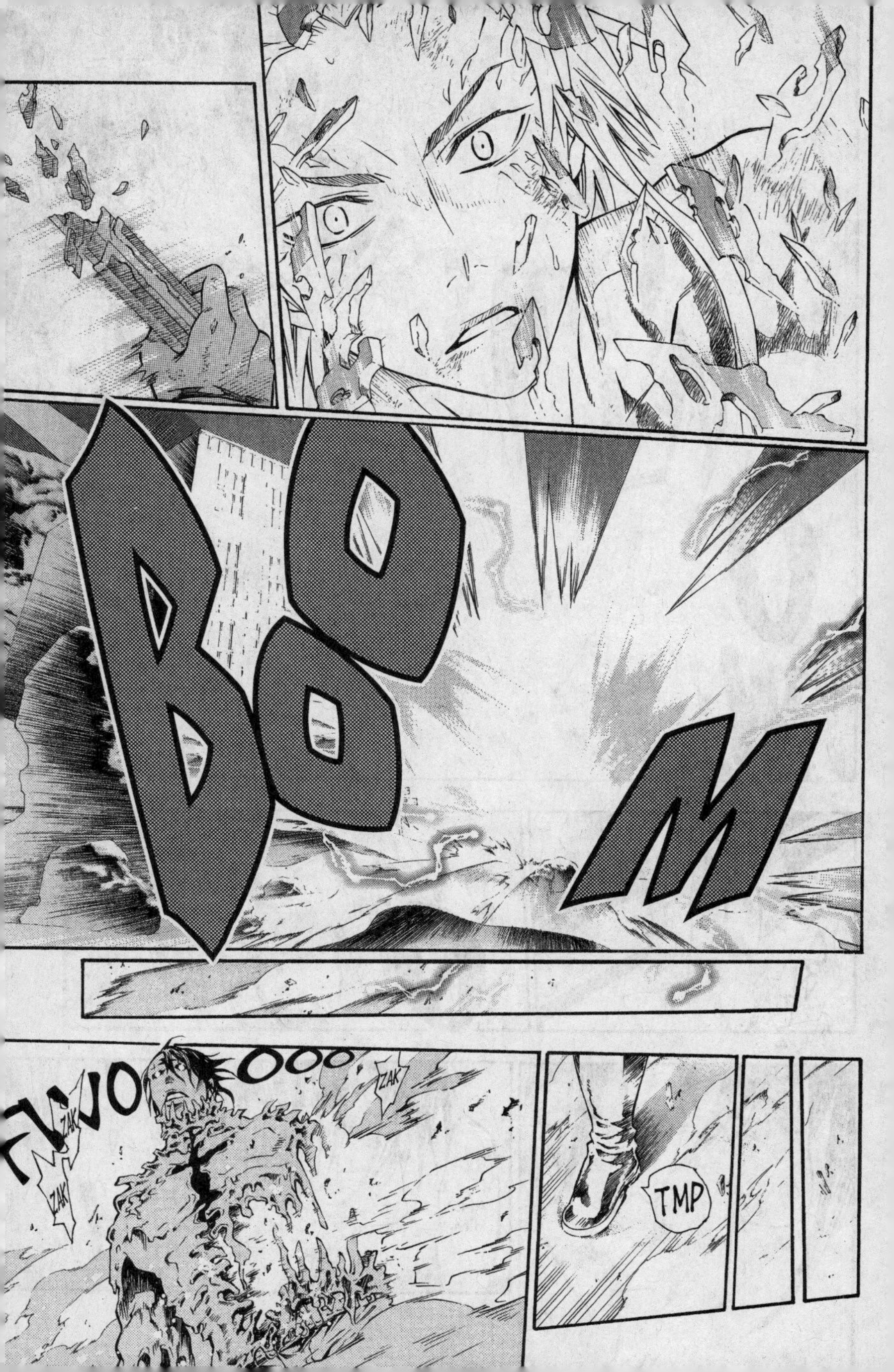
BOOM
TMP
FWOOOOO
ZAK
ZAK
ZAK

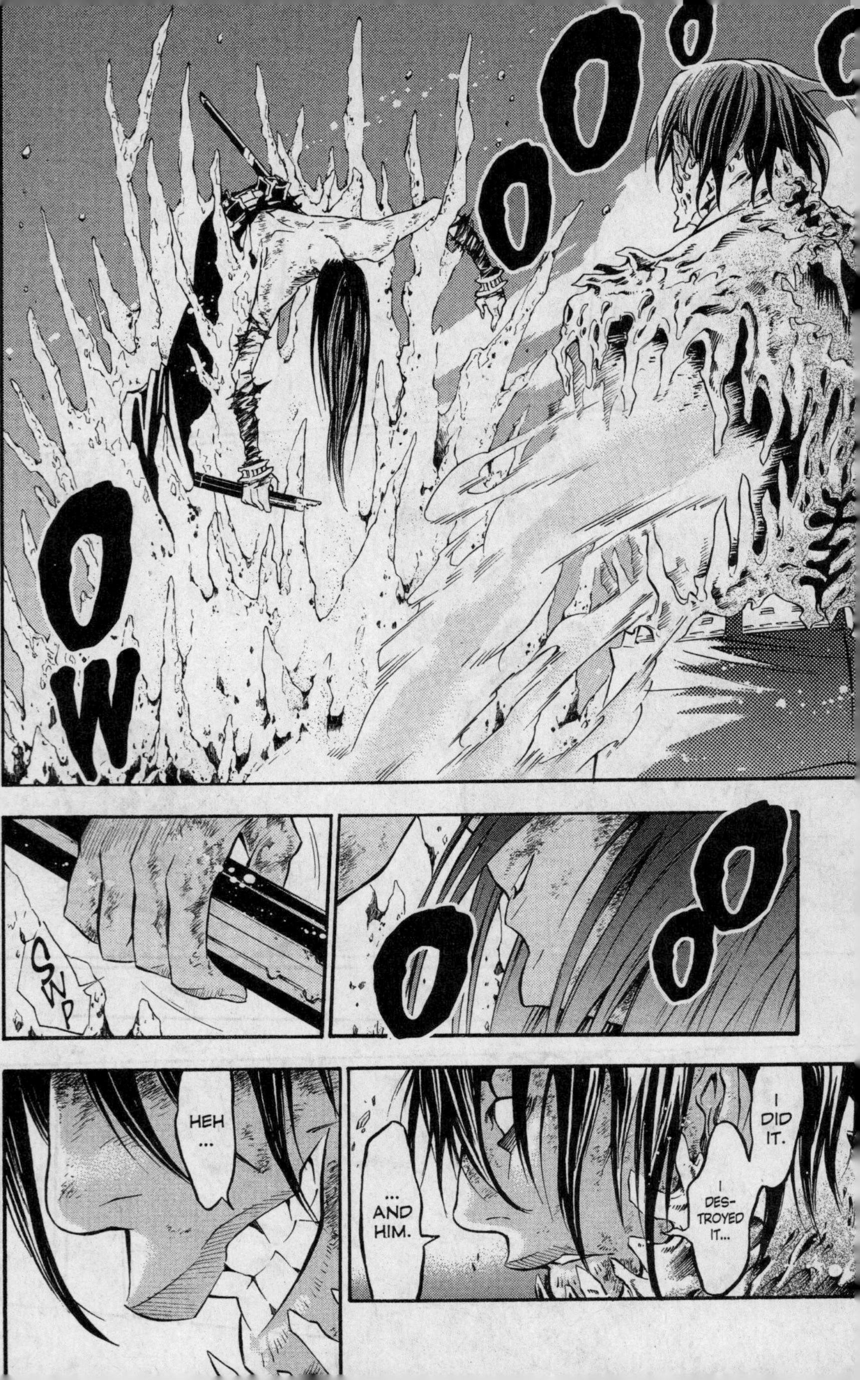
OOOOO
OW
OOOO
SWP
I DID IT.
I DES-TROYED IT...
...AND HIM.
HEH...

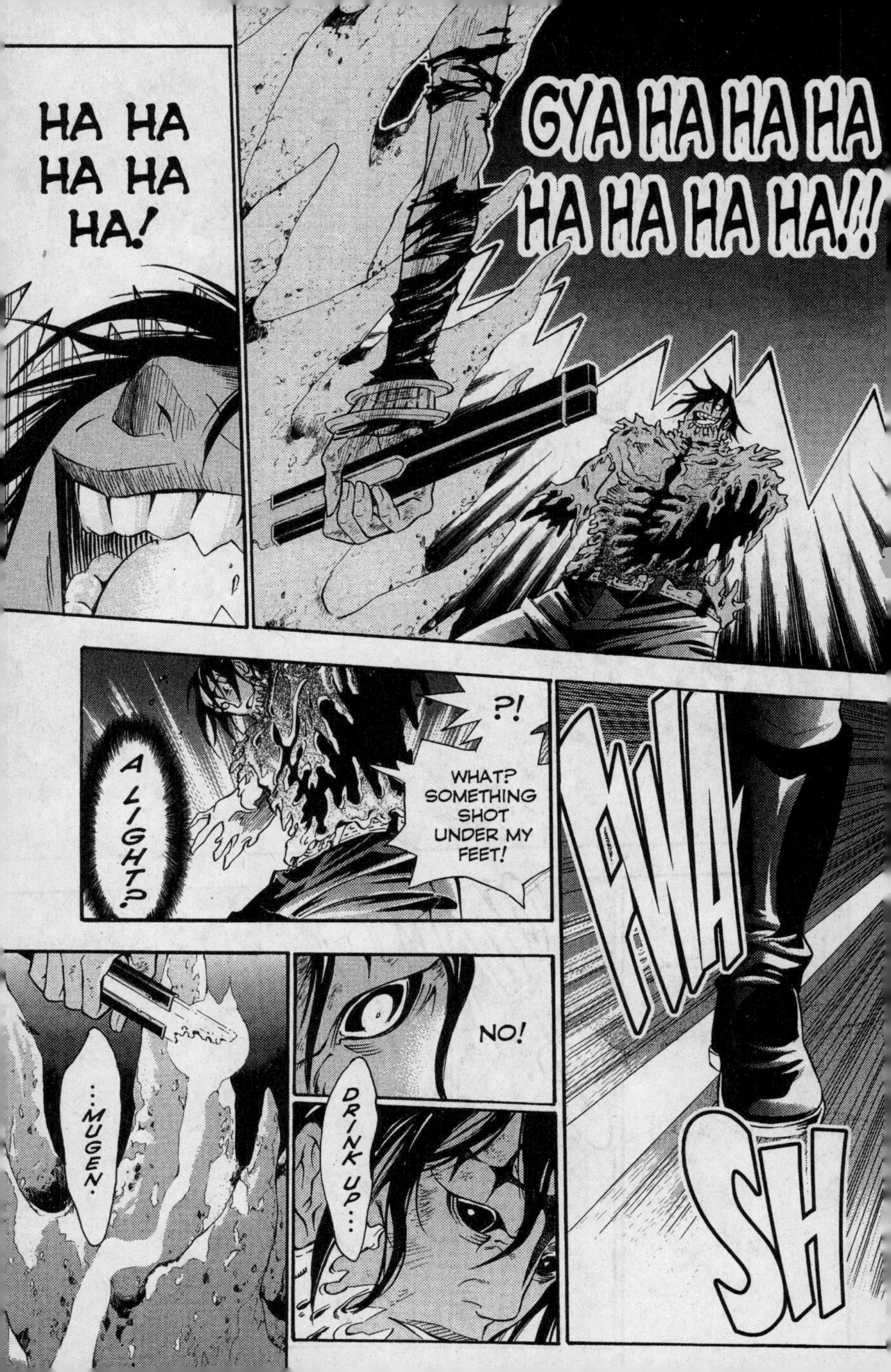
GYA HA HA HA HA HA HA HA HA!!
HA HA HA HA HA!
SWA
SH
?!
WHAT? SOMETHING SHOT UNDER MY FEET!
A LIGHT?
NO!
DRINK UP...
...MUGEN.

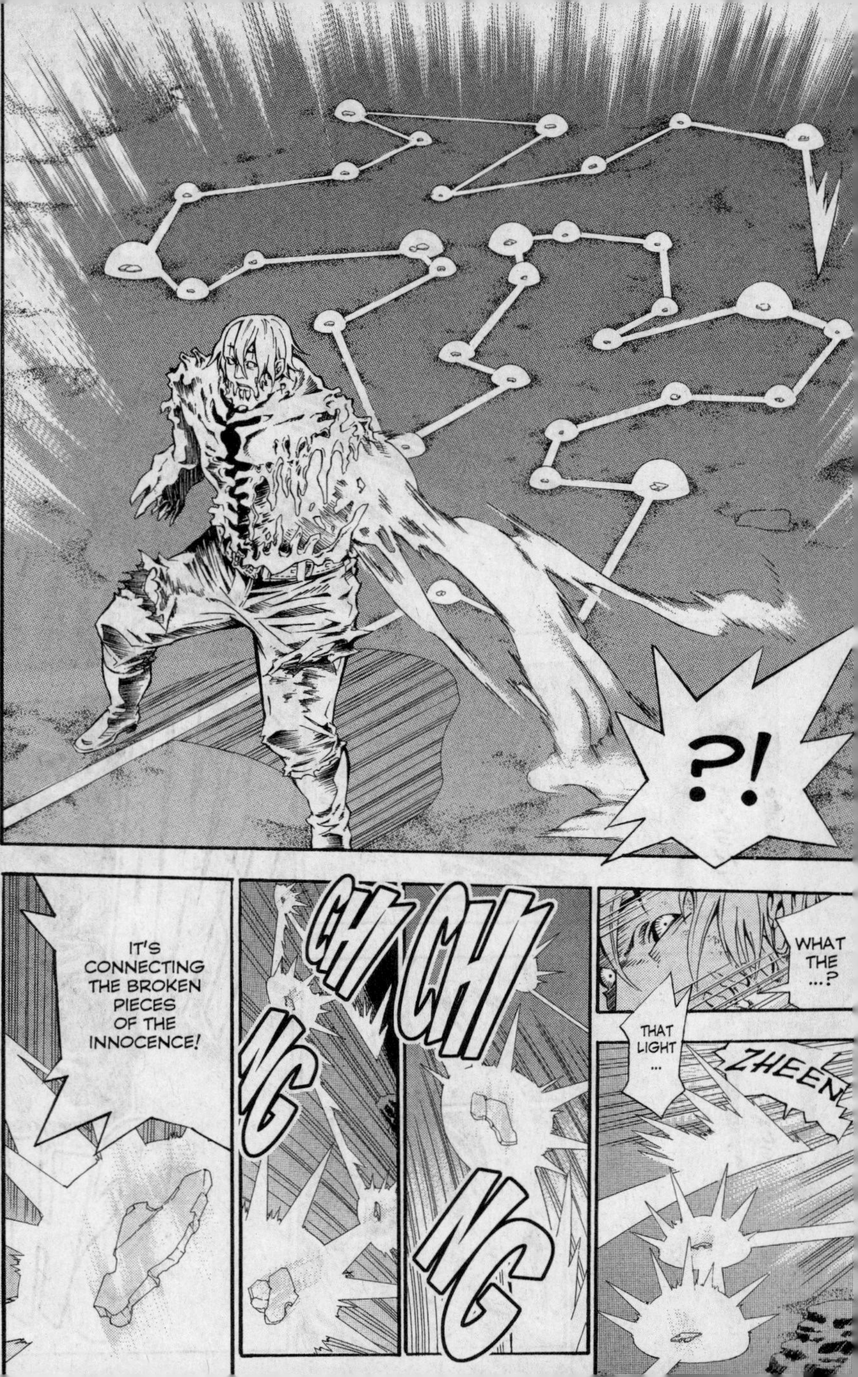
?!
WHAT THE ...?
THAT LIGHT ...
ZHEEN
CHING
CHING
IT'S CONNECTING THE BROKEN PIECES OF THE INNOCENCE!

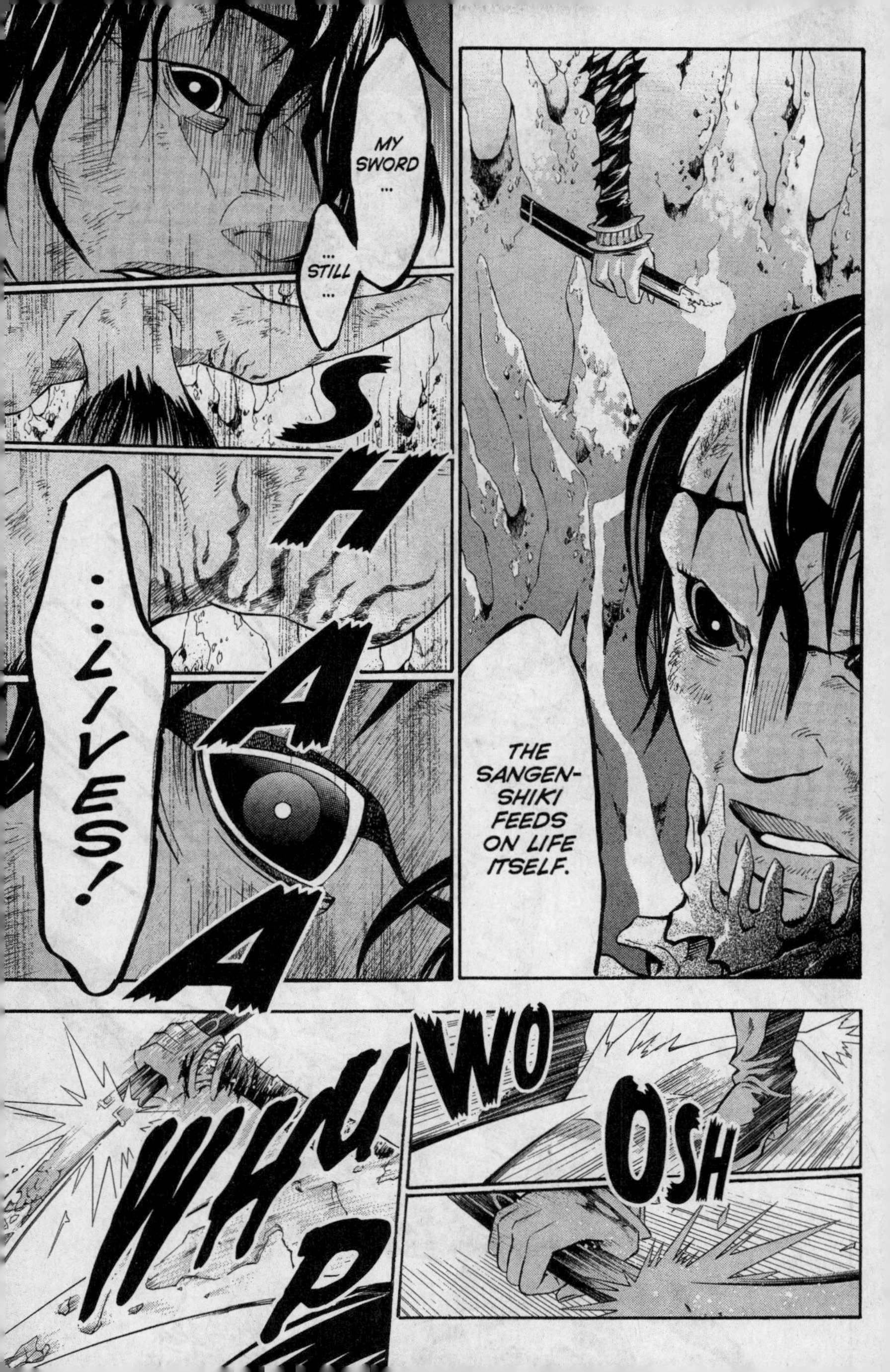
THE SANGEN-SHIKI FEEDS ON LIFE ITSELF.
MY SWORD ...
... STILL ...
...LIVES!
SHAA
WOOSH
WHUMP

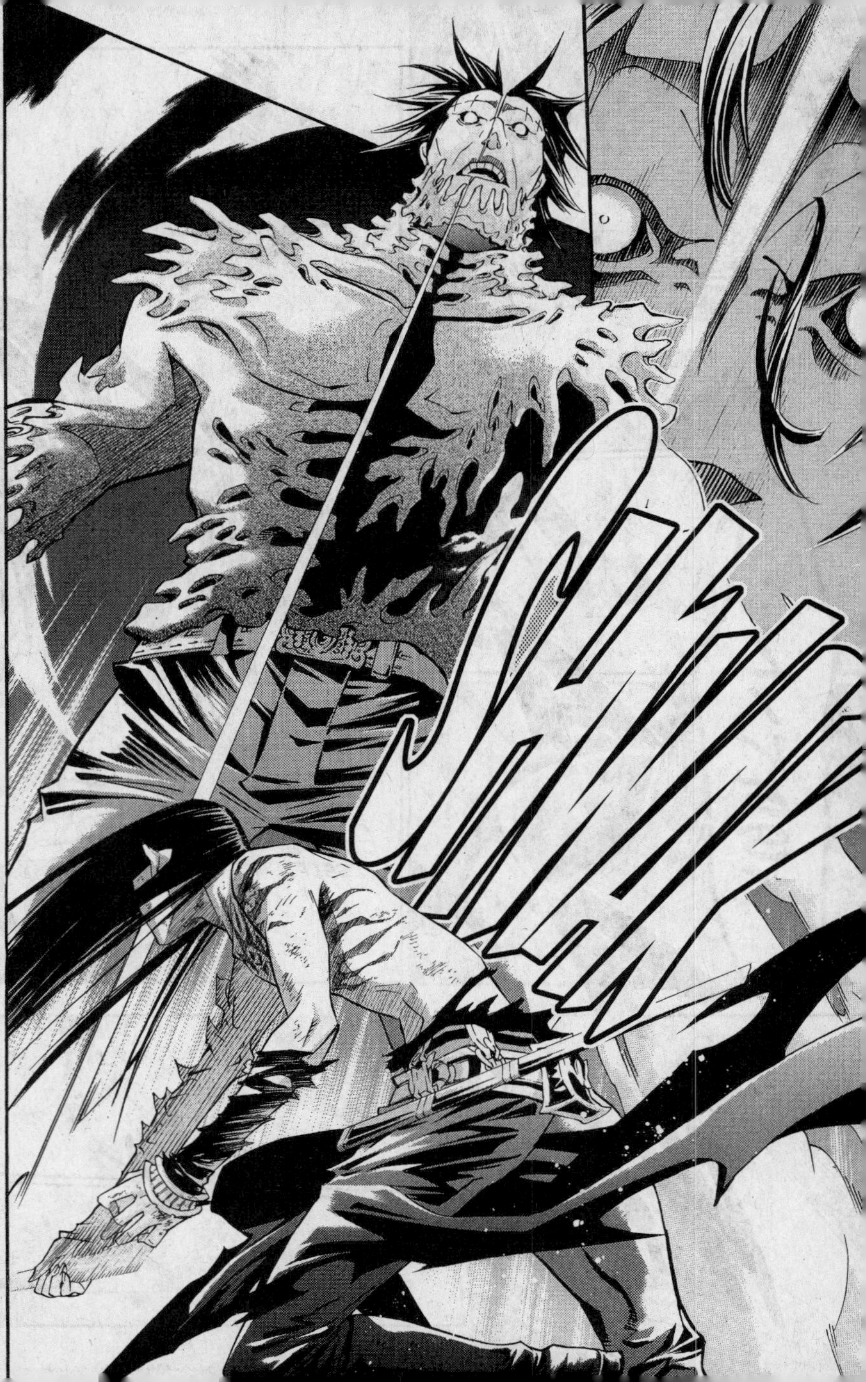

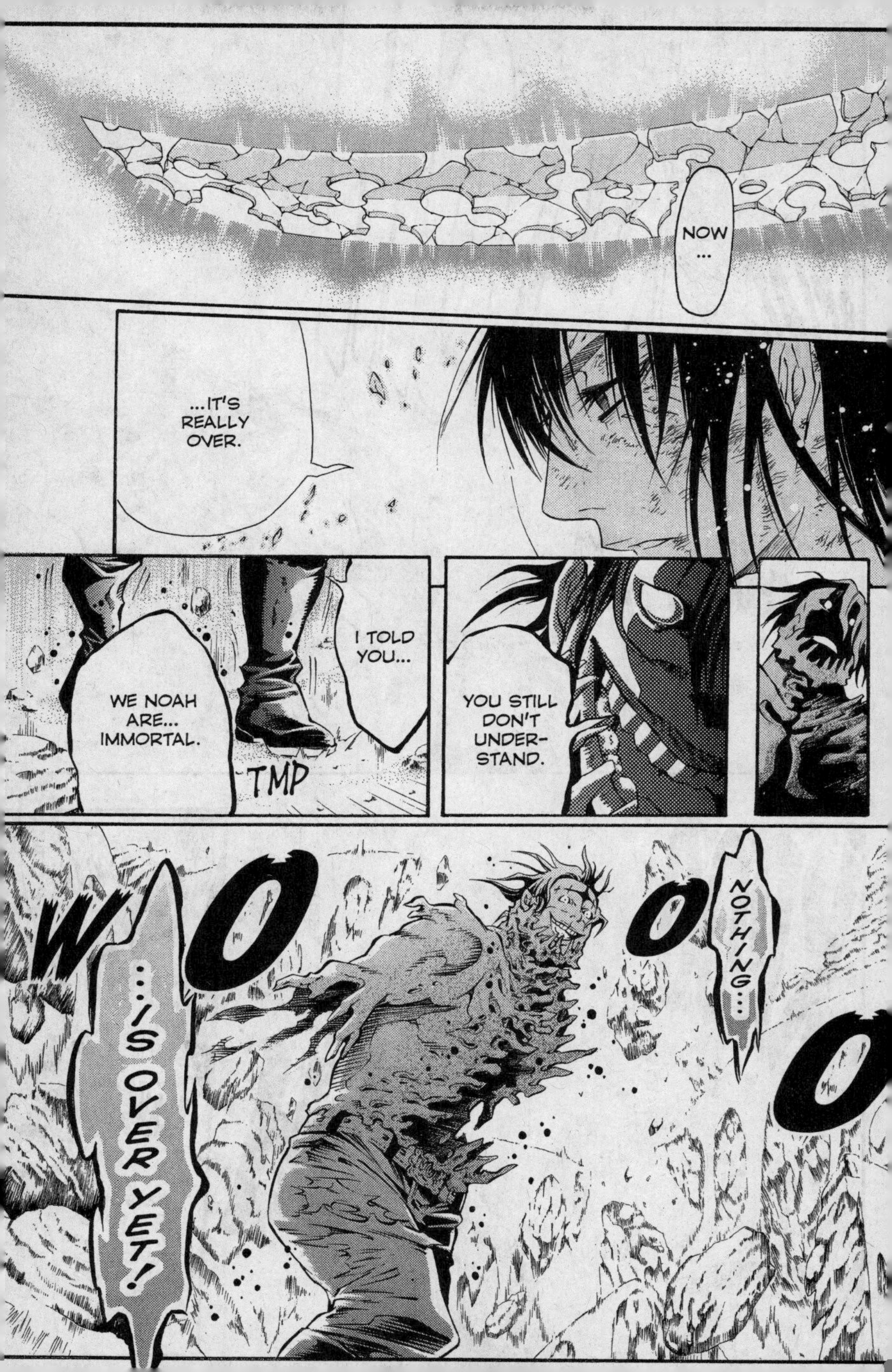
NOW...
...IT'S REALLY OVER.
YOU STILL DON'T UNDER-STAND.
I TOLD YOU...
WE NOAH ARE... IMMORTAL.
TMP
NOTHING...
...IS OVER YET!
WOOOO

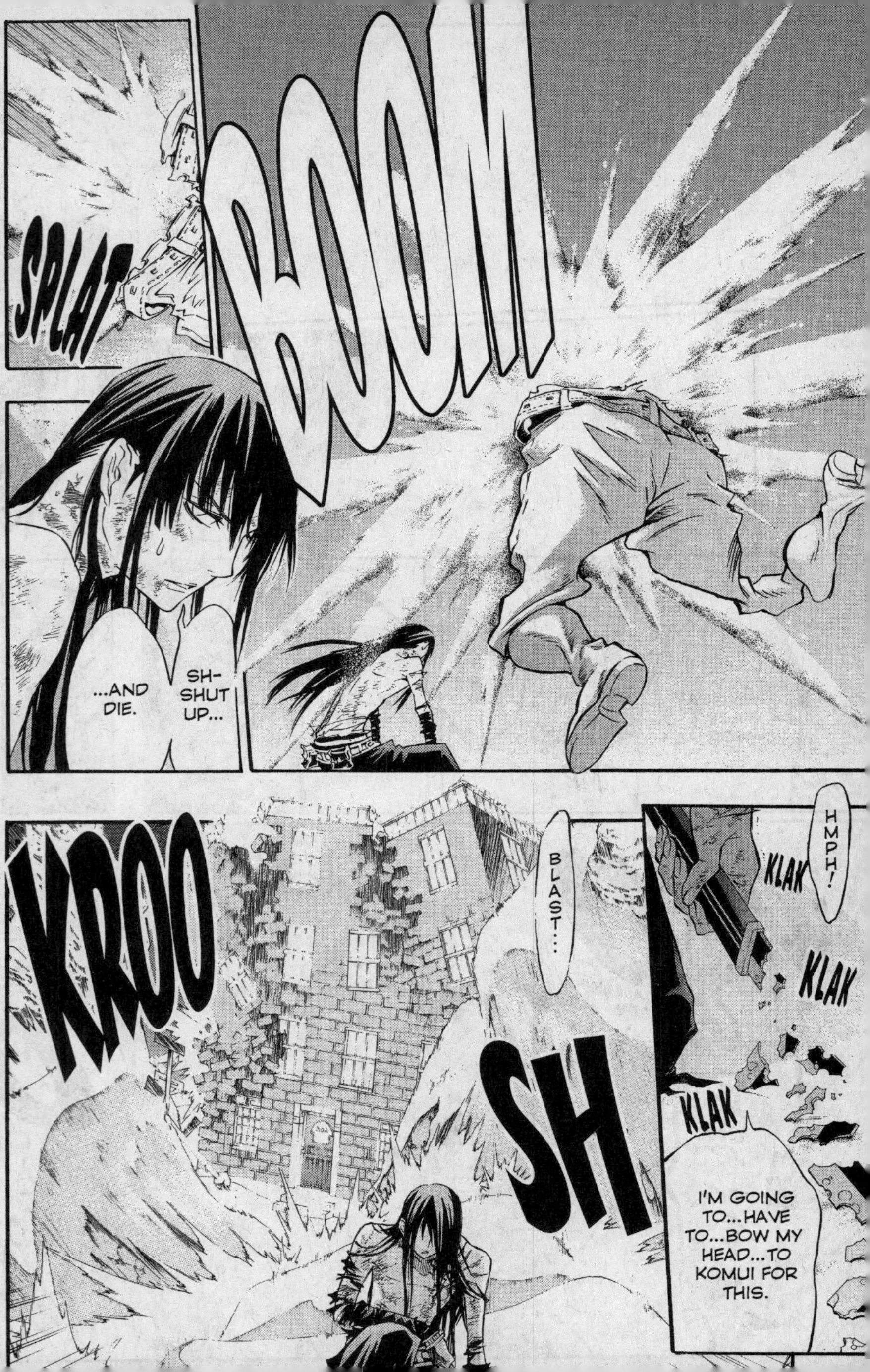
BOOM
SPLAT
SH-SHUT UP...
...AND DIE.
HMPH!
KLAK
KLAK
KLAK
I'M GOING TO...HAVE TO...BOW MY HEAD...TO KOMUI FOR THIS.
BLAST...
KROOSH

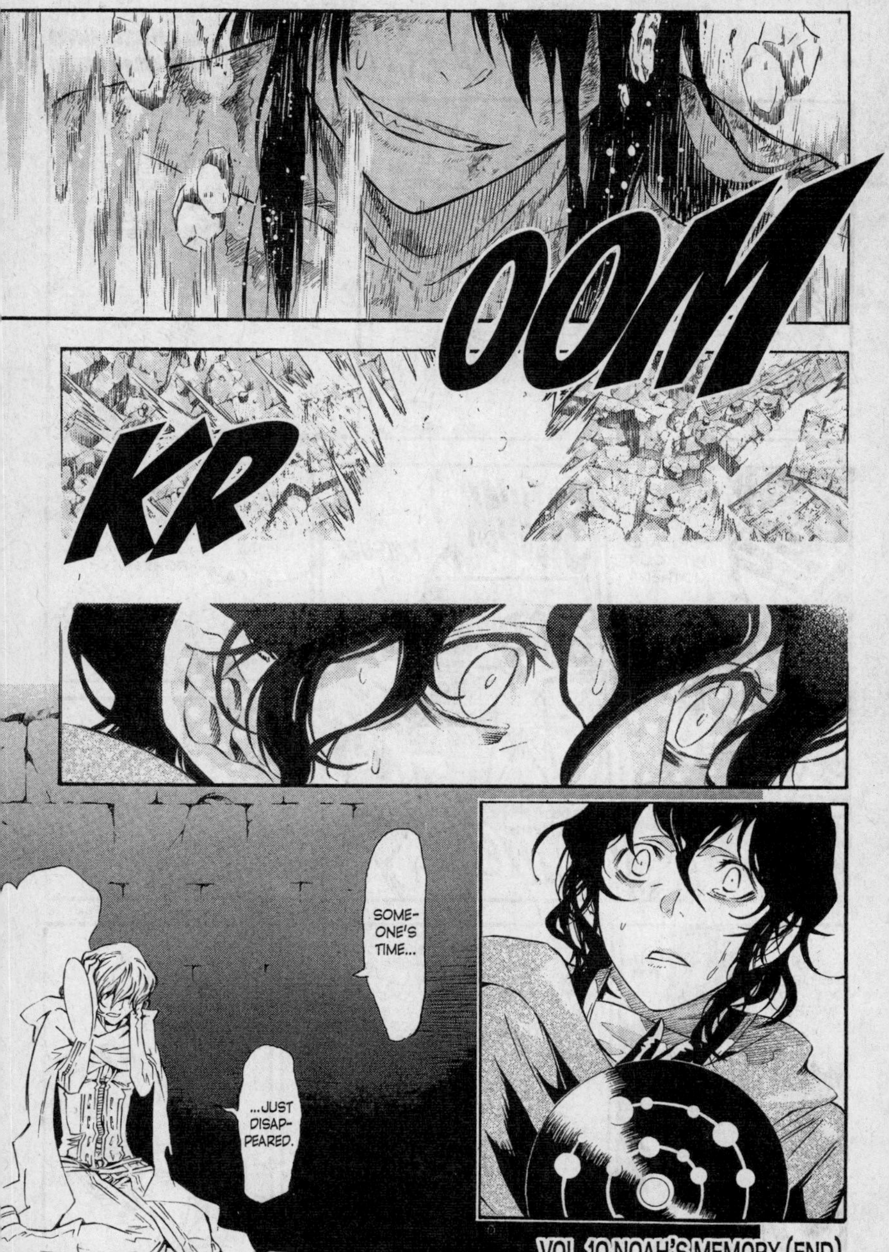
KROOM
SOME-ONE'S TIME...
...JUST DISAP-PEARED.

VOL. 10 NOAH'S MEMORY (END)

D.GRAY THEATER

STORY BY KATSURA HOSHINO
ART BY RANDOM ASSISTANT

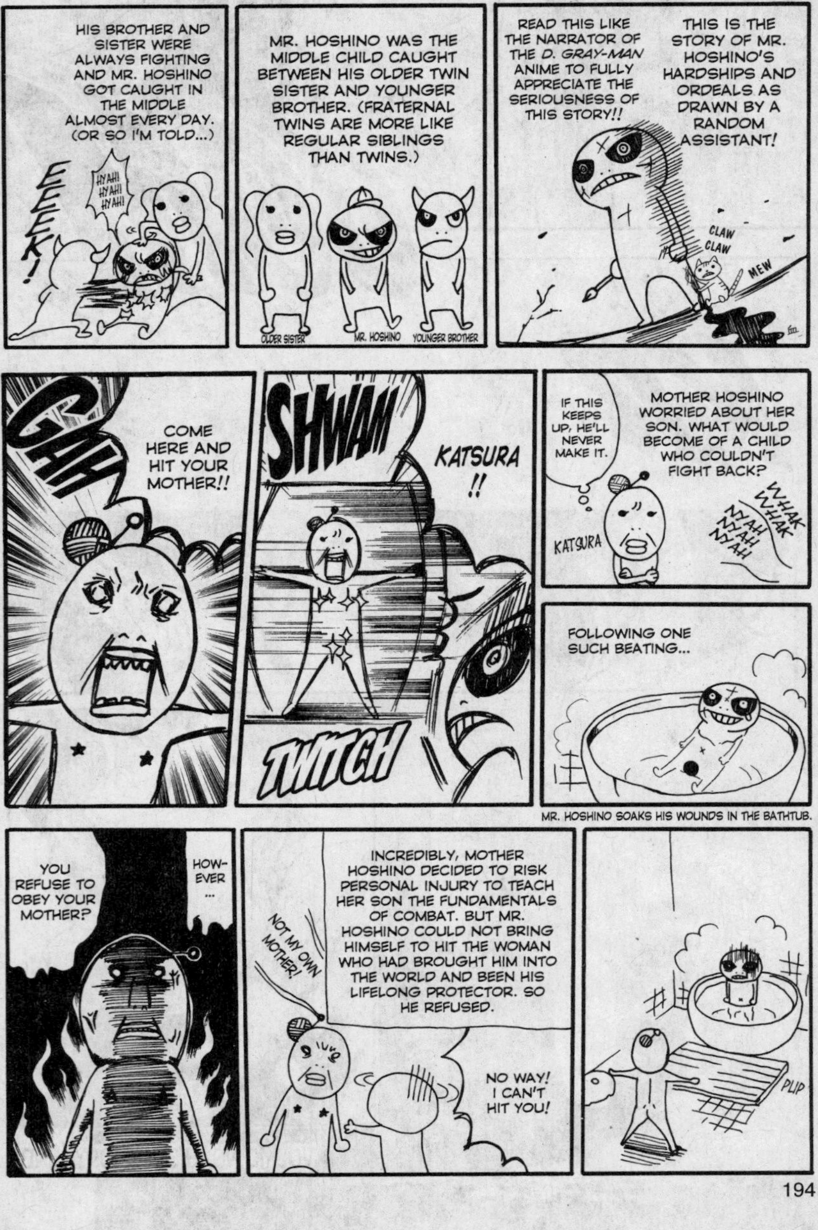

THIS IS THE STORY OF MR. HOSHINO'S HARDSHIPS AND ORDEALS AS DRAWN BY A RANDOM ASSISTANT!
READ THIS LIKE THE NARRATOR OF THE *D. GRAY-MAN* ANIME TO FULLY APPRECIATE THE SERIOUSNESS OF THIS STORY!!
CLAW CLAW
MEW
MR. HOSHINO WAS THE MIDDLE CHILD CAUGHT BETWEEN HIS OLDER TWIN SISTER AND YOUNGER BROTHER. (FRATERNAL TWINS ARE MORE LIKE REGULAR SIBLINGS THAN TWINS.)
YOUNGER BROTHER
MR. HOSHINO
OLDER SISTER
HIS BROTHER AND SISTER WERE ALWAYS FIGHTING AND MR. HOSHINO GOT CAUGHT IN THE MIDDLE ALMOST EVERY DAY. (OR SO I'M TOLD...)
HYAH! HYAH! HYAH!
EEEEK!
MOTHER HOSHINO WORRIED ABOUT HER SON. WHAT WOULD BECOME OF A CHILD WHO COULDN'T FIGHT BACK?
IF THIS KEEPS UP, HE'LL NEVER MAKE IT.
WHAK WHAK
NYAH NYAH NYAH
KATSURA
FOLLOWING ONE SUCH BEATING...
MR. HOSHINO SOAKS HIS WOUNDS IN THE BATHTUB.
KATSURA !!
SHWAM
TWITCH
GAH
COME HERE AND HIT YOUR MOTHER!!
PLIP
INCREDIBLY, MOTHER HOSHINO DECIDED TO RISK PERSONAL INJURY TO TEACH HER SON THE FUNDAMENTALS OF COMBAT. BUT MR. HOSHINO COULD NOT BRING HIMSELF TO HIT THE WOMAN WHO HAD BROUGHT HIM INTO THE WORLD AND BEEN HIS LIFELONG PROTECTOR. SO HE REFUSED.
NOT MY OWN MOTHER!
NO WAY! I CAN'T HIT YOU!
HOW-EVER ...
YOU REFUSE TO OBEY YOUR MOTHER?

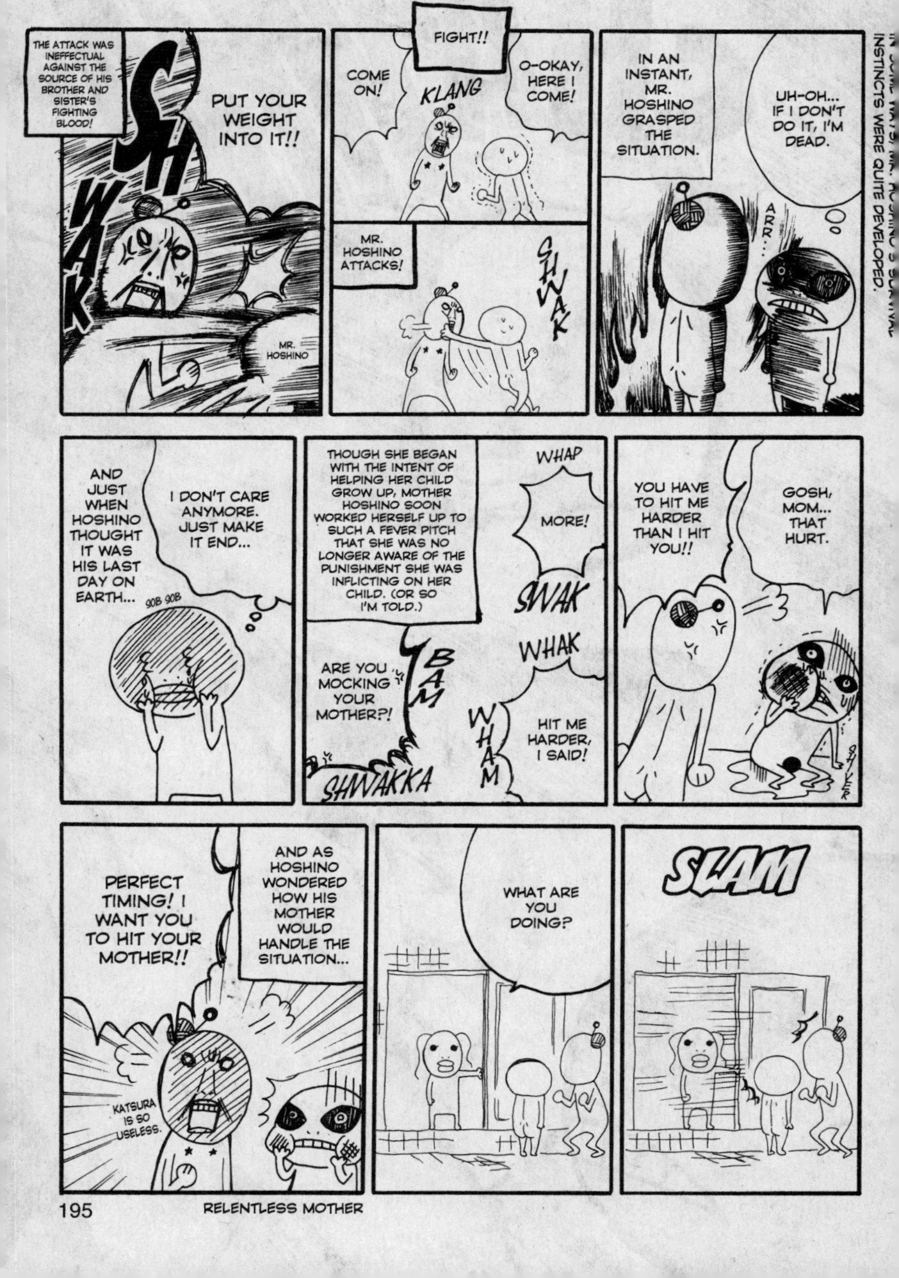
UH-OH... IF I DON'T DO IT, I'M DEAD.
IN AN INSTANT, MR. HOSHINO GRASPED THE SITUATION.
ARR...
FIGHT!!
O-OKAY, HERE I COME!
COME ON!
KLANG
MR. HOSHINO ATTACKS!
SHWAK
THE ATTACK WAS INEFFECTUAL AGAINST THE SOURCE OF HIS BROTHER AND SISTER'S FIGHTING BLOOD!
PUT YOUR WEIGHT INTO IT!!
SHWAK
MR. HOSHINO
GOSH, MOM... THAT HURT.
YOU HAVE TO HIT ME HARDER THAN I HIT YOU!!
SHIVER
WHAP
MORE!
THOUGH SHE BEGAN WITH THE INTENT OF HELPING HER CHILD GROW UP, MOTHER HOSHINO SOON WORKED HERSELF UP TO SUCH A FEVER PITCH THAT SHE WAS NO LONGER AWARE OF THE PUNISHMENT SHE WAS INFLICTING ON HER CHILD. (OR SO I'M TOLD.)
SWAK
WHAK
BAM
ARE YOU MOCKING YOUR MOTHER?!
WHAM
HIT ME HARDER, I SAID!
SHWAKKA
I DON'T CARE ANYMORE. JUST MAKE IT END...
AND JUST WHEN HOSHINO THOUGHT IT WAS HIS LAST DAY ON EARTH...
SOB SOB
SLAM
WHAT ARE YOU DOING?
AND AS HOSHINO WONDERED HOW HIS MOTHER WOULD HANDLE THE SITUATION...
PERFECT TIMING! I WANT YOU TO HIT YOUR MOTHER!!
KATSURA IS SO USELESS.

INSTINCTS WERE QUITE DEVELOPED.

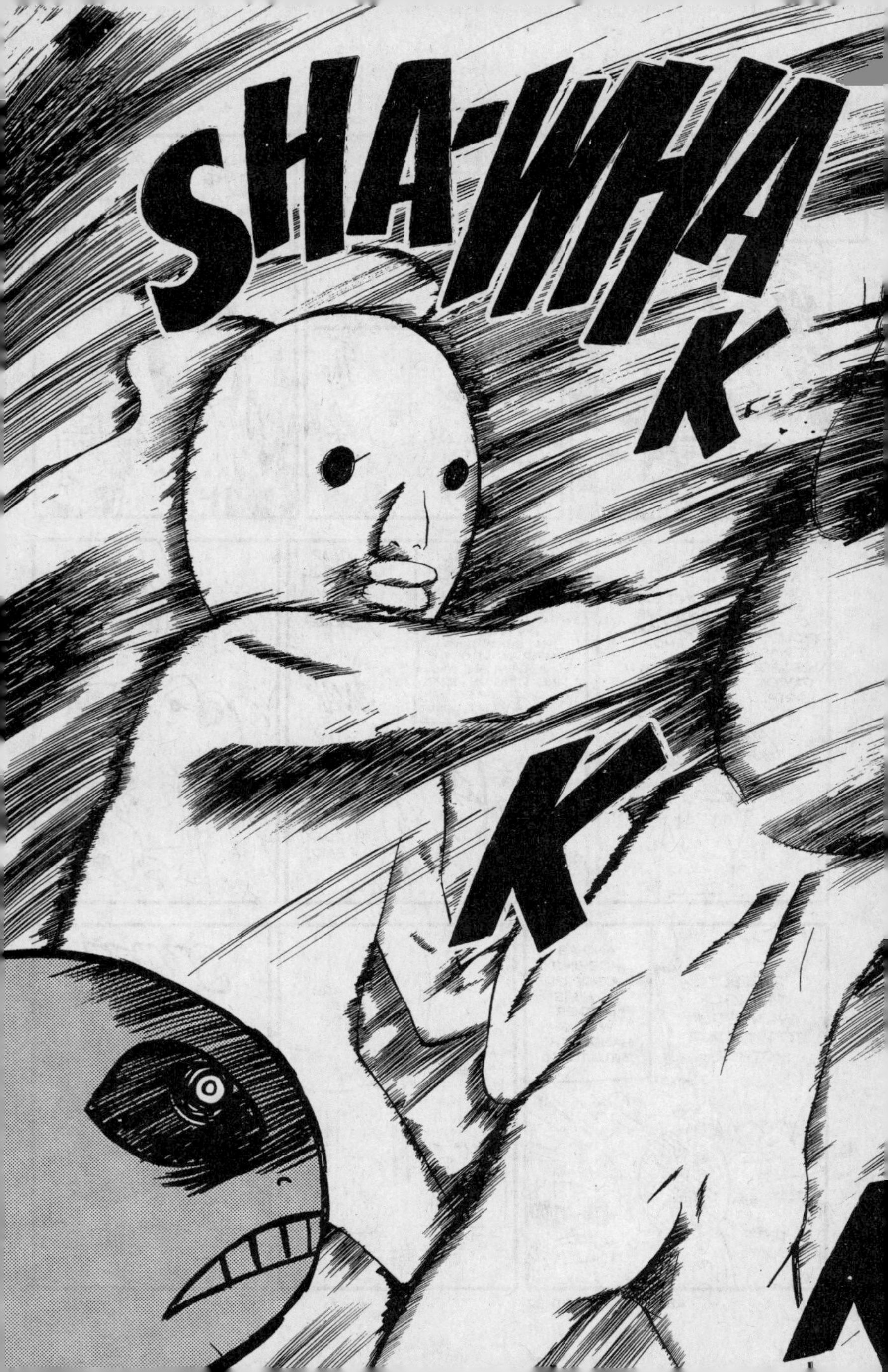
SHA-WHAK
K

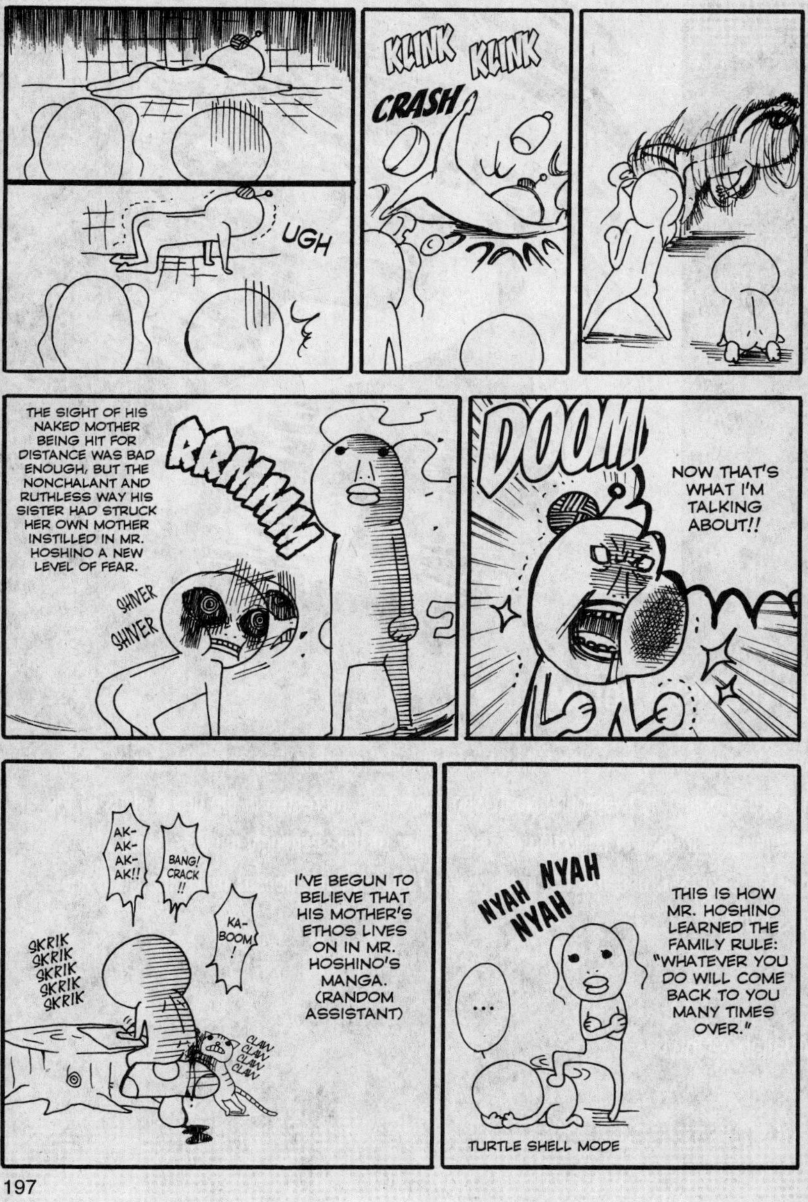
KLINK
KLINK
CRASH
UGH
NOW THAT'S WHAT I'M TALKING ABOUT!!
DOOM
RRMMMM
THE SIGHT OF HIS NAKED MOTHER BEING HIT FOR DISTANCE WAS BAD ENOUGH, BUT THE NONCHALANT AND RUTHLESS WAY HIS SISTER HAD STRUCK HER OWN MOTHER INSTILLED IN MR. HOSHINO A NEW LEVEL OF FEAR.
SHIVER
SHIVER
THIS IS HOW MR. HOSHINO LEARNED THE FAMILY RULE: "WHATEVER YOU DO WILL COME BACK TO YOU MANY TIMES OVER."
NYAH
NYAH
NYAH
...
TURTLE SHELL MODE
I'VE BEGUN TO BELIEVE THAT HIS MOTHER'S ETHOS LIVES ON IN MR. HOSHINO'S MANGA. (RANDOM ASSISTANT)
BANG! CRACK!!
AK-AK-AK-AK!!
KA-BOOM!
SKRIK SKRIK SKRIK SKRIK SKRIK
CLAW CLAW CLAW CLAW

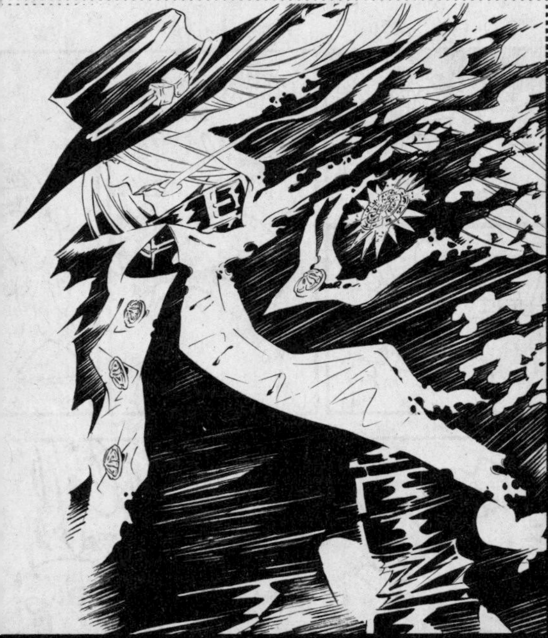

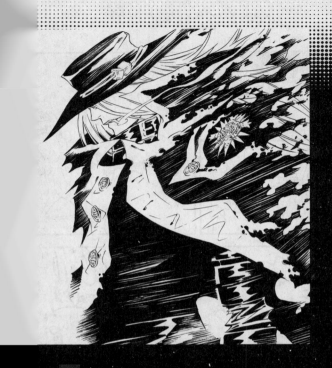

XT VOLUME...

s rejoined his fellow Exorcists, and together they enter the Ark of Noah.
d by two young Noah who seem less interested in the grand plans of the
than in collecting on yet another of the seemingly endless debts Allen's
Cross, has left in his wake. That, however, doesn't make the Noah any

y!

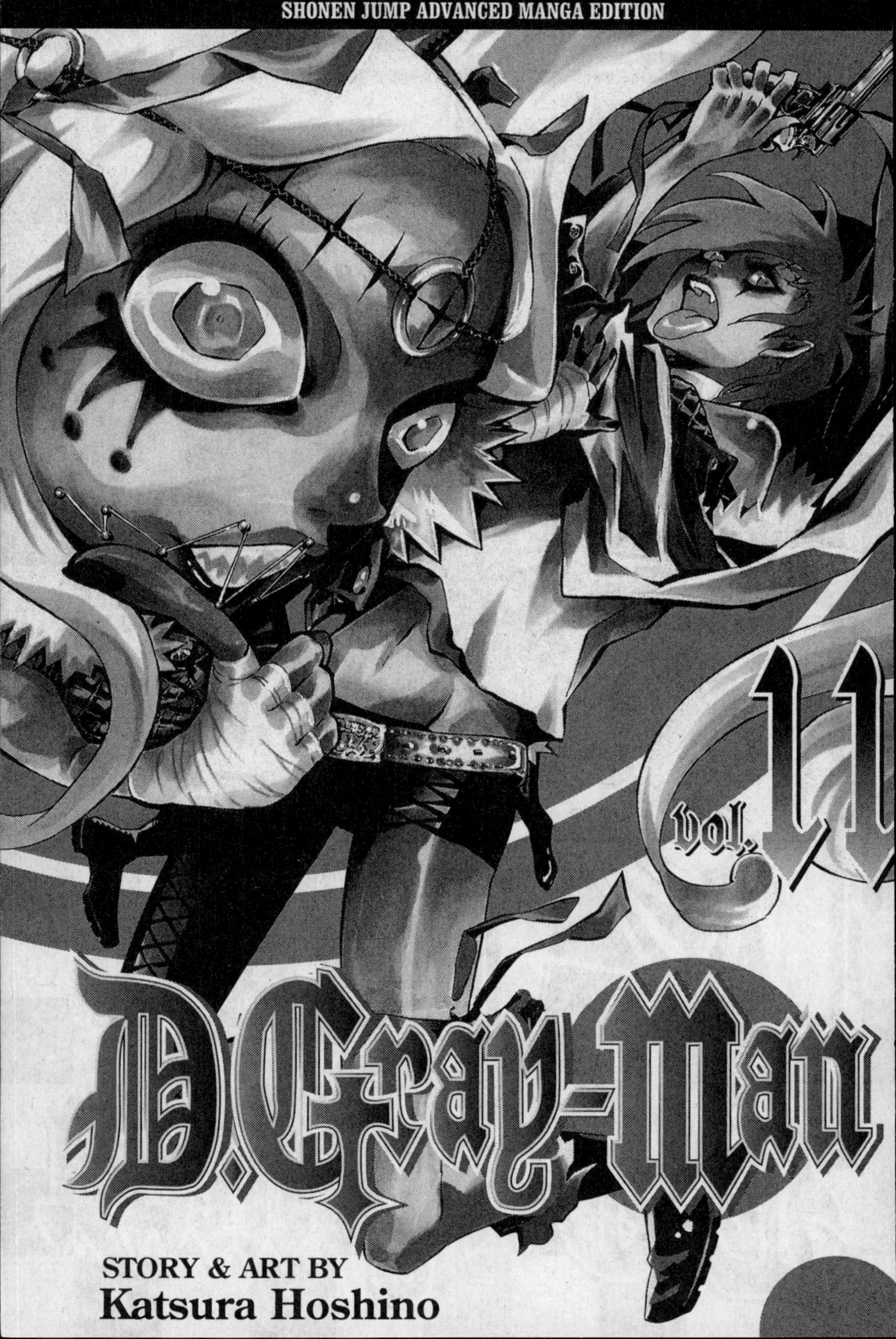
SHONEN JUMP ADVANCED MANGA EDITION
vol. 11
D.Gray-man
STORY & ART BY
Katsura Hoshino

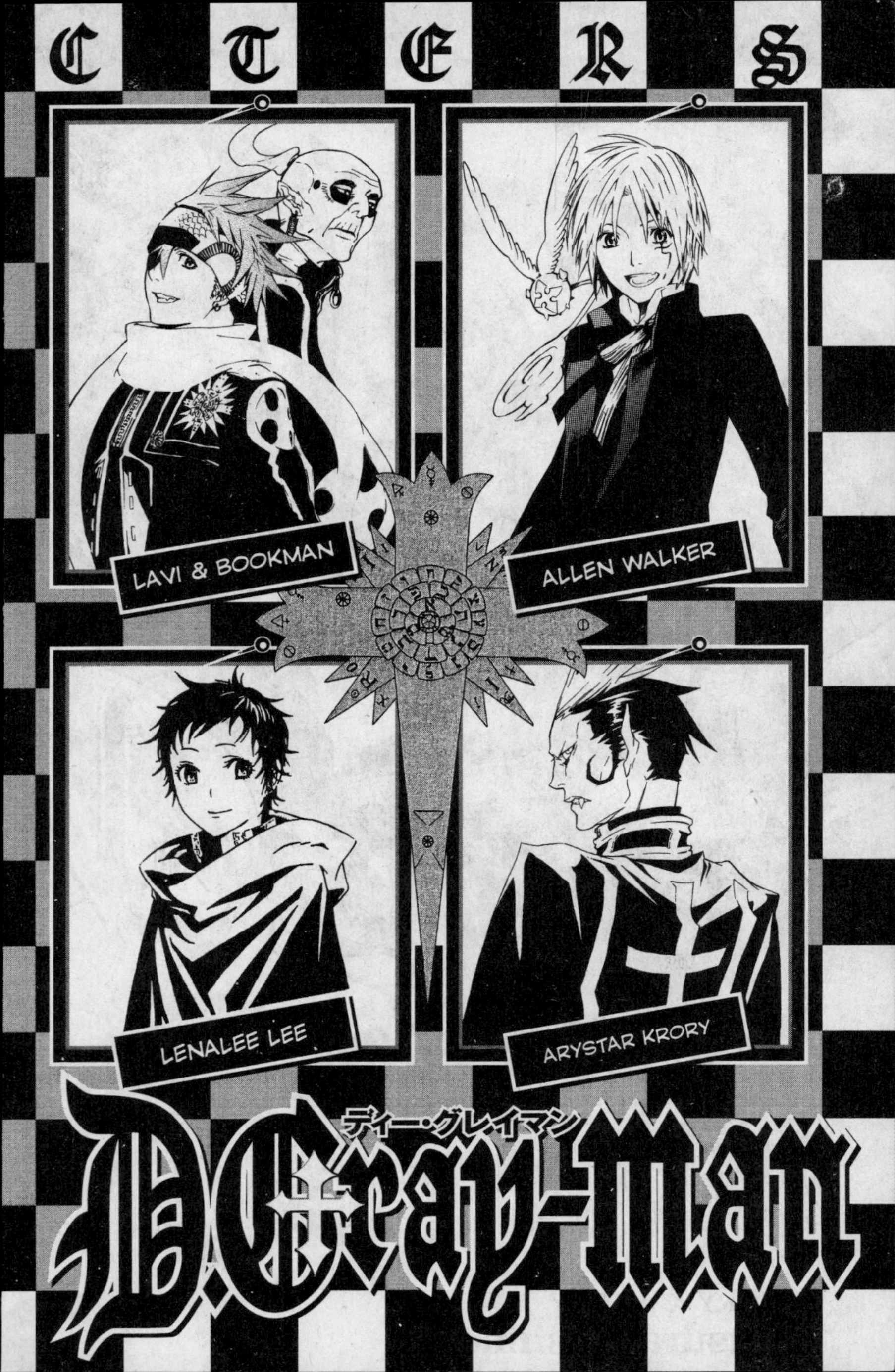
C T E R S
LAVI & BOOKMAN
ALLEN WALKER
LENALEE LEE
ARYSTAR KRORY
ディー・グレイマン
D.Gray-man

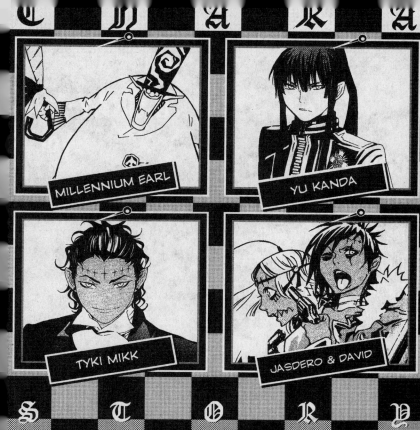

CHARA

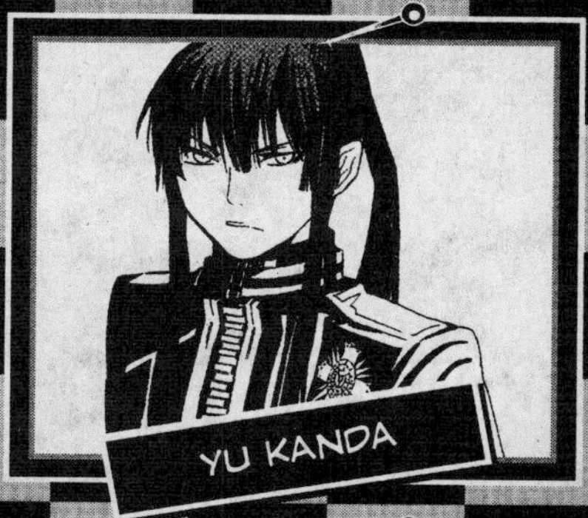
YU KANDA

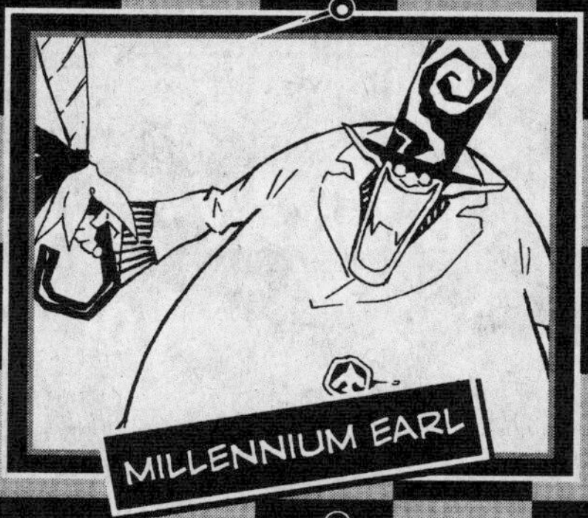
MILLENNIUM EARL

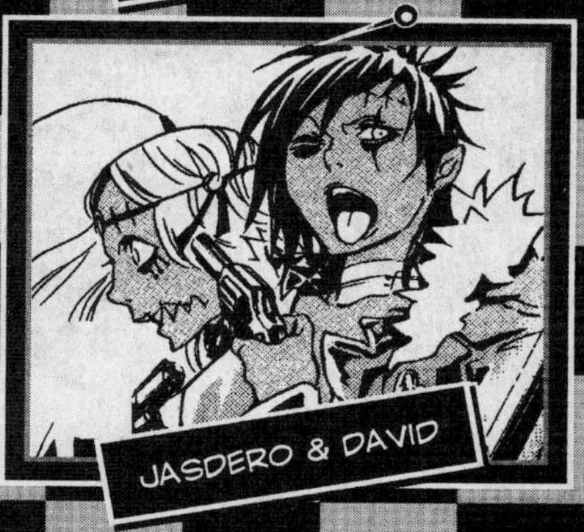
JASDERO & DAVID

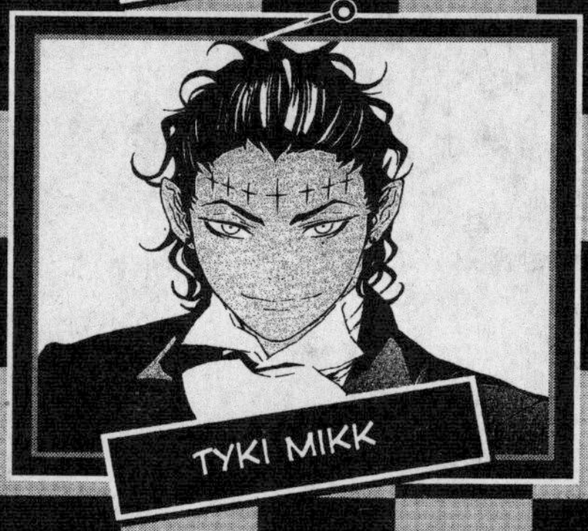
TYKI MIKK

STORY

IT ALL BEGAN CENTURIES AGO WITH THE DISCOVERY OF A CUBE CONTAINING AN APOCALYPTIC PROPHECY FROM AN ANCIENT CIVILIZATION AND INSTRUCTIONS IN THE USE OF INNOCENCE, A CRYSTALLINE SUBSTANCE OF WONDROUS SUPERNATURAL POWER. THE CREATORS OF THE CUBE CLAIMED TO HAVE DEFEATED AN EVIL KNOWN AS THE MILLENNIUM EARL BY USING THE INNOCENCE. NEVERTHELESS, THE WORLD WAS DESTROYED BY THE GREAT FLOOD OF THE OLD TESTAMENT. NOW, TO AVERT A SECOND END OF THE WORLD, A GROUP OF EXORCISTS WIELDING WEAPONS MADE OF INNOCENCE MUST BATTLE THE MILLENNIUM EARL AND HIS TERRIBLE MINIONS, THE AKUMA.

ALLEN ARRIVES IN JAPAN TO JOIN HIS FELLOW EXORCISTS. THEY SOON FIND THEMSELVES TRAPPED INSIDE AN OBSOLETE ARK THAT HAS BEGUN TO DISINTEGRATE. WHILE TRYING TO REACH THE ONLY MEANS OF ESCAPE, THEY ENCOUNTER SKIN BORIC OF THE CLAN OF NOAH. KANDA FORCES THE OTHERS TO GO ON WITHOUT HIM, BUT HE AND BORIC BOTH PERISH IN THE BATTLE THAT FOLLOWS. NOW ALLEN AND THE OTHERS MUST MAKE THEIR WAY OUT OF THE ARK OR BE DESTROYED WITH IT. BUT THE FORCES OF THE EARL HAVE OTHER PLANS.

D.GRAY-MAN
Vol. 11

CONTENTS

THE 98TH NIGHT: TWIN'S ROOM

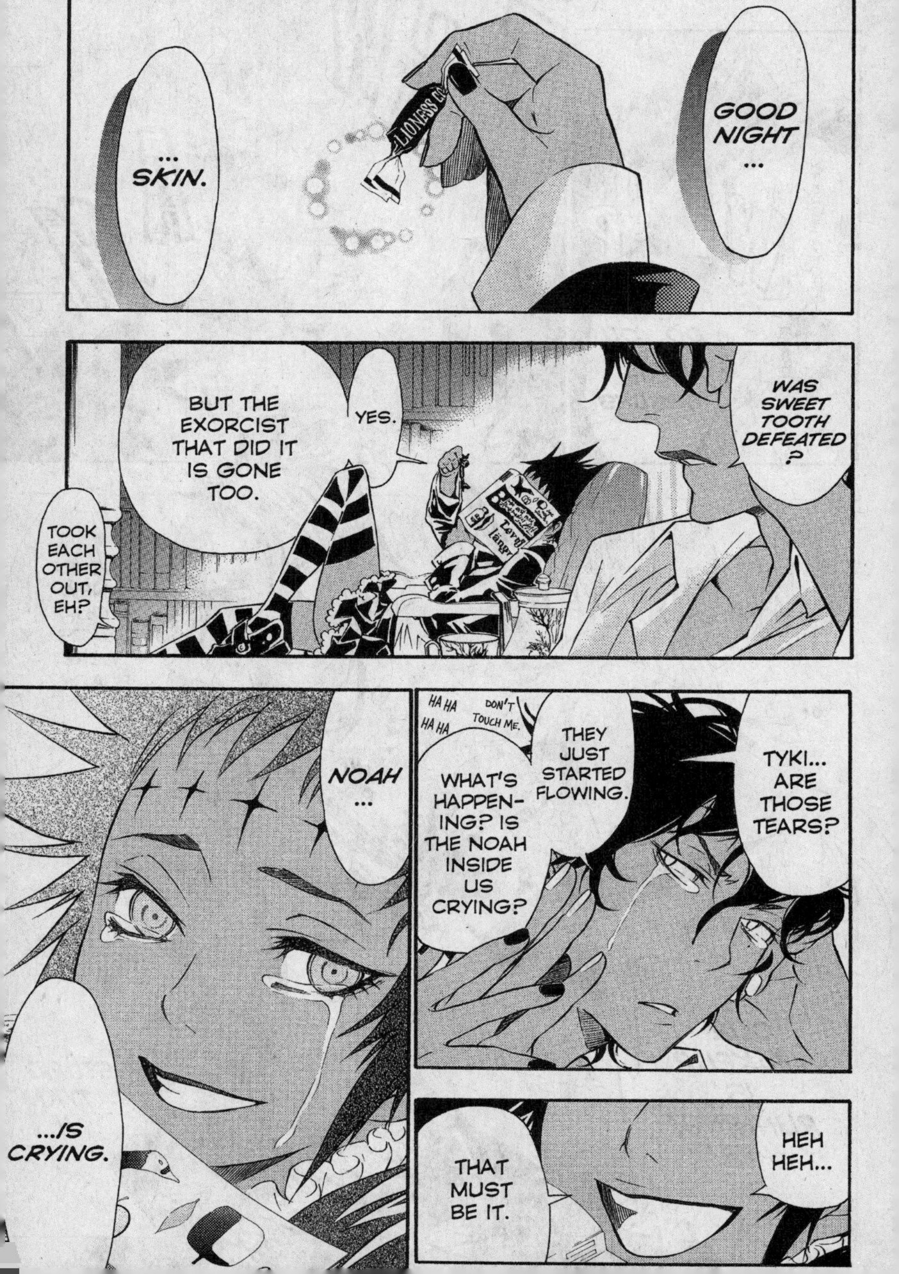
GOOD NIGHT ...
... SKIN.
WAS SWEET TOOTH DEFEATED?
YES.
BUT THE EXORCIST THAT DID IT IS GONE TOO.
TOOK EACH OTHER OUT, EH?
TYKI... ARE THOSE TEARS?
THEY JUST STARTED FLOWING.
DON'T TOUCH ME.
HA HA HA HA
WHAT'S HAPPENING? IS THE NOAH INSIDE US CRYING?
HEH HEH...
THAT MUST BE IT.
NOAH ...
...IS CRYING.

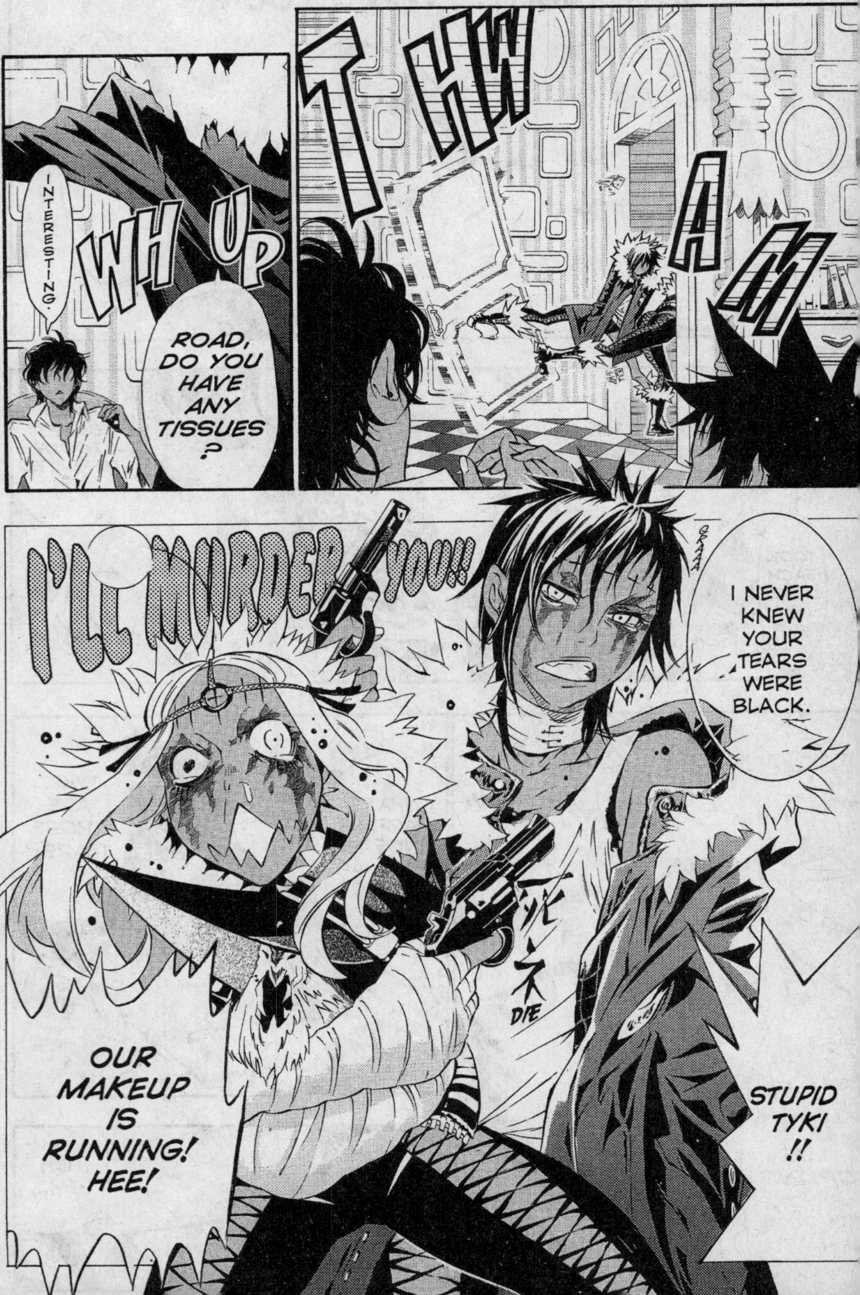
THWAM
WHUP
INTERESTING.
ROAD, DO YOU HAVE ANY TISSUES?
GRAAA
I NEVER KNEW YOUR TEARS WERE BLACK.
STUPID TYKI!!
DIE
I'LL MURDER YOU!!
OUR MAKEUP IS RUNNING! HEE!

THE 98TH NIGHT: TWIN'S ROOM

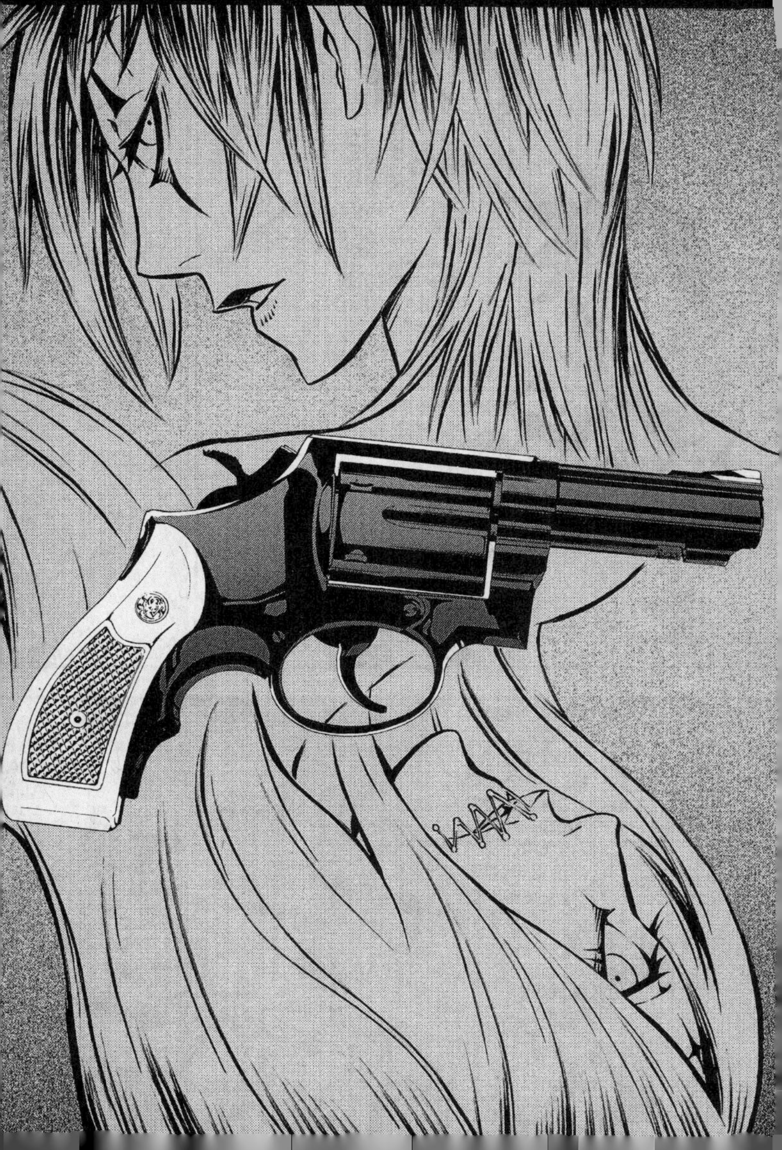

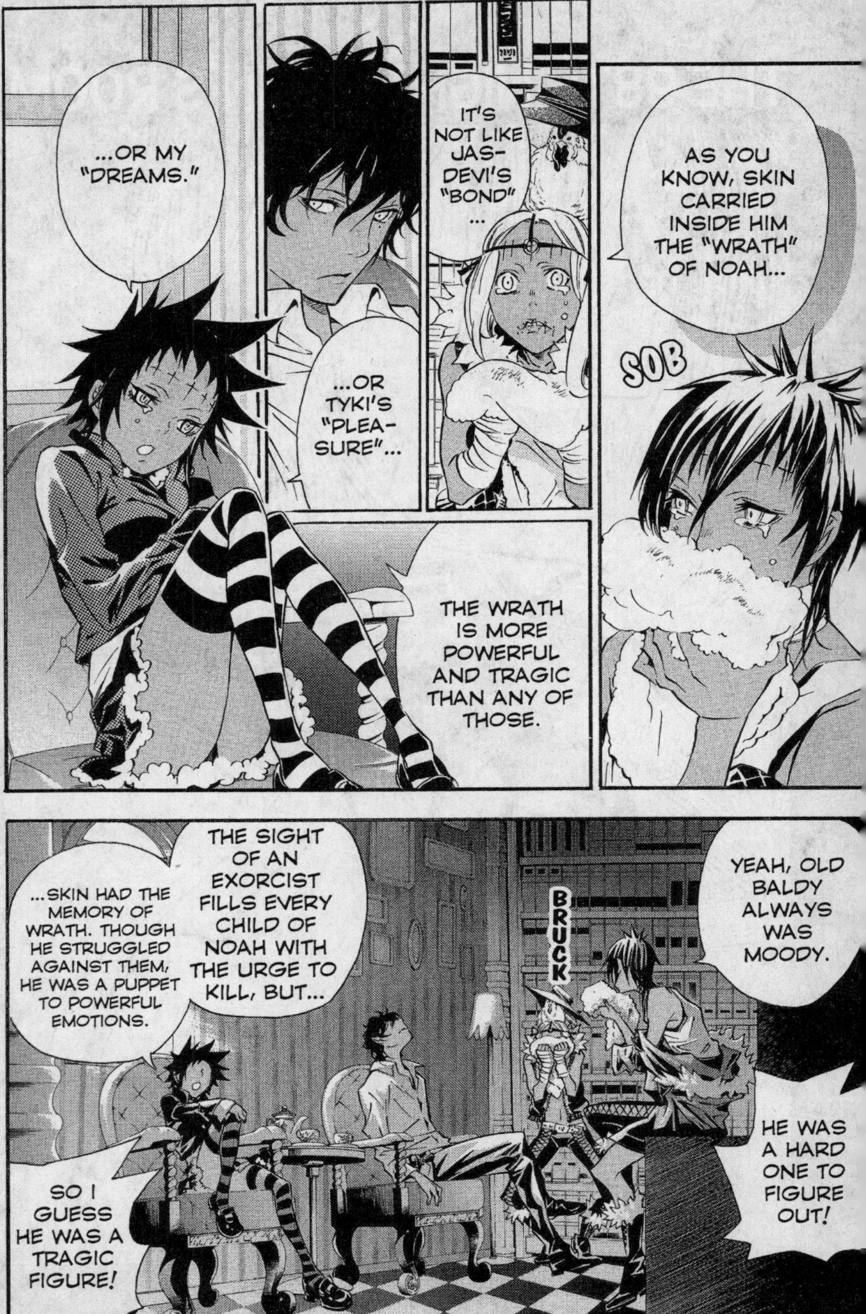
AS YOU KNOW, SKIN CARRIED INSIDE HIM THE "WRATH" OF NOAH...
SOB
IT'S NOT LIKE JAS-DEVI'S "BOND" ...
...OR TYKI'S "PLEA-SURE"...
...OR MY "DREAMS."
THE WRATH IS MORE POWERFUL AND TRAGIC THAN ANY OF THOSE.
YEAH, OLD BALDY ALWAYS WAS MOODY.
HE WAS A HARD ONE TO FIGURE OUT!
BRUCK
THE SIGHT OF AN EXORCIST FILLS EVERY CHILD OF NOAH WITH THE URGE TO KILL, BUT...
...SKIN HAD THE MEMORY OF WRATH. THOUGH HE STRUGGLED AGAINST THEM, HE WAS A PUPPET TO POWERFUL EMOTIONS.
SO I GUESS HE WAS A TRAGIC FIGURE!

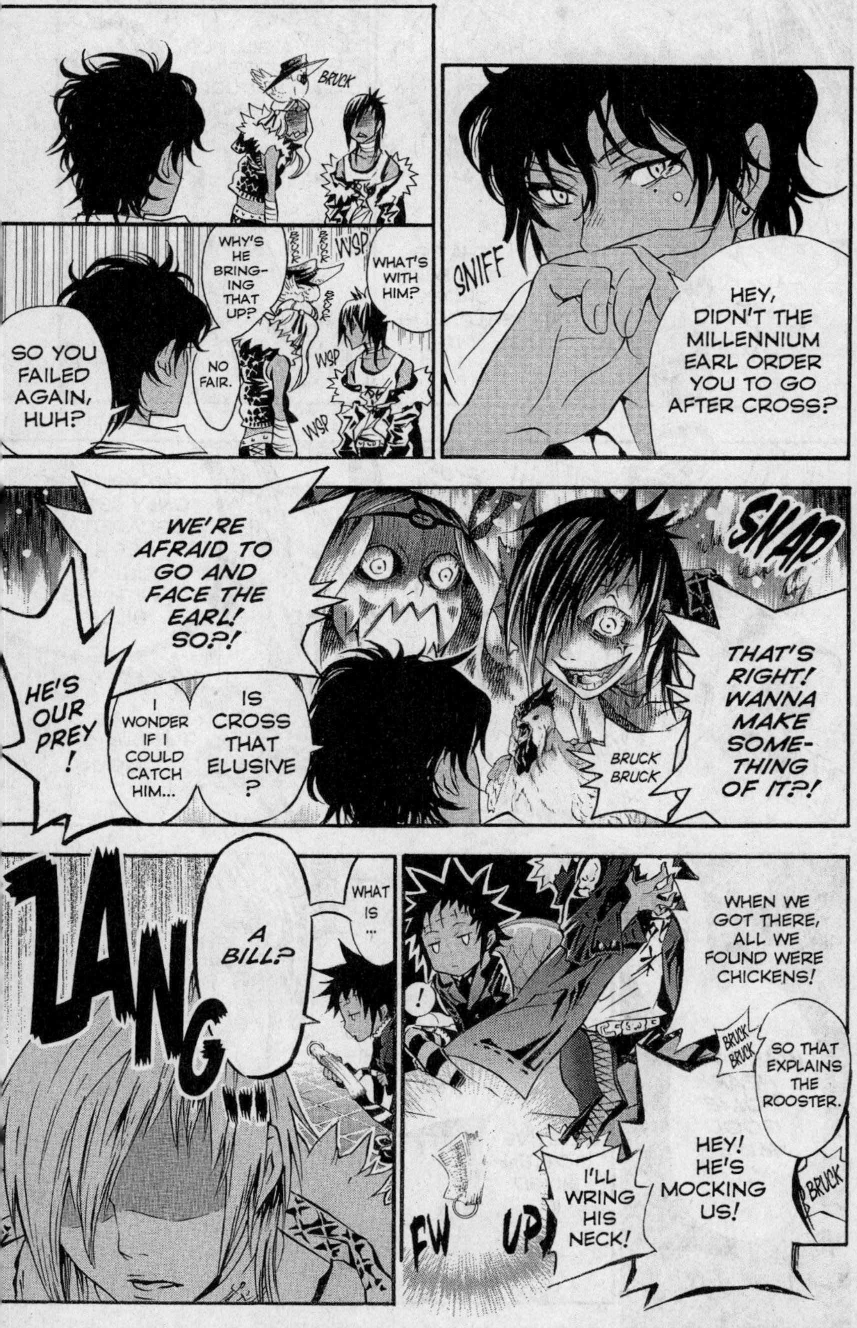
SNIFF
HEY, DIDN'T THE MILLENNIUM EARL ORDER YOU TO GO AFTER CROSS?
BRUCK
WHAT'S WITH HIM?
WSP
BRUCK
BRUCK
WHY'S HE BRINGING THAT UP?
WSP
WSP
NO FAIR.
SO YOU FAILED AGAIN, HUH?
SNAP
THAT'S RIGHT! WANNA MAKE SOMETHING OF IT?!
BRUCK BRUCK
WE'RE AFRAID TO GO AND FACE THE EARL! SO?!
IS CROSS THAT ELUSIVE?
I WONDER IF I COULD CATCH HIM...
HE'S OUR PREY!
WHEN WE GOT THERE, ALL WE FOUND WERE CHICKENS!
BRUCK BRUCK
SO THAT EXPLAINS THE ROOSTER.
HEY! HE'S MOCKING US!
BRUCK
I'LL WRING HIS NECK!
FWUP!
WHAT IS...
A BILL?
ZANG

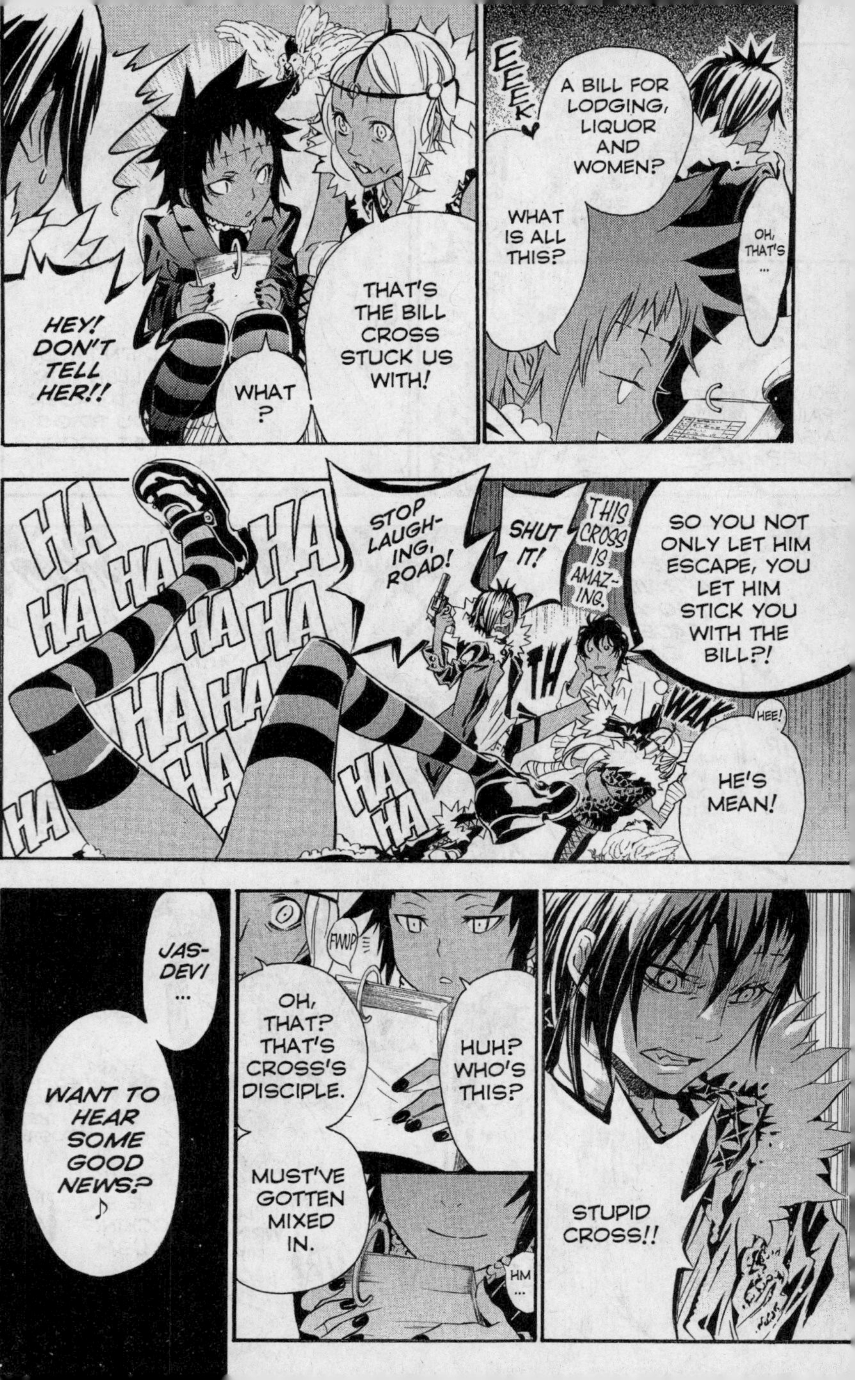
EEEK♥
A BILL FOR LODGING, LIQUOR AND WOMEN?
WHAT IS ALL THIS?
OH, THAT'S ...
THAT'S THE BILL CROSS STUCK US WITH!
WHAT ?
HEY! DON'T TELL HER!!
SO YOU NOT ONLY LET HIM ESCAPE, YOU LET HIM STICK YOU WITH THE BILL?!
THIS CROSS IS AMAZ-ING.
SHUT IT!
STOP LAUGH-ING, ROAD!
HA HA HA HA HA HA HA HA HA HA HA HA HA HA
TH
WAK
HEE!
HE'S MEAN!
STUPID CROSS!!
HUH? WHO'S THIS?
FWUP
OH, THAT? THAT'S CROSS'S DISCIPLE.
HM ...
MUST'VE GOTTEN MIXED IN.
JAS-DEVI ...
WANT TO HEAR SOME GOOD NEWS? ♪

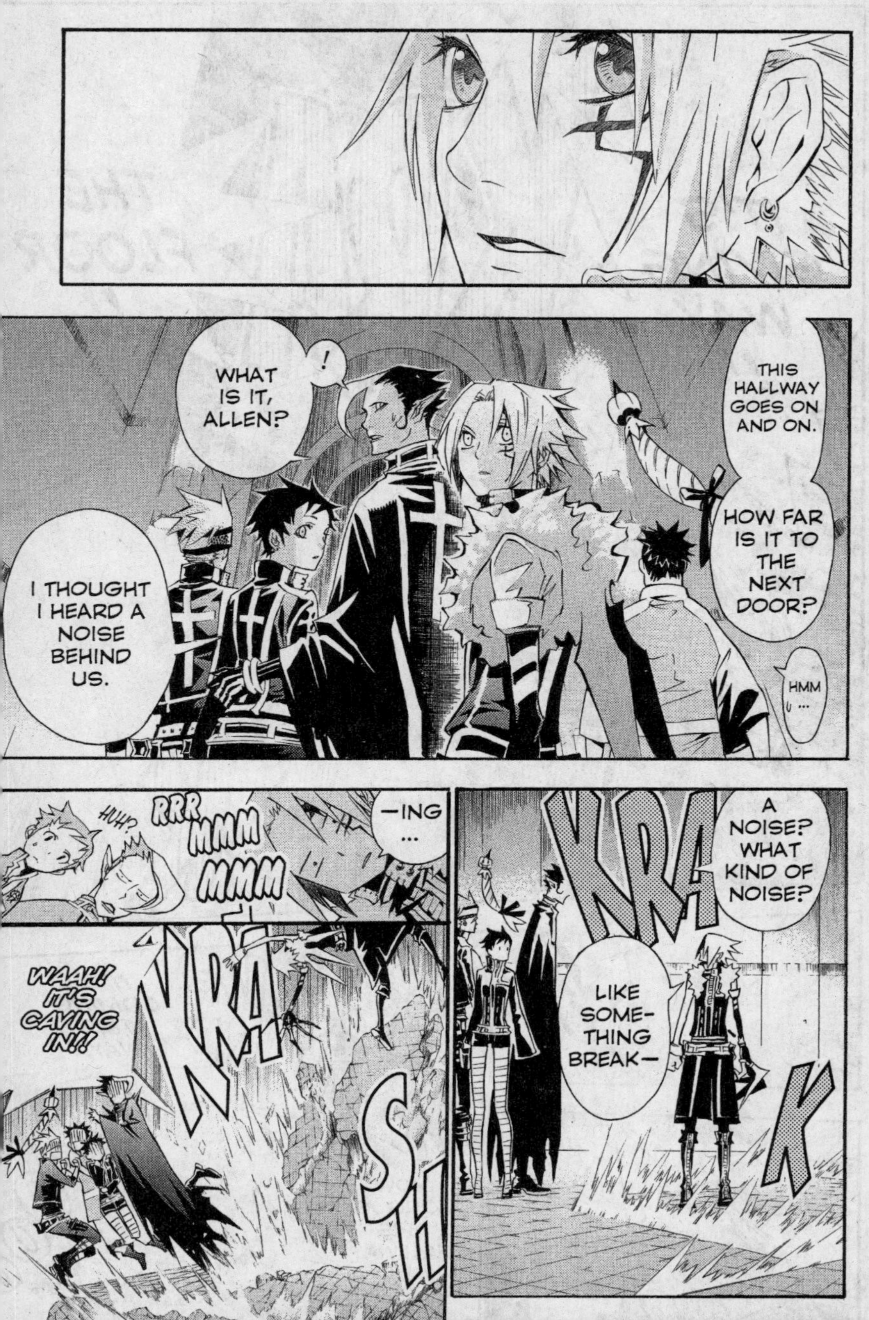
THIS HALLWAY GOES ON AND ON.
HOW FAR IS IT TO THE NEXT DOOR?
HMM...
!
WHAT IS IT, ALLEN?
I THOUGHT I HEARD A NOISE BEHIND US.
KRAK
A NOISE? WHAT KIND OF NOISE?
LIKE SOME-THING BREAK—
—ING ...
RRRMMMMMMM
HUH?
KRASH
WAAH! IT'S CAVING IN!!

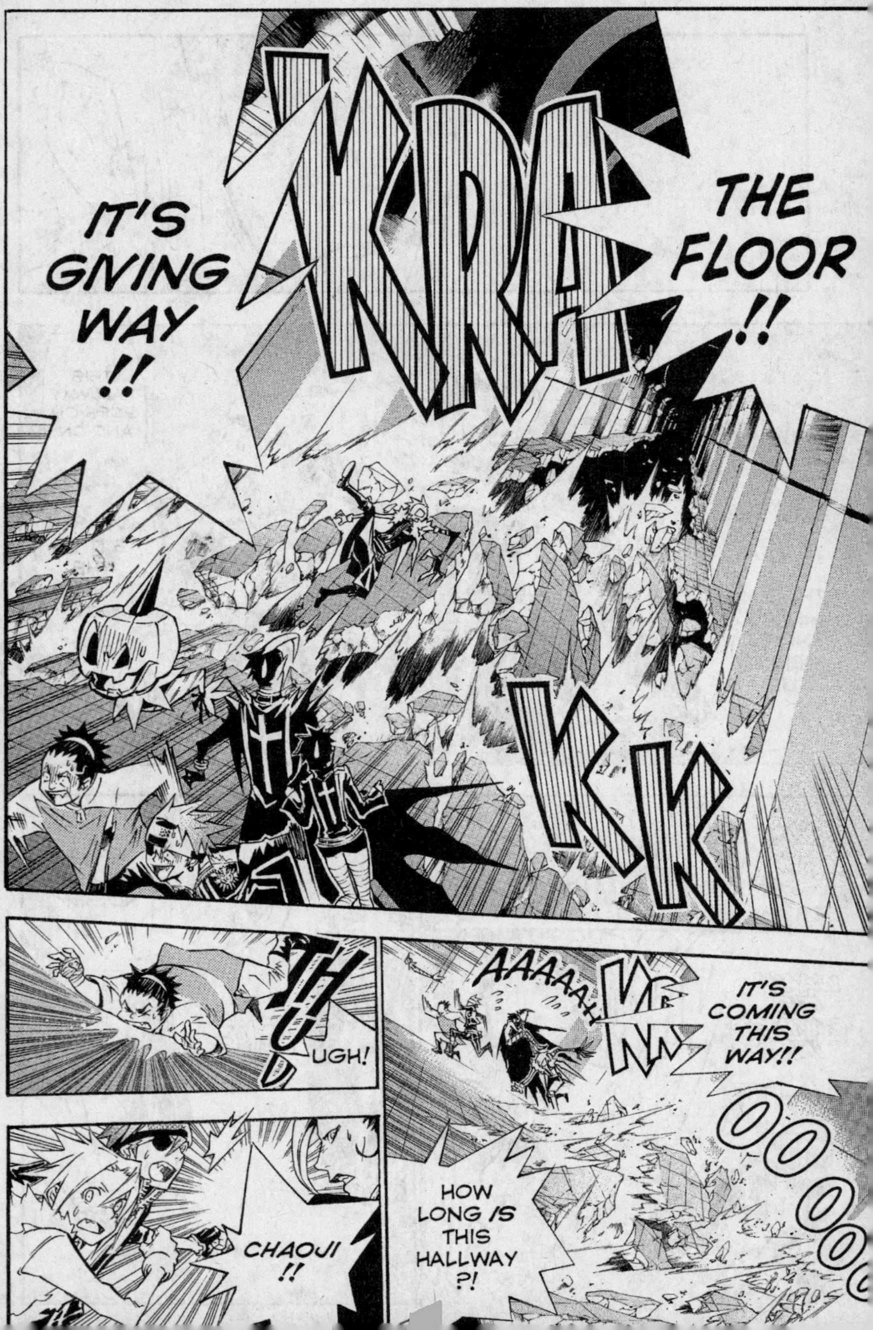
THE FLOOR!!
KRA
IT'S GIVING WAY!!
KK
AAAAAAH
IT'S COMING THIS WAY!!
OOOOO
HOW LONG IS THIS HALLWAY?!
TH
UGH!
CHAOJI!!

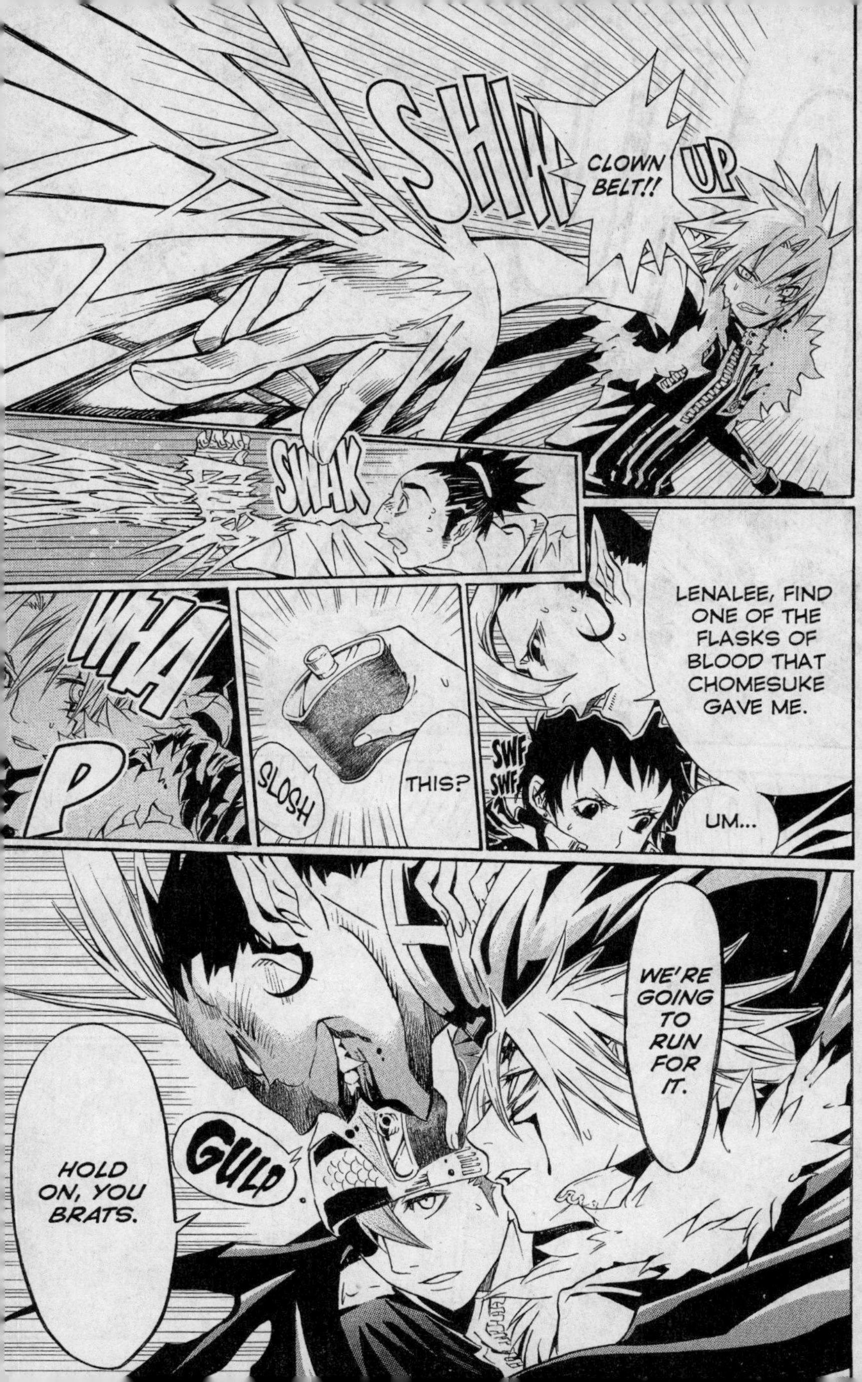
SHIN
UP
CLOWN BELT!!
SWAK
LENALEE, FIND ONE OF THE FLASKS OF BLOOD THAT CHOMESUKE GAVE ME.
SWF SWF
UM...
THIS?
SLOSH
WHAP
WE'RE GOING TO RUN FOR IT.
GULP
HOLD ON, YOU BRATS.

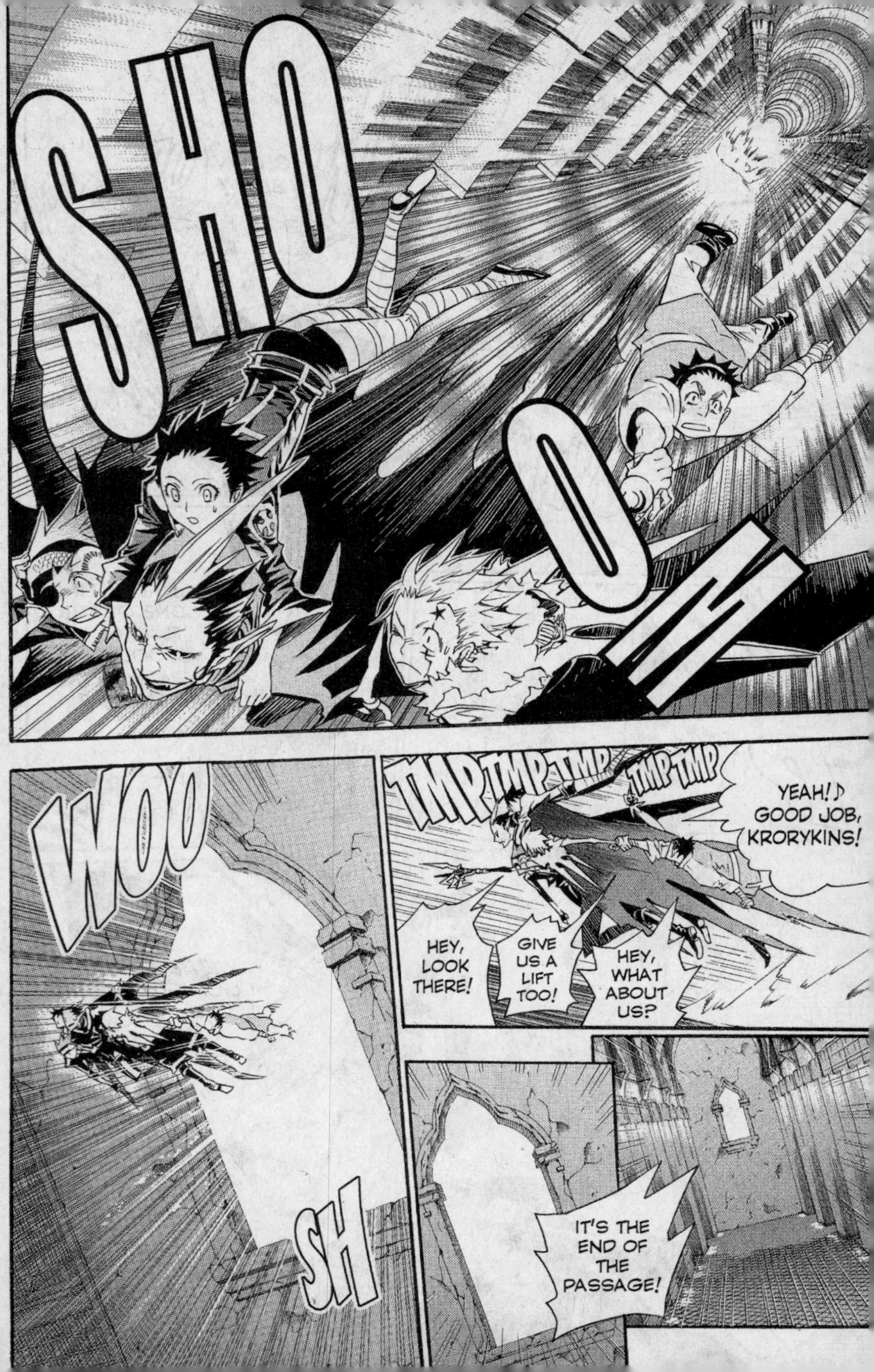
SHO
OM
YEAH! ♪ GOOD JOB, KRORYKINS!
TMP TMP TMP TMP TMP
HEY, WHAT ABOUT US?
GIVE US A LIFT TOO!
HEY, LOOK THERE!
IT'S THE END OF THE PASSAGE!
WOO
SH

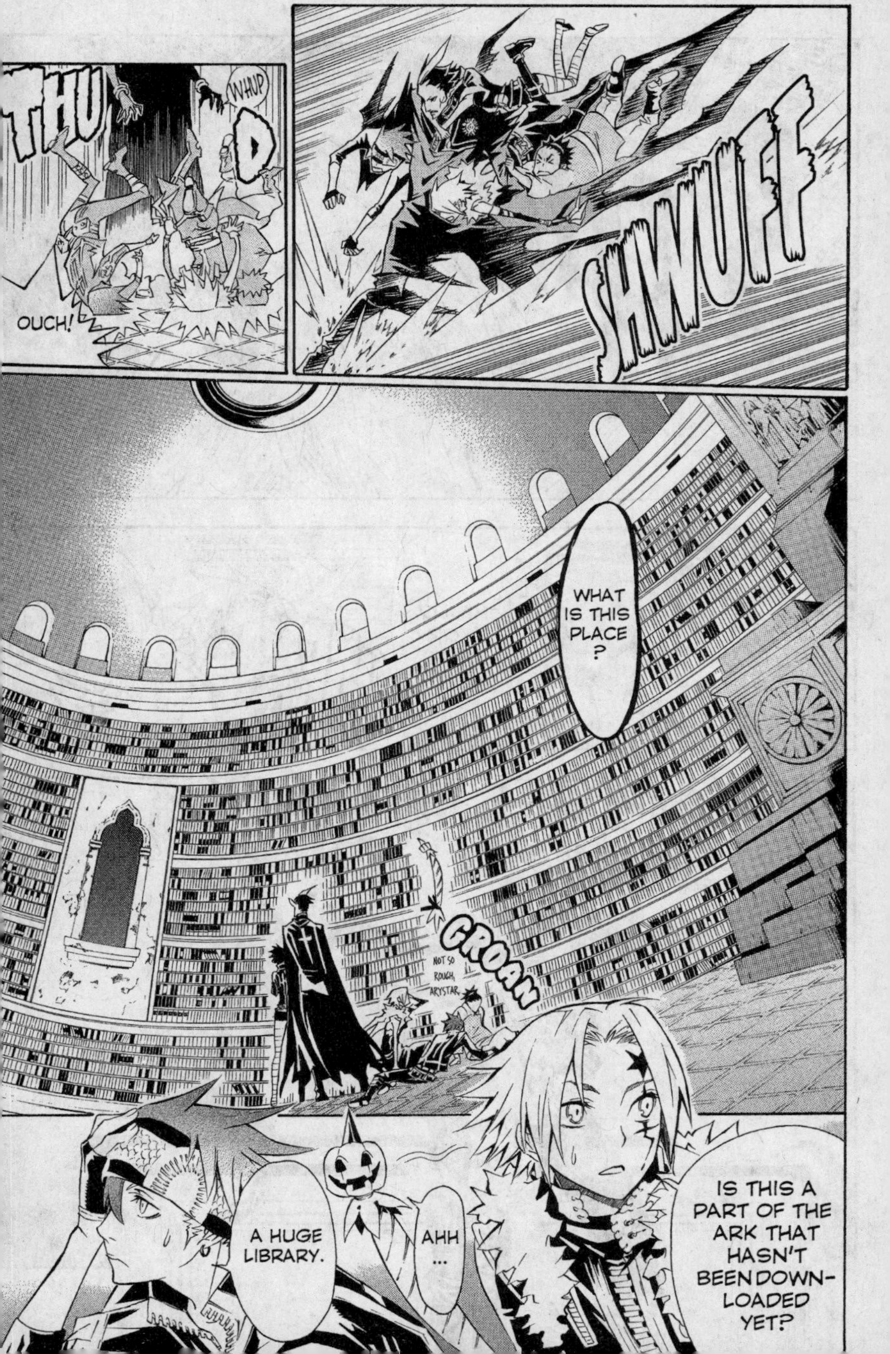
SHWUFF
THUD
WHUP
OUCH!
WHAT IS THIS PLACE?
GROAN
NOT SO ROUGH, ARYSTAR.
IS THIS A PART OF THE ARK THAT HASN'T BEEN DOWN-LOADED YET?
AHH ...
A HUGE LIBRARY.

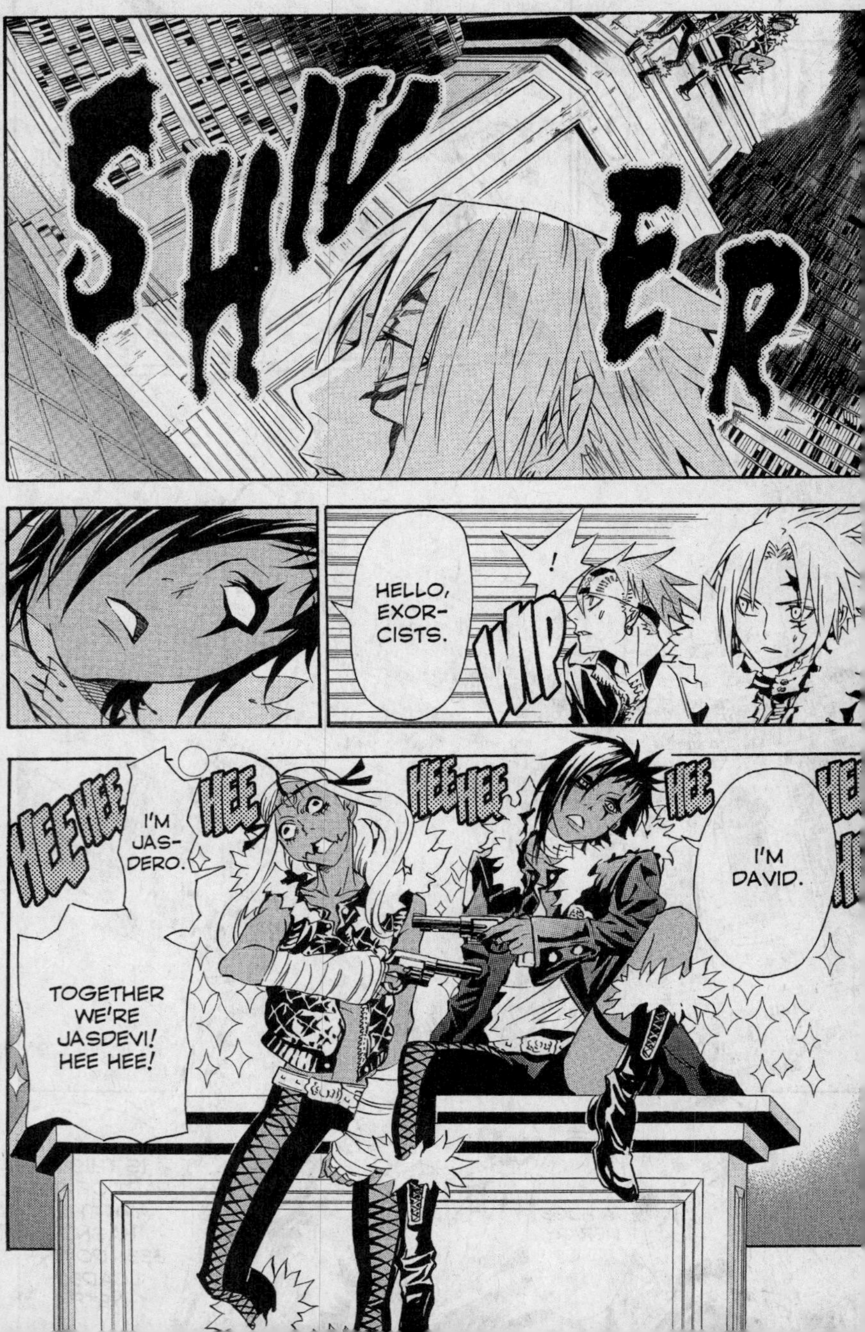
SHIVER
!
HELLO, EXORCISTS.
I'M DAVID.
HEE
HEE HEE
HEE
I'M JASDERO.
HEE HEE
TOGETHER WE'RE JASDEVI! HEE HEE!

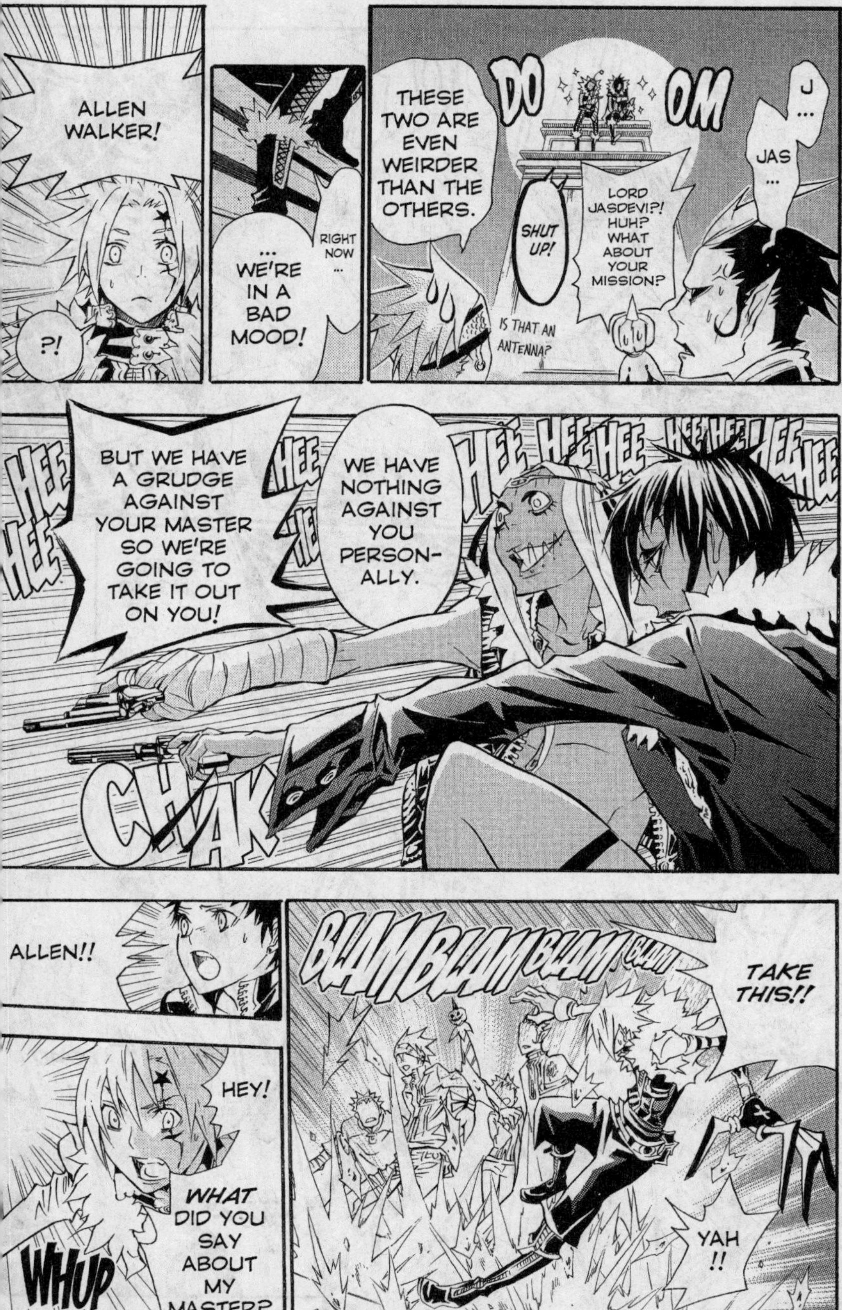
J ... JAS ...
LORD JASDEVI?! HUH? WHAT ABOUT YOUR MISSION?
SHUT UP!
DO OM
THESE TWO ARE EVEN WEIRDER THAN THE OTHERS.
IS THAT AN ANTENNA?
RIGHT NOW ...
... WE'RE IN A BAD MOOD!
ALLEN WALKER!
?!
HEE HEE HEE HEE HEE HEE HEE
WE HAVE NOTHING AGAINST YOU PERSONALLY.
BUT WE HAVE A GRUDGE AGAINST YOUR MASTER SO WE'RE GOING TO TAKE IT OUT ON YOU!
HEE HEE
CHAK
BLAM BLAM BLAM BLAM
TAKE THIS!!
YAH !!
ALLEN!!
HEY!
WHAT DID YOU SAY ABOUT MY MASTER?
WHUP

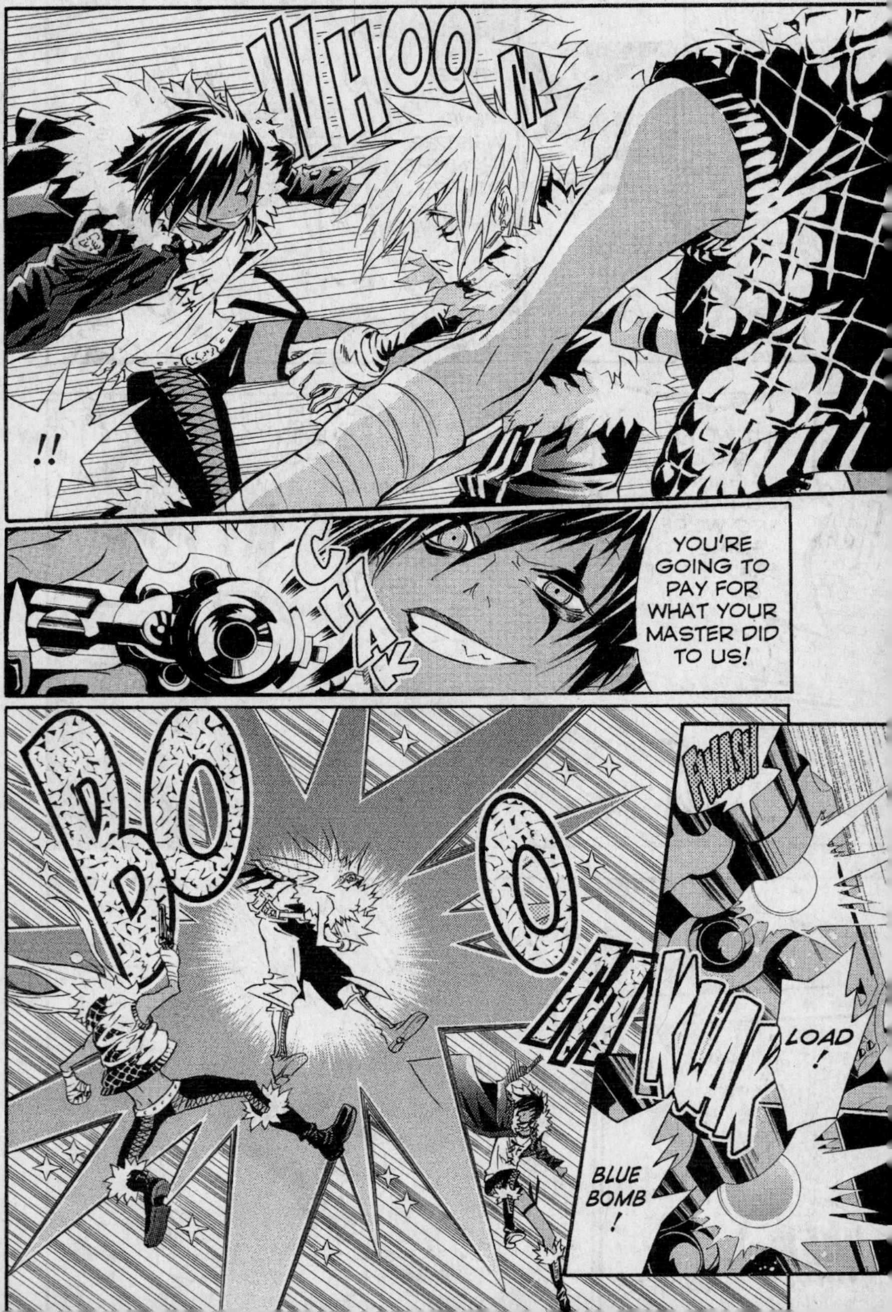
WHOOM
!!
CHAK
YOU'RE GOING TO PAY FOR WHAT YOUR MASTER DID TO US!
FWASH
LOAD!
BLUE BOMB!
BOOM

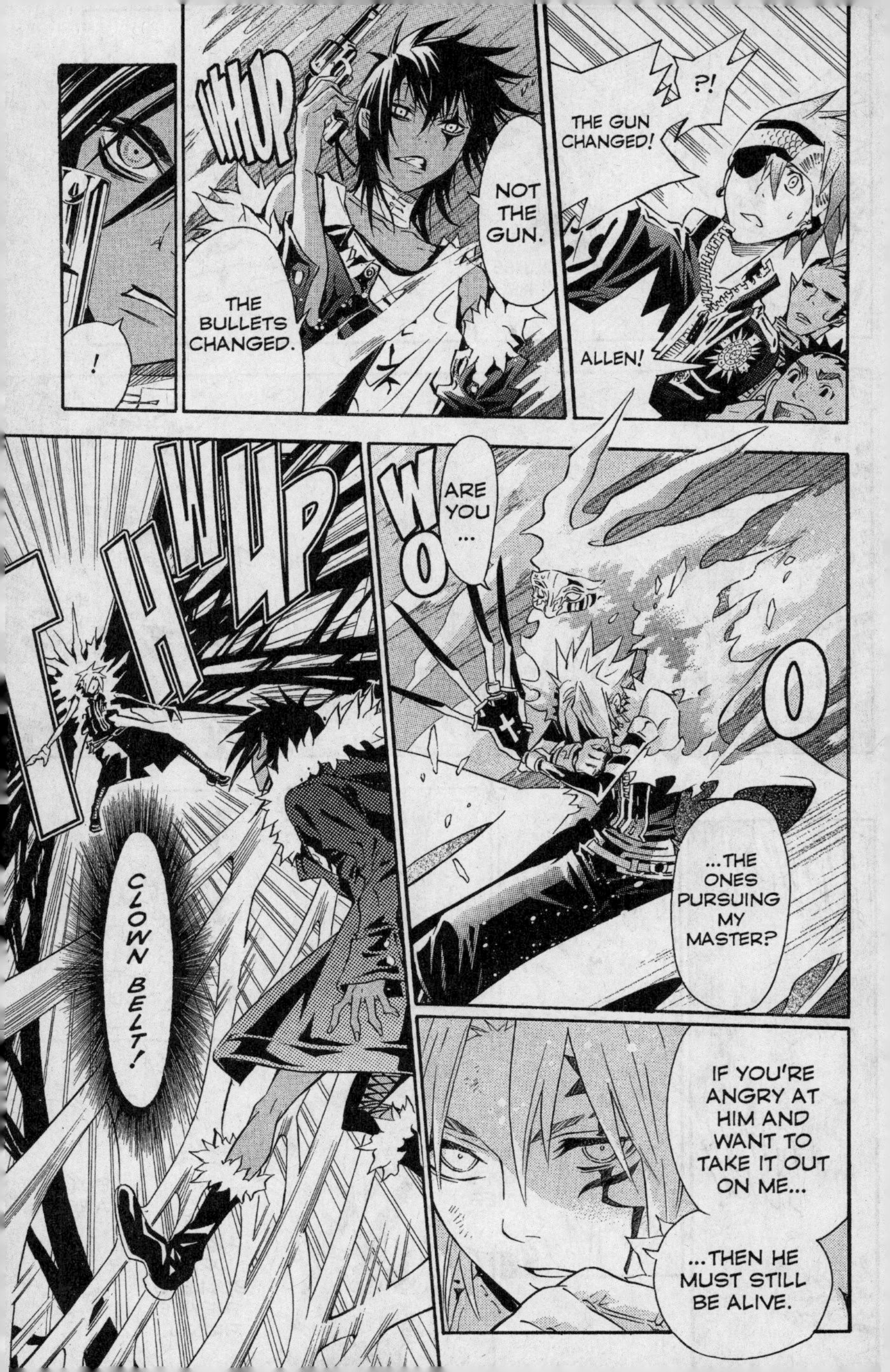

?!
THE GUN CHANGED!
ALLEN!
WHUP
NOT THE GUN.
THE BULLETS CHANGED.
!
WOO
ARE YOU ...
O
...THE ONES PURSUING MY MASTER?
IF YOU'RE ANGRY AT HIM AND WANT TO TAKE IT OUT ON ME...
...THEN HE MUST STILL BE ALIVE.
WHWUP
CLOWN BELT!

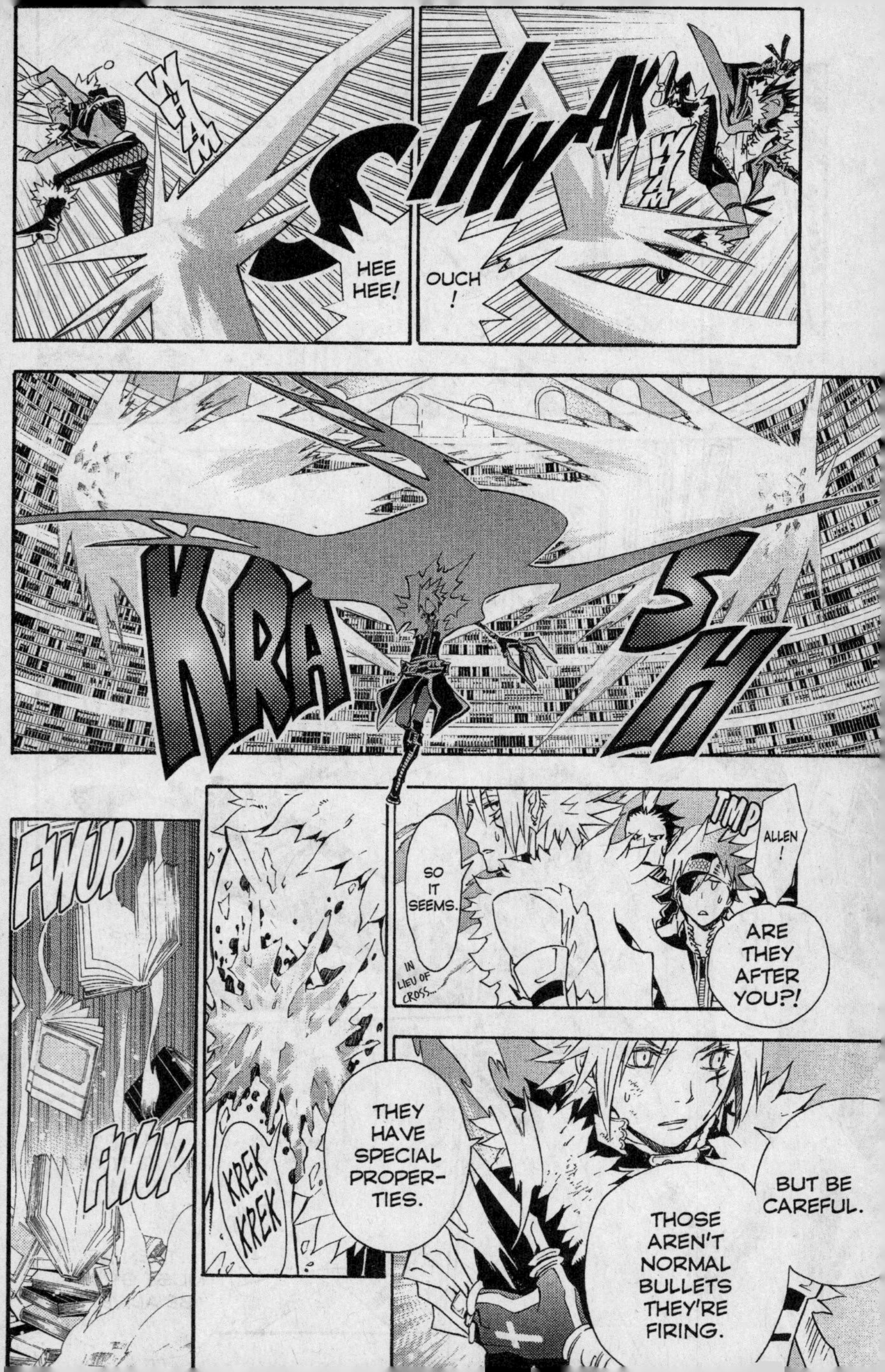
SCHWAK
WHAM
OUCH!
WHAM
HEE HEE!
KRASH
TMP
ALLEN!
ARE THEY AFTER YOU?!
SO IT SEEMS.
IN LIEU OF CROSS...
BUT BE CAREFUL.
THOSE AREN'T NORMAL BULLETS THEY'RE FIRING.
THEY HAVE SPECIAL PROPERTIES.
KREK KREK
FWUP
FWUP

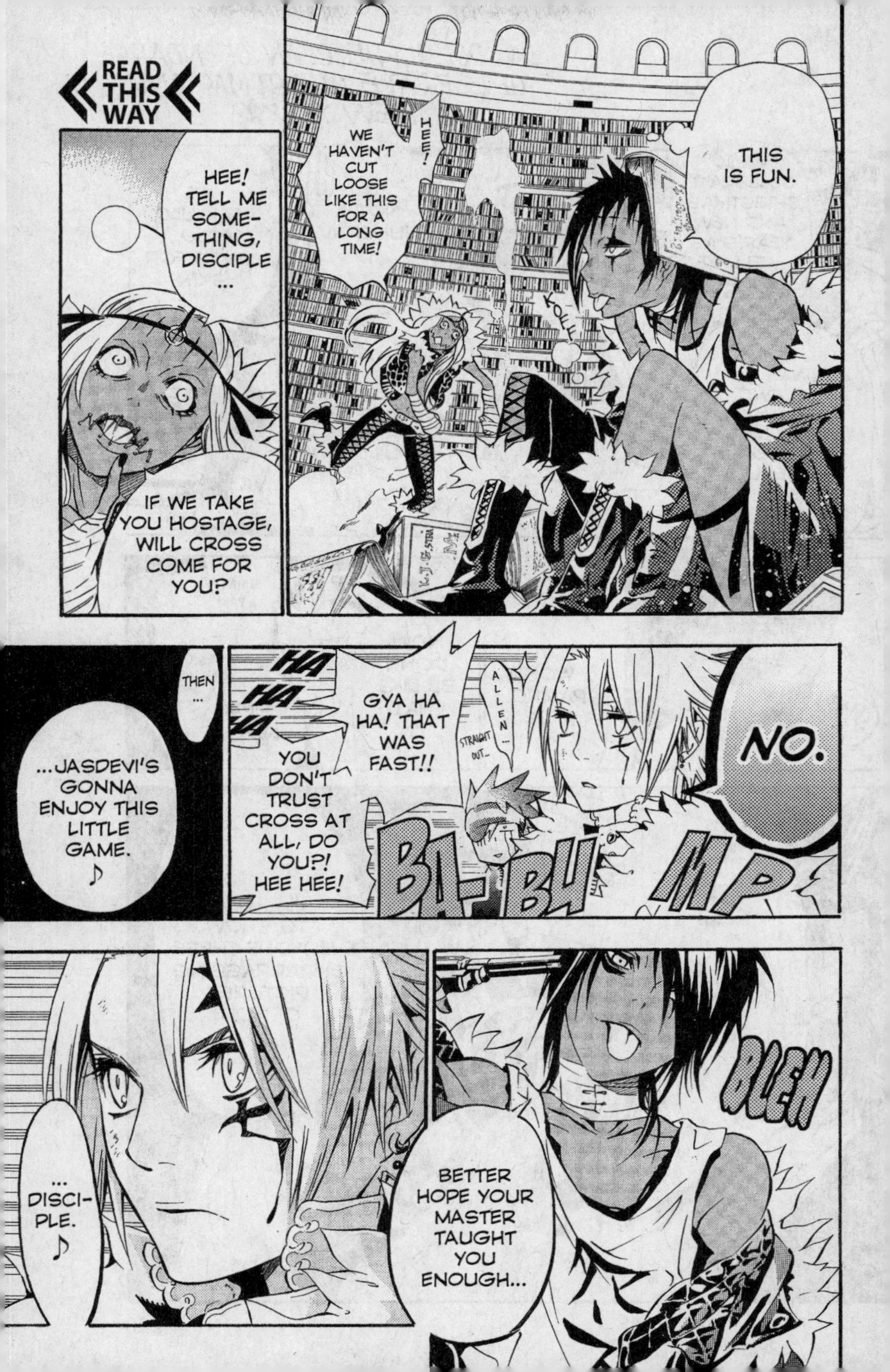
READ THIS WAY
THIS IS FUN.
HEE!
WE HAVEN'T CUT LOOSE LIKE THIS FOR A LONG TIME!
HEE! TELL ME SOME-THING, DISCIPLE ...
IF WE TAKE YOU HOSTAGE, WILL CROSS COME FOR YOU?
NO.
BA-BUMP
ALLEN...
STRAIGHT OUT...
GYA HA HA! THAT WAS FAST!!
HA HA HA
YOU DON'T TRUST CROSS AT ALL, DO YOU?! HEE HEE!
THEN...
...JASDEVI'S GONNA ENJOY THIS LITTLE GAME. ♪
BLEH
BETTER HOPE YOUR MASTER TAUGHT YOU ENOUGH...
... DISCI-PLE. ♪

Q: DOES THE CLAN OF NOAH CELEBRATE CHRISTMAS AND NEW YEAR'S?

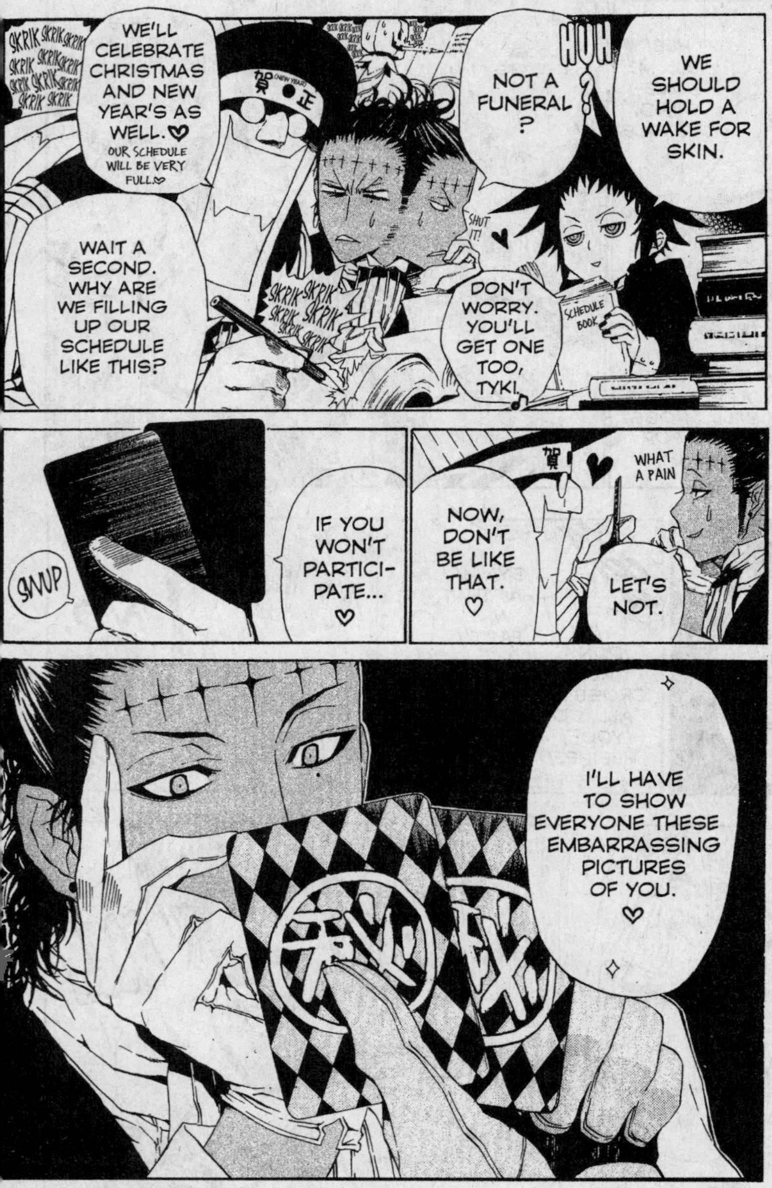
WE SHOULD HOLD A WAKE FOR SKIN.
HUH
NOT A FUNERAL?
WE'LL CELEBRATE CHRISTMAS AND NEW YEAR'S AS WELL. ♡
OUR SCHEDULE WILL BE VERY FULL ♡
(NEW YEAR)
SKRIK SKRIK SKRIK SKRIK SKRIK SKRIK SKRIK SKRIK SKRIK SKRIK
DON'T WORRY. YOU'LL GET ONE TOO, TYKI. ♪
SHUT IT!
SCHEDULE BOOK
SKRIK SKRIK SKRIK SKRIK SKRIK SKRIK
WAIT A SECOND. WHY ARE WE FILLING UP OUR SCHEDULE LIKE THIS?
WHAT A PAIN
NOW, DON'T BE LIKE THAT. ♡
LET'S NOT.
IF YOU WON'T PARTICI-PATE... ♡
SWUP
I'LL HAVE TO SHOW EVERYONE THESE EMBARRASSING PICTURES OF YOU. ♡

THE 99TH NIGHT: DEBT CRISIS

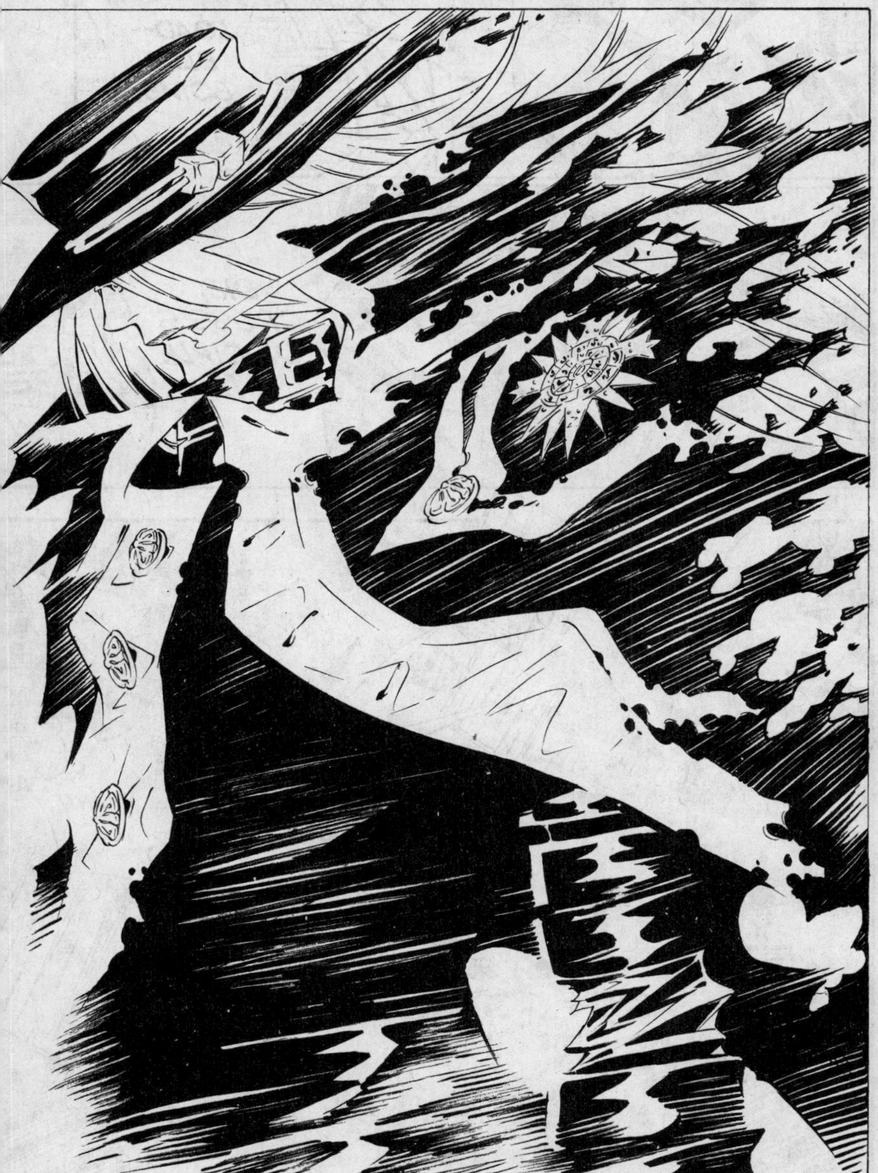

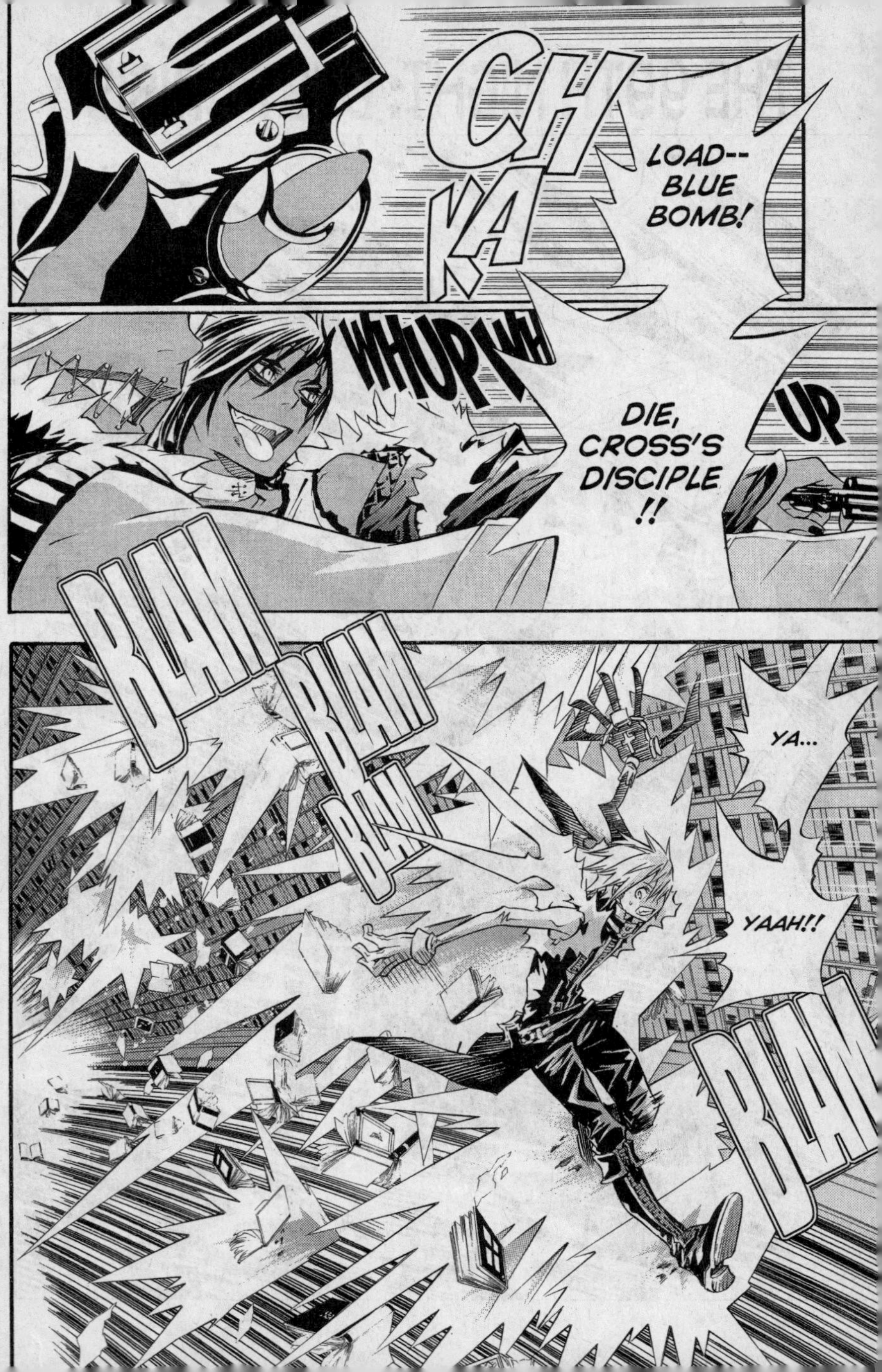
CHAKA
LOAD-- BLUE BOMB!
DIE, CROSS'S DISCIPLE!!
UP
WHUPWH
YA...
YAAH!!
BLAM
BLAM
BLAM
BLAM

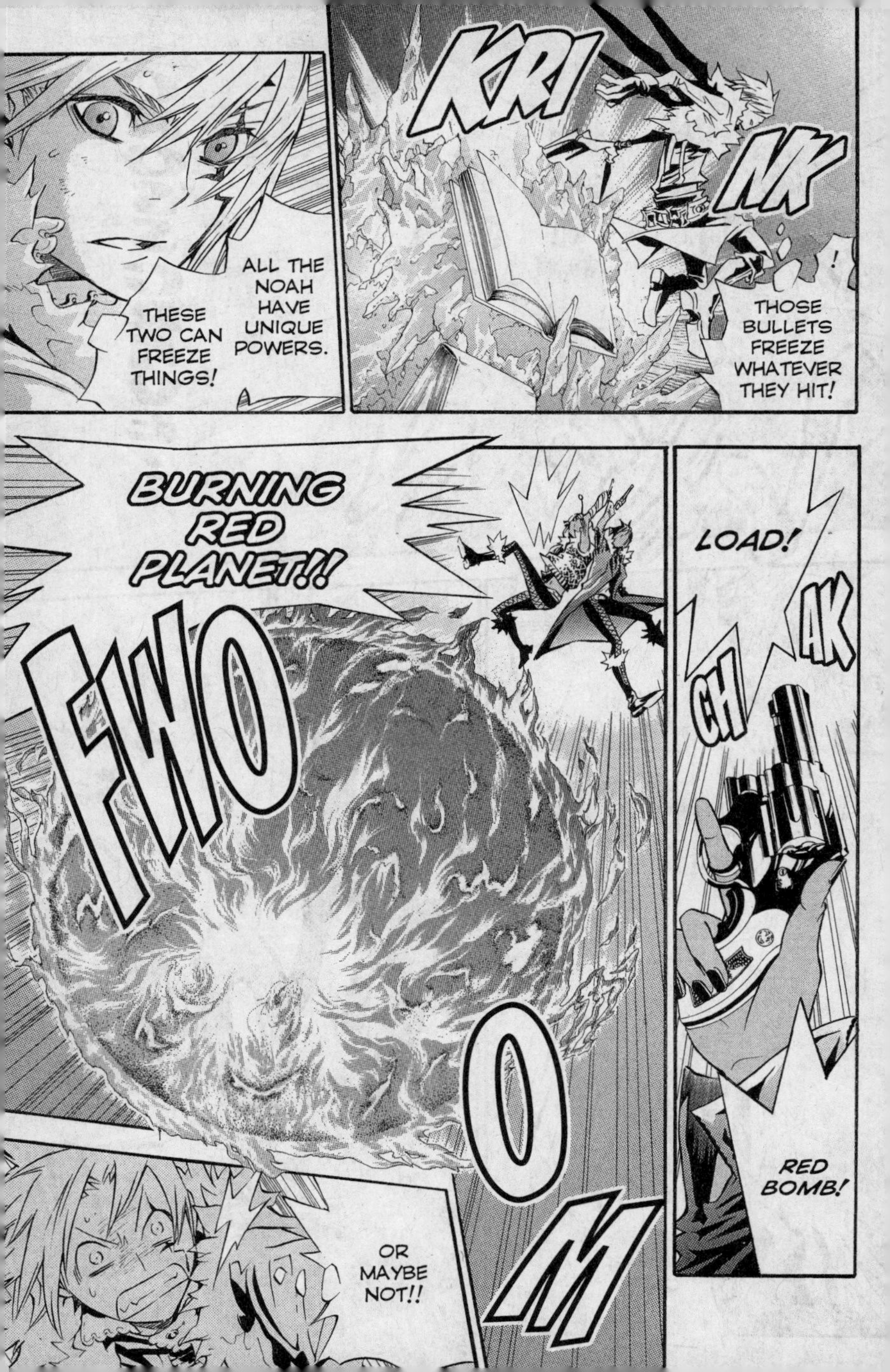
KRINK
THOSE BULLETS FREEZE WHATEVER THEY HIT!
!
ALL THE NOAH HAVE UNIQUE POWERS.
THESE TWO CAN FREEZE THINGS!
LOAD!
CHAK
RED BOMB!
BURNING RED PLANET!!
FWOOM
OR MAYBE NOT!!

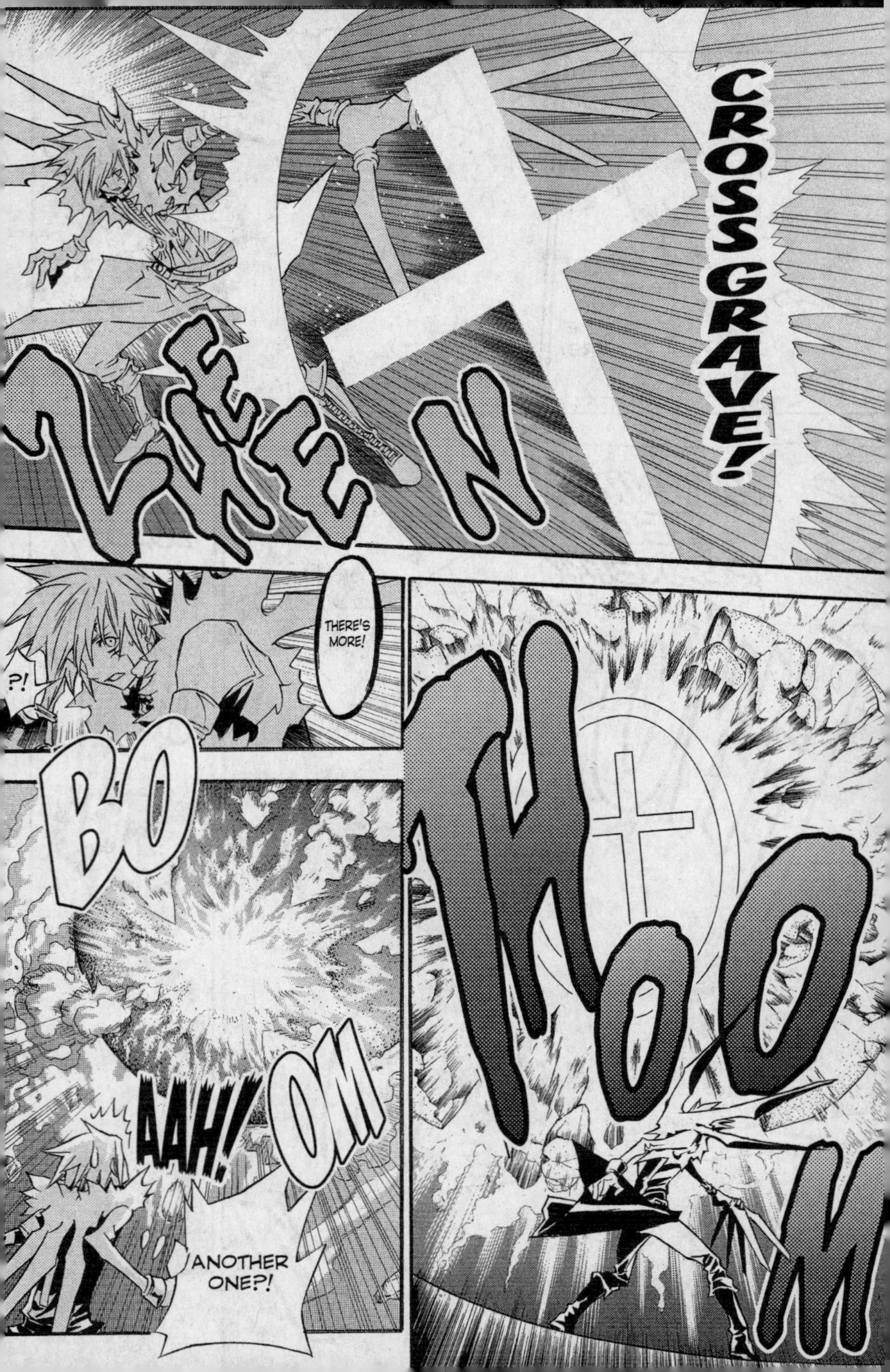

CROSS GRAVE!
ZHEN
THERE'S MORE!
?!
BOOM
AAH!
ANOTHER ONE?!

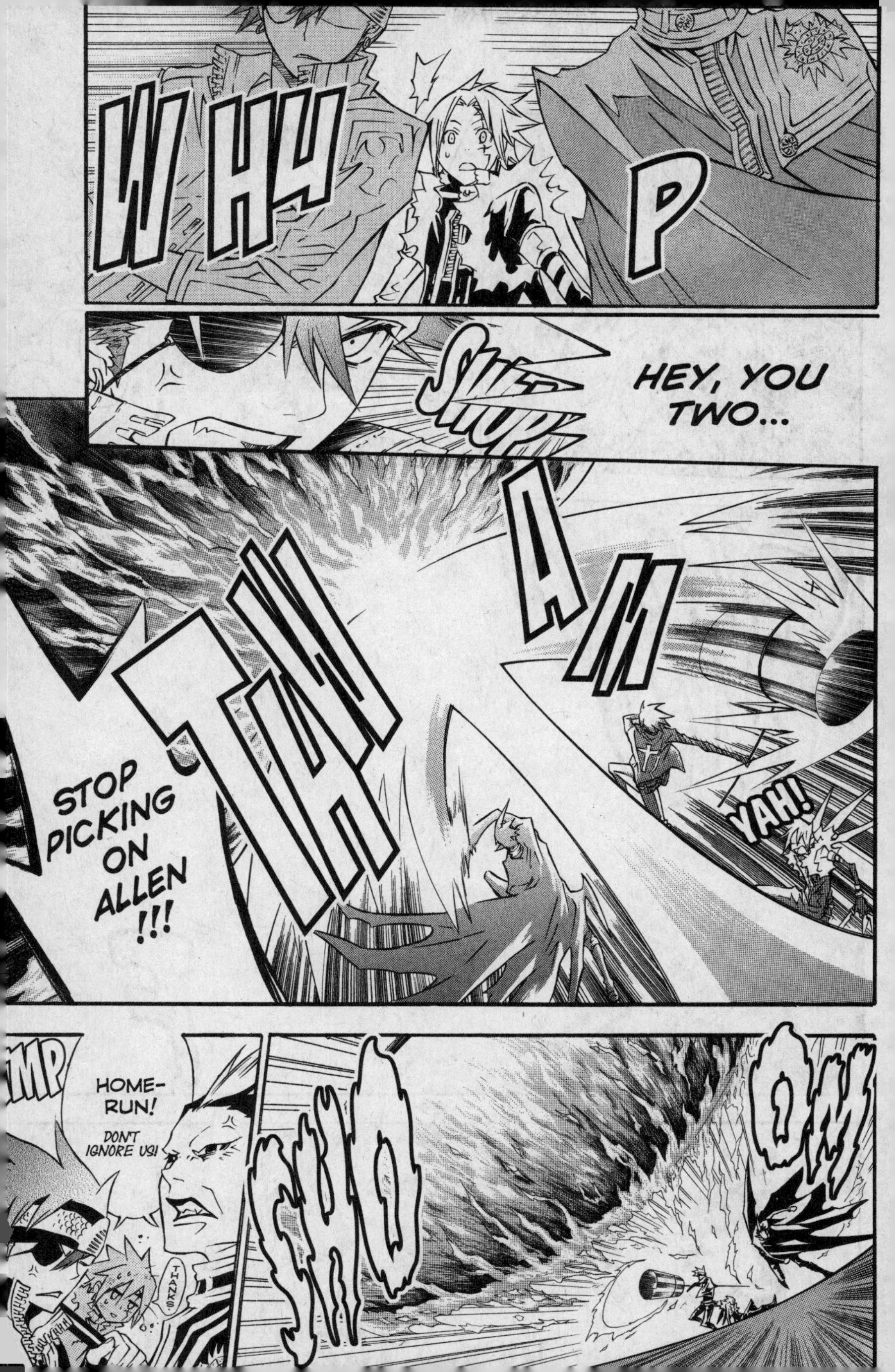
WHUP
HEY, YOU TWO...
THWAM
YAH!
STOP PICKING ON ALLEN!!!
HOME-RUN!
DON'T IGNORE US!
THANKS.

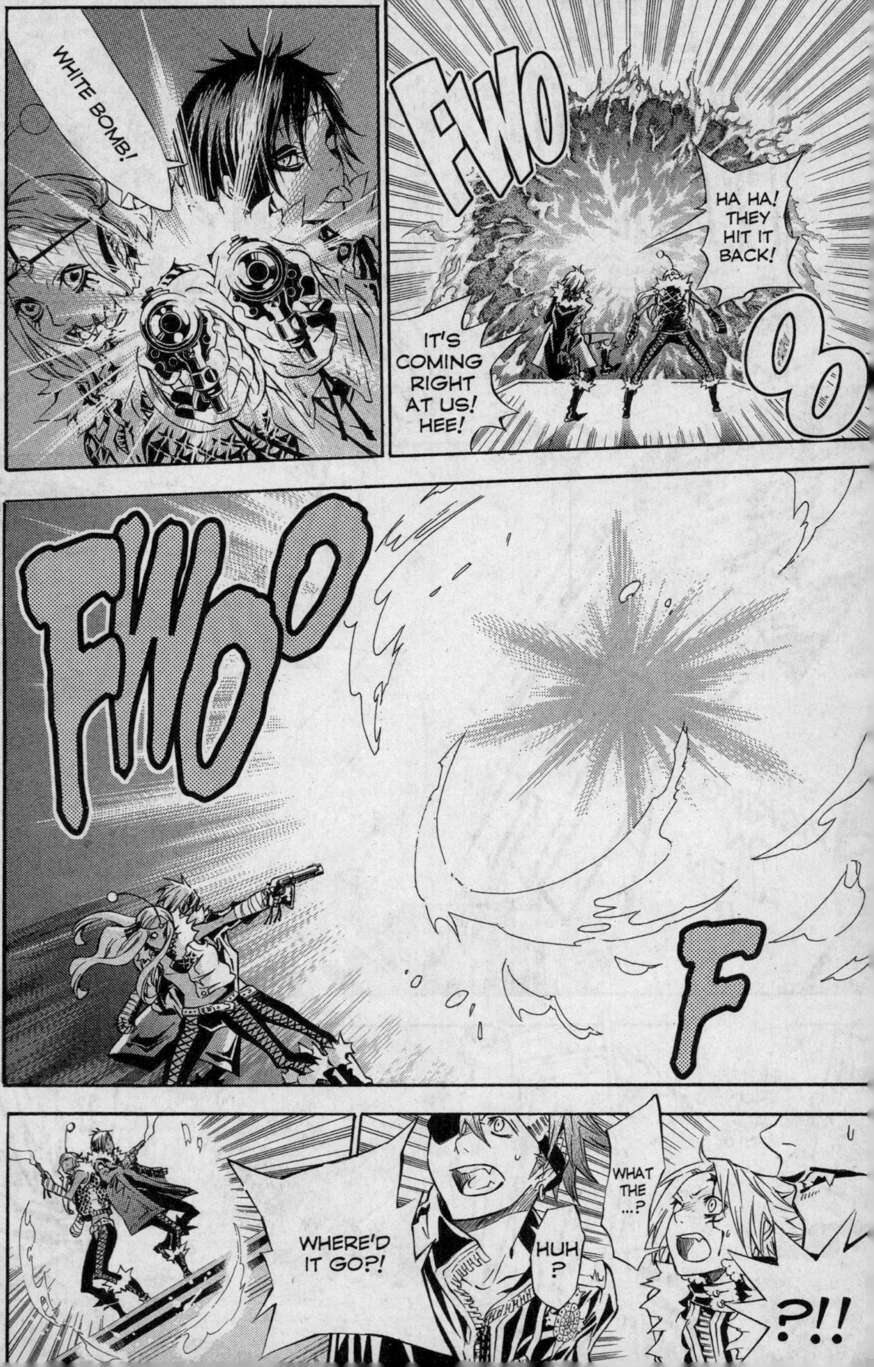

FWO
HA HA! THEY HIT IT BACK!
IT'S COMING RIGHT AT US! HEE!
OO
WHITE BOMB!
FWOO
F
WHAT THE ...?
?!!
HUH?
WHERE'D IT GO?!

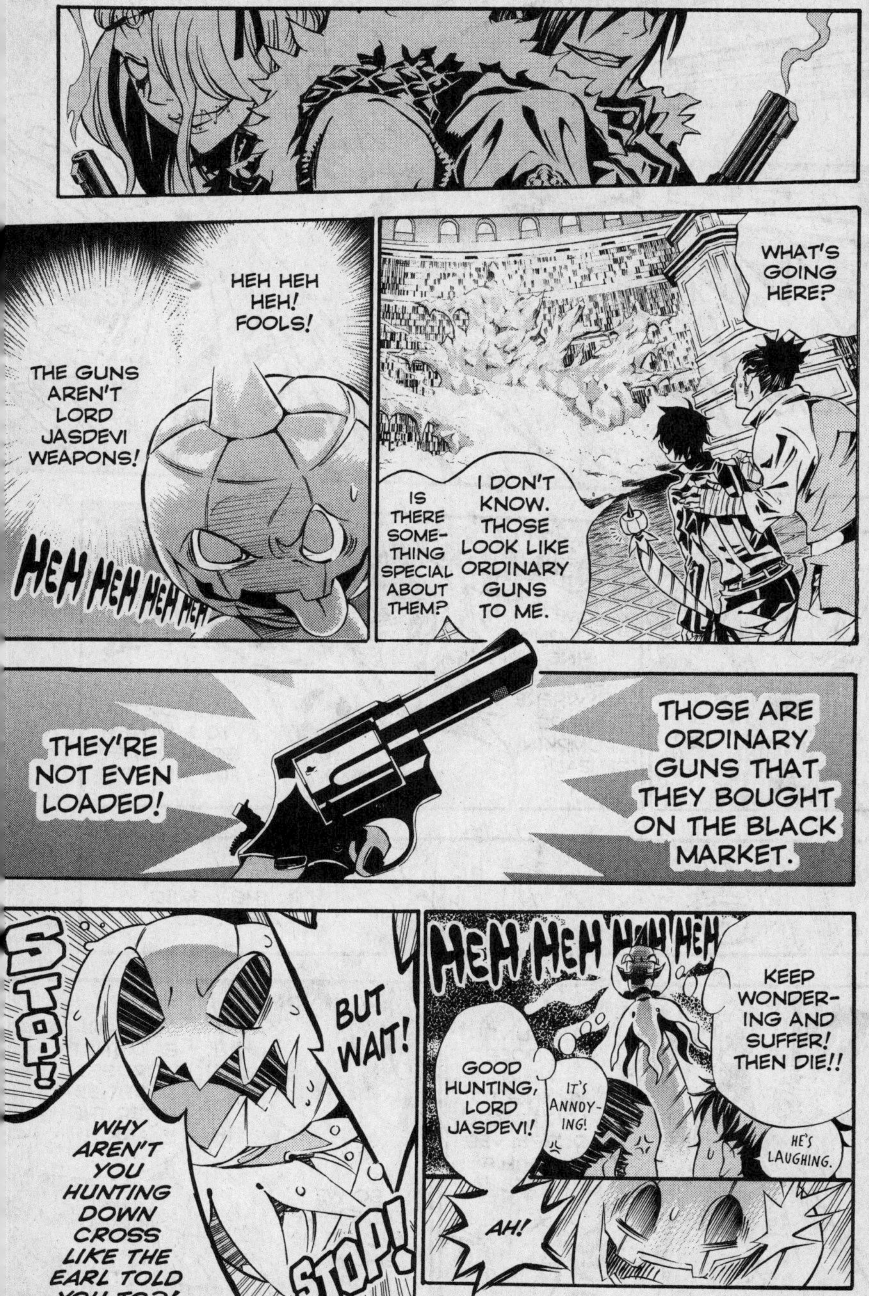
WHAT'S GOING HERE?
I DON'T KNOW. THOSE LOOK LIKE ORDINARY GUNS TO ME.
IS THERE SOMETHING SPECIAL ABOUT THEM?
HEH HEH HEH! FOOLS!
THE GUNS AREN'T LORD JASDEVI WEAPONS!
HEH HEH HEH HEH
THOSE ARE ORDINARY GUNS THAT THEY BOUGHT ON THE BLACK MARKET.
THEY'RE NOT EVEN LOADED!
HEH HEH HEH HEH
KEEP WONDERING AND SUFFER! THEN DIE!!
HE'S LAUGHING.
IT'S ANNOYING!
GOOD HUNTING, LORD JASDEVI!
AH!
BUT WAIT!
STOP!
WHY AREN'T YOU HUNTING DOWN CROSS LIKE THE EARL TOLD YOU TO?!
STOP!

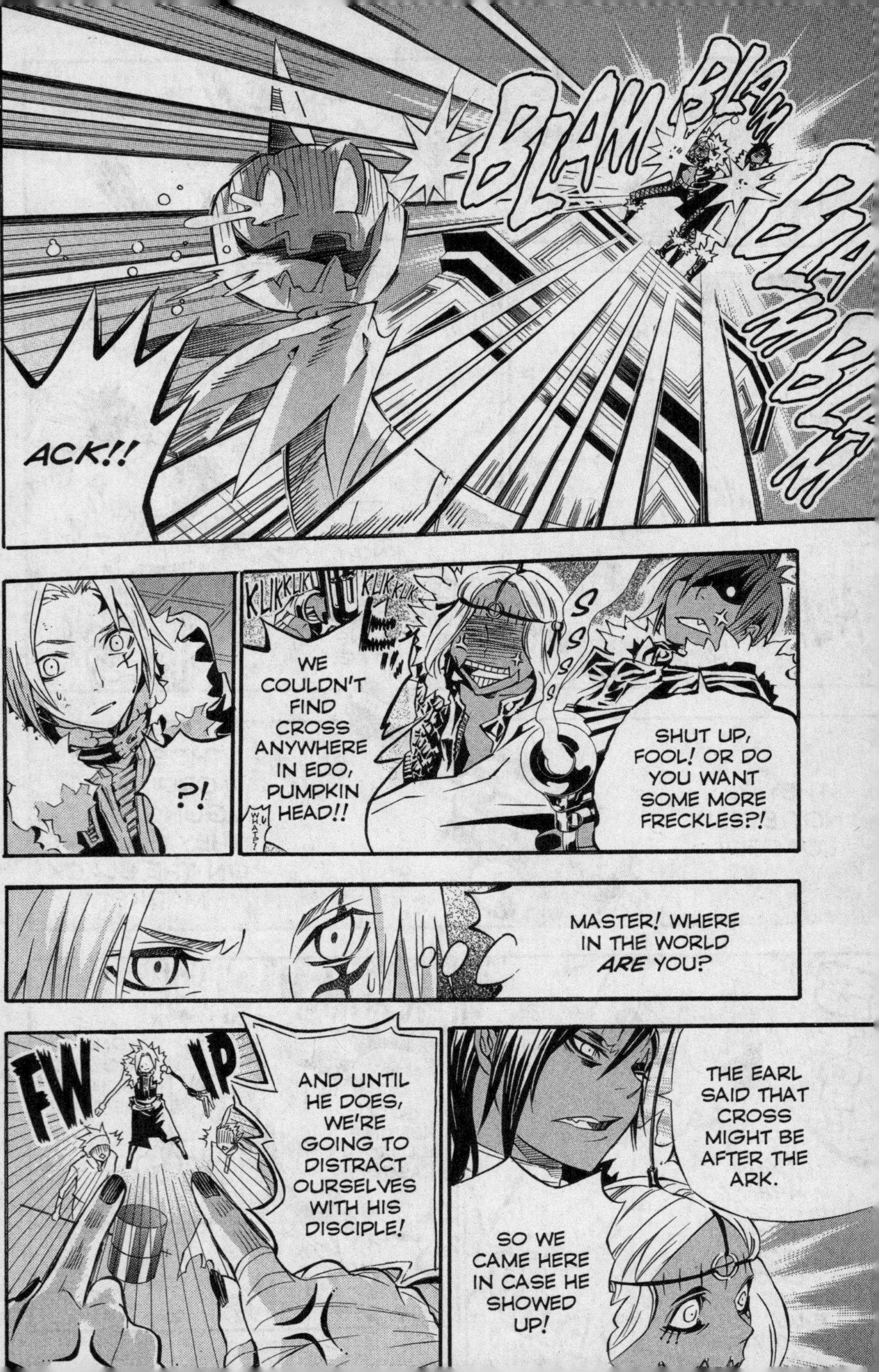
BLAM BLAM
BLAM BLAM
ACK!!
KLIKKLIK KLIKKLIK
WE COULDN'T FIND CROSS ANYWHERE IN EDO, PUMPKIN HEAD!!
WHAT?!
SSSS
SHUT UP, FOOL! OR DO YOU WANT SOME MORE FRECKLES?!
?!
MASTER! WHERE IN THE WORLD *ARE* YOU?
THE EARL SAID THAT CROSS MIGHT BE AFTER THE ARK.
SO WE CAME HERE IN CASE HE SHOWED UP!
FWIP
AND UNTIL HE DOES, WE'RE GOING TO DISTRACT OURSELVES WITH HIS DISCIPLE!

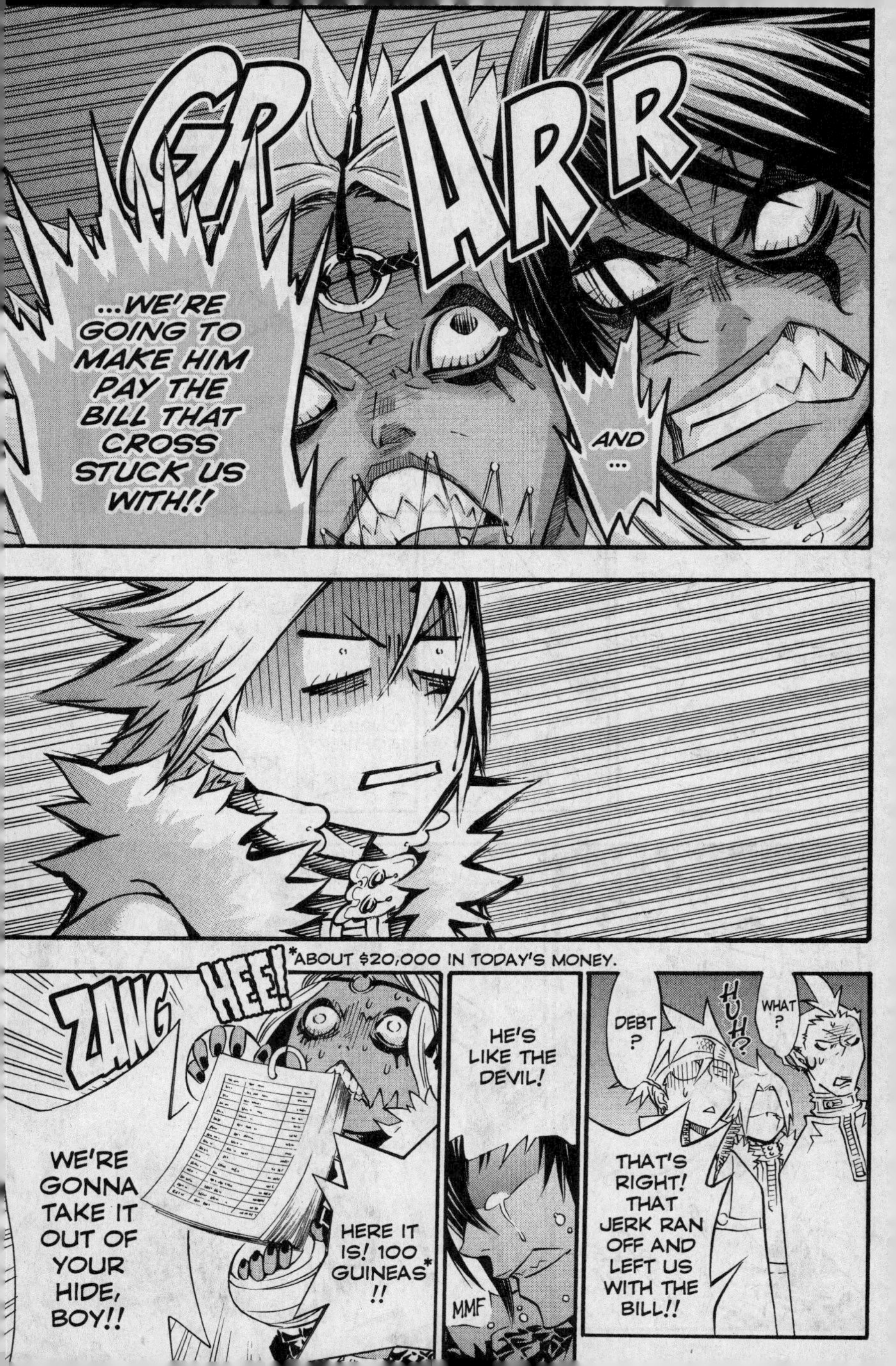
GRARR
AND ...
...WE'RE GOING TO MAKE HIM PAY THE BILL THAT CROSS STUCK US WITH!!
WHAT ?
HUH?
DEBT ?
THAT'S RIGHT! THAT JERK RAN OFF AND LEFT US WITH THE BILL!!
HE'S LIKE THE DEVIL!
MMF
HEE!
ZANG
HERE IT IS! 100 GUINEAS* !!
WE'RE GONNA TAKE IT OUT OF YOUR HIDE, BOY!!
*ABOUT $20,000 IN TODAY'S MONEY.

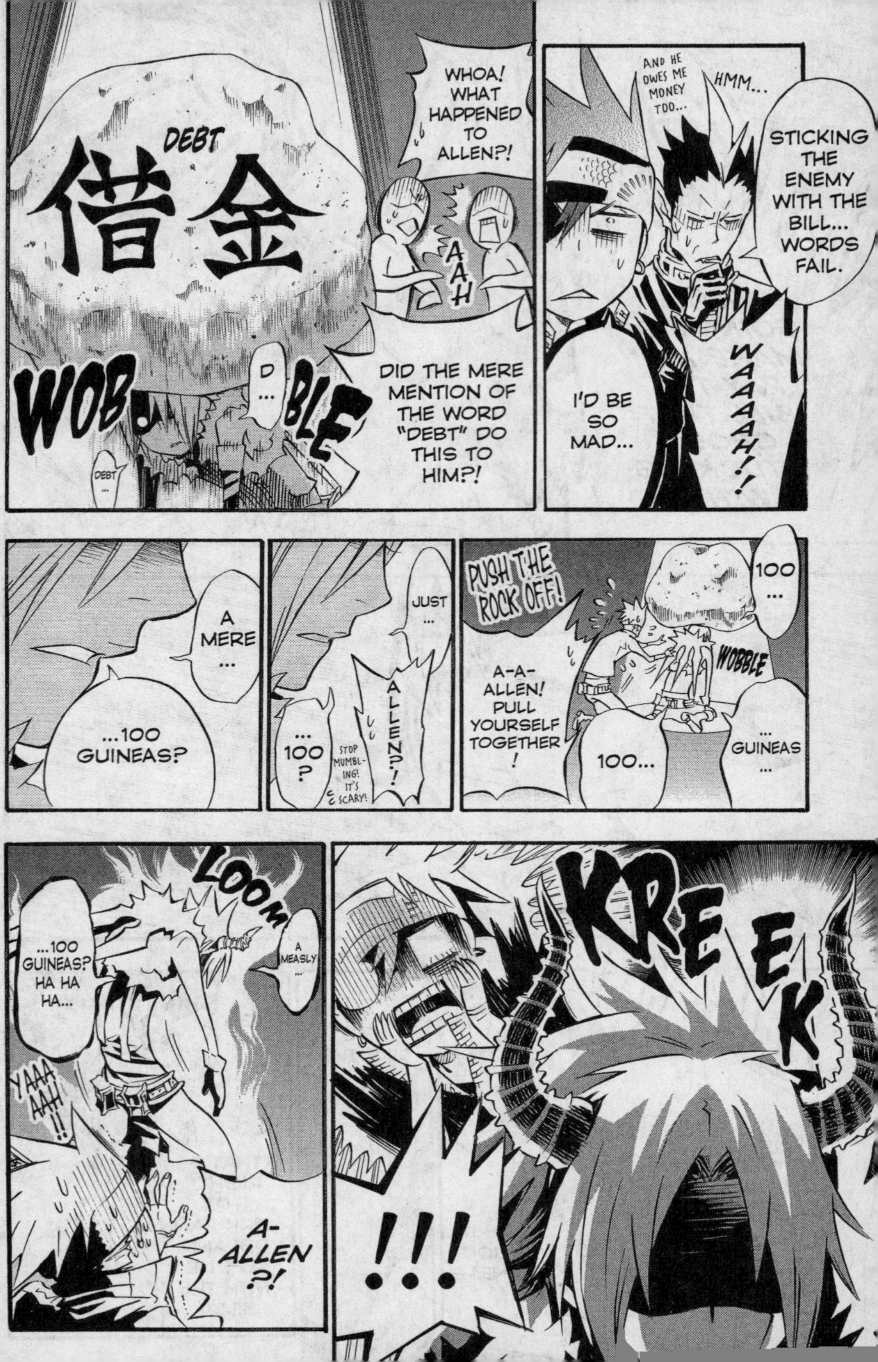
STICKING THE ENEMY WITH THE BILL... WORDS FAIL.
HMM...
AND HE OWES ME MONEY TOO...
WAAAAAH!!
I'D BE SO MAD...
WHOA! WHAT HAPPENED TO ALLEN?!
AAH
DEBT
借金
DID THE MERE MENTION OF THE WORD "DEBT" DO THIS TO HIM?!
D...
WOBBLE
DEBT...
100...
PUSH THE ROCK OFF!
WOBBLE
...GUINEAS...
A-A-ALLEN! PULL YOURSELF TOGETHER!
100...
JUST...
ALLEN?!
...100?
STOP MUMBLING! IT'S SCARY!
A MERE...
...100 GUINEAS?
KREEEK
!!!
LOOM
A MEASLY...
...100 GUINEAS? HA HA HA...
YAAAAAH!!
A-ALLEN?!

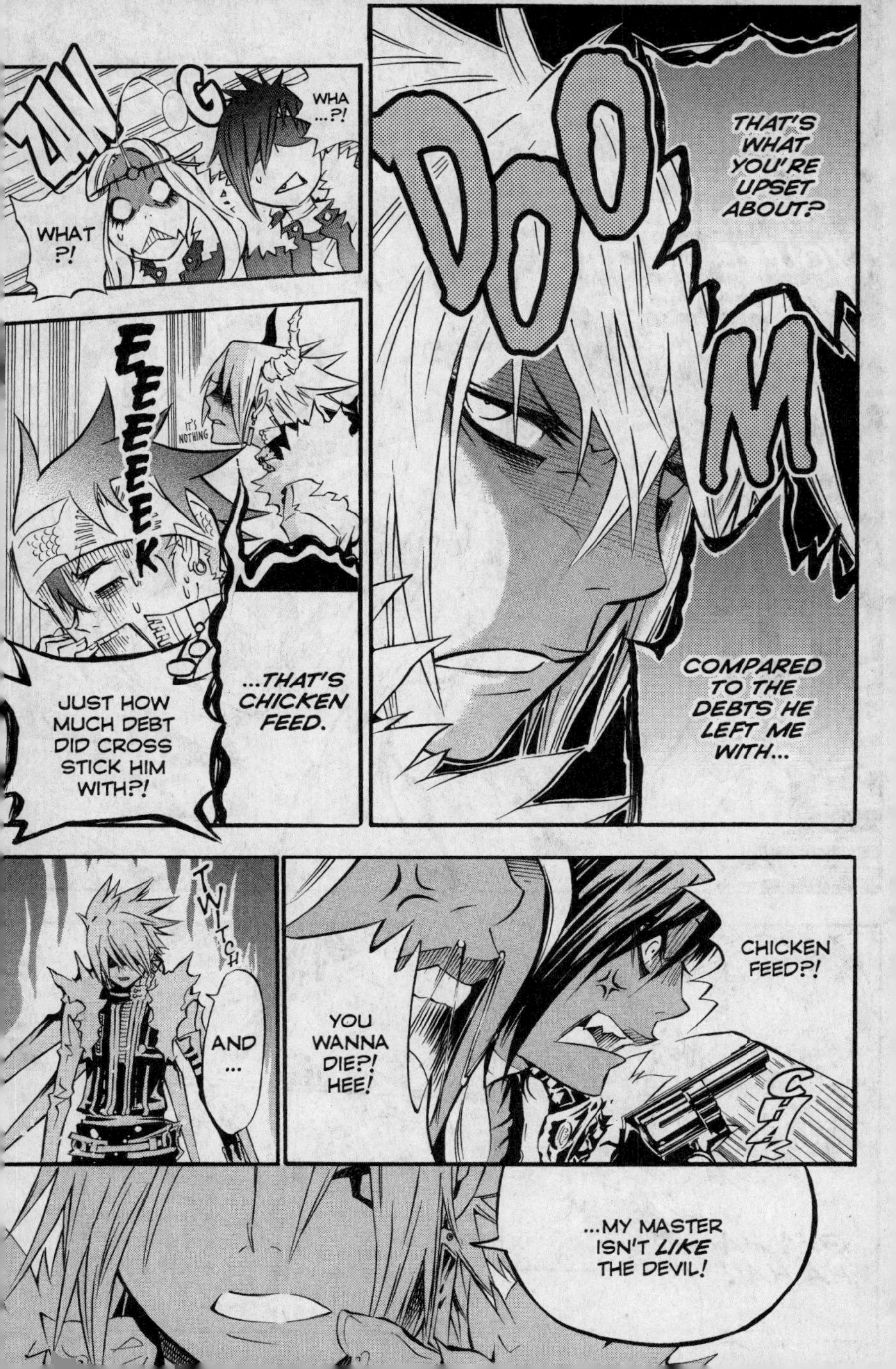
DOOOM
THAT'S WHAT YOU'RE UPSET ABOUT?
COMPARED TO THE DEBTS HE LEFT ME WITH...
ZAWNG
WHA ...?!
WHAT ?!
EEEEEEEK
IT'S NOTHING
...THAT'S CHICKEN FEED.
JUST HOW MUCH DEBT DID CROSS STICK HIM WITH?!
CHICKEN FEED?!
YOU WANNA DIE?! HEE!
CHAK
TWITCH
AND ...
...MY MASTER ISN'T LIKE THE DEVIL!

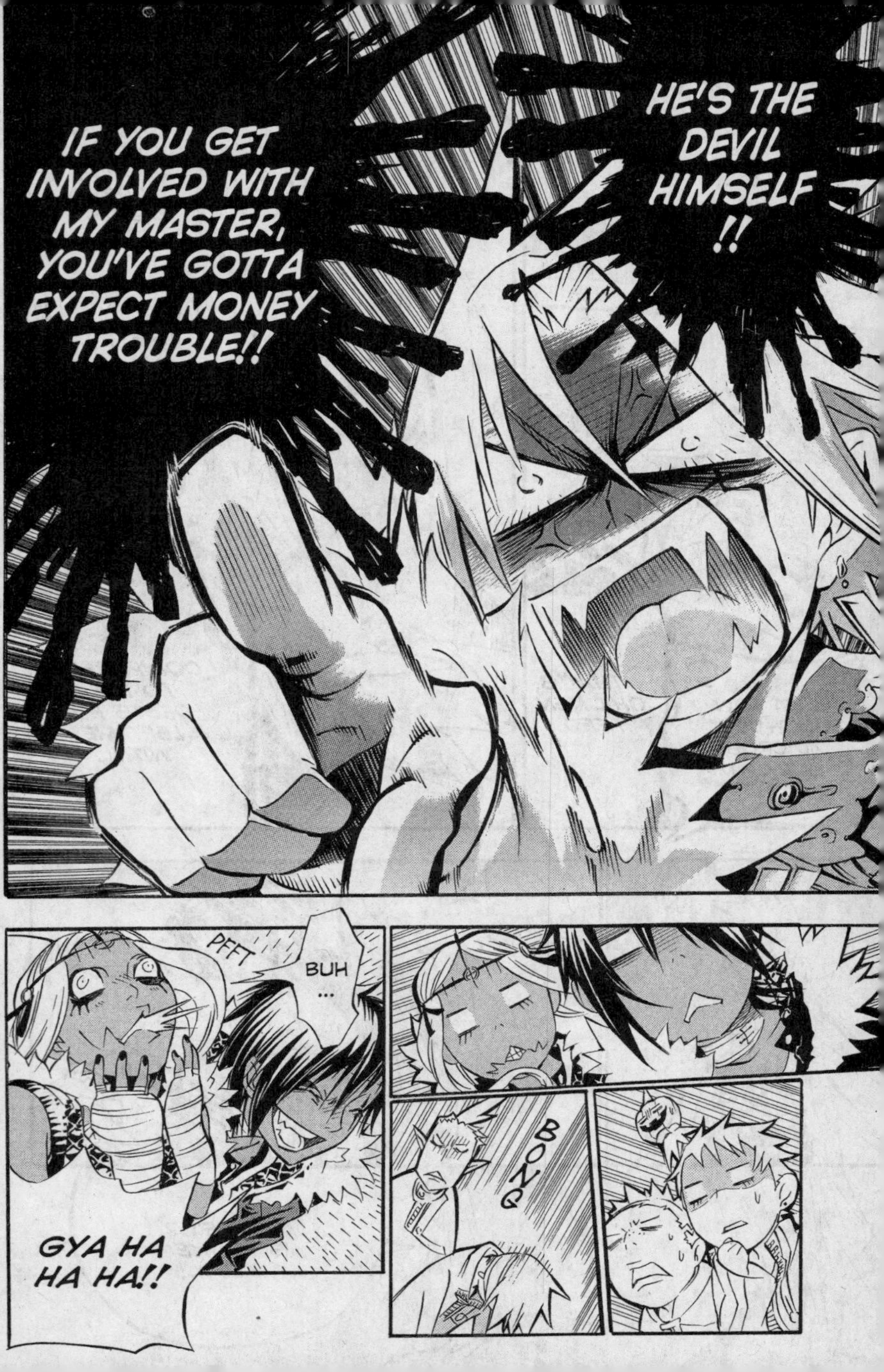
HE'S THE DEVIL HIMSELF!!
IF YOU GET INVOLVED WITH MY MASTER, YOU'VE GOTTA EXPECT MONEY TROUBLE!!
BONG
BUH ...
PFFT
GYA HA HA HA!!

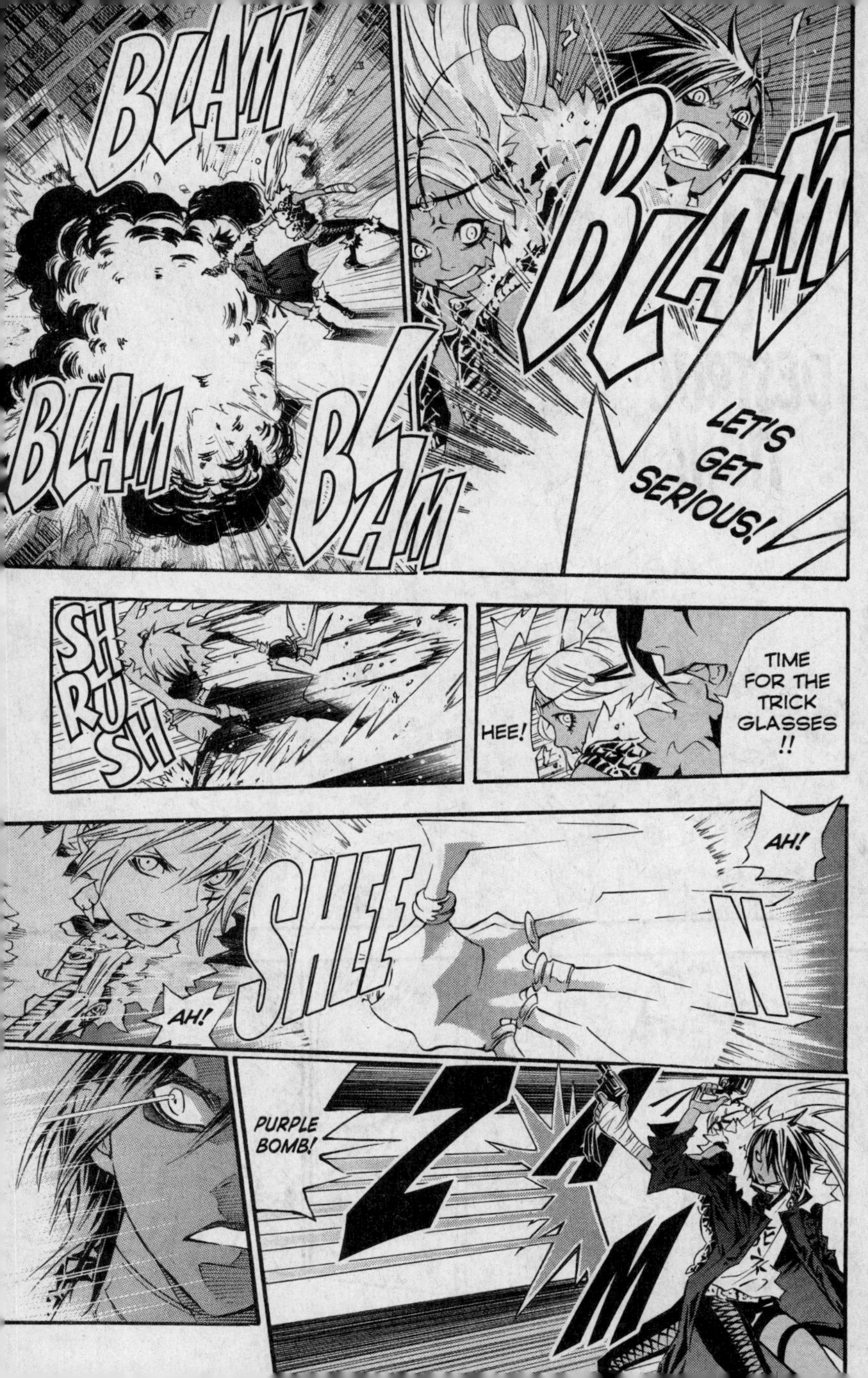
BLAM
LET'S GET SERIOUS!
BLAM
BLAM
BLAM
TIME FOR THE TRICK GLASSES !!
HEE!
SHRUSH
AH!
SHEEN
AH!
ZAM
PURPLE BOMB!

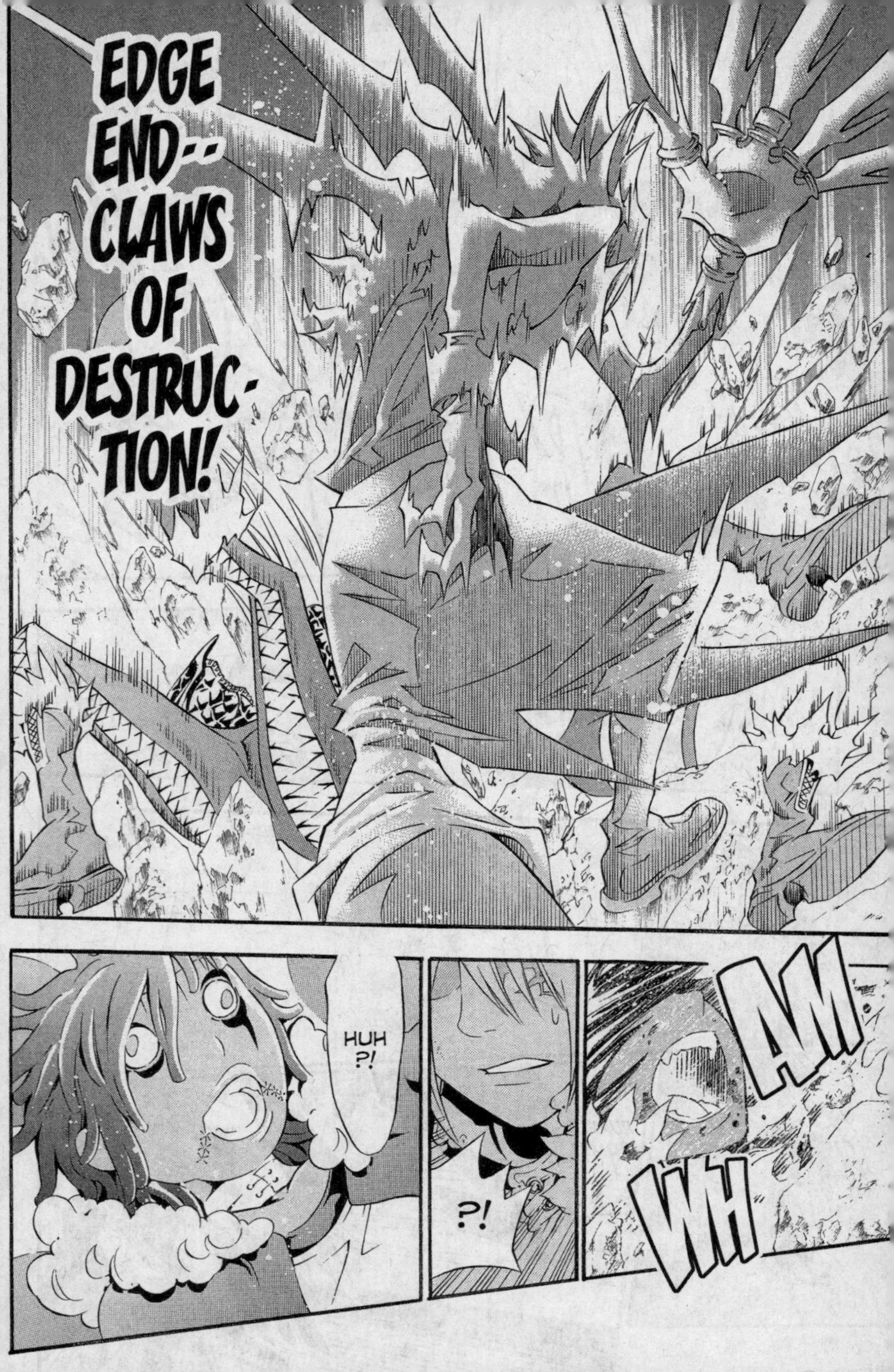
EDGE END--CLAWS OF DESTRUC-TION!
WHAM
?!
HUH ?!

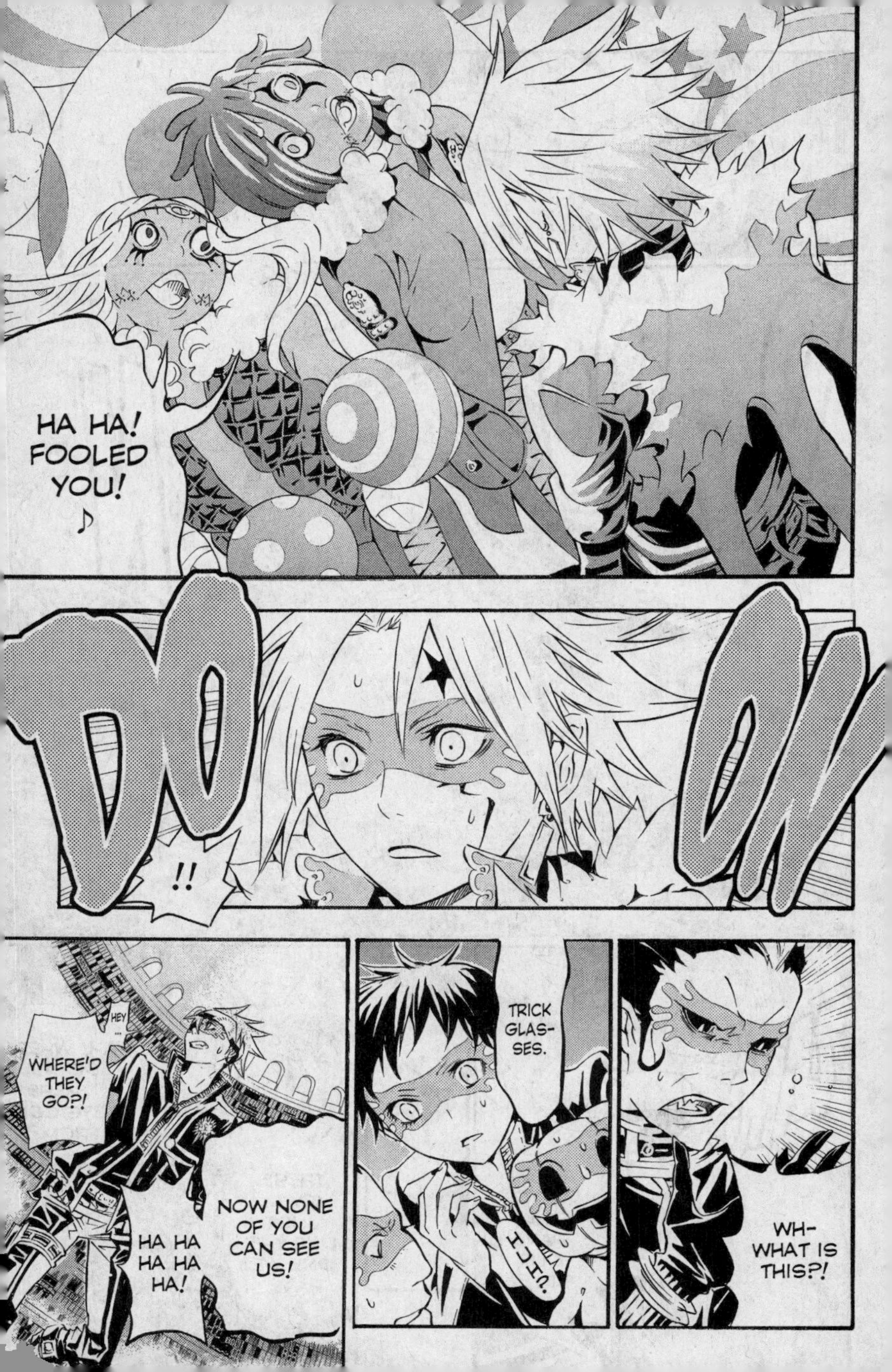
HA HA! FOOLED YOU! ♪
DOON
!!
WH- WHAT IS THIS?!
TRICK GLAS- SES.
HEY ...
WHERE'D THEY GO?!
NOW NONE OF YOU CAN SEE US!
HA HA HA HA HA!

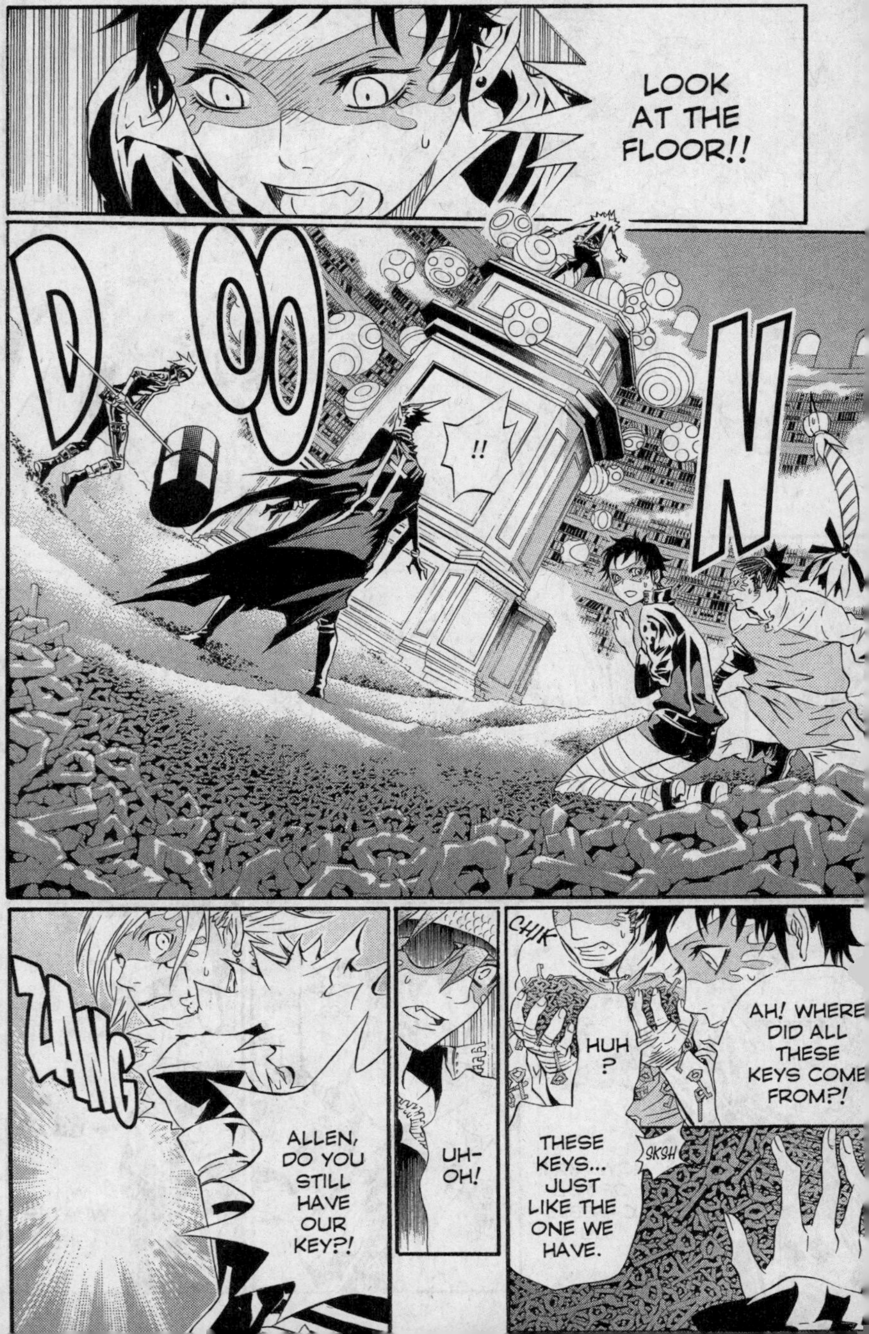
LOOK AT THE FLOOR!!
DOOON
!!
AH! WHERE DID ALL THESE KEYS COME FROM?!
CHIK
HUH?
SKSH
THESE KEYS... JUST LIKE THE ONE WE HAVE.
UH-OH!
ZANG
ALLEN, DO YOU STILL HAVE OUR KEY?!

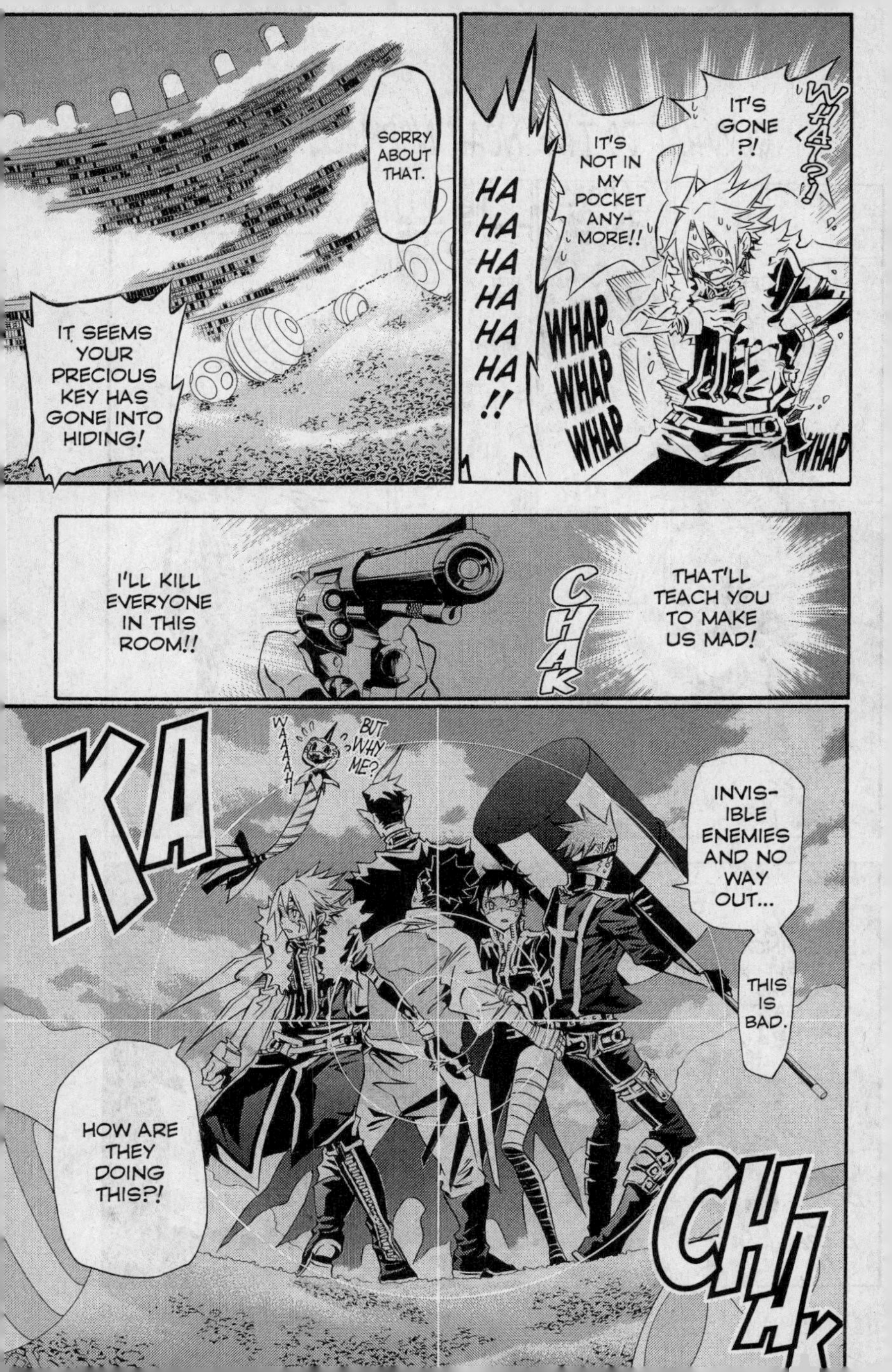
WHAT?!
IT'S GONE?!
IT'S NOT IN MY POCKET ANYMORE!!
HA HA HA HA HA HA!!
WHAP WHAP WHAP
WHAP
SORRY ABOUT THAT.
IT SEEMS YOUR PRECIOUS KEY HAS GONE INTO HIDING!
THAT'LL TEACH YOU TO MAKE US MAD!
CHAK
I'LL KILL EVERYONE IN THIS ROOM!!
INVISIBLE ENEMIES AND NO WAY OUT...
THIS IS BAD.
BUT WHY ME?
WAAAAH!
KA
HOW ARE THEY DOING THIS?!
CHHK

Q: WHAT DO THE NOAH NORMALLY EAT?

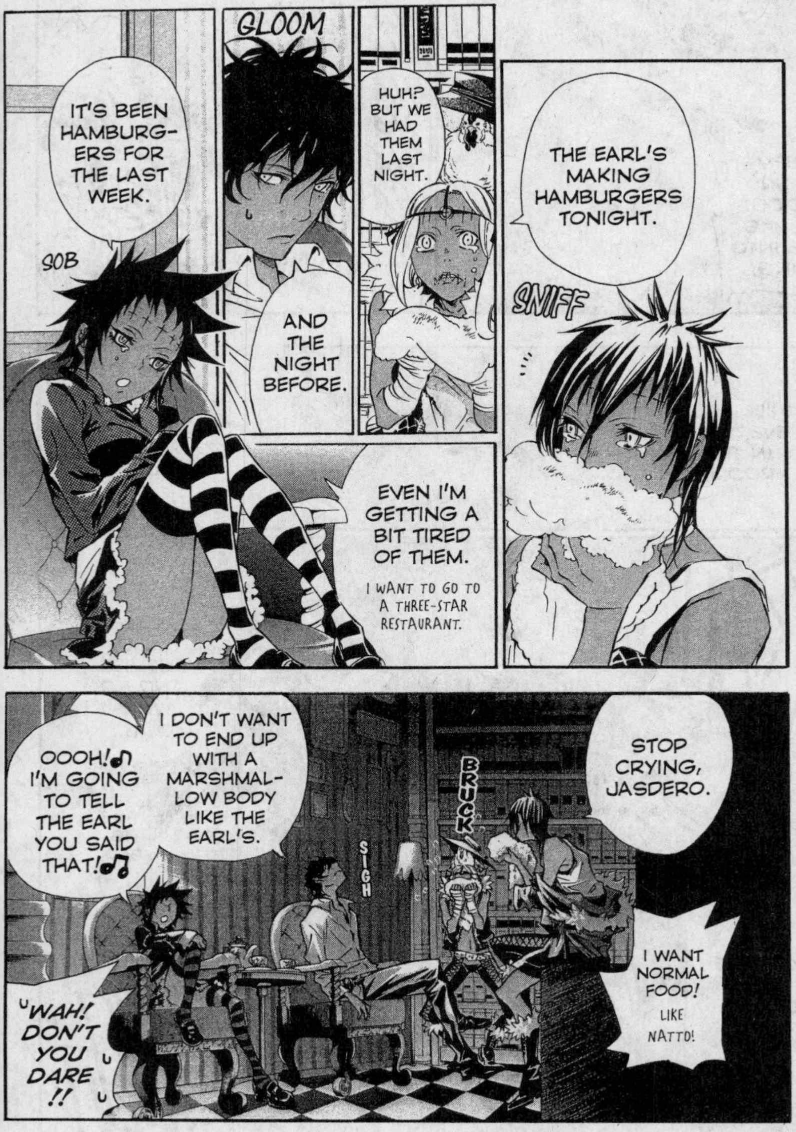

THE EARL'S MAKING HAMBURGERS TONIGHT.
SNIFF
HUH? BUT WE HAD THEM LAST NIGHT.
GLOOM
AND THE NIGHT BEFORE.
EVEN I'M GETTING A BIT TIRED OF THEM.
I WANT TO GO TO A THREE-STAR RESTAURANT.
IT'S BEEN HAMBURGERS FOR THE LAST WEEK.
SOB
STOP CRYING, JASDERO.
I WANT NORMAL FOOD!
LIKE NATTO!
BRUCK
SIGH
I DON'T WANT TO END UP WITH A MARSHMALLOW BODY LIKE THE EARL'S.
OOOH!♫ I'M GOING TO TELL THE EARL YOU SAID THAT!♫
WAH! DON'T YOU DARE!!

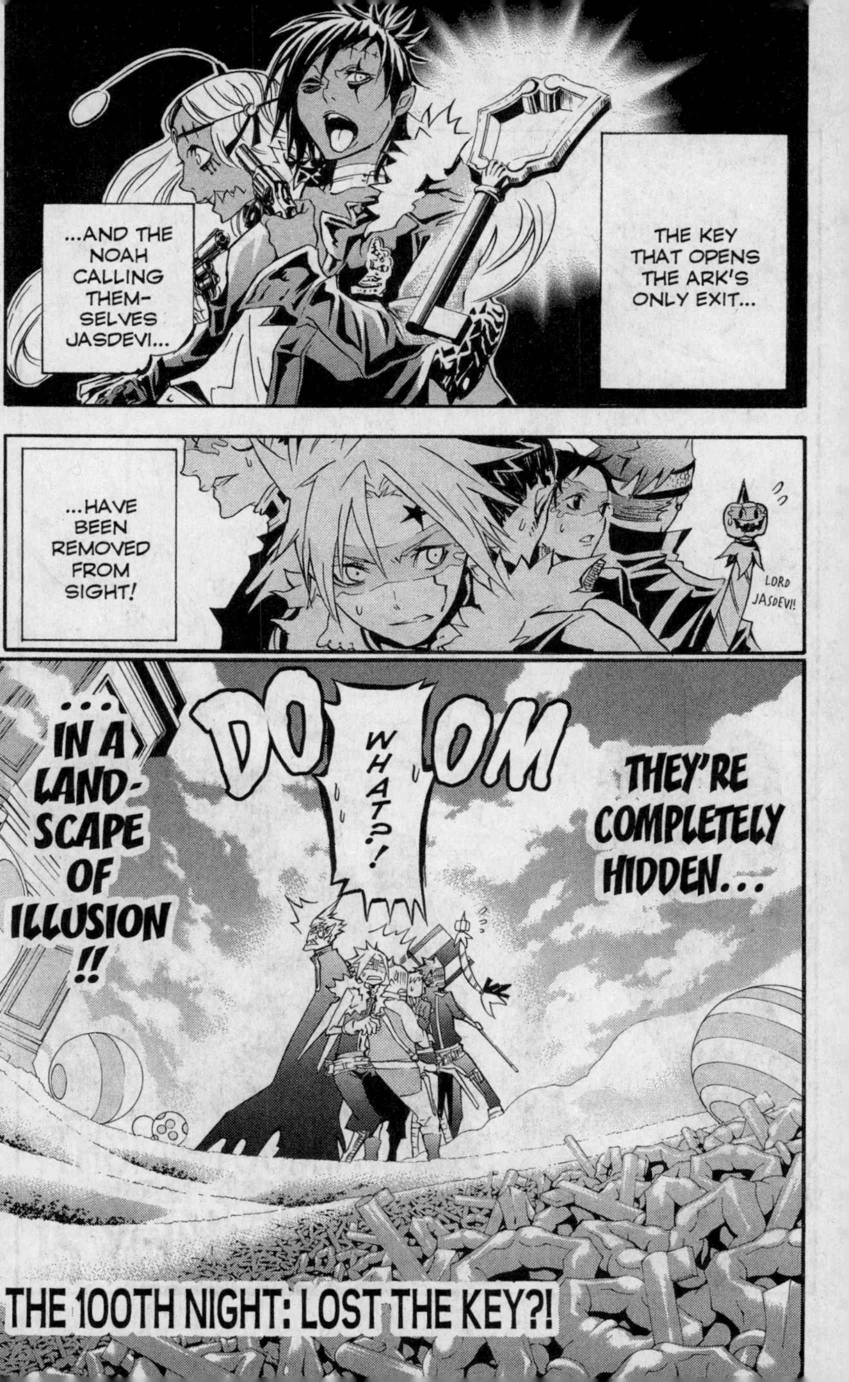
THE KEY THAT OPENS THE ARK'S ONLY EXIT...
...AND THE NOAH CALLING THEM-SELVES JASDEVI...
LORD JASDEVI!
...HAVE BEEN REMOVED FROM SIGHT!
THEY'RE COMPLETELY HIDDEN...
DOOM
WHAT?!
...IN A LAND-SCAPE OF ILLUSION!!
THE 100TH NIGHT: LOST THE KEY?!

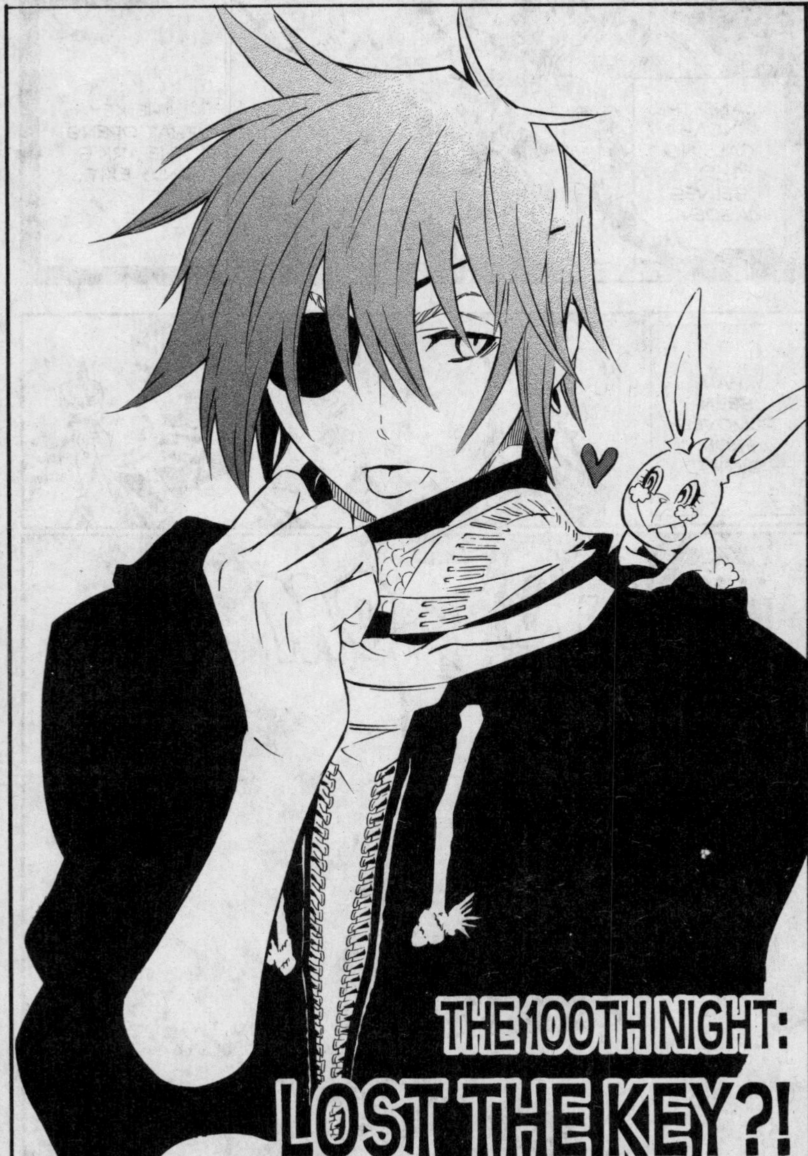
THE 100TH NIGHT:
LOST THE KEY?!

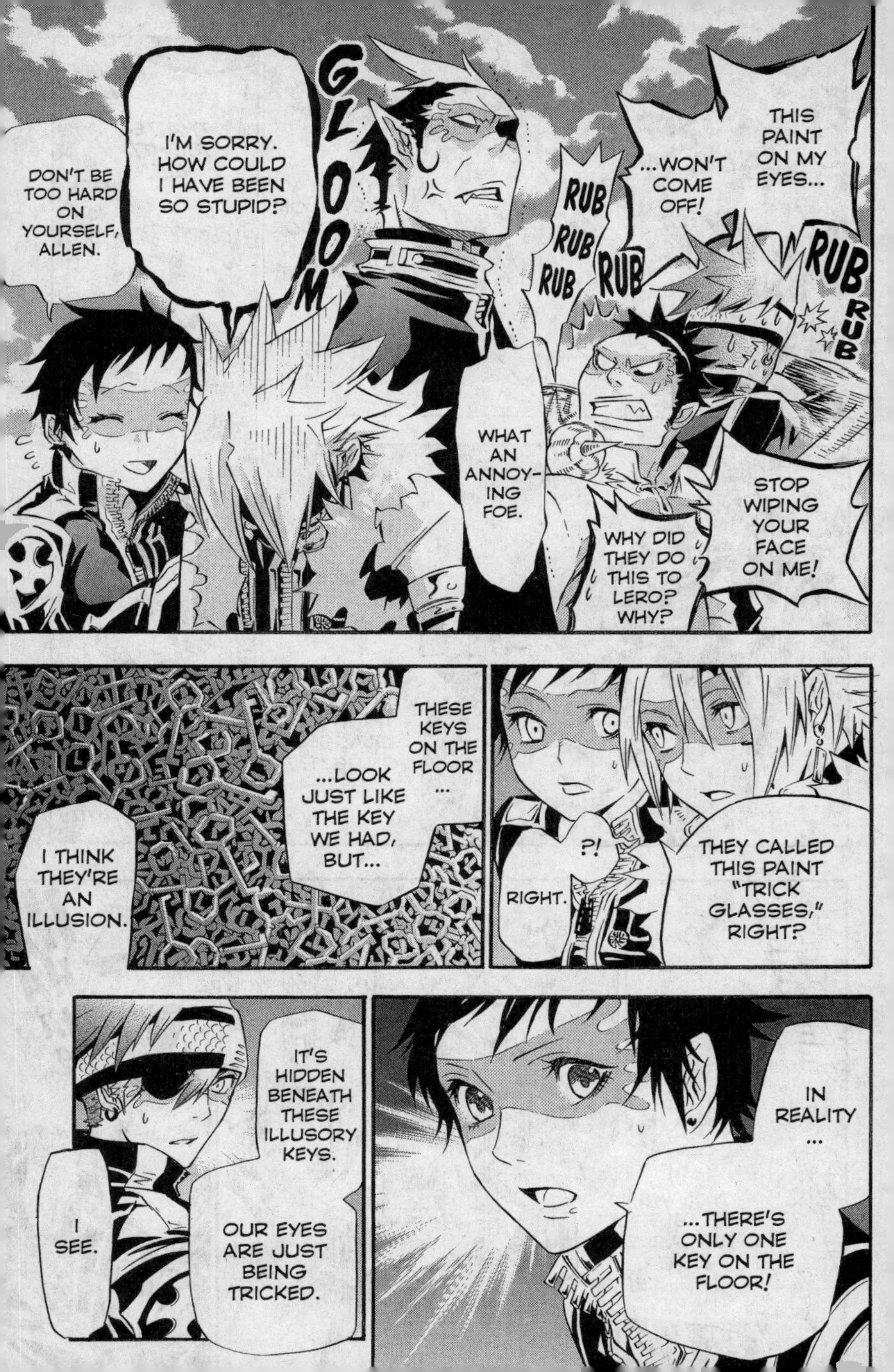
THIS PAINT ON MY EYES...
...WON'T COME OFF!
RUB RUB
RUB RUB RUB RUB
STOP WIPING YOUR FACE ON ME!
WHY DID THEY DO THIS TO LERO? WHY?
WHAT AN ANNOYING FOE.
GLOOM
I'M SORRY. HOW COULD I HAVE BEEN SO STUPID?
DON'T BE TOO HARD ON YOURSELF, ALLEN.
THEY CALLED THIS PAINT "TRICK GLASSES," RIGHT?
?!
RIGHT.
THESE KEYS ON THE FLOOR ...
...LOOK JUST LIKE THE KEY WE HAD, BUT...
I THINK THEY'RE AN ILLUSION.
IN REALITY ...
...THERE'S ONLY ONE KEY ON THE FLOOR!
IT'S HIDDEN BENEATH THESE ILLUSORY KEYS.
OUR EYES ARE JUST BEING TRICKED.
I SEE.

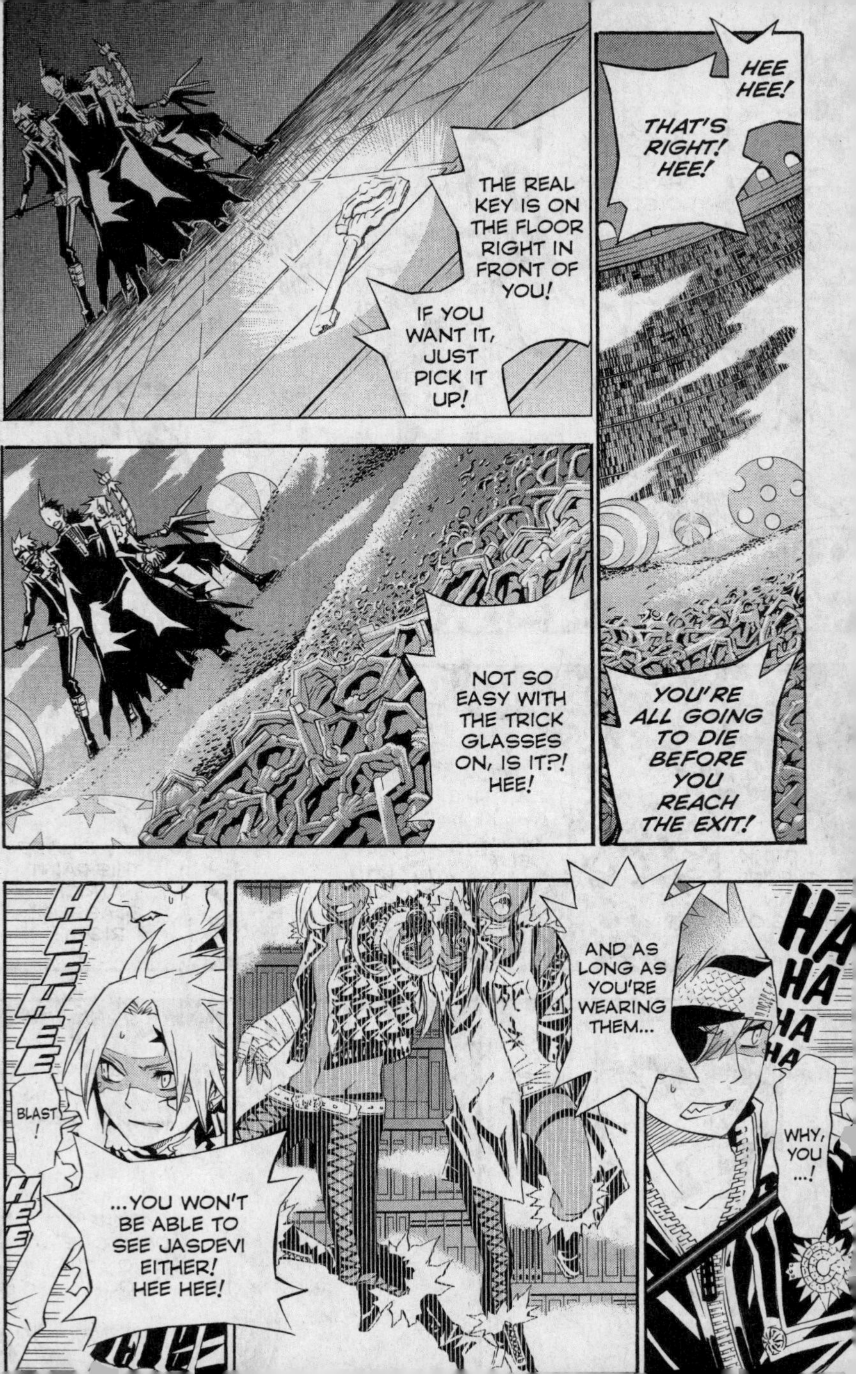

HEE HEE!
THAT'S RIGHT! HEE!
YOU'RE ALL GOING TO DIE BEFORE YOU REACH THE EXIT!
THE REAL KEY IS ON THE FLOOR RIGHT IN FRONT OF YOU!
IF YOU WANT IT, JUST PICK IT UP!
NOT SO EASY WITH THE TRICK GLASSES ON, IS IT?! HEE!
HAHAHAHA
WHY, YOU...!
AND AS LONG AS YOU'RE WEARING THEM...
HEEHEEHEE
BLAST!
...YOU WON'T BE ABLE TO SEE JASDEVI EITHER! HEE HEE!
HEE HEE

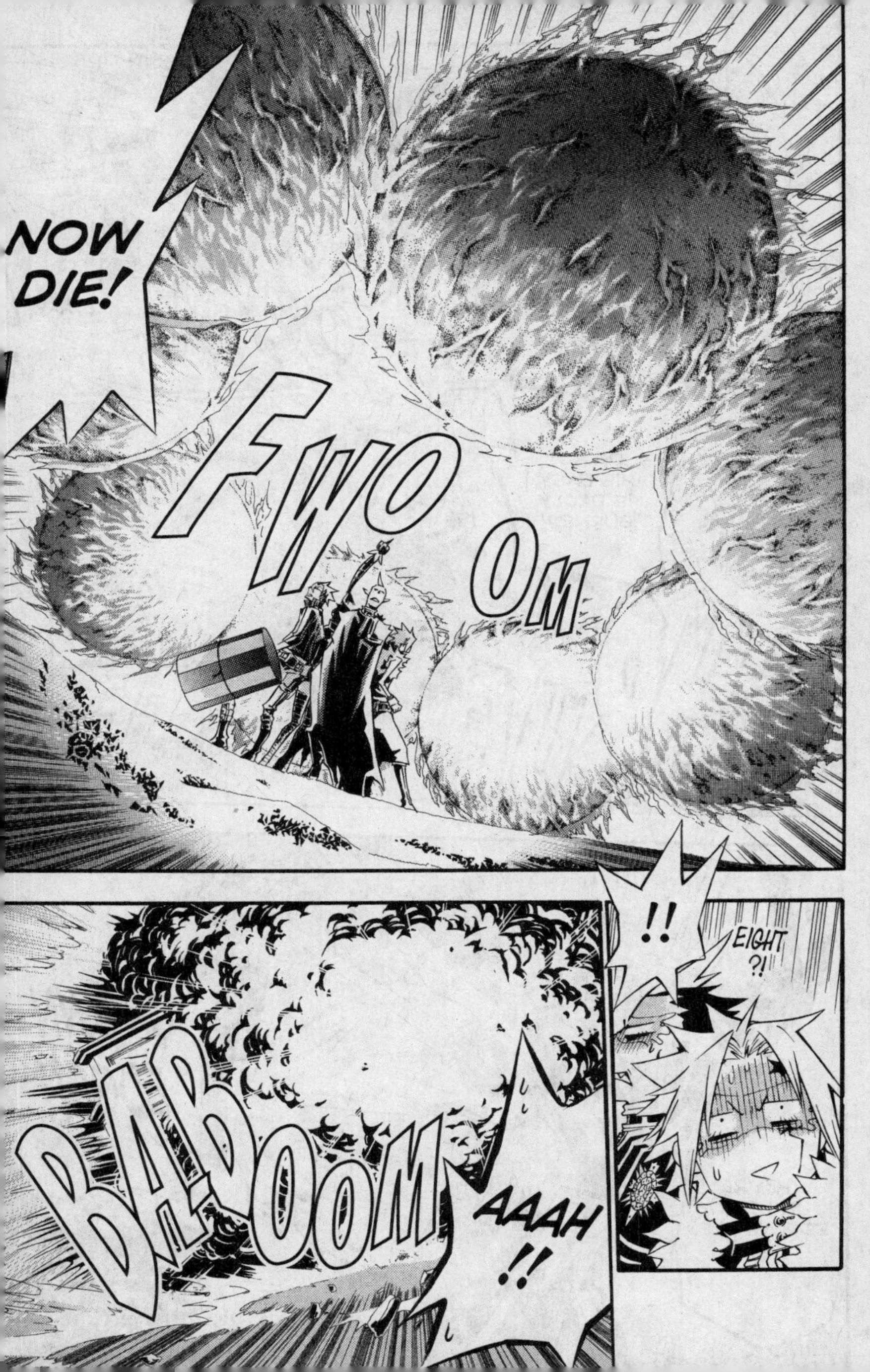
NOW DIE!
FWOOM
!!
EIGHT ?!
BABOOM
AAAH !!

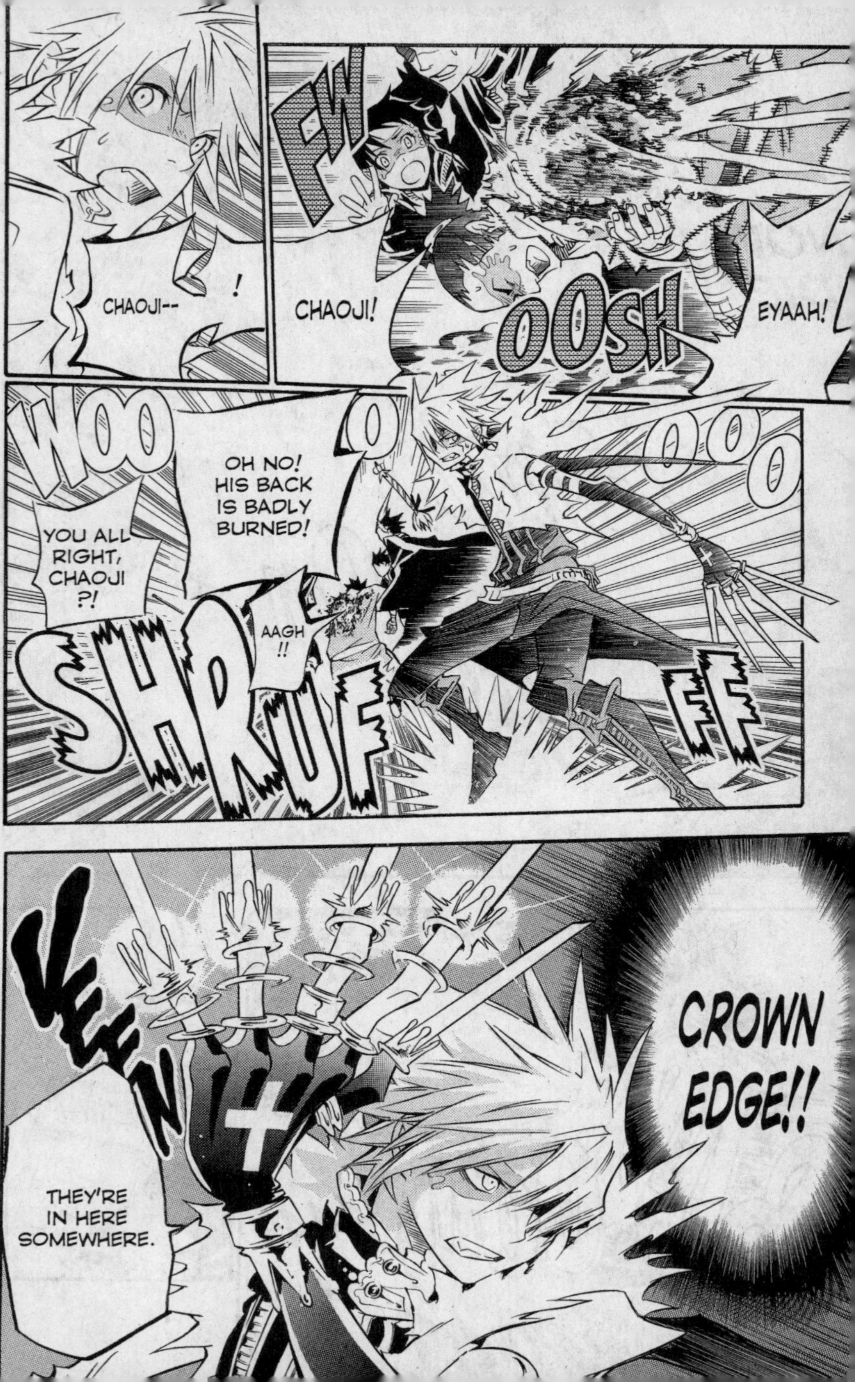

FW
EYAAH!
OOSH
CHAOJI!
!
CHAOJI--
WOOOOOOO
OH NO! HIS BACK IS BADLY BURNED!
YOU ALL RIGHT, CHAOJI?!
AAGH!!
SHRUFF
CROWN EDGE!!
VEEEN
THEY'RE IN HERE SOMEWHERE.

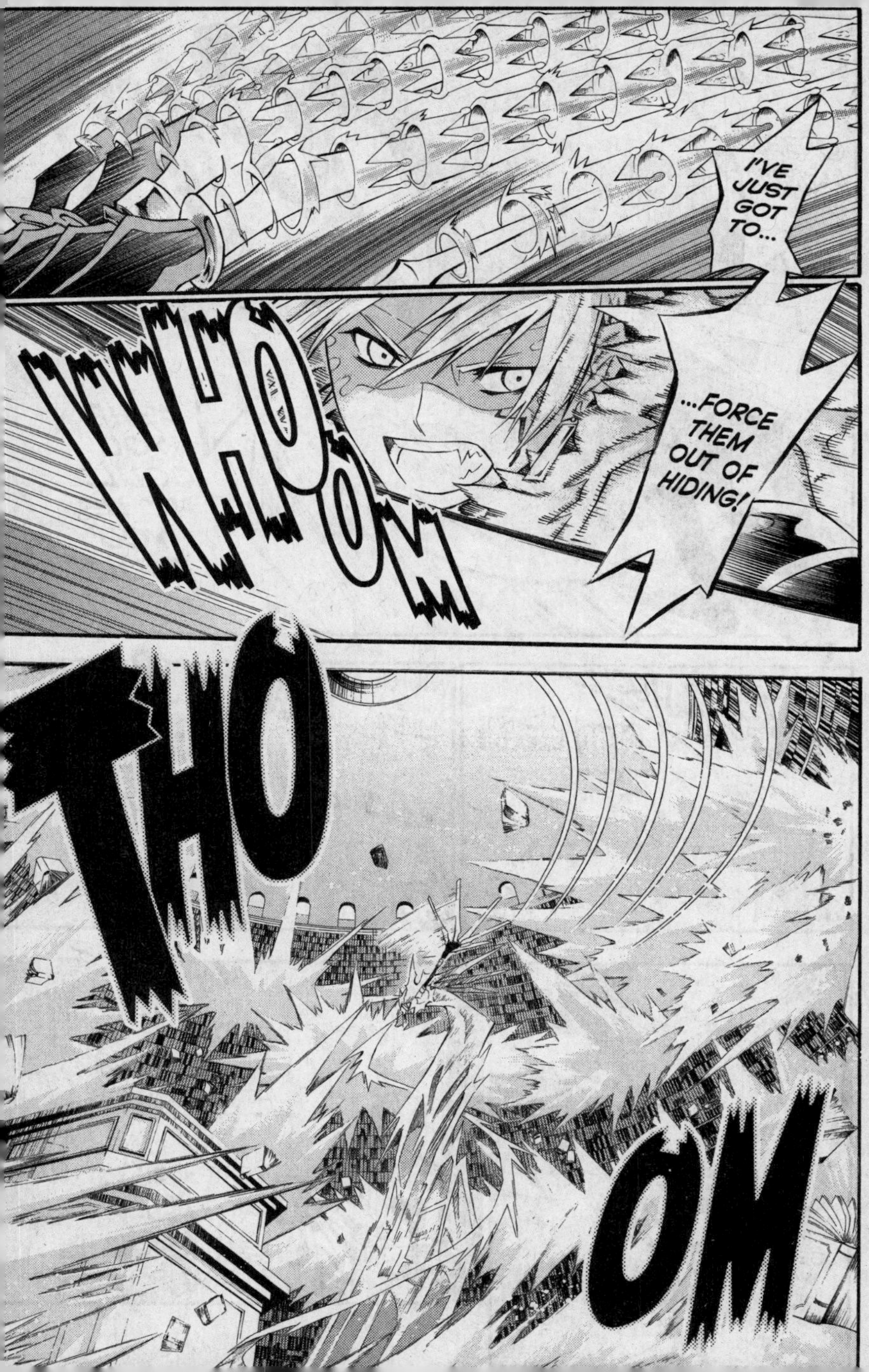
I'VE JUST GOT TO...
...FORCE THEM OUT OF HIDING!
WHOOM
THOOM

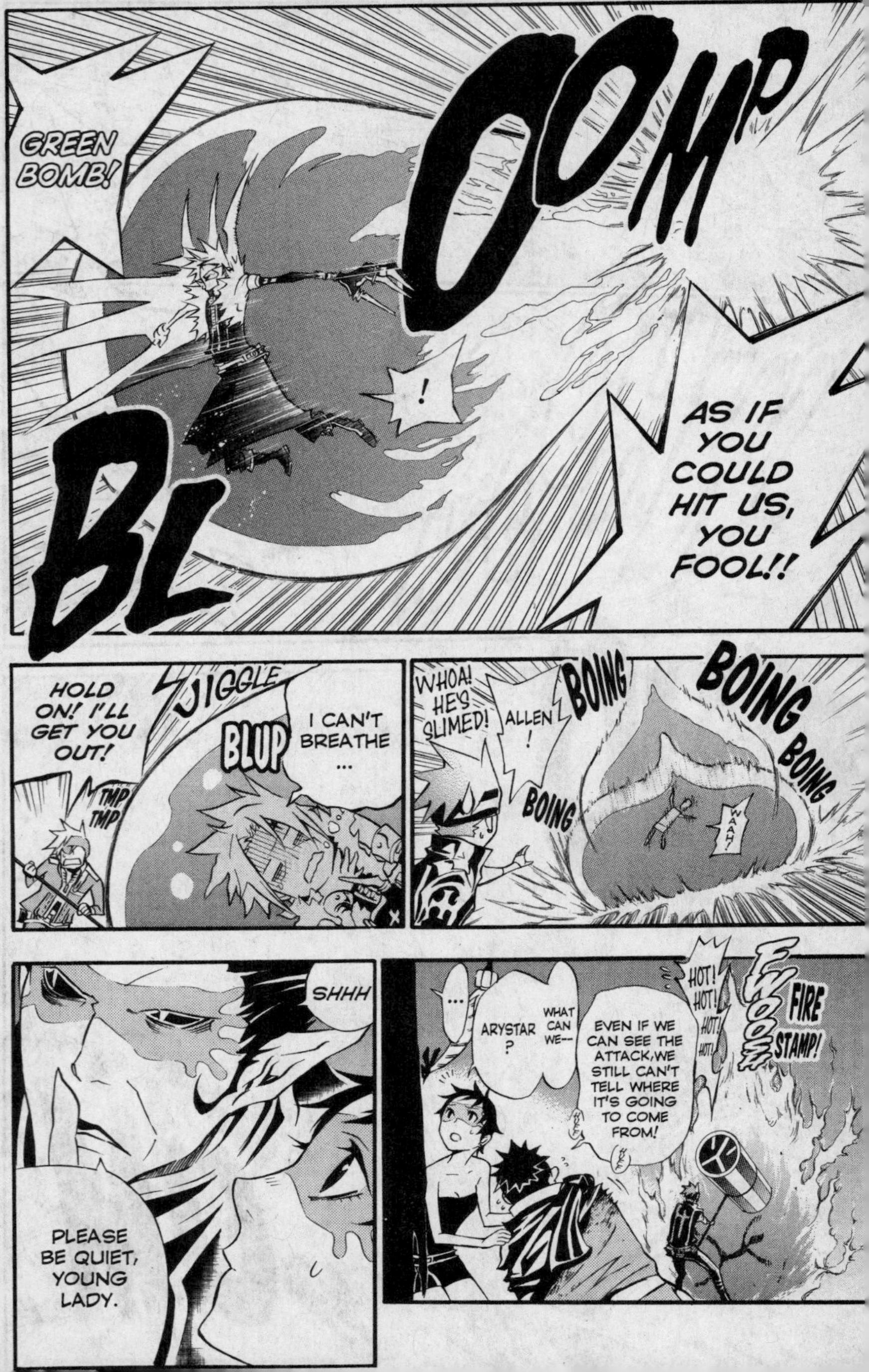
OOMP
AS IF YOU COULD HIT US, YOU FOOL!!
GREEN BOMB!
!
BL
BOING
BOING BOING BOING
ALLEN!
WHOA! HE'S SLIMED!
BOING
WAAH!
JIGGLE
I CAN'T BREATHE ...
BLUP
HOLD ON! I'LL GET YOU OUT!
TMP TMP
FIRE STAMP!
HOT! HOT! HOT! HOT!
EVEN IF WE CAN SEE THE ATTACK, WE STILL CAN'T TELL WHERE IT'S GOING TO COME FROM!
WHAT CAN WE--
ARYSTAR?
...
SHHH
PLEASE BE QUIET, YOUNG LADY.

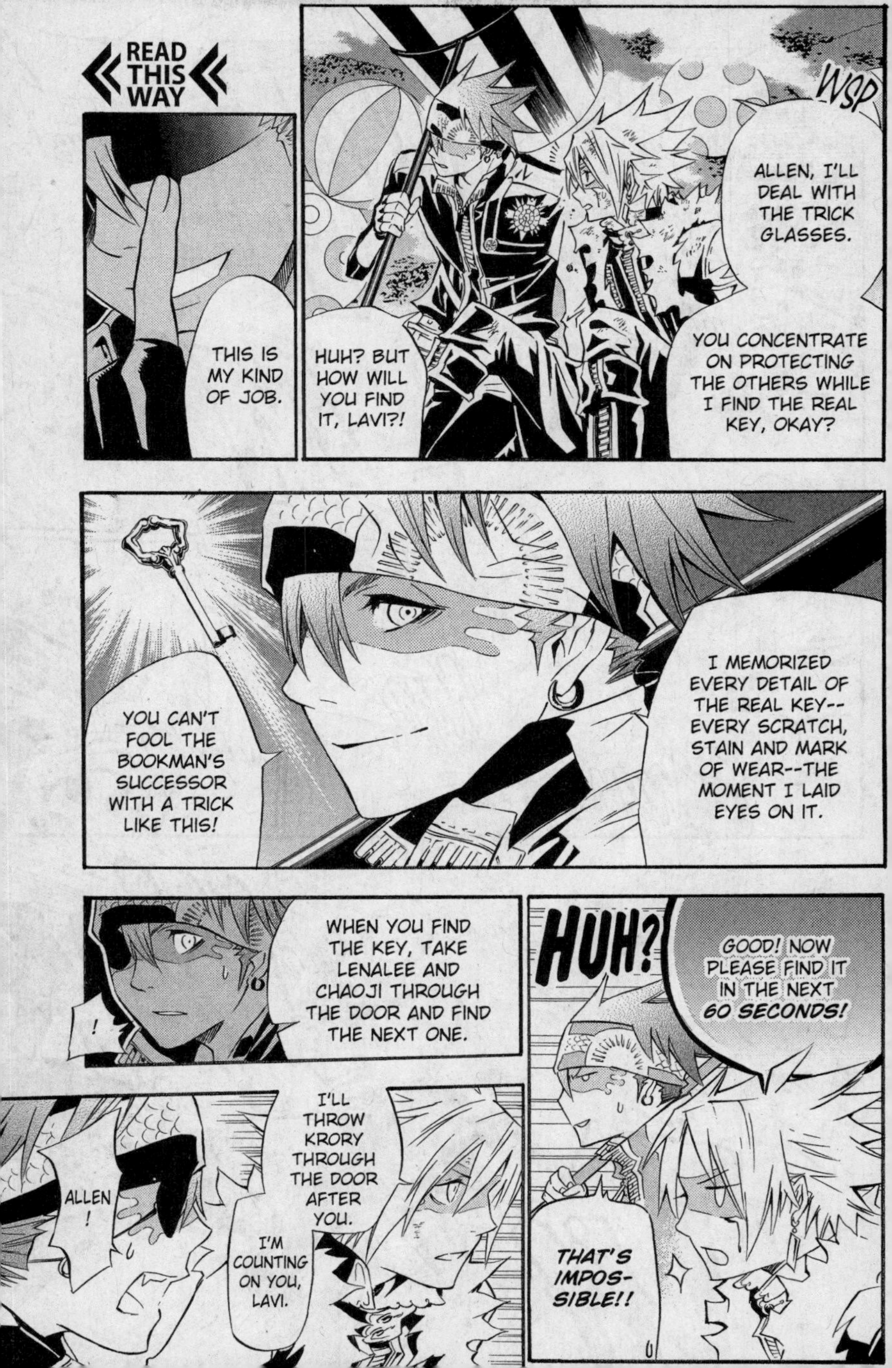
READ THIS WAY
WSP
ALLEN, I'LL DEAL WITH THE TRICK GLASSES.
YOU CONCENTRATE ON PROTECTING THE OTHERS WHILE I FIND THE REAL KEY, OKAY?
HUH? BUT HOW WILL YOU FIND IT, LAVI?!
THIS IS MY KIND OF JOB.
I MEMORIZED EVERY DETAIL OF THE REAL KEY--EVERY SCRATCH, STAIN AND MARK OF WEAR--THE MOMENT I LAID EYES ON IT.
YOU CAN'T FOOL THE BOOKMAN'S SUCCESSOR WITH A TRICK LIKE THIS!
HUH?
GOOD! NOW PLEASE FIND IT IN THE NEXT 60 SECONDS!
THAT'S IMPOSSIBLE!!
WHEN YOU FIND THE KEY, TAKE LENALEE AND CHAOJI THROUGH THE DOOR AND FIND THE NEXT ONE.
!
I'LL THROW KRORY THROUGH THE DOOR AFTER YOU.
I'M COUNTING ON YOU, LAVI.
ALLEN!

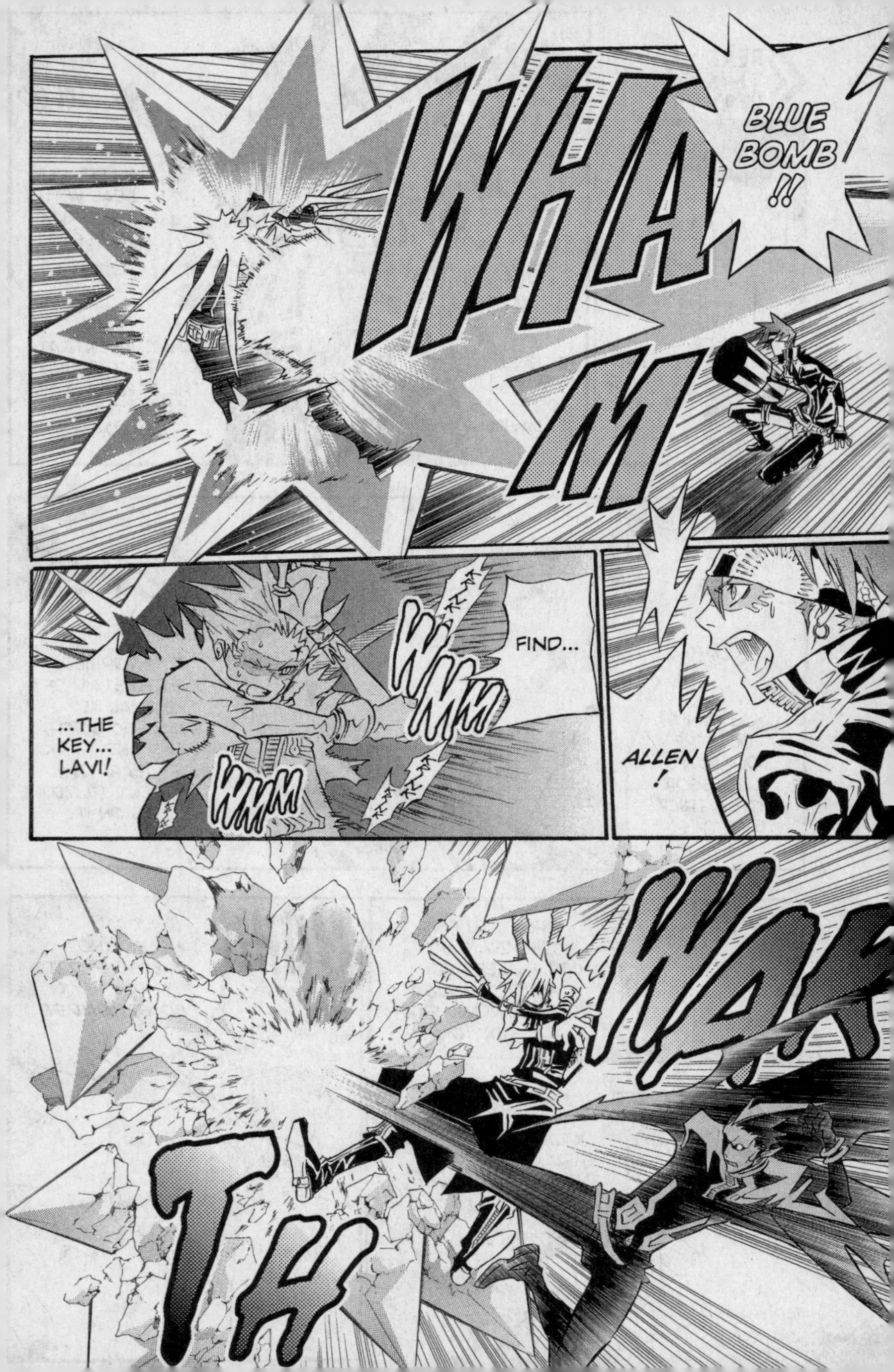
BLUE BOMB !!
WHAM
ALLEN!
FIND...
WMM
WMM
...THE KEY... LAVI!
WHA
TH

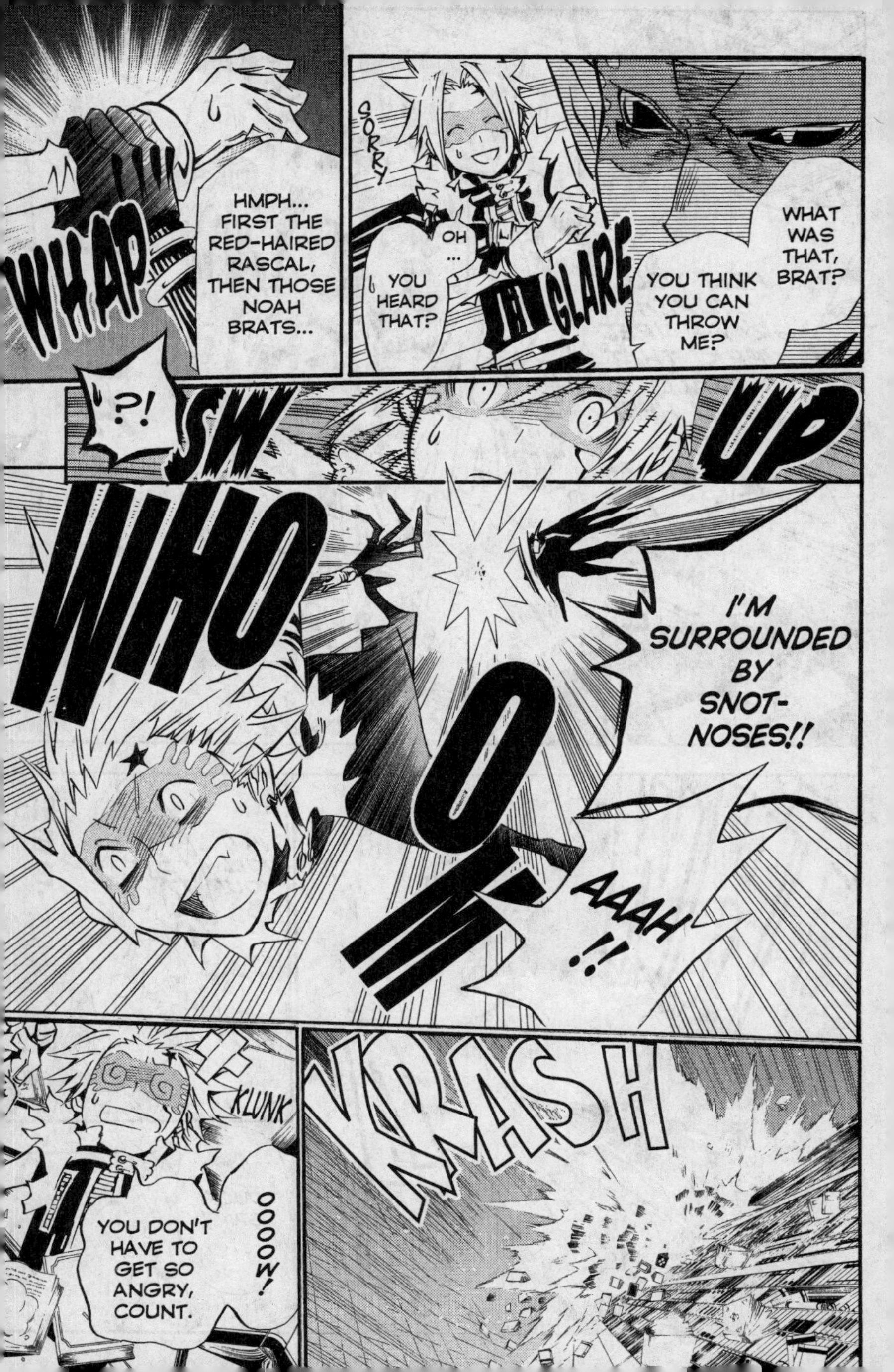
WHAT WAS THAT, BRAT?
YOU THINK YOU CAN THROW ME?
GLARE
SORRY
OH... YOU HEARD THAT?
HMPH... FIRST THE RED-HAIRED RASCAL, THEN THOSE NOAH BRATS...
WHAP
UP
SW
?!
I'M SURROUNDED BY SNOT-NOSES!!
WHOOM
AAAH!!
KRASH
KLUNK
OOOOOW!
YOU DON'T HAVE TO GET SO ANGRY, COUNT.

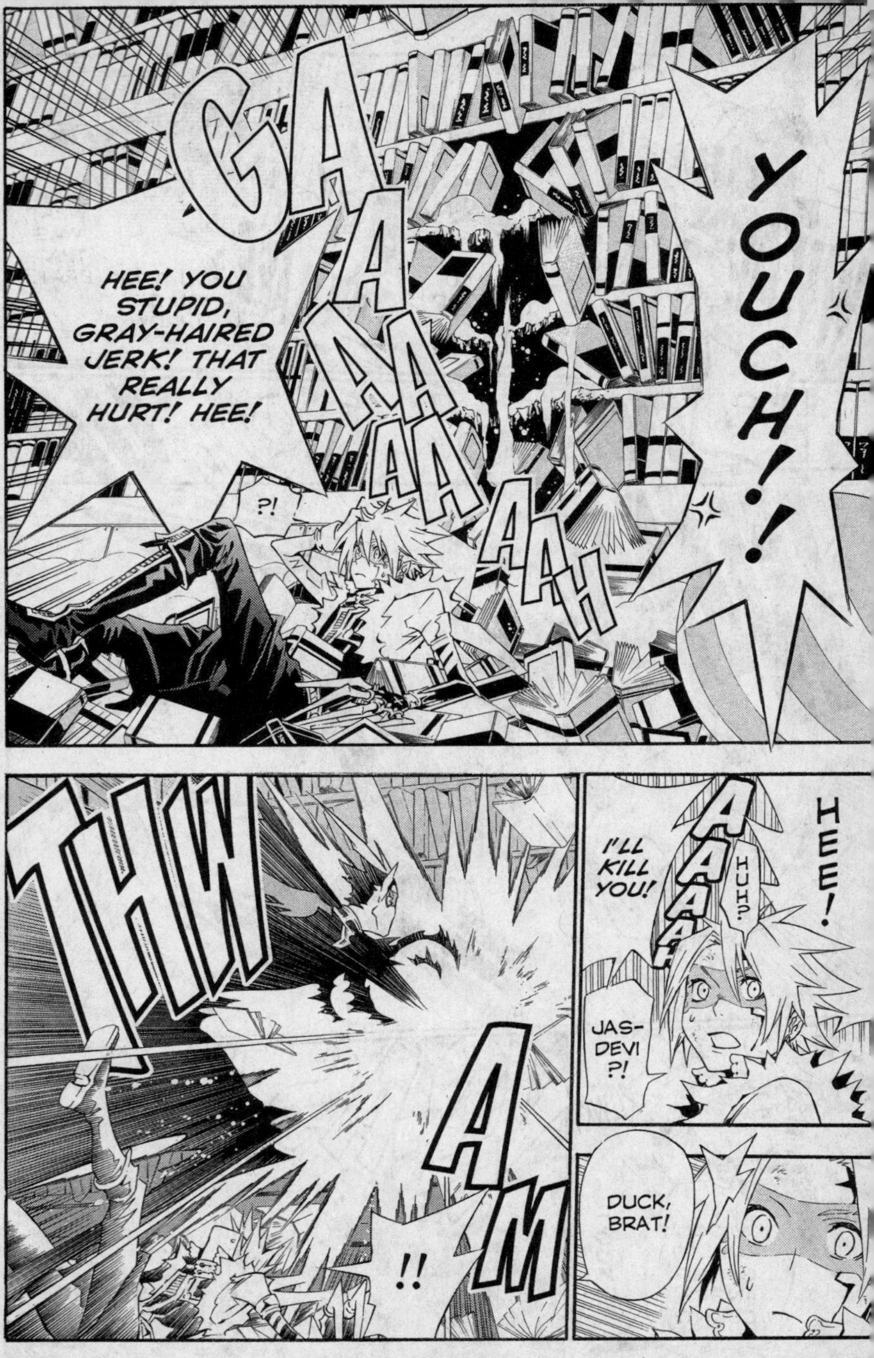
YOUCH!!
GAAAAAAAAH
HEE! YOU STUPID, GRAY-HAIRED JERK! THAT REALLY HURT! HEE!
?!
HEE!
HUH?
AAAA
I'LL KILL YOU!
JAS-DEVI?!
DUCK, BRAT!
THWAAM
!!

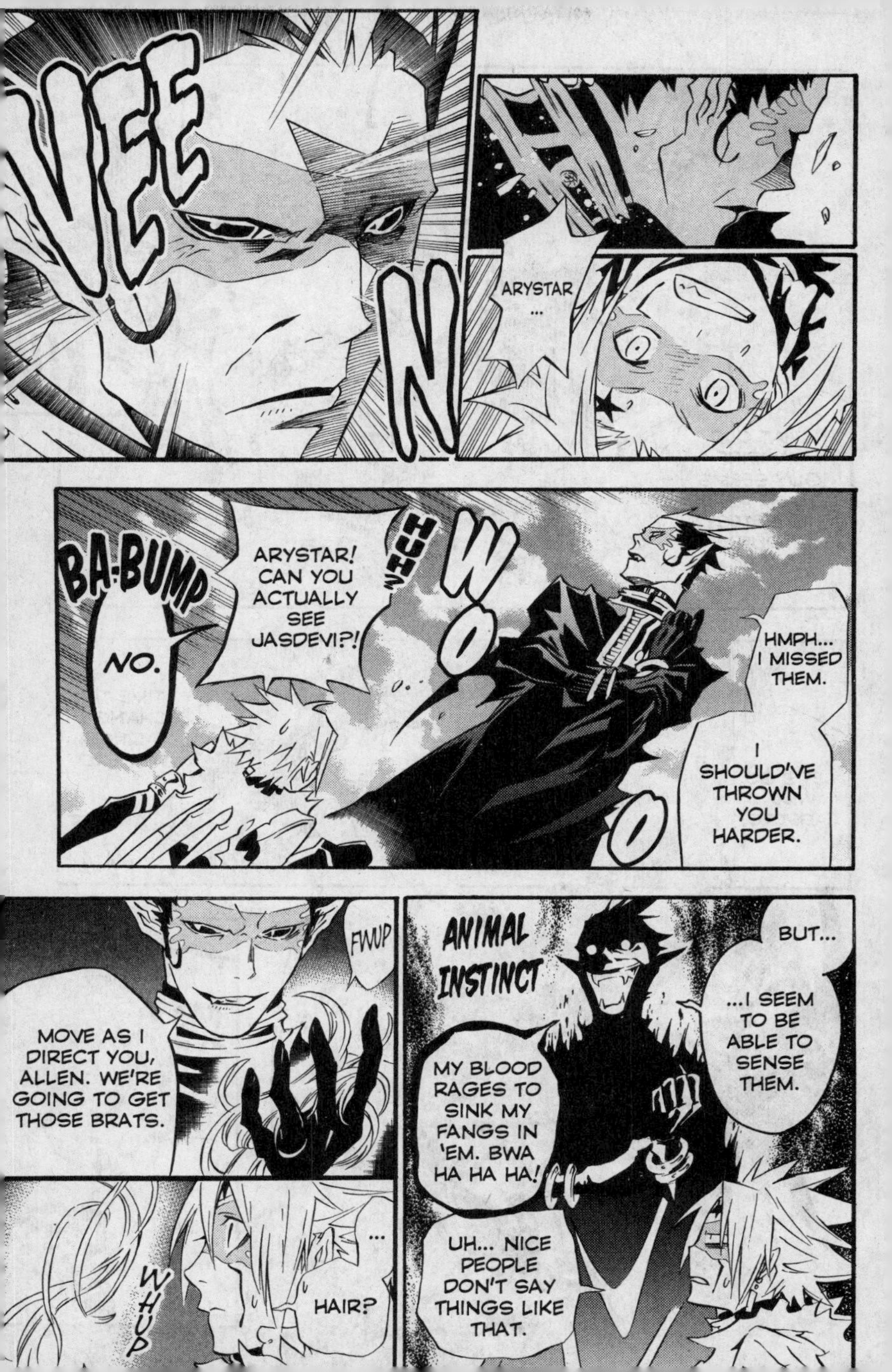
ARYSTAR ...
VEEN
HMPH... I MISSED THEM.
I SHOULD'VE THROWN YOU HARDER.
WOOO
WHUH
ARYSTAR! CAN YOU ACTUALLY SEE JASDEVI?!
BA-BUMP
NO.
BUT...
...I SEEM TO BE ABLE TO SENSE THEM.
ANIMAL INSTINCT
MY BLOOD RAGES TO SINK MY FANGS IN 'EM. BWA HA HA HA!
UH... NICE PEOPLE DON'T SAY THINGS LIKE THAT.
FWUP
MOVE AS I DIRECT YOU, ALLEN. WE'RE GOING TO GET THOSE BRATS.
...
HAIR?
WHUP

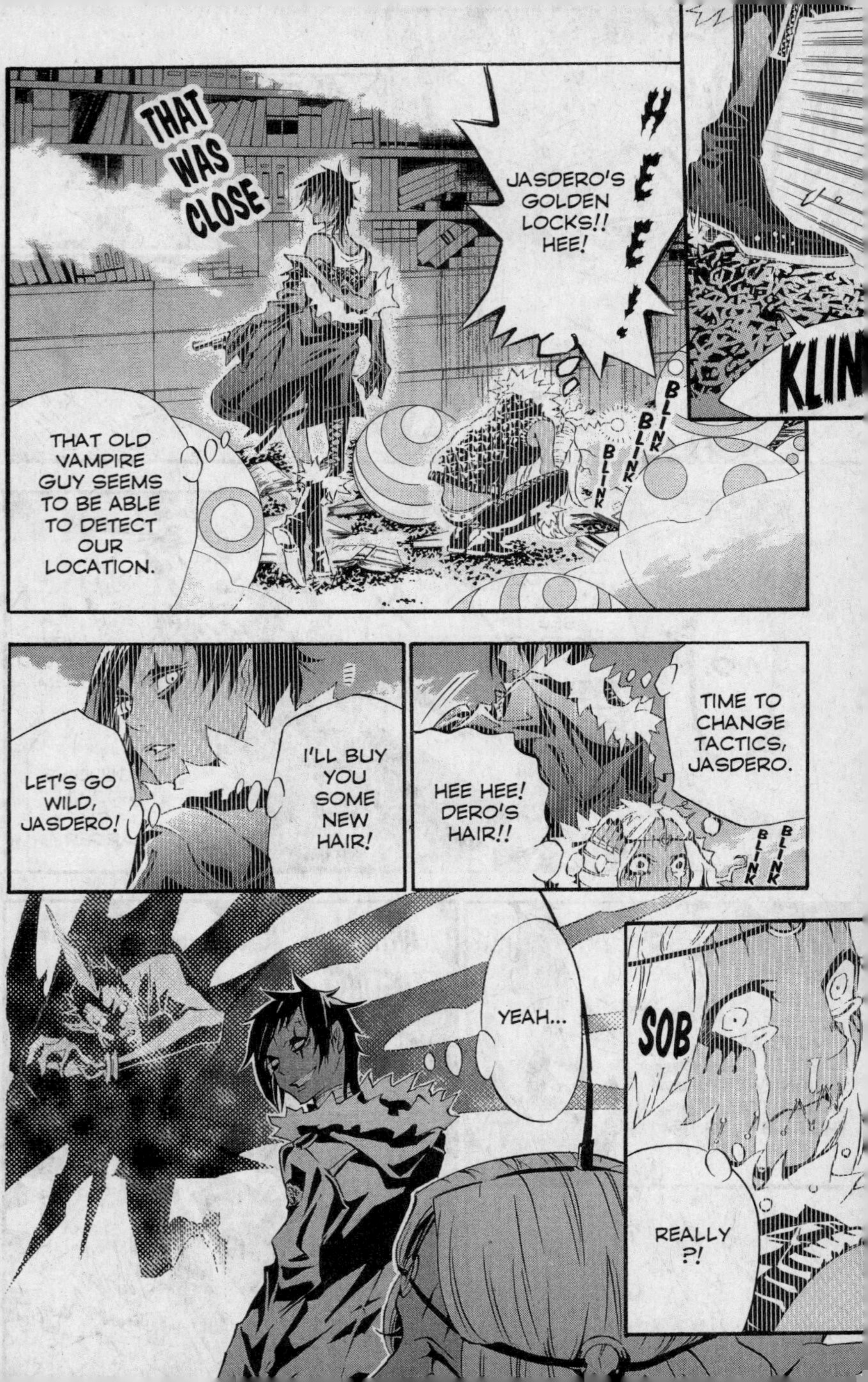
KLIN
HEE!
JASDERO'S GOLDEN LOCKS!! HEE!
THAT WAS CLOSE
BLINK BLINK BLINK
THAT OLD VAMPIRE GUY SEEMS TO BE ABLE TO DETECT OUR LOCATION.
TIME TO CHANGE TACTICS, JASDERO.
HEE HEE! DERO'S HAIR!!
BLINK BLINK
I'LL BUY YOU SOME NEW HAIR!
LET'S GO WILD, JASDERO!
SOB
REALLY ?!
YEAH...

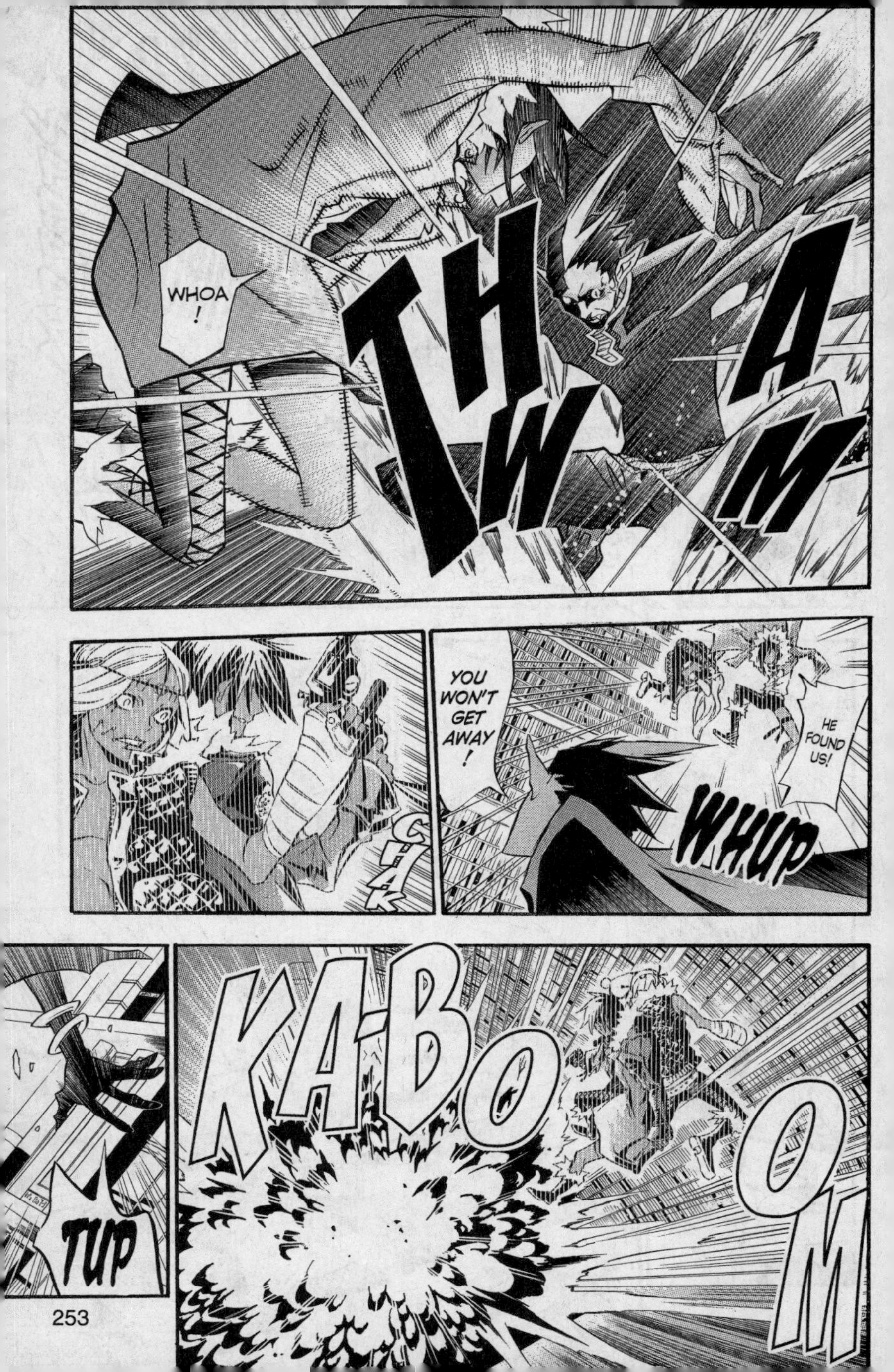
WHOA!
THWAM
HE FOUND US!
YOU WON'T GET AWAY!
WHUP
CHAK
KA-BOOM
TUP

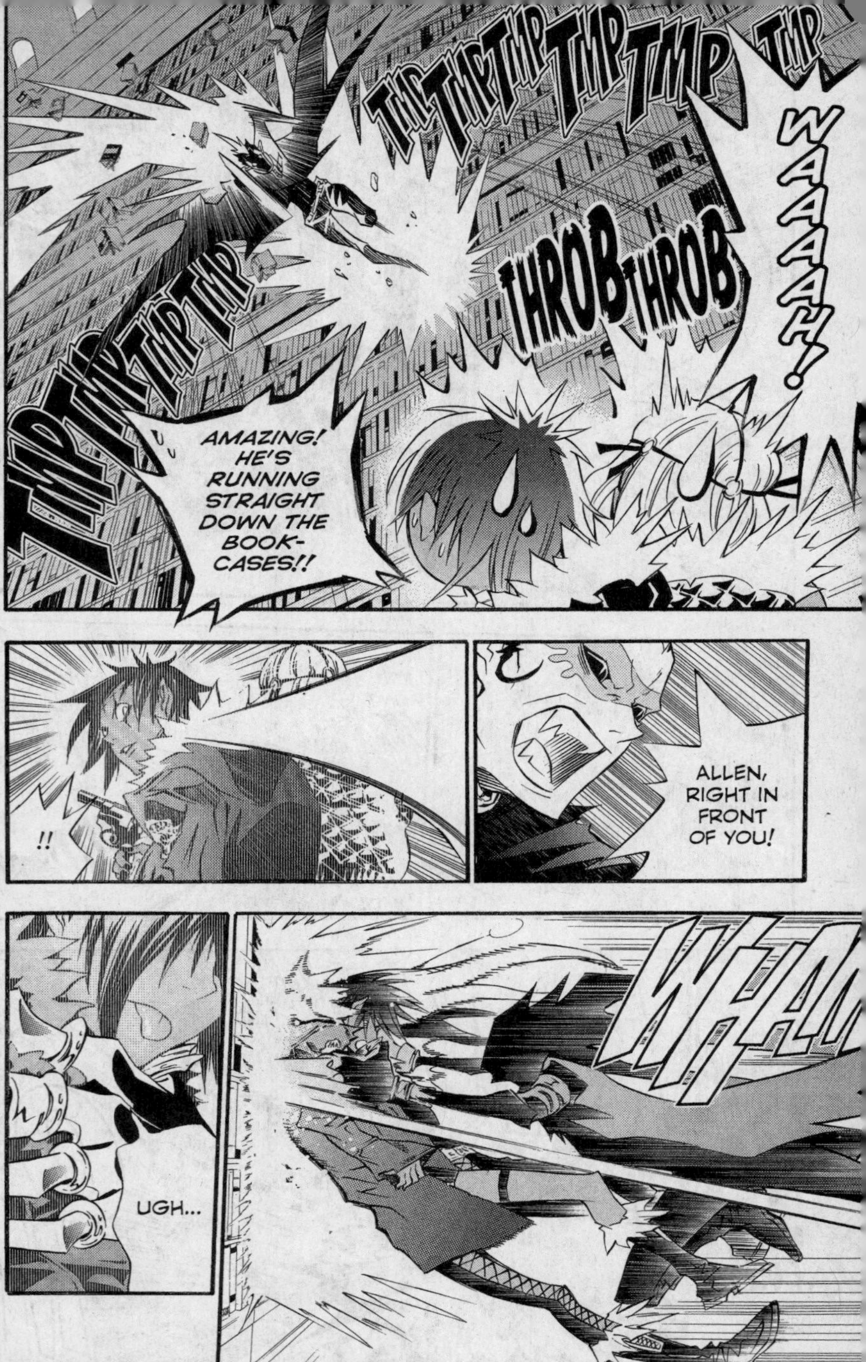

TMP
WAAAAAH!
TMP TMP TMP TMP TMP
THROB THROB
TMP TMP TMP TMP
AMAZING! HE'S RUNNING STRAIGHT DOWN THE BOOK-CASES!!
ALLEN, RIGHT IN FRONT OF YOU!
!!
WHA
UGH...

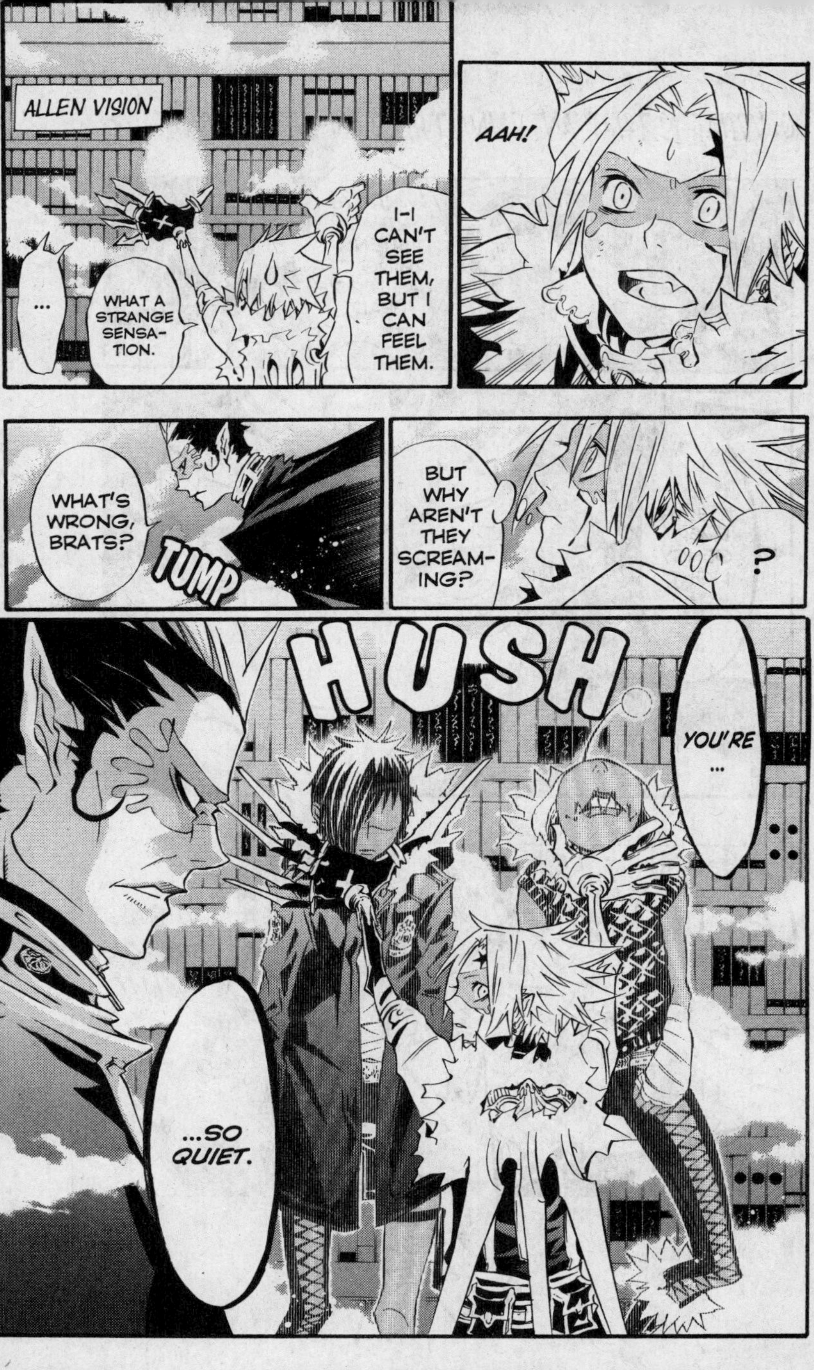
AAH!
I-I CAN'T SEE THEM, BUT I CAN FEEL THEM.
ALLEN VISION
WHAT A STRANGE SENSATION.
...
BUT WHY AREN'T THEY SCREAMING?
?
WHAT'S WRONG, BRATS?
TUMP
YOU'RE ...
HUSH
...SO QUIET.

Q: WHAT IS THAT ANTENNA THING ON JASDERO'S HEAD?

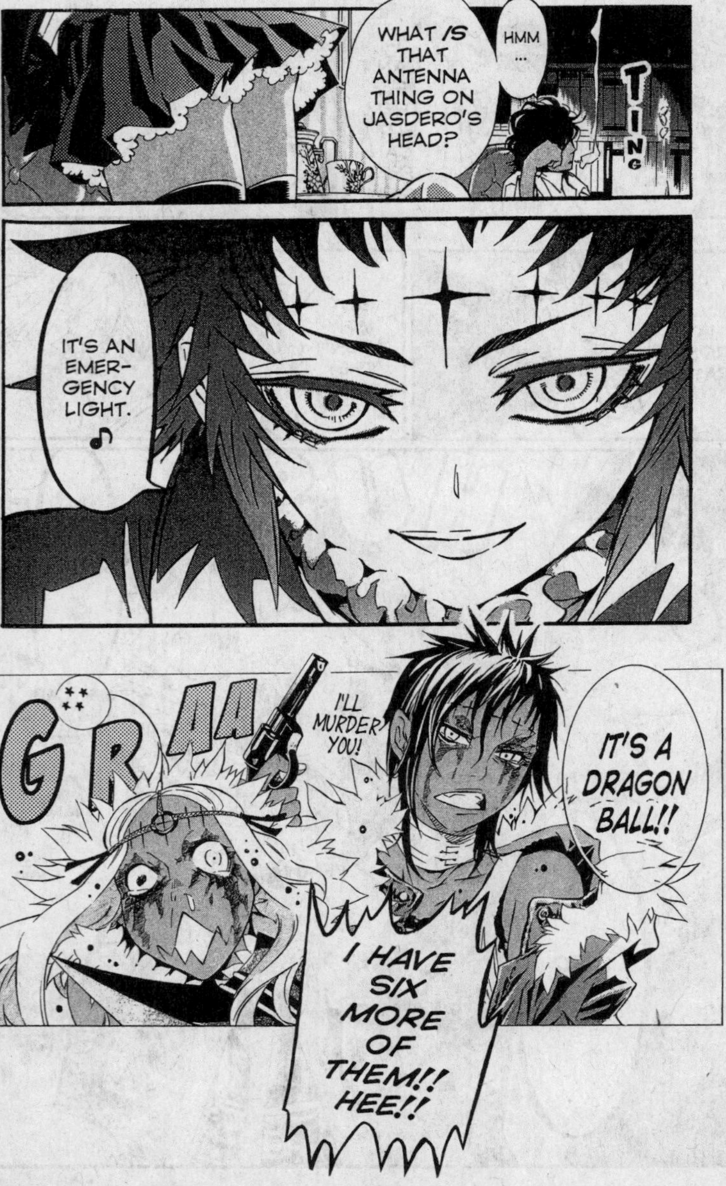
TING
HMM ...
WHAT *IS* THAT ANTENNA THING ON JASDERO'S HEAD?
IT'S AN EMERGENCY LIGHT. ♪
IT'S A DRAGON BALL!!
I'LL MURDER YOU!
I HAVE SIX MORE OF THEM!! HEE!!
GRAA

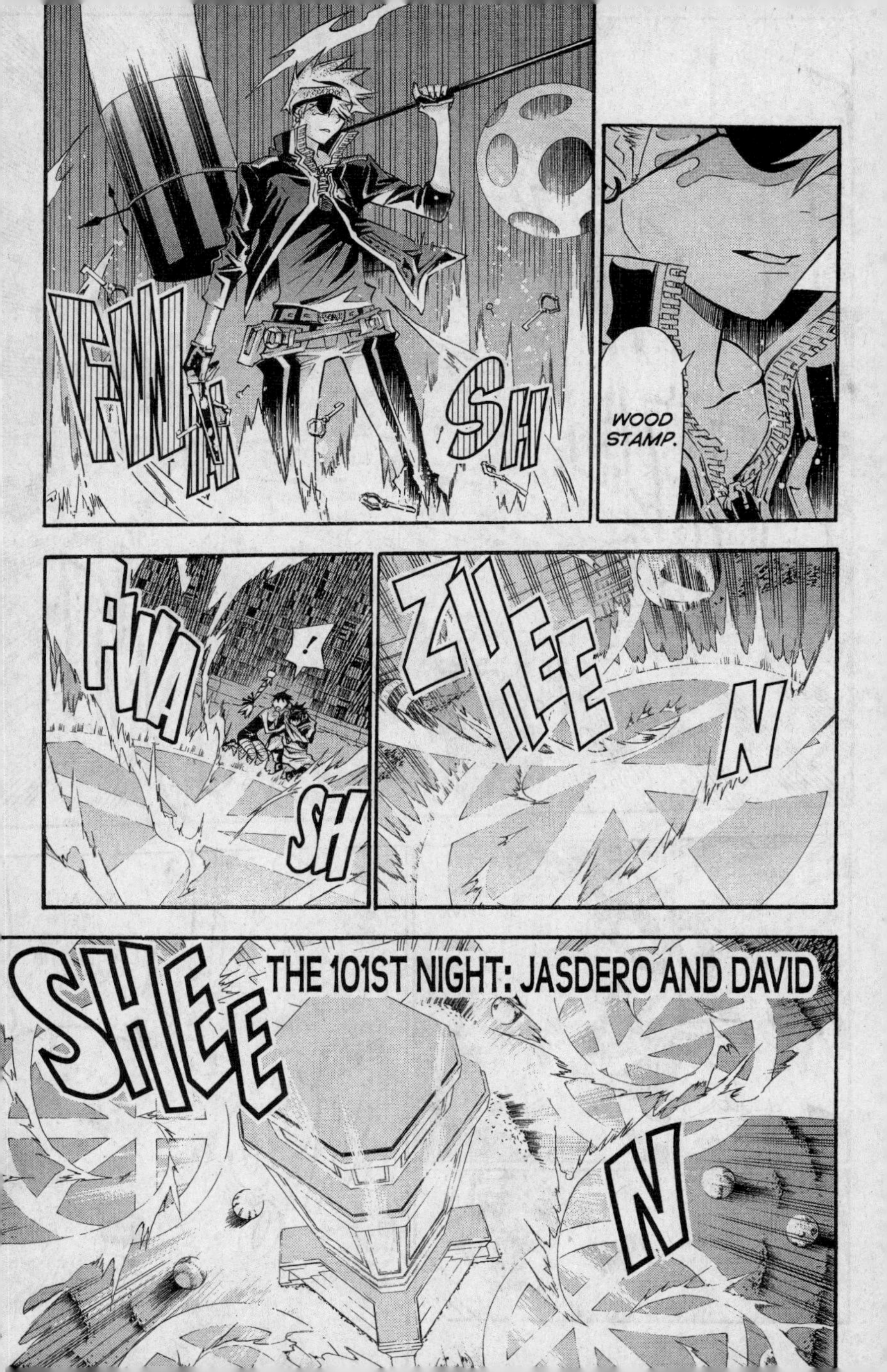
WOOD STAMP.
F-WAA
SH
ZIHEEN
F-WA
!
SH
THE 101ST NIGHT: JASDERO AND DAVID
SHEEEN

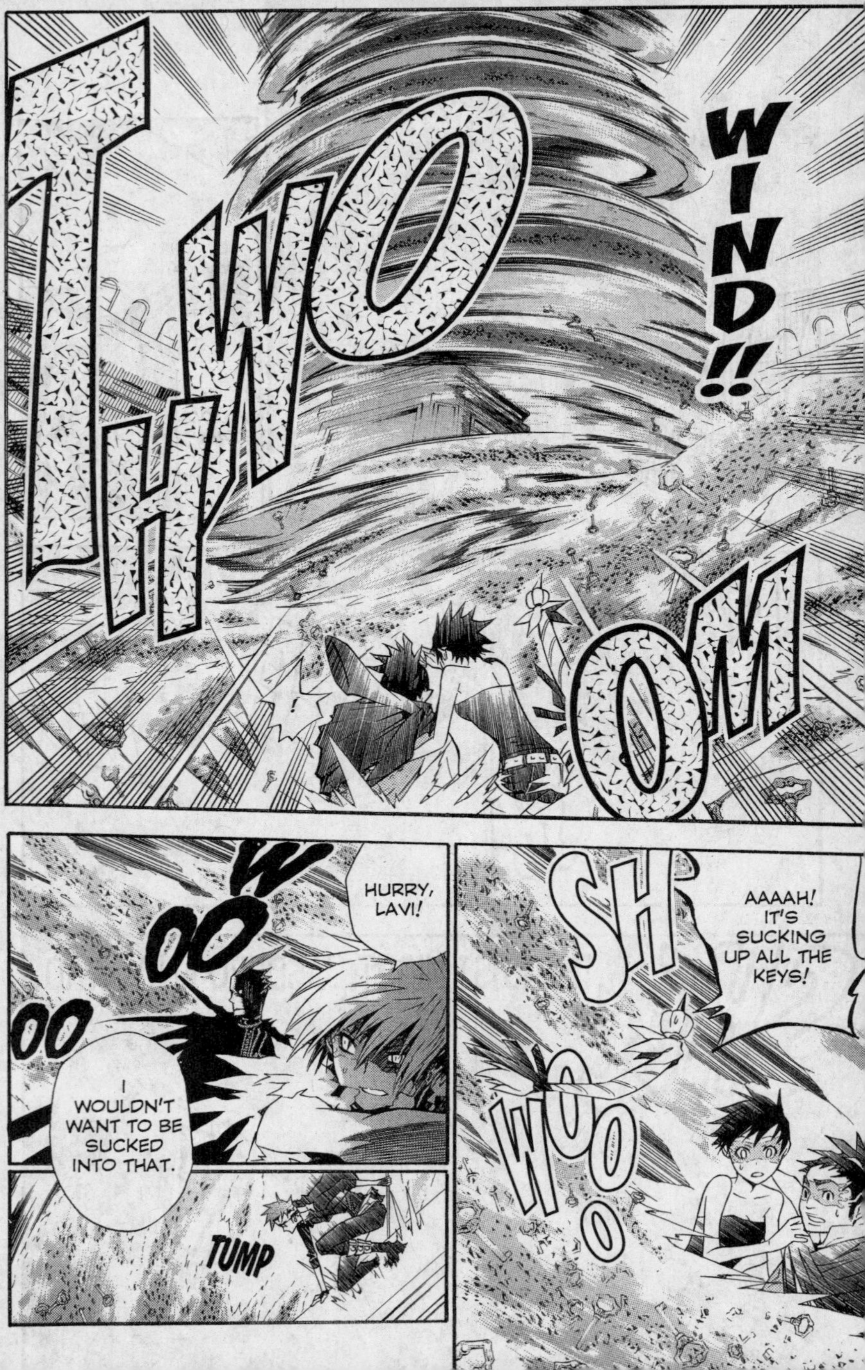
WIND!!
AAAAH! IT'S SUCKING UP ALL THE KEYS!
HURRY, LAVI!
I WOULDN'T WANT TO BE SUCKED INTO THAT.
TUMP

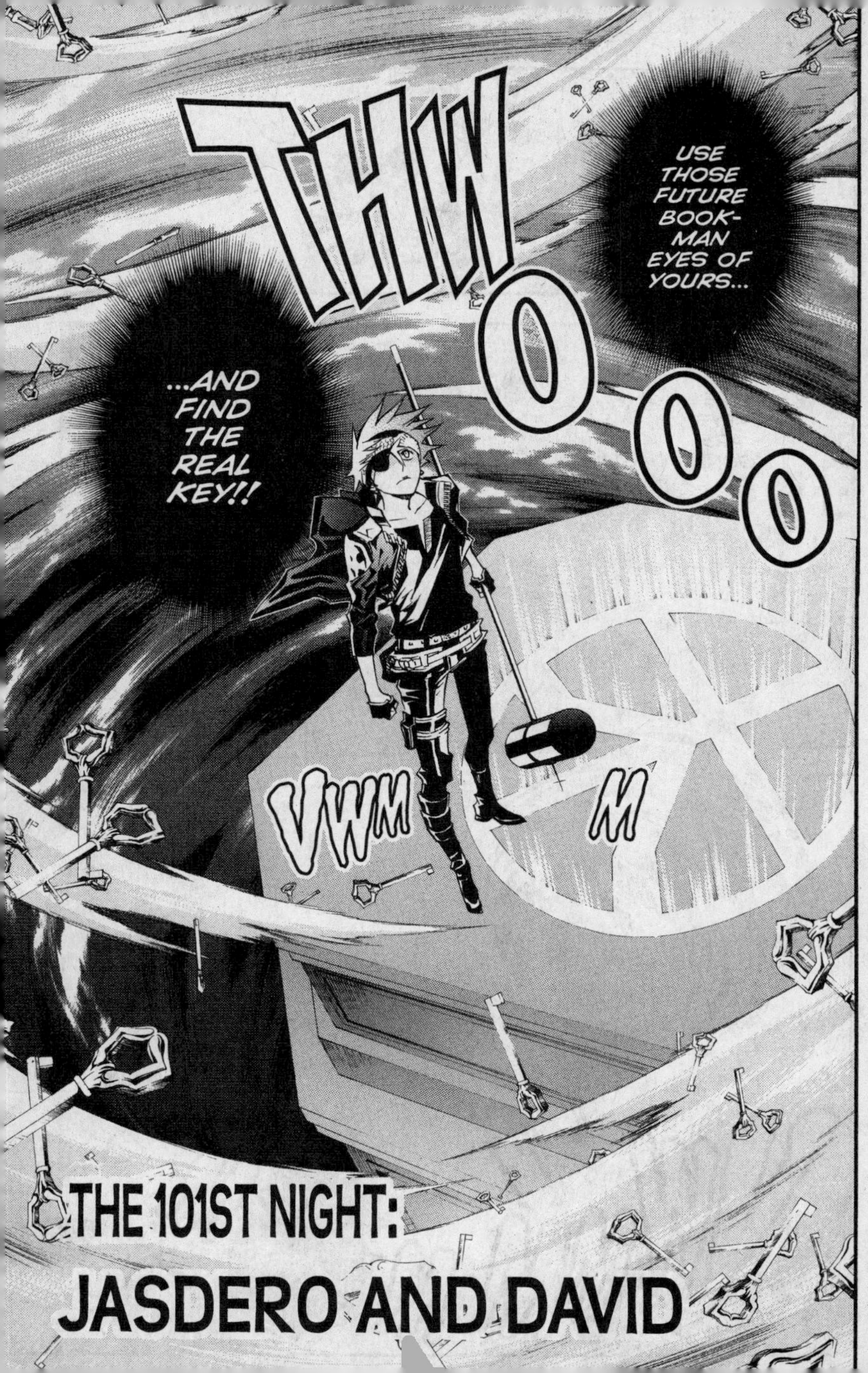
USE THOSE FUTURE BOOK-MAN EYES OF YOURS...
THWOOOO
...AND FIND THE REAL KEY!!
VWMM
THE 101ST NIGHT:
JASDERO AND DAVID

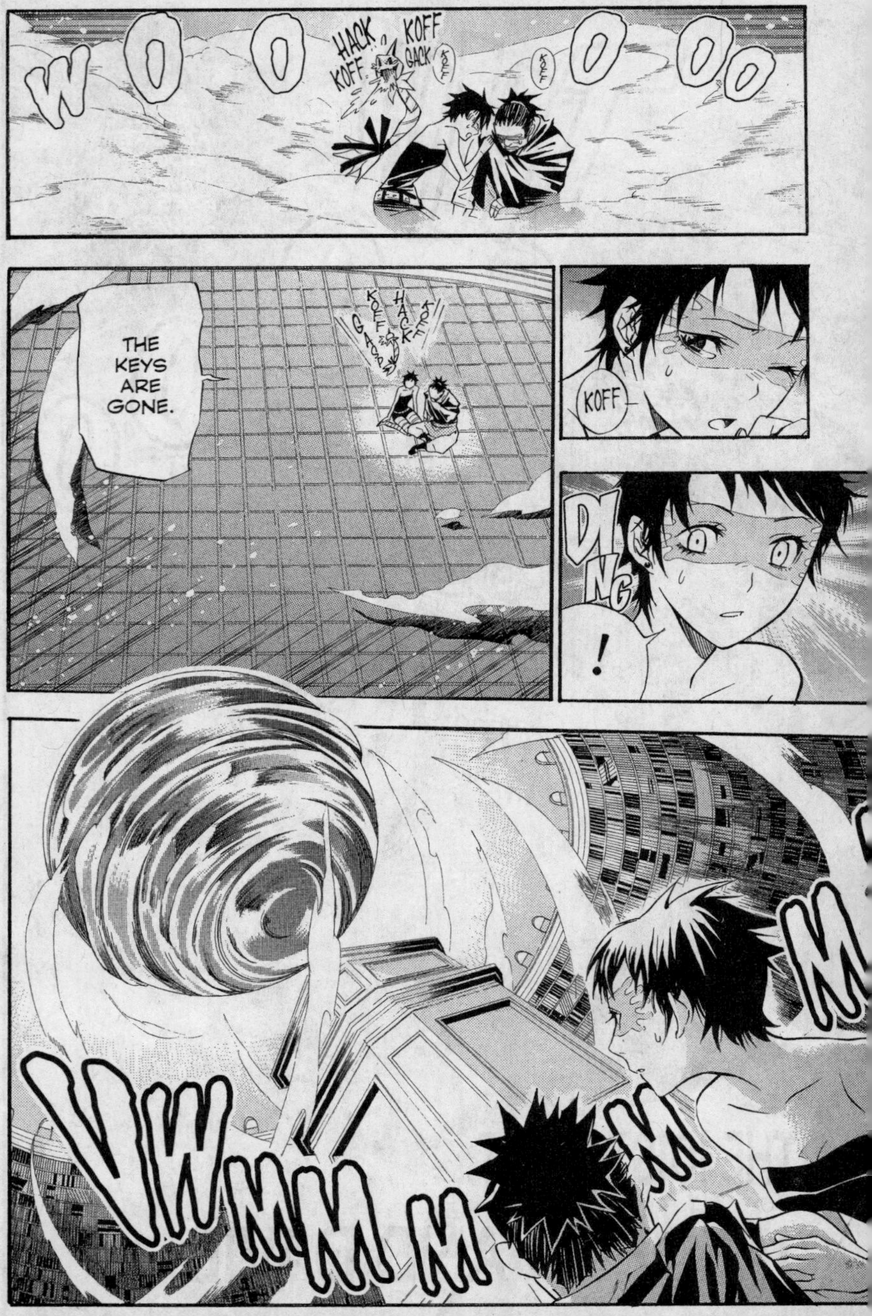
WOOOOOOO
KOFF
KOFF GACK
KOFF
HACK KOFF
KOFF
DING
!
THE KEYS ARE GONE.
KOFF HACK
KOFF GASP
VWMMMMMMMM

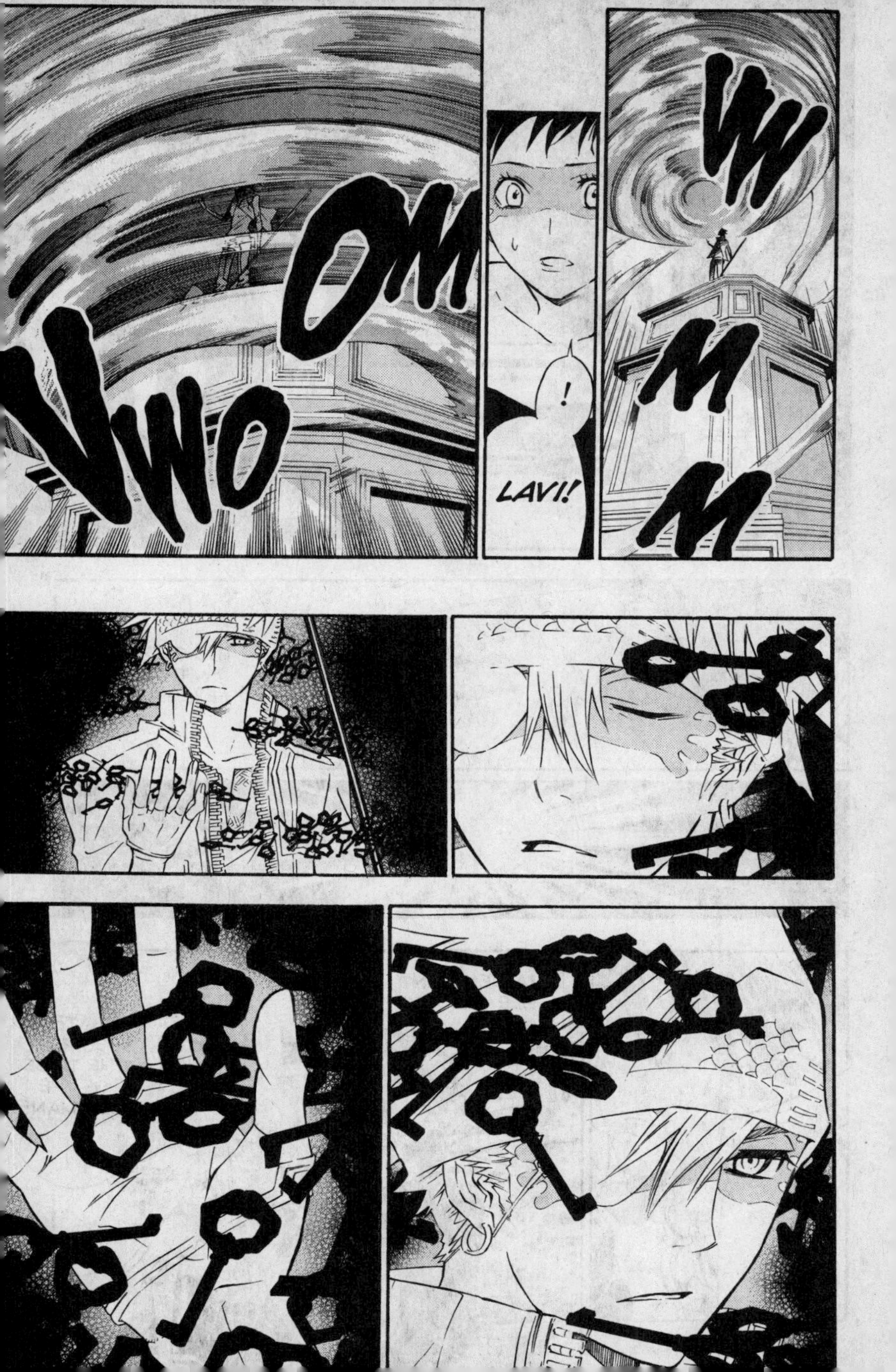
WWMMM
!
LAVI!
VWOOM

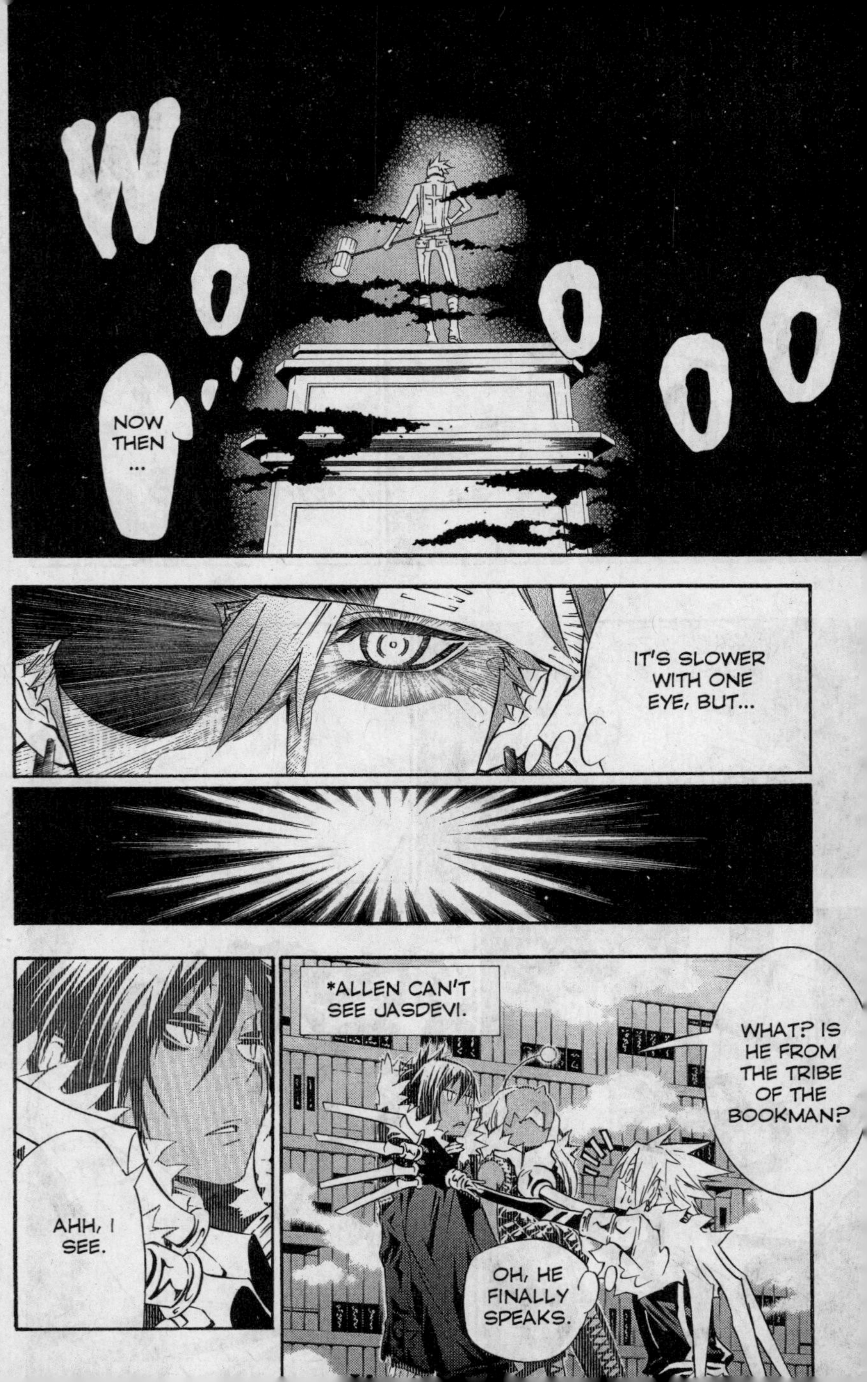
WOOOO
NOW THEN ...
IT'S SLOWER WITH ONE EYE, BUT...
*ALLEN CAN'T SEE JASDEVI.
WHAT? IS HE FROM THE TRIBE OF THE BOOKMAN?
OH, HE FINALLY SPEAKS.
AHH, I SEE.

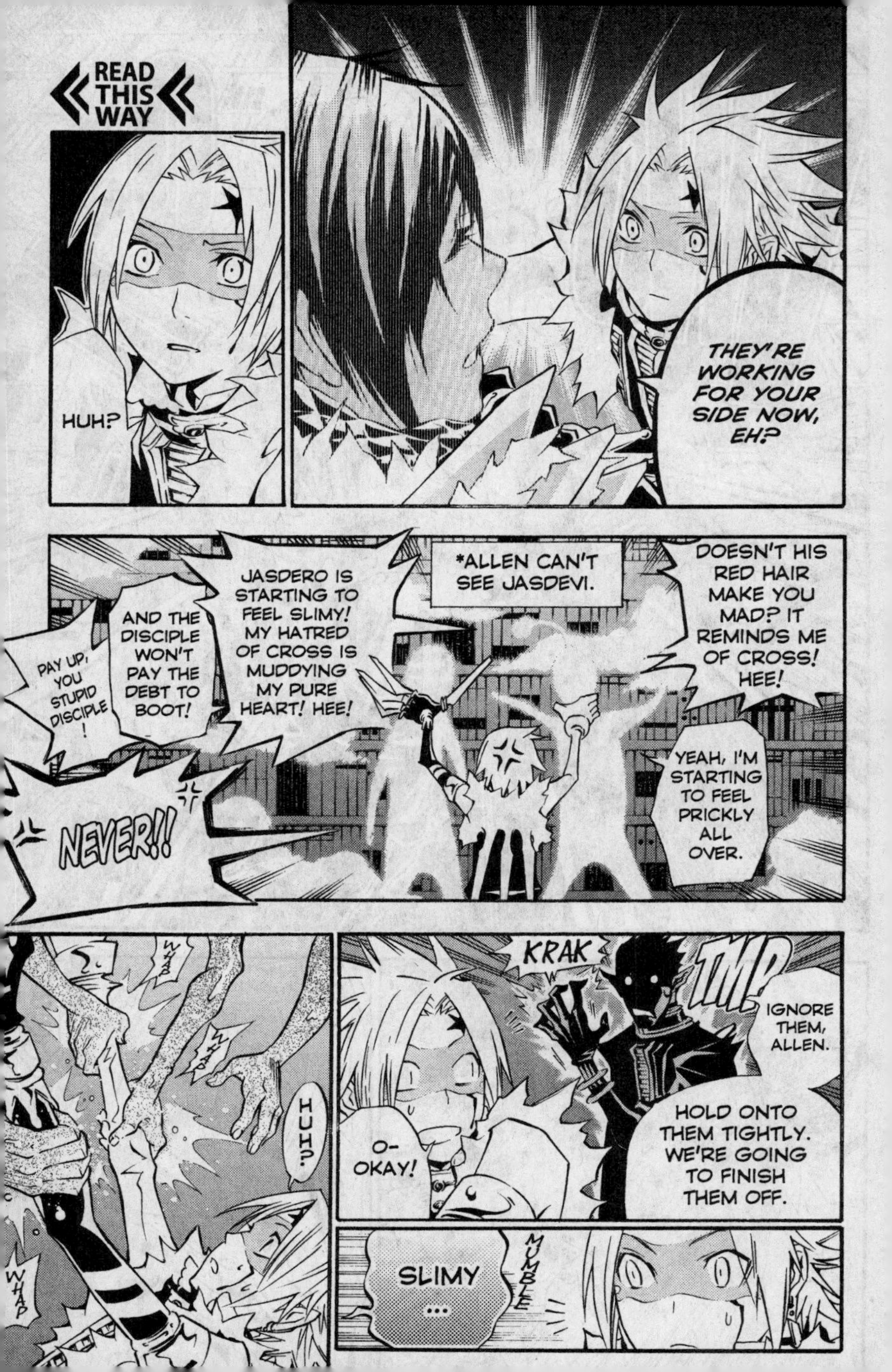
READ THIS WAY
THEY'RE WORKING FOR YOUR SIDE NOW, EH?
HUH?
DOESN'T HIS RED HAIR MAKE YOU MAD? IT REMINDS ME OF CROSS! HEE!
*ALLEN CAN'T SEE JASDEVI.
YEAH, I'M STARTING TO FEEL PRICKLY ALL OVER.
JASDERO IS STARTING TO FEEL SLIMY! MY HATRED OF CROSS IS MUDDYING MY PURE HEART! HEE!
AND THE DISCIPLE WON'T PAY THE DEBT TO BOOT!
PAY UP, YOU STUPID DISCIPLE!
NEVER!!
KRAK
TMP
IGNORE THEM, ALLEN.
HOLD ONTO THEM TIGHTLY. WE'RE GOING TO FINISH THEM OFF.
O-OKAY!
MUMBLE
SLIMY ...
WHAP
WHAP
HUH?
WHAP

VWOOM

!!

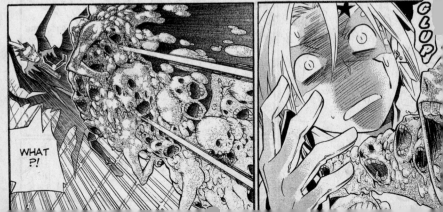

GLUP

WHAT?!

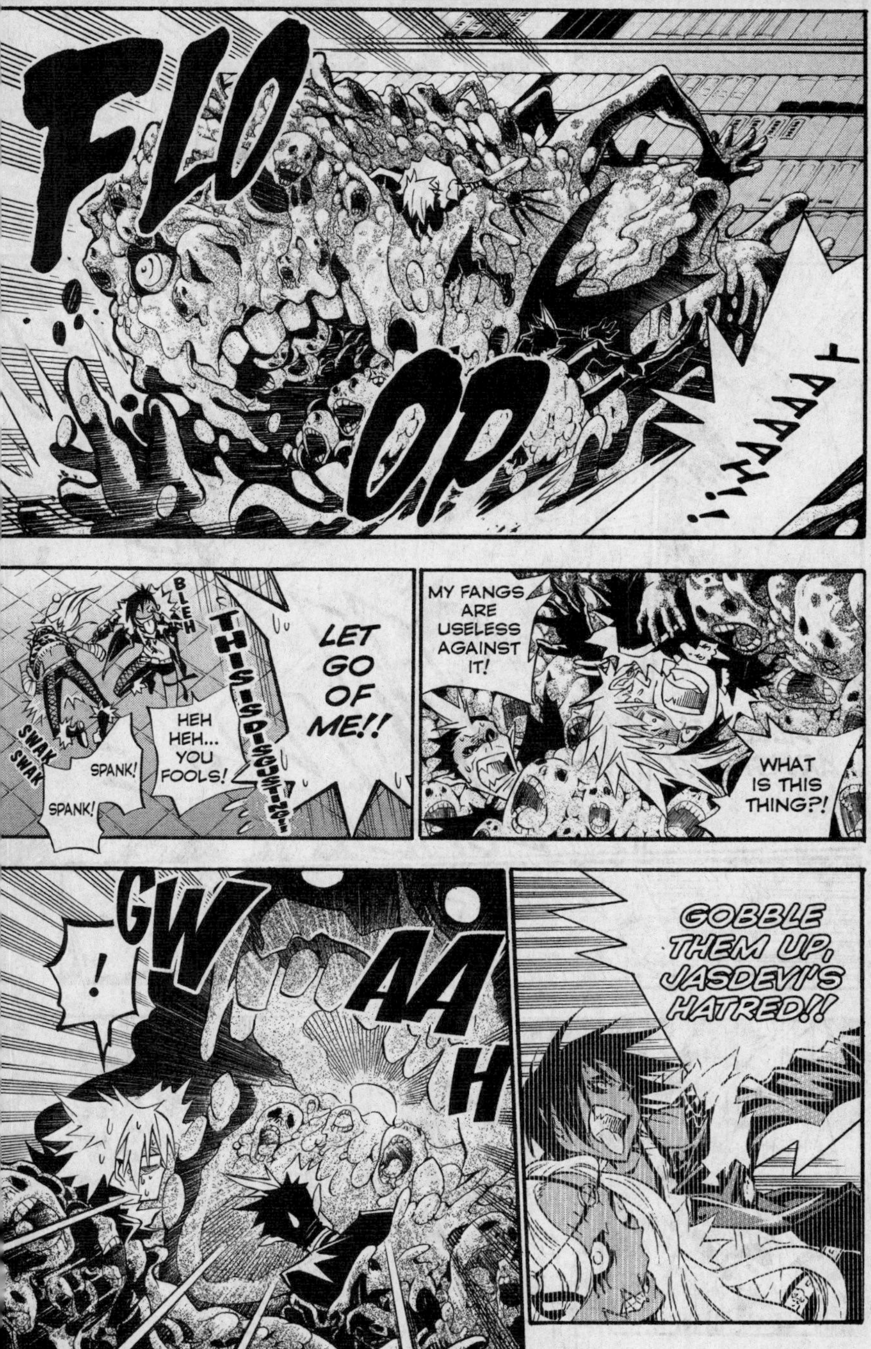
FLOOP
AAAAH!!
MY FANGS ARE USELESS AGAINST IT!
WHAT IS THIS THING?!
LET GO OF ME!!
THIS IS DISGUSTING!!
BLEH
HEH HEH... YOU FOOLS!
SPANK!
SPANK!
SWAK SWAK
GOBBLE THEM UP, JASDEVI'S HATRED!!
GWAAH
!

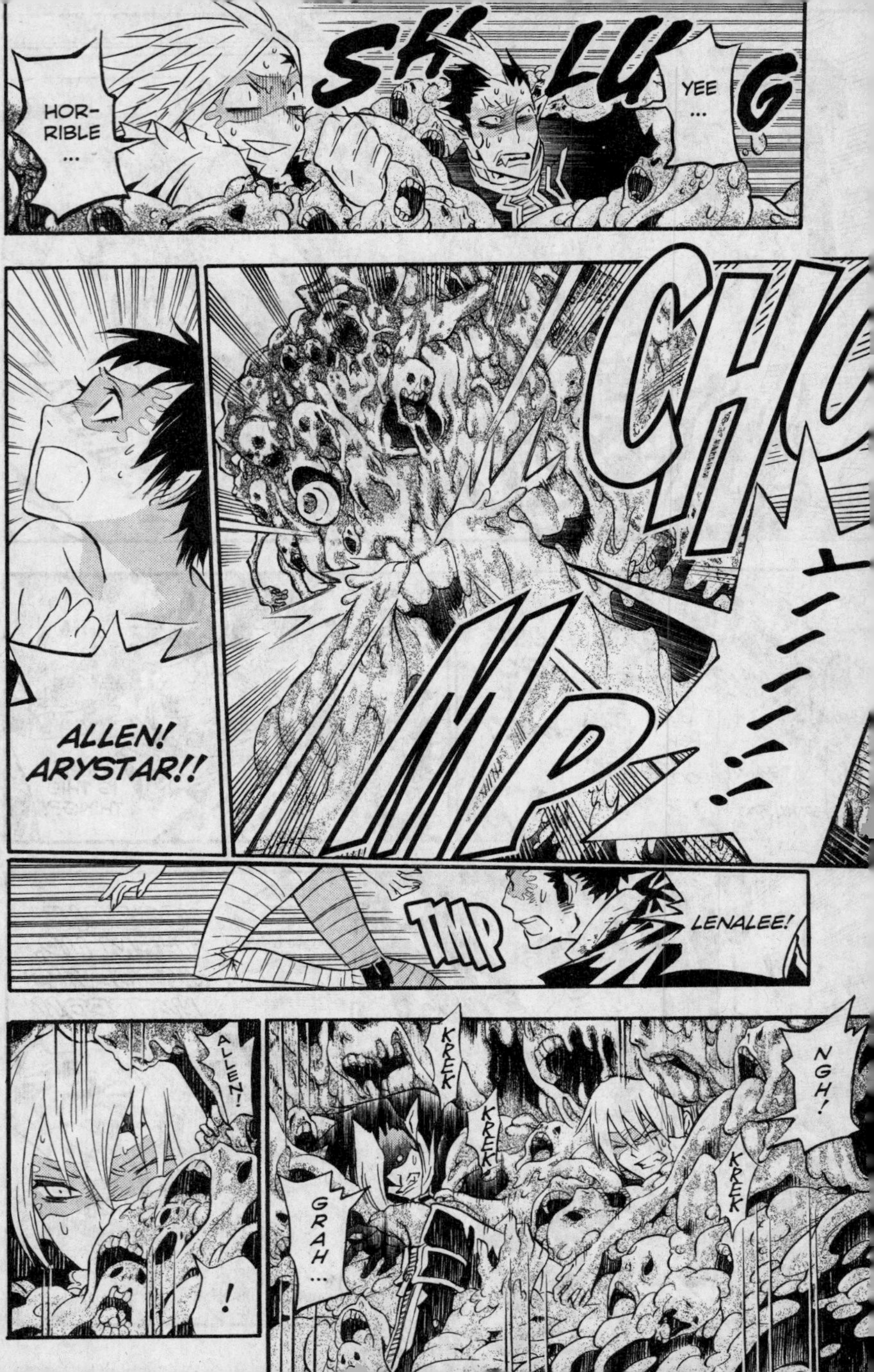
YEE ...
SHLUG
HOR-RIBLE ...
CHOMP
!!
ALLEN! ARYSTAR!!
LENALEE!
TMP
NGH!
KREK
KREK
KREK
GRAH ...
ALLEN!
!

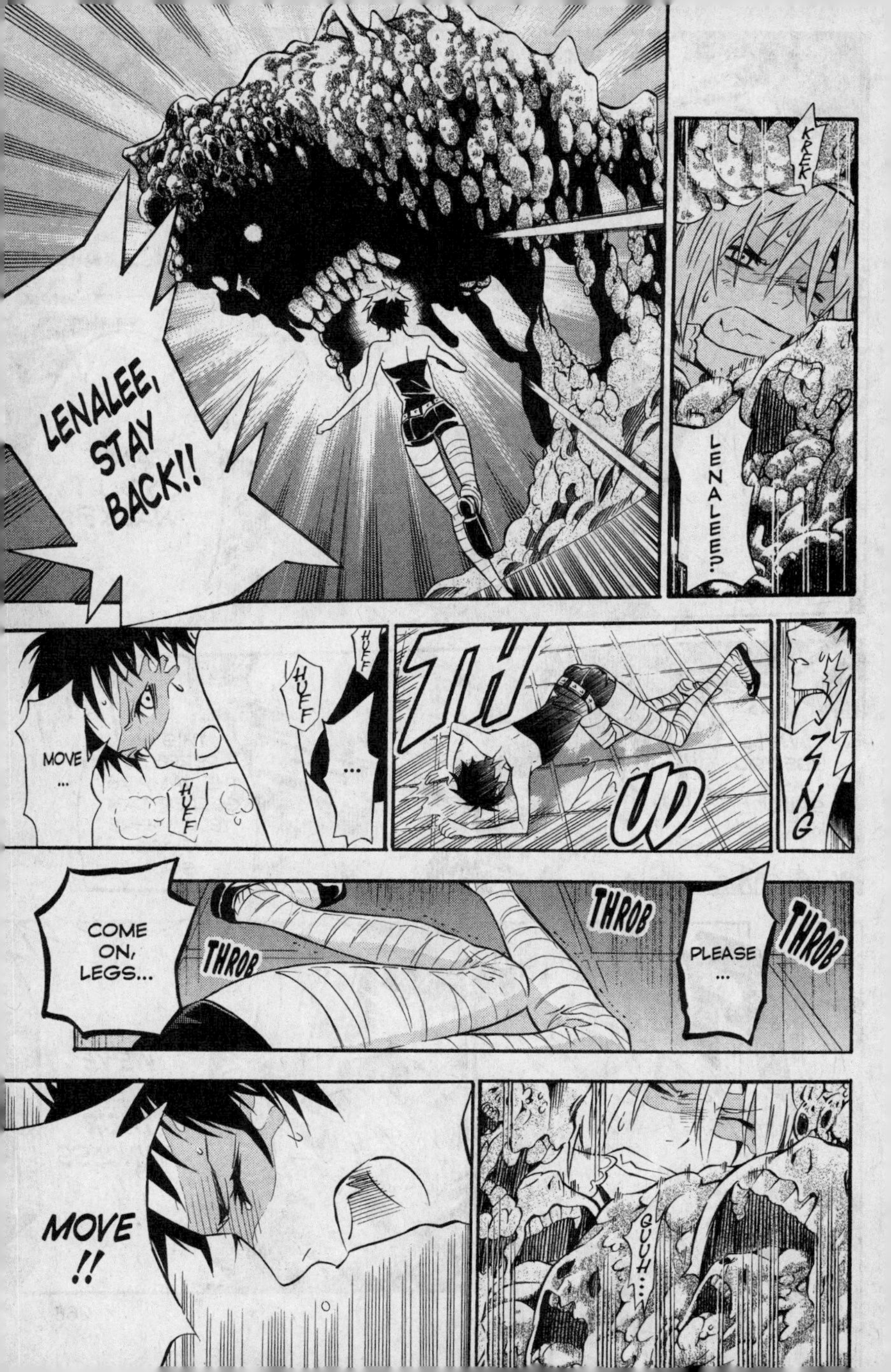
KREK
LENALEE?
LENALEE, STAY BACK!!
ZING
THUD
HUFF HUFF
...
MOVE ...
HUFF HUFF
THROB
PLEASE ...
THROB
COME ON, LEGS...
THROB
GUUH...
MOVE !!

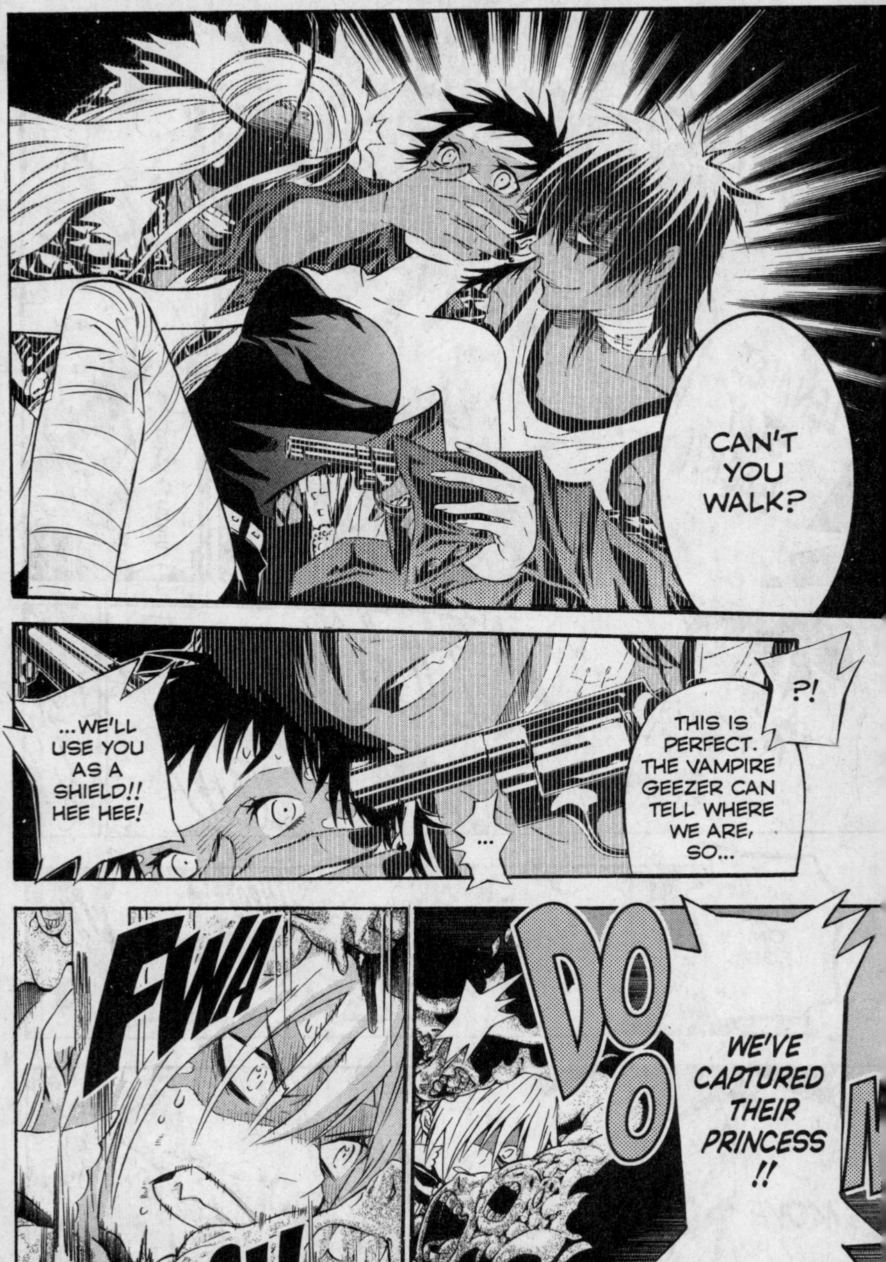
CAN'T YOU WALK?
?!
THIS IS PERFECT. THE VAMPIRE GEEZER CAN TELL WHERE WE ARE, SO...
...
...WE'LL USE YOU AS A SHIELD!! HEE HEE!
DOOO
WE'VE CAPTURED THEIR PRINCESS!!
FWA
SH

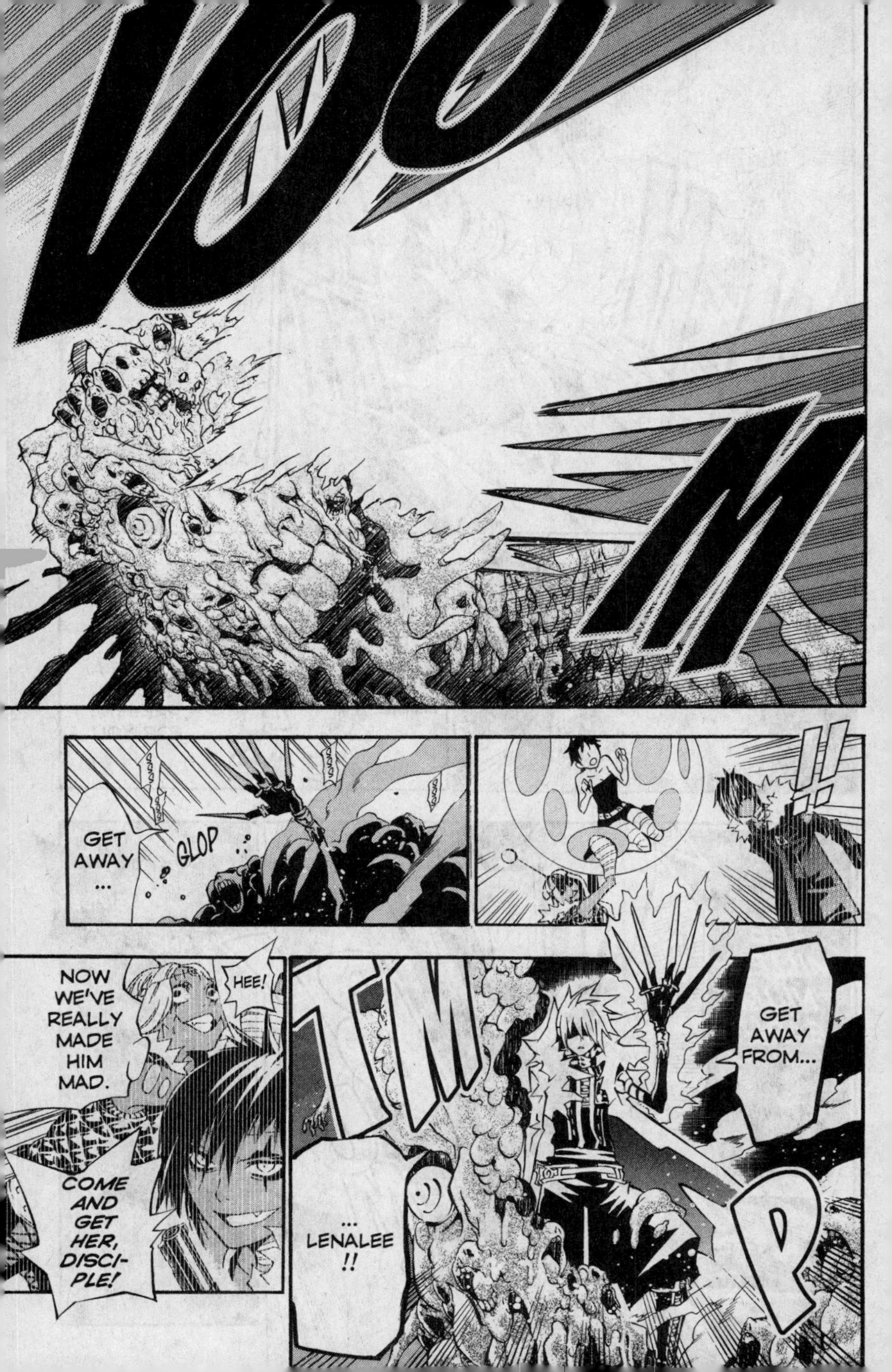
DOOM
!!
GET AWAY ...
GLOP
GET AWAY FROM...
... LENALEE !!
HEE!
NOW WE'VE REALLY MADE HIM MAD.
COME AND GET HER, DISCIPLE!

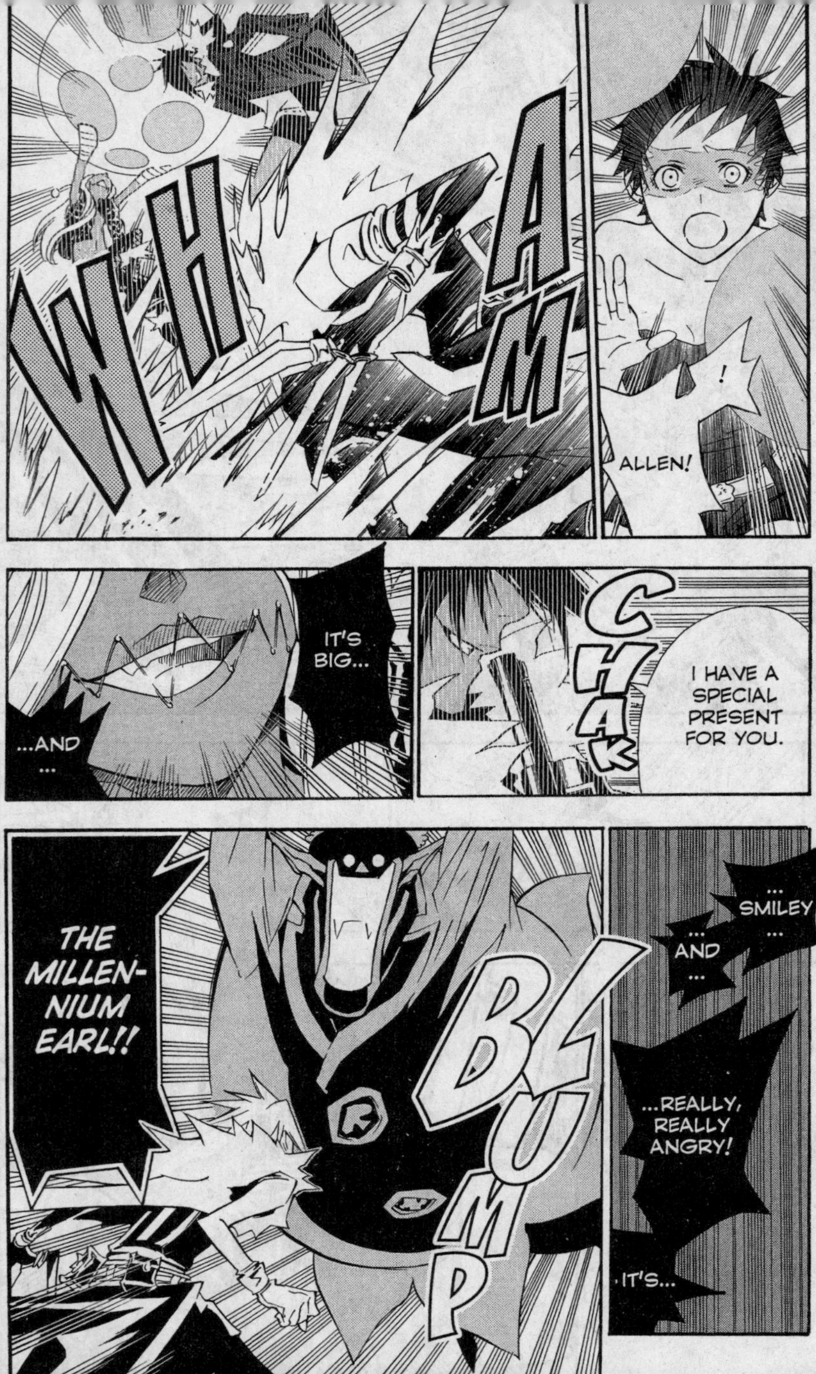
!
ALLEN!
WHAM
CHAK
I HAVE A SPECIAL PRESENT FOR YOU.
IT'S BIG...
...AND ...
... SMILEY ...
... AND ...
...REALLY, REALLY ANGRY!
IT'S...
BLUMP
THE MILLEN-NIUM EARL!!

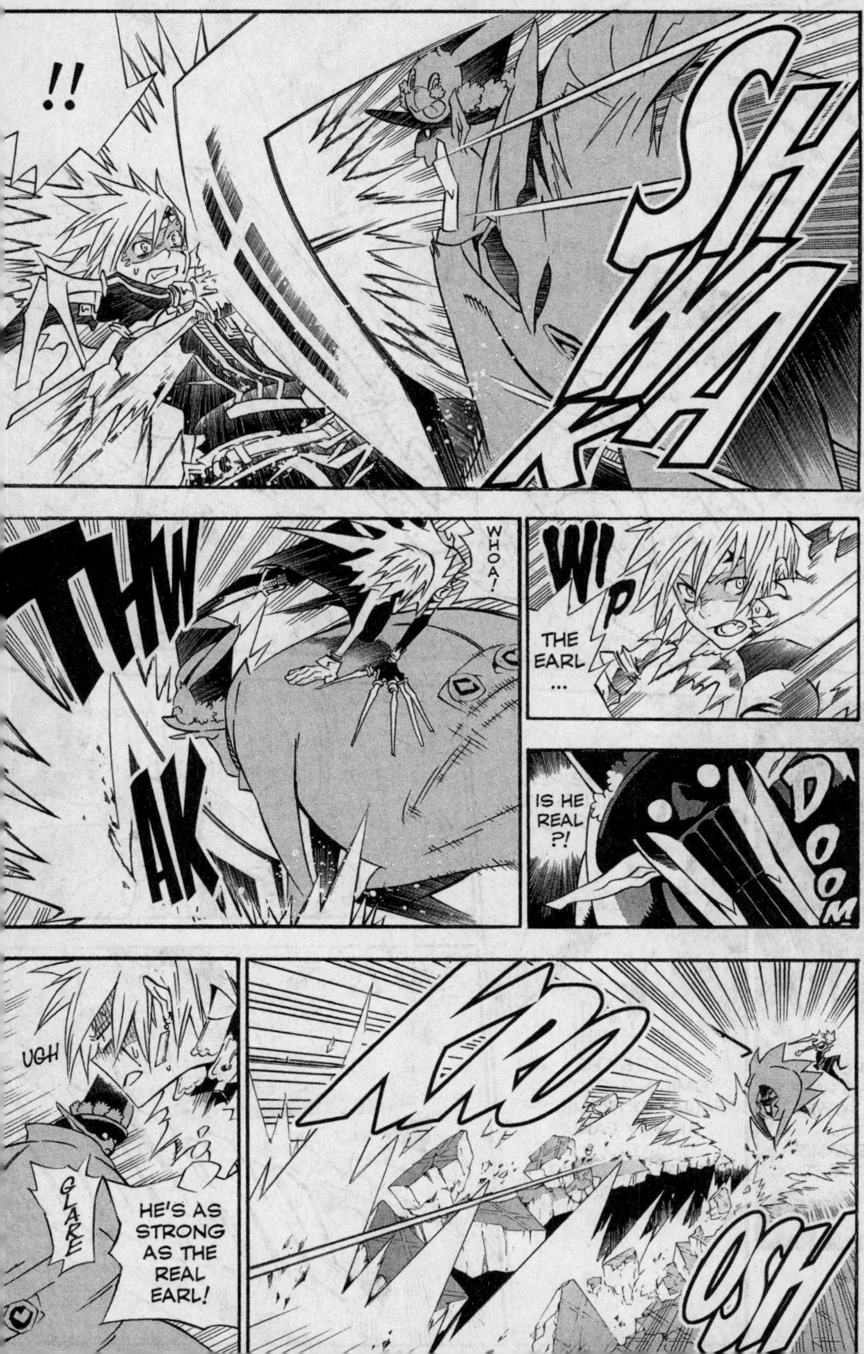
SHAK
!!
WIP
THE EARL...
IS HE REAL?!
DOOOM
WHOA!
THWAK
WOOSH
UGH
HE'S AS STRONG AS THE REAL EARL!
GLARE

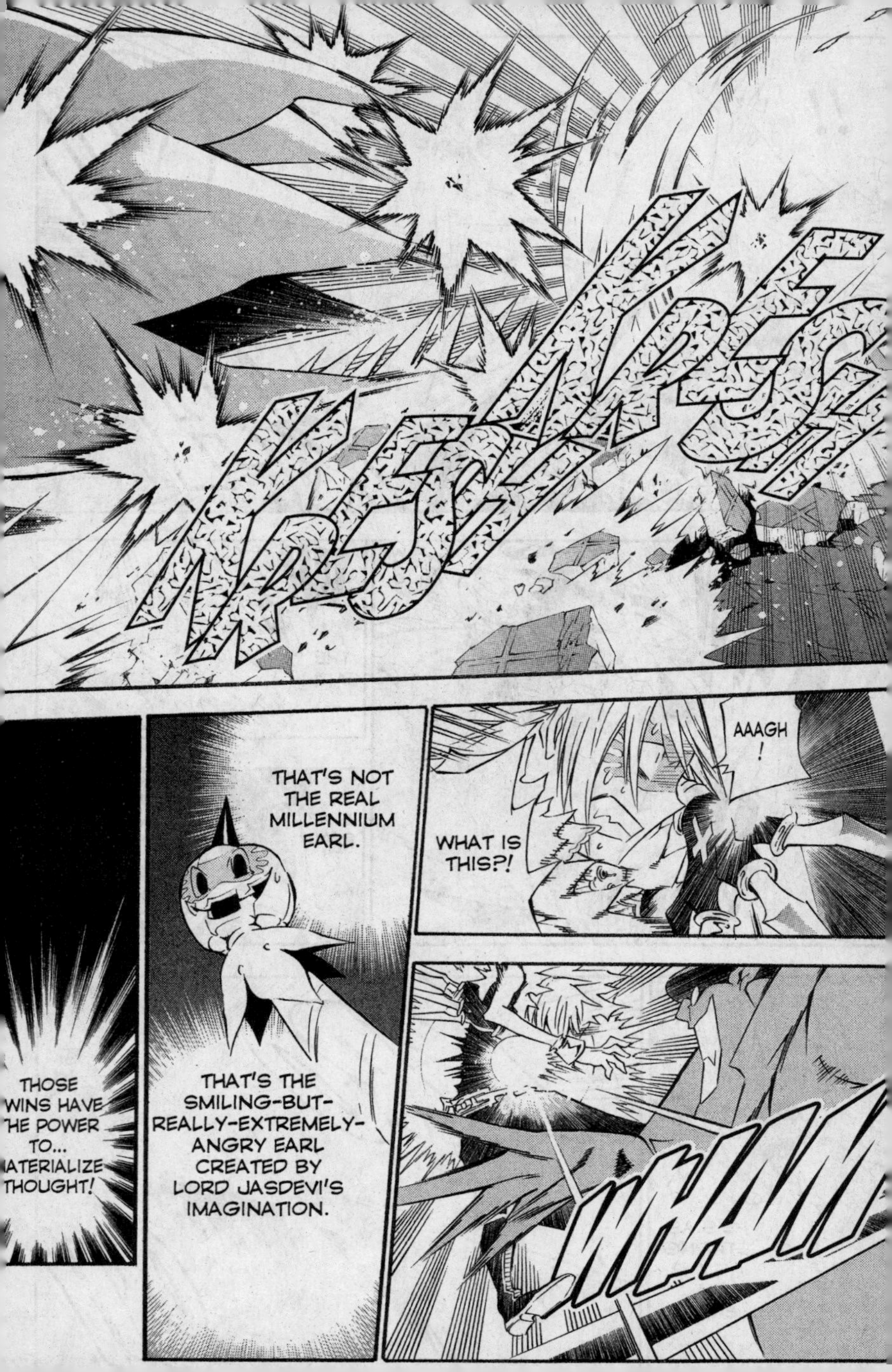
AAAGH!
WHAT IS THIS?!
THAT'S NOT THE REAL MILLENNIUM EARL.
THAT'S THE SMILING-BUT-REALLY-EXTREMELY-ANGRY EARL CREATED BY LORD JASDEVI'S IMAGINATION.
THOSE WINS HAVE HE POWER TO... ATERIALIZE THOUGHT!

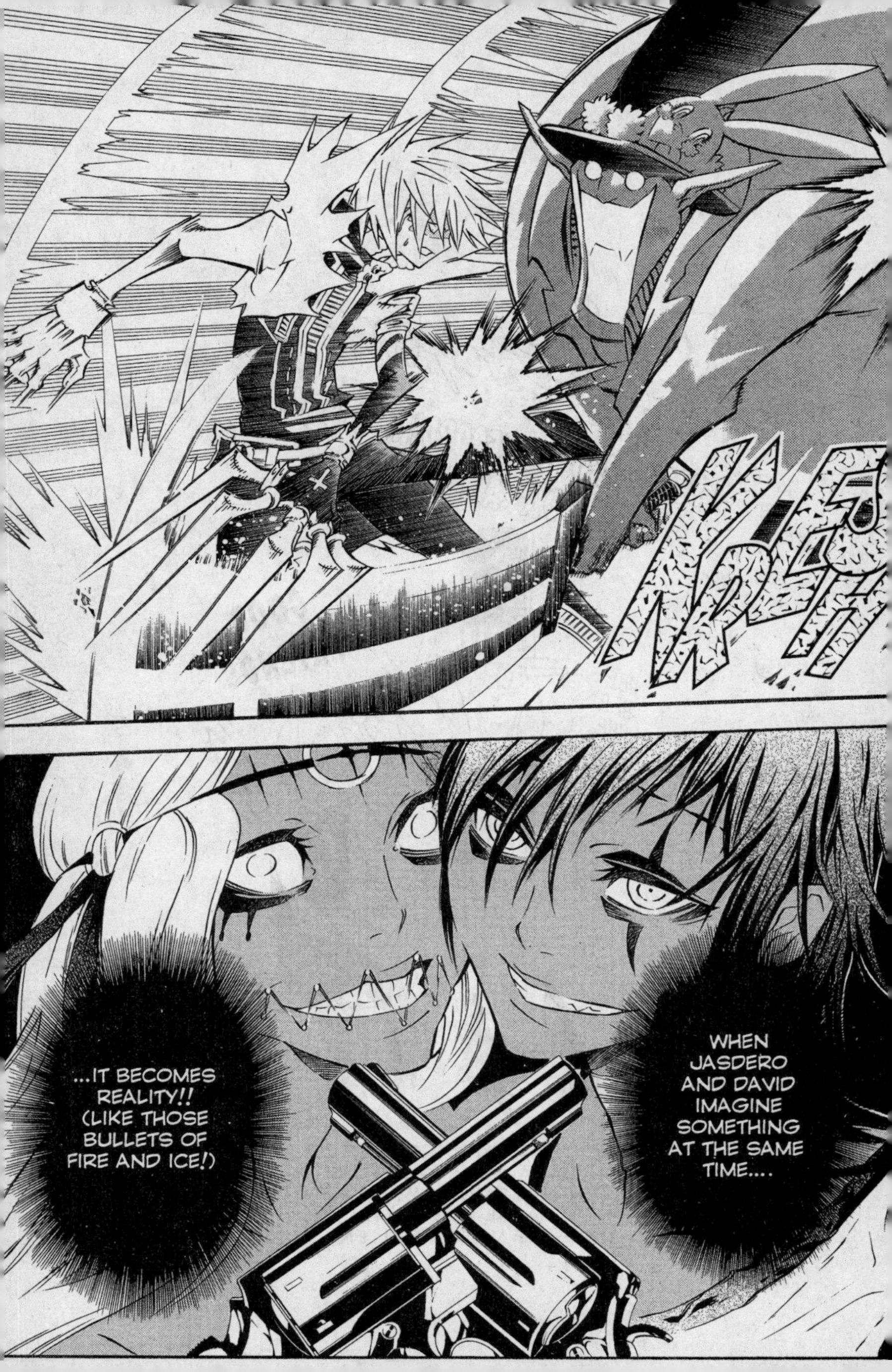
KRASH
WHEN JASDERO AND DAVID IMAGINE SOMETHING AT THE SAME TIME....
...IT BECOMES REALITY!! (LIKE THOSE BULLETS OF FIRE AND ICE!)

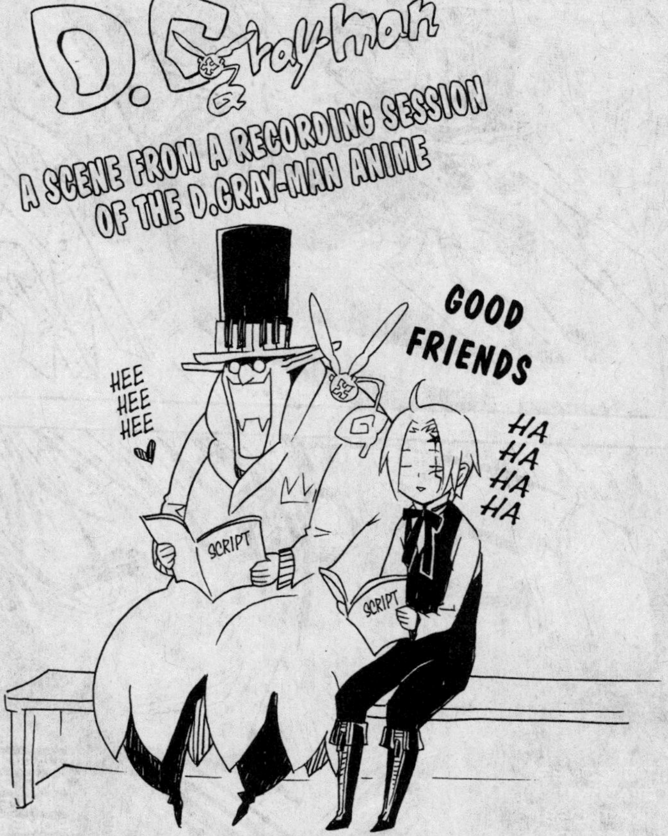
D.Gray-man
A SCENE FROM A RECORDING SESSION OF THE D.GRAY-MAN ANIME
GOOD FRIENDS
HA HA HA HA
HEE HEE HEE
SCRIPT
SCRIPT

DURING THE RECORDING SESSIONS, TAKIZAWA, WHO VOICES THE MILLENNIUM EARL, ALWAYS SITS NEXT TO SANAE KOBAYASHI, WHO DOES THE VOICE OF ALLEN.

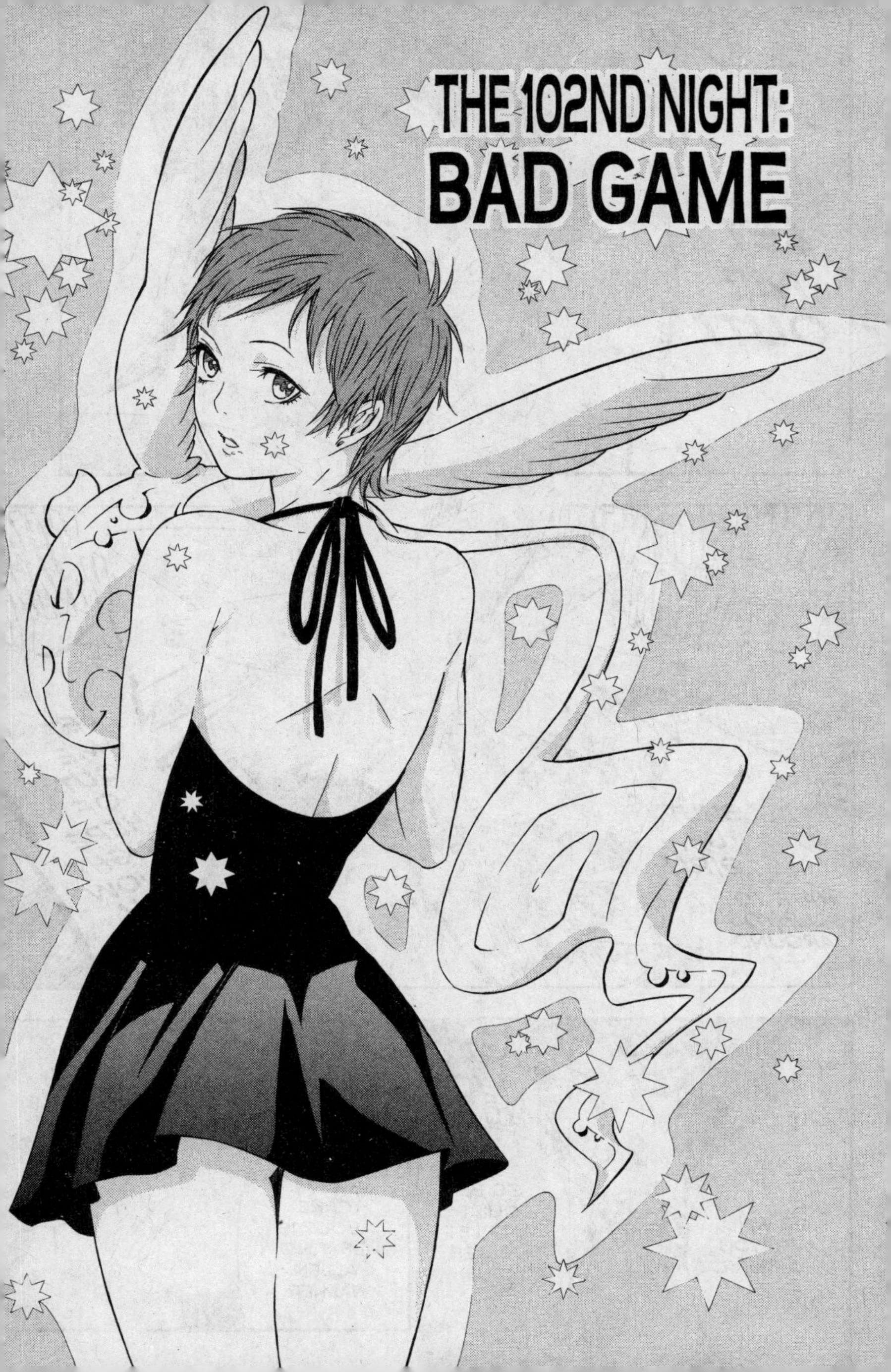
THE 102ND NIGHT:
BAD GAME

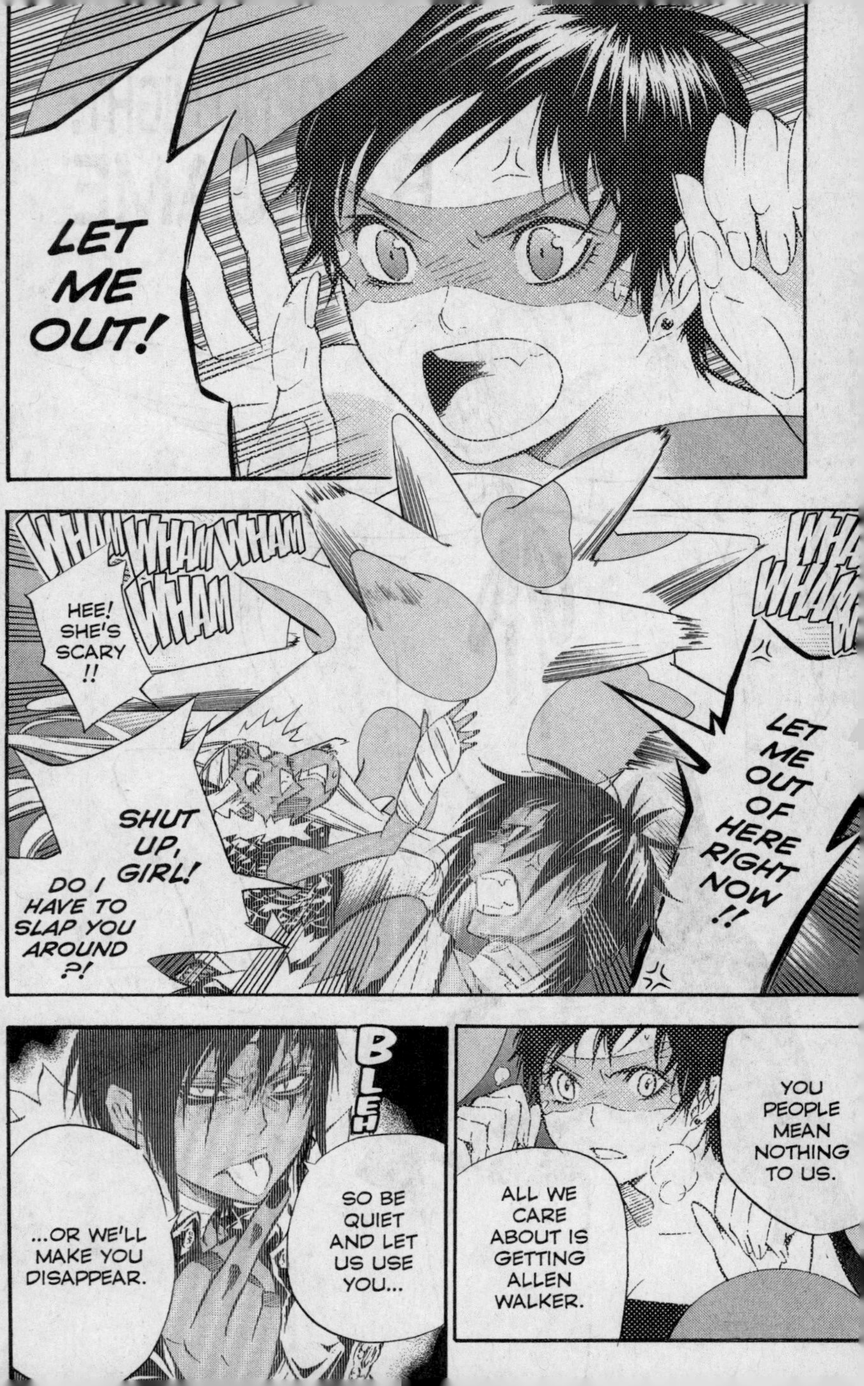
LET ME OUT!
LET ME OUT OF HERE RIGHT NOW!!
WHAM WHAM WHAM WHAM
HEE! SHE'S SCARY!!
SHUT UP, GIRL!
DO I HAVE TO SLAP YOU AROUND?!
YOU PEOPLE MEAN NOTHING TO US.
ALL WE CARE ABOUT IS GETTING ALLEN WALKER.
BLEH
SO BE QUIET AND LET US USE YOU...
...OR WE'LL MAKE YOU DISAPPEAR.

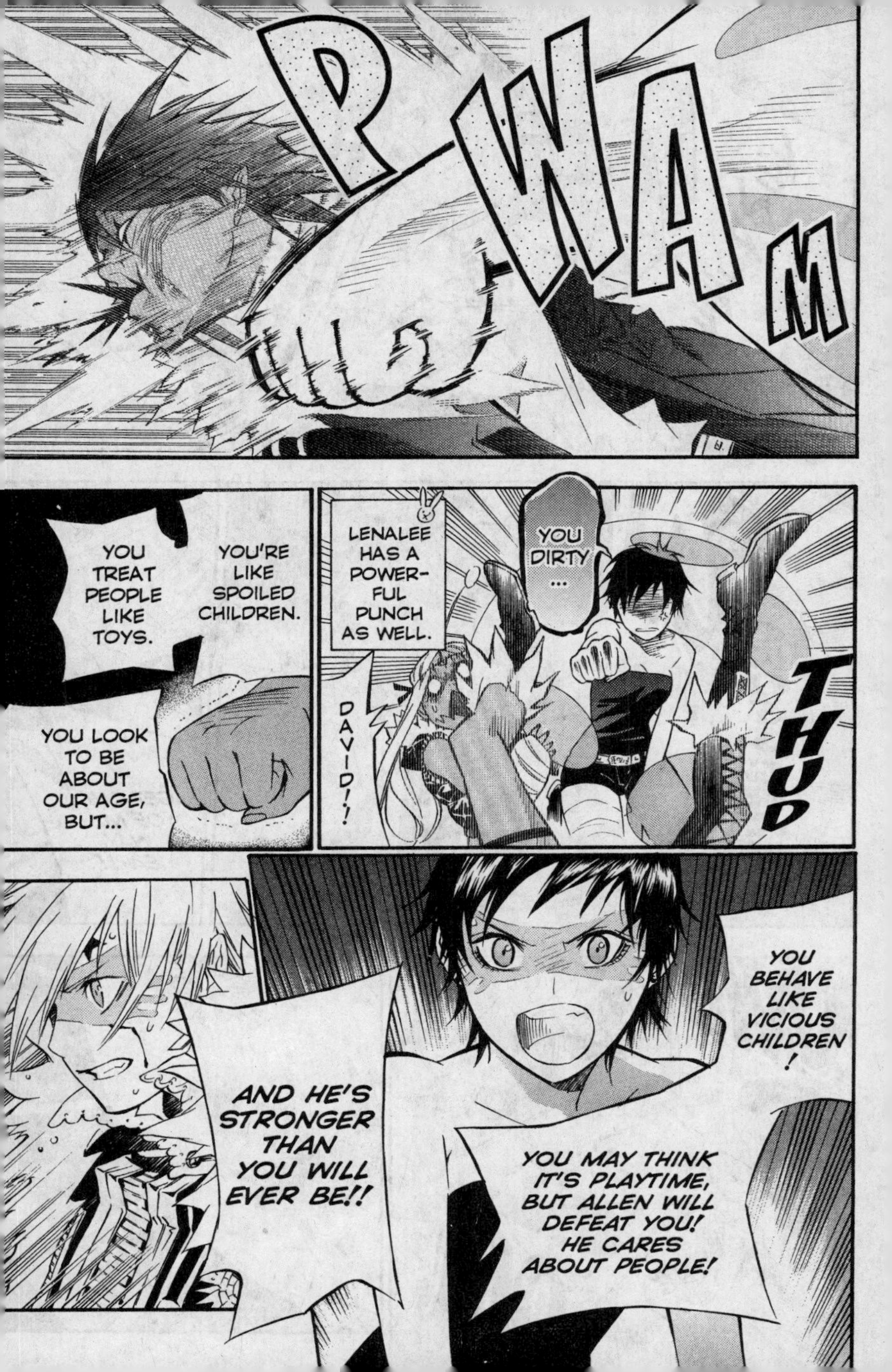
PWAMM
THUD
YOU DIRTY...
LENALEE HAS A POWER-FUL PUNCH AS WELL.
DAVID!!
YOU'RE LIKE SPOILED CHILDREN.
YOU TREAT PEOPLE LIKE TOYS.
YOU LOOK TO BE ABOUT OUR AGE, BUT...
YOU BEHAVE LIKE VICIOUS CHILDREN!
YOU MAY THINK IT'S PLAYTIME, BUT ALLEN WILL DEFEAT YOU! HE CARES ABOUT PEOPLE!
AND HE'S STRONGER THAN YOU WILL EVER BE!!

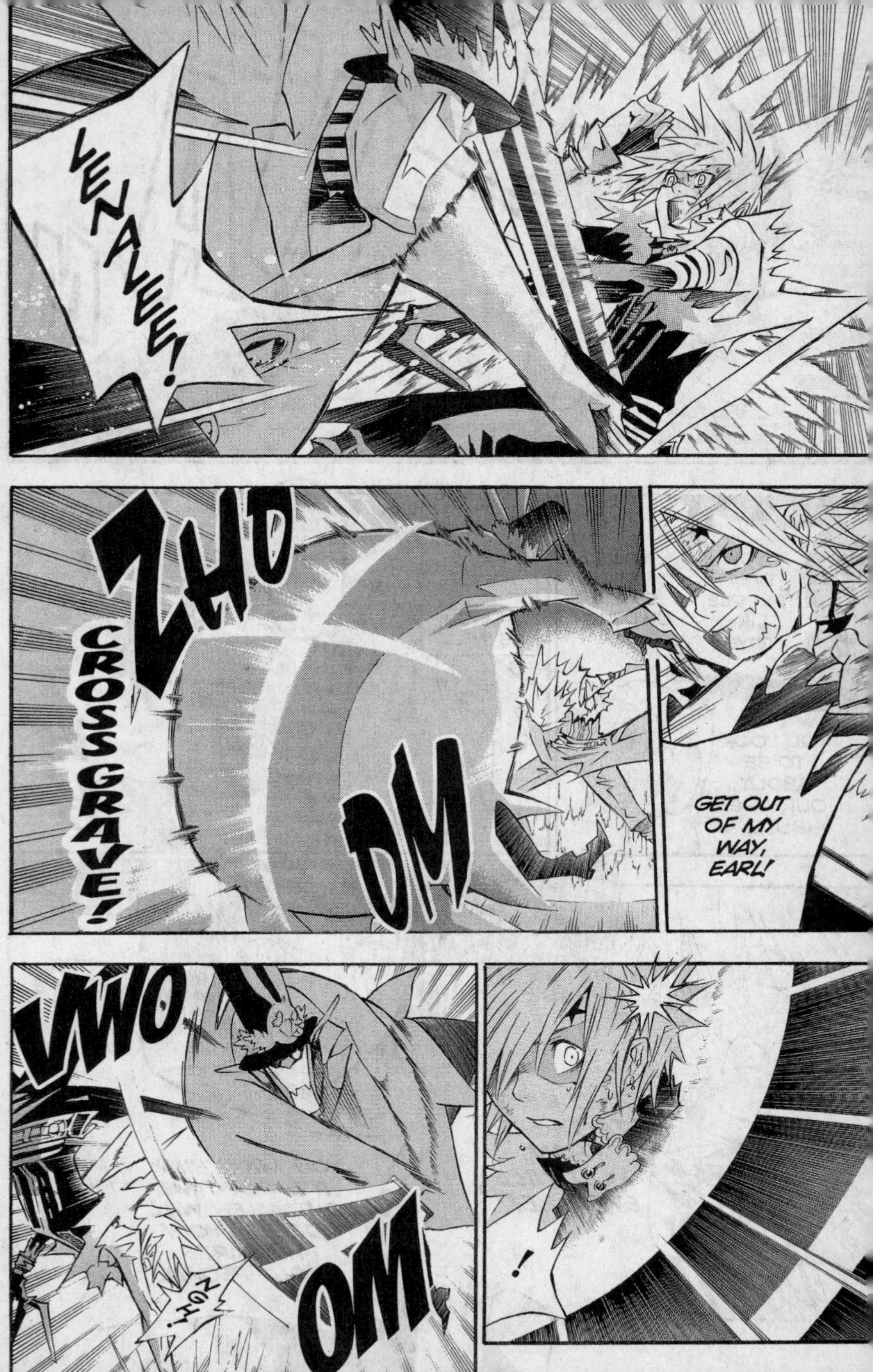
LENALEEE!
GET OUT OF MY WAY, EARL!
ZHO
CROSS GRAVE!
DOM
!
VWO
NGH!
OM

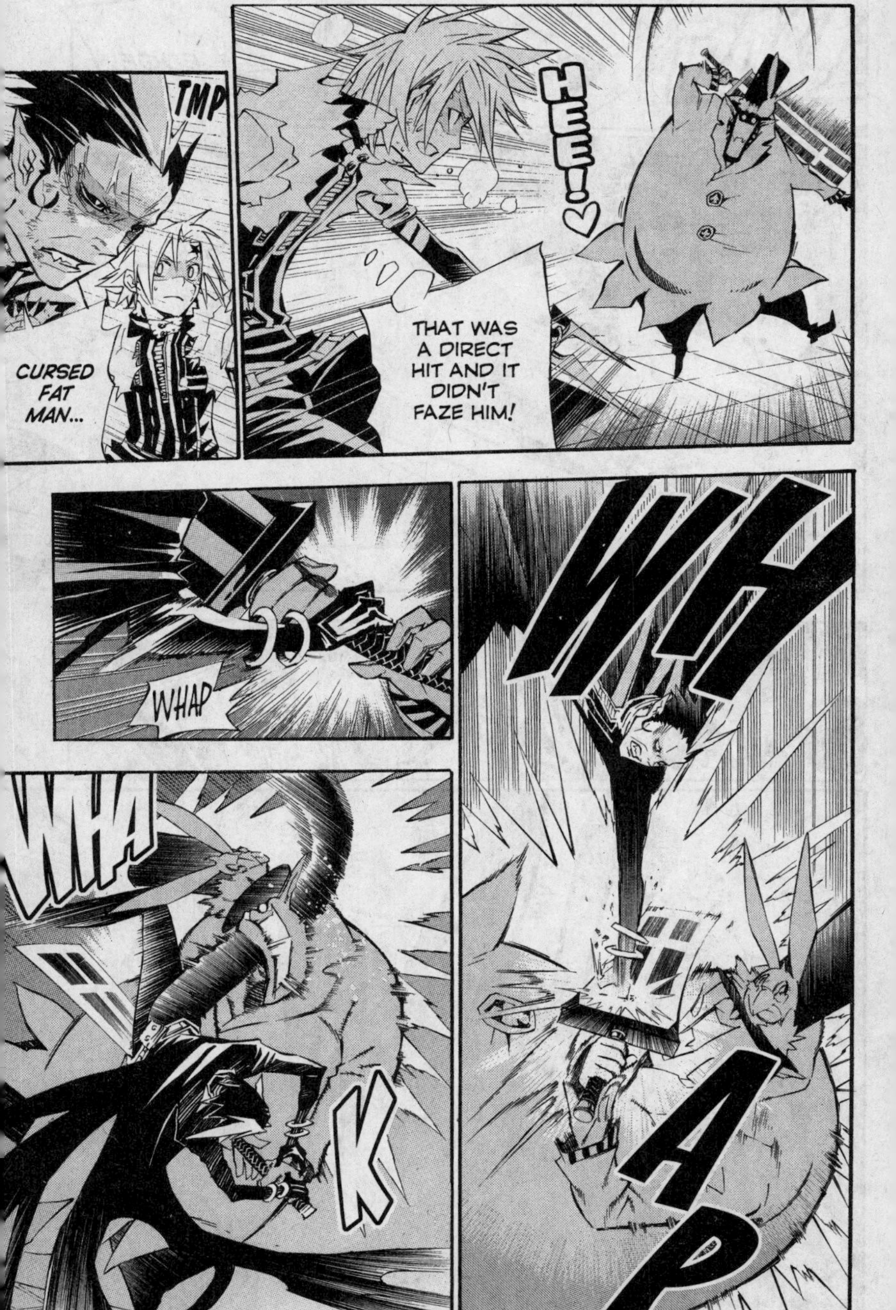
HEEE!♥
THAT WAS A DIRECT HIT AND IT DIDN'T FAZE HIM!
TMP
CURSED FAT MAN...
WH
AP
WHAP
WHA
K

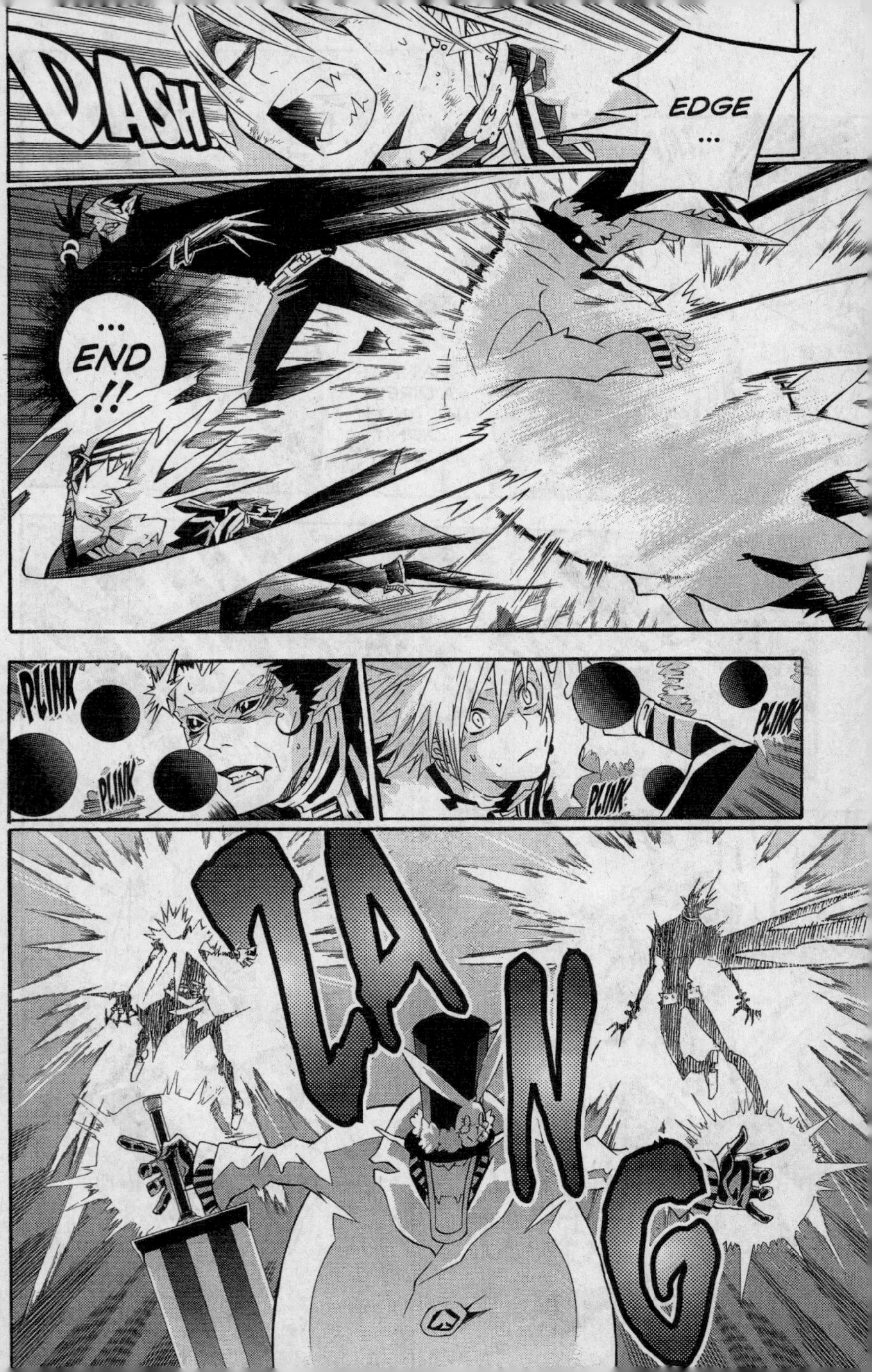
EDGE ...
DASH
... END !!
PLINK
PLINK
PLINK
PLINK
ZANG

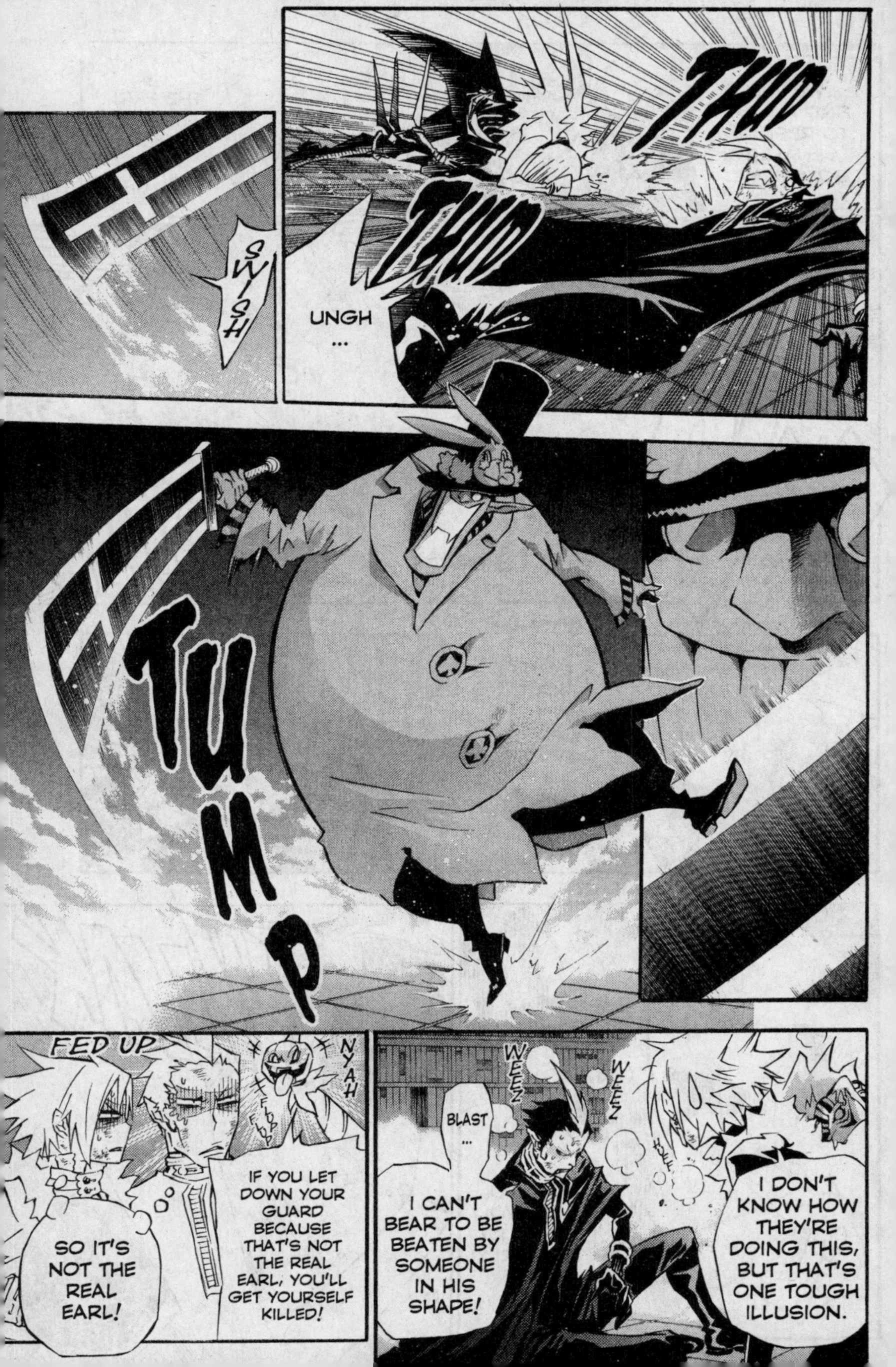
THUD
THUD
UNGH ...
SWISH
TUMP
WEEZ
WEEZ
BLAST ...
I DON'T KNOW HOW THEY'RE DOING THIS, BUT THAT'S ONE TOUGH ILLUSION.
I CAN'T BEAR TO BE BEATEN BY SOMEONE IN HIS SHAPE!
NYAH
FLOP FLOP
FED UP
SO IT'S NOT THE REAL EARL!
IF YOU LET DOWN YOUR GUARD BECAUSE THAT'S NOT THE REAL EARL, YOU'LL GET YOURSELF KILLED!

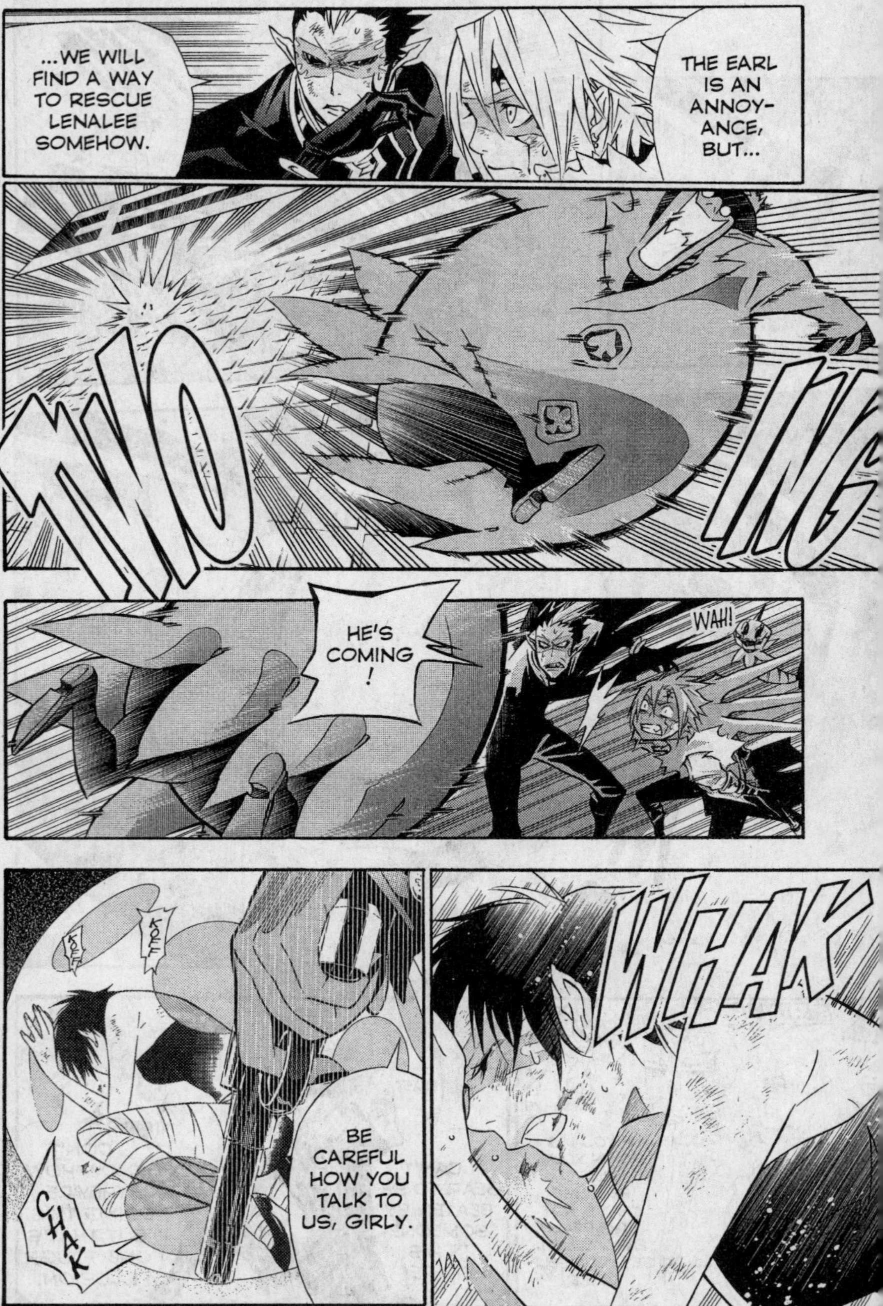
THE EARL IS AN ANNOY-ANCE, BUT...
...WE WILL FIND A WAY TO RESCUE LENALEE SOMEHOW.
TWOING
WAH!
HE'S COMING!
WHAK
KOFF
KOFF
BE CAREFUL HOW YOU TALK TO US, GIRLY.
CHAK

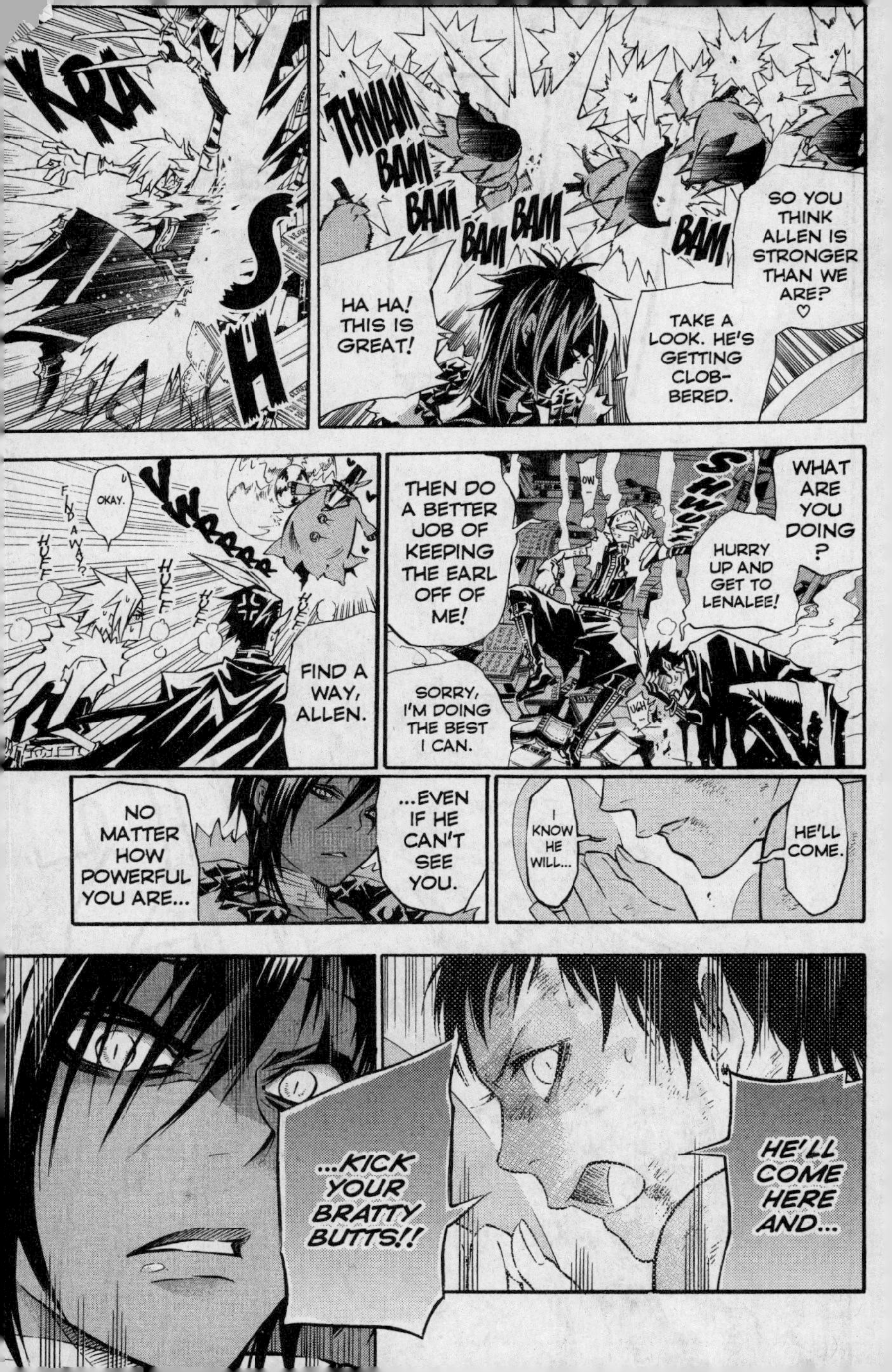
THWAM
BAM
BAM
BAM
BAM
BAM
SO YOU THINK ALLEN IS STRONGER THAN WE ARE? ♡
TAKE A LOOK. HE'S GETTING CLOB-BERED.
HA HA! THIS IS GREAT!
KRASSH
WHAT ARE YOU DOING?
HURRY UP AND GET TO LENALEE!
SHWUK
OW
THEN DO A BETTER JOB OF KEEPING THE EARL OFF OF ME!
UGH
SORRY, I'M DOING THE BEST I CAN.
OKAY.
VWRRRR
FIND A WAY?
HUFF
HUFF
HUFF
HUFF
FIND A WAY, ALLEN.
HE'LL COME.
I KNOW HE WILL...
...EVEN IF HE CAN'T SEE YOU.
NO MATTER HOW POWERFUL YOU ARE...
HE'LL COME HERE AND...
...KICK YOUR BRATTY BUTTS!!

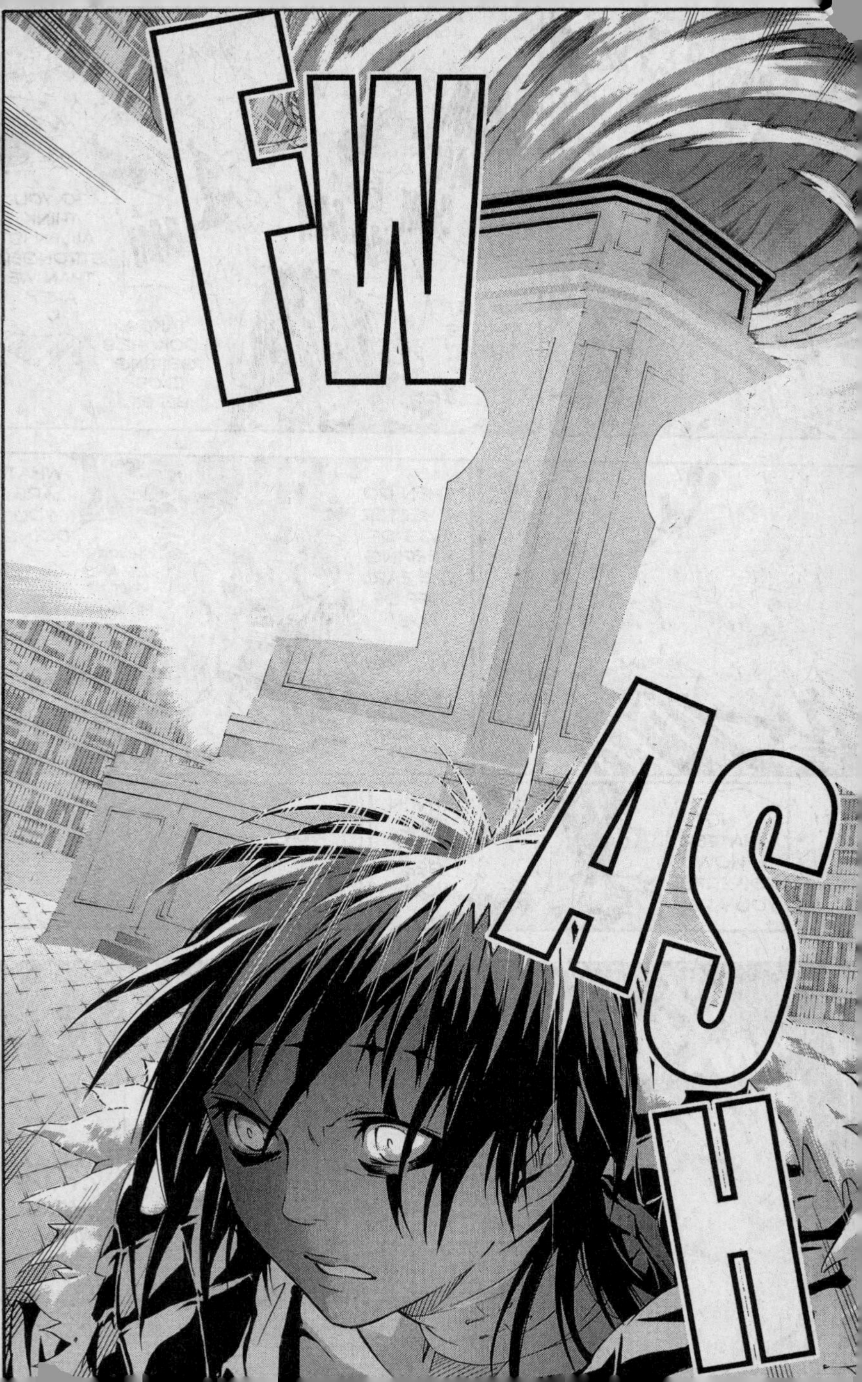
FWASH

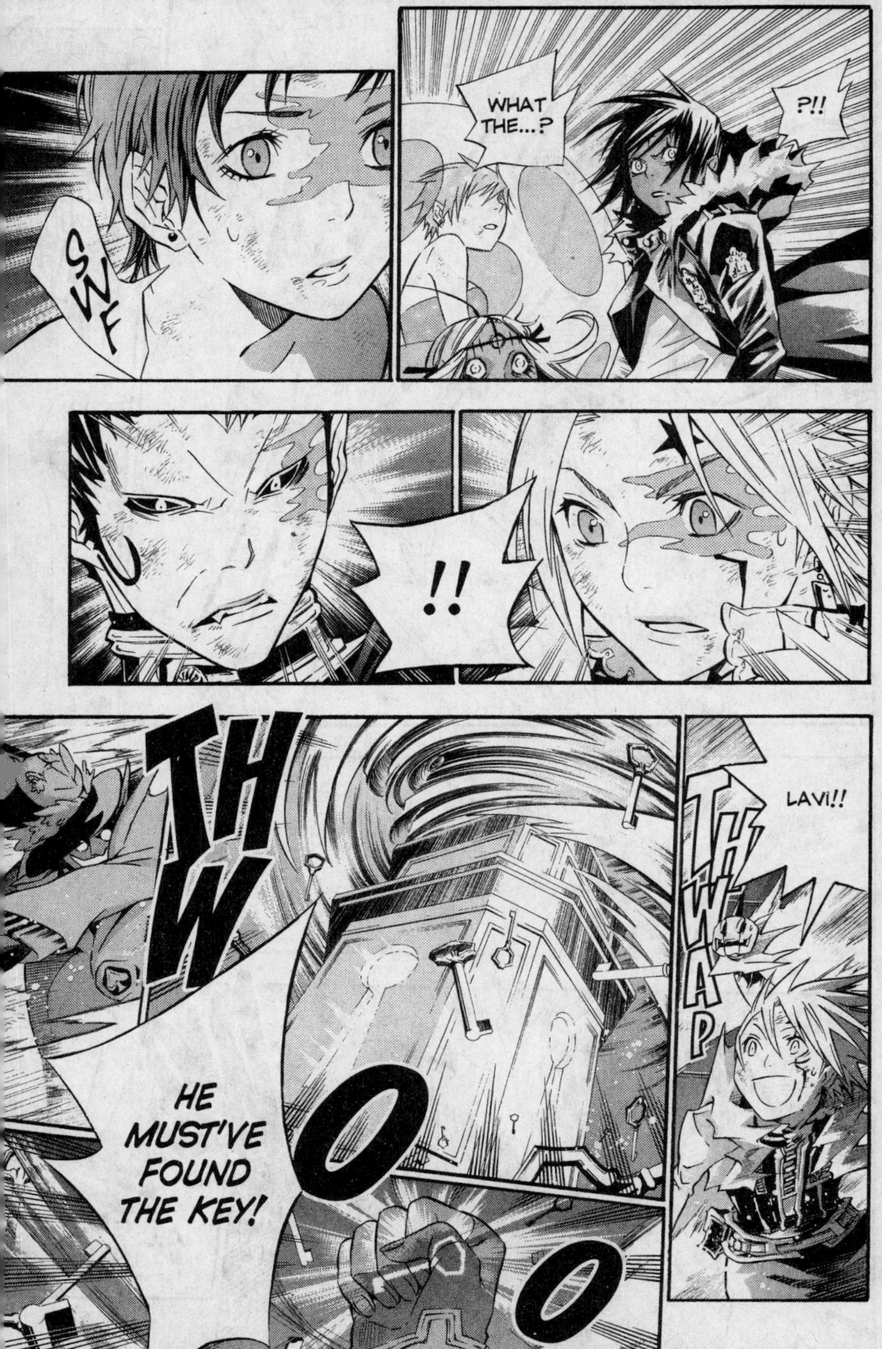

?!!
WHAT THE...?
SWF
!!
LAVI!!
THWAP
THWOO
HE MUST'VE FOUND THE KEY!

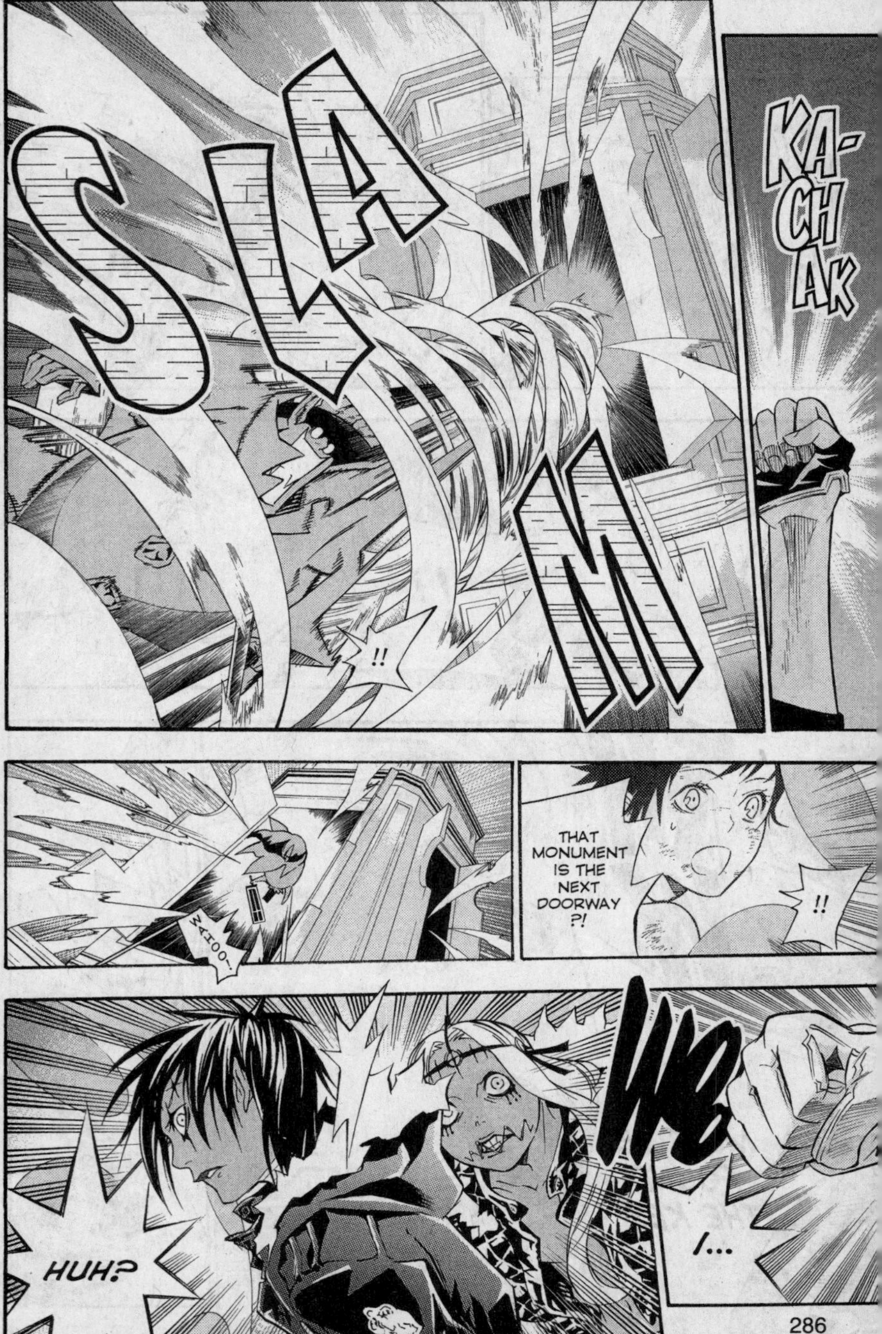
KA-CH AK
SLAM
!!
THAT MONUMENT IS THE NEXT DOORWAY?!
!!
WAIOO-!
WE
I...
HUH?

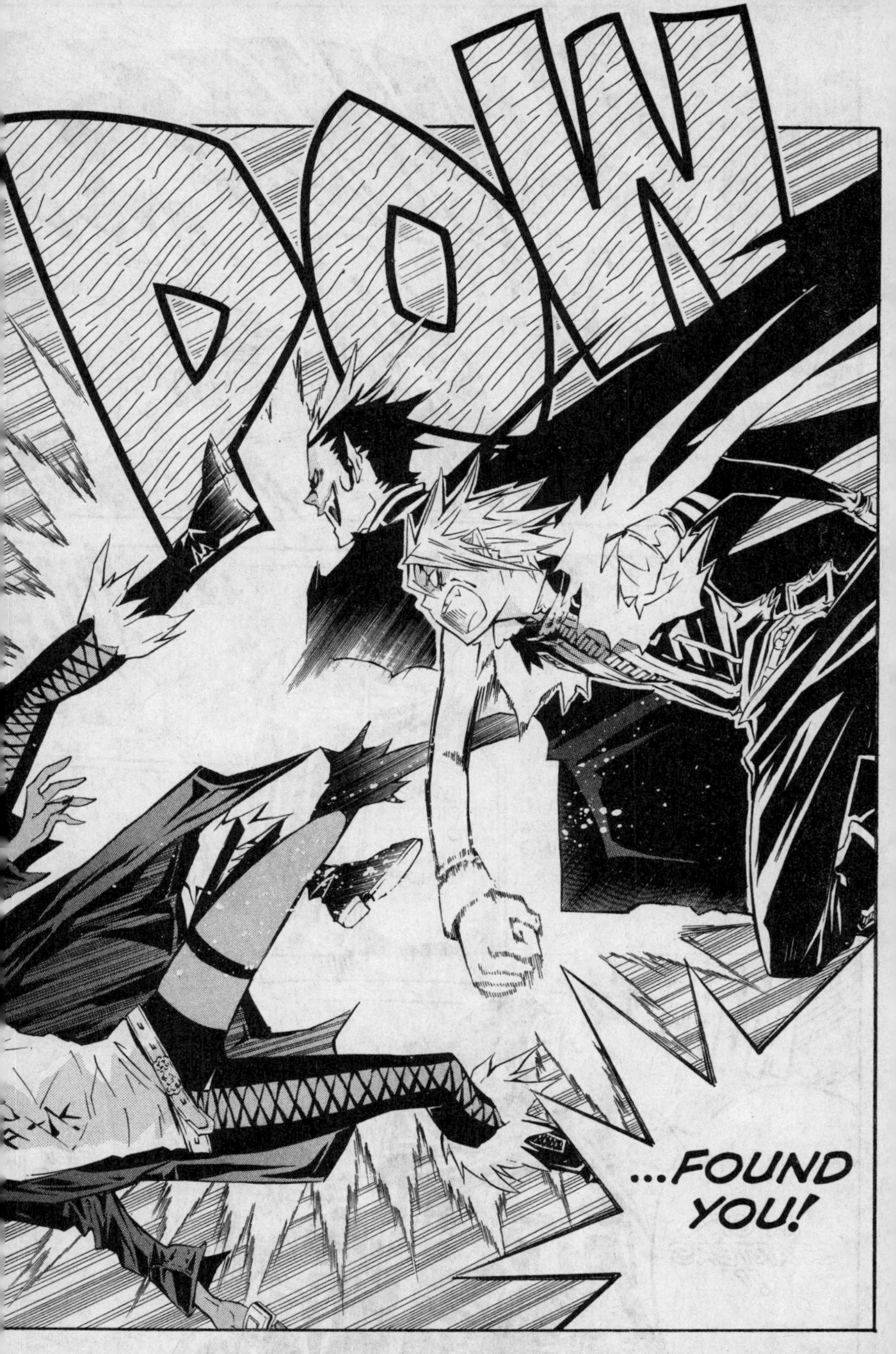
BOOM
...FOUND YOU!

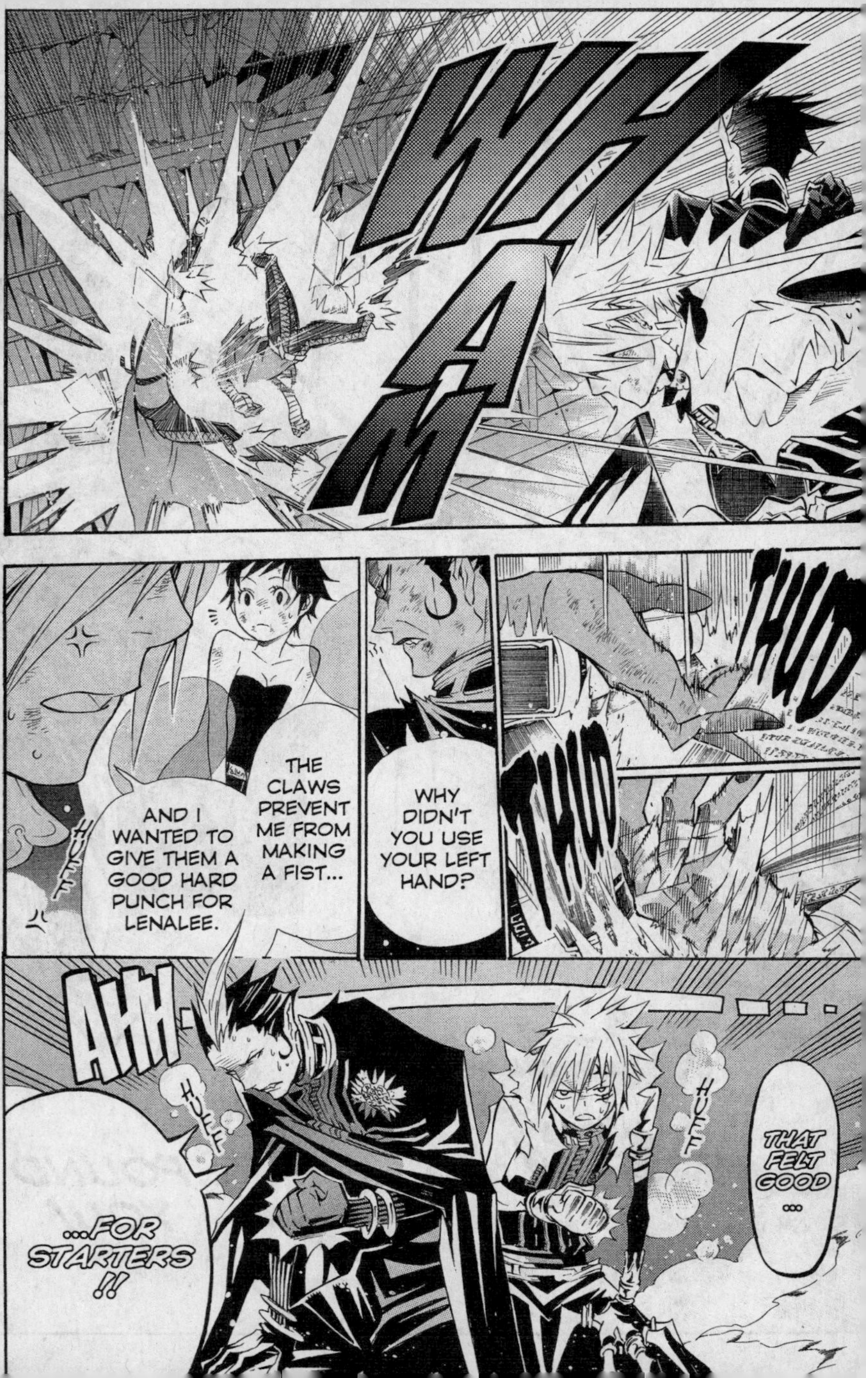
WHAM
THUD
THUD
WHY DIDN'T YOU USE YOUR LEFT HAND?
THE CLAWS PREVENT ME FROM MAKING A FIST...
AND I WANTED TO GIVE THEM A GOOD HARD PUNCH FOR LENALEE.
HUFF
THAT FELT GOOD ...
HUFF
HUFF
AHH-...
...FOR STARTERS!!

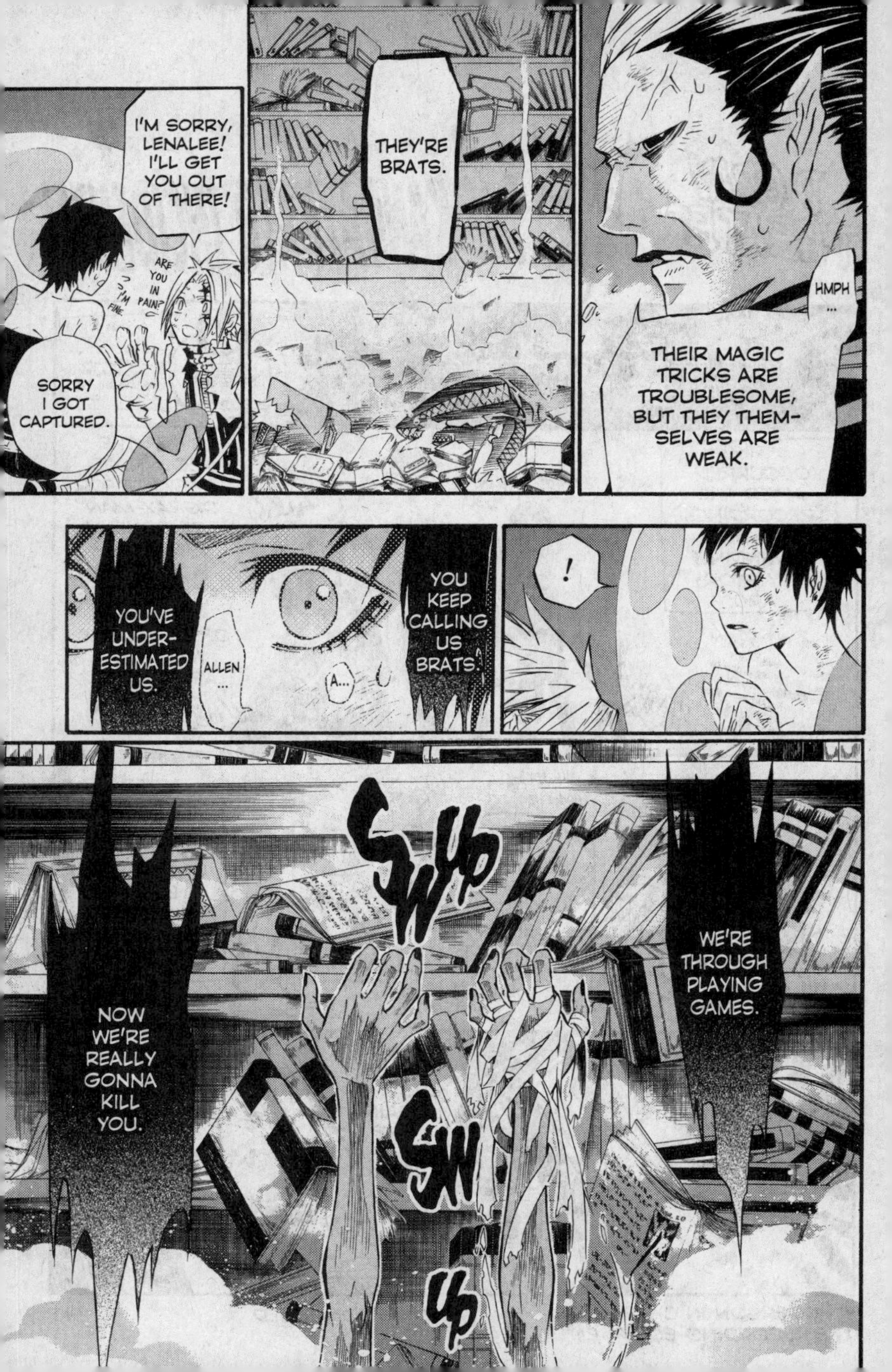
HMPH ...
THEIR MAGIC TRICKS ARE TROUBLESOME, BUT THEY THEM-SELVES ARE WEAK.
THEY'RE BRATS.
I'M SORRY, LENALEE! I'LL GET YOU OUT OF THERE!
ARE YOU IN PAIN?
I'M FINE
SORRY I GOT CAPTURED.
!
YOU KEEP CALLING US BRATS.
A...
ALLEN ...
YOU'VE UNDER-ESTIMATED US.
WE'RE THROUGH PLAYING GAMES.
SWUP
NOW WE'RE REALLY GONNA KILL YOU.
SWUP

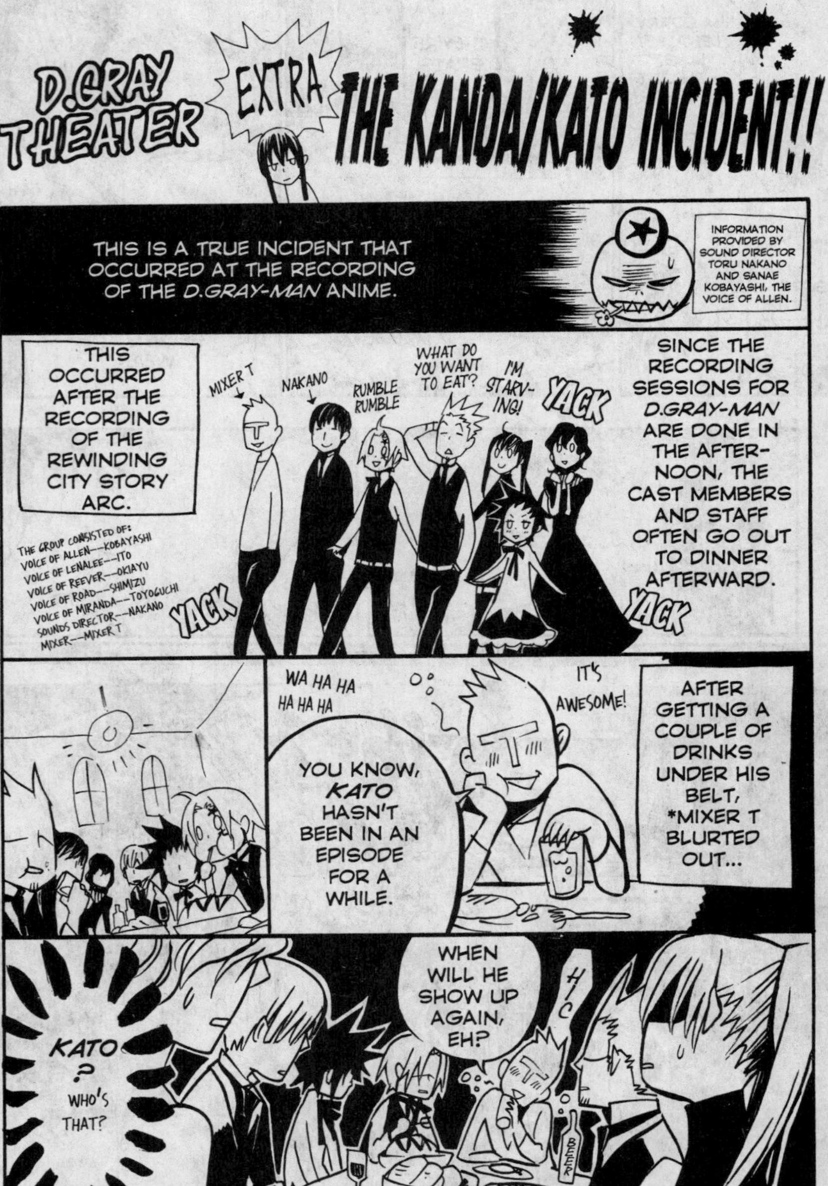
D.GRAY THEATER
EXTRA
THE KANDA/KATO INCIDENT!!
INFORMATION PROVIDED BY SOUND DIRECTOR TORU NAKANO AND SANAE KOBAYASHI, THE VOICE OF ALLEN.
THIS IS A TRUE INCIDENT THAT OCCURRED AT THE RECORDING OF THE D.GRAY-MAN ANIME.
SINCE THE RECORDING SESSIONS FOR D.GRAY-MAN ARE DONE IN THE AFTERNOON, THE CAST MEMBERS AND STAFF OFTEN GO OUT TO DINNER AFTERWARD.
YACK
YACK
I'M STARVING!
WHAT DO YOU WANT TO EAT?
RUMBLE RUMBLE
NAKANO
MIXER T
THIS OCCURRED AFTER THE RECORDING OF THE REWINDING CITY STORY ARC.
YACK
THE GROUP CONSISTED OF:
VOICE OF ALLEN--KOBAYASHI
VOICE OF LENALEE--ITO
VOICE OF REEVER--OKIAYU
VOICE OF ROAD--SHIMIZU
VOICE OF MIRANDA--TOYOGUCHI
SOUNDS DIRECTOR--NAKANO
MIXER--MIXER T
AFTER GETTING A COUPLE OF DRINKS UNDER HIS BELT, *MIXER T BLURTED OUT...
IT'S AWESOME!
WA HA HA HA HA HA
YOU KNOW, KATO HASN'T BEEN IN AN EPISODE FOR A WHILE.
HIC
WHEN WILL HE SHOW UP AGAIN, EH?
KATO?
WHO'S THAT?
BEER

*THE PERSON IN CHARGE OF THE RECORDING EQUIPMENT

TO BE CONTINUED

THE 103RD NIGHT: AN UNRULY CHILD

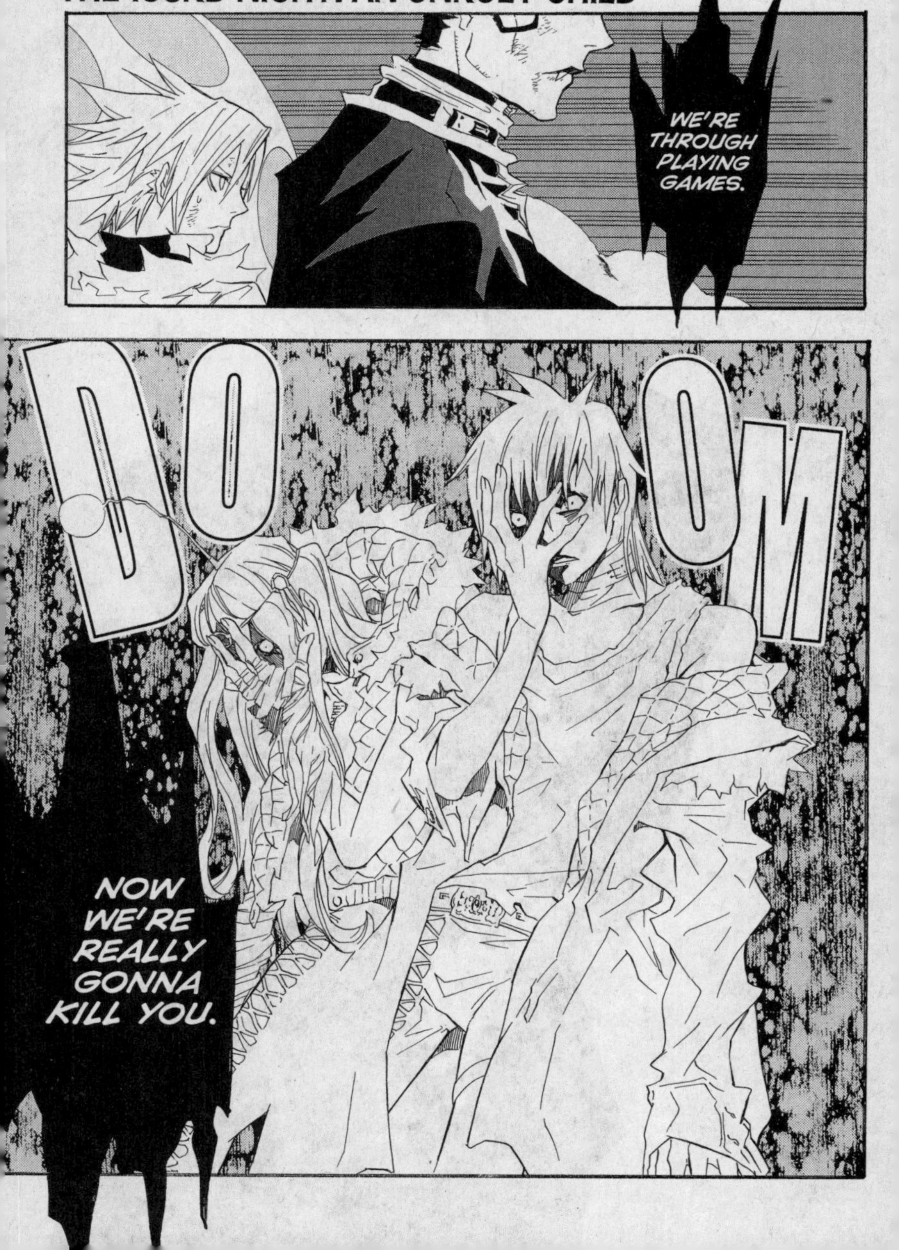
WE'RE THROUGH PLAYING GAMES.
DOOM
NOW WE'RE REALLY GONNA KILL YOU.

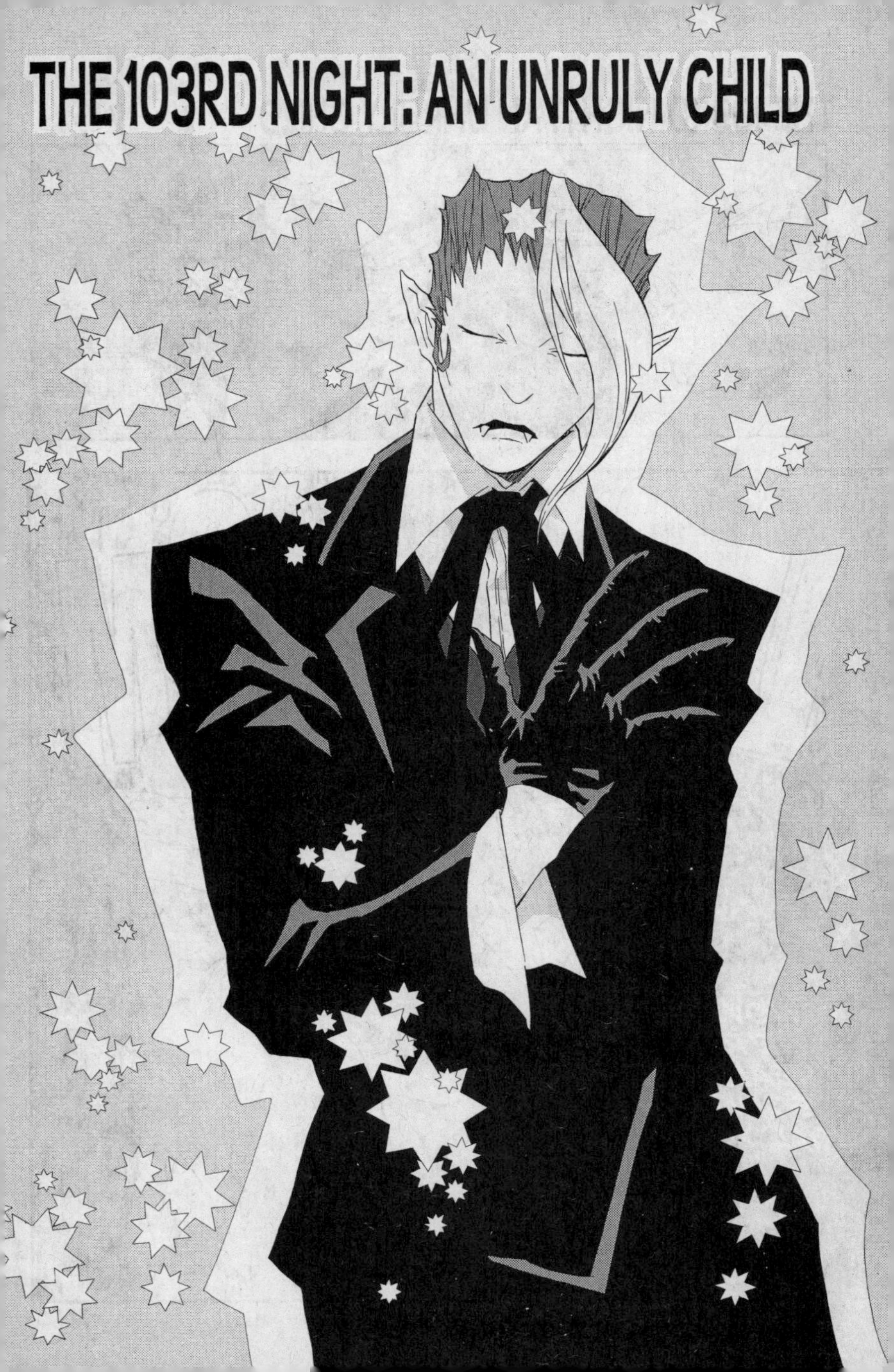
THE 103RD NIGHT: AN UNRULY CHILD

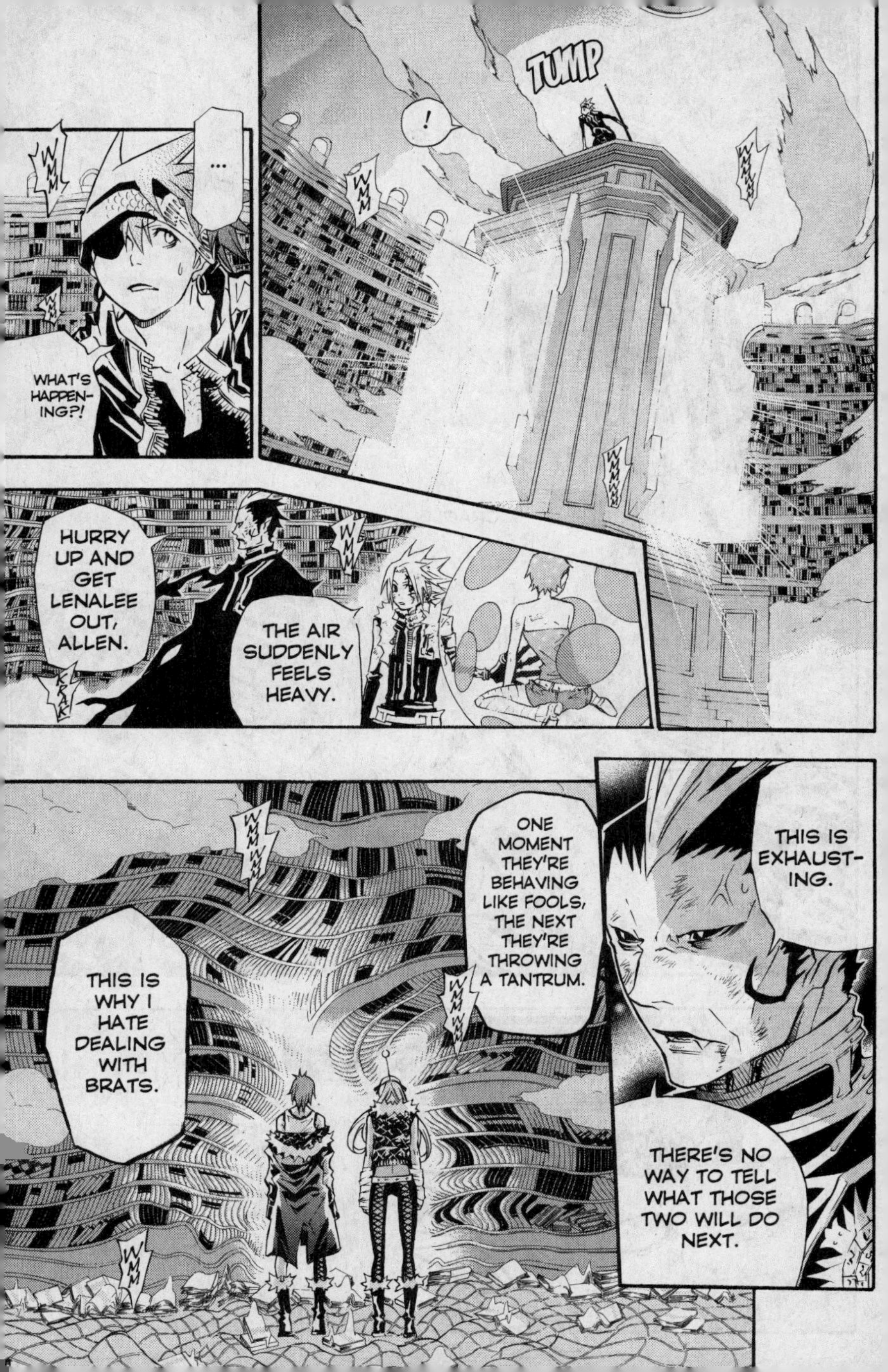
TUMP
!
WMM
...
WMM
WHAT'S HAPPENING?!
THE AIR SUDDENLY FEELS HEAVY.
HURRY UP AND GET LENALEE OUT, ALLEN.
KRAK
THIS IS EXHAUST-ING.
ONE MOMENT THEY'RE BEHAVING LIKE FOOLS, THE NEXT THEY'RE THROWING A TANTRUM.
THERE'S NO WAY TO TELL WHAT THOSE TWO WILL DO NEXT.
THIS IS WHY I HATE DEALING WITH BRATS.
WMM

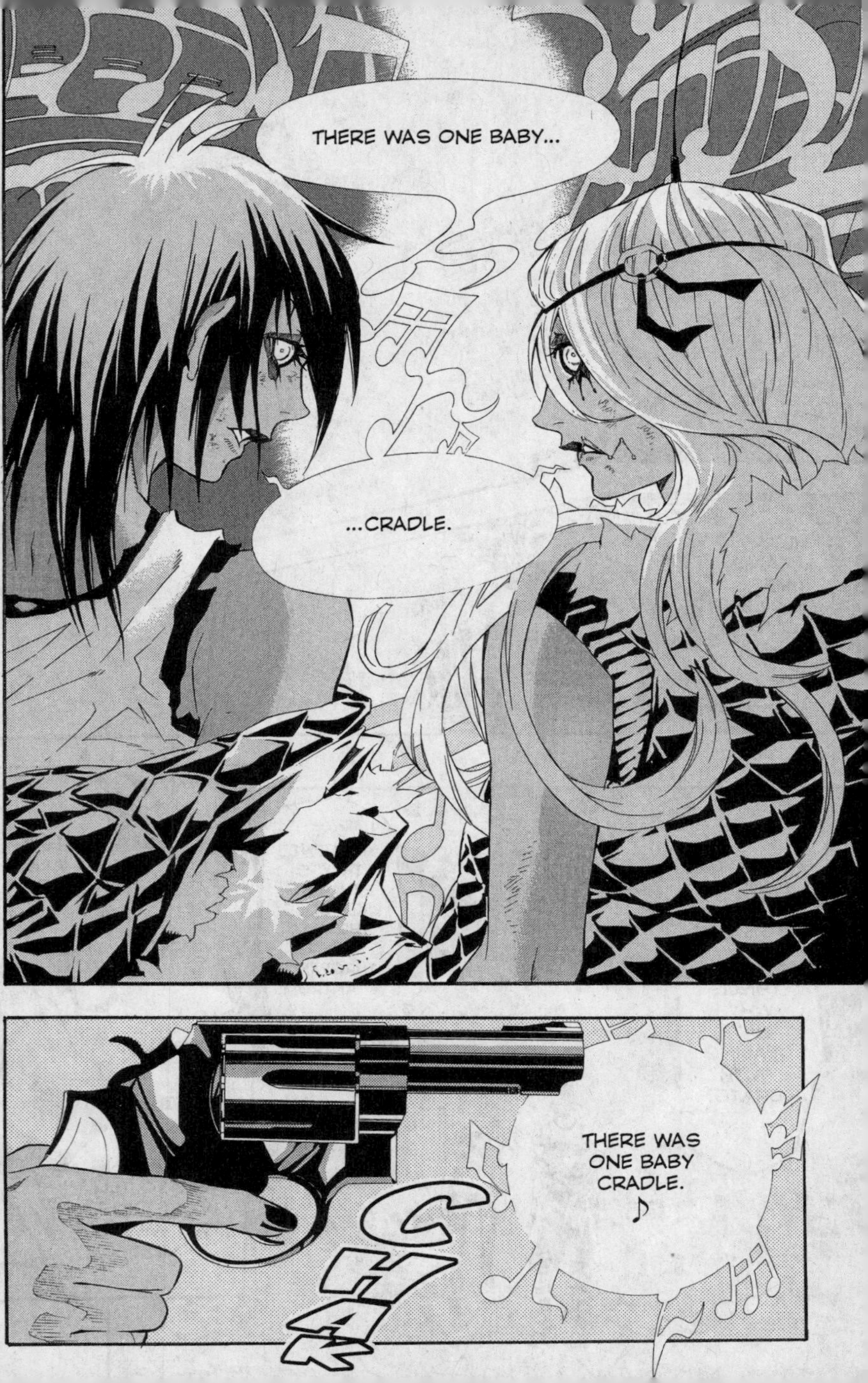
THERE WAS ONE BABY...
...CRADLE.
THERE WAS ONE BABY CRADLE. ♪
CHAK

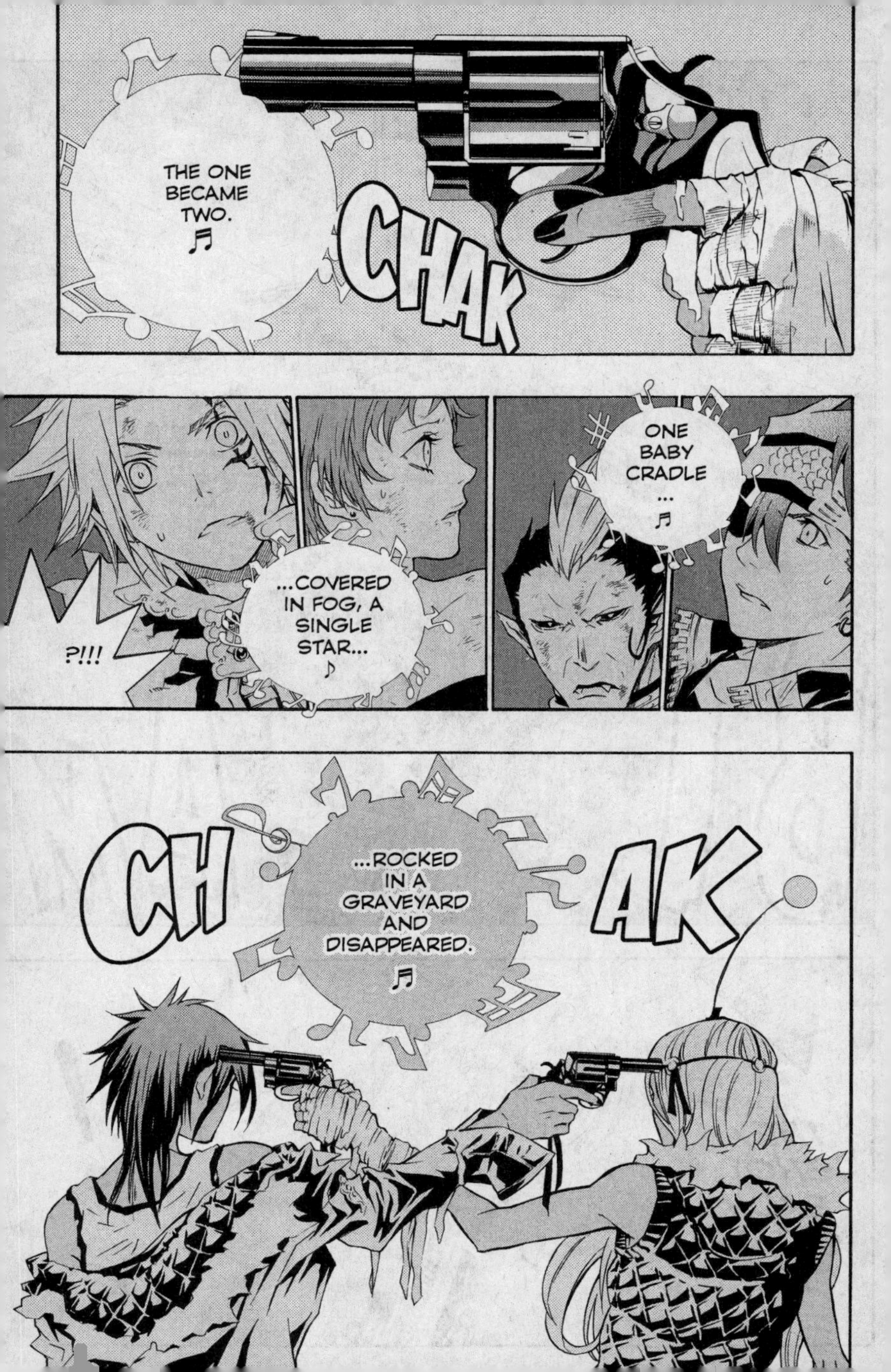
THE ONE BECAME TWO. ♬
CHAK
ONE BABY CRADLE ... ♬
...COVERED IN FOG, A SINGLE STAR... ♪
?!!!
CH
AK
...ROCKED IN A GRAVEYARD AND DISAPPEARED. ♬

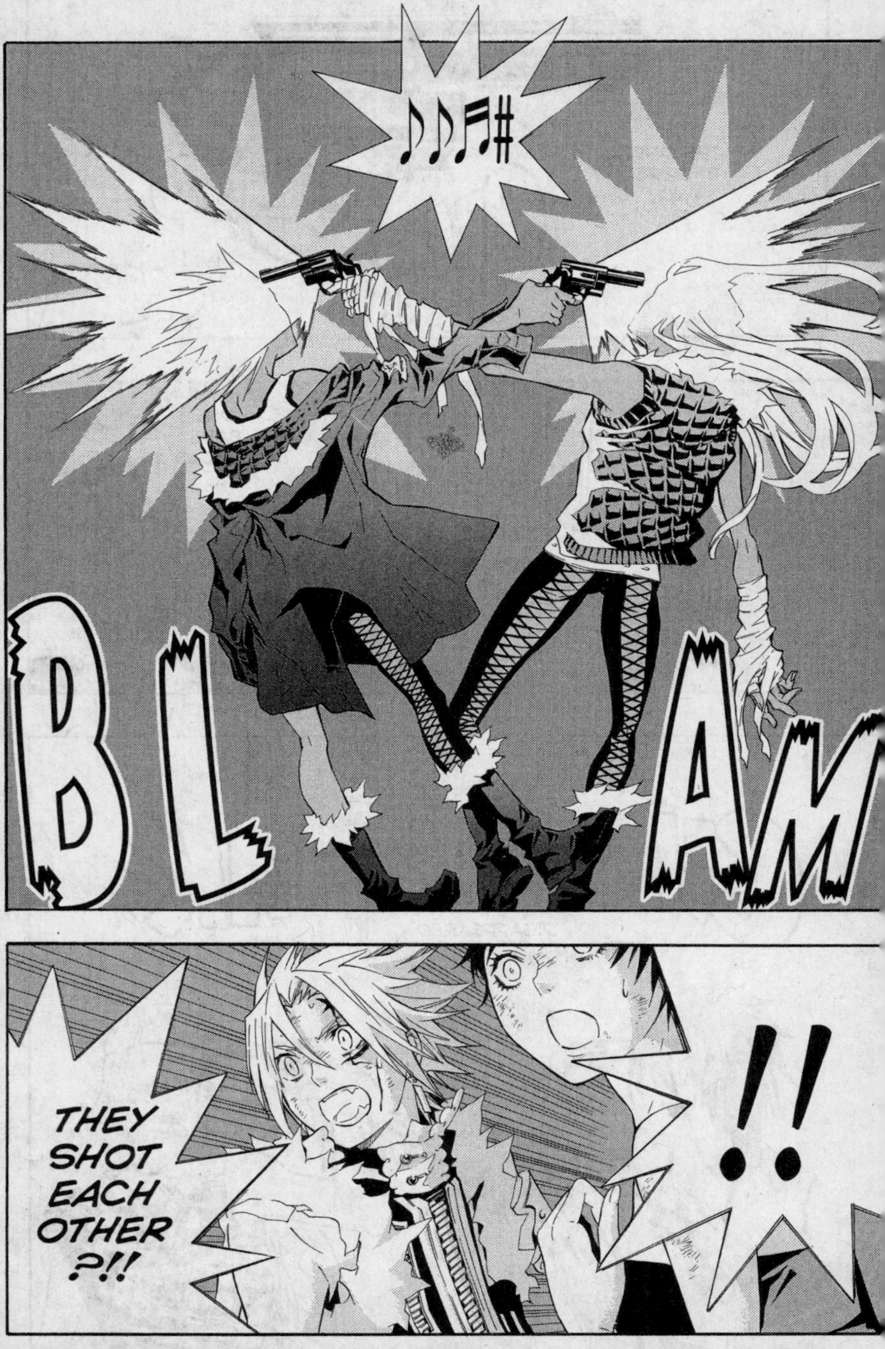
♪♪♫#
BLAM
!!
THEY SHOT EACH OTHER?!!

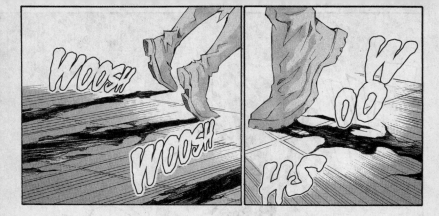

WOOSH

WOOSH

WOOSH

?!!

FWOOOO

THEIR SHA-DOWS...

...ARE MERGING!

297

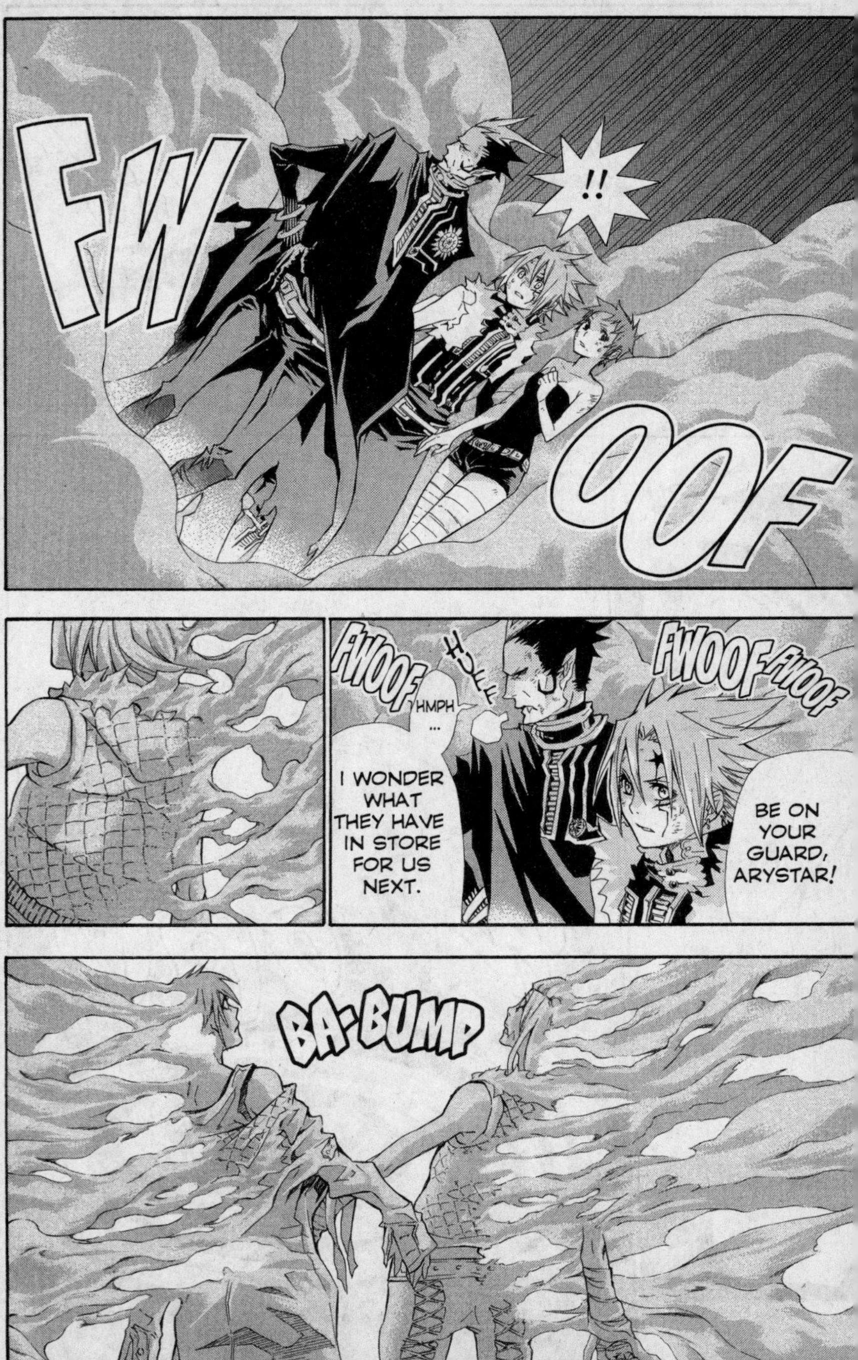
!!
FW
OOF
FWOOF FWOOF
BE ON YOUR GUARD, ARYSTAR!
HUFF
HMPH ...
FWOOF
I WONDER WHAT THEY HAVE IN STORE FOR US NEXT.
BA-BUMP

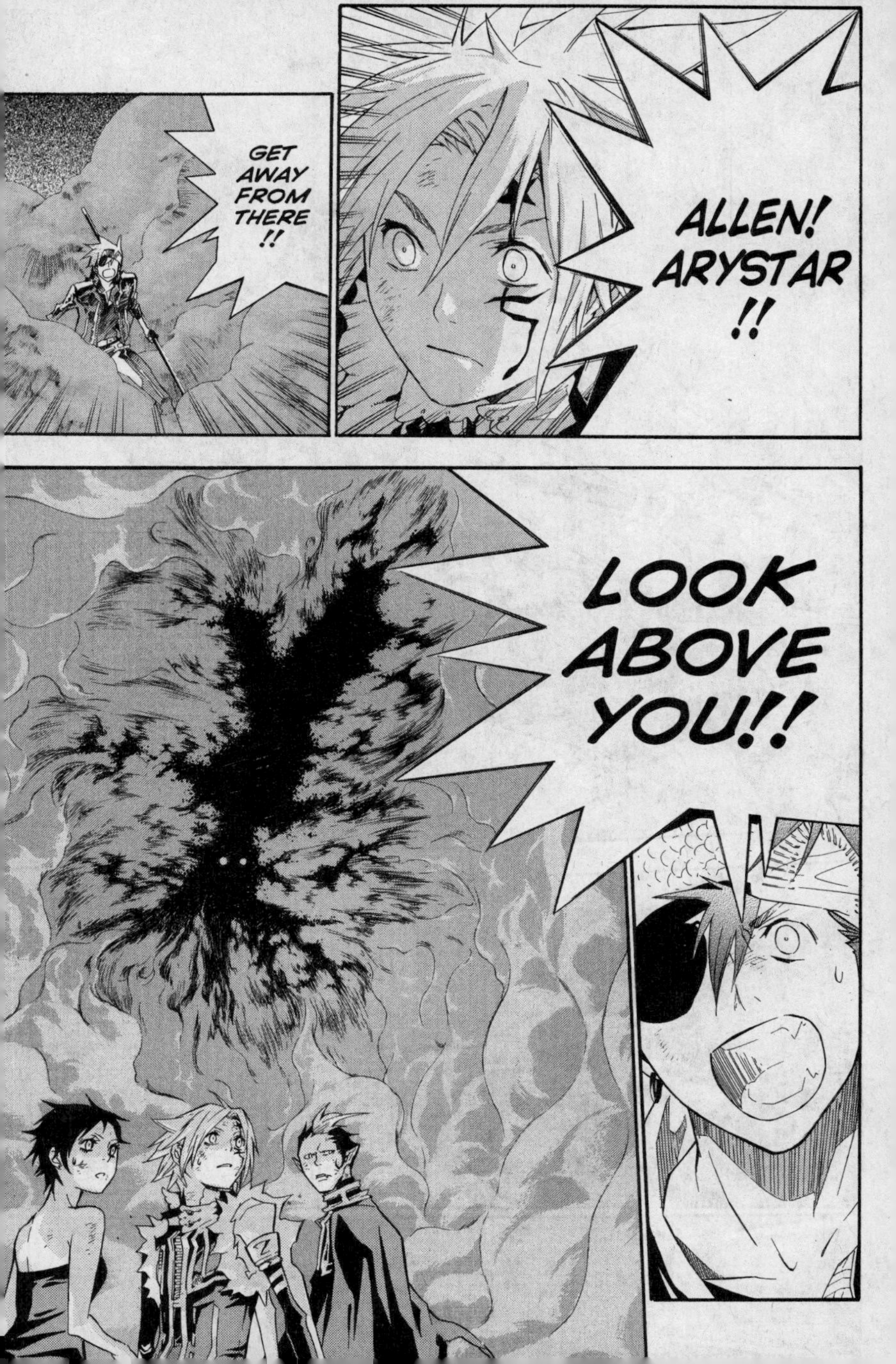
ALLEN! ARYSTAR !!
GET AWAY FROM THERE !!
LOOK ABOVE YOU!!

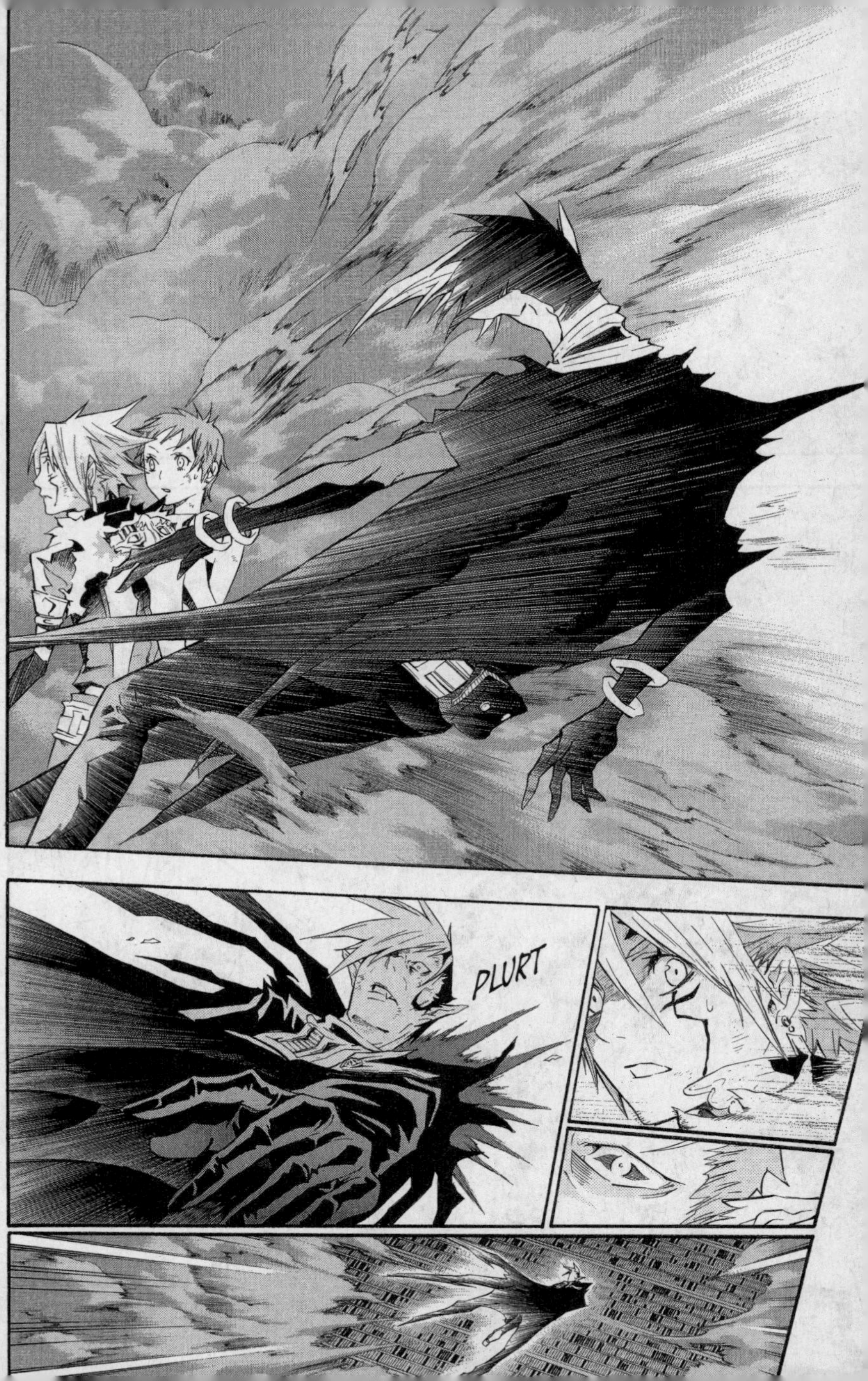
PLURT

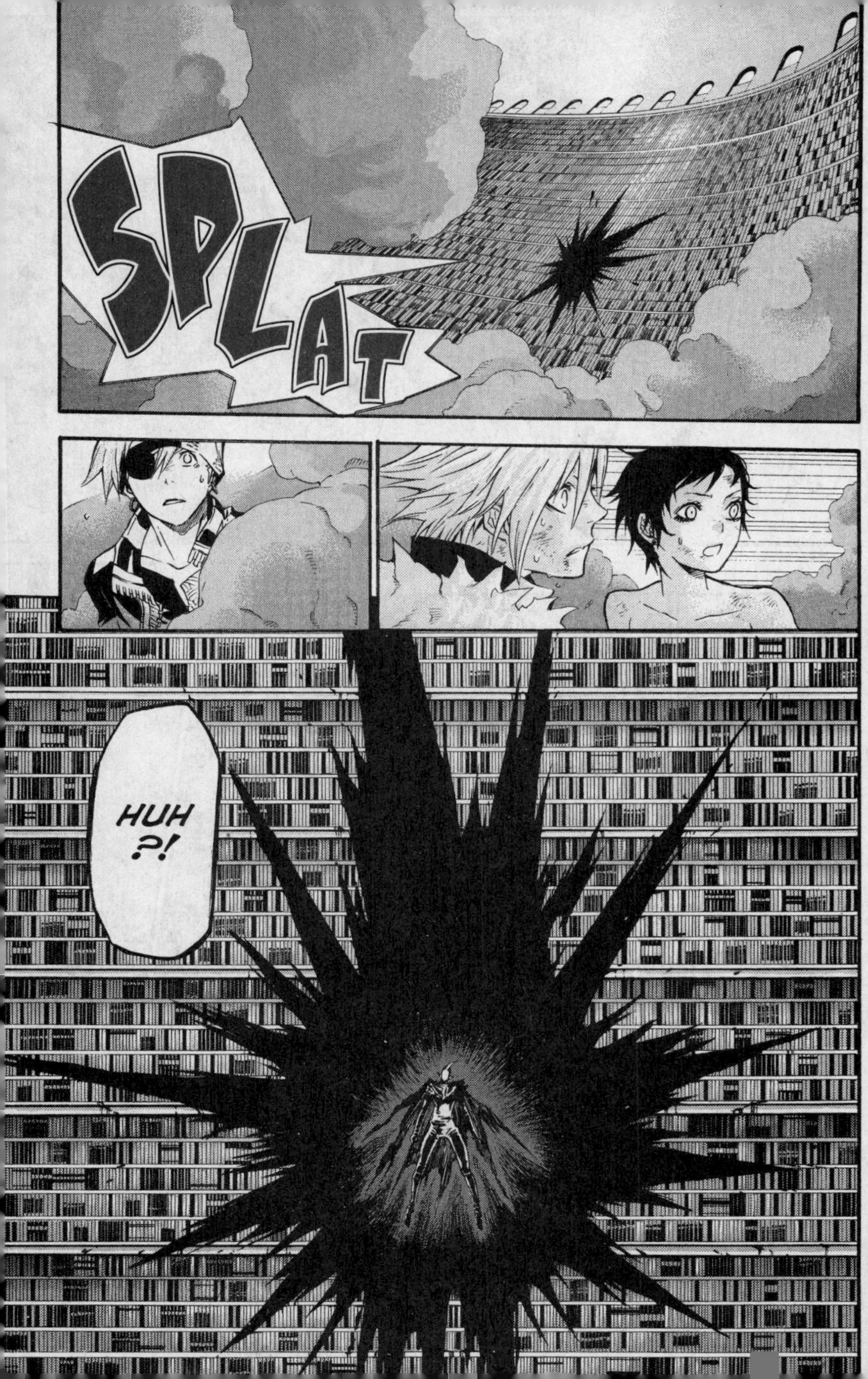
SPLAT
HUH?!

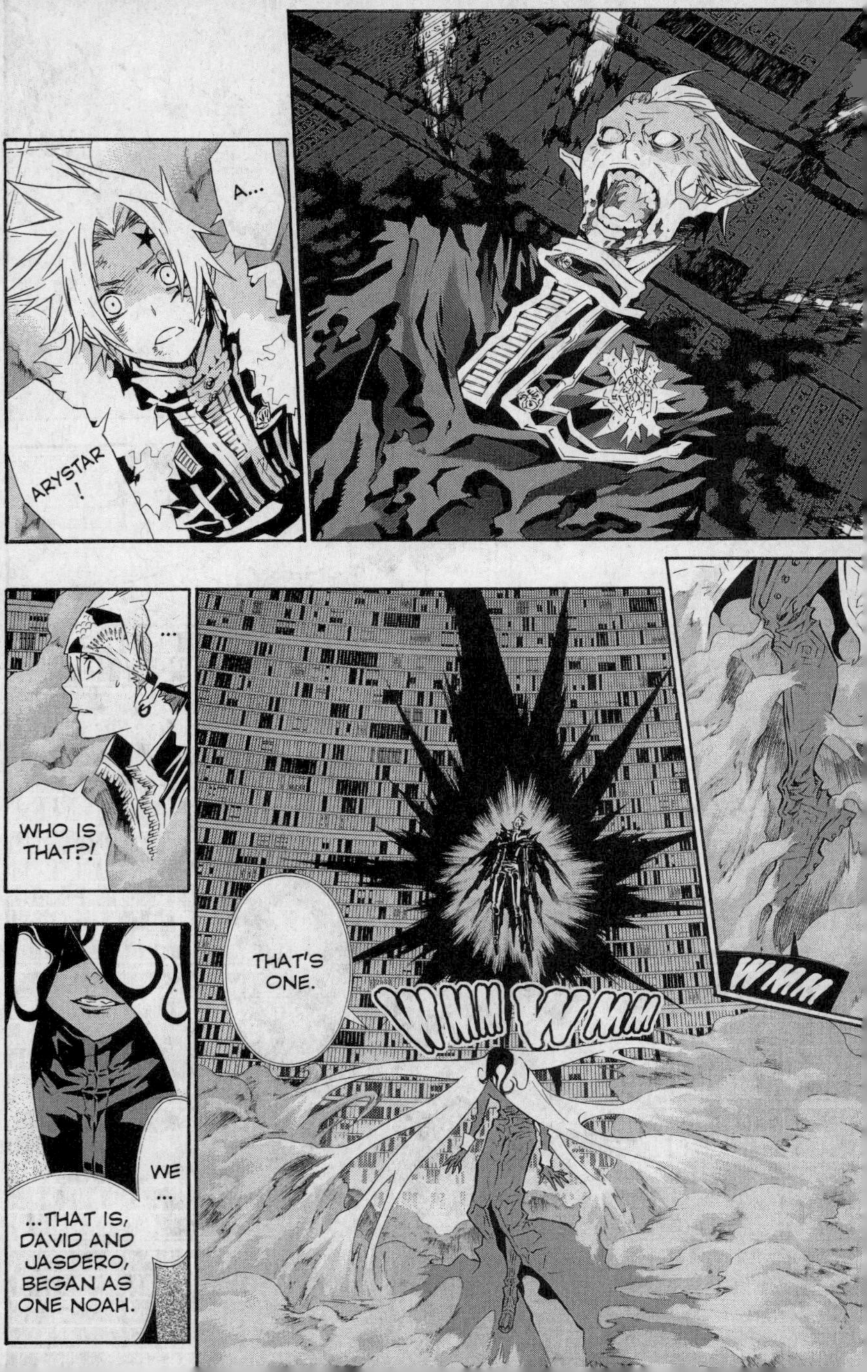
A...
ARYSTAR!
WMM
THAT'S ONE.
WMM WMM
...
WHO IS THAT?!
WE ...
...THAT IS, DAVID AND JASDERO, BEGAN AS ONE NOAH.

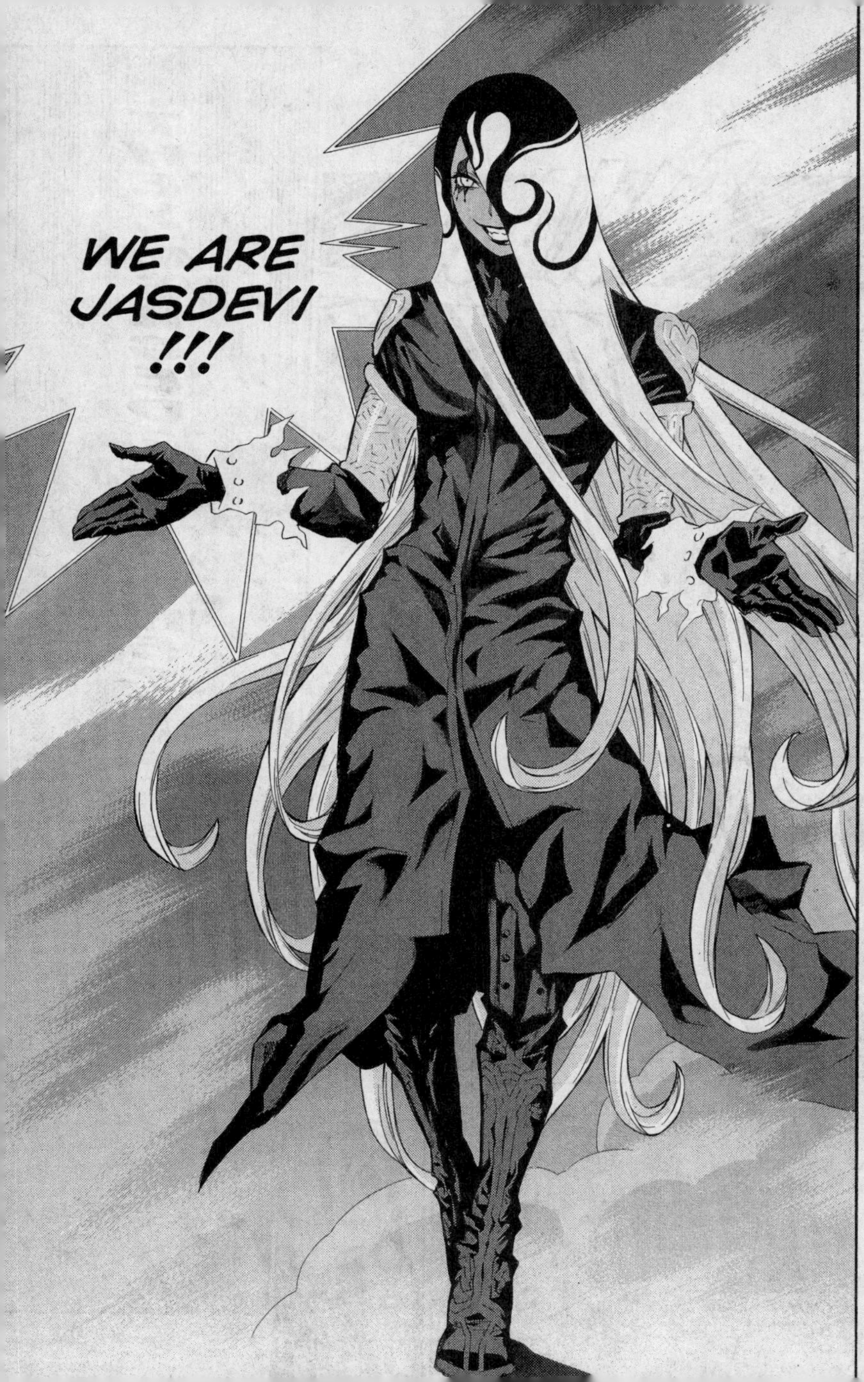
WE ARE JASDEVI !!!

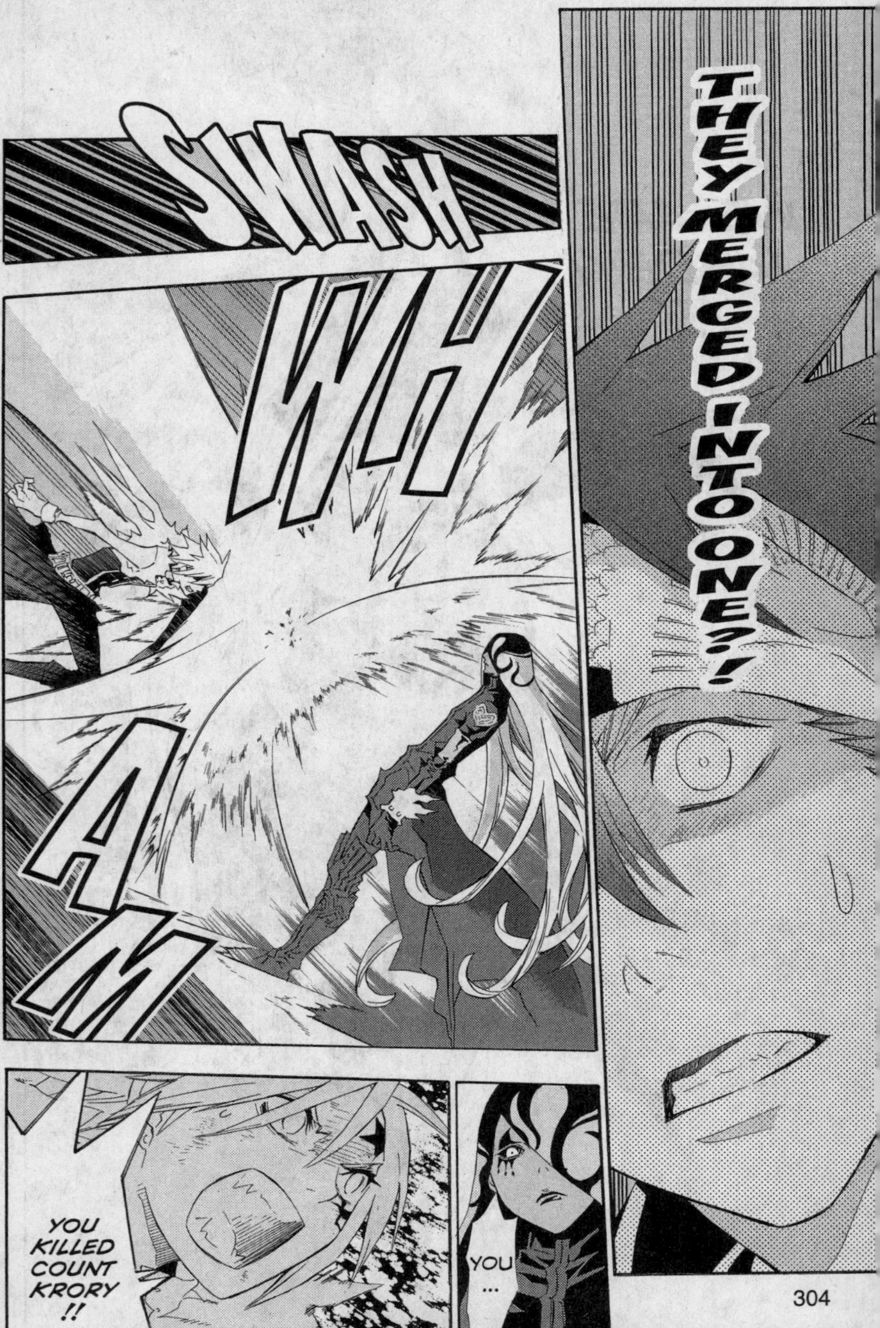
THEY MERGED INTO ONE?!
SWASH
WHAM
YOU ...
YOU KILLED COUNT KRORY!!

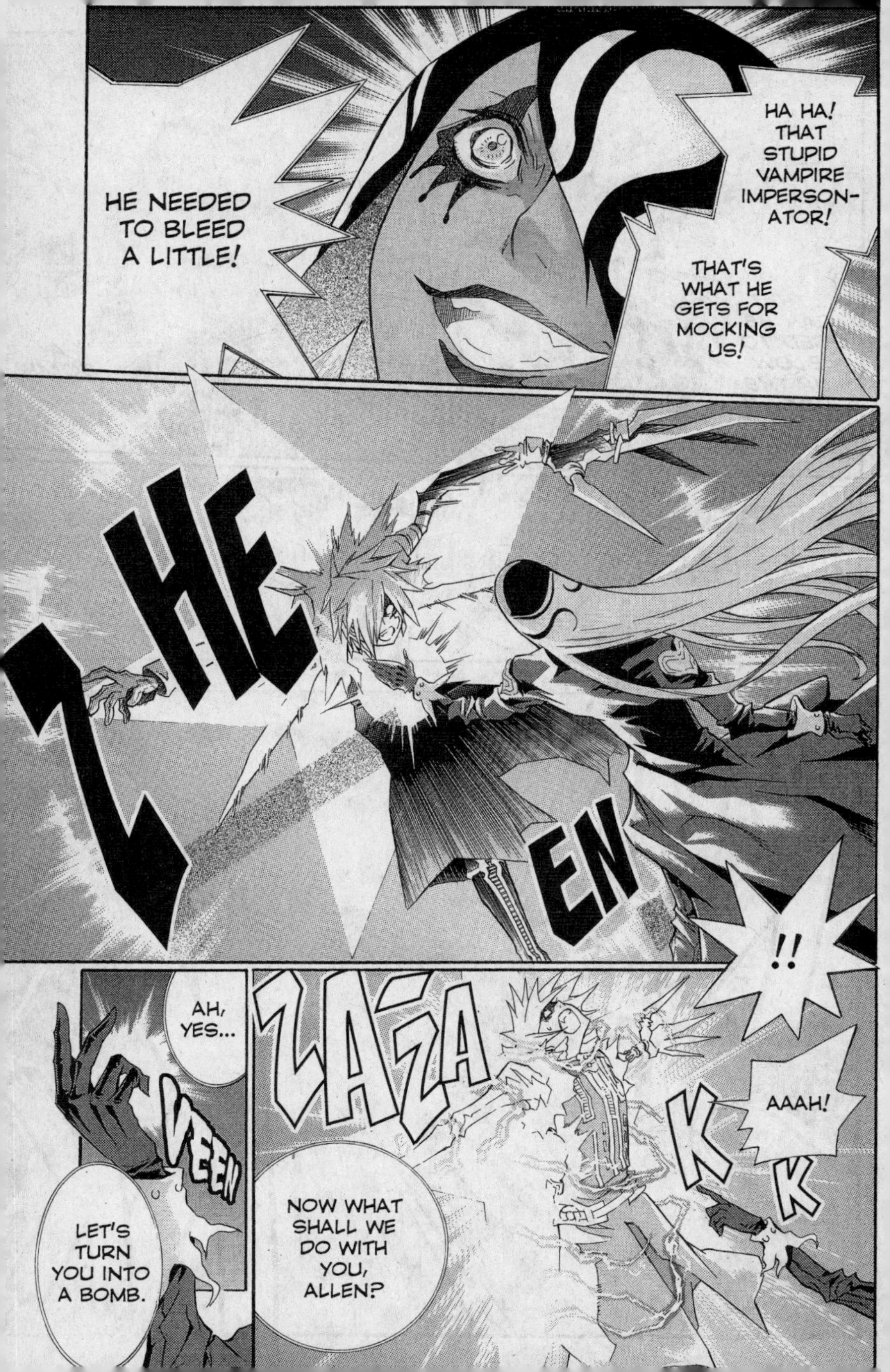
HA HA! THAT STUPID VAMPIRE IMPERSON-ATOR!
THAT'S WHAT HE GETS FOR MOCKING US!
HE NEEDED TO BLEED A LITTLE!
ZHEEN
!!
AAAH!
K K
ZAZA
AH, YES...
NOW WHAT SHALL WE DO WITH YOU, ALLEN?
VEEN
LET'S TURN YOU INTO A BOMB.

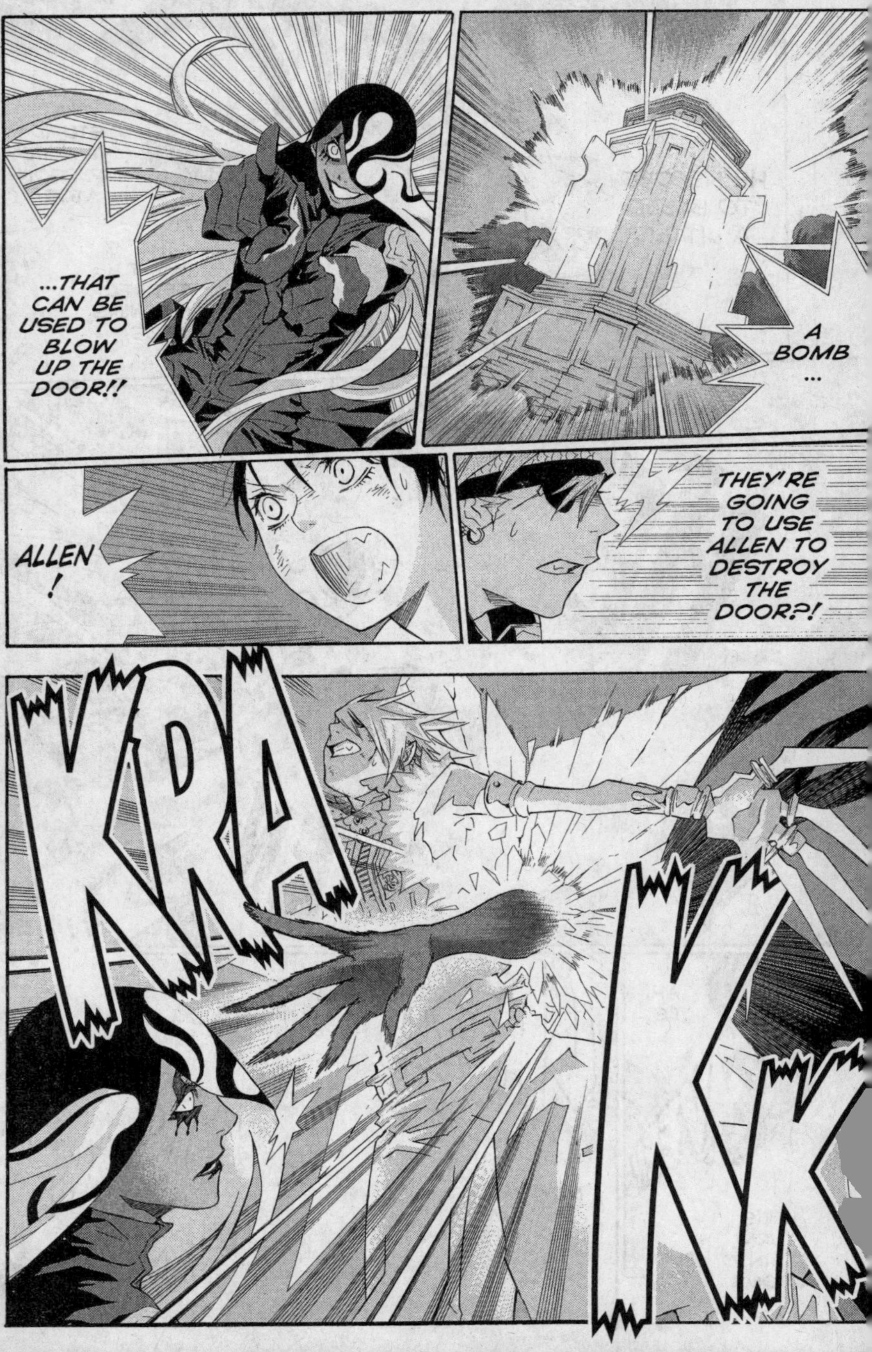
A BOMB ...
...THAT CAN BE USED TO BLOW UP THE DOOR!!
THEY'RE GOING TO USE ALLEN TO DESTROY THE DOOR?!
ALLEN!
KRAKK

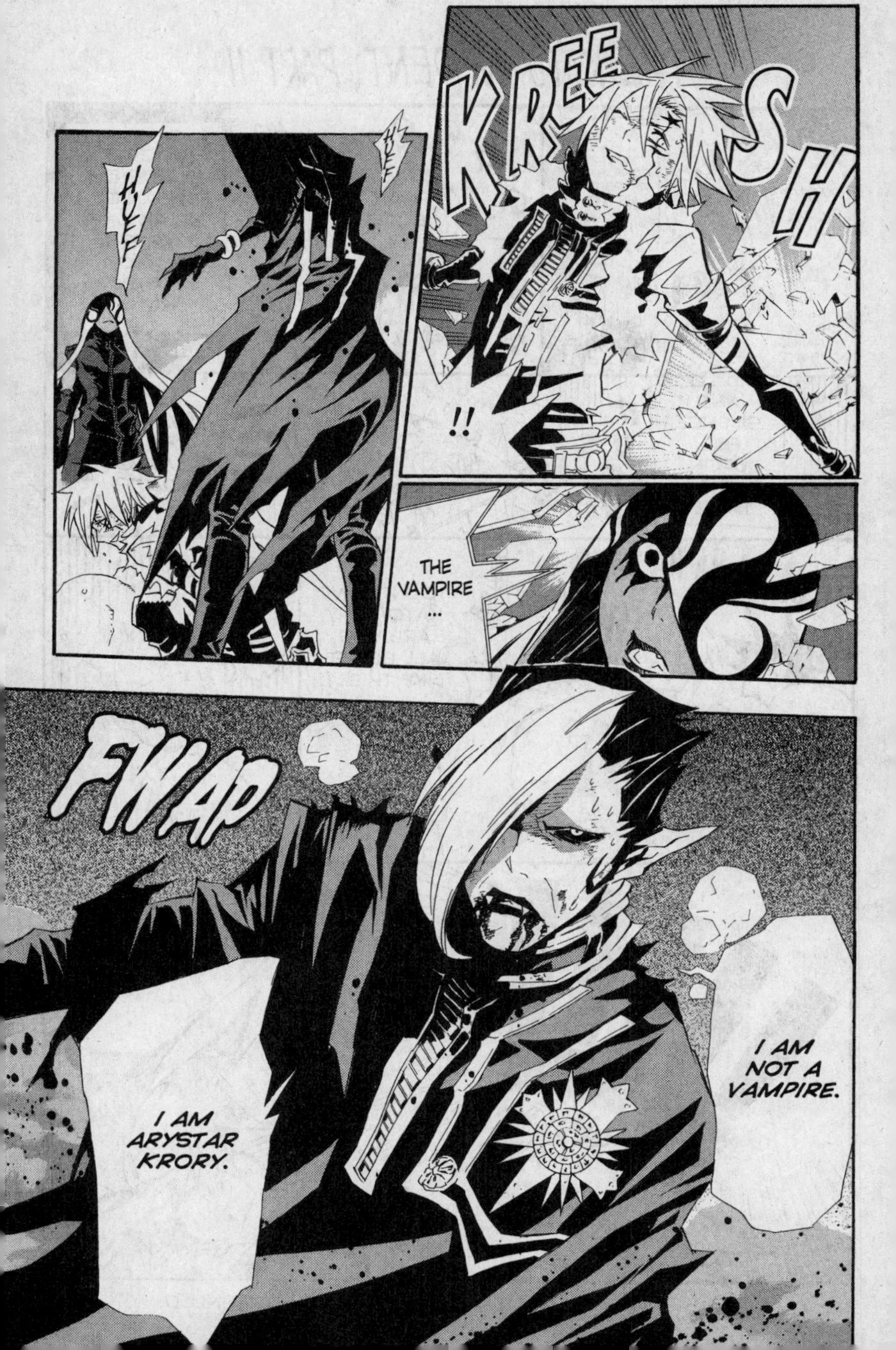
KREESH
!!
THE VAMPIRE ...
HUFF
HUFF
FWAP
I AM NOT A VAMPIRE.
I AM ARYSTAR KRORY.

THE KATO INCIDENT, PART II

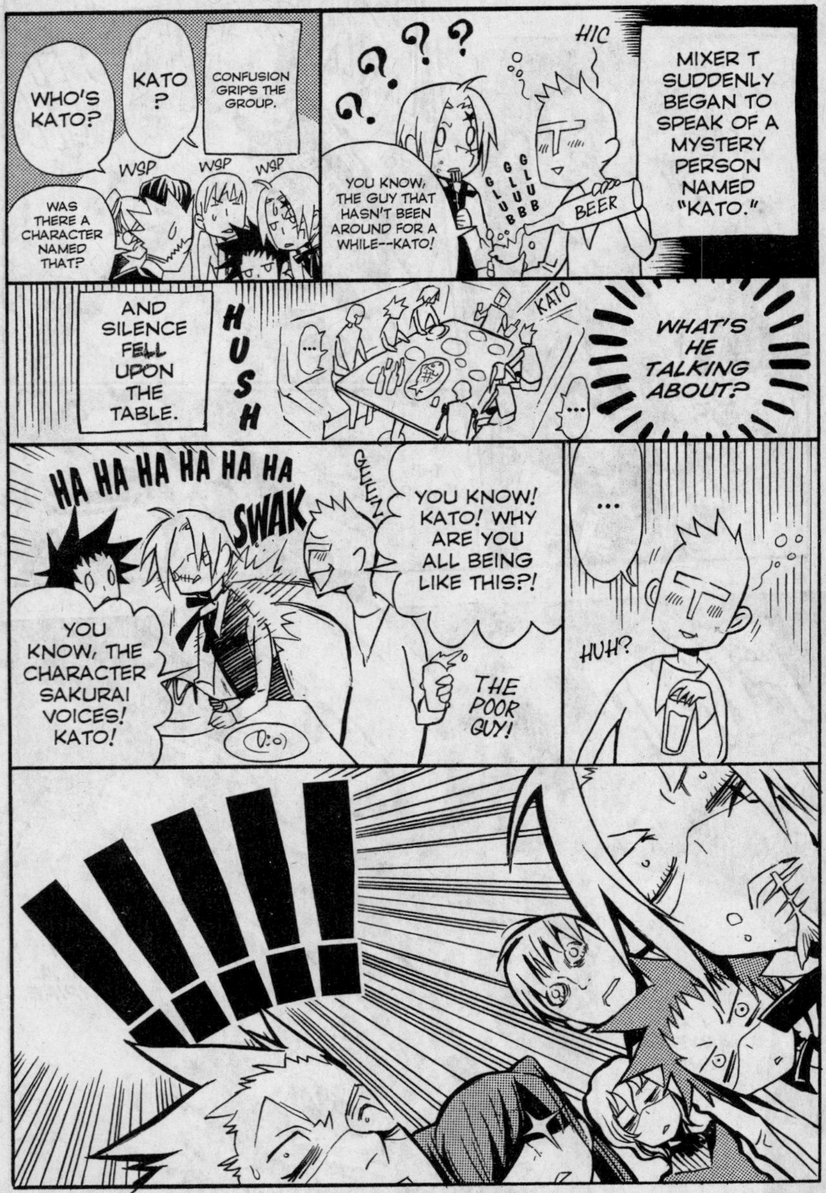
MIXER T SUDDENLY BEGAN TO SPEAK OF A MYSTERY PERSON NAMED "KATO."
HIC
YOU KNOW, THE GUY THAT HASN'T BEEN AROUND FOR A WHILE--KATO!
GLUB GLUB GLUB
BEER
CONFUSION GRIPS THE GROUP.
KATO ?
WHO'S KATO?
WSP
WSP
WSP
WAS THERE A CHARACTER NAMED THAT?
WHAT'S HE TALKING ABOUT?
...
KATO
...
HUSH
AND SILENCE FELL UPON THE TABLE.
...
HUH?
GEEZ
YOU KNOW! KATO! WHY ARE YOU ALL BEING LIKE THIS?!
HA HA HA HA HA HA
SWAK
THE POOR GUY!
YOU KNOW, THE CHARACTER SAKURAI VOICES! KATO!

REALIZATION. STILL TO BE CONTINUED.

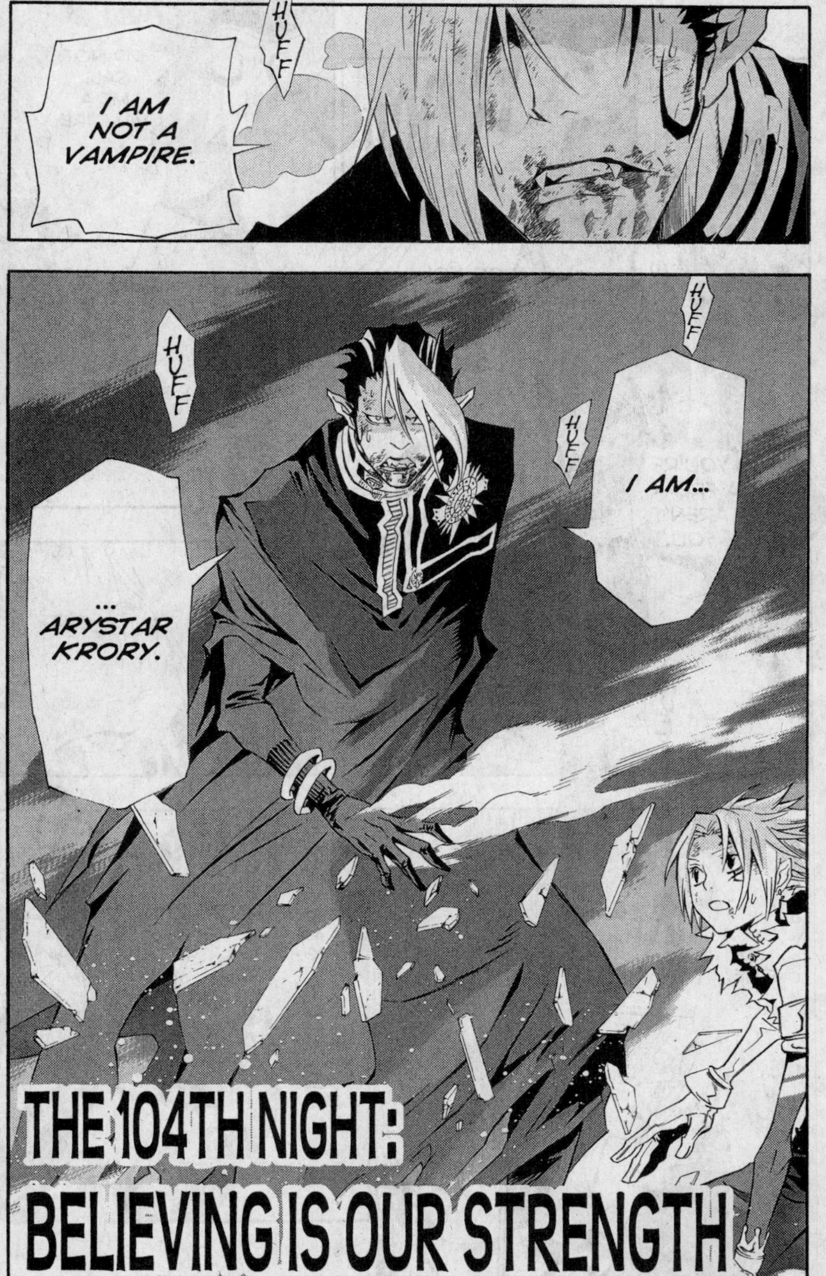
HUFF
I AM NOT A VAMPIRE.
HUFF
HUFF
I AM...
HUFF
... ARYSTAR KRORY.
THE 104TH NIGHT: BELIEVING IS OUR STRENGTH

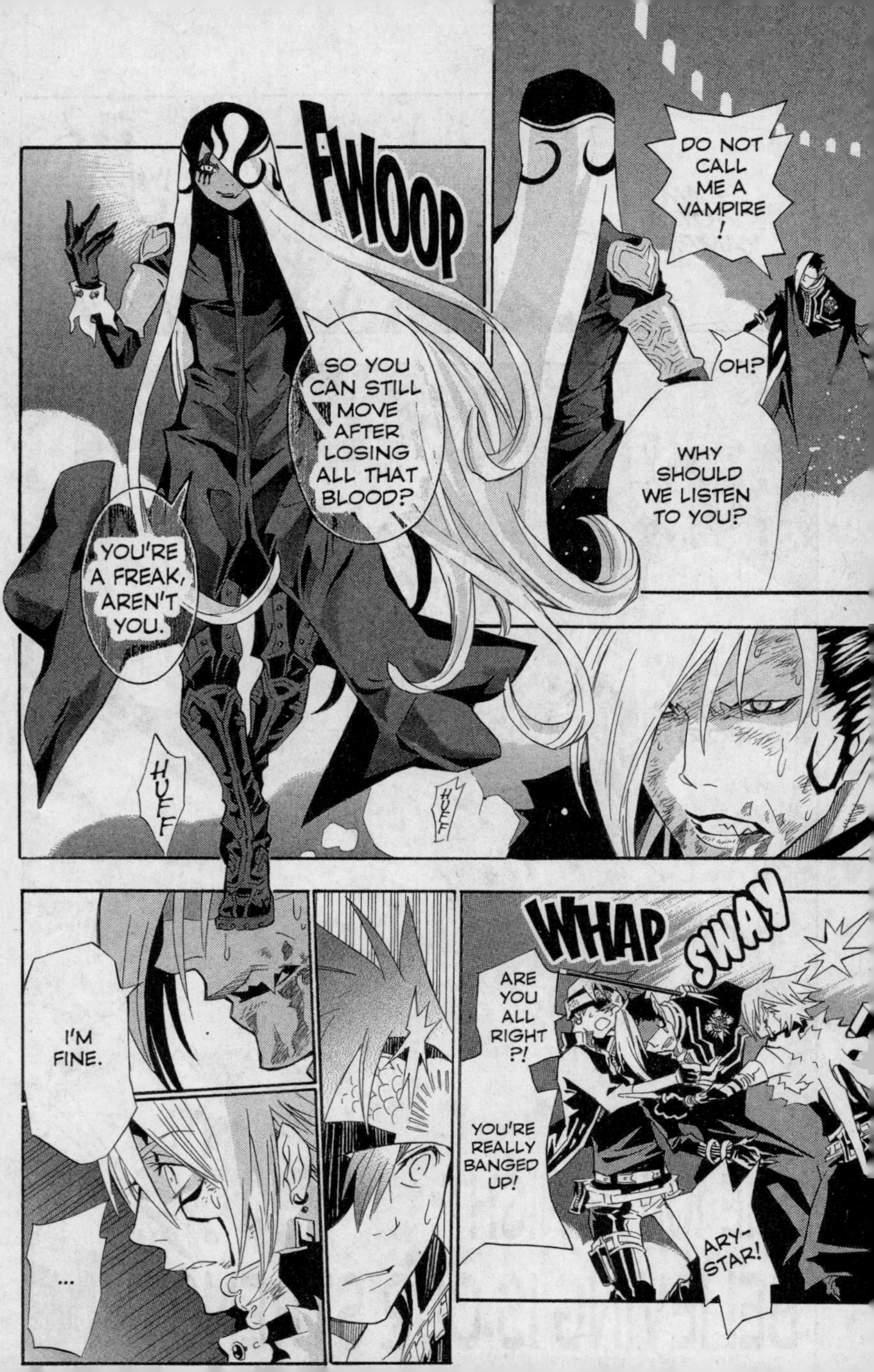
DO NOT CALL ME A VAMPIRE!
OH?
WHY SHOULD WE LISTEN TO YOU?
HUFF
FWOOP
SO YOU CAN STILL MOVE AFTER LOSING ALL THAT BLOOD?
YOU'RE A FREAK, AREN'T YOU.
HUFF
WHAP
SWAY
ARE YOU ALL RIGHT?!
YOU'RE REALLY BANGED UP!
ARY-STAR!
I'M FINE.
...

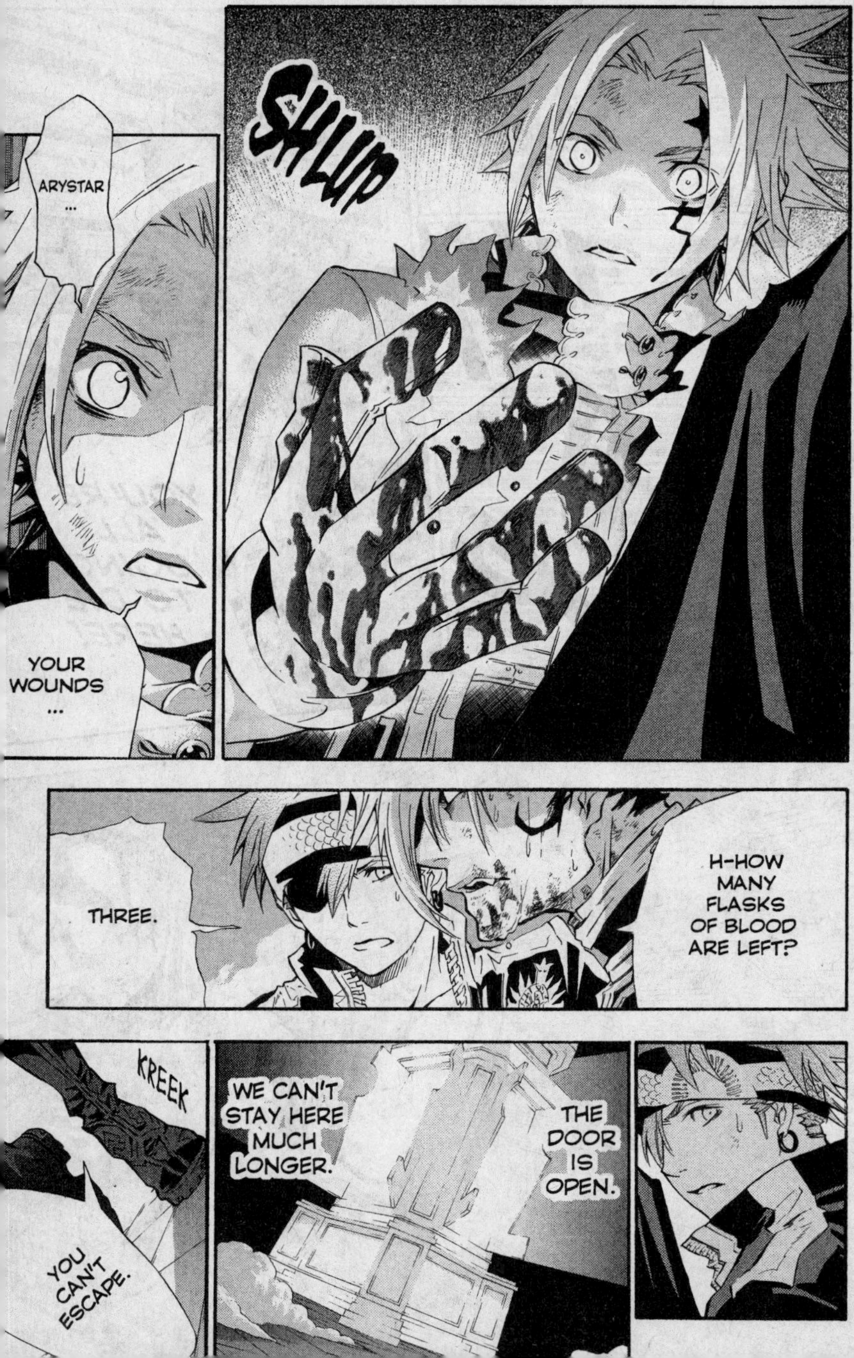
SHLUP
ARYSTAR ...
YOUR WOUNDS ...
H-HOW MANY FLASKS OF BLOOD ARE LEFT?
THREE.
THE DOOR IS OPEN.
WE CAN'T STAY HERE MUCH LONGER.
KREEK
YOU CAN'T ESCAPE.

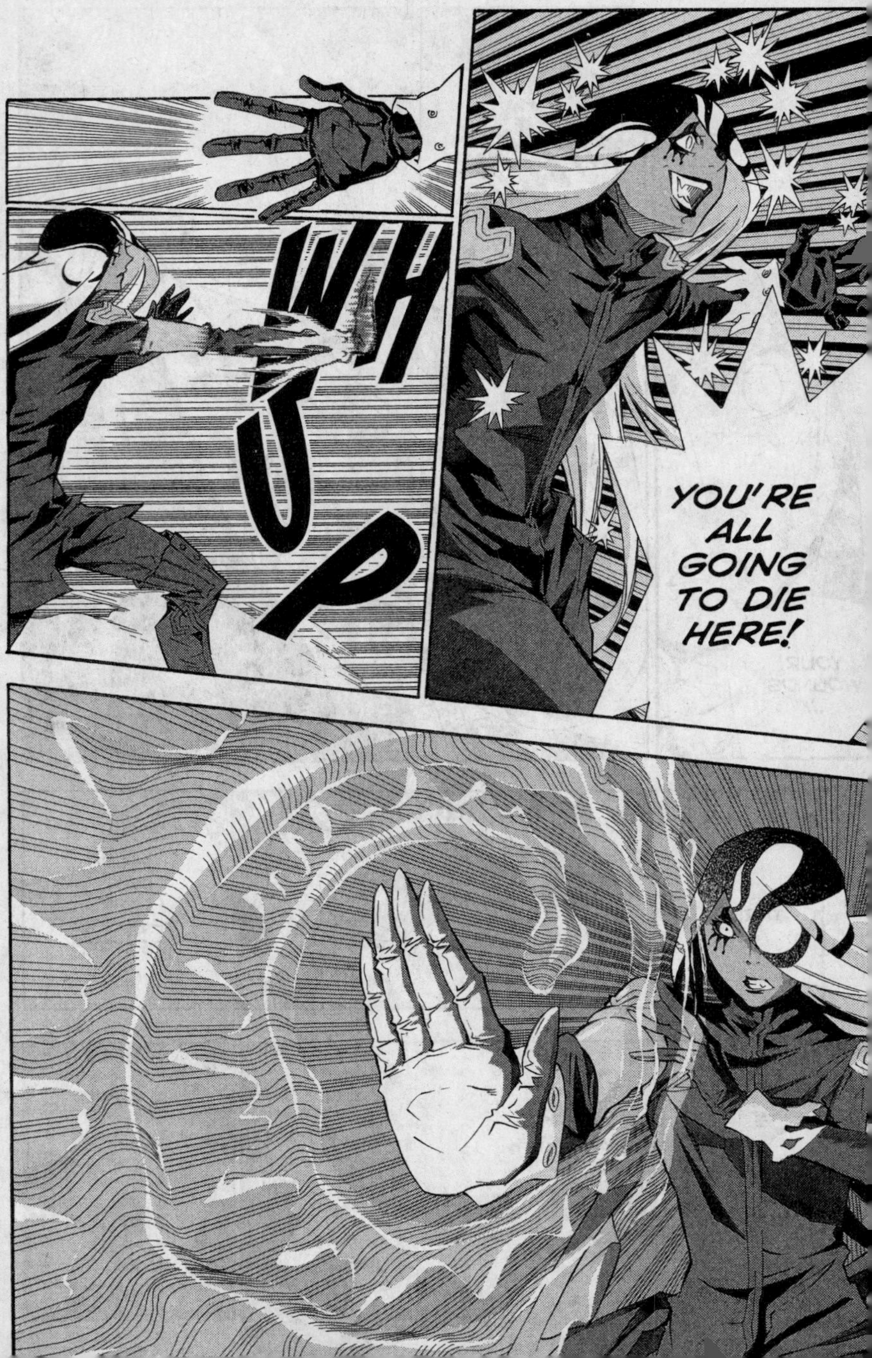
YOU'RE ALL GOING TO DIE HERE!
WHUP

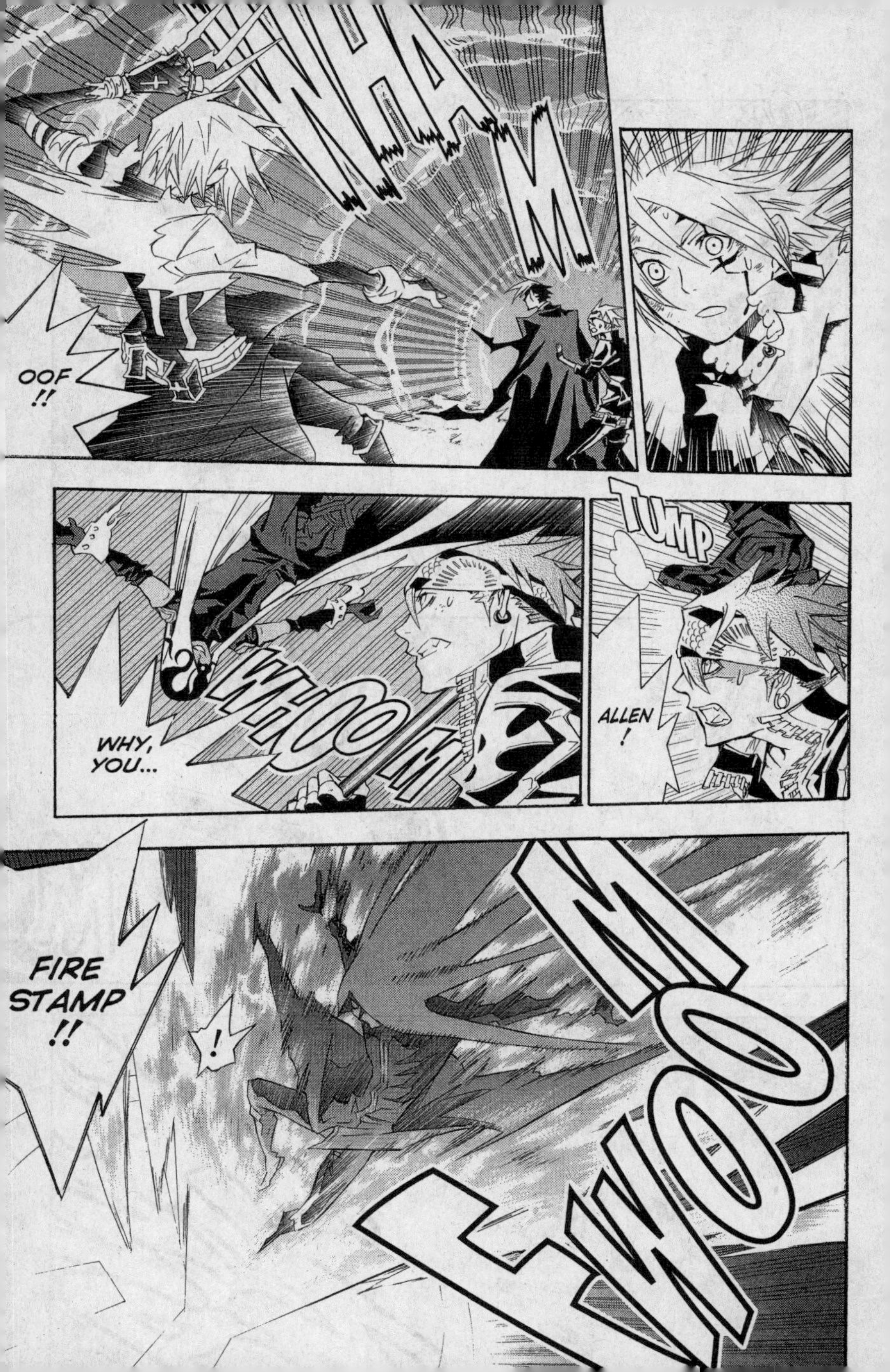
WHAM
OOF !!
TUMP
ALLEN !
WHOOM
WHY, YOU...
FIRE STAMP !!
!
WHOOM

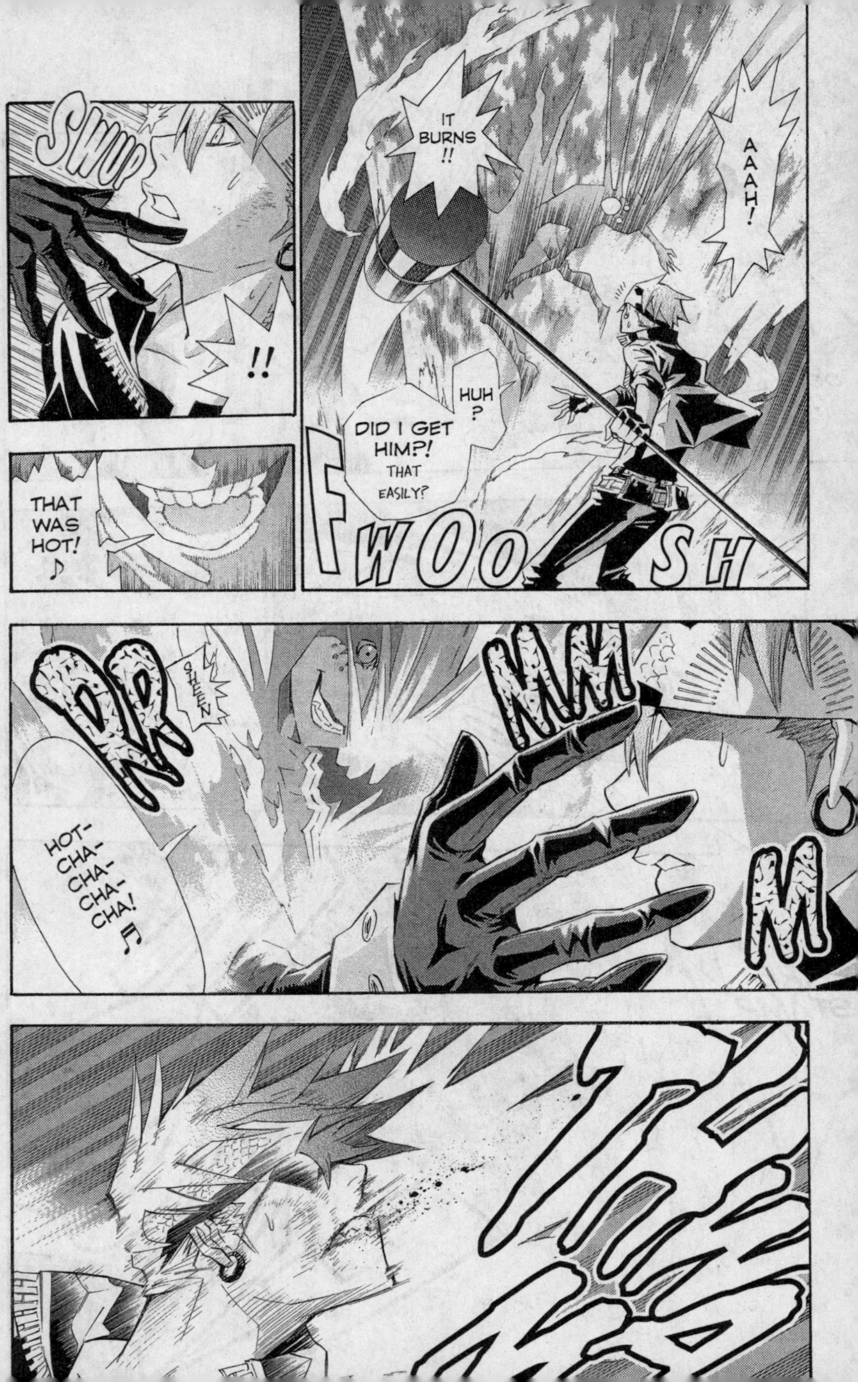
IT BURNS !!
AAAH!
HUH ?
DID I GET HIM?! THAT EASILY?
FWOOSH
SWUP
!!
THAT WAS HOT! ♪
MM
M
SHEEN
DD
HOT-CHA-CHA-CHA-CHA! ♬

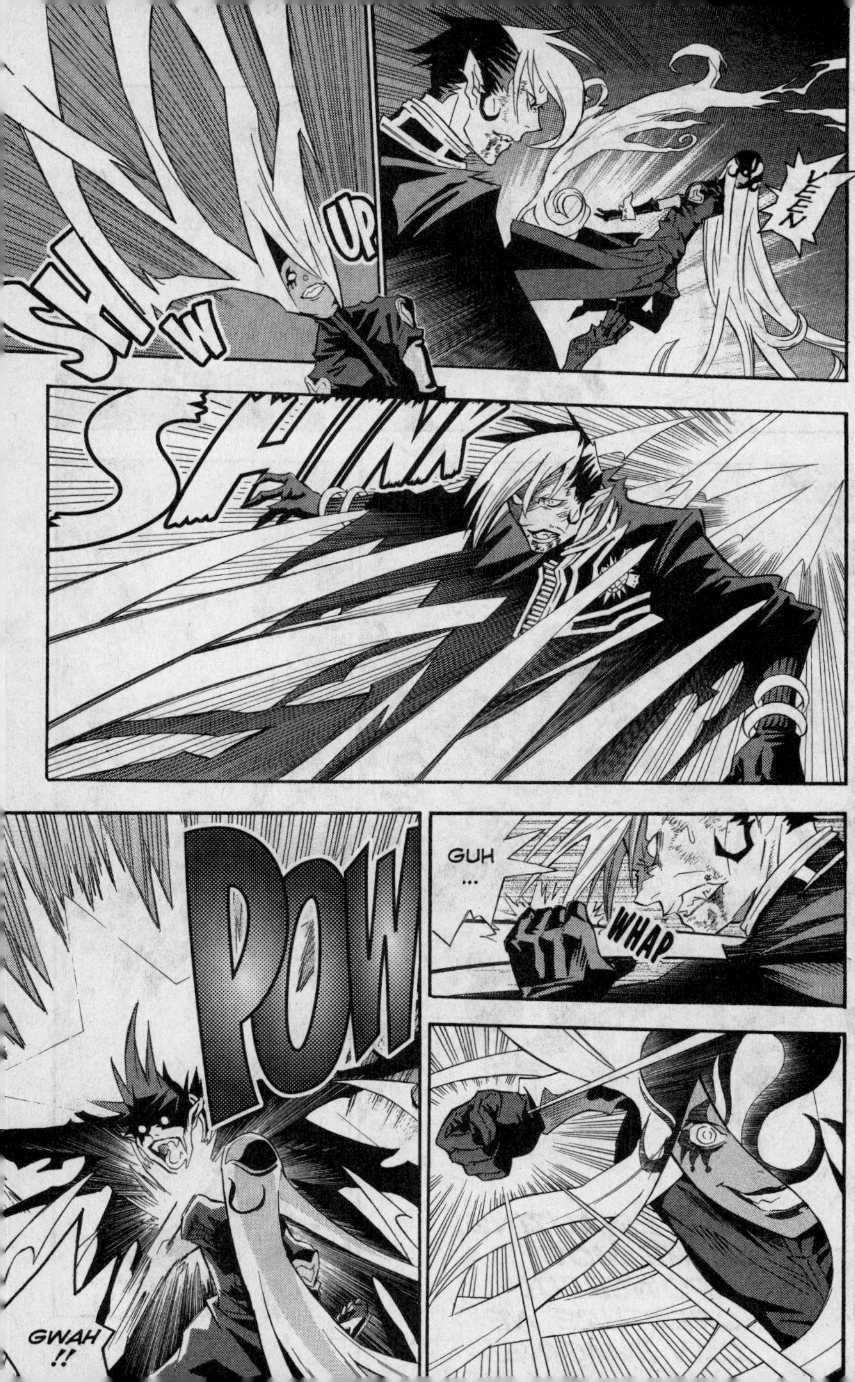
VEEN
SHINK
GUH ...
WHAP
POW
GWAH !!

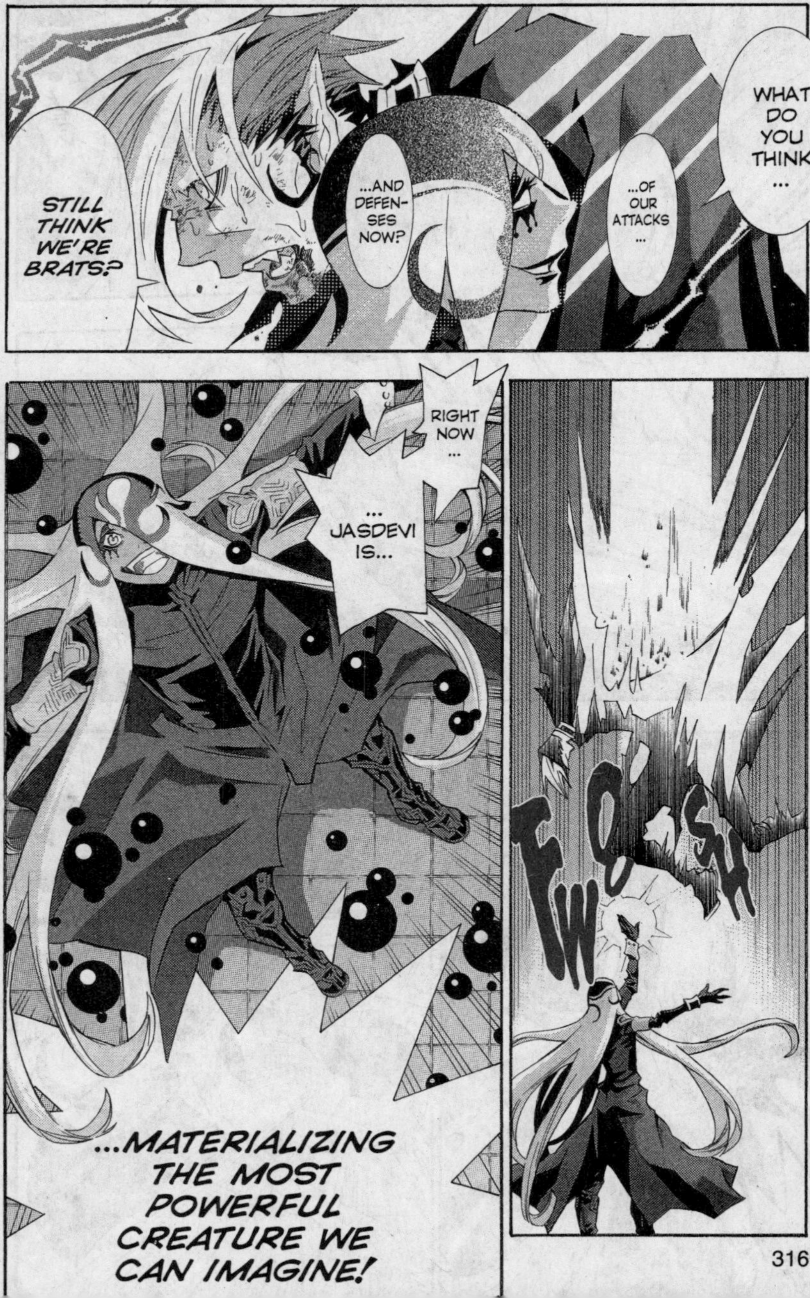
WHAT DO YOU THINK ...
...OF OUR ATTACKS ...
...AND DEFENSES NOW?
STILL THINK WE'RE BRATS?
FWOOSH
RIGHT NOW ...
... JASDEVI IS...
...MATERIALIZING THE MOST POWERFUL CREATURE WE CAN IMAGINE!

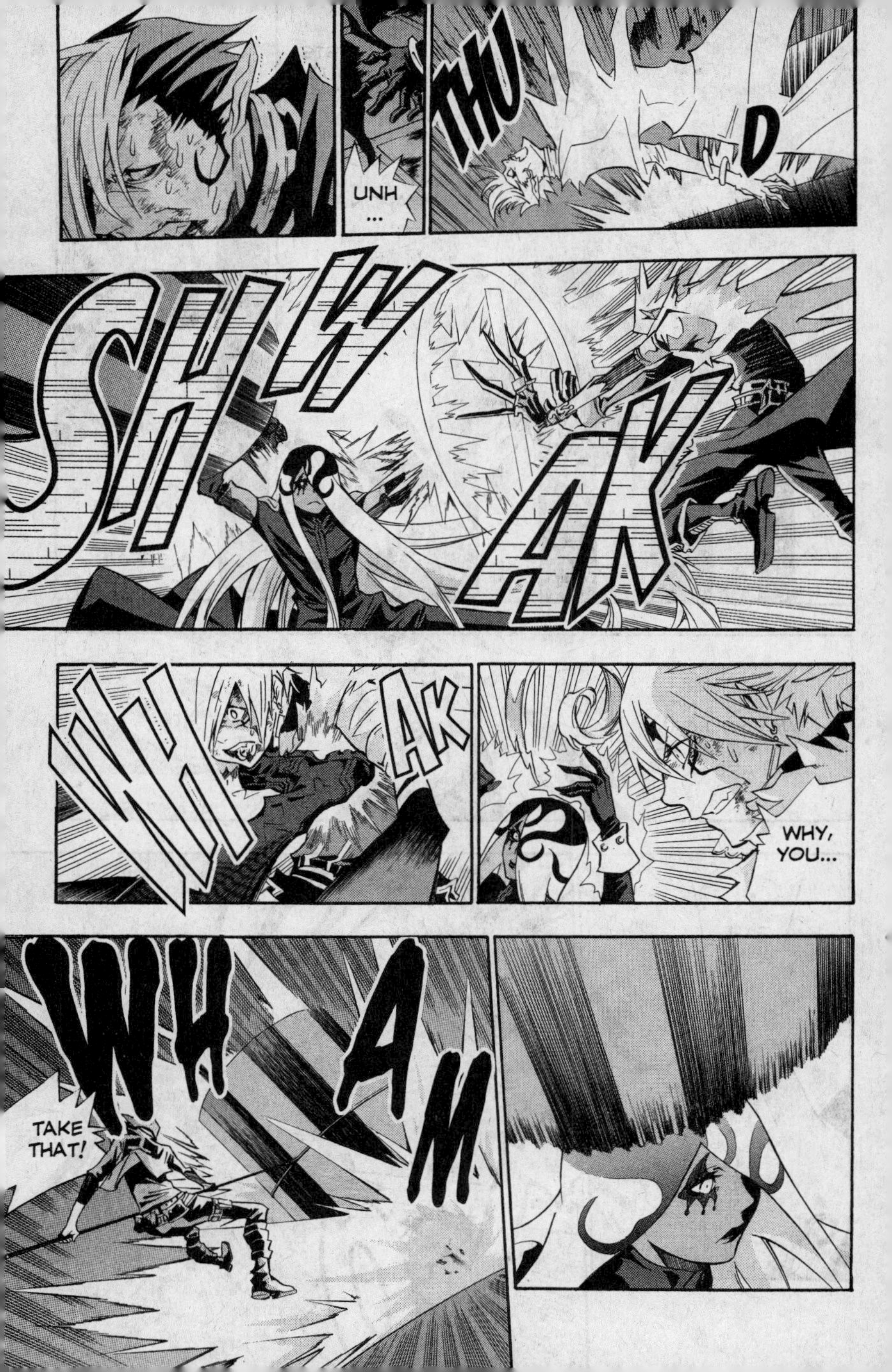

THU
D
UNH
...
SHWAK
WHY, YOU...
WH
AK
WHAM
TAKE THAT!

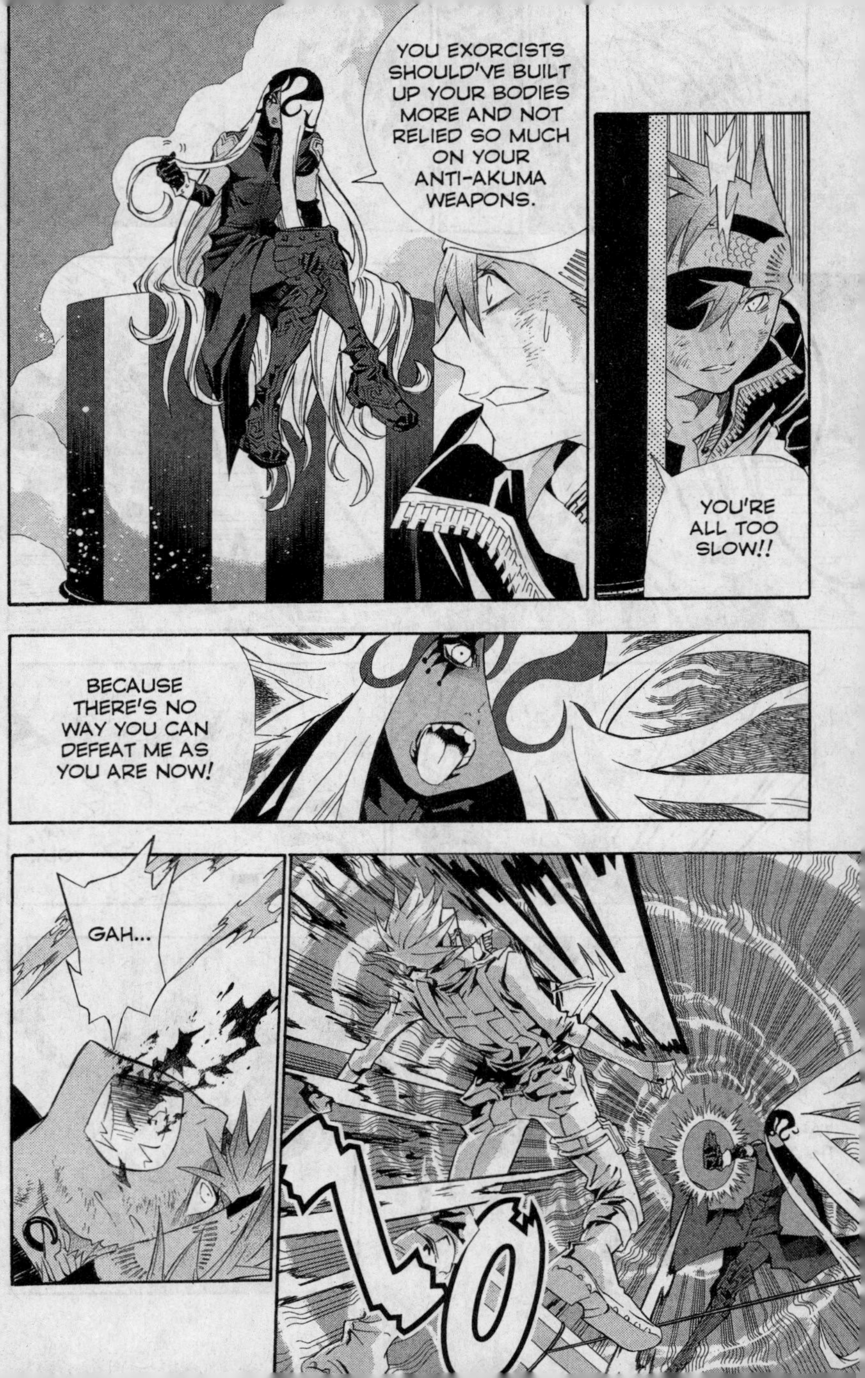

YOU'RE ALL TOO SLOW!!
YOU EXORCISTS SHOULD'VE BUILT UP YOUR BODIES MORE AND NOT RELIED SO MUCH ON YOUR ANTI-AKUMA WEAPONS.
BECAUSE THERE'S NO WAY YOU CAN DEFEAT ME AS YOU ARE NOW!
GAH...

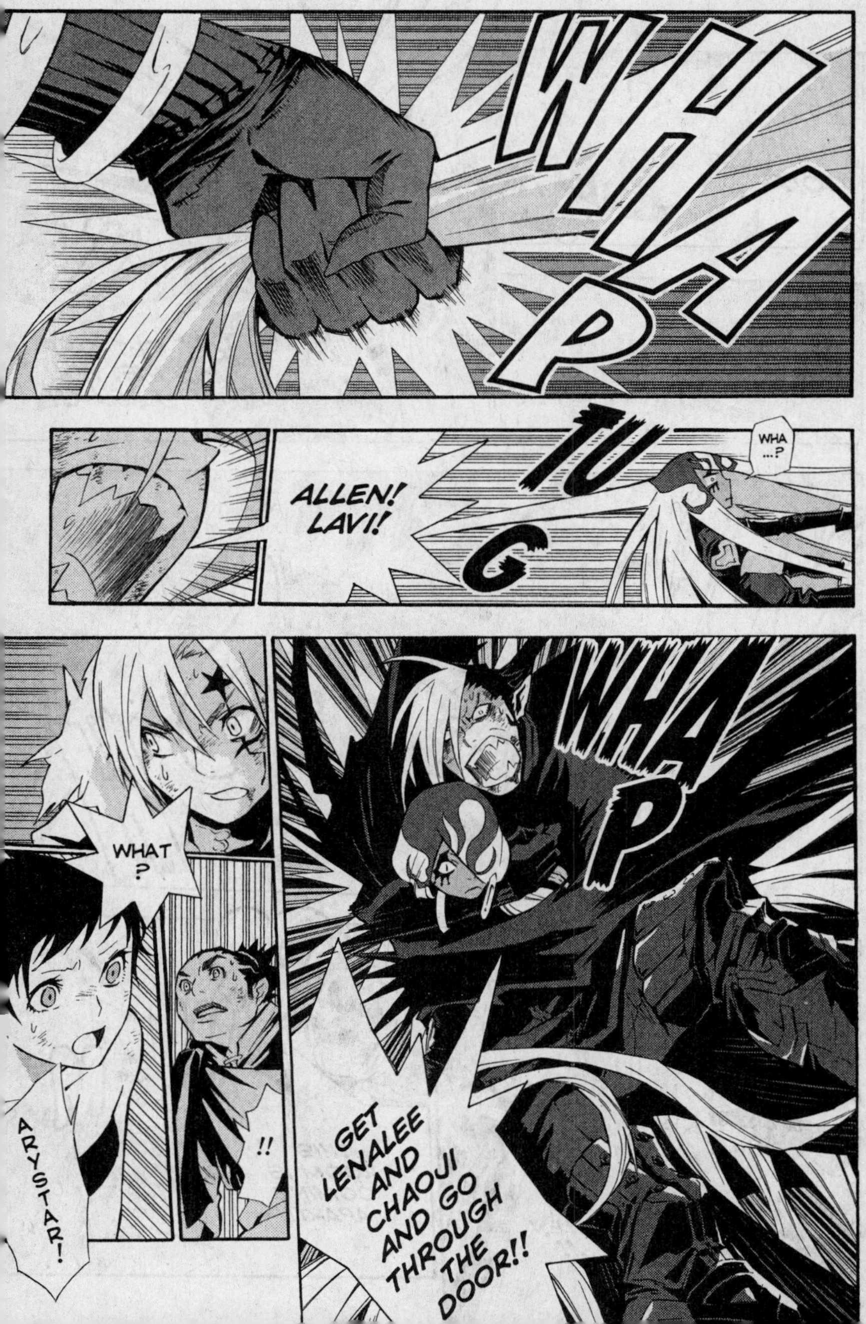
WHAP
WHA ...P
TUG
ALLEN! LAVI!
WHAP
GET LENALEE AND CHAOJI AND GO THROUGH THE DOOR!!
WHAT?
!!
ARYSTAR!

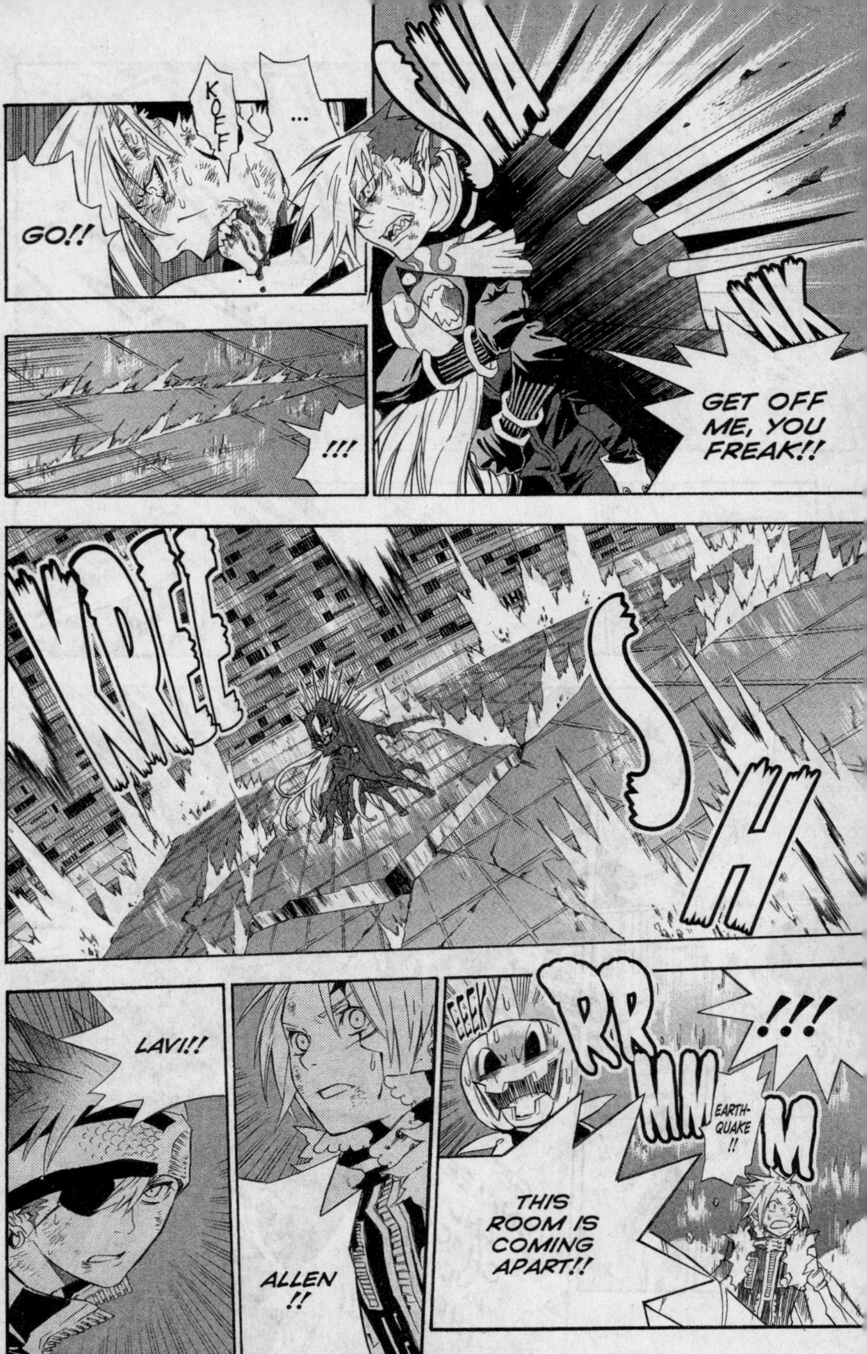
SHA
NK
GET OFF ME, YOU FREAK!!
KOFF
...
GO!!
!!!
EEEK
RR
MM
M
!!!
EARTH-QUAKE!!
THIS ROOM IS COMING APART!!
ALLEN!!
LAVI!!

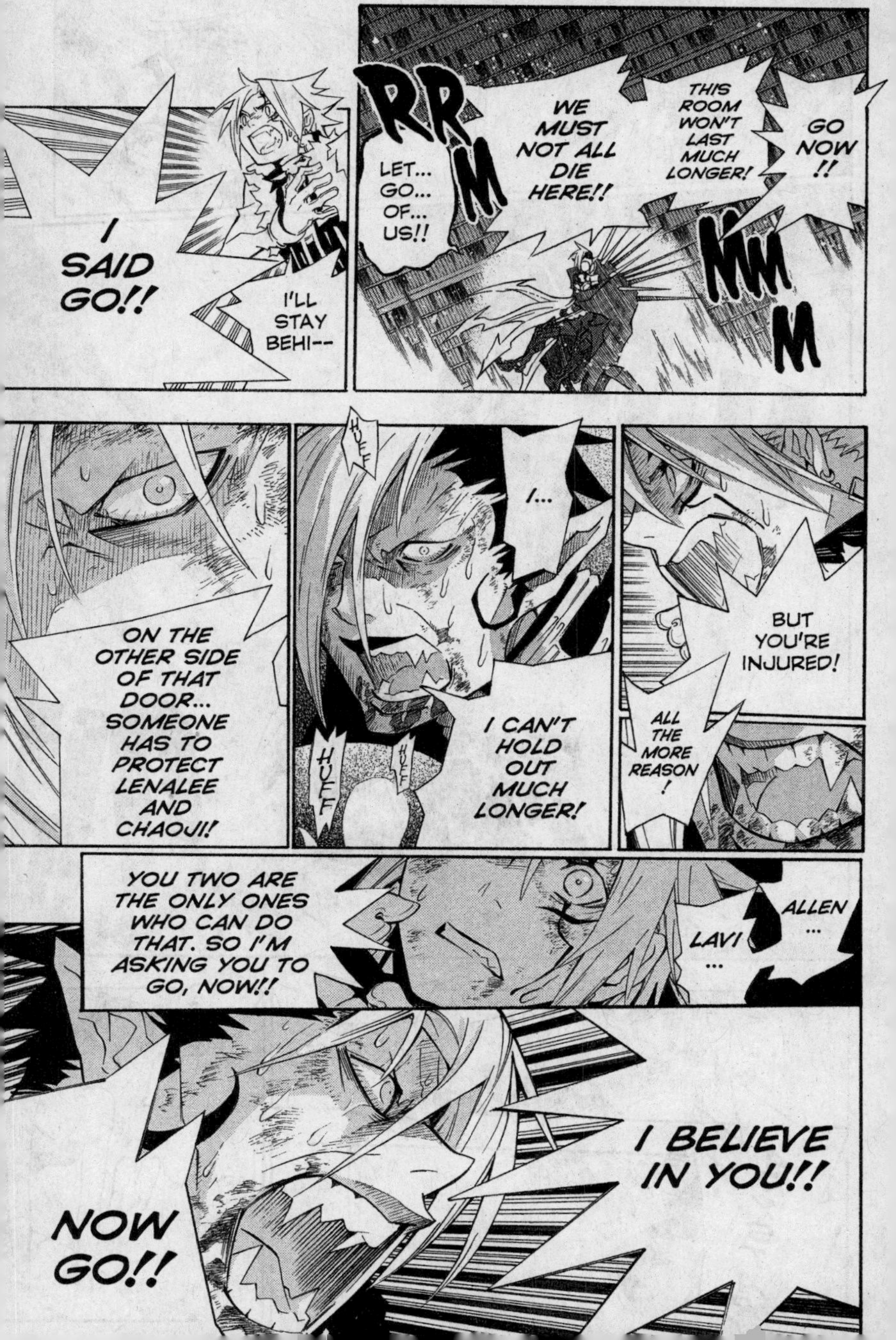
GO NOW!!
THIS ROOM WON'T LAST MUCH LONGER!
WE MUST NOT ALL DIE HERE!!
RRM
LET... GO... OF... US!!
MMM
I'LL STAY BEHI--
I SAID GO!!
BUT YOU'RE INJURED!
ALL THE MORE REASON!
HUFF
I...
I CAN'T HOLD OUT MUCH LONGER!
HUFF
HUFF
ON THE OTHER SIDE OF THAT DOOR... SOMEONE HAS TO PROTECT LENALEE AND CHAOJI!
ALLEN...
LAVI...
YOU TWO ARE THE ONLY ONES WHO CAN DO THAT. SO I'M ASKING YOU TO GO, NOW!!
I BELIEVE IN YOU!!
NOW GO!!

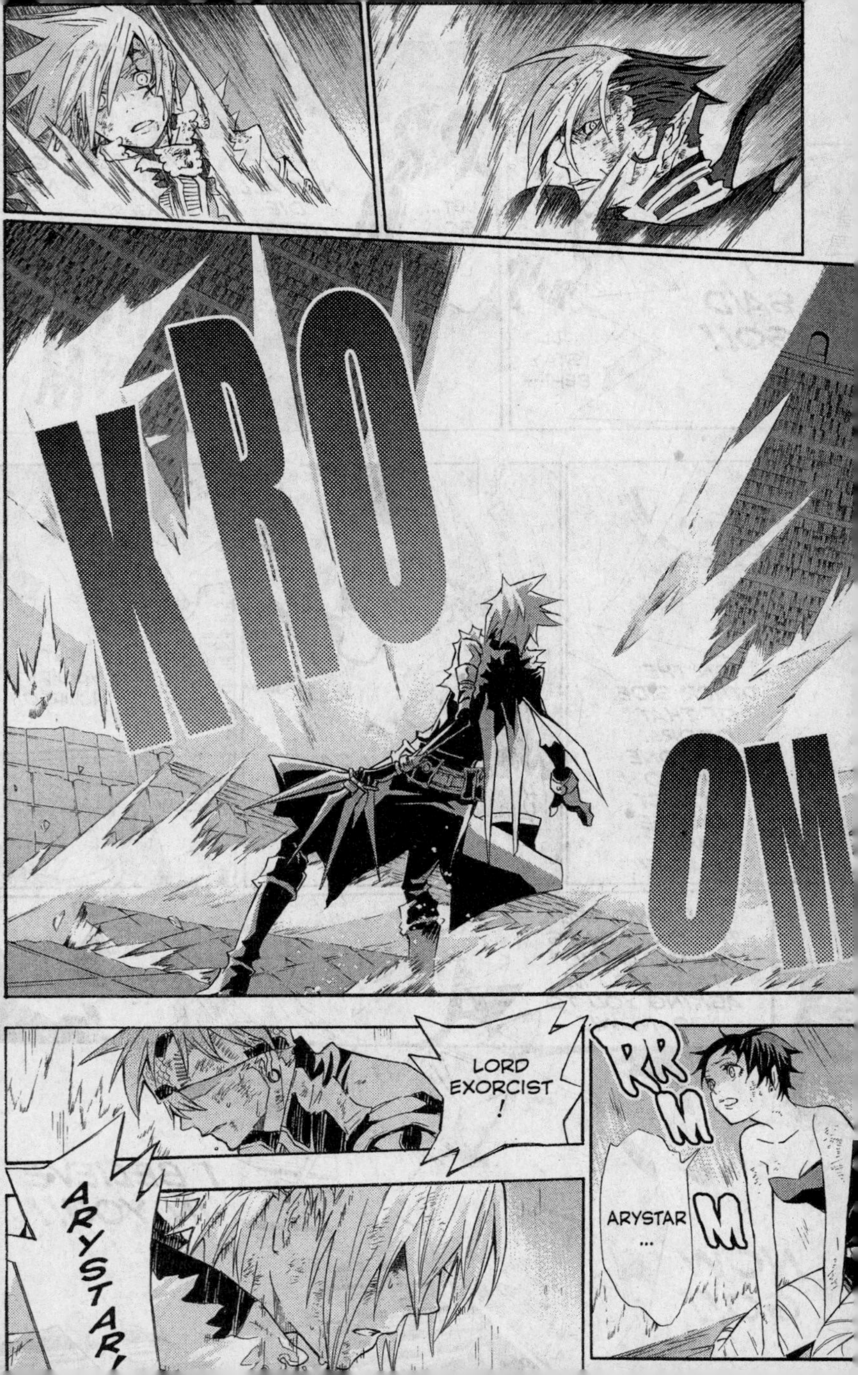
KROOM
RRMM
ARYSTAR ...
LORD EXORCIST !
ARYSTAR!

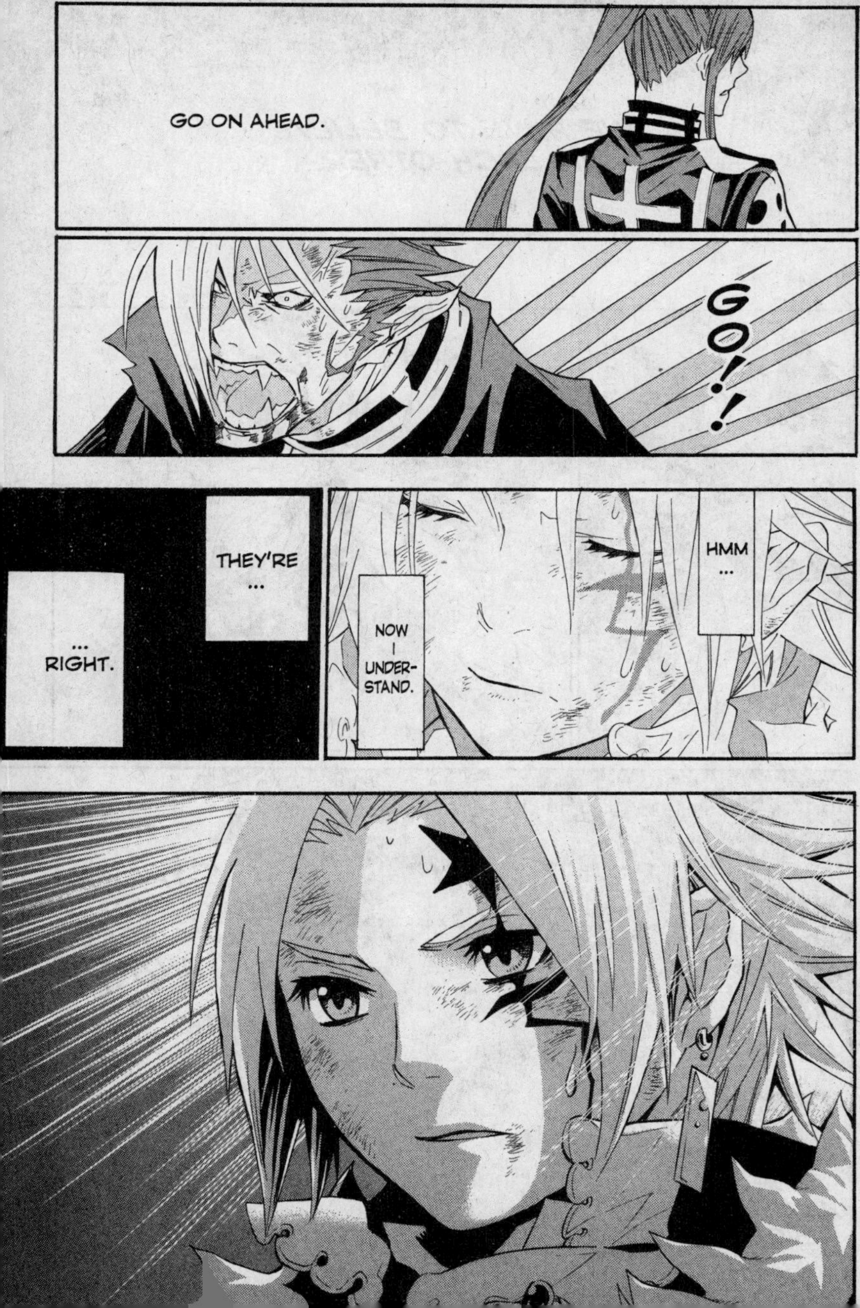
GO ON AHEAD.
GO!!
HMM...
NOW I UNDERSTAND.
THEY'RE...
...RIGHT.

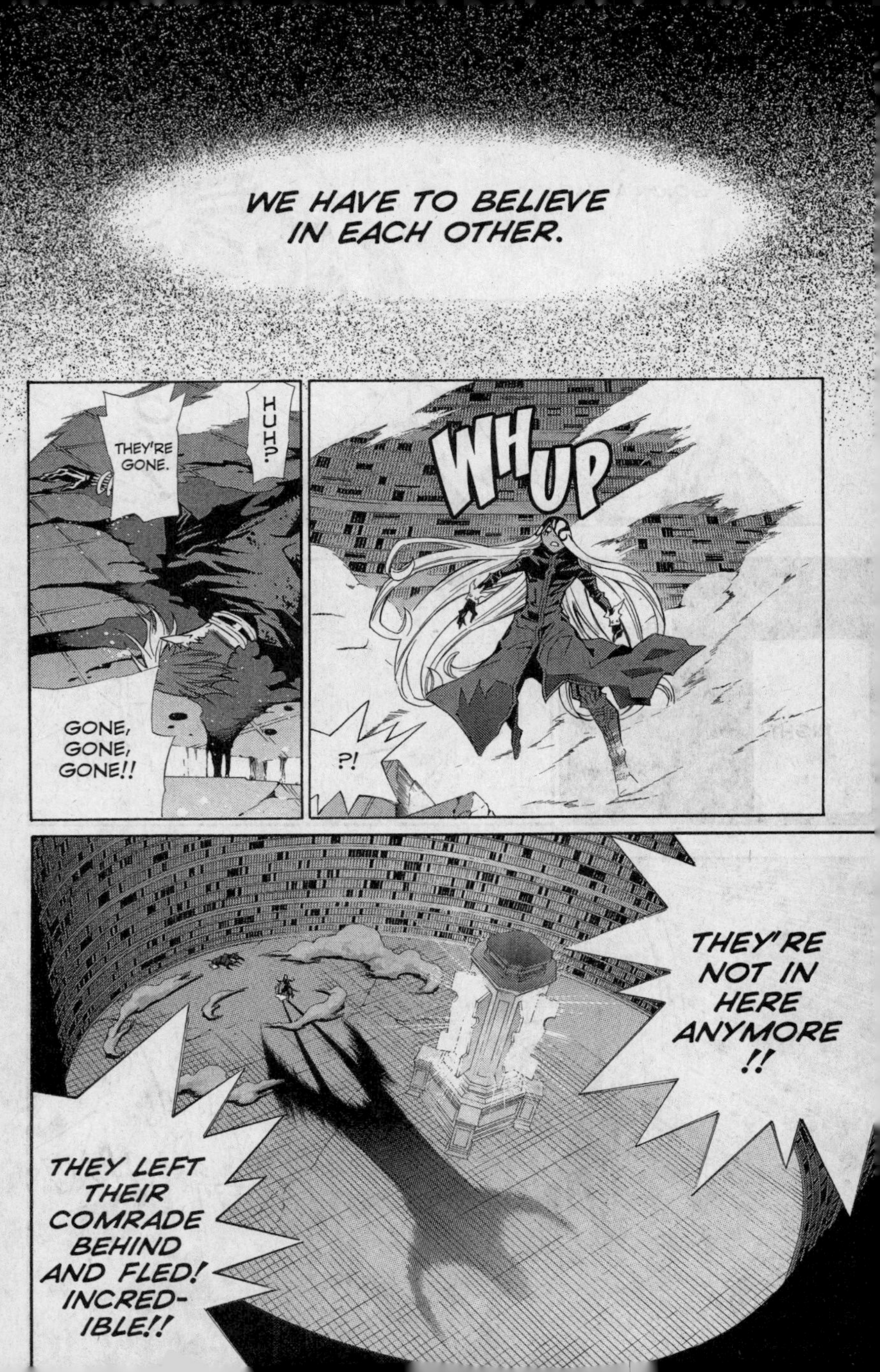
WE HAVE TO BELIEVE IN EACH OTHER.
WHUP
?!
HUH?
THEY'RE GONE.
GONE, GONE, GONE!!
THEY'RE NOT IN HERE ANYMORE!!
THEY LEFT THEIR COMRADE BEHIND AND FLED! INCREDIBLE!!

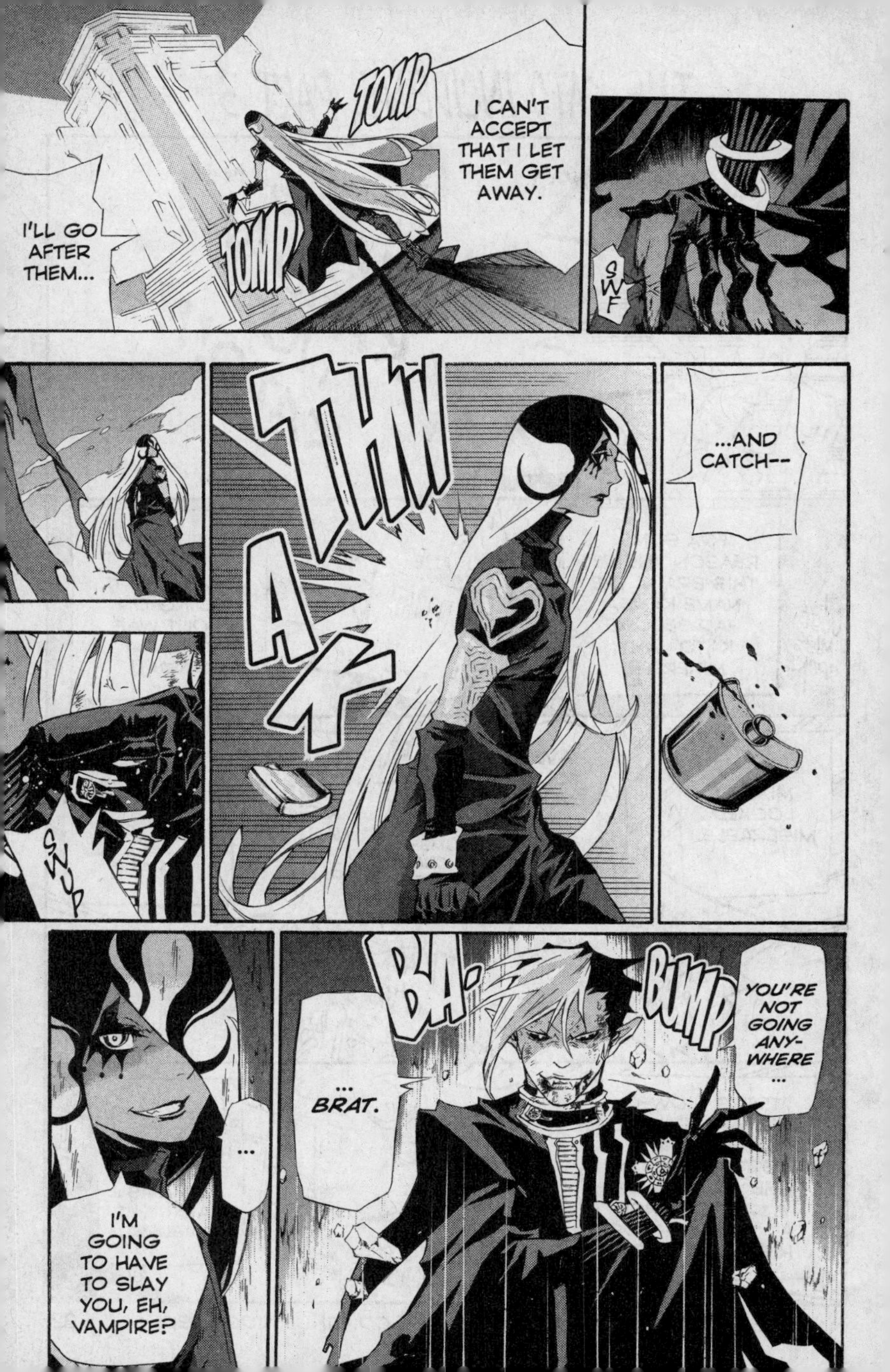
SWF
I CAN'T ACCEPT THAT I LET THEM GET AWAY.
TOMP
TOMP
I'LL GO AFTER THEM...
...AND CATCH--
THWAK
SWUP
BA-
BUMP
YOU'RE NOT GOING ANYWHERE...
...BRAT.
...
I'M GOING TO HAVE TO SLAY YOU, EH, VAMPIRE?

THE KATO INCIDENT, PART 3

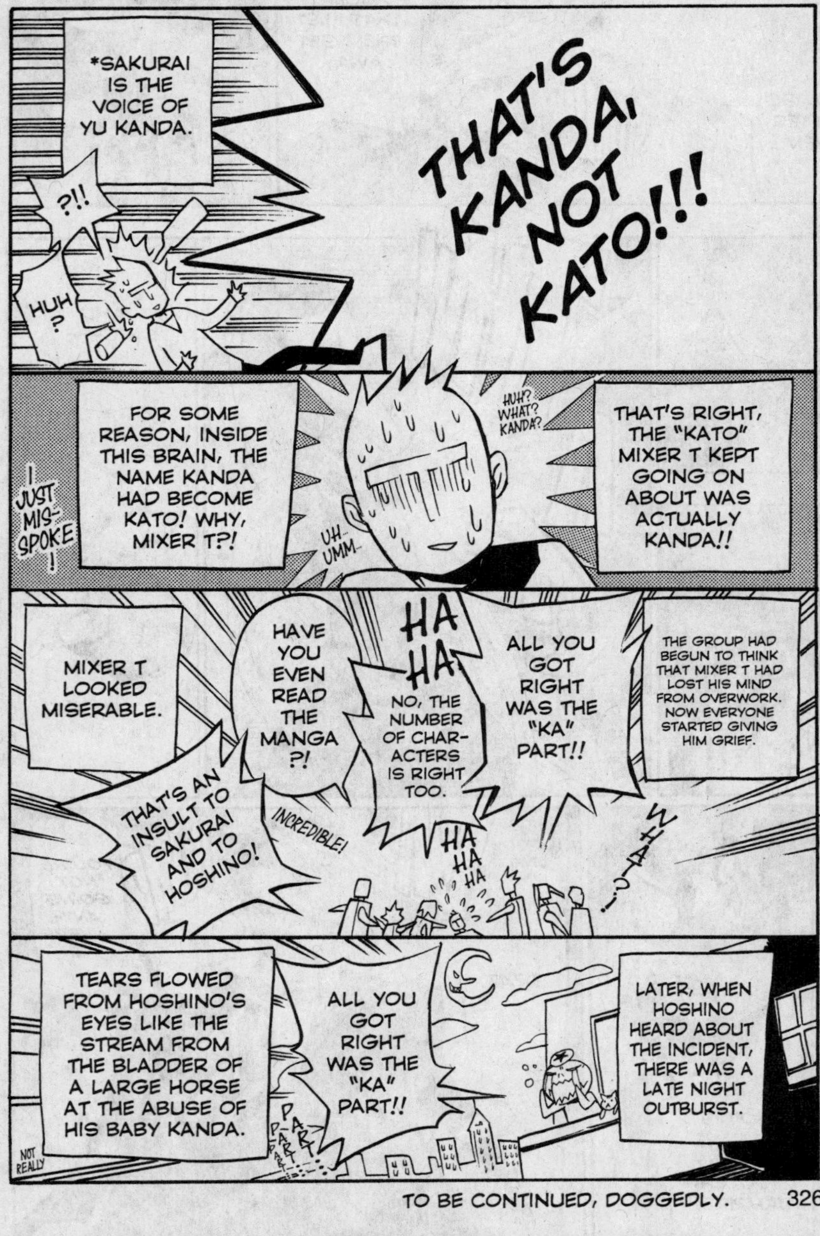
THAT'S KANDA, NOT KATO!!!
*SAKURAI IS THE VOICE OF YU KANDA.
?!!
HUH?
THAT'S RIGHT, THE "KATO" MIXER T KEPT GOING ON ABOUT WAS ACTUALLY KANDA!!
HUH? WHAT? KANDA?
FOR SOME REASON, INSIDE THIS BRAIN, THE NAME KANDA HAD BECOME KATO! WHY, MIXER T?!
UH... UMM...
I JUST MIS-SPOKE!
THE GROUP HAD BEGUN TO THINK THAT MIXER T HAD LOST HIS MIND FROM OVERWORK. NOW EVERYONE STARTED GIVING HIM GRIEF.
ALL YOU GOT RIGHT WAS THE "KA" PART!!
HA HA
NO, THE NUMBER OF CHAR-ACTERS IS RIGHT TOO.
HAVE YOU EVEN READ THE MANGA?!
WHAT...?
HA HA HA
INCREDIBLE!
THAT'S AN INSULT TO SAKURAI AND TO HOSHINO!
MIXER T LOOKED MISERABLE.
LATER, WHEN HOSHINO HEARD ABOUT THE INCIDENT, THERE WAS A LATE NIGHT OUTBURST.
ALL YOU GOT RIGHT WAS THE "KA" PART!!
PART PART PART
TEARS FLOWED FROM HOSHINO'S EYES LIKE THE STREAM FROM THE BLADDER OF A LARGE HORSE AT THE ABUSE OF HIS BABY KANDA.
NOT REALLY

TO BE CONTINUED, DOGGEDLY.

THE 105TH NIGHT: THE ROUGE STAGE

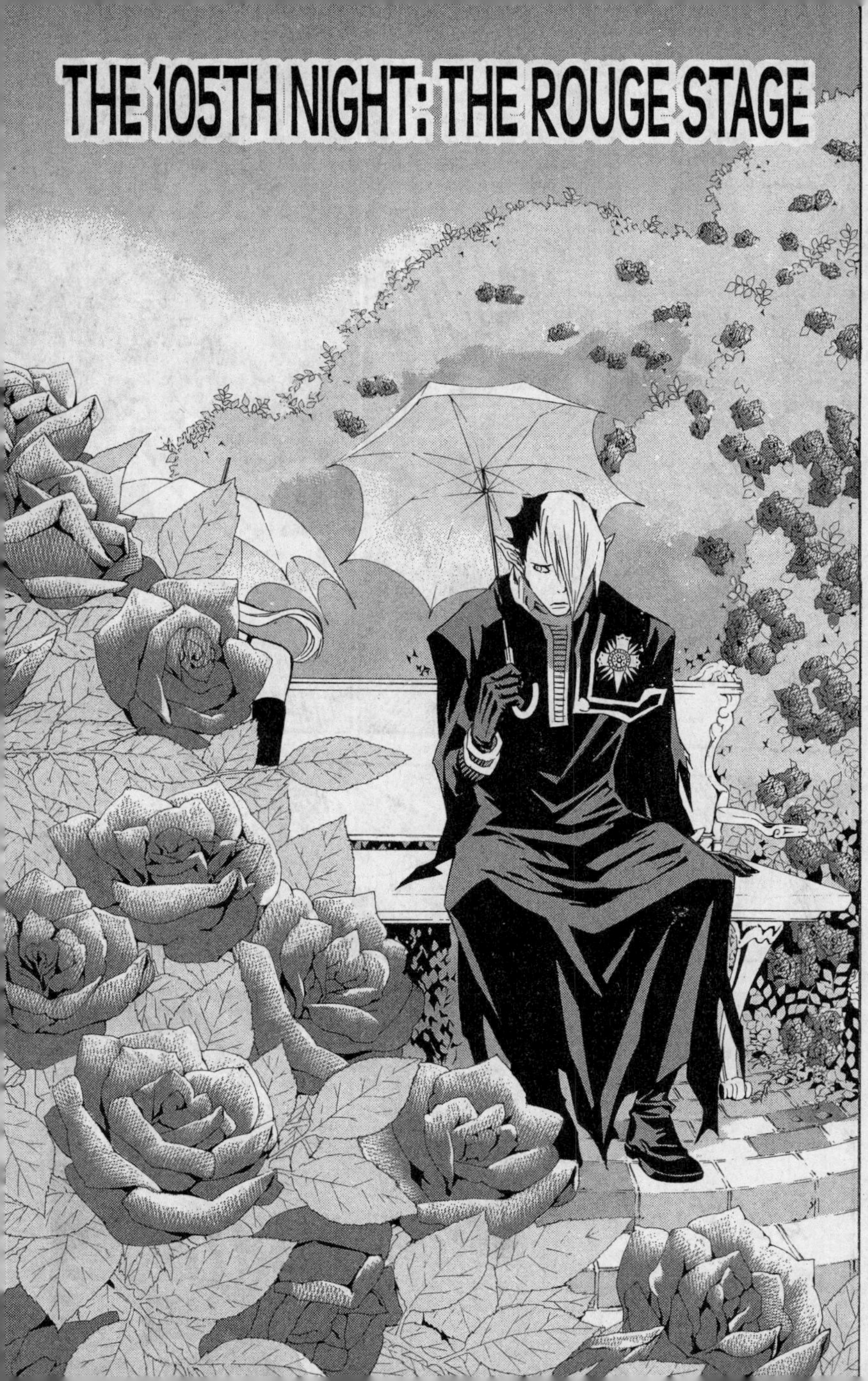

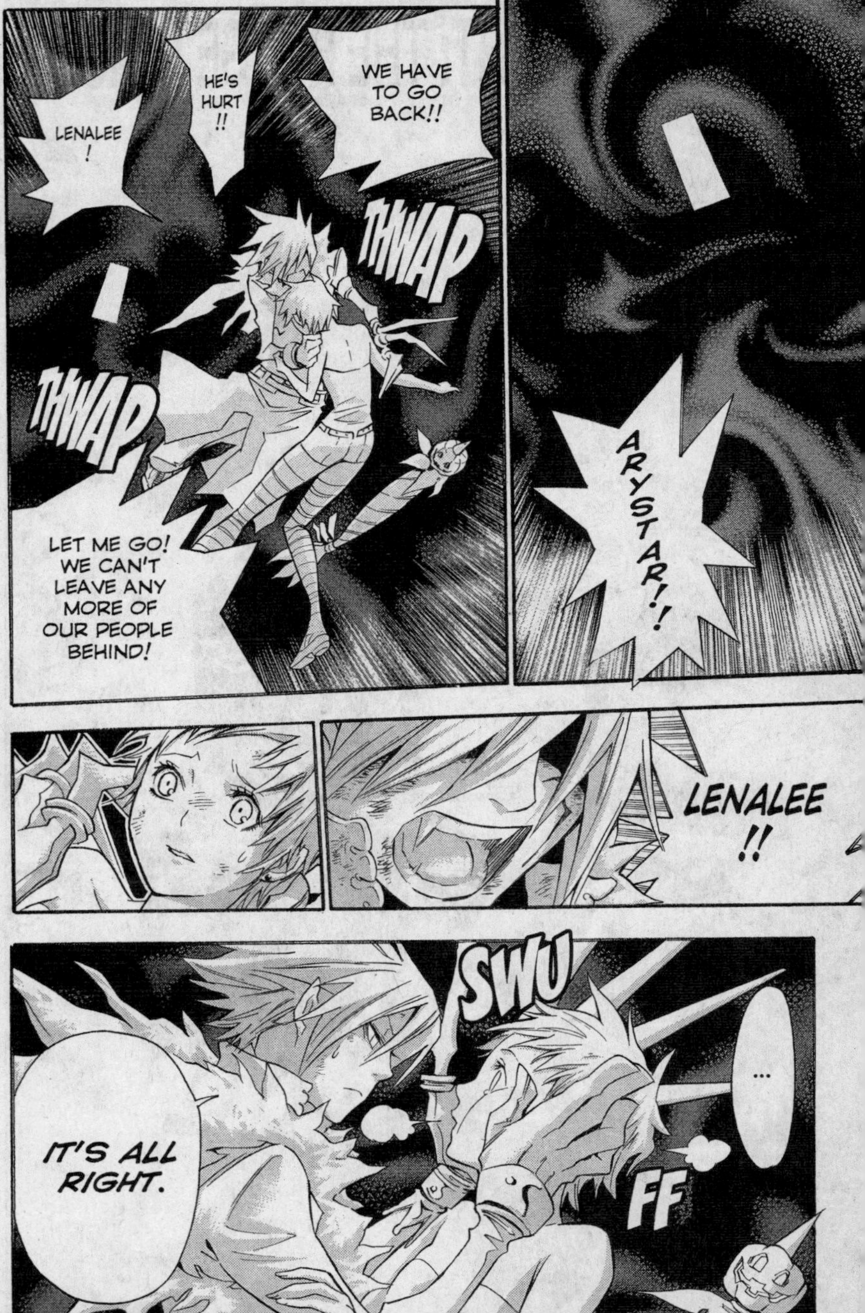

ARYSTAR!!
WE HAVE TO GO BACK!!
HE'S HURT!!
LENALEE!
THWAP
THWAP
LET ME GO! WE CAN'T LEAVE ANY MORE OF OUR PEOPLE BEHIND!
LENALEE!!
SWU
...
FF
IT'S ALL RIGHT.

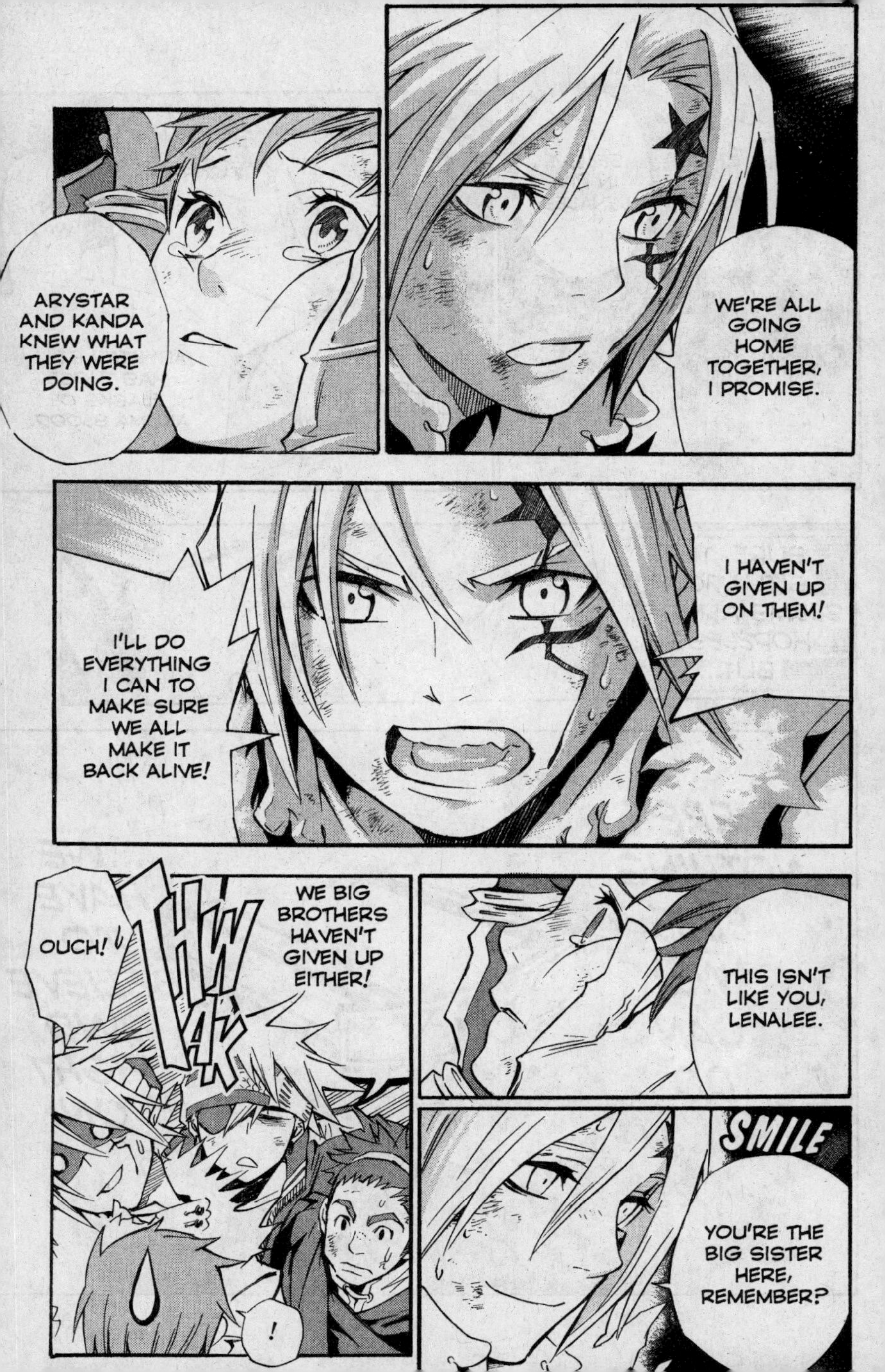

WE'RE ALL GOING HOME TOGETHER, I PROMISE.
ARYSTAR AND KANDA KNEW WHAT THEY WERE DOING.
I HAVEN'T GIVEN UP ON THEM!
I'LL DO EVERYTHING I CAN TO MAKE SURE WE ALL MAKE IT BACK ALIVE!
THIS ISN'T LIKE YOU, LENALEE.
SMILE
YOU'RE THE BIG SISTER HERE, REMEMBER?
WE BIG BROTHERS HAVEN'T GIVEN UP EITHER!
THWAK
OUCH!
!

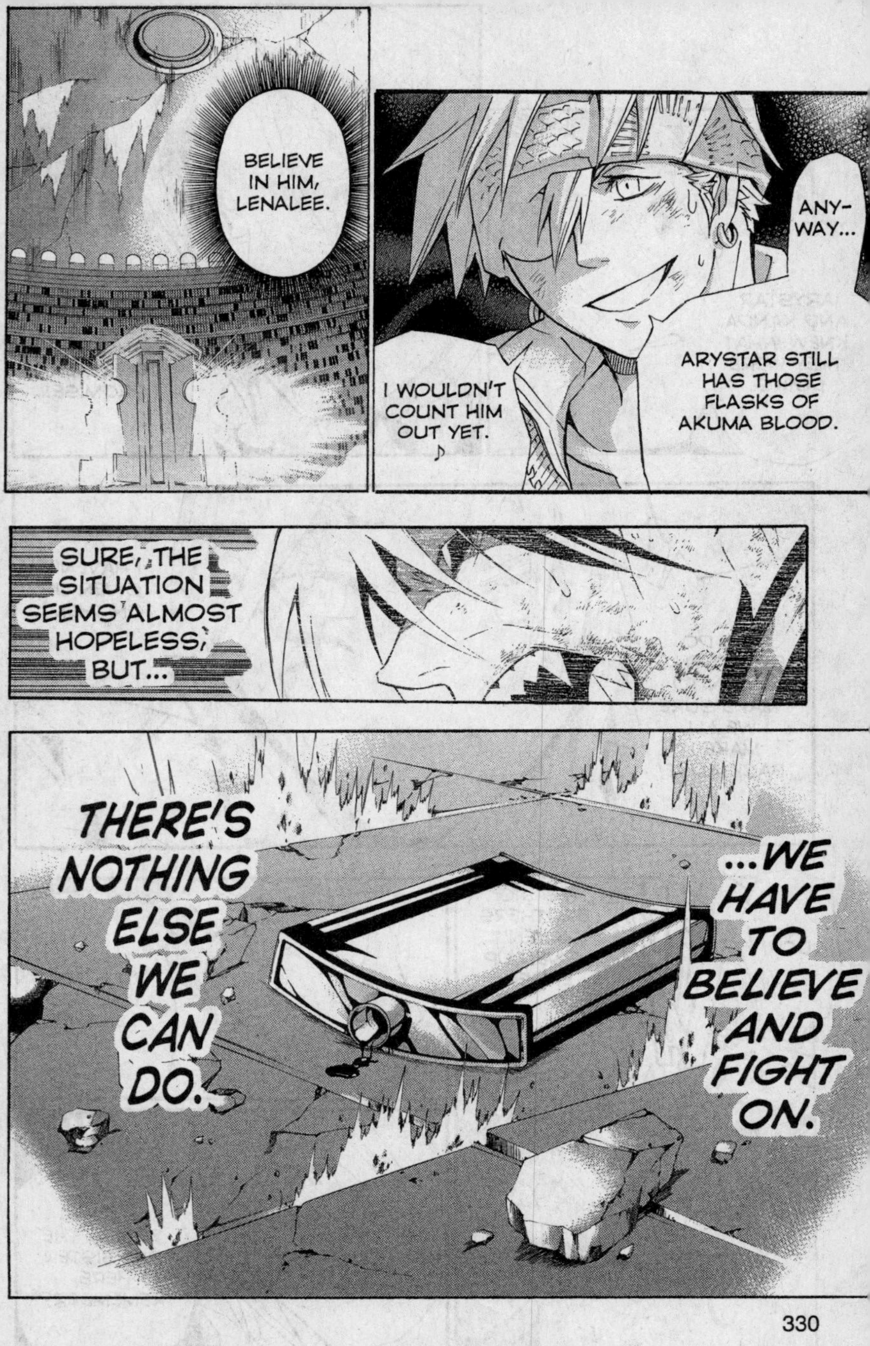
ANY-WAY...
ARYSTAR STILL HAS THOSE FLASKS OF AKUMA BLOOD.
I WOULDN'T COUNT HIM OUT YET. ♪
BELIEVE IN HIM, LENALEE.
SURE, THE SITUATION SEEMS ALMOST HOPELESS, BUT...
THERE'S NOTHING ELSE WE CAN DO.
...WE HAVE TO BELIEVE AND FIGHT ON.

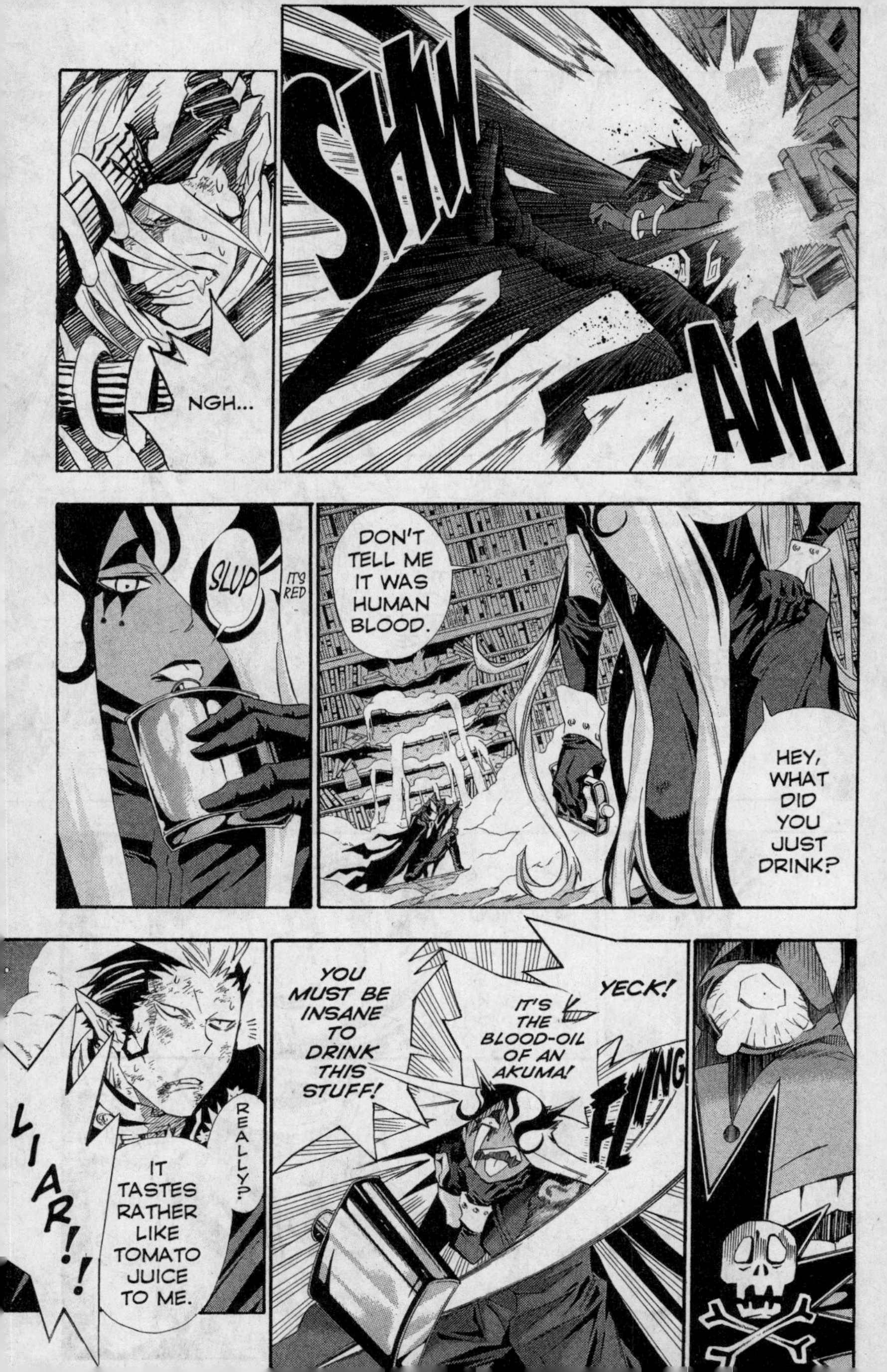
NGH...
HEY, WHAT DID YOU JUST DRINK?
DON'T TELL ME IT WAS HUMAN BLOOD.
SLUP
IT'S RED
YECK!
IT'S THE BLOOD-OIL OF AN AKUMA!
YOU MUST BE INSANE TO DRINK THIS STUFF!
REALLY?
IT TASTES RATHER LIKE TOMATO JUICE TO ME.
LIAR!!

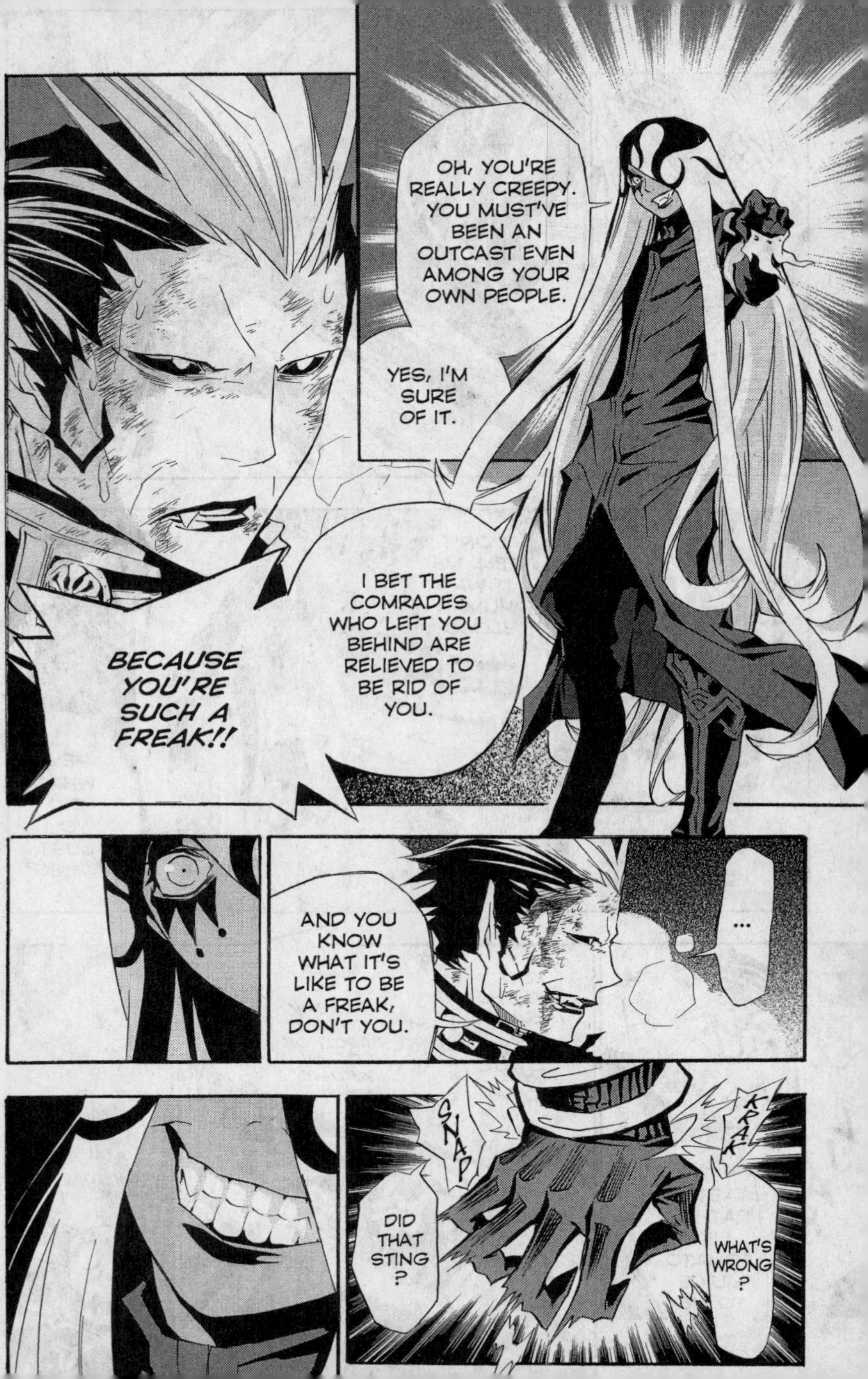
OH, YOU'RE REALLY CREEPY. YOU MUST'VE BEEN AN OUTCAST EVEN AMONG YOUR OWN PEOPLE.
YES, I'M SURE OF IT.
I BET THE COMRADES WHO LEFT YOU BEHIND ARE RELIEVED TO BE RID OF YOU.
BECAUSE YOU'RE SUCH A FREAK!!
...
AND YOU KNOW WHAT IT'S LIKE TO BE A FREAK, DON'T YOU.
KRAK
SNAP
WHAT'S WRONG?
DID THAT STING?

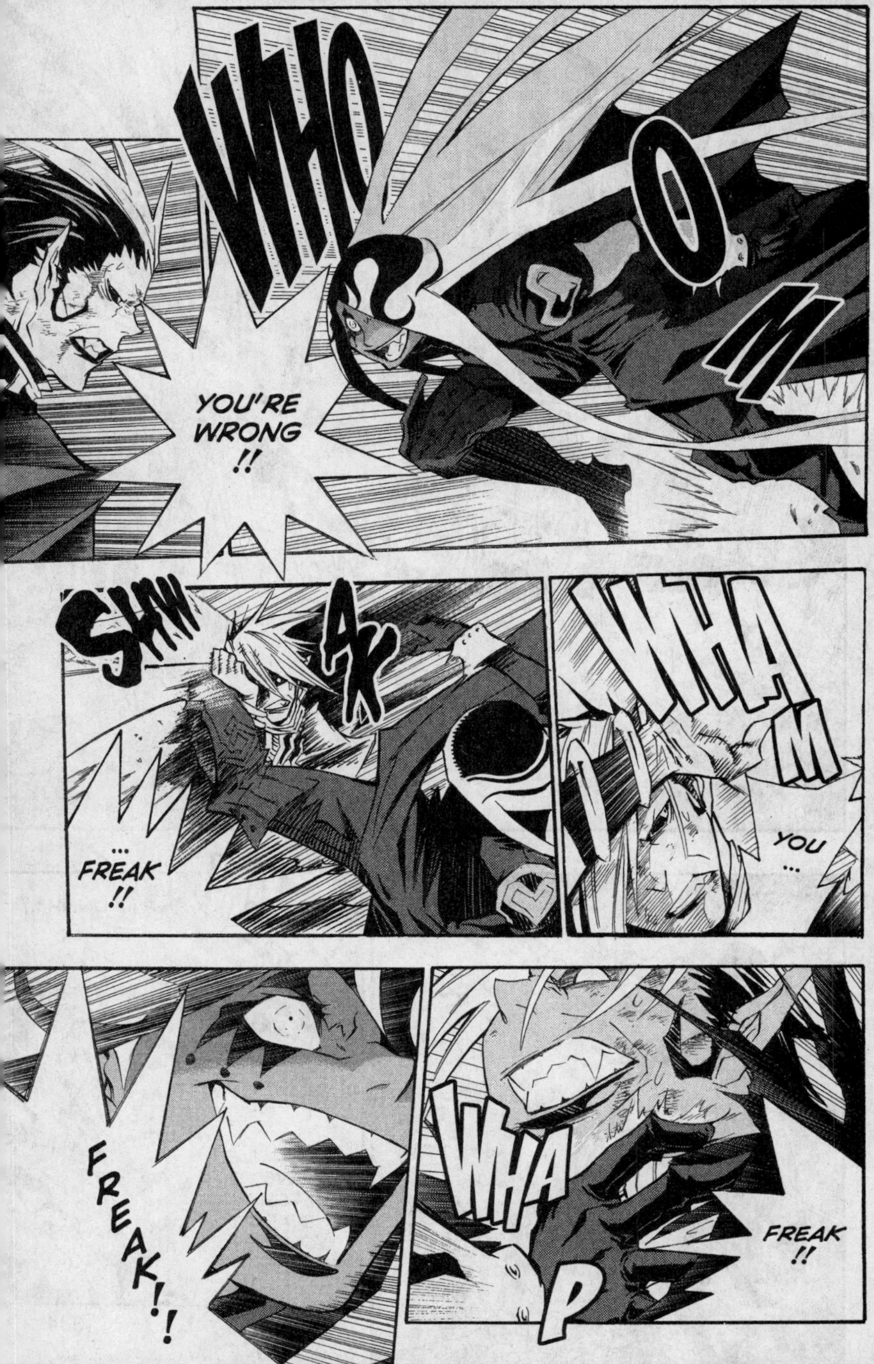
WHOOM
YOU'RE WRONG!!
WHAM
YOU...
SHWAK
...FREAK!!
WHAP
FREAK!!
FREAK!!!

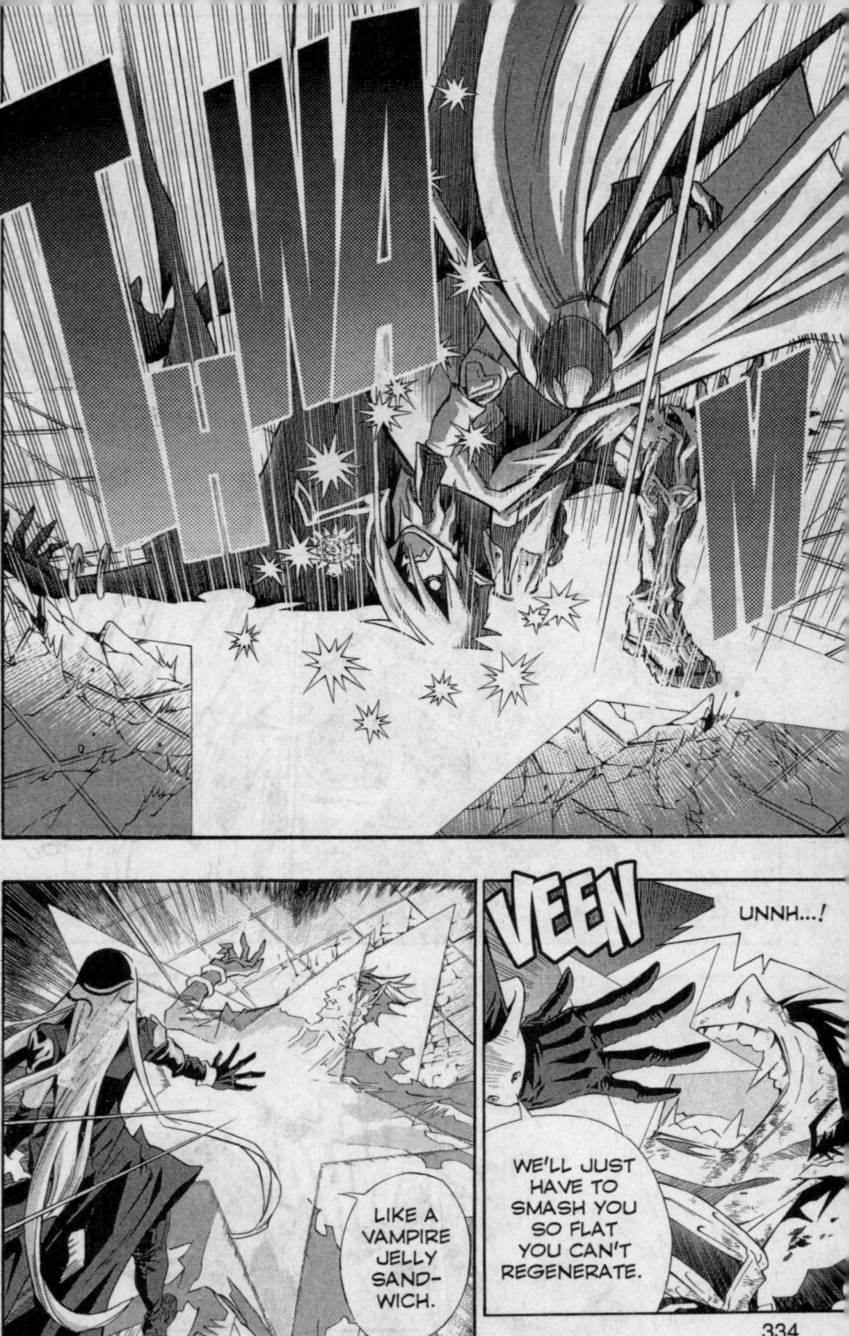
THWAM
VEEN
UNNH...!
WE'LL JUST HAVE TO SMASH YOU SO FLAT YOU CAN'T REGENERATE.
LIKE A VAMPIRE JELLY SAND-WICH.

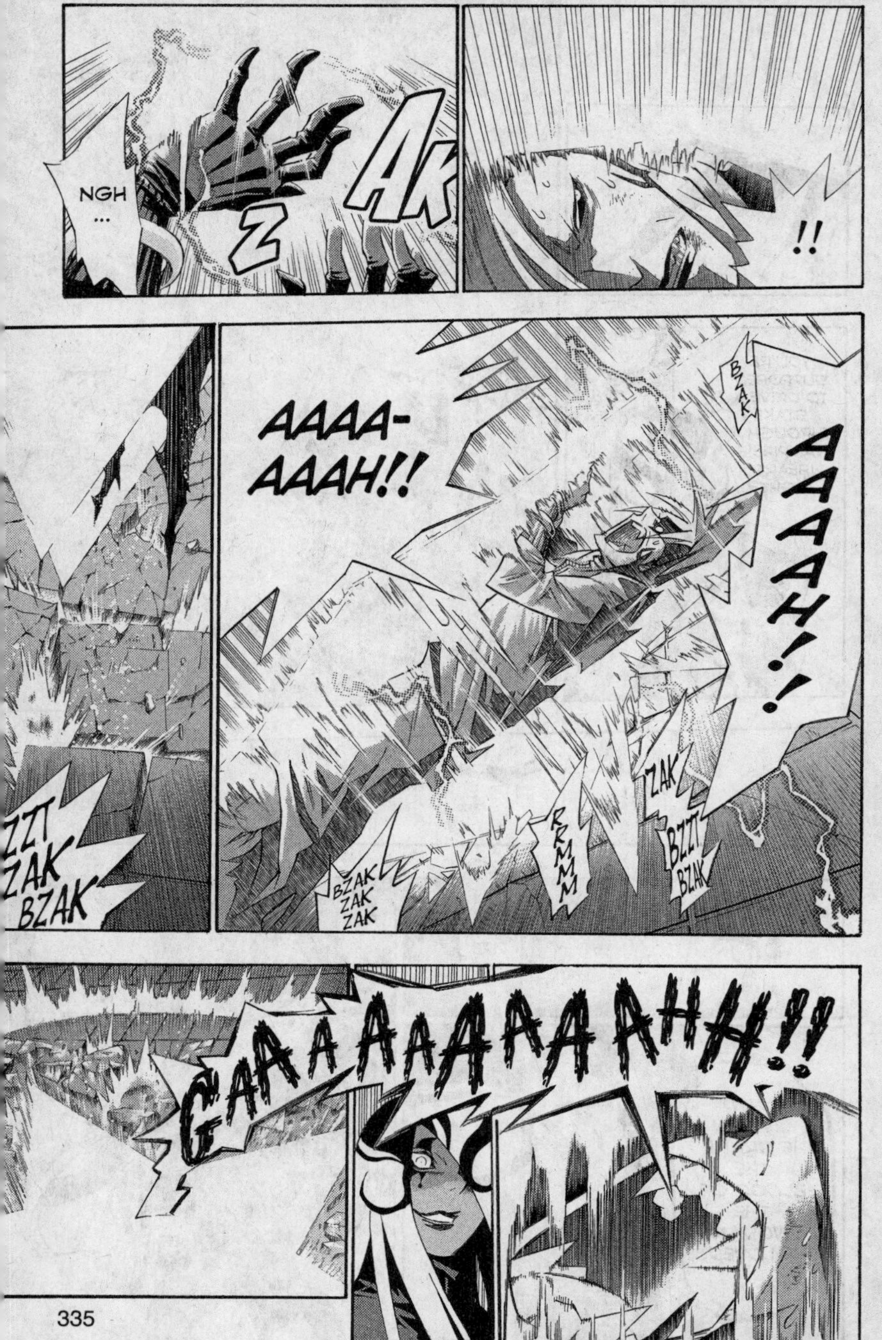
!!
NGH ...
ZAK
AAAAAH!!
BZAK
AAAA-AAAH!!
ZAK
BZZT BZAK
RRMMM
BZAK ZAK ZAK
ZZT ZAK BZAK
GAAAAAAAAHH!!

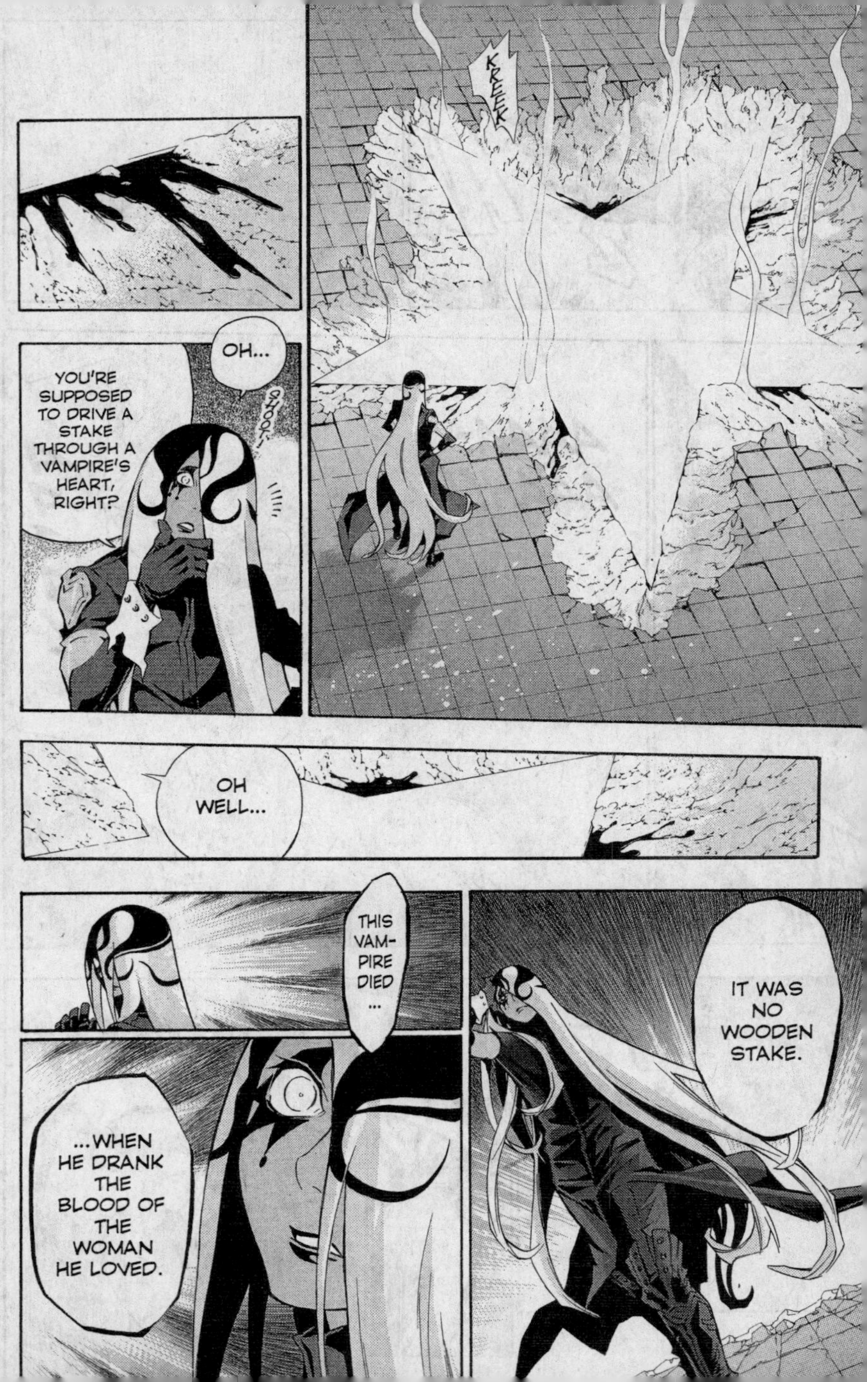
KREEK
OH...
SHOOT!
YOU'RE SUPPOSED TO DRIVE A STAKE THROUGH A VAMPIRE'S HEART, RIGHT?
OH WELL...
IT WAS NO WOODEN STAKE.
THIS VAMPIRE DIED ...
...WHEN HE DRANK THE BLOOD OF THE WOMAN HE LOVED.

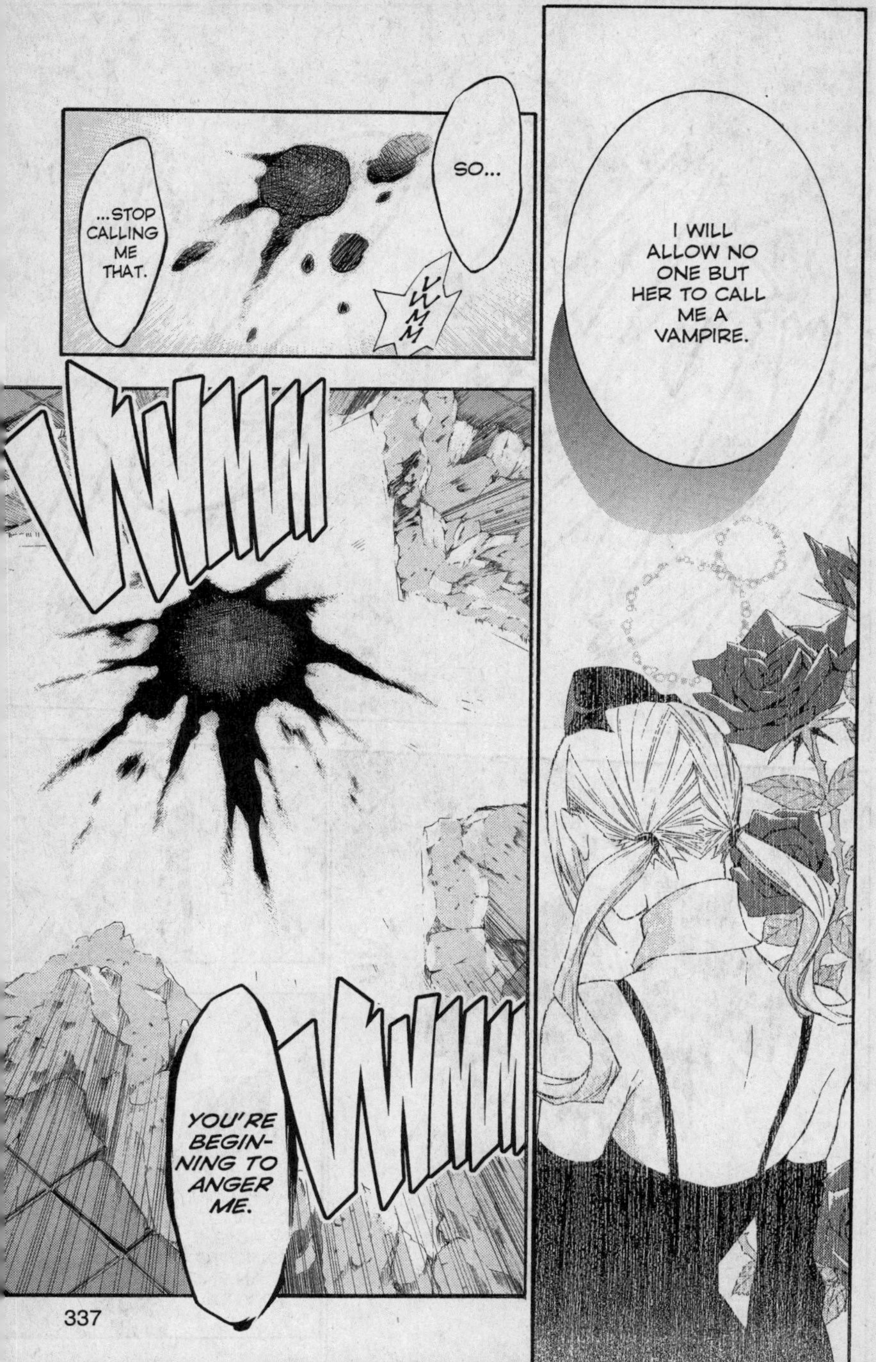
I WILL ALLOW NO ONE BUT HER TO CALL ME A VAMPIRE.
SO...
VWMM
...STOP CALLING ME THAT.
VWMMM
VWMMM
YOU'RE BEGIN-NING TO ANGER ME.

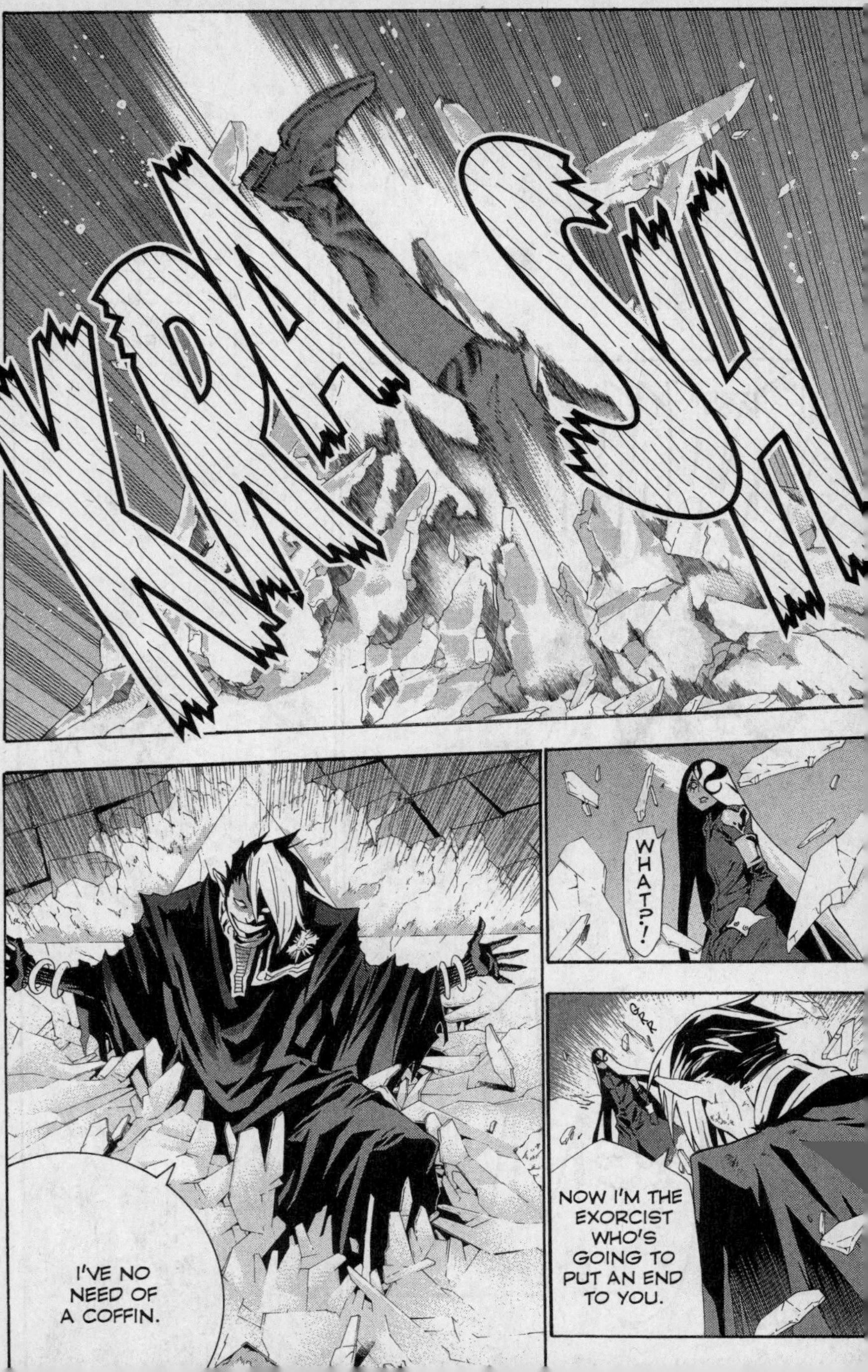
KRASH
WHAT?!
GRR
NOW I'M THE EXORCIST WHO'S GOING TO PUT AN END TO YOU.
I'VE NO NEED OF A COFFIN.

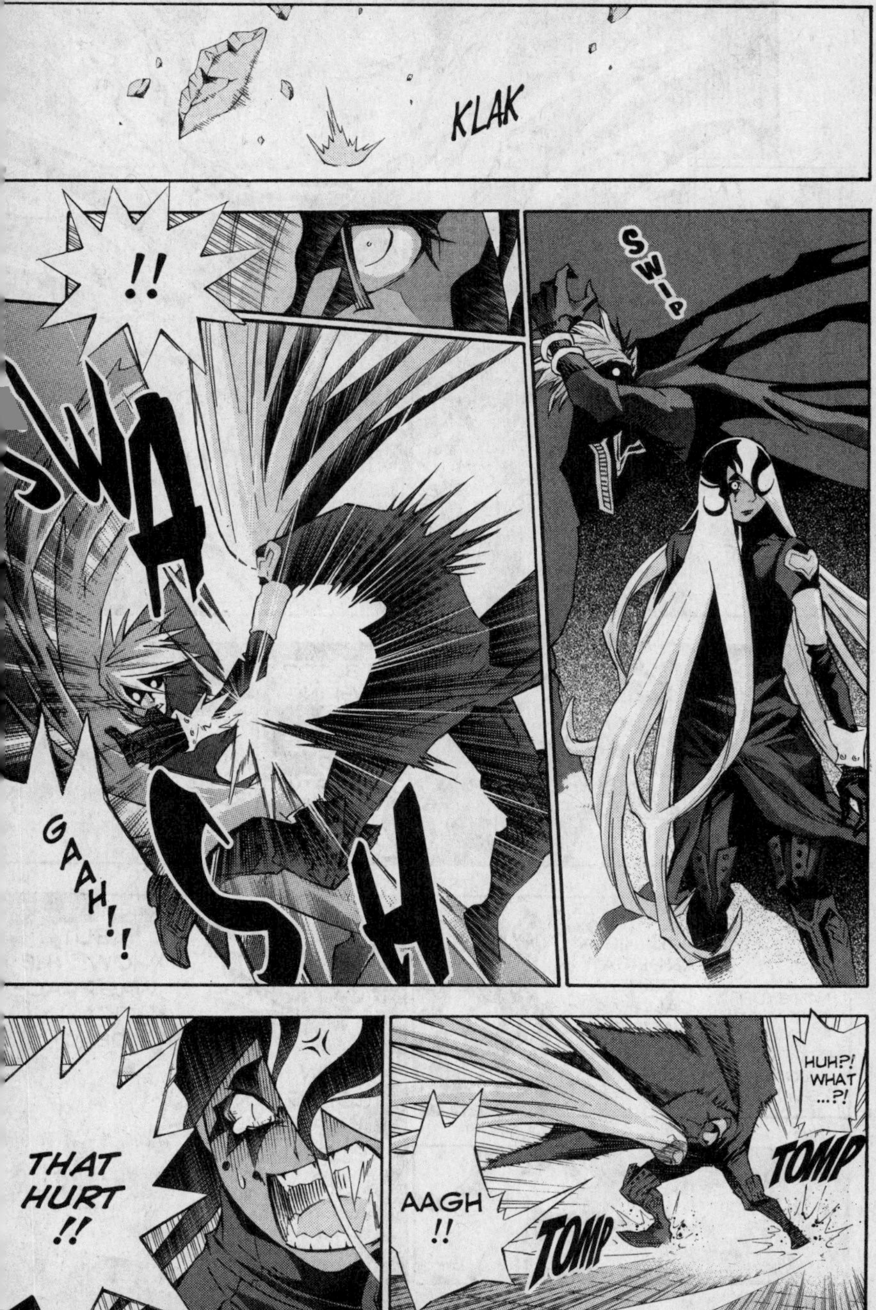
KLAK
SWIP
!!
SWASH
GAAH!!
HUH?! WHAT ...?!
TOMP
AAGH !!
TOMP
THAT HURT !!

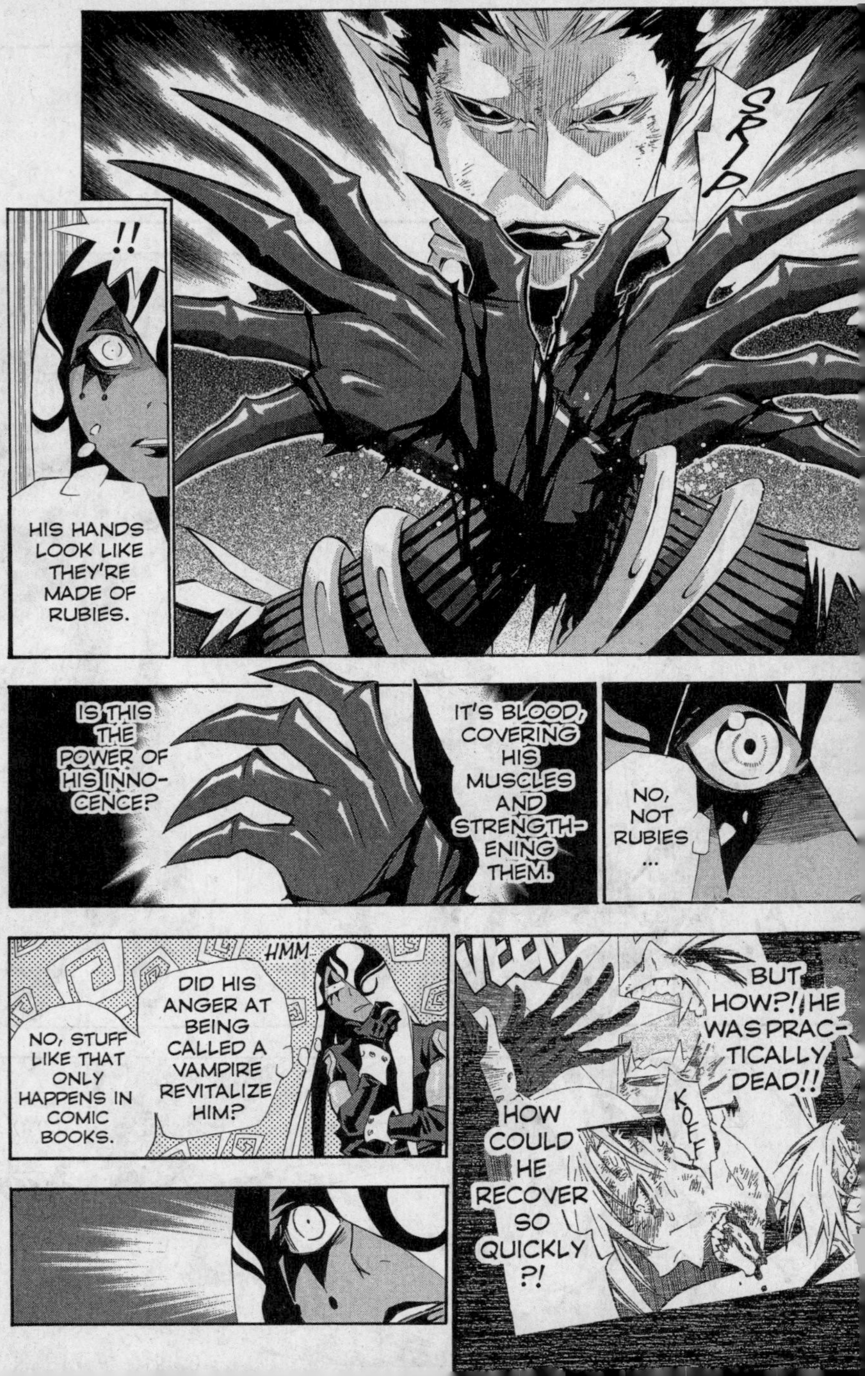
CRIP
!!
HIS HANDS LOOK LIKE THEY'RE MADE OF RUBIES.
NO, NOT RUBIES...
IT'S BLOOD, COVERING HIS MUSCLES AND STRENGTH-ENING THEM.
IS THIS THE POWER OF HIS INNO-CENCE?
BUT HOW?! HE WAS PRAC-TICALLY DEAD!!
KOFF
HOW COULD HE RECOVER SO QUICKLY?!
HMM
DID HIS ANGER AT BEING CALLED A VAMPIRE REVITALIZE HIM?
NO, STUFF LIKE THAT ONLY HAPPENS IN COMIC BOOKS.

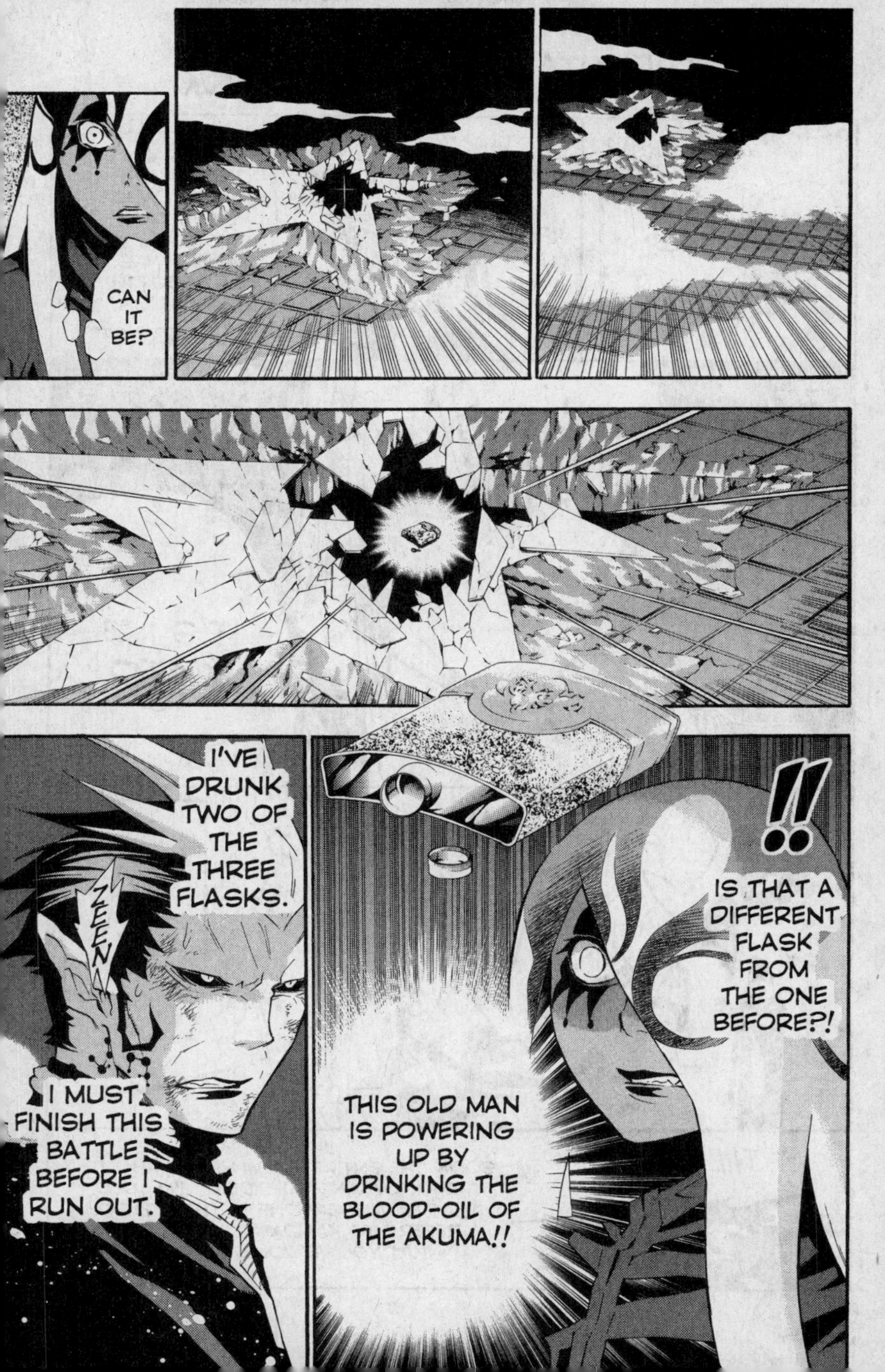
CAN IT BE?
!!
IS THAT A DIFFERENT FLASK FROM THE ONE BEFORE?!
THIS OLD MAN IS POWERING UP BY DRINKING THE BLOOD-OIL OF THE AKUMA!!
I'VE DRUNK TWO OF THE THREE FLASKS.
ZEEN
I MUST FINISH THIS BATTLE BEFORE I RUN OUT.

THE KATO INCIDENT, PART FOUR

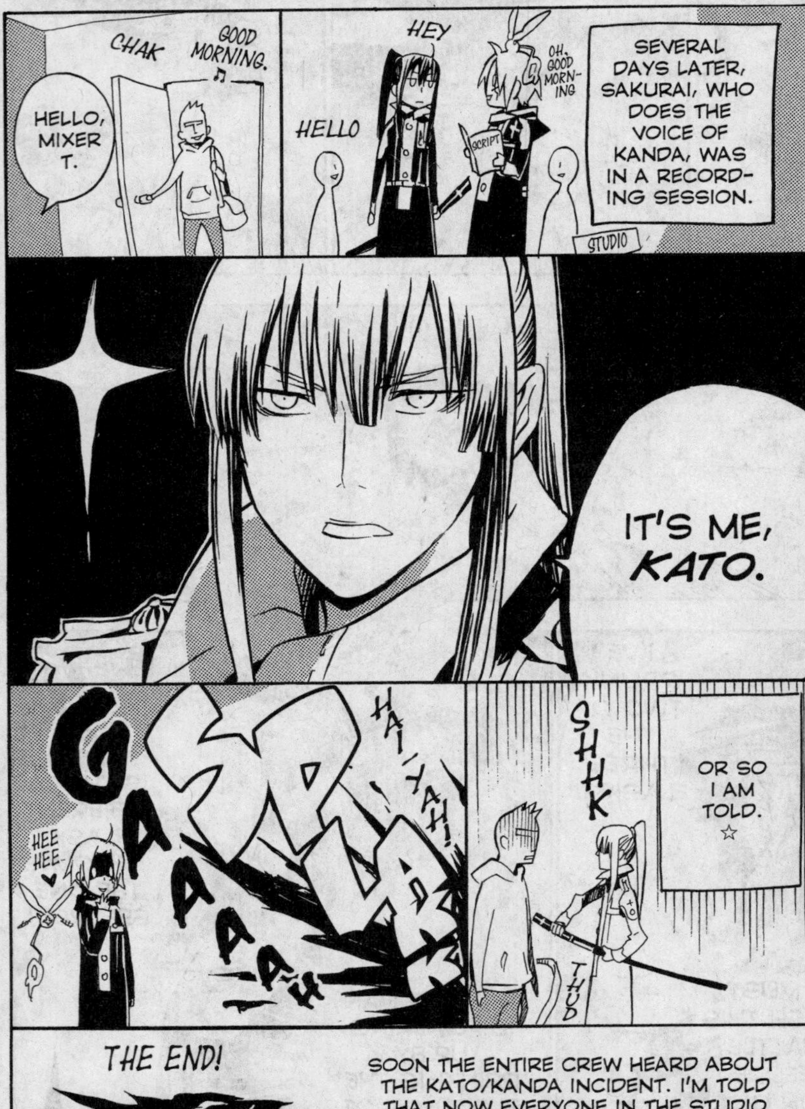
SEVERAL DAYS LATER, SAKURAI, WHO DOES THE VOICE OF KANDA, WAS IN A RECORDING SESSION.
STUDIO
OH, GOOD MORNING
SCRIPT
HEY
HELLO
GOOD MORNING. ♫
CHAK
HELLO, MIXER T.
IT'S ME, KATO.
OR SO I AM TOLD. ☆
SHHK
THUD
HAI-YAH!
GAAAAAH
HEE HEE ♥
SOON THE ENTIRE CREW HEARD ABOUT THE KATO/KANDA INCIDENT. I'M TOLD THAT NOW EVERYONE IN THE STUDIO REFERS TO KANDA AS KATO. SEE WHAT YOU'VE DONE, MIXER T?
THE END!

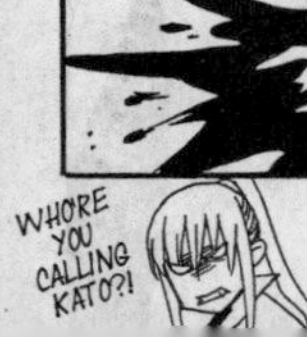
WHO'RE YOU CALLING KATO?!

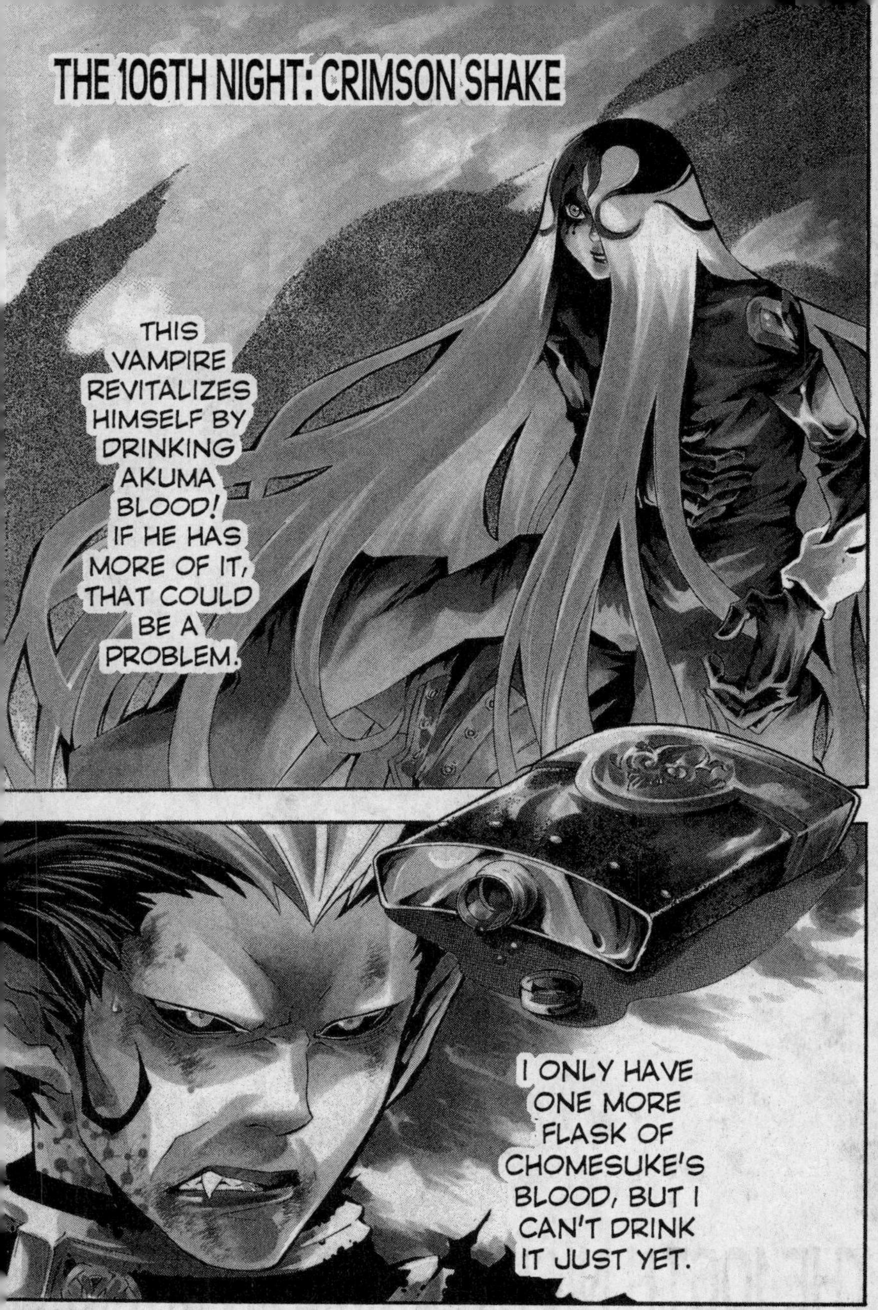
THE 106TH NIGHT: CRIMSON SHAKE
THIS VAMPIRE REVITALIZES HIMSELF BY DRINKING AKUMA BLOOD! IF HE HAS MORE OF IT, THAT COULD BE A PROBLEM.
I ONLY HAVE ONE MORE FLASK OF CHOMESUKE'S BLOOD, BUT I CAN'T DRINK IT JUST YET.

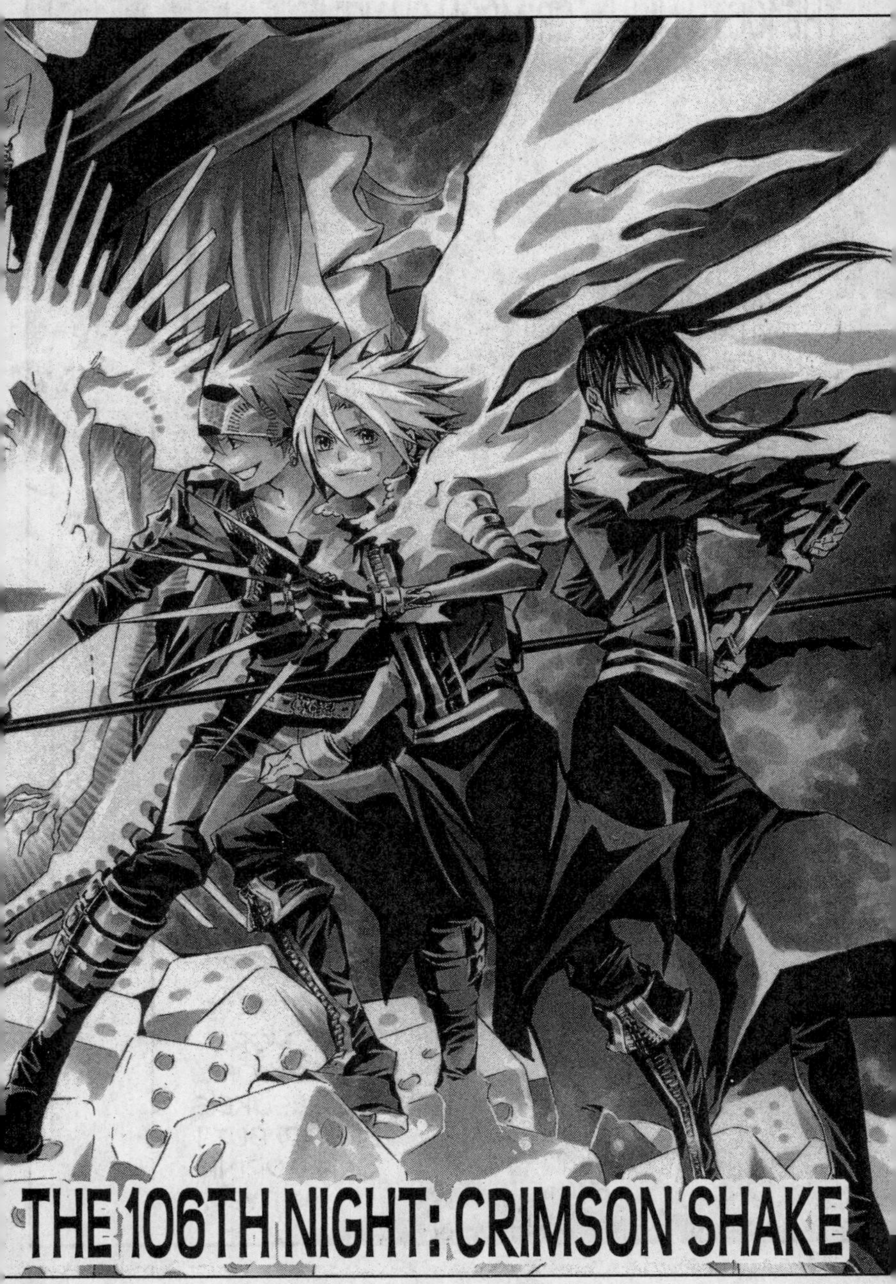
THE 106TH NIGHT: CRIMSON SHAKE

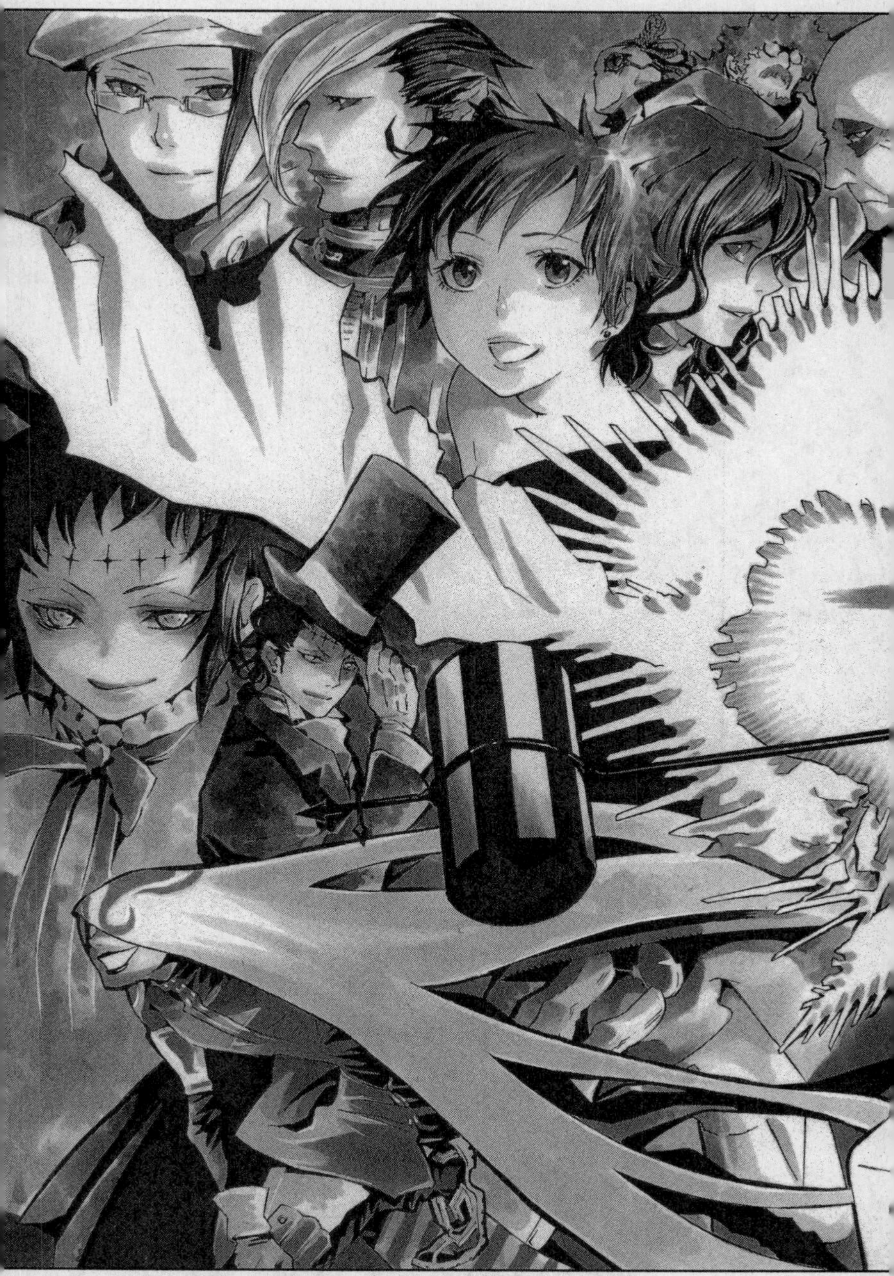

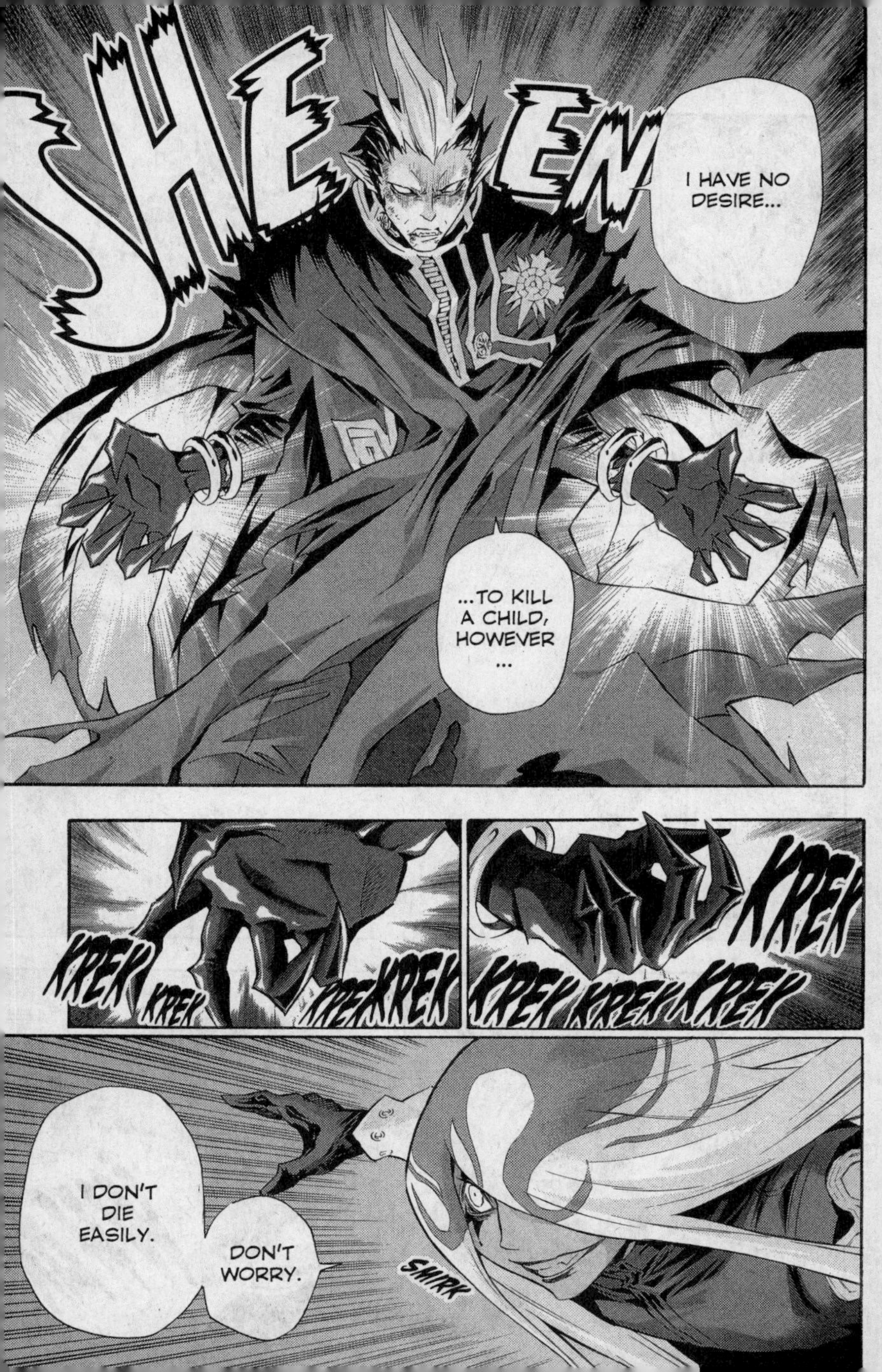
I HAVE NO DESIRE...
SHEEN
...TO KILL A CHILD, HOWEVER ...
KREK
KREK KREK KREK
KREK KREK
KREK KREKKREK
SMIRK
DON'T WORRY.
I DON'T DIE EASILY.

KRK

VWOO

M

SEE
?!

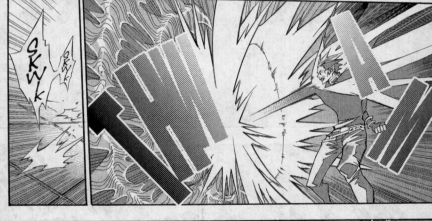

SKWK

SKWK

THW

AM

WHAK

WHAK

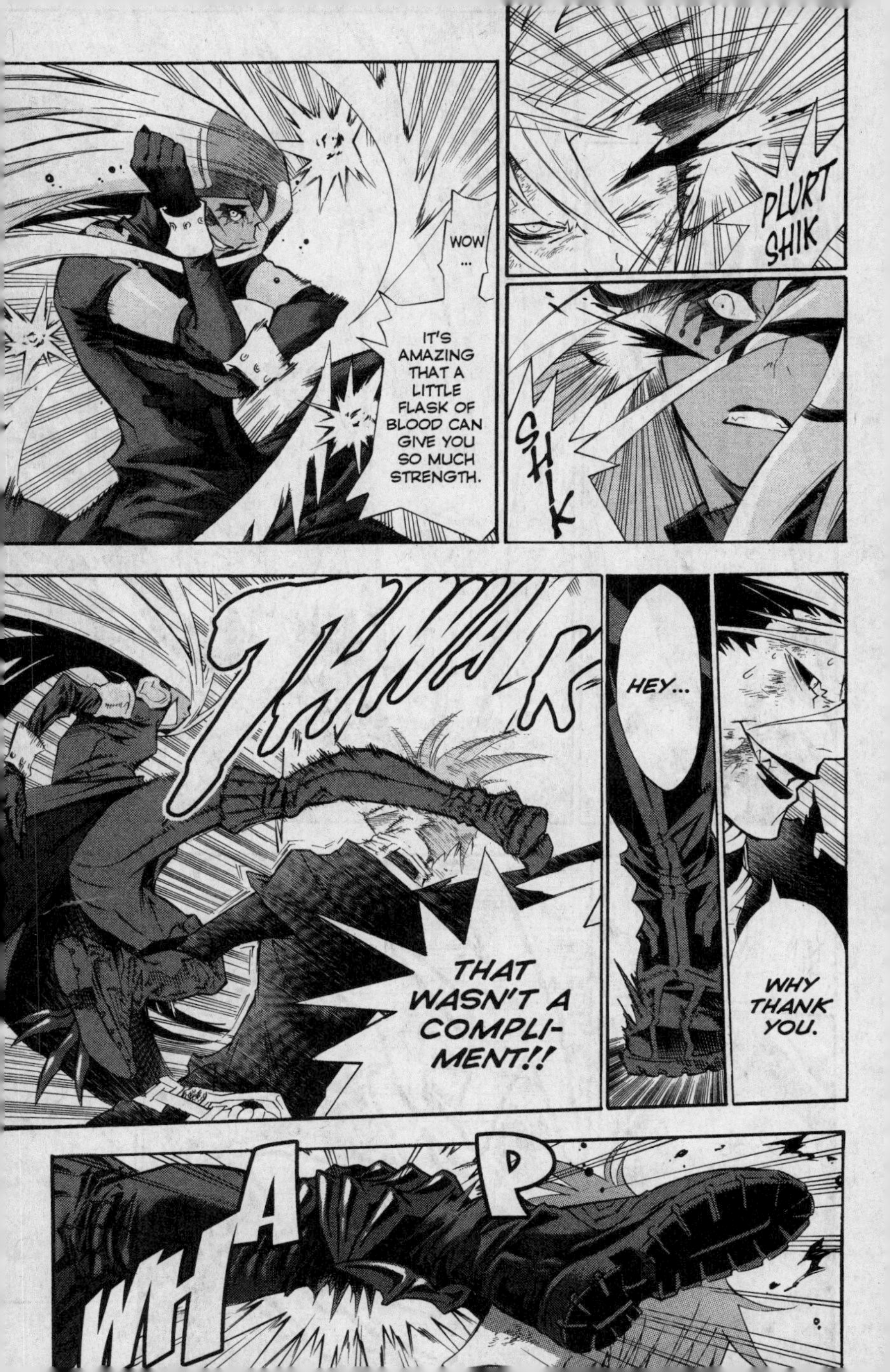
PLURT
SHIK
SHIK
WOW...
IT'S AMAZING THAT A LITTLE FLASK OF BLOOD CAN GIVE YOU SO MUCH STRENGTH.
WHY THANK YOU.
HEY...
THAT WASN'T A COMPLI-MENT!!
WHAP

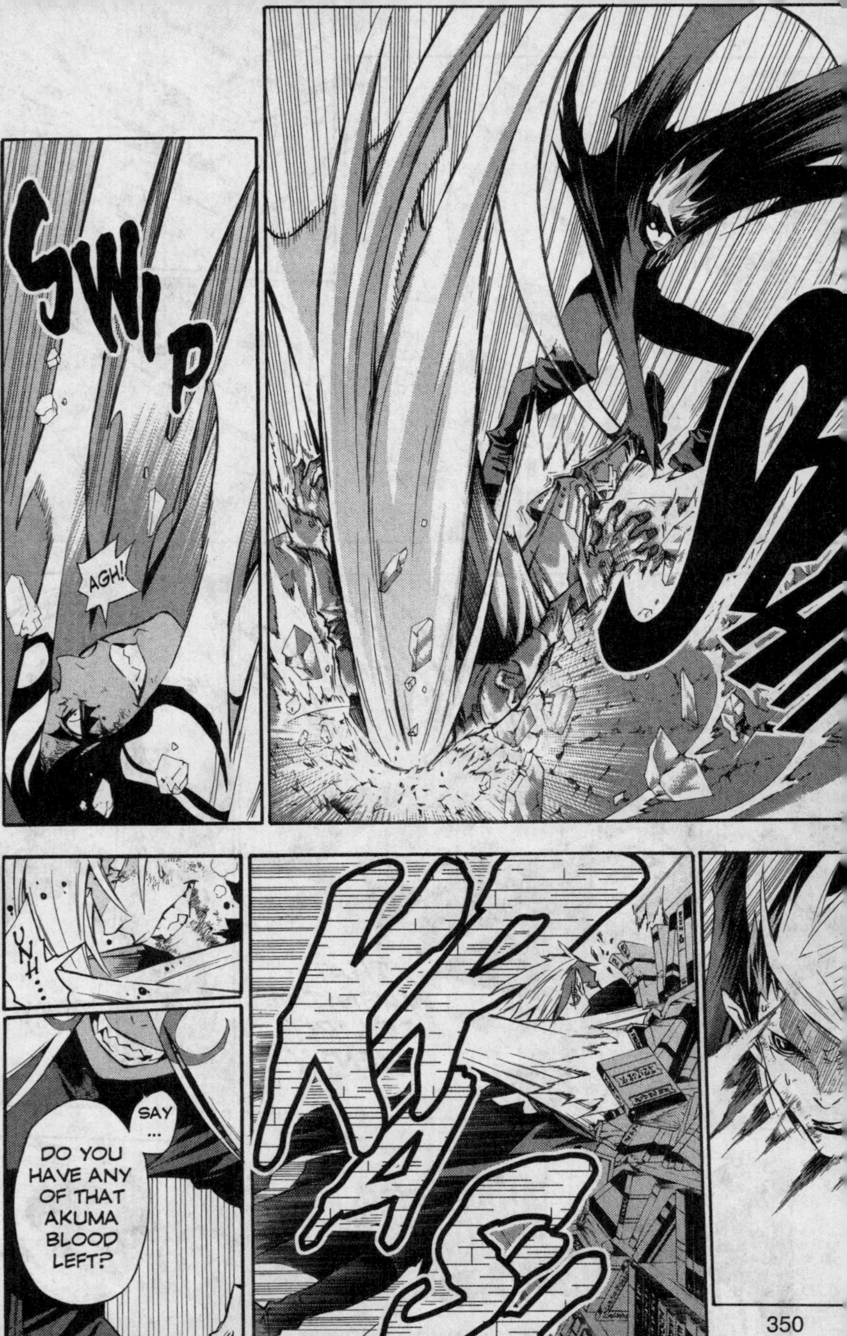
SWIP
AGH!
UNH...
SAY ...
DO YOU HAVE ANY OF THAT AKUMA BLOOD LEFT?

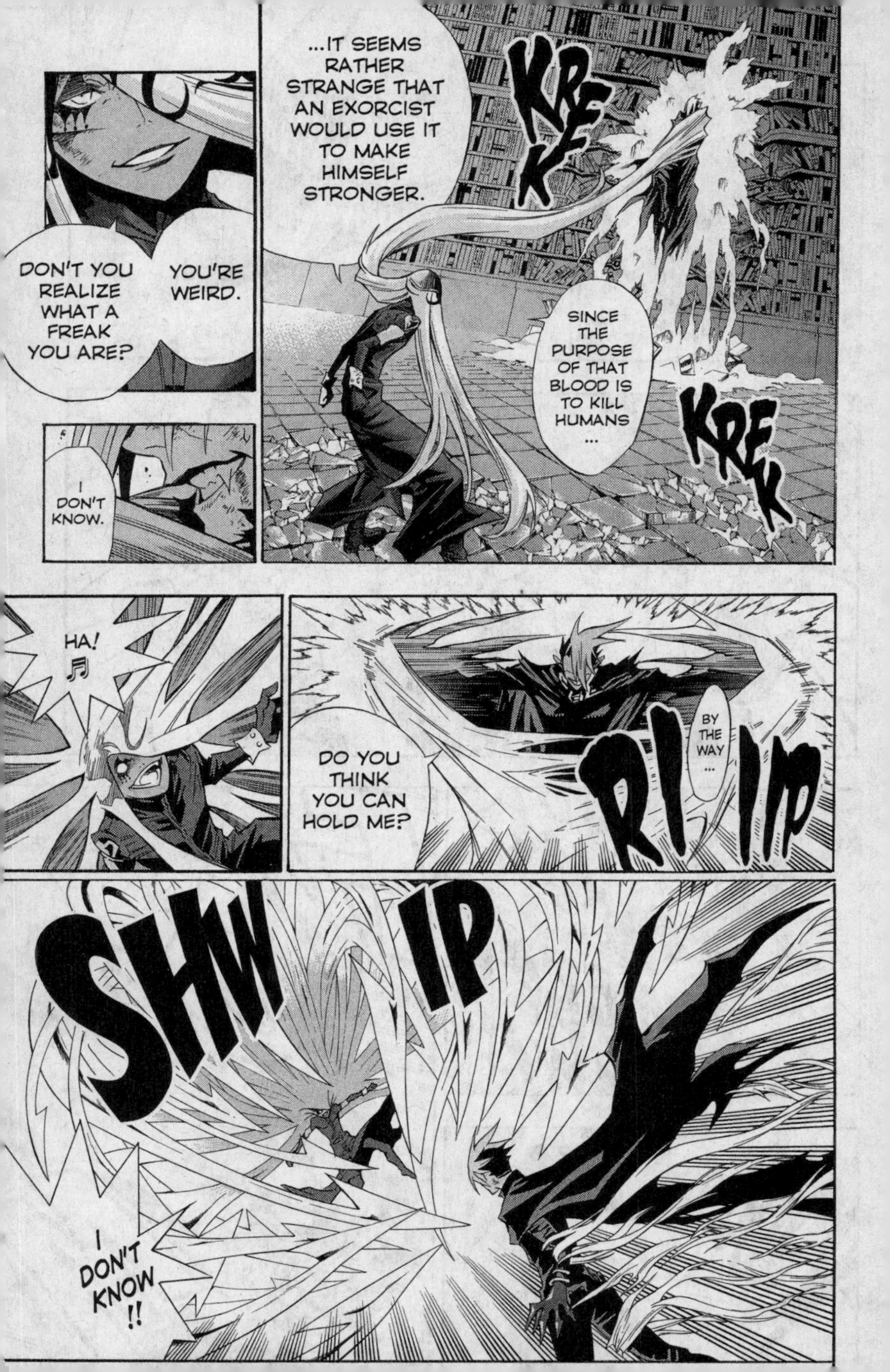
KREK
SINCE THE PURPOSE OF THAT BLOOD IS TO KILL HUMANS ...
...IT SEEMS RATHER STRANGE THAT AN EXORCIST WOULD USE IT TO MAKE HIMSELF STRONGER.
KREK
YOU'RE WEIRD.
DON'T YOU REALIZE WHAT A FREAK YOU ARE?
I DON'T KNOW.
RIIP
BY THE WAY ...
DO YOU THINK YOU CAN HOLD ME?
HA! ♬
SHWIP
I DON'T KNOW !!

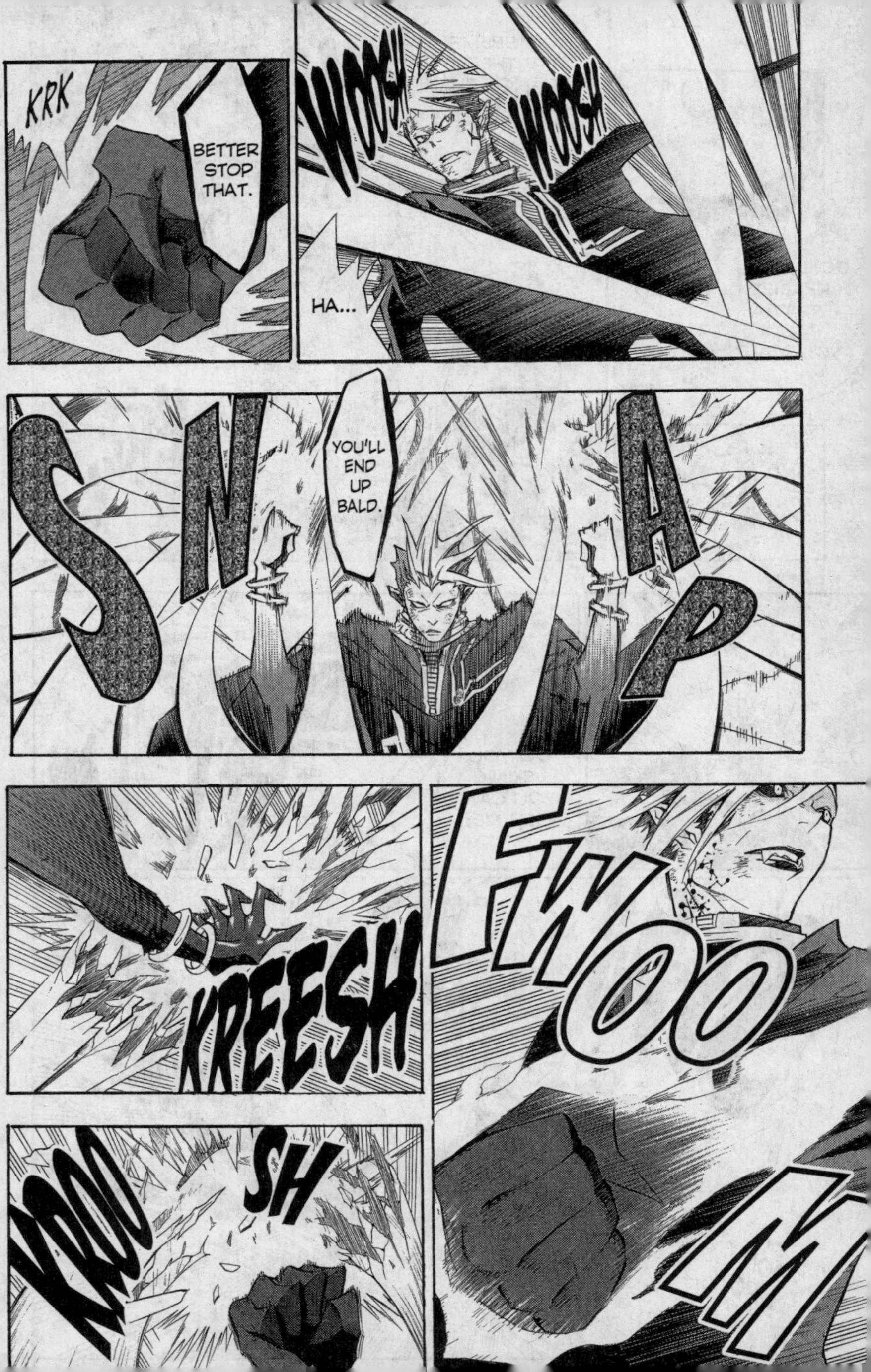
WOOSH
WOOSH
HA...
KRK
BETTER STOP THAT.
SNAP
YOU'LL END UP BALD.
FWOOM
KREESH
WHOOSH

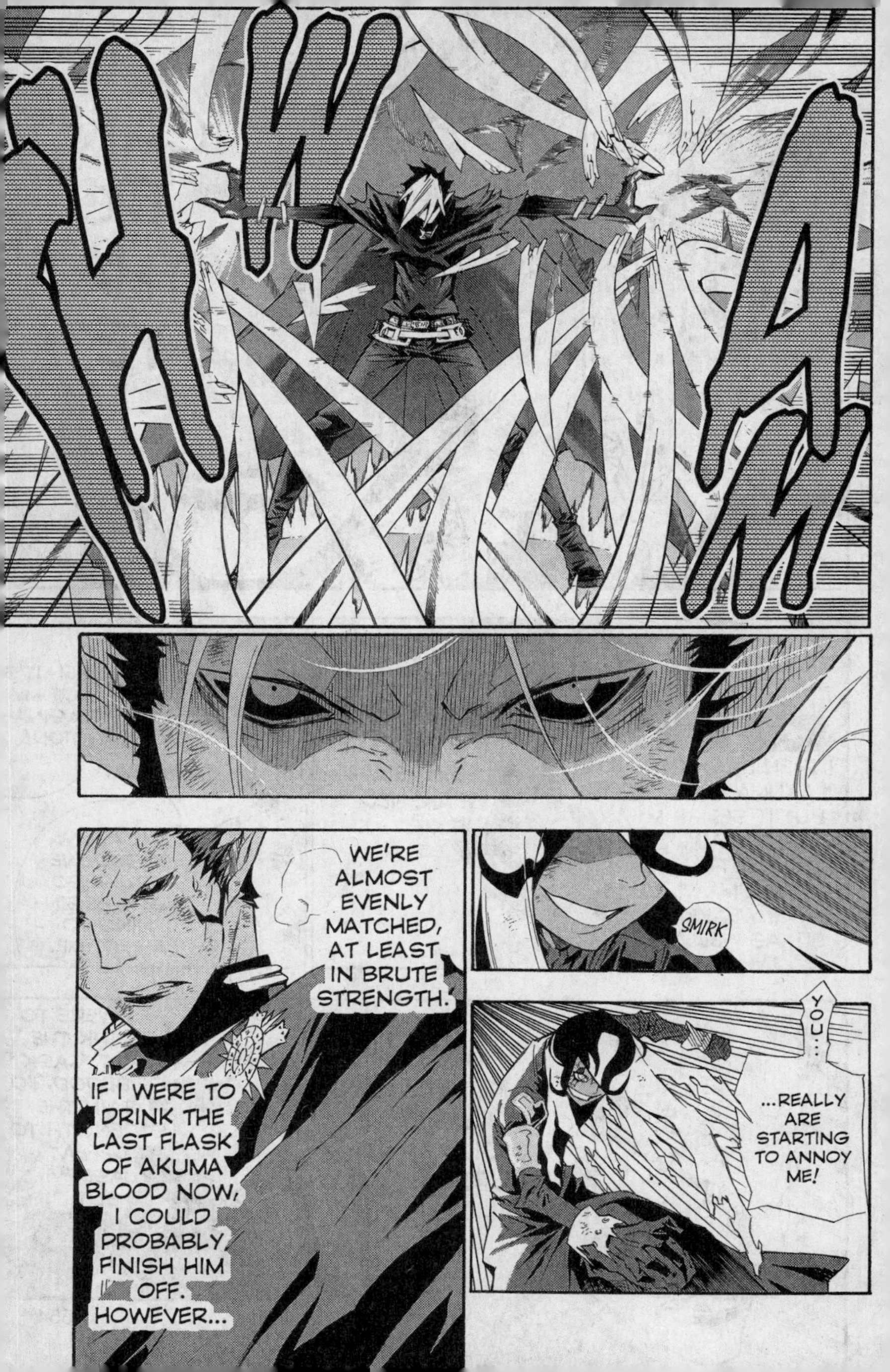
ZWAM
SMIRK
YOU...
...REALLY ARE STARTING TO ANNOY ME!
WE'RE ALMOST EVENLY MATCHED, AT LEAST IN BRUTE STRENGTH.
IF I WERE TO DRINK THE LAST FLASK OF AKUMA BLOOD NOW, I COULD PROBABLY FINISH HIM OFF. HOWEVER...

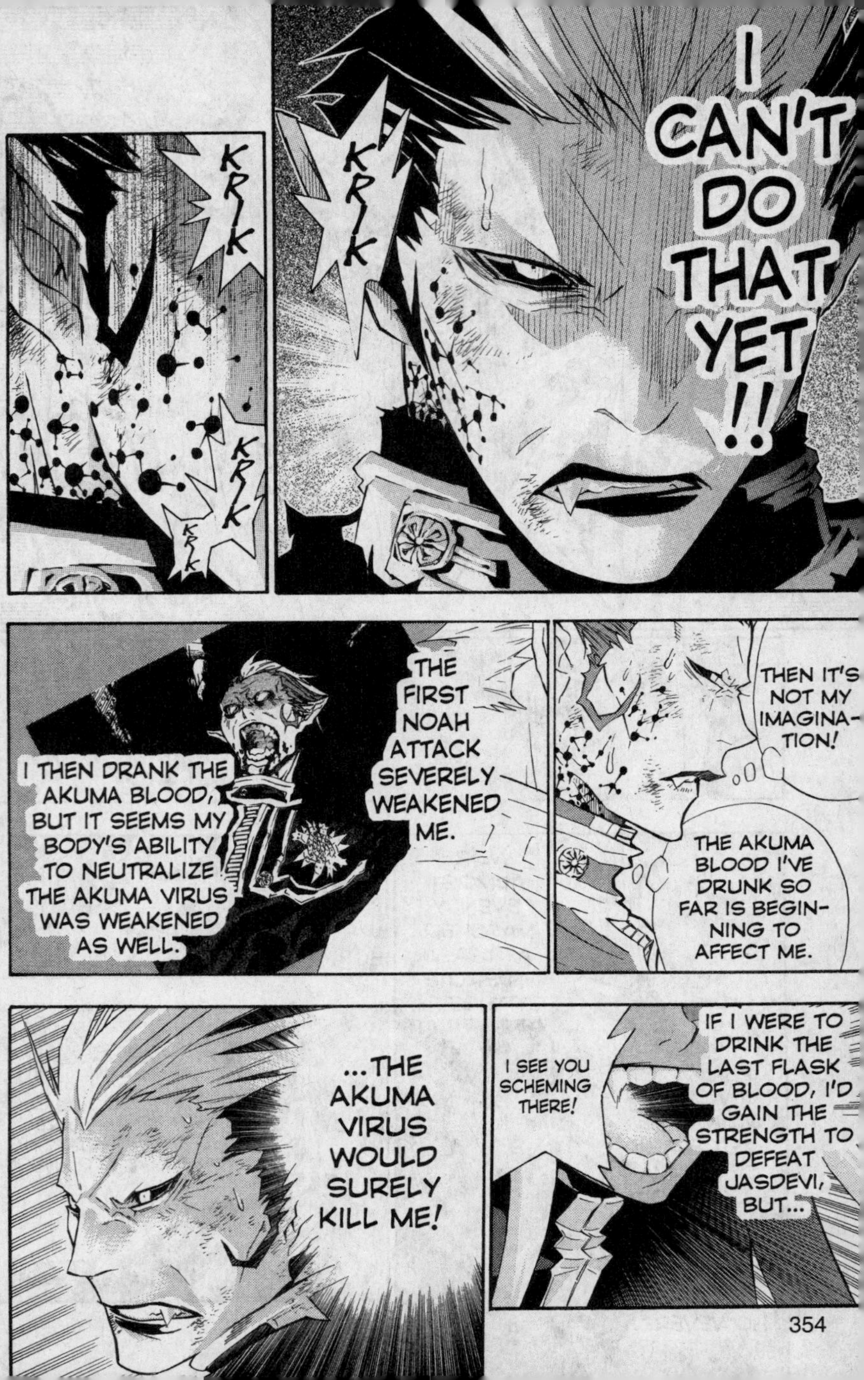
KRIK
I CAN'T DO THAT YET!!
KRIK
KRIK
KRIK
THEN IT'S NOT MY IMAGINATION!
THE AKUMA BLOOD I'VE DRUNK SO FAR IS BEGINNING TO AFFECT ME.
THE FIRST NOAH ATTACK SEVERELY WEAKENED ME.
I THEN DRANK THE AKUMA BLOOD, BUT IT SEEMS MY BODY'S ABILITY TO NEUTRALIZE THE AKUMA VIRUS WAS WEAKENED AS WELL.
IF I WERE TO DRINK THE LAST FLASK OF BLOOD, I'D GAIN THE STRENGTH TO DEFEAT JASDEVI, BUT...
I SEE YOU SCHEMING THERE!
...THE AKUMA VIRUS WOULD SURELY KILL ME!

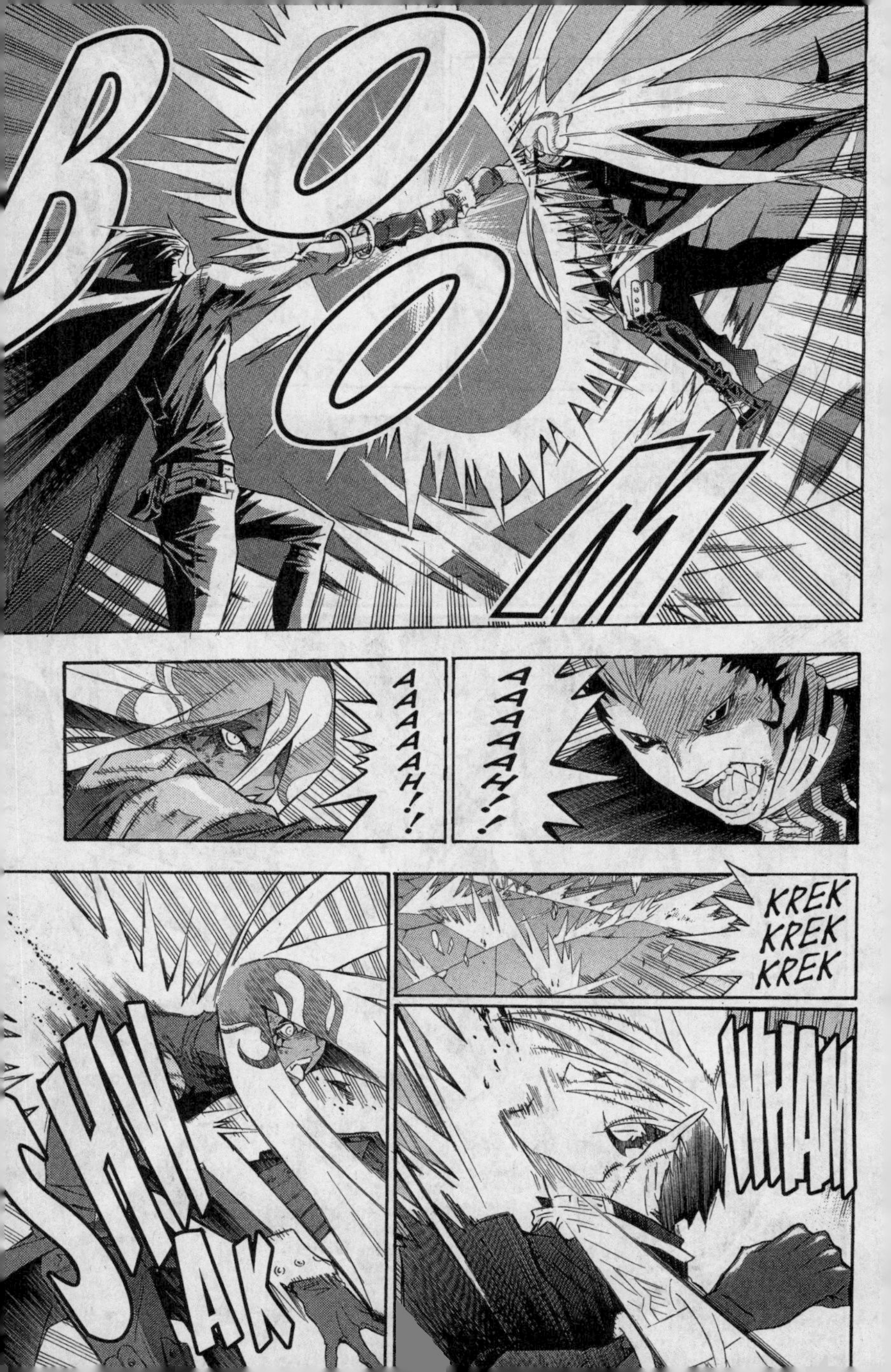
BOOM
AAAAAH!!
AAAAAH!!
KREK
KREK
KREK
WHAM

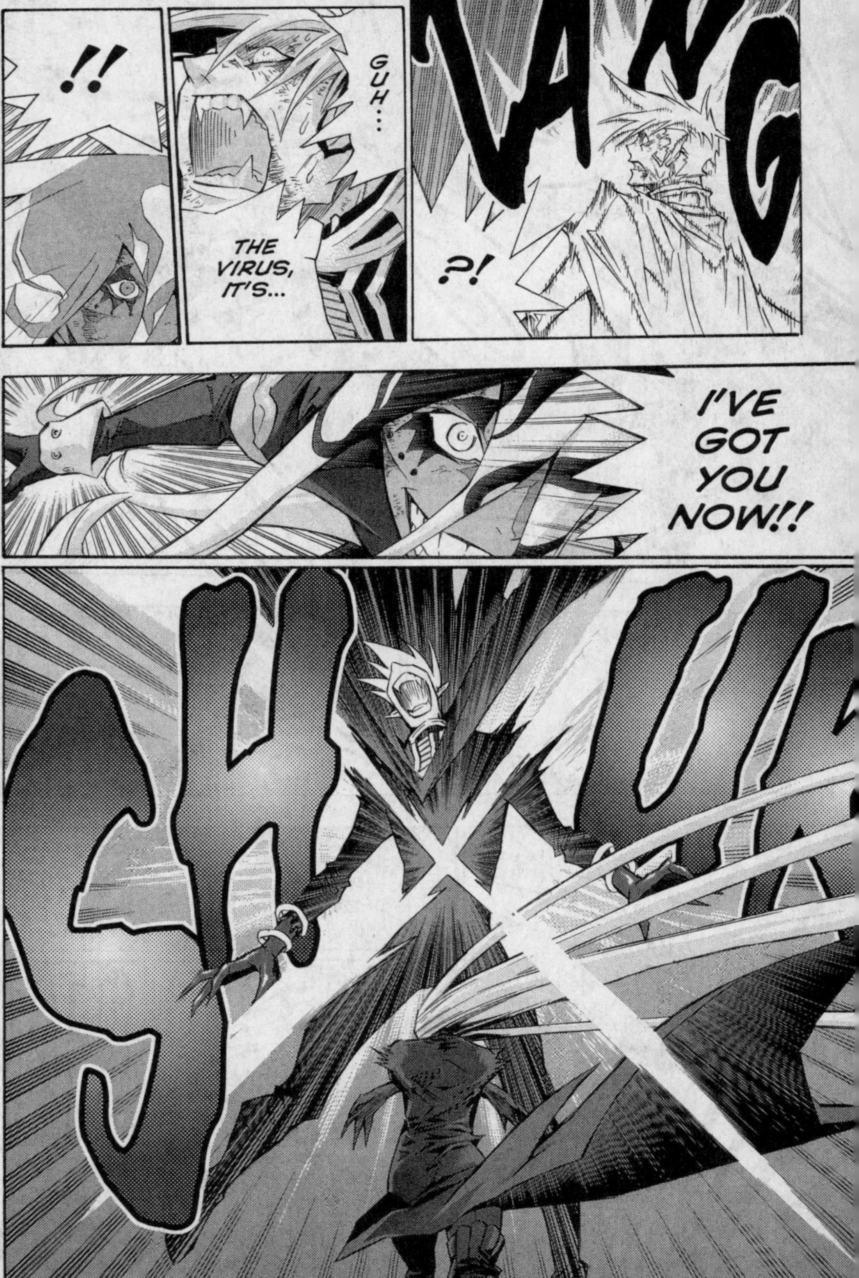
VANG
?!
GUH...
THE VIRUS, IT'S...
!!
I'VE GOT YOU NOW!!
SHU

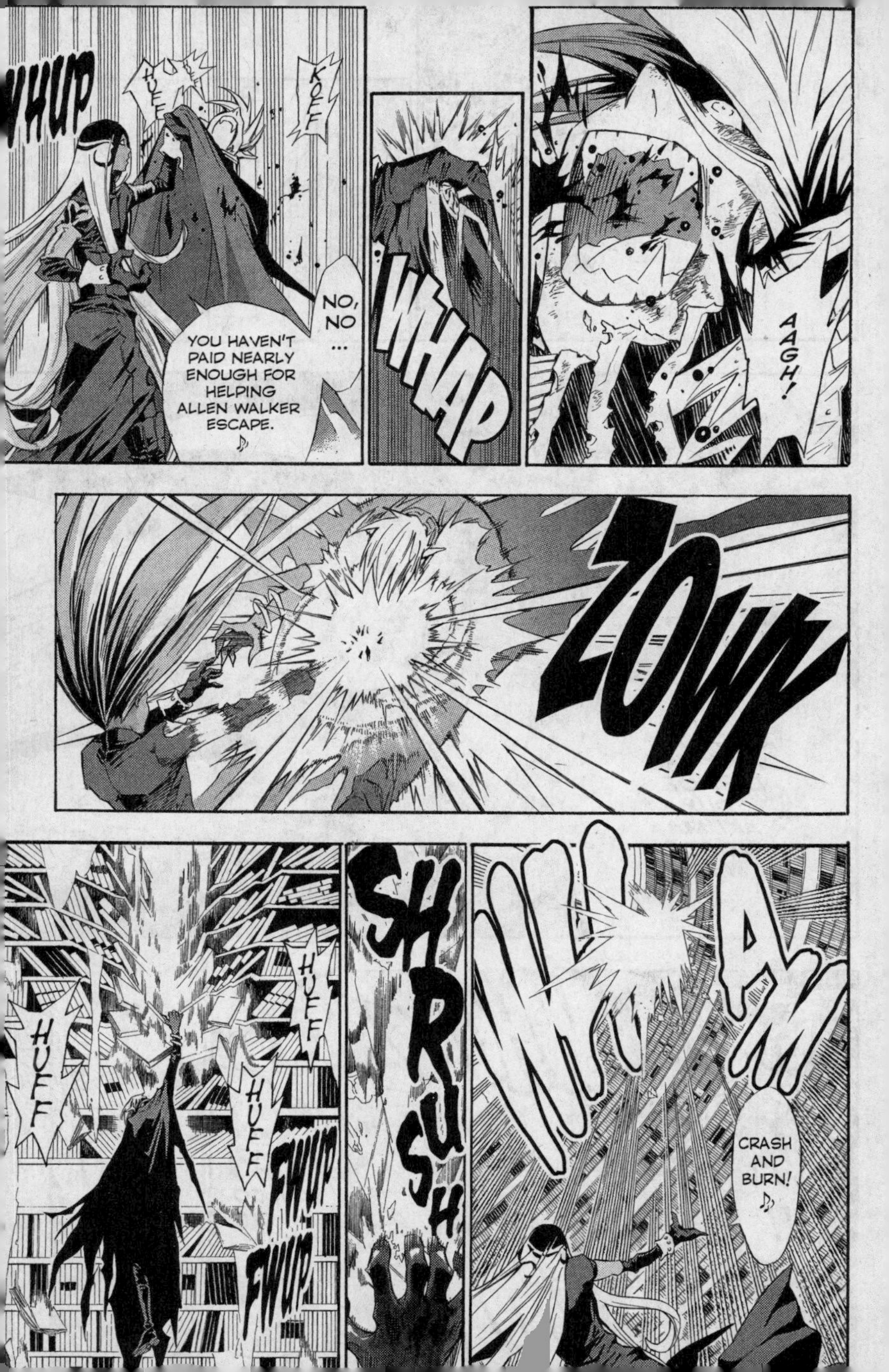
AAGH!
WHAP
KOFF
HUFF
WHUP
NO, NO ...
YOU HAVEN'T PAID NEARLY ENOUGH FOR HELPING ALLEN WALKER ESCAPE. ♪
ZOWK
WHAM
CRASH AND BURN! ♪
SHRUSH
HUFF
HUFF
HUFF
FWUP
FWUP

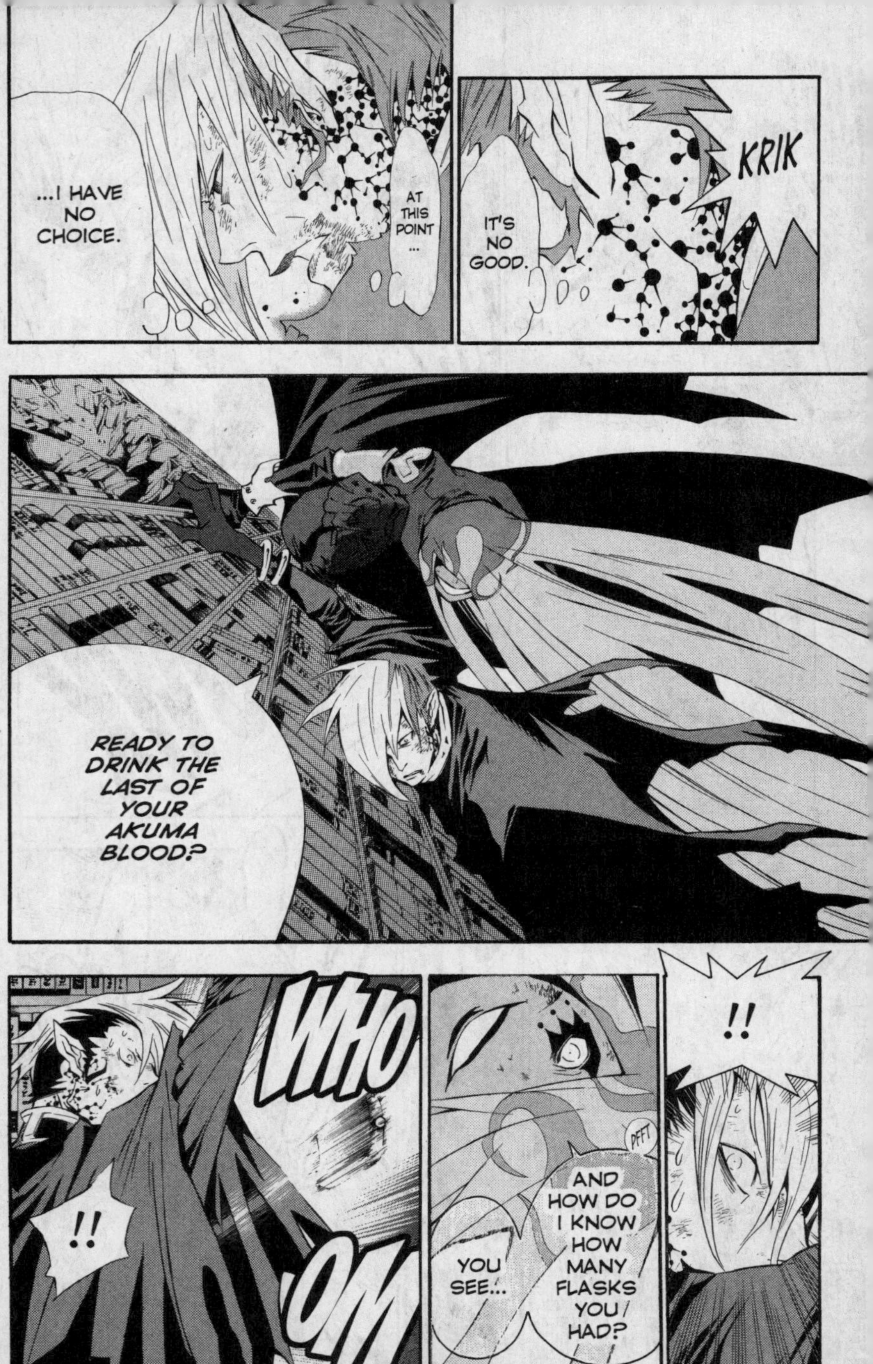
KRIK
IT'S NO GOOD.
AT THIS POINT ...
...I HAVE NO CHOICE.
READY TO DRINK THE LAST OF YOUR AKUMA BLOOD?
!!
PFFT
AND HOW DO I KNOW HOW MANY FLASKS YOU HAD?
YOU SEE...
WHO
OM
!!

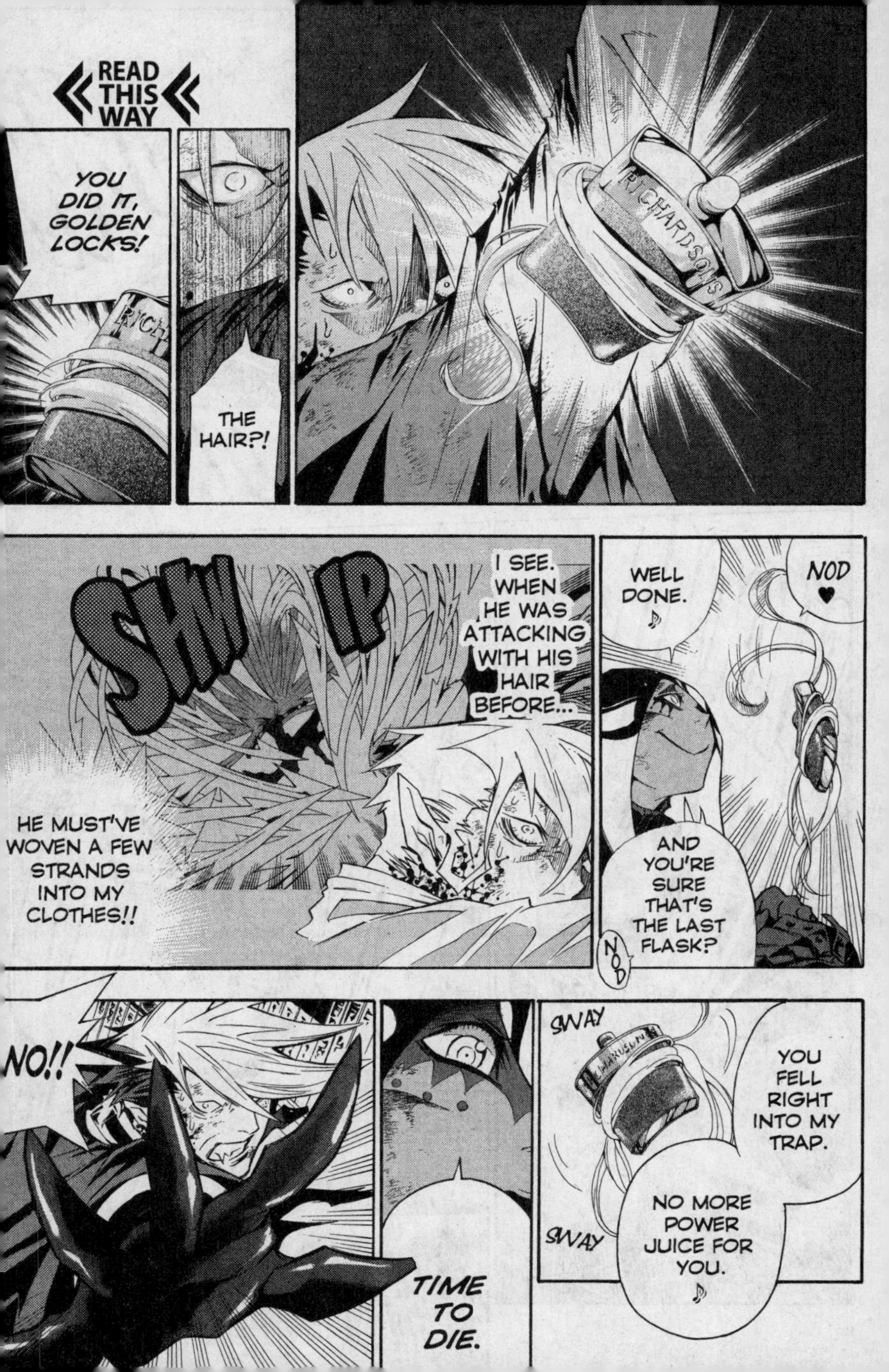
READ THIS WAY
THE HAIR?!
YOU DID IT, GOLDEN LOCKS!
NOD ♥
WELL DONE. ♪
AND YOU'RE SURE THAT'S THE LAST FLASK?
NOD
I SEE. WHEN HE WAS ATTACKING WITH HIS HAIR BEFORE...
SHWIP
HE MUST'VE WOVEN A FEW STRANDS INTO MY CLOTHES!!
SWAY
YOU FELL RIGHT INTO MY TRAP.
SWAY
NO MORE POWER JUICE FOR YOU. ♪
TIME TO DIE.
NO!!

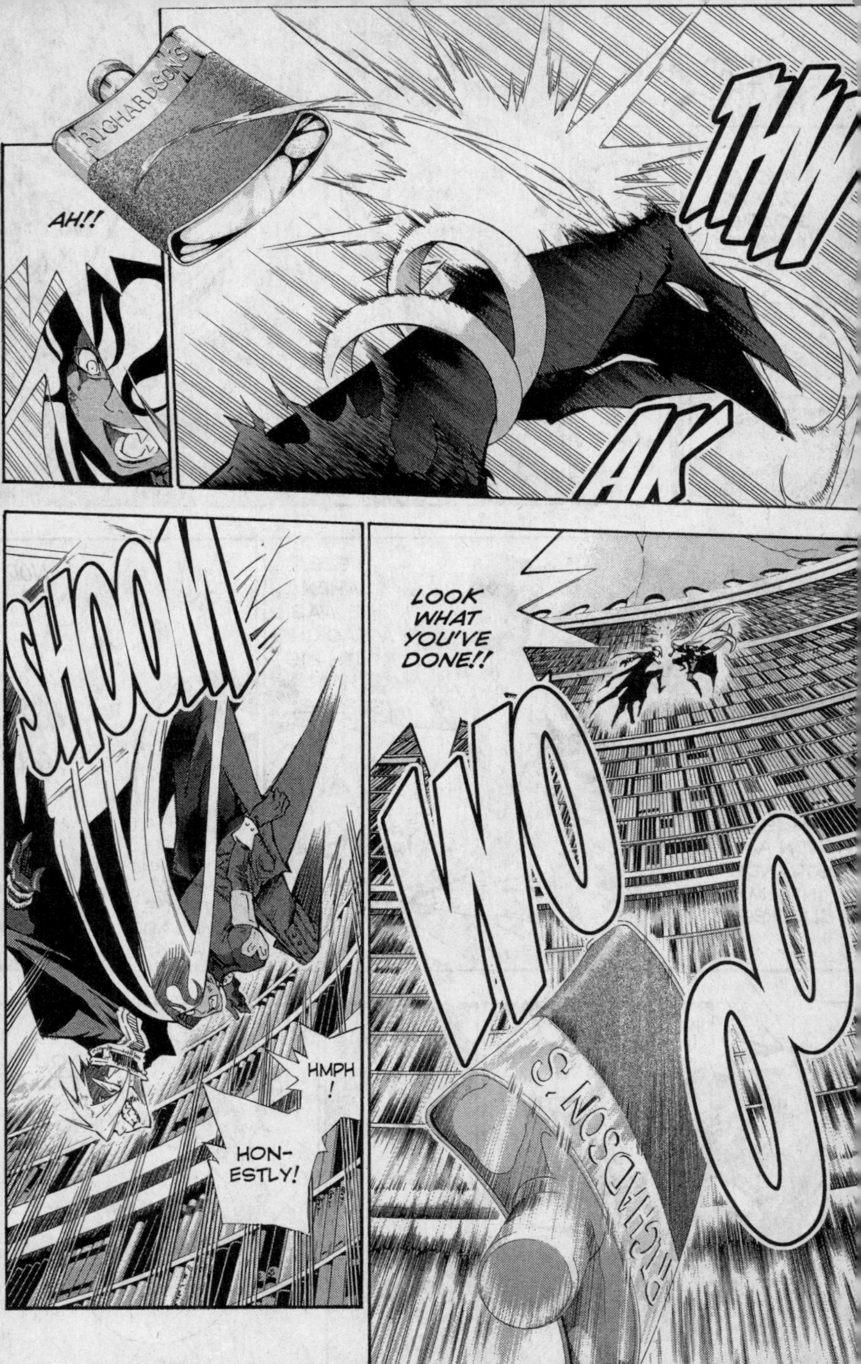
RICHARDSON'S
THW
AK
AH!!
LOOK WHAT YOU'VE DONE!!
WOO
RICHARDSON'S
SHOOM
HMPH!
HON-ESTLY!

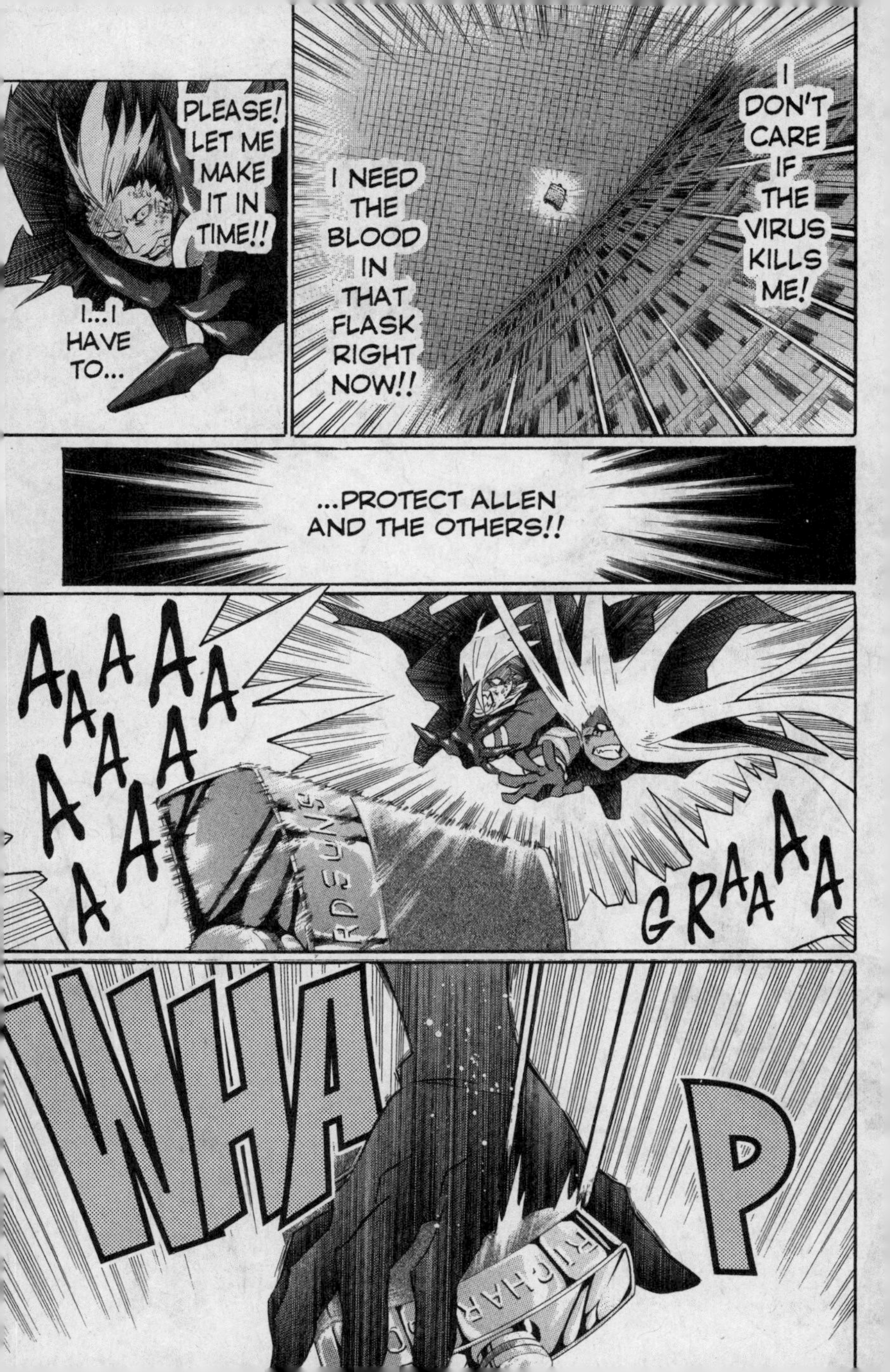
I DON'T CARE IF THE VIRUS KILLS ME!
I NEED THE BLOOD IN THAT FLASK RIGHT NOW!!
PLEASE! LET ME MAKE IT IN TIME!!
I...I HAVE TO...
...PROTECT ALLEN AND THE OTHERS!!
AAAAAAAAAAA
GRAAAA
WHAP

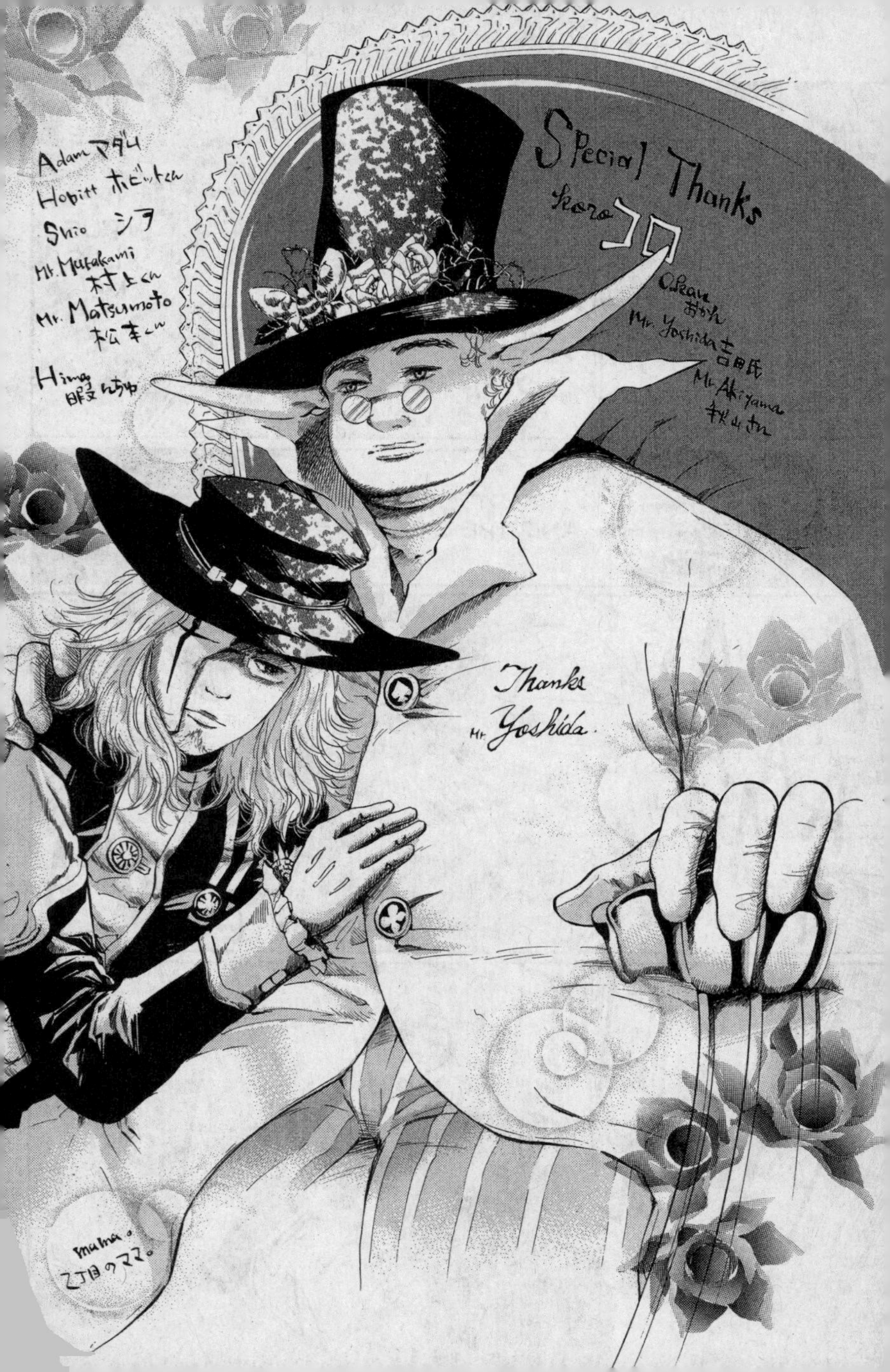
Special Thanks
koro コロ
O.kan おかん
Mr. Yoshida 吉田氏
Mr. Akiyama 秋山さん
Adam アダム
Hobitt ホビットくん
Shio シヲ
Mr. Murakami 村上くん
Mr. Matsumoto 松本くん
Hima 暇んちゃ
Thanks Mr. Yoshida.
mama. 2丁目のママ。

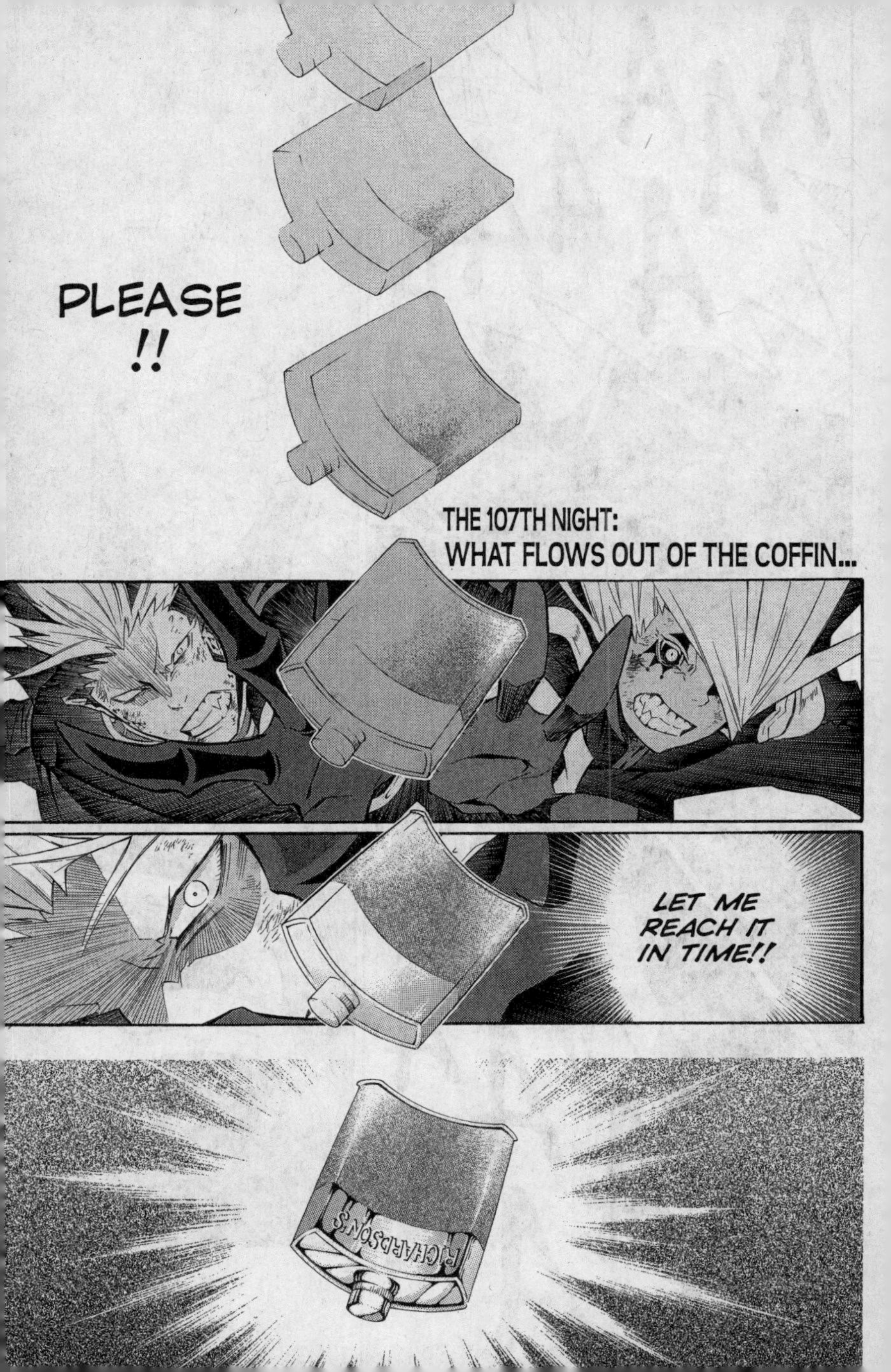
PLEASE !!
THE 107TH NIGHT: WHAT FLOWS OUT OF THE COFFIN...
LET ME REACH IT IN TIME!!
RICHARDSON'S

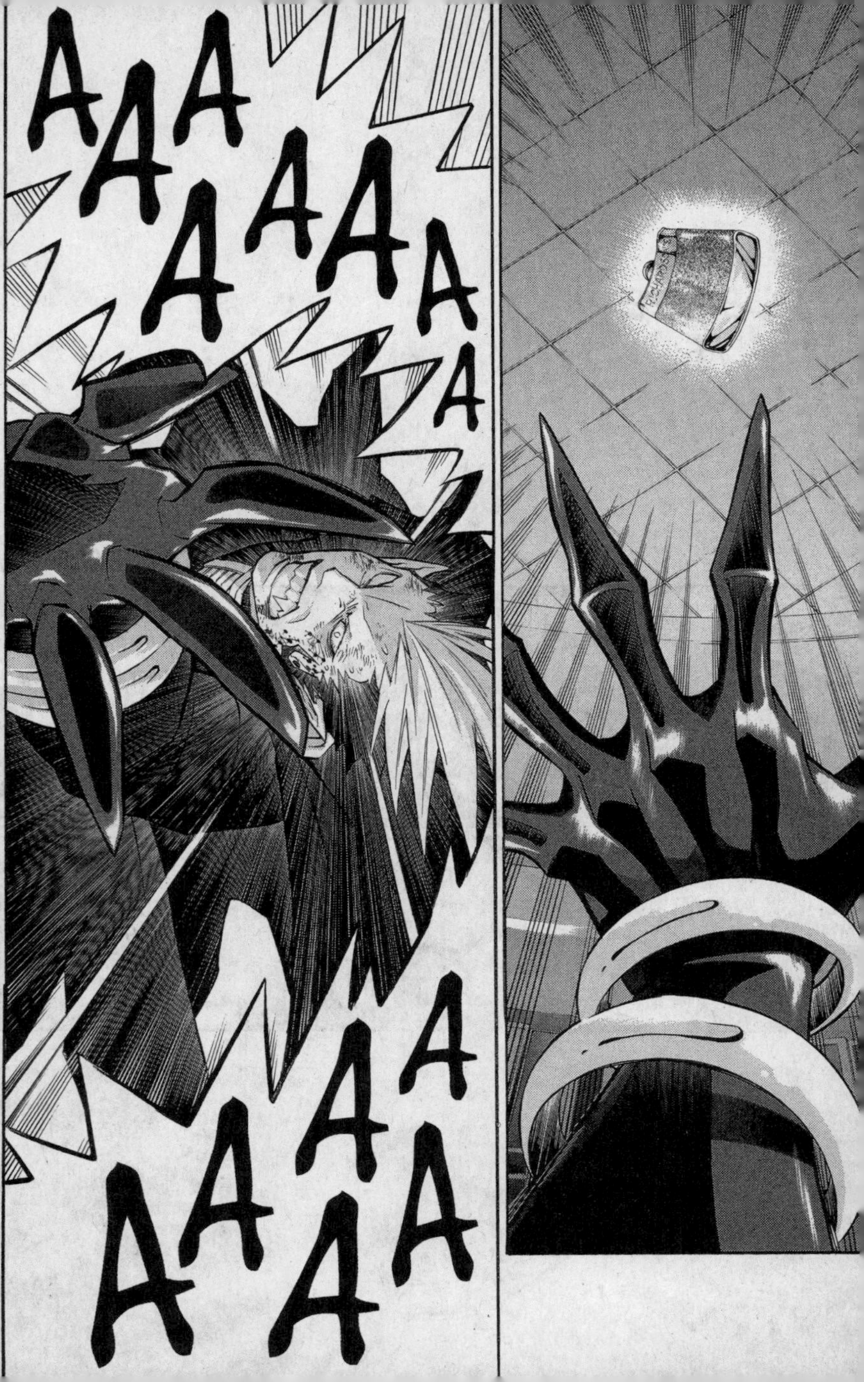
AAAAAAAA
AAAAAAAA

THE 107TH NIGHT: WHAT FLOWS OUT OF THE COFFIN...

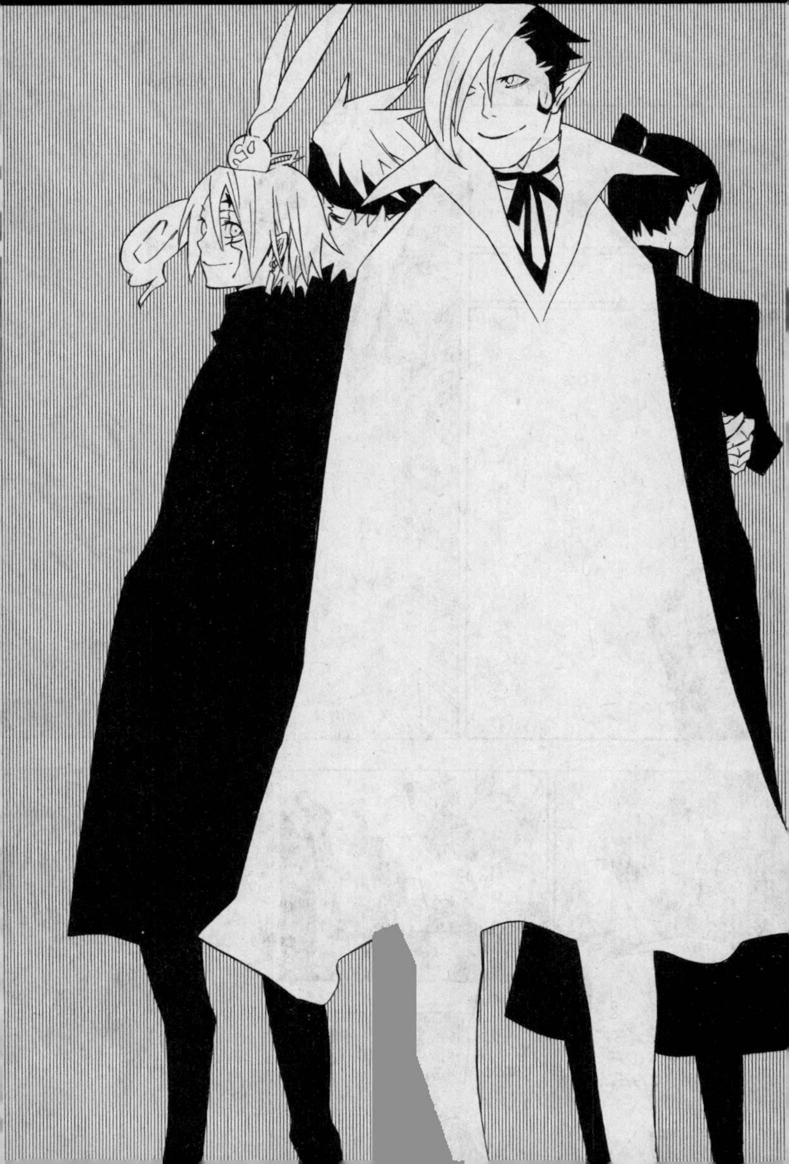

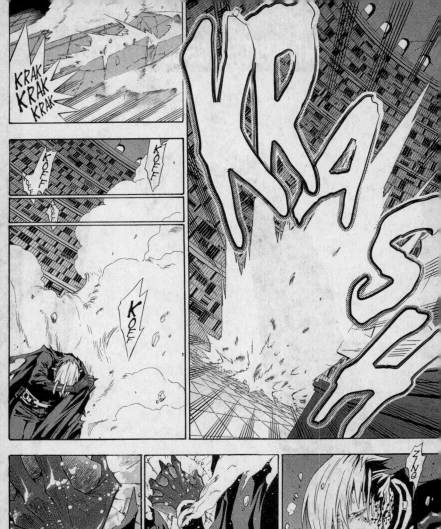

KRAK
KRAK
KRAK

KOFF

KOFF

KOFF

KRASH

ZING

LAST
OF
THE...

BLOOD
...

...!!

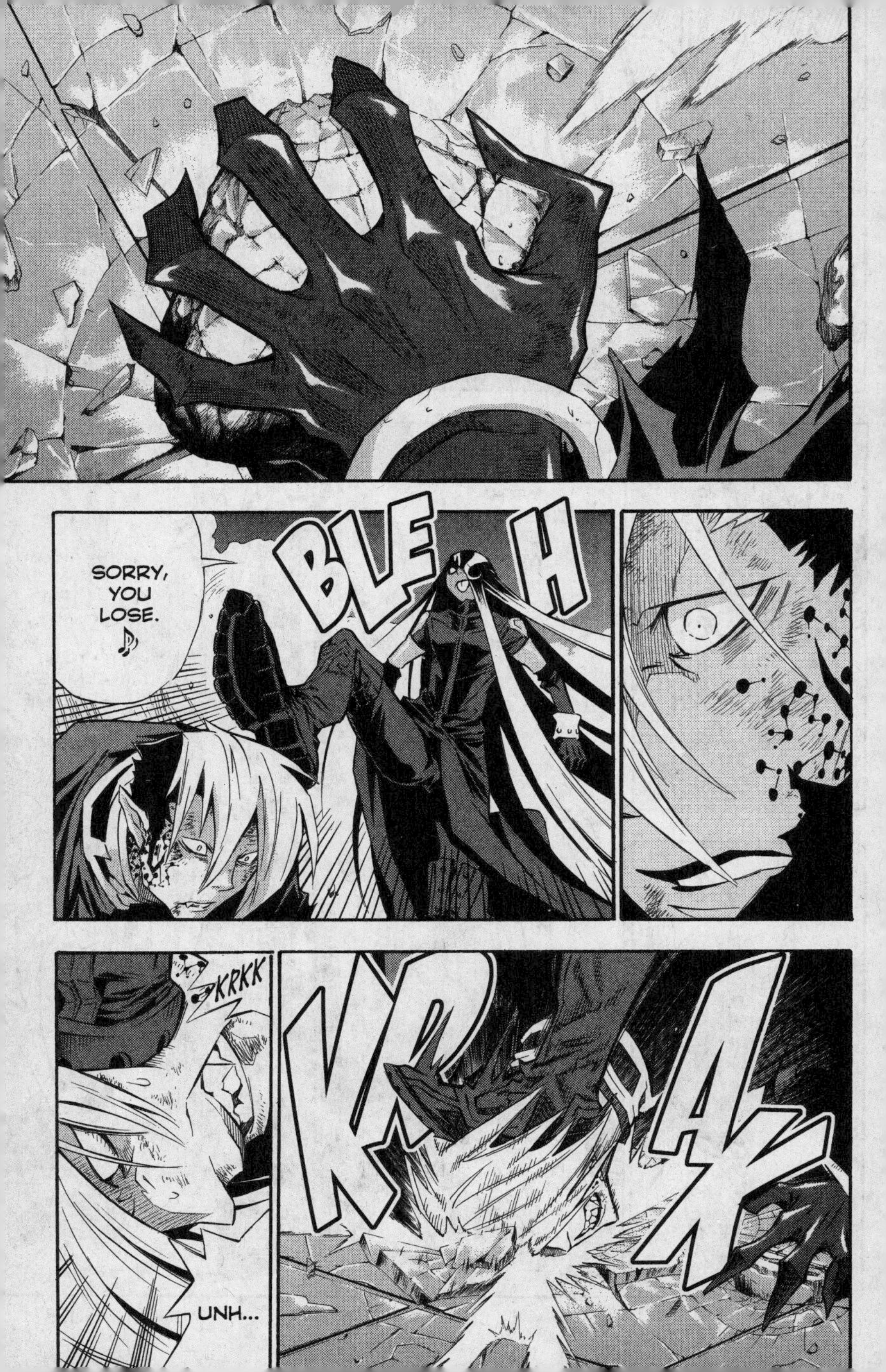
BLE H
SORRY, YOU LOSE. ♪
KRAK
KRKK
UNH...

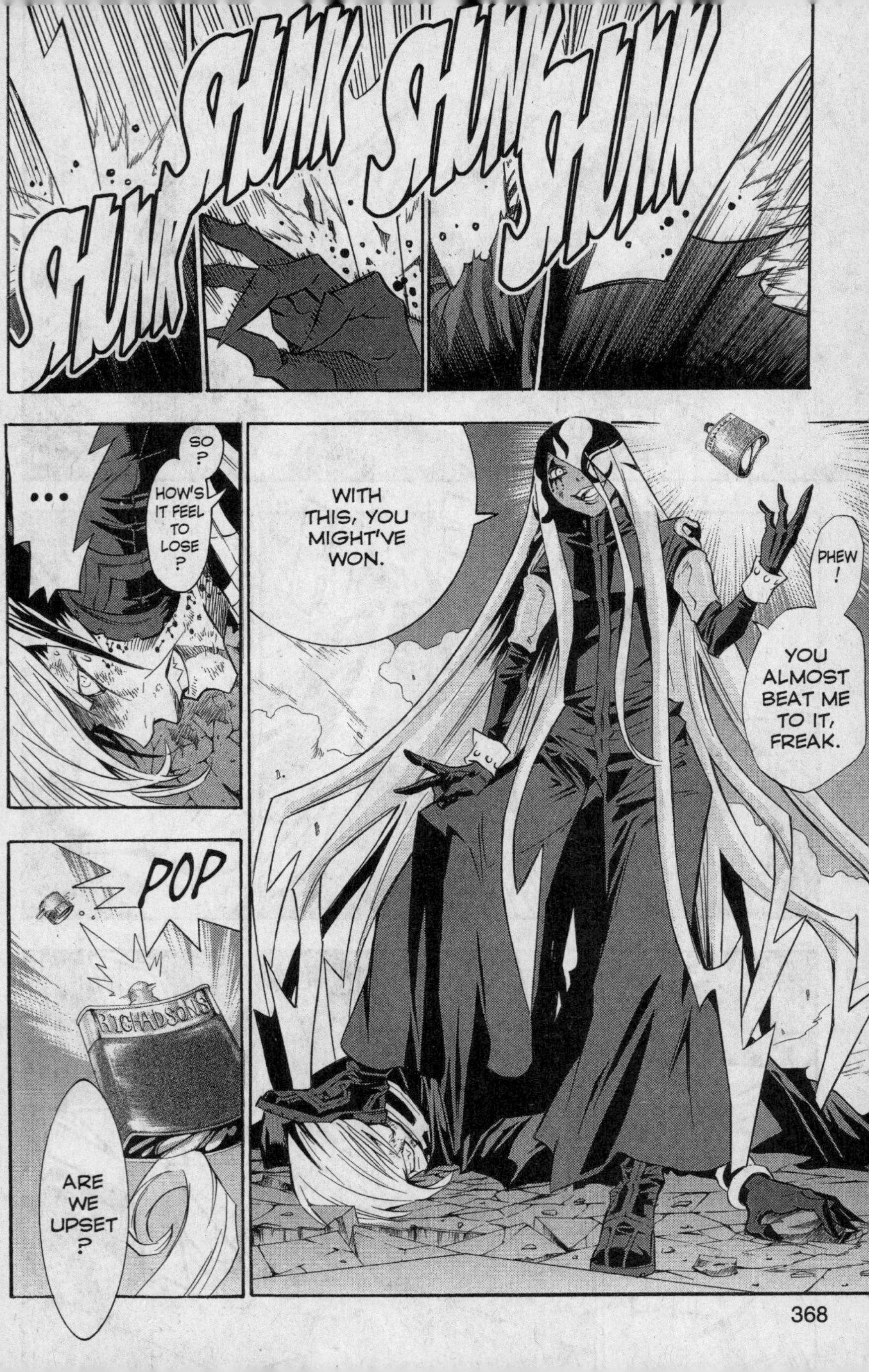
SHUNK
SHUNK
SHUNK
SHUNK
PHEW!
YOU ALMOST BEAT ME TO IT, FREAK.
WITH THIS, YOU MIGHT'VE WON.
SO? HOW'S IT FEEL TO LOSE?
...
POP
RICHADSONS
ARE WE UPSET?

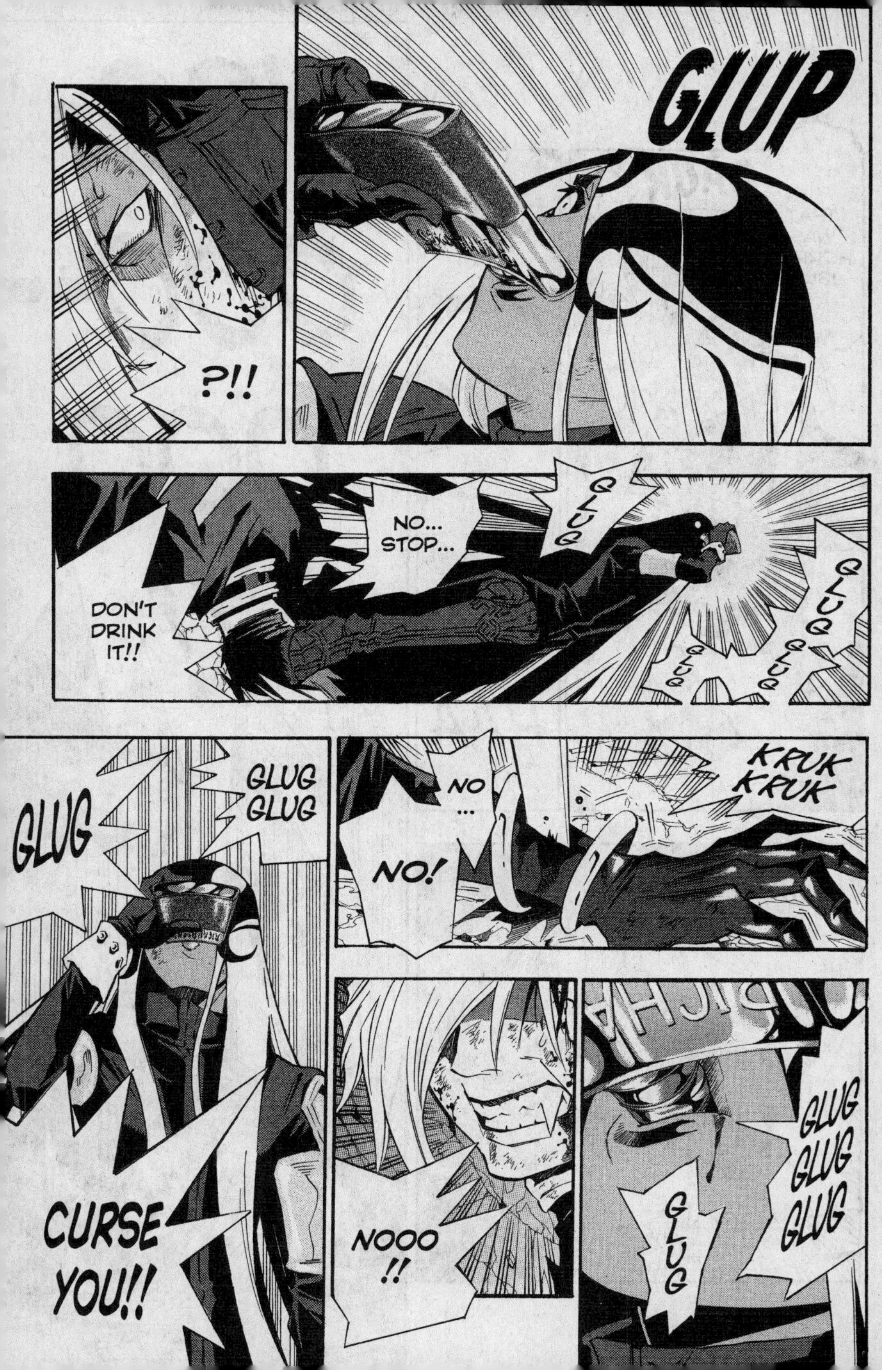
GLUP
?!!
GLUG
NO... STOP...
GLUG
GLUG
GLUG
DON'T DRINK IT!!
KRUK KRUK
NO ...
NO!
GLUG GLUG GLUG
GLUG
NOOO !!
GLUG GLUG
GLUG
CURSE YOU!!

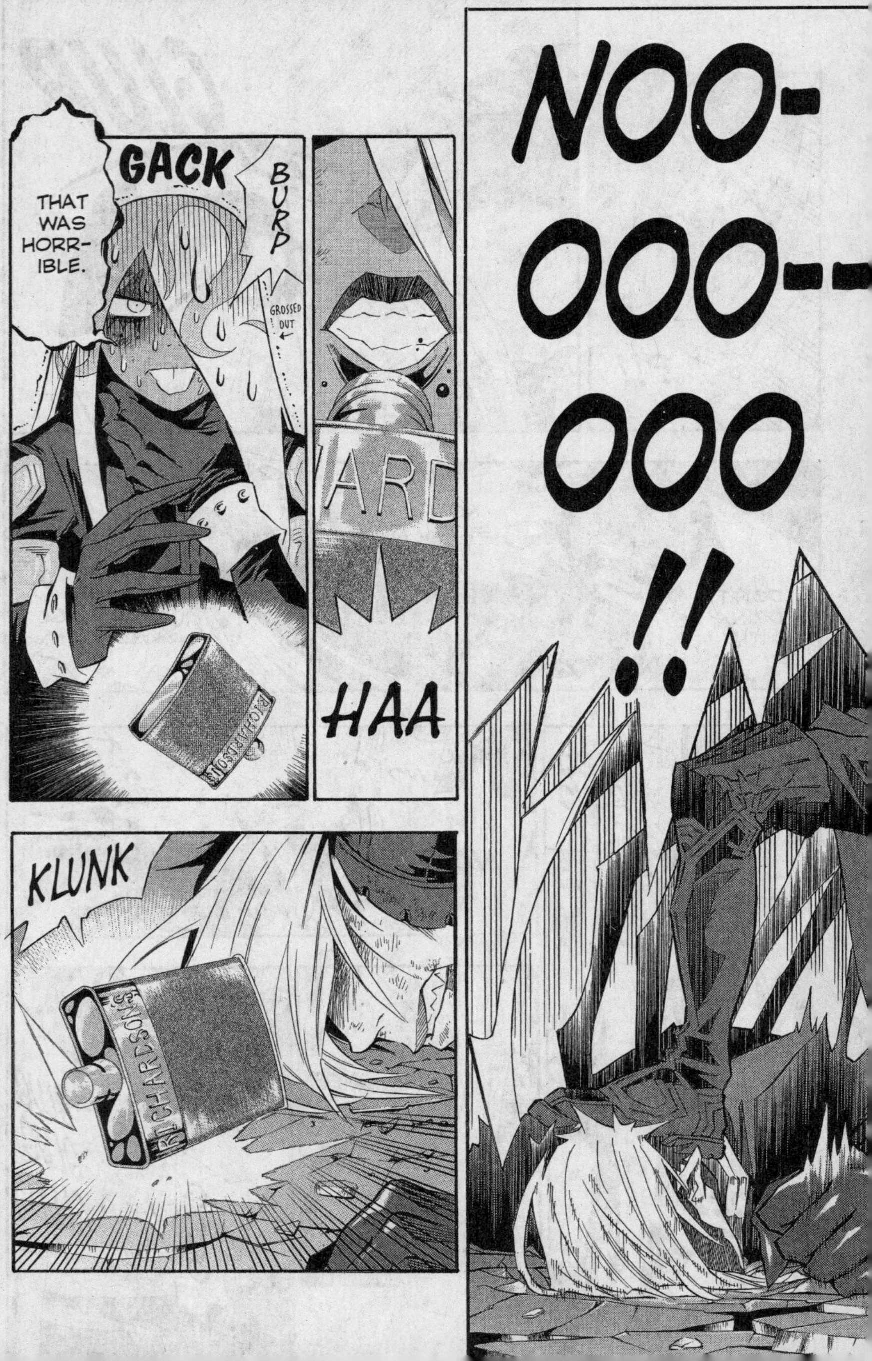
NOO-
OOO--
OOO
!!
ARD
HAA
BURP
GROSSED OUT
GACK
THAT WAS HORRIBLE.
RICHARDSONS
KLUNK
RICHARDSONS

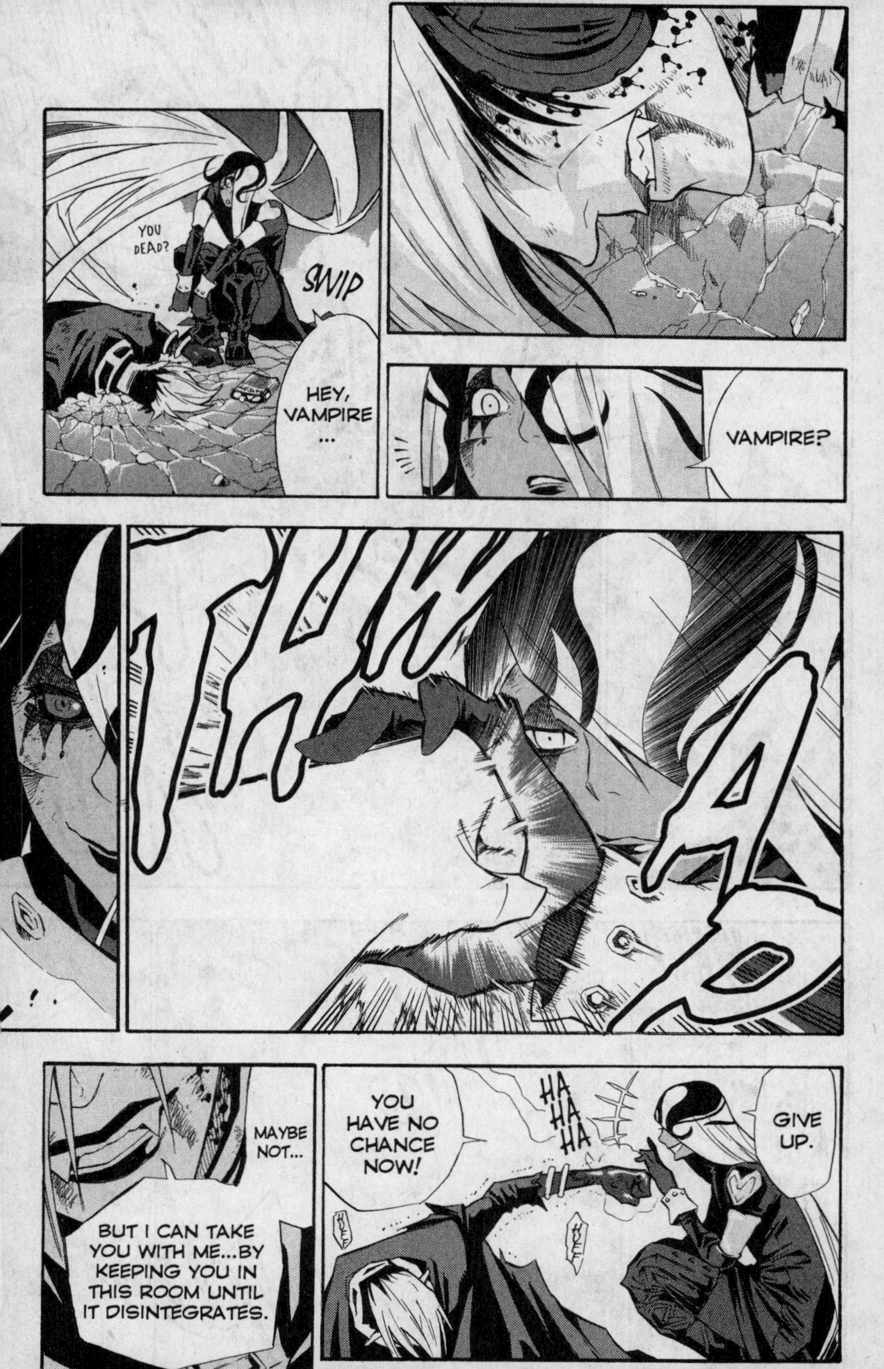
YOU DEAD?
SWIP
HEY, VAMPIRE ...
VAMPIRE?
THWAP
GIVE UP.
HA HA HA
YOU HAVE NO CHANCE NOW!
HUFF
HUFF
MAYBE NOT...
BUT I CAN TAKE YOU WITH ME...BY KEEPING YOU IN THIS ROOM UNTIL IT DISINTEGRATES.

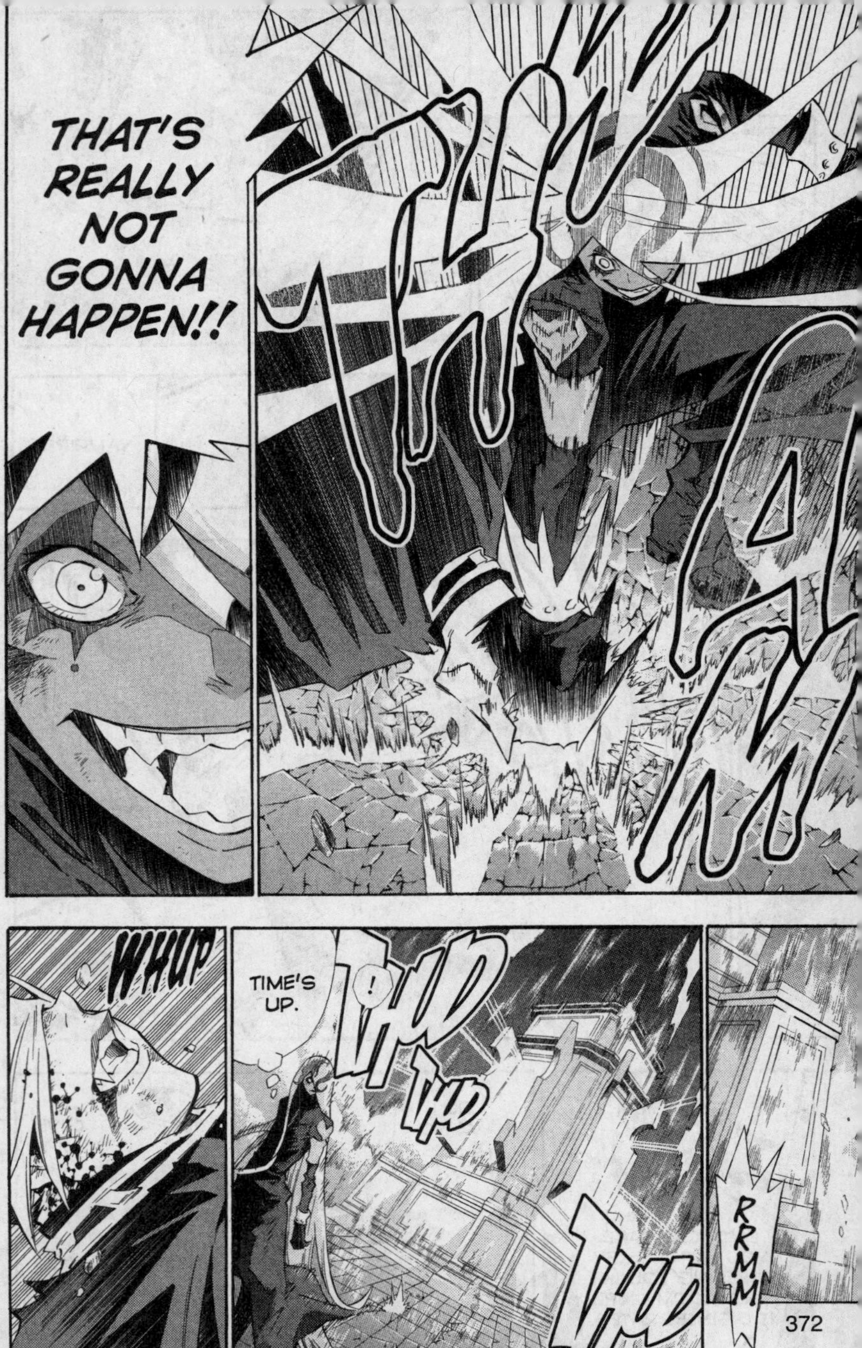
THAT'S REALLY NOT GONNA HAPPEN!!
RRMM
!
TIME'S UP.
THUD
THUD
THUD
WHUP

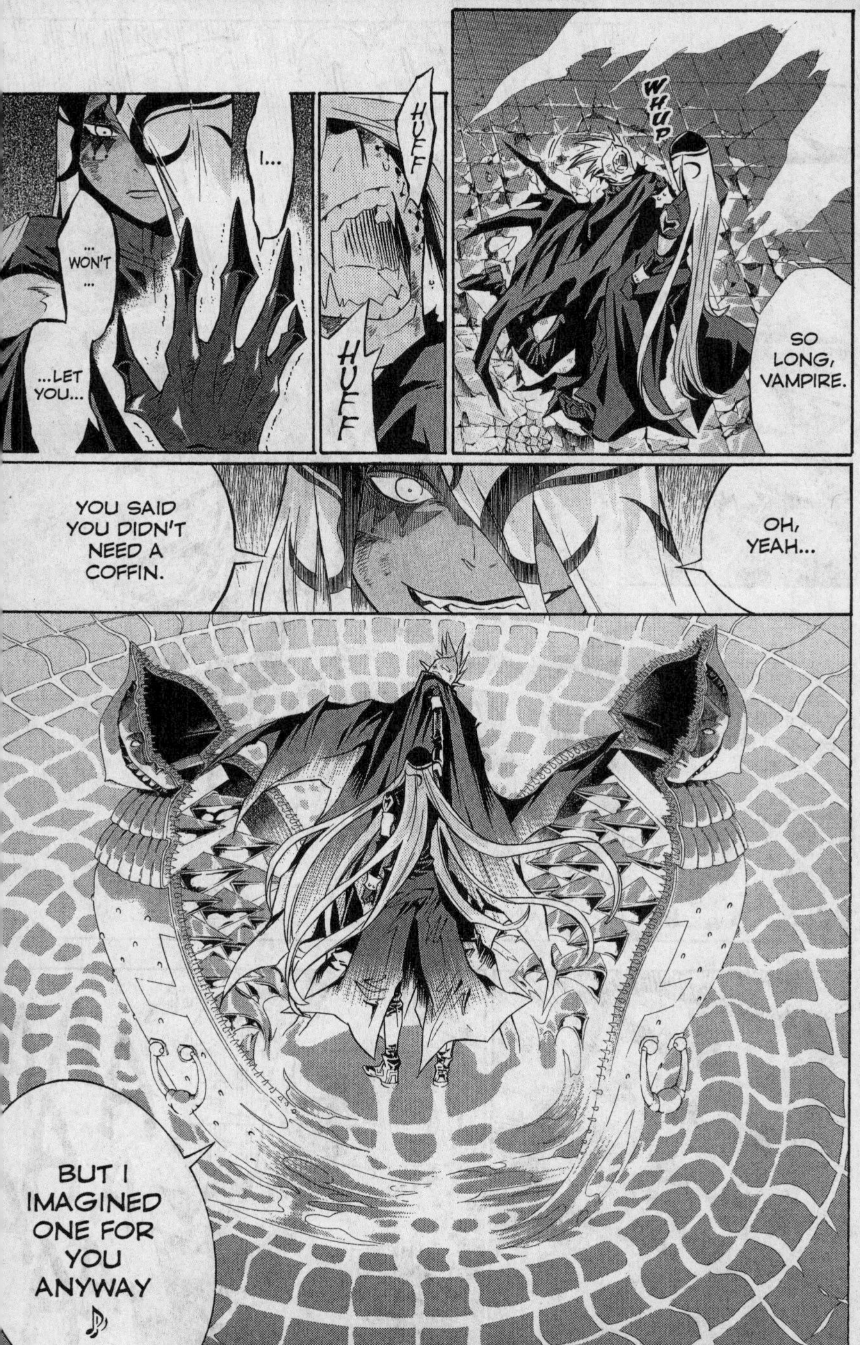
WHUP
SO LONG, VAMPIRE.
HUFF
HUFF
I...
...WON'T...
...LET YOU...
OH, YEAH...
YOU SAID YOU DIDN'T NEED A COFFIN.
BUT I IMAGINED ONE FOR YOU ANYWAY ♪

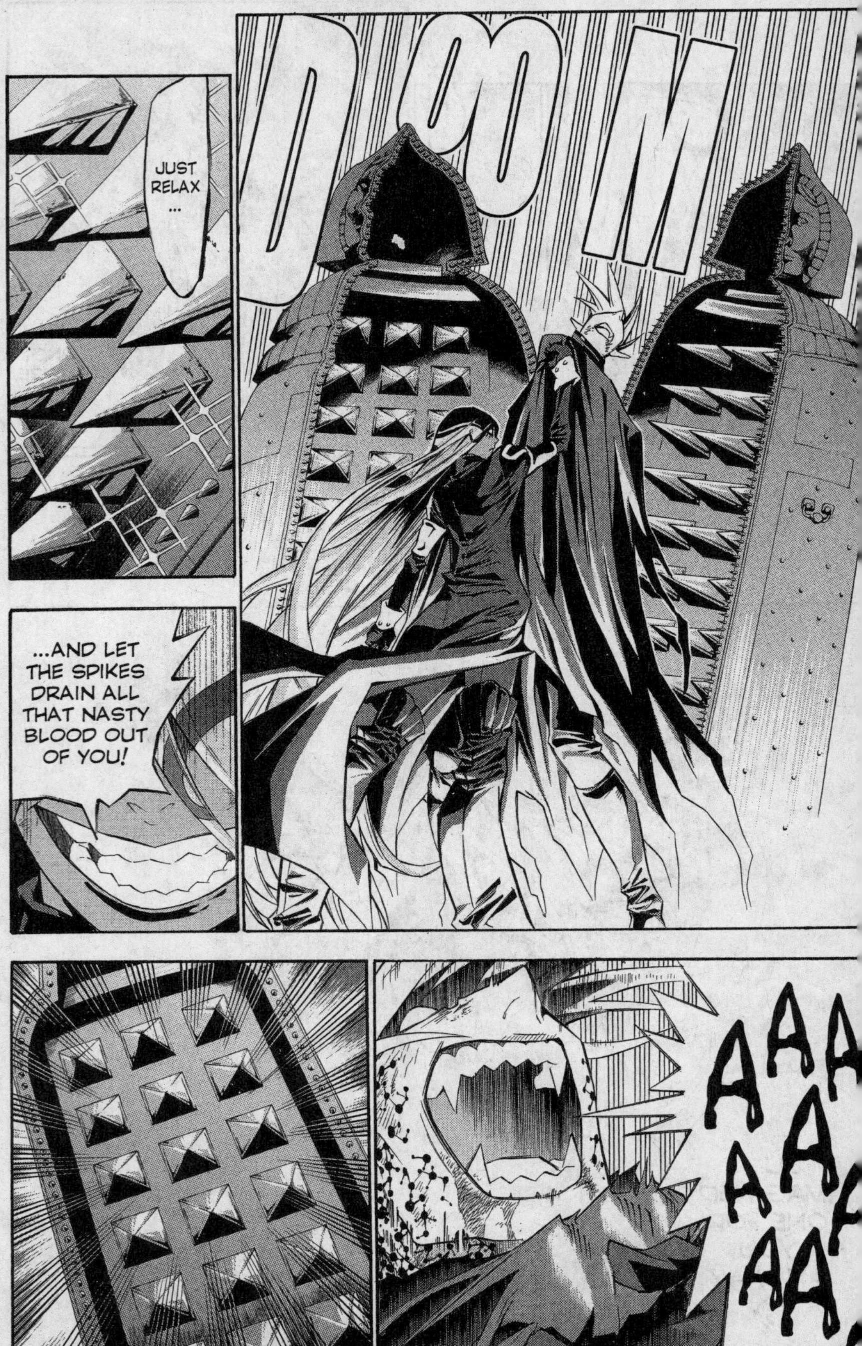
DOOM
JUST RELAX ...
...AND LET THE SPIKES DRAIN ALL THAT NASTY BLOOD OUT OF YOU!
AAAAAAAAAA

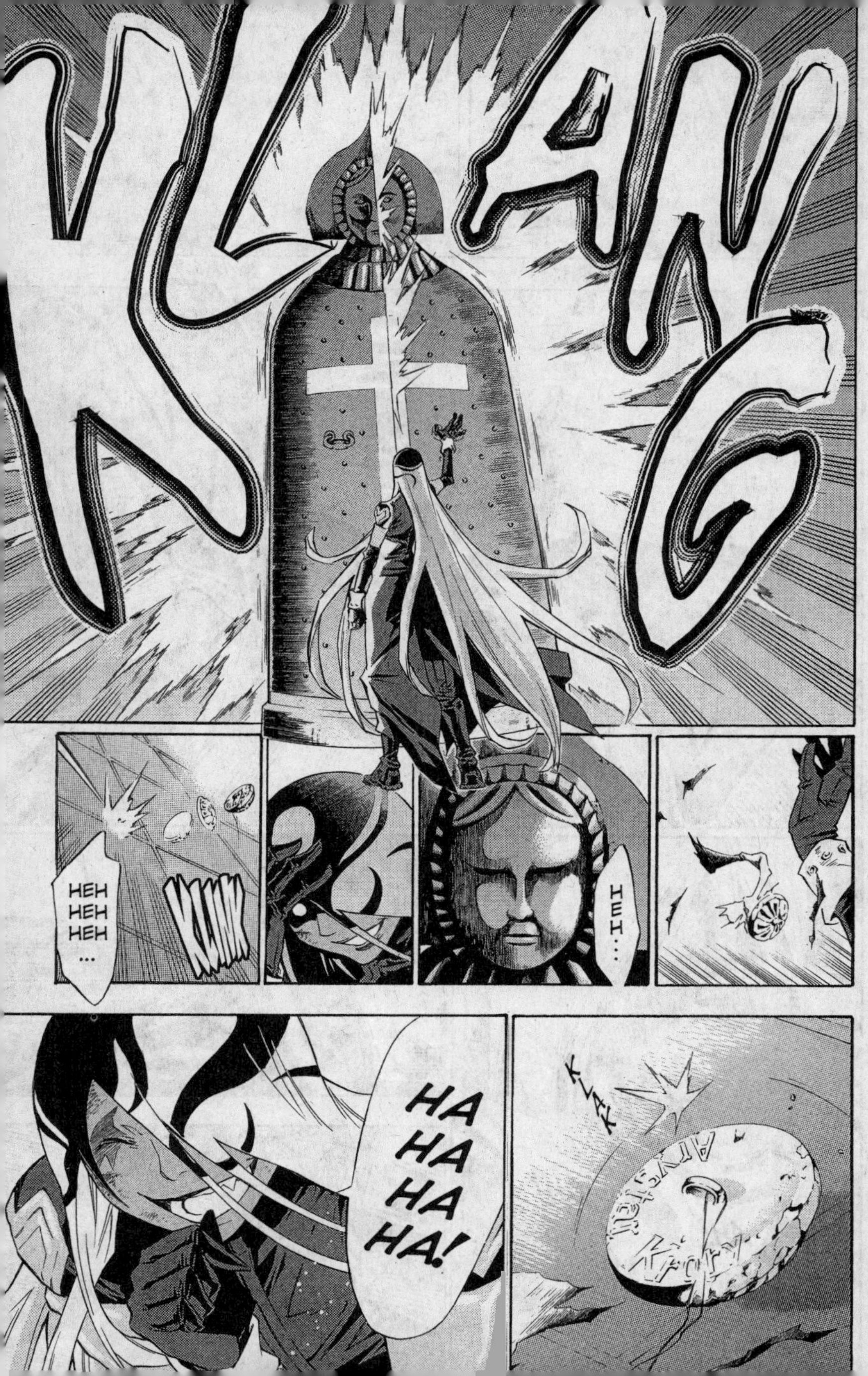
HEH...
HEH HEH HEH ...
K-LAK
HA HA HA HA HA!

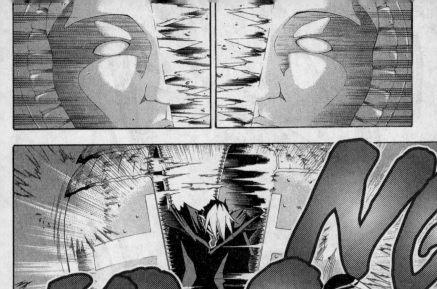

KROO NG

AAAH!

AH!

AH!

AAAH!

HNNGH...

AAAAH...

WROAAH!

!!

GRR...

KRK

KRK

GRAAAH!

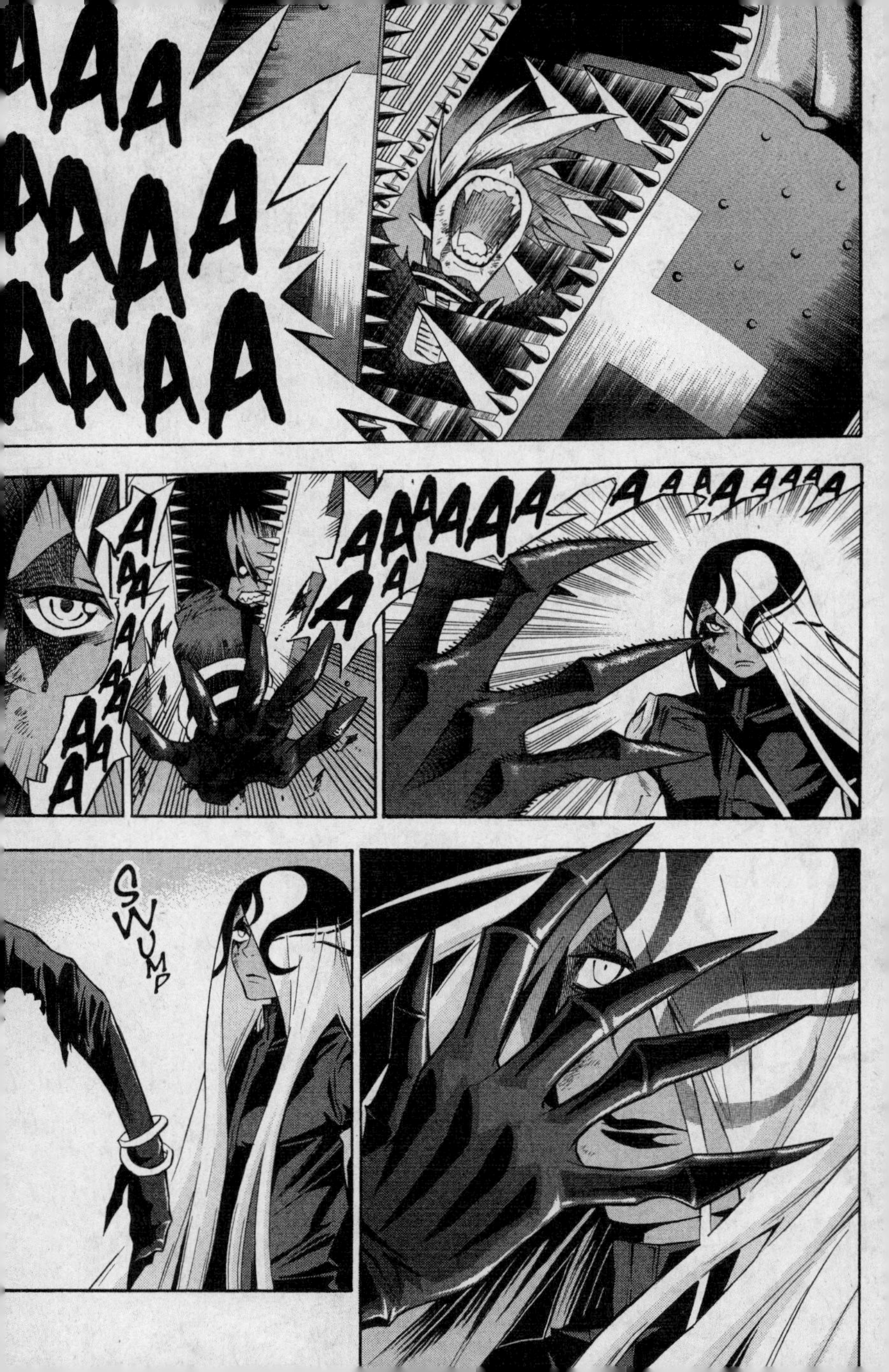
AAAAAAAAAAAAAAAAAA
AAAAAAAAAAAAAAAAAA
AAAAAAAAAAA
SWUMP

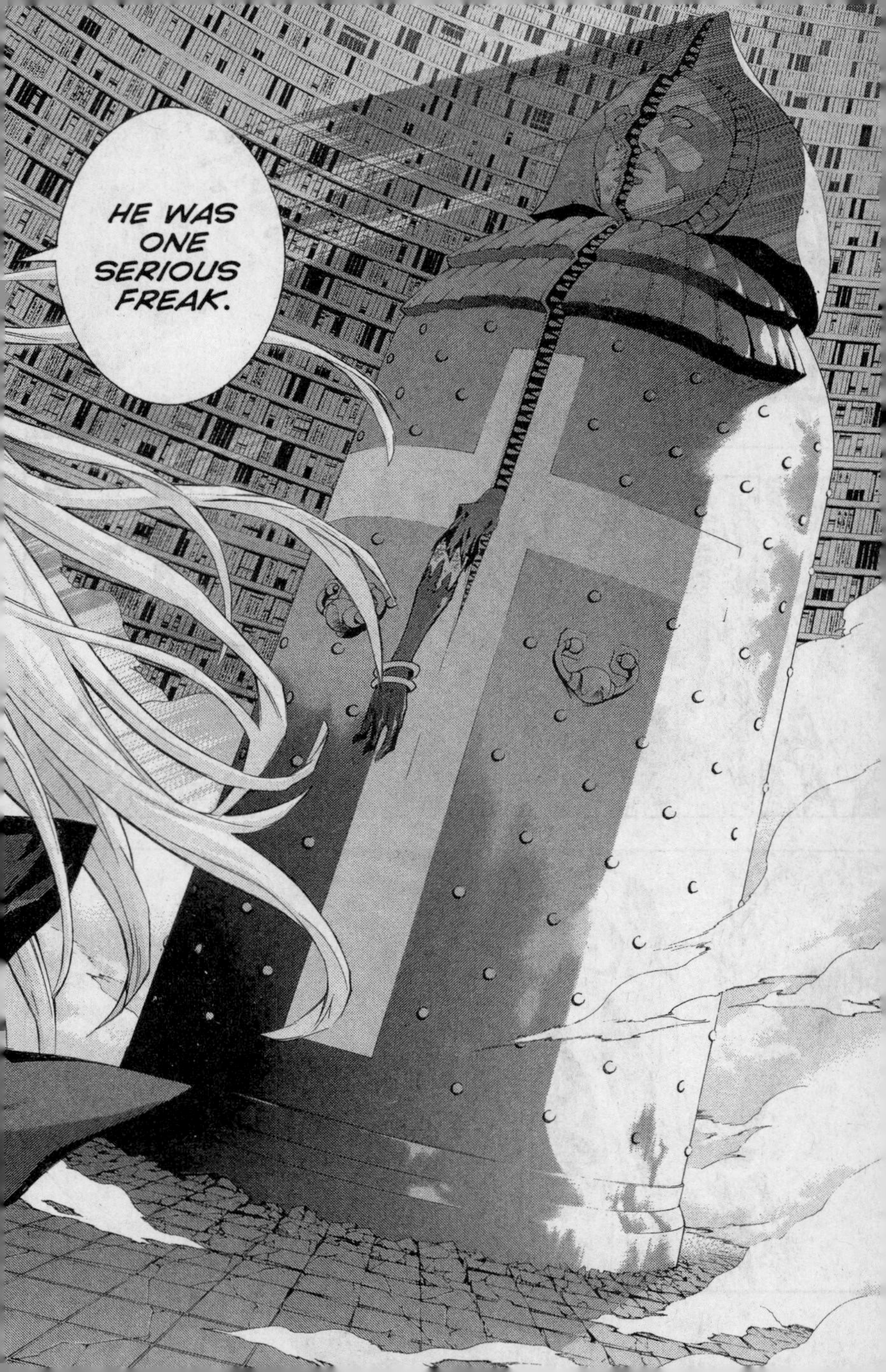
HE WAS ONE SERIOUS FREAK.

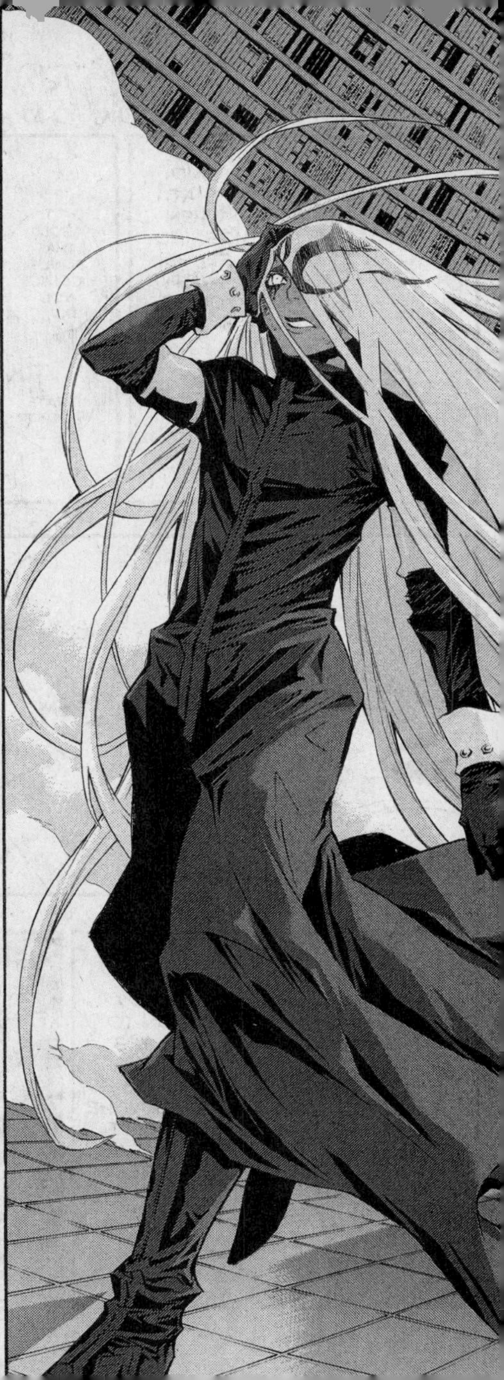

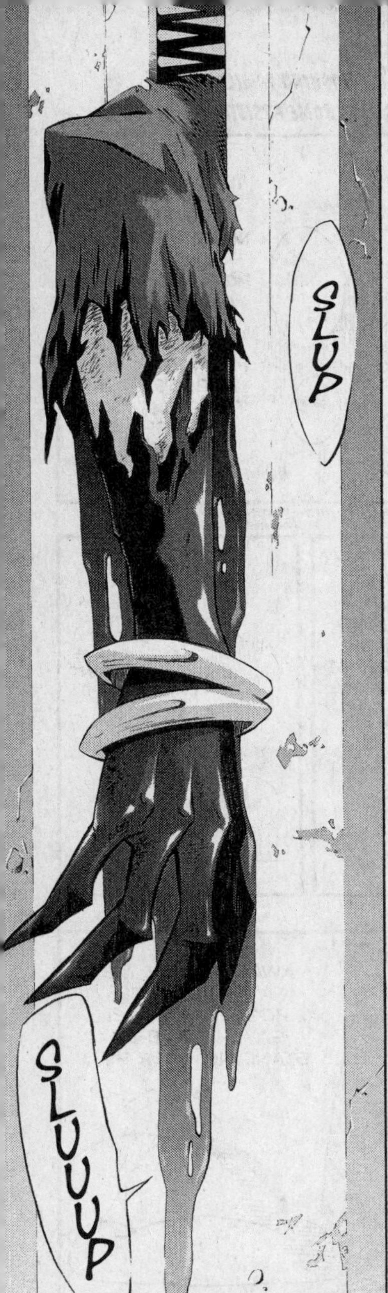
SLUP
SLUUUP

VOL. 11 FIGHT TO THE DEBT (END)

D.GRAY THEATER

THE HOSHINO FAMILY, PART 2
ART BY SOME ASSISTANT

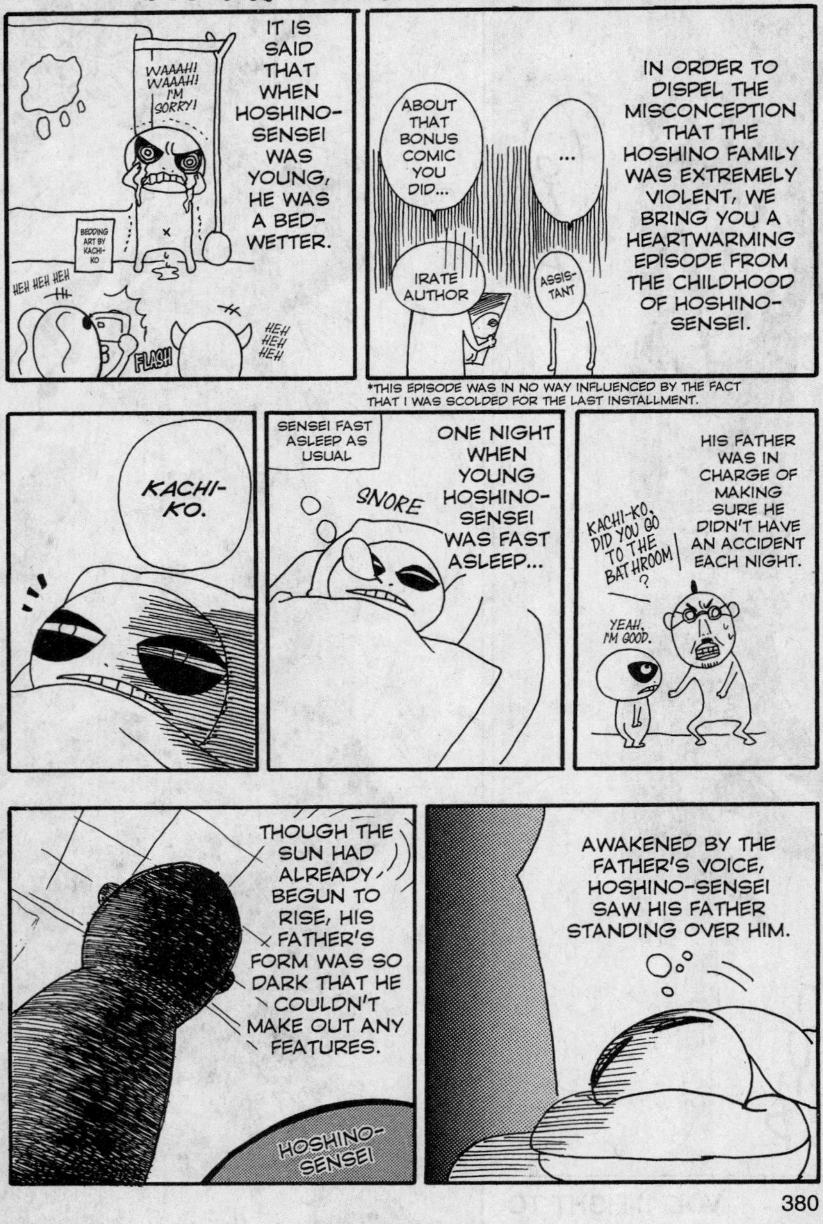

IN ORDER TO DISPEL THE MISCONCEPTION THAT THE HOSHINO FAMILY WAS EXTREMELY VIOLENT, WE BRING YOU A HEARTWARMING EPISODE FROM THE CHILDHOOD OF HOSHINO-SENSEI.
...
ABOUT THAT BONUS COMIC YOU DID...
ASSIS-TANT
IRATE AUTHOR
IT IS SAID THAT WHEN HOSHINO-SENSEI WAS YOUNG, HE WAS A BED-WETTER.
WAAAH! WAAAH! I'M SORRY!
BEDDING ART BY KACHI-KO
HEH HEH HEH
HEH HEH HEH
FLASH
*THIS EPISODE WAS IN NO WAY INFLUENCED BY THE FACT THAT I WAS SCOLDED FOR THE LAST INSTALLMENT.
HIS FATHER WAS IN CHARGE OF MAKING SURE HE DIDN'T HAVE AN ACCIDENT EACH NIGHT.
KACHI-KO, DID YOU GO TO THE BATHROOM?
YEAH, I'M GOOD.
ONE NIGHT WHEN YOUNG HOSHINO-SENSEI WAS FAST ASLEEP...
SENSEI FAST ASLEEP AS USUAL
SNORE
KACHI-KO.
AWAKENED BY THE FATHER'S VOICE, HOSHINO-SENSEI SAW HIS FATHER STANDING OVER HIM.
THOUGH THE SUN HAD ALREADY BEGUN TO RISE, HIS FATHER'S FORM WAS SO DARK THAT HE COULDN'T MAKE OUT ANY FEATURES.
HOSHINO-SENSEI

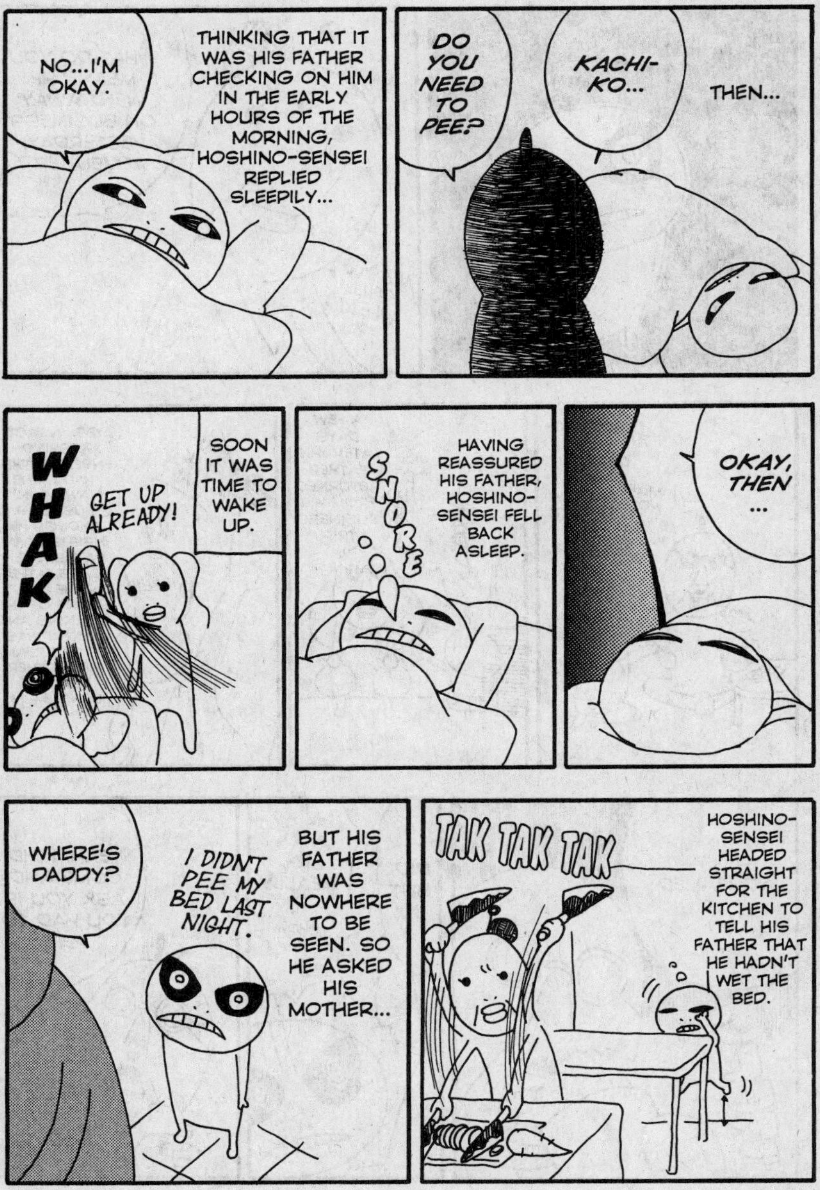
THEN...
KACHI-KO...
DO YOU NEED TO PEE?
THINKING THAT IT WAS HIS FATHER CHECKING ON HIM IN THE EARLY HOURS OF THE MORNING, HOSHINO-SENSEI REPLIED SLEEPILY...
NO...I'M OKAY.
OKAY, THEN ...
HAVING REASSURED HIS FATHER, HOSHINO-SENSEI FELL BACK ASLEEP.
SNORE
SOON IT WAS TIME TO WAKE UP.
GET UP ALREADY!
WHAK
HOSHINO-SENSEI HEADED STRAIGHT FOR THE KITCHEN TO TELL HIS FATHER THAT HE HADN'T WET THE BED.
TAK TAK TAK
BUT HIS FATHER WAS NOWHERE TO BE SEEN. SO HE ASKED HIS MOTHER...
I DIDN'T PEE MY BED LAST NIGHT.
WHERE'S DADDY?

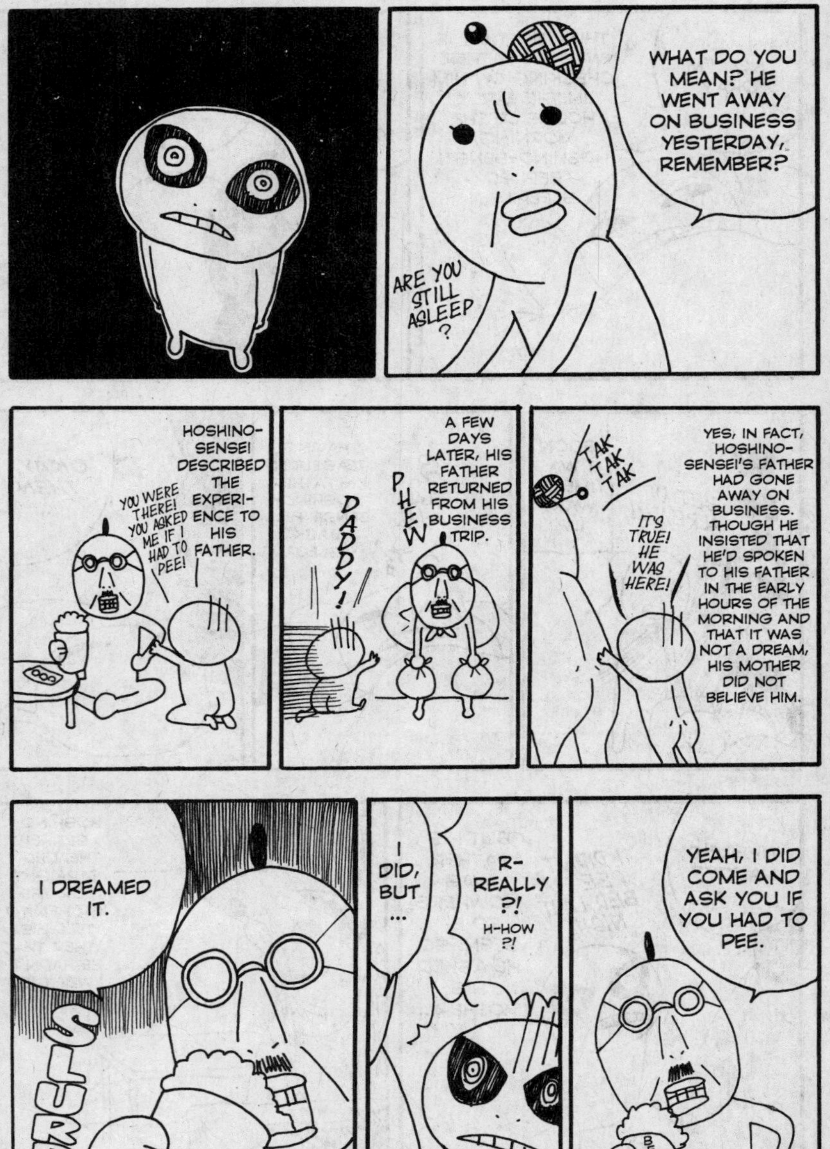
WHAT DO YOU MEAN? HE WENT AWAY ON BUSINESS YESTERDAY, REMEMBER?
ARE YOU STILL ASLEEP?
YES, IN FACT, HOSHINO-SENSEI'S FATHER HAD GONE AWAY ON BUSINESS. THOUGH HE INSISTED THAT HE'D SPOKEN TO HIS FATHER IN THE EARLY HOURS OF THE MORNING AND THAT IT WAS NOT A DREAM, HIS MOTHER DID NOT BELIEVE HIM.
TAK TAK TAK
IT'S TRUE! HE WAS HERE!
A FEW DAYS LATER, HIS FATHER RETURNED FROM HIS BUSINESS TRIP.
PHEW
DADDY!
HOSHINO-SENSEI DESCRIBED THE EXPERIENCE TO HIS FATHER.
YOU WERE THERE! YOU ASKED ME IF I HAD TO PEE!
YEAH, I DID COME AND ASK YOU IF YOU HAD TO PEE.
BEER
R-REALLY?!
H-HOW?!
I DID, BUT...
I DREAMED IT.
SLURP

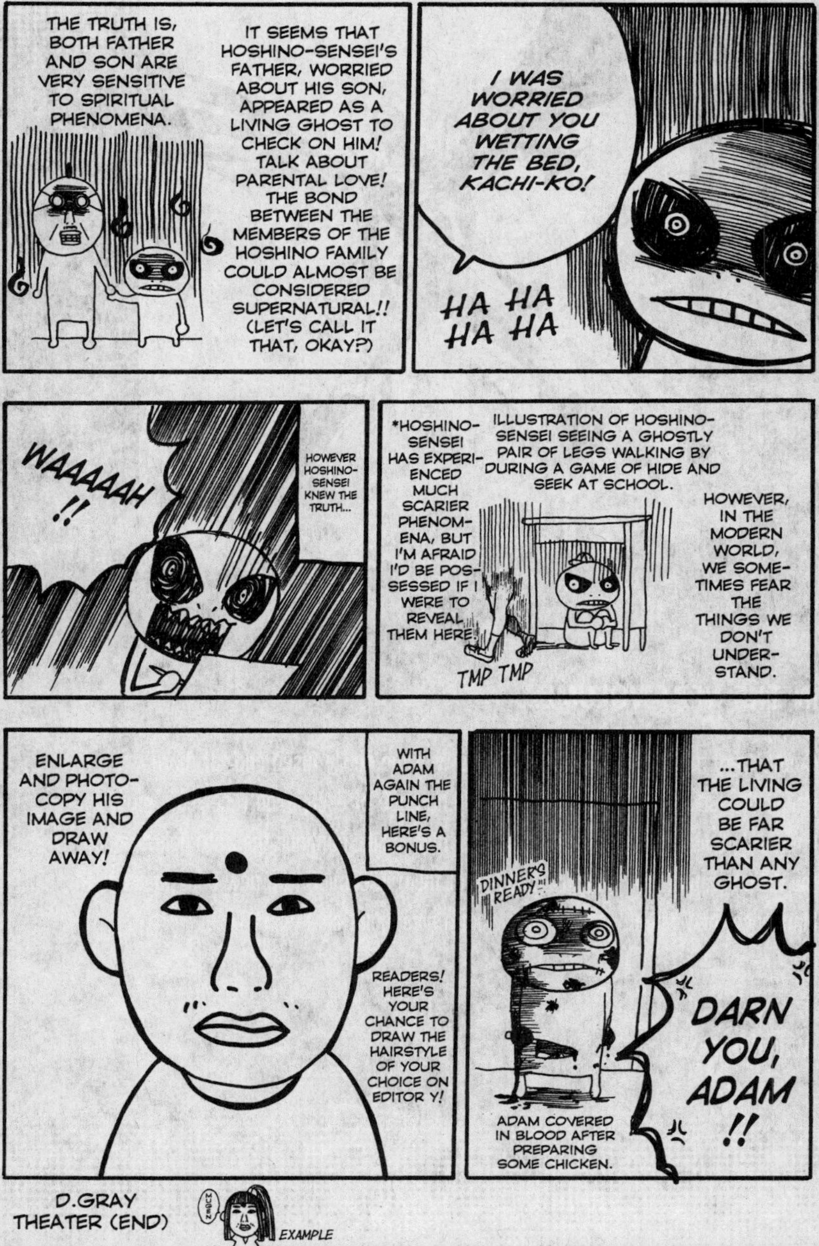
I WAS WORRIED ABOUT YOU WETTING THE BED, KACHI-KO!
HA HA HA HA
IT SEEMS THAT HOSHINO-SENSEI'S FATHER, WORRIED ABOUT HIS SON, APPEARED AS A LIVING GHOST TO CHECK ON HIM! TALK ABOUT PARENTAL LOVE! THE BOND BETWEEN THE MEMBERS OF THE HOSHINO FAMILY COULD ALMOST BE CONSIDERED SUPERNATURAL!! (LET'S CALL IT THAT, OKAY?)
THE TRUTH IS, BOTH FATHER AND SON ARE VERY SENSITIVE TO SPIRITUAL PHENOMENA.
ILLUSTRATION OF HOSHINO-SENSEI SEEING A GHOSTLY PAIR OF LEGS WALKING BY DURING A GAME OF HIDE AND SEEK AT SCHOOL.
HOWEVER, IN THE MODERN WORLD, WE SOMETIMES FEAR THE THINGS WE DON'T UNDERSTAND.
*HOSHINO-SENSEI HAS EXPERIENCED MUCH SCARIER PHENOMENA, BUT I'M AFRAID I'D BE POSSESSED IF I WERE TO REVEAL THEM HERE.
TMP TMP
HOWEVER HOSHINO-SENSEI KNEW THE TRUTH...
WAAAAAH!!
...THAT THE LIVING COULD BE FAR SCARIER THAN ANY GHOST.
DARN YOU, ADAM!!
DINNER'S READY
ADAM COVERED IN BLOOD AFTER PREPARING SOME CHICKEN.
WITH ADAM AGAIN THE PUNCH LINE, HERE'S A BONUS.
ENLARGE AND PHOTOCOPY HIS IMAGE AND DRAW AWAY!
READERS! HERE'S YOUR CHANCE TO DRAW THE HAIRSTYLE OF YOUR CHOICE ON EDITOR Y!
MUGEN
EXAMPLE
D.GRAY THEATER (END)

XT VOLUME...

s been bested in his battle with the newly fused and far more
vi. Trapped, with seemingly no hope of escape, he receives a n
tation! His fellow exorcists, meanwhile, continue their struggle t
g Ark, unaware that one of them is coming to a new understar
why does Tyki Mikk want a nice, quiet chat with Allen?

v!

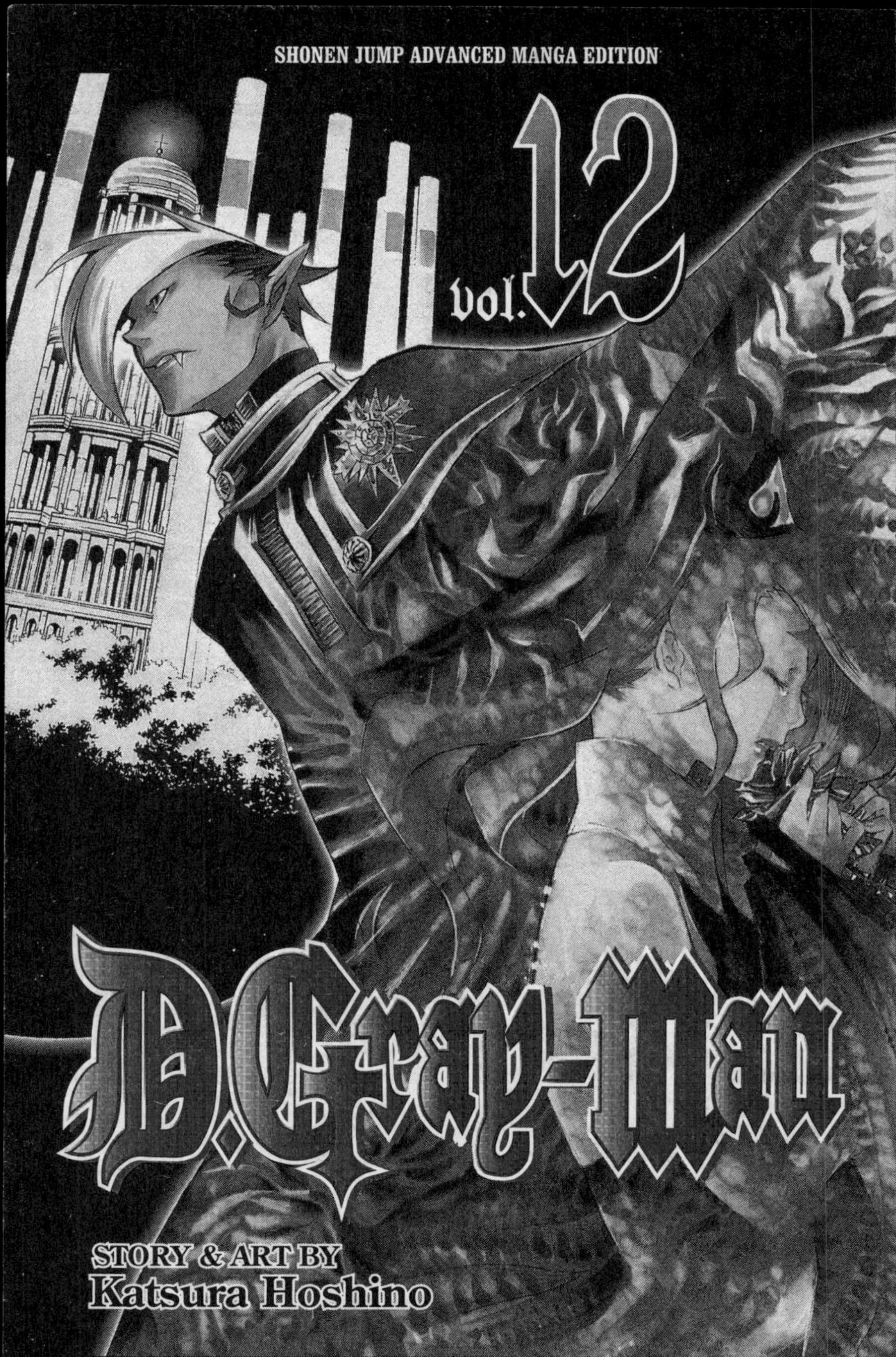
SHONEN JUMP ADVANCED MANGA EDITION
vol. 12
D.Gray-man
STORY & ART BY
Katsura Hoshino

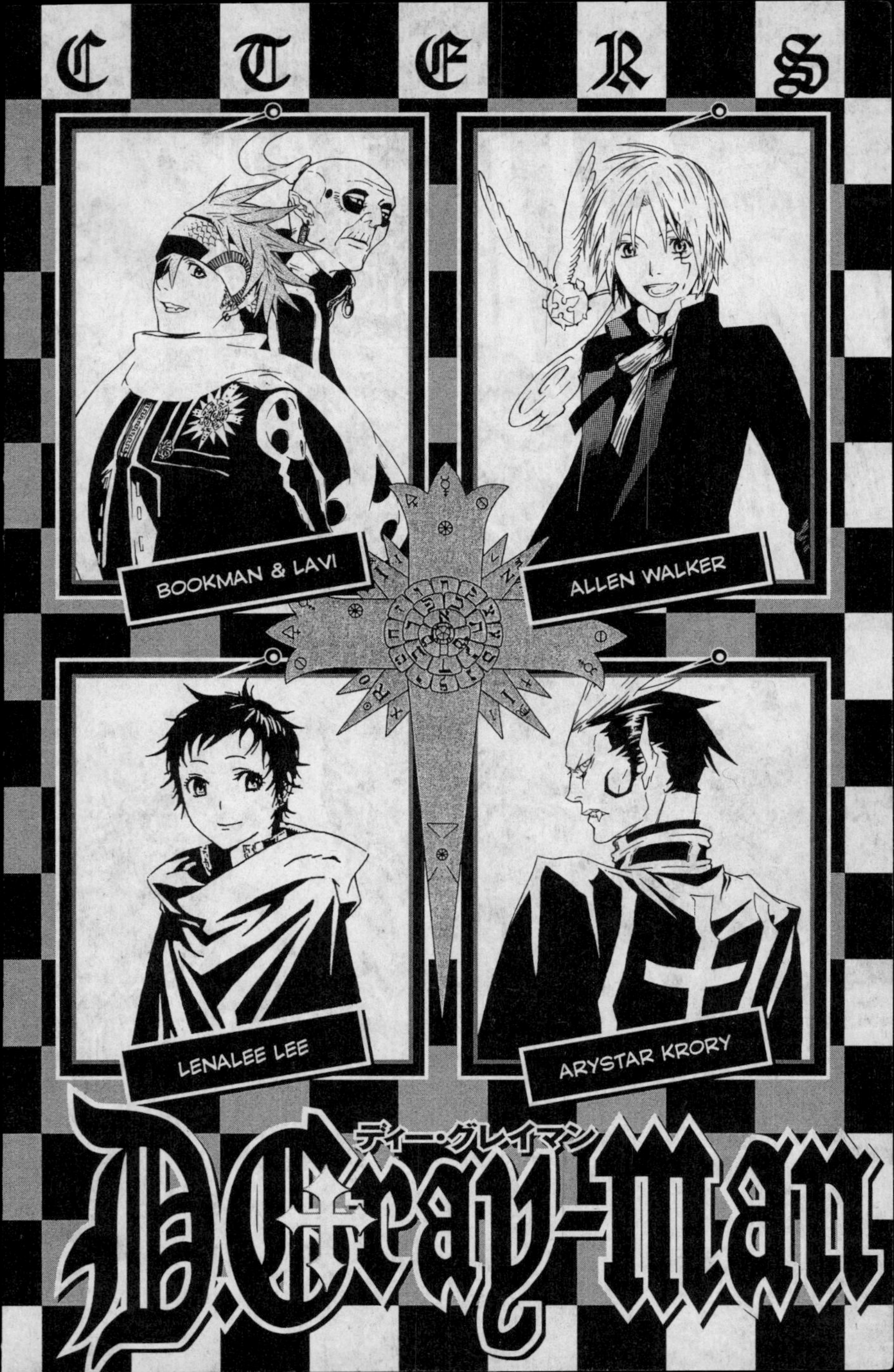

C T E R S
BOOKMAN & LAVI
ALLEN WALKER
LENALEE LEE
ARYSTAR KRORY
ディー・グレイマン
D.Gray-man

MILLENNIUM EARL

ROAD KAMELOT

TYKI MIKK

JASDEVI

STORY

IT ALL BEGAN CENTURIES AGO WITH THE DISCOVERY OF A CUBE CONTAINING AN APOCALYPTIC PROPHECY FROM AN ANCIENT CIVILIZATION AND INSTRUCTIONS IN THE USE OF INNOCENCE, A CRYSTALLINE SUBSTANCE OF WONDROUS SUPERNATURAL POWER. THE CREATORS OF THE CUBE CLAIMED TO HAVE DEFEATED AN EVIL KNOWN AS THE MILLENNIUM EARL BY USING THE INNOCENCE. NEVERTHELESS, THE WORLD WAS DESTROYED BY THE GREAT FLOOD OF THE OLD TESTAMENT. NOW, TO AVERT A SECOND END OF THE WORLD, A GROUP OF EXORCISTS WIELDING WEAPONS MADE OF INNOCENCE MUST BATTLE THE MILLENNIUM EARL AND HIS TERRIBLE MINIONS, THE AKUMA.

STRANDED ON A DISINTEGRATING ARK, ALLEN AND HIS FRIENDS STRUGGLE TO FIND A WAY OFF WHILE BATTLING THE CLAN OF NOAH. THOUGH KANDA AND ARYSTAR VALIANTLY SACRIFICE THEMSELVES, THE OTHERS FIND THEIR ESCAPE BLOCKED BY THE MALEVOLENT JASDEVI, A NOAH WITH A REALLY SPLIT PERSONALITY. WITH TIME RUNNING OUT, CAN THEY DEFEAT THE THREATS THAT STAND IN THEIR WAY, OR WILL THE EXORCISTS CEASE TO EXIST ALONG WITH THE CRUMBLING ARK?

D.GRAY-MAN
Vol. 12

CONTENTS

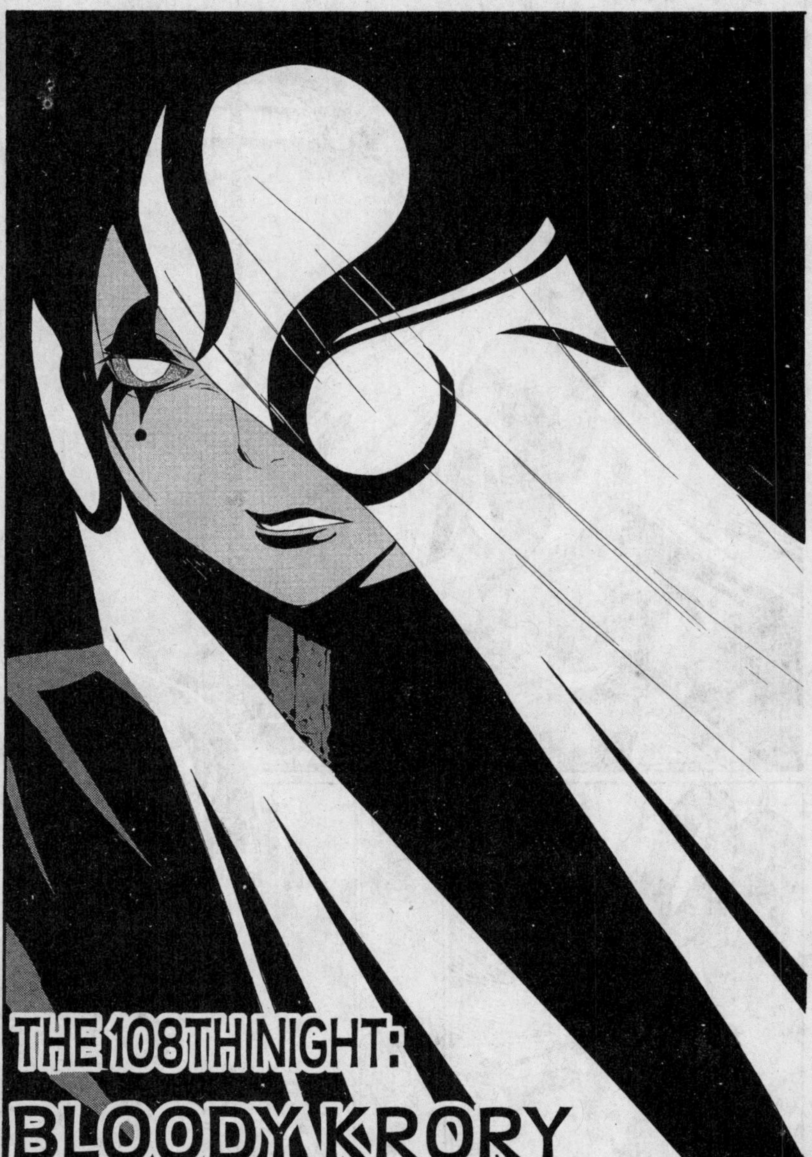
THE 108TH NIGHT:
BLOODY KRORY

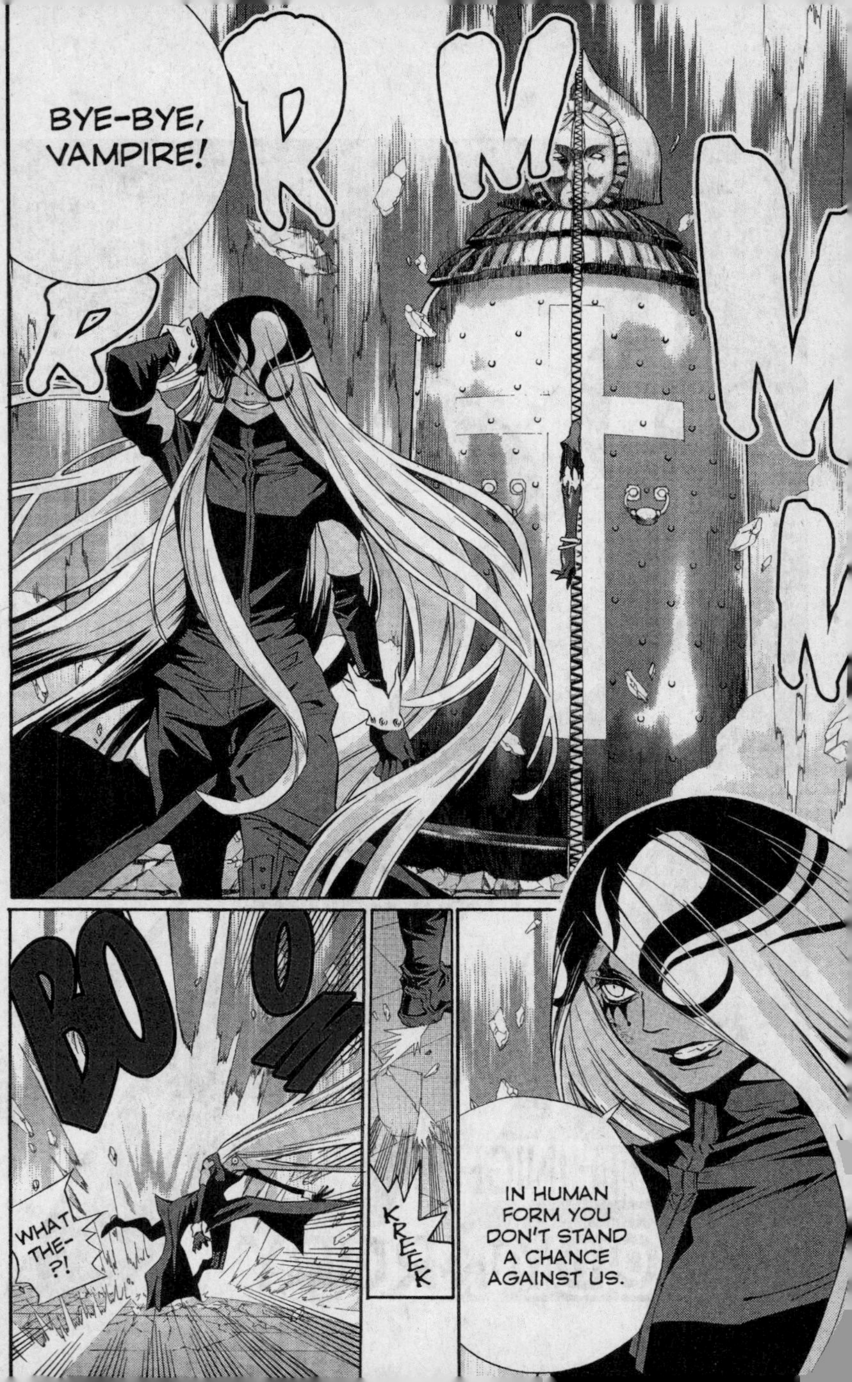
BYE-BYE, VAMPIRE!
IN HUMAN FORM YOU DON'T STAND A CHANCE AGAINST US.
KREEK
WHAT THE-?!

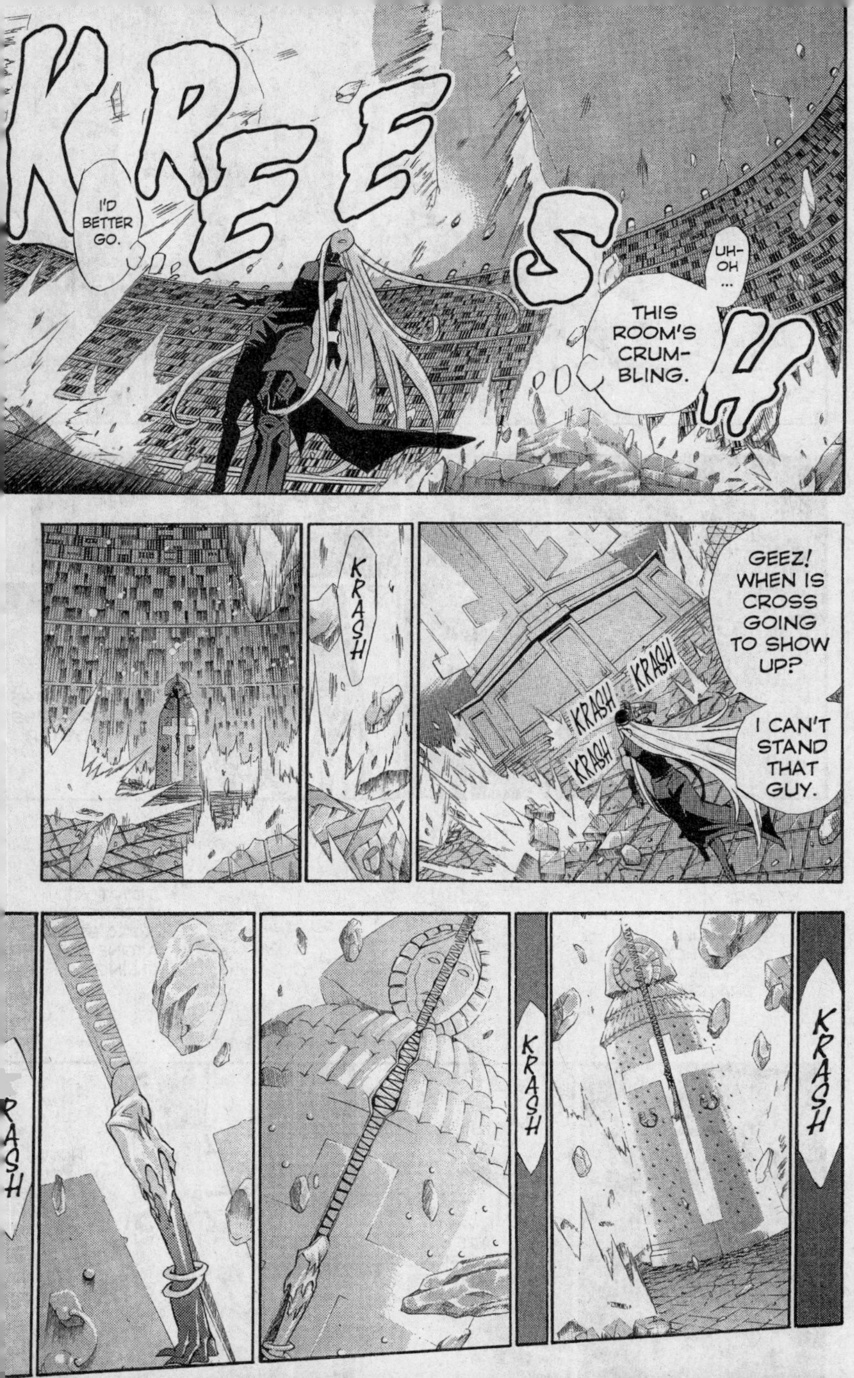
KREESH
UH-OH ...
THIS ROOM'S CRUMBLING.
I'D BETTER GO.
GEEZ! WHEN IS CROSS GOING TO SHOW UP?
I CAN'T STAND THAT GUY.
KRASH
KRASH
KRASH
KRASH
KRASH
KRASH
RASH

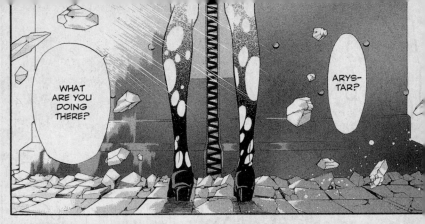

ARYS-TAR?
WHAT ARE YOU DOING THERE?
...
WHO ARE YOU?
YOU REALLY ARE WORTHLESS, ARYSTAR.
THAT VOICE... BUT IT CAN'T BE.
ELIADE?
DIDN'T YOU BECOME AN EXORCIST TO ATONE FOR KILLING ME?
THEN WHY ARE YOU GIVING YOUR LIFE TO PROTECT THOSE BRATS?
HMPH! YOU NEVER SEE THINGS THROUGH.
HEH ...
...
WHAT ARE YOU LAUGHING ABOUT?
HAVE YOU COME...
...TO WELCOME ME?

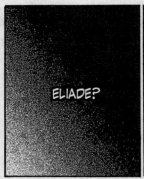

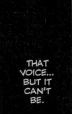

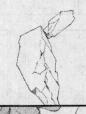

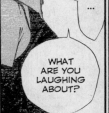

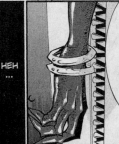

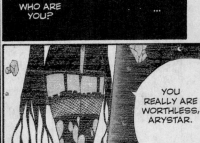

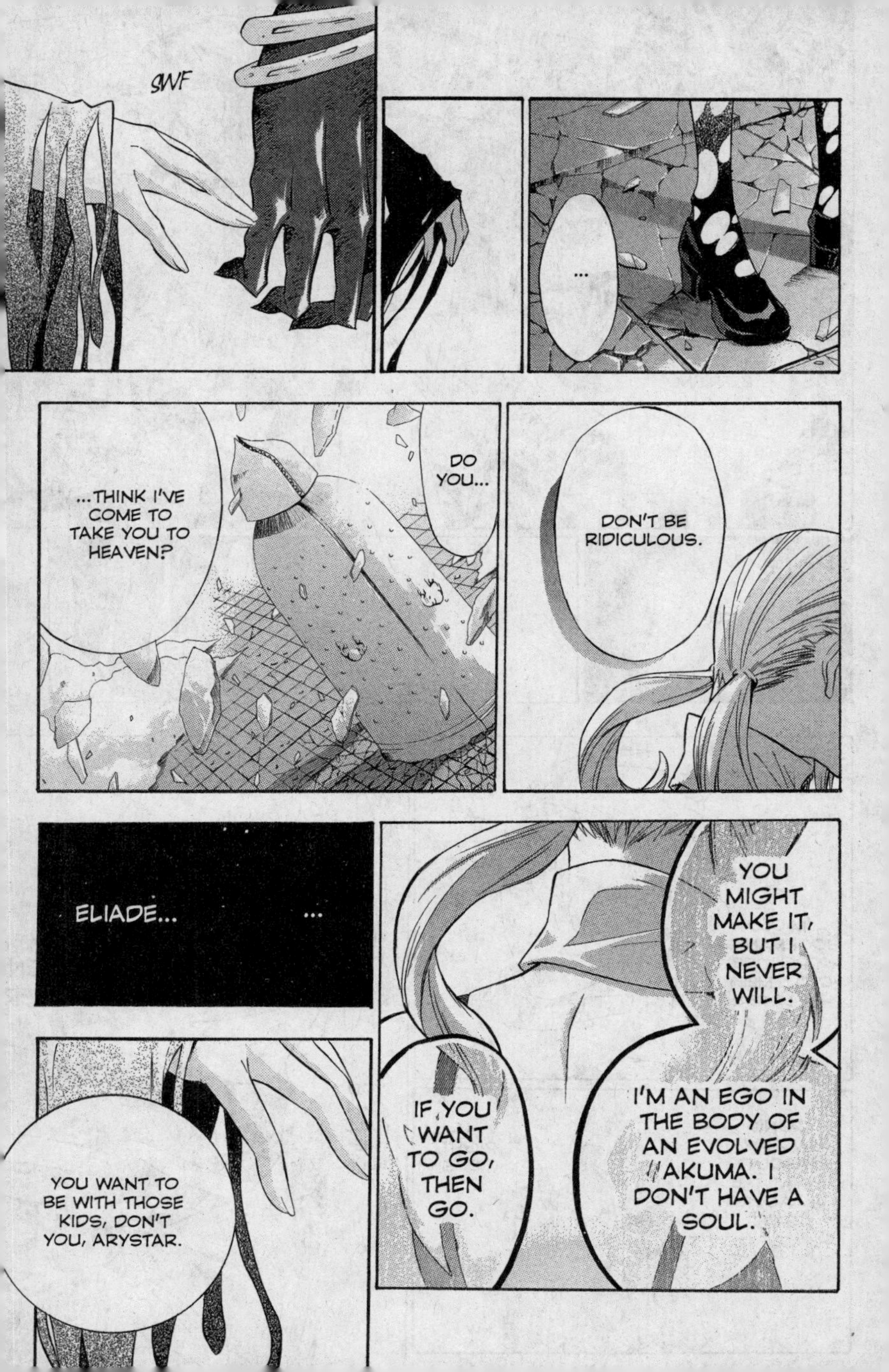
...
SWF
DON'T BE RIDICULOUS.
DO YOU...
...THINK I'VE COME TO TAKE YOU TO HEAVEN?
YOU MIGHT MAKE IT, BUT I NEVER WILL.
I'M AN EGO IN THE BODY OF AN EVOLVED AKUMA. I DON'T HAVE A SOUL.
IF YOU WANT TO GO, THEN GO.
...
ELIADE...
YOU WANT TO BE WITH THOSE KIDS, DON'T YOU, ARYSTAR.

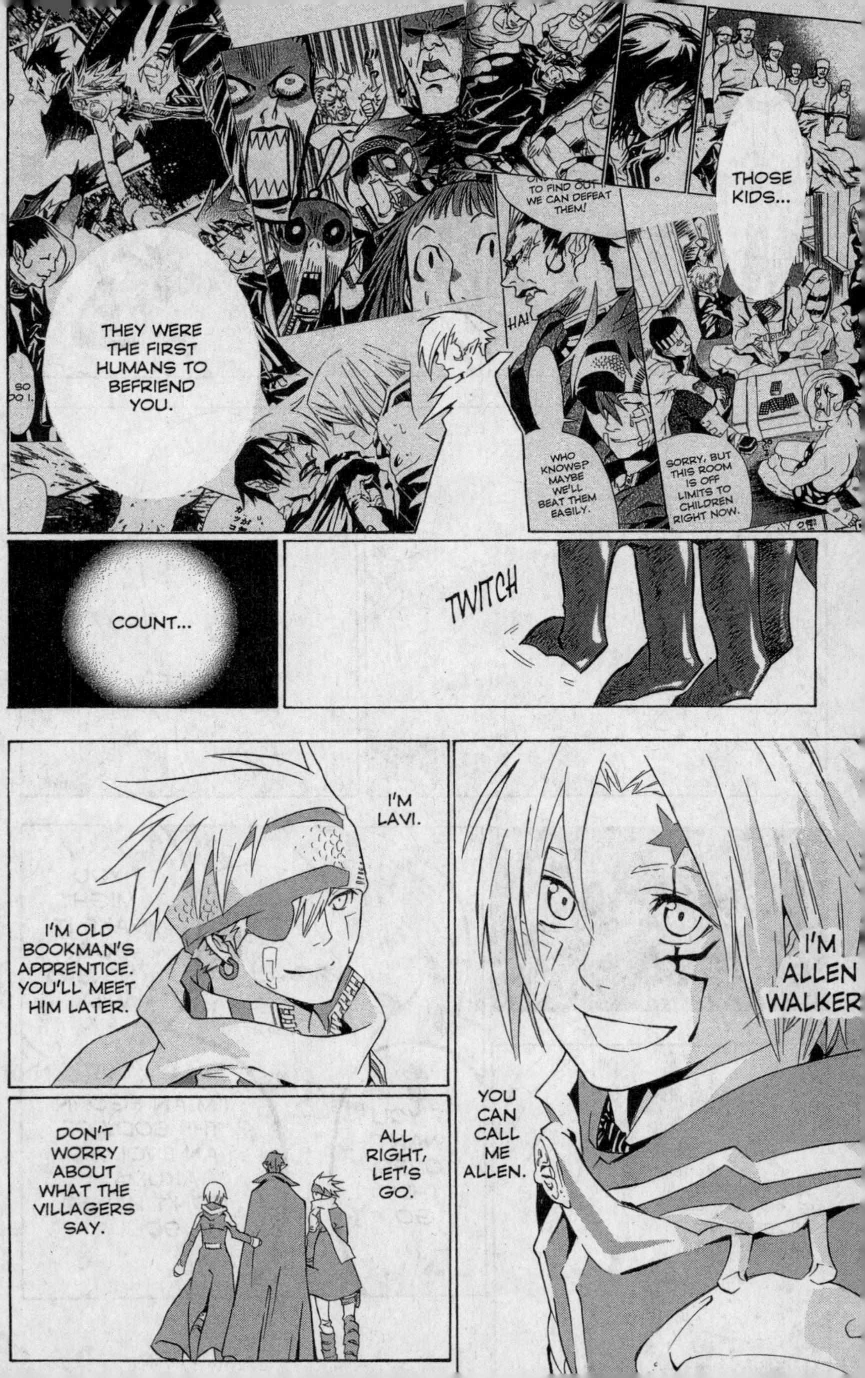
THOSE KIDS...
TO FIND OUT WE CAN DEFEAT THEM!
SORRY, BUT THIS ROOM IS OFF LIMITS TO CHILDREN RIGHT NOW.
WHO KNOWS? MAYBE WE'LL BEAT THEM EASILY.
HA!
THEY WERE THE FIRST HUMANS TO BEFRIEND YOU.
SO DO I.
TWITCH
COUNT...
I'M ALLEN WALKER
YOU CAN CALL ME ALLEN.
I'M LAVI.
I'M OLD BOOKMAN'S APPRENTICE. YOU'LL MEET HIM LATER.
ALL RIGHT, LET'S GO.
DON'T WORRY ABOUT WHAT THE VILLAGERS SAY.

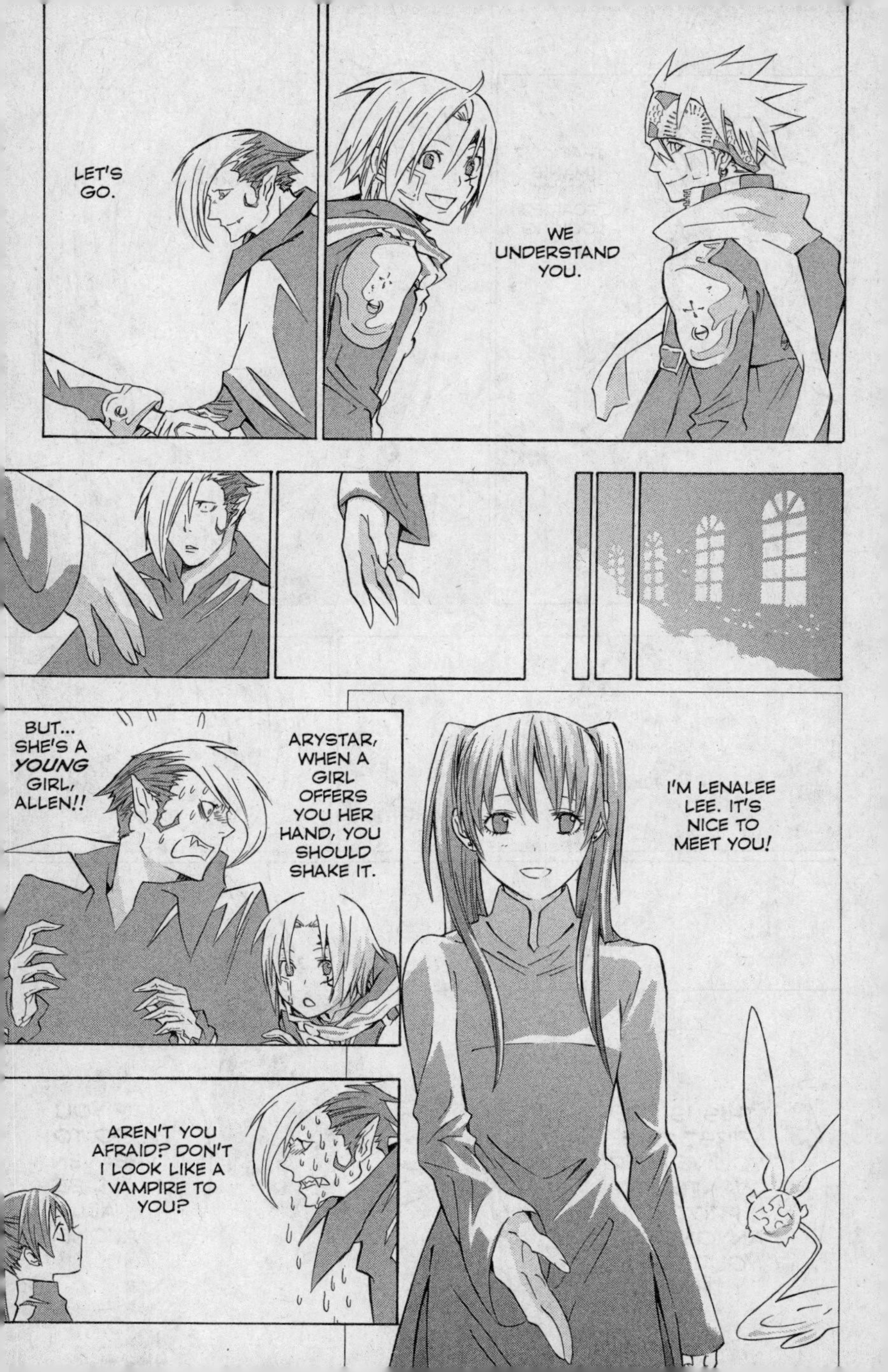

WE UNDERSTAND YOU.
LET'S GO.
I'M LENALEE LEE. IT'S NICE TO MEET YOU!
ARYSTAR, WHEN A GIRL OFFERS YOU HER HAND, YOU SHOULD SHAKE IT.
BUT... SHE'S A *YOUNG* GIRL, ALLEN!!
AREN'T YOU AFRAID? DON'T I LOOK LIKE A VAMPIRE TO YOU?

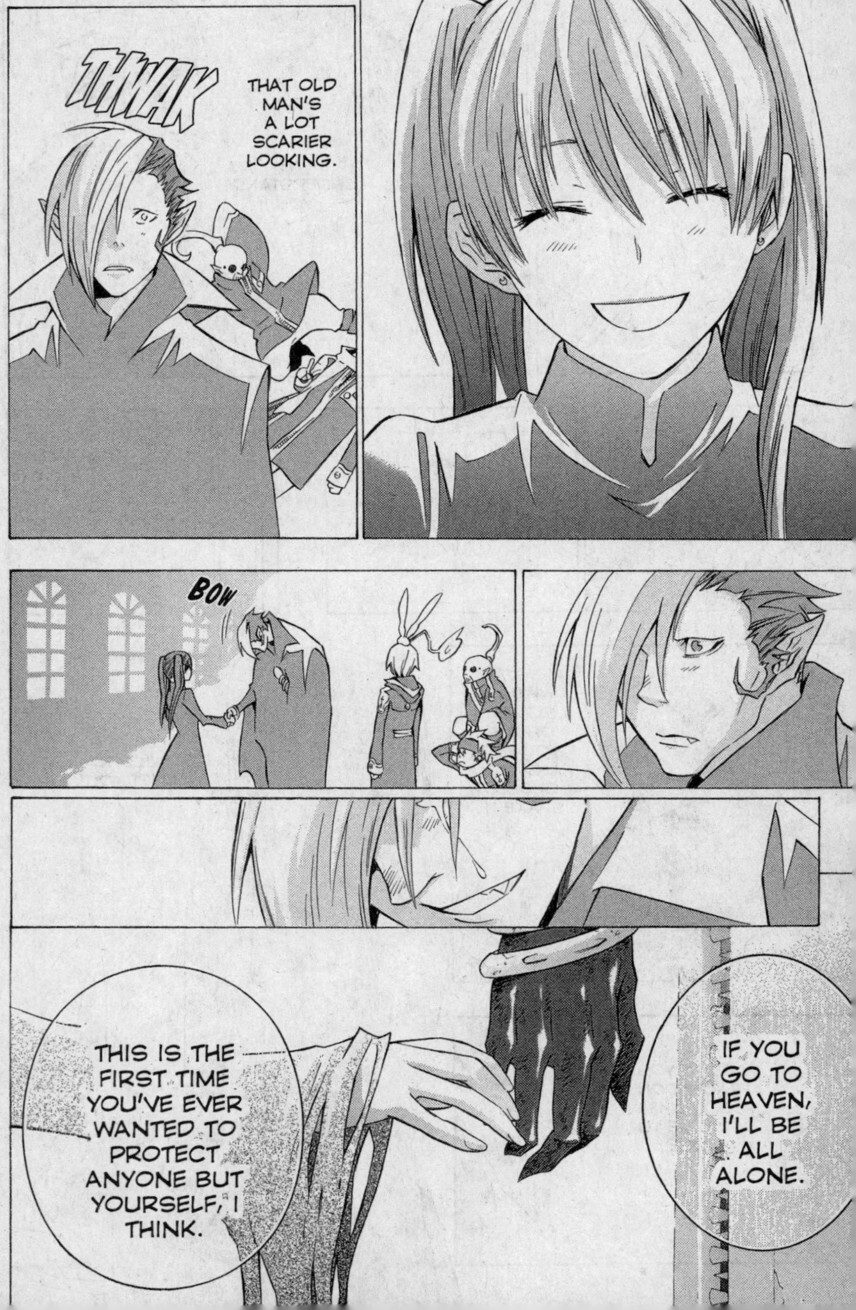
THWAK
THAT OLD MAN'S A LOT SCARIER LOOKING.
BOW
IF YOU GO TO HEAVEN, I'LL BE ALL ALONE.
THIS IS THE FIRST TIME YOU'VE EVER WANTED TO PROTECT ANYONE BUT YOURSELF, I THINK.

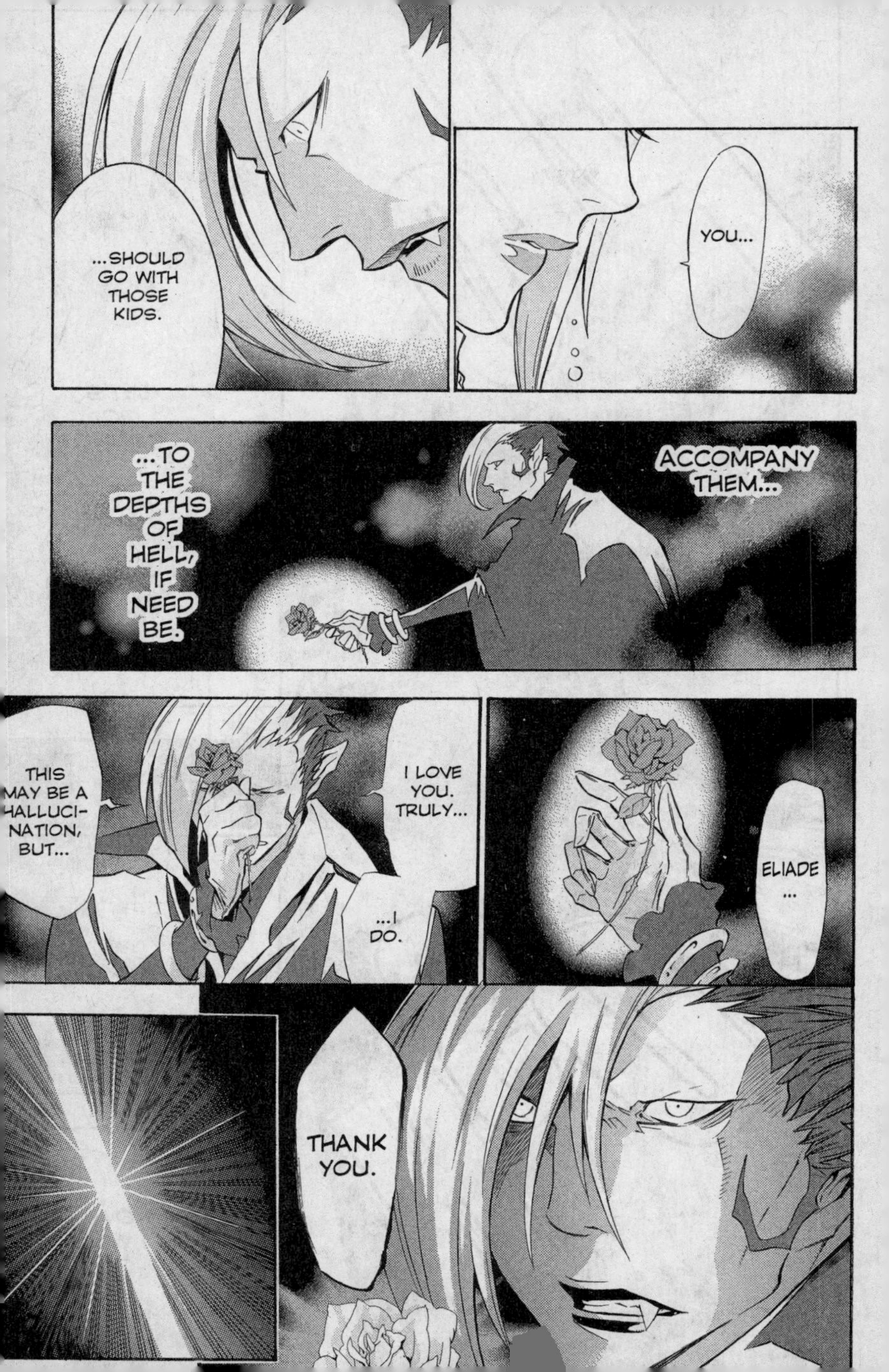
YOU...
...SHOULD GO WITH THOSE KIDS.
ACCOMPANY THEM...
...TO THE DEPTHS OF HELL, IF NEED BE.
ELIADE ...
THIS MAY BE A HALLUCINATION, BUT...
I LOVE YOU. TRULY...
...I DO.
THANK YOU.

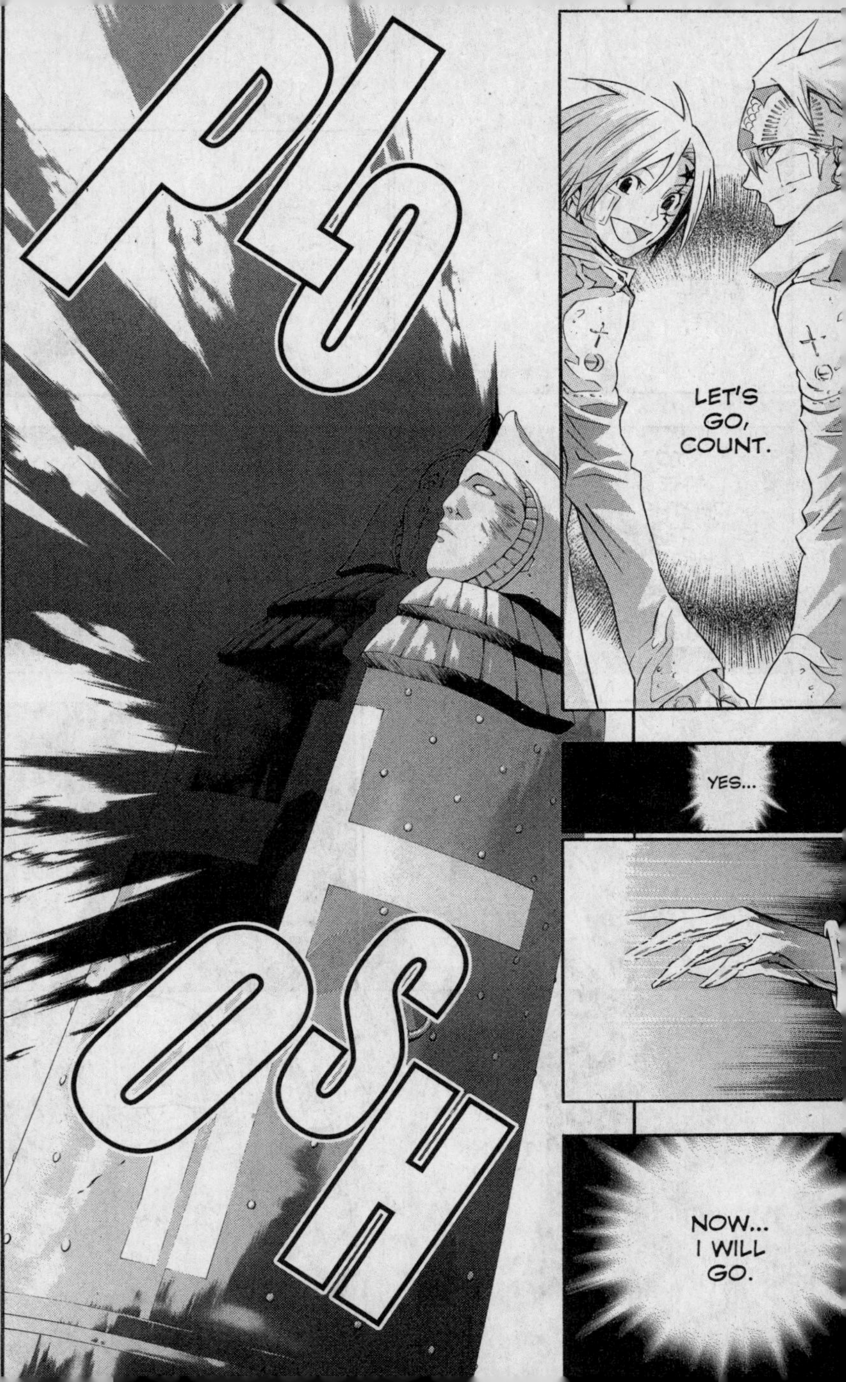
LET'S GO, COUNT.
YES...
NOW... I WILL GO.
PLOOSH

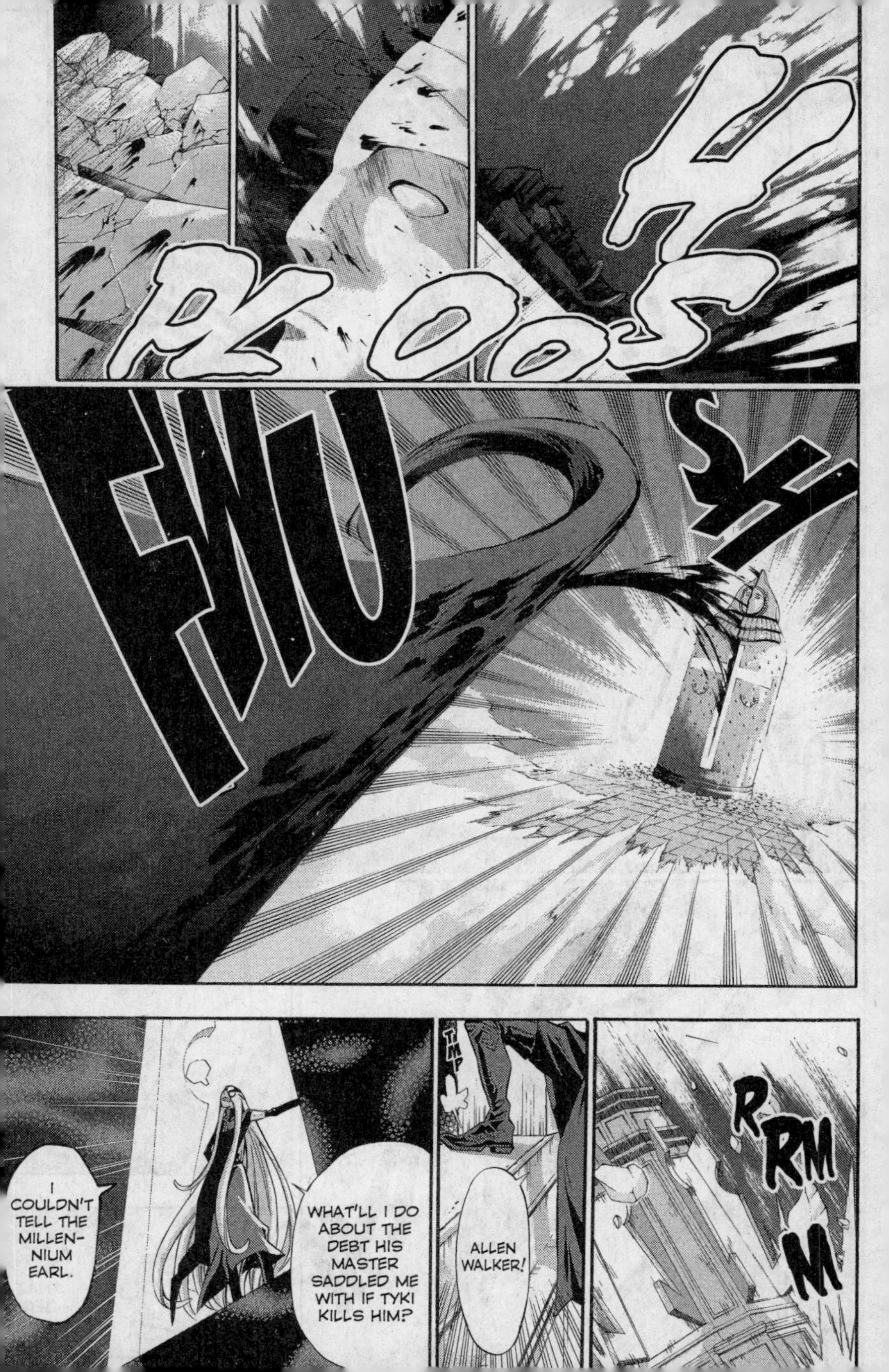
PKOOSH
FWUSH
RRMM
TMP
ALLEN WALKER!
WHAT'LL I DO ABOUT THE DEBT HIS MASTER SADDLED ME WITH IF TYKI KILLS HIM?
I COULDN'T TELL THE MILLEN-NIUM EARL.

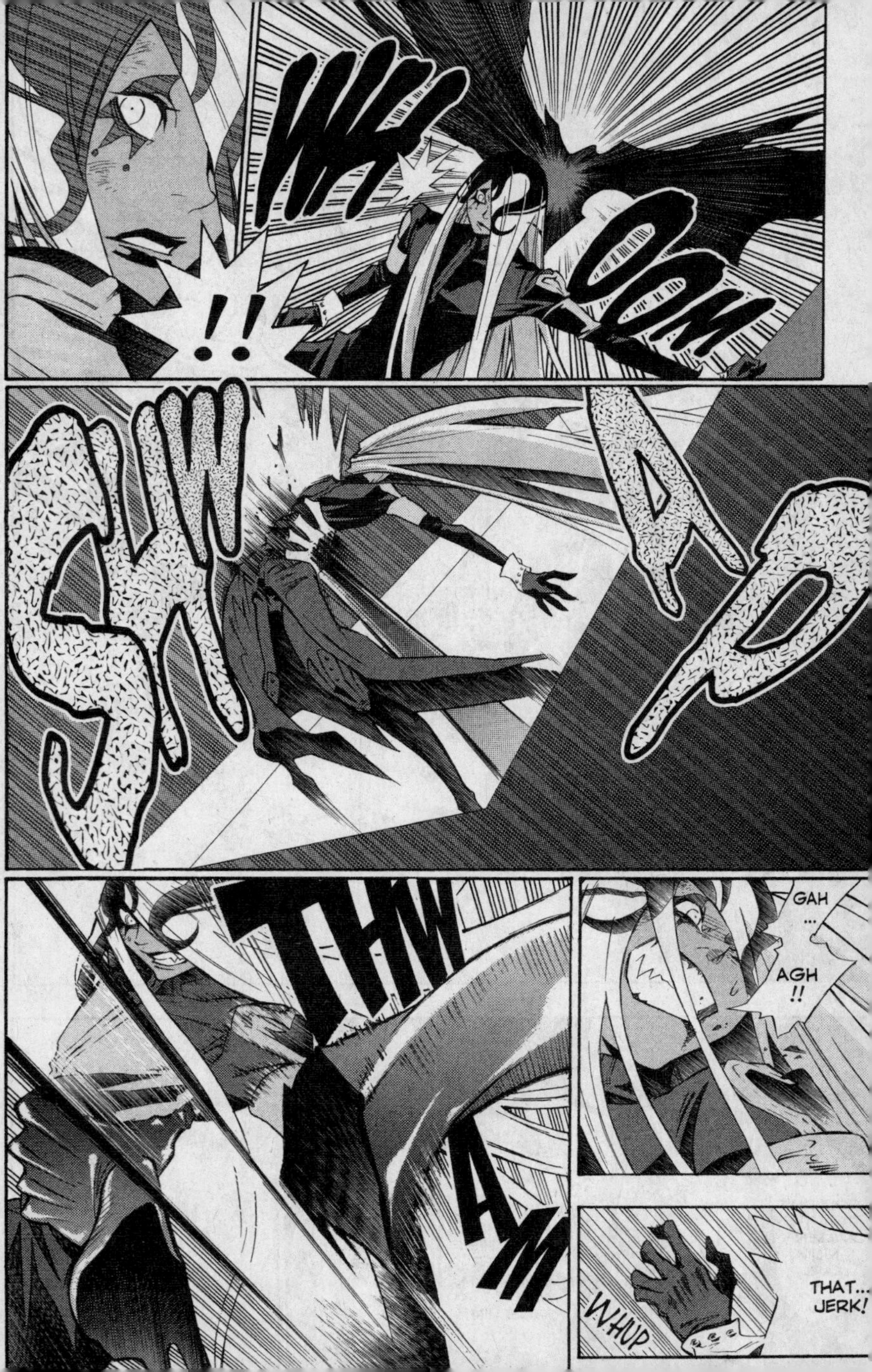
WHOOM
!!
GAH... AGH!!
THAT... JERK!
WHUP
THWAM

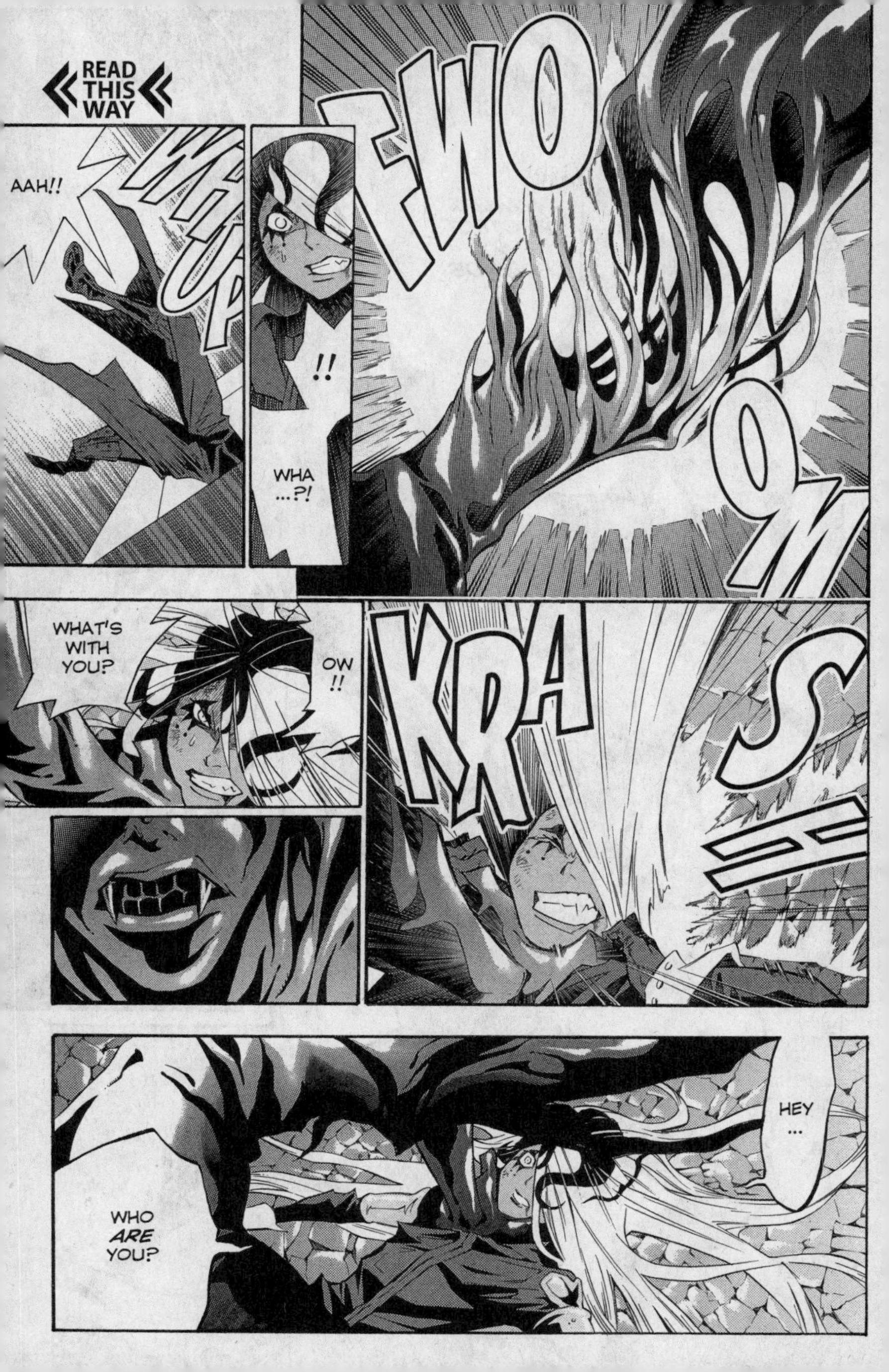

READ THIS WAY
FWOOM
!!
WHA ...?!
WHUP
AAH!!
KRASH
OW !!
WHAT'S WITH YOU?
HEY ...
WHO *ARE* YOU?

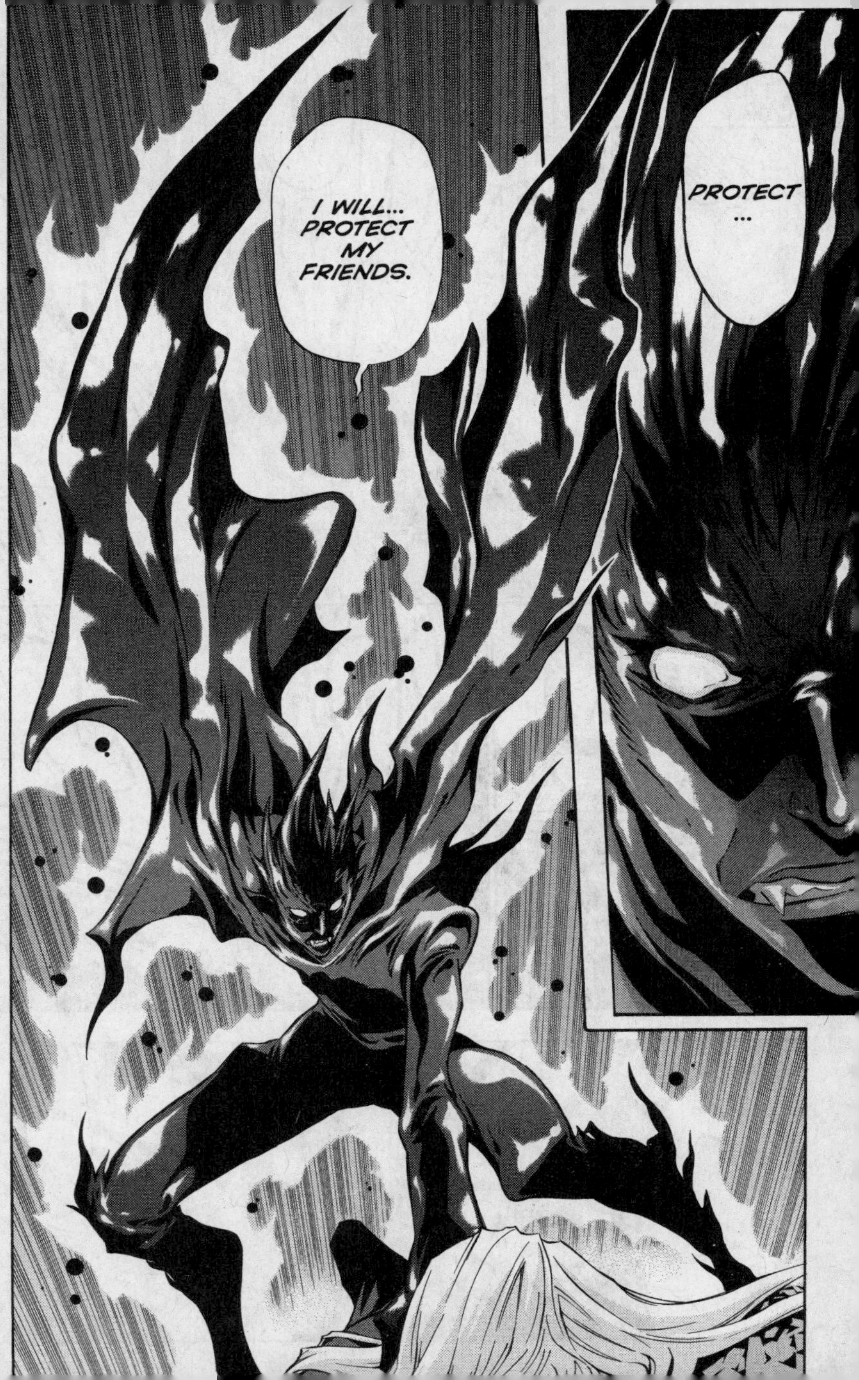
PROTECT ...
I WILL... PROTECT MY FRIENDS.

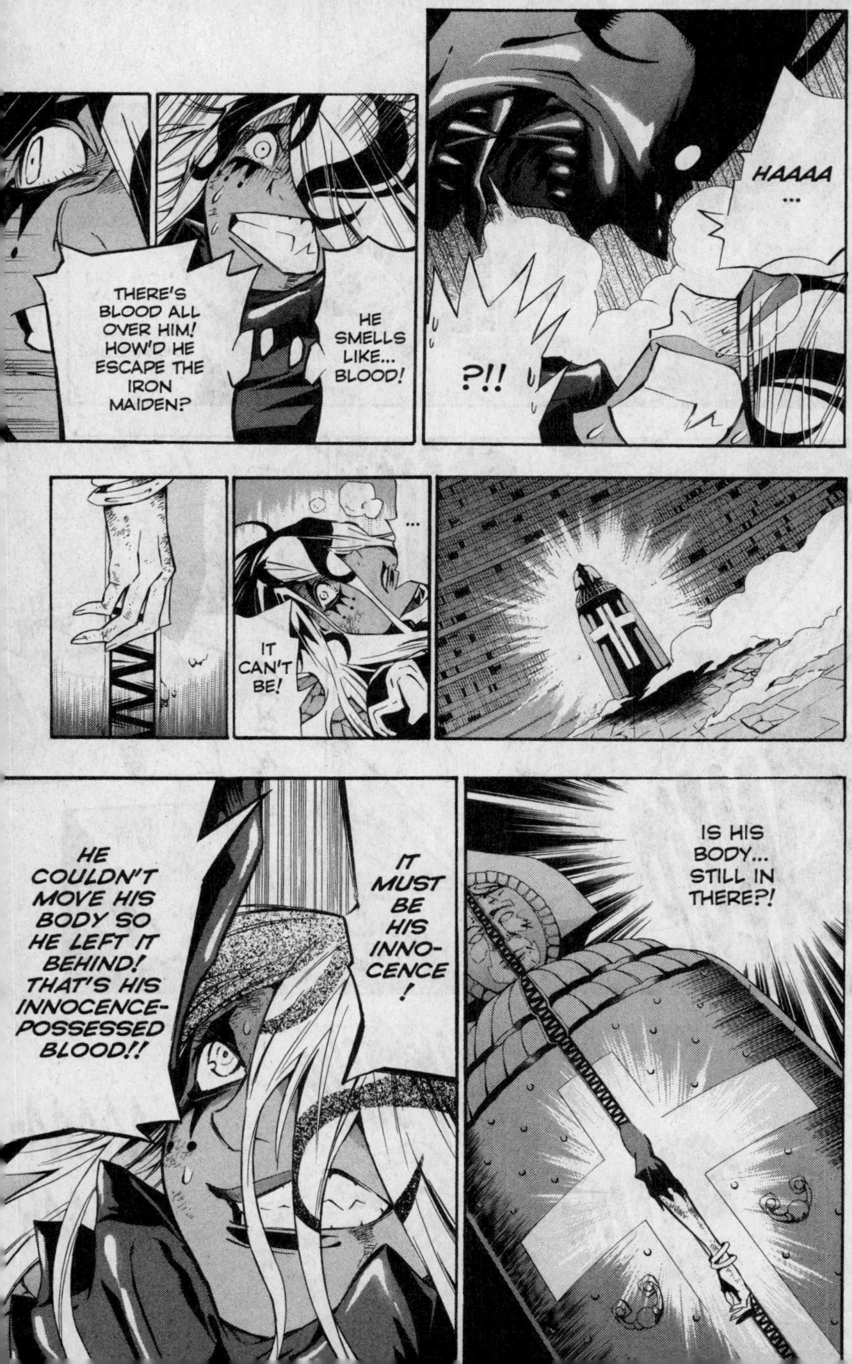
HAAAA ...
?!!
HE SMELLS LIKE... BLOOD!
THERE'S BLOOD ALL OVER HIM! HOW'D HE ESCAPE THE IRON MAIDEN?
...
IT CAN'T BE!
IS HIS BODY... STILL IN THERE?!
IT MUST BE HIS INNOCENCE!
HE COULDN'T MOVE HIS BODY SO HE LEFT IT BEHIND! THAT'S HIS INNOCENCE-POSSESSED BLOOD!!

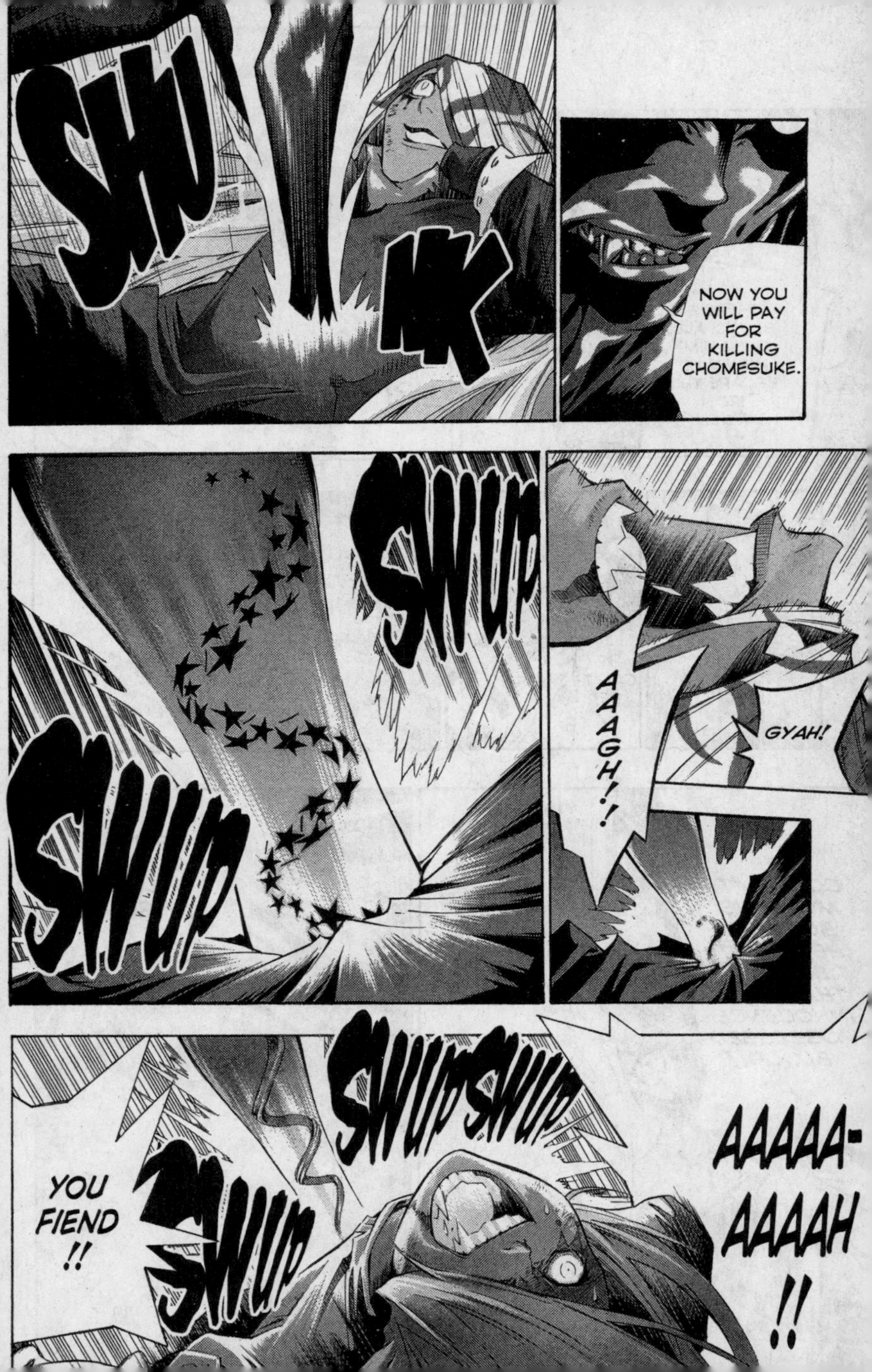
NOW YOU WILL PAY FOR KILLING CHOMESUKE.
SHU
NK
AAAGH!!
GYAH!
SWUP
SWUP
AAAAA-AAAAH!!
SWUP SWUP
SWUP
YOU FIEND!!

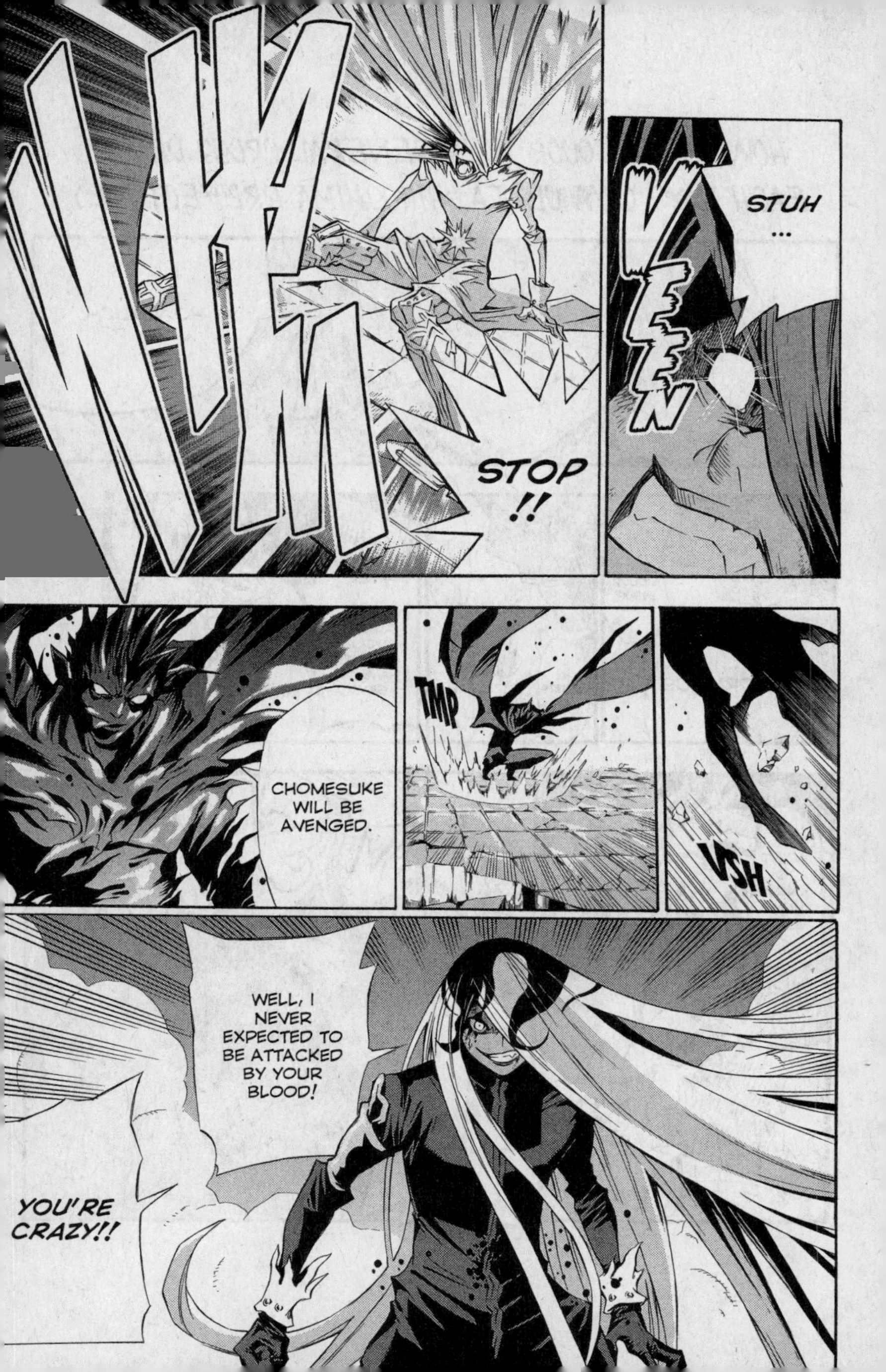
STUH ...
VEEEN
WHAM
STOP !!
VSH
TMP
CHOMESUKE WILL BE AVENGED.
WELL, I NEVER EXPECTED TO BE ATTACKED BY YOUR BLOOD!
YOU'RE CRAZY!!

HOW MUCH LIQUOR DOES GENERAL CROSS DRINK EACH DAY? (AYA UBATA, HIROSHIMA PREFECTURE)

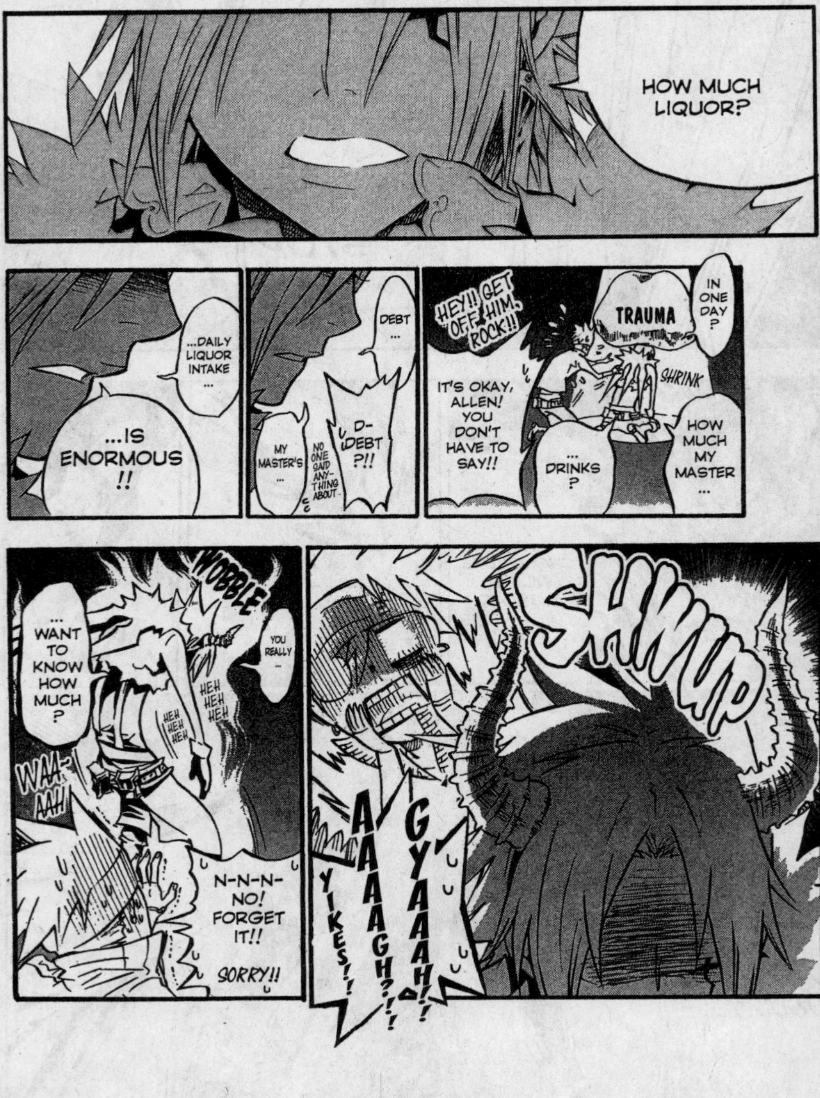
HOW MUCH LIQUOR?
IN ONE DAY?
TRAUMA
SHRINK
HOW MUCH MY MASTER...
...DRINKS?
HEY!! GET OFF HIM, ROCK!!
IT'S OKAY, ALLEN! YOU DON'T HAVE TO SAY!!
DEBT...
D-DEBT?!!
NO ONE SAID ANYTHING ABOUT-
MY MASTER'S...
...DAILY LIQUOR INTAKE...
...IS ENORMOUS!!
SHNUP
GYAAAAH!!
AAAAAGH?!!
YIKES!!
YOU REALLY...
WOBBLE
...WANT TO KNOW HOW MUCH?
HEH HEH HEH
HEH HEH HEH
WAA-AAH
N-N-N-NO! FORGET IT!!
SORRY!!

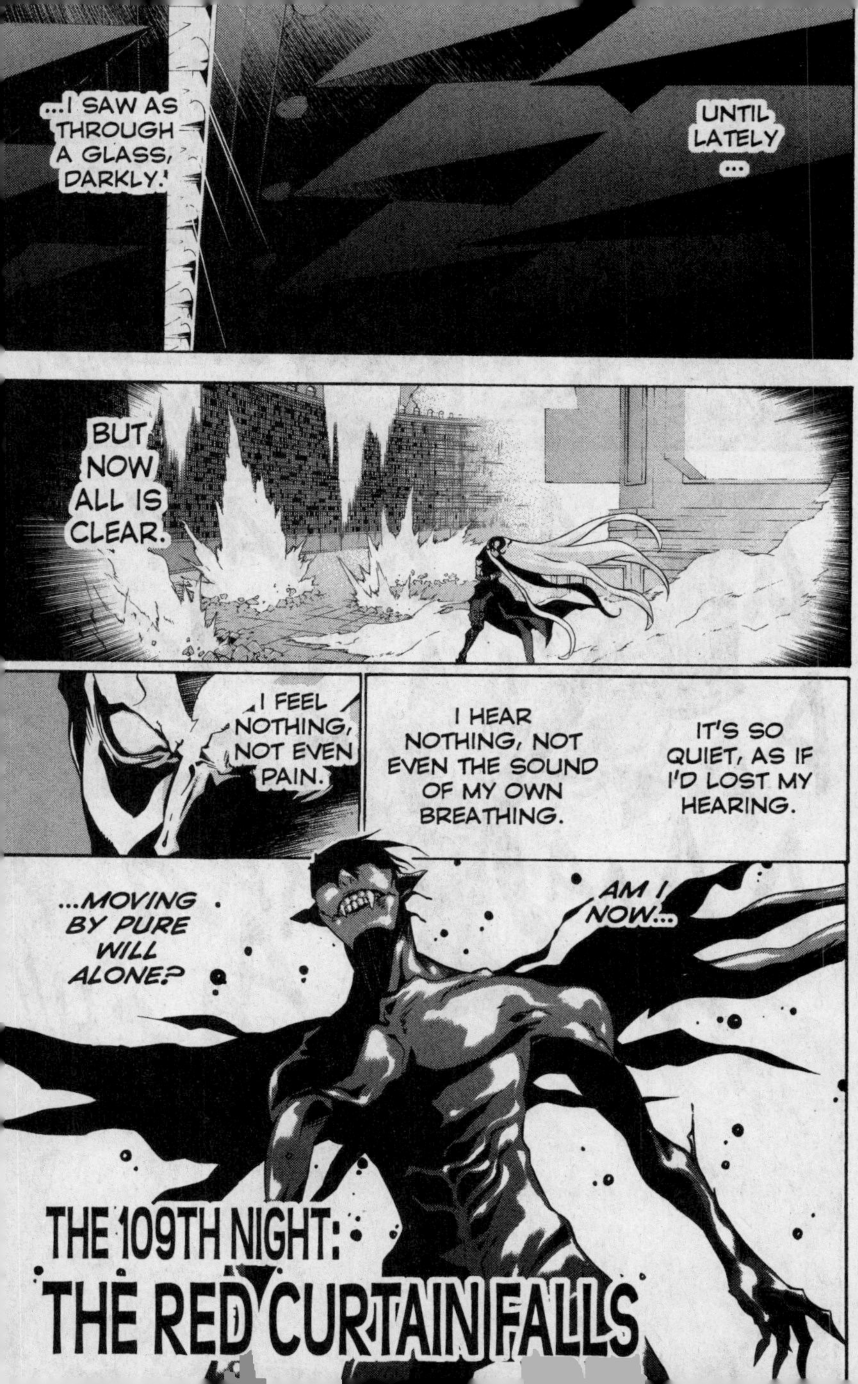
UNTIL LATELY...
...I SAW AS THROUGH A GLASS, DARKLY.
BUT NOW ALL IS CLEAR.
IT'S SO QUIET, AS IF I'D LOST MY HEARING.
I HEAR NOTHING, NOT EVEN THE SOUND OF MY OWN BREATHING.
I FEEL NOTHING, NOT EVEN PAIN.
AM I NOW...
...MOVING BY PURE WILL ALONE?

THE 109TH NIGHT: THE RED CURTAIN FALLS

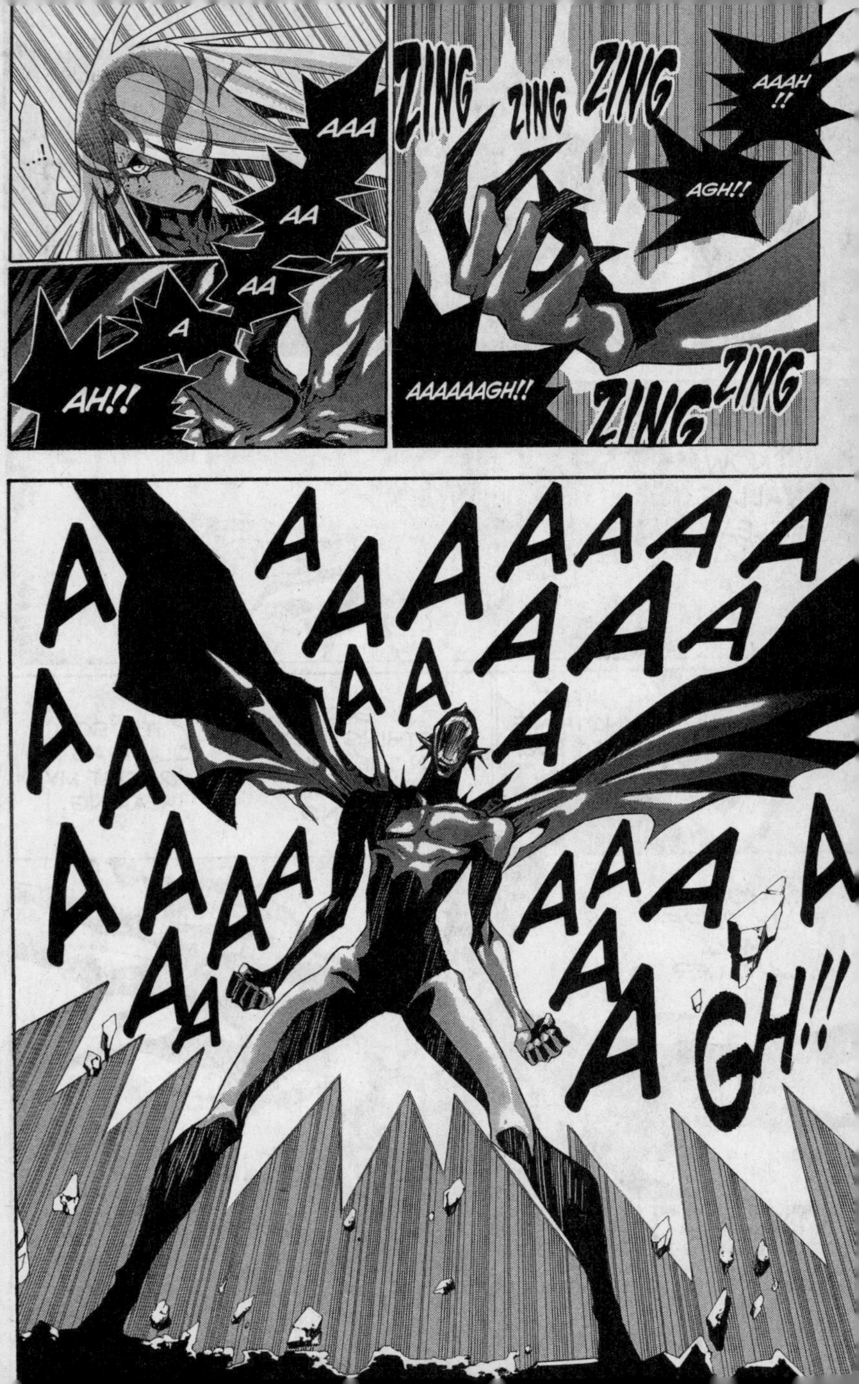

AAAH!!
AGH!!
ZING ZING ZING
AAAAAAGH!!
ZING ZING
...!
AAA
AA
AA
A
AH!!
AAAAAAAAAAAAAAAAAAAAAAAAAAAAAGH!!

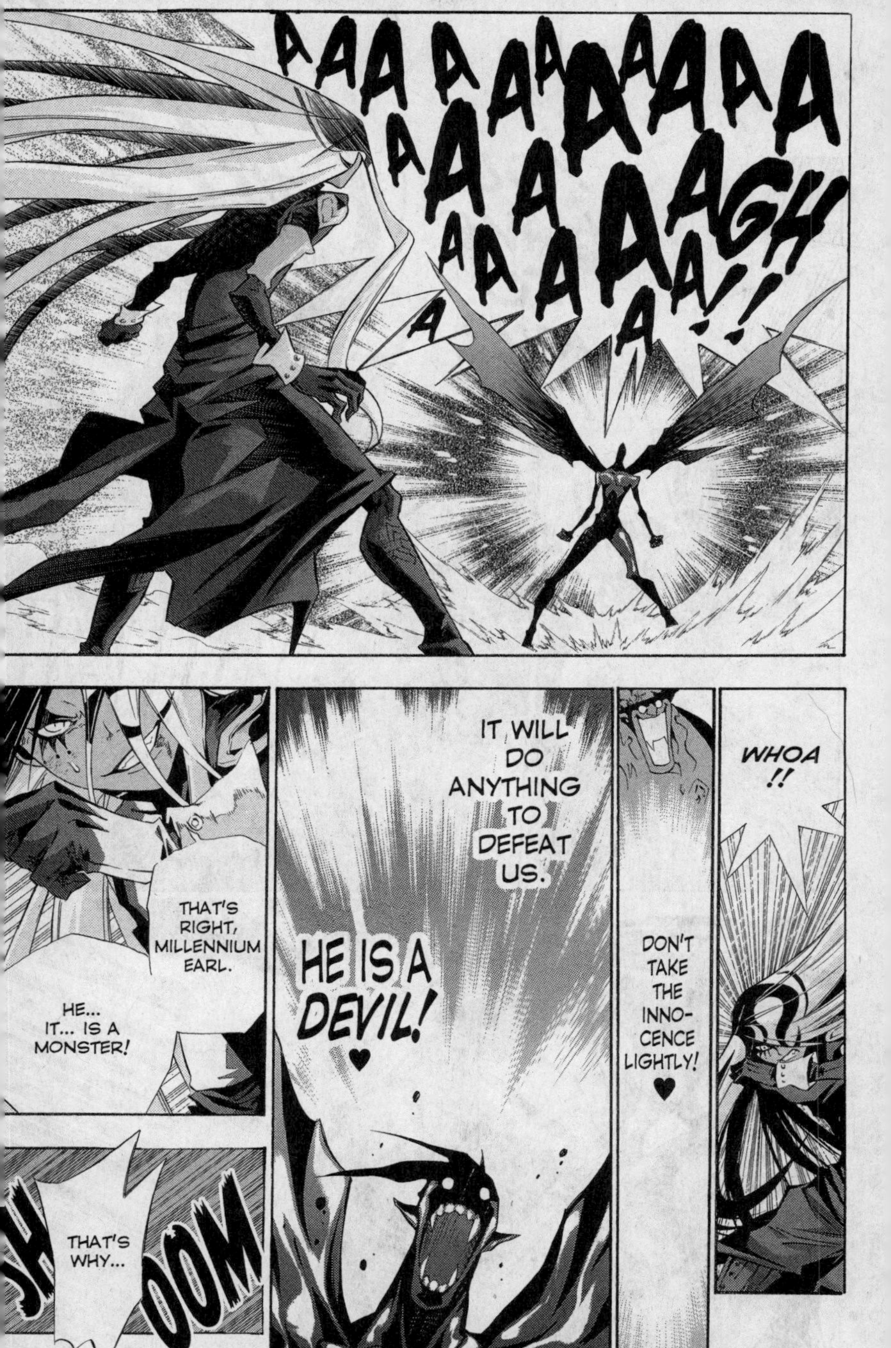
AAAAAAAAAAAAAAAAAAAAAAAAAAAAAGH!!
WHOA !!
DON'T TAKE THE INNOCENCE LIGHTLY! ♥
IT WILL DO ANYTHING TO DEFEAT US.
HE IS A DEVIL! ♥
THAT'S RIGHT, MILLENNIUM EARL.
HE... IT... IS A MONSTER!
THAT'S WHY...
SH
OOM

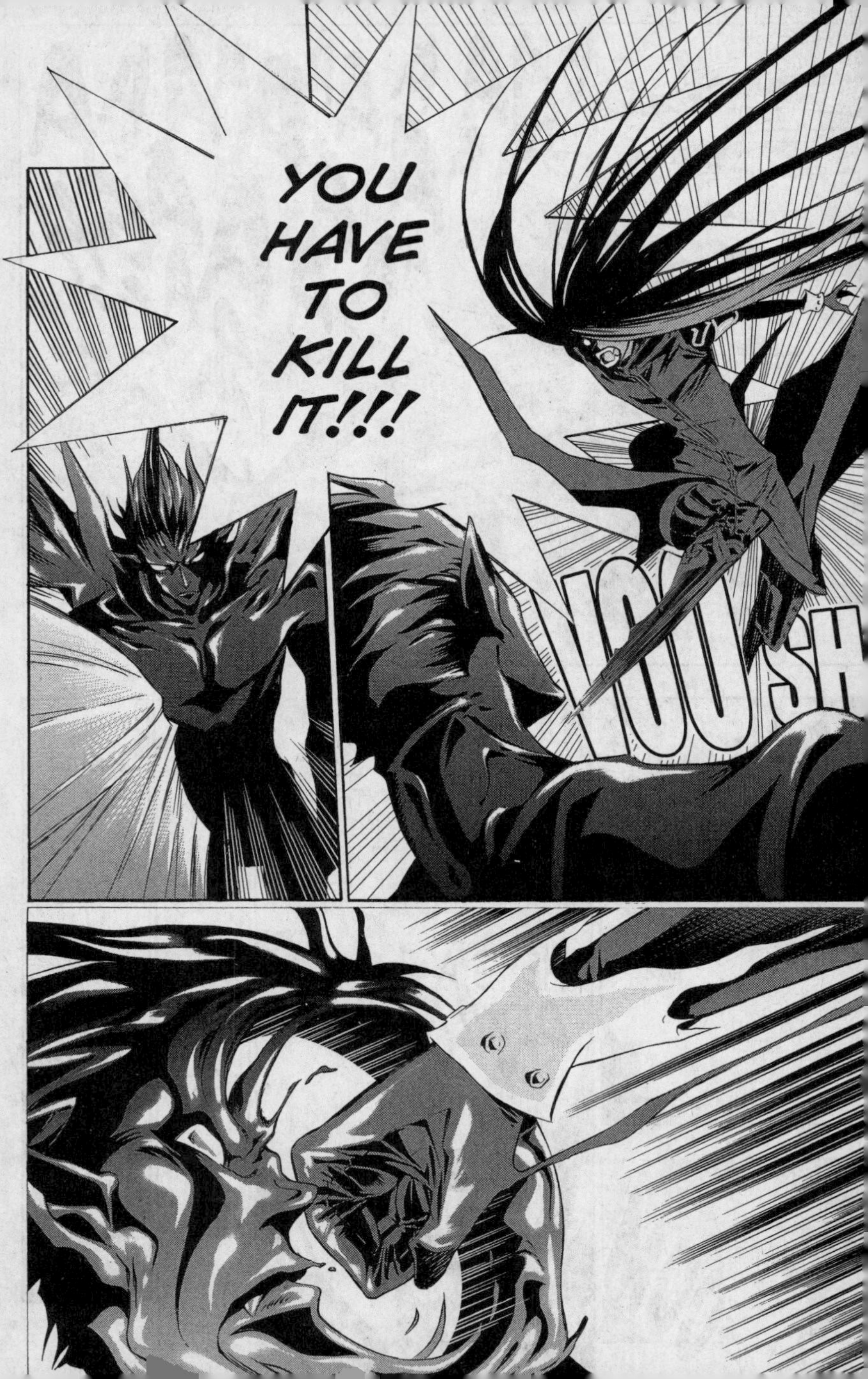
YOU HAVE TO KILL IT!!!

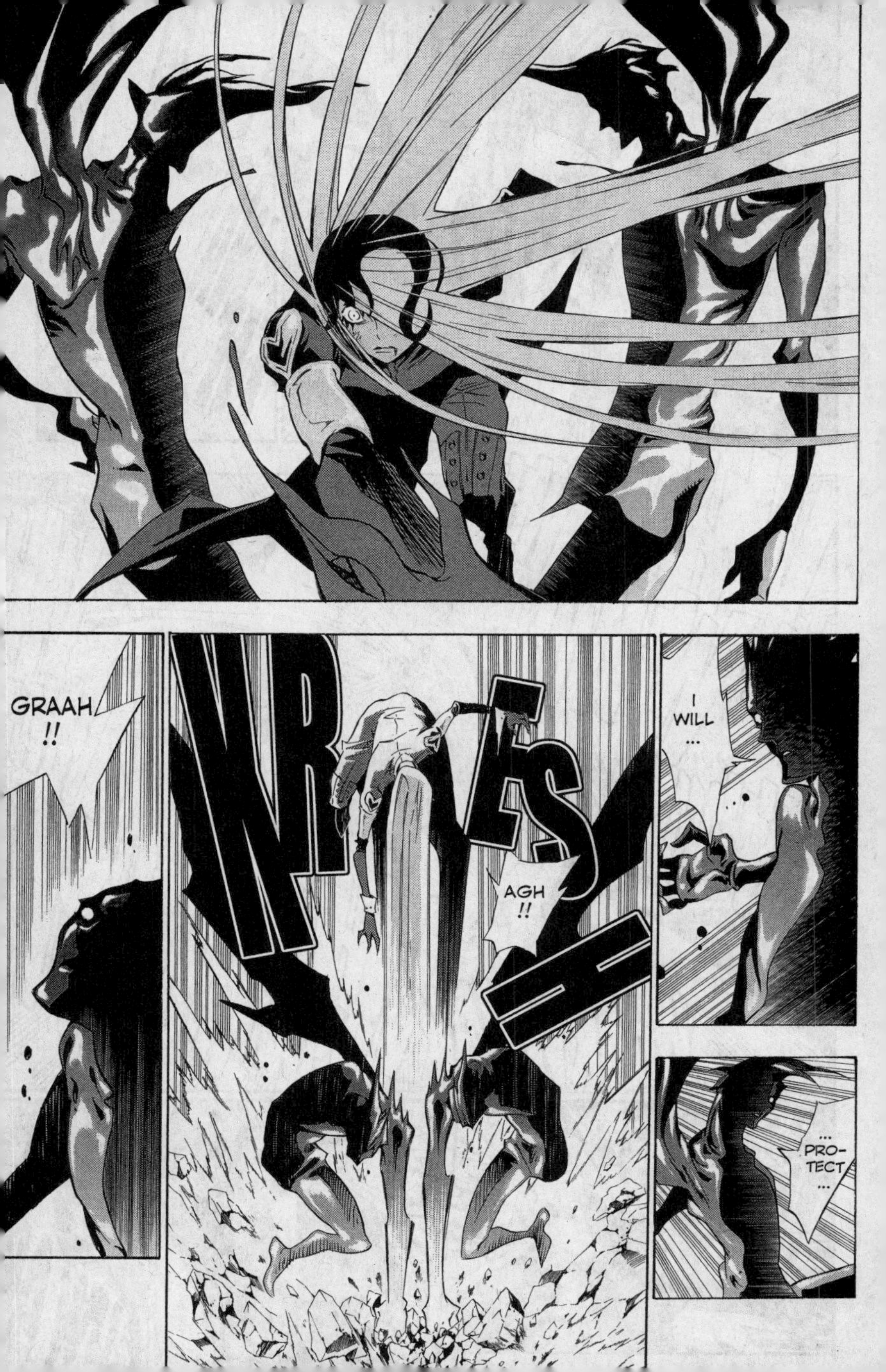
I WILL ...
... PRO-TECT ...
AGH !!
GRAAH !!

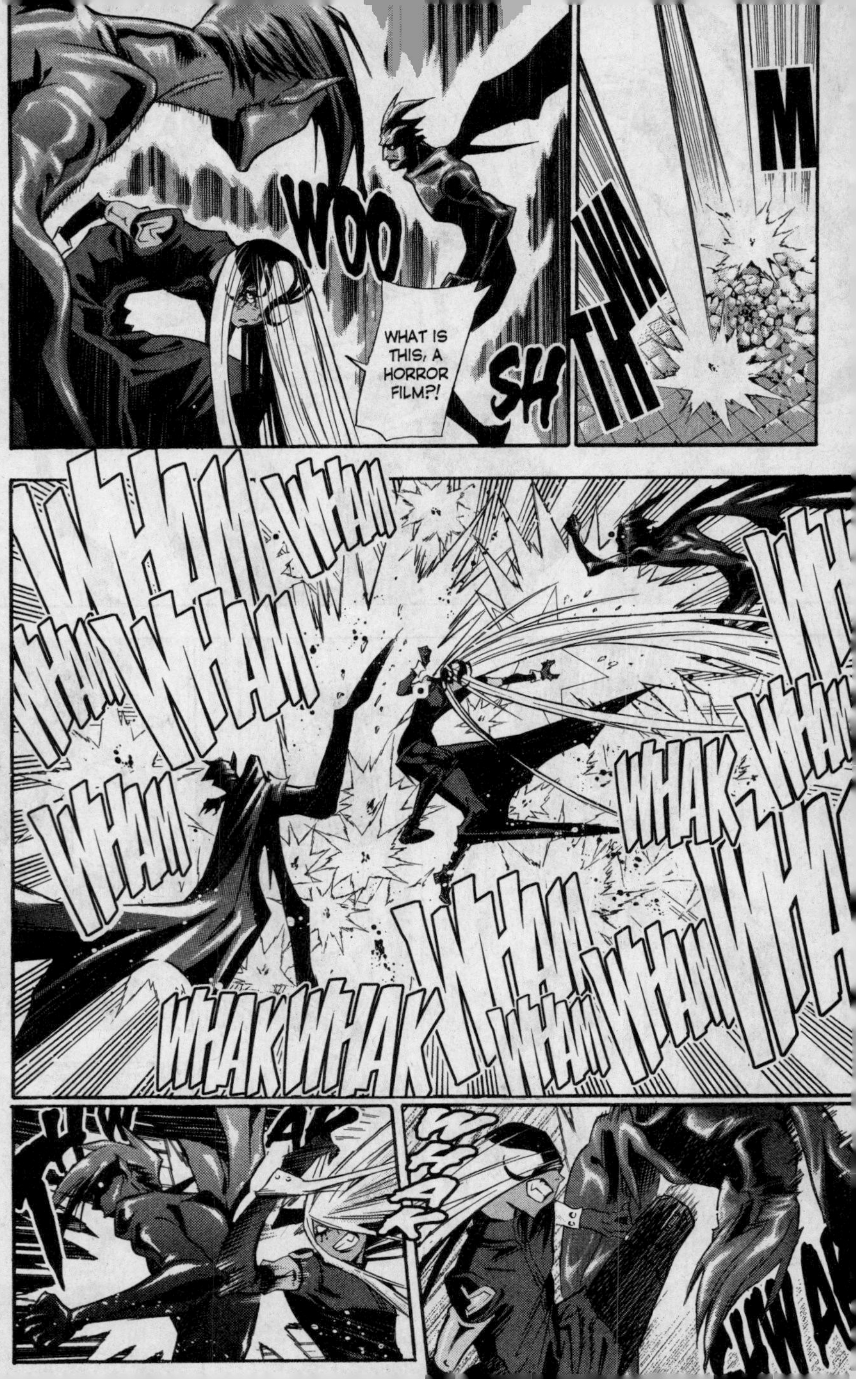
M
WHA
TH
WOO
SH
WHAT IS THIS, A HORROR FILM?!
WHAK
WHAM
WHAM
WHAM
WHAM
WHAM
WHAM
WHAM
WHAKWHAK

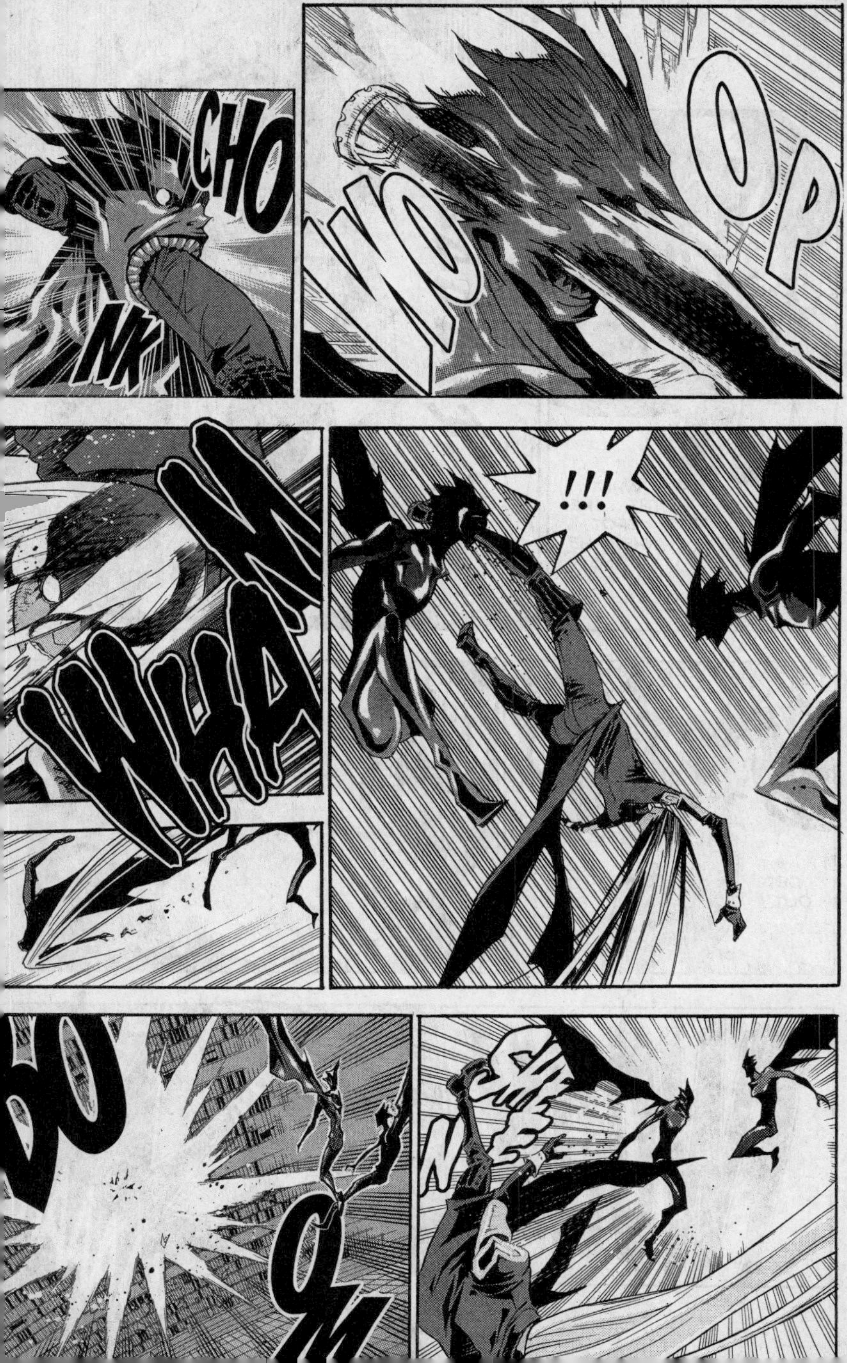
WOOP
CHONK
!!!
WHAM
SHEEN
BOOM

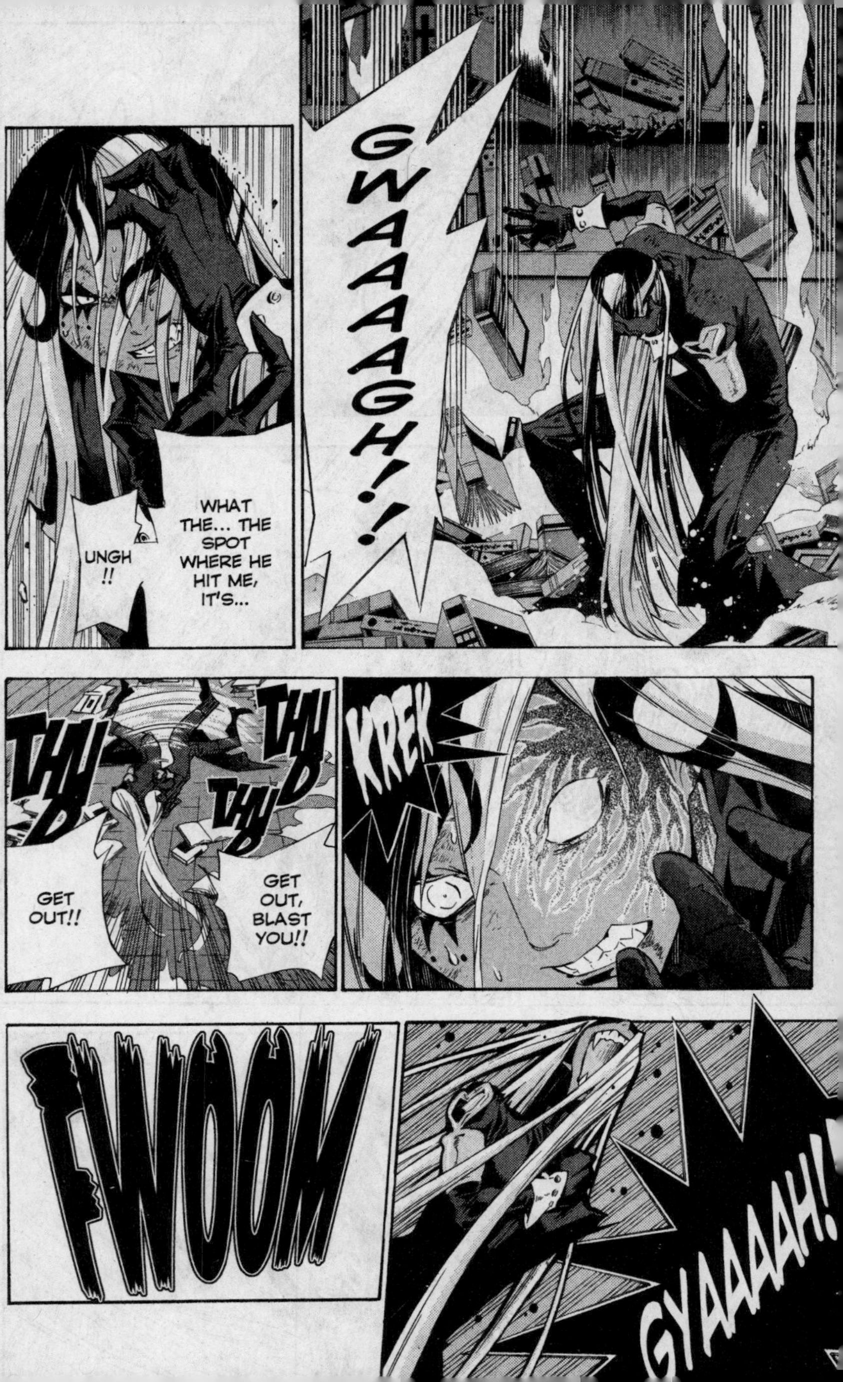
GWAAAAAGH!!
WHAT THE... THE SPOT WHERE HE HIT ME, IT'S...
UNGH !!
KREK
THUD
THUD
THUD
GET OUT, BLAST YOU!!
GET OUT!!
GYAAAAH!
FWOOM

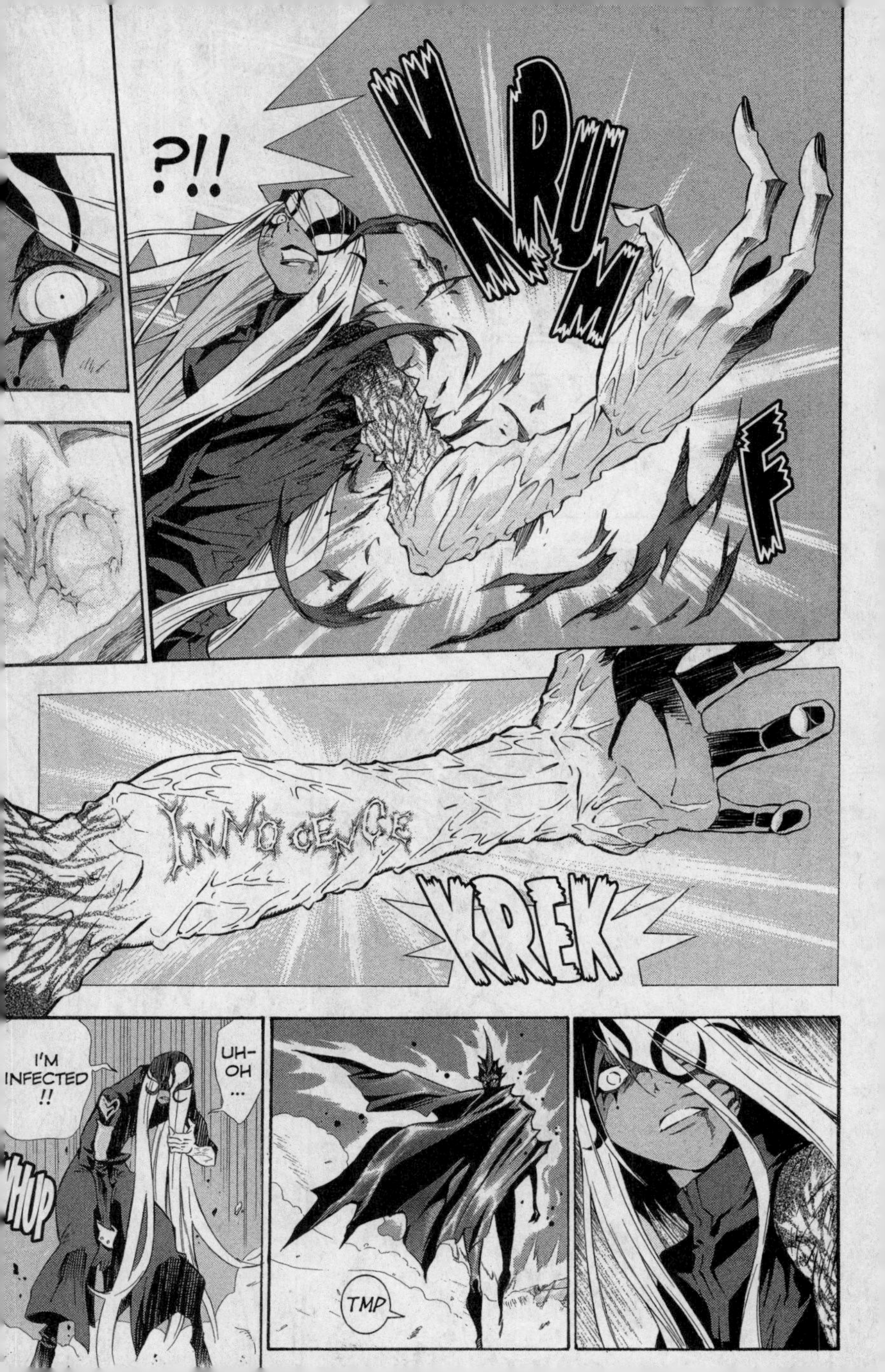

VRUMF
?!!
INNOCENCE
KREK
TMP
UH-OH ...
I'M INFECTED !!
WHUP

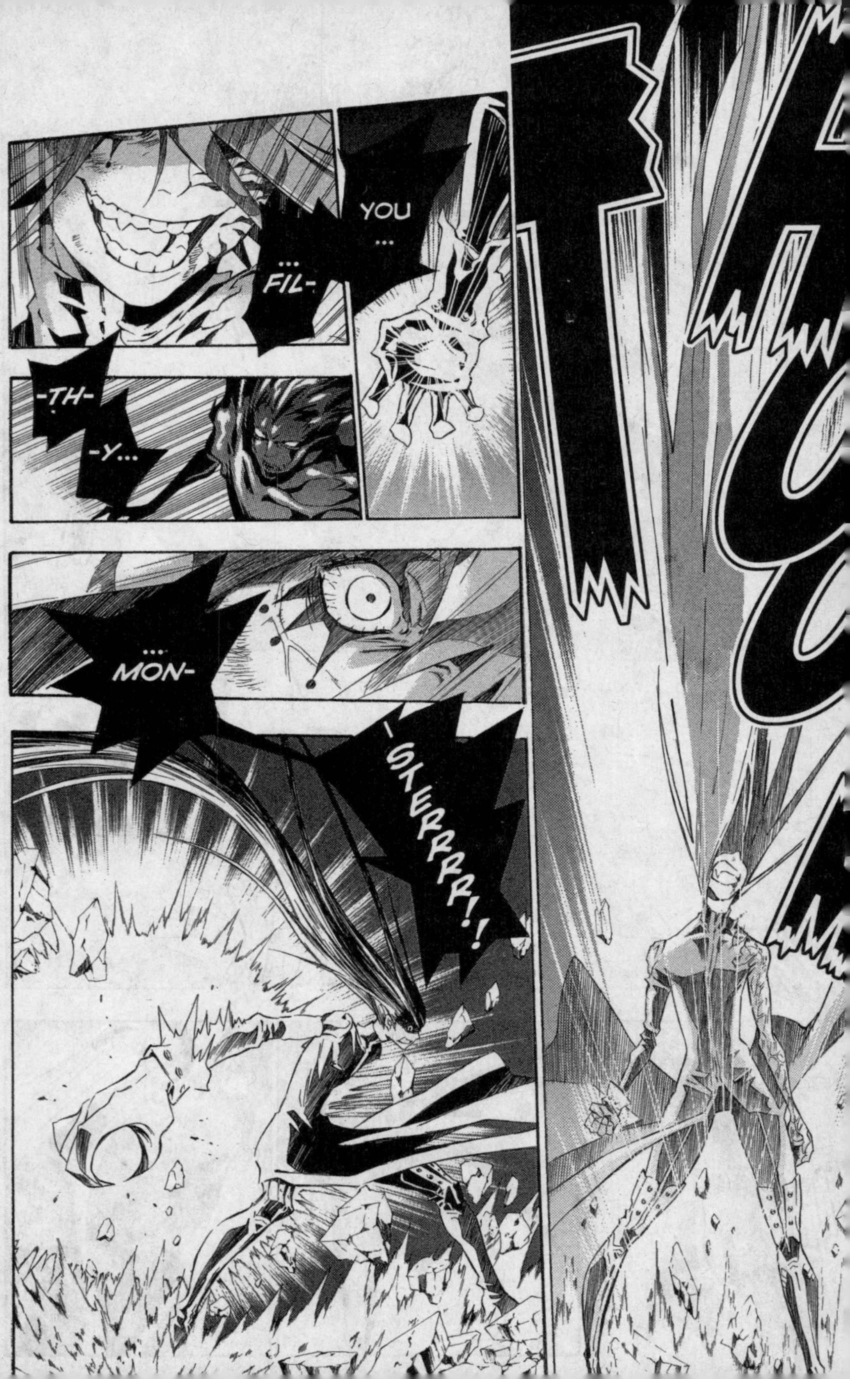
YOU ...
... FIL-
-TH-
-Y...
... MON-
-STERRRR!!

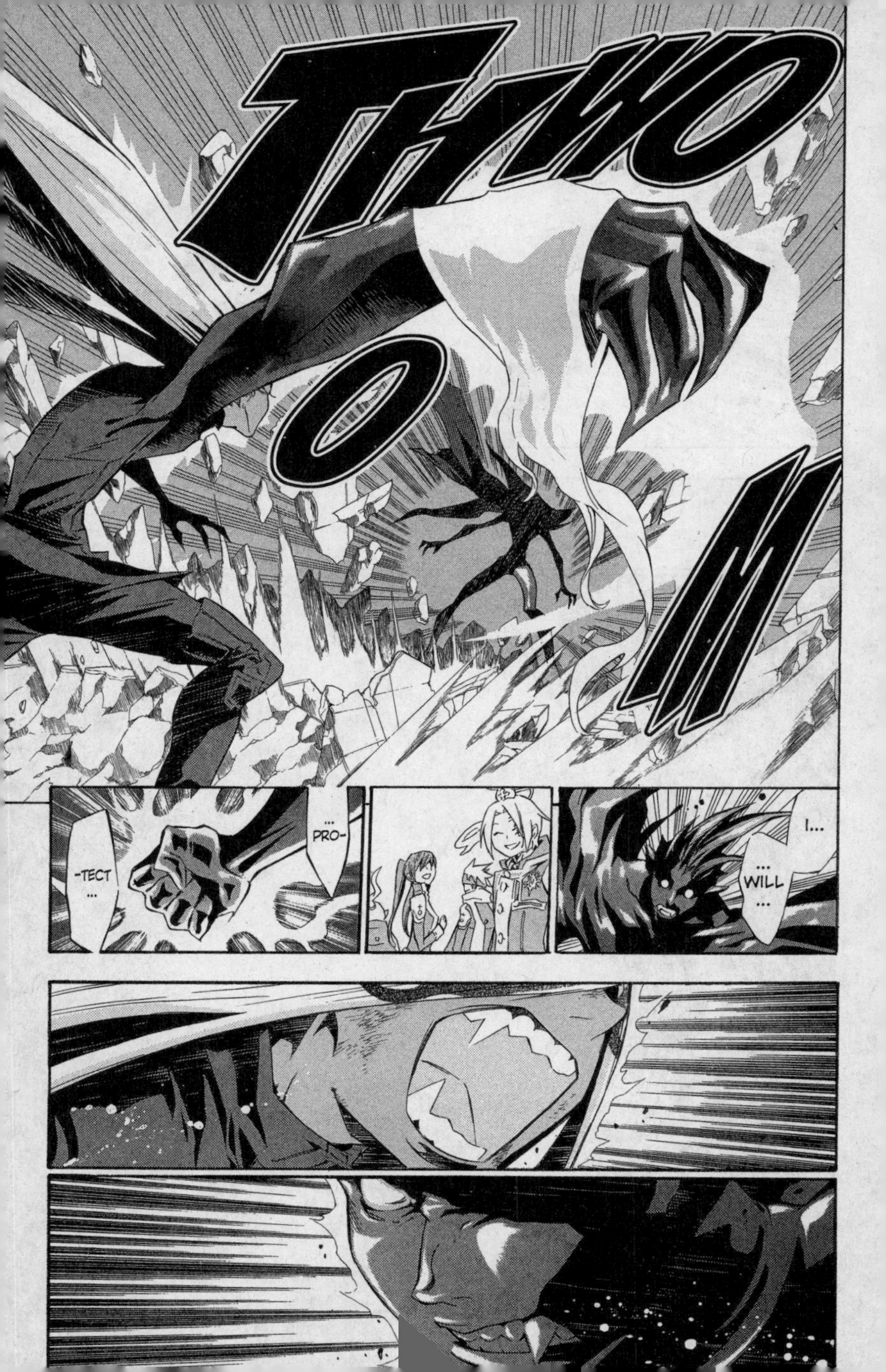
THOOM
I...
... WILL ...
... PRO-
-TECT ...

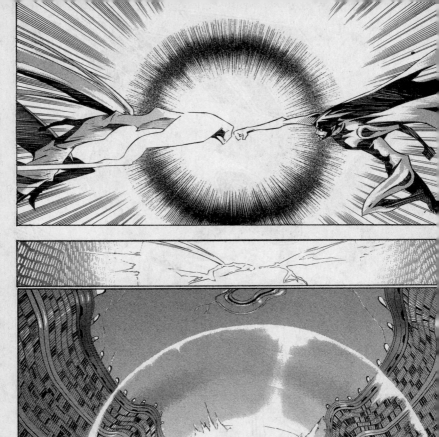

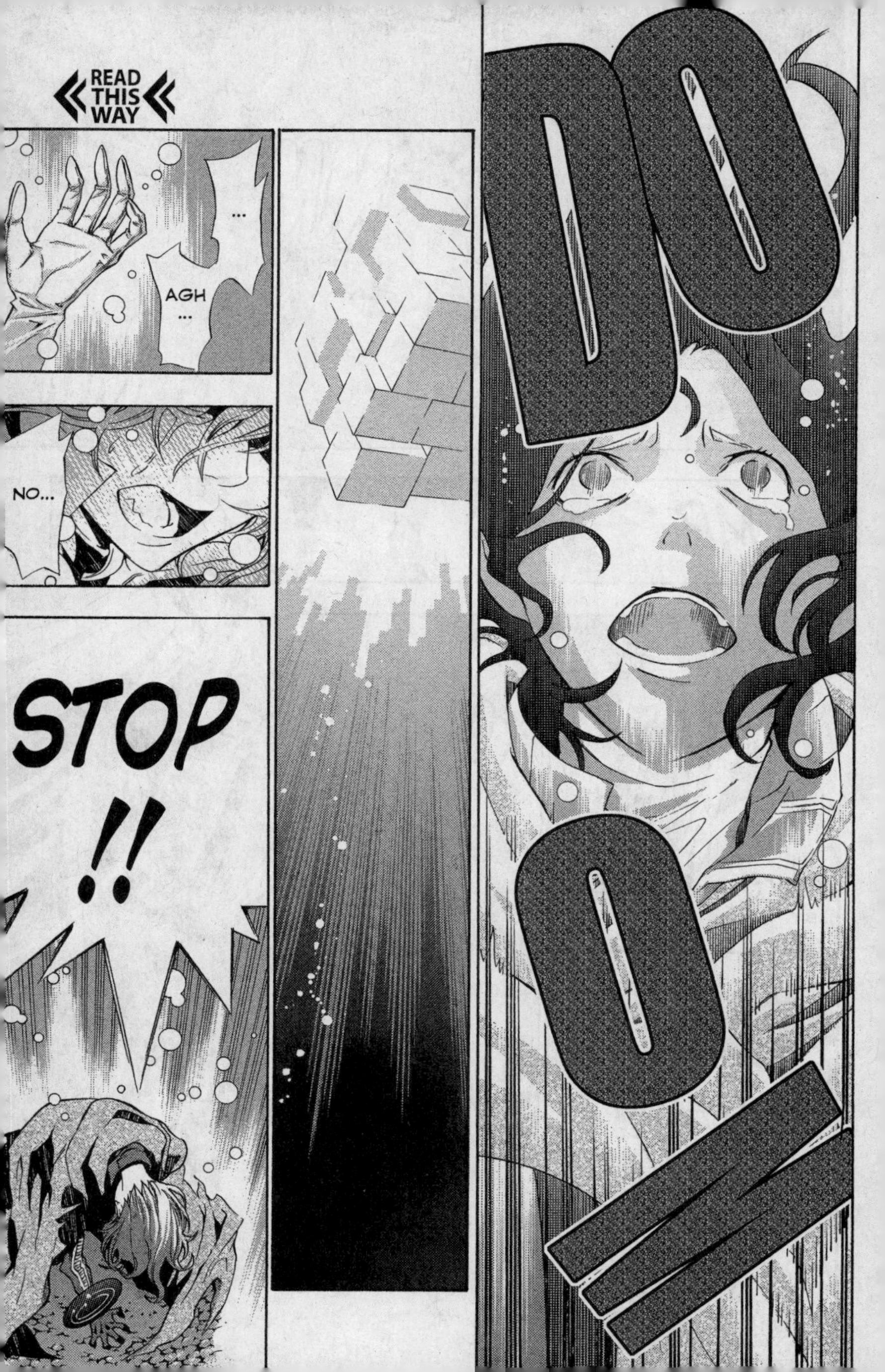
DOO
READ THIS WAY
...
AGH ...
NO...
STOP!!

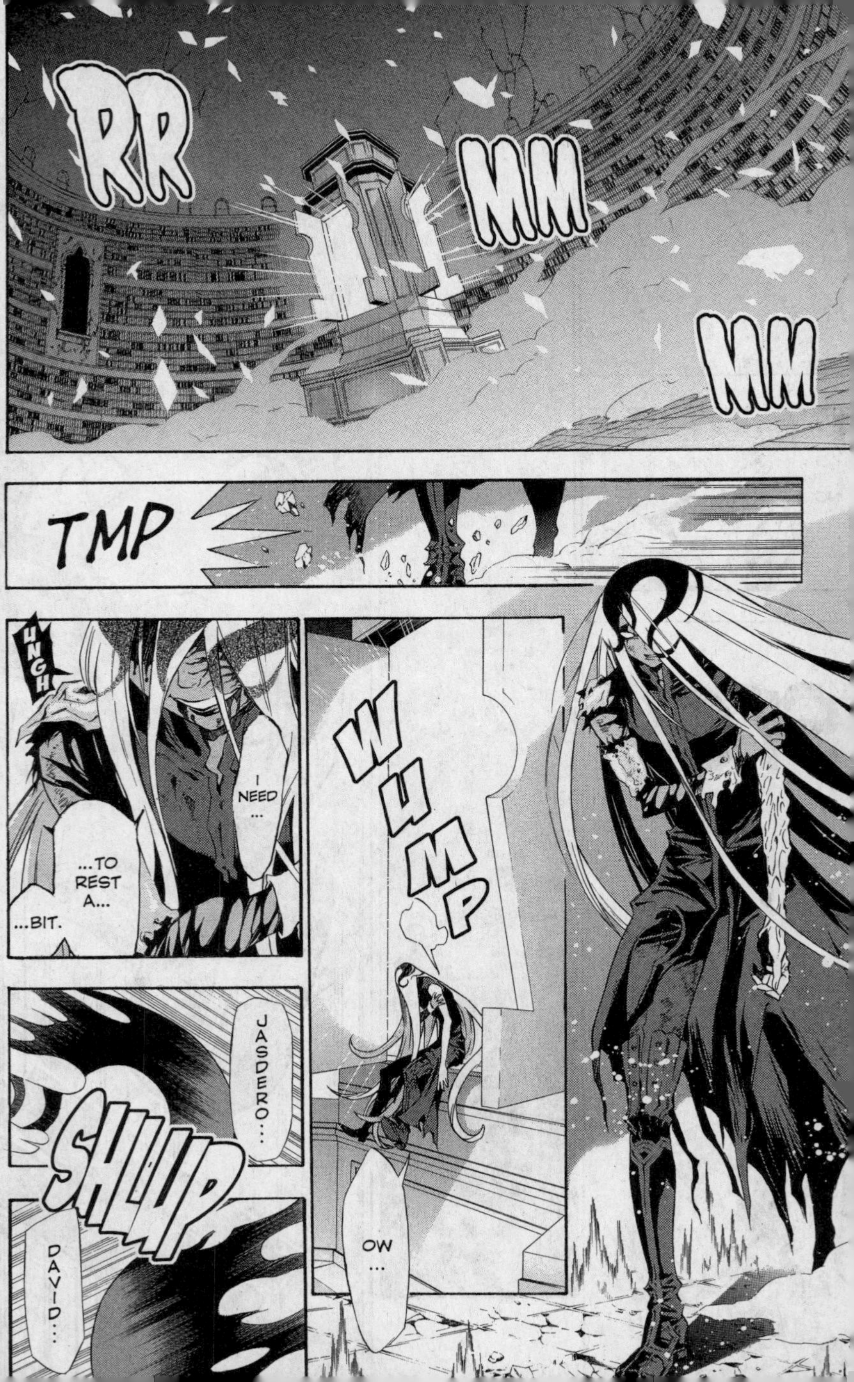
RR
MM
MM
TMP
WUMP
OW...
UNGH
I NEED...
...TO REST A...
...BIT.
JASDERO...
SHLIP
DAVID...

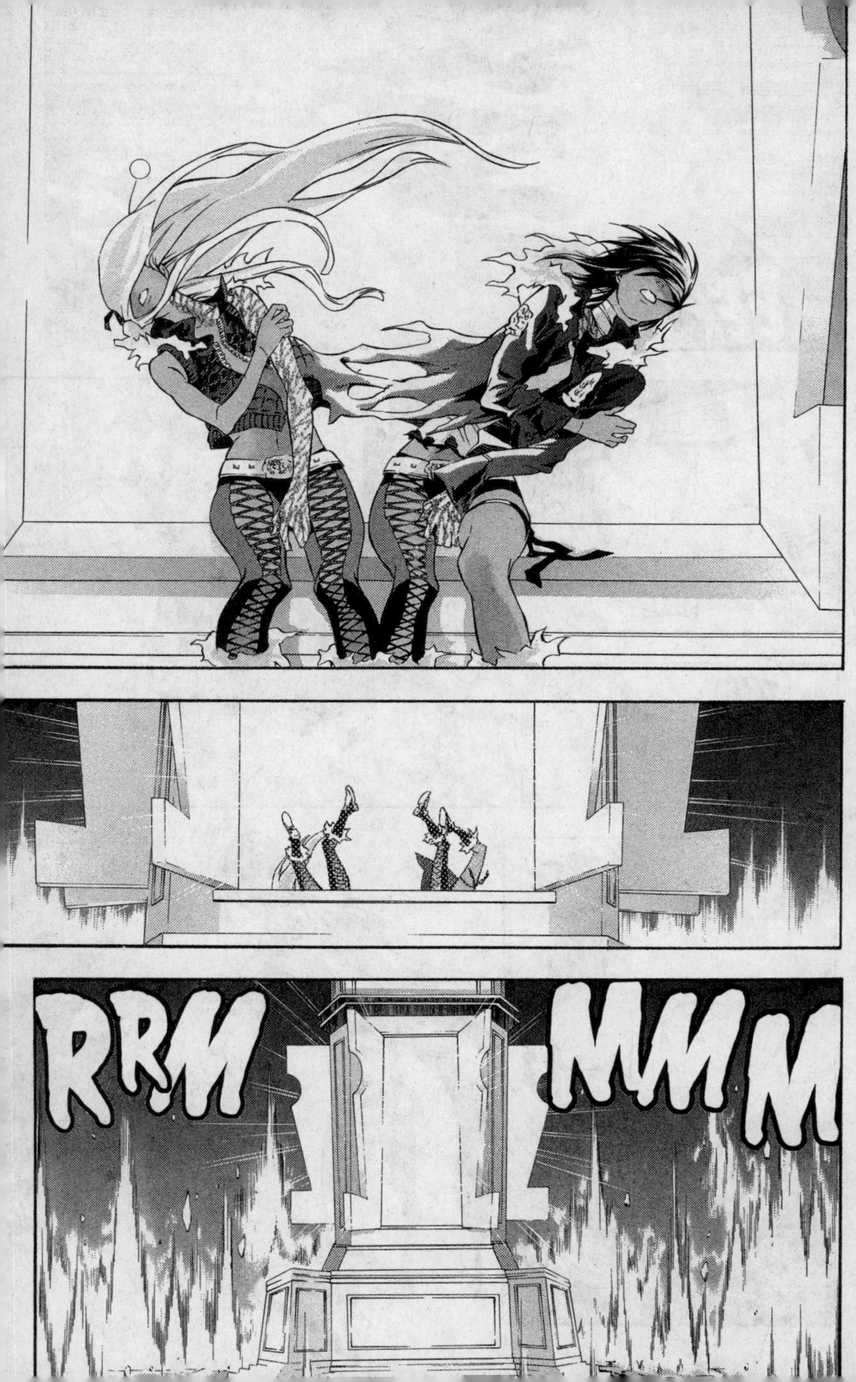
RRM
MMM

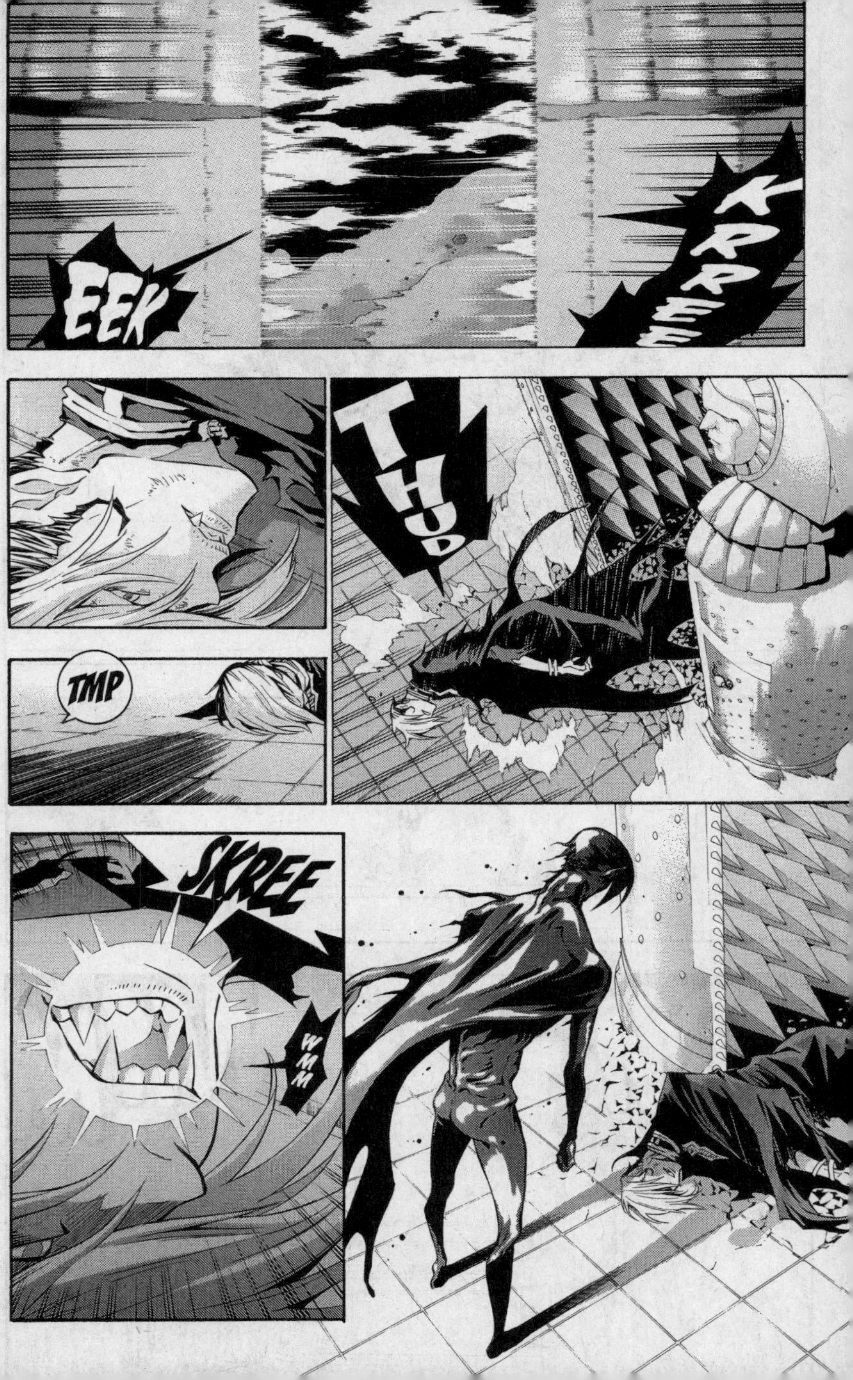
KRREE
EEK
THUD
TMP
SKREE
WMM

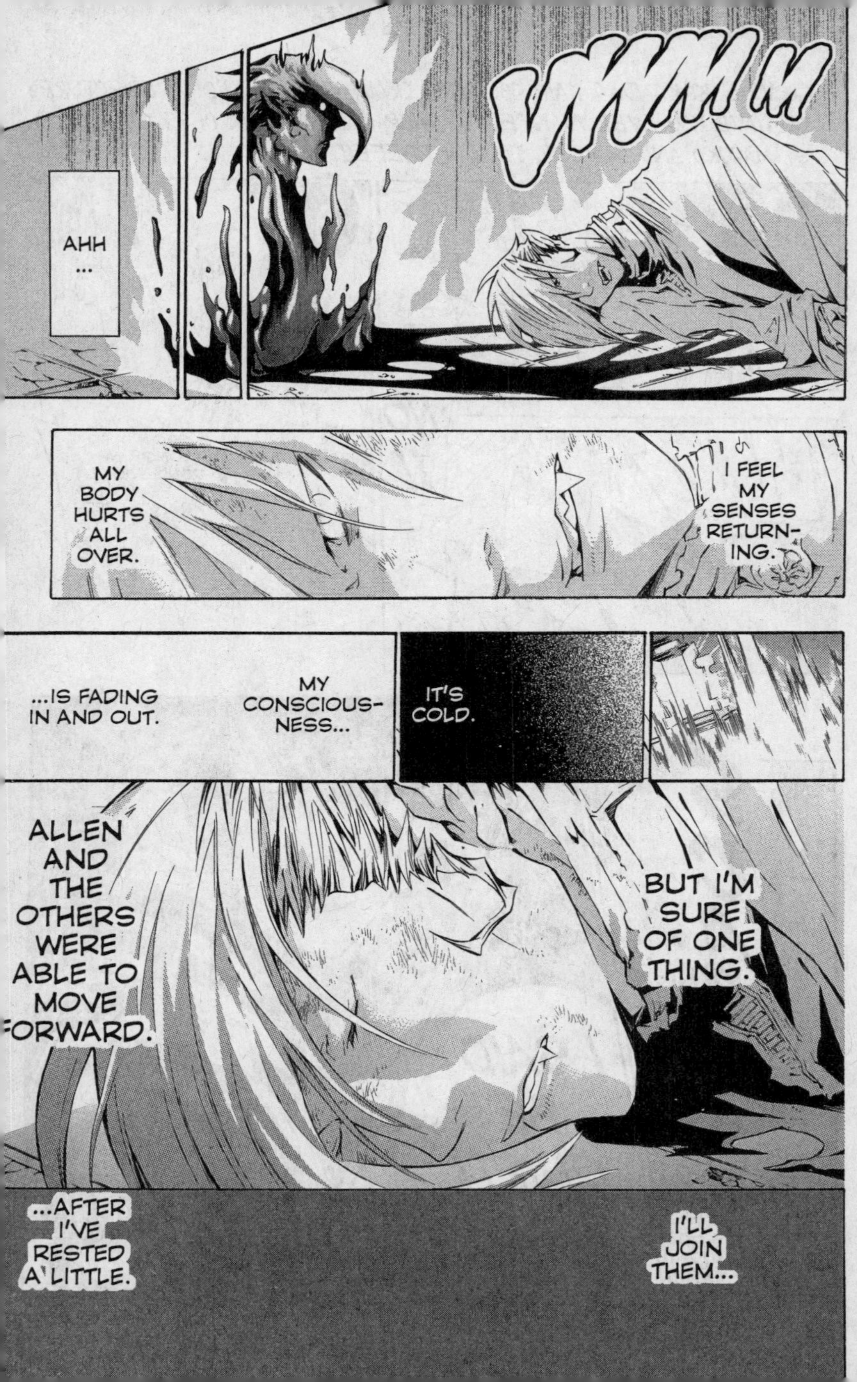
VMMM
AHH ...
I FEEL MY SENSES RETURNING.
MY BODY HURTS ALL OVER.
IT'S COLD.
MY CONSCIOUSNESS...
...IS FADING IN AND OUT.
BUT I'M SURE OF ONE THING.
ALLEN AND THE OTHERS WERE ABLE TO MOVE FORWARD.
I'LL JOIN THEM...
...AFTER I'VE RESTED A LITTLE.

Q. WHY IS KANDA'S HAIR SO LONG? (RAIN-SAN, TOCHIGI PREFECTURE)
Q. HAVE YOU EVER WANTED TO CHOP KANDA'S HAIR OFF? (AKANE MASUKO AND OTHERS, TOCHIGI PREFECTURE)

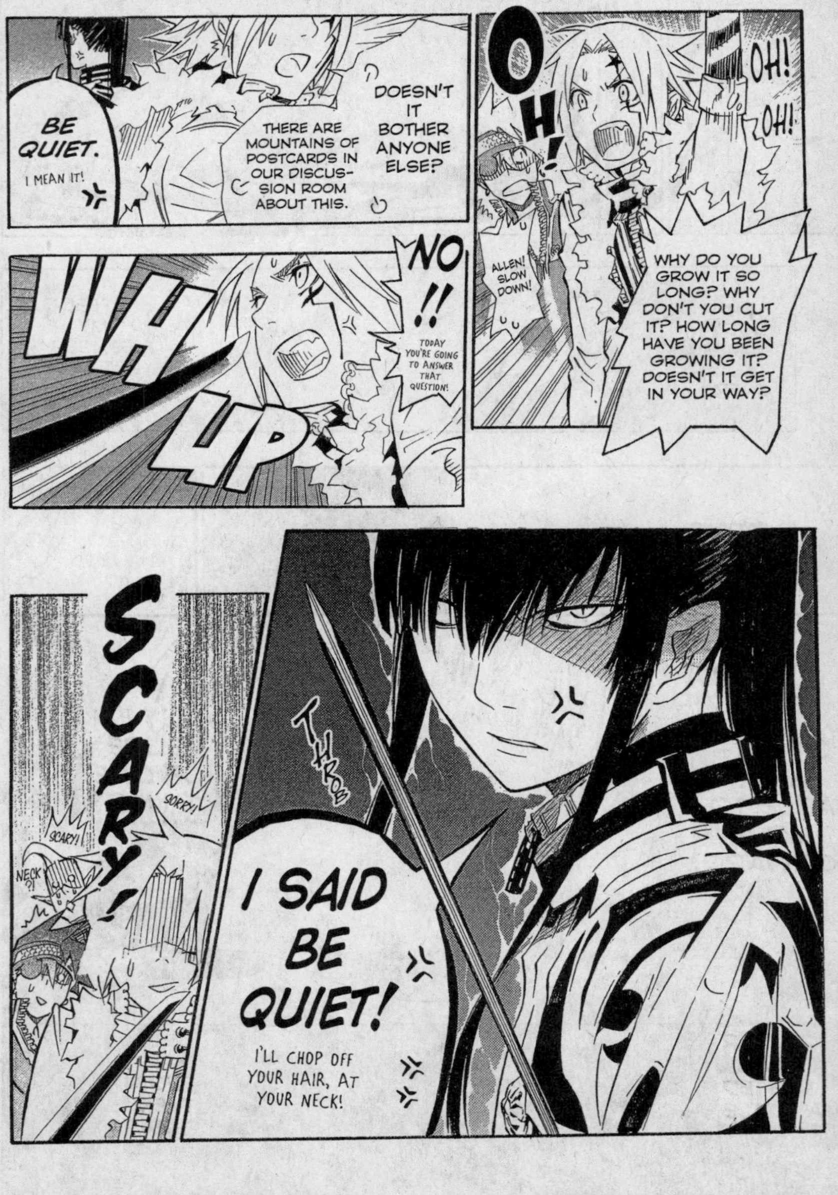
OH!
OH!
OH!
WHY DO YOU GROW IT SO LONG? WHY DON'T YOU CUT IT? HOW LONG HAVE YOU BEEN GROWING IT? DOESN'T IT GET IN YOUR WAY?
ALLEN! SLOW DOWN!
DOESN'T IT BOTHER ANYONE ELSE?
THERE ARE MOUNTAINS OF POSTCARDS IN OUR DISCUSSION ROOM ABOUT THIS.
BE QUIET.
I MEAN IT!
NO!!
TODAY YOU'RE GOING TO ANSWER THAT QUESTION!
WHUP
THROB
I SAID BE QUIET!
I'LL CHOP OFF YOUR HAIR, AT YOUR NECK!
SCARY!
SORRY!
SCARY!
NECK?!

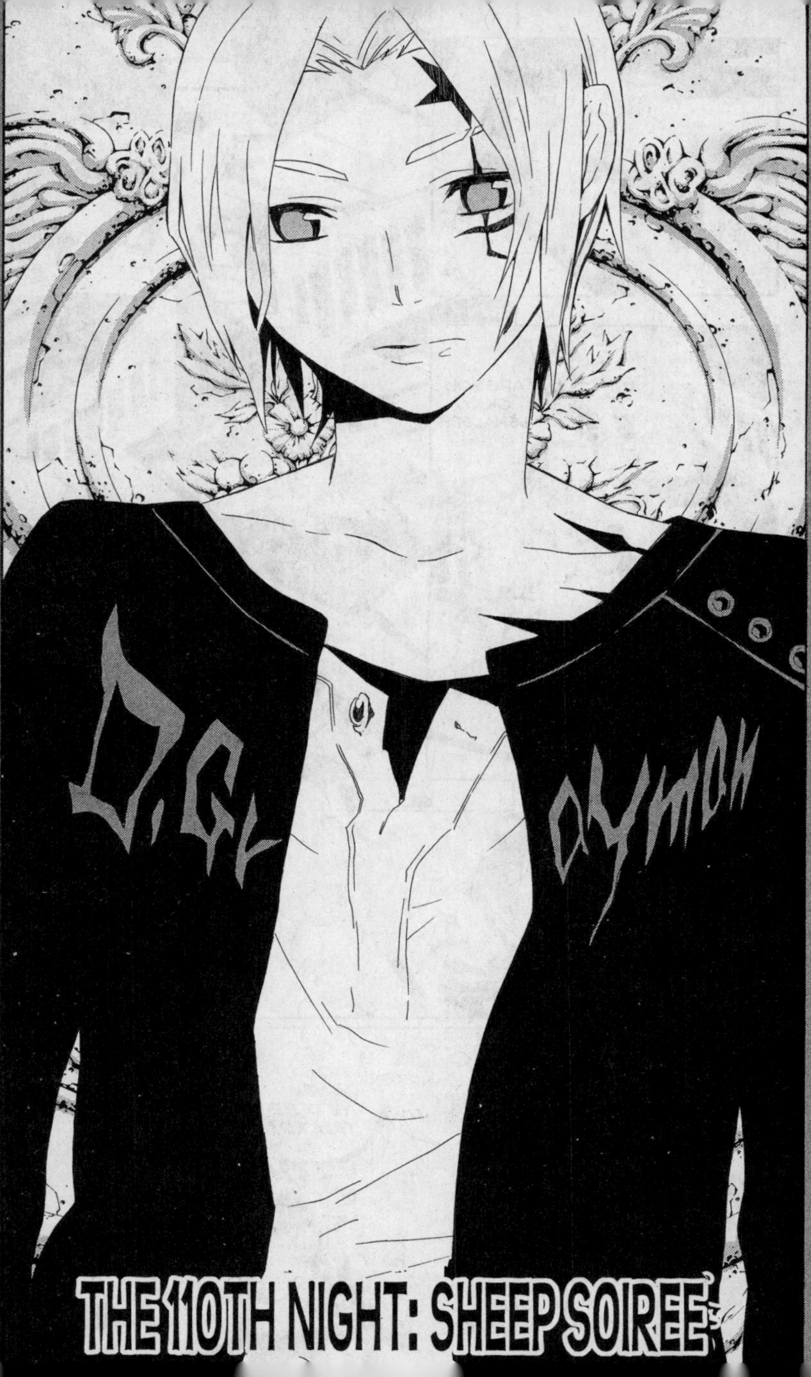

THE 110TH NIGHT: SHEEP SOIREE

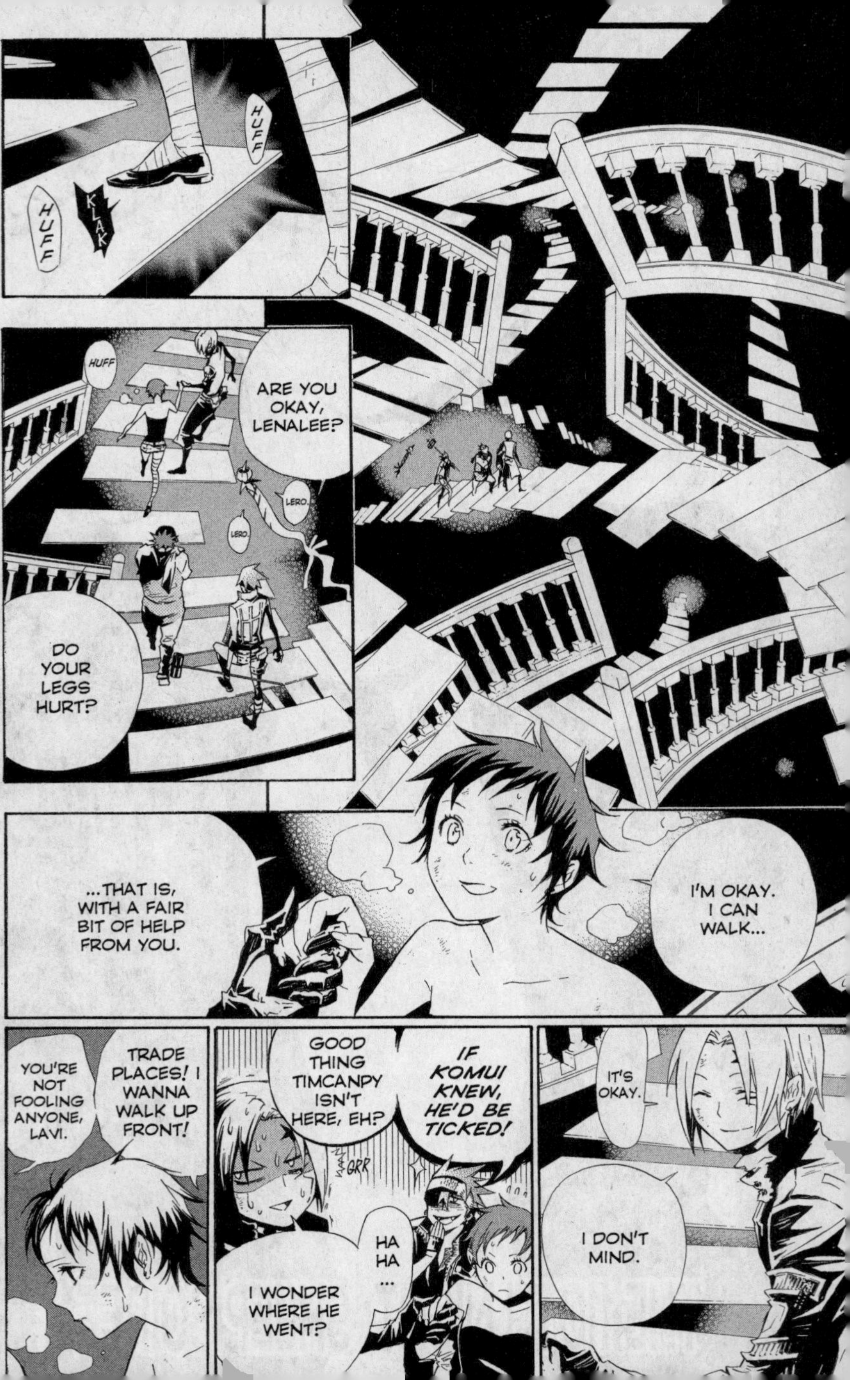
HUFF HUFF
KLAK
HUFF
ARE YOU OKAY, LENALEE?
LERO.
LERO.
DO YOUR LEGS HURT?
I'M OKAY. I CAN WALK...
...THAT IS, WITH A FAIR BIT OF HELP FROM YOU.
IT'S OKAY.
I DON'T MIND.
IF KOMUI KNEW, HE'D BE TICKED!
GOOD THING TIMCANPY ISN'T HERE, EH?
GRR
HA HA ...
I WONDER WHERE HE WENT?
TRADE PLACES! I WANNA WALK UP FRONT!
YOU'RE NOT FOOLING ANYONE, LAVI.

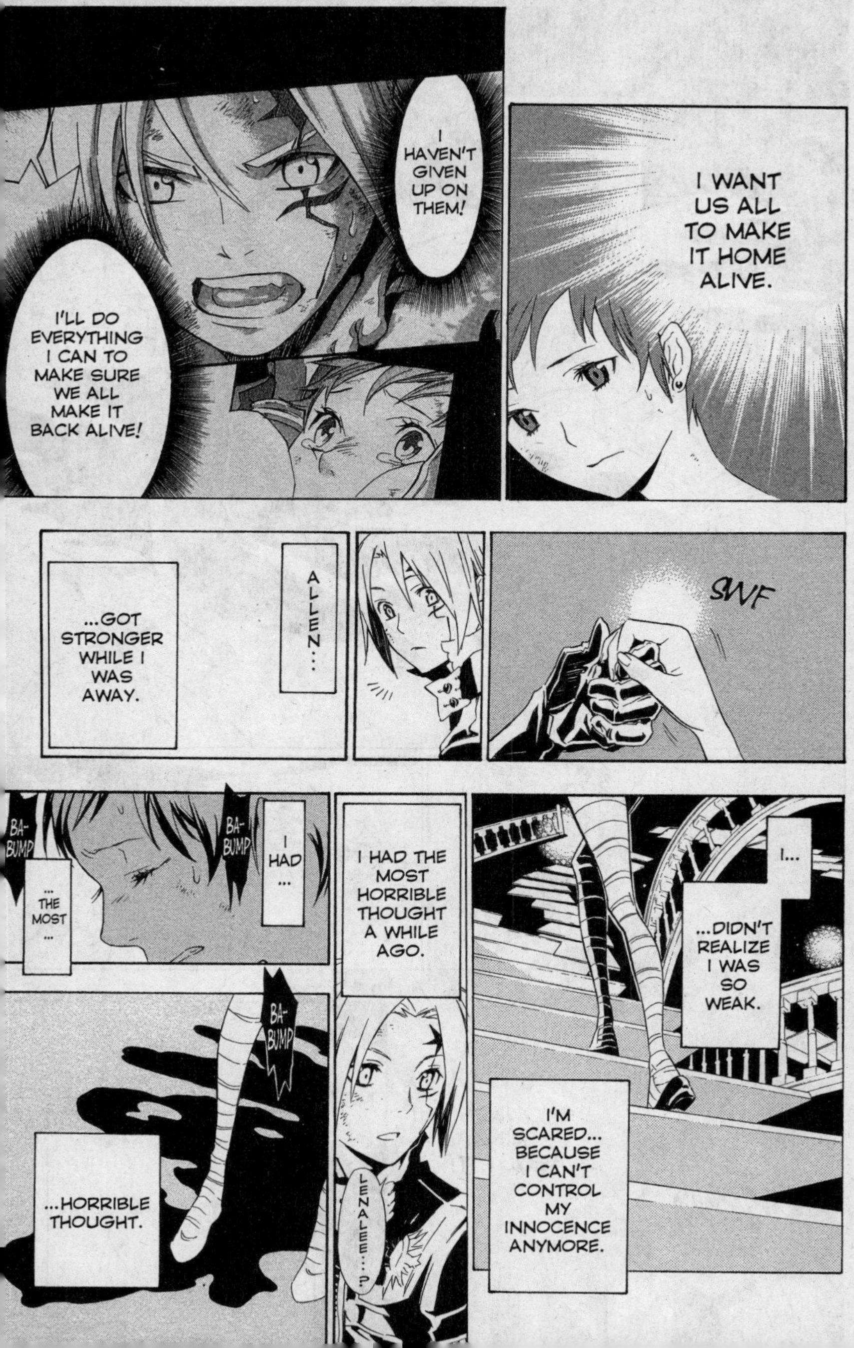
I WANT US ALL TO MAKE IT HOME ALIVE.
I HAVEN'T GIVEN UP ON THEM!
I'LL DO EVERYTHING I CAN TO MAKE SURE WE ALL MAKE IT BACK ALIVE!
SWF
ALLEN...
...GOT STRONGER WHILE I WAS AWAY.
I...
...DIDN'T REALIZE I WAS SO WEAK.
I'M SCARED... BECAUSE I CAN'T CONTROL MY INNOCENCE ANYMORE.
I HAD THE MOST HORRIBLE THOUGHT A WHILE AGO.
LENALEE...?
BA-BUMP
I HAD...
...THE MOST...
BA-BUMP
BA-BUMP
...HORRIBLE THOUGHT.

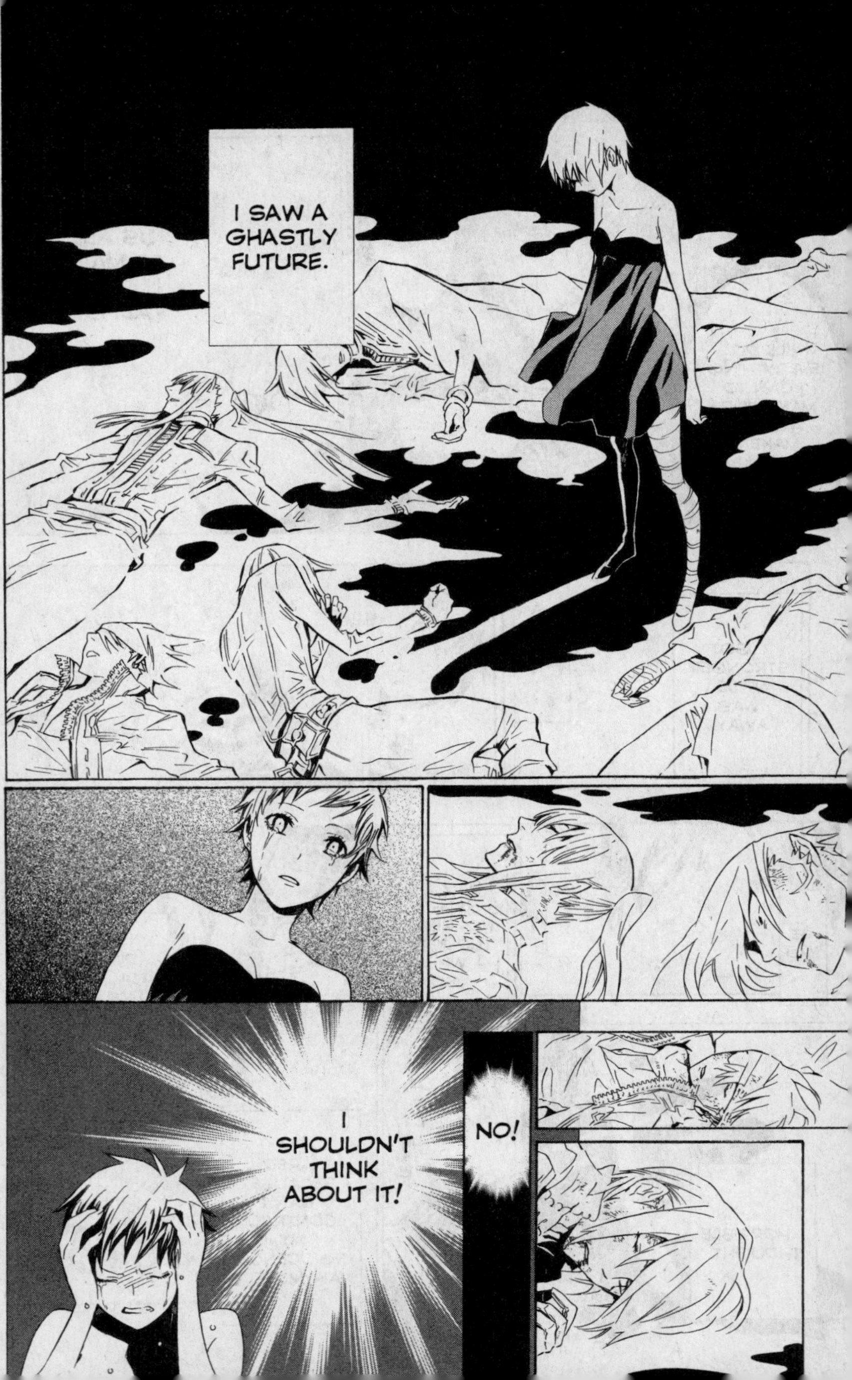
I SAW A GHASTLY FUTURE.
NO!
I SHOULDN'T THINK ABOUT IT!

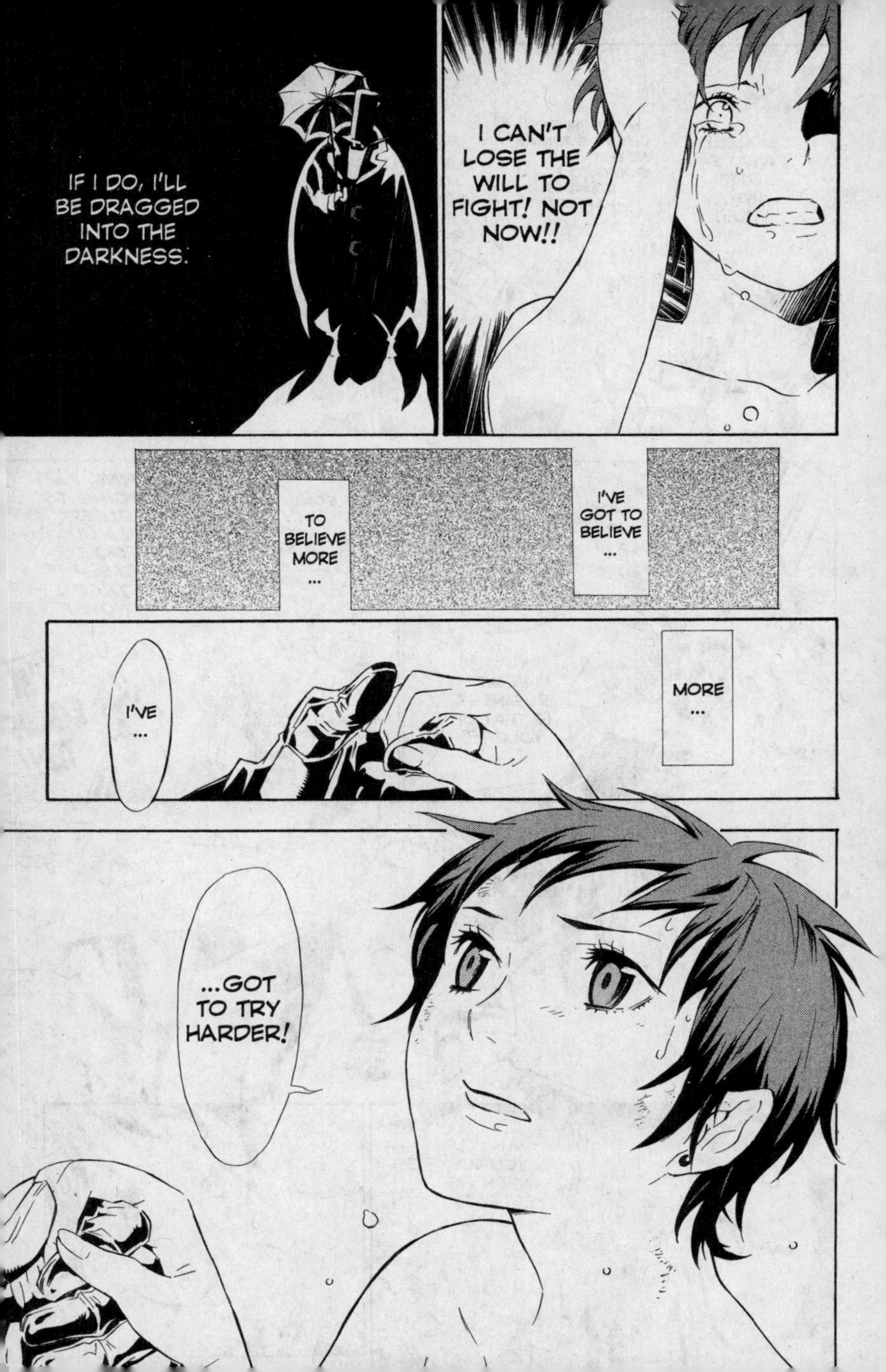
I CAN'T LOSE THE WILL TO FIGHT! NOT NOW!!
IF I DO, I'LL BE DRAGGED INTO THE DARKNESS.
I'VE GOT TO BELIEVE ...
TO BELIEVE MORE ...
MORE ...
I'VE ...
...GOT TO TRY HARDER!

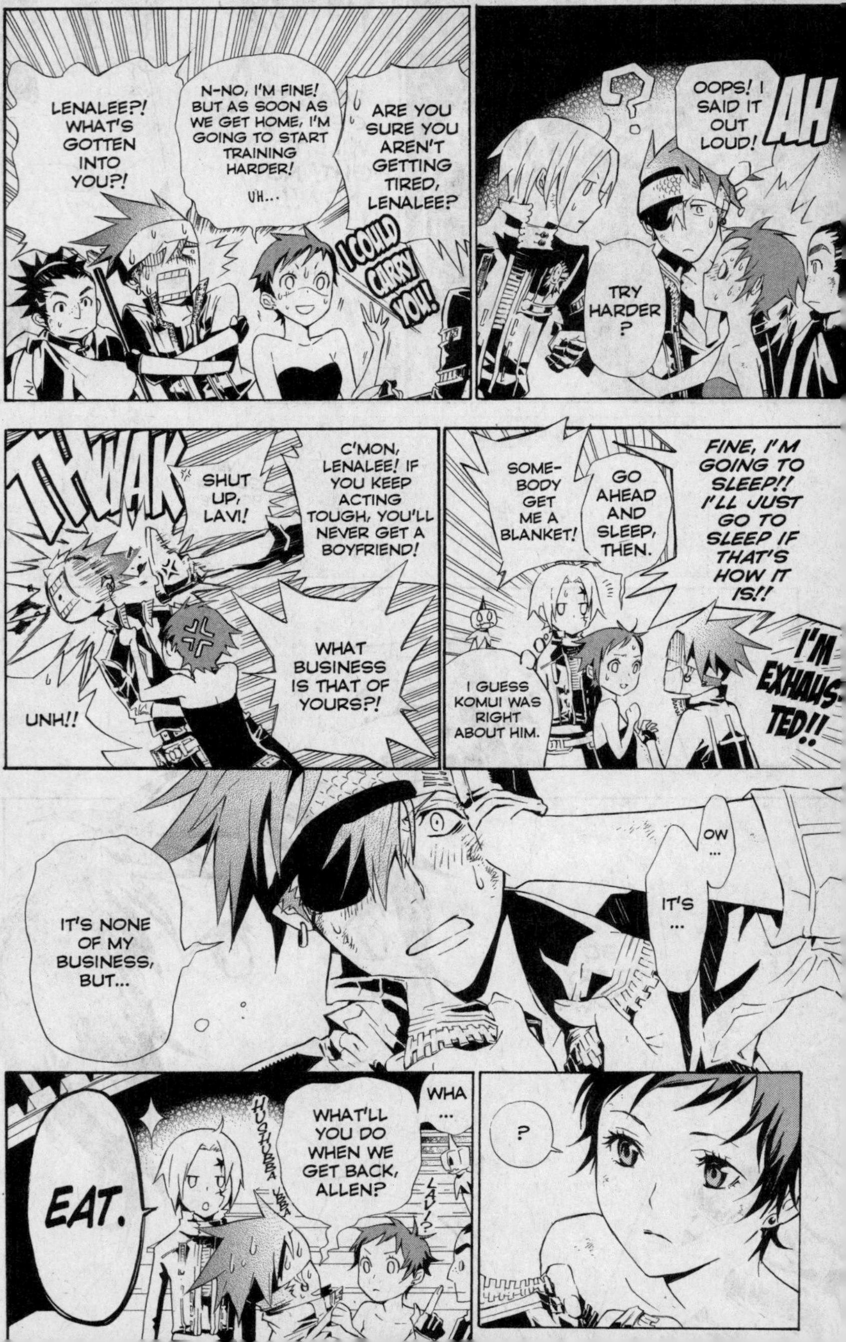
ARE YOU SURE YOU AREN'T GETTING TIRED, LENALEE?
I COULD CARRY YOU!
N-NO, I'M FINE! BUT AS SOON AS WE GET HOME, I'M GOING TO START TRAINING HARDER!
UH...
LENALEE?! WHAT'S GOTTEN INTO YOU?!
TRY HARDER?
?
OOPS! I SAID IT OUT LOUD!
AH
C'MON, LENALEE! IF YOU KEEP ACTING TOUGH, YOU'LL NEVER GET A BOYFRIEND!
THWAK
SHUT UP, LAVI!
WHAT BUSINESS IS THAT OF YOURS?!
UNH!!
I'M EXHAUS-TED!!
FINE, I'M GOING TO SLEEP!! I'LL JUST GO TO SLEEP IF THAT'S HOW IT IS!!
GO AHEAD AND SLEEP, THEN.
SOME-BODY GET ME A BLANKET!
I GUESS KOMUI WAS RIGHT ABOUT HIM.
OW...
IT'S...
IT'S NONE OF MY BUSINESS, BUT...
WHAT'LL YOU DO WHEN WE GET BACK, ALLEN?
HUSHUBBA YUBBA
LAVI?!
WHA...
EAT.
?

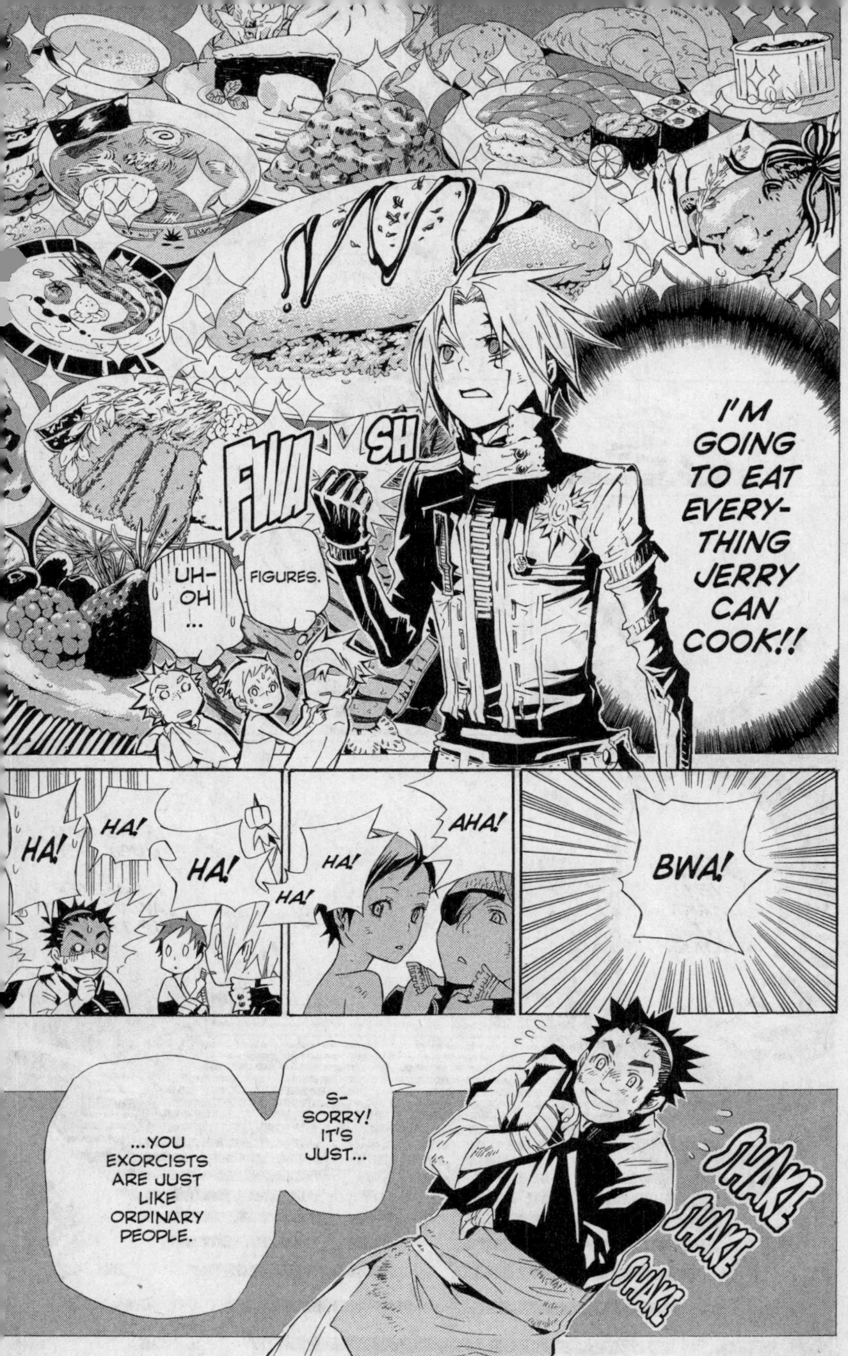

I'M GOING TO EAT EVERY-THING JERRY CAN COOK!!
FWA
SH
FIGURES.
UH-OH ...
BWA!
AHA!
HA!
HA!
HA!
HA!
HA!
SHAKE
SHAKE
SHAKE
S-SORRY! IT'S JUST...
...YOU EXORCISTS ARE JUST LIKE ORDINARY PEOPLE.

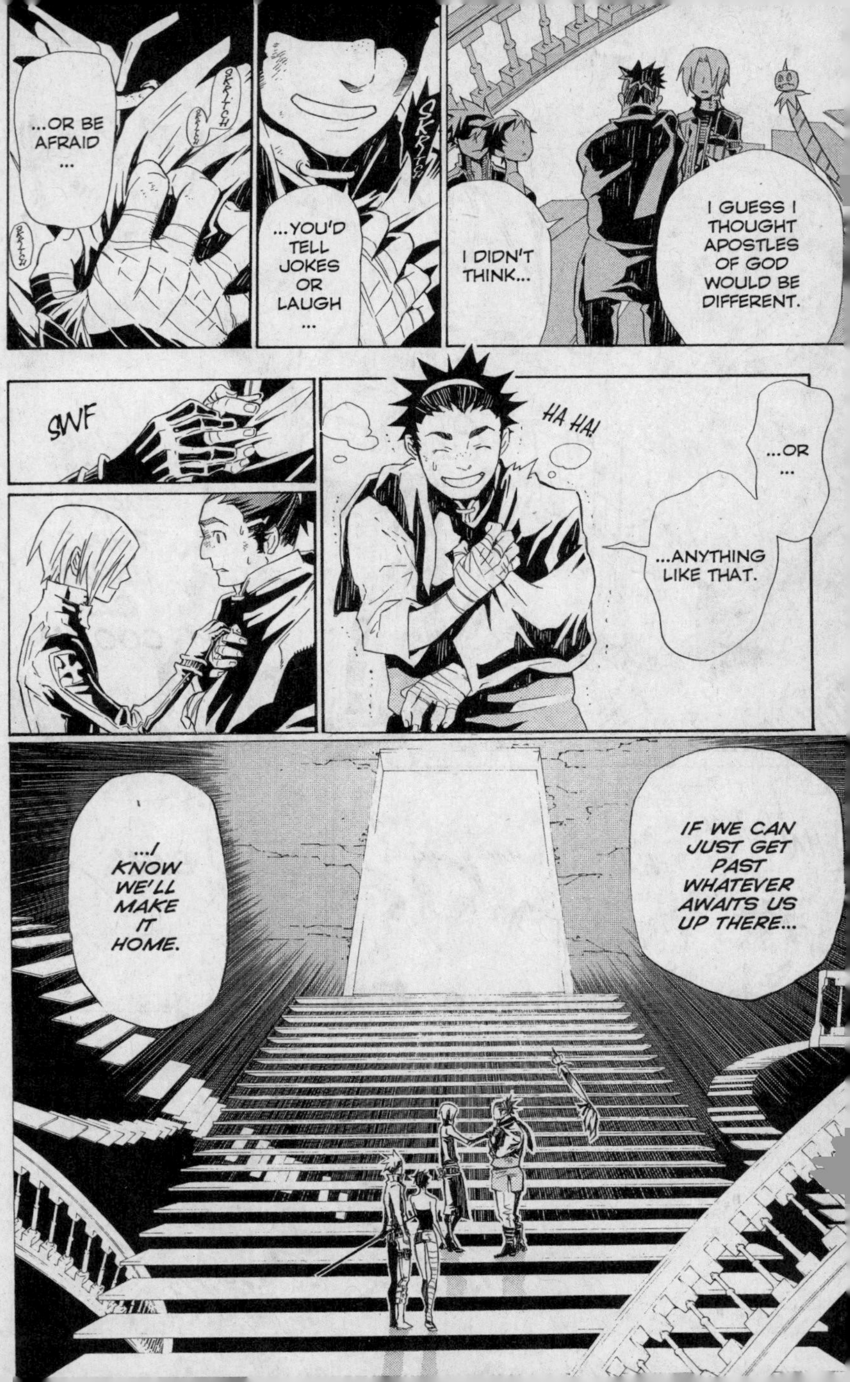
I GUESS I THOUGHT APOSTLES OF GOD WOULD BE DIFFERENT.
I DIDN'T THINK...
SKRITCH
...YOU'D TELL JOKES OR LAUGH ...
...OR BE AFRAID ...
HA HA!
...OR ...
...ANYTHING LIKE THAT.
SWF
IF WE CAN JUST GET PAST WHATEVER AWAITS US UP THERE...
...I KNOW WE'LL MAKE IT HOME.

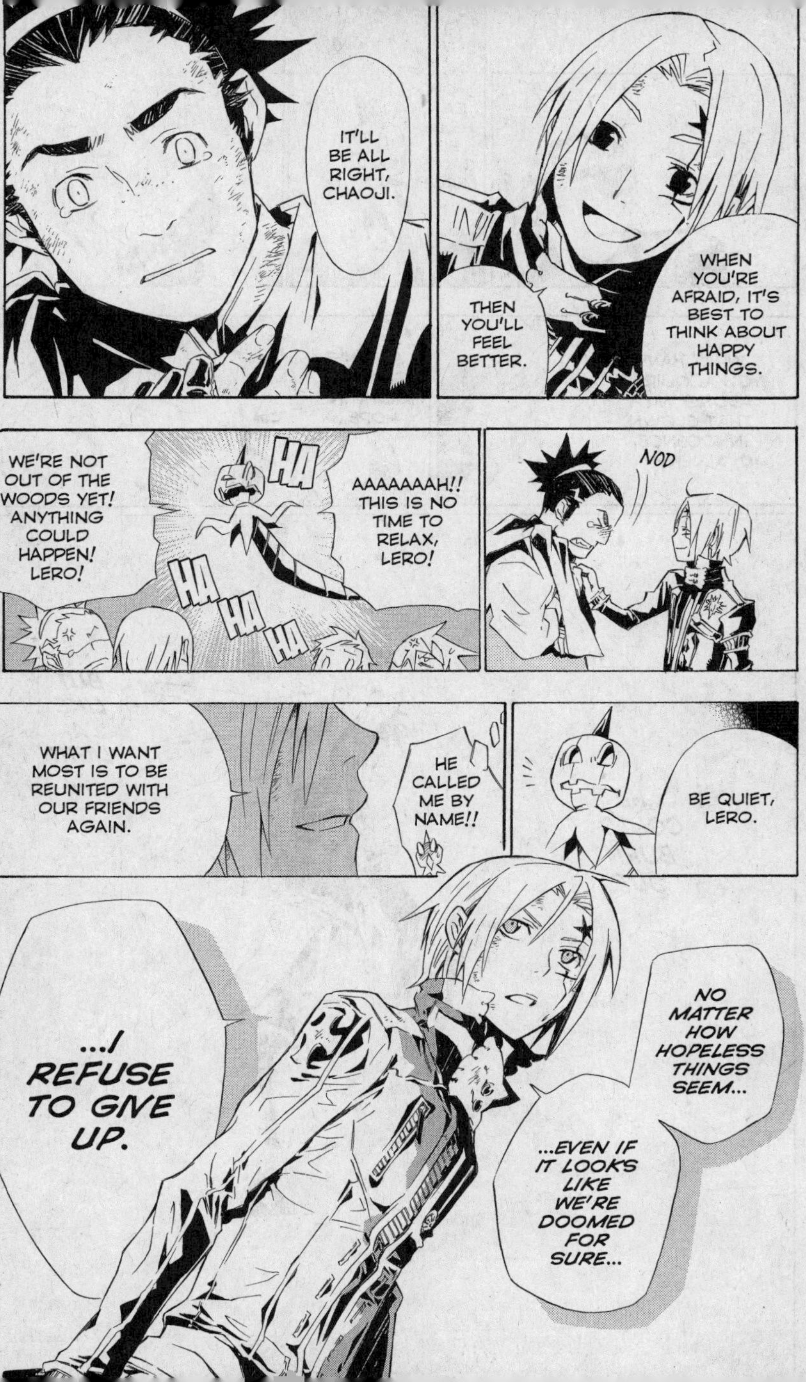
WHEN YOU'RE AFRAID, IT'S BEST TO THINK ABOUT HAPPY THINGS.
THEN YOU'LL FEEL BETTER.
IT'LL BE ALL RIGHT, CHAOJI.
NOD
AAAAAAAH!! THIS IS NO TIME TO RELAX, LERO!
HA HA HA HA
WE'RE NOT OUT OF THE WOODS YET! ANYTHING COULD HAPPEN! LERO!
BE QUIET, LERO.
HE CALLED ME BY NAME!!
WHAT I WANT MOST IS TO BE REUNITED WITH OUR FRIENDS AGAIN.
NO MATTER HOW HOPELESS THINGS SEEM...
...EVEN IF IT LOOKS LIKE WE'RE DOOMED FOR SURE...
...I REFUSE TO GIVE UP.

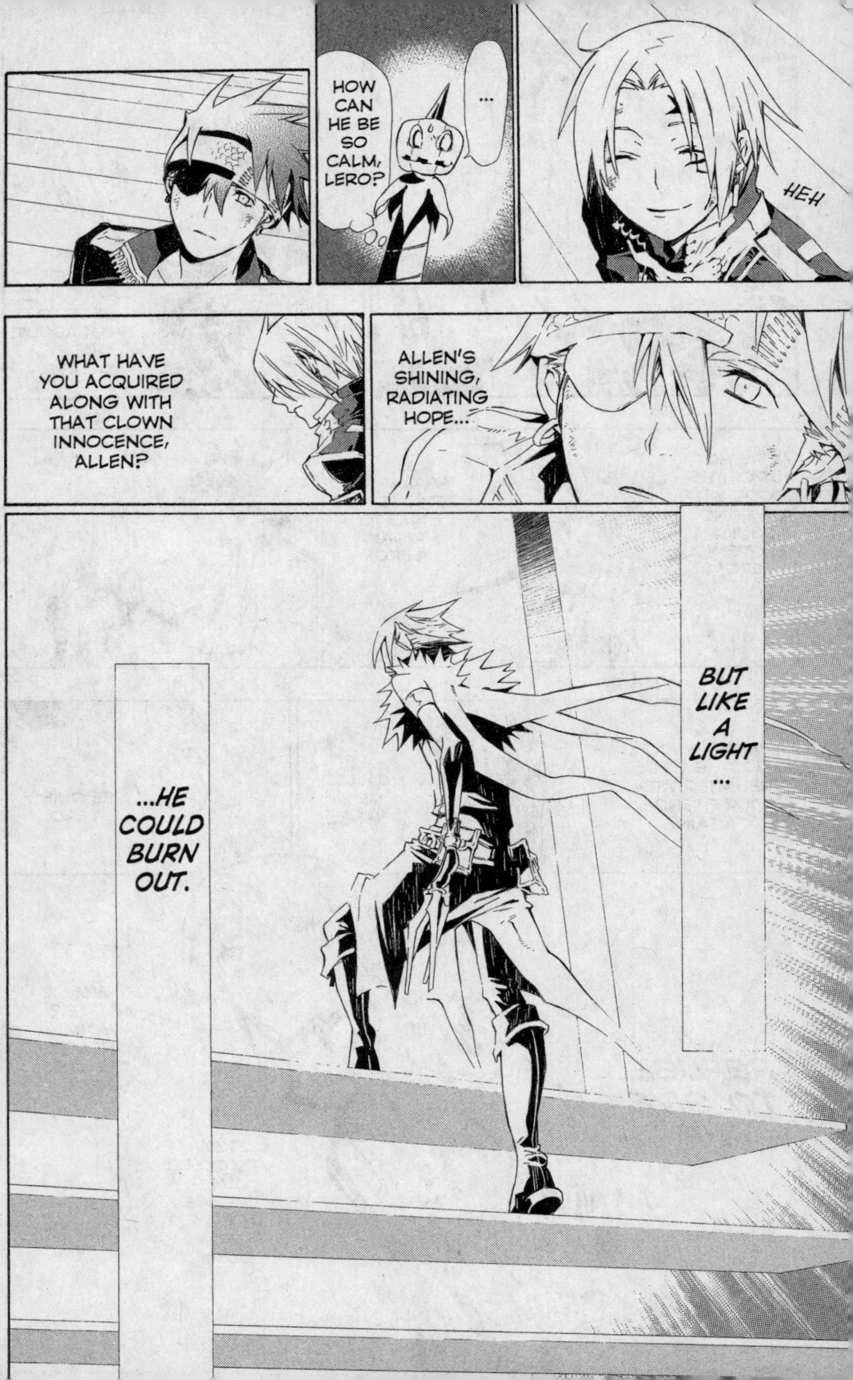
HEH
...
HOW CAN HE BE SO CALM, LERO?
ALLEN'S SHINING, RADIATING HOPE...
WHAT HAVE YOU ACQUIRED ALONG WITH THAT CLOWN INNOCENCE, ALLEN?
BUT LIKE A LIGHT ...
...HE COULD BURN OUT.

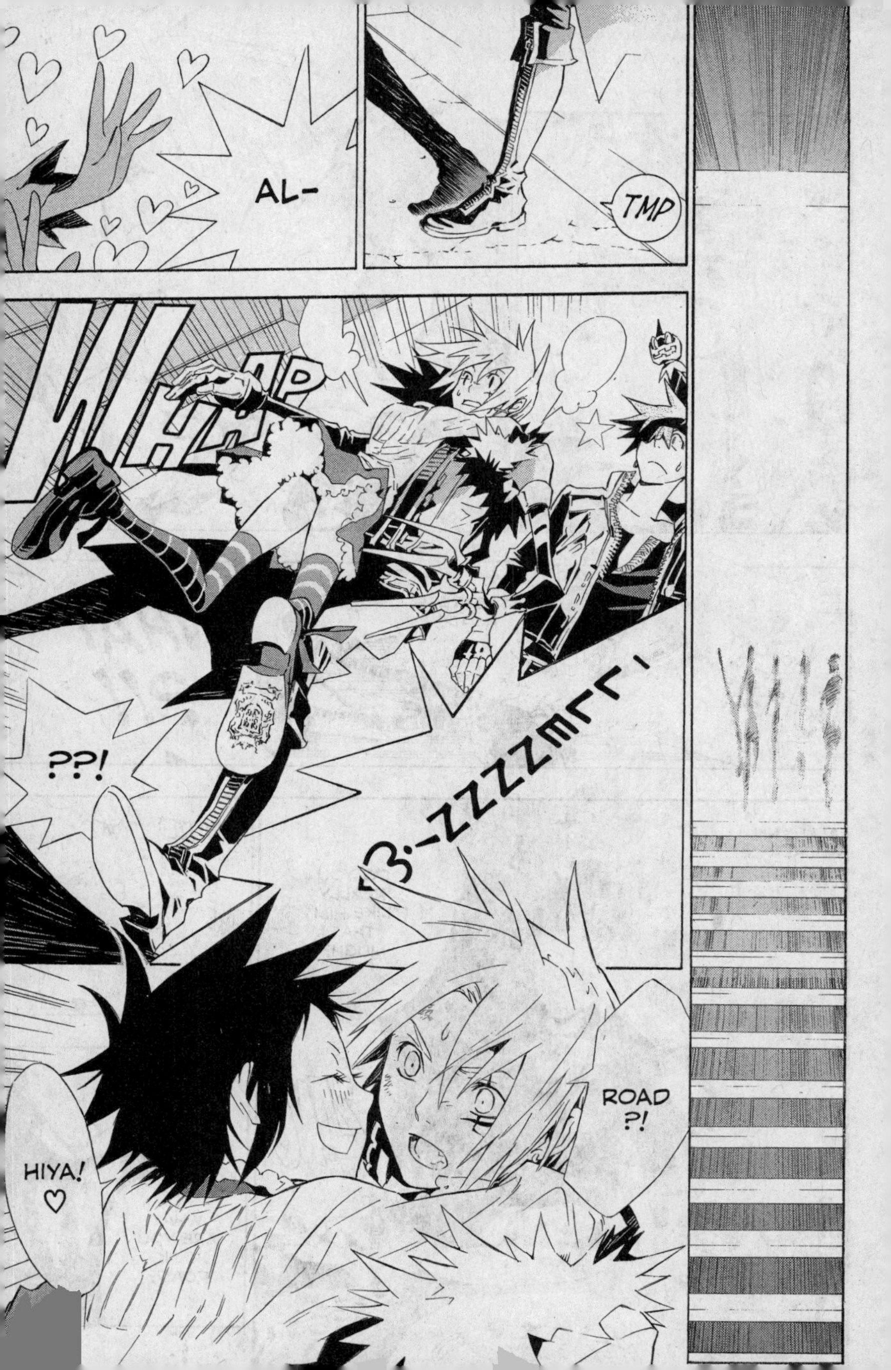
TMP
AL-
WHAP
??!
ROAD ?!
HIYA! ♡

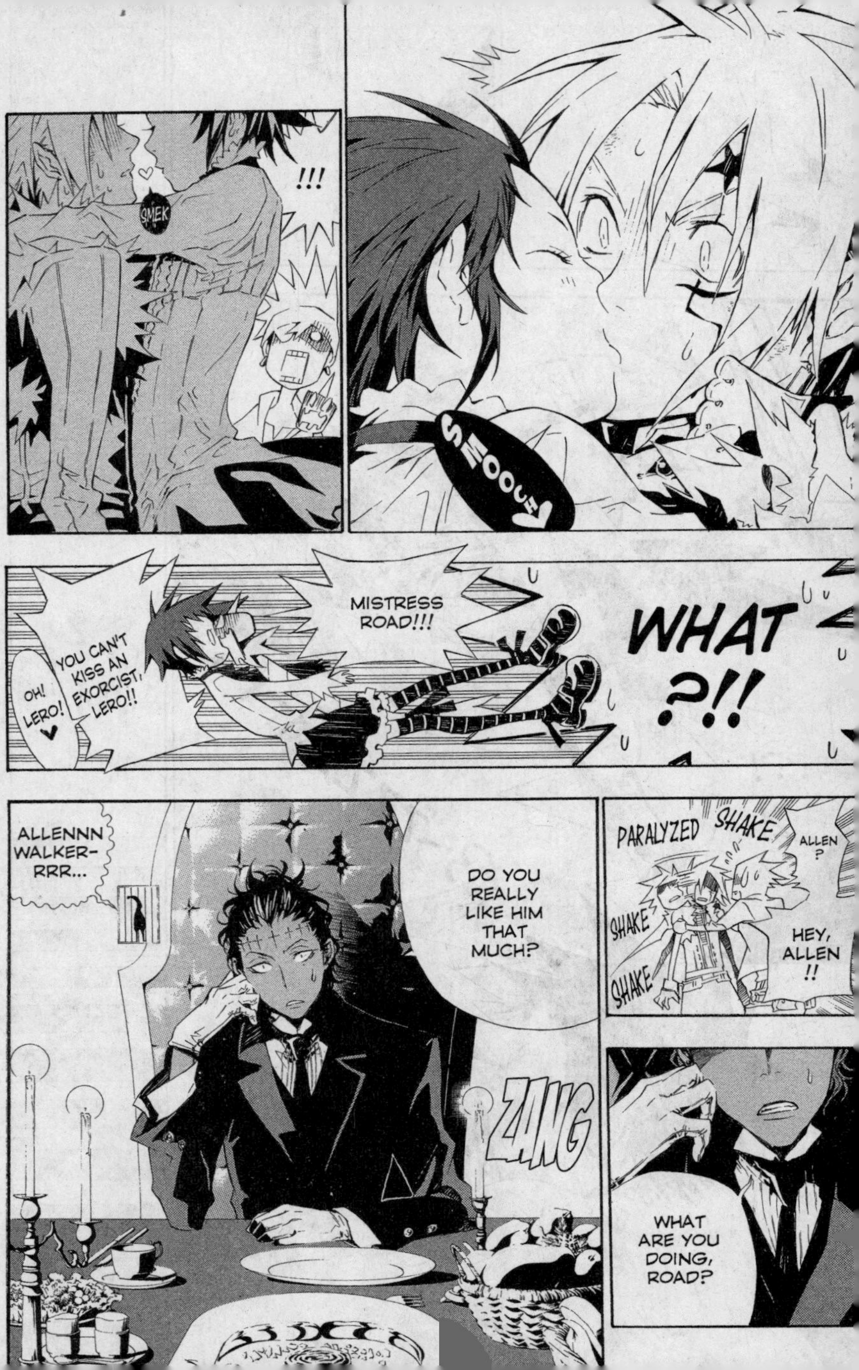
SMOOCH ♥
!!!
SMEK
WHAT ?!!
MISTRESS ROAD!!!
YOU CAN'T KISS AN EXORCIST, LERO!!
OH! LERO! ♥
ALLEN ?
SHAKE
PARALYZED
HEY, ALLEN !!
SHAKE
SHAKE
WHAT ARE YOU DOING, ROAD?
ZANG
DO YOU REALLY LIKE HIM THAT MUCH?
ALLENNN WALKER-RRR...

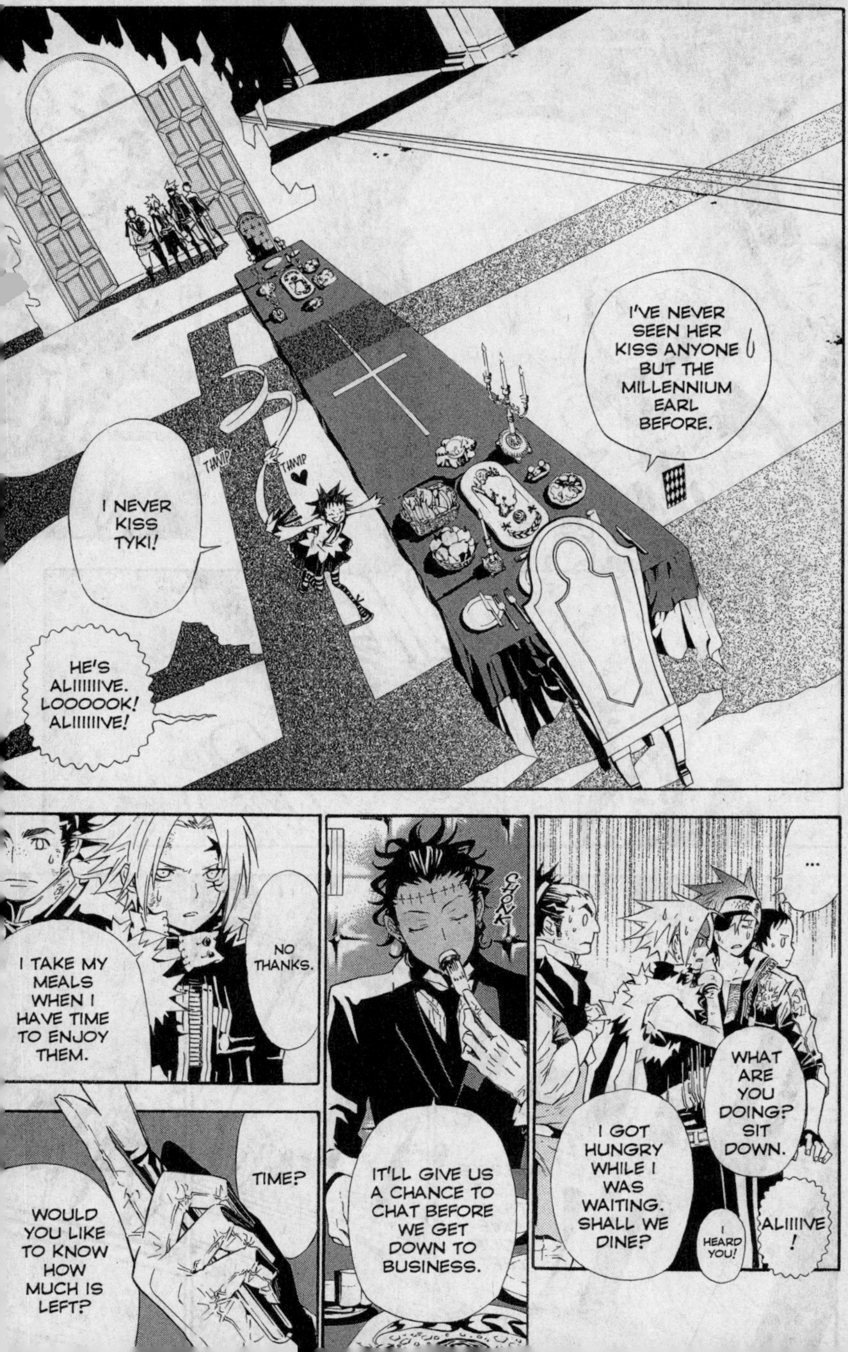
I'VE NEVER SEEN HER KISS ANYONE BUT THE MILLENNIUM EARL BEFORE.
THWIP
THWIP
I NEVER KISS TYKI!
HE'S ALIIIIIIVE. LOOOOOK! ALIIIIIIVE!
...
WHAT ARE YOU DOING? SIT DOWN.
ALIIIIVE!
I HEARD YOU!
CHONK
I GOT HUNGRY WHILE I WAS WAITING. SHALL WE DINE?
IT'LL GIVE US A CHANCE TO CHAT BEFORE WE GET DOWN TO BUSINESS.
NO THANKS.
I TAKE MY MEALS WHEN I HAVE TIME TO ENJOY THEM.
TIME?
WOULD YOU LIKE TO KNOW HOW MUCH IS LEFT?

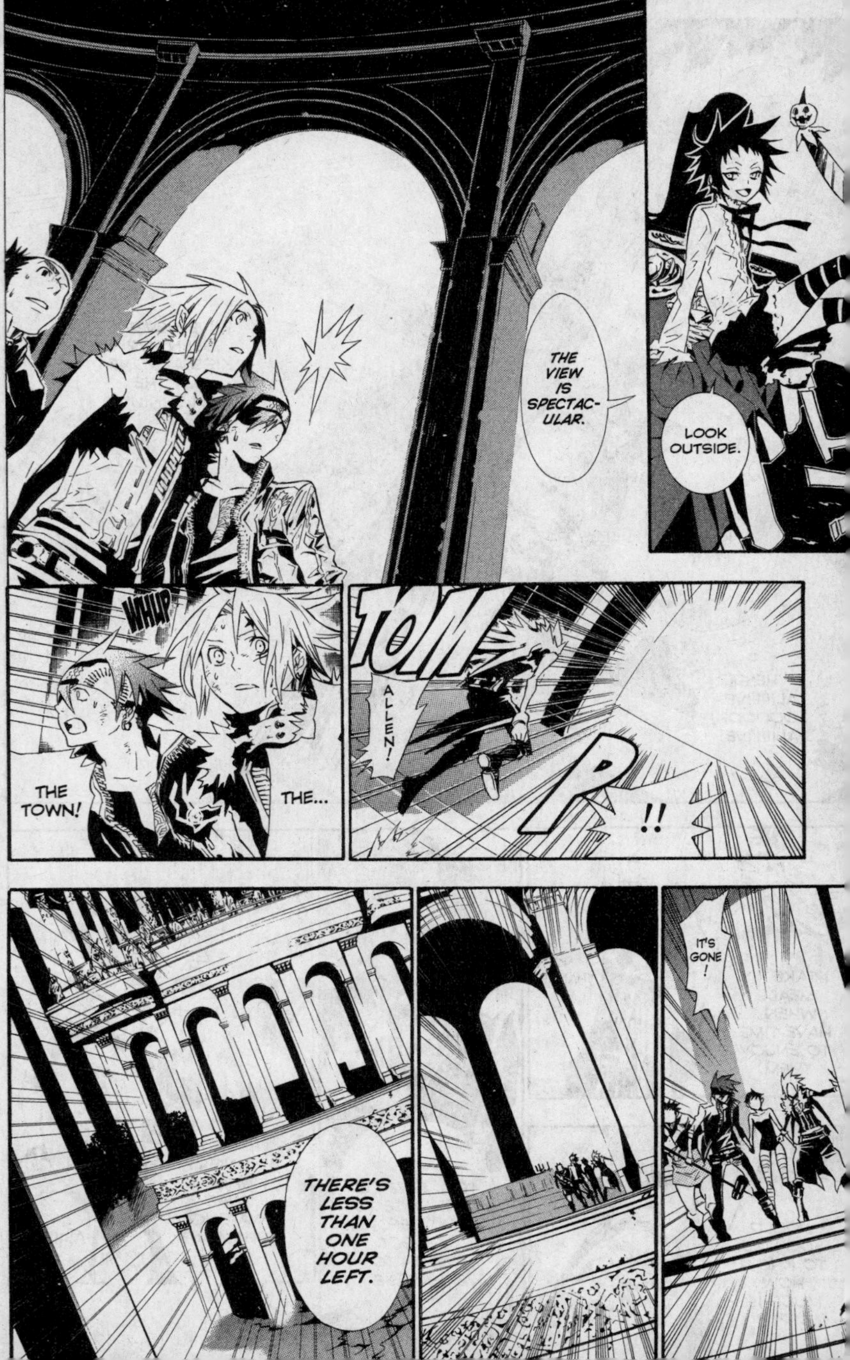
LOOK OUTSIDE.
THE VIEW IS SPECTAC-ULAR.
TOWN
ALLEN!
P
!!
WHUP
THE...
THE TOWN!
IT'S GONE!
THERE'S LESS THAN ONE HOUR LEFT.

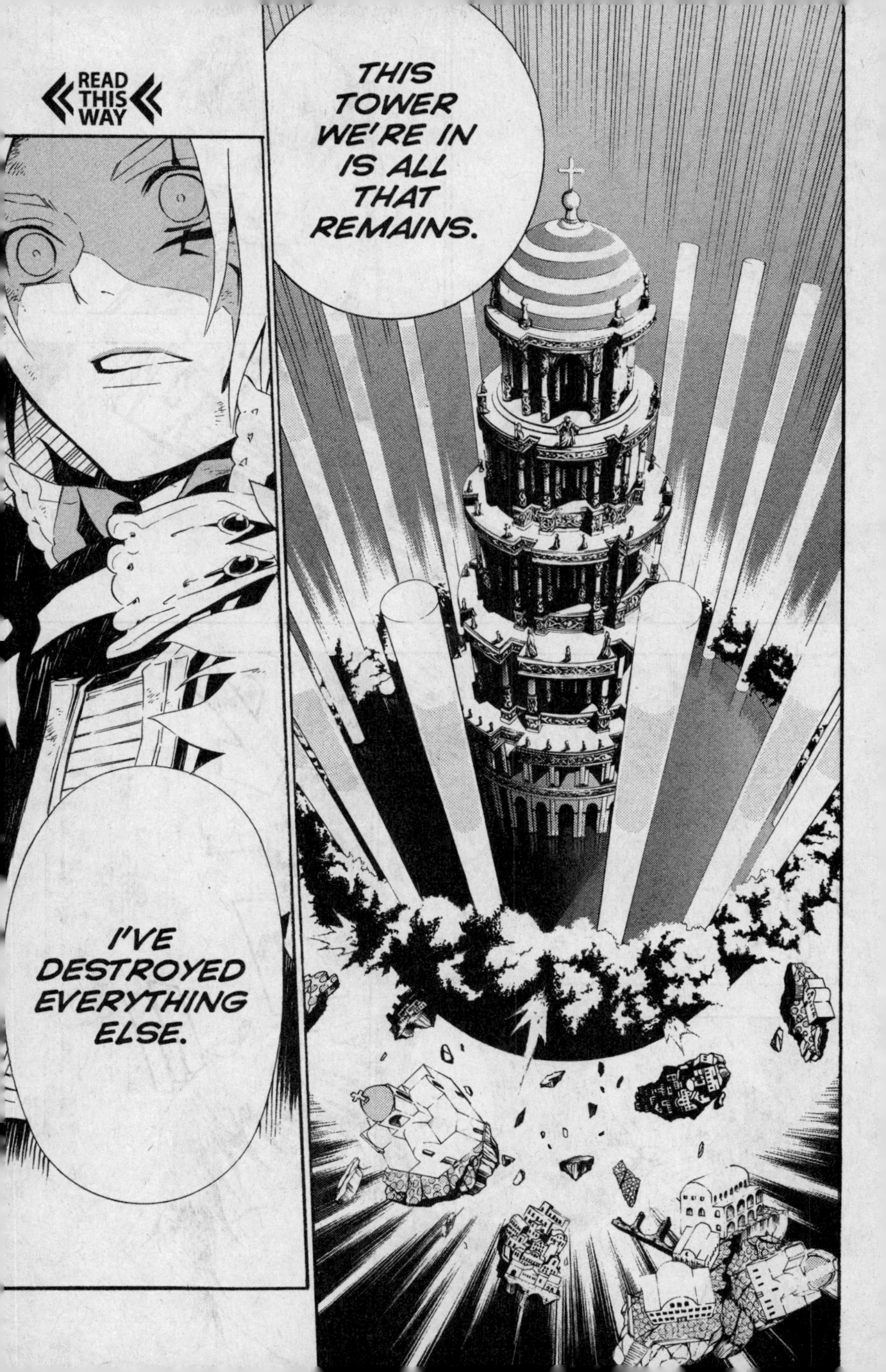
READ THIS WAY
THIS TOWER WE'RE IN IS ALL THAT REMAINS.
I'VE DESTROYED EVERYTHING ELSE.

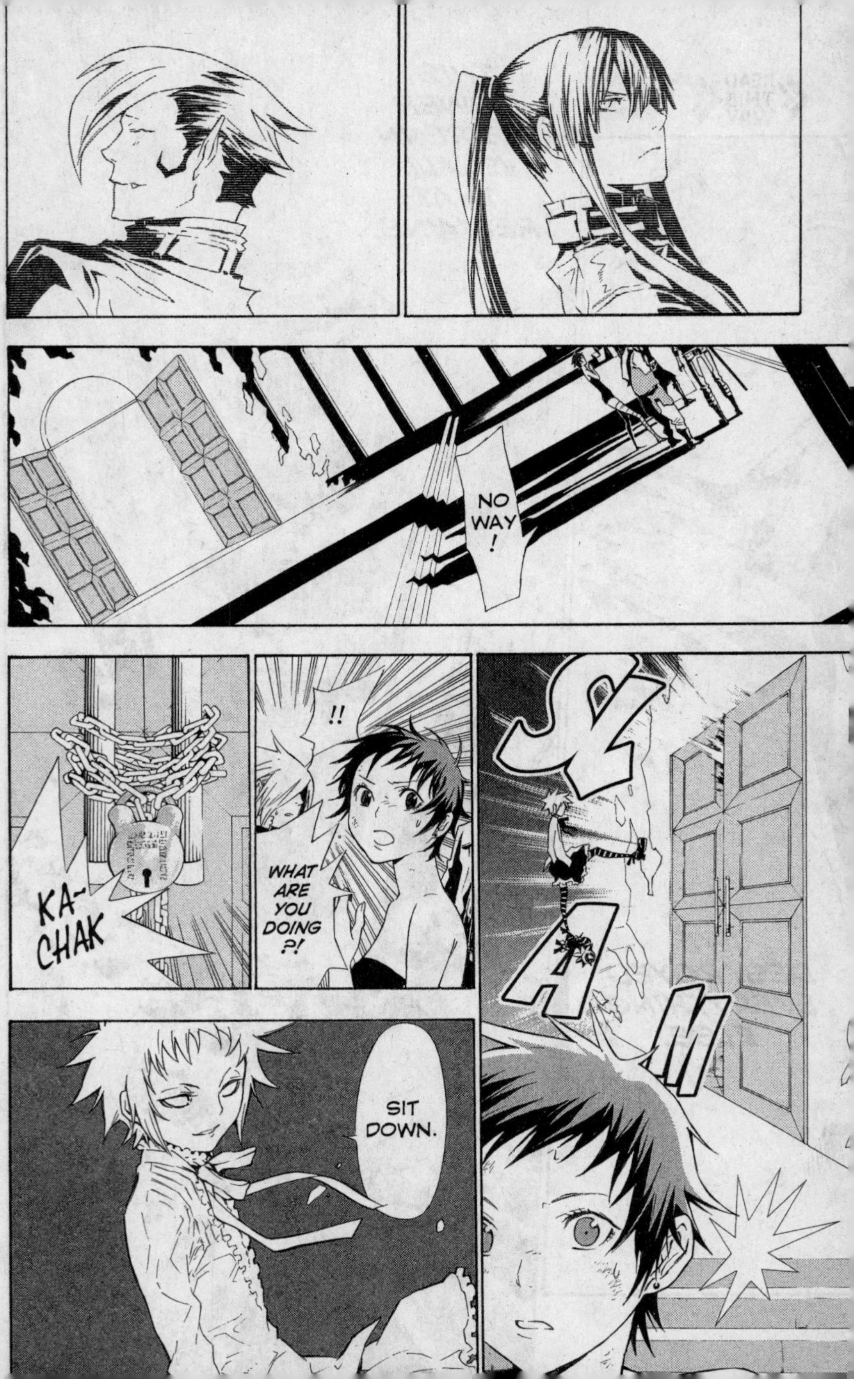
NO WAY!
SLAM
!!
WHAT ARE YOU DOING?!
KA-CHAK
SIT DOWN.

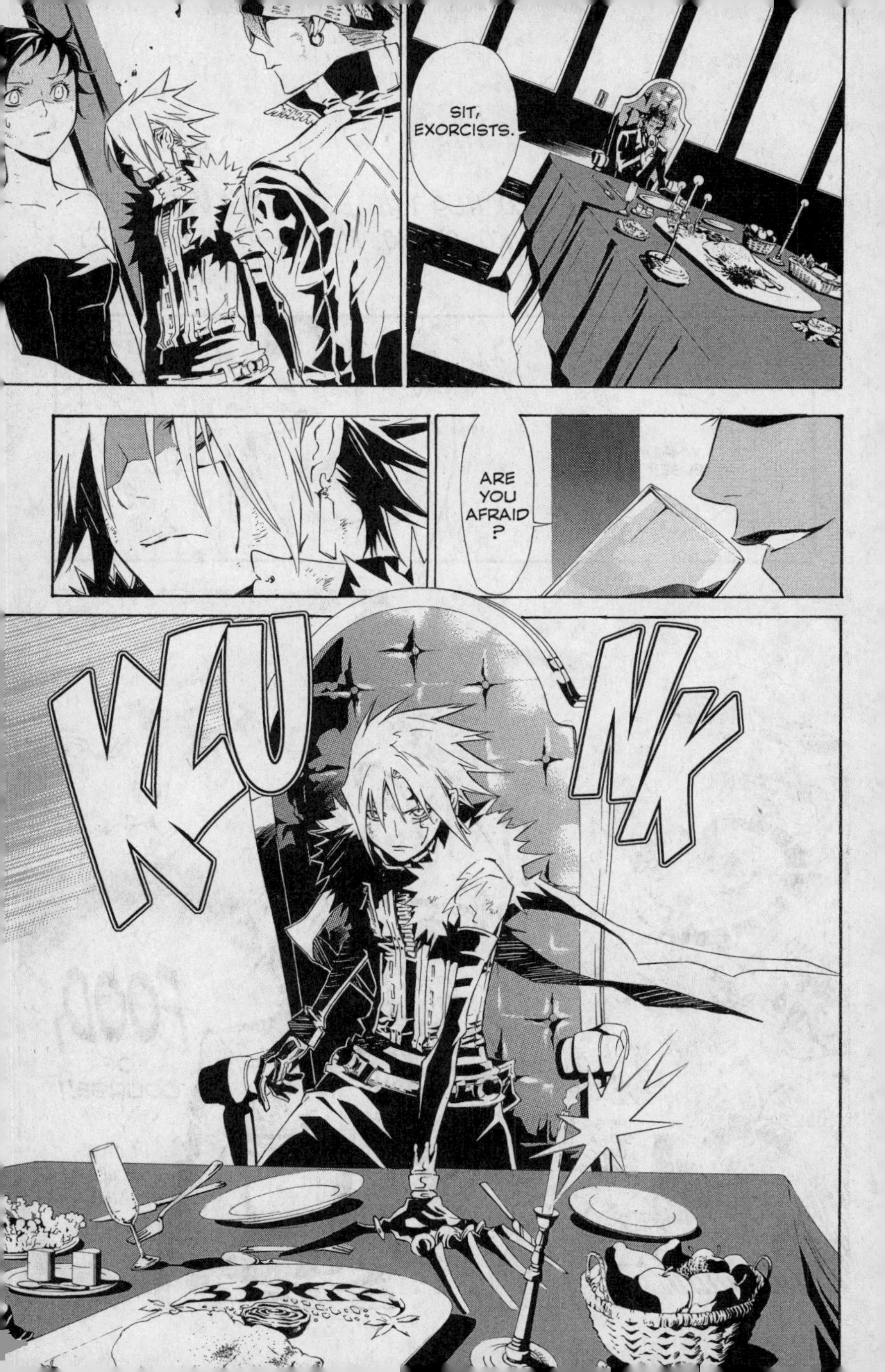
SIT, EXORCISTS.
ARE YOU AFRAID?
KLUNK

Q. WHAT'S IN THE POUCHES THE EXORCISTS WEAR AT THEIR HIPS? (MARIKO, OKUBO, IWATE PREFECTURE)

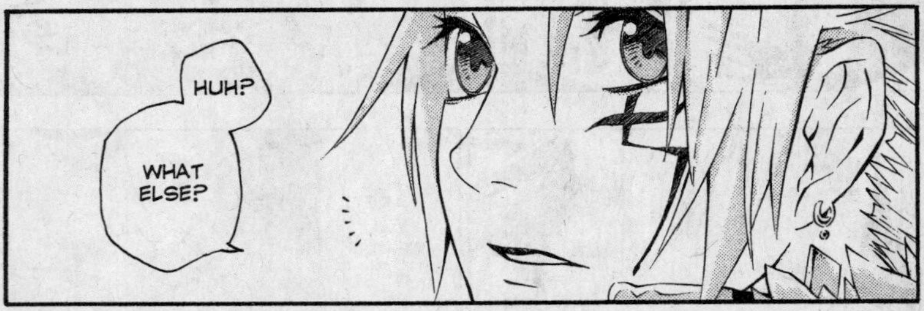
HUH?
WHAT ELSE?

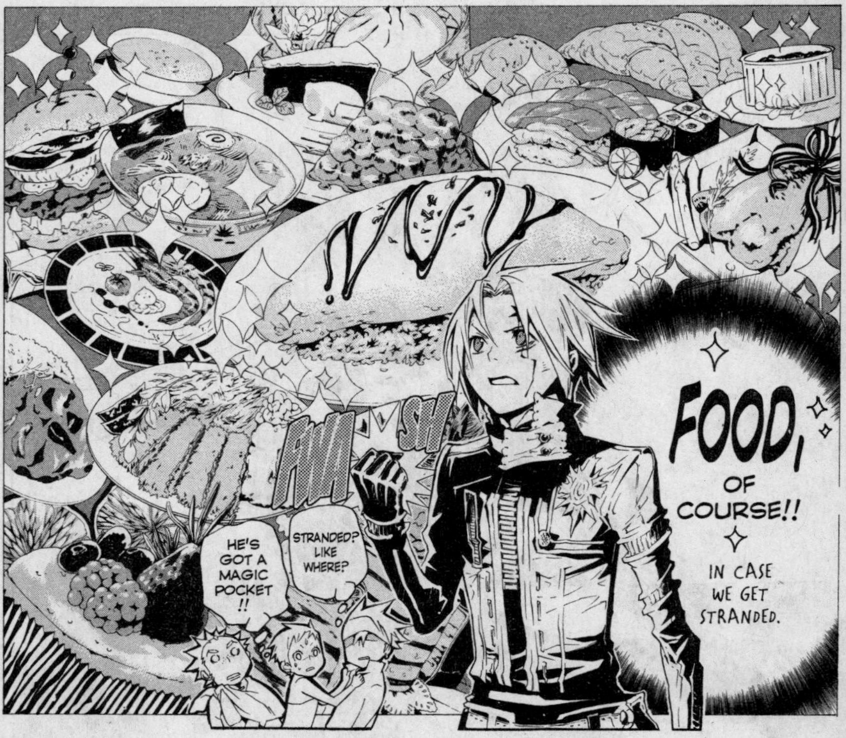
FOOD, OF COURSE!!
IN CASE WE GET STRANDED.
STRANDED? LIKE WHERE?
HE'S GOT A MAGIC POCKET!!

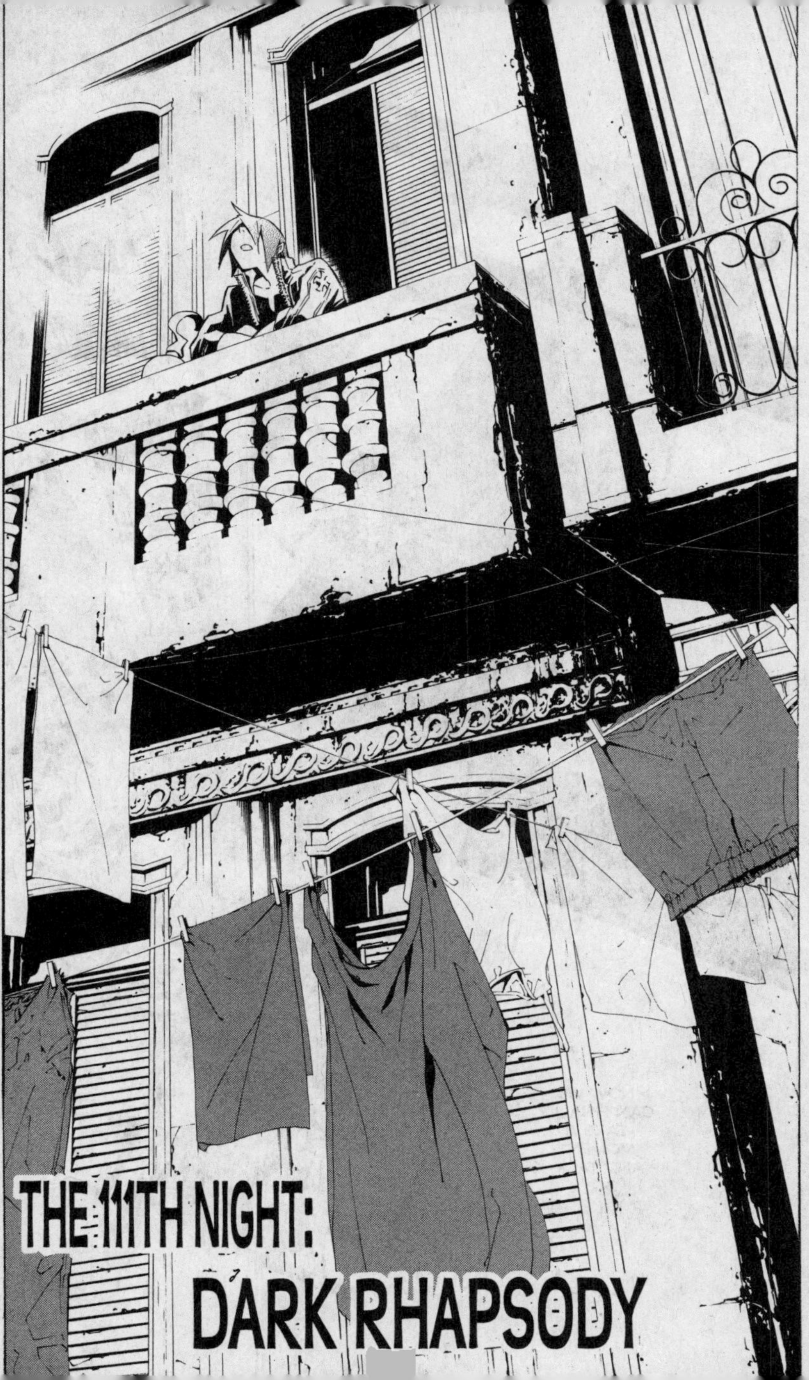
THE 111TH NIGHT:
DARK RHAPSODY

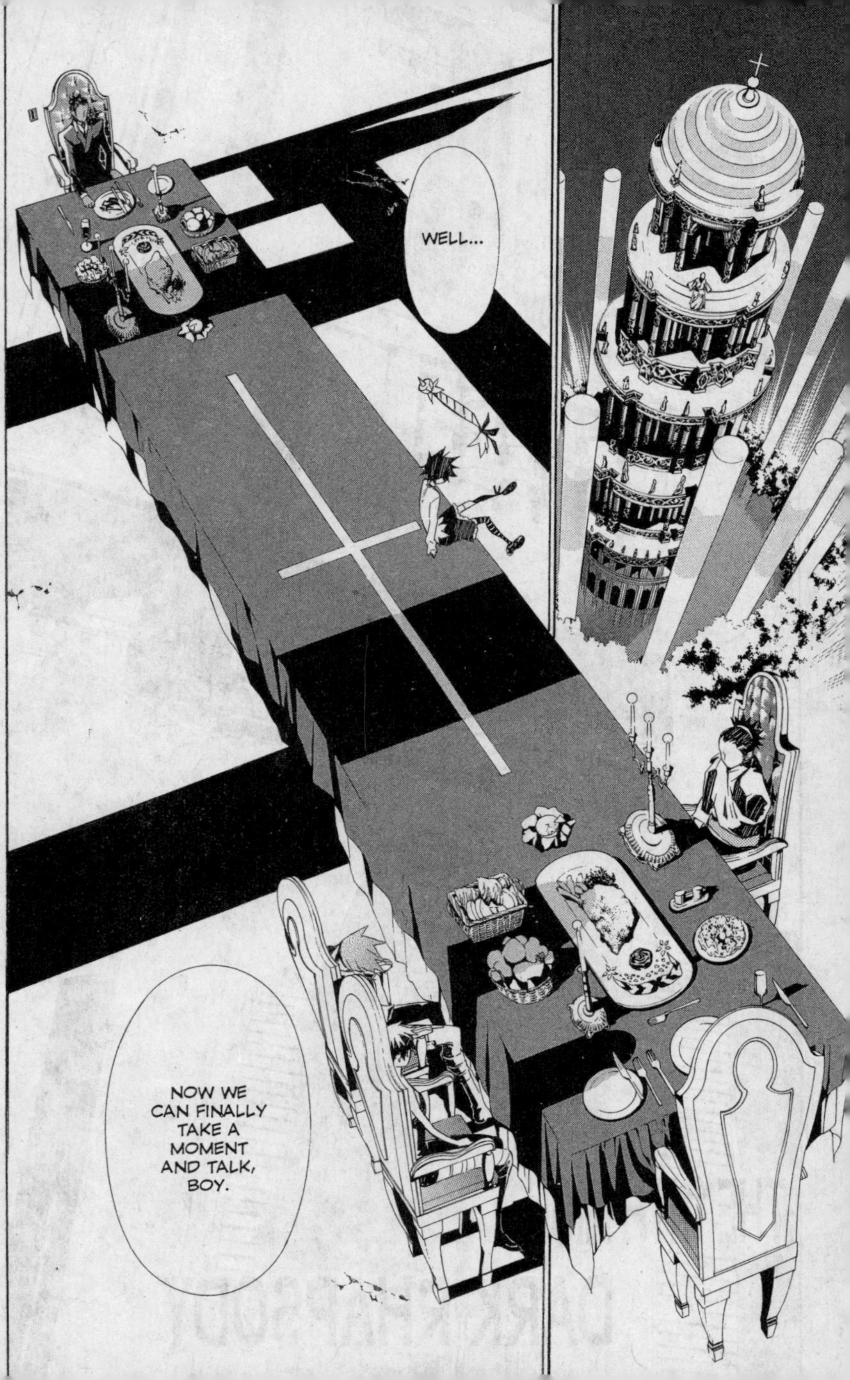
WELL...
NOW WE CAN FINALLY TAKE A MOMENT AND TALK, BOY.

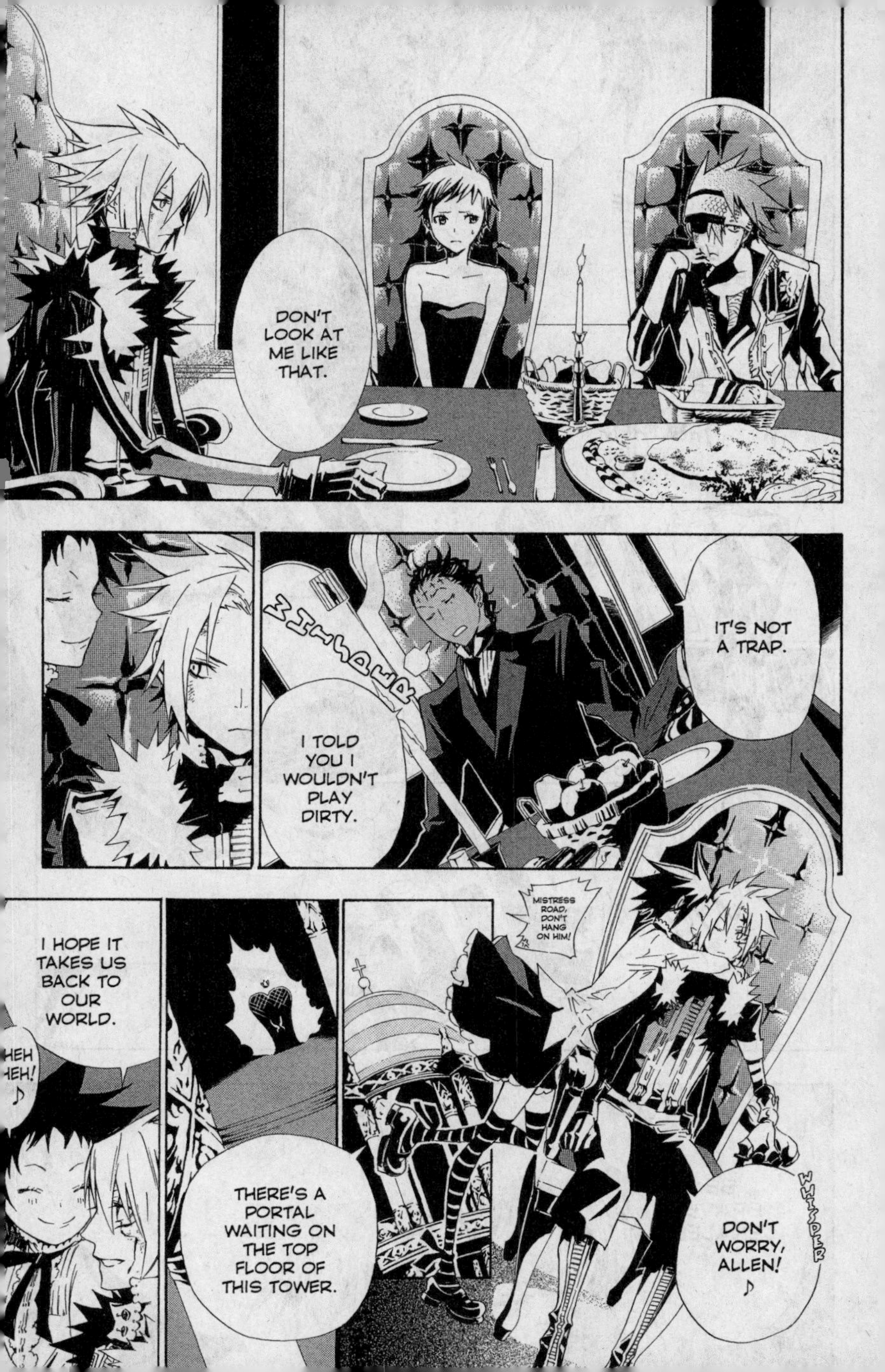
DON'T LOOK AT ME LIKE THAT.
IT'S NOT A TRAP.
WHISPER
I TOLD YOU I WOULDN'T PLAY DIRTY.
MISTRESS ROAD, DON'T HANG ON HIM!
WHISPER
DON'T WORRY, ALLEN! ♪
THERE'S A PORTAL WAITING ON THE TOP FLOOR OF THIS TOWER.
I HOPE IT TAKES US BACK TO OUR WORLD.
HEH HEH! ♪

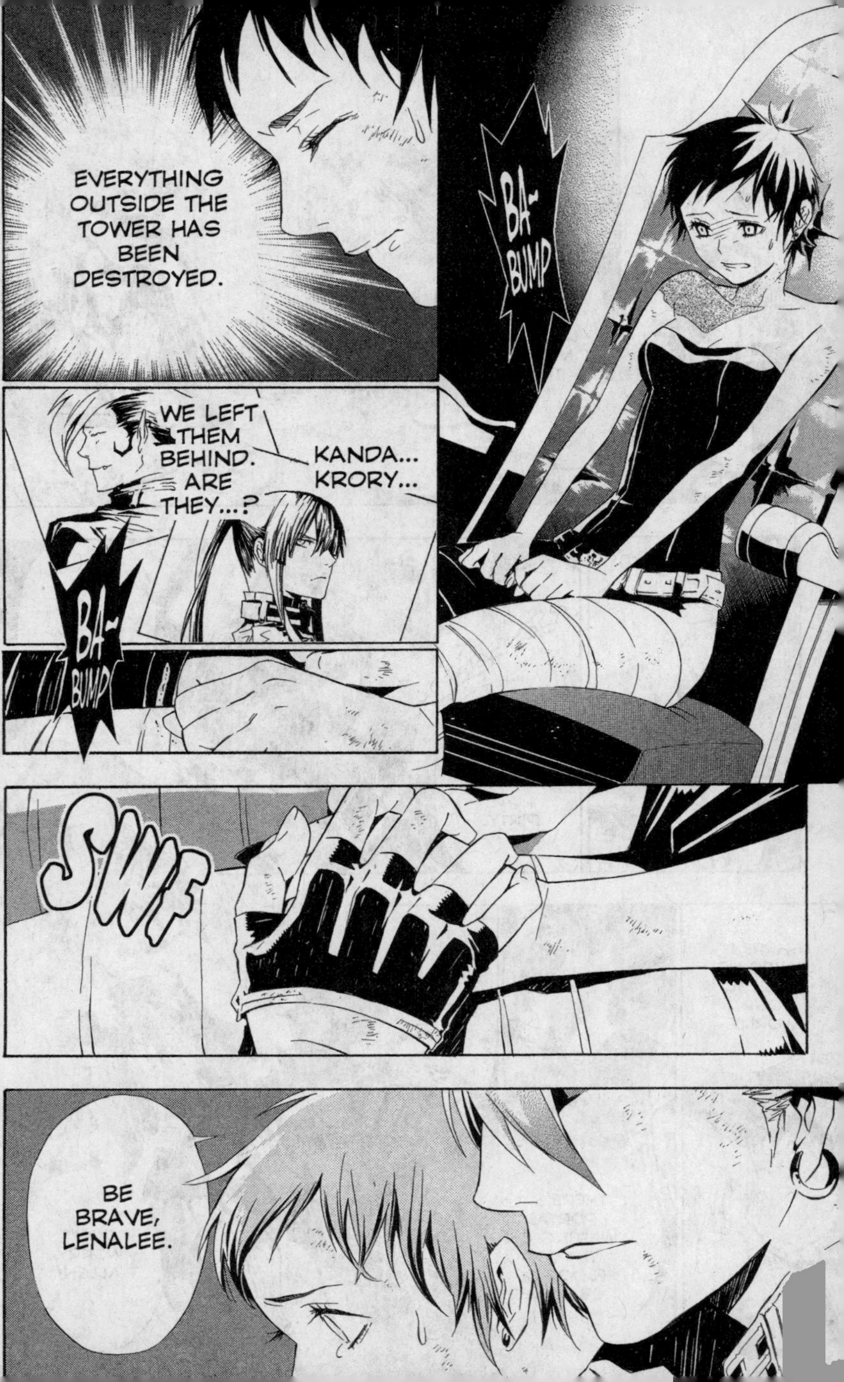
BA-BUMP
EVERYTHING OUTSIDE THE TOWER HAS BEEN DESTROYED.
KANDA... KRORY...
WE LEFT THEM BEHIND. ARE THEY...?
BA-BUMP
SWF
BE BRAVE, LENALEE.

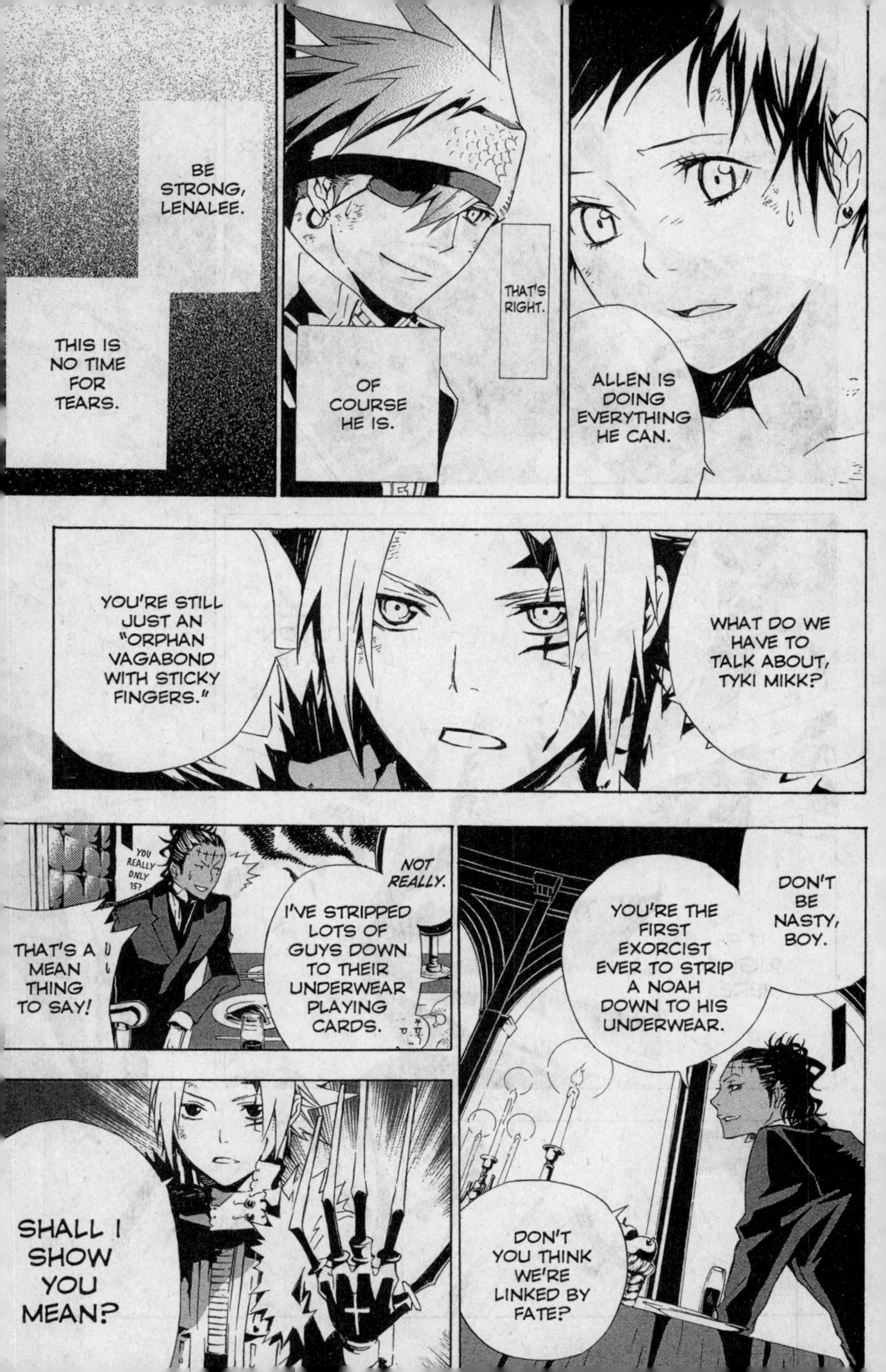
ALLEN IS DOING EVERYTHING HE CAN.
THAT'S RIGHT.
OF COURSE HE IS.
BE STRONG, LENALEE.
THIS IS NO TIME FOR TEARS.
WHAT DO WE HAVE TO TALK ABOUT, TYKI MIKK?
YOU'RE STILL JUST AN "ORPHAN VAGABOND WITH STICKY FINGERS."
DON'T BE NASTY, BOY.
YOU'RE THE FIRST EXORCIST EVER TO STRIP A NOAH DOWN TO HIS UNDERWEAR.
DON'T YOU THINK WE'RE LINKED BY FATE?
NOT REALLY.
I'VE STRIPPED LOTS OF GUYS DOWN TO THEIR UNDERWEAR PLAYING CARDS.
YOU REALLY ONLY 15?
THAT'S A MEAN THING TO SAY!
SHALL I SHOW YOU MEAN?

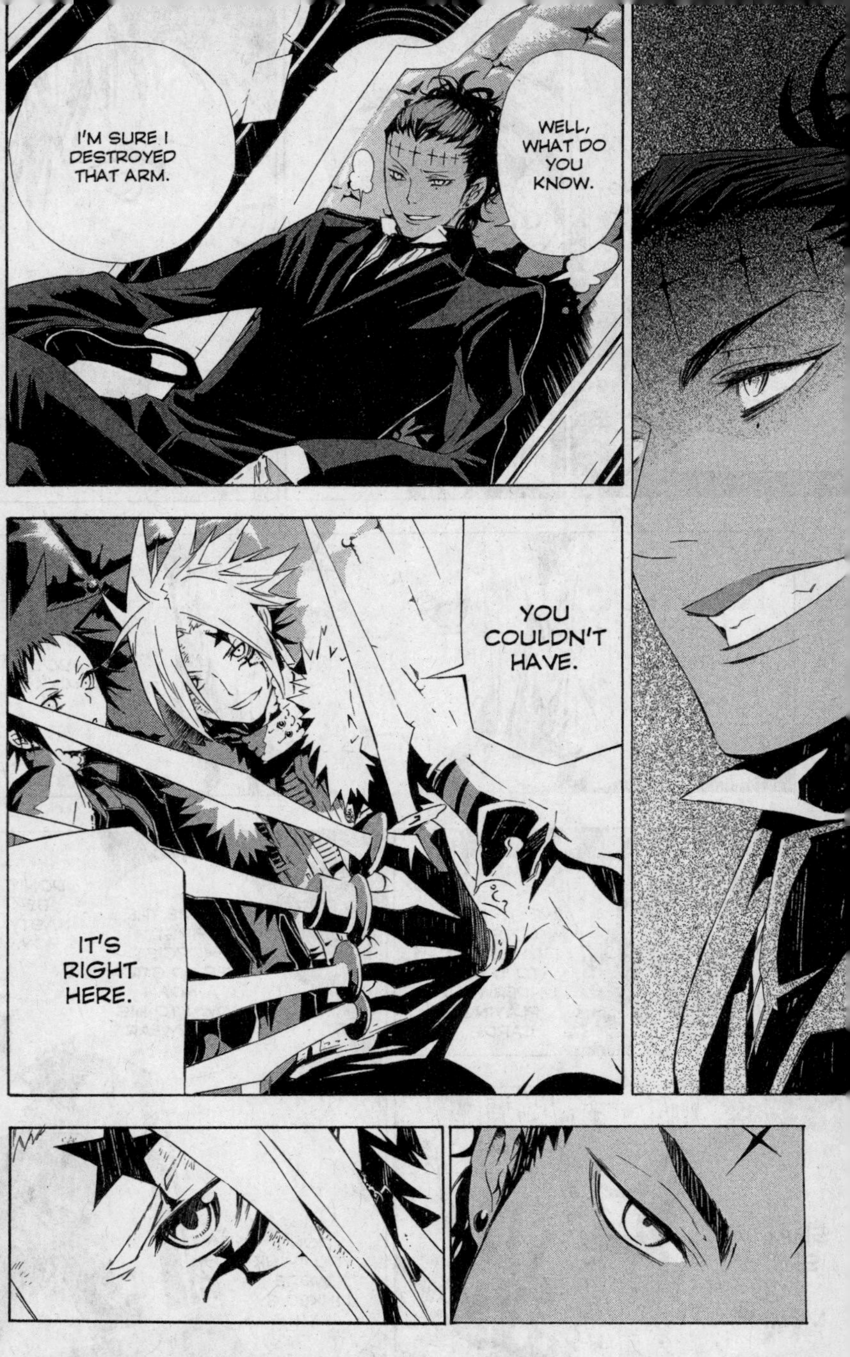
WELL, WHAT DO YOU KNOW.
I'M SURE I DESTROYED THAT ARM.
YOU COULDN'T HAVE.
IT'S RIGHT HERE.

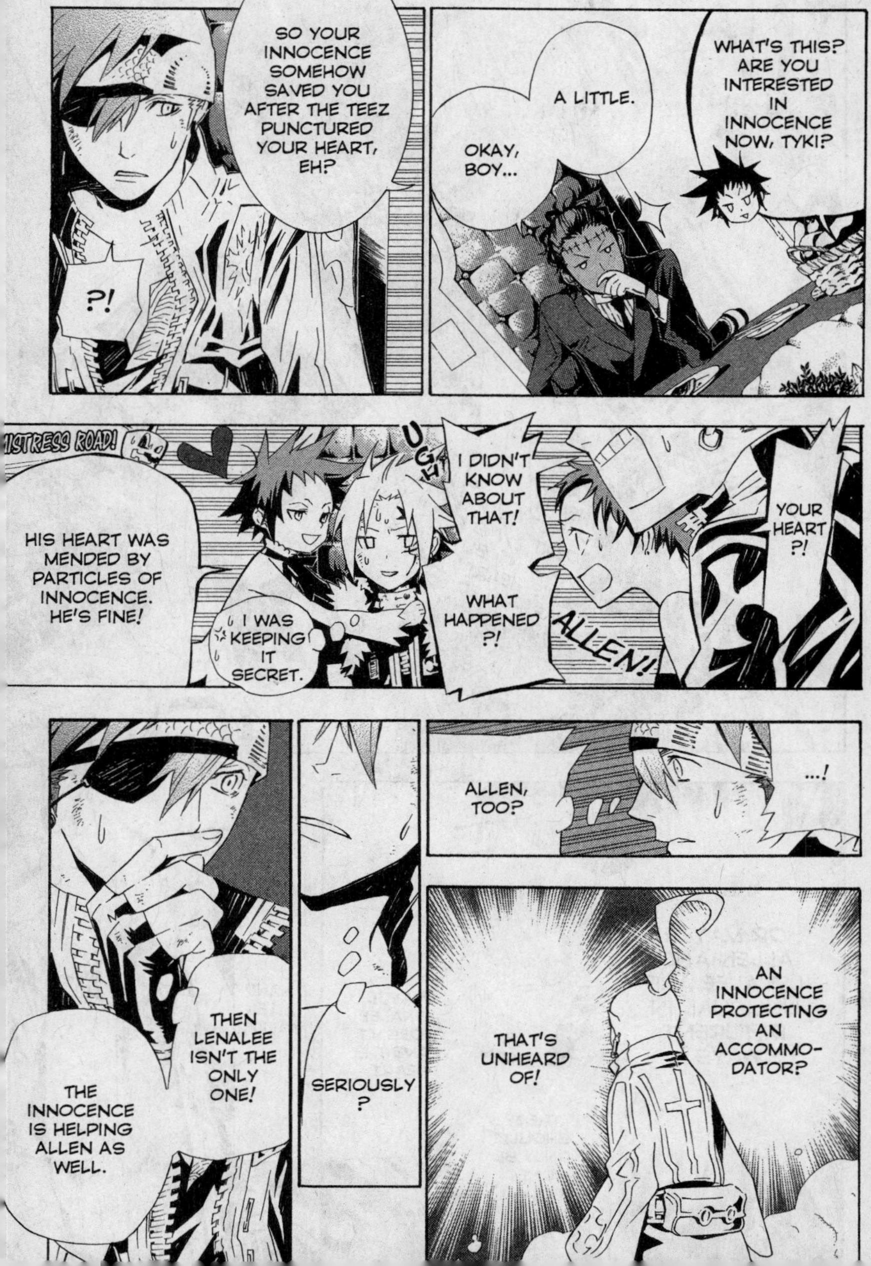
WHAT'S THIS? ARE YOU INTERESTED IN INNOCENCE NOW, TYKI?
A LITTLE.
OKAY, BOY...
SO YOUR INNOCENCE SOMEHOW SAVED YOU AFTER THE TEEZ PUNCTURED YOUR HEART, EH?
?!
YOUR HEART ?!
ALLEN!
I DIDN'T KNOW ABOUT THAT!
WHAT HAPPENED ?!
UGH
I WAS KEEPING IT SECRET.
HIS HEART WAS MENDED BY PARTICLES OF INNOCENCE. HE'S FINE!
ISTRESS ROAD!
...!
ALLEN, TOO?
AN INNOCENCE PROTECTING AN ACCOMMODATOR?
THAT'S UNHEARD OF!
SERIOUSLY ?
THEN LENALEE ISN'T THE ONLY ONE!
THE INNOCENCE IS HELPING ALLEN AS WELL.

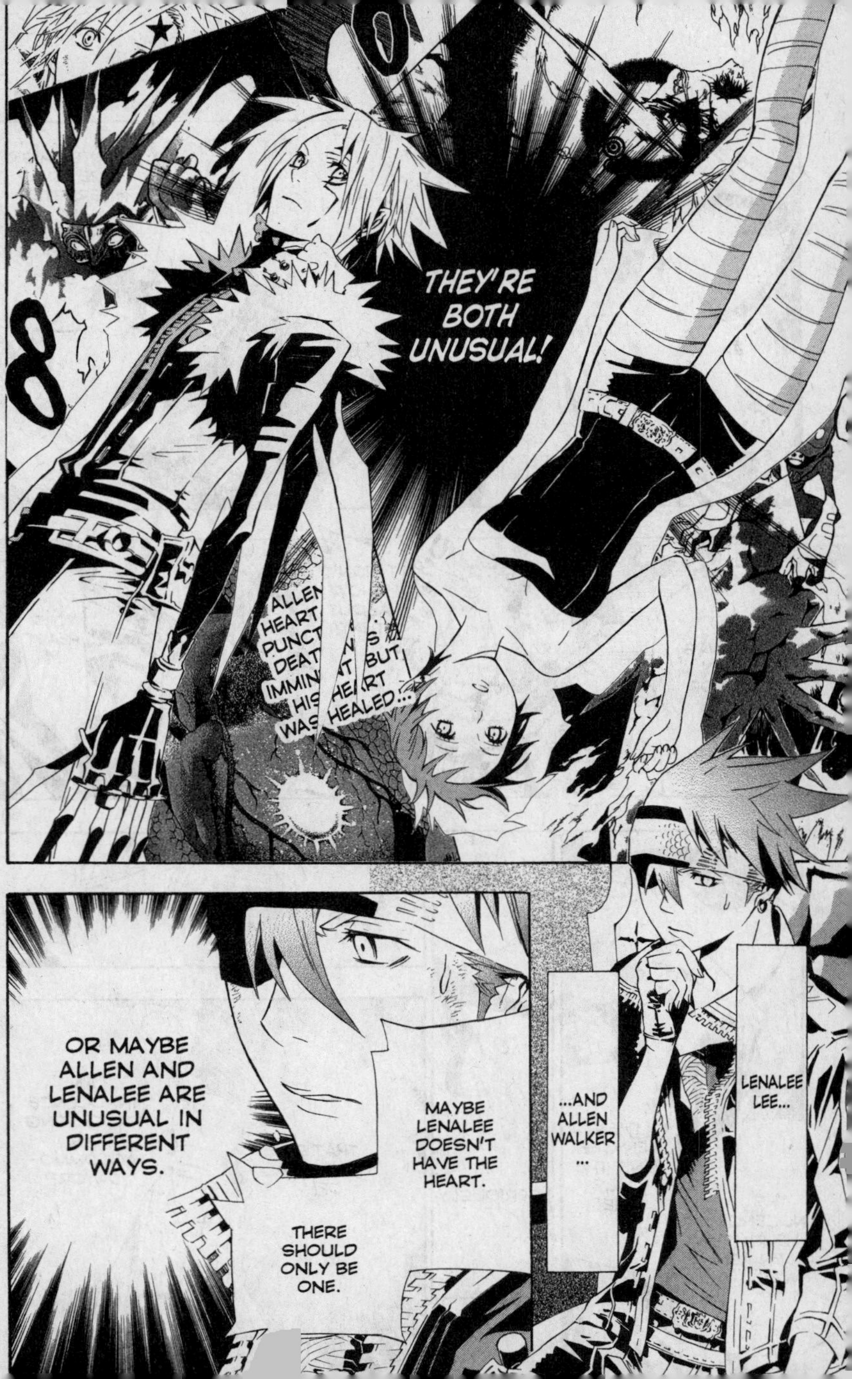
THEY'RE BOTH UNUSUAL!
ALLEN HEART PUNCT S DEAT BUT IMMIN HIS HEART WAS HEALED...
LENALEE LEE...
...AND ALLEN WALKER ...
MAYBE LENALEE DOESN'T HAVE THE HEART.
THERE SHOULD ONLY BE ONE.
OR MAYBE ALLEN AND LENALEE ARE UNUSUAL IN DIFFERENT WAYS.

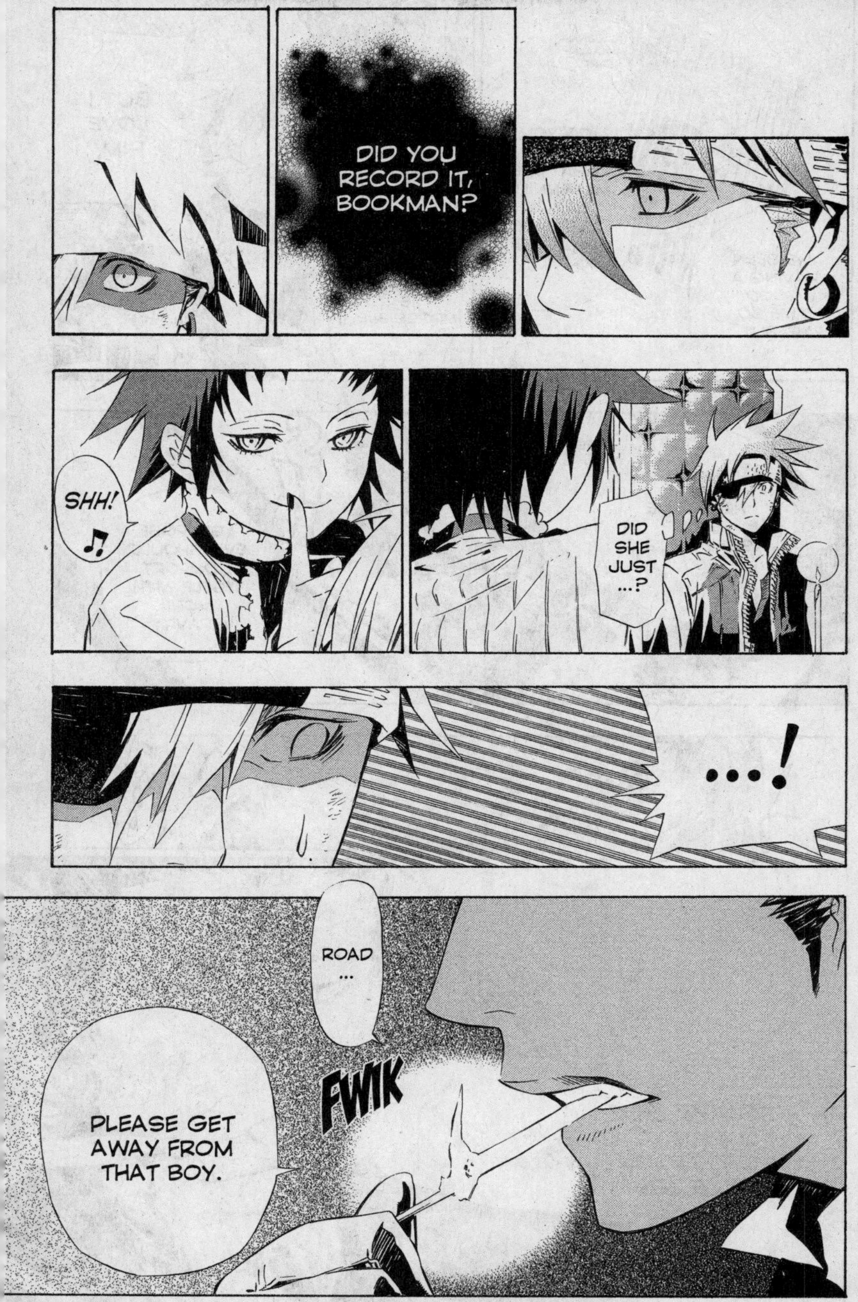
DID YOU RECORD IT, BOOKMAN?
DID SHE JUST ...?
SHH! ♪
...!
ROAD ...
FWIK
PLEASE GET AWAY FROM THAT BOY.

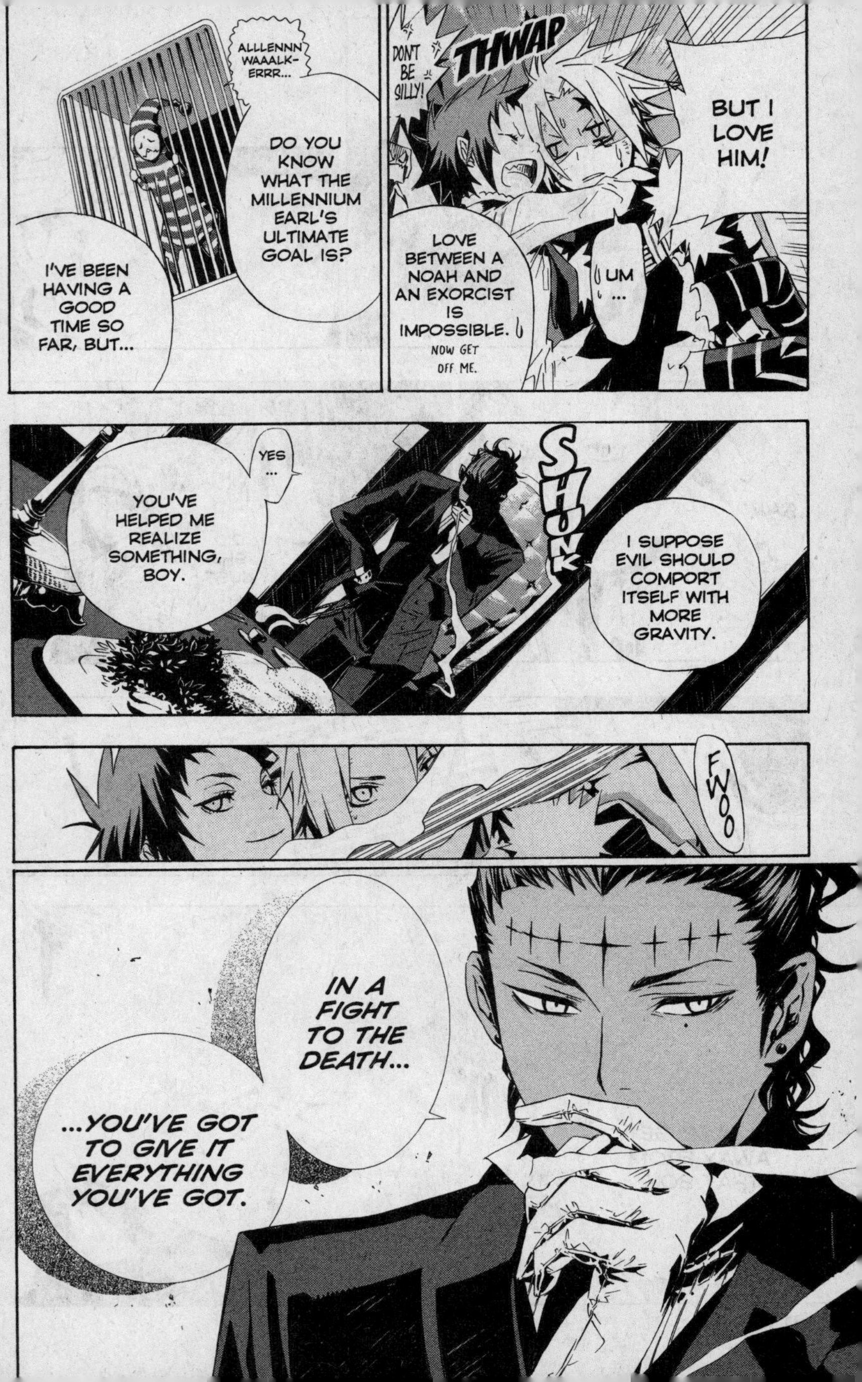
BUT I LOVE HIM!
THWAP
DON'T BE SILLY!
UM ...
LOVE BETWEEN A NOAH AND AN EXORCIST IS IMPOSSIBLE.
NOW GET OFF ME.
ALLLENNN WAAALK-ERRR...
DO YOU KNOW WHAT THE MILLENNIUM EARL'S ULTIMATE GOAL IS?
I'VE BEEN HAVING A GOOD TIME SO FAR, BUT...
SHUNK
I SUPPOSE EVIL SHOULD COMPORT ITSELF WITH MORE GRAVITY.
YES ...
YOU'VE HELPED ME REALIZE SOMETHING, BOY.
FWOO
IN A FIGHT TO THE DEATH...
...YOU'VE GOT TO GIVE IT EVERYTHING YOU'VE GOT.

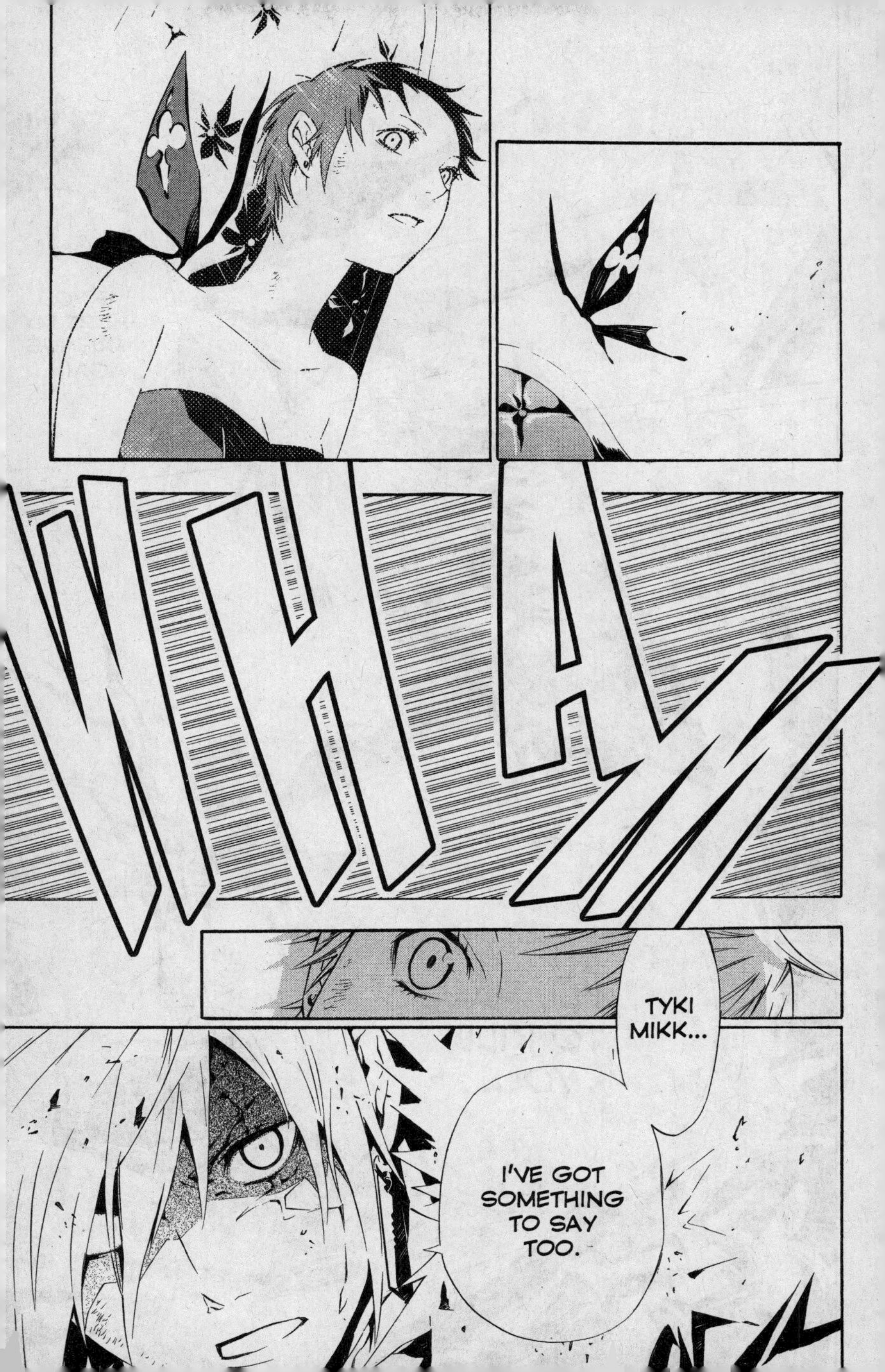
WHAM
TYKI MIKK...
I'VE GOT SOMETHING TO SAY TOO.

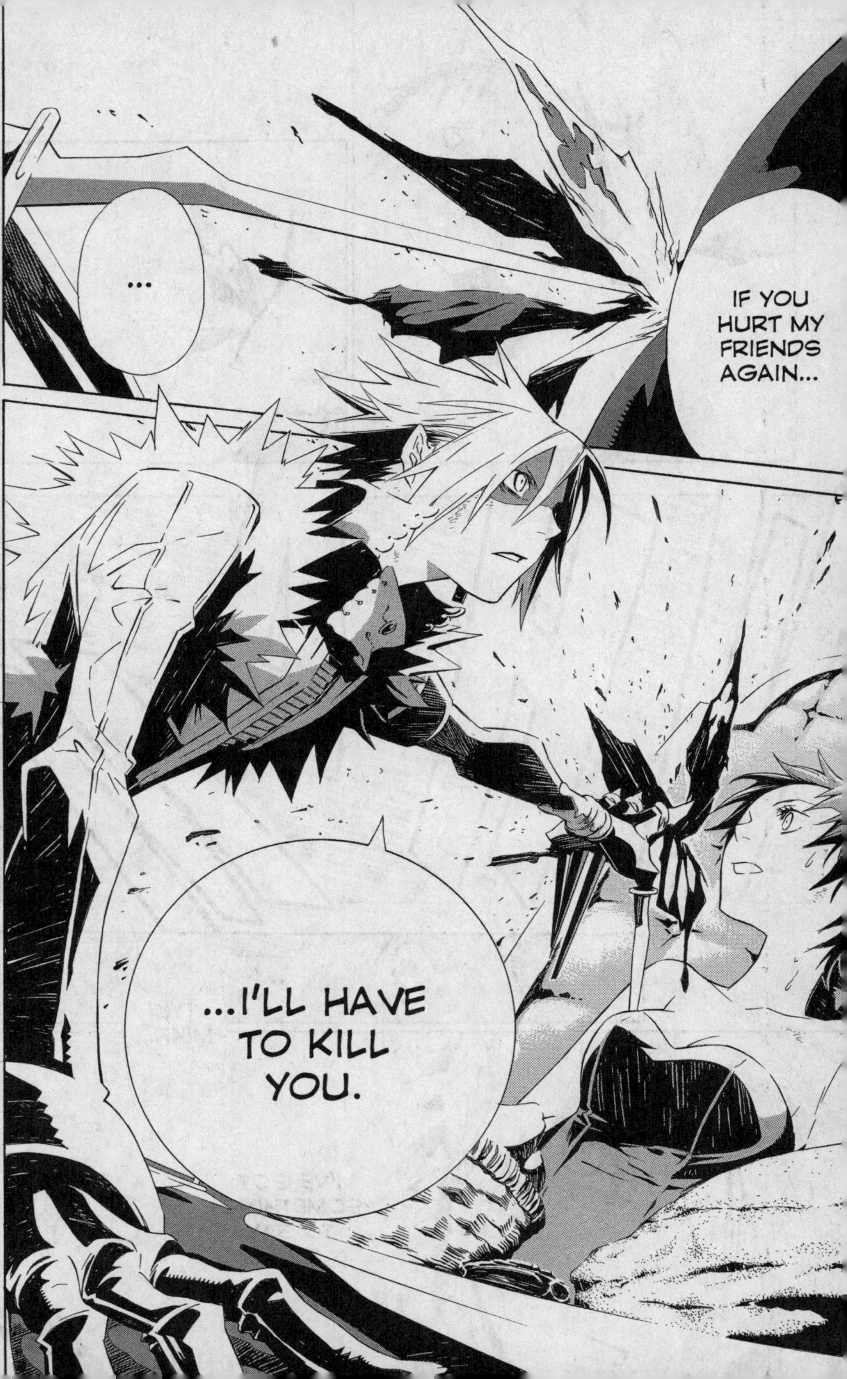
IF YOU HURT MY FRIENDS AGAIN...
...
...I'LL HAVE TO KILL YOU.

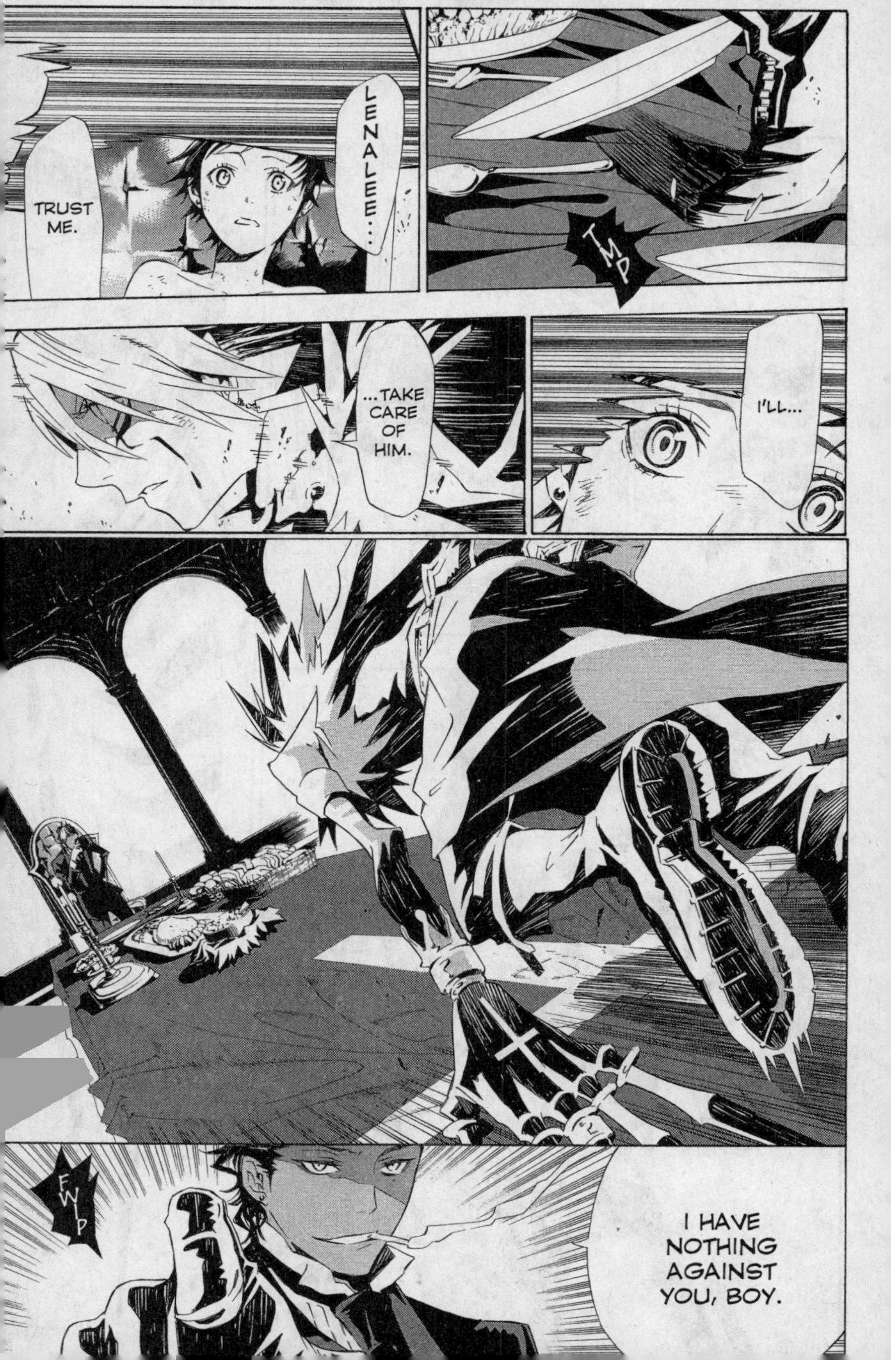
TMP
LENALEE...
TRUST ME.
I'LL...
...TAKE CARE OF HIM.
I HAVE NOTHING AGAINST YOU, BOY.
FWIP

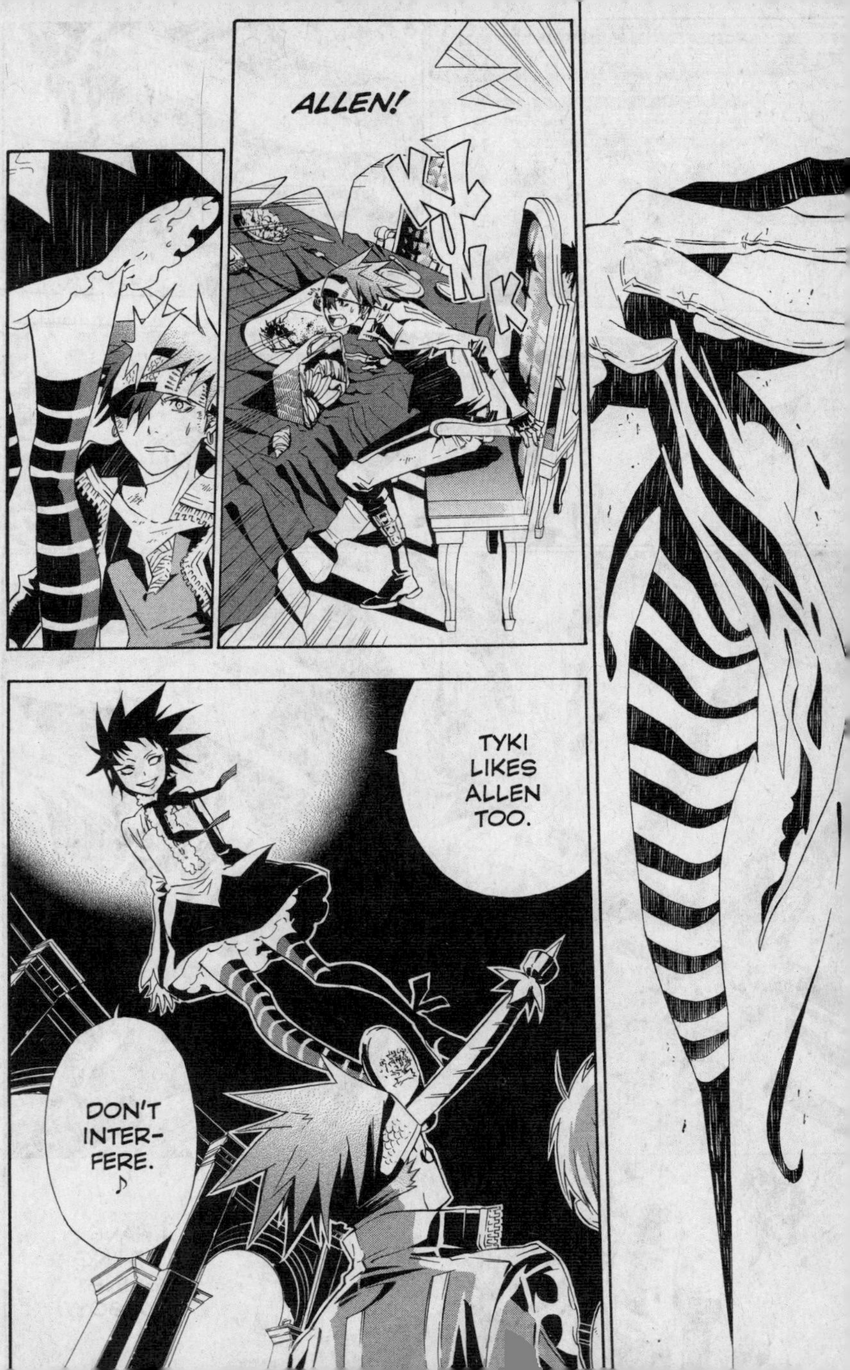
ALLEN!
KLUNK
TYKI LIKES ALLEN TOO.
DON'T INTER-FERE. ♪

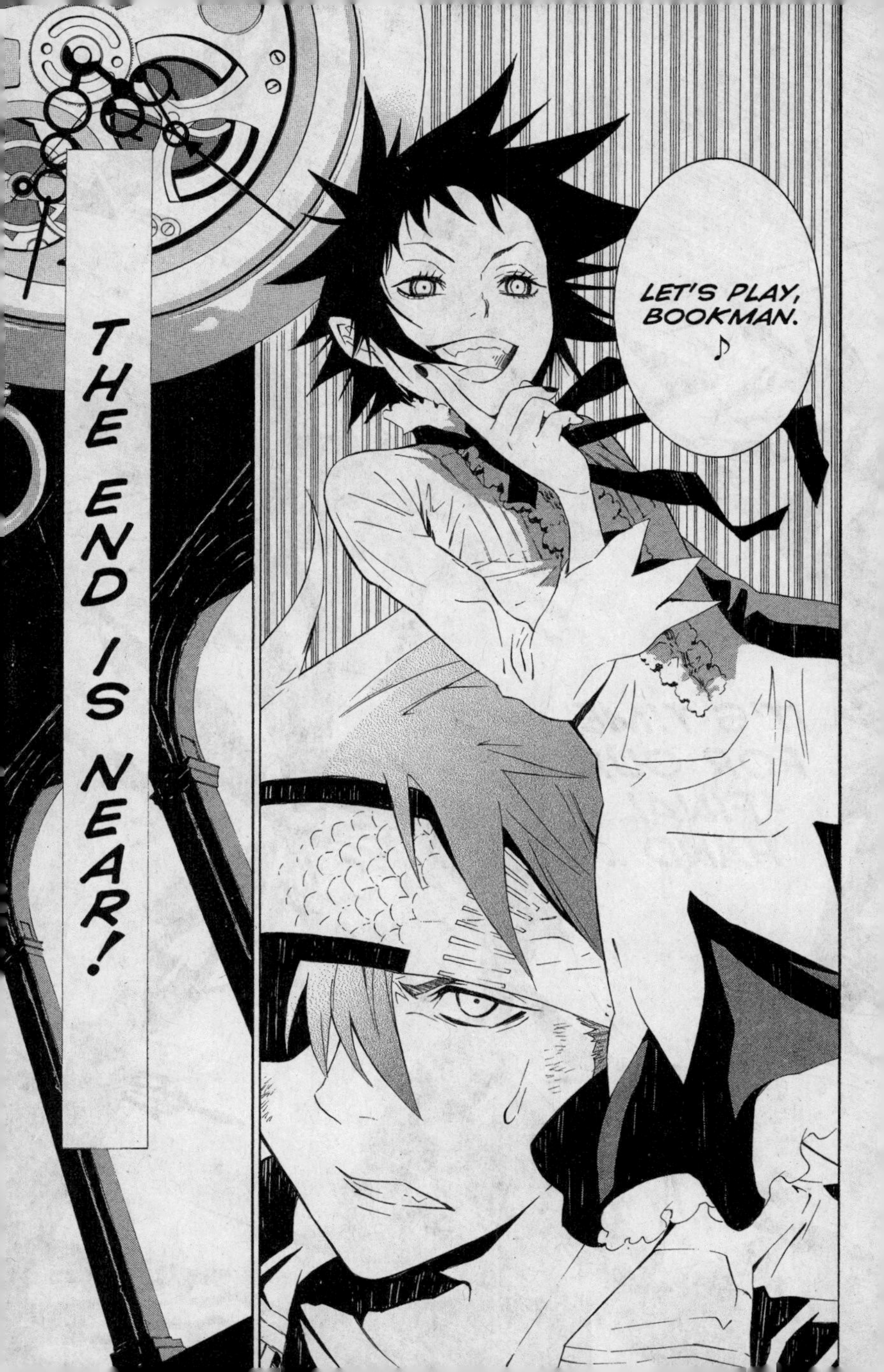
LET'S PLAY, BOOKMAN. ♪
THE END IS NEAR!

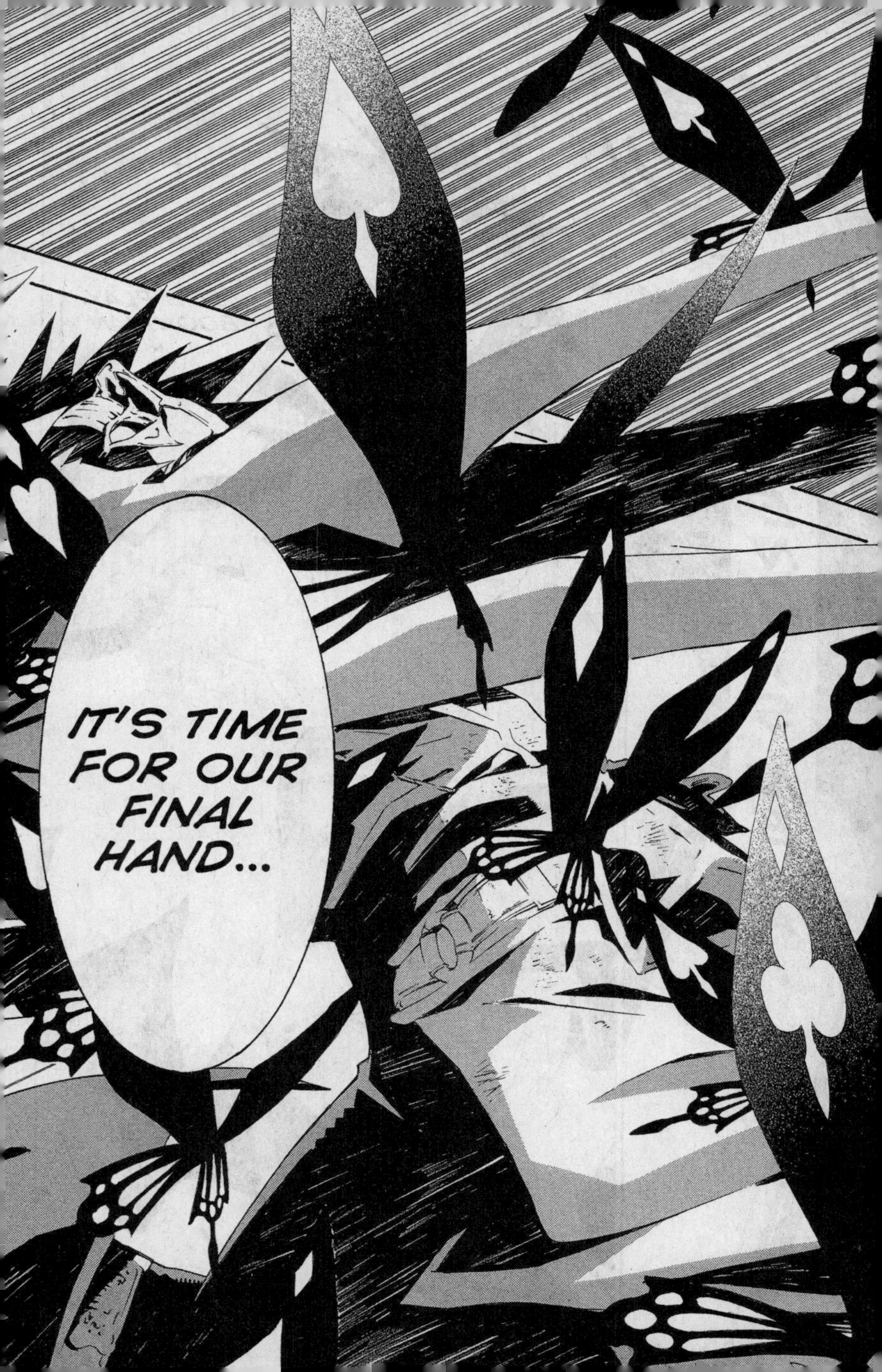
IT'S TIME FOR OUR FINAL HAND...

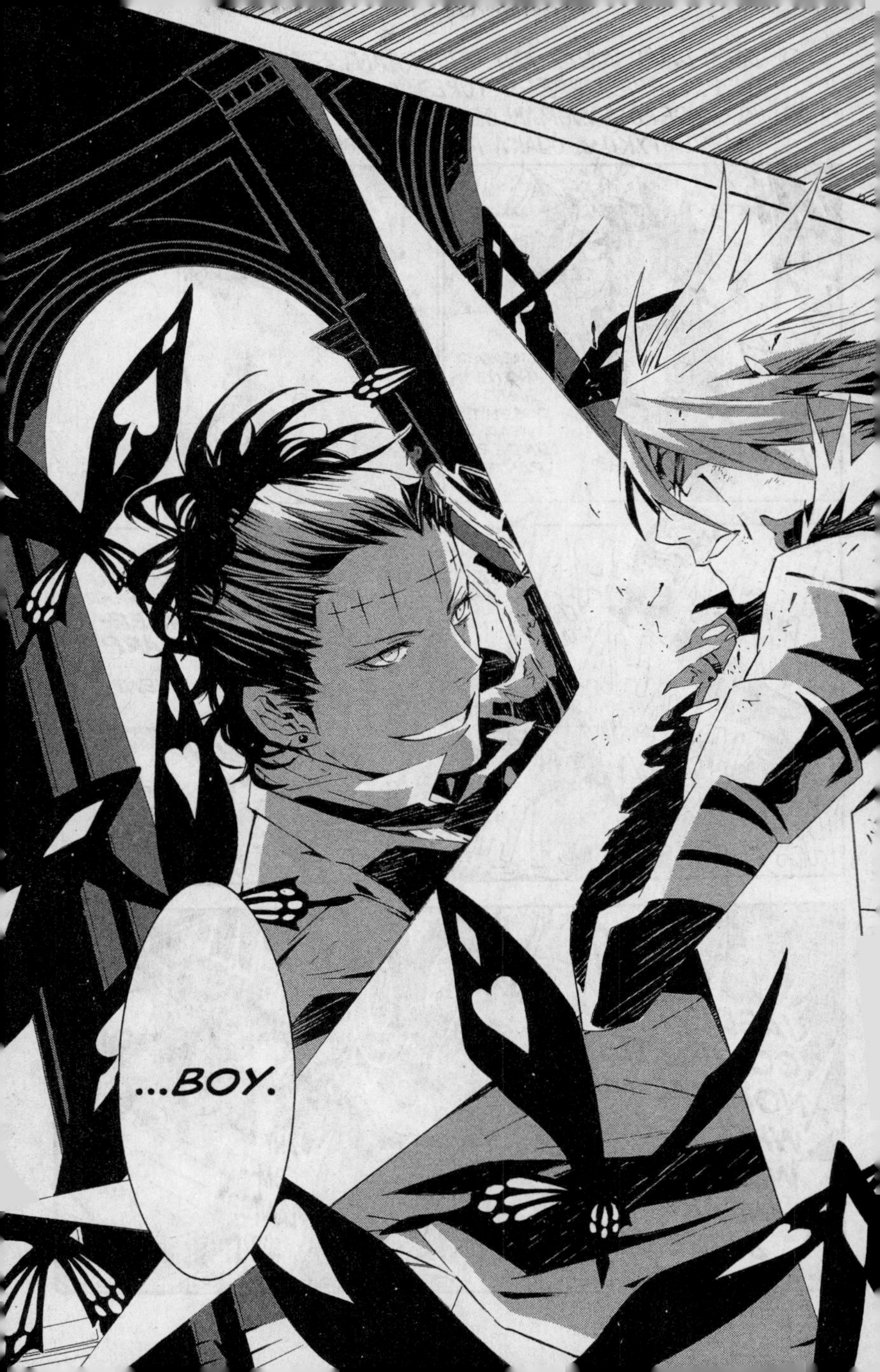
...BOY.

Q. DOES DAVID WEAR ANY UNDERPANTS? (SATOMI SUZUKI, CHIBA PREFECTURE)

Q. IS JASDERO A WOMAN OR A MAN? (I-LOVE-TYKI!♥, OSAKA PREFECTURE)

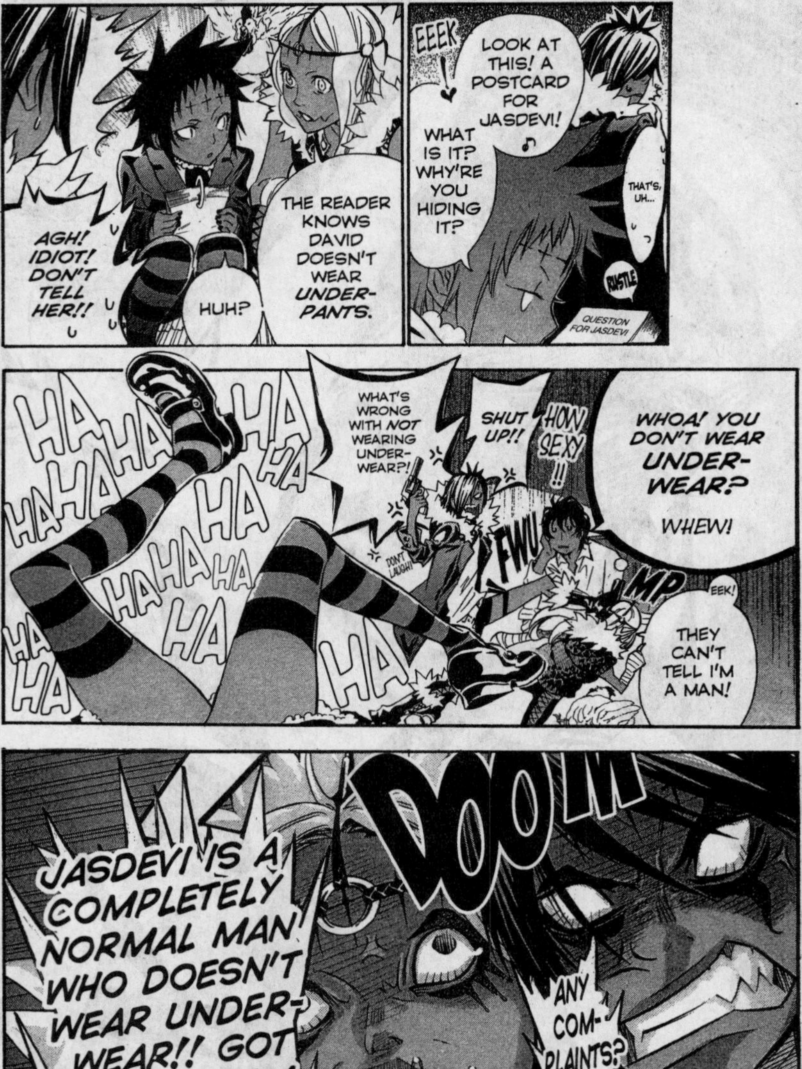
EEEK!
LOOK AT THIS! A POSTCARD FOR JASDEVI! ♪
WHAT IS IT? WHY'RE YOU HIDING IT?
THAT'S, UH...
RUSTLE
QUESTION FOR JASDEVI
THE READER KNOWS DAVID DOESN'T WEAR UNDER-PANTS.
HUH?
AGH! IDIOT! DON'T TELL HER!!
WHOA! YOU DON'T WEAR UNDER-WEAR?
WHEW!
EEK!
THEY CAN'T TELL I'M A MAN!
HOW SEXY!!
SHUT UP!!
FWUMP
WHAT'S WRONG WITH NOT WEARING UNDER-WEAR?!
DON'T LAUGH!
HA HA HA HA HA HA HA HA HA HA HA HA HA HA HA HA
DOOM
ANY COM-PLAINTS? HUH?
JASDEVI IS A COMPLETELY NORMAL MAN WHO DOESN'T WEAR UNDER-WEAR!! GOT A PROBLEM WITH THAT?!

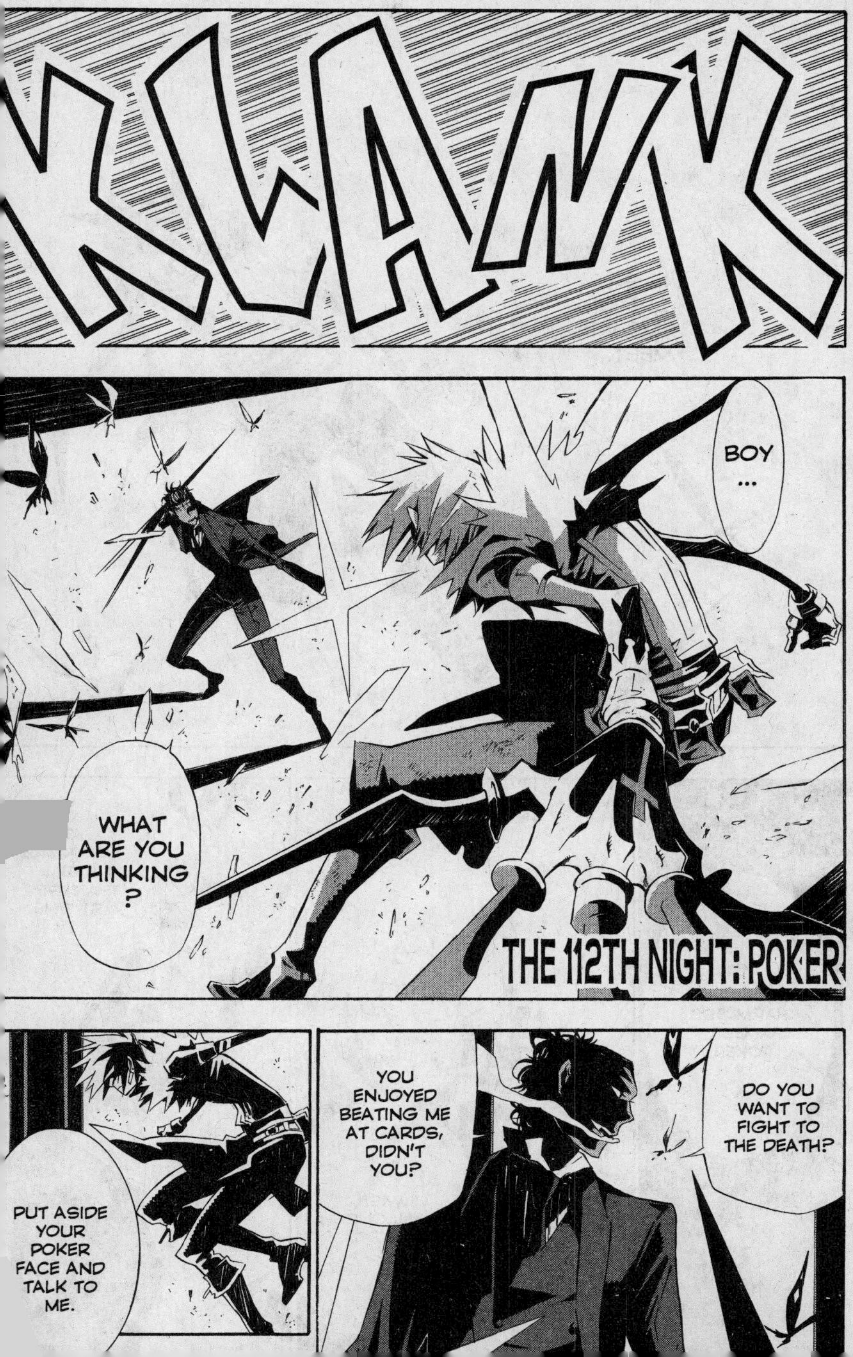
KLANK
BOY ...
WHAT ARE YOU THINKING ?
THE 112TH NIGHT: POKER
DO YOU WANT TO FIGHT TO THE DEATH?
YOU ENJOYED BEATING ME AT CARDS, DIDN'T YOU?
PUT ASIDE YOUR POKER FACE AND TALK TO ME.

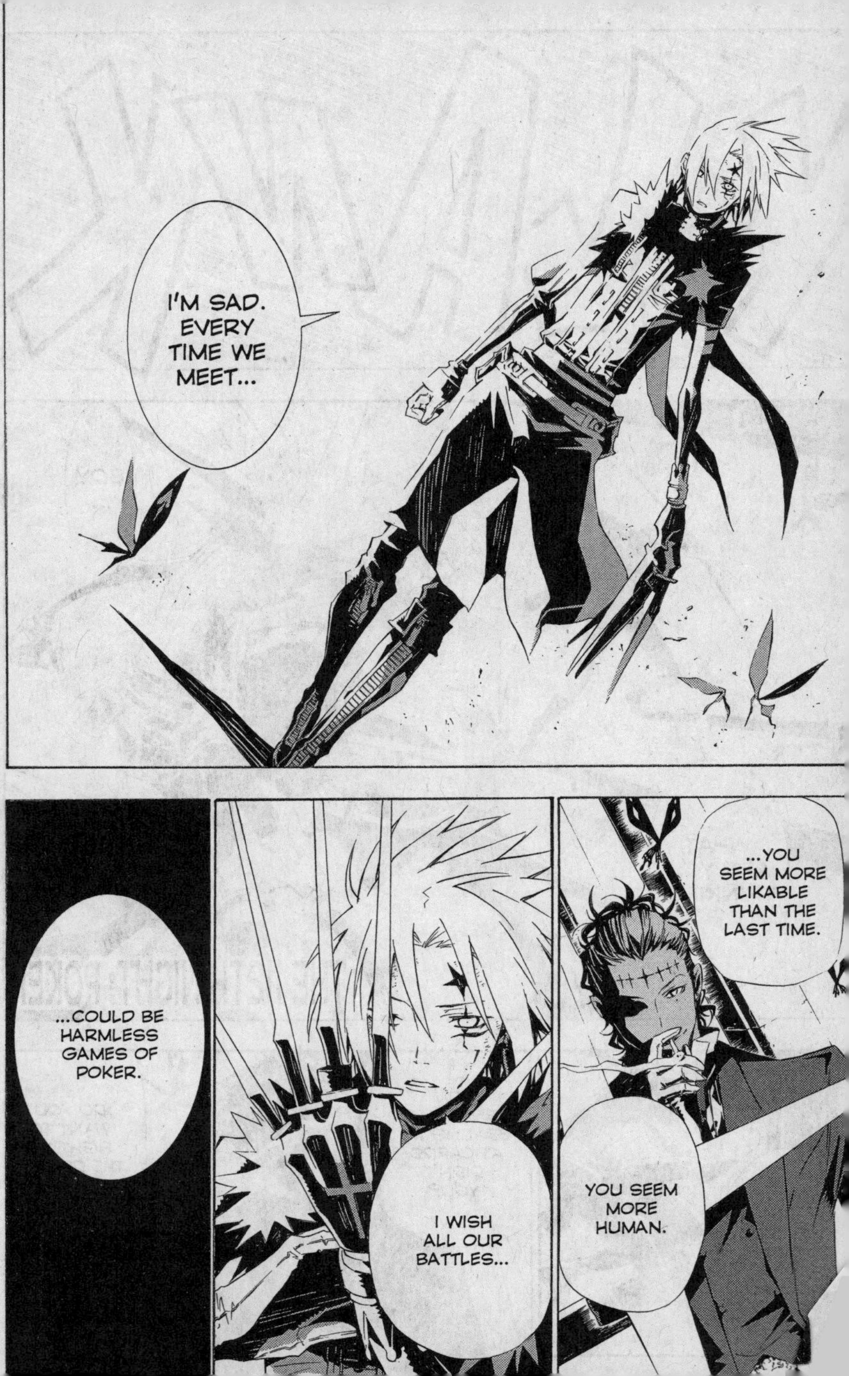
I'M SAD. EVERY TIME WE MEET...
...YOU SEEM MORE LIKABLE THAN THE LAST TIME.
YOU SEEM MORE HUMAN.
I WISH ALL OUR BATTLES...
...COULD BE HARMLESS GAMES OF POKER.

THE 112TH NIGHT: POKER

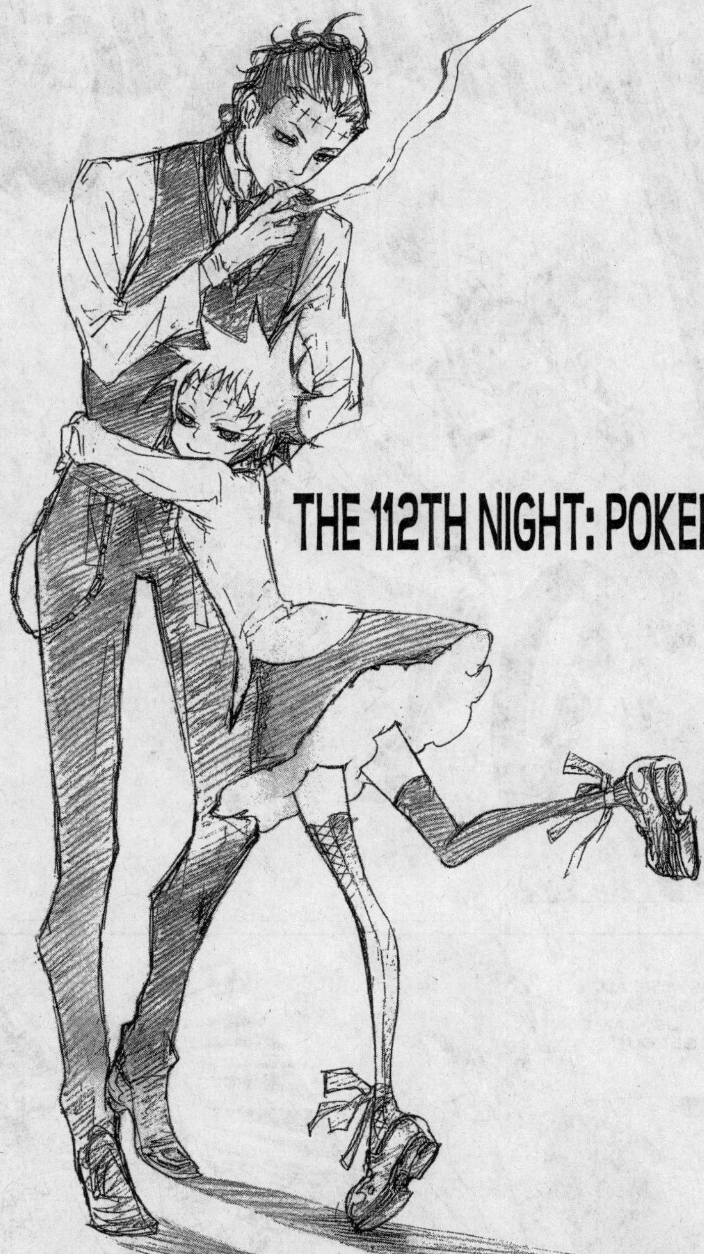

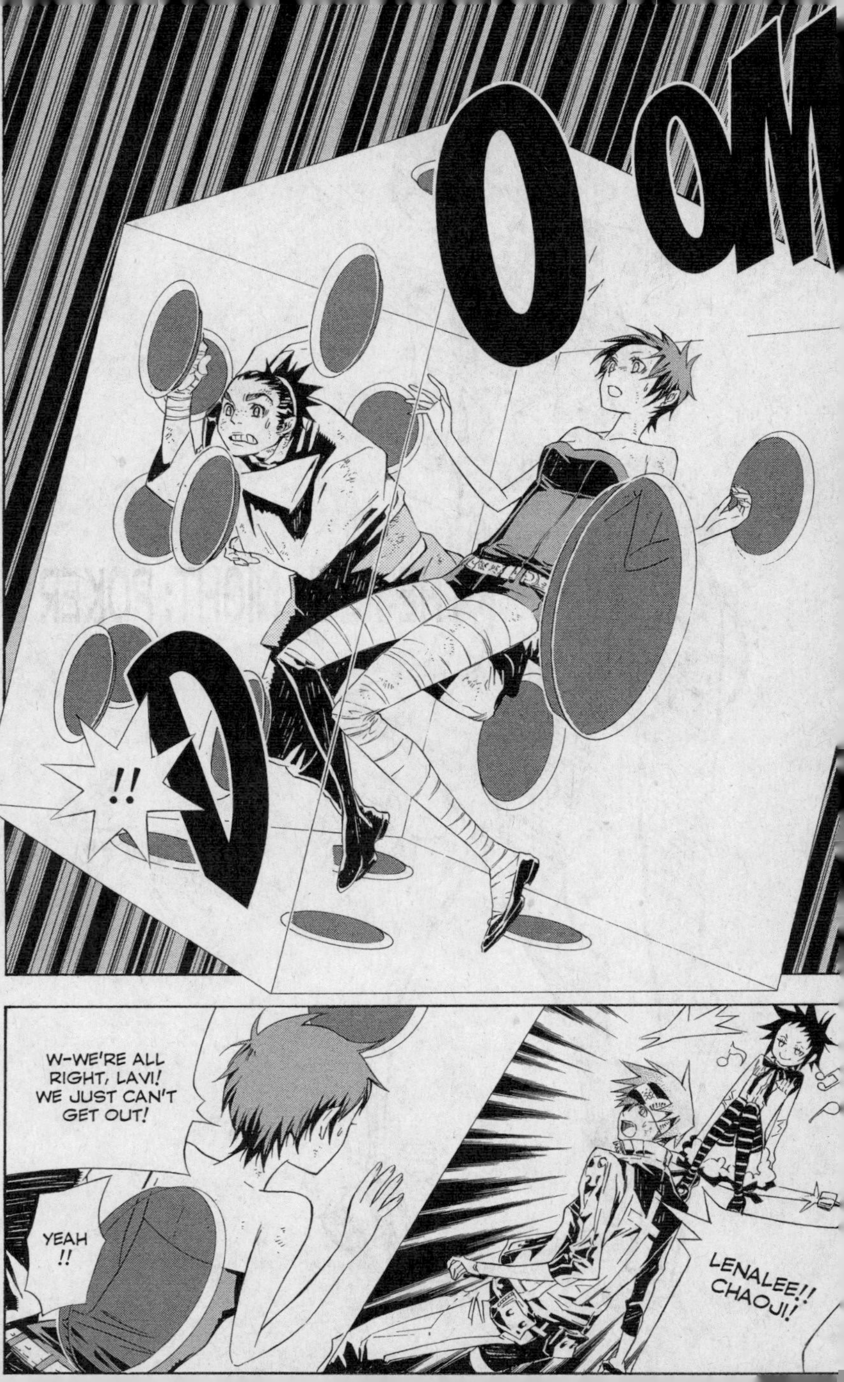
DOOM
!!
LENALEE!! CHAOJI!
W-WE'RE ALL RIGHT, LAVI! WE JUST CAN'T GET OUT!
YEAH !!

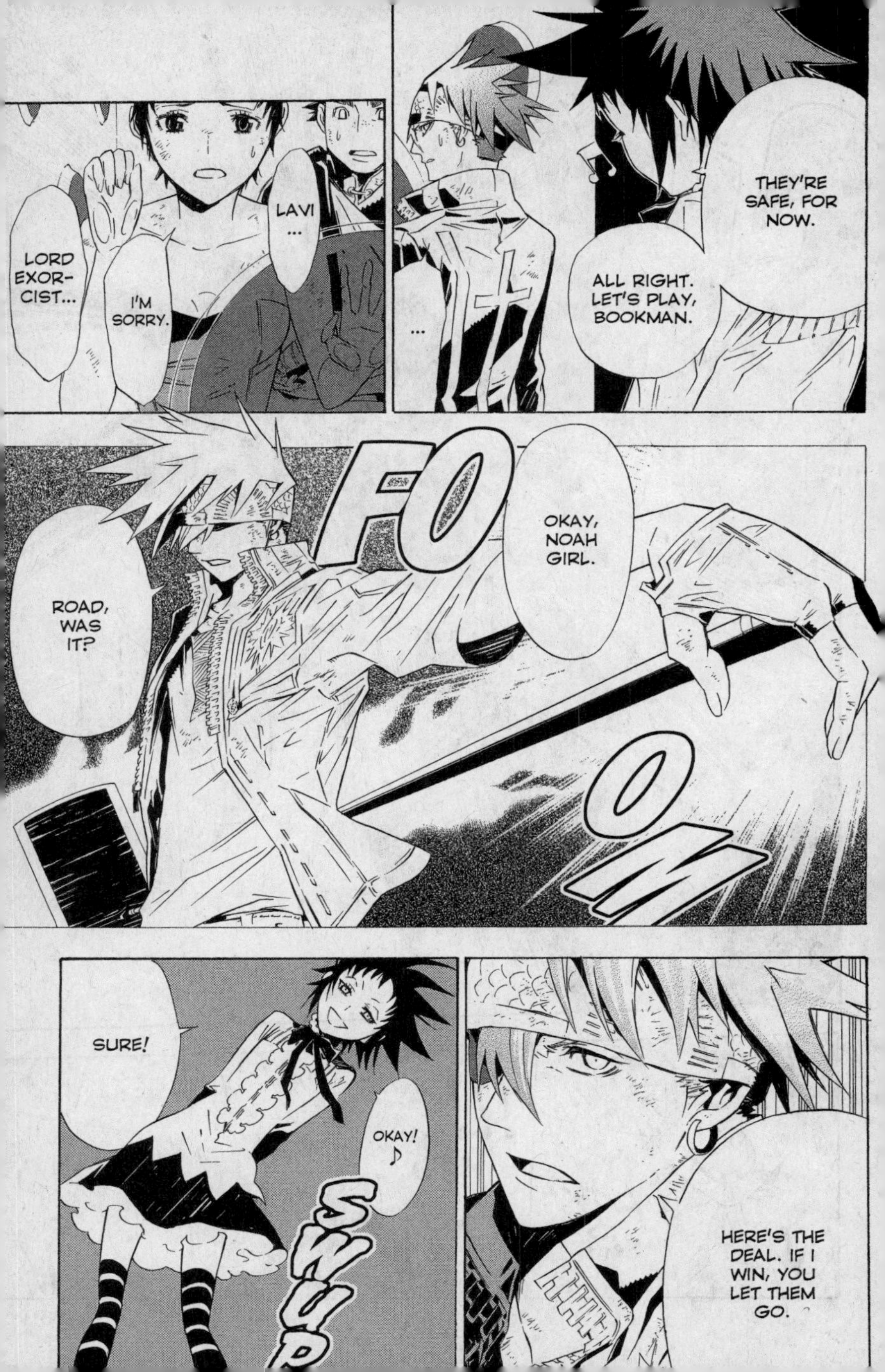
THEY'RE SAFE, FOR NOW.
ALL RIGHT. LET'S PLAY, BOOKMAN.
...
LAVI ...
LORD EXORCIST...
I'M SORRY.
OKAY, NOAH GIRL.
FOOOM
ROAD, WAS IT?
HERE'S THE DEAL. IF I WIN, YOU LET THEM GO.
SURE!
OKAY! ♪
SWUP

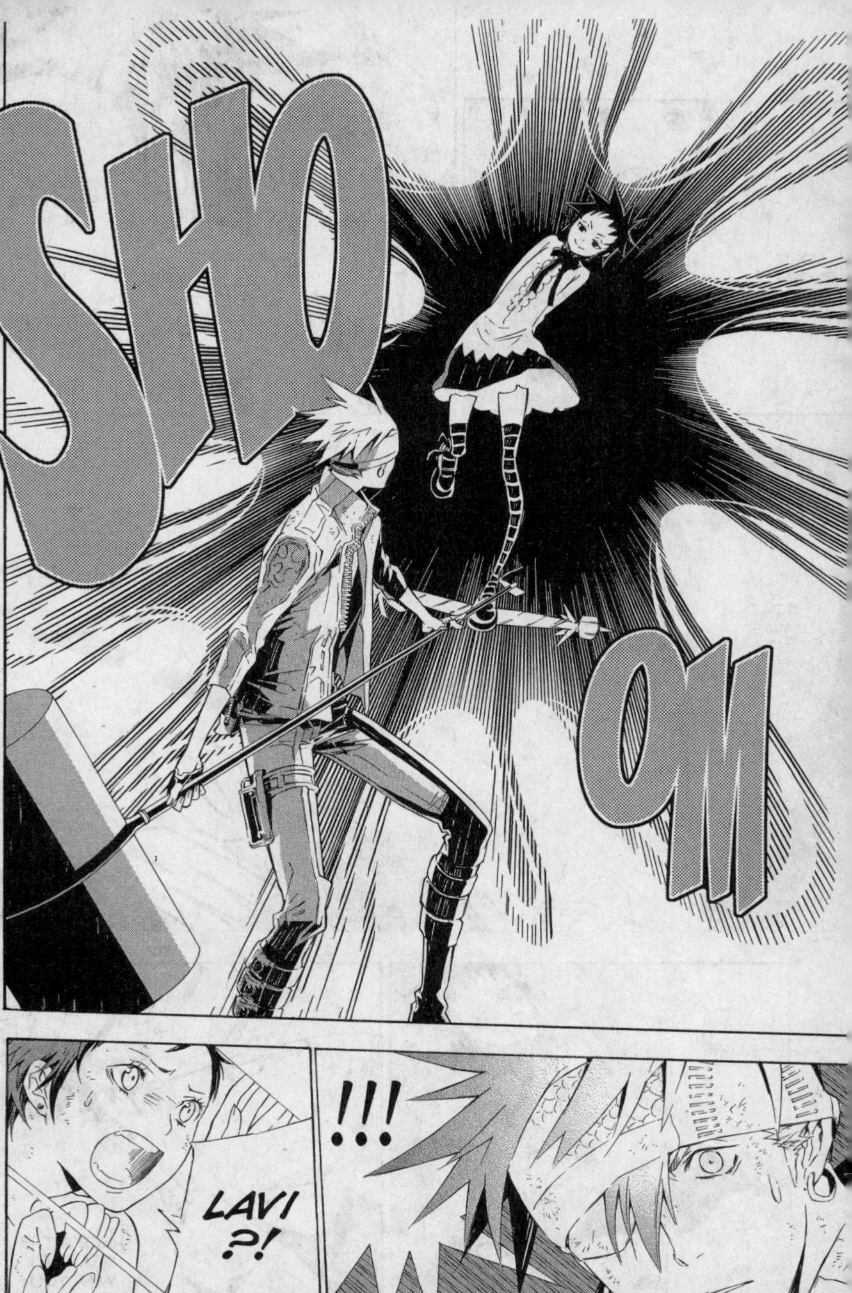
SHO
OM
!!!
LAVI ?!

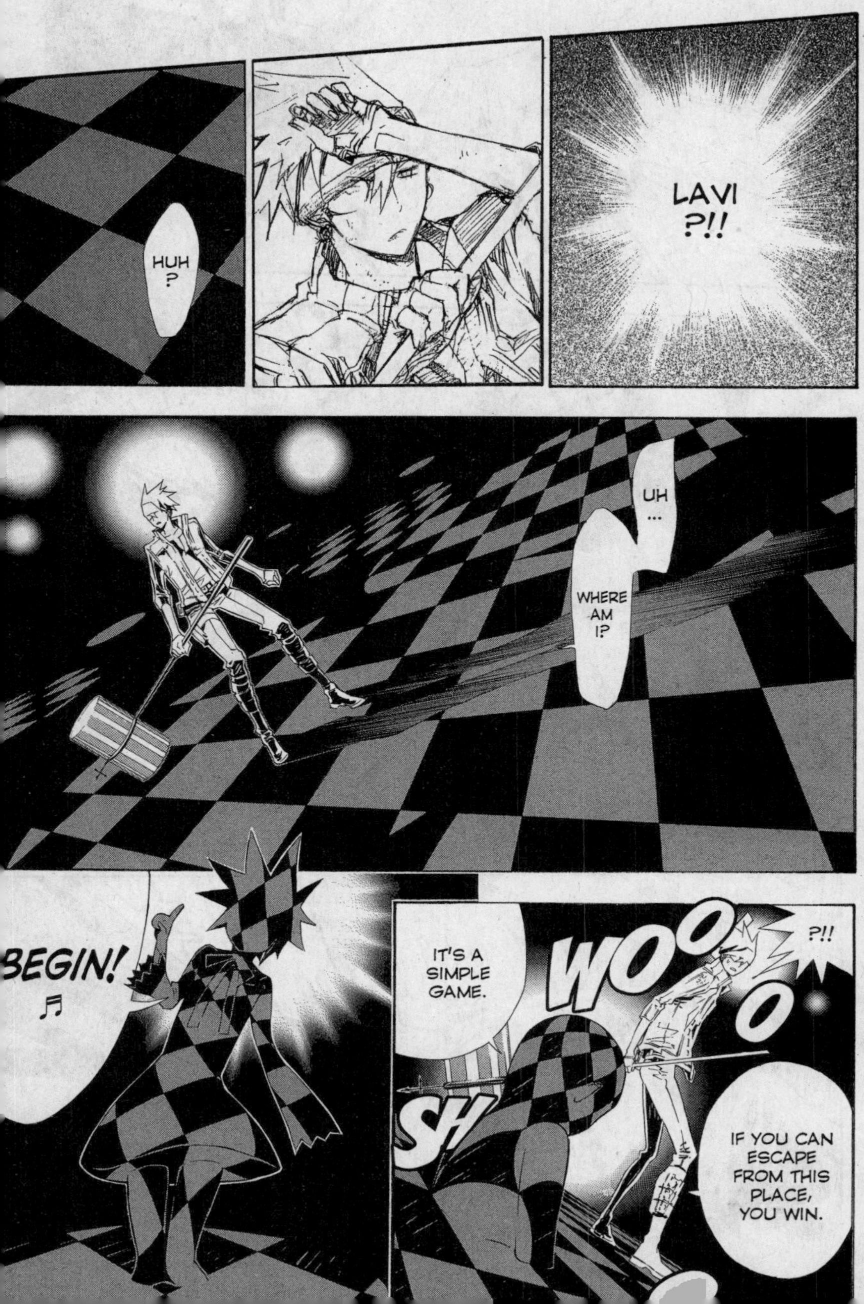
LAVI ?!!
HUH ?
UH ...
WHERE AM I?
?!!
WOOO
IT'S A SIMPLE GAME.
IF YOU CAN ESCAPE FROM THIS PLACE, YOU WIN.
SH
BEGIN! ♬

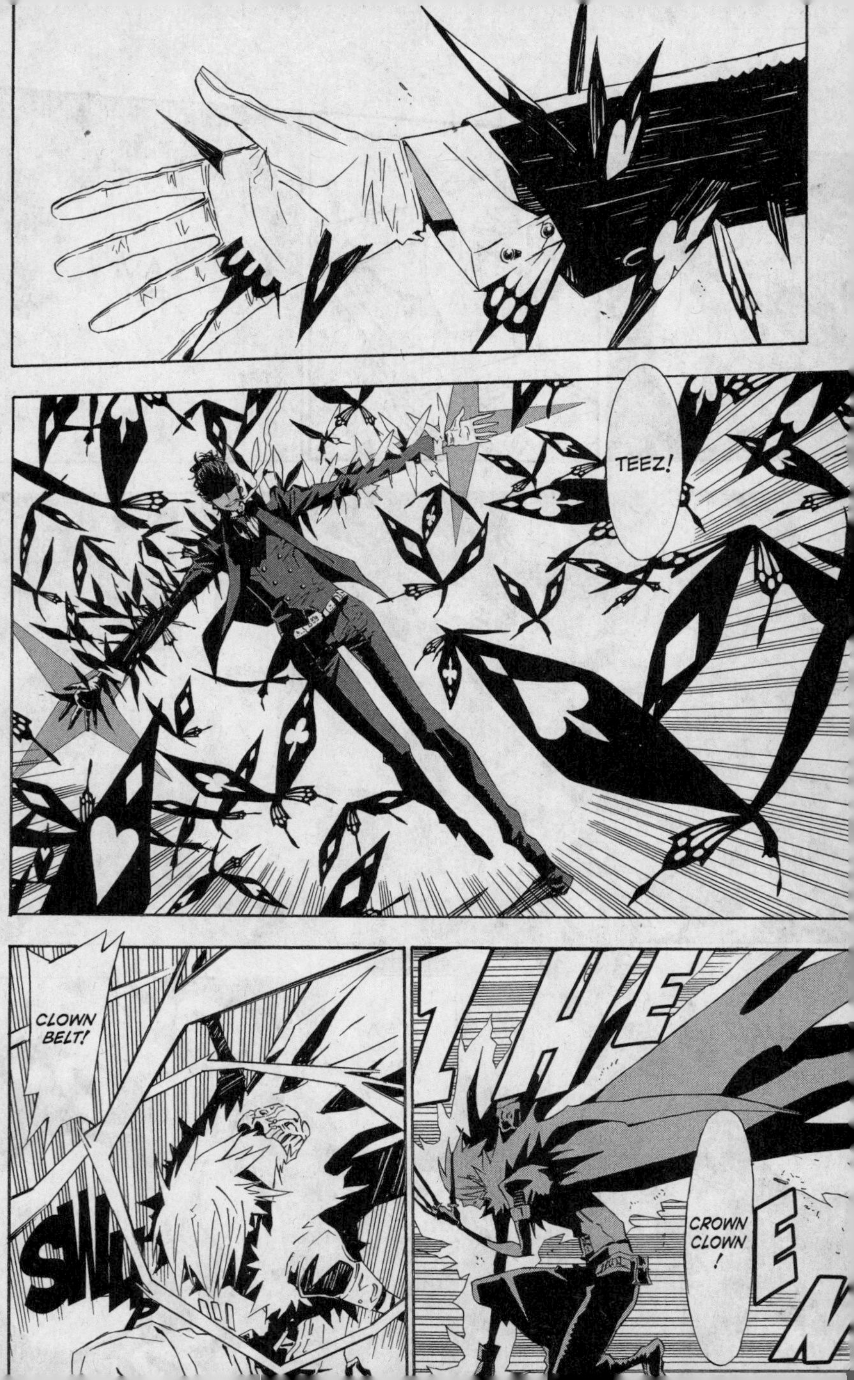
TEEZ!
CROWN CLOWN!
CLOWN BELT!

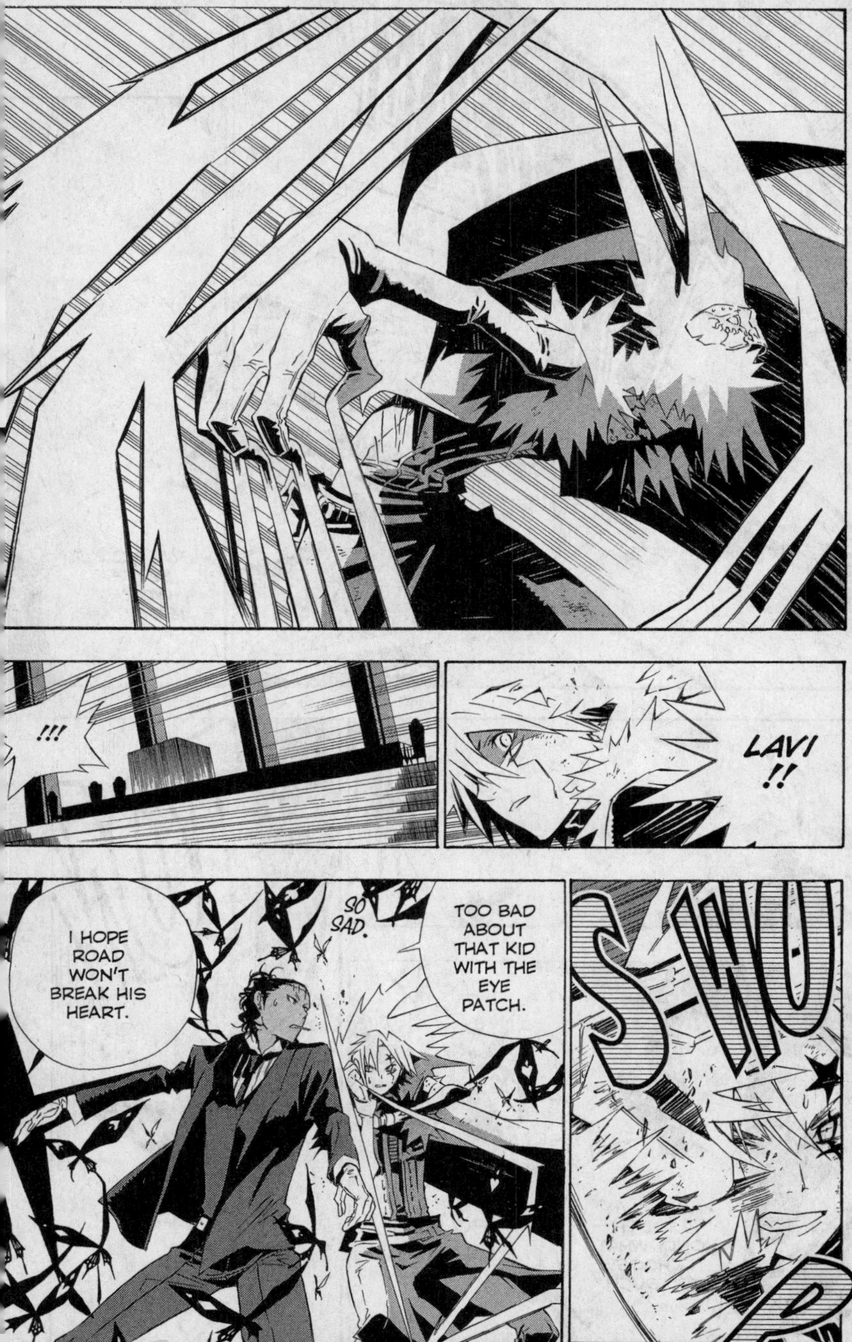
LAVI !!
!!!
TOO BAD ABOUT THAT KID WITH THE EYE PATCH.
SO SAD.
I HOPE ROAD WON'T BREAK HIS HEART.

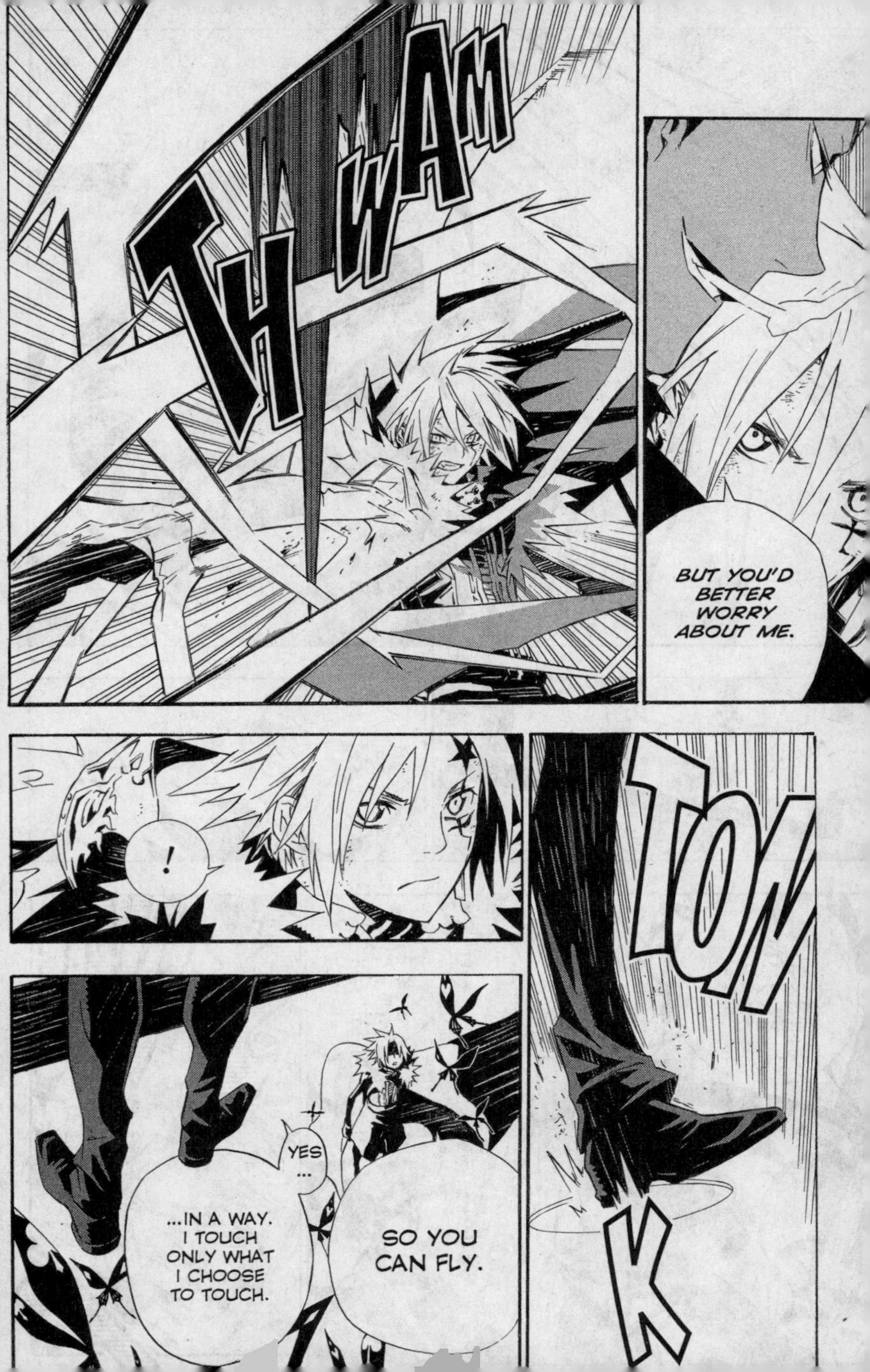
BUT YOU'D BETTER WORRY ABOUT ME.
THWAM
TONK
!
SO YOU CAN FLY.
YES...
...IN A WAY. I TOUCH ONLY WHAT I CHOOSE TO TOUCH.

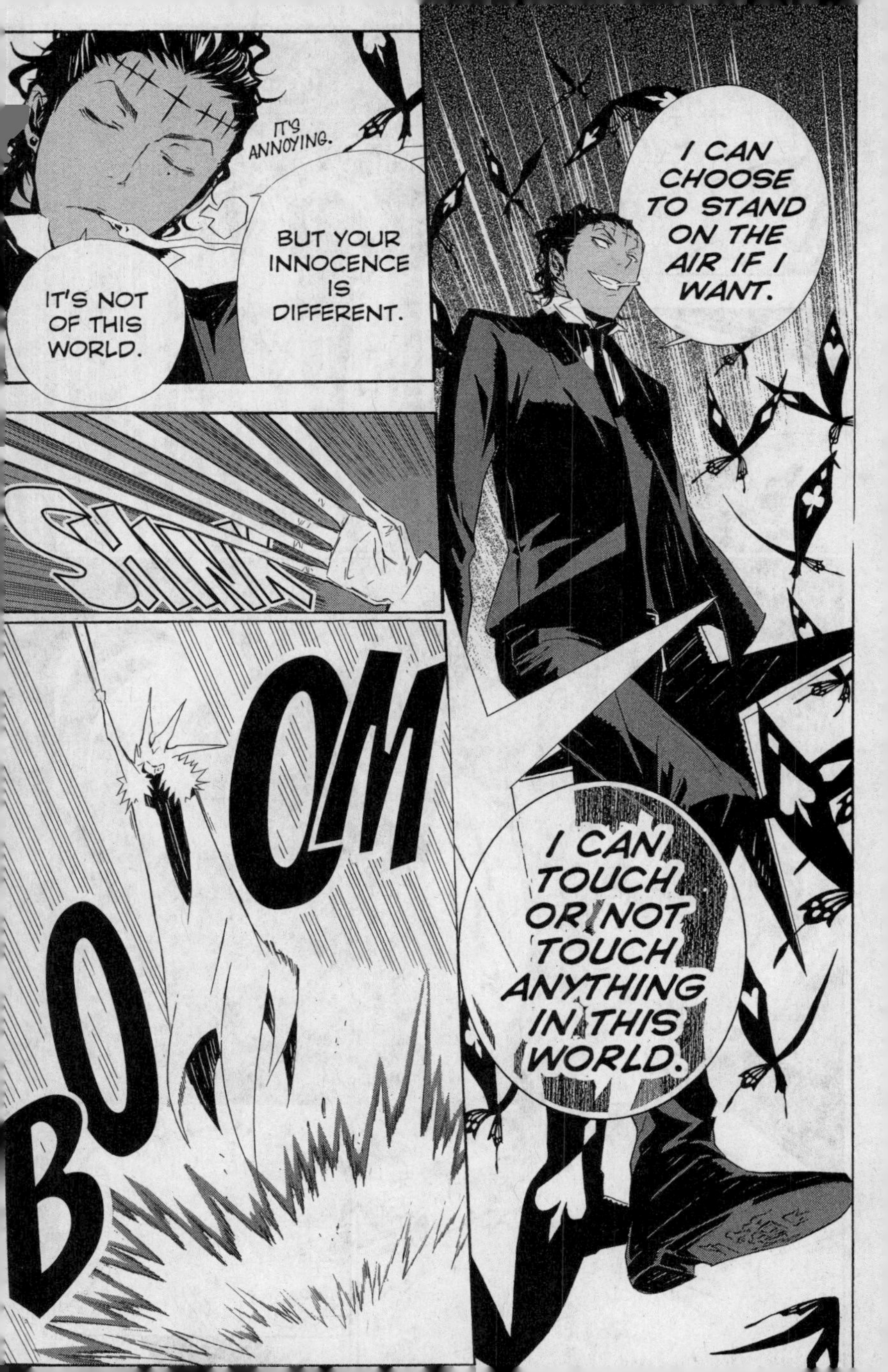
I CAN CHOOSE TO STAND ON THE AIR IF I WANT.
I CAN TOUCH OR NOT TOUCH ANYTHING IN THIS WORLD.
IT'S ANNOYING.
BUT YOUR INNOCENCE IS DIFFERENT.
IT'S NOT OF THIS WORLD.
SHINK
BOOM

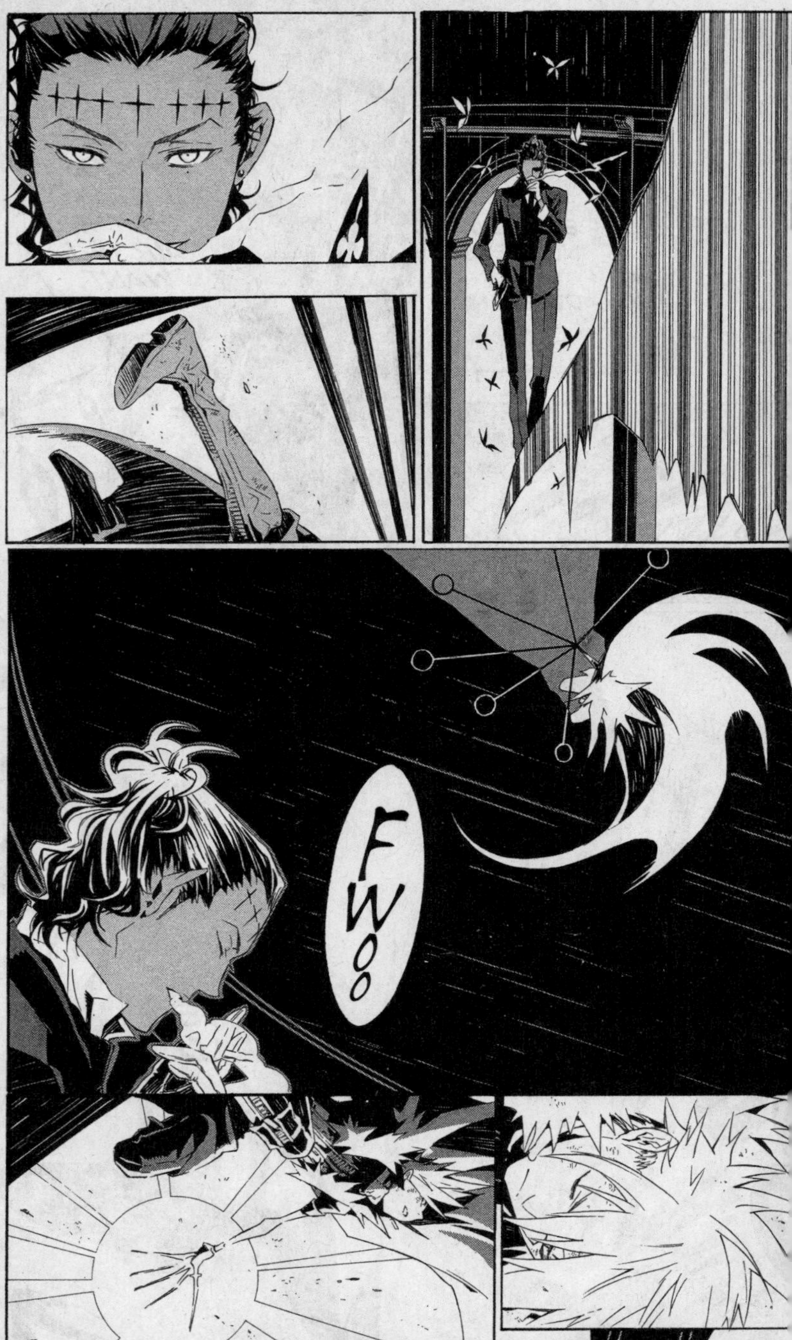
FWOO

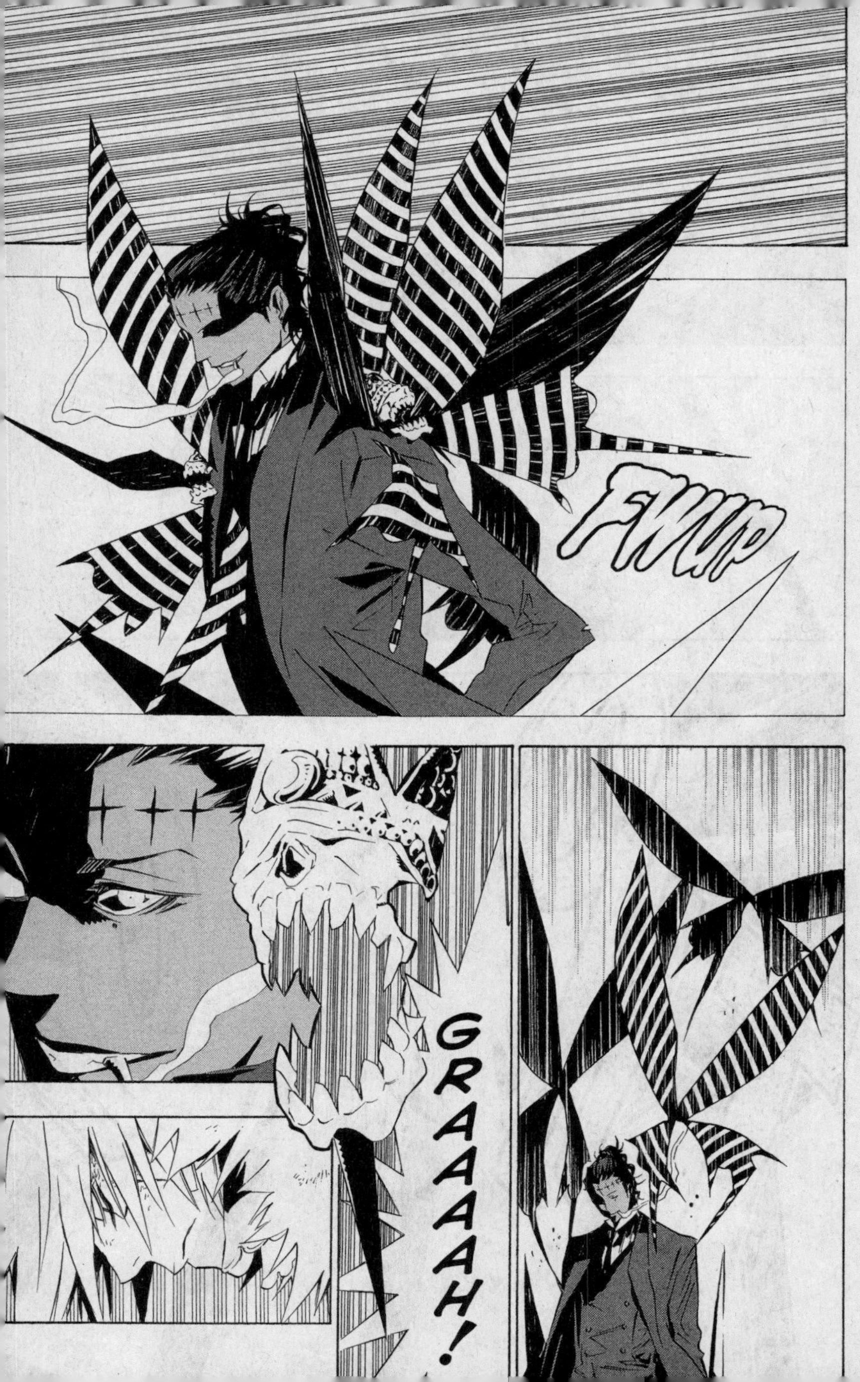
FWUP
GRAAAAH!

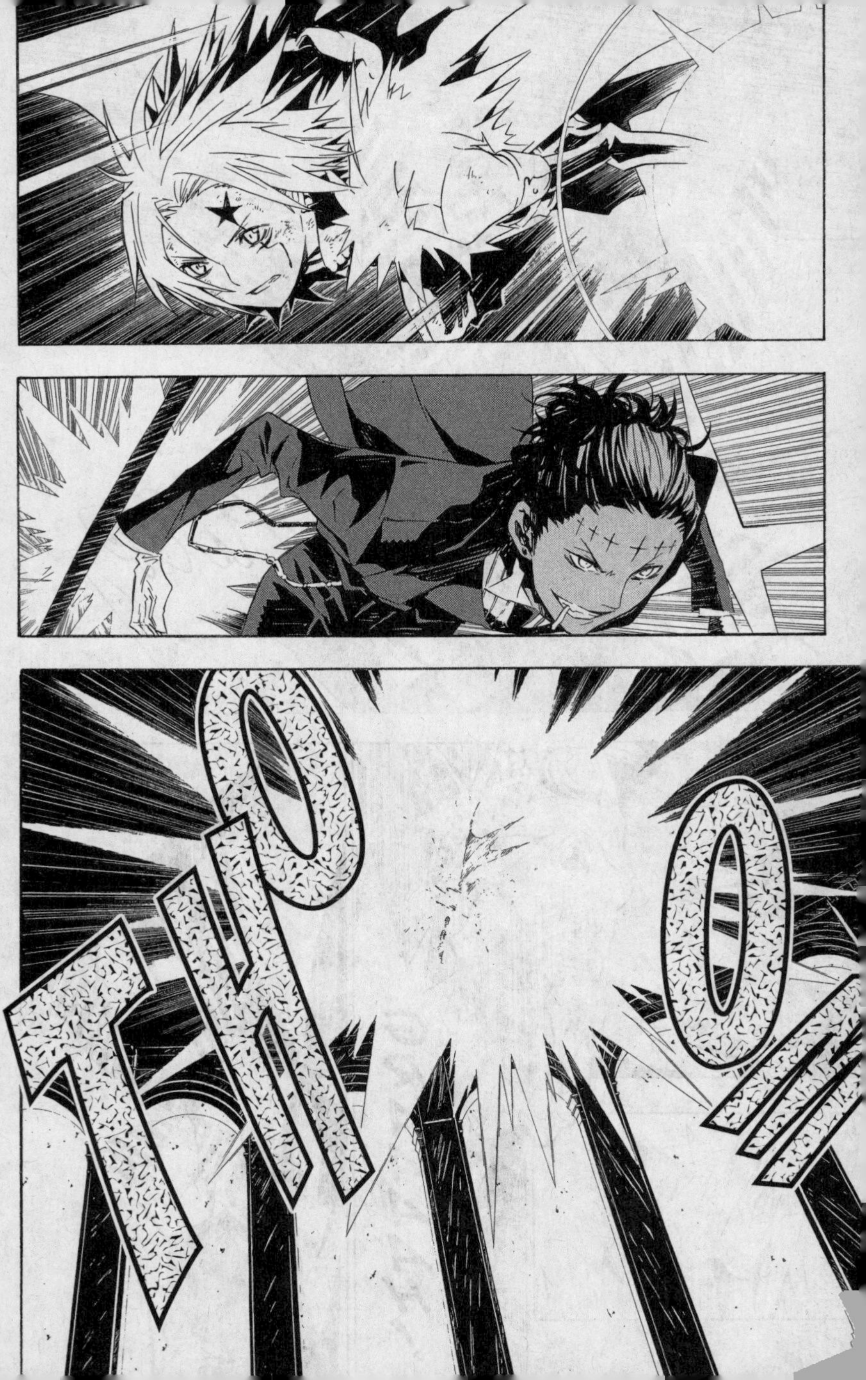
THOOM

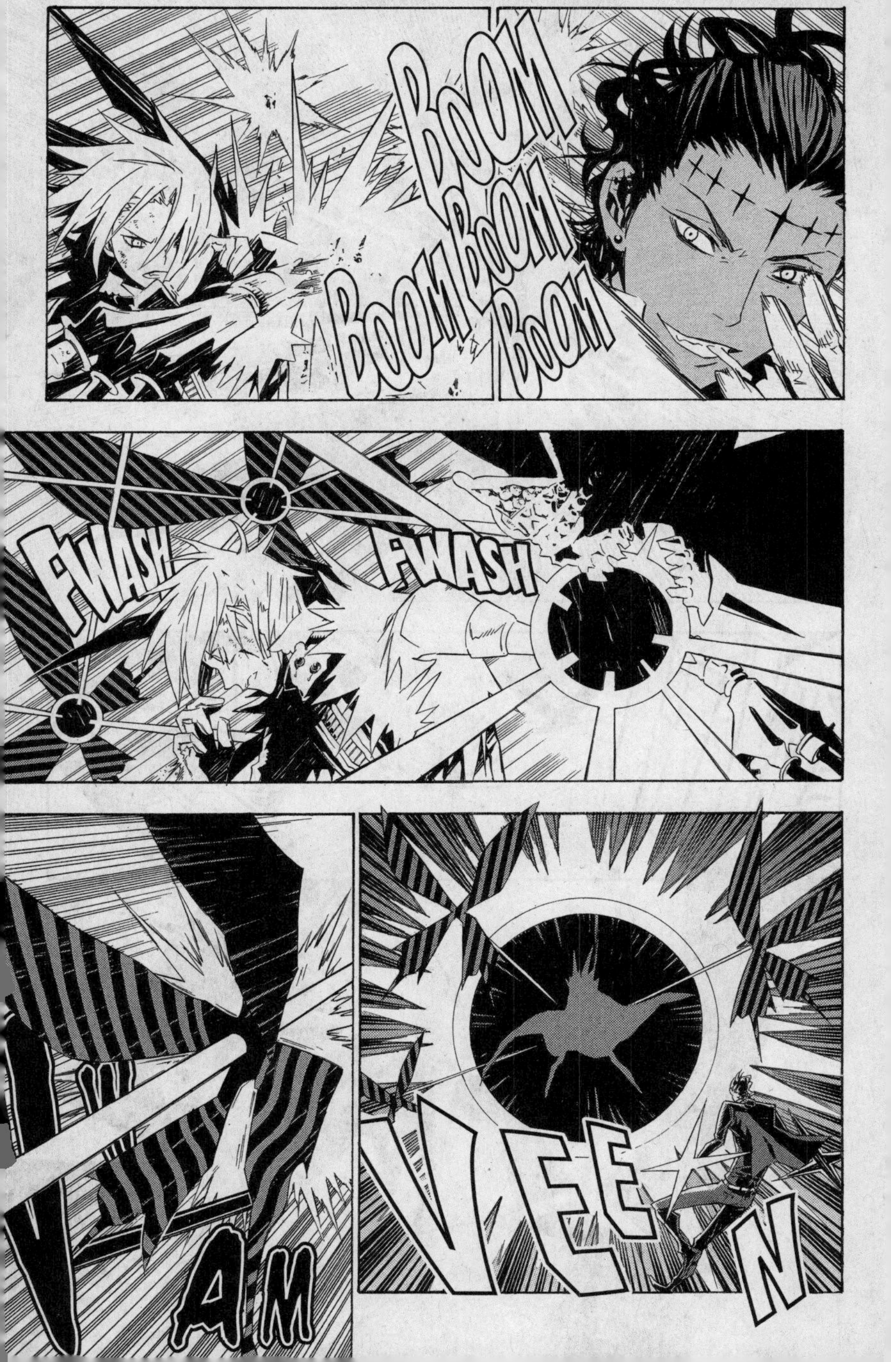
BOOM
BOOM
BOOM
BOOM
FWASH
FWASH
VEEN
A M

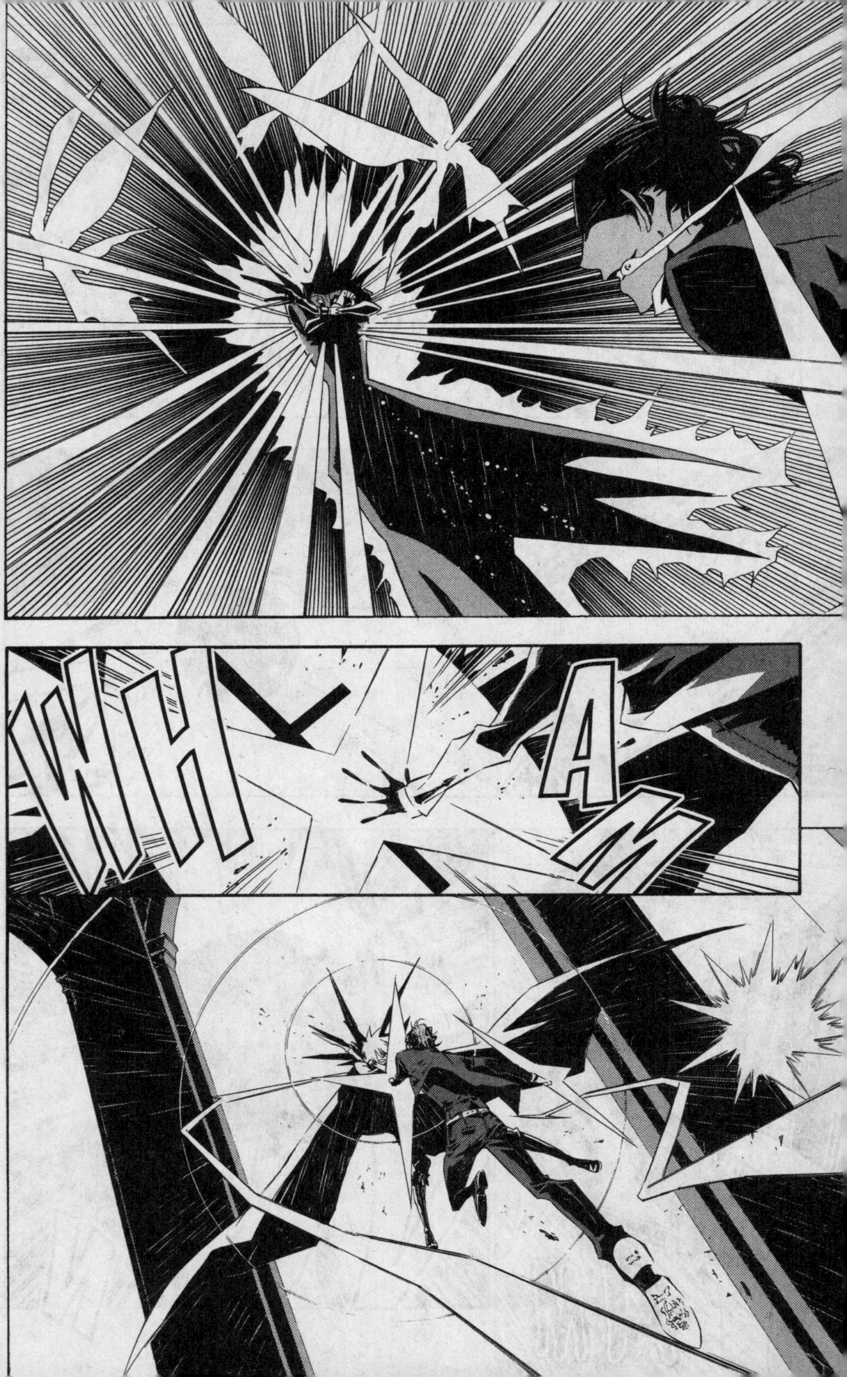
WHAM

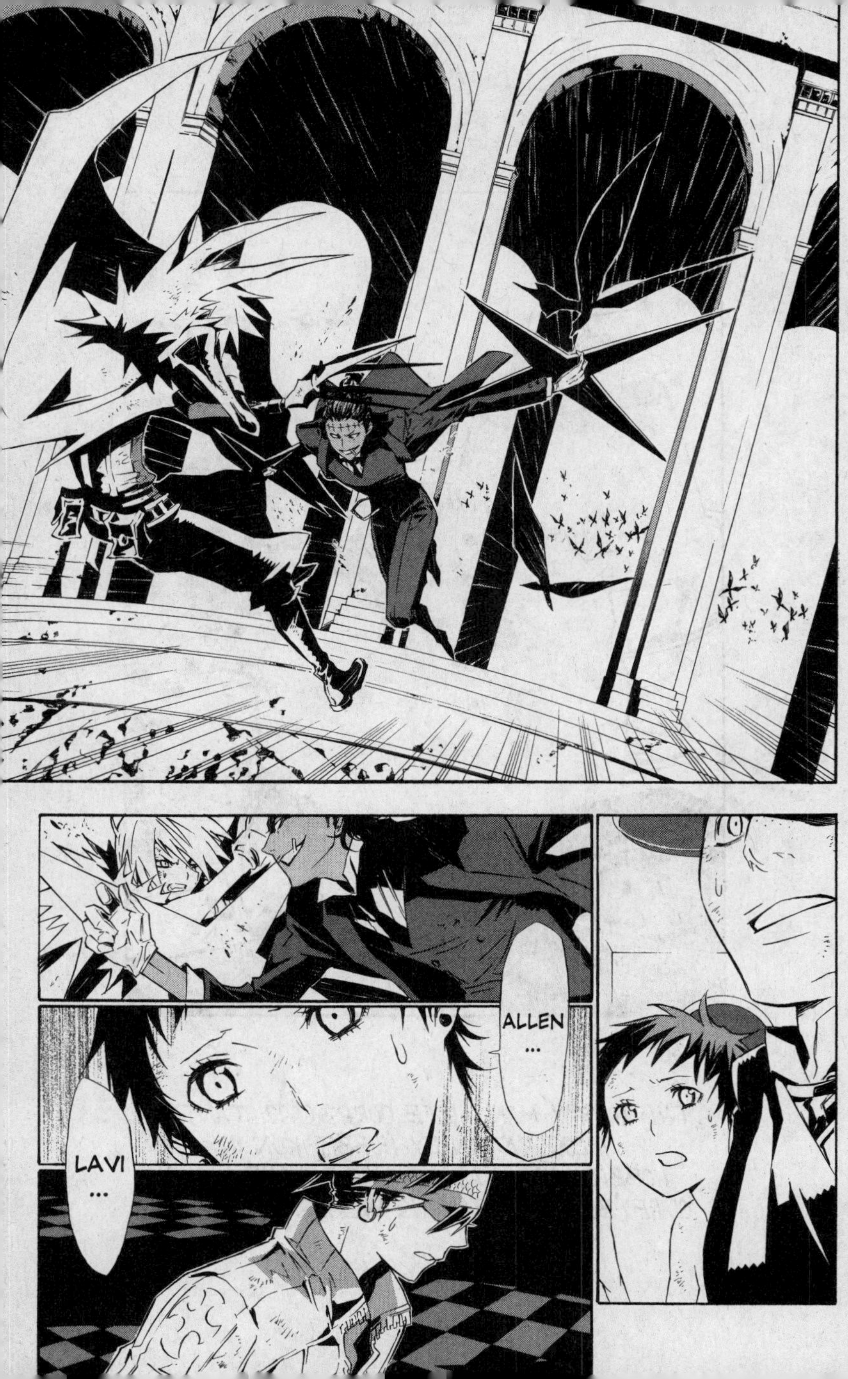
ALLEN ...
LAVI ...

THE D.GRAY-MAN ELITE CORPS (ASSISTANTS)
ILLUSTRATION BY HOBBIT-KUN 1
HOBBIT-KUN IS ABOUT THIS BIG. HE LOOKS
CUTE, BUT HIS HEART IS INCREDIBLY BLACK.

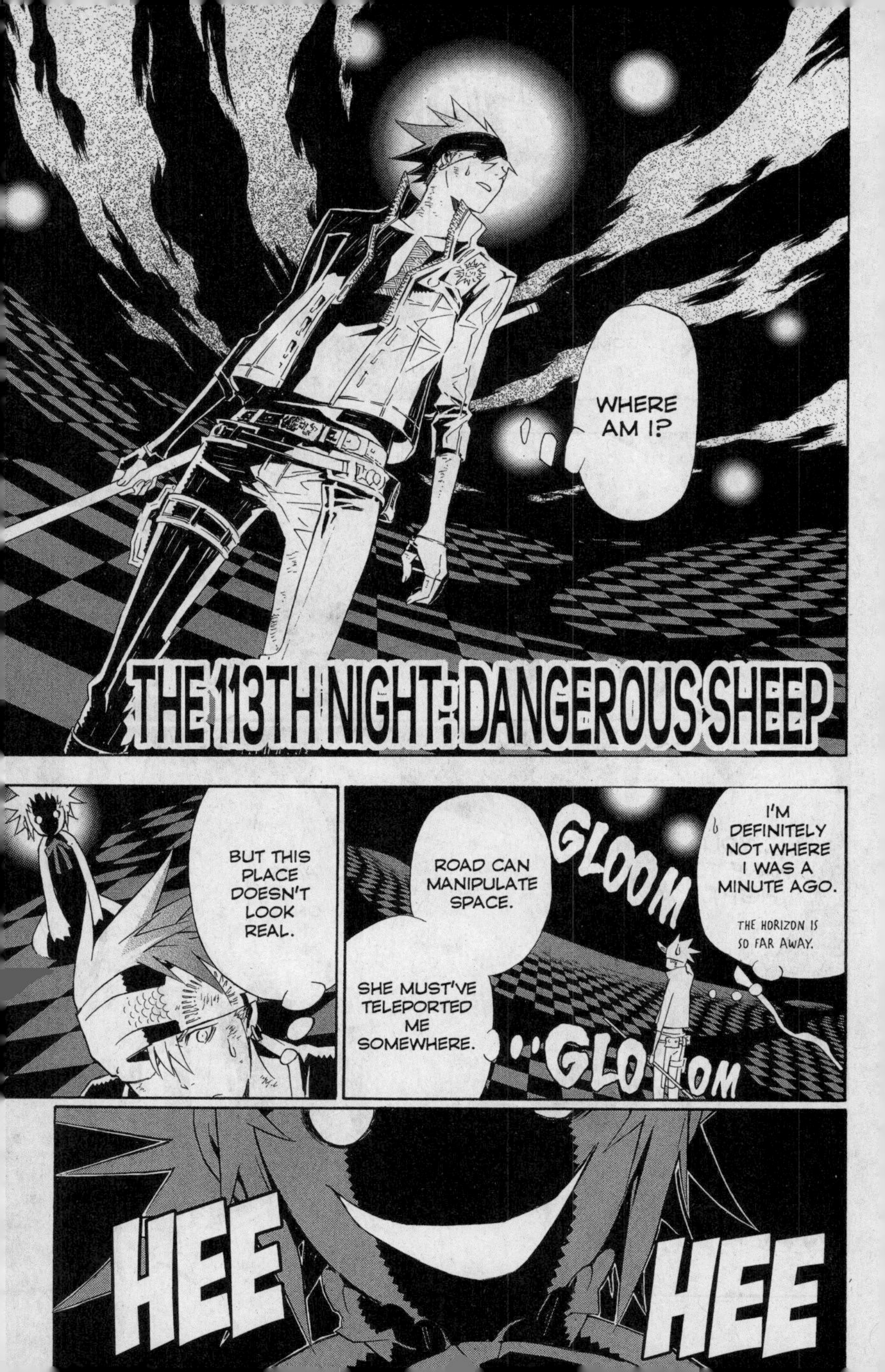
WHERE AM I?
THE 113TH NIGHT: DANGEROUS SHEEP
I'M DEFINITELY NOT WHERE I WAS A MINUTE AGO.
THE HORIZON IS SO FAR AWAY.
GLOOM
ROAD CAN MANIPULATE SPACE.
SHE MUST'VE TELEPORTED ME SOMEWHERE.
GLOOM
BUT THIS PLACE DOESN'T LOOK REAL.
HEE
HEE

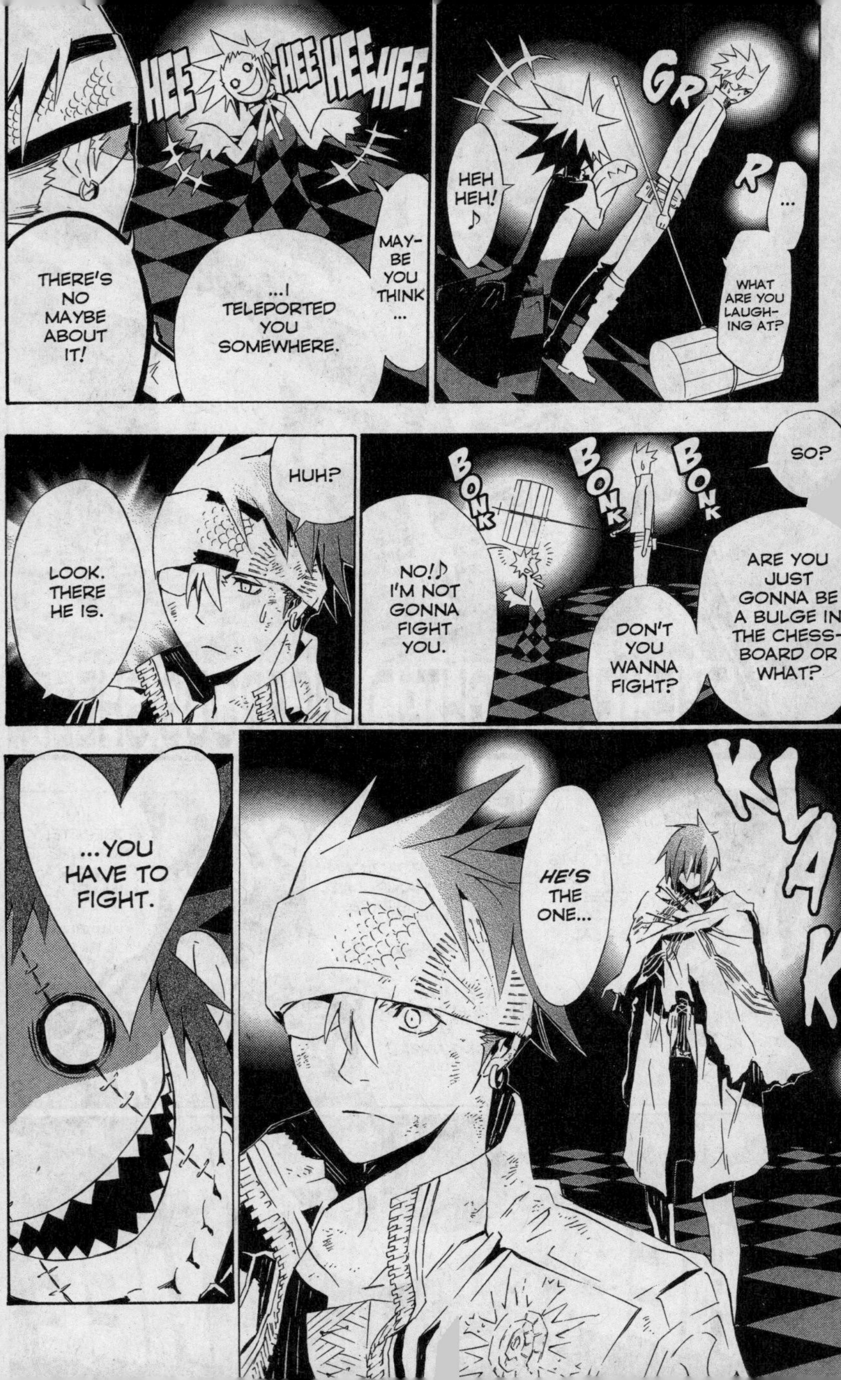
GR
R
...
WHAT ARE YOU LAUGHING AT?
HEH HEH! ♪
HEE HEE HEE HEE
MAYBE YOU THINK ...
...I TELEPORTED YOU SOMEWHERE.
THERE'S NO MAYBE ABOUT IT!
SO?
ARE YOU JUST GONNA BE A BULGE IN THE CHESSBOARD OR WHAT?
DON'T YOU WANNA FIGHT?
BONK
BONK
BONK
NO!♪ I'M NOT GONNA FIGHT YOU.
HUH?
LOOK. THERE HE IS.
KLAK
HE'S THE ONE...
...YOU HAVE TO FIGHT.

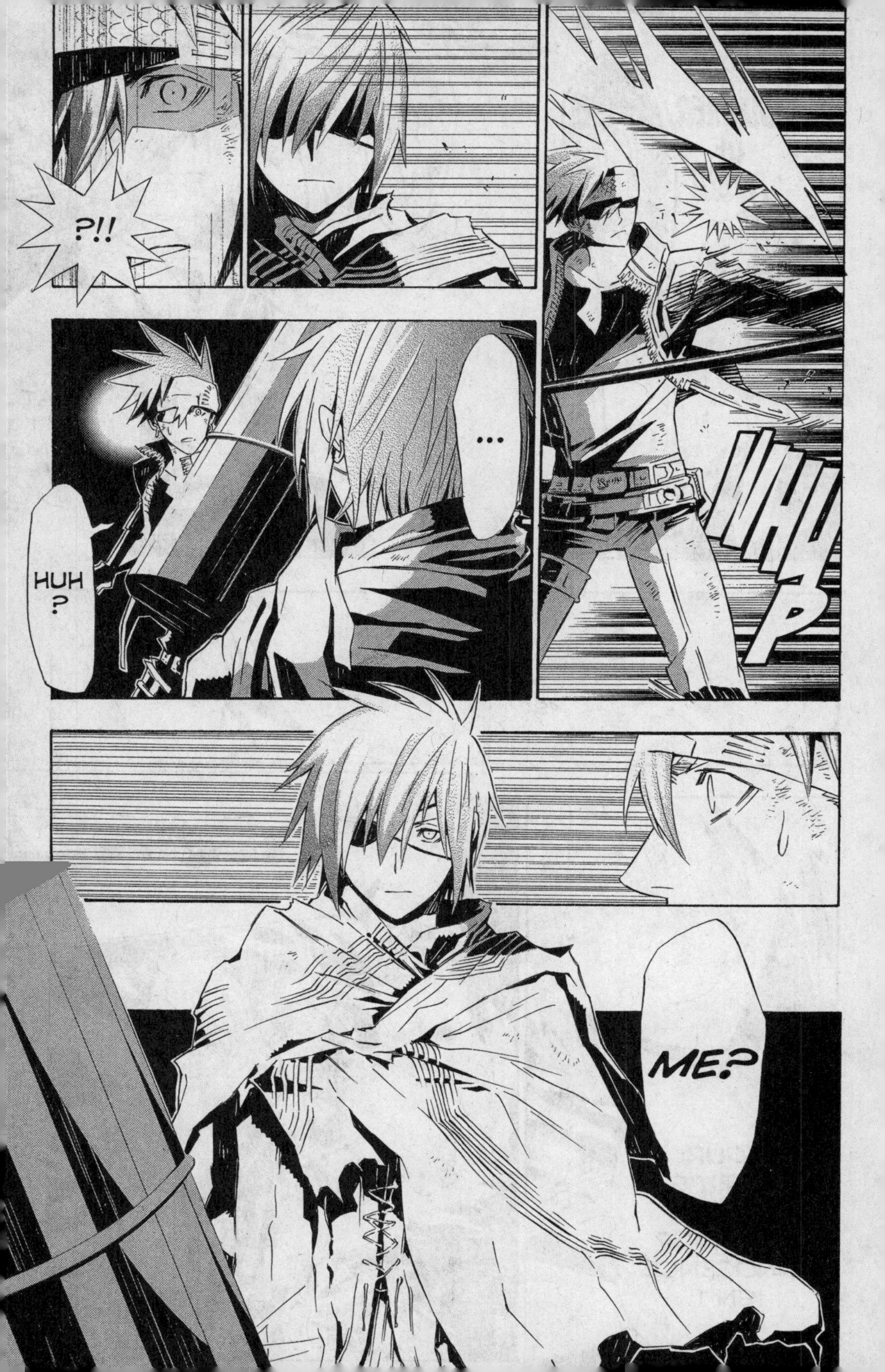
WHUMP
?!!
...
HUH?
ME?

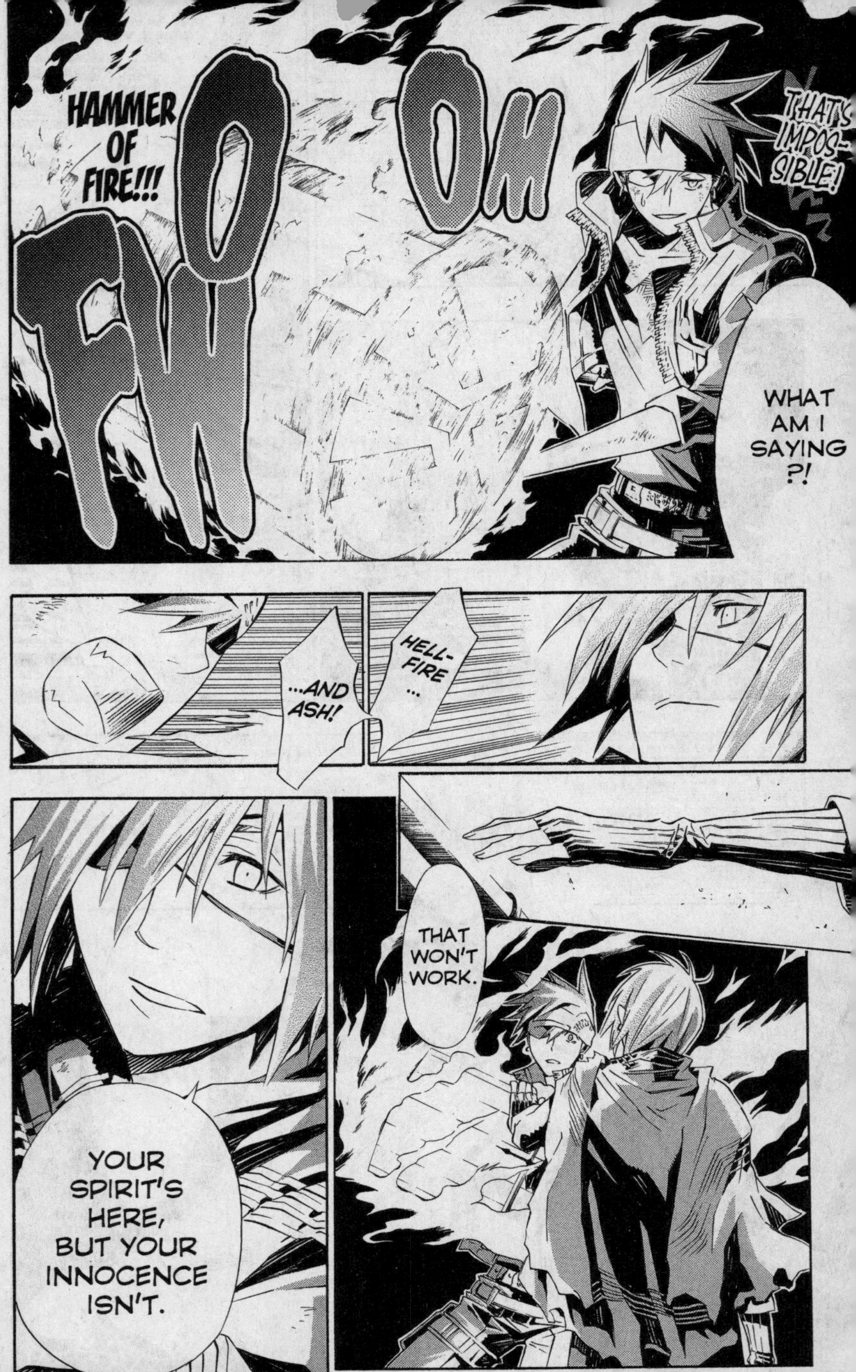
THAT'S IMPOSSIBLE!
HAMMER OF FIRE!!!
FWOOM
WHAT AM I SAYING?!
HELL-FIRE...
...AND ASH!
THAT WON'T WORK.
YOUR SPIRIT'S HERE, BUT YOUR INNOCENCE ISN'T.

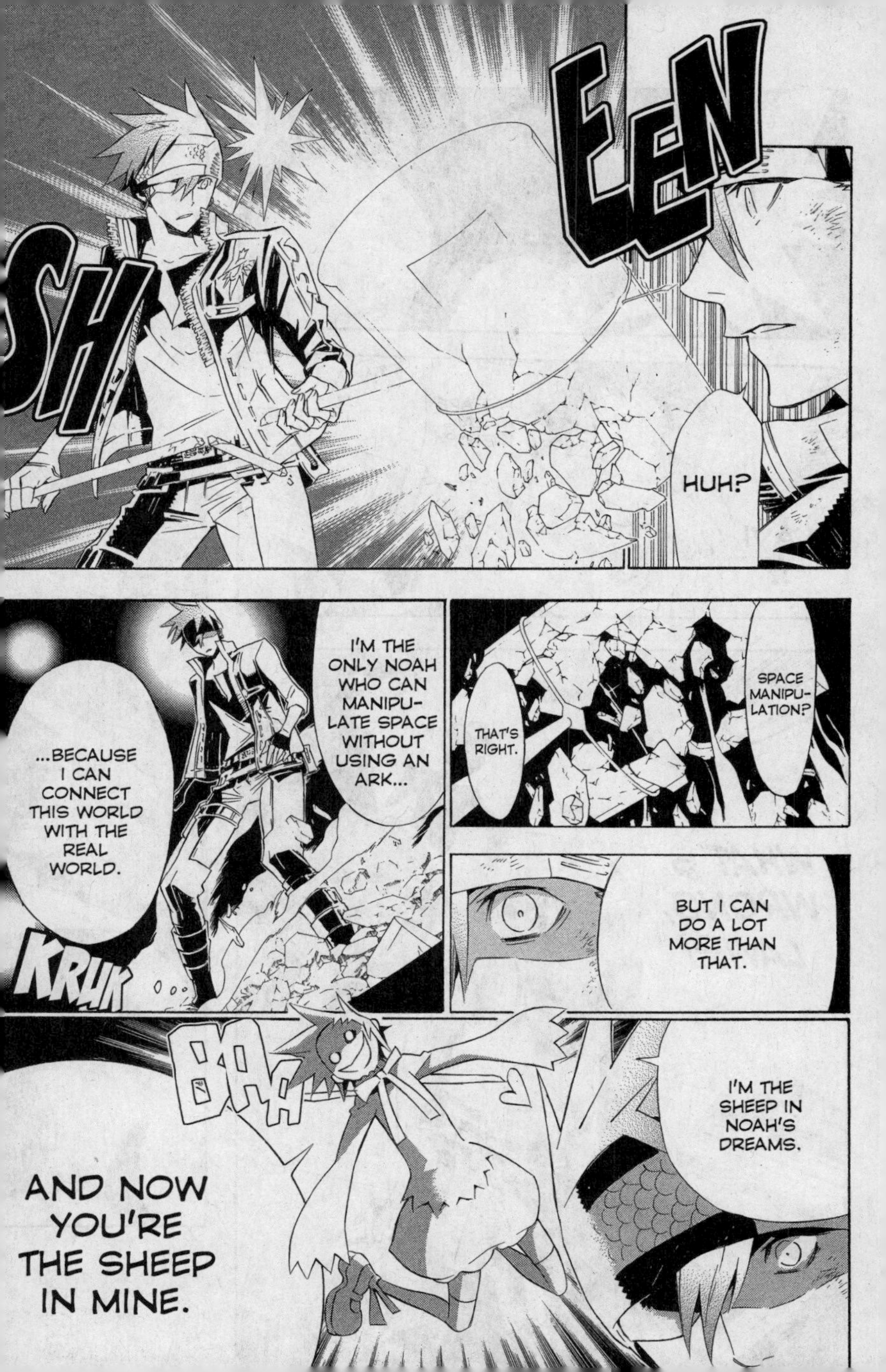
EEN
HUH?
SH
SPACE MANIPU-LATION?
THAT'S RIGHT.
BUT I CAN DO A LOT MORE THAN THAT.
I'M THE ONLY NOAH WHO CAN MANIPU-LATE SPACE WITHOUT USING AN ARK...
...BECAUSE I CAN CONNECT THIS WORLD WITH THE REAL WORLD.
KRUK
I'M THE SHEEP IN NOAH'S DREAMS.
BAA
AND NOW YOU'RE THE SHEEP IN MINE.

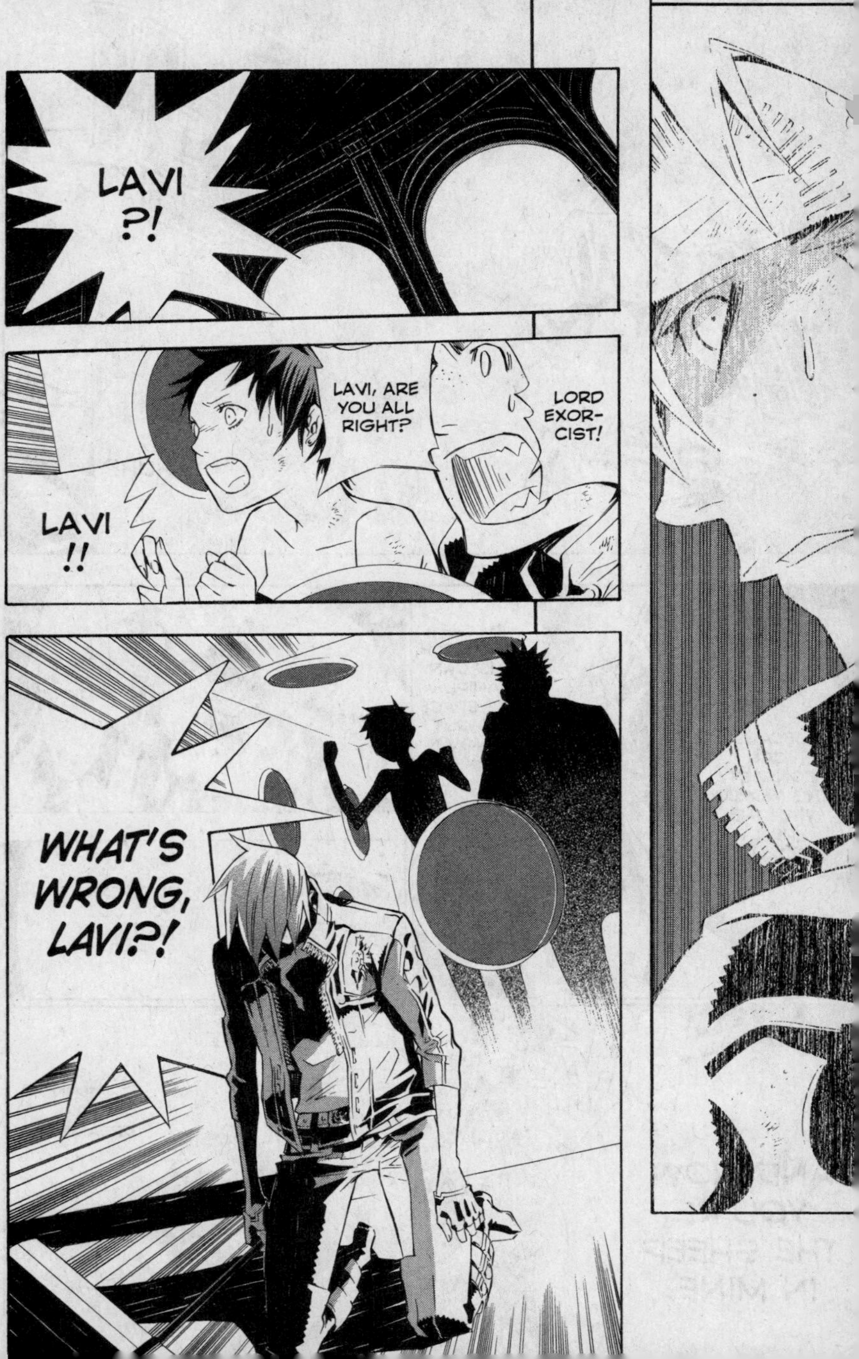

LAVI ?!
LORD EXOR-CIST!
LAVI, ARE YOU ALL RIGHT?
LAVI !!
WHAT'S WRONG, LAVI?!

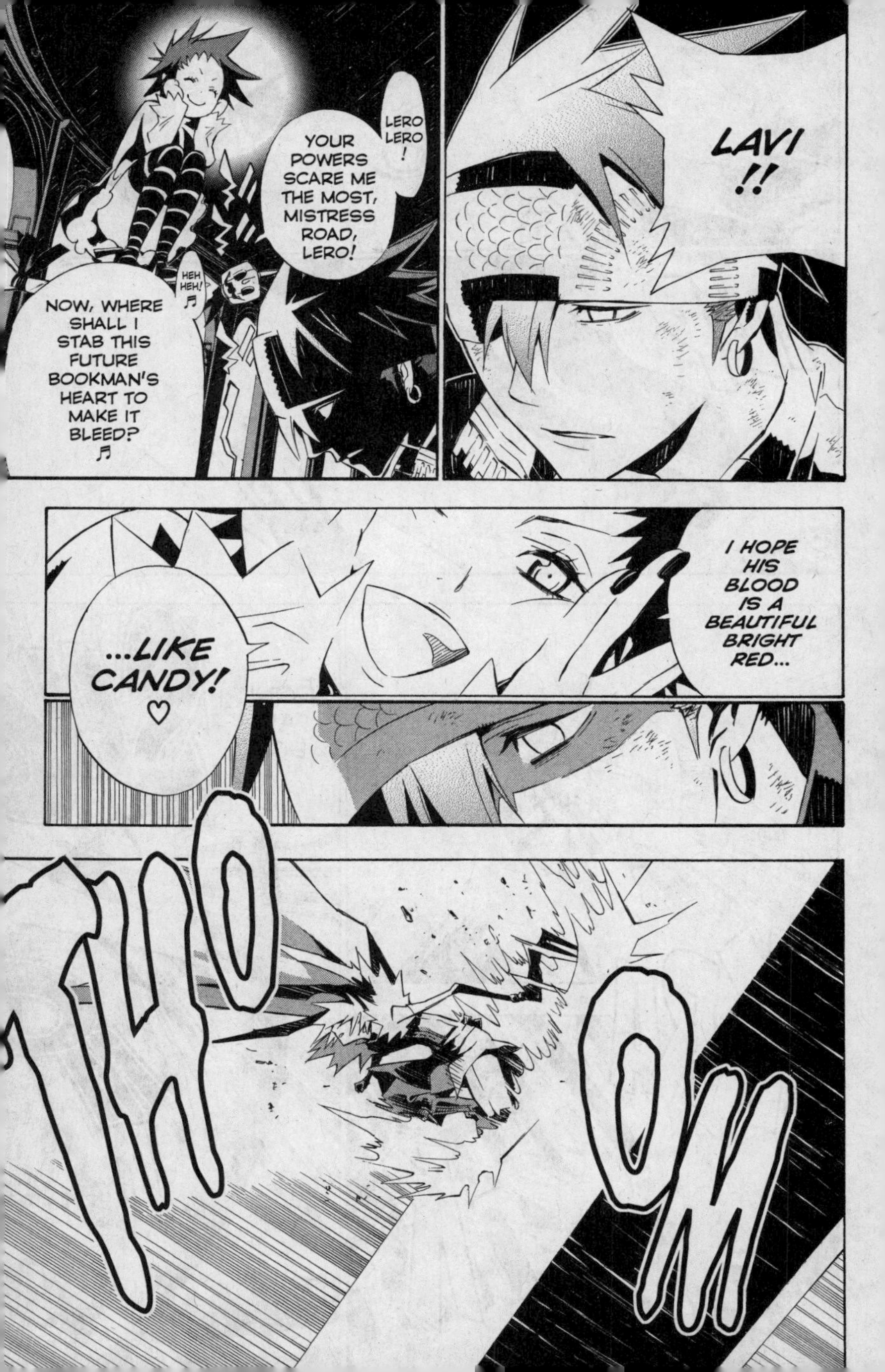
LAVI!!
LERO LERO!
YOUR POWERS SCARE ME THE MOST, MISTRESS ROAD, LERO!
HEH HEH! ♪
NOW, WHERE SHALL I STAB THIS FUTURE BOOKMAN'S HEART TO MAKE IT BLEED? ♬
I HOPE HIS BLOOD IS A BEAUTIFUL BRIGHT RED...
...LIKE CANDY! ♡
THOOM

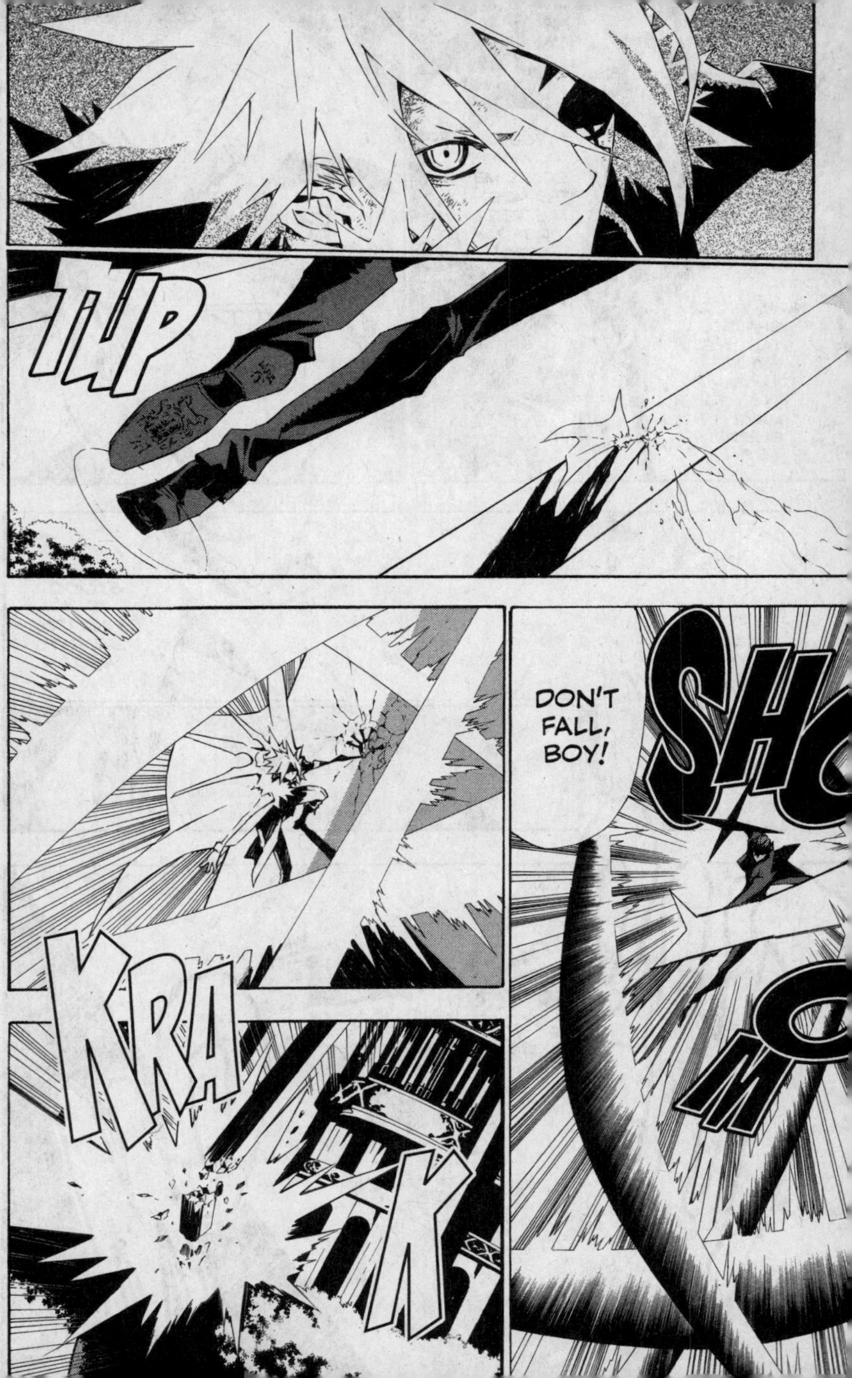
TUP
DON'T FALL, BOY!
KRAK

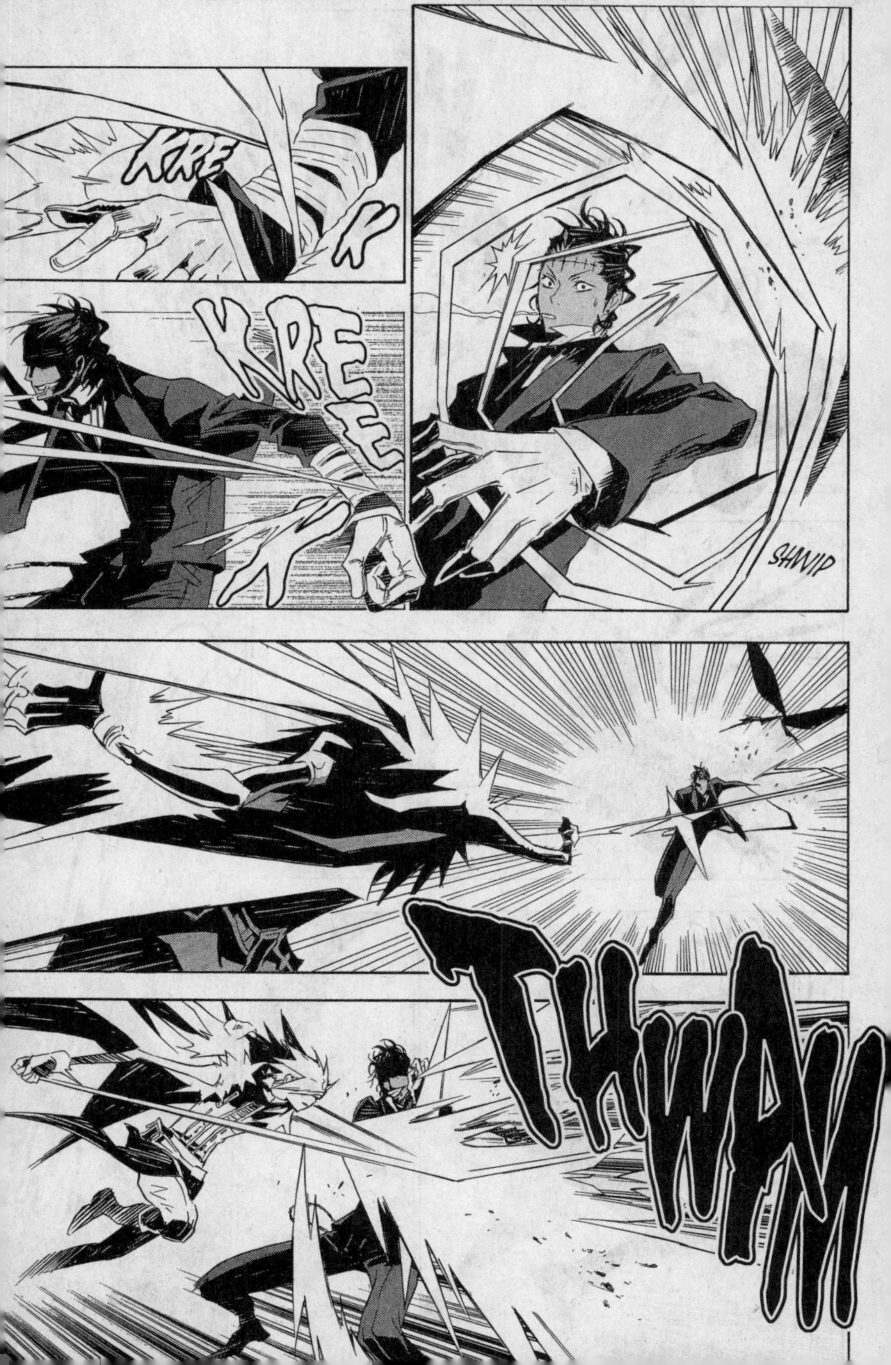
SHWIP
KREK
KREEE
THWAM

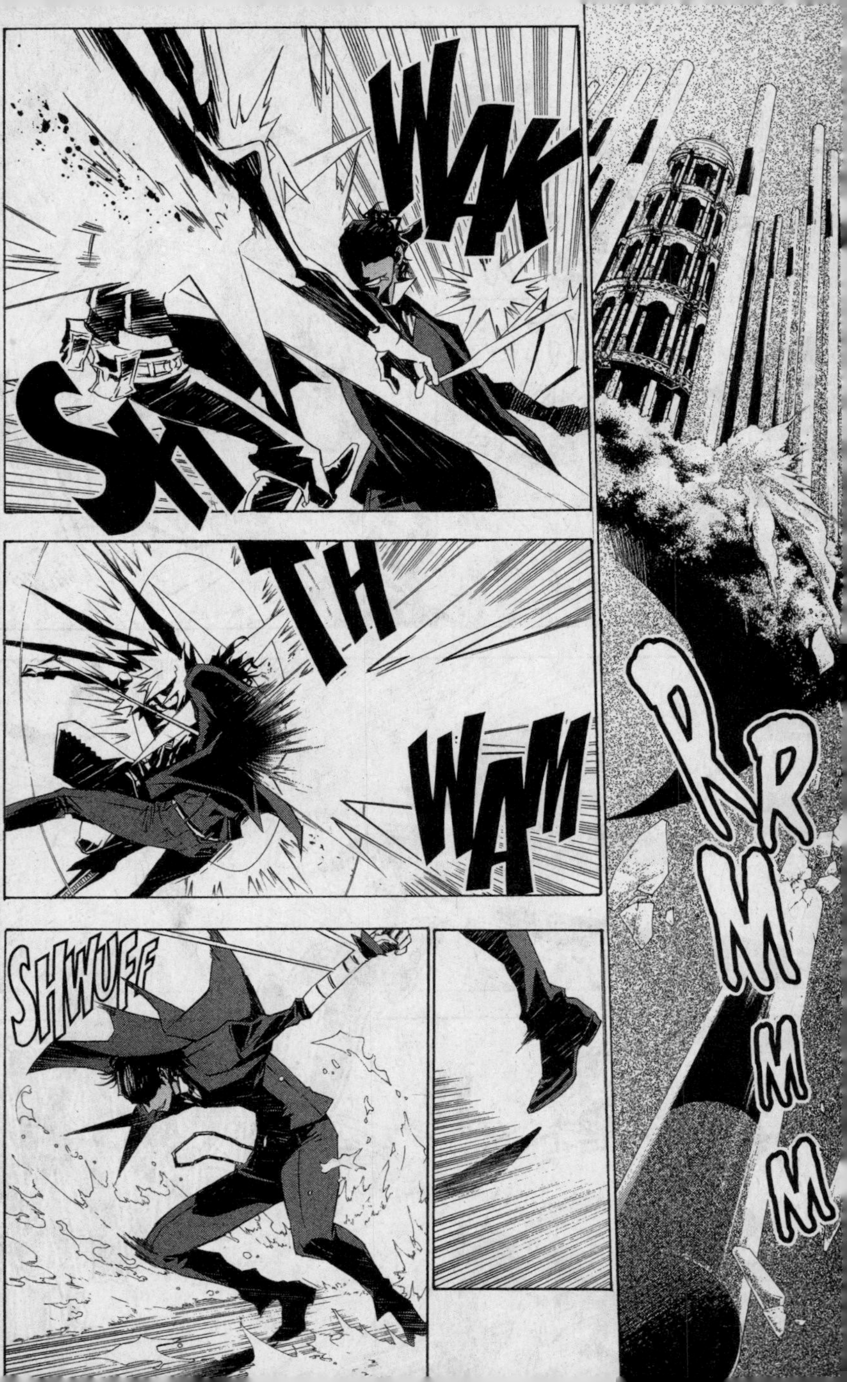

RRMMMM
WAK
SH
TH
WAM
SHWUFF

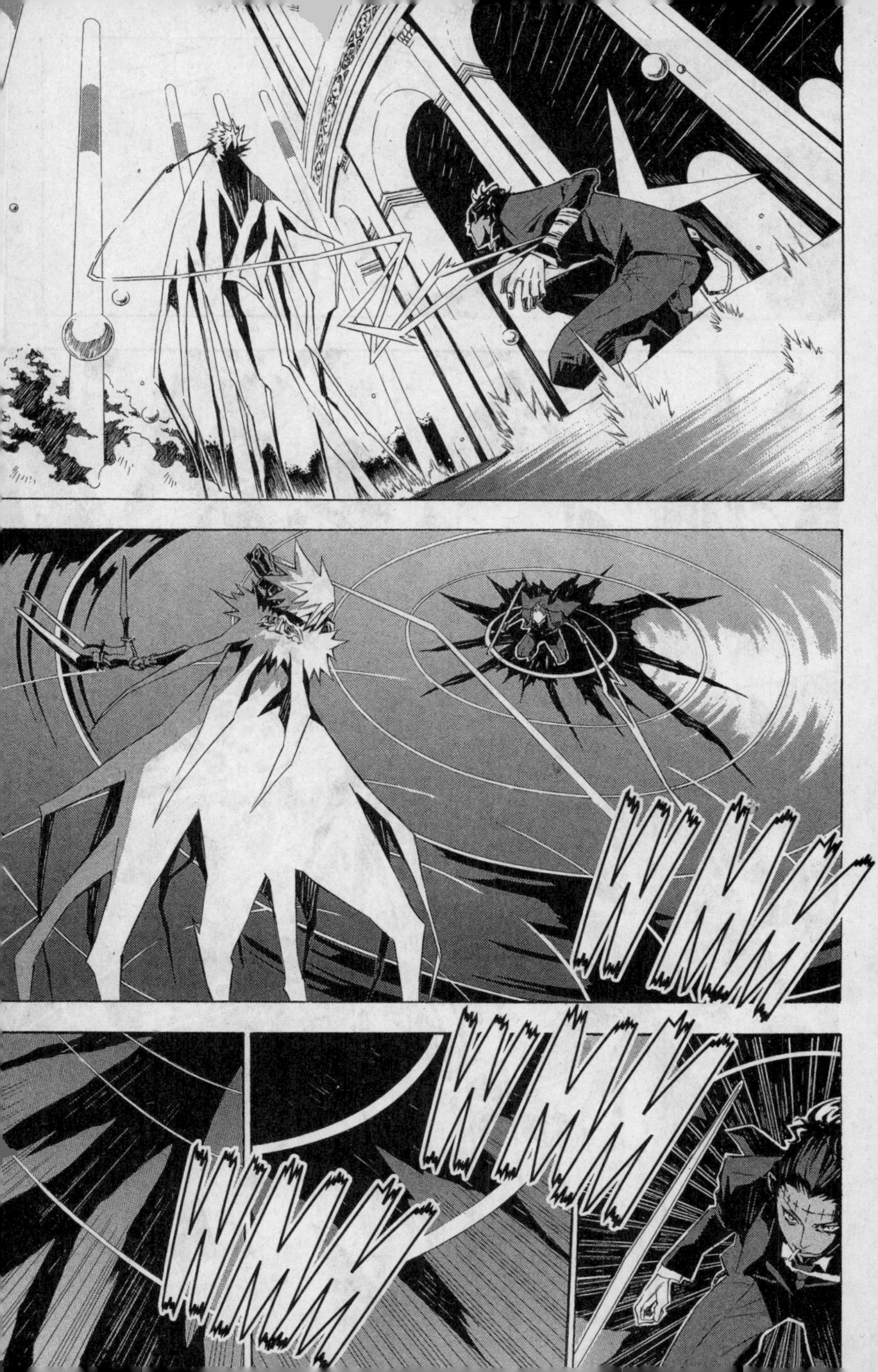

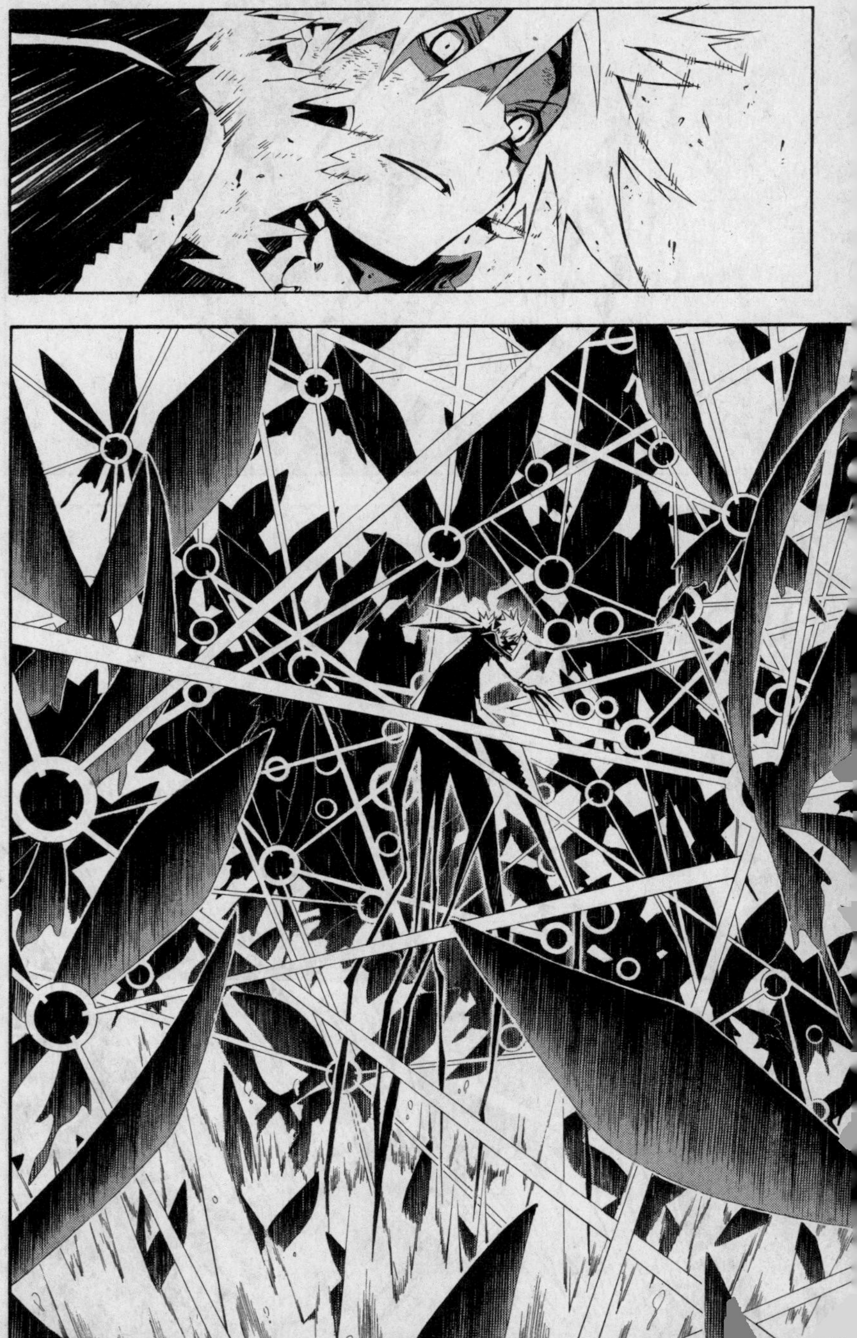

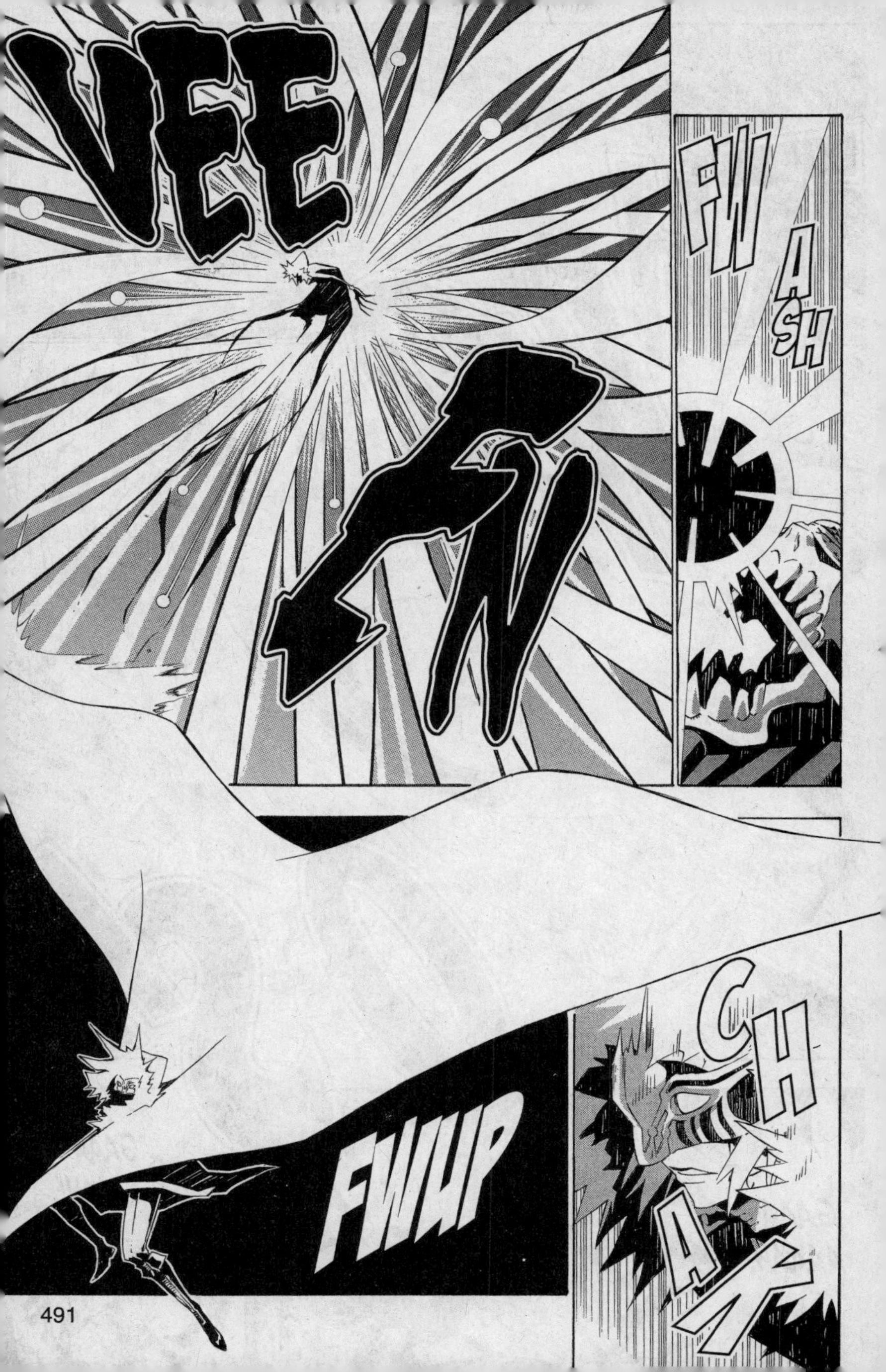
FWASH
VEEN
CHAK
FWHIP

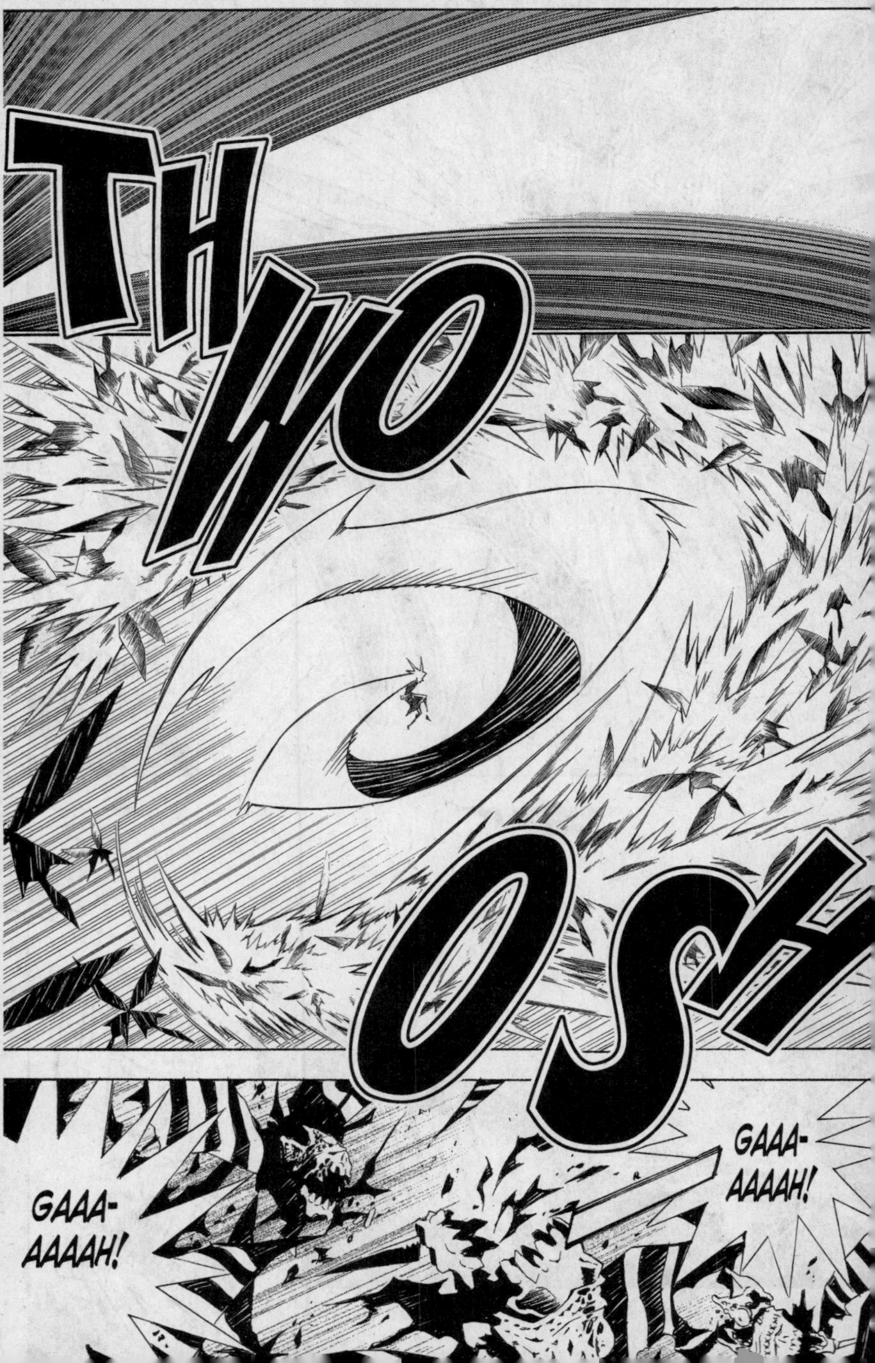
THWOOSH
GAAA-AAAAH!
GAAA-AAAAH!

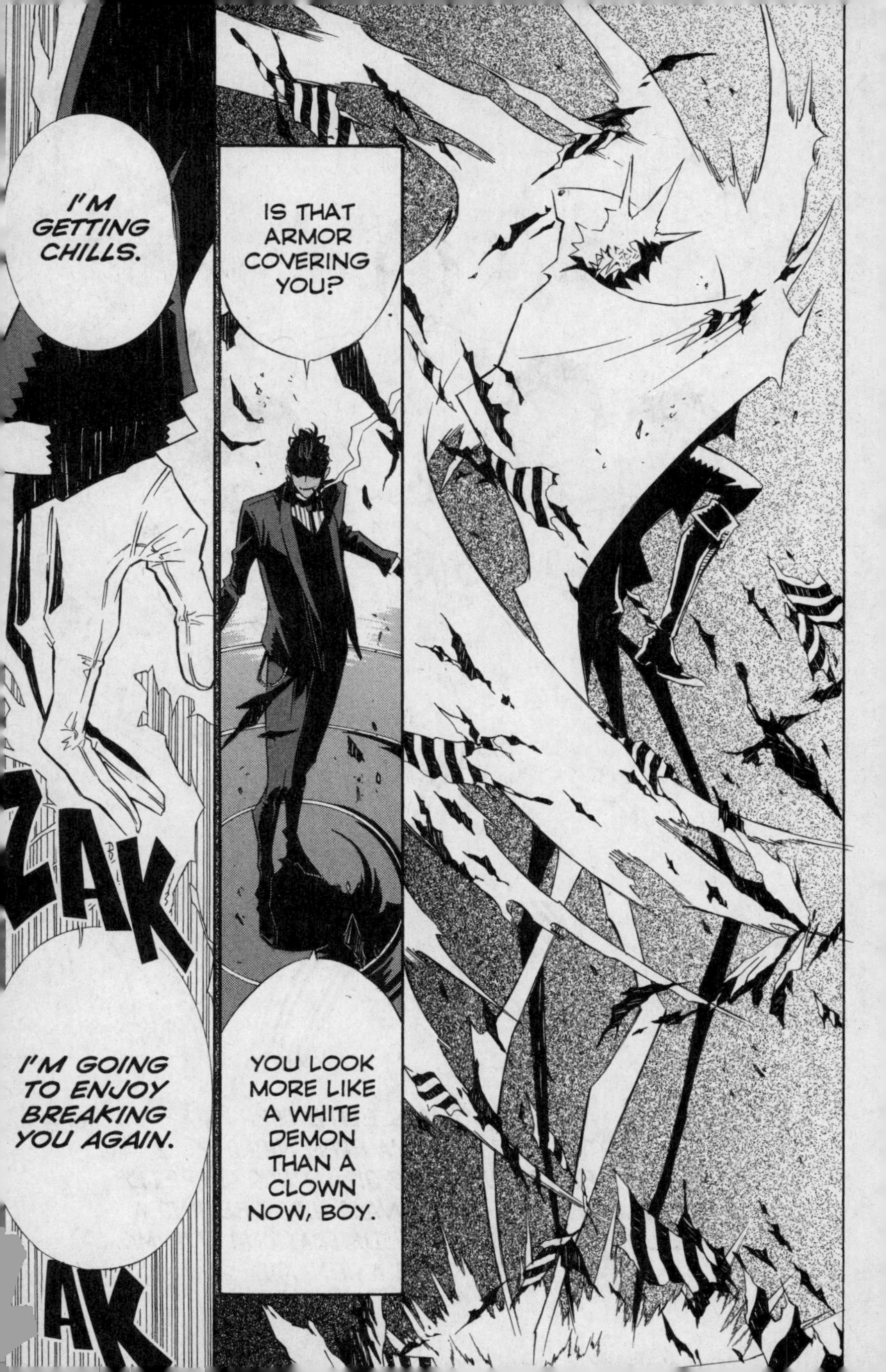
IS THAT ARMOR COVERING YOU?
YOU LOOK MORE LIKE A WHITE DEMON THAN A CLOWN NOW, BOY.
I'M GETTING CHILLS.
ZAK
I'M GOING TO ENJOY BREAKING YOU AGAIN.
AK

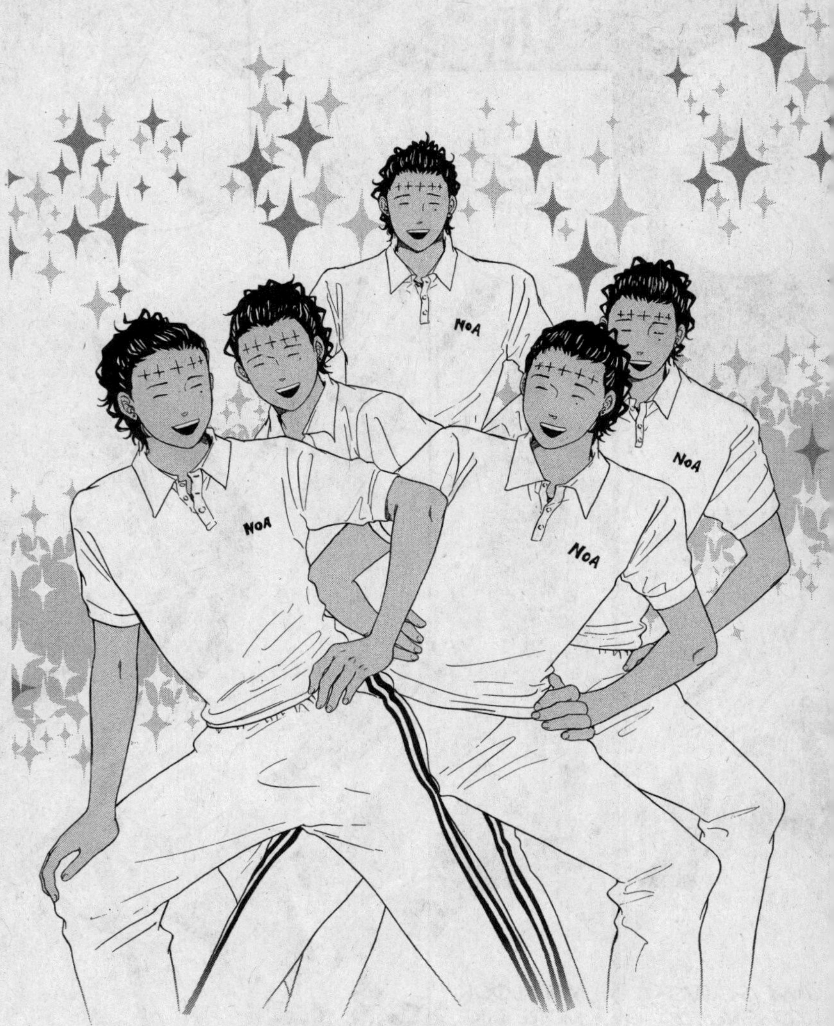
NOA
NOA
NOA
NOA

THE D.GRAY-MAN ELITE CORPS
ILLUSTRATION BY MAMA FROM NICHO-ME 2
SHE'S A BEAUTIFUL YOUNG GIRL WHO'S SECRETLY REALLY WEIRD. SHE ALWAYS HIDES BEHIND A VEIL OF LAUGHTER. HER ILLUSTRATIONS GIVE ME CHILLS. SHE'S A GENIUS!!

THE 114TH NIGHT: TWO STRUGGLES

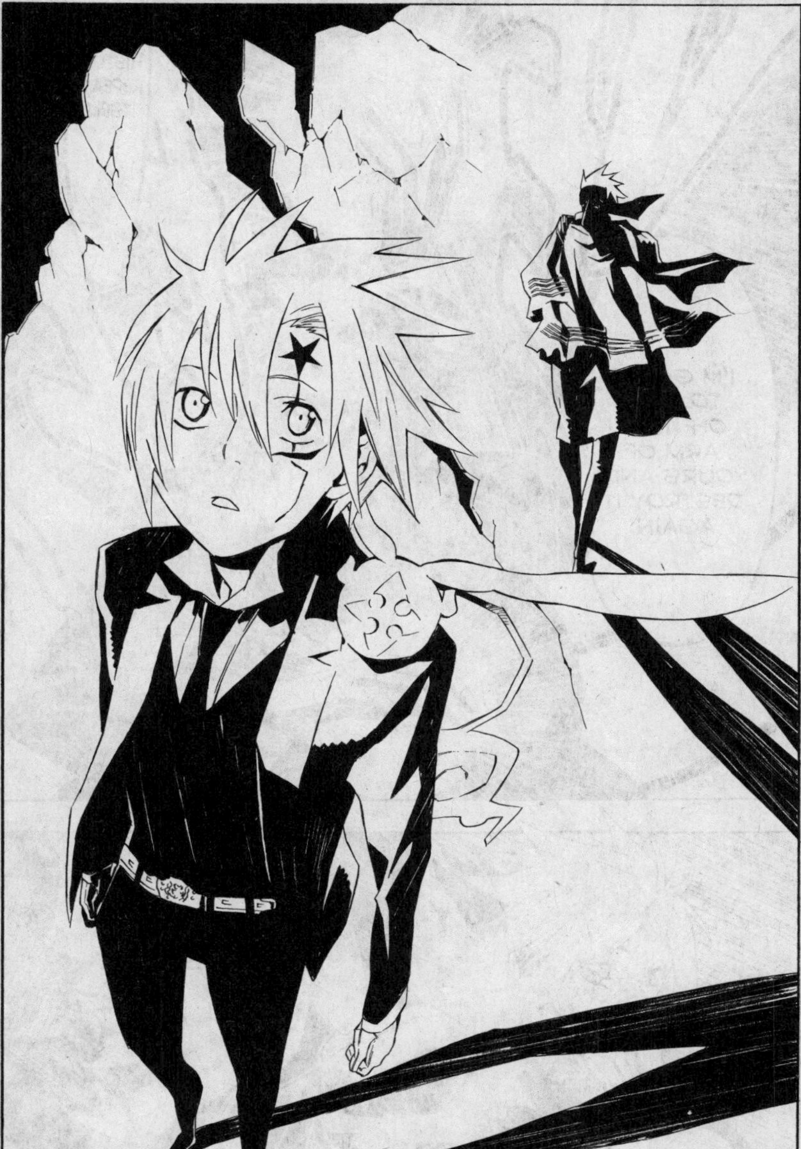

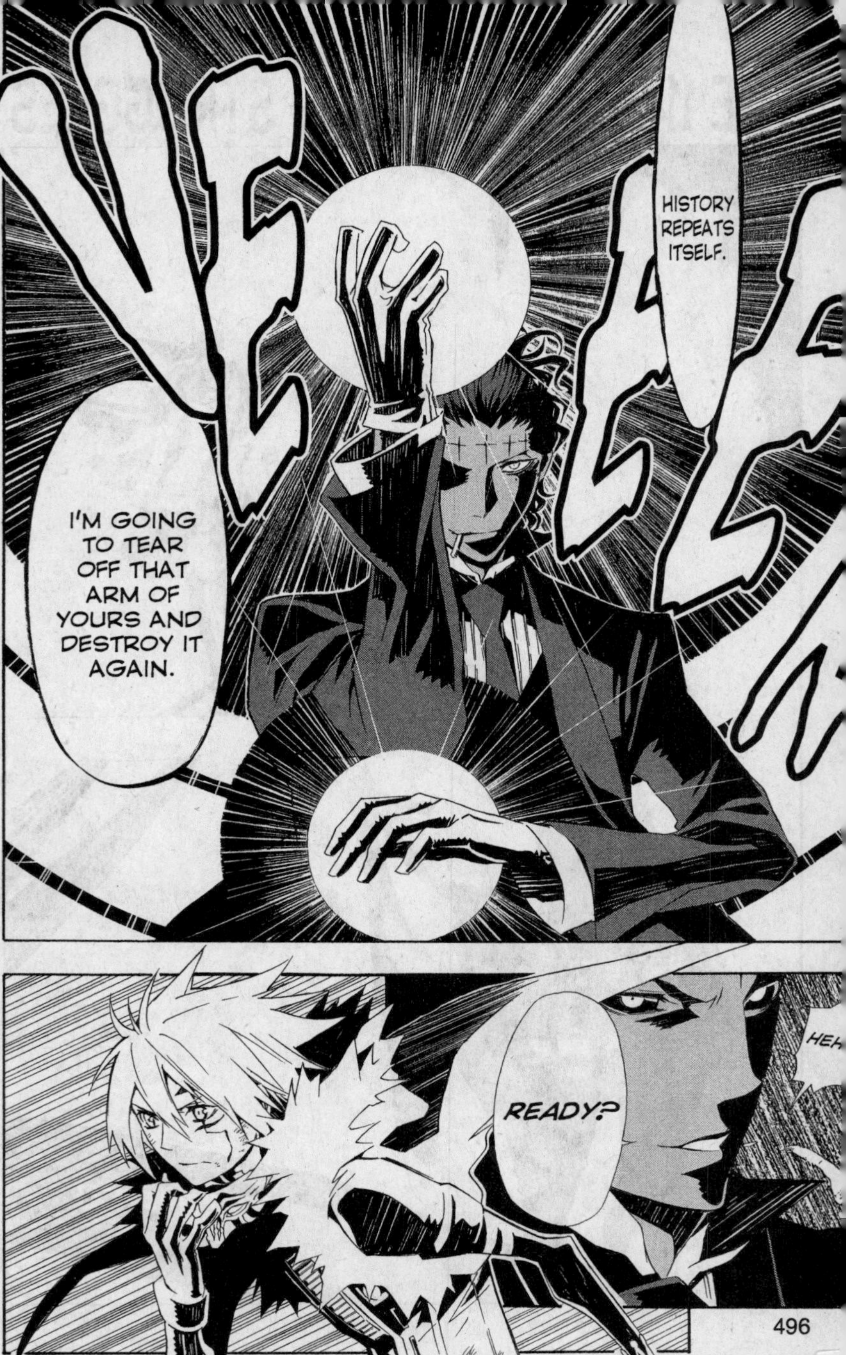
HISTORY REPEATS ITSELF.
I'M GOING TO TEAR OFF THAT ARM OF YOURS AND DESTROY IT AGAIN.
HEH
READY?

READ THIS WAY

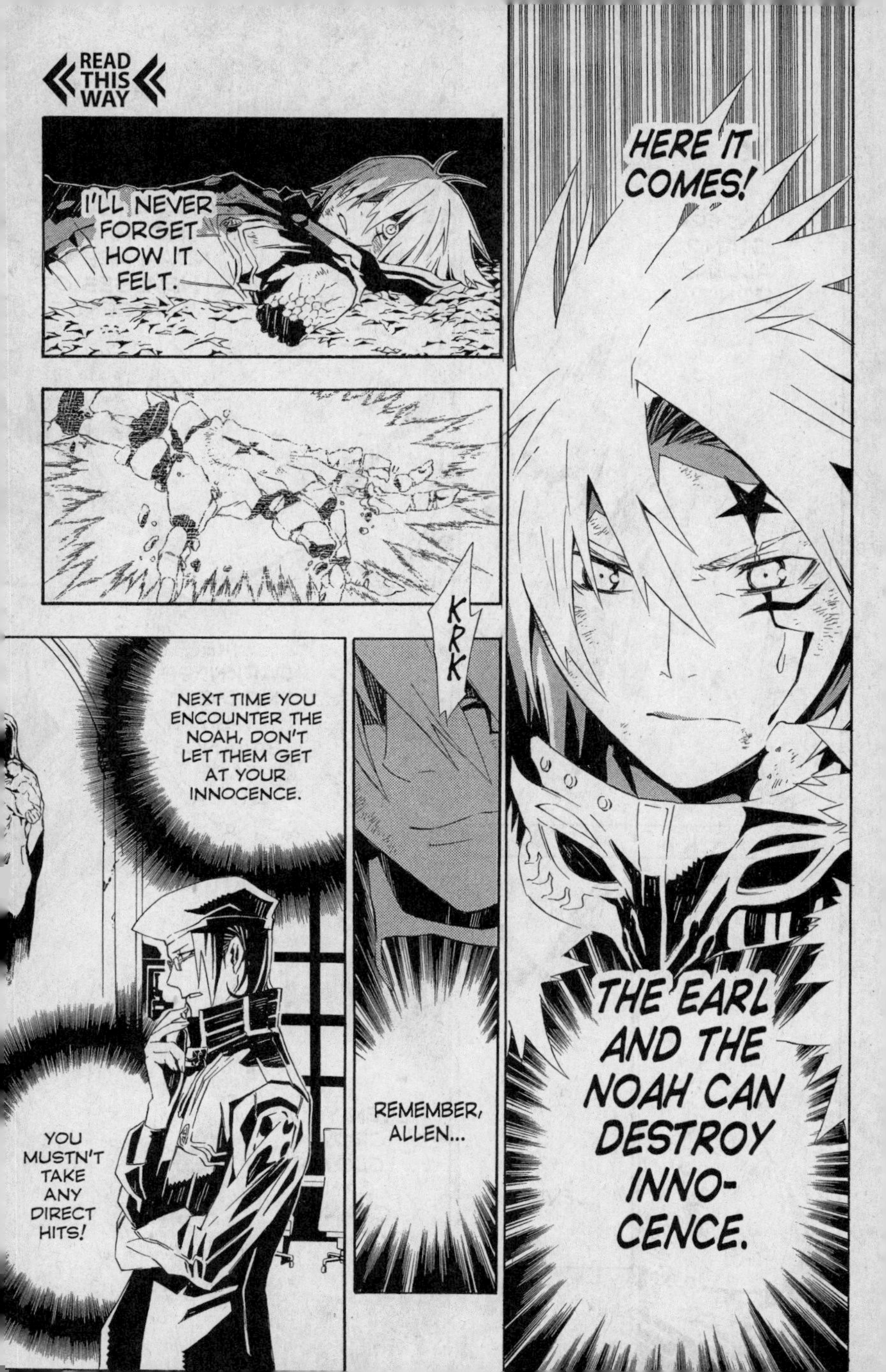
HERE IT COMES!
THE EARL AND THE NOAH CAN DESTROY INNO-CENCE.
I'LL NEVER FORGET HOW IT FELT.
KRK
REMEMBER, ALLEN...
NEXT TIME YOU ENCOUNTER THE NOAH, DON'T LET THEM GET AT YOUR INNOCENCE.
YOU MUSTN'T TAKE ANY DIRECT HITS!

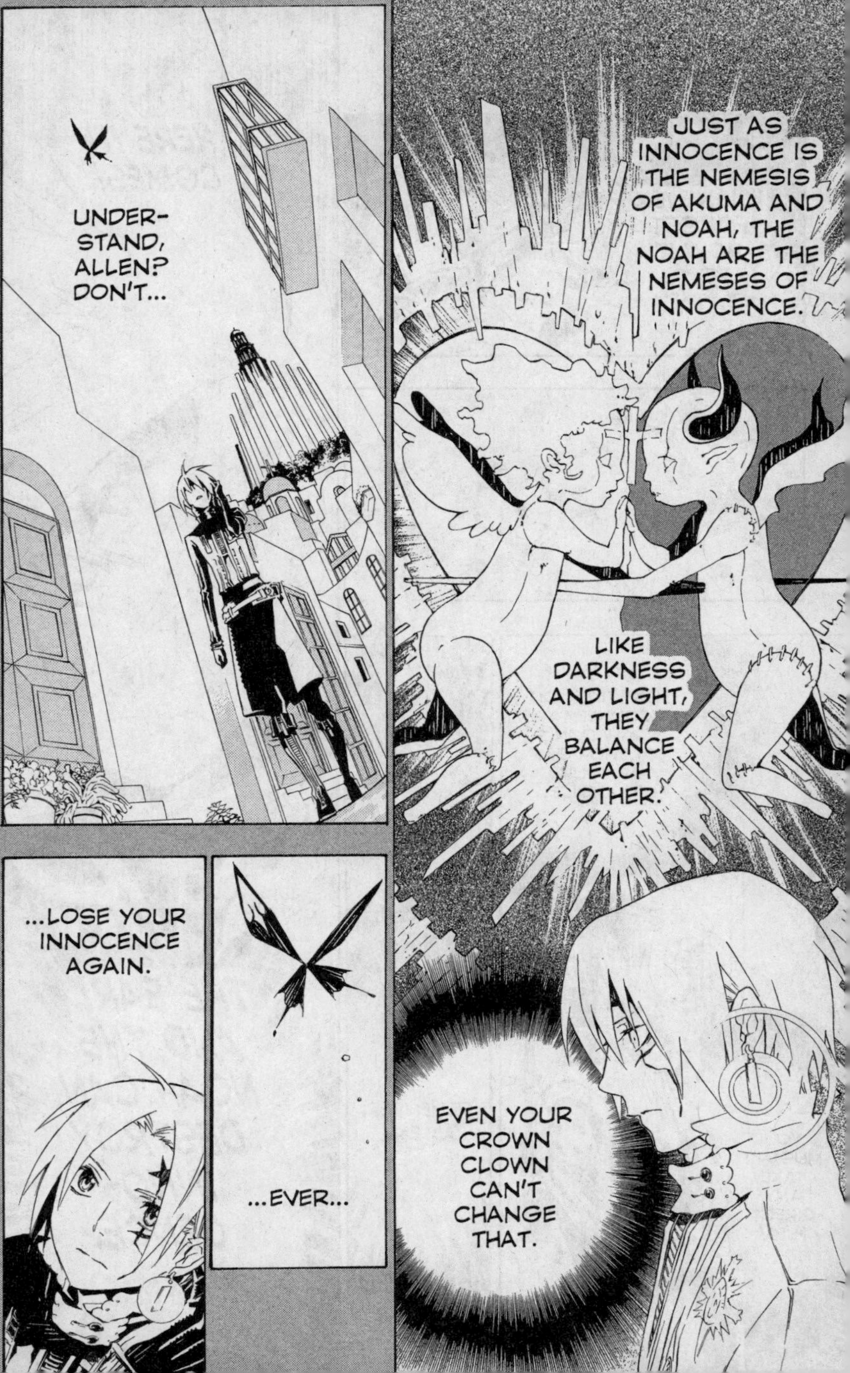
JUST AS INNOCENCE IS THE NEMESIS OF AKUMA AND NOAH, THE NOAH ARE THE NEMESES OF INNOCENCE.
LIKE DARKNESS AND LIGHT, THEY BALANCE EACH OTHER.
EVEN YOUR CROWN CLOWN CAN'T CHANGE THAT.
UNDER-STAND, ALLEN? DON'T...
...EVER...
...LOSE YOUR INNOCENCE AGAIN.

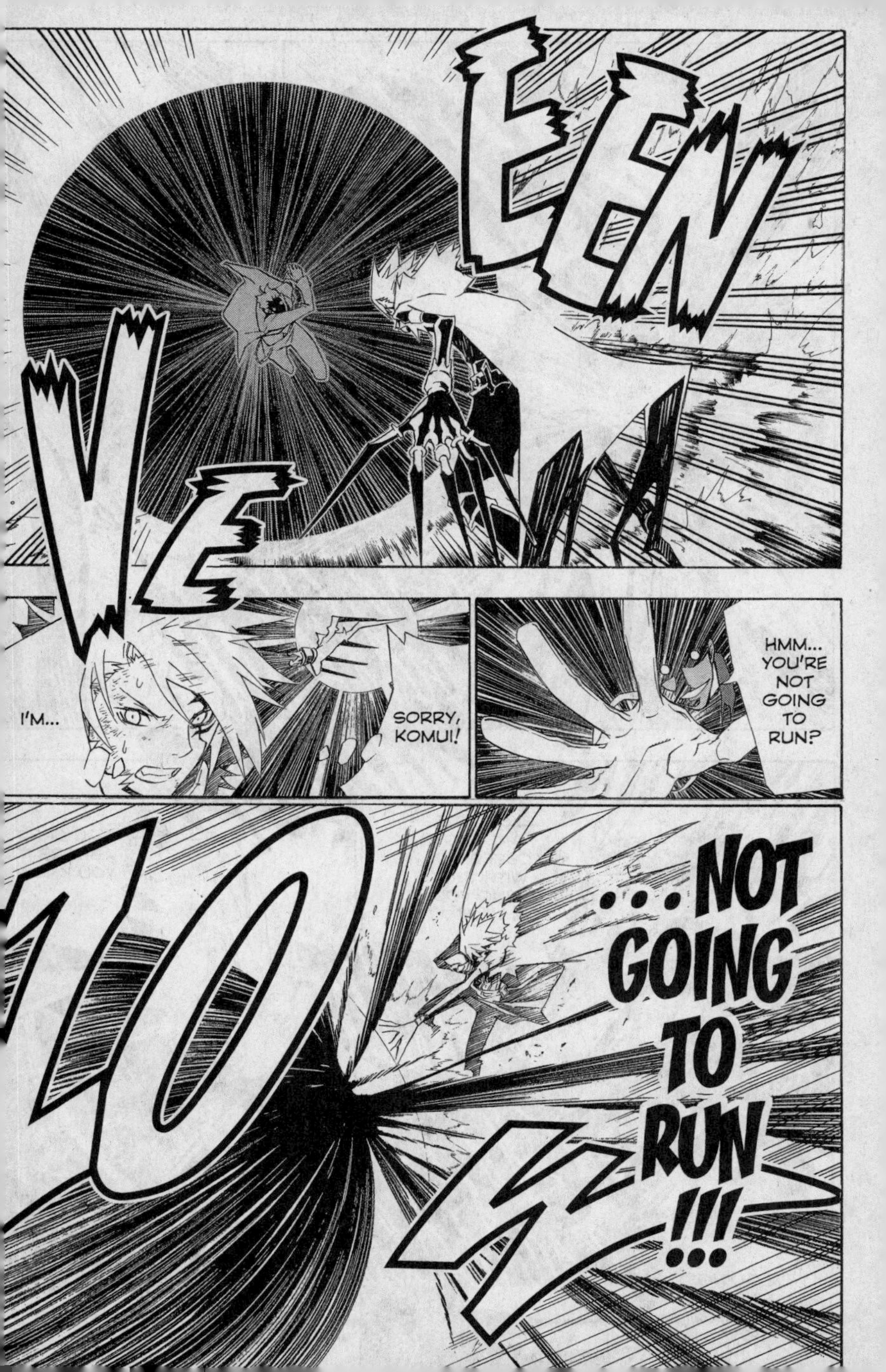
EEN
VE
HMM... YOU'RE NOT GOING TO RUN?
SORRY, KOMUI!
I'M...
...NOT GOING TO RUN!!!

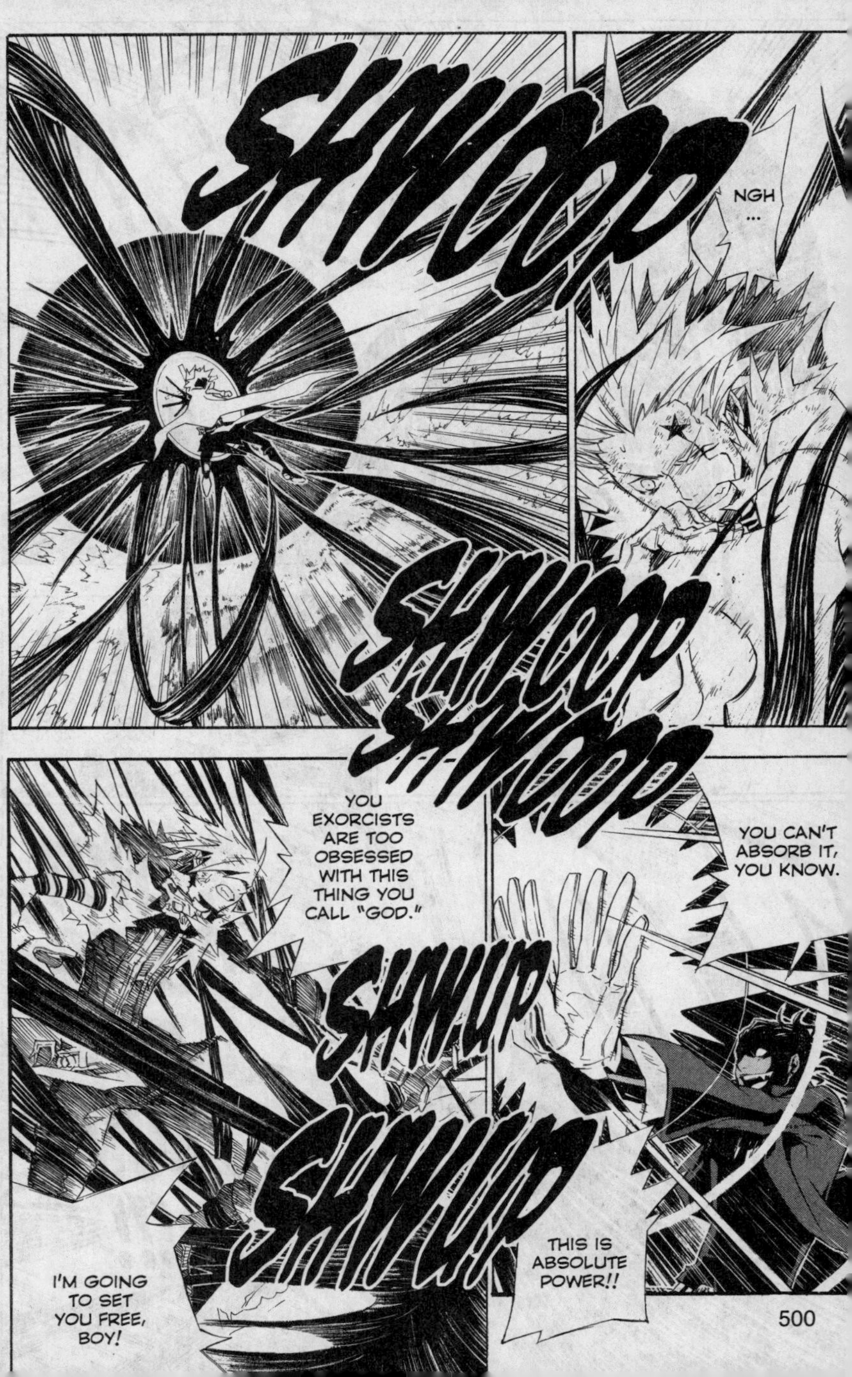
NGH ...
YOU CAN'T ABSORB IT, YOU KNOW.
THIS IS ABSOLUTE POWER!!
YOU EXORCISTS ARE TOO OBSESSED WITH THIS THING YOU CALL "GOD."
I'M GOING TO SET YOU FREE, BOY!

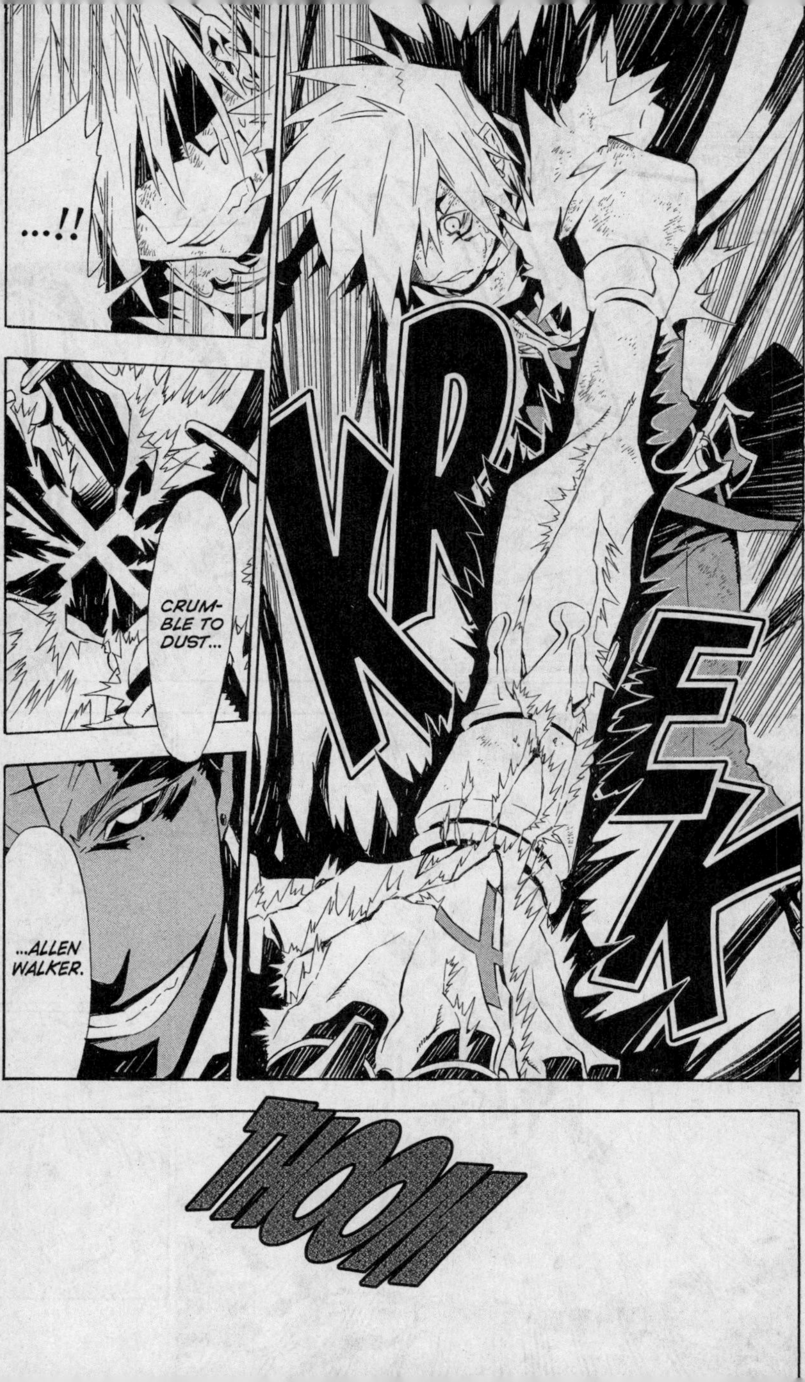
KREEK
...!!
CRUMBLE TO DUST...
...ALLEN WALKER.
THOOM

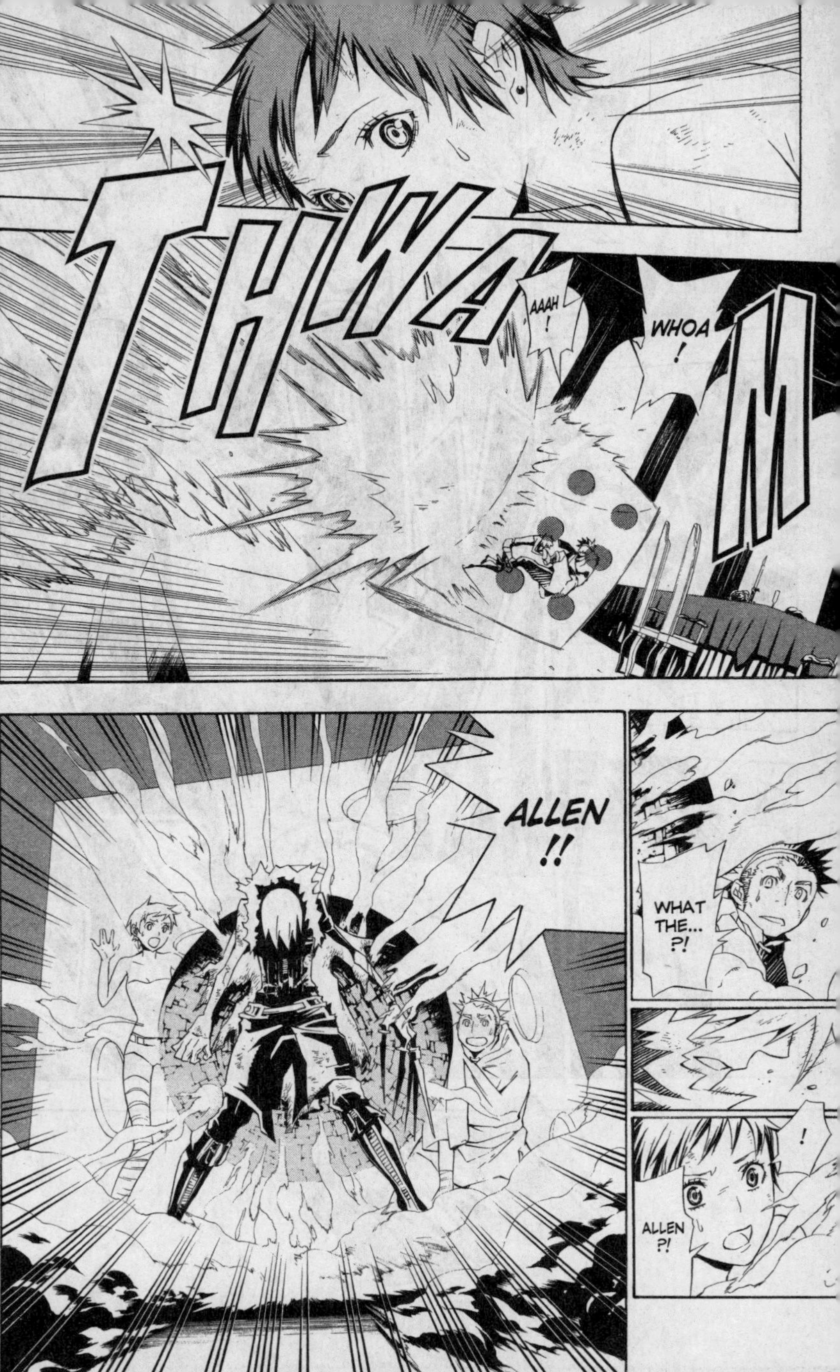
THWAM
WHOA!
AAAH!
WHAT THE...?!
!
ALLEN?!
ALLEN!!

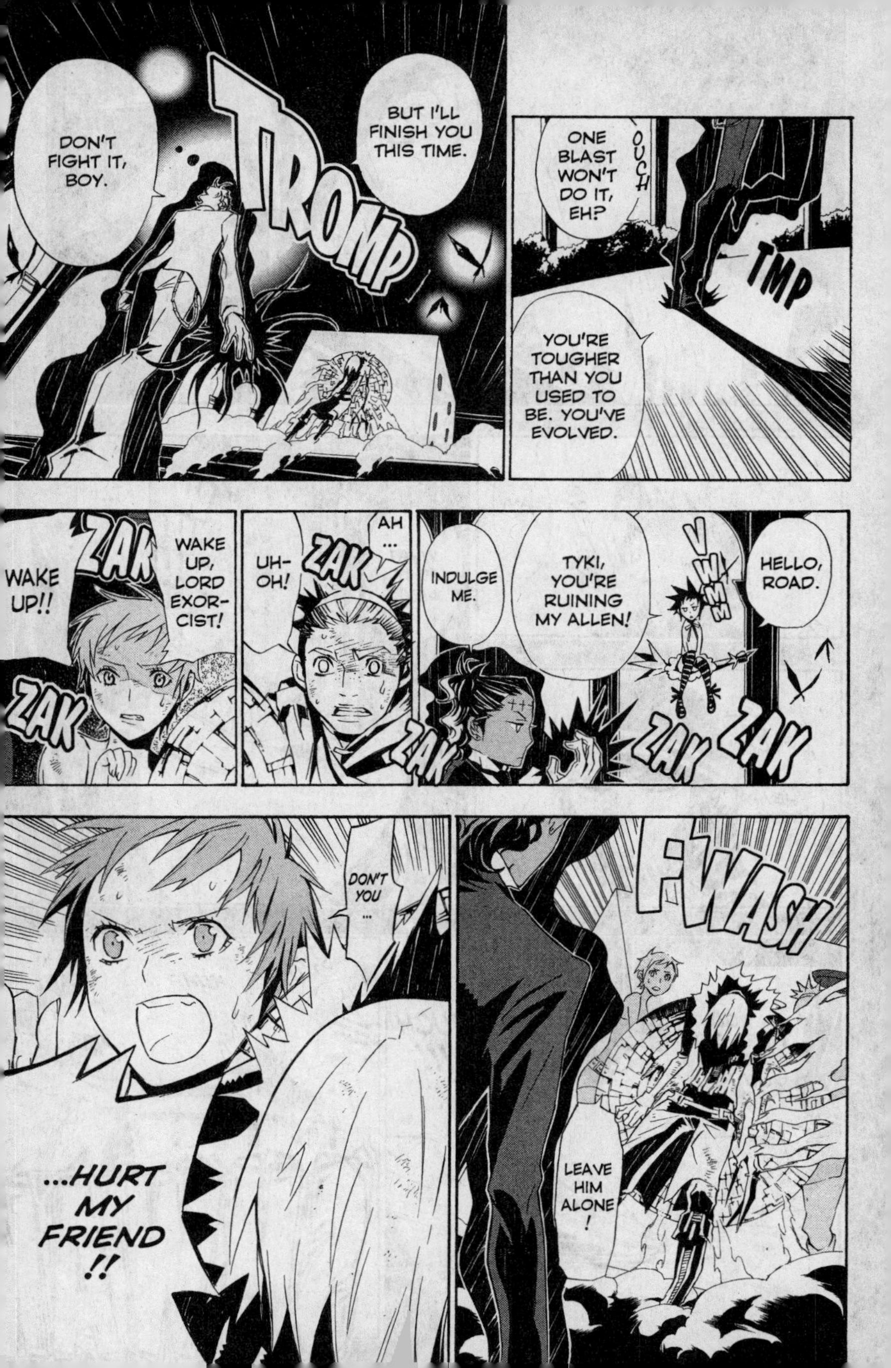
ONE BLAST WON'T DO IT, EH?
OUCH
TMP
YOU'RE TOUGHER THAN YOU USED TO BE. YOU'VE EVOLVED.
BUT I'LL FINISH YOU THIS TIME.
TROMP
DON'T FIGHT IT, BOY.
HELLO, ROAD.
VWMM
TYKI, YOU'RE RUINING MY ALLEN!
INDULGE ME.
ZAK
ZAK
AH ...
ZAK
UH-OH!
ZAK
WAKE UP, LORD EXORCIST!
ZAK
WAKE UP!!
ZAK
F'WASH
LEAVE HIM ALONE!
DON'T YOU ...
...HURT MY FRIEND!!

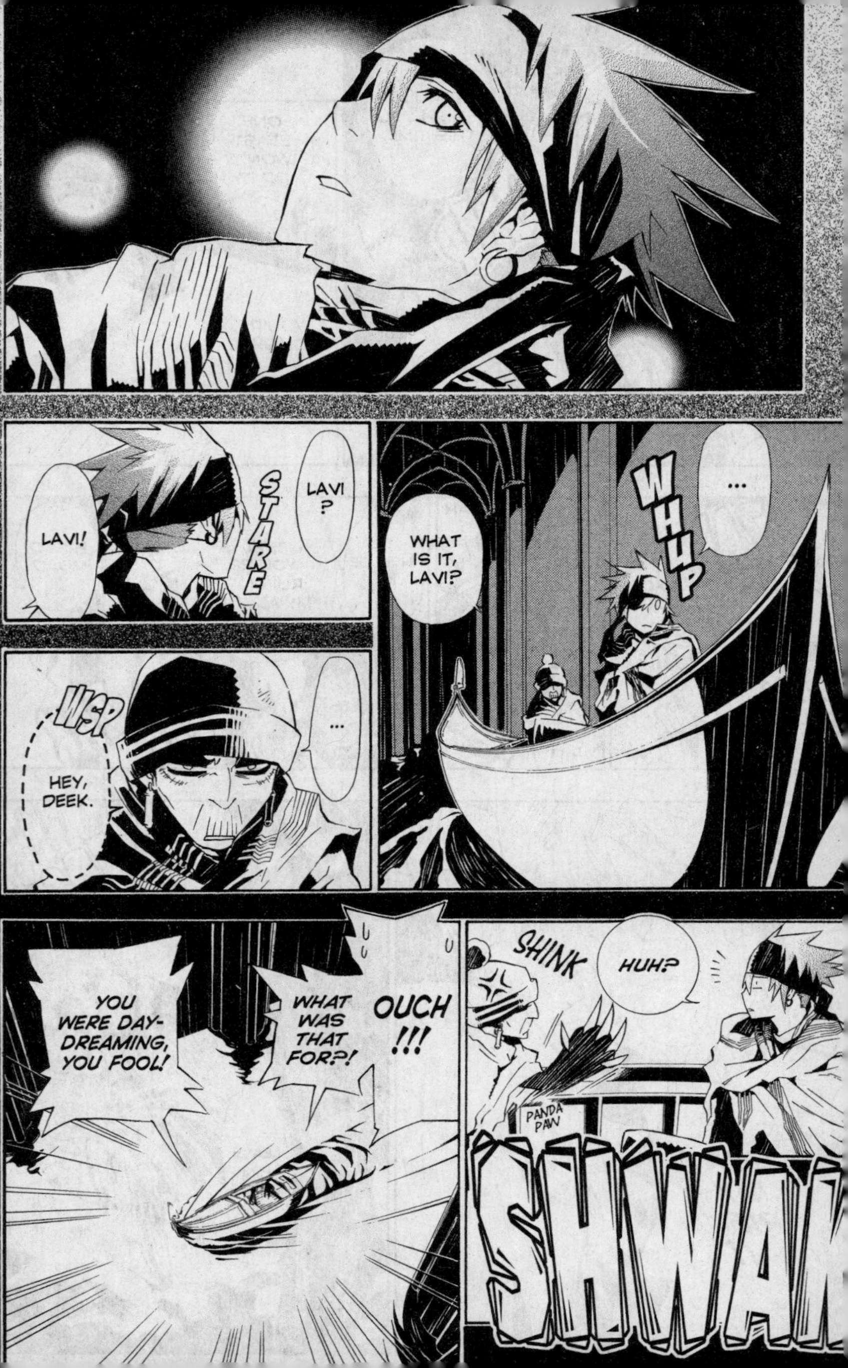
...
WHUP
WHAT IS IT, LAVI?
LAVI ?
STARE
LAVI!
...
WSP
HEY, DEEK.
HUH?
SHINK
PANDA PAW
SHWAK
OUCH !!!
WHAT WAS THAT FOR?!
YOU WERE DAY-DREAMING, YOU FOOL!

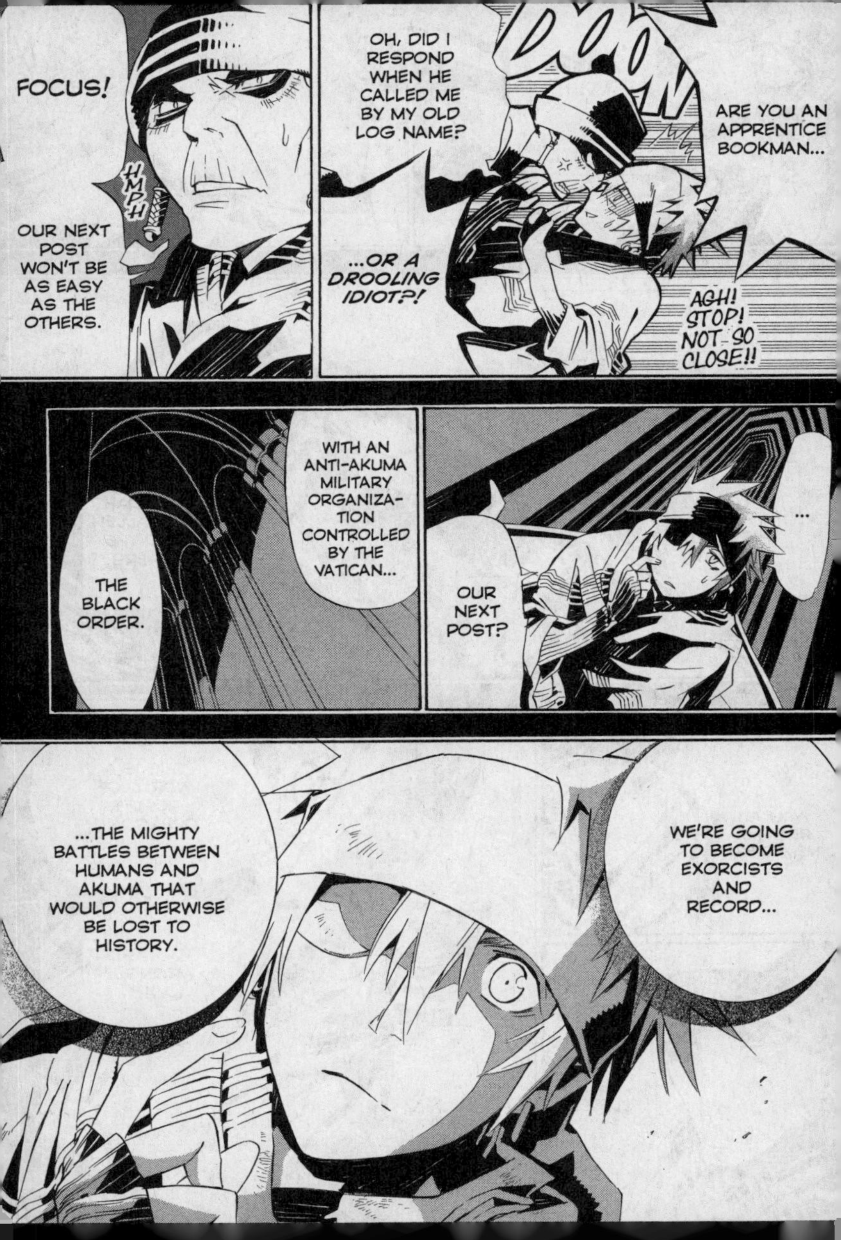
OH, DID I RESPOND WHEN HE CALLED ME BY MY OLD LOG NAME?
ARE YOU AN APPRENTICE BOOKMAN...
...OR A DROOLING IDIOT?!
AGH! STOP! NOT SO CLOSE!!
FOCUS!
HMPH
OUR NEXT POST WON'T BE AS EASY AS THE OTHERS.
...
OUR NEXT POST?
WITH AN ANTI-AKUMA MILITARY ORGANIZA-TION CONTROLLED BY THE VATICAN...
THE BLACK ORDER.
WE'RE GOING TO BECOME EXORCISTS AND RECORD...
...THE MIGHTY BATTLES BETWEEN HUMANS AND AKUMA THAT WOULD OTHERWISE BE LOST TO HISTORY.

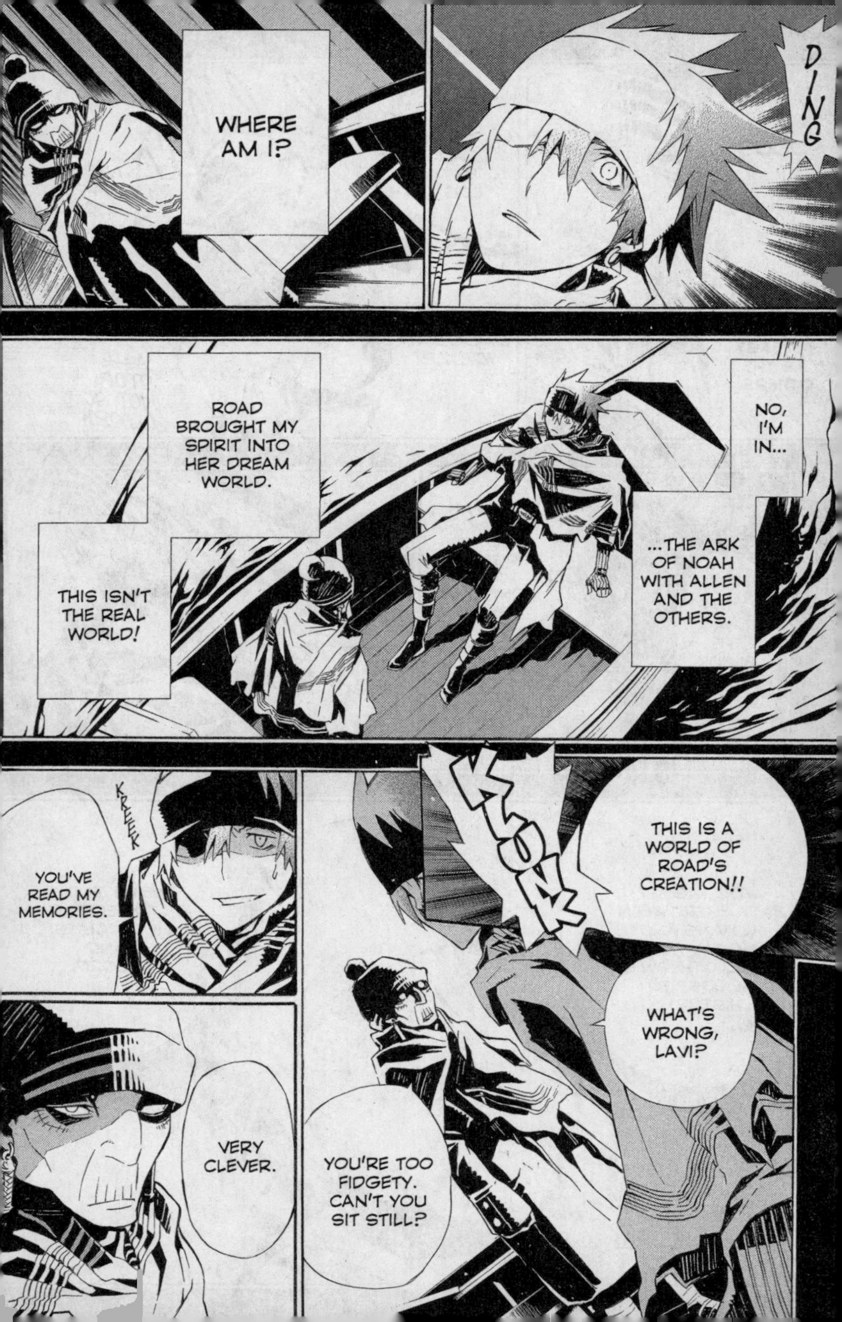
DING
WHERE AM I?
NO, I'M IN...
...THE ARK OF NOAH WITH ALLEN AND THE OTHERS.
ROAD BROUGHT MY SPIRIT INTO HER DREAM WORLD.
THIS ISN'T THE REAL WORLD!
KLUNK
THIS IS A WORLD OF ROAD'S CREATION!!
WHAT'S WRONG, LAVI?
YOU'RE TOO FIDGETY. CAN'T YOU SIT STILL?
KREEK
YOU'VE READ MY MEMORIES.
VERY CLEVER.

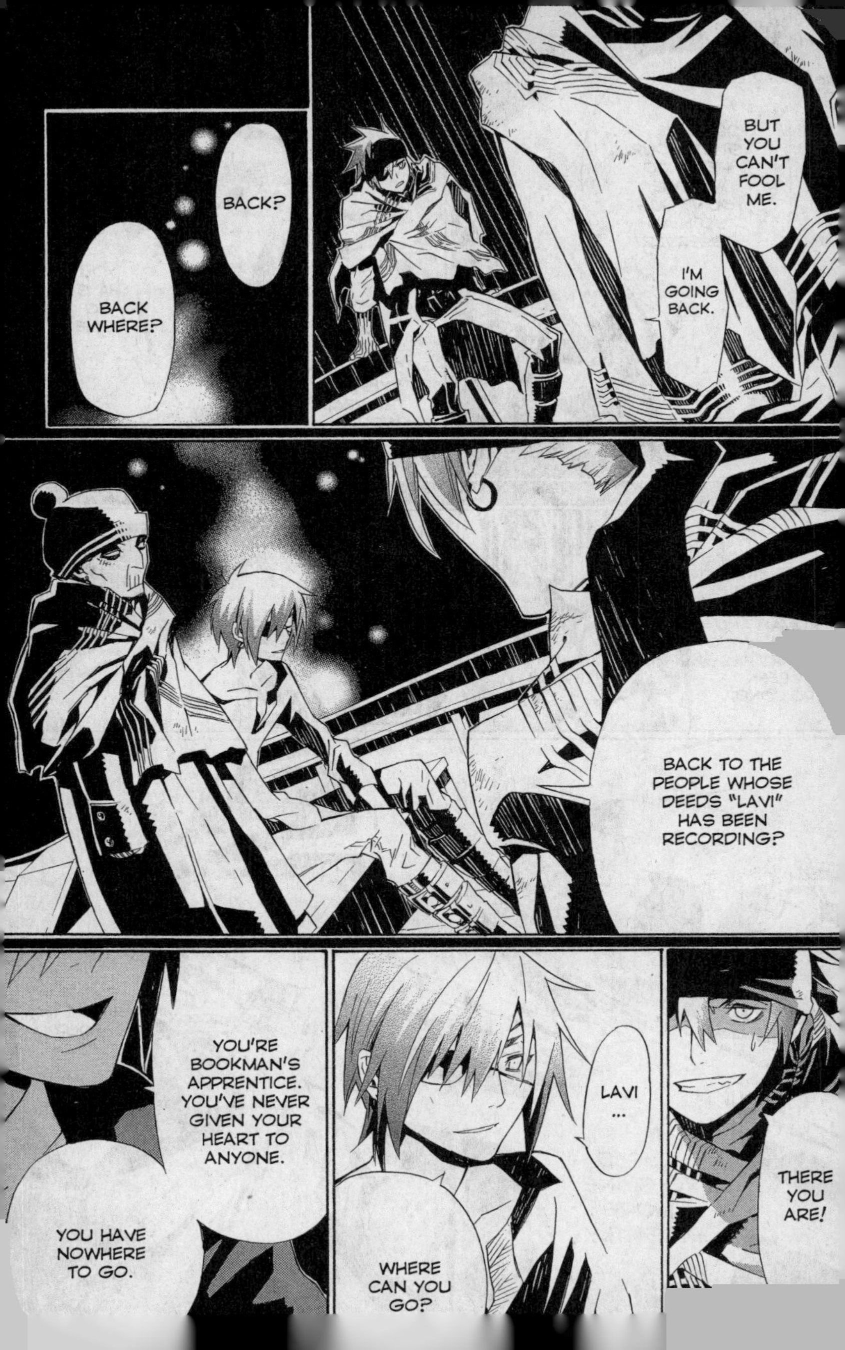
BUT YOU CAN'T FOOL ME.
I'M GOING BACK.
BACK?
BACK WHERE?
BACK TO THE PEOPLE WHOSE DEEDS "LAVI" HAS BEEN RECORDING?
THERE YOU ARE!
LAVI ...
WHERE CAN YOU GO?
YOU'RE BOOKMAN'S APPRENTICE. YOU'VE NEVER GIVEN YOUR HEART TO ANYONE.
YOU HAVE NOWHERE TO GO.

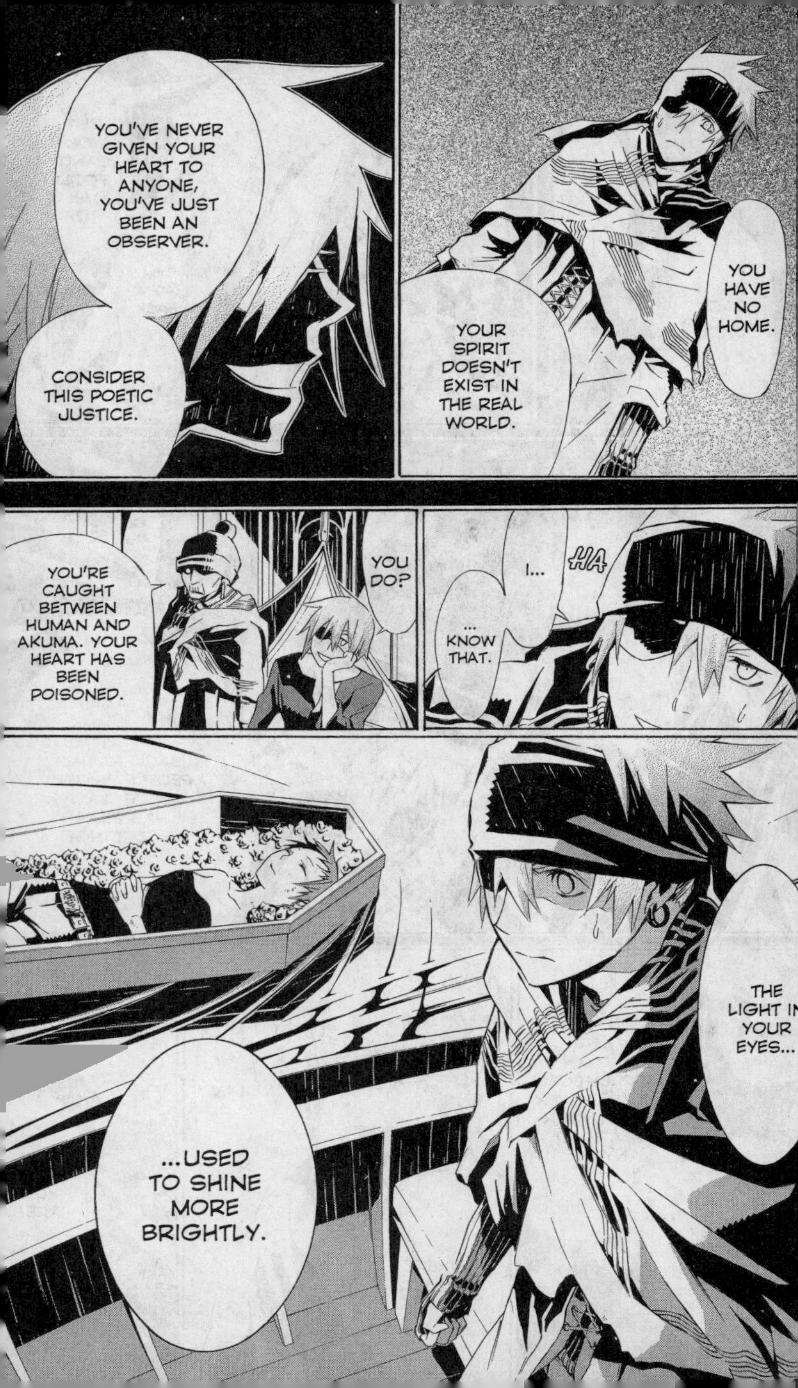
YOU HAVE NO HOME.
YOUR SPIRIT DOESN'T EXIST IN THE REAL WORLD.
YOU'VE NEVER GIVEN YOUR HEART TO ANYONE, YOU'VE JUST BEEN AN OBSERVER.
CONSIDER THIS POETIC JUSTICE.
HA
I...
...KNOW THAT.
YOU DO?
YOU'RE CAUGHT BETWEEN HUMAN AND AKUMA. YOUR HEART HAS BEEN POISONED.
THE LIGHT IN YOUR EYES...
...USED TO SHINE MORE BRIGHTLY.

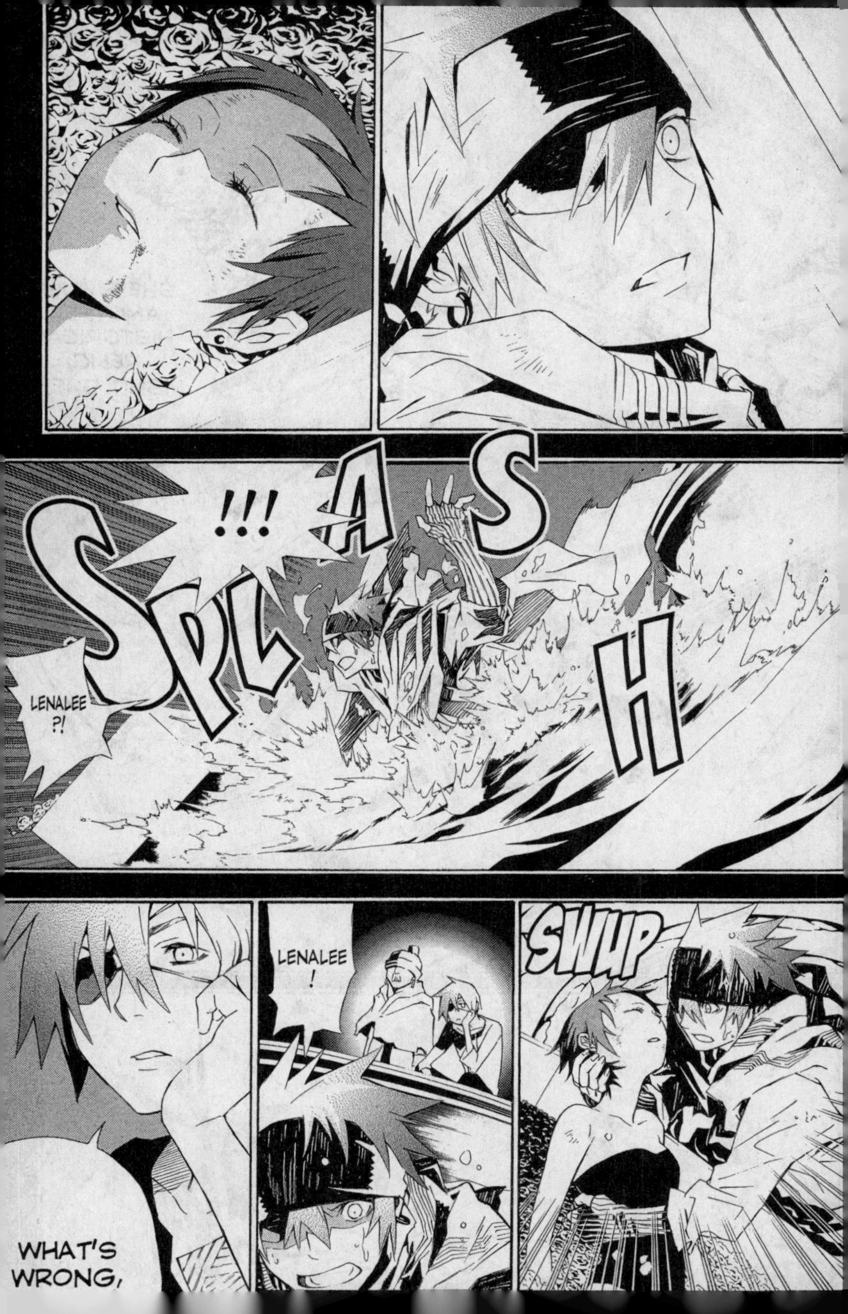
SPLASH
!!!
LENALEE ?!
SWUP
LENALEE !
WHAT'S WRONG,

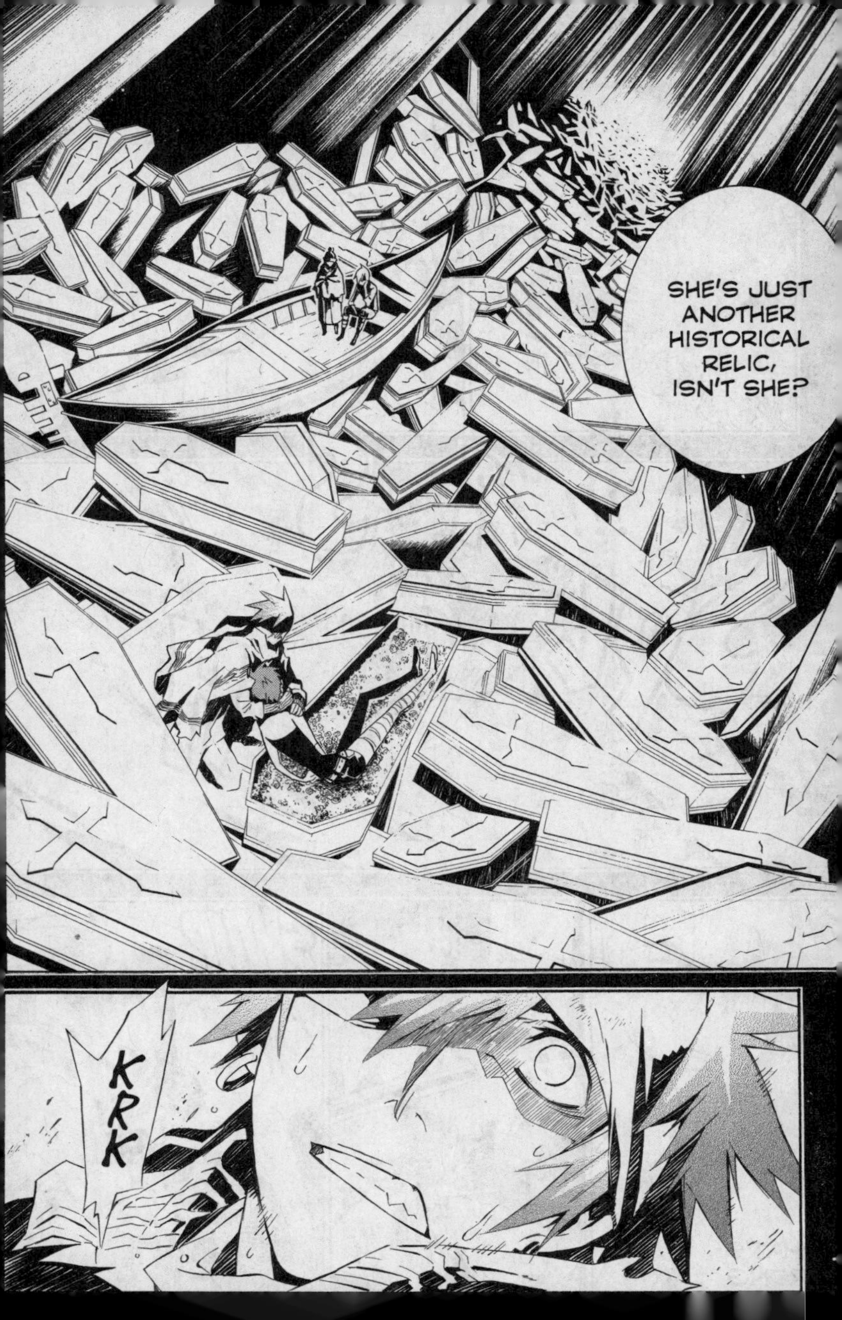
SHE'S JUST ANOTHER HISTORICAL RELIC, ISN'T SHE?
KRK

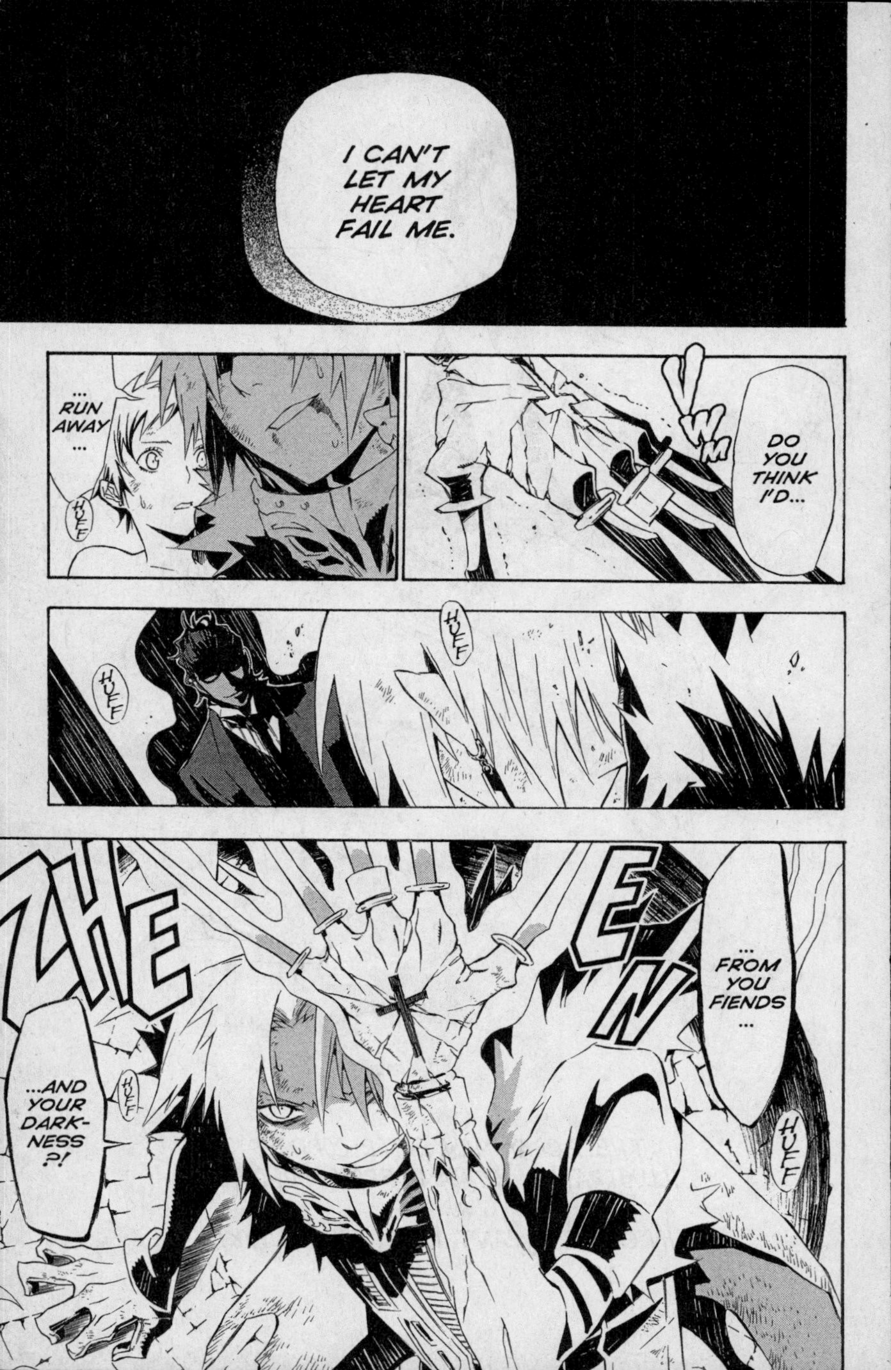
I CAN'T LET MY HEART FAIL ME.
VWM
DO YOU THINK I'D...
...RUN AWAY...
HUFF
HUFF
HUFF
...FROM YOU FIENDS...
EN
HUFF
ZHE
...AND YOUR DARKNESS?!
HUFF

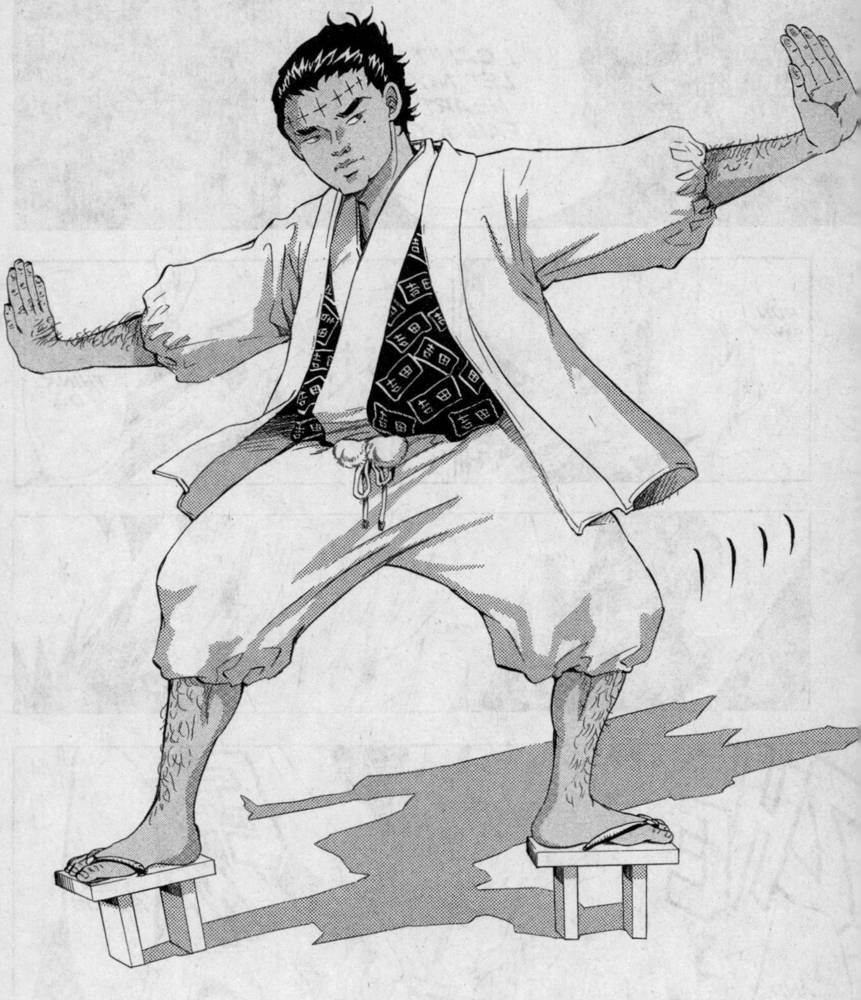

THE D.GRAY-MAN ELITE CORPS 3
ILLUSTRATION BY MAMA FROM NICHO-ME
HUH?
IN CASE YOU CAN'T TELL, THIS IS TYKI.

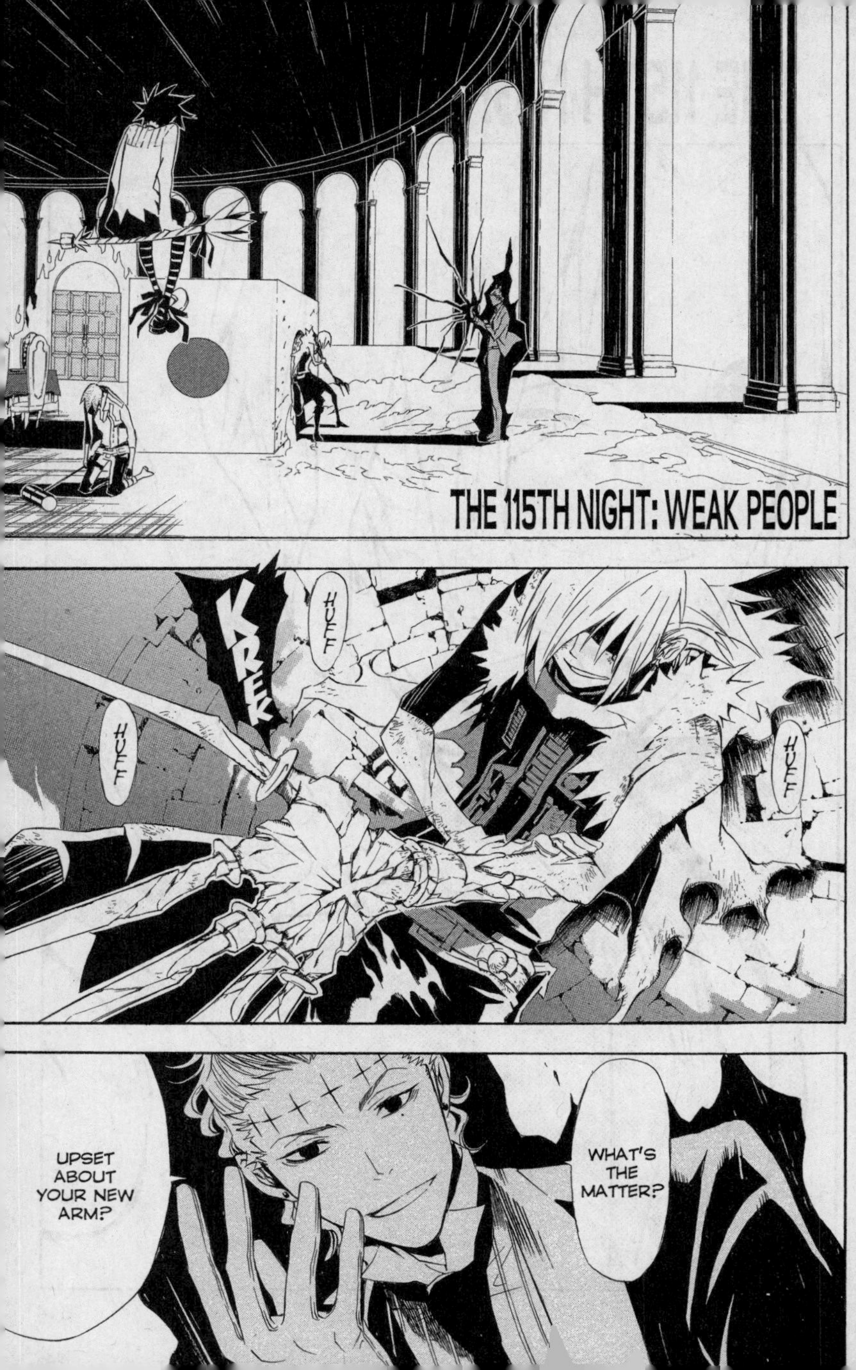
THE 115TH NIGHT: WEAK PEOPLE
HUFF
KREK
HUFF
HUFF
WHAT'S THE MATTER?
UPSET ABOUT YOUR NEW ARM?

THE 115TH NIGHT: WEAK PEOPLE

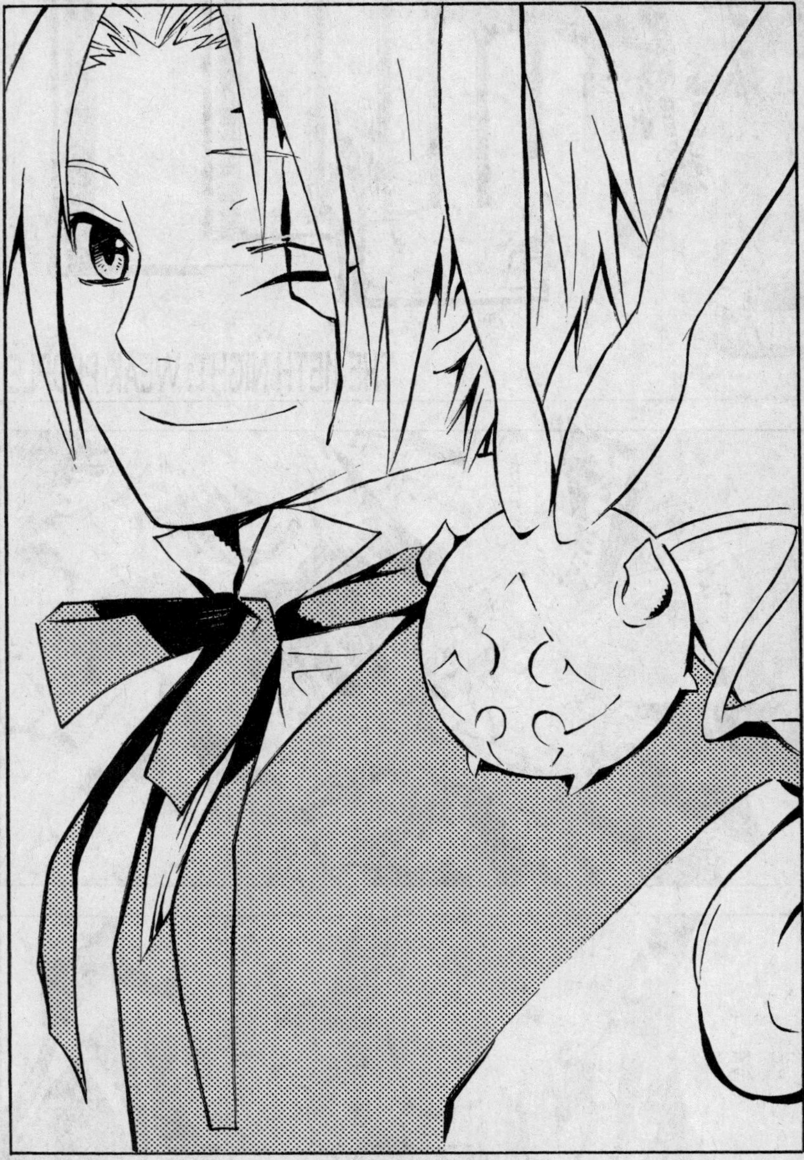

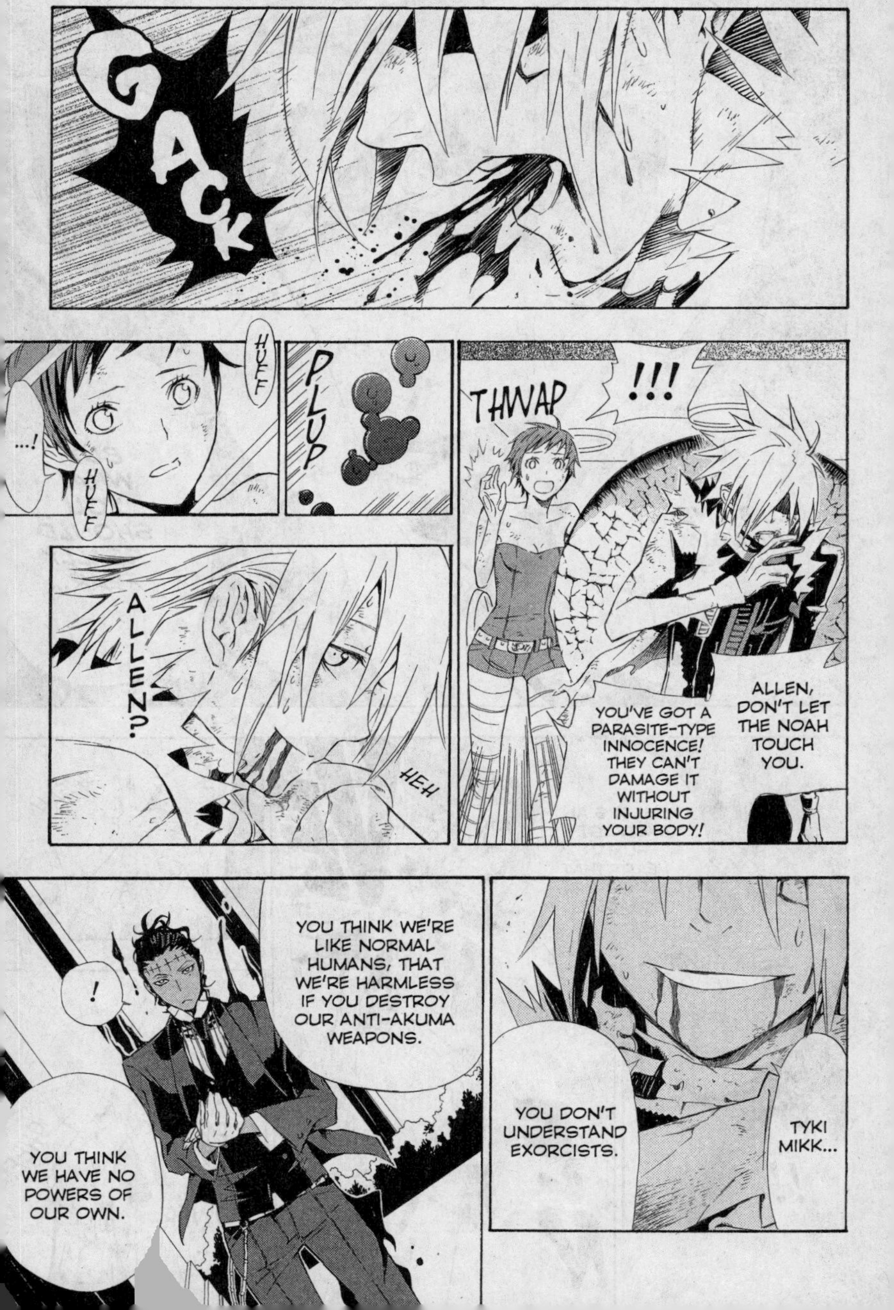
GACK
THWAP
!!!
ALLEN, DON'T LET THE NOAH TOUCH YOU.
YOU'VE GOT A PARASITE-TYPE INNOCENCE! THEY CAN'T DAMAGE IT WITHOUT INJURING YOUR BODY!
PLUP
HUFF
...!
HUFF
ALLEN?
HEH
TYKI MIKK...
YOU DON'T UNDERSTAND EXORCISTS.
YOU THINK WE'RE LIKE NORMAL HUMANS, THAT WE'RE HARMLESS IF YOU DESTROY OUR ANTI-AKUMA WEAPONS.
!
YOU THINK WE HAVE NO POWERS OF OUR OWN.

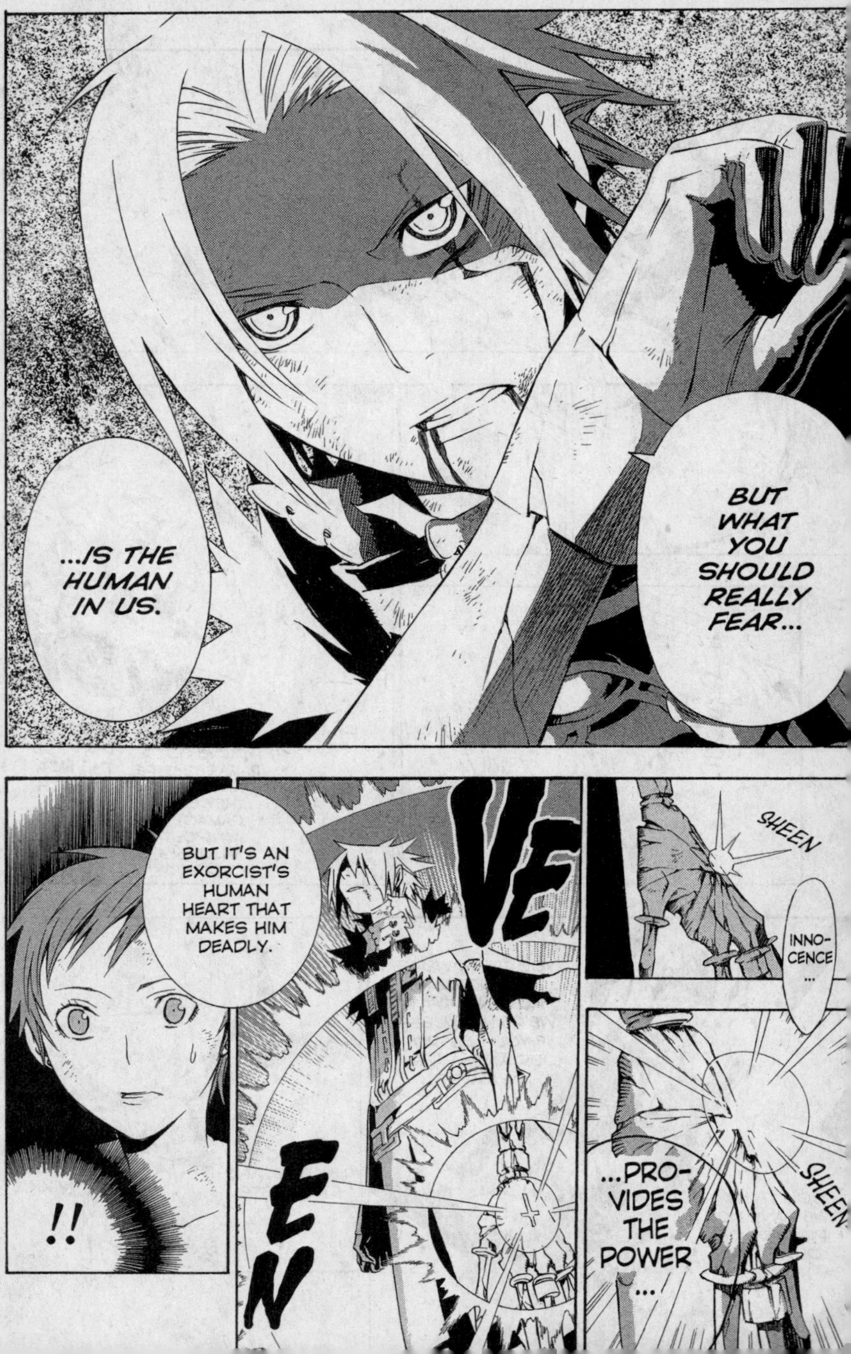
BUT WHAT YOU SHOULD REALLY FEAR...
...IS THE HUMAN IN US.
SHEEN
INNO-CENCE ...
SHEEN
...PRO-VIDES THE POWER ...
VE
BUT IT'S AN EXORCIST'S HUMAN HEART THAT MAKES HIM DEADLY.
EN
!!

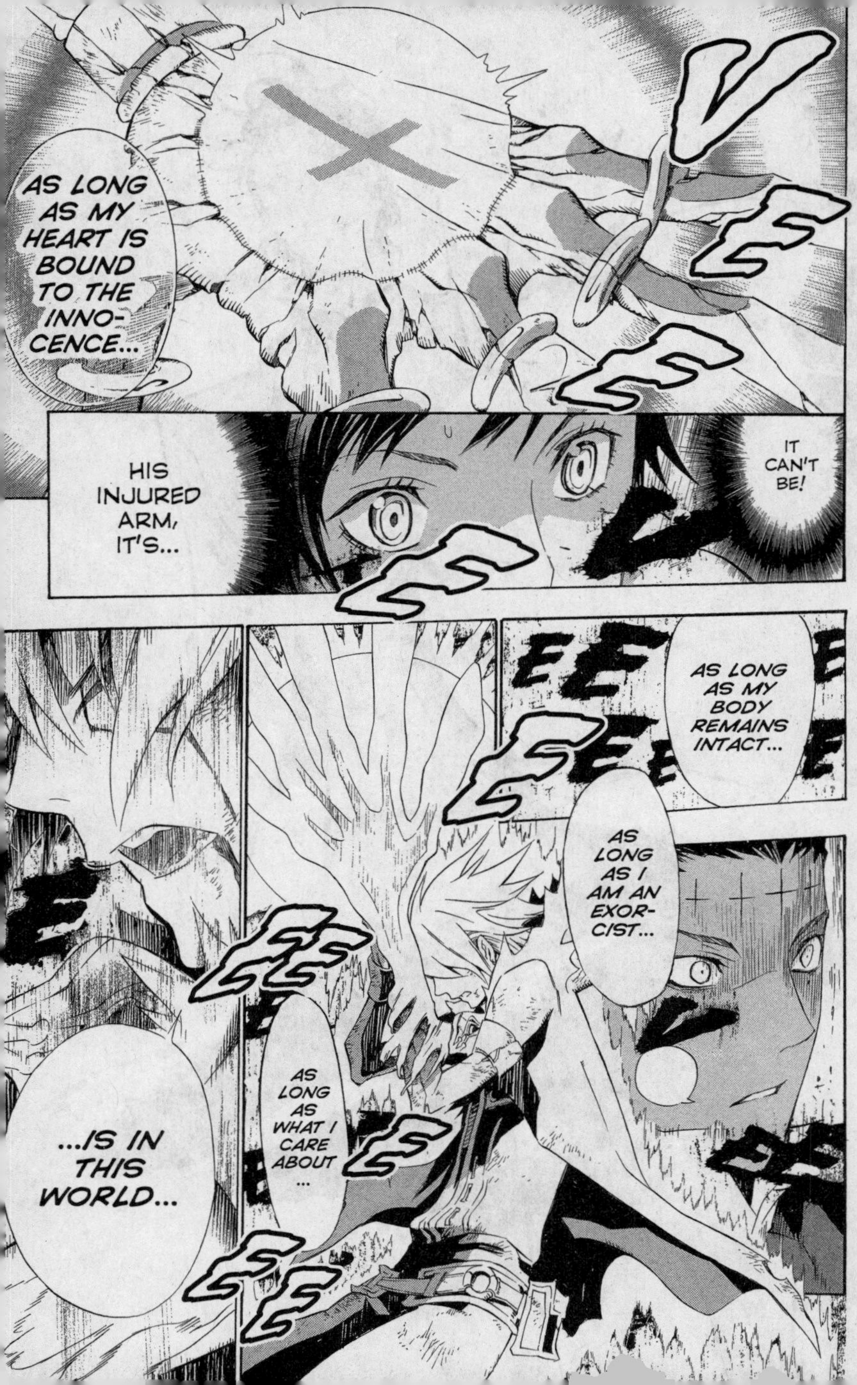
AS LONG AS MY HEART IS BOUND TO THE INNO-CENCE...
IT CAN'T BE!
HIS INJURED ARM, IT'S...
AS LONG AS MY BODY REMAINS INTACT...
AS LONG AS I AM AN EXOR-CIST...
AS LONG AS WHAT I CARE ABOUT ...
...IS IN THIS WORLD...

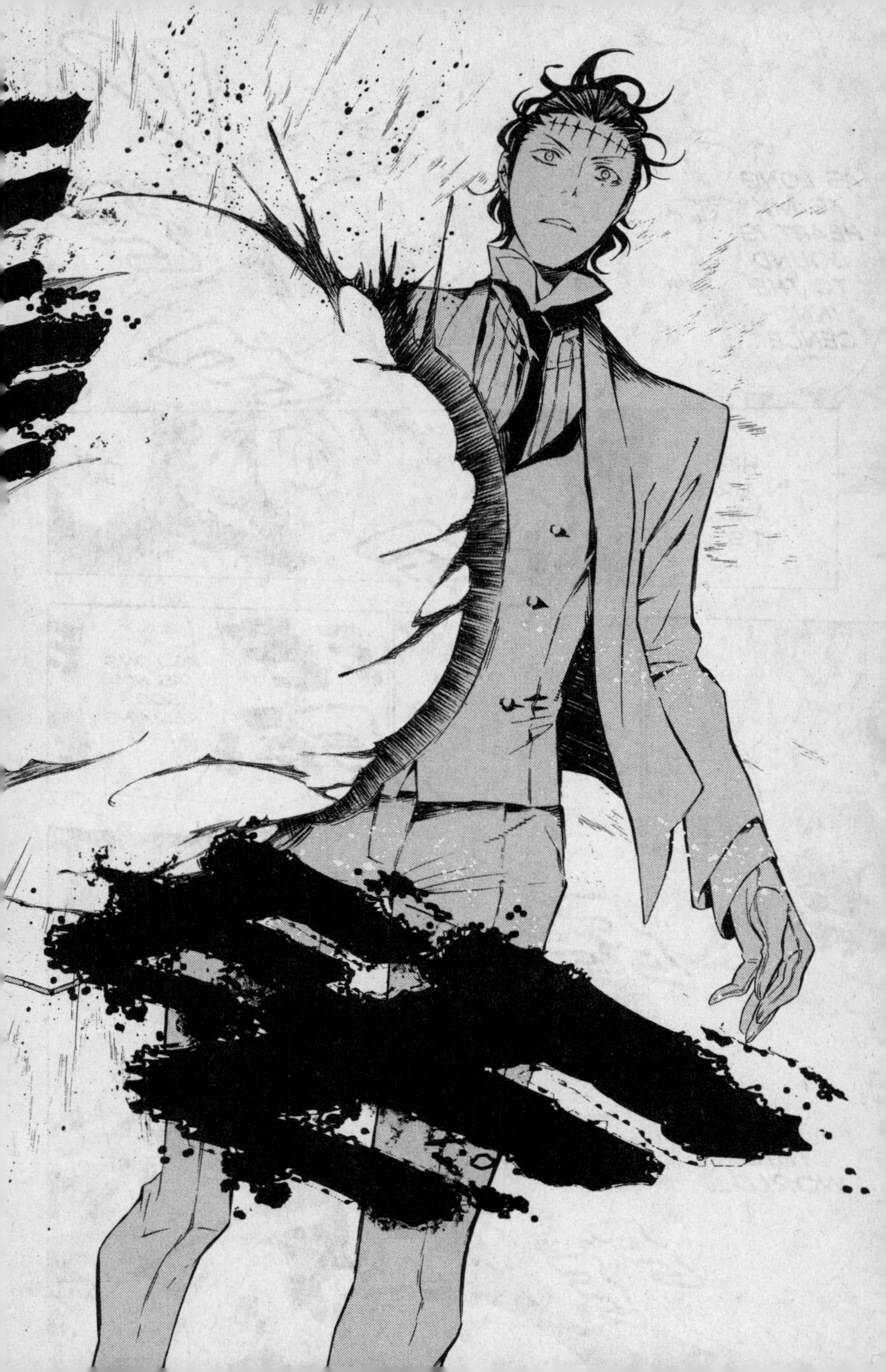

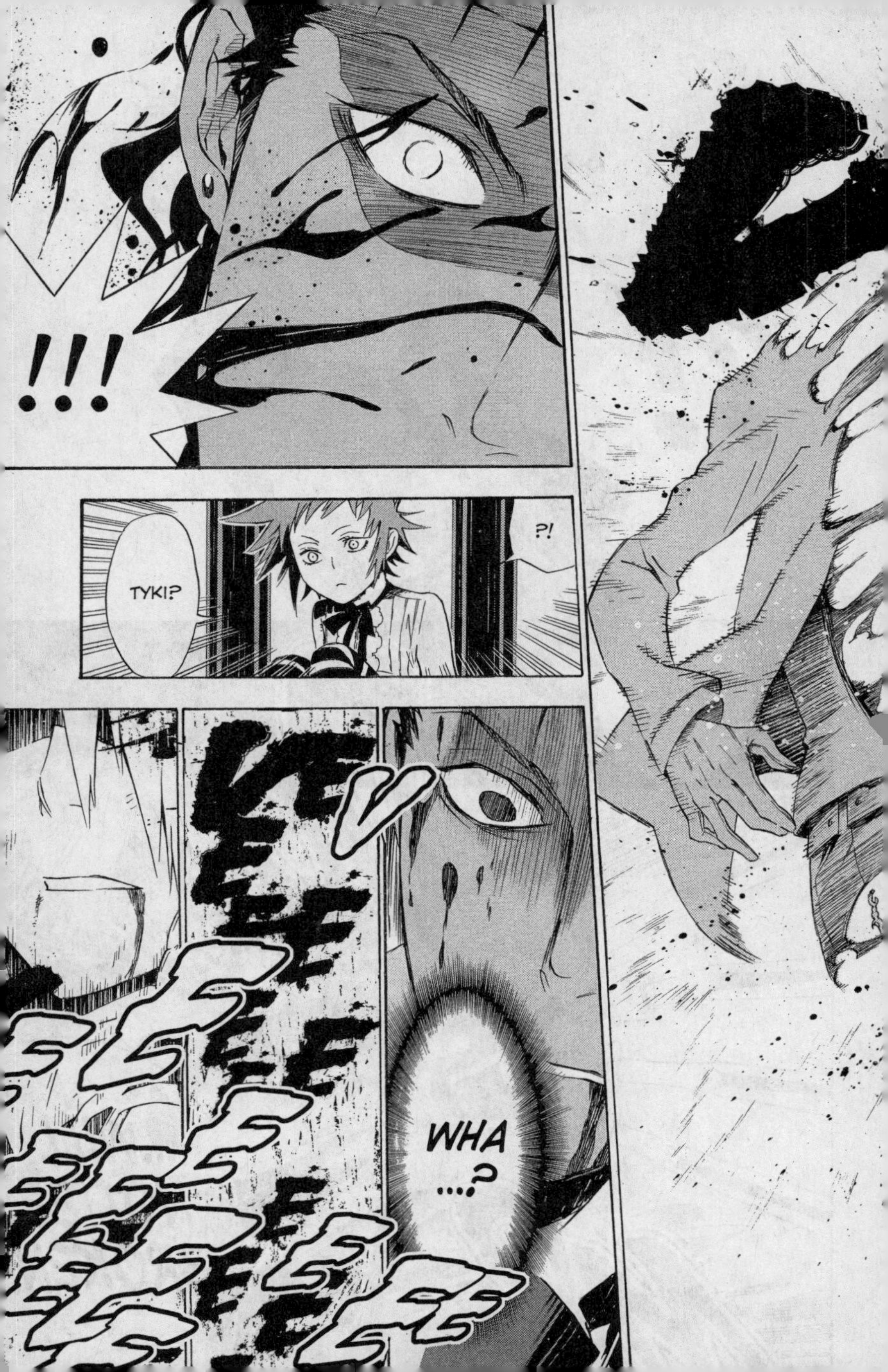
!!!
?!
TYKI?
WHA ...?

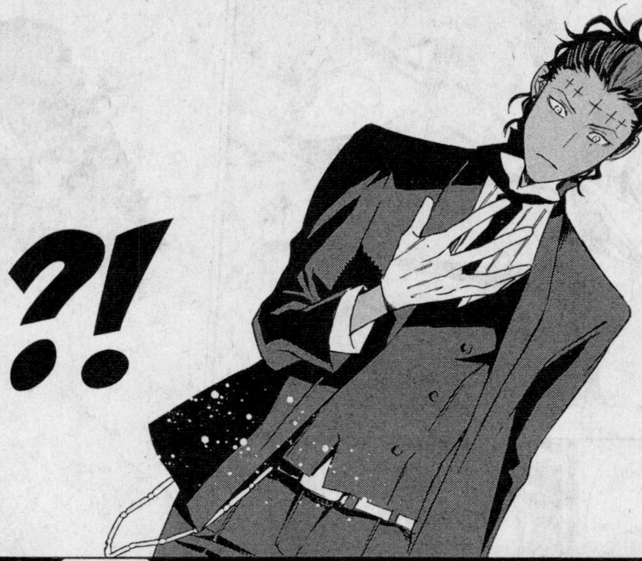
?!

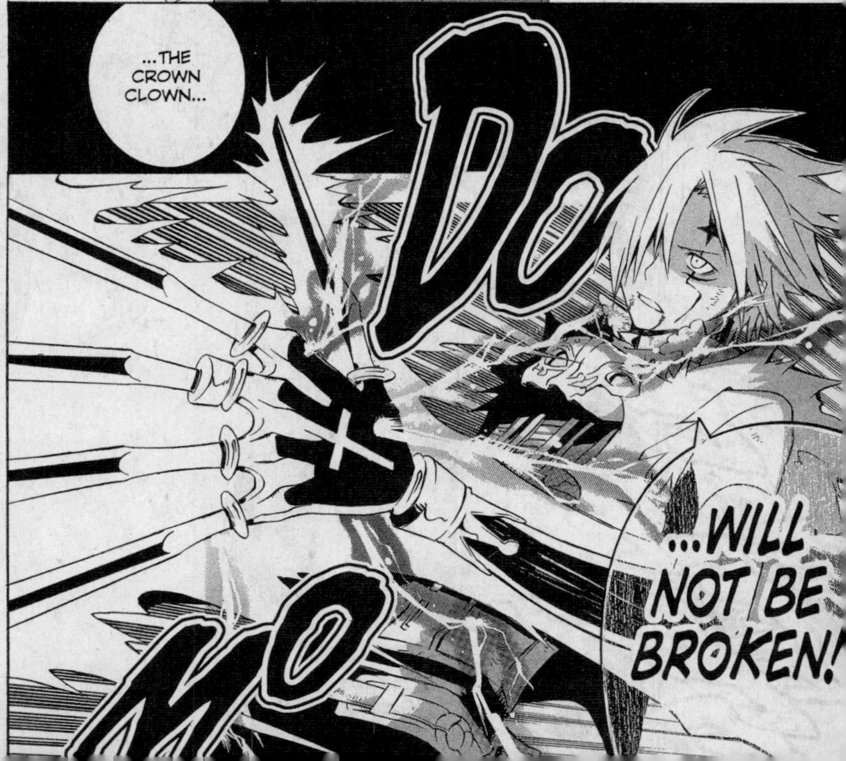
...THE CROWN CLOWN...
...WILL NOT BE BROKEN!

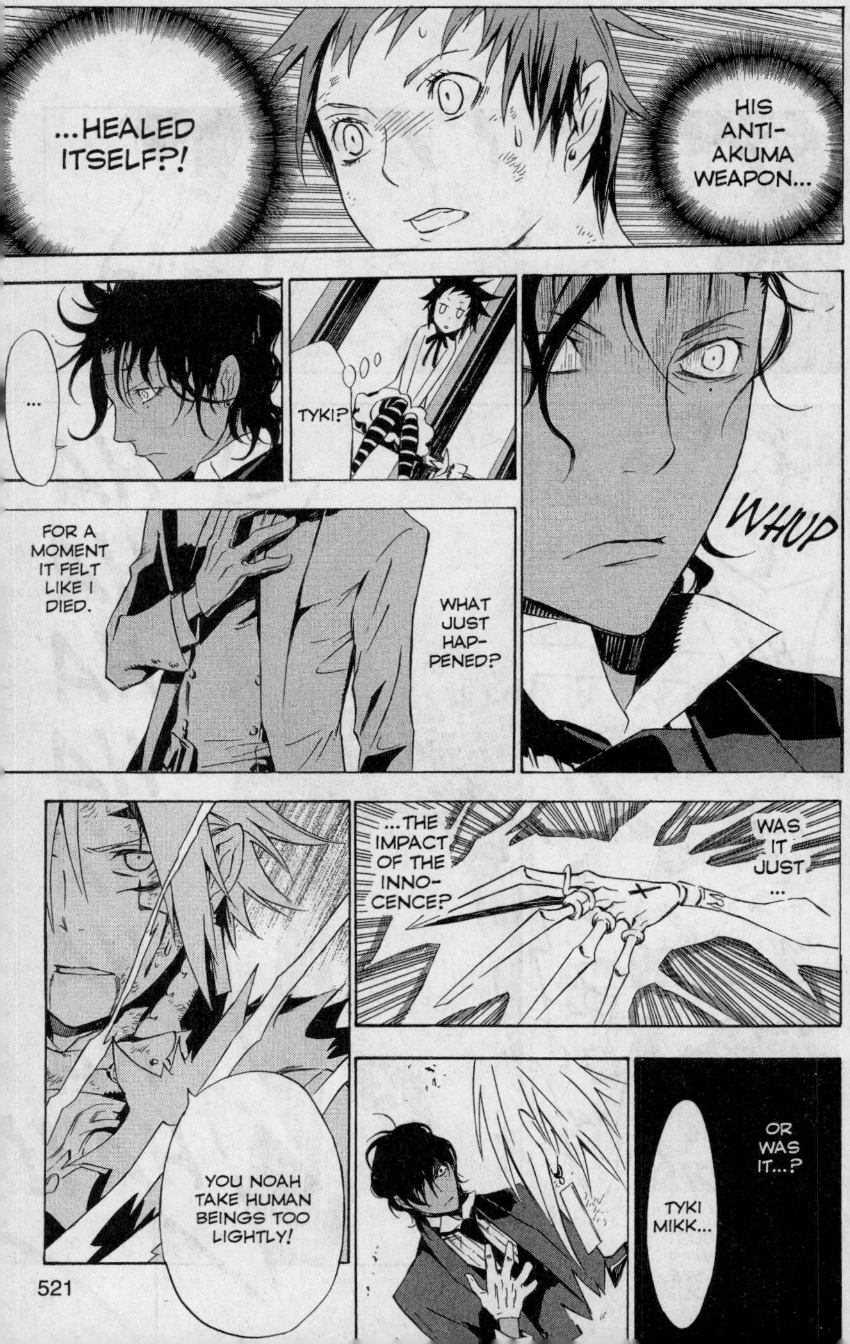
HIS ANTI-AKUMA WEAPON...
...HEALED ITSELF?!
WHUP
TYKI?
...
WHAT JUST HAPPENED?
FOR A MOMENT IT FELT LIKE I DIED.
WAS IT JUST...
...THE IMPACT OF THE INNOCENCE?
OR WAS IT...?
TYKI MIKK...
YOU NOAH TAKE HUMAN BEINGS TOO LIGHTLY!

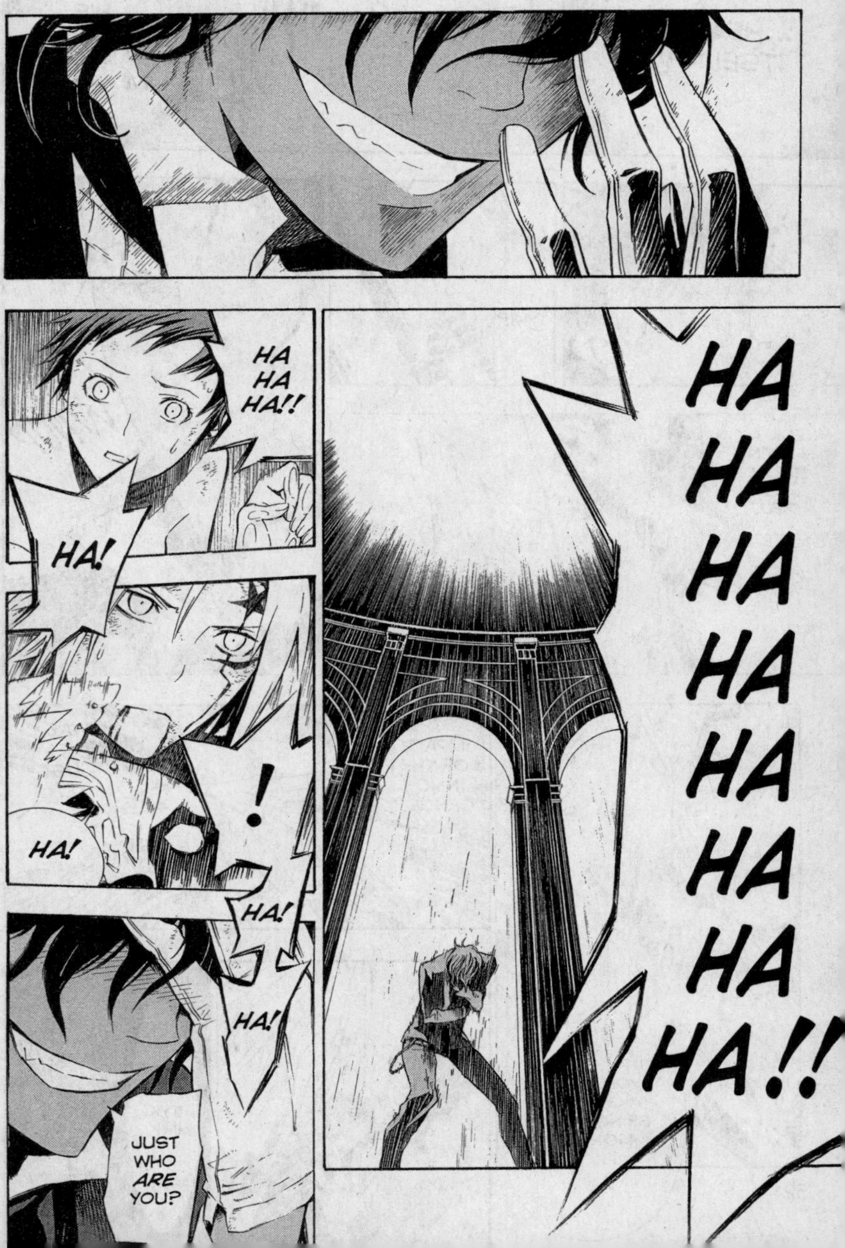
HA HA HA HA HA HA HA HA HA HA HA!!
HA HA HA!!
HA!
HA!
HA!
HA!
JUST WHO *ARE* YOU?

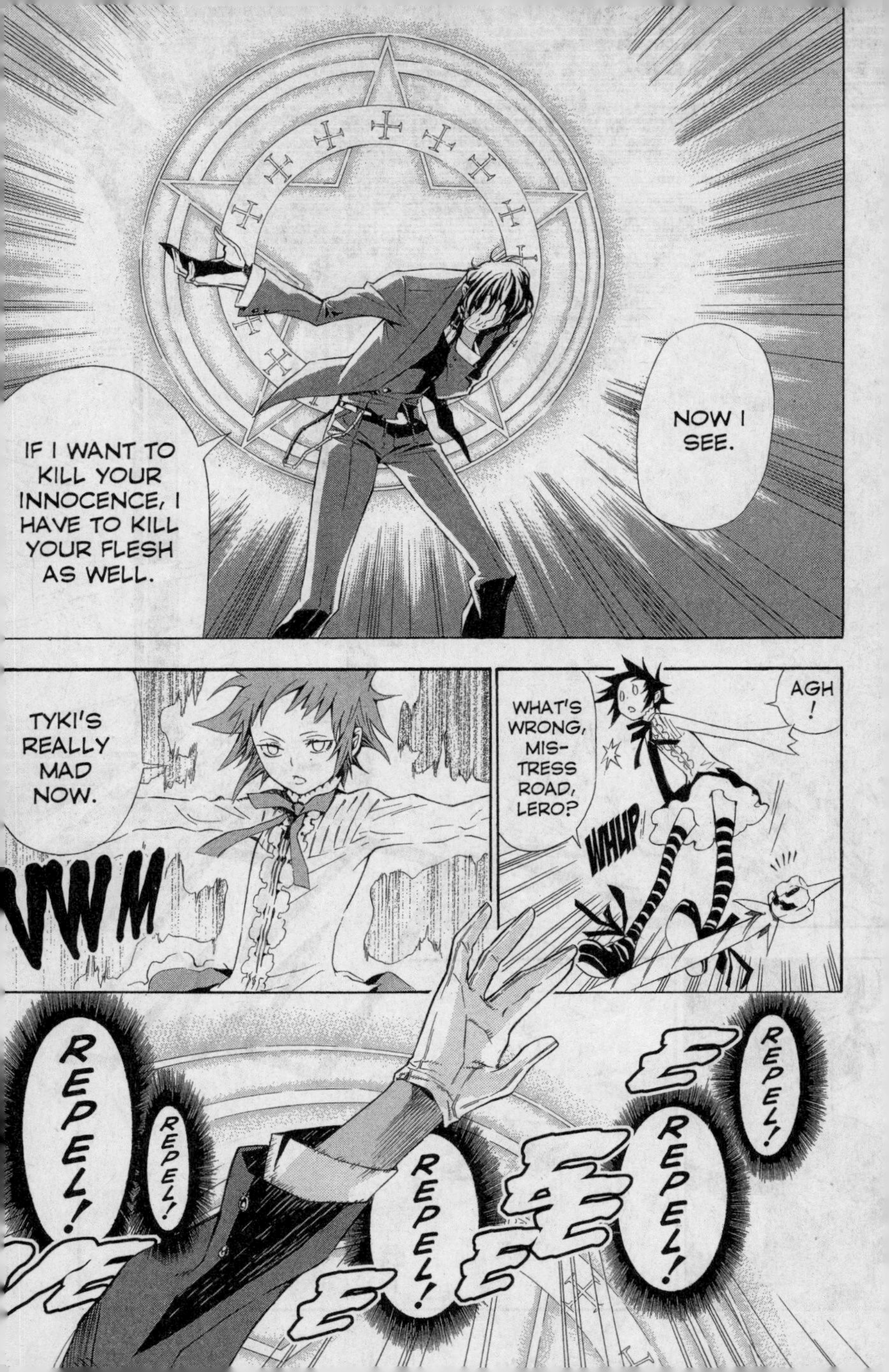
NOW I SEE.
IF I WANT TO KILL YOUR INNOCENCE, I HAVE TO KILL YOUR FLESH AS WELL.
AGH!
WHAT'S WRONG, MISTRESS ROAD, LERO?
WHUP
TYKI'S REALLY MAD NOW.
VWM
REPEL!
REPEL!
REPEL!
REPEL!
REPEL!

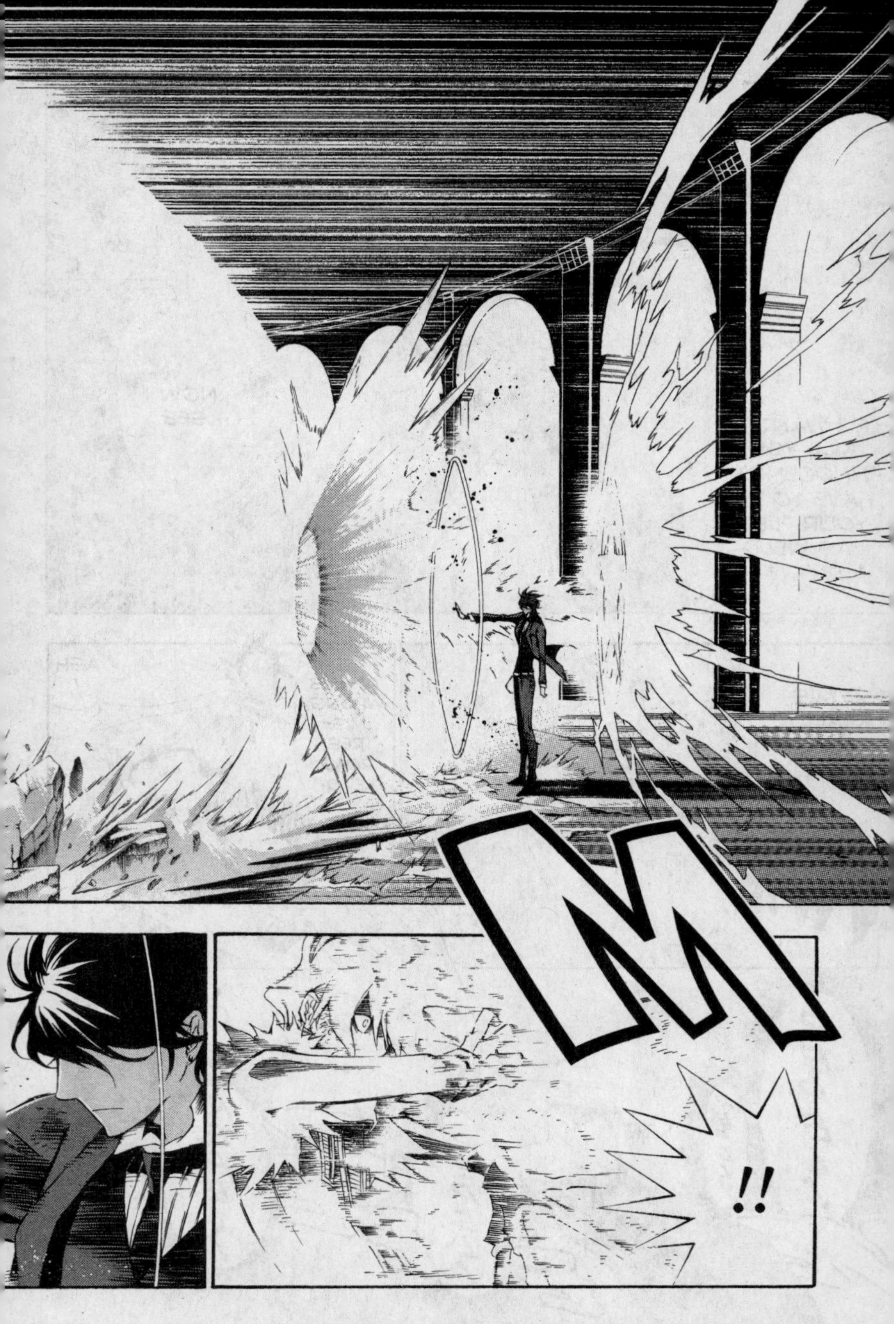
M
!!

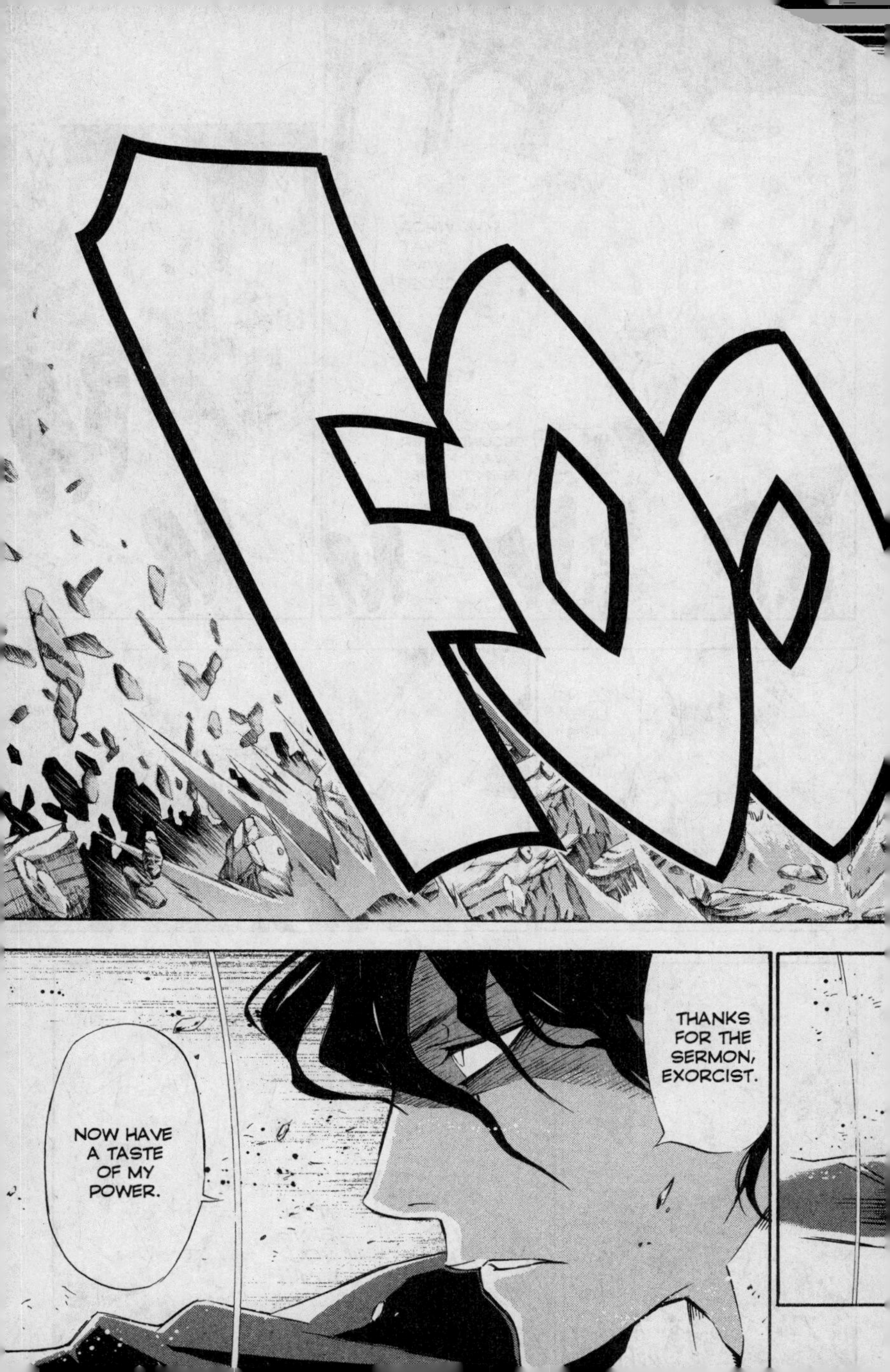
THANKS FOR THE SERMON, EXORCIST.
NOW HAVE A TASTE OF MY POWER.

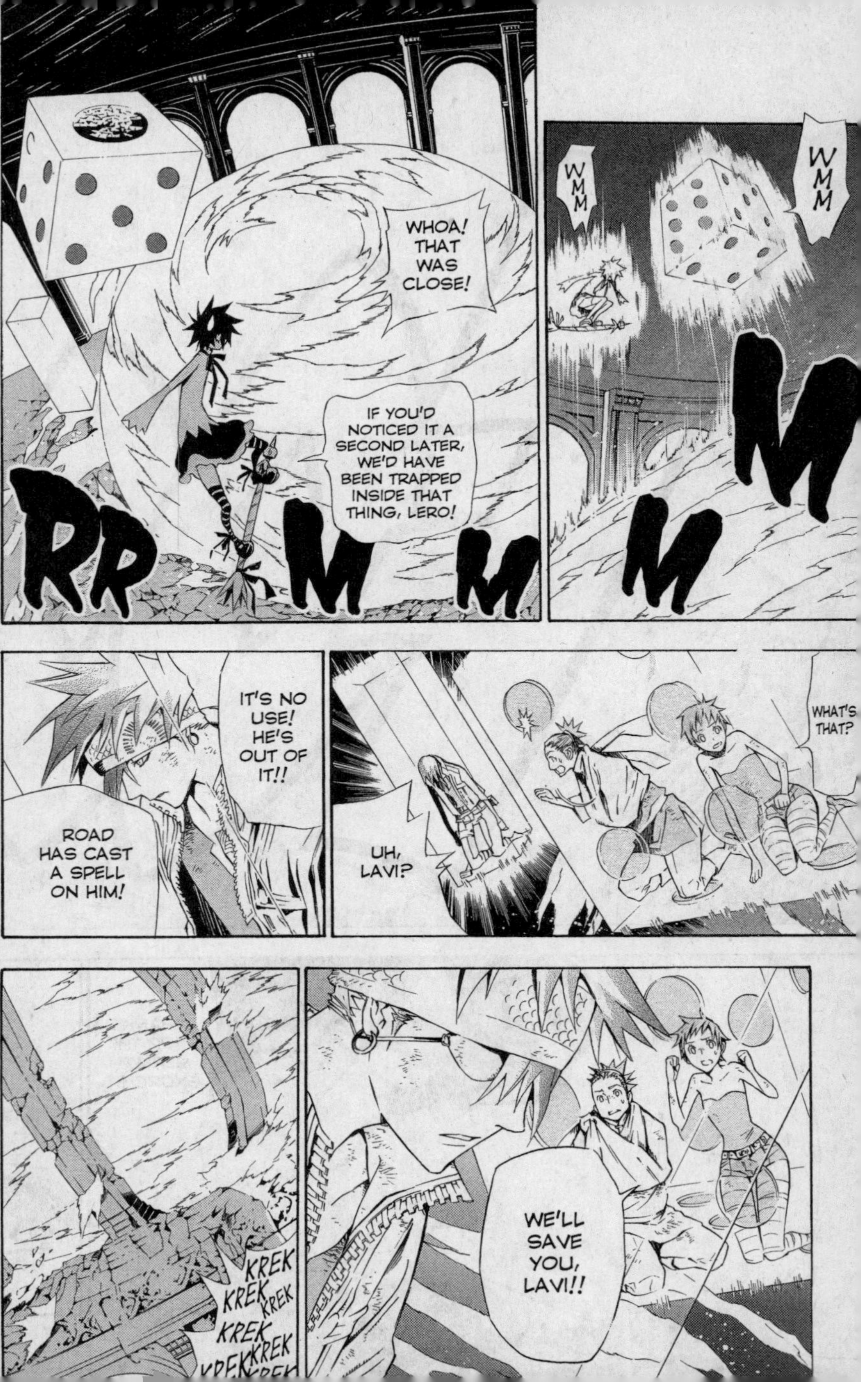

WMM
WMM
M M M
WHOA! THAT WAS CLOSE!
IF YOU'D NOTICED IT A SECOND LATER, WE'D HAVE BEEN TRAPPED INSIDE THAT THING, LERO!
RR M M
WHAT'S THAT?
UH, LAVI?
IT'S NO USE! HE'S OUT OF IT!!
ROAD HAS CAST A SPELL ON HIM!
WE'LL SAVE YOU, LAVI!!
KREK KREK KREK KREK KREK

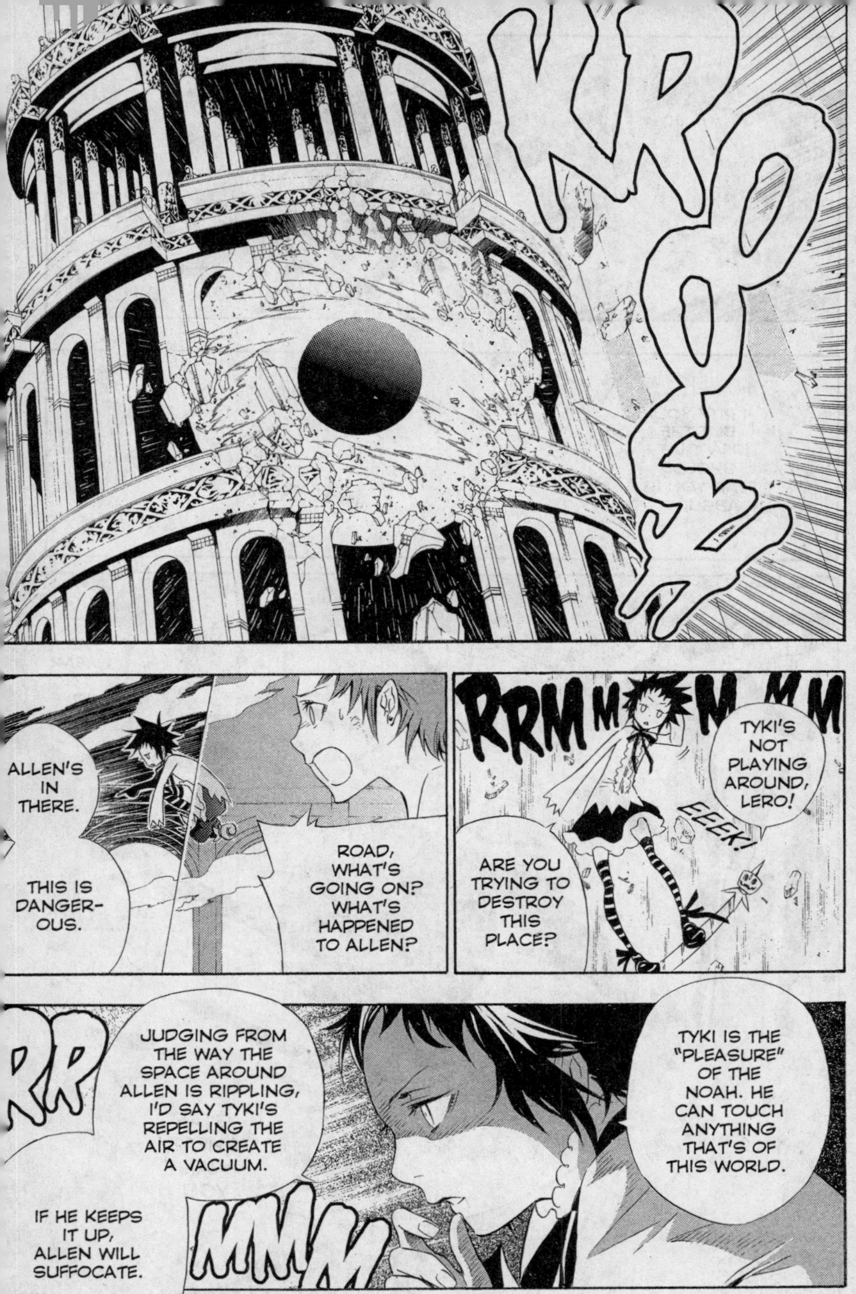
RRMMMMMM
TYKI'S NOT PLAYING AROUND, LERO!
EEEK!
ARE YOU TRYING TO DESTROY THIS PLACE?
ROAD, WHAT'S GOING ON? WHAT'S HAPPENED TO ALLEN?
ALLEN'S IN THERE.
THIS IS DANGER-OUS.
TYKI IS THE "PLEASURE" OF THE NOAH. HE CAN TOUCH ANYTHING THAT'S OF THIS WORLD.
RR
JUDGING FROM THE WAY THE SPACE AROUND ALLEN IS RIPPLING, I'D SAY TYKI'S REPELLING THE AIR TO CREATE A VACUUM.
MMM
IF HE KEEPS IT UP, ALLEN WILL SUFFOCATE.

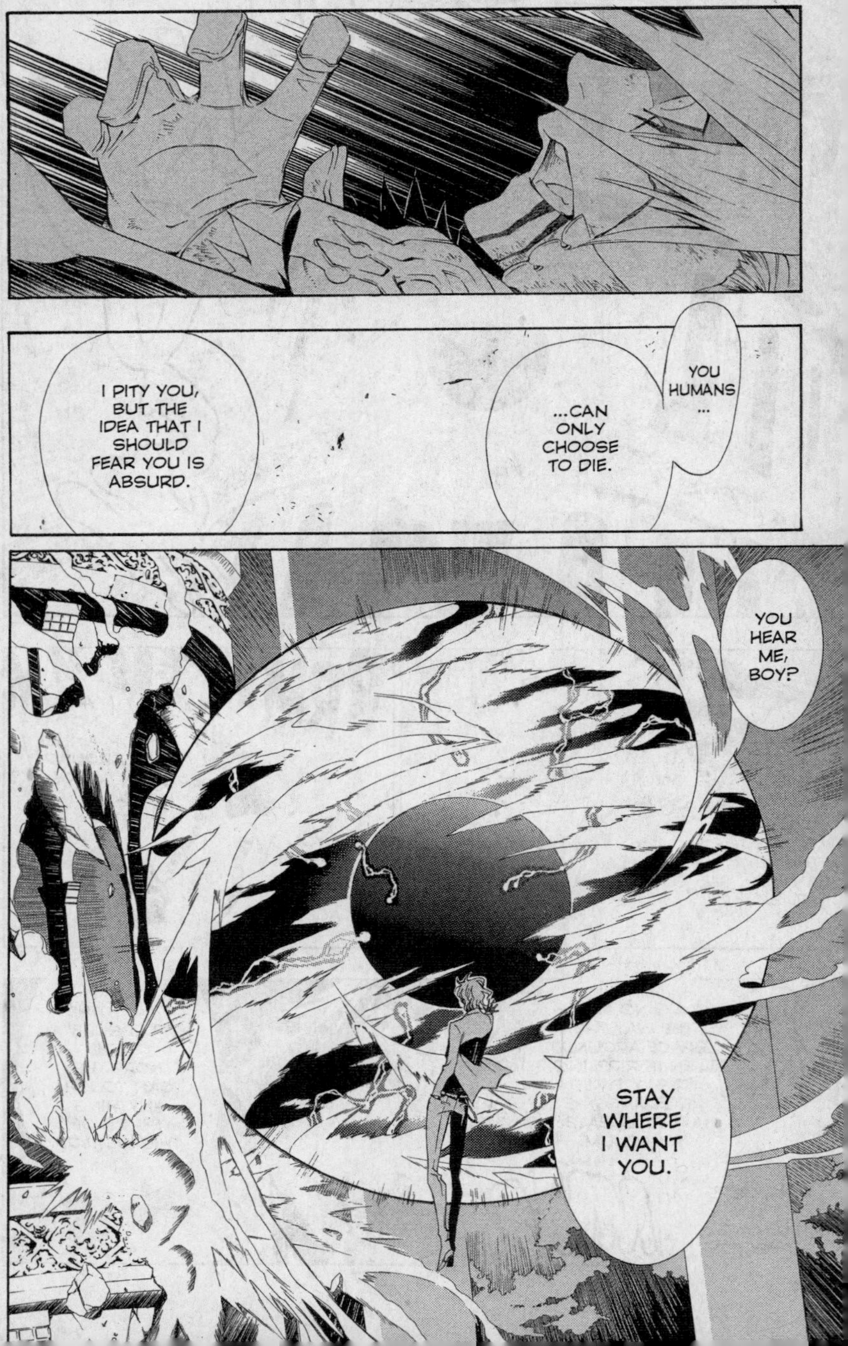
YOU HUMANS...
...CAN ONLY CHOOSE TO DIE.
I PITY YOU, BUT THE IDEA THAT I SHOULD FEAR YOU IS ABSURD.
YOU HEAR ME, BOY?
STAY WHERE I WANT YOU.

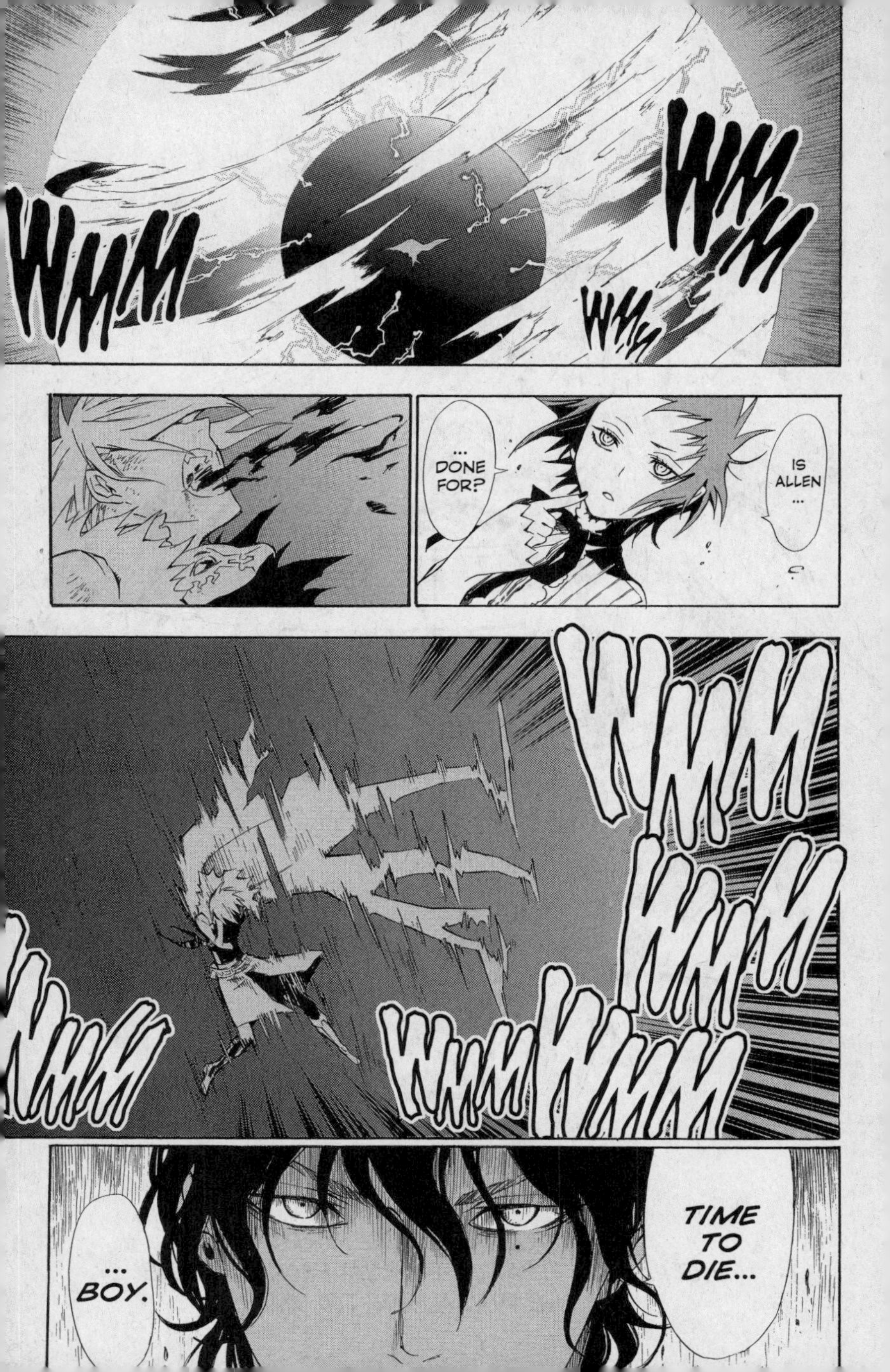
WMM
WMM
WMM
IS ALLEN ...
... DONE FOR?
WMM
WMM
WMMWMM
WMM
TIME TO DIE...
... BOY.

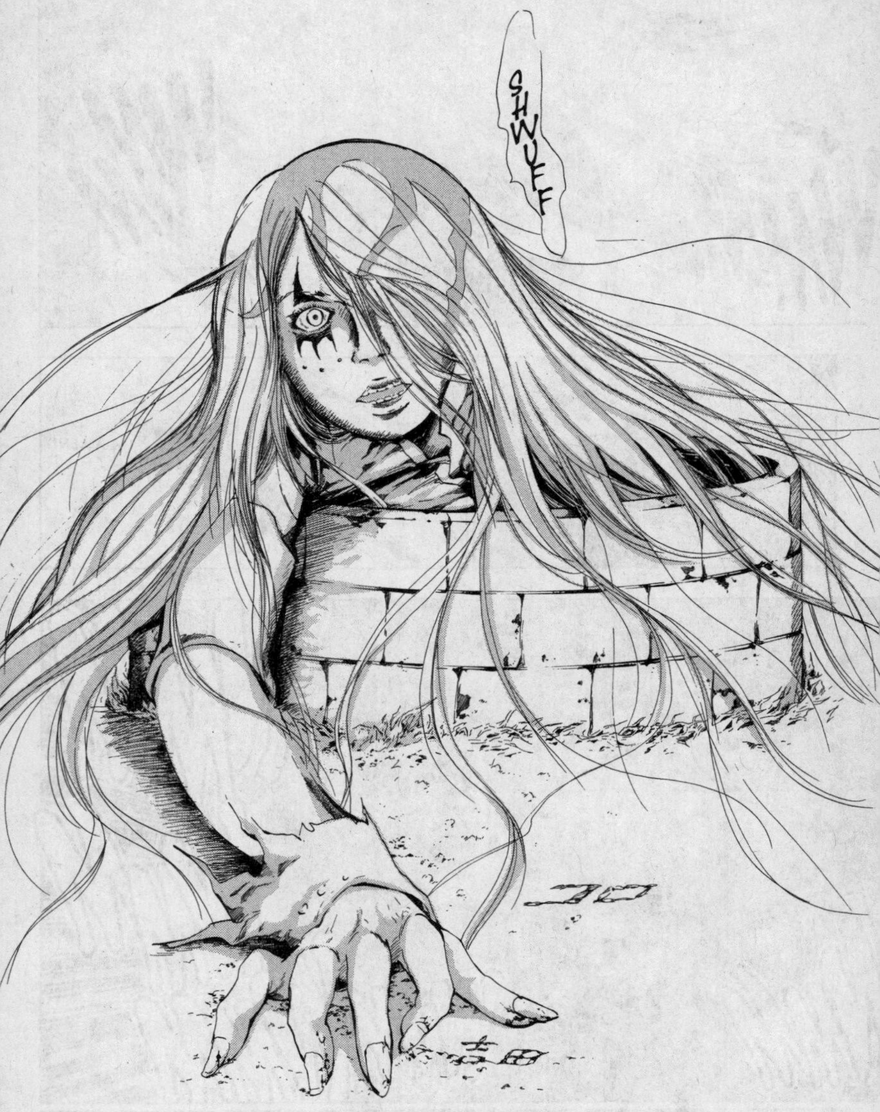
SHWUFF

THE D.GRAY-MAN ELITE CORPS 4
ANOTHER ILLUSTRATION BY MAMA FROM NICHO-ME
THIS ONE WAS ALMOST TOO SCARY.

THE 116TH NIGHT: THE TRANSCENDENT ONE

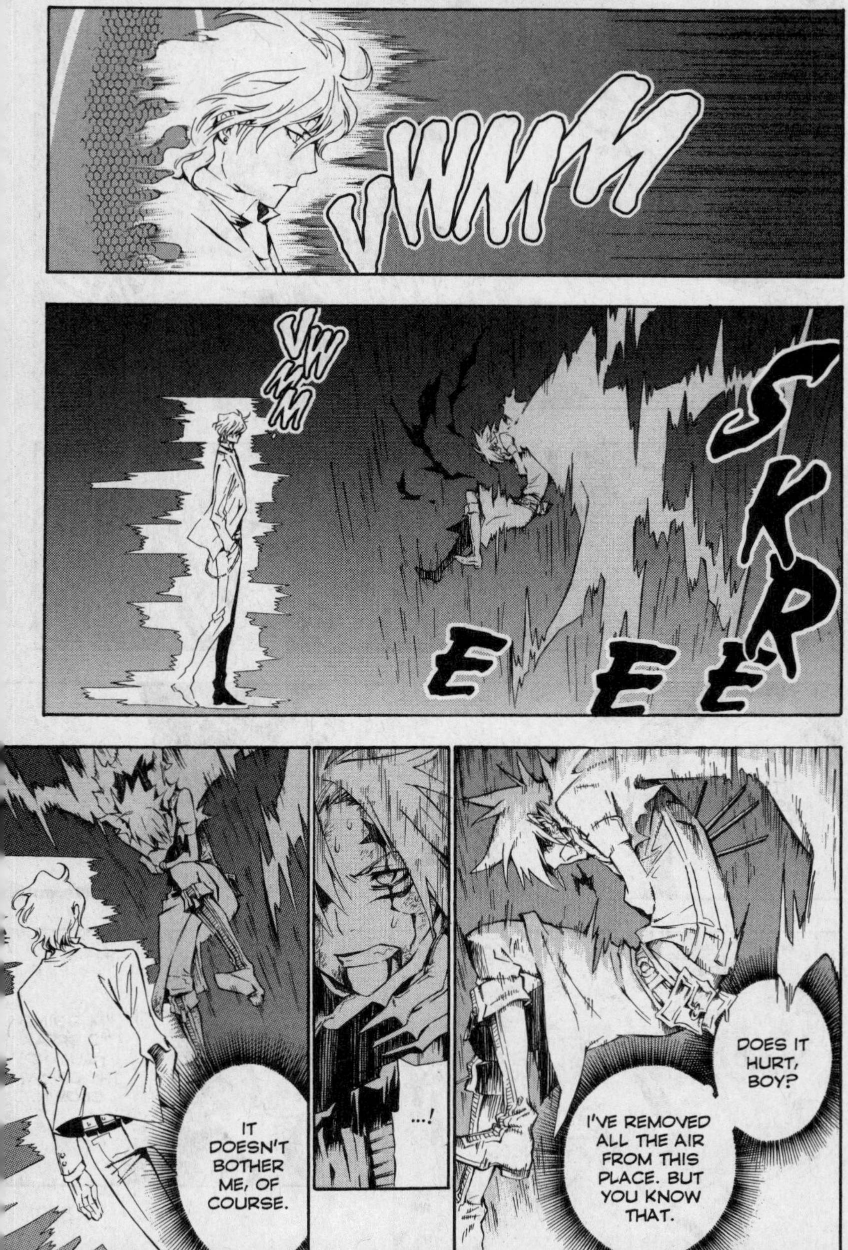
VWMM
SKREEE
VWMM
DOES IT HURT, BOY?
I'VE REMOVED ALL THE AIR FROM THIS PLACE. BUT YOU KNOW THAT.
...!
IT DOESN'T BOTHER ME, OF COURSE.

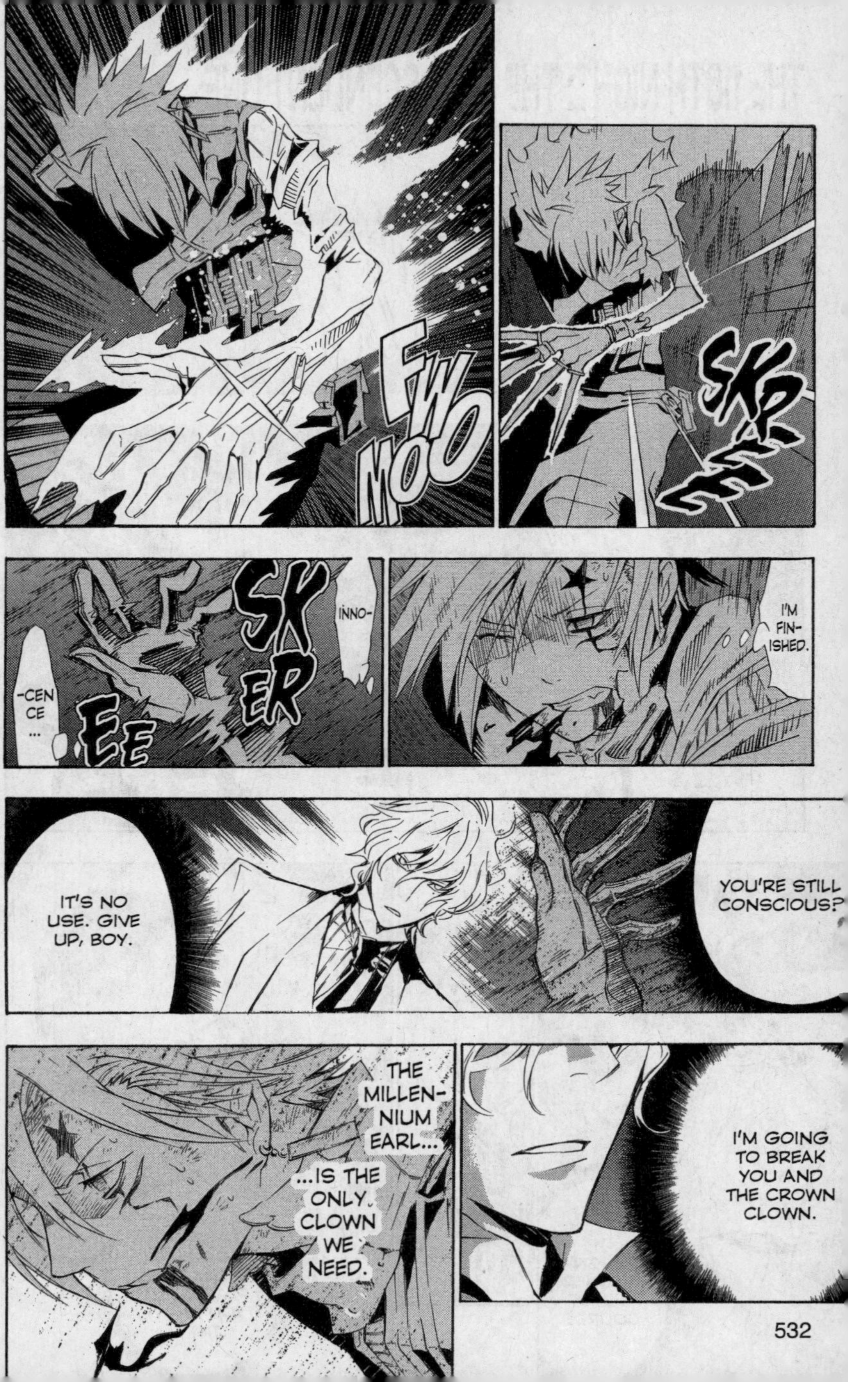
SKREEE
FWOOMM
I'M FIN-ISHED.
SKREE
INNO-
-CENCE ...
YOU'RE STILL CONSCIOUS?
IT'S NO USE. GIVE UP, BOY.
I'M GOING TO BREAK YOU AND THE CROWN CLOWN.
THE MILLEN-NIUM EARL...
...IS THE ONLY CLOWN WE NEED.

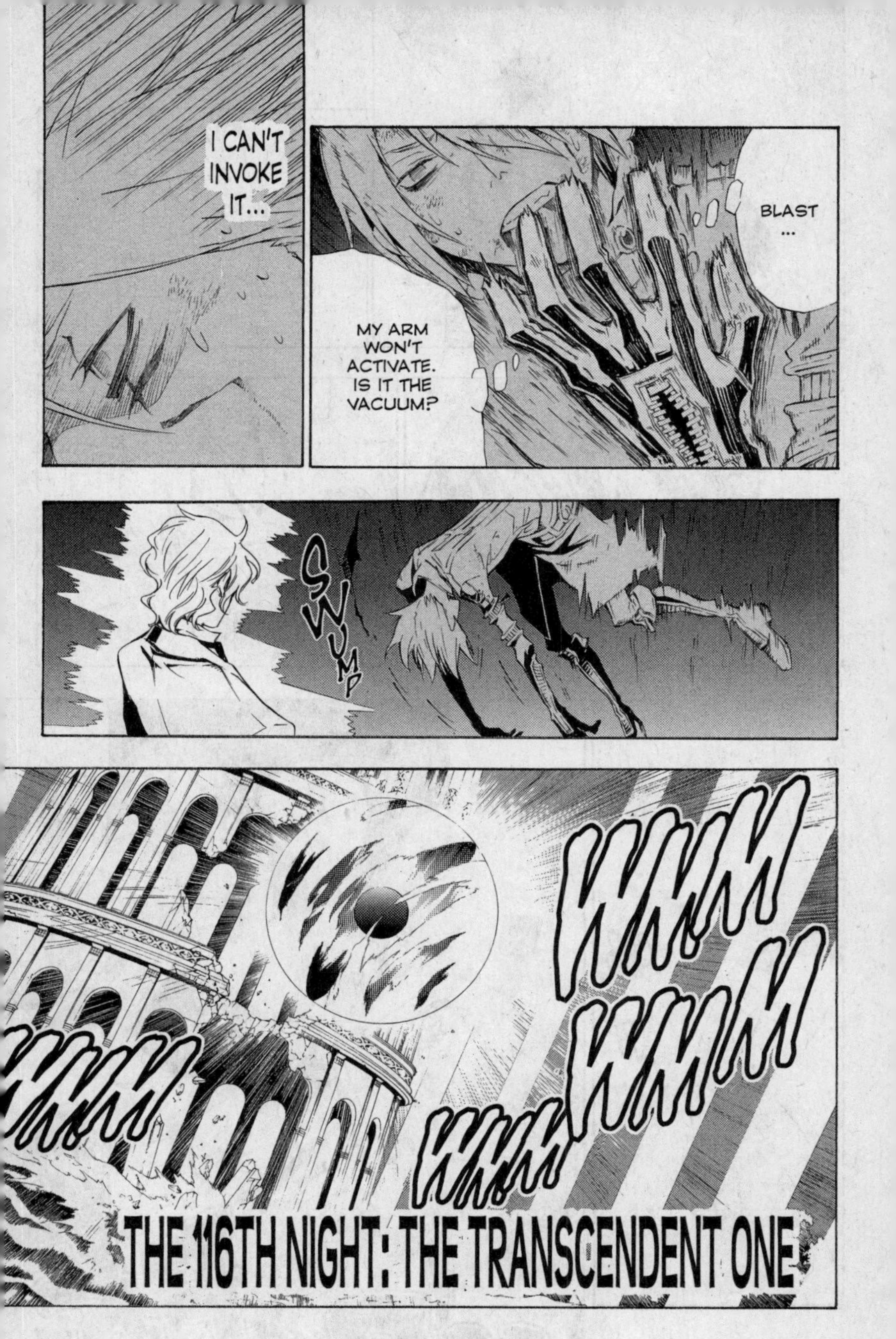
BLAST ...
MY ARM WON'T ACTIVATE. IS IT THE VACUUM?
I CAN'T INVOKE IT...
SWUMP
THE 116TH NIGHT: THE TRANSCENDENT ONE

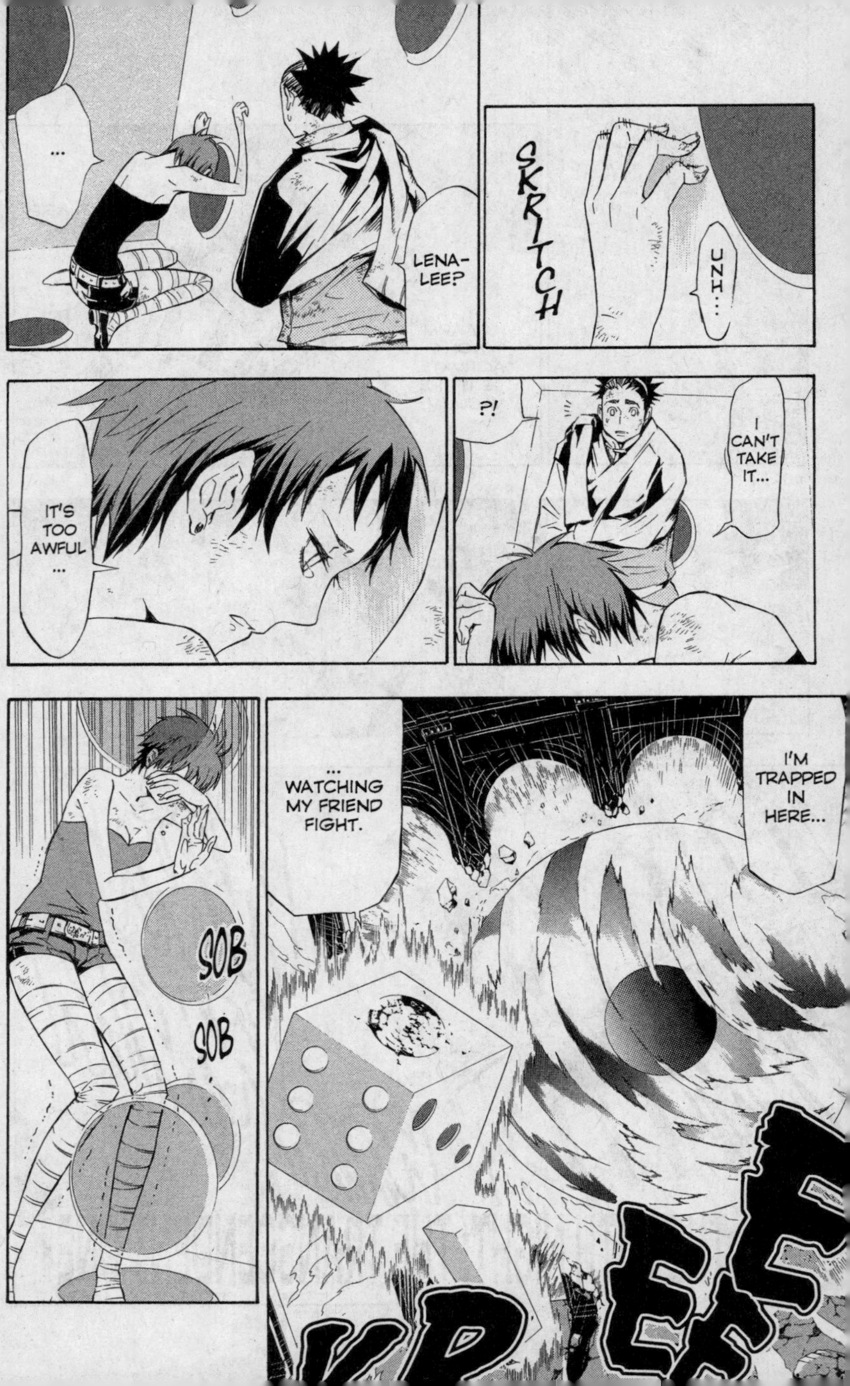
SKRITCH
UNH...
...
LENA-LEE?
I CAN'T TAKE IT...
?!
IT'S TOO AWFUL...
I'M TRAPPED IN HERE...
... WATCHING MY FRIEND FIGHT.
SOB
SOB

READ THIS WAY

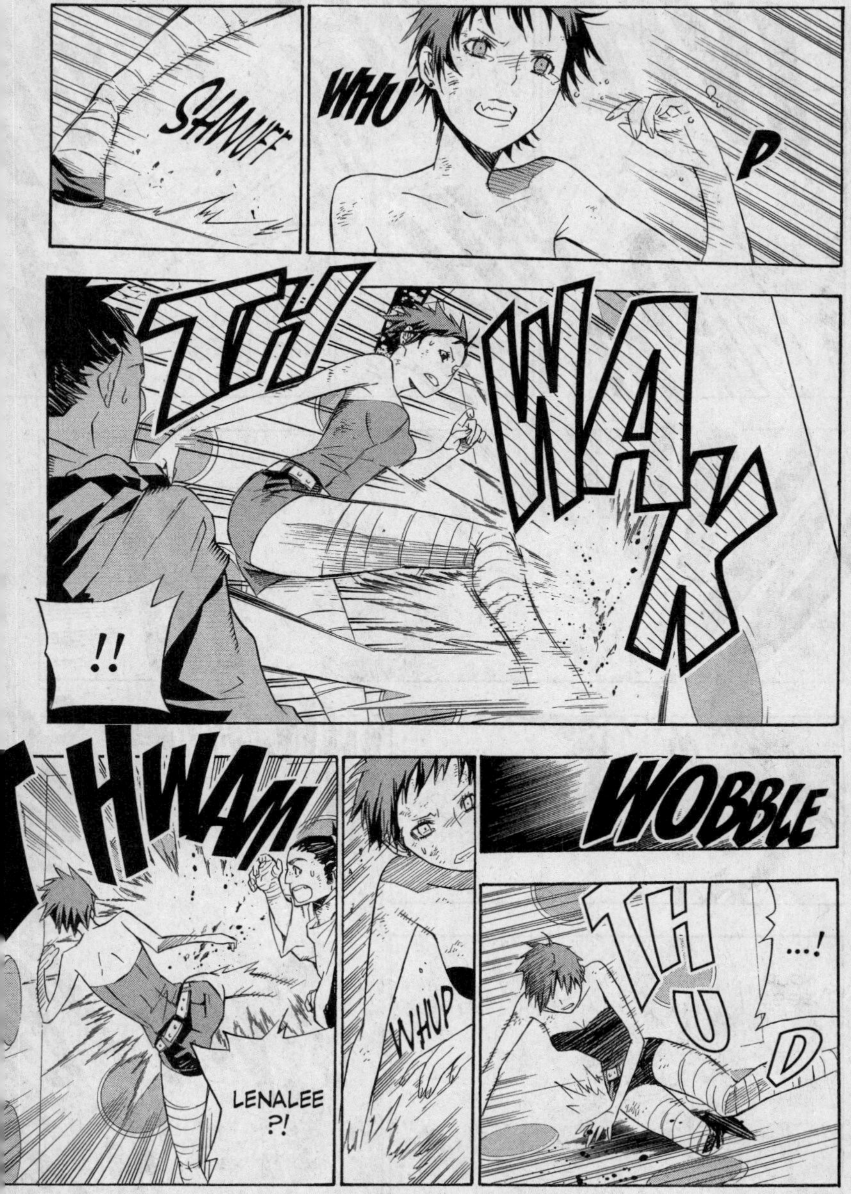
WHU
P
SHWUFF
TCH
WAK
!!
WOBBLE
TH
U
D
...!
WHUP
THWAM
LENALEE ?!

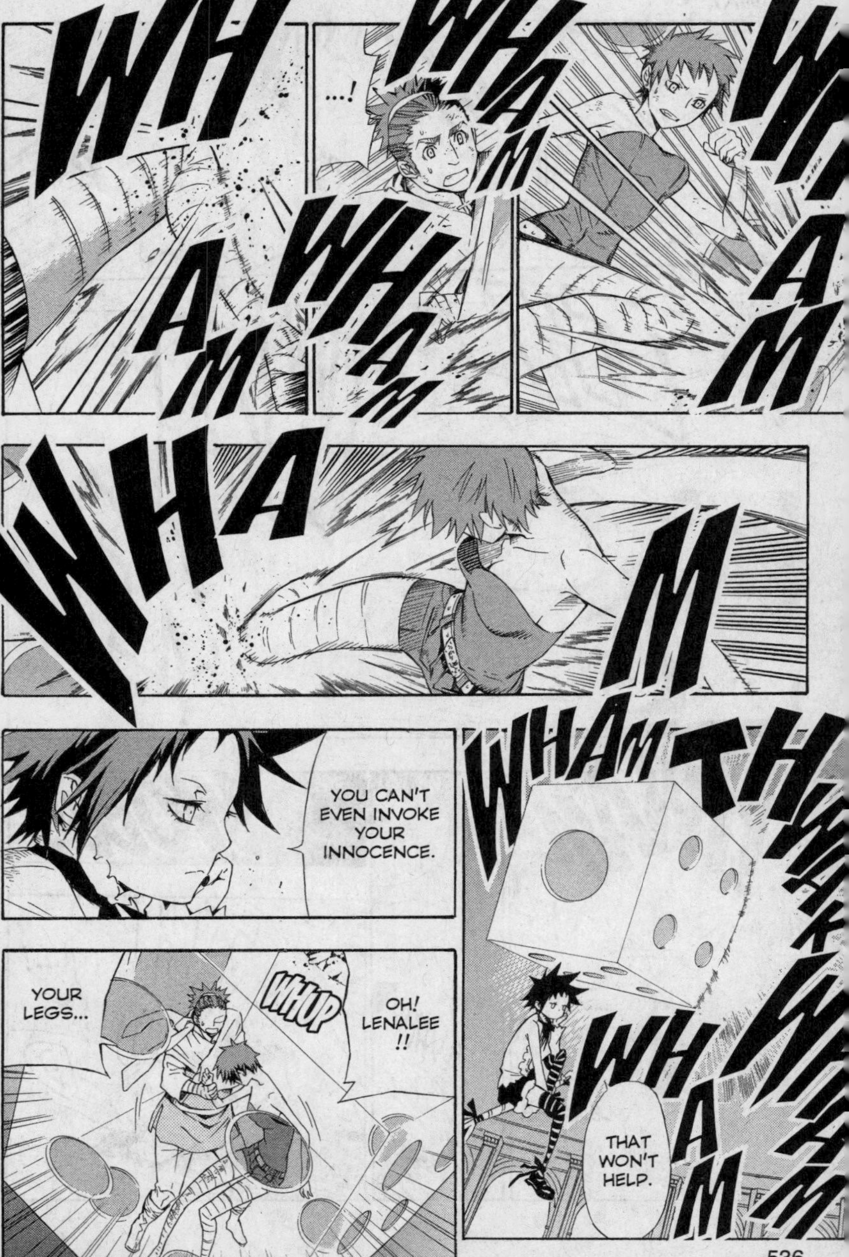
WHAM
...!
WHAM
WHAM
WHAM
WHAM
WHAM
WHAM
THAT WON'T HELP.
YOU CAN'T EVEN INVOKE YOUR INNOCENCE.
OH! LENALEE !!
WHUP
YOUR LEGS...

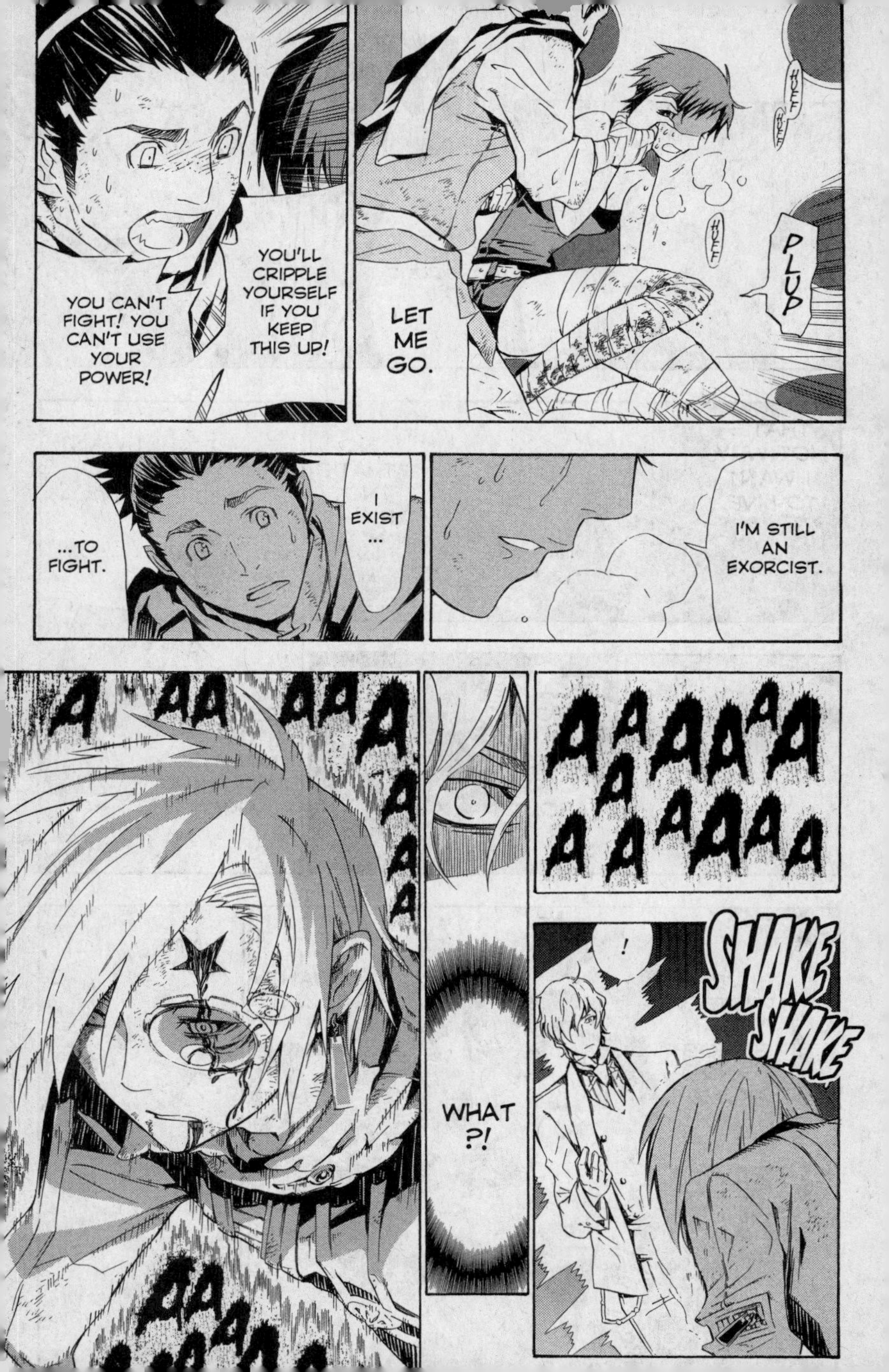

HUFF HUFF
HUFF
PLUP
LET ME GO.
YOU'LL CRIPPLE YOURSELF IF YOU KEEP THIS UP!
YOU CAN'T FIGHT! YOU CAN'T USE YOUR POWER!
I'M STILL AN EXORCIST.
I EXIST...
...TO FIGHT.
AAAAAAAAAAAAA
SHAKE SHAKE
!
WHAT?!
AAAAAAAAAA
AAAA

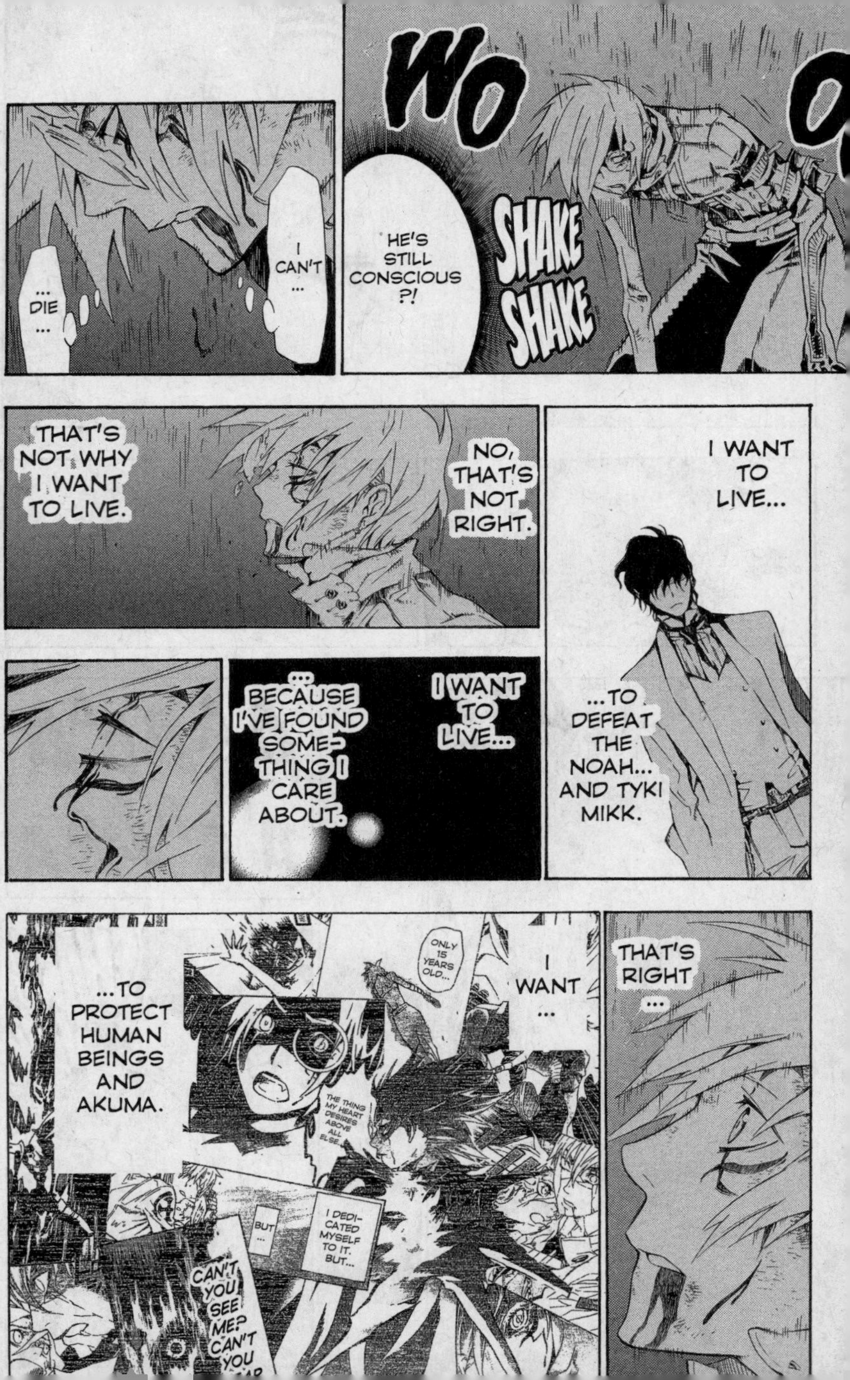

WO O
SHAKE SHAKE
HE'S STILL CONSCIOUS?!
I CAN'T ...
... DIE ...
I WANT TO LIVE...
...TO DEFEAT THE NOAH... AND TYKI MIKK.
NO, THAT'S NOT RIGHT.
THAT'S NOT WHY I WANT TO LIVE.
I WANT TO LIVE...
...BECAUSE I'VE FOUND SOME-THING I CARE ABOUT.
THAT'S RIGHT ...
I WANT ...
ONLY 15 YEARS OLD...
...TO PROTECT HUMAN BEINGS AND AKUMA.
THE THING MY HEART DESIRES ABOVE ALL ELSE...
I DEDI-CATED MYSELF TO IT. BUT...
BUT ...
CAN'T YOU SEE ME? CAN'T YOU

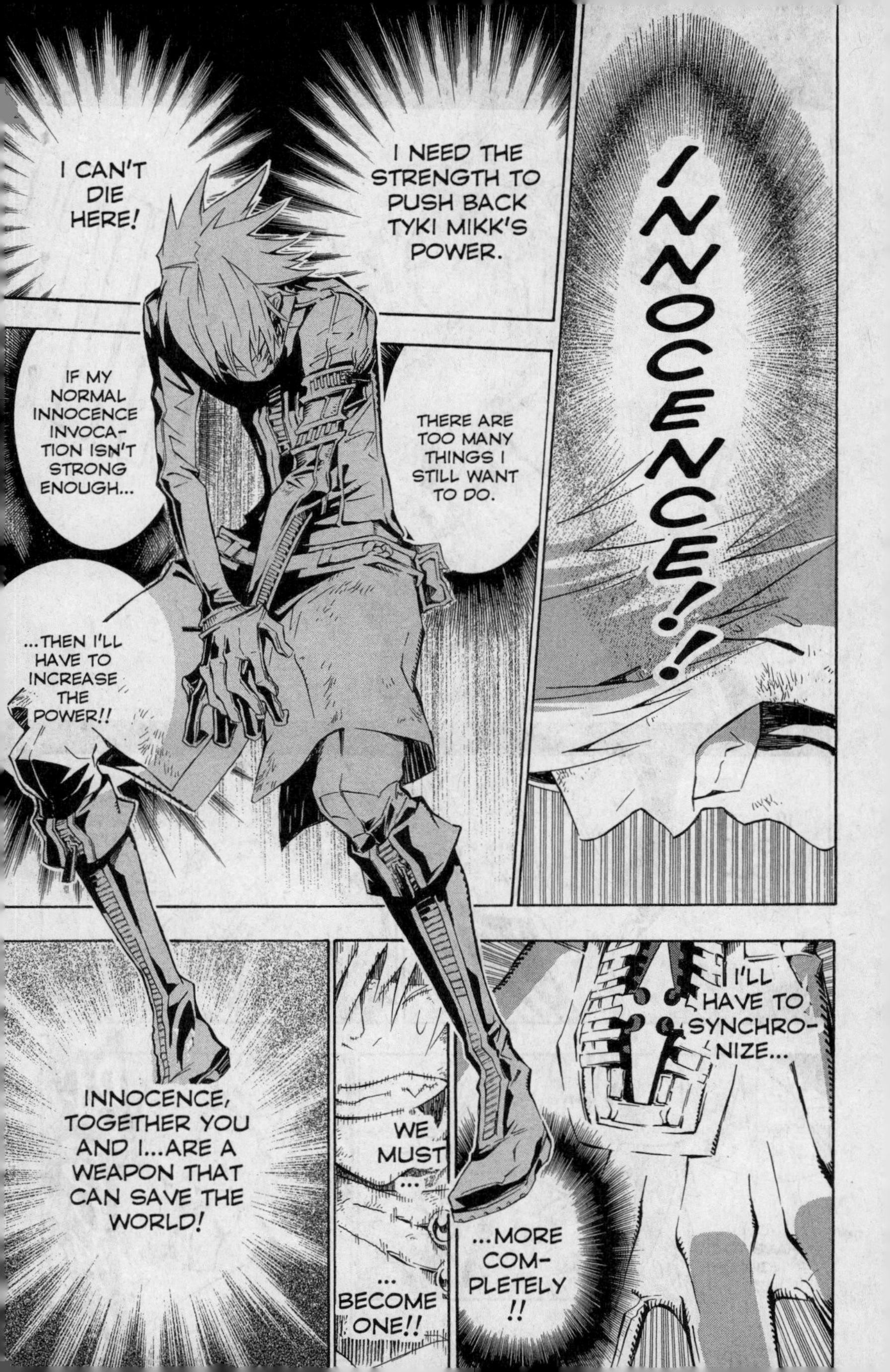
INNOCENCE!!
I NEED THE STRENGTH TO PUSH BACK TYKI MIKK'S POWER.
I CAN'T DIE HERE!
THERE ARE TOO MANY THINGS I STILL WANT TO DO.
IF MY NORMAL INNOCENCE INVOCATION ISN'T STRONG ENOUGH...
...THEN I'LL HAVE TO INCREASE THE POWER!!
I'LL HAVE TO SYNCHRONIZE...
WE MUST...
...BECOME ONE!!
...MORE COMPLETELY!!
INNOCENCE, TOGETHER YOU AND I...ARE A WEAPON THAT CAN SAVE THE WORLD!

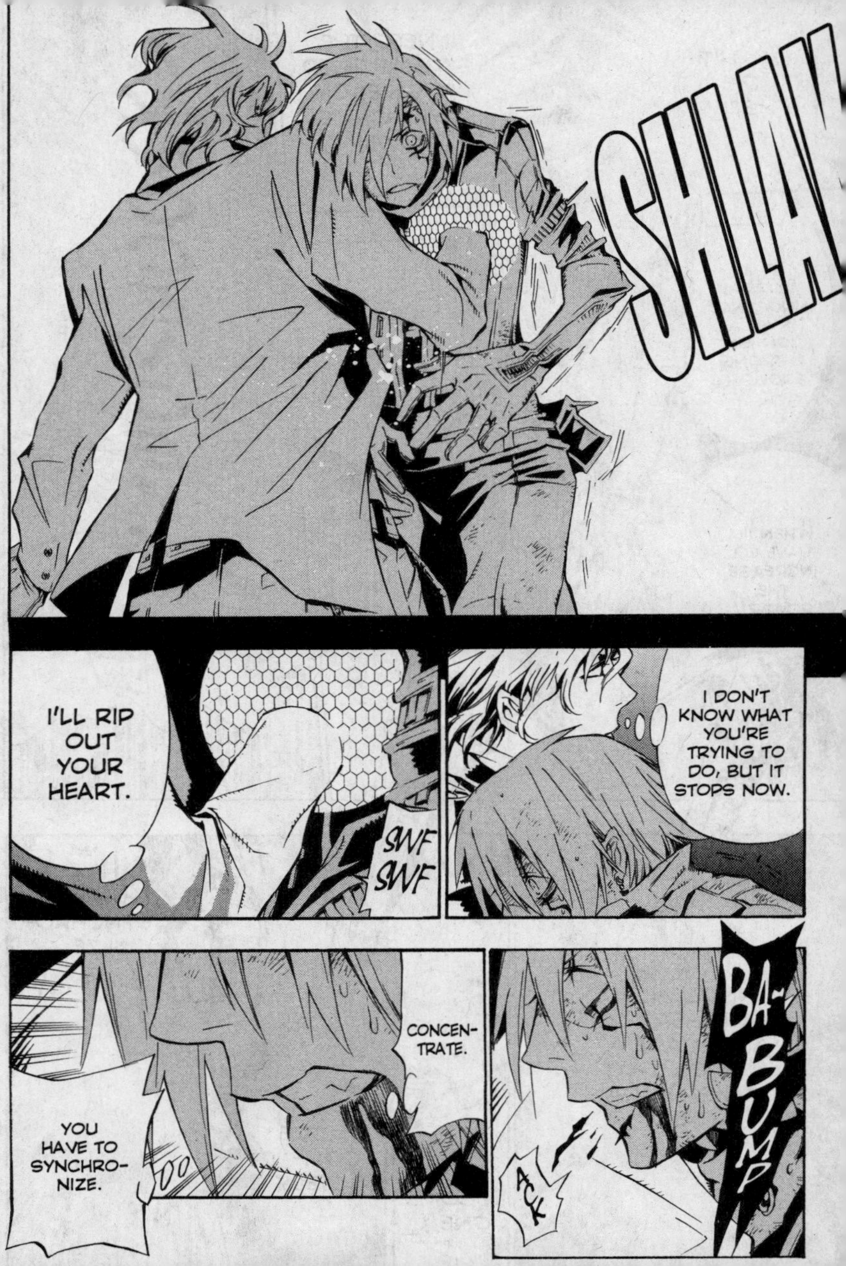
SHLA
I DON'T KNOW WHAT YOU'RE TRYING TO DO, BUT IT STOPS NOW.
I'LL RIP OUT YOUR HEART.
SWF SWF
BA-BUMP
ACK
CONCEN-TRATE.
YOU HAVE TO SYNCHRO-NIZE.

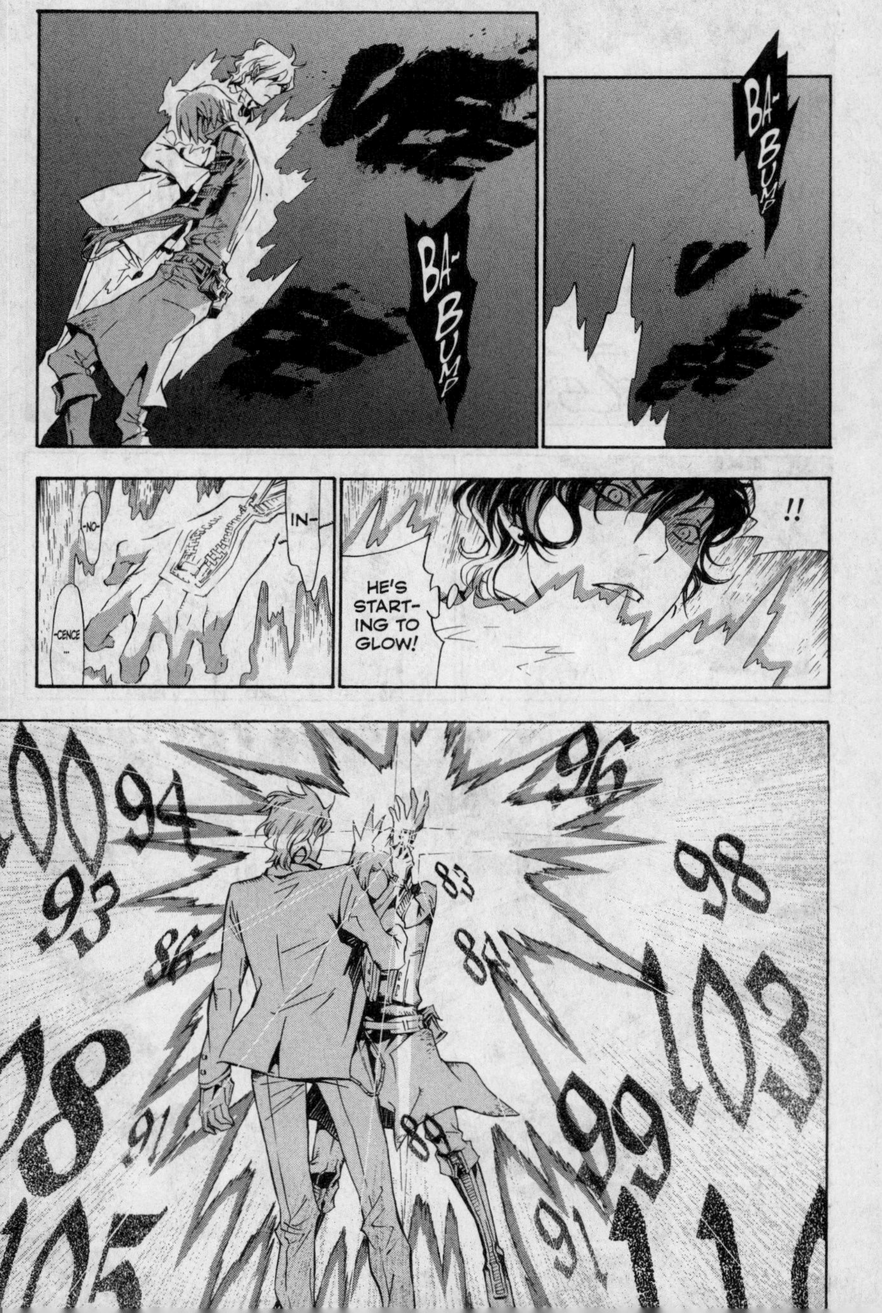

BA-BUMP
BA-BUMP
!!
HE'S STARTING TO GLOW!
IN-
-NO-
-CENCE ...
96
98
103
83
84
99
91
89
94
93
86
91
105

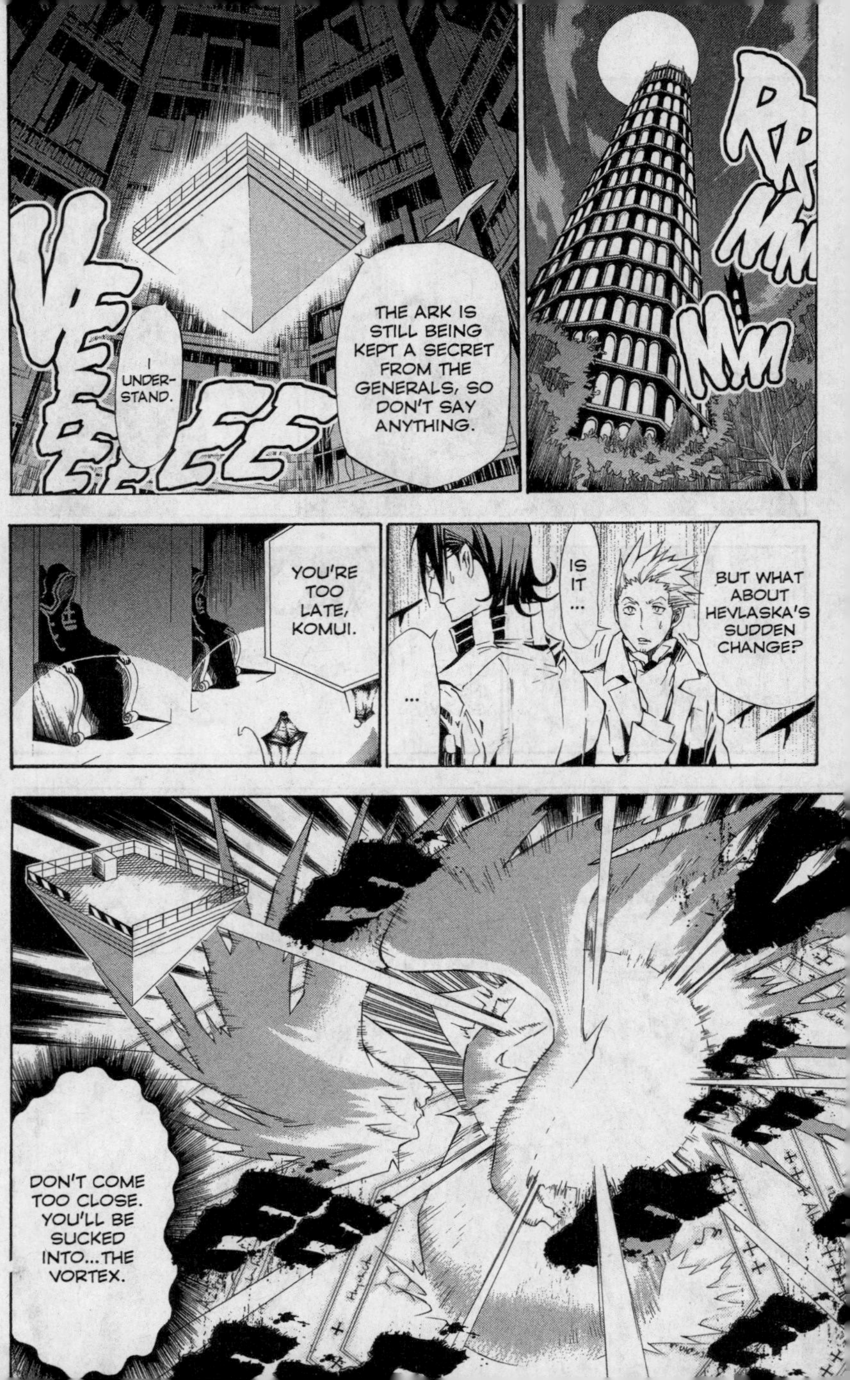
THE ARK IS STILL BEING KEPT A SECRET FROM THE GENERALS, SO DON'T SAY ANYTHING.
I UNDER-STAND.
BUT WHAT ABOUT HEVLASKA'S SUDDEN CHANGE?
IS IT ...
...
YOU'RE TOO LATE, KOMUI.
DON'T COME TOO CLOSE. YOU'LL BE SUCKED INTO...THE VORTEX.

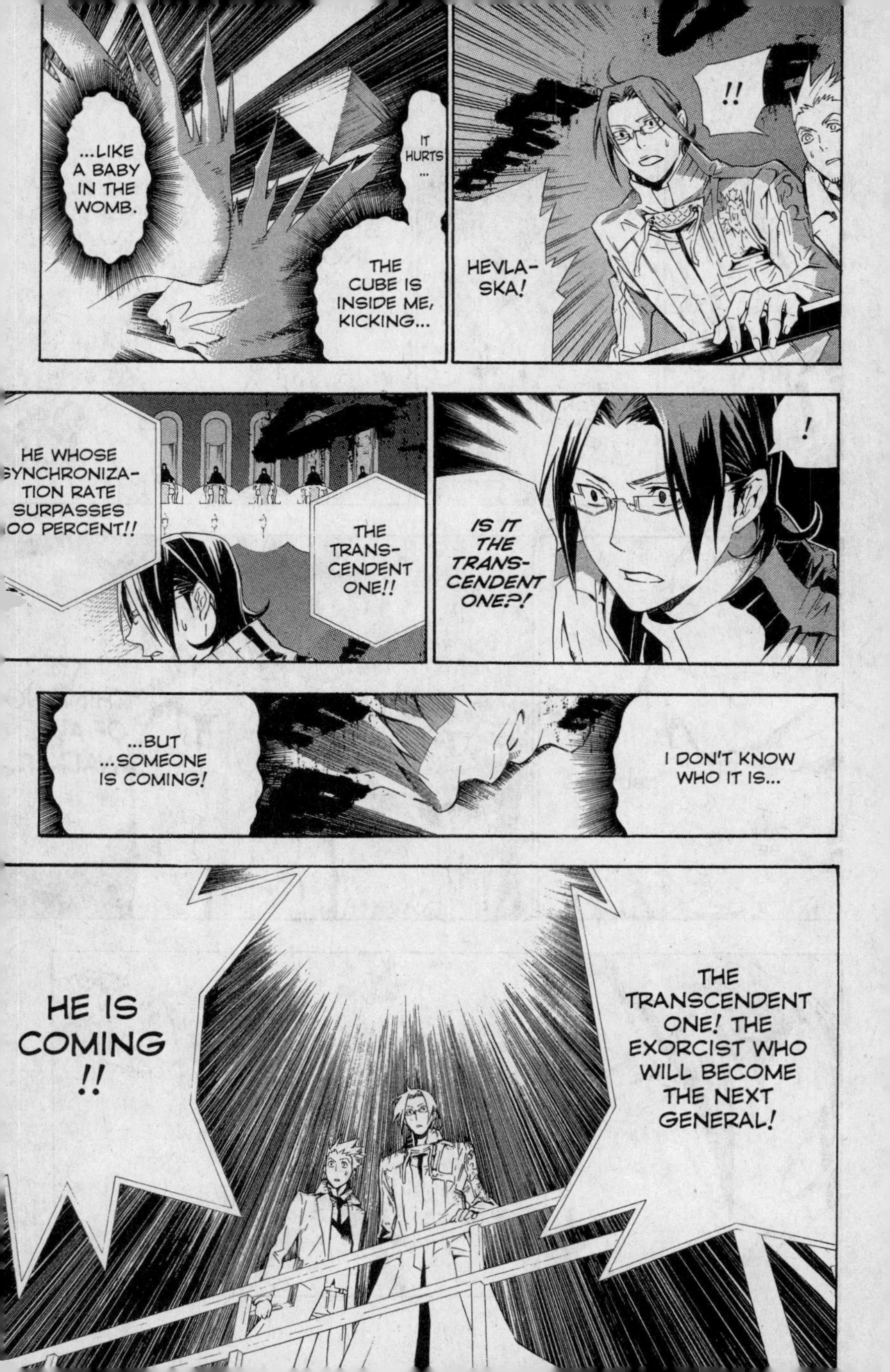
!!
HEVLA-SKA!
IT HURTS ...
THE CUBE IS INSIDE ME, KICKING...
...LIKE A BABY IN THE WOMB.
!
IS IT THE TRANS-CENDENT ONE?!
THE TRANS-CENDENT ONE!!
HE WHOSE SYNCHRONIZA-TION RATE SURPASSES 00 PERCENT!!
I DON'T KNOW WHO IT IS...
...BUT ...SOMEONE IS COMING!
THE TRANSCENDENT ONE! THE EXORCIST WHO WILL BECOME THE NEXT GENERAL!
HE IS COMING !!

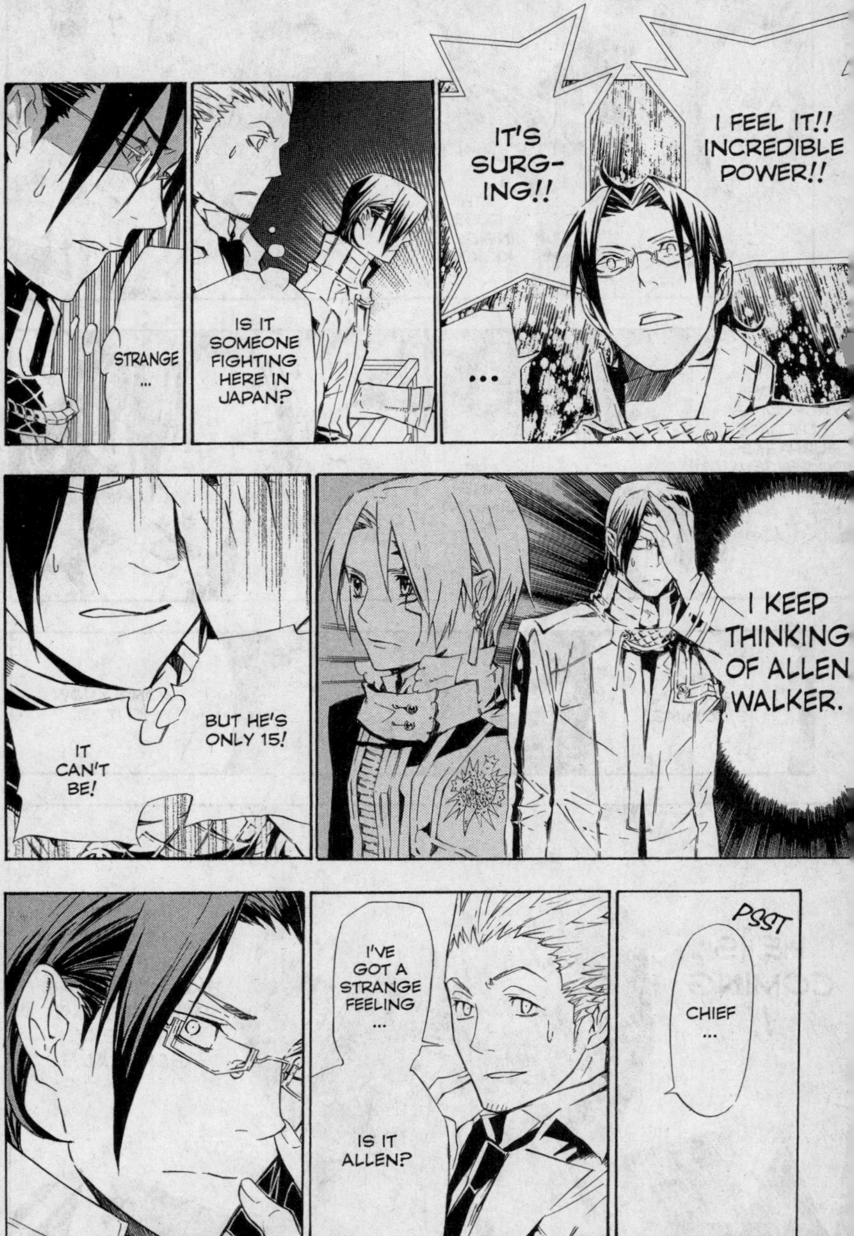
I FEEL IT!! INCREDIBLE POWER!!
IT'S SURG-ING!!
...
IS IT SOMEONE FIGHTING HERE IN JAPAN?
STRANGE ...
I KEEP THINKING OF ALLEN WALKER.
BUT HE'S ONLY 15!
IT CAN'T BE!
PSST
CHIEF ...
I'VE GOT A STRANGE FEELING ...
IS IT ALLEN?

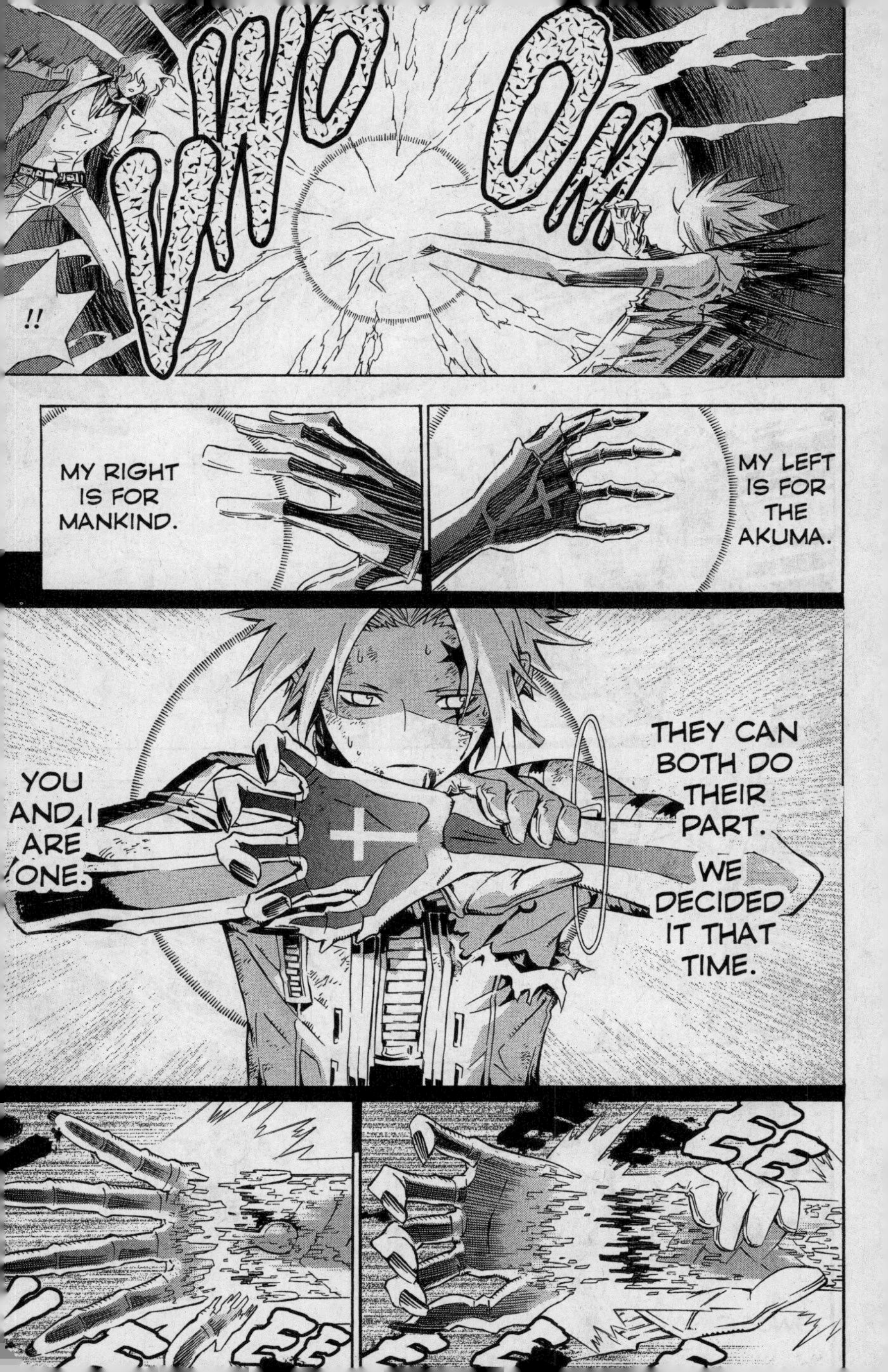
VWOOM
!!
MY LEFT IS FOR THE AKUMA.
MY RIGHT IS FOR MANKIND.
THEY CAN BOTH DO THEIR PART.
WE DECIDED IT THAT TIME.
YOU AND I ARE ONE.

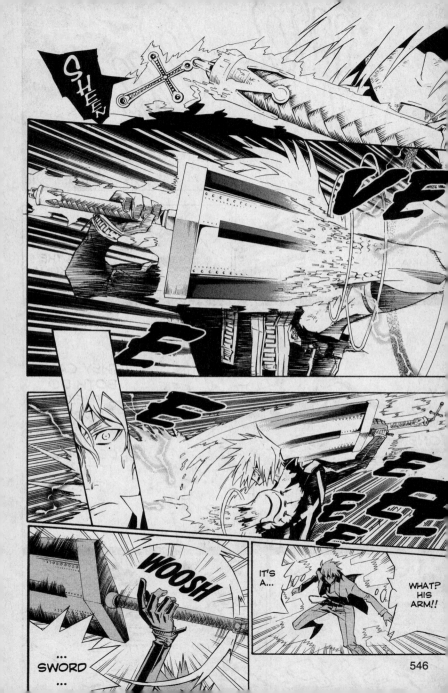

SHEER

VE

EE

WOOSH

...SWORD...

IT'S A...

WHAT? HIS ARM!!

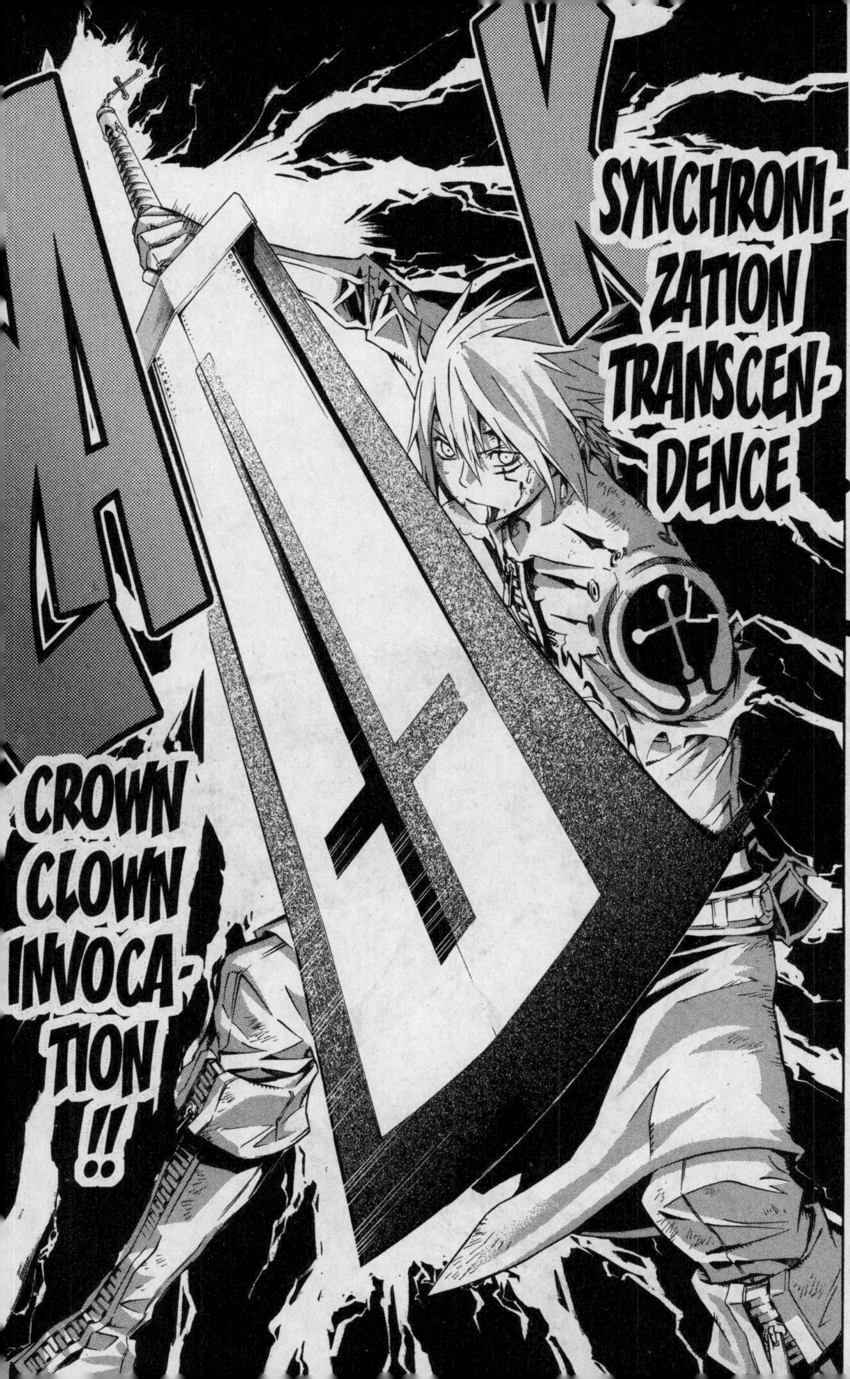
SYNCHRONI-ZATION TRANSCEN-DENCE
CROWN CLOWN INVOCA-TION!!

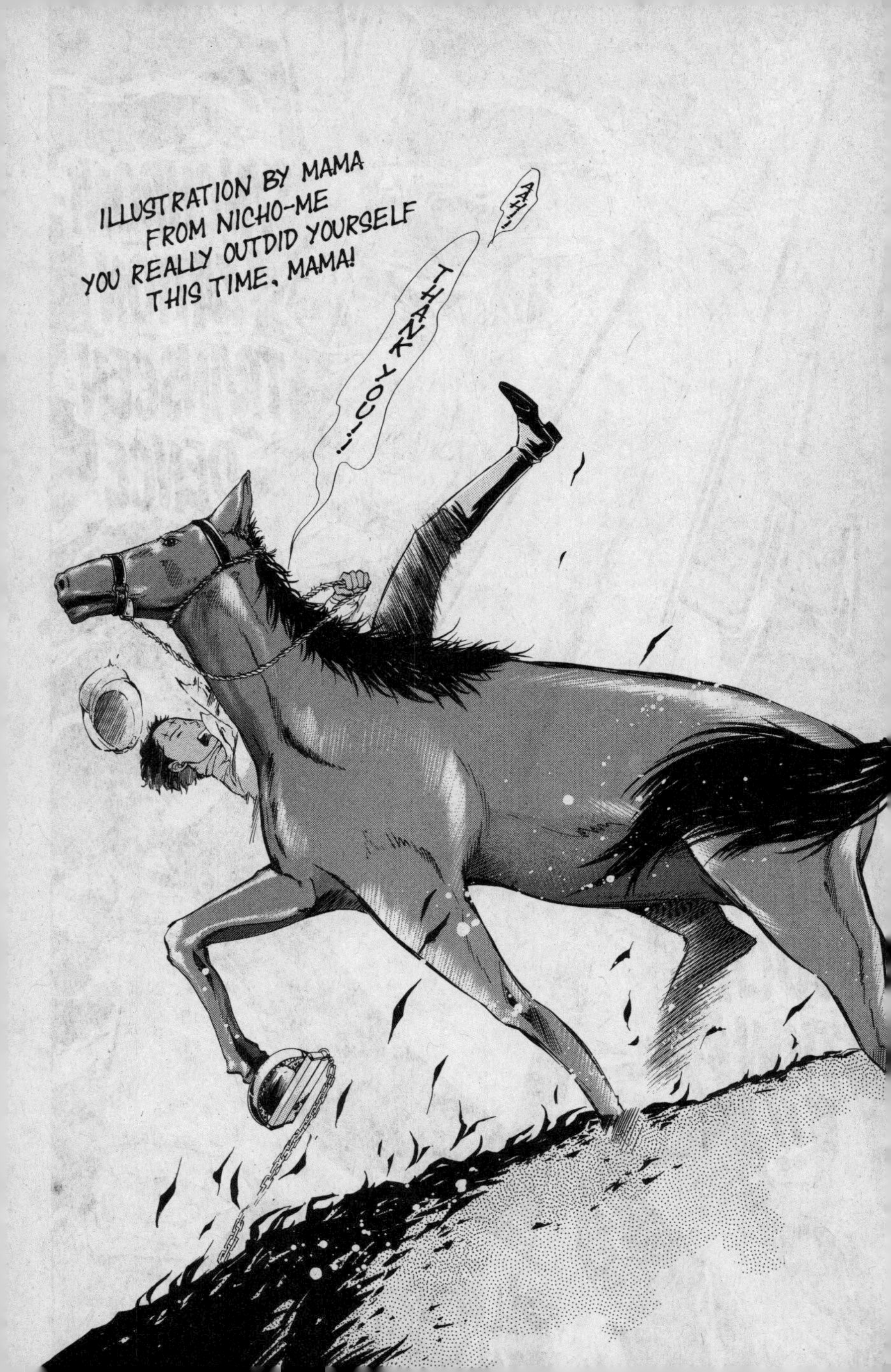
ILLUSTRATION BY MAMA
FROM NICHO-ME
YOU REALLY OUTDID YOURSELF
THIS TIME, MAMA!
AAH!!
THANK YOU...!!

THE 117TH NIGHT: KINDNESS AND STRENGTH

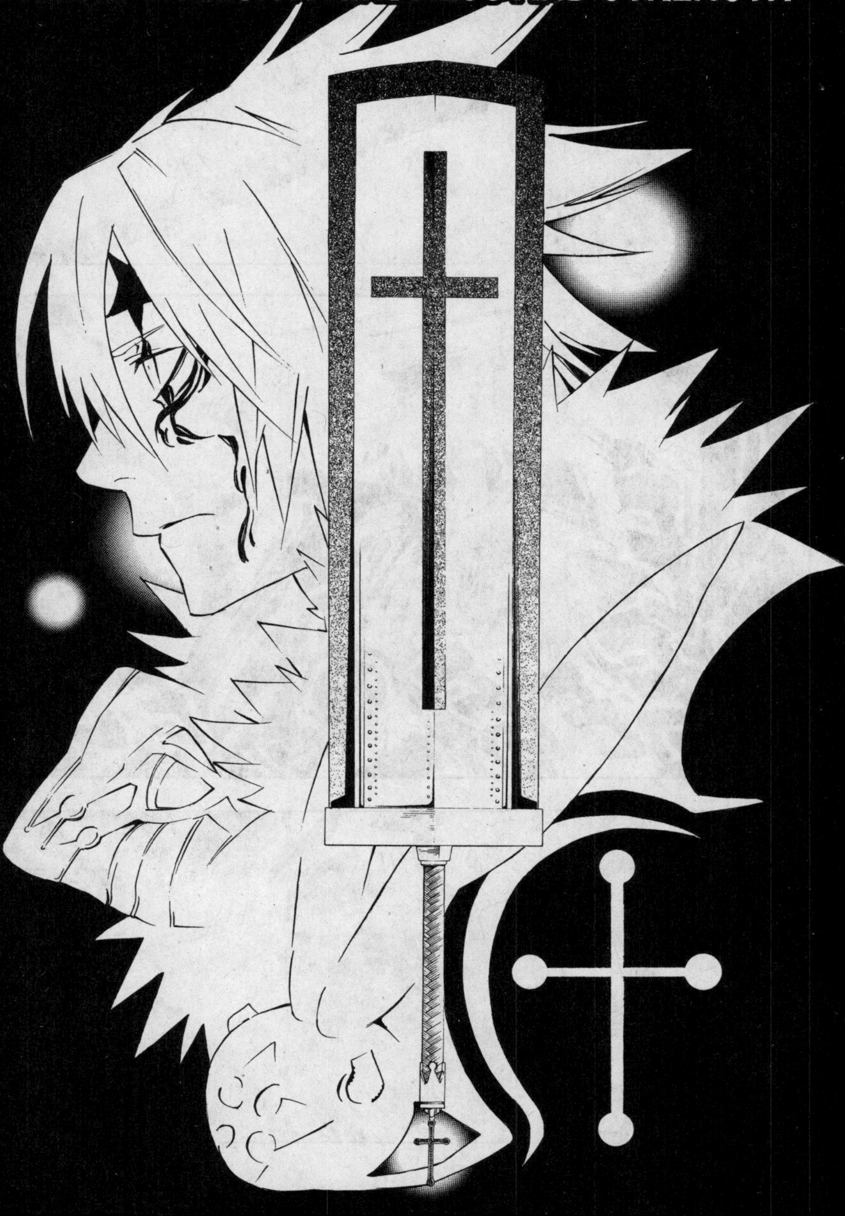

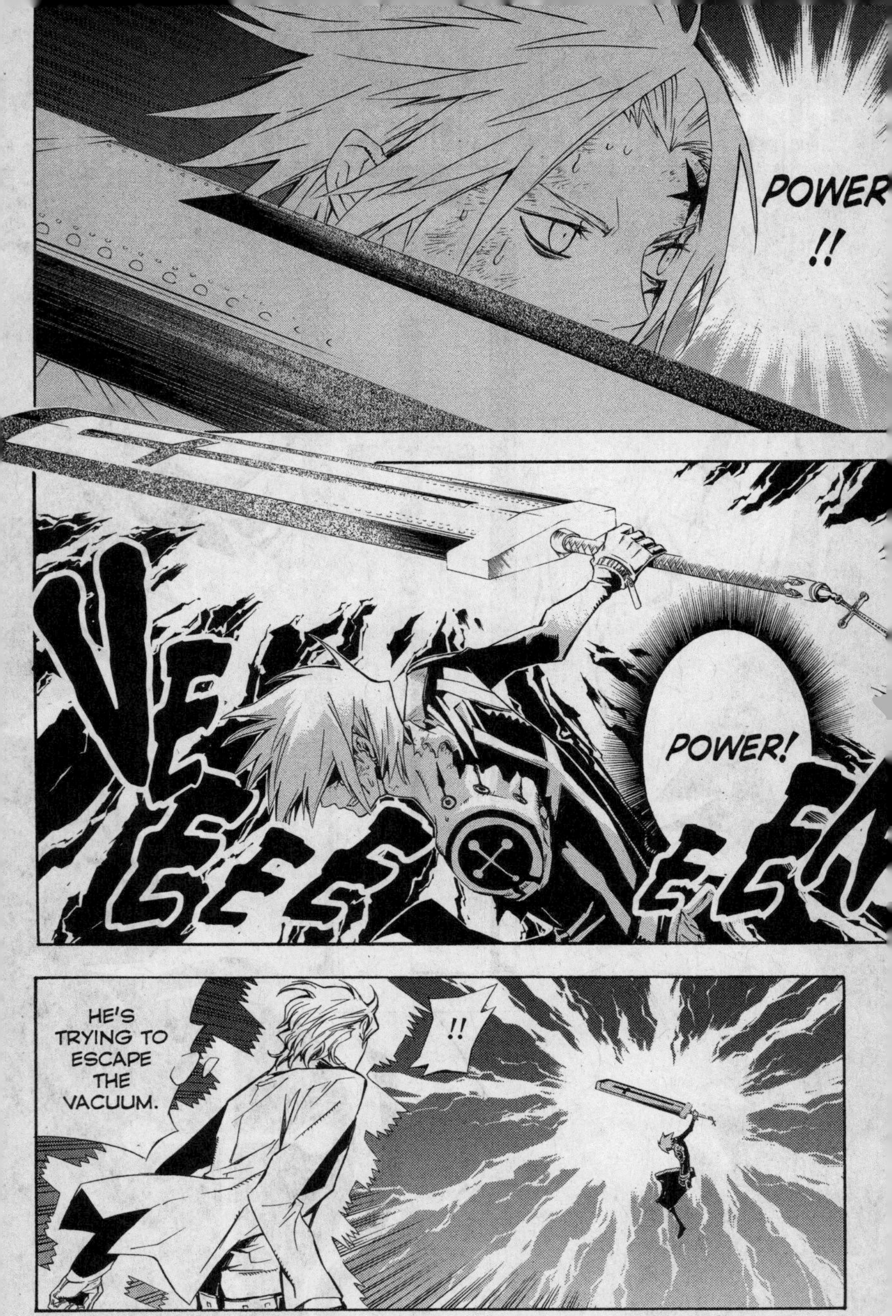
POWER !!
POWER!
!!
HE'S TRYING TO ESCAPE THE VACUUM.

READ THIS WAY

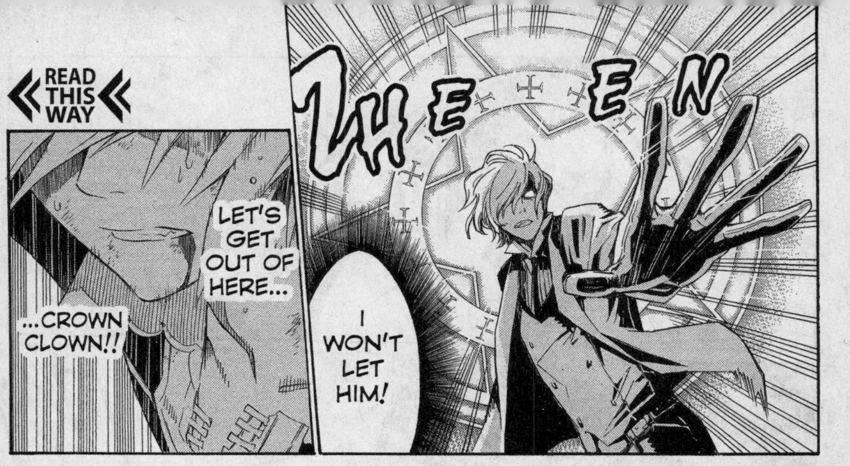

ZHEEN
I WON'T LET HIM!
LET'S GET OUT OF HERE...
...CROWN CLOWN!!

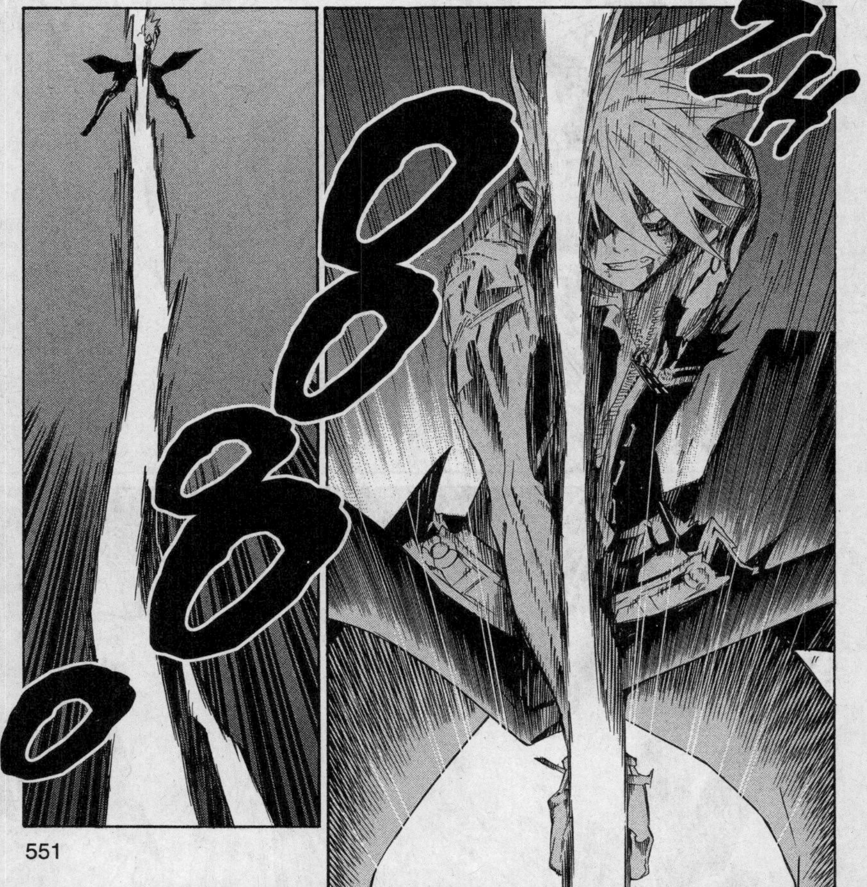

ZH

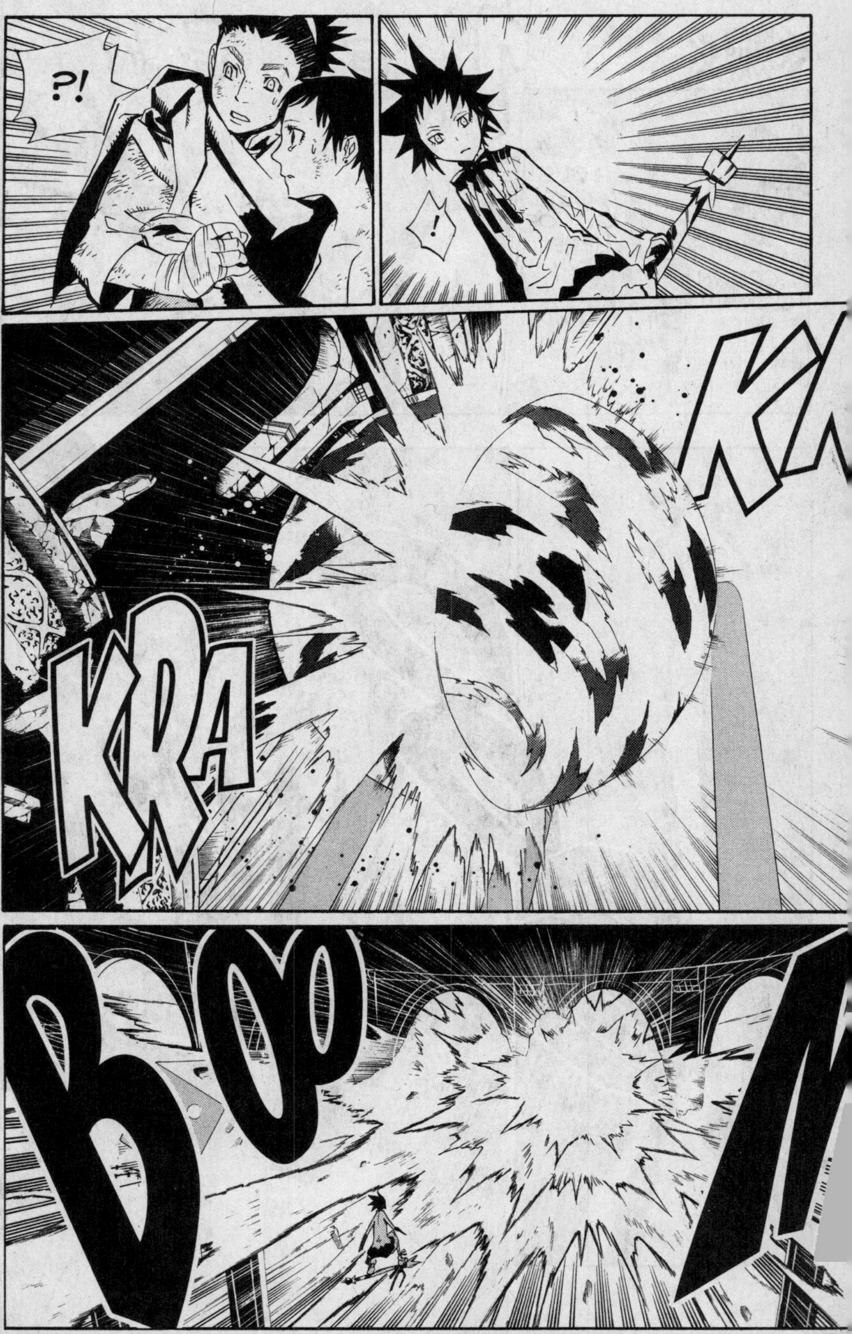
!
?!
KRA

READ THIS WAY

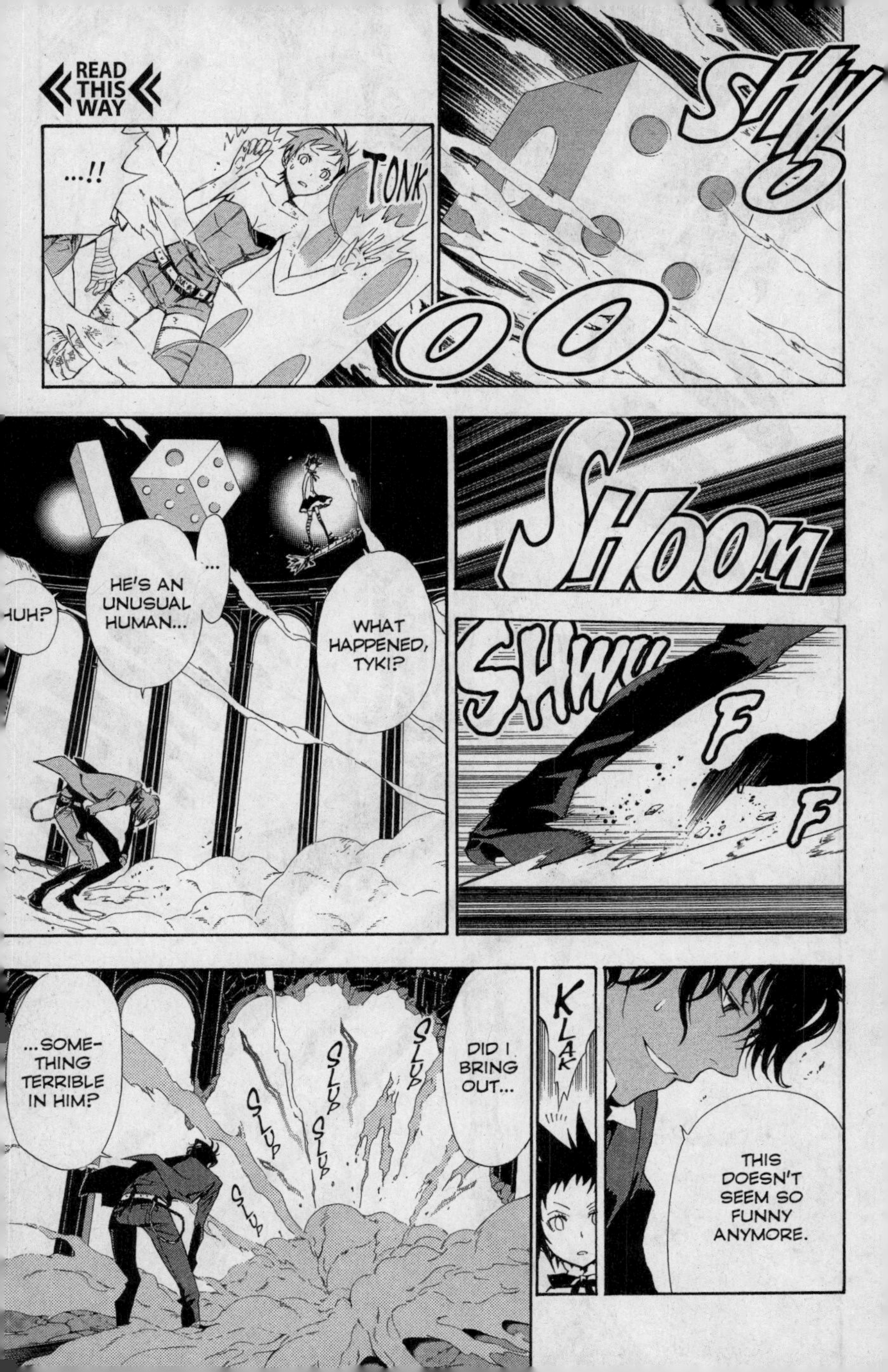
SHYOOO
...!!
TONK
SHOOM
SHWUFF
WHAT HAPPENED, TYKI?
...
HE'S AN UNUSUAL HUMAN...
HUH?
THIS DOESN'T SEEM SO FUNNY ANYMORE.
KLAK
DID I BRING OUT...
SLUP SLUP SLUP SLUP SLUP SLUP
...SOME-THING TERRIBLE IN HIM?

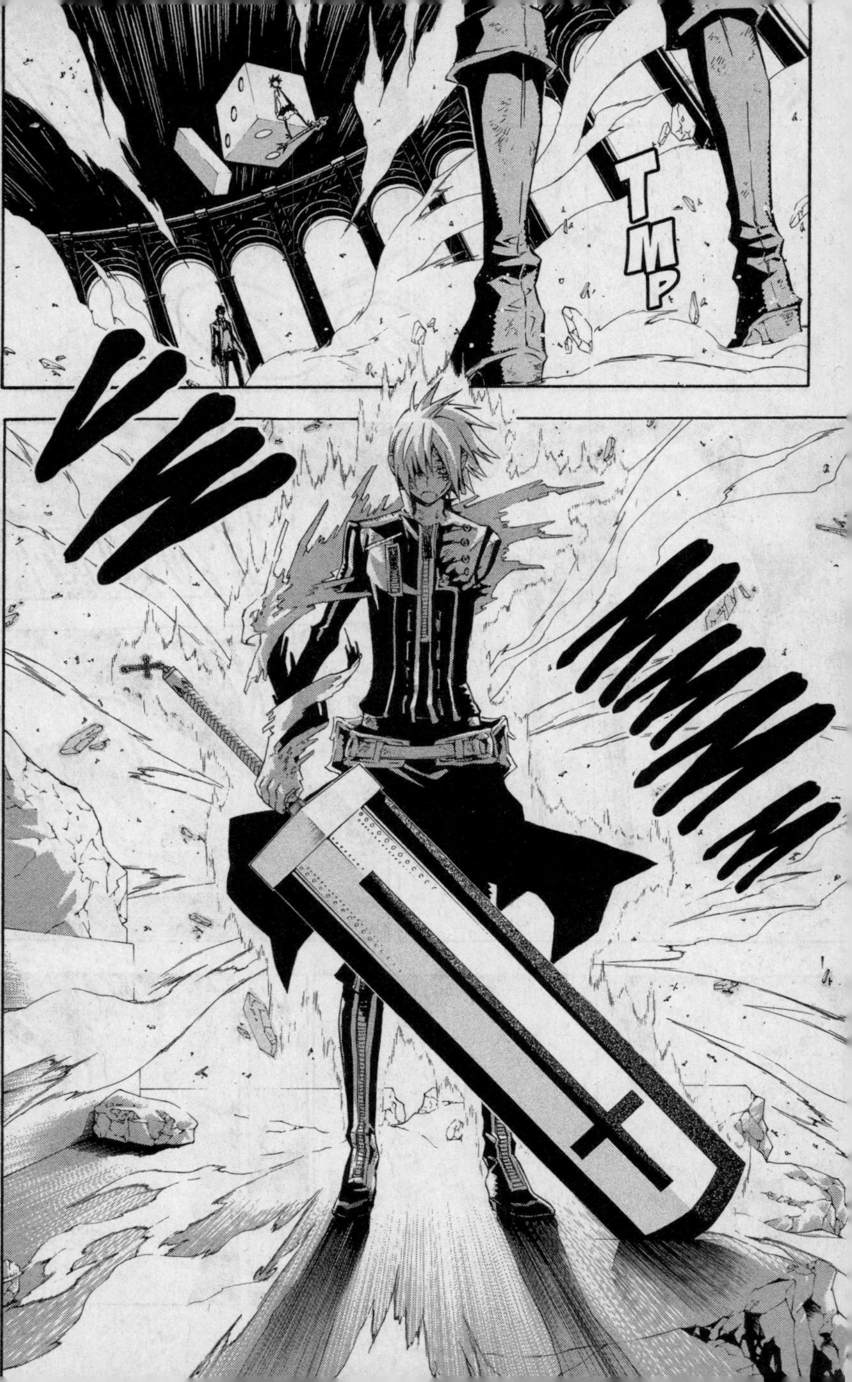
TMP
VWMMMN

READ THIS WAY

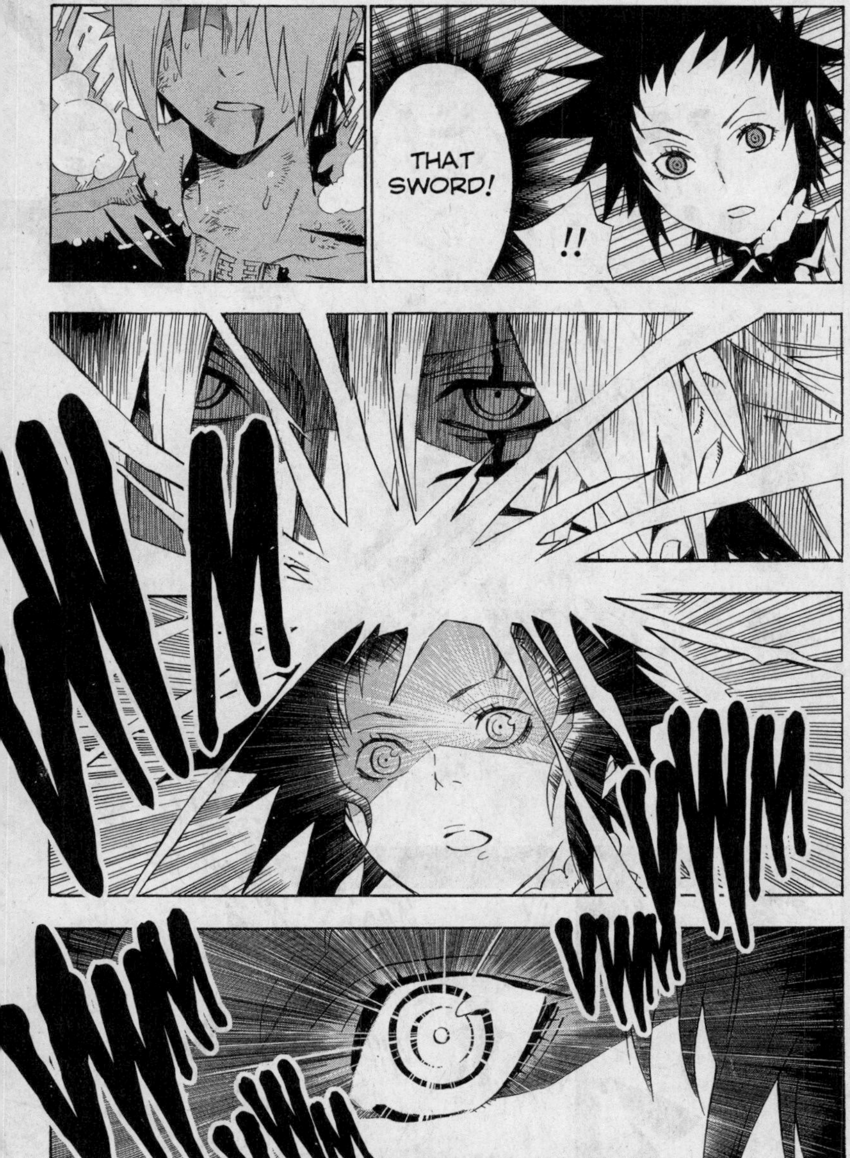
THAT SWORD!
!!

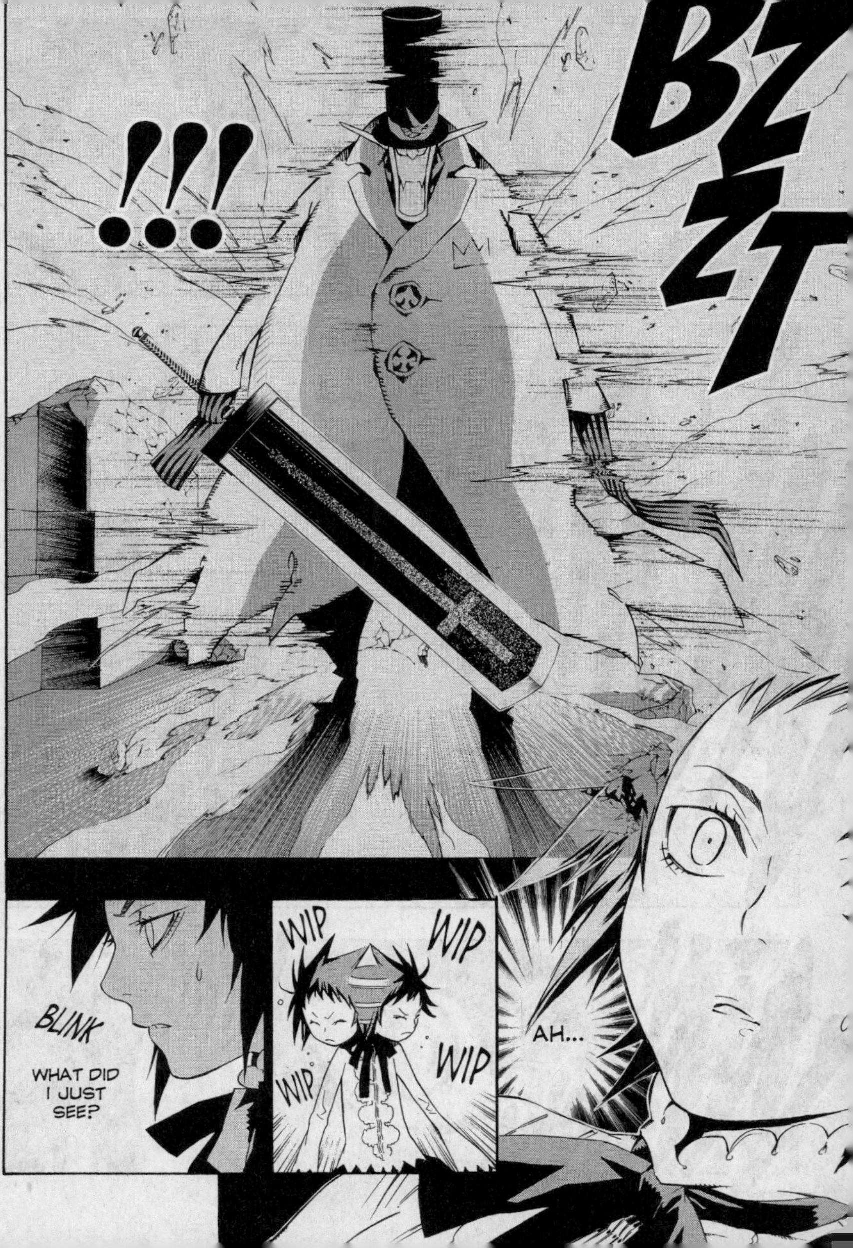
BZZT
!!!
AH...
WIP
WIP
WIP
WIP
BLINK
WHAT DID I JUST SEE?

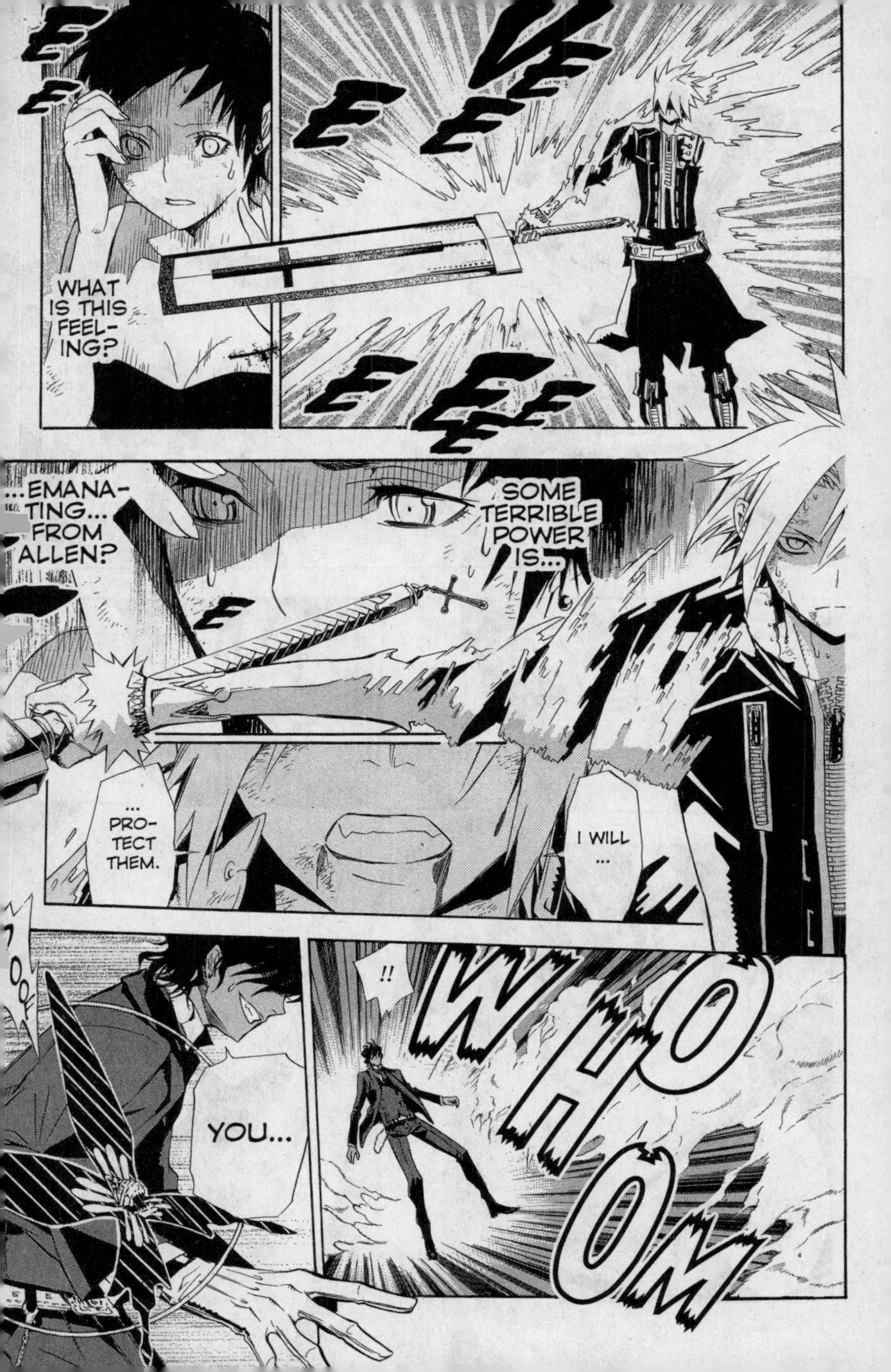
WHAT IS THIS FEEL-ING?
SOME TERRIBLE POWER IS...
...EMANA-TING... FROM ALLEN?
I WILL ...
... PRO-TECT THEM.
!!
WHOOM
YOU...

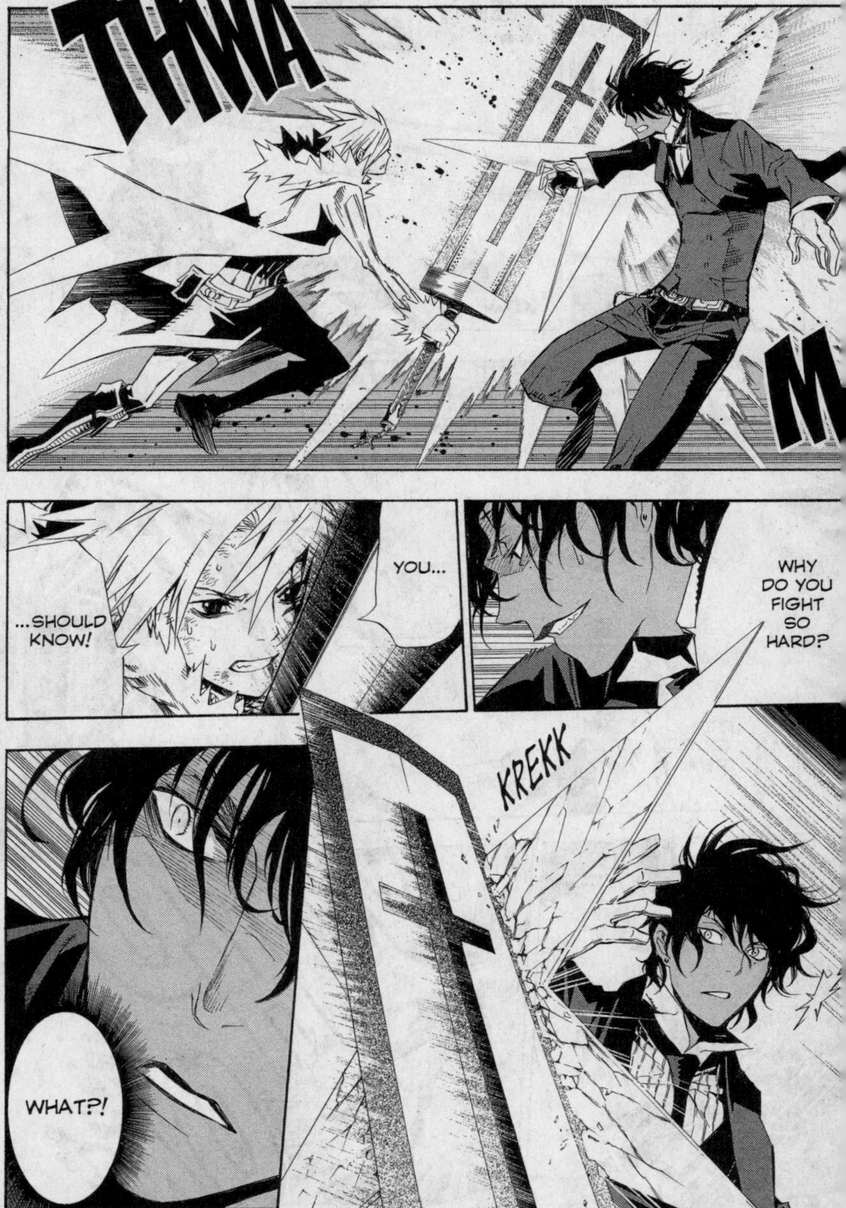
THWA
M
WHY DO YOU FIGHT SO HARD?
YOU...
...SHOULD KNOW!
KREKK
WHAT?!

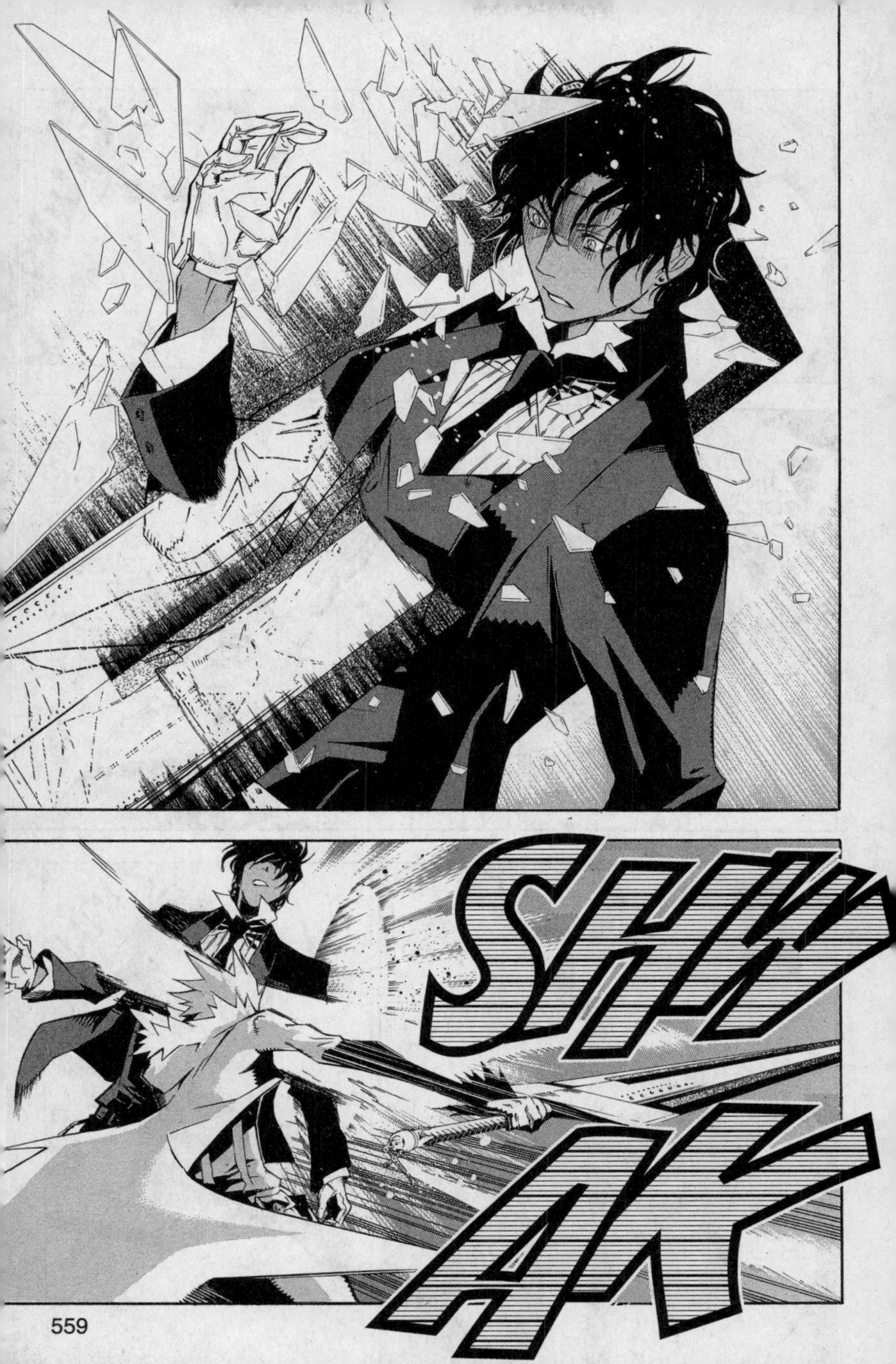
SHHAK

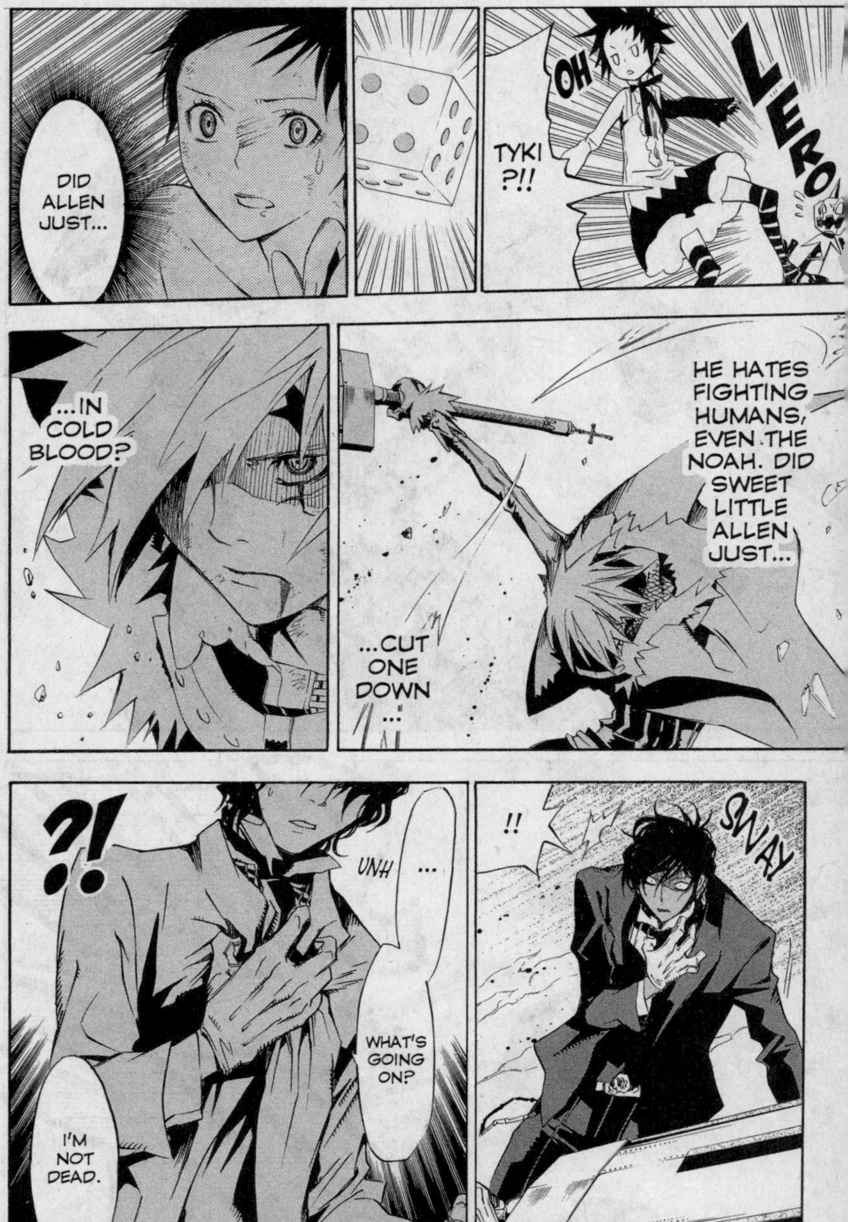
OH
LERO
TYKI ?!!
DID ALLEN JUST...
HE HATES FIGHTING HUMANS, EVEN THE NOAH. DID SWEET LITTLE ALLEN JUST...
...CUT ONE DOWN ...!
...IN COLD BLOOD?
SWAY
!!
?!
UNH ...
WHAT'S GOING ON?
I'M NOT DEAD.

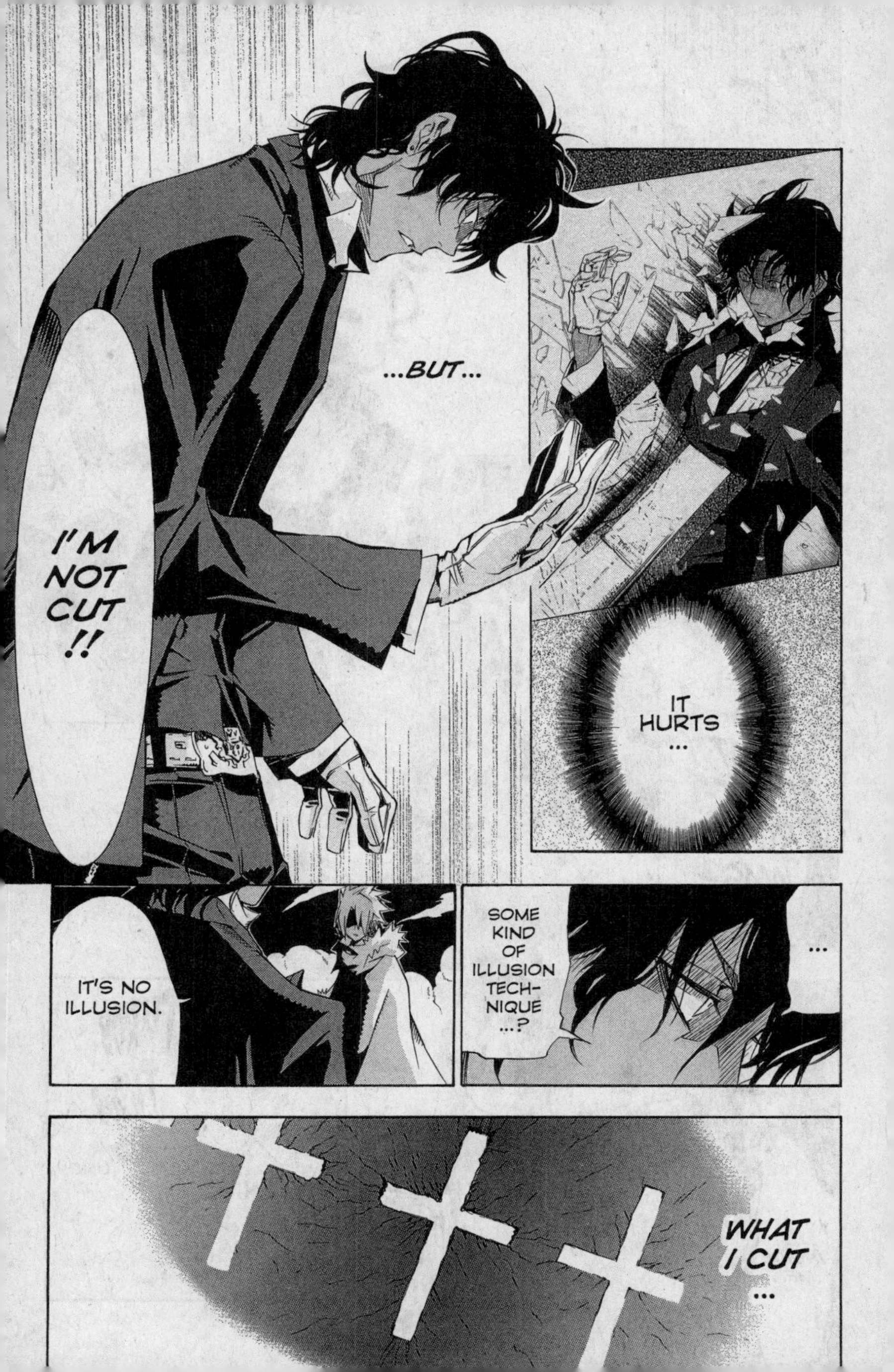
IT HURTS ...
...BUT...
I'M NOT CUT !!
...
SOME KIND OF ILLUSION TECHNIQUE ...?
IT'S NO ILLUSION.
WHAT I CUT ...

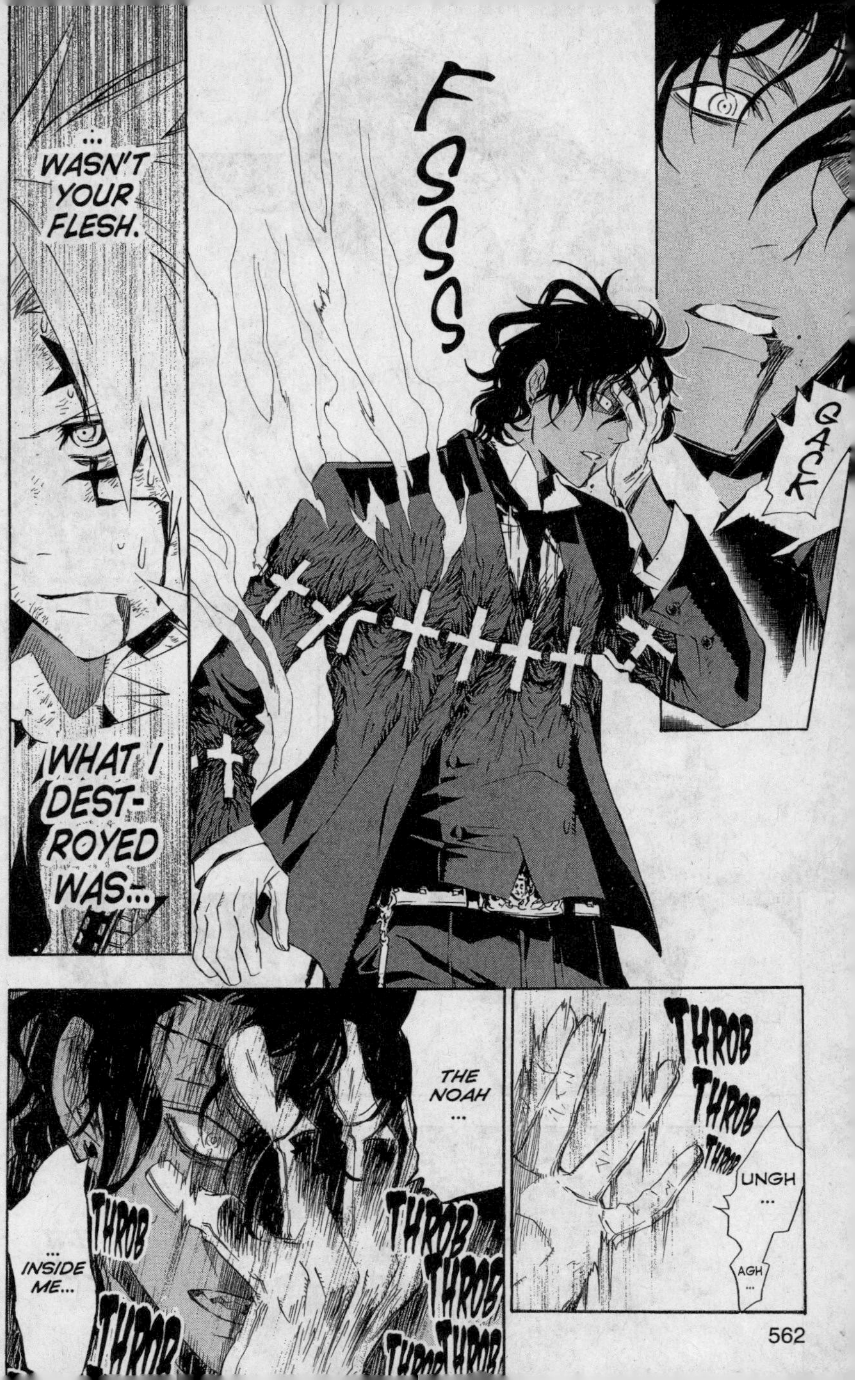
GACK
FSSSS
...WASN'T YOUR FLESH.
WHAT I DEST-ROYED WAS...
THROB THROB THROB
UNGH...
AGH...
THE NOAH...
...INSIDE ME...
THROB
THROB
THROB THROB THROB THROB

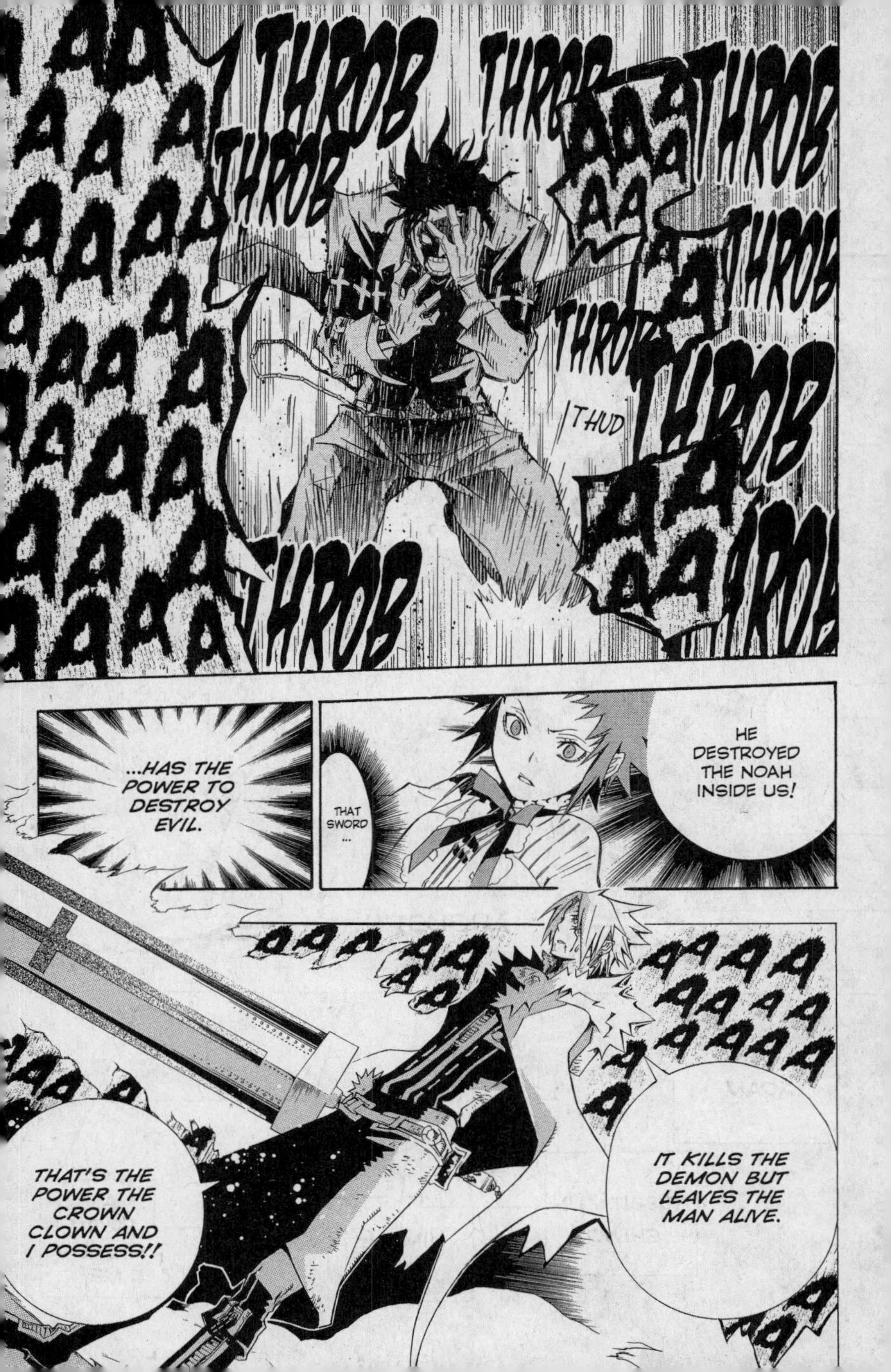
THROB
THROB
THROB
THROB
THROB
THROB
THROB
THROB
THUD
AAAAAAAAAAAAAAAAAAAAAAAAAAAAAA
HE DESTROYED THE NOAH INSIDE US!
THAT SWORD ...
...HAS THE POWER TO DESTROY EVIL.
AAAAAAAAAAAAAAAAAAAA
IT KILLS THE DEMON BUT LEAVES THE MAN ALIVE.
THAT'S THE POWER THE CROWN CLOWN AND I POSSESS!!

OKAN!
NAKAJI!
7:52
Special Thanks
おはようテレビ
AUGUST 4
CORO
MAMA FROM NICHO-ME!
AKIYAMA!
HIMAN-CHU!
MURAKAMI-KUN
MATSUMOTO-SAN
HOBBIT-KUN
SHIWO
ADAM

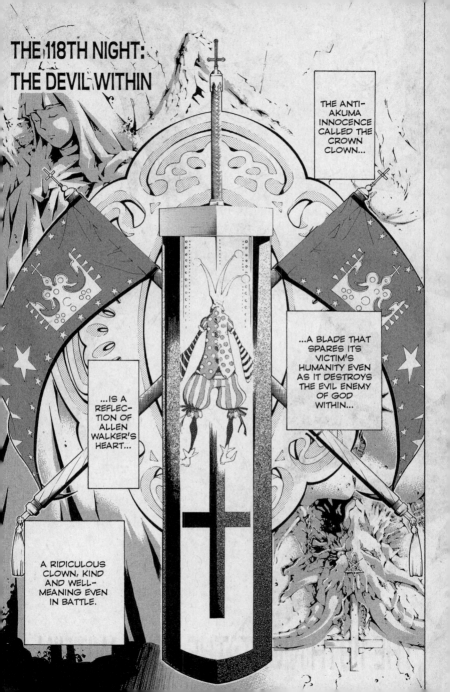

THE 118TH NIGHT: THE DEVIL WITHIN

THE ANTI-AKUMA INNOCENCE CALLED THE CROWN CLOWN...

...A BLADE THAT SPARES ITS VICTIM'S HUMANITY EVEN AS IT DESTROYS THE EVIL ENEMY OF GOD WITHIN...

...IS A REFLECTION OF ALLEN WALKER'S HEART...

A RIDICULOUS CLOWN, KIND AND WELL-MEANING EVEN IN BATTLE.

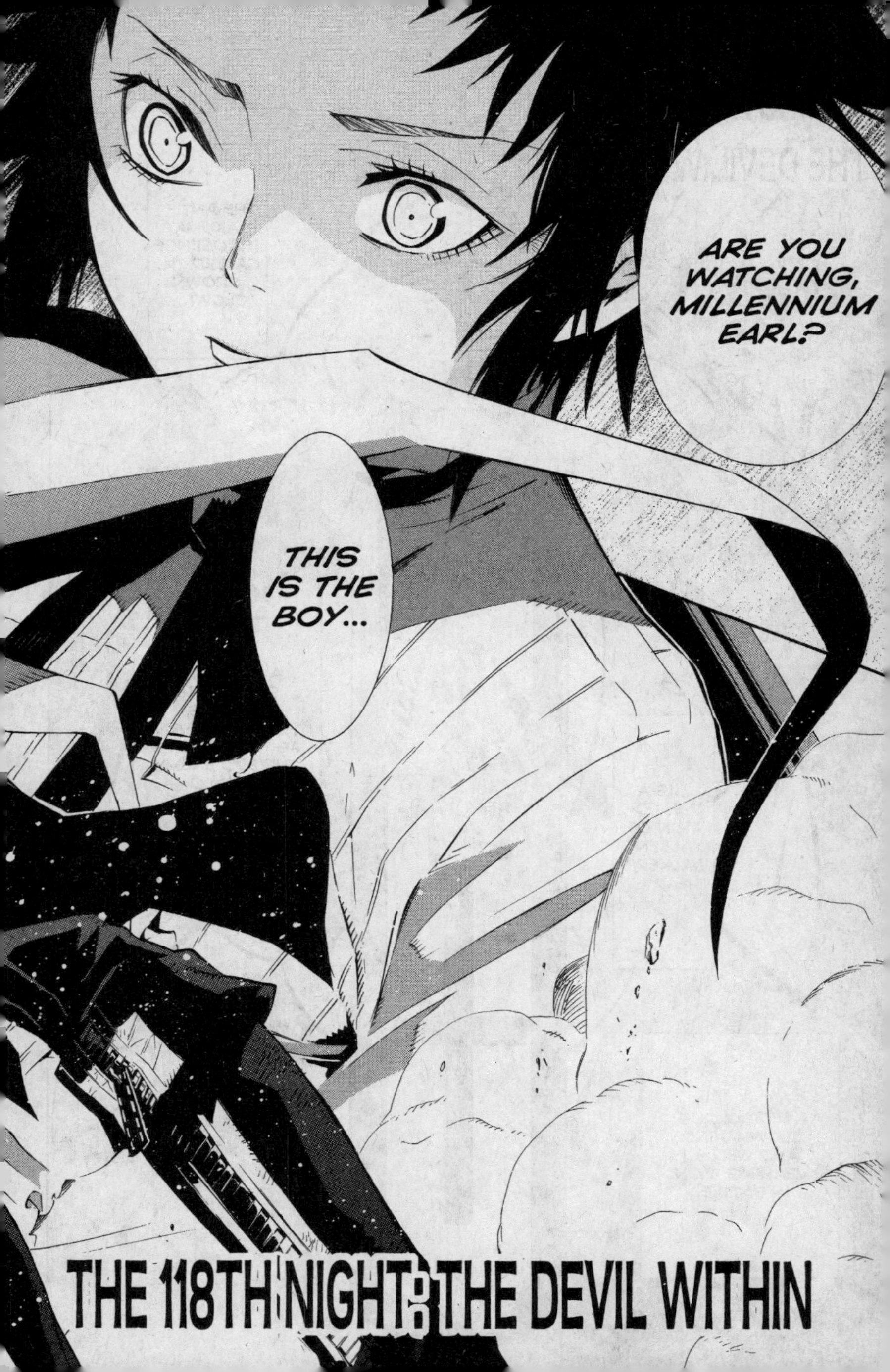
ARE YOU WATCHING, MILLENNIUM EARL?
THIS IS THE BOY...
THE 118TH NIGHT: THE DEVIL WITHIN

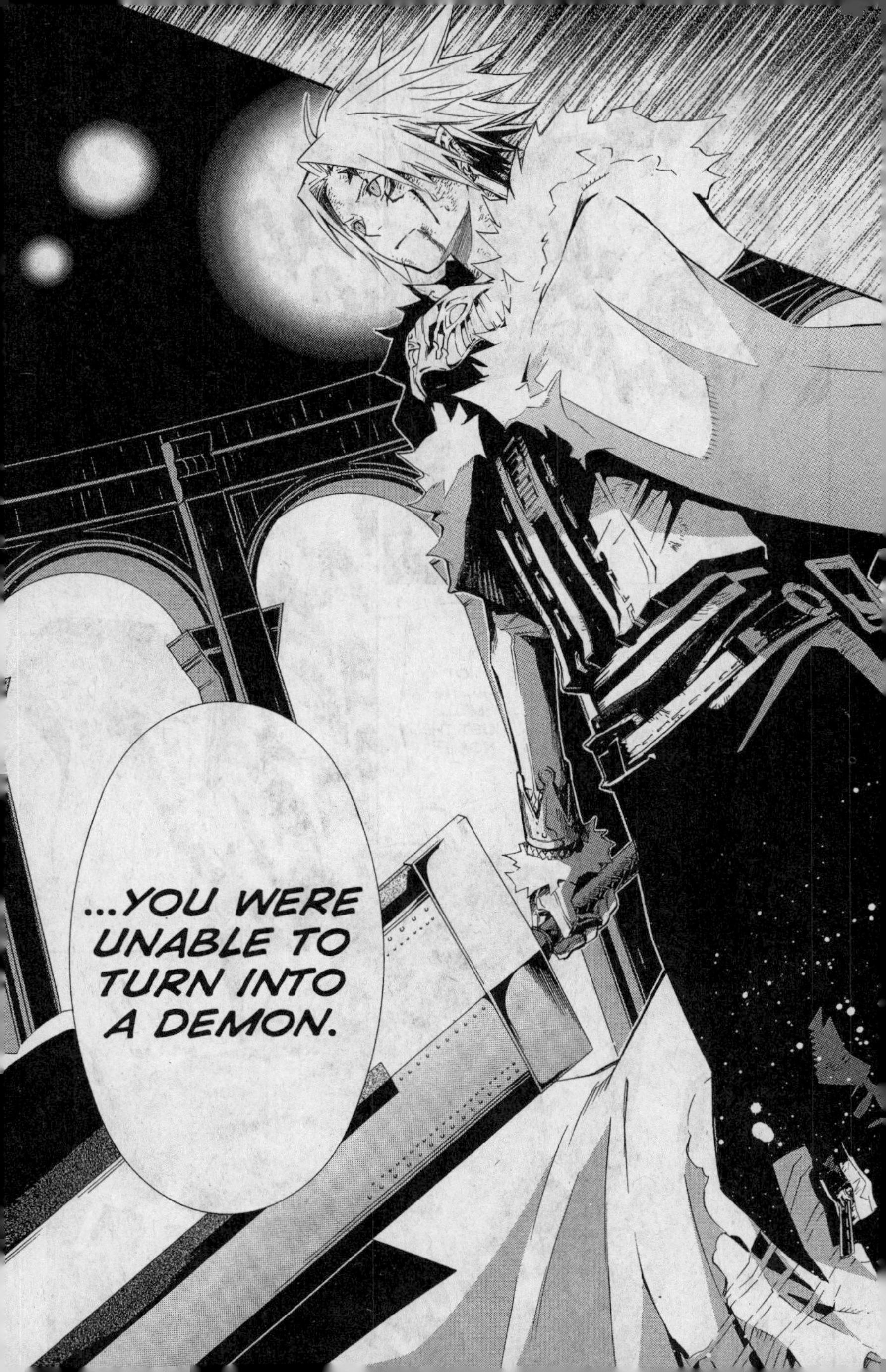
...YOU WERE UNABLE TO TURN INTO A DEMON.

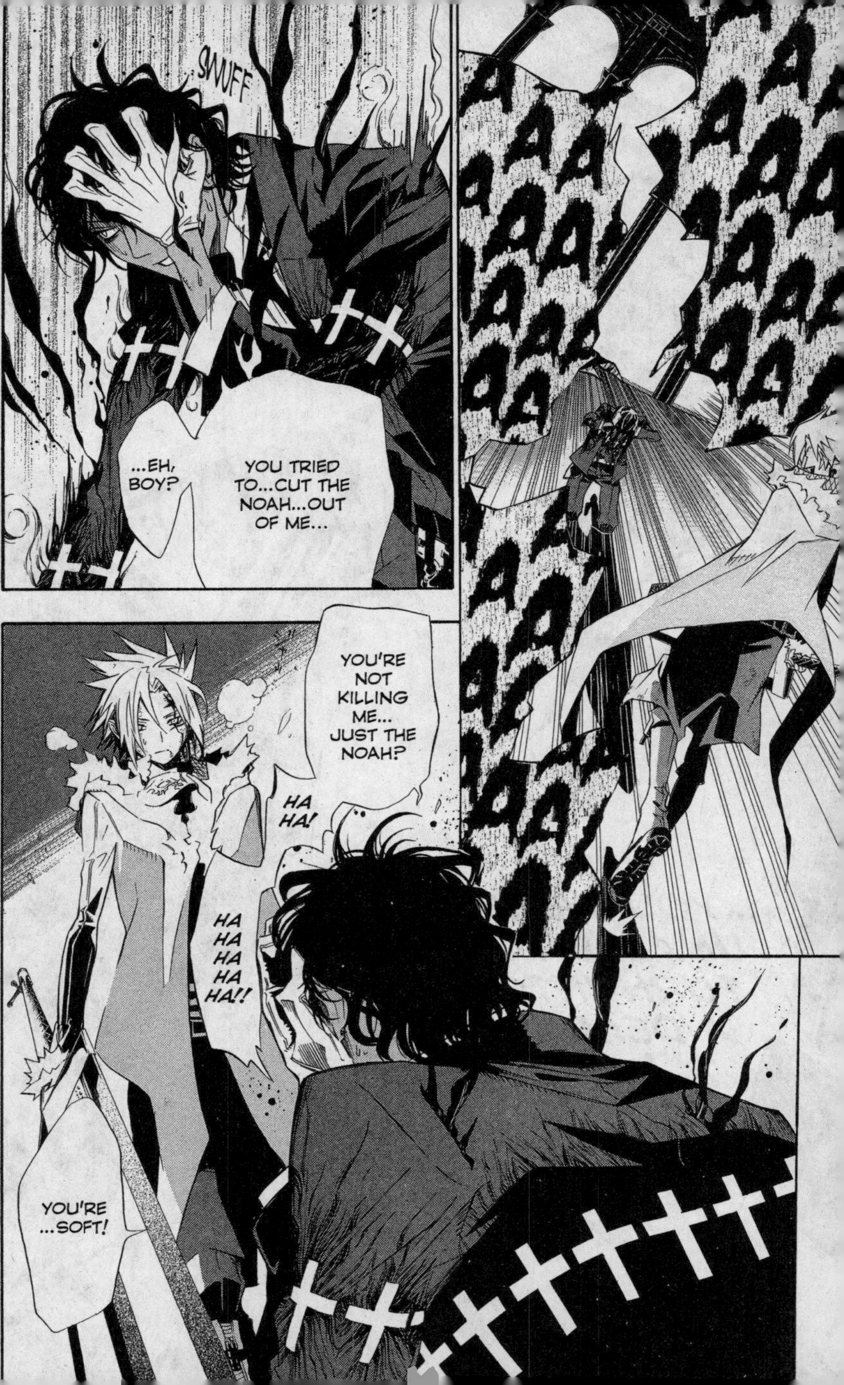
AAAAAAAAAAAAAAAAAAAA
SNUFF
YOU TRIED TO...CUT THE NOAH...OUT OF ME...
...EH, BOY?
YOU'RE NOT KILLING ME... JUST THE NOAH?
HA HA!
HA HA HA HA HA!!
YOU'RE ...SOFT!

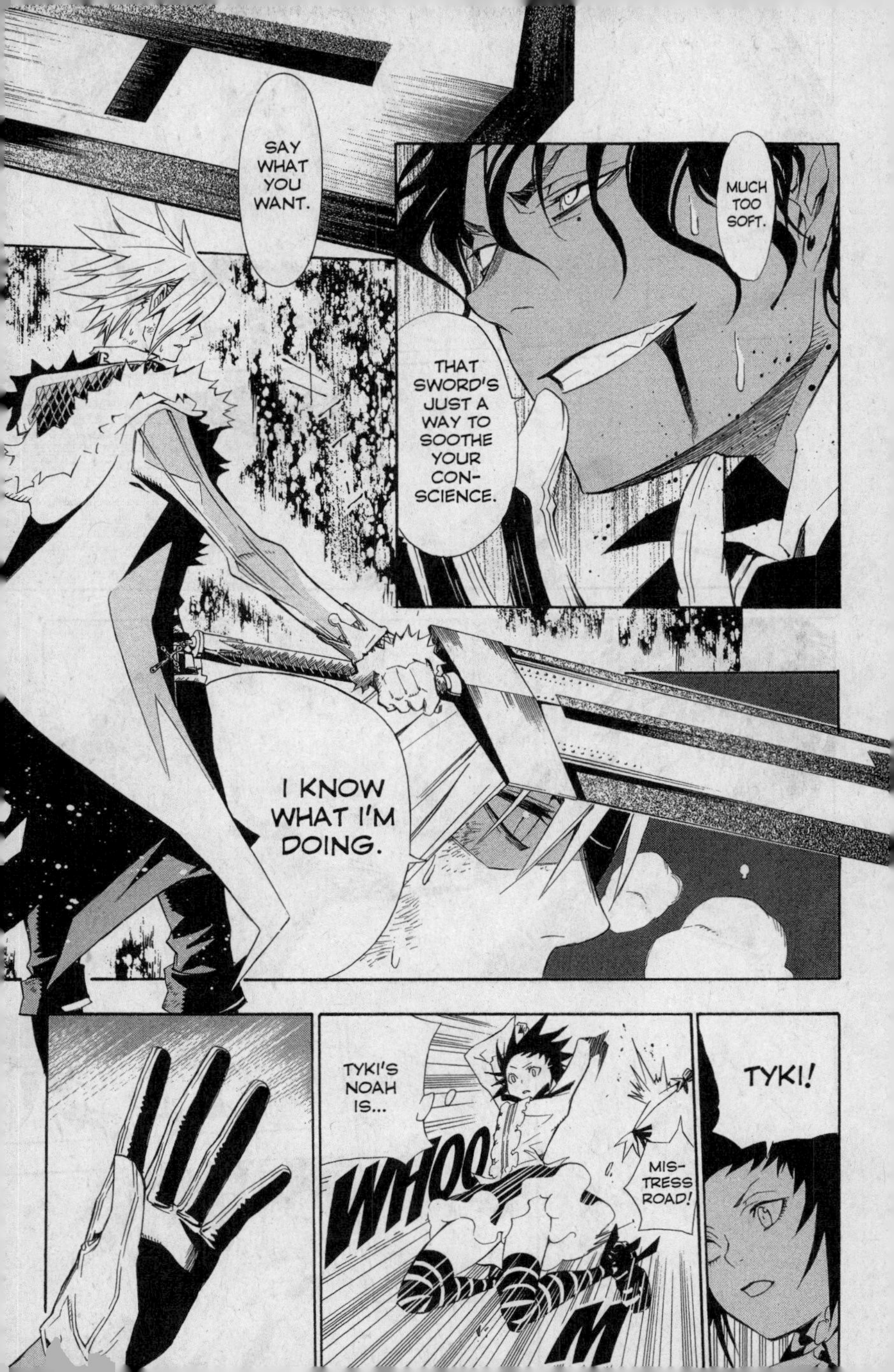
MUCH TOO SOFT.
THAT SWORD'S JUST A WAY TO SOOTHE YOUR CON-SCIENCE.
SAY WHAT YOU WANT.
I KNOW WHAT I'M DOING.
TYKI!
TYKI'S NOAH IS...
MIS-TRESS ROAD!
WHOOM

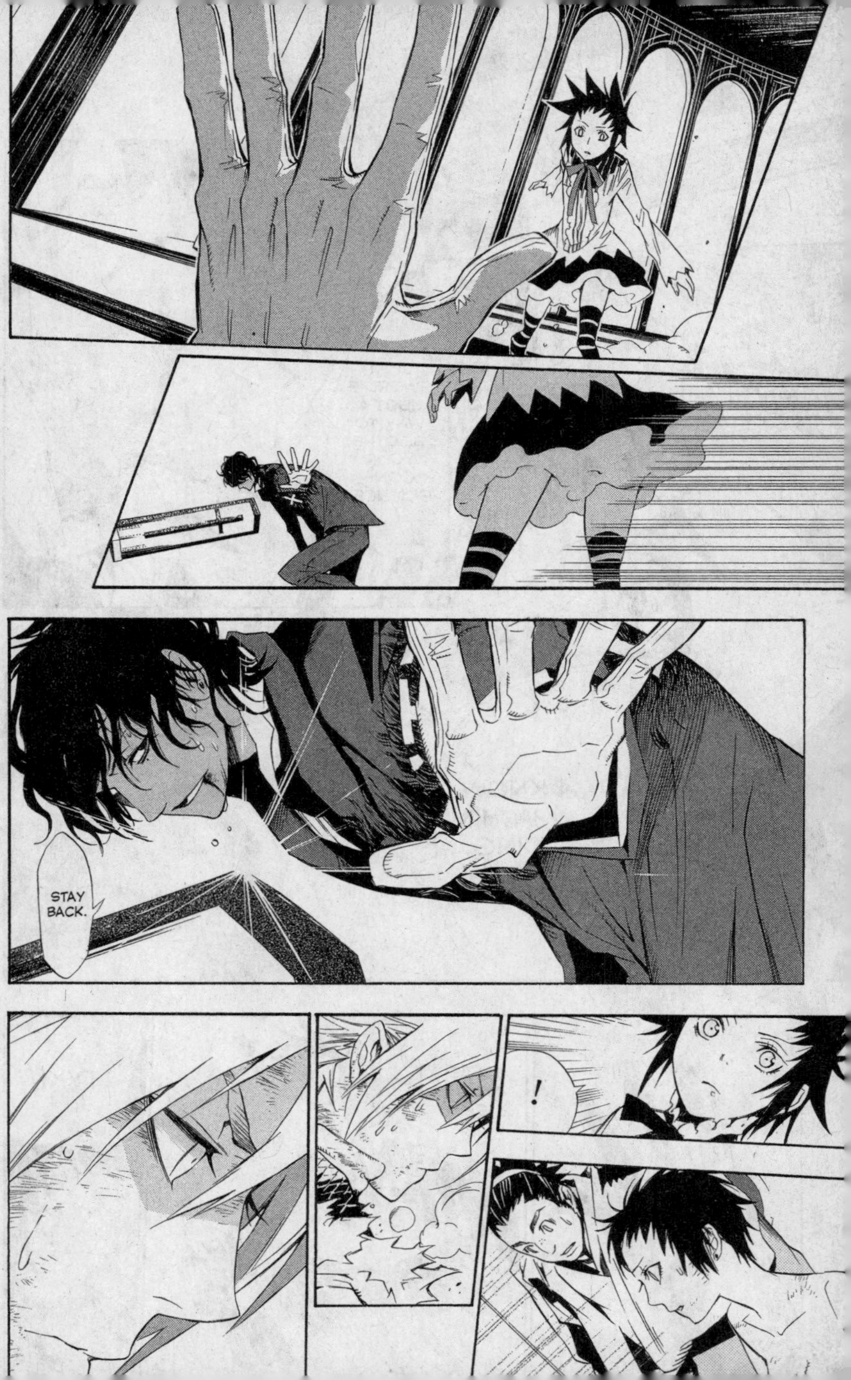
STAY BACK.
!

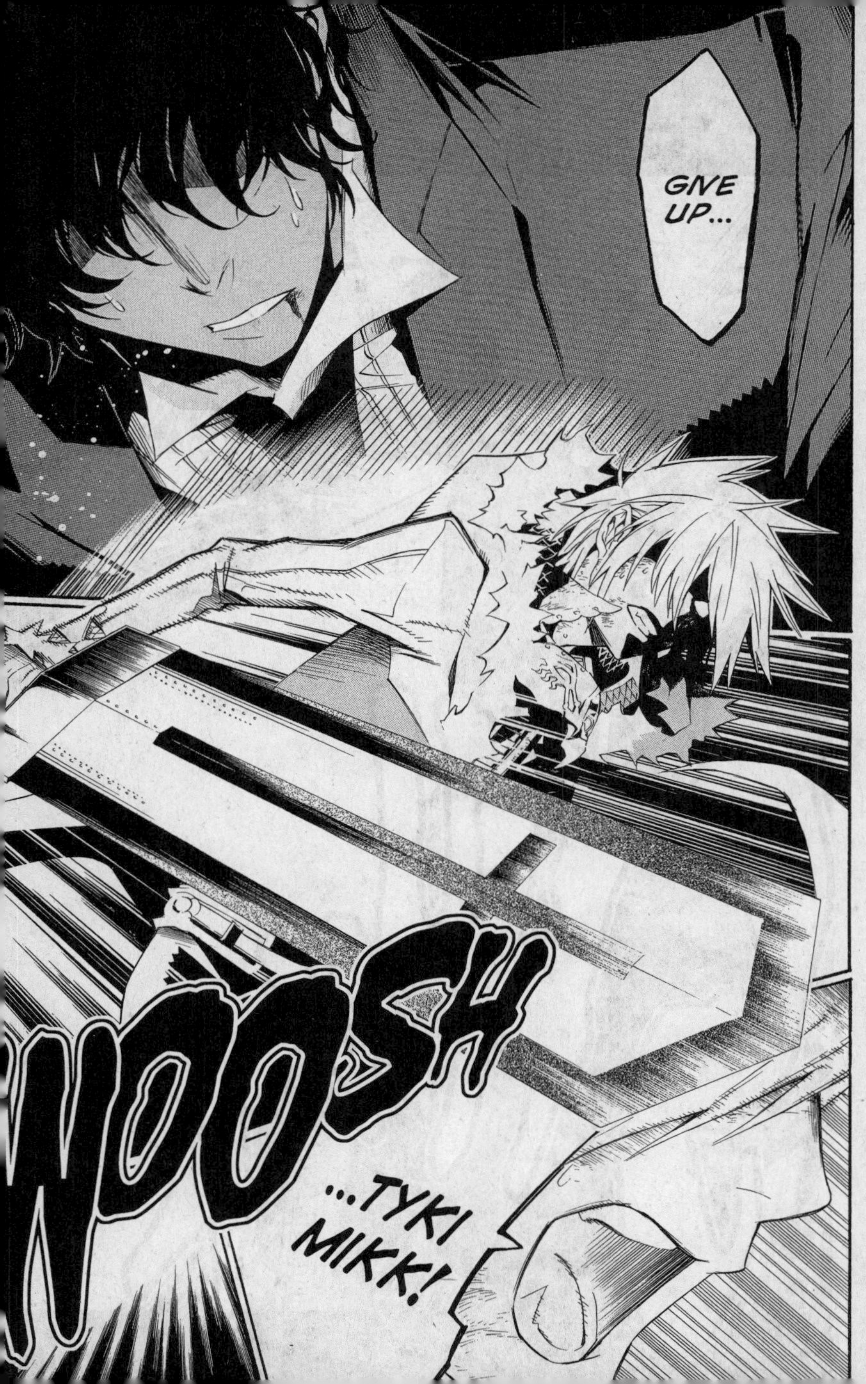
GIVE UP...
WHOOSH
...TYKI MIKK!

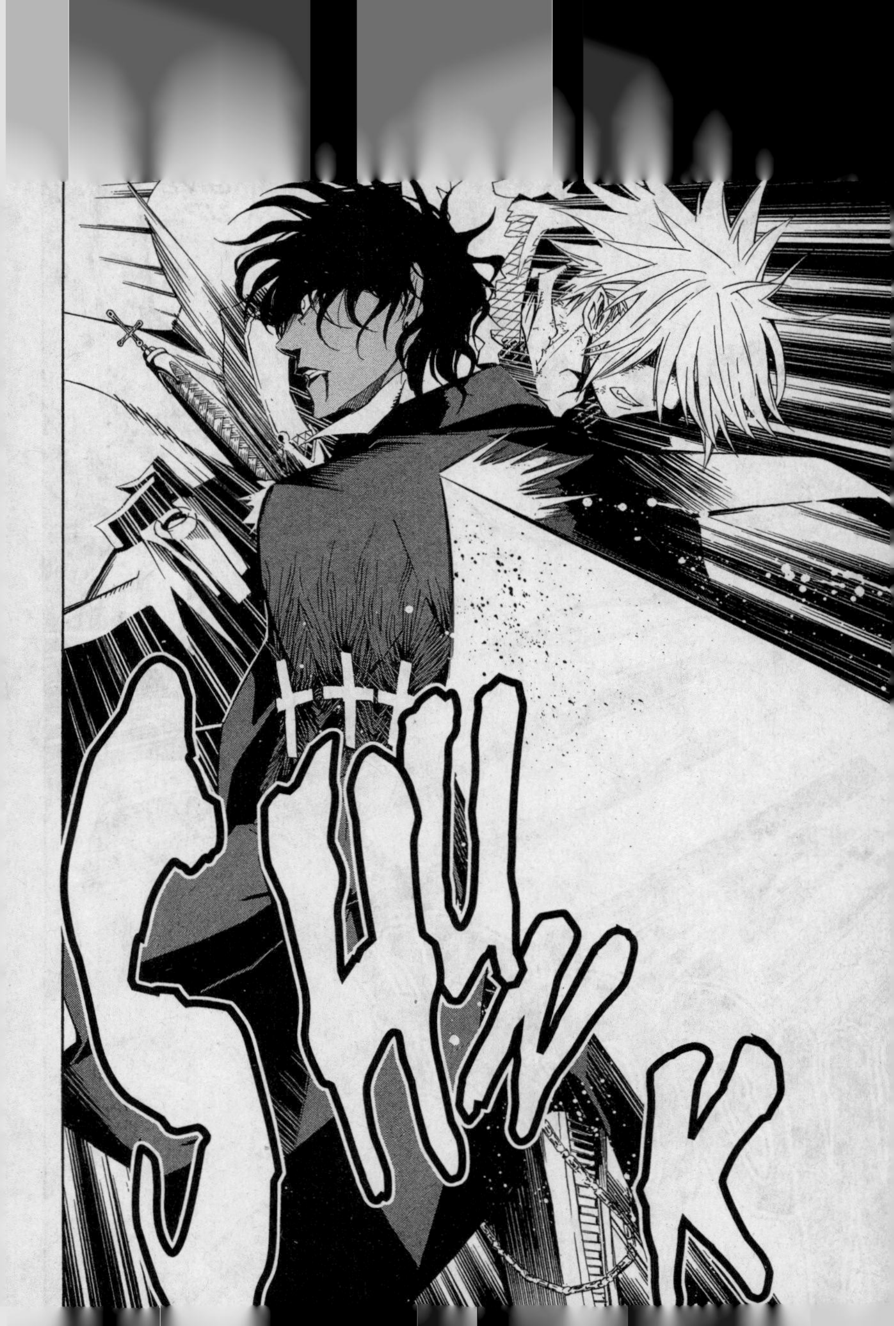
SHUK

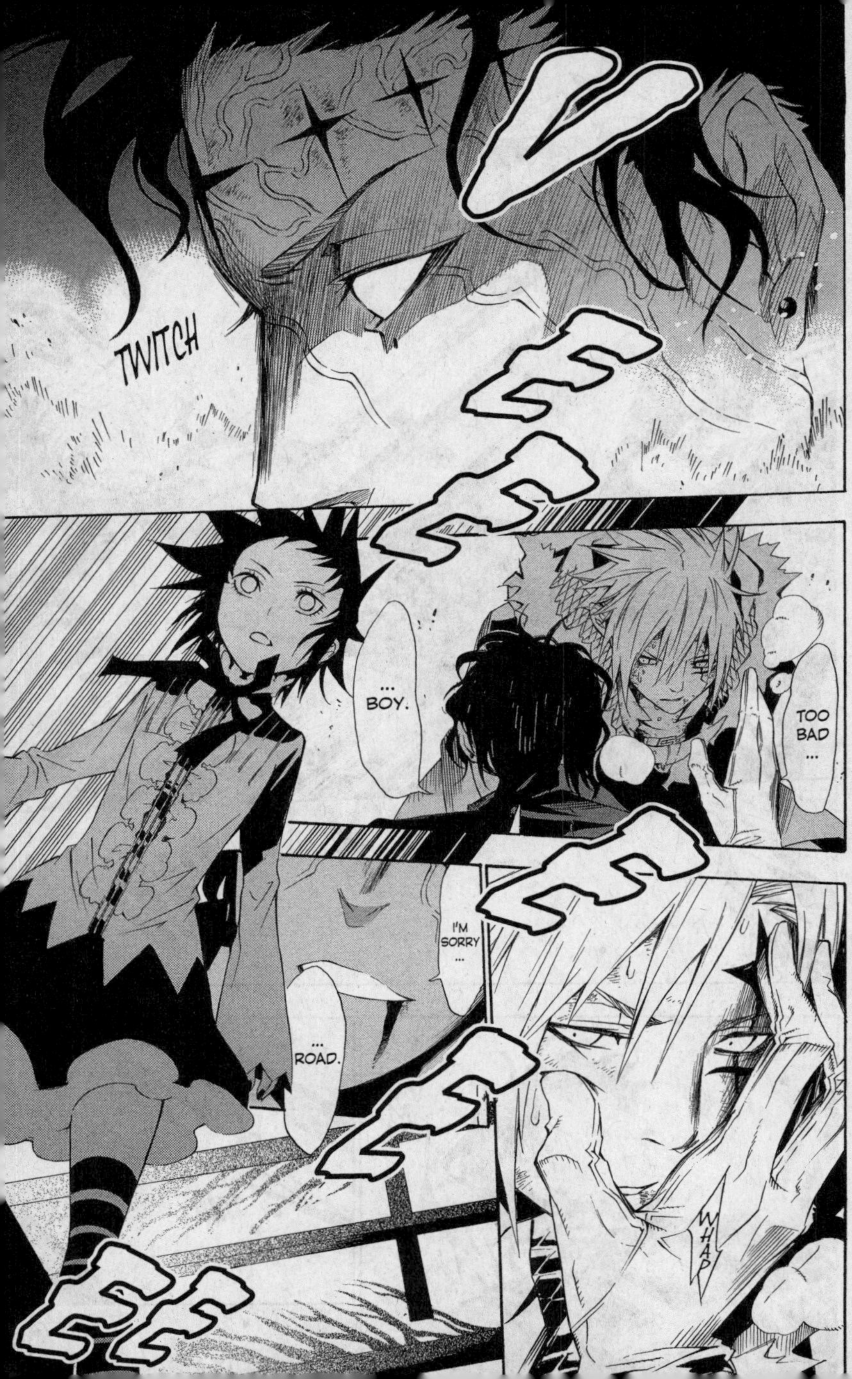
TWITCH
TOO BAD ...
... BOY.
I'M SORRY ...
WHAP
... ROAD.

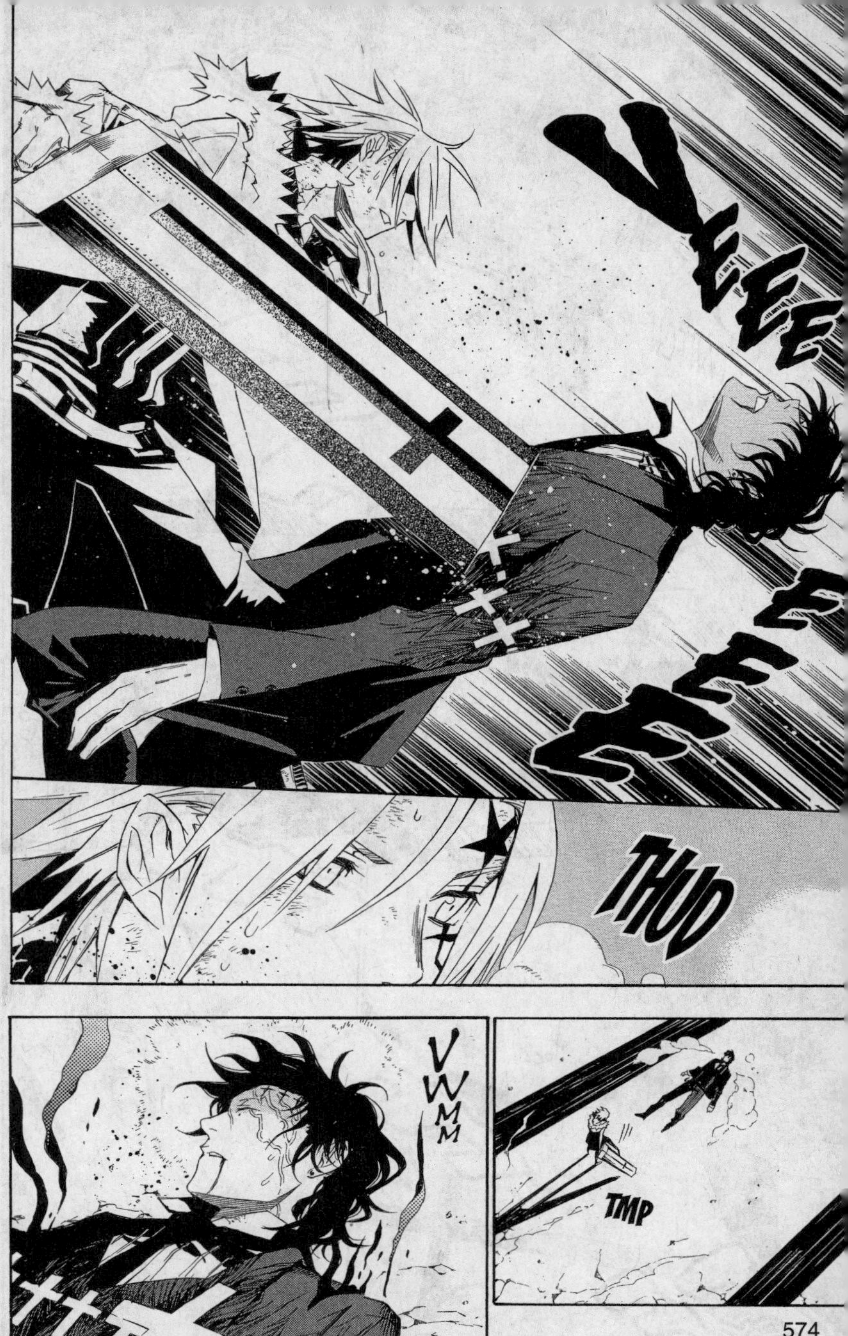
VEEEEEEE
THUD
TMP
VWMM

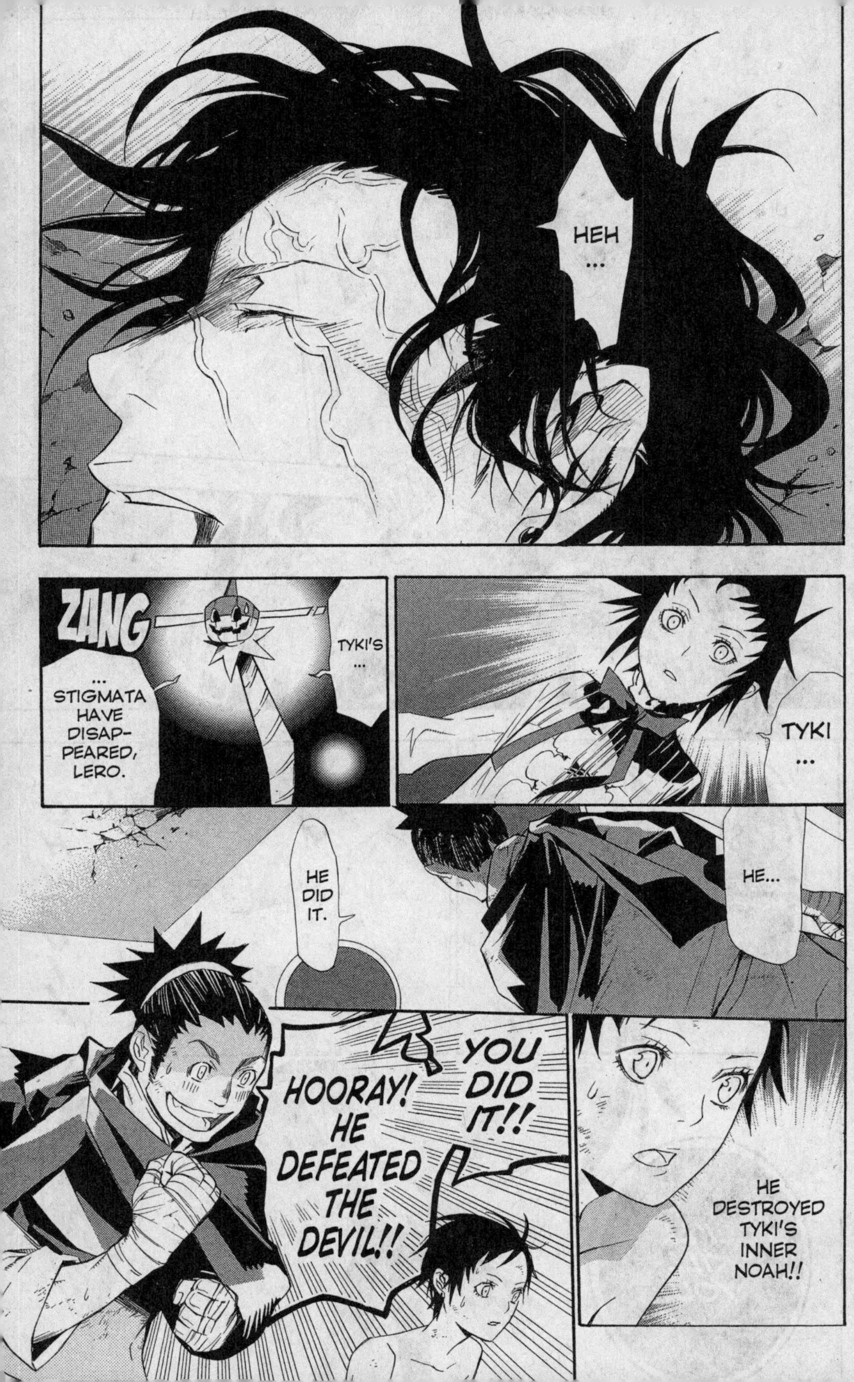
HEH ...
TYKI ...
ZANG
TYKI'S ...
... STIGMATA HAVE DISAPPEARED, LERO.
HE...
HE DID IT.
HE DESTROYED TYKI'S INNER NOAH!!
YOU DID IT!!
HOORAY! HE DEFEATED THE DEVIL!!

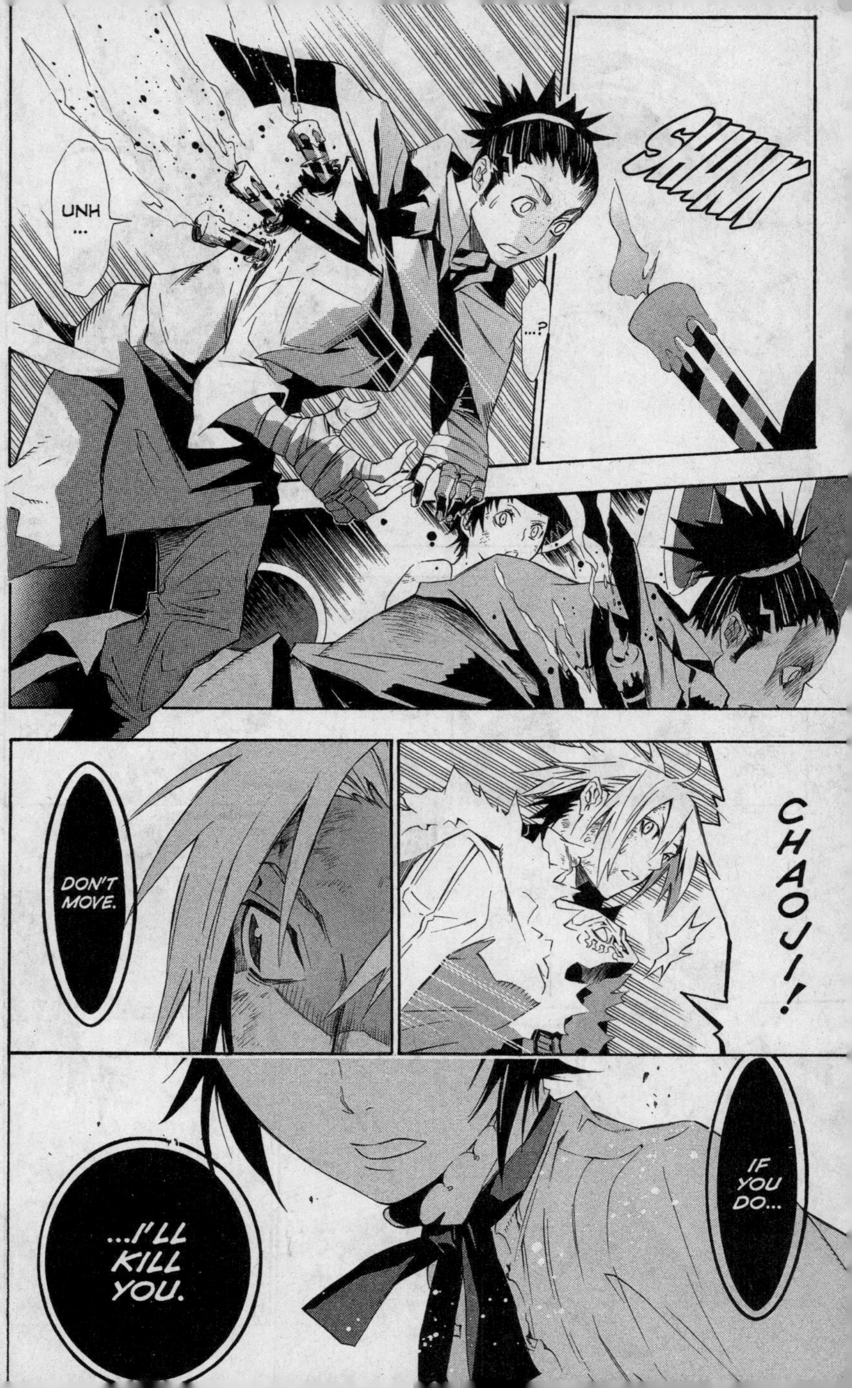
SHUNK
...?
UNH ...
CHAOJI!
DON'T MOVE.
IF YOU DO...
...I'LL KILL YOU.

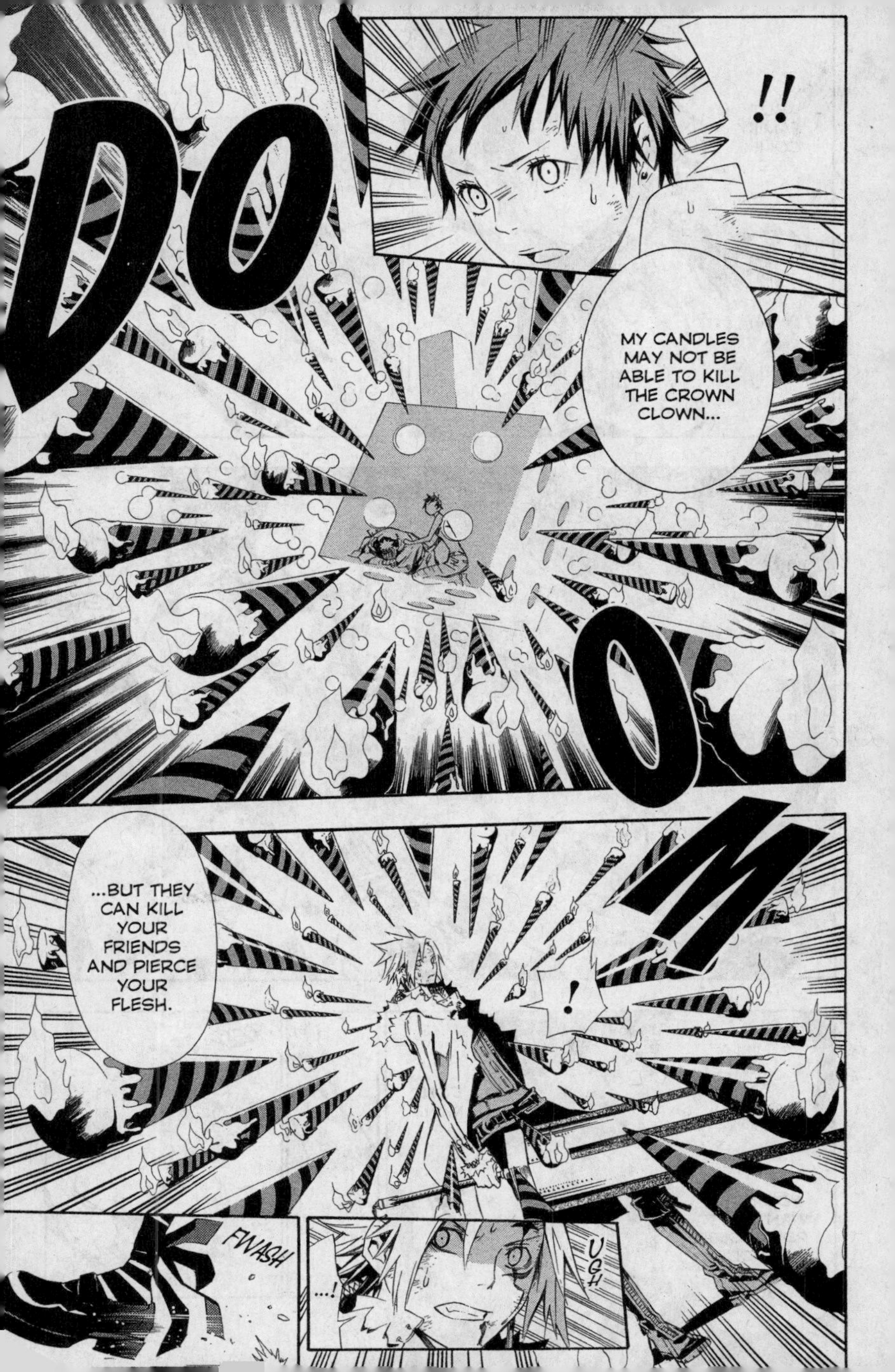
!!
DO
MY CANDLES MAY NOT BE ABLE TO KILL THE CROWN CLOWN...
O
M
...BUT THEY CAN KILL YOUR FRIENDS AND PIERCE YOUR FLESH.
!
UGH
...!
FWASH

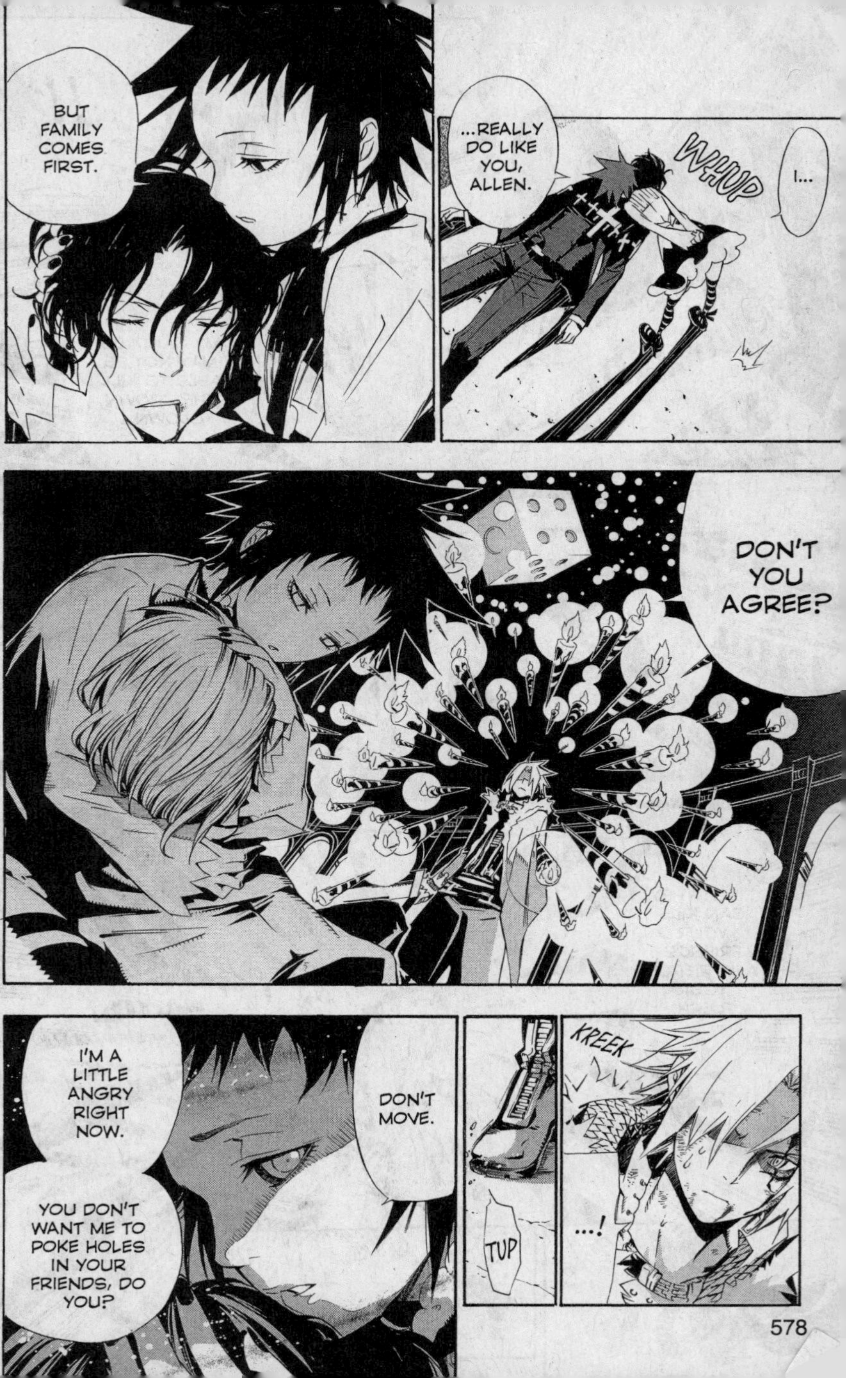
I...
WHUP
...REALLY DO LIKE YOU, ALLEN.
BUT FAMILY COMES FIRST.
DON'T YOU AGREE?
KREEK
...!
TUP
DON'T MOVE.
I'M A LITTLE ANGRY RIGHT NOW.
YOU DON'T WANT ME TO POKE HOLES IN YOUR FRIENDS, DO YOU?

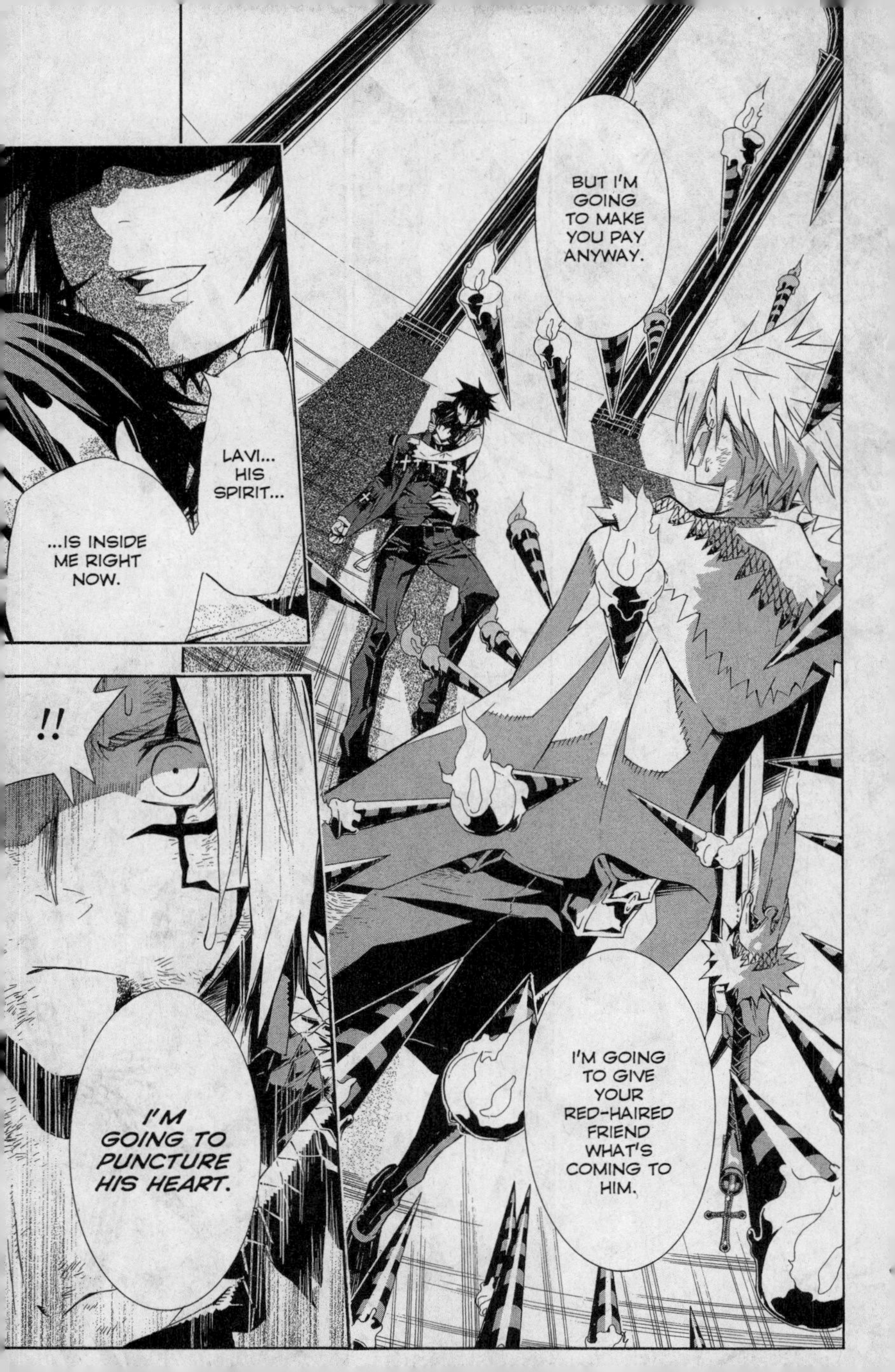
BUT I'M GOING TO MAKE YOU PAY ANYWAY.
I'M GOING TO GIVE YOUR RED-HAIRED FRIEND WHAT'S COMING TO HIM.
LAVI... HIS SPIRIT...
...IS INSIDE ME RIGHT NOW.
!!
I'M GOING TO PUNCTURE HIS HEART.

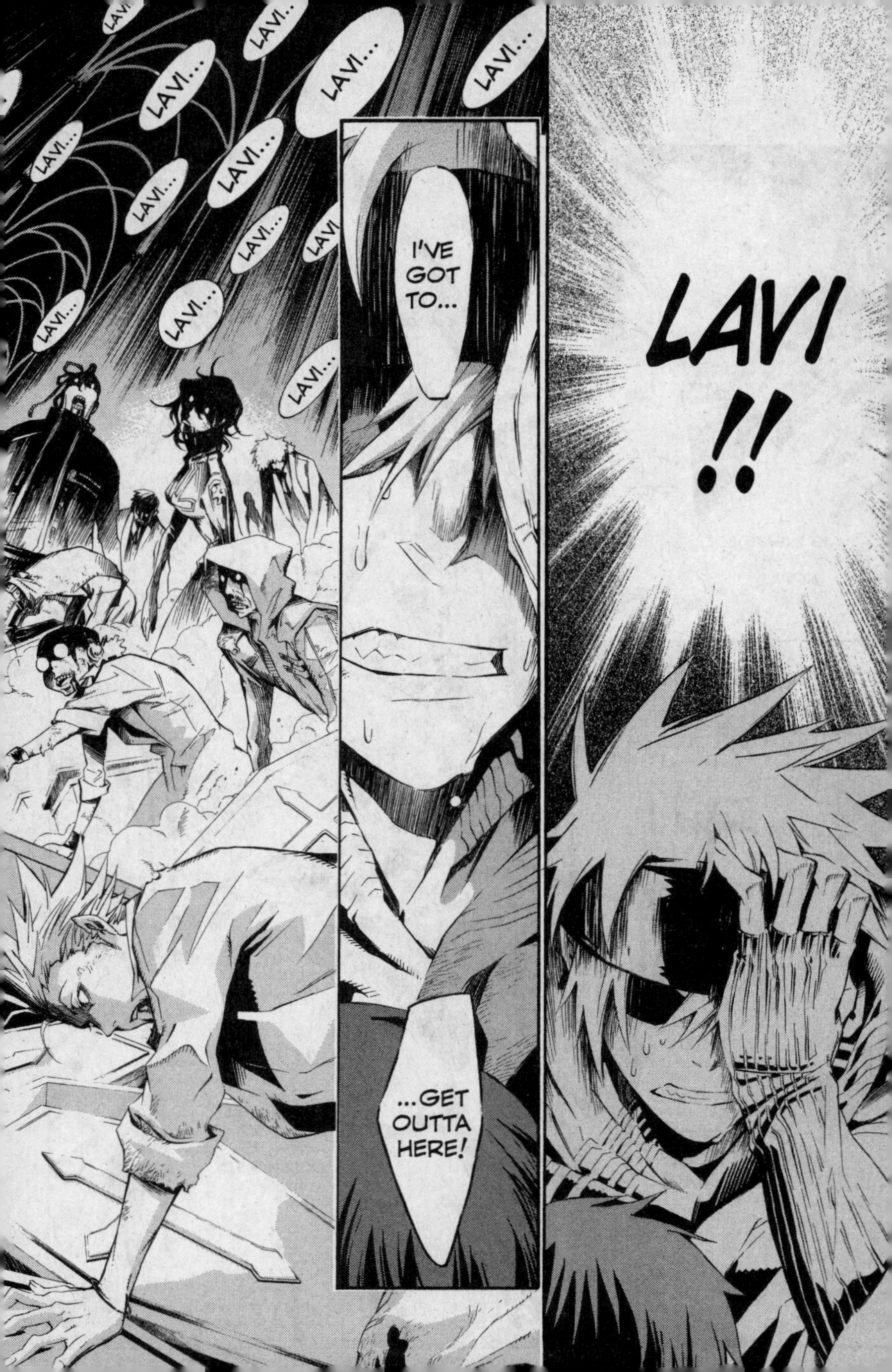
LAVI !!
I'VE GOT TO...
...GET OUTTA HERE!
LAVI...
LAVI...
LAVI...
LAVI...
LAVI...
LAVI...
LAVI...
LAVI...
LAVI...
LAVI...
LAVI...
LAVI...
LAVI

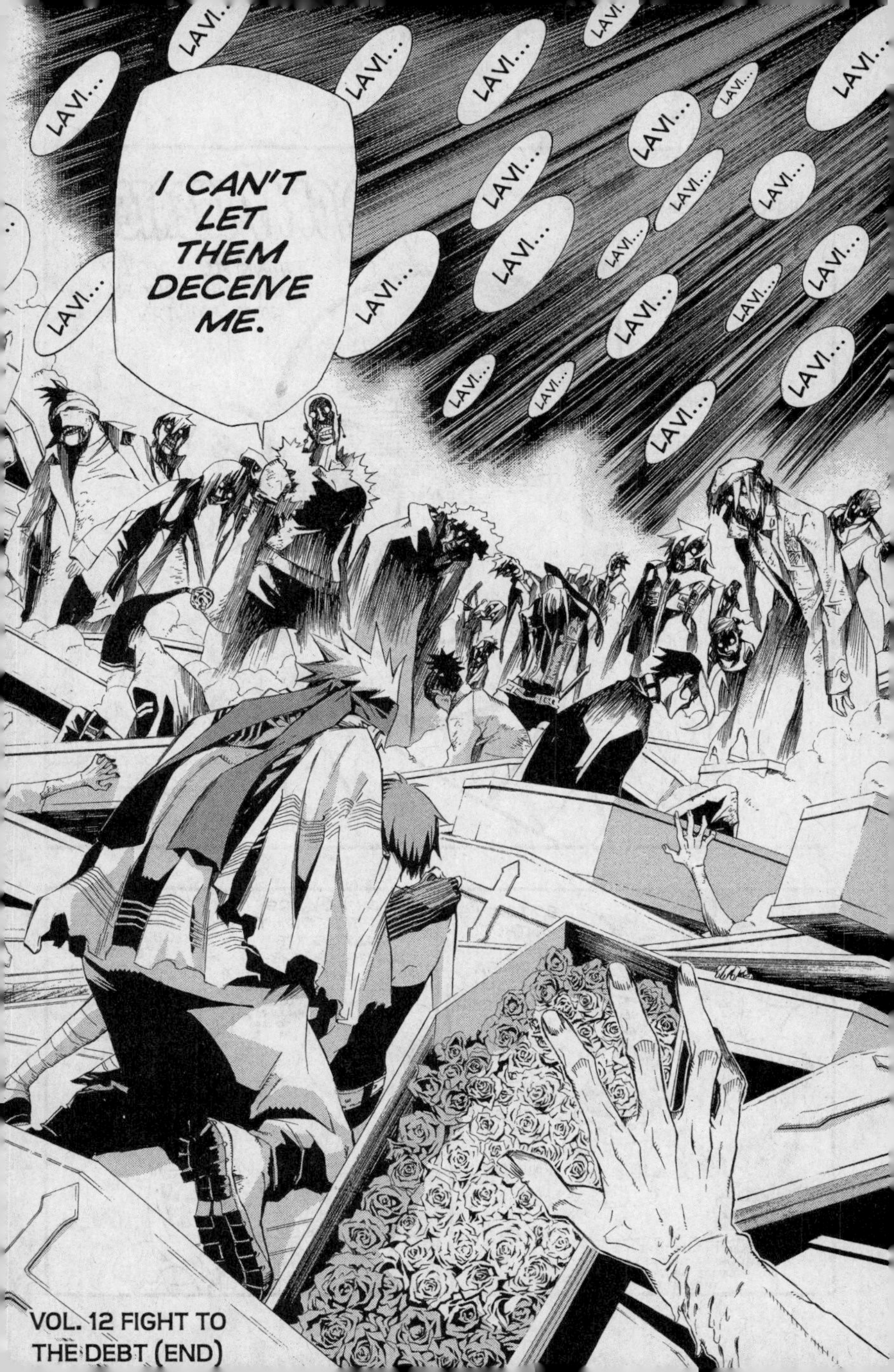
LAVI...
LAVI...
LAVI...
LAVI...
LAVI...
LAVI...
LAVI...
LAVI...
LAVI...
LAVI...
LAVI...
LAVI...
LAVI...
LAVI...
LAVI...
LAVI...
LAVI...
I CAN'T LET THEM DECEIVE ME.
LAVI...
LAVI...
LAVI...
LAVI...
LAVI...

VOL. 12 FIGHT TO THE DEBT (END)

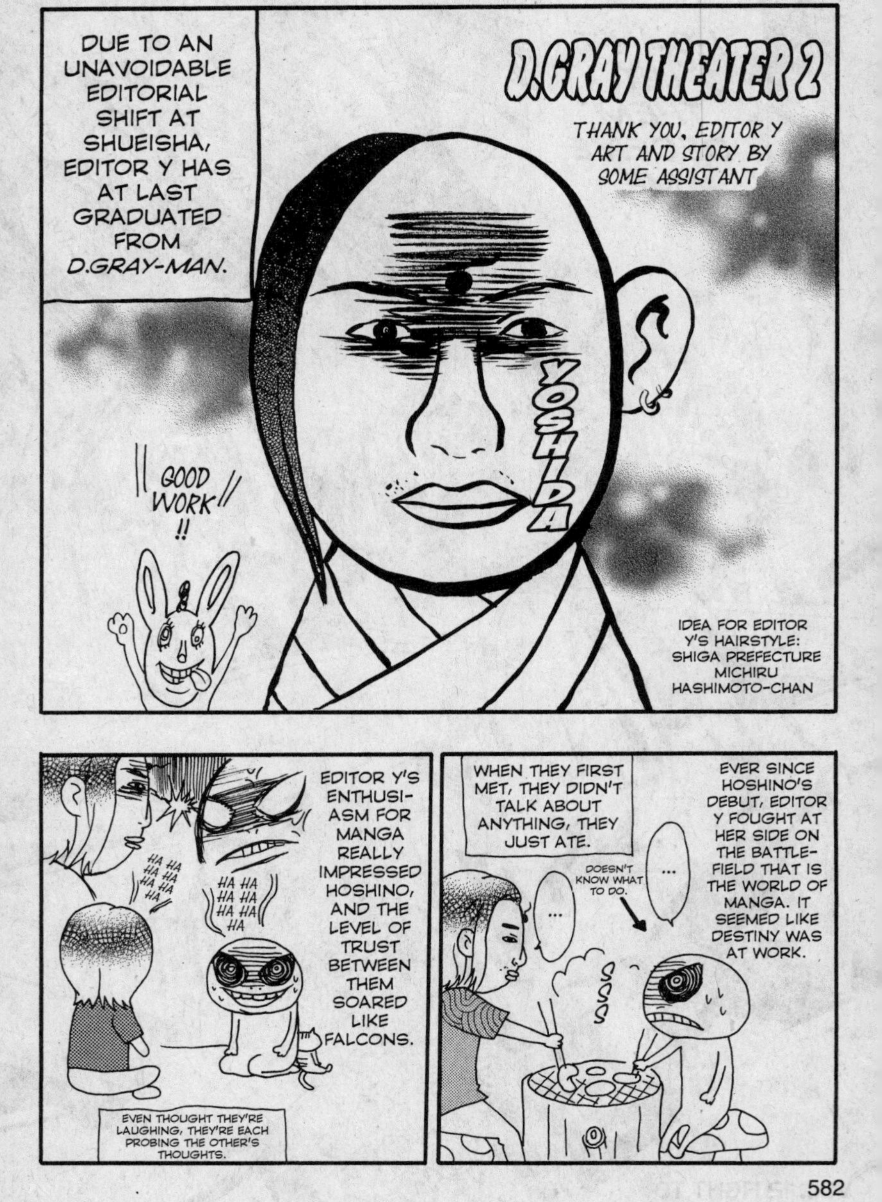
D.GRAY THEATER 2
THANK YOU, EDITOR Y
ART AND STORY BY SOME ASSISTANT
DUE TO AN UNAVOIDABLE EDITORIAL SHIFT AT SHUEISHA, EDITOR Y HAS AT LAST GRADUATED FROM D.GRAY-MAN.
YOSHIDA
GOOD WORK!!
IDEA FOR EDITOR Y'S HAIRSTYLE: SHIGA PREFECTURE MICHIRU HASHIMOTO-CHAN
EVER SINCE HOSHINO'S DEBUT, EDITOR Y FOUGHT AT HER SIDE ON THE BATTLE-FIELD THAT IS THE WORLD OF MANGA. IT SEEMED LIKE DESTINY WAS AT WORK.
WHEN THEY FIRST MET, THEY DIDN'T TALK ABOUT ANYTHING, THEY JUST ATE.
...
DOESN'T KNOW WHAT TO DO.
...
SSSS
EDITOR Y'S ENTHUSI-ASM FOR MANGA REALLY IMPRESSED HOSHINO, AND THE LEVEL OF TRUST BETWEEN THEM SOARED LIKE FALCONS.
HA HA HA HA HA HA HA
HA HA HA HA HA HA HA
EVEN THOUGHT THEY'RE LAUGHING, THEY'RE EACH PROBING THE OTHER'S THOUGHTS.

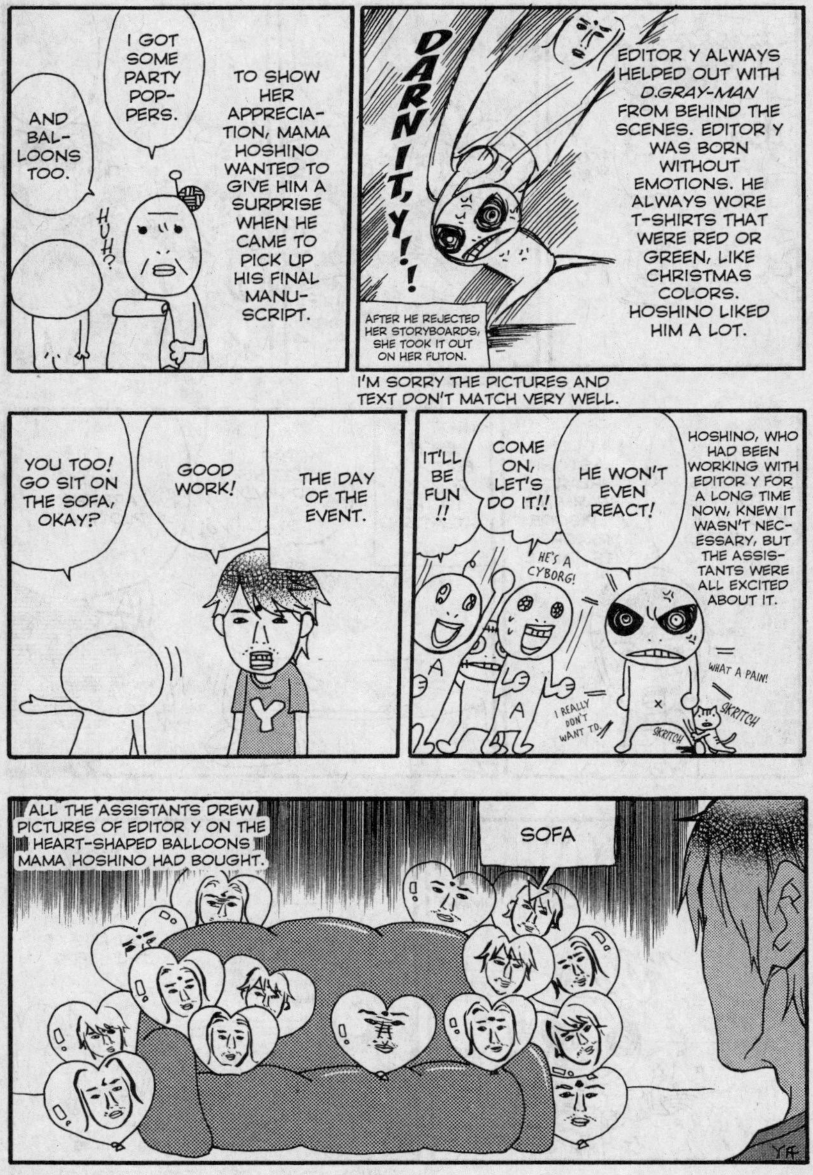
EDITOR Y ALWAYS HELPED OUT WITH *D.GRAY-MAN* FROM BEHIND THE SCENES. EDITOR Y WAS BORN WITHOUT EMOTIONS. HE ALWAYS WORE T-SHIRTS THAT WERE RED OR GREEN, LIKE CHRISTMAS COLORS. HOSHINO LIKED HIM A LOT.
DARNIT, Y!!
AFTER HE REJECTED HER STORYBOARDS, SHE TOOK IT OUT ON HER FUTON.
I'M SORRY THE PICTURES AND TEXT DON'T MATCH VERY WELL.
TO SHOW HER APPRECIATION, MAMA HOSHINO WANTED TO GIVE HIM A SURPRISE WHEN HE CAME TO PICK UP HIS FINAL MANUSCRIPT.
I GOT SOME PARTY POPPERS.
AND BALLOONS TOO.
HUH?
HOSHINO, WHO HAD BEEN WORKING WITH EDITOR Y FOR A LONG TIME NOW, KNEW IT WASN'T NECESSARY, BUT THE ASSISTANTS WERE ALL EXCITED ABOUT IT.
HE WON'T EVEN REACT!
COME ON, LET'S DO IT!!
IT'LL BE FUN!!
HE'S A CYBORG!
WHAT A PAIN!
SKRITCH
I REALLY DON'T WANT TO.
SKRITCH
THE DAY OF THE EVENT.
GOOD WORK!
YOU TOO! GO SIT ON THE SOFA, OKAY?
SOFA
ALL THE ASSISTANTS DREW PICTURES OF EDITOR Y ON THE HEART-SHAPED BALLOONS MAMA HOSHINO HAD BOUGHT.

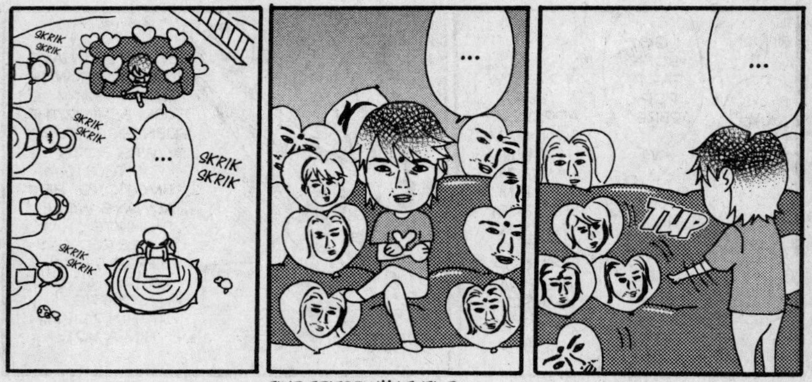
...
THP
...
SKRIK SKRIK
SKRIK SKRIK
...
SKRIK SKRIK
SKRIK SKRIK

FIND EDITOR Y!! LEVEL 3

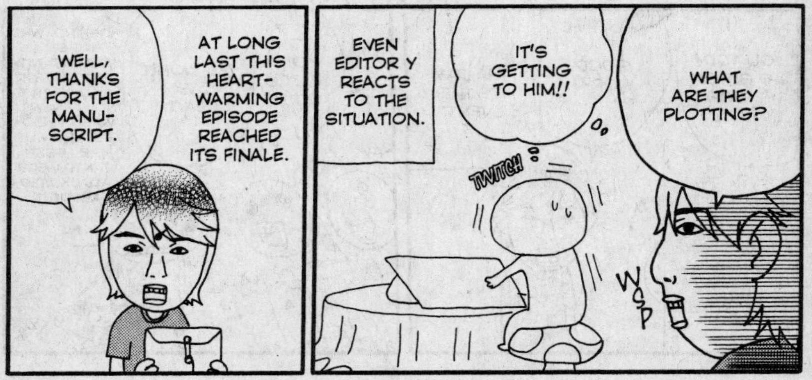
WHAT ARE THEY PLOTTING?
WSP
IT'S GETTING TO HIM!!
EVEN EDITOR Y REACTS TO THE SITUATION.
TWITCH
AT LONG LAST THIS HEART-WARMING EPISODE REACHED ITS FINALE.
WELL, THANKS FOR THE MANU-SCRIPT.

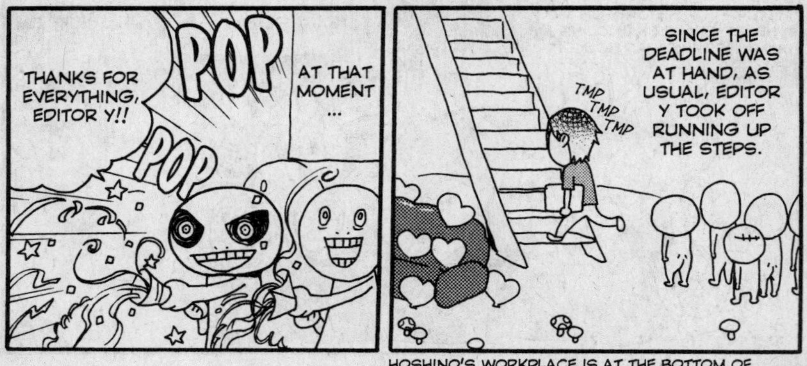
SINCE THE DEADLINE WAS AT HAND, AS USUAL, EDITOR Y TOOK OFF RUNNING UP THE STEPS.
TMP TMP TMP
AT THAT MOMENT ...
POP
THANKS FOR EVERYTHING, EDITOR Y!!
POP

HOSHINO'S WORKPLACE IS AT THE BOTTOM OF A STAIRWELL WITH THE ENTRANCE UPSTAIRS.

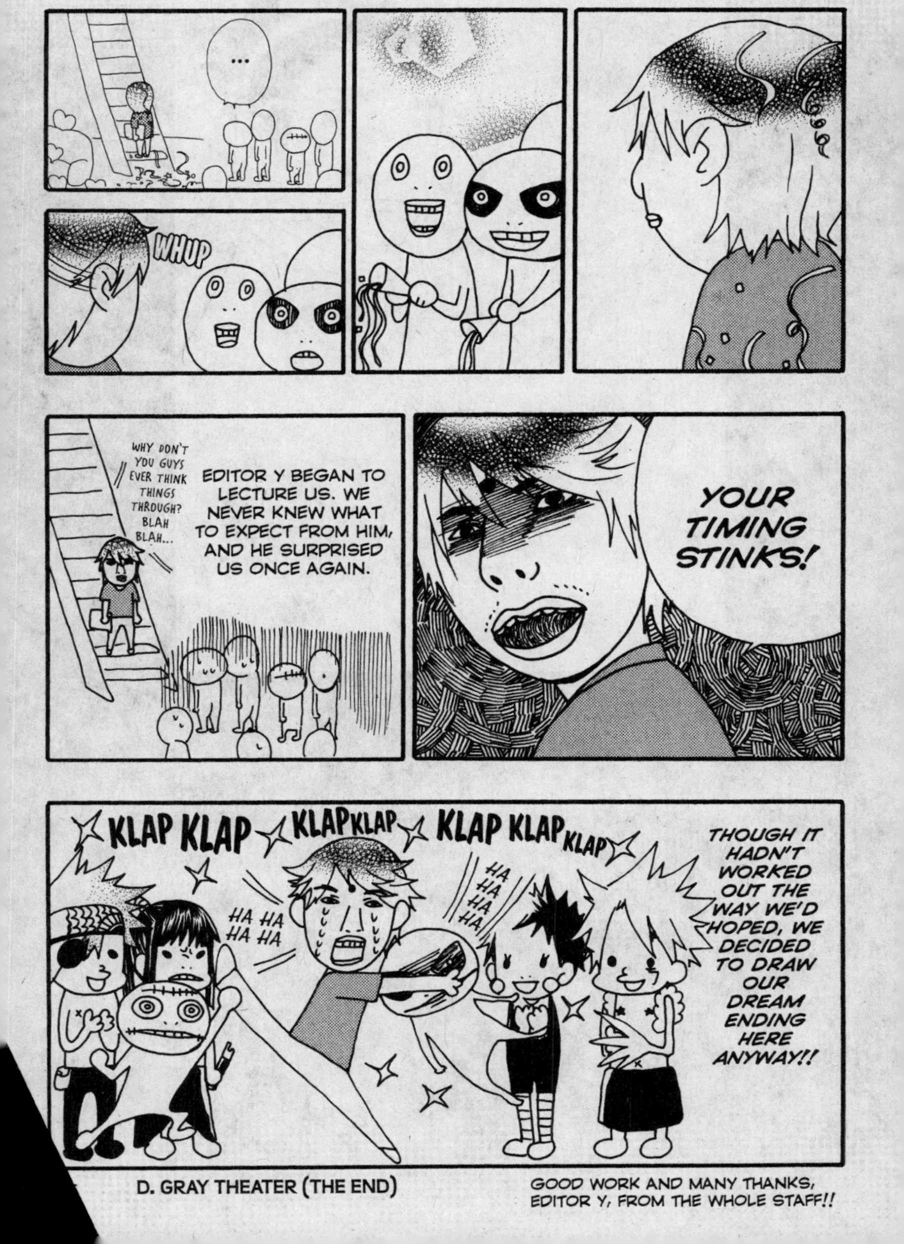
...
WHUP
YOUR TIMING STINKS!
EDITOR Y BEGAN TO LECTURE US. WE NEVER KNEW WHAT TO EXPECT FROM HIM, AND HE SURPRISED US ONCE AGAIN.
WHY DON'T YOU GUYS EVER THINK THINGS THROUGH? BLAH BLAH...
THOUGH IT HADN'T WORKED OUT THE WAY WE'D HOPED, WE DECIDED TO DRAW OUR DREAM ENDING HERE ANYWAY!!
KLAP KLAP KLAP
HA HA HA HA HA
KLAP KLAP
HA HA HA HA
KLAP KLAP

D. GRAY THEATER (THE END)

GOOD WORK AND MANY THANKS, EDITOR Y, FROM THE WHOLE STAFF!!

XT VOLUME...

...aken care of Tyki Mikk at last, Allen is brought up short by Roa ...vith a stark choice—if he wishes to rescue Lenalee and Chaoji, ...nd Lavi! Lavi himself has other ideas, but just getting Allen's atte ...s battle rages, Allen finds himself attending a most unexpected

...v!

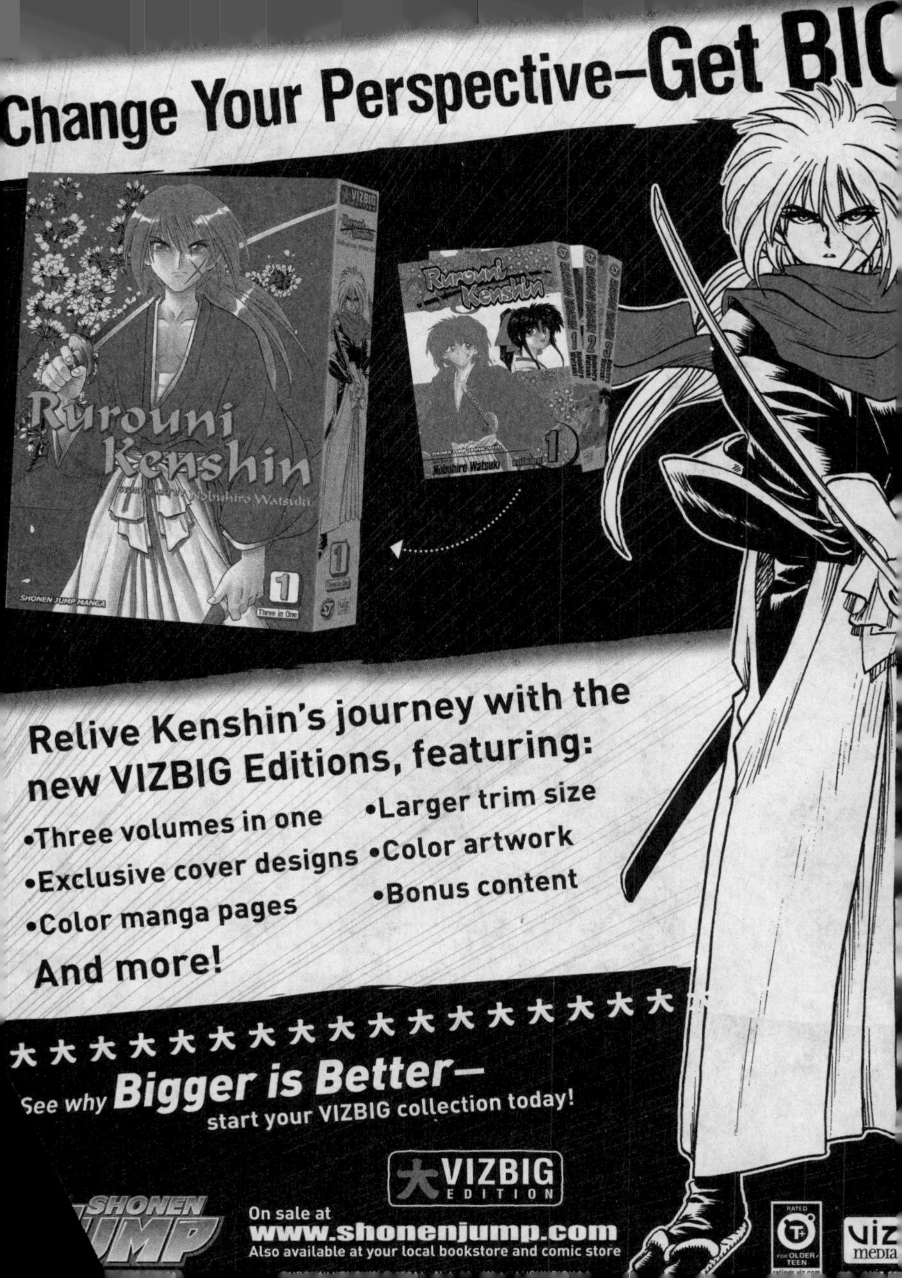

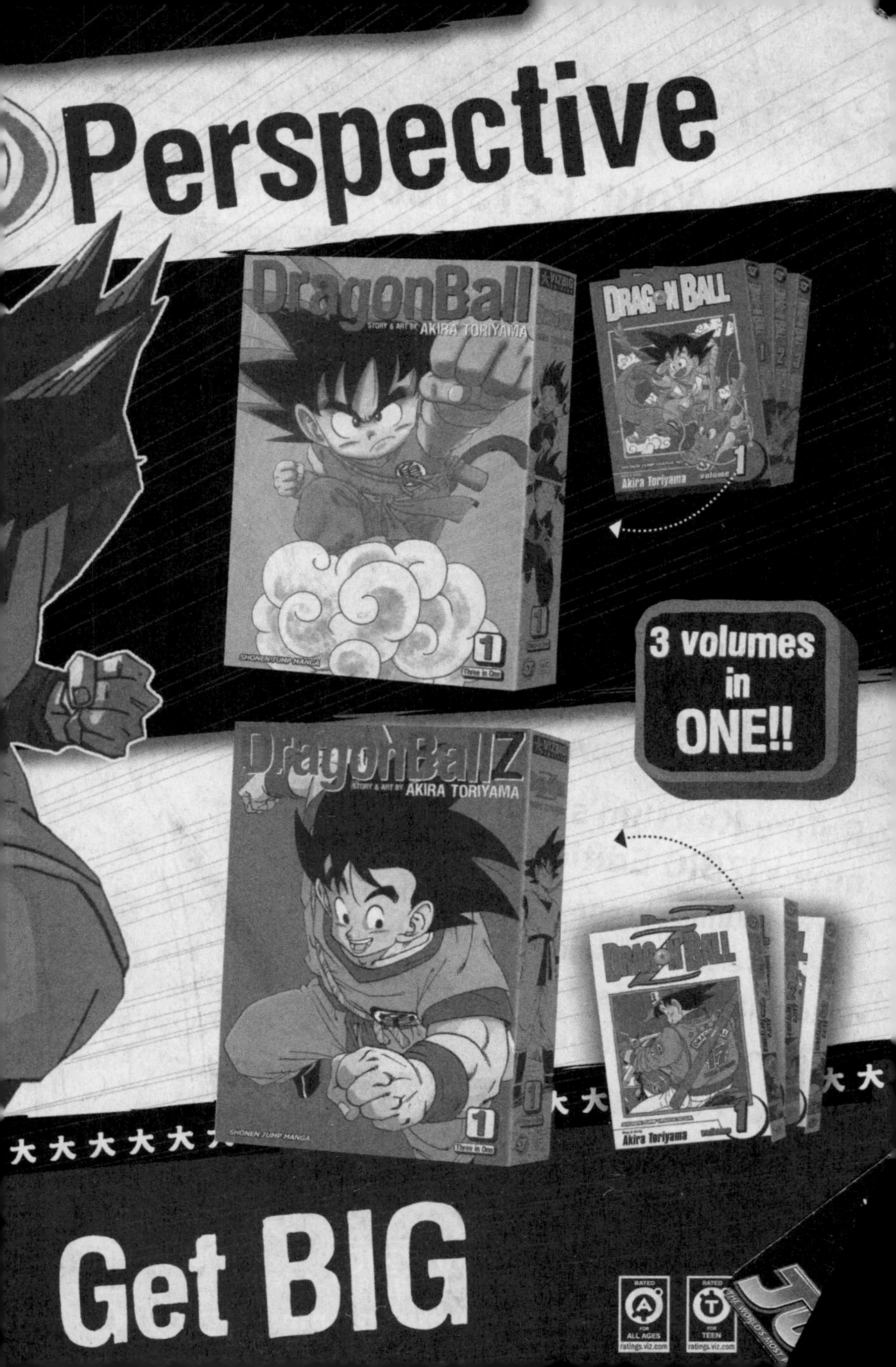
Perspective
DragonBall
STORY & ART BY AKIRA TORIYAMA
1
Three in One
SHONEN JUMP MANGA
DRAGON BALL
Akira Toriyama volume 1
3 volumes in ONE!!
DragonBall Z
STORY & ART BY AKIRA TORIYAMA
1
Three in One
SHONEN JUMP MANGA
DRAGON BALL Z
Akira Toriyama volume 1
Get BIG
RATED A FOR ALL AGES ratings.viz.com
RATED T FOR TEEN ratings.viz.com

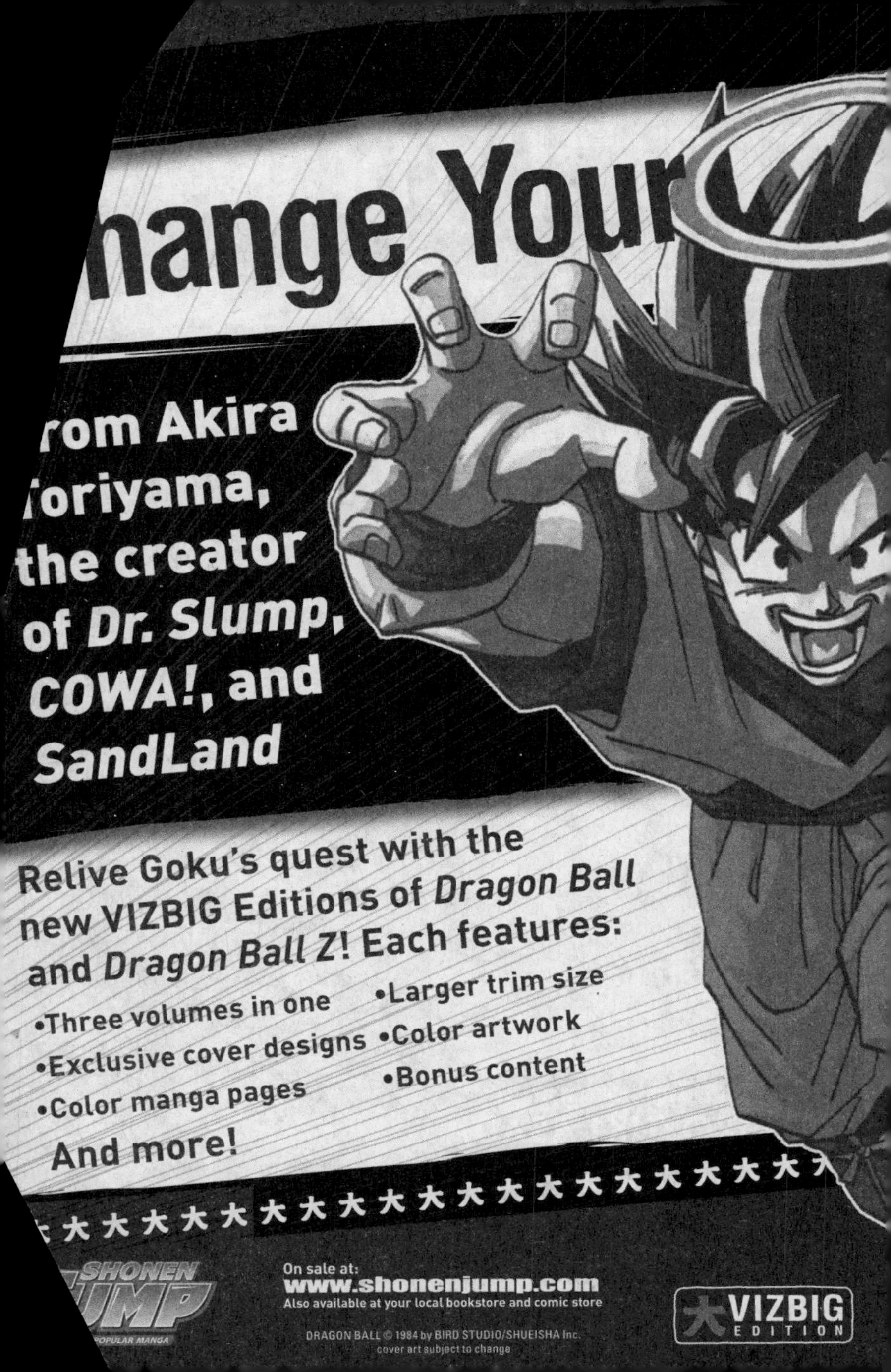

hange Your
rom Akira
oriyama,
the creator
of Dr. Slump,
COWA!, and
SandLand
Relive Goku's quest with the
new VIZBIG Editions of Dragon Ball
and Dragon Ball Z! Each features:
•Three volumes in one
•Exclusive cover designs
•Color manga pages
•Larger trim size
•Color artwork
•Bonus content
And more!
SHONEN JUMP
On sale at:
www.shonenjump.com
Also available at your local bookstore and comic store
VIZBIG EDITION
DRAGON BALL © 1984 by BIRD STUDIO/SHUEISHA Inc.
cover art subject to change

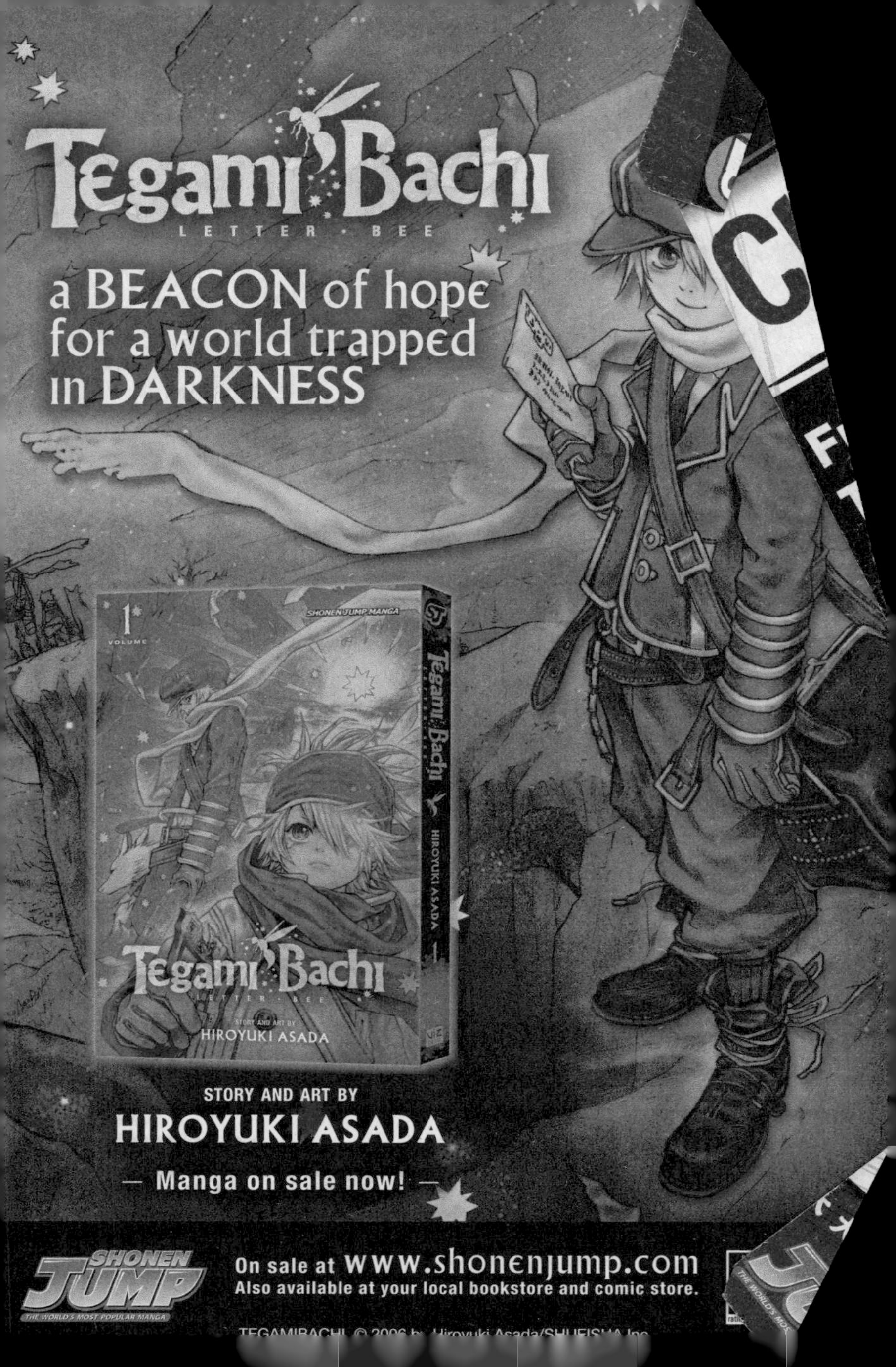
Tegami Bachi
LETTER BEE
a BEACON of hope
for a world trapped
in DARKNESS
1
VOLUME
SHONEN JUMP MANGA
Tegami Bachi
LETTER BEE
STORY AND ART BY
HIROYUKI ASADA
STORY AND ART BY
HIROYUKI ASADA
— Manga on sale now! —
SHONEN JUMP
THE WORLD'S MOST POPULAR MANGA
On sale at www.shonenjump.com
Also available at your local bookstore and comic store.
TEGAMIBACHI © 2006 by Hiroyuki Asada/SHUEISHA Inc.

VIZMANGA

Read manga anytime, anywhere!

From our newest hit series to the classics you know and love, the best manga in the world is now available digitally. Buy a volume* of digital manga for your:

- iOS device (**iPad®, iPhone®, iPod® touch**) through the **VIZ Manga** app

- Android-powered device (**phone or tablet**) with a browser by visiting **VIZManga.com**

Mac or PC computer by visiting **VIZManga.com**

VIZ Digital has loads to offer:

- 500+ ready-to-read volumes
- New volumes each week
- FREE previews
- Access on multiple devices! Create a log-in through the app so you buy a book once, and read it on your device of choice!*

To learn more, visit www.viz.com/apps

* Some series may not be available for multiple devices.
Check the app on your device to find out what's available.

viz.com/app

You're Reading in the Wrong Direction!

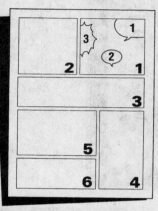

Whoops! Guess what? starting at the wrong end o comic!

It's true! In keeping with the origin Japanese format, **D.Gray-man** is meant to be read from right to left, starting in the upper-right corner.

Unlike English, which is read from left to right, Japanese is read from right to left, meaning action, sound effects and word-balloon order are completely reversed… something which can make readers unfamiliar with Japanese feel pretty backwards themselves. For this reason, manga or Japanese comics published in the U.S. in English have sometimes been published "flopped"—that is, printed in exact reverse order, as though seen from the other side of a mirror.

By flopping pages, U.S. publishers can avoid confusing readers, but the compromise is not without its downside. For one thing, a character in a flopped manga series who once wore in the original Japanese version a T-shirt emblazoned with "M A Y" (as in "the merry month of") now wears one which reads "Y A M"! Additionally, many manga creators in Japan are themselves unhappy with the process, as some feel the mirror-imaging of their art skews their original intentions.

We are proud to bring you Katsura Hoshino's **D.Gray-man** in the original unflopped format. For now, though, turn to the other side of the book and let the adventure begin…!

—Editor